W9-BJK-805

123

invent 4 digit
mã
tên bưu
hang np.
_____

124 - 4 digit - 0 - #

South India

Footprint

The travel guide

Handbook

Robert & Roma Bradnock

Fruit sellers and beedi-and-betel sellers cried themselves hoarse. Latecomers pushed, shouted and perspired. The engine added to the general noise with the low monotonous hum of its boiler; the first bell rang, the guard looked at his watch. Mr. Rajam Iyer arrived on the platform at a terrific pace, with a small roll of bedding under one arm and an absurd yellow trunk under the other. He ran to the first third-class compartment that caught his eye, peered in and, since the door could not be opened on account of the congestion inside, flung himself in through the window.

From *Malgudi Days* by R.K. Narayan

South India Handbook

First edition
© Footprint Handbooks Ltd 2000

Published by Footprint Handbooks

6 Riverside Court
Lower Bristol Road
Bath BA2 3DZ. England
T +44 (0)1225 469141
F +44 (0)1225 469461
Email discover@footprintbooks.com
Web www.footprintbooks.com

ISBN 1 900949 81 4
CIP DATA: A catalogue record for this
book is available from the British Library

In USA, published by
NTC/Contemporary Publishing Group
4255 West Touhy Avenue, Lincolnwood
(Chicago), Illinois 60712-1975, USA
T 847 679 5500 F 847 679 2494
Email NTCPUB2@AOL.COM

ISBN 0-658-01453-6
Library of Congress Catalog Card
Number 00-135726

® Footprint Handbooks and the
Footprint mark are a registered
trademark of Footprint Handbooks Ltd.

All rights reserved. No part of this
publication may be reproduced, stored
in a retrieval system, or transmitted, in
any form or by any means, electronic,
mechanical, photocopying, recording,
or otherwise, without the prior
permission of Footprint Handbooks Ltd.

Neither the black and white nor
coloured maps are intended to have
any political significance.

Credits

Series editors
Patrick Dawson and Rachel Fielding

Editorial
Editor: Stephanie Lambe
Maps: Sarah Sorensen

Production
Typesetting: Richard Ponsford, Leona
Bailey and Emma Bryers
Maps: Robert Lunn, Claire Benison, and
Alasdair Dawson
Colour maps: Robert Lunn
Cover: Camilla Ford

Design
Mytton Williams

Photography
Front cover: Travel Ink
Back cover: Travel Ink
Inside colour section: Travel Ink, Eye
Ubiquitous, James Davis Travel
Photography.

Print
Manufactured in Italy by LEGOPRINT

Every effort has been made to ensure
that the facts in this Handbook are
accurate. However, travellers should still
obtain advice from consulates, airlines
etc about current travel and visa
requirements before travelling. The
authors and publishers cannot accept
responsibility for any loss, injury or
inconvenience however caused.

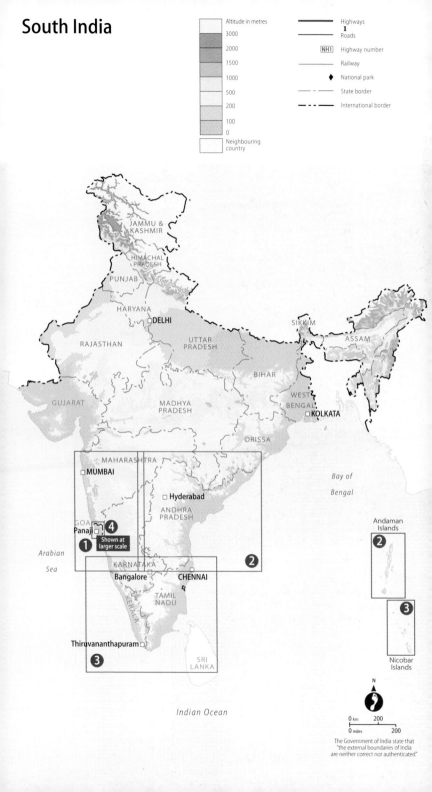

South India

Altitude in metres
3000
2000
1500
1000
500
200
100
0

Neighbouring country

Highways
Roads
NH1 Highway number
Railway
National park
State border
International border

JAMMU & KASHMIR

HIMACHAL PRADESH

PUNJAB

HARYANA

□DELHI

RAJASTHAN

UTTAR PRADESH

SIKKIM

ASSAM

BIHAR

GUJARAT

MADHYA PRADESH

WEST BENGAL

□KOLKATA

ORISSA

MAHARASHTRA

□MUMBAI

Bay of Bengal

GOA

Panaji □ ❶ ❹

Shown at larger scale

□Hyderabad

ANDHRA PRADESH

Andaman Islands

❷

Arabian Sea

KARNATAKA

Bangalore □ □CHENNAI

❸

KERALA

TAMIL NADU

❸

Nicobar Islands

Thiruvananthapuram □

SRI LANKA

Indian Ocean

N

0 km   200
0 miles   200

The Government of India state that "the external boundaries of India are neither correct nor authenticated"

Contents

Right: A Holy Man, or Sadhu, in Tamil Nadu

A foot in the door

Highlights

A tasty prospect South India boasts such a full and flavoursome diversity of landscape, culture and history it leaves most countries seeming bland and uninteresting by comparison. In the southeastern corner, the hot, dusty plains of Tamil Nadu are scattered with emerald green paddy fields and teeming with life. This landscape, rich in history, is the centre of Tamil culture and full of temples with their towering, ornately decorated gopurams, or gateways. From the east, the once densely forested high slopes, in places long since cleared for tea, rubber or coffee, run down through a series of hill ranges to the narrow coastal strip of western India, with its rich luxuriance of vegetation.

Across lowland Kerala the towering coconut palms cover what seems to be one gigantic village, without beginning or end. From Kerala to Goa and beyond, a string of little ports still witness to the vibrant trade which has linked southern India with the world to the west across the Arabian Sea. Arab traders have brought both their goods and their cultures to these west coast towns, while in Goa, innumerable white painted churches which were built in the heart of the Old Portuguese Territories have given their wholly distinctive character to another of South India's cultural enclaves.

The spice is right Traders valued the Kerala coast for its spices, and the wet, shady groves are still major producers of some of the world's most widely used. Pepper, once known as black gold, can still be seen, the vines spiralling round tree trunks, suspended strings of deep green corns hanging in the shade. Harvested and dried, pepper is still traded in bulk in the Kochi market. Other spices like cardamom and vanilla have found markets round the world. Further north into Karnataka and Goa, with a longer dry season and less reliable rainfall, cashew takes over as the most valuable item of trade for many coastal villages.

A peach of a beach The whole coastline of South India is lined with golden and silver beaches. The vast majority are used exclusively by local fishing communities, selling their catch to neighbouring towns and villages. Especially along the west coast, small ports have rapidly modernized and sell their fish to the wider Indian market and beyond. Yet there are also some spectacular stretches of sand, where visitors can swim and chill out. Goa's coastline has the most developed, but away from the established centres such as Anjuna, there is a string of superb beaches down the west coast, from Arambol in the north of Goa, , to Varkala and Kovalam in the south of Kerala.

Party animals Every month is brightened by the riot of colour, sound and feasting that mark religious or seasonal festivals. They offer the visitor a chance to experience the region's rich heritage of traditional customs, music, dance and folk theatre. In Tamil Nadu, *Pongal*, celebrated at Makar Sankranti in mid-January, is a thanksgiving for a good harvest when the cattle are specially honoured. Decorated with brightly painted horns, they are festooned with balloons and garlands of flowers and paraded along town and village roads accompanied by bands of musicians. In Kerala, the magnificent eight-day *Pooram*, is a grand spectacle staged by rival temples with elaborately decorated elephants with golden ornaments and carrying glittering parasols which are joined by skilled drummers and horn players and magnificent displays of fireworks. In common with the rest of India, some major Hindu and Muslim festivals also have their place in the south. Particularly spectacular are *Dasara* in October which celebrates the triumph of Good over Evil, and Diwali, the striking festival of lights which follows soon after on the dark night of the new moon, when the night sky bursts out with spectacular displays of fire works.

Left: A fisherman at work on his boat on beautiful Kovalam Beach in Kerala.
Right: Train passengers watching the world go by at Cochin.

Above: A street vendor enjoying a welcome breather in Hampi, in Karnataka. *Left*: It's horses for courses at Puttan Malika Palace at Trivandrum

Heavenly pursuits

The landscapes of South India are divine in more than one sense. Like the church spires of medieval European cities, its temple gateways carry a wealth of spiritual significance. They are one of the South's most resonant images and the major temple towns continue to pulse with the life of Hindu belief and practice. Chidambaram, Madurai, Thanjavur and the other towns of the Kaveri delta, contain some of the finest monuments to the skill of South Indian temple architects and craftsmen. Others are a still increasingly powerful draw to Hindu pilgrims from around the world.

Tiny treasures   While the great gopurams of Tamil Nadu's temples may catch the eye, South India has contributed far more to Hindu architecture than plaster decorated towers. You can trace the evolution of the northern and southern schools of Hindu temple building through a series of tiny gems of temple building in Aihole, Badami and Pattadakal, remote in northern Karnataka, or see the immaculate workmanship on Hindu and Jain temples at Belur and Halebid on the edge of Karnataka's western Ghats, or the still little-visited 13th century masterpiece of Somnathpur.

Big is beautiful   Not all South India's architectural treasures are in miniature. The great shore temple of Mahabalipuram, a short distance south of Chennai, has magnificent rock cut sculptures and one of the south's oldest standing temples which has been designated a World Heritage Site. Thanjavur, in the heart of the Kaveri delta, is home to another World Heritage monument, the Brihadishvara temple, built by the great Chola king Rajaraja I at the end of the 10th century. In the north of Karnataka is one of the greatest monuments of all, the now deserted city of Vijayanagar at Hampi, northern Karnataka. From this centre the last great Hindu kingdom stretched its power to most of the southern peninsula, and the city's ruins still demonstrate the dramatic scope of its economic and political influence.

The great Ghats   The quaint hill resorts developed by the British in the high hills of the Western Ghats may be changing, but they still capture something of the wholly different world of tropical life more than 2000 metres above the plains. From their beautiful shola forests to the high level grasslands, the peace and silence of the uplands comes as an astonishing contrast to the heat and pressure of the plains. The cool freshness of the air of Kodaikanal, Ooty or Coonoor in Tamil Nadu or Munnar in Kerala may not have the backdrop of snow covered mountains characteristic of the Himalayan colonial hill stations, but they are still a world in microcosm, and a wonderful base to explore.

Royal riches   The former Raja of Travancore's palace of Padmanabhapuram is a world apart from the dynastic palaces of Rajput India to the north, yet is just one of the reminders of a royal past in which South India had its own rich traditions. Some of the palaces - Mattancherry in Kochi, the Palace at Mysore or Tipu Sultan's summer palace on the banks of the Kaveri River at Srirangapatnam – may be modest in scale, but they have fine workmanship and often wonderful murals. And while South India has none of the majestically sited forts of India's northwest, Golconda, on the outskirts of Hyderabad in Andhra Pradesh, Bijapur in northern Karnataka or Gingee and Tiruchirappalli in Tamil Nadu are all evocative of centuries of struggle for military and political supremacy.

Right: The 17ᵗʰ century Nandi bull shrine, on Chamandi Hill near Mysore. **Next page**: Now that's a lot of old bull! A hole in your bucket? Well, this guy's certainly got the answer.

Essentials

2

Essentials

Planning your trip

Where to go

First time visitors are often at a loss when faced with the vast possibilities for travel in India. We have made a few suggestions here for two to three week trips on the basis that some journeys will be flown and that air or rail tickets have been booked in advance. Reliable travel agencies are listed through the book, who can make the necessary arrangements for a relatively small fee saving you time and bother.

    South India offers an almost daunting range of possibilities for travellers. From the mountain ranges of the Western Ghats, which run like a spine just inland of the west coast, with their cool climates and unique vegetation, down to the steamy heat of the east coast lowlands, rich in culture. You can travel for weeks without seeing it all. Travel networks of road, rail and air are so interconnected that you can combine parts of the routes given below. We suggest below a small sample of the wide range of possible tours, ranging from short two to three week trips, to options for a much longer stay. Figures in brackets are the approximate number of nights we suggest you spend.

The Konkan railway has brought **Mumbai** (1) within comfortable reach of **Goa** (3). You can stay in one of the beach centres and visit the Portuguese churches of **Old Goa**, before continuing south to **Mangalore** (1). From the coast you can then go through the forest clad Western Ghats to **Hassan** (2) to see the wonderful Hindu and Jain temples at Belur and Halebid. The old Kodagu (Coorg) capital **Madikeri** (3), south of Hassan, is an excellent place to relax and get a feel of the unspoilt hill country. Mysore is within easy reach via the national park at **Nagarhole** (2). **Mysore** (3) itself is an excellent base from which to see Tipu Sultan's palace at Srirangapatnam and there is a choice of other rewarding sights, including the Maharajah's palace, a gem of a medieval Hindu temple at Somnathpur, and the magnificent Falls of the River Kaveri at Sivasamudram. The tour can end at the dynamic modern city of **Bangalore** (2), directly connected by air with **Mumbai** (1).

1. South India circuit - western route 18 days

From **Mumbai** (1) you can go by train or plane to the capital of Andhra Pradesh, **Hyderabad** (3). The rapidly modernising city has the impressive Golconda fort and Qutb Shahi tombs nearby. You can then go south to see some of the greatest treasures of southern culture. Flying to **Chennai** (2) you can visit Mahabalipuram's shore temple before stopping at **Pondicherry** (1) where the French left their mark. Great Hindu temples are scattered across Tamil Nadu's central plains, and **Trichy** (1) with Srirangam nearby, and **Madurai** (2) offer access to some of the most spectacular. From Madurai it is

2. South Indian circuit - eastern route 16 days

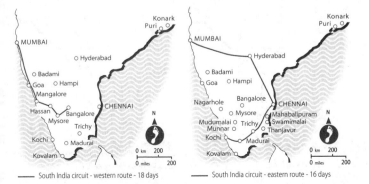

— South India circuit - western route - 18 days   — South India circuit - eastern route - 16 days

Essentials

possible to experience a complete change of climate and scenery by climbing the Western Ghats to the National Park at **Periyar (1)**. From Periyar, a day's journey takes you to Kerala's west coast port of **Kochi** (2). where the Jewish and Dutch connections can be traced before the British arrived. From here you can sample the idyllic backwaters in a punted wooden boat before returning by plane to **Mumbai** (1).

3. Temple towns
14 days

Starting at **Chennai** (1) which has many art treasures in its museum, visit **Mahabalipuram** (3) by the sea with its rock cut and structural temples. If you are feeling energetic you can take a day trip to see either the great temples of Kanchipuram, also famous as a silk making town, or the fort at Gingee and the magnificent temple at Tiruvannamalai. Continue to the centres of ancient Tamil culture with remarkable temples at **Chidambaram** (1), and stop at **Swamimalai** (2) where exquisite deities are still cast in solid bronze, to visit Darasuram and Kumbakonam, Gangaikondacholapuram en route to **Thanjavur** (2) and **Madurai** (2). Return via **Trichy** (2) and Srirangam to **Chennai** (1).

4. Making more
of a Kerala
beach package
14 or 21 days

Fly to Thiruvananthapuram on a charter and take advantage of the good value package holiday on the beach at **Kovalam** for 14-21 days. From there you can visit the museums in the Kerala capital and venture further south along the coast. A long day allows you to visit the atmospheric old wooden palace at **Padmanabhapuram**, the crowded **Suchindram** temple and to the very tip of the peninsula at **Kanniyakumari** with the Vivekananda Rock out at sea. Take a few days away from your beach hotel and explore the interior travelling by car or bus through rubber plantations beyond Kottayam, the heart of Christian Kerala, up to the tea gardens on the high hills at **Munnar** (2). Go and see the rich mixture of East and West in **Kochi** (2) and sample the backwaters on a punted wooden boat, before driving back to Kovalam.

5. Wildlife tours

South India's distinctive habitats are home to outstanding reserves which offer many oppportunities for seeing wildlife. The suggested tours take you to the most popular of these and also allow excursions to cultural sites. Most national parks charge foreigners Rs 100-350 per head for entry. Camera fees, vehicle charges and guides, usually compulsory, can add a lot to the cost.

Start in **Chennai** (2) to visit the bird sanctuary of **Vedanthangal** and **Mahabalipuram** (2), by the sea, with its ancient temples. Then travel down to **Trichy** (2) to climb up the rock fort and see the great temple of Srirangam on the banks of the Kaveri. From there the route continues to the hill station of **Coonoor** (2) going up to **Udhagamandalam** (Ooty) (1) on the Blue Mountain railway (if it is running), then on to the rich wildlife

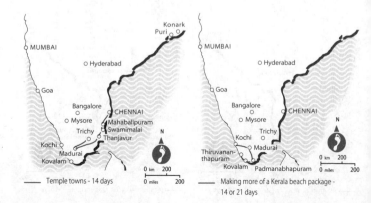

Temple towns - 14 days

Making more of a Kerala beach package - 14 or 21 days

Essentials

sanctuary of **Mudumalai-Bandipur** (3). Travelling north into Karnataka, you can visit the beautiful national park of **Nagarhole** (3). A stop in **Mysore** (3) gives a chance to visit and stay in palaces, and to see Tipu Sultan's **Srirangapatnam** before ending the tour at **Bangalore** (2). 20 days.

From **Chennai** (Madras, 2) drive to **Swamimalai** (2) known for traditional bronze casting and continue south to the ancient Tamil temples at **Thanjavur** (2) and **Madurai** (2). A morning start allows a stop at **Padmanabhapuram Palace** on the way across to Kerala on the west coast to relax by the beach at **Kovalam** (3) near Thiruvananthapuram. Take a boat along the backwaters as you move to **Kochi** (3), a fascinating meeting point of Eastern and European cultures. Then drive across to the tea estates of **Munnar** (2), high in the Western Ghats before dropping to the Tamil plains to visit the ancient fort and temples at **Trichy** (2) and **Srirangam**. Before returning home from Chennai, stop by the sea for the rock-cut cave temples at **Mahabalipuram** (3). 21 days.

6. Sampling the south 21 days

Although six weeks gives you longer to explore, it also gives time to take things more gently. The best way to take advantage of the extra time is to take plenty of rest breaks with longer in each place - far better than trying to cram everything possible in.

7. Six week tours

After a common route for the first two weeks, we offer alternative routes for the remaining four, described as A, B and C.

Mahabalipuram can be a great place to recover after a long flight and to get settled in with its beach and temples, and other fascinating sights are within easy reach. You can go north to Tirupati and Tirumalai, possible in a day trip from Chennai, but staying one night away for comfort. Close to Mahabalipuram are the bird sanctuary at Vedanthangal, and the silk weavers and medieval temples at Kanchipuram.

Week 1
Chennai and Mahabalipuram

Stop in the former French colonial town Pondicherry (3) with its Aurobindo Ashram and the ideologically planned city of Auroville nearby. It is a good base to explore the historic fort of Gingee, and the extraordinary temple town of Tiruvannamalai. Travel south to some of the great temples of Tamil Nadu. Active religious centres like Chidambaram, Kumbakonum and Trichy contrast with the now deserted but remarkable temples of Thanjavur, Gangakondaicholapuram or Darasuram. You can stay in Trichy or Thanjavur 2 or 3 nights.

Week 2
Pondicherry and the Kaveri delta

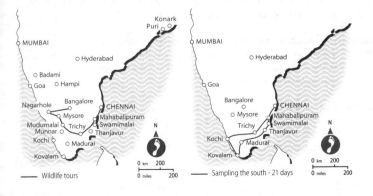

Route A

Week 3
To Coonoor/Ooty

If you have seen enough temples - for now at least - you can head straight for the Nilgiris, staying at Coonoor or Ooty after travelling by road or the narrow gauge train. There are plenty of relaxing walks, some opportunity to visit tribal Toda groups, and catch something of the atmosphere of the colonial hill towns.

Week 4
EITHER To Mysore via Kochi

From the hills, you can head south to Kochi on Kerala's coast (4). The fort is fascinating, with its Jewish quarter, spice market and palaces, but you also have the chance to see the Kerala dances Kathakali or Theyyam in live performance and sample the quiet of the backwaters. Then head north up the coast to Kannur (1) before climbing to the the the National Park at Nagarhole (2) to Mysore.

OR To Mysore via the National Parks

For a much less hectic travel schedule you can go down the Ghats to the National Parks at Mudumalai/Bandipur (3) and Nagarhole (2) en route for the Coorg capital of Madikeri (2), ending in the relaxed and attractive city of Mysore.

Week 5
Mysore and Bangalore

Mysore (3) is an excellent base for gentle exploration of sites like Srirangapatnam and Somnathpur, close by. A longer trip to Belur and Halebid needs an overnight stay at Hassan or Chikmagalur (1). If you take that option, go straight on to Bangalore, stopping for a visit to Sravanbelagola. Otherwise from Mysore go to the dynamic and rapidly modernising city of Bangalore (3) for a feel of a quite different India.

Week 6
From Bangalore to Mumbai

Travel north to Hampi (2) then to Goa (4). Stay in a beach resort in either north or south Goa, giving the opportunity to see both the Portuguese colonial churches in the territory of the Old Conquests and the distinctive Goan Hindu temples, or just relax on the beach. Train or flight to Mumbai.

Route B

Week 3
To Kodai and Munnar

An alternative from Thanjavur/Trichy is to travel south to Madurai (2) and then head up to Kodaikkanal (2). There is no direct road to Munnar, but it is a very attractive day's journey down the Palani Ghat to Palani then through two national parks to the delightful small hill resort of Munnar (3). Excursions to Maduppatti, Eravikulam or Top Station offer fantastic scenery, and a chance to see the endangered Nilgiri Tahr, and to visit a tea plantation and factory.

Week 4
Munnar to Bangalore via Kochi

From Munnar you can descend to Kochi on the coast (4). The fort is fascinating, with its Jewish quarter, spice market and palaces, but you also have the chance to see the Kerala dances Kathakali or Theyyam in live performance. You can also sample the quiet of the backwaters. Travel direct to Bangalore (3).

Week 5
Bangalore to Bijapur

From Bangalore travel north to Hospet for Hampi, capital of the 15th century Vijayanagar empire (3). Then continue to three of the most atmospheric centres of Hindu architectural development Badami, Aihole and Pattadakal (2) and the former regional Muslim capital of Bijapur (2).

Week 6
Bijapur to Hyderabad

Continue north east to the capital of Andhra Pradesh, Hyderabad (4). The distinctive imprint of the Muslim Zizam of Hyderabad is felt both on old forts such as Golconda and more modern public buildings. You can take a long day trip to the medieval fortress town of Bidar. Travel by train or plane to Mumbai (2) or return to Chennai.

Route C

From Thanjavur/Trichy travel through the Chettiar country to Madurai (3), with its vibrantly active Meenakshi Temple. A wonderfully scenic road climbs the Western Ghats to one of South India's best known National Parks at Thekkadi/Periyar (3). Then allow a day's travel to the coast at Kovalam.

Week 3
To Kovalam via Periyar

The beach resort of Kovalam (5) is close to Kerala's capital of Thiruvananthapuram. This is an attractive place just to rest for a couple of days and take in the palace at Padmanabhapuram of the old rajahs of Travancore. From Kovalam go north to Kollam and cruise on the backwaters to Alappuzha (2) to Kochi.

Week 4
Kovalam to Kochi

Stay in Kochi (3) to explore the sights of the old Fort, with its Jewish synagogue, spice markets and palaces. Head north from Kochi up the coast, visiting one of Kerala's most important pilgrimage sites, Guruvayur en route to the capital of the former Zamorin of Calicut, Kozhikode (2) If you are there at the time of the Thrissur Pooram arrange to visit for a day. Continue north via Mahe and Thalassery and Kannur (1). To visit a still undeveloped beach, stop off at Bekal en route to Mangalore (1).

Week 5
The coastal route north to Goa

You can take the Konkan railway up the coast all the way to Mumbai, stopping off at Canacona for the magnificent Palolem beach in southern Goa, or Margao for a central Goa beach (or get there by road). There are other interesting places on the route, including the important Hindu pilgrimage centre of Udupi, famous for its vegetarian cuisine, and Jog Falls, the highest in India. In Goa there is plenty to see away from the beaches, so you can allocate this final week to your taste, flying back from Goa to Mumbai or Chennai.

Week 6
Mangalore to Goa

A much longer tour gives you the chance to see something of all the strands that give richness to peninsular India, including getting right off the beaten track. You might choose to combine elements of the routes described above. For example, from Kannur (A4 or C5) travel to Madikeri and then explore Karnataka (A5), and Andhra Pradesh (B5,6) at leisure. From Mangalore (C5) it is easy to get to Hassan for a trip around Karnataka before returning to Chennai. Or from Goa (C6) venture out to Hampi and then north to Bijapur and Hyderabad, before returning south to Bangalore to see the rest of Karnataka.

Three months

When to go

South India is very warm to hot throughout the year. Coastal regions are generally humid. In Kerala and Karnataka the main rainy season is June to September, but in Tamil Nadu and central Andhra the rains come later, between October-December. The hill stations in the Western Ghats are beautiful in the drier months from January to early June though they can be quite cold from January to March. The chart above gives an idea of which areas can be visited comfortably during any particular month. Because local variations are important, the handbook gives temperatures and rainfall details for all regions and many cities, indicating the best times to visit.

Some of India's great festivals such as *Dasara* and *Diwali* are celebrated in autumn and winter. In Tamil Nadu Pongal is a January harvest festival, which in Kerala is known as Onam, a great rainy season festival.

Essentials

	Tamil Nadu		Kerala		Karnataka and Goa		Andhra Pradesh	
	Hills	Plains	Hills	Coast	Interior	Coast	Interior	Coast
January	✓	✓	✓	✓	✓	✓	✓	✓
	Very warm and dry; cool in hills		Very warm and dry; cool in hills		Very warm and dry; cool in hills		Very warm and dry	
February	✓	✓	✓	✓	✓	✓	✓	✓
	Very warm and dry; cool in hills		Very warm and dry; cool in hills		Very warm and dry; cool in hills		Very warm and dry	
March	✓	✓	✓	✓	✓	✓	✓	✓
	Getting hot in plains; dry and pleasant in hills		Coast hot; dry and pleasant in hills		Hot and dry on coast and in interior		Getting very hot in interior and coast; dry	
April	✓		✓	✓	✓	✓	✓	✓
	Very hot in plains; beautiful in hills		Very hot on coast; beautiful in hills		Very hot on coast and interior		Very hot and dry	
May	✓		✓	✓	✓			
	Very hot in plains; beautiful high in hills		Very hot on coast; beautiful high in hills		Very hot on coast and hot in interior		Very hot and dry	
June					✓			
	Hot, showery, humid on coast; often windy; hills in cloud		Breaking rains; very wet on coast; hills in cloud		Rains begin to break; hot, windy on coast but cooler in south		Slightly cooler; some heavy bursts of rain; cloud	
July					✓			
	Hot, showery, humid on coast, often windy; hills in cloud		Heavy rains, especially in centre and north; hills in cloud		Southern interior often pleasant; coast and hills very wet		Occasional heavy rain, cloud, humid	
August					✓			
	Hot, showery, humid on coast, often windy; hills in cloud		Still very wet on coast and cloudy on hills		Warm and wet; pleasant in southern interior		Occasional heavy rain, cloud, humid	
September			✓		✓	✓	✓	✓
	Hot, showery, humid on coast; often windy; hills in cloud		Rains easing off; hills often still cloudy		Rains easing off; still very warm in interior		Still hot, though getting drier	
October			✓		✓	✓	✓	
	Monsoon rains start; risk of cyclones on coast		Very warm; heavy showers on coast; hills cloudy		Very warm; coast becoming drier		Interior very warm but drying; risk of cyclones on coast	
November			✓		✓	✓	✓	
	Monsoon, with risk of cyclones; often wet, cloudy and windy		Warm and some rain, but clear spells; hills sometimes cloudy		Very warm; coast dry and pleasant; some rain further east		Very warm; interior pleasant; risk of cyclones along coast	
December	✓	✓	✓	✓	✓	✓	✓	✓
	Risk of cyclones in first half of month, otherwise warm and pleasant		Clearing; very warm; generally clear on coast and hills		Warm; dry on coast, generally very pleasant		Risk of cyclones in first half of month, otherwise warm and pleasant	

Tours and tour operators

You may choose to try an inclusive package holiday or let a specialist operator quote for a tailor-made tour. Out of season these can be worth exploring. The lowest prices quoted for 2000 from the UK vary from about US$550 for a week (flights, hotel and breakfast) in the low season, to over US$3,000 for three weeks during the peak season. Most will chalk out individual itineraries and cover the major sights with small groups. Tour companies are listed here who arrange anything from general tours to wildlife safaris to ashram.

Ace, T01223-835055, ace@studytours.org Cultural study tours, expert led; *Adventures Abroad*, T0114-2473400 (USA & Canada, T800 665 3998, Australia T800 890 790), info@adventures-abroad.org Outward bound; *Asian Journeys*, T01604 234401, F234866, www.asianjourneys.com Fairs, festivals, culture, religion, *Andrew Brock* (*Coromandel*), T01572-821330, abrock@aol.com Special interest (crafts, textiles, botany etc). *Banyan Tours*, T01672-564090, www.india-traveldirect.com BanyanUK@ compuserve.com Tailored tours, local contact. *Cox & Kings* (Taj Group), T020-78735001, F6306038. Palaces, forts, tourist high spots. *Discovery Initiatives*, T020-79786341, www.discoveryinitiatives.com Wildlife safaris, *Dragoman*, T01728-861133, www.dragoman.co.uk, st@dragoman.co.uk Overland, adventure, camping. *Exodus Travels*, T020-87723822, sales@exodustravels.co.uk *Gateway to India*, T0870-4423204, F0870-4423205, specialist-travel@gateway-to-india.co.uk Tailor-made, off-the-beaten-track, local reps. *Greaves Tours*, T020-74879111, F74860722, sbriggs@greavesuk.com Railways, cities, heritage. *Indian Magic*, T020-84274848, sales@indiamagic.co.uk Homestays, small-scale, pulse of India. *Myths and Mountains*, USA T800-6706984, www.mythsandmountains.com Culture, crafts, religion. *Paradise Holidays*, Delhi,

Essentials

sightseeing.

exodus.co.uk
The Different Holiday
Leaders in small group Walking & Trekking, Discovery & Adventure Holidays, Biking Adventures, European Destinations and Overland Expeditions Worldwide.

Tel 020 8772 3822 for brochure.
e-mail: sales@exodustravels.co.uk

Exodus Travels Ltd ATOL 2582/AITO

www.exodus.co.uk

EXPERIENCE IS EVERYTHING

Specialists in Student &
Young Independent Travel

250 Branches Worldwide

Low Cost Flights ∗ Adventure Tours ∗ Ski Insurance
Travel Passes ∗ Accommodation ∗ Car Hire

BOOKINGS &
ENQUIRIES: 0870 160 6070

www.statravel.co.uk

STA Travel Ltd.   ATOL 3206   ABTA TRAVEL AGENT 99209

India Tourist Offices Overseas

Australia Level 1, 2 Picadilly, 210 Pitt St, Sydney, NSW 2000, T612-292644855, F92644860.

Canada 60 Bloor St, West Suite No 1003, Toronto, Ontario, T416-9623787, F9626279.

France 11-13 Bis Boulevard Hausmann, F75009, Paris T45233045, F45233345.

Germany Baserler St 48, 60329, Frankfurt AM-Main 1, T069-2429490, F24294977.

Italy Via Albricci 9, Milan 20122, T8053506, F72021681.

Japan Pearl Building, 9-18 Chome Ginza, Chuo Ku, Tokyo 104, T33-5715062, F5715235.

The Netherlands Rokin 9-15, 1012 Amsterdam, T020-6208891, F6383059.

Singapore 20 Kramat Lane, 01-01A United House, Singapore 0922. T2353800, F2358677.

Sweden Sveavagen 9-11 1st Flr, S-III 57 Stockholm 11157, T468-101187, F210186.

Switzerland 1-3 rue de Chantepoulet, 1201 Geneva, T41-227321813, F7315660.

Thailand 3rd Flr, KFC Bldg, 62/5 Thaniya Rd, Bangkok 10500, T662-2352585, F2368411.

UK 7 Cork St, London W1X 2AB, T020-74373677, F74941048.

USA 3550 Wilshire Blvd, Room 204, Los Angeles, California 90010. T213-3808855, F3806111; Suite 1808, 1270 Avenue of Americas, New York, NY 10020, T212-5864901, F5823274.

Essentials

T0091-11-6145116, F0091-11-6145112, www.paradiseholidays.com.in paradise@del2.vsnl.net.in *Pettitts*, T01892-515966, F521500, www.pettitts.co.uk, pettitts@ centrenet.co.uk Unusual locations, activities, wildlife. *Royal Expeditions*, Delhi, T0091-11-6238545, F0091-11-6475954, www.royalexpeditions.com, vss@royalexpeditions. com *Spirit of India*, USA T888-3676147, inquire@spirit-of-india.com Focussed, local experts. *STA Travel*, T020-73616100, F020-73680075, www.statravel.co.uk *Trans Indus*, T020-85662729, F88405327, www.transindus.co.uk, trans.indus@dial.pipex.com Activities, wildlife. *USIT Campus*, 52 Grosvenor Gardens, London, T0870-2401010, www.usitcampus.co.uk *Western & Oriental*, T020-73136611, F73136601, enquiries@westernoriental.com Upmarket, unique heritage hotels.

Know what's so erotic about Khajuraho?

Take a peek. Dragoman takes you overland in top quality secure vehicles to explore AFRICA, S. & C. AMERICA, **ASIA & INDIA**, THE MIDDLE EAST, CHINA, HIMALAYAS OR ANTARCTICA. Choose camping or hotel accommodation, from 2 to 37 weeks.

dragoman

ATOL 4157

Call 01728 861133
www.dragoman.co.uk
st@dragoman.co.uk

Essentials

INDIA
Culture • Wildlife • Adventure

With over 10 years experience in organising escorted groups, individual itineraries and tailor made tours, our expertise for the widest range of India holidays is unmatched in the UK.

TRANS INDUS

020 8566 2729
www.transindus.co.uk
ABTA V0705   ATOL 3429

Experience the delights & grandeur of India with
Royal Expeditions
Under the guidance of our patron
Rani Chandresh Kumari, *Princess of Jodhpur*

We are renowned for **tailor-made** culture, wildlife, riding, fishing, beach & other special-interest holidays for **discerning yet adventurous traveller**
Royal Expeditions Private Limited

R-184, Greater Kailash-I, New Delhi - 110048. Tel: 91 (11) 623 8545 Fax: 91 (11) 647 5954
Email:vss@royalexpeditions.com   Web site: www.royalexpeditions.com

Book directly or via our fully bonded / licensed representative in U.K. or Australia

---

Paradise Holidays

★ Cultural, adventure, wildlife & incentive tours
★ Experienced, professionally qualified & multilingual staff
★ Special rates with hotels throughout year
★ Fully computerised communication system

★ Own fleet of air conditioned cars and coaches with experienced drivers and multilingial guides/escorts.
★ International/domestic air ticketing with various CRS - Galileo, Sabre, Amadeus etc and Indian Airlines

(APPROVED TOUR OPERATOR BY GOVT OF INDIA MEMBER - IATO, PATA, TAAI, AFTA, ASTA,UFTAA)

For individual and personal care please contact us at:
20-B, Basant Lok, Community Centre, Vasant Vihar, New Delhi - 110057.
Telephone: 6145116, 6145117, 6146712, 6148597. Fax 6145112, 6147122. Email: paradise@del2.vsnl.net.in
For more information visit our website: www.paradiseholidays.com.in

---

usit CAMPUS

for students and young travellers

THE PLANET IN YOUR POCKET

● Adventure Tours
● Low Cost Travel Insurance
● International Identity Cards
● Low Cost Air, Sea, Rail Fares & Passes
● Round the World Flights
● Worldwide Budget Accommodation

●●●●●●●●●●●●●●●●●●●●●●●●●●

CALL CENTRE **0870 240 1010**   www.usitcampus.co.uk

ATOL 3839   51 BRANCHES NATIONWIDE...265 BRANCHES WORLDWIDE

Finding out more

There are Government of India Tourist offices in the state capitals, as well as State Tourist Offices (sometimes Tourism Development Corporations) in the major cities and a few important sites. They produce their own tourist literature, either free or sold at a nominal price, and some also have lists of city hotels and paying guest options. The quality of material is improving though maps handed out are often inadequate. Many offer tours of the city, neighbouring sights and overnight and regional packages. Some run modest hotels and mid-way motels with restaurants, and may also arrange car hire and guides. The staff in the regional and local offices are usually helpful.

Don't take advice from unofficial 'Tourist Offices' at airports or railway stations

Essentials

Language

Hindi, spoken as a mother tongue by over 400 million people, is India's official language. The use of English is also enshrined in the Constitution for a wide range of official purposes, notably communication between Hindi and non-Hindi speaking states. South India is the region of the Dravidian languages, a quite different language family from that of the Indo-European languages of North India. Each of the four states has its own dominant language, with its own distinctive script. Tamil, the oldest living language of India, reaches back over two thousand years and is spoken by 7% of India's population. Telugu (8.2%), the language of Andhra Pradesh, Kannada (4.2%), spoken in Karnataka, and Malayalam (3.5%) the seemingly unpronounceable language of Kerala to anyone other than a native Malayali speaker, each contribute to a rich cultural tradition of literature, poetry, song and film. In this Handbook many town names are written in the appropriate script as many place names on sign boards, buses and stations are only given in the regional script.

It is possible to study a number of Indian languages at language centres. Some are listed on page 547

Before you travel

Getting in

Virtually all foreign nationals require a visa to enter India. Nationals of Bhutan and Nepal only require a suitable means of identification. The rules regarding visas change frequently and arrangements for application and collection also vary from town to town so it is essential to check details and costs with the relevant office. These remain closed on Indian national holidays. In London, applications are processed in a couple of hours (0800-1200). Visitors from countries which do not have an Indian representation may apply to the resident British representative, or enquire at the *Air India* office. An application on the prescribed form should be accompanied by three passport photographs and your passport which should be valid three months beyond the period of the visit.

Documents
For overseas embassies & consulates, see page 19, & India tourist offices, see page 68

Visa fees vary according to nationality. In mid-2000 the following visa rules applied: **Transit** For passengers en route to another country. **Tourist** One month visa (entry must be within a month of issue), or six month visa, from the date of issue with multiple entry. Same fee. **Business** Up to one year from the date of issue. A letter from company giving the nature of business is required. **Five year** For those of Indian origin only, who have held Indian passports. **Student** Valid up to one year from the date of issue. Attach a letter of acceptance from Indian institution, and an AIDS test certificate. Allow up to three months for approval. **Visa extensions** Applications should be made to the Foreigners' Regional Registration Offices at New Delhi, Mumbai, Kolkata or Chennai, or an office of the Superintendent of Police in the District Headquarters. After 6 months, you must leave India and apply for a new visa – the Nepal office is known to be difficult.

Visas

Restricted & protected areas

Some areas are politically sensitive. The border regions, tribal areas and Himalayan zones are subject to restrictions and special permits may be needed to visit them though the government is relaxing its regulations.

In the south special permits are required for the following: **Andaman Islands** Permits are issued for 30 days to visit some of the islands on arrival at Port Blair, see page 192. **Lakshadweep Islands** Foreigners may visit Bangaram and Suheli Islands only; permits from the Lakshadweep Administration, Willingdon Island, Harbour Rd, Cochin 3.

No foreigner needs to **register** within the 180 day period of their tourist visa. All foreign visitors who stay in India for more than 180 days are required to get an **income tax clearance** exemption certificate from the Foreign Section of the Income Tax Dept in Delhi, Mumbai, Kolkata or Chennai.

Work permits

Foreigners should apply to the Indian representative in their country of origin for the latest information about work permits.

Liquor permits

Periodically some Indian states have tried to enforce prohibition. States which have some degree of prohibition in force are Gujarat, Mizoram and Manipur. When applying for your visa you can ask for an All India Liquor Permit. You can also get the permit from any Govt of India Tourist Office in Delhi or the state capitals.

What to take

Travel light. Most essentials are available in the larger cities, items are cheap and laundry services are generally speedy. Here are some items you might find particularly helpful in India:

Loose-fitting, light cotton **clothes** are good for travelling almost anywhere at any time of year, being cool and comfortable with the added advantage of being quick drying. Pale colours may give some protection against mosquitoes. Sarongs are useful – they can be used as a skirt, scarf, towel etc. Women should dress modestly. Brief shorts and tight vest tops are best avoided, though on the beach 'modest' swimwear is fine. Locally bought, inexpensive and cool *kurta pyjama* for men, and *shalwar kameez* for women are excellent options on the plains but it can be cold in the north between December and February and also everywhere at heights above 1,500 m, where some heavier clothing is essential. Comfortable shoes, sandals or trainers are essential and difficult to replace in India. Take high-factor sun screen and a sun hat.

It is best to take a sufficient supply of personal **medicines** from home, including inhalers and anti-malarial drugs (Proguanil is not available from pharmacists). For protection against mosquitoes, take *Mosiguard* repellent which is recommended by MASTA. Most **toiletries**, contact lens cleaners, tampons and barrier contraceptives are available in the larger cities.

Photocopies of essential **documents**, passport identification and visa pages, and spare photos are useful when applying for permits or in case of loss or theft.

Budget travellers Nets are not always provided in cheap hotels so try to take an impregnated mosquito net. Earplugs come in handy when a hotel room is particularly noisy, especially during festivals when loudspeakers playing film music tend to work overtime. On overnight journeys, blocking out the perpetual light is effective with eyeshades (given away by the airlines). Take a good padlock to secure your budget room too. A cotton, sheet sleeping bag which can cover a pillow, makes all the difference when you can't be sure of clean linen. Toilet paper, soap, towel and the washbasin plug may all be missing so be prepared.

Money matters

It can be difficult to use torn or very worn currency notes. Check notes carefully when you are given them and refuse any that are damaged.

A good supply of small denomination notes always comes in handy for bus tickets, cheap meals and tipping. Remember that if offered a large note, the recipient will never have any change!

Carry a few clean, new sterling or dollar notes for use where travellers' cheques and credit cards are not accepted.

Money

Prices in the handbook are quoted in Rupees, although top hotels often quote rates in US$. Very few people are familiar with international currencies apart from currency touts on city street corners. Visitors do best to think in Rupee terms.

Currency

Indian currency is the Indian Rupee (Re/Rs). It is **not** possible to purchase these before you leave. If you want cash on arrival it is best to get it at the airport bank. Rupee notes are printed in denominations of Rs 500, 100, 50, 20, 10. The Rupee is divided into 100 Paise. Coins are minted in denominations of Rs 5, 2, 1, and 50, 25, 20, 10 and 5 Paise, though coins below 50 paise are rarely seen. **NB** Carry money, mostly as TCs, in a money belt worn under clothing. Have a small amount in an easily accessible place.

Travellers' cheques

Travellers' cheques issued by reputable companies (eg Thomas Cook, American Express) are accepted without difficulty. Travellers' cheques nearly always have to be exchanged in banks or hotels, and can only very rarely be used directly for payment. Identification documents – usually a passport – need to be shown. Except in hotels, encashing travellers' cheques nearly always takes up to 30 minutes or longer, so it is worth taking larger denomination travellers' cheques and changing enough money to last for some days. Most banks, but not all, will accept US$ travellers' cheques. Many will also accept sterling so it is a good idea to carry some of each. Other major currency travellers' cheques are also accepted in some larger cities. A traveller warns that replacement of lost AmEx travellers' cheques may take weeks. If you are travelling to remote areas it can be worth buying Indian Rupee travellers' cheques from a major bank, as these are more widely accepted than foreign currency ones.

Credit cards

Major credit cards are increasingly acceptable in the main centres, though in smaller cities and towns it is still rare to be able to pay by credit card. Payment by credit card can sometimes be more expensive than payment by cash. **Visa** have a growing number of ATMs in major cities (see below), but many ATMs only deal with local account holders. It is however straightforward to obtain a cash advance against a credit card. Railway Reservation centres in 17 major cities are now taking payment for train tickets by Visa card which can be very quick as the queue is very short.

Changing money

The *State Bank of India* and several others in major towns are authorized to deal in foreign exchange. Some give cash against **Visa/Master cards** (eg *ANZ, Bank of Baroda* who print a list of their participating branches, *Andhra Bank*). **American Express** cardholders can use their cards to get either cash or travellers' cheques in the four major cities. They also have offices in Coimbatore, Goa, Hyderabad, and Thiruvananthapuram. The larger cities have **licensed money changers** with offices usually in the commercial sector. Changing money through unauthorized dealers is illegal. Premiums on the currency black market are very small and highly risky. Large **hotels** change money 24 hours a day for guests, but banks often give a substantially better rate of exchange than hotels.

Request some Rs 100 & 50 notes. If you cash sterling, always make certain that you have been given Rupees at the sterling & not at the dollar rate

Exchange rates

	Rs			Rs
Aus $	26.62		Japanese Yen	0.42
Dutch G	18.85		NZ $	20.71
Euro	41.57		Swiss Fr	26.85
French Fr	6.34		UK £	68.48
German DM	21.25		US $	45.77

It is best to get exchange on arrival at the airport bank or the Thomas Cook counter. Thomas Cook has a high reputation for excellent service. Many international flights arrive during the night, and it is generally far easier and less time consuming to change money at the airport than in the city.

You should be given a foreign currency **encashment certificate** when you change money through a bank or authorized dealer, ask for one if it is not automatically given. It allows you to change Indian Rupees back to your own currency on departure. It also enables you to use Rupees to pay hotel bills or buy air tickets for which payment in foreign exchange may be required. The certificates are only valid for three months.

Transferring money to India   *HKSB*, *Barclays* and *ANZ Grindlays* and others can make 'instant' transfers to their offices in India but charge a high fee (about US$30). *Standard Chartered Bank* issues US$ travellers' cheques. Sending a bank draft (up to US$1,000) by post (four to seven days by Speedpost) is the cheapest option.

Cost of living   The cost of living in India remains well below that in the West. The average wage is about Rs 10,000 per month (US$220) for government employees according to government statistics – manual workers, unskilled labourers (women are often paid less than men), farmers and others in rural areas earn considerably less.

Cost of travelling   Most food, accommodation and public transport, especially rail and bus, are exceptionally cheap. There is a widening range of moderately priced but clean hotels and restaurants outside the big cities, making it possible to get a great deal for your money. Budget travellers sharing a room, eating in local restaurants, and using the cheapest means of travel can expect to spend around Rs 420-500 (about US$10-12) a day, though you can each get by on less in the south. Those looking for the comfort of the occasional night in a simple a/c room, and using reserved seats on trains and luxury buses, should budget for about US$25-30 a day. However, if you travel alone and are looking for reasonably comfortable a/c rooms, use taxis and second class a/c train berths, expect to spend US$60-70 a day. When shopping or hiring an unmetered vehicle, bargaining is expected, and essential.

Getting there

Air

South India is accessible from virtually every continent. There are some direct flights from Europe and elsewhere in Asia to cities such as Chennai, Bangalore and Tiruvananthapuram, but it can be much cheaper to fly in via Mumbai or Delhi, which have far more international flights. At the end of 2000 the cheapest return flights to Chennai from London were around £600 ($900), while it was still possible to get return tickets at under £400 to Mumbai or Delhi, though internal flights can add an extra £100 (US$150) to that price to reach the far south. It is easy to fly to Chennai, Trichy or Tiruvananthapuram from Colombo, and costs under US$150. Singapore also has direct flights to Chennai and Bangalore. Some carriers permit 'open-jaw' travel, arriving in, and departing from, different cities in India. Some (eg *Air India, British Airways*) have convenient non-stop flights from Europe, from London to Delhi or Mumbai taking only nine hours, and to Chennai between 11 and 12 hours.

Charter flights Several tour operators from Europe, especially from Britain (eg *JMC, Jewel in the Crown, Manos, Somak, Tropical Places*) flying from Gatwick and Manchester, offer package holidays between October and April to Kerala and Goa. They are often exceptional value (especially in November and from mid-January to mid-March).

The following rules apply:
■ They are not available to Indian nationals.
■ The deal must include accommodation. If you take the cheap 'dorm house' option, it may be necessary to change to a more comfortable room. It may be difficult to find a room during the peak Christmas and New Year period so it is worth paying a little extra on booking, to ensure accommodation of a reasonable standard.
■ Officially, charter passengers can only stay for a maximum of 45 days, although this restriction can be bent somewhat if you have a valid visa to cover the duration of your proposed extension.

Stop-overs & Round-the-World tickets You can arrange several stop-overs in India on Round-the-World and long distance tickets. RTW tickets allow you to fly in to one and out from another international aiport. You may be able to arrange some internal flights using international carriers eg *Air India*, www.airindia.com sometimes allows stop-overs within India for a small extra charge.

Rajasthan–Kerala–Himalaya
Cultural and
Adventure Tours
Specialist, Individual and
Tailor-made tours arranged by
experts to all areas for all interests.

GATEWAY TO INDIA

Tel: 0044 (0)870 442 3204
Fax: 0044 (0)870 442 3205
Email:specialist-travel@gateway-to-india.co.uk

Agt for ATOL Holder
AETA W043X

Essentials

Essentials

Discounts	The cheapest fares from Europe tend to be with Central European, Central Asian or Middle Eastern airlines. You can also get good discounts from Australasia, Southeast Asia and Japan.
	If you plan to visit two or more South Asian countries within three weeks, you may qualify for a 30% discount on your international tickets. Ask your National Tourist office. International air tickets can be bought in India though payment must be made in foreign exchange.
Ticket agents	Companies dealing in volume and taking reduced commissions for ticket sales can offer better deals than the airlines themselves. The national press carry their advertisements. *Usit*, T0870-2401010, www.usitcampus.co.uk, *Campus* is good for students and have offices in several university cities. *Trailfinders* of London, T020-79383939, worldwide agencies; *STA*, in London, T020-79379962, T0870-1606070, www.statravel.co.uk with over 100 offices worldwide, offers special deals for under-26s; *Travelbag*, T01420-541007, www.travelbag. adventures.co.uk quotes competitive fares. **General Sales Agents** (GSAs) for specific airlines can sometimes offer attractive deals: *Jet Airways*, 188 Hammersmith Rd, London W6 7DJ, T020-89701500, for *Gulf Air, Kuwait Airways* etc; *Welcome Travels*, 58 Wells St, London W1P 3RA, T020-74363011, for *Air India*. *Orient International (Travels) Ltd*, 91 Charlotte Street, London W1P 1LB, T020-76371330, 76370037, F73239755, offer good discounts.
Airline security	International airlines vary in their arrangements and requirements for security, in particular the carrying of equipment like radios, tape-recorders, lap-top computers and batteries. Ring the airline in advance to confirm what their current regulations are. **Internal airlines often have different rules from the international carriers**. You are strongly advised not to pack valuables in your luggage. Avoid repacking at the airport.
From the UK, Continental Europe & the Middle East	The best deals are offered from the UK. You can pick up attractive deals on *Air India* which flies direct to Delhi and Mumbai throughout the year with direct connections to Chennai, Hyderabad, Bangalore, Thiruvananthapuram and other South Indian cities. A few European airlines (eg *Lufthansa, KLM*) and several from the Middle East (eg *Emirates, Gulf Air, Kuwait Airways, Royal Jordanian*) offer good discounts to Mumbai and some state capitals from London, but fly via their hub cities, so adding to the journey time. Good deals can be offered by **General Sales Agents** (GSAs), see above. Consolidators in UK quote competetive fares: *Bridge the world*, T020-79110900, www.b-t-w.co.uk *Flightbookers*, T020-77573000, www.ebookers.com *North South Travel*, T01245-492882 (profits to charity).
From Australasia via the Far East	*Qantas, Singapore Airlines, Thai Airways, Malaysian Airlines, Cathay Pacific* and *Indian Airlines* are the principal airlines connecting the continents. They fly to one of the Indian regional capitals. *STA* and *Flight Centres* offer discounted tickets from their branches in major cities in Australia and New Zealand. *Abercrombie & Kent, Adventure World, Peregrine*, and *Travel Corporation of India*, organize tours.
From North America	From the east coast, it is best to fly direct to India from New York via London by *Air India* (18 hours), or pick up a direct charter from UK to Goa or Thiruvananthapuram but this will usually involve a stopover in London. Discounted tickets on *British Airways, KLM, Lufthansa, Gulf Air* and *Kuwait Airways* are sold through agents although they will invariably fly via their country's capital cities. From the west coast, it is best to fly via Hong Kong, Singapore or Bangkok to Mumbai using one of those countries' national carriers. *Hari World Travels*, www.hariworld.com and *STA*, www.sta-travel.co.uk have offices in New York, Toronto and Ontario. Student fares are also available from *Council Travel*, www.counciltravel.com, with several offices in the USA and *Travel Cuts*, www.travelcuts.com, in Canada.

Sea

No regular passenger liners operate to India. A few cruise ships stop at some ports like Mumbai, Marmagao, Kochi and Chennai. Operators include *Swan Hellenic*, 77 New Oxford St, London WC1A 1PP, T020-7800 2200, reservations@swanhellenic.com

It is very unusual for foreign tourists to arrive by sea but shipping agents in Colombo (Sri Lanka) or Male (Maldives), may, in exceptional circumstances, allow passengers on their cargo boats to Tuticorin in Tamil Nadu.

From Sri Lanka & Maldives

Essentials

Touching down

Airport information

Tourists are allowed to bring in all personal effects 'which may reasonably be required', without charge. The official customs allowance includes 200 cigarettes or 50 cigars, 0.95 litres of alcohol, a camera with five rolls of film and a pair of binoculars. Valuable personal effects or professional equipment must be registered on a Tourist Baggage Re-Export Form (TBRE), including jewellery, special camera equipment and lenses, lap-top computers, sound and video recorders. These forms require the serial numbers of such equipment. It saves considerable frustration if you know the numbers in advance and are ready to show the serial numbers on the equipment. In addition to the forms, details of imported equipment may be entered into your passport. Save time by completing the formalities while waiting for your baggage. **It is essential to keep these forms** for showing to the customs when leaving India, otherwise considerable delays are very likely at the time of departure.

Duty free allowance
Some airports have duty free shops though the range of goods is very limited

There are no restrictions on the amount of foreign currency or travellers' cheques a tourist may bring into India. If you were carrying more than US$10,000 or its equivalent in cash or travellers' cheques you need to fill in a currency declaration form. This could change with a relaxation in the currency regulations. You may not take out Rs 500 notes into Nepal.

Currency regulations

The import of dangerous drugs, live plants, gold coins, gold and silver bullion and silver coins not in current use are either banned or subject to strict regulation. It is illegal to import firearms into India without special permission. Enquire at consular offices abroad for details.

Prohibited items

Export of gold jewellery purchased in India is allowed up to a value of Rs 2,000 and other jewellery (including settings with precious stones) up to a value of Rs 10,000. Export of antiquities and art objects over 100 years old is restricted. Ivory, skins of all animals, *toosh* and *pashmina* wool, snake skin and articles made from them are banned, unless you get permission for export. For further information enquire at the Indian High Commission or consulate, or access the Government of India at www.indiagov.org or the customs at konark.ncst.ernet.in/customs/

Export restrictions

The formalities on arrival in India have been increasingly streamlined during the last five years and the facilities at the major international airports greatly improved. However, arrival can still be a slow process. Disembarkation cards, with an attached customs declaration, are handed out to passengers during the inward flight. The immigration form should be handed in at the immigration counter on arrival. The customs slip will be returned, for handing over to the customs on leaving the baggage collection hall. The Immigration formalities can be very slow. You may well find that

Documentation & tax

Essentials

Touching down

Electricity 220-240 volts AC. Some top hotels have transformers. There may be pronounced variations in the voltage, and power cuts are common. Socket sizes vary so you are advised to take a universal adaptor (available at most airports). Many hotels even in the higher categories don't have electric razor sockets. During power cuts, diesel generators are often used in the medium and higher category hotels to provide power for essential equipment but this may not always cover air-conditioning.

Hours of business Banks: 1030-1430, Monday-Friday; 1030-1230, Saturday. Top hotels sometimes have a 24-hour service. **Post offices:** Usually 1000-1700, Monday-Friday; Saturday mornings.

Government offices: 0930-1700, Monday- Friday; 0930-1300, Saturday (some open on alternate Saturday only). **Shops:** 0930-1800, Monday-Saturday. Bazars keep longer hours. **NB** There are regional variations.

IDD 91. A double ring repeated regularly means it is ringing. Equal tones with equal pauses means engaged.

Official time GMT +5½ hours throughout the year (USA, EST +10½ hours).

Weights and measures The metric system has come into universal use in the cities. In remote rural areas local measures are sometimes used.

there are delays of over an hour in processing passengers passing through immigration who need help with filling forms.

Departure tax Rs 500 is payable for all international departures other than those to neighbouring SAARC countries, when the tax is Rs 250 (not reciprocated by Sri Lanka). This must be paid in Rupees in India unless it is included in your international ticket; check when buying. (To save time 'Security Check' your baggage before checking-in at Departure.)

Public transport to and from airport

Bus Chennai international airport has special bus services into the town centre from early morning to around midnight.

Pre-paid taxis
See detailed advice under international airports

Pre-paid taxis to the city are available at all major airports. Some airports have up to three categories, 'limousine', 'luxury' and ordinary. The first two usually have prominent counters, so you may have to insist if you want to use the standard service. Insist on being taken to your chosen destination even if the driver claims the city is unsafe or the hotel has closed down.

Tourist information

Disabled travellers India is not geared up specially for making provisions for the physically handicapped or wheelchair bound traveller. Access to buildings, toilets (sometimes 'squat' type), pavements, kerbs and public transport can prove frustrating, but it is easy to find people to give a hand with lifting and carrying. Provided there is an able-bodied companion to scout around and arrange help, and so long as you are prepared to pay for at least mid-price hotels or guest houses, private car-hire and taxis, India should be perfectly rewarding, even if in a somewhat limited way.

Some travel companies are beginning to specialize in exciting holidays, tailor-made for individuals depending on their level of disability. For those with access to the internet, a Global Access – Disabled Travel Network Site is www.geocities.

com/Paris/1502 It is dedicated to providing travel information for 'disabled adventurers' and includes a number of reviews and tips from members of the public. You might also want to read *Nothing Ventured*, editied by Alison Walsh (Harper Collins), which gives personal accounts of worldwide journeys by disabled travellers, plus advice and listings.

Indian law forbids homosexual acts for men (but not women) and carries a maximum sentence of life imprisonment. Although it is common to see young males holding hands in public, it doesn't necessarily indicate a gay relationship and is usually an expression of friendship.

Gay & lesbian travellers

Essentials

Full time students qualify for an ISIC (International Student Identity Card) which is issued by student travel and specialist agencies (eg *Usit, Campus, STA*) at home. A card allows certain travel benefits (eg reduced prices) and acts as proof of student status within India allowing ticket concessions into a few sites. For details contact *STIC* in Imperial Hotel, Janpath, New Delhi, T3327582. Those intending to study in India may get a one year student visa (see above).

Student travellers

Children of all ages are widely welcomed, being greeted with a warmth in their own right which is often then extended to those accompanying them. However, care should be taken when travelling to remote areas where health services are primitive since children can become more rapidly ill than adults. It is best to visit South India in the cooler months since you need to protect children from the sun, heat, dehydration and mosquito bites. Cool showers or baths help, and avoid being out during the hottest part of the day. Diarrhoea and vomiting are the most common problems, so take the usual precautions, but more intensively. Breastfeeding is best and most convenient for babies. In the big cities you can get safe baby foods and formula milk. It doesn't harm a baby to eat an unvaried and limited diet of familiar food carried in packets for a few weeks if the local dishes are not acceptable, but it may be an idea to give vitamin and mineral supplements. Wet wipes, always useful, are sometimes difficult to find in India as are disposable nappies. The biggest hotels provide babysitting.

Travelling with children
See also the health section, page 59

It is best to arrange voluntary work well in advance with organisations in South India, alternatively, contact an organisation abroad. In the UK: *International Voluntary Service*, St John's Centre, Edinburgh EH2 4BJ, or *VSO*, 317 Putney Bridge Rd, London SW15 2PN www.sci.ivs.org Students may spend part of their 'year off' helping in a school through 'GAP' or teach English through '1 to 1' Notre Dame SFC, St Mark's Ave, Leeds LS2 9BN. In the USA: *Council for International Programs* 1101 Wilson Blvd Ste 1708, Arlington, VA 22209. www.voluntarywork.org is an international directory of organizations.

Volunteering

Although it is relatively safe for women to travel around South India, most people find it an advantage to travel with a companion. Even so, privacy is rarely respected and there can be a lot of hassle, pressure and intrusion on your personal space, as well as outright harassment. If you are blonde, you are quite naturally likely to attract more attention. Some seasoned travellers find that dying their hair dark helps. See below and page 33.

Women travellers

Rules, customs and etiquette

Most travellers experience great warmth and hospitality in India. You may however, be surprised that with the warm welcome comes an open curiosity about personal matters. Total strangers on a train, for example, may ask for details about your job, income and family circumstances, or discuss politics and religion.

Essentials

 First impressions

On arrival at any of South India's major cities the first impressions can take you aback. The exciting images of an ancient and richly diverse culture which draw many visitors to India can be completely overwhelmed by the immediate sensations which first greet you. You need to be prepared for:

Pollution All the cities suffer from bad air pollution, especially from traffic fumes.

Noise Be prepared – radios, videos and loudspeakers seem to blare in unlikely places at all times of day and night.

Smells An almost baffling mixture of smells, from the richly pungent and unpleasant to the delicately subtle, assaults the nose.

Pressure From stepping out of the airport or hotel everybody seems to clamour to sell you their services. Taxi and rickshaw drivers are always there when you don't want them, much less often when you do. There often seems to be no sense of personal space or privacy. Young women are often stared at and sometimes touched.

Public hygiene – or lack of it. It is common to see people urinating in public places (eg roadside), and defecating in the open countryside. These can all be daunting and make early adjustment difficult. Even on a short visit you need to give yourself time and space to adjust!

Conduct Respect for the foreign visitor should be reciprocated by a sensitivity towards local customs and culture. How you dress is mostly how people judge you. Clean, modest clothes and a smile go a long way. Scanty, tight clothing draws unwanted attention. Nudity is not permitted on beaches in India and although there are some places where this ban is ignored, it causes widespread offence. Displays of intimacy are not considered suitable in public.

You may at times be justifiably frustrated by delays, bureaucracy and inefficiency, but displays of anger and rudeness will not achieve anything positive, and may in fact make things worse. We suggest you remain patient and polite. The concept of time and punctuality is also rather vague so be prepared to be kept waiting.

Courtesy It takes little effort to learn and use common gestures of courtesy but they are greatly appreciated by Indians. The **greeting** when meeting or parting, used universally among the Hindus across India, is the palms joined together as in prayer, sometimes accompanied with the word *namaste* (North and West), *namoshkar* (East) or *vanakkam* in Tamil. Muslims use the greeting *assalām aleikum*, with the response *waleikum assalām*, meaning 'peace be with you'; **"please"** is **mehrbani-se**; **"thank you"** is often expressed by a smile, or with the somewhat formal **dhannyabad**, **shukriya** (Urdu), and **nandri** in Tamil.

Hands & eating Traditionally, Indians use the right hand for eating, cutlery being alien at the table except for serving spoons. In rural India, don't expect table knives and forks though you might find small spoons. Use your right hand for giving, receiving, eating or shaking hands as the left is considered to be unclean since it is associated with washing after using the toilet.

Women Indian women in urban and rural areas differ in their social interactions with men. Certainly, to the westerner, Indian women may seem to remain in the background and appear shy when approached, often hiding their face and avoiding eye contact. Yet you will see them working in public, often in jobs traditionally associated with men in the West, in the fields, in construction sites or in the market place. Even from a distance, men should not photograph women without their consent.

Women do not, in general, shake hands with men since physical contact is not traditionally acceptable between acquaintances of the opposite sex. A westernized city woman, however, may feel free to shake hands with a foreign visitor. In traditional rural circles, it is still the custom for men to be offered food first, separately, so don't be surprised if you, as foreign guest (man or woman), are awarded this special status when invited to an Indian home, and never set eyes on your hostess.

Visitors to all religious places should be dressed in clean, modest clothes; shorts and vests are inappropriate. Always remove shoes before entering (and all leather items in Jain temples). Take thick socks for protection when walking on sun-baked stone floors. Menstruating women are considered 'unclean' and should not enter places of worship. **Visiting religious sites**

Non-Hindus are sometimes excluded from the inner sanctum of **Hindu** temples and occasionally even from the temple itself. Look for signs or ask. In certain temples, and on special occasions, you may only enter if you wear unstitched clothing such as a *dhoti*.

In **Buddhist** shrines, walk clockwise around shrines and stupas (keeping them to your right), and turn Buddhist prayer wheels in a clockwise direction.

In **Muslim** mosques, visitors should only have their face, hands and feet exposed; women should also cover their heads. Mosques may be closed to non-Muslims shortly before formal prayers.

Some temples have a register or a receipt book for **donations** which works like an obligatory entry fee. The money is normally used for the upkeep and services of the temple or monastery. In some pilgrimage centres, priests can become unpleasantly persistent. In general, if you wish to leave a donation, put money in the donation box; priests and Buddhist monks often do not handle money. It is also not customary to shake hands with a priest or monk. **Alms** *Sanyasis* (holy men), and some pilgrims, depend on gifts of money.

Beggars are often found in busy street corners in large Indian cities, as well as at bus and train stations where they often target foreigners for special attention. Visitors usually find this very distressing, especially the sight of severely undernourished children or those displaying physical deformity. You may be particularly affected when some persist on making physical contact. In the larger cities, beggars are often exploited by syndicates which cream off most of their takings. Yet those seeking alms near religious sites are another matter, and you may see Indian worshippers giving freely to those less fortunate than themselves, since this is tied up with gaining 'merit'. How you deal with begging is a matter of personal choice but it is perhaps better to give to a recognized charity than to make largely ineffectual handouts to individuals. **Begging**

Young children sometimes offer to do 'jobs' such as call a taxi, carry shopping or pose for a photo. You may want to give a coin in exchange. However, it is not helpful to hand out sweets, 'school pens' (which are often sold) and money indiscriminately to open-palmed children who tag on to any foreigner. Some visitors prefer to give fruit.

A pledge to donate a part of one's holiday budget to a local charity would be an effective formula for 'giving'. Some visitors like to support self-help co-operatives, orphanages, refugee centres, disabled or disadvantaged groups, or international charities like *Oxfam*, *Save the Children* or *Christian Aid* which work with local partners, by either making a donation or by buying their products. Some of these are listed under the appropriate towns. A few (which also welcome volunteers) are listed here. www//Indiacharitynet.com is useful. *Novartis*, T0044-616977200, novartis. foundations@group.novartis.com (sustainable development, leprosy). Oxfam, Sushil Bhawan, 210 Shahpur Jat, New Delhi 110049, T011-6491774; 274 Banbury Rd, Oxford OX2 7D2, UK, oxindia@giasdl01.vsnl.net.in (400 grassroots projects). *SOS Children's* **Charitable giving**

Essentials

Villages, A-7 Nizamuddin (W), New Delhi 110013, T011-4647835, www//pw2.netcom/ sanjayd/sos.html (over 30 poor and orphaned children's projects in India eg opposite Pital Factory, Jhotwara Rd, Jaipur 302016, T0141-322393).

Tipping A tip of Rs 10 to a bell-boy carrying luggage in a modest **hotel** (Rs 20 in a higher category) would be appropriate. In up-market **restaurants**, a 10% tip is acceptable when 'Service' is not already included, while in places serving very cheap meals, round off the bill with small change. Indians don't normally tip **taxi drivers** but a small extra amount over the fare is welcomed. **Porters** at airports and railway stations often have a fixed rate displayed but will usually press for more. Ask fellow passengers what the fair rate is – they will nearly always advise.

Photography Given the dusty conditions, a UV filter is best left on the lens permanently and a polarising filter can often give you stronger colours, better contrast and a bluer sky. Although good quality films are available in all major cities and tourist centres, it is best to take rolls of films from home and certainly any specialist camera batteries. In India, only buy films from a reputable shop since hawkers and roadside stalls may not be reliable; check the carton carefully as well as the expiry date.

Many monuments now charge a camera fee ranging from Rs 20 to Rs 50 for still cameras, and as much as Rs 500 for video cameras (more for professionals). Special permits are needed from the Archaeological Survey of India, New Delhi for using tripods and artificial lights. When photographing people, it is polite to first ask – they will usually respond warmly with smiles. Visitors often promise to send copies of the photos – don't unless you really mean to do so. Photography of airports, military installations, bridges and in tribal and 'sensitive border areas', is not permitted.

Safety

Personal security In general the threats to personal security for travellers in India are remarkably small. In most areas it is possible to travel either individually or in groups without any risk of personal violence. However, care is necessary in some places, and basic common sense needs to be used with respect to looking after valuables.

Some parts of South India are subject to political violence. A few areas are noted for banditry. However in the great majority of places visited by tourists, violent crime and personal attacks are extremely rare.

Theft Theft is not uncommon. It is best to keep travellers' cheques, passports and valuables with you at all times since you can't regard hotel rooms as automatically safe; even hotel safes don't guarantee secure storage. Avoid leaving valuables near open windows even when you are in the room. Use your own padlock in a budget hotel when you go out. Pickpockets and other thieves operate in the big cities. Crowded areas are particularly high risk. Take special care of your belongings when getting on or off public transport. Never accept food or drink from casual acquaintances. Travellers have reported being drugged and then robbed.

Confidence tricksters These are particularly common where people are on the move, notably around railway stations or places where budget tourists gather. A common plea is some sudden and desperate calamity; sometimes a letter will be produced in English to back up the claim. The demands are likely to increase sharply if sympathy is shown. See also page 52, shopping.

Security on trains It can be difficult to keep an eye on your belongings when travelling. Nothing of value should be left close to open train windows. First class a/c compartments are self-contained and normally completely secure. Second class a/c compartments, which have much to recommend them especially in the summer, are larger, allowing more movement of passengers but are not so secure. Attendants may take little notice of what is going on, so luggage should be chained to a seat for security overnight. Locks and chains are easily available at main stations and bazars.

If you have items stolen, they should be reported to the police as soon as possible. Keep a separate record of vital documents, including passport details and travellers' cheques numbers. Larger hotels will be able to assist in contacting and dealing with the police.

    Dealings with the police can be very difficult and in the worst regions such as Bihar even dangerous. The paperwork involved in reporting losses can be time consuming and irritating, and your own documentation (eg passport and visas) may be demanded. In some states the police themselves sometimes demand bribes, though tourists should not assume, however, that if procedures move slowly they are automatically being expected to offer a bribe. The **traffic police** are tightening up very hard on traffic offences in some places. They have the right to make on-the-spot fines for speeding and illegal parking. If you face a demand for a fine, insist on a receipt. If you have to go to a police station, try to take someone with you. If you face really serious problems, for example in connection with a driving accident, you should contact your consular office as quickly as possible. You should ensure you always have your International driving licence and motorbike or car documentation with you.

Police
Some states have introduced special Tourist Police to help the foreign traveller

Certain areas have become associated with foreigners taking drugs such as Goa's beaches, Kovalam (Kerala), Gokarna and Hampi (Karnataka). These are likely to attract local and foreign drug dealers but be aware that the government takes the misuse of drugs very seriously. Anyone charged with the illegal posession of drugs risks facing a fine of Rs 100,000 and a minimum 10 years imprisonment. Several foreigners have been imprisoned for drugs related offences in the last decade.

Drugs

There are some problems to watch out for and some simple precautions to take, to avoid both personal harassment and giving offence. Modest dress is always advisable: loose-fitting non-see-through clothes, covering the shoulders, and skirts, dresses or shorts of a decent length. Many find the *shalwar-kameez*-scarf ideal. In mosques women should be covered from head to ankle. Unaccompanied women are most vulnerable in major cities, crowded bazars, beach resorts and tourist centres where men may follow them and touch them. "Eve teasing" is the euphemism for physical harassment. If you are harassed, it can be effective to make a scene. As one woman traveller wrote, "they should not get away with it, and in many public places other people will quickly take your side". Be firm and clear if you don't wish to speak to someone. Some buses have seats reserved for women. Most railway booking offices have separate women's ticket queues or ask women to go to the head of the general queue. It is best to be accompanied at night, especially when travelling by rickshaw or taxi in towns. Be prepared to raise an alarm if anything unpleasant threatens. Women have reported that they have been molested while being measured for clothing in tailors' shop. If possible, take a friend with you.

Women travelling alone

It is better to seek advice on security from your own consulate than from travel agencies. Before you travel you can contact: British Foreign & Commonwealth Office, Travel Advice Unit, Consular Division, 1 Palace Street, London SW1E 5HE, UK, T020-72384503 (Pakistan desk T020-72702385), F020-72384545, www.fco.gov.uk/. US State Department's Bureau of Consular Affairs, Overseas Citizens Services, Room 4800, Department of State, Washington, DC 20520-4818, USA, T202-6474225, F-6473000, http://travel.state.gov/travel_warnings. html Australian Department of Foreign Affairs, Canberra, Austrailia, T06-62613305, www.dfat.gov.au/consular/advice.html Canadian official advice is on www.dfait-maeci.gc.ca/travelreport/menu_e.htm

Advice

Where to stay

South India has an enormously wide range of accommodation. You can stay safely and very cheaply by western standards in all four states. In all the major cities there are also high quality hotels, offering a full range of personal and business facilities. In small centres even the best hotels are far more variable. In the peak season (December to April for most of South India, May for the hill resorts) bookings can be extremely heavy in popular destinations. It is sometimes possible to book in advance by phone, fax or email either from abroad or in India itself. However, double check your reservation, and always try to arrive as early as possible in the day.

Hotels

Hotels in beach resorts and hill-stations, because of their location and special appeal, often deviate from the description of our different categories. Unmarried couples sharing hotel rooms usually causes no difficulty. Some cheaper hotels in India attracting tourists don't allow Indian guests in order to avoid 'unwanted harassment'.

Price categories The categories are based on prices of double rooms excluding taxes. They are **not** star ratings, and individual facilities vary considerably. Modest hotels may not have their own restaurant but will often offer 'room service', bringing in food from outside. Some restaurants may only serve vegetarian food. Many hotels operate a '24 hour check-out' system. Make sure that this means that you can stay 24 hours from the time of check-in.

Regional variation Expect to pay more in Mumbai, and to a lesser extent in Chennai and Bangalore for all categories. Prices away from large cities tend to be lower for comparable hotels. Away from the metropolitan cities, in South India, room rates tend to be lower than the North, and the standard of cleanliness is higher.

Off-season rates Large reductions are made by hotels in all categories out-of-season in many resort centres. Always ask if any is available. You may also request the 10% agent's commission to be deducted from your bill if you book direct. Clarify whether the agreed figure includes all taxes.

Taxes In general most hotel rooms rated at Rs 1,200 or above are subject to an expenditure tax of 10%. Many states levy an additional luxury tax of between 10 and 25%, and some hotels add a service charge of 10%. Taxes are not necessarily payable on meals, so it is worth settling the meals bill separately from the room bill. Most hotels in the **C** category and above accept payment by credit card. Check your final bill carefully. Visitors have complained of **incorrect bills**, even in the most expensive hotels. The problem particularly afflicts groups, when last-minute extras appear mysteriously on some guests' bills. Check the evening before departure, and keep all receipts.

Hotel facilities You have to be prepared for difficulties which are uncommon in the West. It is best to inspect the room and check that all equipment (a/c, TV, water heater, flush) works before checking in at a modest hotel.

Power supply In some states power cuts are common, or hot water may be restricted to certain times of day. The largest hotels have their own generators but it is best to carry a good torch.

Hotel categories

In category B hotels and above, you are likely to be charged in dollars and may have to pay in foreign currency. In category C and below it is usual to pay in Rupees.

***LL** and **L** ($150+) These are exceptional hotels. They are in the metropolitan cities or in exclusive locations such as a commanding coastal promontory, a lake island or a scenic hilltop, with virtually nothing to fault them. They have high class business facilities, specialist restaurants and well-stocked bars, several pools, sports.*

***AL** ($100-150) and **A** ($50-100) Most major towns have at least some in these categories which too reach high international standards but are less exclusive. Many quote an inflated 'dollar price' to foreigners.*

***B** ($25-50) Comfortable but not plush, choice of restaurants, pool, some have a gym. These are often aimed at the business client.*

***C** (Rs 750-1000) and **D** In many small towns the best hotel is in the **C** category, but they are not necessarily the best value. Some charge higher prices for a flash reception area, usually central a/c, restaurant, satellite TV, foreign exchange and travel desk. **D** (Rs 400-750) hotels often offer very good value though quality and cleanliness can vary widely. Most have some a/c rooms with bath, satellite TV, restaurants. **D** hotels may have some rooms in the **E** price range, so if you are looking for good but cheap accommodation, start here!*

***E** (Rs 200-400) Simple room with fan (occasionally air-cooler or a/c), often shared toilet and shower. May not have a restaurant or provide bed linen, towel etc. **F** (Under Rs 200) Very basic, shared toilet (often 'squat'), bucket and tap, variable cleanliness and hygiene. **E** and **F** category hotels are often in busy parts of town. They may have some rooms for under Rs 100, and dormitory beds for under Rs 50. (Some only have four or six beds.)*

Essentials

Air-conditioning (a/c) Usually, only category **C** and above have central a/c. Elsewhere a/c rooms are cooled by individual units and occasionally by large 'air-coolers' which can be noisy and unreliable. When they fail to operate tell the management as it is often possible to get a rapid repair done, or to transfer to a room where the unit is working. During power cuts generators may not be able to cope with providing air-conditioning. Fans are provided in all but the cheapest of hotels.

Heating Hotels in hill stations often supply wood fires in rooms. Usually there is plenty of ventilation, but ensure that there is always good air circulation, especially when charcoal fires are provided in a basket.

Toilets Apart from those in the **A** category and above, 'attached bath' does not necessarily refer to a bathroom with a bathtub. Most will provide a bathroom with a toilet, basin and a shower. In the lower priced hotels and outside large towns, a bucket and tap may replace the shower, and an Indian 'squat' toilet instead of a Western WC (squat toilets are very often the cleaner). Even mid-price hotels, which are clean and pleasant, don't always provide towels, soap and toilet paper.

Water supply In some regions water supply is rationed periodically. Keep a bucket filled to use for flushing the toilet during water cuts. Occasionally, tap water may be discoloured due to rusty tanks. During the cold weather and in hill stations, **hot water** will be available at certain times of the day, sometimes in buckets, but is usually very restricted in quantity. Electric water heaters may provide enough for a shower but not enough to fill a bath tub! For details on drinking water see page 50.

Essentials

Laundry can be arranged very cheaply (eg a shirt washed and pressed for Rs 10-20 in **C-D** category; Rs 50 in luxury hotels) and quickly in 12-24 hours. It is best not to risk delicate fibres, though luxury hotels can usually handle these and also dry-clean items.

Insects At some times of the year and in some places mosquitoes can be a real problem, and not all hotels have mosquito-proof rooms or mosquito nets. If you have any doubts check before confirming your room booking. In cheap hotels you need to be prepared for a wider range of insect life, including flies, cockroaches, spiders, ants and geckos (harmless house lizards). Poisonous insects, including scorpions, are extremely rare in towns. Hotel managements are nearly always prepared with insecticide sprays. Many small hotels in mosquito-prone areas supply nets. Remember to shut windows and doors at dusk. Electrical mat and pellets are now widely available, as are mosquito coils which burn slowly. Dusk and early evening are the worst times for mosquitoes so trousers and long-sleeved shirts are advisable, especially out of doors. At night, fans can be very effective in keeping mosquitoes off. A traveller recommends Dettol soap to discourage mosquitoes.

Service Where staff training is lacking, the person who brings up your cases may proceed to show you light switches, room facilities, TV tuning, and hang around waiting for a tip. Room boys may enter your room without knocking or without waiting for a response to a knock. Both for security and privacy, it is a good idea to lock your door when you are in the room. It is worth noting these failings in the comments book when leaving as the management may take action.

Noise Hotels close to temples can be very noisy, especially during festivals. Music blares from loudspeakers late at night and from very early in the morning, often making sleep impossible. Mosques call the faithful to prayers at dawn. Some find earplugs helpful.

Tourist 'Bungalows' The different State Tourism Development Corporations run their own hotels and hostels which are often located in places of special interest. These are very reasonably priced, though they may be rather dated, restaurant menus may be limited and service is often slow. Upkeep varies and in some states it is sadly well below standard.

Railway & airport retiring rooms Railway stations often have 'Retiring Rooms' or 'Rest Rooms' which may be hired for periods of between one and 24 hours by anyone holding an onward train ticket. They are cheap and simple though some stations have a couple of a/c rooms, which are often heavily booked. They are convenient for short stops, though some can be very noisy. Some major airports (eg Mumbai) have similar facilities.

Indian style hotels These, catering for Indian businessmen, are springing up fast in or on the outskirts of many small and medium sized towns. Most have some air-conditioned rooms and attached showers. They are variable in quality but it is increasingly possible to find excellent value accommodation even in remote areas.

Hostels The Department of Tourism runs 16 youth hostels, each with about 50 beds, usually organized into dormitory accommodation. The YHA also have a few sites all over India. Travellers may also stay in religious hostels (*dharamshalas*) for up to three days. These are primarily intended for pilgrims and are sometimes free, though voluntary offerings are welcome. Usually only vegetarian food is permitted; smoking and alcohol are not.

Camping Mid-price hotels with large grounds are sometimes willing to allow camping. Regional tourist offices have details of new developments. For information on YMCA camping facilities contact: *YMCA*, The National General Secretary, National Council of YMCAs of India, PB No 14, Massey Hall, Jai Singh Rd, New Delhi 1.

Getting around

Air

India has a comprehensive network linking the major cities of the different states. In addition to *Indian Airlines* (the nationalized carrier) www.nic.in/indianairlines and its subsidiary *Alliance Air*, there are several private airlines such as *Jet Airways* www.jetairways.com Competition from the efficiently run private sector has, in general, improved the quality of services provided by the nationalized airlines. The Airports Authorities too have made efforts to improve handling on the ground.

Although flying is expensive, for covering vast distances or awkward links on a route, it is an option worth considering, although delays and re-routing can be irritating. However, for short distances, and on some routes (eg Chennai to Trichy or Bangalore) it makes more sense to travel by train.

Air tickets All the major airlines are connected to the central reservation system and there are local travel agents who will book your tickets for a fee if you don't want to spend precious time waiting in a queue. Remember that tickets are in great demand in the peak season on some sectors so it is essential to get them months ahead. If you are able to pre-plan your trip, it is even possible to ask if the internal flights can be booked at the time you buy your international air ticket at home through an agent (eg *Trailfinders, SD Enterprises*, London) or direct (eg *Jet Airways*). You can also book internal flights on the internet, www.welcometravel.com and collect and pay for them on your arrival in India.

Payment Foreign passport holders buying air tickets in India must pay the 'US dollar rate' and pay in foreign exchange (major credit cards, travellers' cheques accepted), or in rupees against an encashment certificate which will be endorsed accordingly. There is very little difference in prices quoted by competing airlines.

Special fares *Indian Airlines*, www.nic.in/indian-airlines and *Jet Airways*, www.jetairways.com offer special 7, 15 and 21 day unlimited travel, deals from around US$300 to US$750 (some are limited to one sector) which represent good savings. **Youth fares** 25% discount is given on US$ fares for anyone between 12 and 30 years. **Night savers** 25% discount fares are being introduced on late night flights between some metropolitan cities.

Air travel tips **Security** Indian airlines don't permit batteries in cabin baggage, and once confiscated, you may never see your batteries again. You may need to identify your baggage after they have been checked in and just before they are loaded onto the plane.
Telephone There is a free telephone service at major airports (occasionally through the tourist office counter), to contact any hotel of your choice.
Wait-lists If you don't have a confirmed booking and are 'wait-listed' it pays to arrive early at the airport and be persistent in enquiring about your position.

Road

Road travel is often the only choice for reaching many of the places of outstanding interest in which India is so rich. For the uninitiated, travel by road can also be a worrying experience because of the apparent absence of conventional traffic regulations and also in the mountains, especially during the rainy season when landslides are possible. Vehicles drive on the left – in theory. Routes around the major cities are usually crowded with lorry traffic, and the main roads are often poor and slow. There are no motorways, and many main roads are single track. Some district

Essentials

Essentials

 Indian Airlines: approximate economy fares on popular routes

Sector	US$
From Ahmadabad to:	
Bangalore	205
Chennai	220
Hyderabad	155
From Bangalore to:	
Ahmadabad	205
Chennai	65
Cochin[3]	75
Delhi	235
Goa	95
Hyderabad	95
Kolkata[4]	240
From Bhubaneshwar to:	
Chennai	185
From Bhuj to:	
Mumbai	105

Sector	US$
From Kolkata[4] to:	
Port Blair	200
Visakhapatnam	135
From Calicut[2] to:	
Chennai	85
Mumbai	145
From Chennai to:	
Cochin[3]	110
Coimbatore	85
Delhi	240
Goa	130
Hyderabad	110
Madurai	85
Mangalore	100
Mumbai	150
Port Blair	200
Trichy	75
Trivandrum[1]	110

Sector	US$
From Cochin[3] to:	
Goa	115
Mumbai	155
From Coimbatore to:	
Bangalore	95
From Delhi to:	
Trivandrum[1]	330
From Goa to:	
Mumbai	95
From Hyderabad to:	
Mumbai	110
Nagpur	110
From Mangalore to:	
Mumbai	120
From Mumbai to:	
Trivandrum[1]	180
From Trivandrum to:	
Delhi	330
Mumbai	180

Alternative names:
[1] Thiruvananthapuram
[2] Kozhikode
[3] Kochi
[4] Calcutta

roads are quiet, and although they are not fast they can be a good way of seeing the country and village life if you have the time.

Bus Buses now reach virtually every part of South India, offering a cheap, if often uncomfortable means of visiting places off the rail network. Very few villages are now more than 2 or 3 km from a bus stop. Services are run by the State Corporation from the State Bus Stand (and private companies which often have offices nearby). The latter allow advance reservation and though tickets prices are a little higher, they have fewer stops and are a bit more comfortable.

There are three categories. **A/c luxury coaches**: though comfortable for sight-seeing trips, apart from the very best 'sleeper coaches', even these can be very uncomfortable for really long journeys. Journeys over 10 hours can be extremely tiring so it is better to go by train if there is a choice. **Express buses**: run over long distances (frequently overnight), these are often called 'video coaches' and can be an appalling experience unless you appreciate loud film music blasting through the night. Ear plugs and eye masks may ease the pain. They rarely average more than 45 km per hour. **Local buses**: these are often very crowded, quite bumpy and slow and usually poorly maintained. However, over short distances, they can be a very cheap, friendly and easy way of getting about. Even where signboards are not in English someone will usually give you directions. Many larger towns have **minibus** services which charge a little more than the buses and pick up and drop passengers on request. Again very crowded, and with restricted headroom, they are the fastest way of getting about many of the larger towns.

Bus travel tips Some towns have different bus stations for different destinations. Booking on major long-distance routes is now computerized. Book in advance and avoid the back of the bus where it can be very bumpy. If your destination is only served by a local bus you may do better to take the Express bus and 'persuade' the driver, with a tip in advance, to stop where you want to get off. You will have to pay the full fare to the first stop beyond your destination but you will get there faster and more comfortably.

A car provides a chance to travel off the beaten track, and give unrivalled opportunities **Car** for seeing something of India's great variety of villages and small towns. The most widely used hire car, the Hindustan Ambassador is often very unreliable, and although they still have their devotees, many find them uncomfortable for long journeys. For a similar price, Maruti cars and vans (Omni) are much more reliable. Gypsy 4WDs and Jeeps are also available, especially in the hills, where a few Sumos have made an appearance. Maruti Esteems are comfortable and have optional reliable a/c, so are recommended in the hot weather. A specialist operator can be very helpful in arranging itineraries and car hire in advance. Try *Andrew Brock*, 54 High St, Uppingham, LE5 9PZ, T/F01572-821072.

Car hire, with a driver, is often cheaper than in the West. A car shared by three or four can be very good value. Two or three-day trips from main towns can also give excellent opportunities for sightseeing off the beaten track in reasonable comfort. Local drivers often know their way much better than drivers from other states, so where possible it is a good idea to get a local driver who speaks the state language, in addition to being able to communicate with you. Drivers may sleep in the car overnight, though hotels sometimes provide a bed for them. They are responsible for all their expenses, including their meals. A tip at the end of the tour of Rs 100 per day in addition to their daily allowance is perfectly acceptable. Check beforehand if fuel and inter-state taxes are included in the hire charge.

Cars can be hired through private companies. International companies such as *Hertz*, *Europcar* and *Budget* operate in some major cities and offer reliable cars; their rates are generally higher than those of local firms (eg *Sai Service, Wheels*). The price of an imported car can be three times that of the Ambassador.

Car hire rates

Car with driver	Economy Maruti 800 Ambassador	Regular A/C Maruti 800 Ambassador	Premium A/C Maruti 1000 Contessa	Luxury A/C Esteem Opel etc
8 hrs/80 km	Rs 800	Rs 1,000	Rs 1,400	Rs 1,800+
Extra km	Rs 7	Rs 9	Rs 13	Rs 18
Extra hour	Rs 40	Rs 50	Rs 70	Rs 100
Out of town				
Per km	Rs 7	Rs 9	Rs 13	Rs 18
Night halt	Rs 160	Rs 200	Rs 250	Rs 250

Importing a car Tourists may import their own vehicles into India with a Carnet de Passage (Triptyques) issued by any recognized automobile association or club affiliated to the Alliance Internationale de Tourisme in Geneva.

Self-drive car hire is still in its infancy and many visitors may find the road conditions difficult and sometimes dangerous. If you drive yourself it is essential to take great care. Pedestrians, cattle and a wide range of other animals roam at will. This can be particularly dangerous when driving after dark especially as even other vehicles often carry no lights.

Essentials

The hazards of road travel

On most routes it is impossible to average more than 50-60 kph in a car. Journeys are often very long, and can seem an endless succession of horn blowing, unexpected dangers, and unforeseen delays. Villages are often congested – beware of the concealed spine-breaking speed bumps – and cattle, sheep and goats may wander at will across the road. Directions can also be difficult to find. Drivers frequently don't know the way, maps are often hopelessly inaccurate and map reading is an almost entirely unknown skill. Training in driving is negligible and the test often a farce. You will note a characteristic side-saddle posture, one hand constantly on the horn, but there can be real dangers from poor judgement, irresponsible overtaking and a general philosophy of 'might is right'.

When booking emphasize the importance of good tyres & general roadworthiness

Car travel tips Fuel: on main roads across India petrol stations are reasonably frequent, but some areas are poorly served. Some service stations only have diesel pumps though they may have small reserves of petrol. Always carry a spare can. Diesel is widely available and normally much cheaper than petrol. Petrol is rarely above 92 octane. **Insurance**: drivers must have third party insurance. This may have to be with an Indian insurer, or with a foreign insurer who has a national guarantor. **Asking the way**: can be very frustrating as you are likely to get widely conflicting advice each time you stop to ask. On the main roads, 'mile' posts periodically appear in English and can help. Elsewhere, it is best to ask directions often. **Accidents**: often produce large and angry crowds very quickly. It is best to leave the scene of the accident and report it to the police as quickly as possible thereafter. **Provisions**: ensure that you have adequate food and drink, and a basic tool set in the car.

The **Automobile Association** offers a range of services to members. **Mumbai**: Western India AA, Lalji Naranji Memorial Bldg, 76, Vir Nariman Rd; **Chennai**: AA of Southern India, 187 Anna Salai.

Taxis 'Yellow-top' taxis in cities and large towns are metered, although tariffs change frequently. These changes are shown on a fare chart which should be read in conjunction with the meter reading. Increased night time rates apply in some cities, and there is a small charge for luggage, insist on the taxi meter being 'flagged' in your presence. If the driver refuses, the official advice is to call the police. This may not work, but it is worth trying. When a taxi doesn't have a meter, you will need to fix the fare before starting the journey. Ask at the hotel desk for a guide price.

Taxi tips At stations and airports it is often possible to share taxis to a central point. It is worth looking for fellow passengers who may be travelling in your direction and get a pre-paid taxi. At night, always have a clear idea of where you want to go and insist on being taken there. Taxi drivers may try to convince you that the hotel you have chosen 'closed three years ago', is 'completely full' or is an 'unsafe den'. You may have to say that you have an advance reservation. See individual city entries for more details.

Rickshaws
It is best to walk a short distance away from a hotel gate before picking up an auto to avoid paying an inflated rate

Auto-rickshaws ('autos') are almost universally available in towns across India and are the cheapest convenient way of getting about. In addition to using them for short journeys it is often possible to hire them by the hour, or for a half or full day's sight-seeing. In some areas younger drivers who speak some English and know their local area well, may want to show you around. However, rickshaw drivers are often paid a commission by hotels, restaurants and gift shops, so advice is not always impartial. Drivers sometimes refuse to use a meter, quote a ridiculous price or attempt to stop short of your destination. If you have real problems it can help to threaten to go to the police.

Cycle-rickshaws and horse-drawn tongas These are more common in the more rustic setting of a small town or the outskirts of a large one. You will need to fix a price by bargaining. The animal attached to a tonga usually looks too undernourished to have the strength to pull the driver, leave alone passengers.

Cycling is an excellent way of seeing the quiet by-ways of India and particularly enjoyable if you travel with a companion. It is easy to hire bikes in most small towns for about Rs 15-20 per day. Indian bikes are heavy and without gears, but on the flat they offer a good way of exploring comparatively short distances outside towns. It is also quite possible to tour more extensively and you may then want to buy a cycle.

Cycling

Buying a bicycle There are shops in every town and the local Raleighs are considered the best, with Atlas and BSA good alternatives; expect to pay around Rs 1,200-1,500 for a second-hand Indian bike but remember to bargain. At the end of your trip you can usually sell it quite easily at half that price. Imported bikes have the advantage of lighter weight and gears, but are more difficult to get repaired, and carry the much greater risk of being stolen or damaged. If you wish to take your own, it is quite easy if you dismantle it and pack it in its original shipping carton; be sure to take all essential spares including a pump. All cyclists should take bungy cords (to strap down a backpack) and good lights from home; take care not to leave your machine parked anywhere with your belongings though. Bike repair shops are universal and charges are nominal.

It is possible to cover 50 to 80 km a day quite comfortably – "the National Highways are manic but country roads, especially along the coast, can be idyllic, if rather dusty and bumpy". You can even put your bike on a boat for the backwater trip or on top of a bus. Should you wish to take your bike on the train, allow plenty of time for booking it in on the brake van at the Parcels office, and for filling in forms.

It is best to start a journey early in the morning, stop at mid-day and resume cycling in the late afternoon. Night-riding, though cooler, can be hazardous because of lack of lighting and poor road surfaces. Try to avoid the major highways as far as possible. Fortunately foreign cyclists are usually greeted with cheers, waves and smiles and truck drivers are sometimes happy to give lifts to cyclists (and their bikes). This is a good way of taking some of the hardship out of cycling round India.

Motorcycling is particularly attractive for bike enthusiasts. It is easy to buy new Indian-made motorcycles including the Enfield Bullet and several 100cc Japanese models, including Suzukis and Hondas made in collaboration with Indian firms. Buying new ensures greater reliability and fixed price – (Indian Rajdoots are less expensive but have a poor reputation for reliability). Buying second hand in Rupees takes more time but is quite possible; expect to get a 30-40% discount. You can get a broker to help with the paper-work involved (certificate of ownership, insurance etc) for a fee. They charge about Rs 5,000 for a 'No Objection Certificate' (NOC) which is essential for reselling; it is easier to have the bike in your name.

Motorcycling
See under Car & Cycling above for general advice

When selling, don't be in a hurry, and only negotiate with "ready cash" buyers. A black bike is easier to sell than a coloured one! Repairs are usually easy to arrange and quite cheap. Bring your own helmet and an International Driving Permit.

Peter and Friends Classic Adventures, an Indo-German company based in Goa at Casa Tres Amigos, Socol Vado 425, Assagao (4 km west on Anjuna road), T0832-273351, F276124, runs organized motorbike tours in Goa, Rajasthan, Himachal Pradesh and South India ranging from four days to three weeks. They also hire out Enfield motorbikes in Goa (US$120-US$165/week). Tours with full back up are also offered by Royal Enfield Motors, Chennai, T0445-43300, F543253: South India (about US$1,200-1,600 for 14 days). For expert advice contact Cyclists' Touring Club, Cotterel House, 69 Meadowgrow, Godalming, Surrey, UK, T01483-417217.

Essentials

 On the road on a motorbike

An experienced motorbiker writes: unless you bring your own bike (Carnet de passage, huge deposit) the only acceptable machine is the legendary Enfield Bullet 350 or 500 cc. Humming along the Indian roads or tracks this lovely four stroke classic machine is a must. Also available in diesel version (1.5 litres per 100 km and much cheaper fuel) the 500 cc is much better for travelling with luggage and easier to take home as brakes and 12v lights conform with EC regulations.

Expect a cruising speed of around 60 kph. Riding above 80 gets very tiring due to the lack of silent blocks and the nerve-wracking Indian roads. A good average distance is 200 km per day. Riding at night furthers the excitement – practise at home on a death race video first, but bear in mind that accidents can turn into a first-hand lynching experience! If you stop, prepare to settle quickly in cash, but while third party insurance is cheap (Rs 53 per year!) refunds are less than guaranteed.

Buying You can now find good helmets at a fraction of the European price (Studds Rs 300-Rs 2,000 for a full face type), also goggles, sturdy panniers and extras. A Bullet will cost from Rs 25,000 to Rs 40,000 second hand, or Rs 50,000-Rs 60,000 new.

Allow plenty of time to shop around.

Papers Many Indians and tourists don't bother changing the name on the ownership papers. If you are driving through more than one state this is rash, as it is essential to have the papers in your name, plus the NOC (No Objection Certificate) from the Motor Vehicles Department if you intend to export the vehicle home. Regardless of the dealer's assertions to the contrary, demand the NOC as otherwise you will have to apply for it in the state of origin. You have to allow 15 days.

Spares Before buying, negotiate the essential extras: mirrors, luggage carriers, better saddle, battery. Spares are cheap and readily available for the 350cc model. Take along a spare throttle and clutch cable, a handful of nuts and bolts, puncture repair kit and pump or emergency canister so you don't have to leave the bike unattended while hitching a lift to the nearest puncture wallah – and of course a full set of tools. Check the oil level daily. Finally, remember that for long distances you can load your bike on a night train (Rs 100 per 100 km). Just turn up at the parcel office with an empty petrol tank at least two hours before departure.

Hitchhiking Hitchhiking is uncommon in India, partly because public transport is so cheap. If you try, you are likely to spend a very long time on the roadside. However, getting a lift on motorbikes/scooters and on trucks in areas with little public transport can be worthwhile. It is not recommended for women on their own.

Train

Trains can still be the cheapest and most comfortable means of travelling long distances saving you hotel expenses on overnight journeys. It gives access to booking station Retiring Rooms, which can be useful from time to time. Above all, you have an ideal opportunity to meet local travellers and catch a glimpse of life on the ground although the dark glass fitted on a/c coaches does restrict vision.

High-speed trains There are several air-conditioned 'high-speed' *Shatabdi* (or 'Century') for day travel, and *Rajdhani Express* ('Capital City') for overnight journeys which connect major South Indian cities. As these are in high demand you need to book them well in advance – up to 60 days. Meals and drinks are usually included.

Riding the rails

High class, comfortable, and by Indian standards fast Express trains have brought many journeys within daytime reach. But while they offer an increasingly functional means of covering long distances in comfort, it is the overnight trips which still retain something of the early feel of Indian train travel. The bedding carefully prepared – and now available on a/c Second Class trains – the early morning light illuminating another stretch of hazy Indian landscape, the spontaneous conversations with fellow travellers – these are still on offer, giving a value far beyond the still modest prices. Furthermore, India still has a complete guide to its rail timetables. The Trains at a Glance available at stations (Rs 25) lists all important trains.

For rail enthusiasts, the steam-hauled narrow-gauge trains between Mettupalayam **Steam** and Coonoor, and a special one between Ooty and Runnymede in the Nilgiris, are an attraction. *Williams Travel*, 18/20 Howard St, Belfast, BT1 6FQ, Northern Ireland, T01232-329477, and *SD Enterprises* (address below) are recommended for tailor-made trips.

A/c First Class, available only on main routes and cheaper than flying, is very **Classes** comfortable (bedding provided). It will also be possible for tourists to reserve special coaches (some a/c) which are normally allocated to senior railway officials only. *A/c Sleeper* two and three-tier, are clean and comfortable and good value. *A/c Executive Class*, with wide reclining seats are available on many *Shatabdi* trains at double the price of the ordinary *a/c Chair Car* which are equally comfortable. *2nd Class* (non-a/c) two and three-tier, provides exceptionally cheap travel but can be crowded and uncomfortable, and toilet facilities can be unpleasant. It is nearly always better to use the Indian style toilets as they are better maintained.

These allow travel across the network without having to pay extra reservation fees **Indrail passes** and sleeper charges but you have to spend a high proportion of your time on the train to make it worthwhile (see boxes). However, the advantages of pre-arranged reservations and automatic access to 'Tourist Quotas' can tip the balance in their favour for some travellers.

Tourists (foreigners and Indians resident abroad) may buy these passes for periods ranging from seven to 90 days from the tourist sections of principal railway booking offices, and pay in foreign currency, major credit cards, travellers' cheques or rupees with encashment certificates. Rail-cum-air tickets are also to be made available.

Indrail passes can also conveniently be bought abroad from special agents. For most people contemplating a single long journey soon after arriving in India, the Half or One day Pass with a confirmed reservation is worth the peace of mind; 2 or 4 Day Passes are also sold. The **UK** agent is *SD Enterprises Ltd*, 103, Wembley Park Drive, Wembley, Middx HA9 8HG, England, T020-89033411, F89030392, dandpani@dircon.co.uk They make all necessary reservations and offer excellent advice. They can also book *Indian Airlines* and *Jet Airways* internal flights.

Other **international agents** are: Australia: *Adventure World*, PO Box 480, North Sydney NSW 2060, T9587766, F9567707. **Bangladesh**: *Omnitrans International*, National Scouts Bhavan, 4th Flr, 70/1 Inner Circular Rd, Kakrail Dhaka, T9121053057, **Canada**: *Hari World Travels*, 1 Financial Place, 1 Adelaide St East, Concou Level, Toronto, T3662000, F3666020. **Denmark**: *Danish State Railways*, DSW Travel Agency Div, Reventlowsgade – 10, DK 1651 Kobenhaven V. **Finland**: *Intia-Keskus*, Yrjonkatu 8-10, 00120 Helsinki, Finland, T46856-266000, F100946. **France**: *Le Monde de L'Inde et de L'Asie*, 15 Rue Des Ecoles, Paris 75005. **Germany**: *Asra-Orient*, Kaiserstrasse 50, D-6000

Shatabadi Expresses

No	From	To	Days	Dep	Arr	One-way Fare (Rs)	
						Chair Car	Exec
2023	Chennai C	Coimbatore	Daily (ex W)	1510	2200	675	1,335
2024	Coimbatore	Chennai C	Daily (ex W)	0725	1410	"	"
2007	Chennai C	Mysore	Daily (ex Tu)	0600	1300	630	1,270
2008	Mysore	Chennai C	Daily (ex Tu)	1410	2115	"	"
2035	Chennai C	Tirupati	Daily	0545	0815	400	800
2036	Tirupati	Chennai C	Daily	1945	2215	"	"
2033	Raja	Sec	Daily	0500	1200	650	1335
2034	Sec	Raja	Daily	1740	0040	"	"

M = Monday; **Tu** = Tuesday; **W** = Wednesday; **Th** = Thursday; **F** = Friday; **Sa** = Saturday; **Su** = Sunday; **ex** = except

C = Central; **Chennai** = Madras; **Haora** = Howrah (Kolkata [Calcutta]); **Mumbai** = Bombay; **ND** = New Delhi; **Raja** = Rajahmundry; **Sec** = Secunderabad

Frankfurt/M, T069253098, F69232045, asra-orient@t-online-d **Hong Kong:** *Cheung Hung*, B1&2 Carnarvon Mansion, 12 Carnarvon Rd,Tisimshatsui, Kowloon, Hong Kong, T852-2369-5333, F2739-9899. **Israel:** *Teshet*, 32 Ben Yehuda St, Tel Aviv 63805, T6290972, F6295126. **Japan:** *Japan Travel Bureau*, Overseas Travel Div, 1-6-4 Marunouchi, Chiyoda-ku, Tokyo-100, T031-284739. **Malaysia:** *City East West Travels*, 23 Jalan Yapah Shak, 50300, Kuala Lumpur, T2930569, F2989214. **Oman:** *National Travel & Tourism* , PO Box 962, Muttrah, Muscat, T968566046, T968566125. **South Africa:** *MK Bobby Naidoo*, PO Box 2878, Durban, T3094710. **Thailand:** *SS Travel*, 10/12-13 Convent Rd, SS Building, Bangkok, T2367188, F2367186. **UAE:** *Sharjah National Travels*, PO Box 17, Sharjah, T/F97165- 374968. **USA:** *Hari World Travels*, 25W 45th St, 1003, New York, NY 10036, T9573000, F9973320.

A White Pass allows first class a/c travel; a Green, a/c two-tier Sleepers and Chair Cars; and the Yellow, only second class travel. Special half and one day passes are only sold abroad.

Cost A/c first class costs about double the rate for two-tier shown below, and non a/c second class about half. Children (five to 12) travel at half the adult fare. The young (12-30) and senior citizens (65+) are allowed a 30% discount on journeys over 500 km (just show passport).

Period	A/c 2-tier US$	Period	A/c 2-tier US$
½ day	26	21 days	198
1 day	43	30 days	248
7 days	135	60 days	400
15 days	185	90 days	530

Fares for individual journeys are based on distance covered and reflect both the class and the type of train. Higher rates apply on the Mail and Express trains and the air conditioned *Shatabdi* and *Rajdhani Expresses*.

Rajdhani Trains

No	From	To	Days	Dep	Arr	Fare (Rs)[1] 2-Tier	3-Tier
2434	HN	Chennai	W, F	1530	2005**	3,335	2,045
2433	Chennai	HN	F, Su	1100	0630**	"	"
2432	HN	Trivandrum	W, Th	1100	0610**	4,235	2,765
2431	Trivandrum	HN	F, Sa	1915	1350**	"	"
2430	HN	Bangalore	M, Sa	2050	0655**	3,470	2,205
2429	Bangalore	HN	M, W	1835	0505**	"	"
2438	HN	Secunderabad	Su	1530	1330*	2,795	1,665
2437	Secunderabad	HN	M	1920	1645*	"	"

M = Monday; *Tu* = Tuesday; *W* = Wednesday; *Th* = Thursday; *F* = Friday; *Sa* = Saturday;
Su = Sunday; *ex* = except

C = Central; *Chennai* = Madras; *HN* = Hazrat Nizamuddin (N Delhi) Station;
Haora = Howrah (Kolkatta [Calcutta]); *Mumbai* = Bombay (also Chair Car);
ND = New Delhi Station; *Trivandrum* = Thiruvananthapuram

Sat = 2424 terminates in Dibrugarh at 2030

Wt = 2423 originates in Dibrugarh

[1] = First class fares are about 70-80% higher than 2-Tier

* Next day ** Third day

Rail travel tips

Food and drink: it is best to carry some though tea and snacks are sold on the platforms (through the windows). On long distance trains, the restaurant car is often near the upper class carriages (or bogies) as they are still called in India.

Timetables: regional timetables are available cheaply from station bookstalls; the monthly 'Indian Bradshaw' is sold in principal stations, while the handy 'Trains at a Glance' (Rs 25) lists popular trains likely to be used by most foreign travellers.

Delays: always allow time for booking and for making connections. Delays are common on all types of transport.

Tickets: you can save a lot of time and effort by asking a travel agent to get yours for a small fee. Non-Indrail Pass tickets can be bought over the counter. It is always best to book as far in advance as possible (usually up to 60 days). Avoid touts at the station offering tickets, hotels or money changing.

Ladies' queues: separate (much shorter) ticket queues may be available for women.

Credit cards: some main stations now have separate credit card booking queues – even shorter than women's queues!

Quotas: a large number of seats are technically reserved as 'quotas' for various groups of travellers (civil servants, military personnel, foreign tourists etc). In addition, many stations have their own quota for particular trains so that a train may be 'fully booked' when there are still some tickets available from the special quota of other stations. These are only sold on the day of departure so wait-listed passengers are often able to travel at the last minute. Ask the Superintendent on duty to try the 'Special' or 'VIP Quota'.

Reservations: ask for the separate Tourist Quota counter at main stations, and while queuing fill up the Reservation Form which requires the number, name, departure time of the train, and the passenger's name, age and sex; you can use one form for up to four passengers. If you don't have a reservation for a particular train but carry an Indrail Pass, you may get one by arriving about three hours early.

Porters: carry prodigious amounts of luggage. Rates vary from station to station but are usually around Rs 5 per item of luggage (board on the station platform). They can be quite aggressive particularly on the main tourist routes: be firm but polite and remember that they will always leave the train when it pulls out of the station!

Getting a seat: it is usually impossible to make seat reservations at small 'intermediate' stations as they don't have an allocation. You can sometimes use a porter to get you a seat in a 2nd class carriage. For about Rs 20 he will take the luggage and ensure that you get a seat!

Main railways

Note: indications about gauges are approximate

—— Broad gauge

- - - Metre gauge

········ Mountain railway

Adilabad A2	Erode C2	Latur A2	Parli Vaijnath A1	Tirunelveli C2
Arsikere B1	Gadag B1	Lonavla A1	Pondicherry B2	Tirupati B2
Arkonam B2	Giddalur B2	Londa B1	Pune A1	Tiruvarur C2
Bagalkot A1	Gudur B2	Madgaon/Margao B1	Puri A3	Vasco da Gama B1
Bangalore B2	Guntakal B2	Madurai C2	Purna A2	Vijayawada A2
Belgaum A1	Hassan B1	Manamadurai C2	Rajahmundry A3	Vikarabad A2
Bellary B2	Hospet B1	Mangalore B1	Rameswaram C2	Villupuram C2
Berhampur A3	Hubli B1	Masulipatnam A2	Ranigunta B2	Virudhunagar C2
Bijapur A1	Hyderabad A2	Matheran A1	Sagar Talguppa B1	Vishakapatnam A3
Birur B1	Jolarpettai B2	Miraj A1	Salem B2	Vizianagaram A3
Chamrajnagar B1	Kanniyakumari C2	Mudkhed A2	Secunderabad A2	Vriddhachalam C2
Chennai B2	Karwar B1	Mumbai A1	Shoranur C1	Wadi A2
Coimbatore C2	Katpadi B2	Mysore B1	Solapur A1	Waltair A3
Dhond A1	Kirandul A3	Nasik A1	Talguppa B1	Warangal A2
Dharmavaram B2	Kochi C1	Nasik Road A1	Tenkasi C2	
Dindigul C2	Kodangalur C2	Neral A1	Thanjavur C2	
Dronachallam B2	Kolhapur A1	Ooty C1	Thiruvananthapuram C1	
Ernakulam C1	Kollam C1	Parbhani A2	Tiruchirapalli C2	

Train touts

Many railway stations – and some bus stations and major tourist sites – are heavily populated with touts. Self-styled 'agents' will board trains before they enter the station and seek out tourists, often picking up their luggage and setting off with words such as "Madam!/Sir! Come with me madam/sir! You need top class hotel ..." They will even select porters to take your luggage without giving you any say. If you have succeeded in getting off the train or even in obtaining a trolley you will find hands eager to push it for you. For a first time visitor such touts can be more than a nuisance. You need to keep calm and firm. Decide in advance where you want to stay. If you need a porter on trains, select one yourself and agree a price **before** the porter sets off with your baggage. If travelling with a companion one can stay guarding the luggage while the other gets hold of a taxi and negotiates the price to the hotel. It sounds complicated, and sometimes it feels it. The most important thing is to behave as if you know what you are doing!

Essentials

Berths: it is worth asking for upper berths, especially in second class three-tier sleepers, as they can also be used during the day time when the lower berths are used as seats, and which may only be used for lying down after 2100.

Overbooking: passengers with valid tickets but no berth reservations are sometimes permitted to travel overnight, causing great discomfort to travellers occupying lower berths.

Bedding: travelling at night in the winter can be very cold in North India and in a/c coaches. Bedding is provided on second class a/c sleepers. On others it can be hired for Rs 30 from the Station Baggage Office for second class.

Ladies' compartments: a woman travelling alone, overnight, on an unreserved second class train can ask if there is one of these.

Security: keep valuables close to you, securely locked, and away from windows. For security, carry a good lock and chain to attach your luggage.

Left-luggage: bags left in station cloakrooms must be lockable. Don't leave any food in them.

Pre-paid taxis: many main stations have a pre-paid taxi (or auto-rickshaw) service which offers a reliable, fair-price service.

Keeping in touch

Internet Access is becoming increasingly available in major cities as cyber cafés mushroom and PCOs (Public Call Office) are beginning to offer the service, but in small towns the machines can be woefully slow. Alternatively, you can ask a large hotel or a travel agent if they will allow you to use their system.

Post The post is frequently unreliable, and delays are common. It is advisable to use a post office where it is possible to hand over mail for franking across the counter, or a top hotel post box. Valuable items should only be sent by **Registered Mail**. Government Emporia or shops in the larger hotels will send purchases home if the items are difficult to carry. **Airmail** service to Europe, Africa and Australia takes at least a week and a little longer for the Americas. **Speed post** (which takes about four days to the UK) is available from major towns. Specialist shippers deal with larger items, normally approximately US$150 per cubic metre. **Courier services** (eg *DHL*) are available in the larger towns. At some main post offices you can send small packages under 2 kg as Letter Post (rather than parcel post) which is much cheaper at Rs 220. 'Book Post' (for printed paper) is cheaper still, approximately Rs 170 for 5 kg. Book parcels must be sewn in cloth (best over see-through plastic) with a small open 'window' slit for contents to be seen.

The email explosion

As the internet shrinks the world, travellers are increasingly using emails to keep in touch with home. Their free accounts are invariably with **hotmail.com**, **yahoo.com**, **email.com** or **backpackers.com**; usually the less common the provider, the quicker the access.

India has its own set of problems which can be frustrating: very few machines which may also be out-dated; untrained staff and poor technical support; the server may be unreliable; the system may be clogged with users, especially during day; there may be frequent power cuts ... There are exceptions, of course.

New offices are opening weekly and new towns are getting connected. To track down the most reliable and best value internet service, ask other travellers. The length of the queue can be a good indicator. On the web, you can get a list from **www.netcafeguide.com**. Don't always head for the cheapest since they may also have the oldest and slowest equipment. Rates vary, but in 2000, it cost around Rs 50 for 30 minutes.

Hot Tips

Use the folder facility to save mail

Keep your in-box clear to reduce loading time

Avoid junk mail by not giving your address to on-line companies

Avoid downloading and using scanned pictures and documents

Save files and back up regularly

The system can be efficient and satisfying but it can also become an expensive habit with more than its fair share of frustrations. As one sending an email to us mused, "many a hard-up traveller will wax lyrical about 'getting away from it all' and escaping 'the pressure of western society'. They will then spend hours and several hundred rupees a week slaving over a computer keyboard in some hot and sticky back street office".

Parcels The process can take up to two hours. Check that the post office holds necessary customs declaration forms (two/three copies needed). Write 'No commercial value' if returning used clothes, books etc. Air mail is expensive; sea mail slow but reasonable (10 kg, Rs 800). 'Packers' outside post offices will do all necessary cloth covering, sealing etc for Rs 20-50; you address the parcel, obtain stamps from a separate counter; stick stamps and one customs form to the parcel with glue available (the other form/s must be partially sewn on). Post at the Parcels Counter and obtain a Registration slip. **Maximum dimensions:** height 1 m, width 0.8 m, circumference 1.8 m. Cost: sea mail, about Rs 775 for first kilogram, Rs 70 each extra kilogram. Air mail also Rs 775 first kilogram, Rs 200 each subsequent kilogram.

Warning Many people complain that private shops offering a postal service actually send cheap substitutes. It is usually too late to complain when the buyer finds out. It is best to buy your item and then get it packed and posted yourself.

Poste restante facilities are widely available in even quite small towns at the GPO where mail is held for one month. Ask for mail to be addressed to you with your surname in capitals and underlined. When asking for mail at Poste Restante check under surname as well as Christian name. Any special issue foreign stamps are likely to be stolen from envelopes in the Indian postal service and letters may be thrown away. Advise people who are sending you mail to India to use only definitive stamps (without pictures).

Best short-wave frequencies

BBC World service: *Signal strength varies throughout the day, with lower frequencies better during the night. The nightly "South Asia Report" offers up to the minute reports covering the sub-continent. Try 15310, 17790 or 1413, 5975, 11955, 17630, 17705. More information on www.bbc.uk/worldservice/sasia*

Voice of America: *1400-1800 GMT; 1575, 6110, 7125, 9645, 9700, 9760, 15255,15395 Mhz. www.voa.gov/sasia*

Deutsche Welle: *0600-1800 GMT; 6075, 9545, 17845; other frequencies include 17560, 12000 and 21640.*

Essentials

International Direct Dialling is now widely available in privately run call 'booths', usually labelled on yellow boards with the letters 'PCO-STD-ISD'. You dial the call yourself, and the time and cost are displayed on a computer screen. They are by far the best places from which to telephone abroad. Cheap rate (2100-0600) means long queues may form outside booths. Telephone calls from hotels are usually much more expensive (check price before calling).

Telephone
International code: 00 91. Phone codes for towns are printed after the town name

Ringing tone: double ring, repeated regularly; **Engaged**: equal length, on and off. Both are similar to UK ringing and engaged tones.

One disadvantage of the tremendous pace of the telecommunications revolution is the fact that millions of telephone numbers go out of date every year. Current telephone directories themselves are often out of date and some of the numbers given in the Handbook will have been changed even as we go to press. Directory enquiries, **197**, can be helpful but works only for the local area code.

Fax services are available from many PCOs and larger hotels, who charge either by the minute or per page.

Newspapers International newspapers (mainly English language) are sold in the bookshops of top hotels in major cities, and occasionally by booksellers elsewhere. India has a large English language press. They all have extensive analysis of contemporary Indian and some international issues. The major papers now have internet sites which are excellent for keeping daily track on events, news and weather. The best known are *The Hindu*, www.hinduonline.com/today/. *The Hindustan Times* www.hindustantimes.com *The Independent, The Times of India* www.timesofindia.com/, and *The Statesman* www.thestates man.org/ *The Economic Times* is possibly the best for independent reporting and world coverage. *The Telegraph* published in Kolkata, www.telegraphindia.com/, has good foreign coverage. The *Indian Express* www.expressindia.com/ has stood out as being consistently critical of the Congress Party and Government. *The Asian Age* is now published in the UK and India simultaneously and gives good coverage of Indian and international affairs. Of the fortnightly magazines, some of the most widely read are *Sunday, India Today* and *Frontline*, all of which are current affairs journals on the model of *Time* or *Newsweek*. To check weather conditions, try www.wunderground.com

Media

Television and radio India's national radio and television network, *Doordarshan*, broadcasts in national and regional languages but things have moved on. The advent of satellite TV has hit even remote rural areas. The 'Dish' can help travellers keep in touch through Star TV from Hong Kong (accessing BBC World, CNN etc), VTV (music) and Sport, now available even in some modest hotels in the smallest towns.

Food and drink

Food
See footnotes for a food glossary

You find just as much variety in dishes and presentation crossing South India as you would on an equivalent journey across Europe. Combinations of spices give each region its distinctive flavour.

The larger hotels, open to non-residents, often offer **buffet** lunches with Indian, Western and sometimes Chinese dishes. These can be good value (Rs 250-300; but around Rs 450 in the top grades), and can provide a welcome, comfortable break in the cool. The health risks, however, of food kept warm for long periods in metal containers are considerable, especially if turnover at the buffet is slow. We have received several complaints of stomach trouble following a buffet meal, even in five star hotels.

It is essential to be very careful since food hygiene may be poor, flies abound and refrigeration in the hot weather may be inadequate and intermittent because of power cuts. It is best to eat only freshly prepared food by ordering from the menu (especially meat and fish dishes); avoid salads and cut fruit.

If you are unused to spicy food, go slow! Stick to Western or mild Chinese meals in good restaurants, and try the odd Indian dish to test your reaction. Those used to Indian spices may choose to be more adventurous. Popular local restaurants are obvious from the number of people eating in them. Try a traditional *thali*, which is a complete meal served on a large stainless steel plate (or very occasionally on a banana leaf). Several preparations, placed in small bowls, surround the central serving of wholewheat *chapati* and rice. A vegetarian *thali* would include *daal* (lentils), two or three curries (which can be quite hot), and crisp poppadums, although there are regional variations. A variety of pickles are offered – mango and lime are two of the most popular. These can be exceptionally hot, and are designed to be taken in minute quantities alongside the main dishes. Plain *dahi* (yoghurt) usually acts as a bland 'cooler'.

Western food Many city restaurants offer some so-called European options such as toasted sandwiches, stuffed pancakes, apple pies, crumbles and cheese cakes. Italian favourites (pizzas, pastas) can be very different from what you are used to. Western confectionery, in general, is disappointing. Ice creams, on the other hand, can be exceptionally good (there are excellent Indian ones as well as international brands such as *Cadbury's* and *Walls*).

Fruit India has many delicious tropical fruits. Some are highly seasonal (eg mangoes, pineapples and lychees), while others (eg bananas, grapes, oranges) are available throughout the year. It is safe to eat the ones you can wash and peel.

Drink
Drinking water used to be regarded as one of India's biggest hazards. It is still true that water from the tap or a well should never be considered safe to drink since public water supplies are often polluted. Bottled water is now widely available although not all bottled water is mineral water; some is simply purified water from an urban supply. Buy from a shop or stall, check the seal carefully (some companies now add a second clear plastic seal around the bottle top) and avoid street hawkers; when disposing bottles puncture the neck which prevents misuse but allows recycling for storage. There is growing concern over the mountains of plastic bottles that are collecting and the waste of resources to produce them, so travellers are encouraged to use alternative methods of getting safe drinking water. In some towns purified water is now sold for refilling your own container. Travellers may wish to purify water themselves (see above). A portable water filter is a good option, carrying the drinking water in a plastic bottle in an insulated carrier. Always carry enough drinking water with you when travelling. It is important to use pure water for cleaning teeth.

A cup of chai!

Not long ago, when you stopped at a road side tea stall nearly anywhere in India and asked for a cup of chai, the steaming hot sweet tea would be poured out into your very own, finely handthrown, beautifully shaped clay cup! Similarly, whenever a train drew into a railway station, almost any time of day or night, and you heard the familiar loud call of "chai garam, garam chai!" go past your window, you could have the tea served to you in your own porous clay cup.

True, it made the tea taste rather earthy but it added to the romance of travelling. Best of all, when you had done with it, you threw it away and it would shatter to bits on the road side (or down on the railway track) – returning 'earth to earth'. It was

the eco-friendly "disposable" cup of old – no question of an unwashed cup which someone else had drunk out of, hence unpolluted and 'clean'. And, of course, it was good business for the potter.

But, time moves on, and we have now advanced to tea stalls that prefer thick glass tumblers (which leave you anxious when you glance down at the murky rinsing water). A step ahead – those catering for the transient customer now offer the welcome hot chai in an understandably convenient, light, hygienic, easy-to-stack, thin plastic cup which one gets the world over, sadly lacking the biodegradability of the earthen pot. With the fast disappearing terracotta cup we will lose a tiny bit of the magic of travelling in India.

Essentials

Hot drinks Tea and coffee are safe and widely available. Both are normally served sweet, and with milk. If you wish, say 'no sugar' (*chini nahin*), 'no milk' (*dudh nahin*) when ordering. Alternatively, ask for 'Set Tea' for a pot of tea, milk and sugar brought separately; a 'Full Set' with four cups, a 'Half Set' with two. Freshly brewed coffee is a common drink in South India. Even in aspiring smart cafés, *Espresso* or *Capuccino* may not turn out quite as one would expect in the West.

Soft drinks Bottled carbonated drinks such as 'Coke', 'Pepsi', 'Teem' and 'Gold Spot' are universally available but always check the seal when you buy from a street stall. There are now also several brands of fruit juice sold in cartons, including mango, pineapple and apple. Don't add ice cubes as the water source may be contaminated.

Alcohol Indians rarely drink alcohol with a meal, water being on hand. In the past wines and spirits were generally either imported and extremely expensive, or local and of poor quality. Now, the best Indian whisky, rum and brandy (IMFL or 'Indian Made Foreign Liquor') are widely accepted, as are good Champagnoise and other wines from Maharashtra. If you hanker after a bottle of imported wine, you will only find it in the top restaurants and have to pay Rs 800-1,000 at least.

For the urban elite, cooling Indian beers are popular when eating out and so are widely available, though you may need to check the 'chill' value. The 'English Pub' has appeared in the major cities, where the foreign traveller too would feel comfortable. Elsewhere, seedy, all male drinking dens in the larger cities are best avoided. Head for the better hotel bar instead. In rural India, local rice, palm, cashew or date juice *toddy* and *arak* should be treated with great caution.

Most states have alcohol free 'dry' days, or enforce degrees of Prohibition. For 'dry' states and Liquor Permits, see page 22. Some up-market restaurants may serve beer even if it's not listed so it's worth asking.

Essentials

 Two masala dosai and a pot of tea!

A traveller reported that a hotel bar prohibition has had some unexpected results. One traveller to Ooty reported that the hotel bar had closed for good. He found however that it was still possible to obtain alcoholic drinks from the restaurant. Having ordered and been served a beer, he was intrigued that when the bill came it was made out for "2 masala dosai". The price was, of course, correct for the beer!

Another traveller found that a well-known hotel also appeared to have been forced to adapt its attitude to serving alcohol to the prevailing laws. Asked in the early evening for a double whisky the barman was very happy to comply until he was asked to serve it in the garden. On being told that he could only drink it in the bar the visitor expressed great disappointment, on which the barman relented, whispering that if the visitor really wanted to drink it outside he would serve it to him in a tea pot!

If you are thirsting for alcohol in a prohibitionist area perhaps you need to order two masala dosai and a pot of tea.

Shopping

India excels in producing fine crafts at affordable prices through the tradition of passing down of ancestral skills. You can get handicrafts of different states from the government emporia in the major cities which guarantee quality at fixed prices (no bargaining), but many are poorly displayed, not helped by reluctant and unenthusiastic staff. Private upmarket shops and top hotel arcades offer better quality, choice and service but at a price. Vibrant and colourful local bazars (markets) are often a great experience but you must be prepared to bargain.

Bargaining Bargaining can be fun and quite satisfying. It is best to get an idea of prices being asked by different stalls for items you are interested in, before taking the plunge. Some shopkeepers will happily quote twice the actual price to a foreigner showing interest, so you might well start by halving the asking price. On the other hand it would be inappropriate to do the same in an established shop with price-tags, though a plea for the "best price" or a "special discount" might reap results even here. Remain good humoured throughout. Walking away slowly might be the test to ascertain whether your custom is sought and you are called back!

The country is a vast market place but there are regional specializations. If you are planning to travel widely, wait to find the best places to buy specific items. Export of certain items is controlled or banned (see page 27).

Carpets & dhurries The handicrafts of India are widely available across the four southern states. The superb hand-knotted carpets of Kashmir, using old Persian designs woven in wool or silk or both, are hard to beat for their beauty and quality. Kashmiri traders can now be found throughout India, wherever there is a hint of foreign tourism. Agra too has a long tradition of producing wool carpets and welcomes visitors to their factories. Tibetan refugees in Karnataka produce excellent carpets which are less expensive but of very high quality.

Jewellery Whether it is chunky tribal necklaces from the Himalaya, heavy 'silver' bangles from Rajasthan, fine Orissan filigree, legendary pearls from Hyderabad, Jaipuri uncut gems set in gold or semi-precious stones in silver, or glass bangles from Varanasi, the visitor is drawn to the arcade shop window as much as the way-side stall. It is best to buy from reputable shops as street stalls often pass off fake ivory, silver, gems, stones and coral as real.

The choice is vast – from brass, copper and white-metal plates and bowls in the North, **Metal work** with ornate patterns or plain polished surfaces, exquisite Jaipuri enamelled silver pill boxes, tribal lost-wax *dhokra* toys from Orissa, Bihar and Bengal, Nawabi silver-on-gun metal Bidri pieces from around Hyderabad, to exceptional copies of Chola bronzes cast near Thanjavur.

Coveted contemporary Indian art is exhibited in modern galleries in the state capitals **Paintings** often at a fraction of London or New York prices. Traditional 'Mughal' miniatures, sometimes using natural pigments on old paper (don't be fooled) and new silk, are reaching mass production levels in Rajasthan's back alleys. Fine examples can still be found in good crafts shops (eg Taj hotels' *Khazanas*, Central Cottage Industries).

Artisans in Agra inspired by the Taj Mahal continue the tradition of inlaying tiny pieces **Stoneware** of gem stones on fine white marble, to produce something for every pocket, from a small coaster to a large table top. Softer soap stone is cheaper. Stone temple carvings are produced for sale in Tamil Nadu (try Mahabalipuram), Orissa (Puri, Konark) and Uttar Pradesh (near Hamirpur).

Handlooms produce rich shot silk from Kanchipuram, skillful *ikat* from Gujarat, Orissa **Textiles** and Andhra, brocades from Varanasi, golden *muga* from Assam, printed silks and batiks from Bengal or opulent *Himroo* shawls from Aurangabad. *Sober* handspun *khadi*, colourful Rajasthani block-printed cottons using vegetable dyes, tribal weaving from remote Himalayan villages, and tie-and-dye Gujarati *bandhni* are easier on the pocket. Kashmiri embroidery on wool, Lucknowi *chickan* shadow work on fine voil or *zari* (gold/silver thread) work on silk, produce unique pieces.

Each region has its special wood – walnut in Kashmir, sandalwood in Mysore, rosewood **Wood craft** in the South, sheesham in the North. Carving, inlay and lacquer work are specialities.

Taxi/rickshaw drivers and tour guides sometimes insist on recommending certain **Pitfalls** shops where they expect a commission, but prices there are invariably inflated. Some shops offer to pack and post your purchases but small private shops can't always be trusted. Unless you have a specific recommendation from a person you know, only make such arrangements in government emporia or a large store. Don't enter into any arrangement to help 'export' marble items, jewellery etc which a shopkeeper may propose by making tempting promises of passing on some of the profits to you. Several have been cheated through misuse of their credit card accounts, and being left with unwanted purchases. Make sure that credit cards are not run off more than once when making a purchase.

Holidays and festivals

Every month is brightened by the riot of colour, sound and feasting that mark religious **Festivals for** or seasonal festivals. These usually follow the lunar calendar, so are movable feasts. **all seasons** They offer the visitor a chance to experience the region's rich heritage of traditional customs, music, dance and folk theatre.

In Tamil Nadu, *Pongal*, celebrated at Makar Sankranti (14th January), is a thanksgiving for a good harvest. A sweet milk and 'first rice' dish is prepared and the cattle are specially honoured. Decorated with brightly painted horns, they are festooned with balloons and garlands of flowers and paraded along town and village roads accompanied by bands of rustic musicians and cheering children.

Essentials

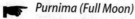

Purnima (Full Moon)

Many religious festivals depend on the phases of the moon. Full moon days are particularly significant and can mean extra crowding and merrymaking in temple towns throughout India, and are sometimes public holidays.

In Kerala, the magnificent eight-day *Pooram* at Thrissur in April-May, is a grand spectacle staged by rival temples with elaborately decorated elephants with golden ornaments and carrying glittering parasols which are joined by skilled drummers and horn players and magnificent displays of fireworks. The summer harvest festival is *Thiruvonam* (*Onam*) in August-September which is marked with grand elephant processions, Kathakali dances, fireworks and the famous Snake Boat races in some coastal towns along the backwaters.

In common with the rest of India, some major Hindu and Muslim festivals have their place in the the south too. Particularly spectacular are *Dasara* in October which celebrates the triumph of Good over Evil, and Diwali, the striking festival of lights which follows soon after on the dark night of the new moon, when the night sky bursts out with spectacular displays of fire works. In Karnataka, *Mahanavami* in October is marked with great pomp during its spectacular *dasara* celebrations at the Mysore palace and at Chamundi Hill.

The Hindu Calendar
For the Hindu & the corresponding Gregorian calendar months, see page 538

Hindus follow two distinct eras: The *Vikrama Samvat* which began in 57 BC and the *Salivahan Saka* which dates from 78 AD and has been the official Indian calendar since 1957. The *Saka* new year starts on 22 March and has the same length as the Gregorian calendar. In most of South India, the New Year is celebrated in the first month, *Chaitra* (corresponding to March-April). However, in Tamil Nadu it is celebrated in the second month of *Vaishakh*. The 29½ day lunar month with its 'dark' and 'bright' halves based on the new and full moons, are named after 12 constellations, and total a 354 day year. The calendar cleverly has an extra month (*adhik maas*) every two and a half to three years, to bring it in line with the solar year of 365 days coinciding with the Gregorian calendar of the West. The year is divided into six seasons: *Vasant* (spring), *Grishha* (summer), *Varsha* (rains), *Sharat* (early autumn), *Hemanta* (late autumn) and *Shishir* (winter).

Some major national and regional festivals are listed below; details of these and others appear under the particular state or town. A few count as national holidays: **26 January**: *Republic Day*; **15 August**: *Independence Day*; **2 October**: *Mahatma Gandhi's Birthday*; **25 December**: *Christmas Day*.

Major festivals & fairs

1 January *New Year's Day* is accepted officially when following the Gregorian calendar but there are regional variations which fall on different dates, often coinciding with spring/harvest time in March and April: *Ugadi* in Andhra and *Vishu* in Kerala. **January 14** *Makar Sankranti* marks the end of winter and is celebrated with kite flying. **26** *Republic Day Parade*.

February *Vasant Panchami*, the Spring (Vasant) festival when people wear bright yellow clothes to mark the advent of the season with singing, dancing and feasting.

February-March *Maha sivaratri* marks the night when Siva danced his celestial dance of destruction (*Tandava*) celebrated with feasting and fairs at Siva temples, but preceded by a night of devotional readings and hymn singing. Orthodox Saivites fast during the day and offer prayers every three hours; devotees who remain awake through the night believe they will win the Puranic promise of prosperity and salvation. Carnival – Goa. Spectacular costumes, music and dance, float processions and feasting mark the three day event.

March *Holi*, the festival of colours, marks the climax of spring. Although this festival is celebrated more widely in North India it is also commonly enjoyed in parts of the south. The previous night bonfires are lit in parts of North India symbolizing the end of winter (and conquering of evil). People have fun throwing coloured powder and water at each other and in the evening some gamble with friends. If you don't mind getting covered in colours, you can risk going out but celebrations can sometimes get rowdy. Some link the festival to worship of Kama the god of pleasure; some worship Krishna who defeated the demon Putana.

April/May *Buddha Jayanti*, the first full moon night in April/May marks the birth of the Buddha. Celebrations are held in several parts of the country. *International Spice Festival* – Kochi (Cochin), Kerala. *Pooram* – Thrissur, Kerala.

July/August *Raksha (or Rakhi) Bandhan* (literally 'protection bond') commemorates the wars between *Indra* (the King of the Heavens) and the demons, when his wife tied a silk amulet around his wrist to protect him from harm. The festival symbolizes the bond between brother and sister, celebrated mainly at full-moon. A sister says special prayers for her brother and ties coloured (silk) threads around his wrist to remind him of the special bond. He in turn gives a gift and promises to protect and care for her. Sometimes *rakshas* are exchanged as a mark of friendship. *Narial Purnima* on the same full-moon. Hindus particularly in coastal areas of South India make offerings of *narial* (coconuts) to the Vedic god Varuna (Lord of the waters) by throwing them into the sea. **15 August** *Independence Day*, a national secular holiday. In cities it is marked by special events. *Ganesh Chaturthi*, unlike most Hindu festivals, was established just over 100 years ago by the Indian nationalist leader Tilak. The elephant-headed God of good omen is shown special reverence. On the last of the five-day festival after harvest, clay images of Ganesh (Ganpati) are taken in procession with dancers and musicians, and are immersed in the sea, river or pond.

August/September *Janmashtami*, the birth of Krishna is celebrated at midnight at Krishna temples.

September/October *Dasara* has many local variations. In parts of South India, celebrations for the nine nights *(navaratri)* are marked with *Ramlila*, various episodes of the Ramayana story (see section on Hinduism, page 532) are enacted and recited, with particular reference to the battle between the forces of good and evil. In some parts of India it celebrates *Rama*'s victory over the Demon king *Ravana* of Lanka with the help of loyal *Hanuman* (Monkey). Huge effigies of *Ravana* made of bamboo and paper are burnt on the 10th day (*Vijaya dasami*) of *Dasara* in public open spaces. In other regions the focus is on Durga's victory over the demon *Mahishasura*. *Onam* – Kerala.

October/November 2 October *Gandhi Jayanti*, Mahatma Gandhi's birthday is remembered with prayer meetings and devotional singing. Diwali/Deepavali (from the Sanskrit Dipa lamp, the festival of lights, is celebrated in Karnataka and other parts of South India. Some Hindus celebrate Krishna's victory over the demon Narakasura, some Rama's return after his 14 years' exile in the forest when citizens lit his way with earthen oil lamps (see also page 542). If the festival is properly celebrated it is believed that gods may visit the earth. It falls on the dark *chaturdasi* (14th) night (the one preceding the new moon), when rows of lamps or candles are lit in remembrance, and *rangolis* are painted on the floor as a sign of welcome. Fireworks have become an integral part of the celebration which are often set off days before Diwali. Equally, Lakshmi, the Goddess of Wealth (as well as Ganesh) is worshipped by merchants and the business community, who open the new year's account on the day. Most people wear new clothes; some play games of chance.

25 December *Christmas Day*, Indian Christians celebrate the birth of Christ in much the same way as in the West; many churches hold services/mass at midnight. There is an air of festivity in city markets which are specially decorated and illuminated. **December** *New Year's Eve* In Kerala specially designed and brightly lit paper stars decorate homes for a month before the festival. Some churches mark the night with a *Midnight Mass. Hampi-Vijaynagar Festival* – Karnataka.

Muslim holy days These are fixed according to the lunar calendar, see page 541. According to the Gregorian calendar, they tend to fall 11 days earlier each year, dependent on the sighting of the new moon.

Ramadan Start of the month of fasting when all Muslims (except young children, the very elderly, the sick, pregnant women and travellers) must abstain from food and drink, from sunrise to sunset.

Id ul Fitr (**28 December 2000**) The three-day festival marks the end of Ramadan.

Id-ul-Zuha/Bakr-Id Muslims commemorate Ibrahim's sacrifice of his son according to God's commandment; the main time of pilgrimage to Mecca (the Hajj). It is marked by the sacrifice of a goat, feasting and alms giving.

Muharram when the killing of the Prophet's grandson, Hussain, is commemorated by Shi'a Muslims. Decorated *tazias* (replicas of the martyr's tomb) are carried in procession by devout wailing followers who beat their chests to express their grief. Hyderabad is famous for their grand *tazias*. Shi'as fast for the 10 days.

Entertainment

Despite an economic boom in cities like Chennai, Hyderabad and Bangalore and the rapid growth of a young business class, India's night life remains meagre, focused on club discos in the biggest hotels. In Goa, beach raves and parties, which usually take place in make-shift venues, continue to attract large groups of foreigners particularly during Christmas and the New Year. However the Government has threatened to close down these venues, and the beaches may soon be silenced. More traditional, popular entertainment is widespread across Indian villages in the form of folk drama, dance and music, each region having its own styles, and open air village performance being common. The hugely popular local film industry comes largely out of this tradition. It's always easy to find a cinema, but prepare for a long sitting with a standard story line and set of characters and lots of action. See also pages 58 and 555 for spectator sports.

Sport and special interest travel

Adventure sports familiar in Europe or the US are still rare in South India. Despite the great lengths of sandy beach surfing is unheard of, though there are some good swimming beaches. The hills of the Western Ghats offer excellent walking and treks.

Bird watching South India is wonderfully rich in bird life. Visitors can enjoy spotting Oriental species whether it is in towns and cities, in the country side or more abundantly in the national parks and sanctuaries. There are spectacular sanctuaries for migrating birds, such as Vedanthangal in Tamil Nadu or Ranganathittoo in Karnataka, but every village tank is home to a wide variety of local and migratory birds.

A Birdwatcher's Guide to India by Krys Kazmierczak and Raj Singh, published by Prion Ltd, Sandy, Bedfordshire, UK, 1998, is well researched and comprehensive with helpful practical information and maps.

There has been a growing Western interest in the ancient life-disciplines in search of **Yoga &** physical and spiritual wellbeing, as practised in ancient India. Yoga is supposed to **mediatation** regulate the nervous system and aims to attain perfect equilibrium through the practice of *asanas* (body postures), breath control, discipline, cleansing, contemplation and awareness. It seeks to achieve moral purification through abstinence and restraint (dietary and sexual). Meditation which complements yoga to relieve stress, increase awareness and bring inner peace prescribes *dhyana* (purposeful concentration) by withdrawing oneself from external distractions and focusing ones attention to consciousness itself, which leads ultimately to *samadhi* (release from worldly bonds). At the practical level *Hatha Yoga* has captured the Western imagination as it promises good health through postural exercises, while the search for inner peace and calm drive others to learn meditation techniques.

Centres, especially in Kerala, offer courses for beginners and practitioners. Some are at special resort hotels which offer all inclusive packages in idyllic locations, some advocate simple communal living in an ashram while others may require rigorous discipline in austere monastic surroundings. Whether you wish to embark on a serious study of yoga or sample an hour's introductory meditation session, India offers opportunities for all, though you may need to apply in advance for some popular courses.

Cycling offers a peaceful – not to mention healthy – alternative to cars, buses or trains. **Cycling** Touring on locally hired bicycles is possible along country roads in many parts of South India – ideal if you want to see village life and the lesser known wildlife parks. Consult a good Indian agent for advice.

For those keen on moving faster along the road, discover the joys of travelling on the **Biking** two wheels of a motorbike (preferably a 'Bullet'). See page 41.

Sun, sand and warm waters for safe swimming are not the only attractions along the **Watersports** long stretches of unspoilt coastal India. Select beaches in Goa, and the crystal clear waters around the Andamans and the Laccadive islands, are excellent for diving. Snorkelling is possible more widely, as well as parasailing, wind surfing and water skiing. The scuba diving centres are on Vainguinim Beach and Bogmalo in Goa, on Havelock Island and the Marine National Park in the Andamans, and on Bangaram in the Laccadives. Courses are well-run and cost around US$75 for an introductory dive, $350 for 4 days, or $600 for a 2-week Dive Master course. To check details of approved courses contact *PADI International*, Head Office, Unit 6, Unicorn Park, Whitby Road, Bristol, BS4 4EX, T0117-9711717, F9721821, general@padi.co.uk or *PADI Europe*, Oberwilerstrasse 3, CH-8442, Hettlingen, Switzerland, T52-3041414, F3041499, admin@padi.ch In addition, coastal resorts in Kerala and Goa offer fishing trips and dolphin viewing during the season, sometimes combining these with a beach barbecue.

The Hill Stations of the Western Ghats where the Nilgiri hills, the 'blue mountains' rise **Trekking** to 2,500 m are ideal for walking and 'trekking'. At the same time the wide range of habitat from dense cover of shola forests to scrub and meadow grassland, offer a rich variety of birdlife, some wildlife. The May to November monsoon months can be too wet and overcast to make trekking worthwhile.

The easily accessible parts of the National Parks and Reserved Forests provide ample opportunity for walking but if you want to venture deeper you'll need to take a local guide as paths can soon become indistinct and confusing. Some areas (Silent Valley in Kerala) require a permit to visit since the authorities wish to keep disturbance to wildlife and tribal communities to a minimum . The government Wildlife and Forestry Departments and private tour operators will be able to set you on the right path but you need to make ask, sometimes as much as a month, in advance. There are simple

Leeches

When walking or trekking in the hills during the monsoon, beware of leeches. They usually stay on the ground waiting for a passerby and get in boots when you are walking. Then when they are gorged with blood they drop off.

Don't try pulling one off as the head will be left behind and cause infection. Put some salt (or hold a lighted cigarette to it) which will make it quickly fall off. It helps to spray socks and bootlaces with an insect repellent before starting off in the morning.

lodges and guest houses in most areas including tribal villages, but comfortable jungle camps and luxury safari lodges also exist in the National Parks, which can be used as a base for day treks.

Good areas to explore are around Madikeri, Ooty and Munnar as well as the National Parks at Mudumalai-Bandipur, Nagarhole, Annamalai, Periyar and Bilgiri. Local agents include **Clipper Holidays**, 4 Magrath Rd, Bangalore, Karnataka, T080-5592023, F5599833, clipper@bangalore.wipro.net.in **Chalukya**, Vadayakadu, Kunnukzhy, Thiruvananthapuram, Kerala, T0471-444618, **Indian Adventures**, T022-6408742, F6458401, www.indianadventures.com **Jungle Lodges and Resorts**, T080-5597025, F5586163, jungle@giasbg01.vsnl.net.in **Jungle Retreat**, Bokkapuram, Mudumalai, Tamil Nadu, T/F0423-56469, peres@giasbg01.vsnl.net.in **Seagull**, by 8 Ramanashree Complex, Hardinge Circle, Mysore, Karnataka, T0821-529732, F520535.

Western Ghats Madikere Tala cauvery, Igutappa, Tadiandamole, Virajpet, Ponnampet, Srimangala, Nagarhole.

Nilgiris Around Udhagamandalam (Ooty) Coonoor, Pollachi, Topslip, Monamboli, Valparai, Grass Hills, Vaguvarai, Chanduvarai, Kilavarai, Kodaikkanal. The hills can be damp during November-December and are best from January to May.

Kerala On the Ghats, from Munnar and Ponmudi.

Spectator sports

Cricket — Sport has become one of India's greatest popular entertainment. Cricket has an almost fanatical following across South India. Reinforced by satellite TV and radio, and a national side that enjoys high world rankings and much outstanding individual talent, cricket has become a national obsession. Stars have cult status, and you can see children trying to model themselves on their game on any and every open space.

Soccer — Soccer is played from professional level to kickabout in any open space. Professional matches are played in Goa in large stadia attracting vast crowds; the latter holds 40,000 spectators and is also popular in Kerala. The season is from October to March and details of matches are published in the local papers. The top class game tickets are Rs 25, but they are sold for much more on the black market. The crowds generate tremendous fervour for the big matches, and standards are improving. African players are now featuring more frequently with Indian teams and monthly salaries have risen to over Rs 40,000 per month, a very good wage by Indian standards.

Health

Travellers to South India are exposed to health risks not encountered in Western Europe or North America. Because much of the area is economically underdeveloped, serious infectious diseases are common, as they were in the West some decades ago. Obviously, business travellers staying in international hotels and tourists on organized tours face different health risks to travellers backpacking through rural areas. There are no absolute rules to follow; you will often have to make your own judgement on the healthiness of your surroundings. With suitable precautions you should stay healthy.

There are many well qualified doctors in India, most of whom speak English, but the quality and range of medical care diminishes rapidly as you leave the major cities. If you are in a major city, your embassy may be able to recommend a list of doctors. If you are a long way from medical help, some self-treatment may be needed. You are more than likely to find many drugs with familiar names on sale. Always buy from a reputable source, and check date stamping. Vaccines in particular have a much reduced shelf-life if not stored properly. Locally produced drugs may be unreliable because of poor quality control and the substitution of inert ingredients for active drugs.

Before you go

Take out good medical insurance. Check exactly what the level of cover is for specific eventualities, in particular whether a flight home is covered in case of an emergency, whether the insurance company will pay any medical expenses directly or whether you have to pay and then claim them back, and whether specific activities such as trekking or climbing are covered. If visiting for a while have a dental check up. Take spare glasses (or a glasses prescription) and/or lenses, if you wear them. If you have a long-standing medical problem such as diabetes, heart trouble, chest trouble or high blood pressure, get advice from your doctor, and carry sufficient medication to last the full duration of your trip. You may want to ask your doctor for a letter explaining your condition.

Self-medication may be forced on you by circumstances so the following text contains the names of drugs and medicines which you may find useful in an emergency or in out-of-the-way places. You may like to take some of the following items with you from home: **anti-infective ointment** eg cetrimide; **dusting powder** for feet, containing fungicide; **antacid tablets**; **antibiotics** (ask your GP); **anti-malarial tablets**; **painkillers** (paracetamol or aspirin); **rehydration salts** packets plus anti-diarrhoea preparations; **travel sickness tablets**; **first aid kit** including a couple of sterile syringes and needles and disposable gloves (available from camping shops) in case of an emergency.

Travelling with children Children get dehydrated very quickly in hot countries and can become drowsy and uncooperative unless cajoled to drink water or juice plus salts. The treatment of diarrhoea is the same for adults, except that it should start earlier for children and be continued with more persistence. Colds, catarrh and ear infections are also common so take suitable antibiotics. To help young children to take anti-malarial tablets, one suggestion is to crush them between spoons and mix with a teaspoon of dessert chocolate (for cake-making) bought in a tube.

Vaccination & immunization If you require travel vaccinations see your doctor well in advance of your travel. Most courses must be completed in a minimum of four weeks. Travel clinics may provide rapid courses of vaccination, but are likely to be more expensive. The following vaccinations are recommended:

Typhoid This disease is spread by the insanitary preparation of food. A single dose injection is now available (*Typhim Vi*) that provides protection for up to three years. A vaccine taken by mouth in three doses is also available, but the timing of doses can be a problem and protection only lasts for one year.

Polio Protection is by a live vaccine generally given orally, and a full course consists of three doses with a booster every five years.

Tetanus If you have not been vaccinated before, one dose of vaccine should be given with a booster at six weeks and another at six months. Ten yearly boosters are strongly recommended. Children should, in addition, be properly protected against diphtheria, mumps and measles.

Infectious Hepatitis If you are not immune to hepatitis A already, the best protection is vaccination with *Havrix*. A single dose gives protection for at least a year, while a booster taken six months after the initial injection extends immunity to at least 10 years. If you are not immune to hepatitis B, the vaccine Energix is highly effective. It consists of three injections over six months before travelling. A combined hepatitis A & B vaccine is now licensed and available.

Malaria For details of malaria prevention, see below.

The following vaccinations may also be considered:

Tuberculosis The disease is still common in the region. Consult your doctor for advice on BCG inoculation.

Meningococcal Meningitis and Diphtheria If you are staying in the country for a long time, vaccination should be considered.

Japanese B Encephalitis (JBE) Immunization (effective in 10 days) gives protection for around three years. There is an extremely small risk in India, though it varies seasonally and from region to region. Consult a travel clinic or your family doctor.

Rabies Vaccination before travel gives anyone bitten more time to get treatment (so particularly helpful for those visiting remote areas), and also prepares the body to produce antibodies quickly. The cost of the vaccine can be shared by three persons receiving vaccination together.

Smallpox, **Cholera** and **Yellow Fever** Vaccinations are not required, although you may be asked to show a vaccination certificate if you have been in a country affected by yellow fever immediately prior to travelling to India.

You can get all your injections done at your local surgery for a fee but you will need to give them some notice. If you are in London, you have a choice. *Nomad*, c/o STA, 40 Bernard St, Russell Square, London WC1, T020-78334114, and 3-4 Wellington Terrace, Turnpike Lane, London N8, T020-88897014, operates a small clinic with a visiting pharmacist twice a week, free advice on preventative treatment; medicines and vaccinations are available at the Dispensary. *British Airways Travel Clinic*, Harrow, Middx, offers a similar service on weekdays. All this is cheaper at the *Hospital for Tropical Diseases*, 4 St Pancras Way, London, N1 0PE, T020-72889600, 0900-1630 (call for an appointment).

On the road

Intestinal upsets Intestinal upsets are due, most of the time, to the insanitary preparation of food. Do not eat uncooked fish, vegetables or meat (especially pork, though this is highly unlikely in India), fruit with the skin on (always peel fruit yourself), or food that is exposed to flies (particularly salads).

Shellfish eaten raw are risky and at certain times of the year some fish and shellfish concentrate toxins from their environment and cause various kinds of food poisoning.

Tap water should be assumed to be unsafe, especially in the monsoon; the same goes for stream or well water. Bottled mineral water is now widely available, although not all bottled water is mineral water; some is simply purified water from an urban supply. If your hotel has a central hot water supply, this is generally safe to drink after cooling. Ice for drinks should be made from boiled water but rarely is, so stand your drink on the ice cubes rather than putting them in your drink. For details on water purification, see box.

Heat treated **milk** is widely available, as is ice cream produced by the same methods. Unpasteurized milk products, including cheese, are sources of tuberculosis, brucellosis, listeria and other food poisoning germs. You can render fresh milk safe by heating it to 62°C for 30 minutes, followed by rapid cooling or by boiling. Matured or processed cheeses are safer than fresh varieties.

Diarrhoea is usually the result of food poisoning, occasionally from contaminated water. There are various causes: viruses, bacteria or protozoa (like amoeba and giardia). It may take one of several forms, coming on suddenly, or rather slowly. It may be accompanied by vomiting or by severe abdominal pain and the passage of blood or mucus with stools. How do you know which type you have and how do you treat them?

All kinds of diarrhoea, whether or not accompanied by vomiting, respond favourably to the replacement of water and salts taken as frequent small sips of some kind of rehydration solution. Proprietary preparations, consisting of sachets of powder which you dissolve in water (ORS, or Oral Rehydration Solution) are widely available in India, although it is recommended that you bring some of your own. They can also be made by adding half a teaspoonful of salt (3½ g) and four tablespoonfuls of sugar (40 g) to a litre of safe drinking water.

If you can time the onset of diarrhoea to the minute, then it is probably viral or bacterial, and/or the onset of dysentery. The treatment, in addition to rehydration, is Ciprofloxacin (500 mg every 12 hours). The drug is now widely available. If the diarrhoea has come on slowly or intermittently, then it is more likely to be protozoal (ie caused by amoeba or giardia). These cases are best treated by a doctor, as should any diarrhoea continuing for more than three days. If medical facilities are remote a short course of high dose Metronidazole (*Flagyl*) may provide relief. This drug is widely available in India, although it is best to bring a course with you after discussion with your family doctor. If there are severe stomach cramps, the following drugs may sometimes help: *Loperamide* (*Imodium, Arret*) and *Diphenoxylate* with *Atropine* (*Lomotil*).

Thus, the lynch pins of treatment for diarrhoea are rest, fluid and salt replacement, antibiotics such as Ciprofloxacin for some bacterial types and special diagnostic tests and medical treatment for amoeba and giardia infections.

Salmonella infections and **cholera** can be devastating diseases and it would be wise to get to a hospital as soon as possible if these were suspected. Fasting, peculiar diets and the consumption of large quantities of yoghurt have not been found to be useful in calming travellers' diarrhoea or in rehabilitating inflamed bowels. As there is some evidence that alcohol and milk might prolong diarrhoea, they should probably be avoided during and immediately after an attack. Antibiotics to prevent diarrhoea are ineffective and some, such as Entero-vioform, can have serious side effects if taken for long periods.

Heat & cold

Full acclimatization to high temperatures takes about two weeks. During this period it is normal to feel relatively apathetic, especially if the relative humidity is high. Drink plenty of water and avoid extreme exertion. When you are acclimatized you will feel more comfortable, but your need for plenty of water will continue. Tepid showers are more cooling than hot or cold ones. Remember that especially in the mountains, deserts and the highlands, there can be a large and sudden drop between temperatures in the sun and shade, and between night and day. Large hats do not cool you down, but do prevent sunburn. Warm jackets or woollens are essential after dark at high altitude. Loose cotton is still the best material when the weather is hot.

The burning power of the tropical sun is phenomenal, especially at altitude. Always wear a wide brimmed hat and use some form of sun cream or lotion. Normal temperate sun tan lotions (up to factor seven) are not much good. You will need to use the types designed specifically for the tropics or for mountaineers/skiers, with a protection factor between seven and 25 (dependent on skin type). Glare from the sun can cause conjunctivitis, so wear good quality UV protection sunglasses on beaches and snowy areas. There are several variations of 'heat stroke'. The most common cause is severe dehydration, so drink plenty of non-alcoholic fluid. Sun-block and cream is not widely available in India, so you should bring adequate supplies with you.

Insects These can be a great nuisance. Some of course are carriers of serious disease. The best way to keep mosquitoes away at night is to sleep off the ground with a mosquito net, and to burn mosquito coils containing Pyrethrum (available in India). Aerosol sprays or a 'flit' gun may be effective, as are insecticidal tablets which are heated on a mat which is plugged into a wall socket. These devices, and the refills, are not widely available in India, so if you are taking your own make sure it is of suitable voltage with the right adaptor plug. Bear in mind also that there are regular power cuts in many parts of India.

A better option is to use a personal insect repellent of which the best contain a high concentration of Diethyltoluamide (DEET). Liquid is best for arms, ankles and face (take care around eyes and make sure you do not dissolve the plastic of your spectacles). These are available in India (eg *Mospel, Repel*), although it is recommended that you bring your own supply. Aerosol spray on clothes and ankles deter mites and ticks. Liquid DEET suspended in water can be used to impregnate cotton clothes and mosquito nets. MASTA recommends *Mosiguard* which does not contain DEET as an insect repellent.

If you are bitten, itching may be relieved by cool baths and anti-histamine tablets (care with alcohol or driving), corticosteroid creams (great care and never use if hint of infection or on the face) or by judicious scratching. Calamine lotion and cream are of no real use, and anti-histamine creams may sometimes cause skin allergies so use with caution.

Bites which do become infected (common in India) should be treated with a local antiseptic or antibiotic cream such as Cetrimide, as should infected scratches. Skin infestations with body lice, crabs and scabies are unfortunately easy to pick up, particularly by those travelling cheaply or trekking to mountain grazing pastures. Use Gamma benzene hexachloride for lice and Benzylbenzoate for scabies. Crotamiton cream alleviates itching and also kills a number of skin parasites. Malathion five percent is good for lice, but avoid the highly toxic full strength Malathion used as an agricultural insecticide.

Malaria In South India malaria was once theoretically confined to coastal and jungle zones, but is now on the increase again. It remains a serious disease and you are strongly advised to protect yourself against mosquito bites and to take prophylactic (preventive) drugs. Certain areas are badly affected particularly by the highly dangerous falciparum strain. Mosquitos do not thrive above 2,500 m, so you are safe at altitude. Recommendations on prevention change, so consult your family doctor or see the further information at the end of this section. However, the current combination of anti-malarial drugs for use in India requires a daily dosage of *Proguanil* (brands such as *Paludrine*) and a weekly dosage of *Chloroquine* (various brands). Start taking the tablets one week before exposure and continue to take them for four weeks after leaving the malarial zone. For those unable to use these particular drugs, your doctor may suggest *Mefloquine*, although this tends to be more expensive, less well tried, and may cause more serious side effects so it is best to try two doses before leaving.

The subject of malaria prevention is becoming more complex as the malaria parasite becomes immune to some of the older drugs. In particular, there has been an increase in the proportion of cases of falciparum malaria which is particularly dangerous. Some of the preventive drugs can cause side effects, especially if taken for long periods of time, so before you travel you must check with a reputable agency the likelihood and type of malaria in the areas you intend to visit. Take their advice on prophylaxis, but be prepared to receive conflicting advice. Do not use the possibility of side effects as an excuse not to take drugs.

Essentials

You can catch malaria even when taking prophylactic drugs, although it is unlikely. If you do develop symptoms (high fever, shivering, severe headache, sometimes diarrhoea) seek medical advice immediately. The risk of disease is obviously greater the further you move from the cities into rural areas with primitive facilities and standing water.

Infectious hepatitis (jaundice)

Medically speaking there are two types. The less serious but more common is **hepatitis A**, a disease frequently caught by travellers, and common in India. The main symptoms are yellowness of eyes and skin, lack of appetite, nausea, tiredness and stomach pains. The best protection is careful preparation of food, the avoidance of contaminated drinking water and scrupulous attention to toilet hygiene.

The other, more serious version is **hepatitis B**, which is acquired as a sexually transmitted disease, from blood transfusions or injection with an unclean needle, or possibly by insect bites. The symptoms are the same as hepatitis A, but the incubation period is much longer.

You may have had jaundice before or you may have had hepatitis of either type without becoming jaundiced, in which case it is possible that you could be immune to either form. This immunity can be tested for before you travel. There are various other kinds of viral hepatitis (C, E etc) which are fairly similar to A and B, but currently vaccines do not exist for these.

AIDS

AIDS is increasing in prevalence with a pattern typical of developing societies. Thus, it is not wholly confined to the well known high risk sections of the population ie homosexual men, intravenous drug abusers, prostitutes and the children of infected mothers. Heterosexual transmission is now the dominant mode and so the main risk to travellers is from casual unprotected sex. The same precautions should be taken as when encountering any sexually transmitted disease.

The AIDS virus (HIV) can be passed via unsterile needles which have previously been used to inject a HIV positive patient, but the risk of this is very small. It would, however, be sensible to check that needles have been properly sterilized, or better still, disposable needles used. The chance of picking up hepatitis B in this way is much more of a danger. If disposable needles are carried as part of a proper medical kit, customs officials in India are not generally suspicious.

The risk of receiving a blood transfusion with blood infected with the HIV virus is greater than from dirty needles because of the amount of fluid exchanged. Supplies of blood for transfusion are now usually screened for HIV in reputable hospitals, so the risk may be small. Catching the AIDS virus does not necessarily produce an illness in itself; the only way to be sure if you feel you have been at risk is to have a blood test for HIV antibodies on your return to a place where there are reliable laboratory facilities. The test does not become positive for many weeks and you are advised to be re-tested after 6 months.

Bites & stings

The best precaution against a snake bite is not to walk in snake territory with bare feet, sandals or shorts & not to touch snakes even if assured they are harmless

If you are unlucky enough to be bitten by a venomous snake, spider, scorpion, centipede or sea creature, try (within limits) to catch the animal for identification. Failing this, an accurate description will aid treatment. See the information on rabies (below) for other animal bites.

The reactions to be expected are fright, swelling, pain and bruising around the bite, soreness of the regional lymph glands (eg armpits for bites to hands and arms), nausea, vomiting and fever. If, in addition, any of the following symptoms supervene get the victim to a doctor without delay: numbness, tingling of face, muscular spasm, convulsions, shortness of breath or haemorrhage. Commercial snake bile or scorpion sting kits may be available but are only useful for the specific type of snake or scorpion for which they are designed. The serum has to be given by injection into a vein, so it is not much good unless you have some practice in making and giving such injections. If the bite is on a limb, immobilize the limb and apply a tight bandage (not a tourniquet) between the bite and the body. Be sure to release it for 90 seconds every 15 minutes. Do not try to slash the bite and suck out the poison because this will do more harm than good. Reassurance of the bitten person is important. Death from snake-bite is extremely rare. Hospitals usually hold stocks of snake-bite serum, though it is important to have a good description of the snake, or where possible, the creature itself.

If swimming in an area where there are poisonous fish such as stone or scorpion fish (also called by a variety of local names) or sea urchins on rocky coasts, tread carefully or wear footwear. The sting of such fish is intensely painful but can be helped by immersing the stung part in water as hot as you can bear for as long as it remains painful. This is not always very practical and you must take care not to scald yourself. At certain times of the year, coincidental with the best surfing season, stinging jelly-fish can be a problem.

Avoid spiders and scorpions by keeping your bed away from the wall, look under lavatory seats and inside your shoes in the morning. Dark dusty rooms are popular with scorpions. In the event of being bitten, consult a doctor quickly.

Other afflictions **Rabies** is endemic. If you are bitten by a domestic or wild animal, do not leave things to chance. Scrub the wound immediately with soap and water/disinfectant. Try to capture the animal (within limits). Treatment depends on whether you have already been vaccinated against rabies. If you have (and this is worthwhile if you are spending lengths of time in developing countries) then some further doses of vaccine are all that is needed. Human diploid cell vaccine is best, but expensive; other, older types of vaccine such as that made of duck embyos may be the only type available. These are effective, much cheaper and interchangeable generally with the human derived types. If not already vaccinated then anti-rabies serum (immunoglobulin) may be required in addition. It is wise to finish the course of treatment whether the animal survives or not.

Dengue fever is present in India. It is a viral disease, transmitted by mosquito bites, presenting severe headache, fevers and body pains. Complicated types of dengue known as haemorrhagic fevers occur throughout Asia, but usually in persons who have caught the disease a second time. Thus, although it is a very serious type, it is rarely caught by visitors. There is no treatment; you must just avoid mosquito bites as much as possible.

Athlete's foot and other fungal infections are best treated by sunshine and a proprietary preparation such as Canesten or Ecostatin.

Influenza and respiratory diseases are common, perhaps made worse by polluted cities and rapid temperature and climatic changes.

Intestinal worms are common, and the more serious ones such as hook worm can be contracted by walking barefoot on infested earth.

Prickly heat is a very common itchy rash, and can be avoided by frequent washing and wearing loose clothing. It is helped by the use of talcum powder to allow the skin to dry thoroughly after washing.

Returning home

It is important to take your anti-malaria tablets for four weeks after you return. Malaria can develop up to one year after leaving a malaria area. If you do become ill with fever or the other symptoms listed above, make sure your doctor knows about your travel. If you have had attacks of diarrhoea, it may be worth having a stool specimen tested in

Essentials

case you have picked up amoebic dysentery, giardiaisis or other protozoal infections. If you have been living rough, a blood test may be worthwhile to detect worms and other parasites.

Further information

The following organizations give information regarding well trained English speaking physicians throughout the world: *International Association for Medical Assistance to Travellers*, 745, 5th Avenue, New York, 10022; *Intermedic*, 777, Third Avenue, New York, 10017. Information regarding country by country malaria risk can be obtained from: *Malaria Reference Laboratory*, UK, T0891-600350; *Liverpool School of Tropical Medicine*, UK, T0891-172111 (both have recorded messages, premium rate); and *Centre for Disease Control*, Atlanta, USA, T404-3324555. The organization MASTA (Medical Advisory Service to Travellers Abroad), T020-78375540, F0113-2387575, www.masta.org and *Travax* (Glasgow, T0141-9467120 ext 247) will provide up to date country by country information on health risks.

Further information on medical problems abroad can be obtained from: "*Travellers' Health: How To Stay Healthy Abroad*", edited by Richard Dawood (Oxford University Press), recently updated. A new edition of the HMSO publication "Health Information for Overseas Travel" is available. The London School of Hygiene and Tropical Medicine, Keppel Street, London, WC1E 7HT, UK, publishes a strongly recommended book titled "*The Preservation of Personal Health in Warm Climates*".

This information has been compiled by Dr David Snashall, Senior Lecturer in Occupational Health, United Medical Schools of Guy's and St Thomas' Hospitals and Chief Medical Advisor, Foreign and Commonwealth Office, London. Added comments and recommendations specific to India are from Dr Martin Taylor, Kensington Street Health Centre, Bradford, West Yorkshire and Dr Anthony Bryceson, Emeritus Professor of Tropical Medicine at the London School of Hygiene and Tropical Medicine.

Further reading

The literature on India is as huge and varied as the subcontinent itself. India is a good place to buy English language books as foreign books are often much cheaper than the published price. There are also cheap Indian editions and occasionally reprints of out-of-print books. There are excellent bookshops in all the major Indian cities. Below are a few suggestions.

Art & architecture T Richard Burton *Hindu Art* British Museum P. A well illustrated paperback; a broad view of art and religion. **Ilay Cooper and Barry Dawson** *Traditional Buildings of India*, Thames & Hudson. **George Michell** *The Hindu Temple*, Univ of Chicago Press, 1988. An authoritative account of Hindu architectural development. **Henri Sterlin** *Hindu India*. Köln, Taschen, 1998. Traces the development from early rock-cut shrines, detailing famous examples; clearly written, well illustrated, *Buddhist India* to follow. *The tradition of Indian architecture*, Yale 1989. Superbly clear writing on development of Indian architecture under Rajputs, Mughals and the British.

Current affairs & politics Patrick French *Liberty or Death*. Harper Collins, 1997. Well researched and serious yet reads like a story. **Sunil Khilnani** *The idea of India*, Penguin, 1997. Excellent introduction to contemporary India, described by the Nobel prize winner Amartya Sen as "spirited, combative and insight-filled, a rich synthesis of contemporary India". **James Manor (ed)** *Nehru to the Nineties: the changing office of Prime Minister in India*,

Hurst, 1994. An excellent collection of essays giving an insider's view of the functioning of Indian democracy.

History: pre-history & early history
Bridget and Raymond Allchin *Origins of a civilisation*, Viking, Penguin Books, 1997. The most authoritative up to date survey of the origins of Indian civilizations. **AL Basham** *The Wonder that was India*, London, Sidgwick & Jackson, 1985. Still one of the most comprehensive and readable accounts of the development of India's culture.

History: medieval & modern
Mohandas K Gandhi *An Autobiography*, London, 1982. **Jawaharlal Nehru** *The discovery of India*, New Delhi, ICCR, 1976. **John Keay** *India: a History*, Harper Collins. A major new popular history of the subcontinent. **Francis Robinson** (ed) *Cambridge Encyclopaedia of India*, Cambridge, 1989. An introduction to many aspects of South Asian society. **Percival Spear & Romila Thapar** *A history of India*, 2 vols, Penguin, 1978.

Language
H Yule and AC Burnell (eds), *Hobson-Jobson*, 1886. New paperback edition , 1986. A delightful insight into Anglo-Indian words and phrases.

Literature
Nirad Chaudhuri Four books give vivid, witty and often sharply critical accounts of India across the 20th century. *The autobiography of an unknown Indian*, Macmillan, London; *Thy Hand, Great Anarch!*, London, Chatto & Windus, 1987. **VS Naipaul** *A million mutinies now*, Penguin, 1992. Naipaul's 'revisionist' account of India turns away from the despondency of his earlier two India books (*An Area of darkness* and *India: a wounded civilisation*) to see grounds for optimism at India's capacity for regeneration. **RK Narayan** has written many gentle and humorous novels and short stories of South India. *The Man-eater of Malgudi* and *Under the Banyan tree and other stories*, *Grandmother's stories*, among many, London, Penguin, 1985. **Arundhati Roy** *The God of Small Things*. Indian Ink/Harper Collins, 1997. Excellent first novel about family turmoil in a Syrian Christian household in Kerala. **Salman Rushdie** The Moor's Last Sigh (Viking 1996) is of particular interest to those travelling to Kochi and Mumbai. **Salman Rushdie** and **Elizabeth West** *The Vintage book of Indian writing*, Random House, 1997. **Paul Scott** *The Raj Quartet*, London, Panther, 1973; *Staying on*, Longmans, 1985. Outstandingly perceptive novels of the end of the Raj. **Vikram Seth** *A Suitable Boy*, Phoenix House London 1993. Prize winning novel of modern Indian life. **Simon Weightman** (ed) *Travellers Literary Companion: the Indian Sub-continent*. An invaluable introduction to the diversity of Indian writing.

Music
Raghava R Menon *Penguin Dictionary of Indian Classical Music*, Penguin New Delhi 1995.

People & places
Elizabeth Bomiller *May you be the mother of 100 sons*, Penguin, 1991. An American woman journalists' account of coming to understand the issues that face India's women today. **Lakshmi Holmstrom** *The Inner Courtyard*, a series of short stories by Indian women, translated into English, Rupa, 1992.

Religion
W Theodore de Bary (ed) *Sources of Indian Tradition: Vol 1*. Columbia U.P. Traces the origins of India's major religions through illustrative texts. **Wendy Doniger O'Flaherty** *Hindu Myths*, London, Penguin, 1974. A sourcebook translated from the Sanskrit. **IH Qureshi** *The Muslim Community of the Indo-Pakistan Sub-Continent 610-1947*, OUP, 1977, Karachi. **Walpola Rahula** *What the Buddha Taught*. **RC Zaehner** *Hinduism*, OUP.

Travel
Alexander Frater *Chasing the monsoon*, London, Viking, 1990. An attractive and prize winning account of the human impact of the monsoon's sweep across India. **John Hatt** *The tropical traveller: the essential guide to travel in hot countries*, Penguin, 3rd ed 1992. Excellent, wide ranging and clearly written common sense, based on extensive

experience and research. **John Keay** *Into India*. London, John Murray, 1999. A seasoned traveller's introduction to understanding and enjoying India; with a new foreword.

Salim Ali *Indian hill birds*, OUP. **Salim Ali and S. Dillon Ripley** *Handbook of the birds of India & Pakistan* (compact ed); also in five volumes. **DV Cowen** *Flowering Trees and Shrubs in India*. **RE Hawkins** *Encyclopaedia of Indian Natural History*, Bombay Natural History Soc/OUP. **Krys Kazmierczak & Raj Singh** *A birdwatcher's guide to India*. Prion, 1998, Sandy, Beds, UK. Well researched and carrying lots of practical information for all birders. **SM Nair** *Endangered animals of India*, New Delhi, NBT, 1992. **SH Prater** *The Book of Indian Animals*. **Martin Woodcock** *Handguide to Birds of the Indian Sub-Continent*, Collins.

Wildlife & vegetation

Maps

For anyone interested in the geography of India, or even simply getting around, trying to buy good maps is a depressing experience. For security reasons it is illegal to sell large scale maps of any areas within 80 km of the coast or national borders.

The export of large scale maps from India is prohibited

The **Bartholomew** 1:4 m map sheet of India is the most authoritative, detailed and easy to use map available. It can be bought worldwide. *GeoCenter* World Map 1:2 m, covers India in three regional sections and are clearly printed. *Nelles'* regional maps of India at the scale of 1:1.5 m offer generally clear route maps, though neither the road classifications nor alignments are wholly reliable. The same criticism applies to the attractively produced and easy to read **Lonely Planet** *Travel Atlas of India and Bangladesh* (1995, 162 pp).

State maps and town plans are published by the **TT Company**. These are updated and improved and are often the best available, but also have numerous mistakes. For the larger cities they provide the most compact yet clear map sheets (generally 50 mm x 75 mm format).

Sources of maps outside India: **Australia:** *The Map Shop*, 16a Peel St, Adelaide, SA 5000, T08-82312033. **Canada:** *Worldwide Books*, 552 Seymore St. Vancouver, BC. **Germany:** *Geo Buch Verlag*, Rosenthal 6, D-6000 München 2; *GeoCenter GmbH*, Honigwiessenstrasse 25, Postfach 800830, D-7000 Stuttgart 80; *Zumsteins Landkartenhaus*, Leibkerrstrasse 5, 8 München 22. **Italy:** *Libreria Alpina*, Via C Coroned-Berti, 4 40137 Bologna, Zona 370-5. **Switzerland:** *Travel Bookshop*, Rindermarkt, 8001 Zurich. **UK:** *Blackwell's*, 53 Broad St, Oxford, T01865-792792, www.bookshop.blackwell.co.uk *Stanfords*, 12-14 Long Acre, London WC2E 9LP, T020-78361321, www.stanfords.co.uk **USA:** *Michael Chessler*, PO Box 2436, Evergreen, CO 80439, T800-6548502, 303-6700093; *Ulysses*, 4176 St Denis Montreal, T0524-8439447.

The Survey of India publishes large scale 1:10,000 town plans of approximately 70 cities. These detailed plans are the only surveyed town maps in India, and some are over 20 years old. The Survey also has topographic maps at the scale of 1:25,000 and 1:50,000 in addition to its 1:250,000 scale coverage, some of which are as recent as the late 1980s. However, maps are regarded as highly sensitive and it is only possible to buy these from main agents of the Survey of India.

India on the web

www.tourindia.com The official government promotional site with useful information but no objective evaluation of problems and difficulties. Has separate state entries within it. 'India Travel Online' is informative and issued fortnightly.

General sites

www.indiacurrentaffairs.com/ Regularly updated cuttings from Indian national dailies.
www.fco.gov Advice from the Foreign Office, London.
www.travel.indiamart.com Commercial site Online bookings for selected hotels.
www.india.org The sites on India section contains excellent information on the

Essentials

structure of Indian government. Tourism Information is less useful.

www.123india.com Wide ranging current affairs and general India site.
www.tourismindia.com Yellow pages for major cities.
www.wunderground.com An excellent weather site, world wide, city specific, fast.

State specific sites www.tamilnadutourism, www.keralatourism.org, www.ktdc.com Carries ktdc accommodation and tour information, www.goanet.com/india.html A very personal site on Goa.

Indian embassies & consulates

Australia, 3-5 Moonah Place, Yarralumla, Canberra T6273-3999; Level 2, 210 Pitt St, Sydney T9264-4855; Melbourne T9386-7399. **Austria,** Kärntner Ring 2, A-1015 Vienna, T50-58666669, F50-59219. **Bangladesh,** 2 Chanmodi RA, House 129, Dhaka-2, T503606, Chittagong T507670. **Belgium,** 217-Chaussée de Vleurgat, 1050 Brussels, T6409802, F6489638. Consulates: Ghent T091-263423, Antwerp T03-2341122. **Bhutan,** India House Estate, Thimpu, T2162. **Canada,** 10 Springfield Rd, Ottawa, Ontario K1M 1C9, T613-7443751. Consulates: Toronto T416-9600751, Vancouver T9266080. **Denmark,** Vangehusvej 15, 2100 Copenhagen, T3918-2888, F3927-0218. **Finland,** Satamakatu 2 A8, 00160 Helsinki-16, T608927. **France,** 15 Rue Alfred Dehodencq, Paris, T45203930. **Germany,** Adenauerallee, 262/264, 5300 Bonn-1, T0228-54050. Consulates: Berlin T8817068, Frankfurt T069-271040, Hamburg T338036, Munich T089-92562067, Stuttgart T0711-297078. **Ireland,** 6 Lesson Park, Dublin 6, T01-4970843. **Israel,** 4 Kaufmann St, Sharbat, Tel Aviv 68012, T0368-580585, F510143. **Italy,** Via XX Settembre 5, 00187 Rome, T4884642. Consulates: Milan T02-8690314, Genoa T54891. **Japan,** 2-11, Kudan Minami 2-Chome, Chiyoda-ku, Tokyo 102, T03-2622391. Consulate: Kobe T078-2418116. **Korea,** 37-3, Hannam-dong, Yongsan-Ku, Seoul, T7984257, F7969534. **Malaysia,** 19 Malacca St, Kuala Lumpur, T221766. **Maldives,** Mafabbu Aage 37, Orchid Magu, Male 20-02, T323015. **Nepal,** Lainchour, PO Box No 292, Kathmandu, T211300. **Netherlands,** Buitenrustweg 2, The Hague (2517KD), T070-3469771. **New Zealand,** 10th Flr, Princess Tower, 180 Molesworth St (PO Box 4045), Wellington, T4736390. **Norway,** 30 Niels Jules Gate, 0272 Oslo-2, T443194. **Pakistan,** G5 Diplomatic Enclave, Islamabad, T050-8144731, Karachi T021-814371. **Singapore,** India House, 31 Grange Rd, Singapore 0923, T7376777. **Spain,** Avda Pio XII 30-32, 28016 Madrid, T457-0209. Consulate: Barcelona T93-2120422. **Sri Lanka,** 36-38 Galle Rd, Colombo 3, T421605 Kandy, T446430. **Sweden,** Adolf Fredriks Kyrkogata 12, Box 1340, 11183 Stockholm, T08-107008, F08-248505. **Switzerland,** Kirchenfeldstrasse 28 CH - 3005 Bern, T031-351 1110. **Thailand,** 46, Soi 23 (Prasarn Mitr) Sukhumvit 23, Bangkok 10110, T2580300. Also in Chiang Mai. **UK,** India House, Aldwych, London WC2B 4NA, T020-78368484 (0930-1300, 1400-1730; visas 0800-1200), www.Hcilondon.org Consulates: The Spencers, 19 Augusta St, Hockley, Birmingham, B18 6DS, T0121-2122782; 6th Flr, 134 Renfrew St, Glasgow 3 7ST, T0141-3310777, F331-0666. (Send SAE for postal applications.) **USA,** 2107 Massachusetts Ave, Washington DC 20008, T202-9397000. Consulates: New Orleans T504-5828105, New York T212-8797800, San Francisco T415-6680662, Chicago T312-781680, Cleveland T216/696.

Tamil Nadu

3

Tamil Nadu

Tamil Nadu, once known as the Coromandel coast, has a language over 2,000 years old and poetry dating back to before the birth of Christ. It also boasts some of the most remarkable temple architecture in India, and, with a living tradition of music and dance, is culturally very rich. Temple towns and historic sites are dotted across the plains, especially in the fertile Thanjavur delta, while the hill stations of the Western Ghats are within easy reach. Together with the former French territory of Pondicherry with its own distinctive colonial inheritance, Tamil Nadu is one of India's most rewarding states to visit.

★ *A foot in the door*

Stand facing the sea at **Mahabalipuram's** shore temple at dawn, then walk down to the rock carving, the descent of the Ganges, to catch it in the early morning sun

Look out over the Tamil nadu plains from Pillar rocks, **Kodaikkanal**

Wander into the **Meenakshi Temple** Madurai during the ten day Chitrai festival in April/May

Watch the ritual bathing by pilgrims in the Kaveri at **Srirangam** temple near Trichy

Try a 'Brahmin meals ready' at a small town restaurant

Clamber on board first class front coach of the narrow guage Blue Mountain railway to see the **Nilgiris** at their best

Watch the silk weavers of **Kanchipuram**

Talk your way into a trip on a fishing catamaran

Background

The land
Population: 55.6 mn
Area: 130,000 sq km

Tamil Nadu rises from the flat coastal plains in the east to the magnificent Western Ghats – the Nilgiris in the north and the Palani, Cardamom and Anamalai hills in the south. The Nilgiris – 'blue mountains' – rise like a wall above the haze of the plains to heights of over 2,500 m, with Dodabetta the second highest mountain in South India.

The plains are hot, often dry and dusty, with isolated blocks of granite forming often bizarre shapes on the ancient eroded surface. The coast itself is a flat alluvial plain, with deltas at the mouths of major rivers.

The river Kaveri (formerly Cauvery), the vital life blood of agriculture in the state, rises in Karnataka. The only virtually perennial river, its waters irrigate the rice bowl of South India, the Thanjavur delta. The medieval rulers in Tamil Nadu often created tanks which now add a beautiful touch to the landscape.

History
Early history Tamil Nadu's cultural identity has been shaped by the Dravidians, who have inhabited the south since at least the fourth millennium BC. Tamil, India's oldest living language, developed from the earlier languages of people who were probably displaced from the north by the Aryans from 2000 BC to 1500 BC.

By the fourth century BC Tamil Nadu was under the rule of three dynasties. The **Cholas** occupied the coastal area east of Thanjavur and inland to the head of the Kaveri Delta at Tiruchi. Periodically they were a strong military power, one of their princes, Elara, for example conquering the island of Sri Lanka in the second century BC. The south – Madurai, Tirunelveli and a part of southern Kerala were under the **Pandiyas** while the **Cheras** controlled much of what is now Kerala on the west coast of the peninsula. The three kingdoms are mentioned in Asokan edicts of circa 257 BC. Western classical sources and Chinese records show that from at least the second century BC South Indians traded by sea. Indian merchants organized themselves in guilds, trading with the Kra Isthmus and other Southeast Asian ports.

The **Pandiyas** returned to power in the Tamil area after the decline of the Cholas and ruled from 1175 to 1300. In the 13th century, international trade flourished under their control and was only superseded by the rise of Vijayanagar.

The **Pallavas** of Kanchi came to power in the fourth century AD and were dominant between AD 550-869. Possibly of northern origin, under their control Mahabalipuram (Mahabalipuram) became an important port in the seventh century. Narasimhavarman II built the great Kailasanatha Temple at Kanchipuram which for 150 years was both their administrative and literary capital.

The **Cholas** returned to power in 850 and were a dominant political force until 1173. During the reign of **Rajaraja I**, their great empire at one time embraced Sri Lanka, Andhra, Southern Karnataka and the islands of Lakshadweep and the Maldives. During the 11th-century Rajendra Chola (1013-44) extended Chola power to the River Ganga in Bengal. His naval expeditions to the Malayan Peninsula resulted in Chola domination over the trade routes of the Indian Ocean to Java, Sumatra and China until the resumption of Pandiya power for a further century.

Subsequently the warring kingdoms of peninsular India spread their influence south. The defeat of the great Vijayanagar Empire by a confederacy of Muslim states in 1565 forced their leaders south. As the Nayaka kings they continued to rule from as far south as Madurai well into the 17th century. Ultimately when Muslim political control finally reached Tamil Nadu it was as brief as it was tenuous.

Best time to visit

Tamil Nadu receives most of its rain between October and December, often associated with cyclonic depressions. This is the worst time to travel, but from mid-December to early March dry sunny weather sets in – the best time to visit, before the heat gets too crushing. The hills can then be really cold, especially at night. In the rainshadow of the Western Ghats, temperatures never fall much below 21°C except in the hills, but although humidity is often very high maximum temperatures rarely exceed 42°C.

The British It was more than 150 years after their founding of Fort St George at Madras in 1639 before the East India Company could claim political supremacy in South India. **Haidar Ali**, who mounted the throne of Mysore in 1761, and his son **Tipu Sultan**, allied with the French, won many battles against the English. The Treaty of Versailles in 1783 brought the French and English together and Tipu was forced to make peace. The English took Malabar in 1792, and in 1801 Lord Wellesley brought together most of the south under the Madras Presidency, see page 322.

The French acquired land at Pondicherry in 1673. In 1742, Dupleix was named Governor of the French India Company and took up residence at **Pondicherry**. He seized Madras within a few years but in 1751 **Clive** attacked Arcot. His victory was the beginning of the end French ambitions in India. The Treaty of Paris brought their Empire to a close in 1763 although they retained five counting houses.

People The great majority of Tamilians are Dravidians, with Mediterranean ethnic origins. They have been settled in Tamil Nadu for several thousand years. Tamil, the main language of the State, is spoken by over 85% of the population. In the north, especially around Chennai, are many Telugu speakers, who make up a further 10% of the population. Hindus make up nearly 90% of the population, and over 5% are Christian, a group especially strong in the south where Roman Catholic and Protestant missions have been active for over 500 years. There are also small but significant minorities of Muslims, Jains and Parsis.

Culture

Tribal groups There are isolated groups of as many as 18 different types of tribal people who live in the Nilgiri Hills. Some of them are of aboriginal stock although local archaeological discoveries suggest that an extinct race preceded them.

The **Todas'** life and religion revolve around their long-horned buffalo which are a measure of their wealth. In physical appearance the Todas stand out with their sharp features, the men with their close cropped hair, and the women who wear theirs in long shiny ringlets. Both wrap the traditional *puthukuli* toga-style shawl which is brightly patterned. Their small villages are called *munds* with half a dozen or so igloo- like, windowless bamboo and dried grass huts. The animist temples and 'cathedrals' or *boa*, which only men are allowed to enter, are of similar construction but larger.

Their chief goddess 'Tiekirzi', the creator of the indispensable buffalo, and her brother 'On', rule the world of the dead and the living. There are only about 1,000 Todas left. Many young people now leave their munds while others take advantage of their close contact with 'civilization' and produce articles such as silver jewellery and shawls for the tourist market.

The **Badagas** are the main tribal group and probably came from Karnataka. Like the Kotas and Kurumbas, they speak a mixture of Kannada and Tamil and

The terrifying guardian deities

Many Hindu villagers in Tamil Nadu believe in guardian deities of the village – Ayyanar, Muneeswaram, Kaliamman, Mariamman and many more. Groups of larger than life images built of brick, wood or stone and covered in brightly painted lime plaster (chunam) guard the outskirts of several villages. They are deliberately terrifying, designed to frighten away evil spirits from village homes, but villagers themselves are also very frightened of these gods and try to keep away from them.

The deities are supposed to prevent epidemics, but if an epidemic does strike special sacrifices are offered, mainly of rice. Firewalking, often undertaken in fulfilment of a vow, is a feature of the special festivals at these shrines. Disease is also believed to be held at bay by other ceremonies, including piercing the cheeks and tongue with wire and the carrying of kavadis (special carriages or boxes, sometimes designed like a coffin). Swamy says that those who undertake vows may be bathed, dressed in a cloth dipped in turmeric and carried through the village streets as though dead, to 'come to life' when the procession enters the temple.

their oral tradition is rich in folktales, poetry, songs and chants. Agriculturalists, their villages are mainly in the upper plateau, with rows of three-roomed houses. They worship Siva and observe special tribal festivals including an unusual fire feast in honour of the gods of harvest. Progressive and adaptable, they are being absorbed into the local community faster than the others.

The **Kotas** who live mainly in the Kotagiri/Tiruchigadi area are particularly musical and artistic, and are distinguished by their colourful folk dances. Their villages are also on the upper plateau, with a few detached huts or rows of huts, the place of worship marked out in a large square with a loose stone wall. Being the artisan tribe, they are the blacksmiths, gold and silver smiths, carpenters, potters and tanners to the other groups.

The **Kurumbas** live in the lower valleys and forests in villages called 'mothas'. They collect fruit, particularly bananas, honey, resin, medicinal herbs and hunt and trap big game. Most of their dead are buried in a sitting position, except the very old who are cremated. They used to practise black magic but, when they claimed to conjure up elephants and tigers at will and reduce rocks to powder with their magic herbs, were murdered by the other tribes.

The **Irulas** are the second largest group and in many ways similar to the Kurumbas. They live on the lower slopes in huts made of bamboo and thatch cultivating small areas to grow ragi, and fruit (plantains, oranges, pumpkins, jackfruit). They also hunt and ensnare wild animals. They take produce such as honey, beeswax, gum, dyes and fruit down to towns in the plains to trade. The Irulas worship Vishnu, especially in the form of Rangaswamy, and their temples are simple circles of stone which enclose an upright stone with a trident.

Literature Tamil is the oldest of India's living languages, with a literature stretching back to the early centuries before Christ. The poet and thinker Thiruvalluvar, whose work the 'Thirukkural' (written between first century BC and second century AD) is still revered today. From around the second century AD a poets' academy known as the **Sangam** was established in Madurai.

Tamil *Sangam* literature underwent an extraordinary test, see page 162. Books would be thrown into the sacred tank of the Minakshi Temple at Madurai and those that floated would be deemed worthy, while those that were useless would sink. (A large enough body of worthy literature was ensured by books being were written on leaves of the Palmyra palm!) See page 548.

Right- and left-handed castes

In India today the left hand is universally regarded as 'unclean'. Yet for over 800 years from the 11th century there was a major social group for whom the left hand was pure and the right unclean. The "right handed" and "left handed" castes, given the Tamil names Valangai and Idangai respectively, were often in conflict. No one knows exactly how or why the division came about. At times the left-hand groups were identified with particular types of artisan activity, in contrast with the right-handed groups more commonly engaged in agricultural work.

The impurity associated with left-handedness may suggest ritual connections, though why those called 'left-handed' should have accepted such a damaging description is not clear. Burton Stein suggests that perhaps the usefulness of the label came to outweigh the underlying stigma of its associations, and that alliances across wide regions gave a measure of security and political leverage to disadvantaged groups.

Sangam literature suggests that life in Tamil society had a social hierarchy with the sages at the top, followed by peasants, hunters, artisans, soldiers, fishermen and scavengers – quite different from the caste system that existed in the rest of the subcontinent.

From the beginning of the Christian era Tamil religious thinkers began to transform the image of Krishna from the remote and heroic figure of the epics into the focus of a new and passionate devotional worship – *bhakti*. Jordens has written that this new worship was "emotional, ardent, ecstatic, often using erotic imagery". From the 7th to the 10th century there was a surge of writing new hymns of praise, sometimes referred to as 'the Tamil *Veda*'. Attention focused on the 'marvels of Krishna's birth and infancy and his heroic and amorous exploits as a youth among the cowherds and cowherdesses of Gokula'. In the ninth century Vaishnavite Brahmans produced the *Bhagavata Purana*, which, through frequent translation into all India's major languages, became the vehicle for the new worship of Krishna. Its 10th book has been called "one of the truly great books of Hinduism". There are over forty translations into Bengali alone.

Religious orders Followers of both Siva and Vishnu (*Saivites* and *Vaishnavites*) formed religious orders. Monks travelled all over India, preaching and converting, giving the lie to the widely held view that Hinduism is not a proselytizing religion. The Vaishnava mystic and saint **Ramanuja**, the first and perhaps the greatest of these, is believed to have lived between 1017 and 1137. Fleeing from the Saivite Cholas in Tamil Nadu he founded the *Srivaishnava* sect. **Madhva**, a Kanarese Brahmin, founded the Madhva sect in the 13th century. The Telugu Brahmins **Nimbarka** (13th century) and **Vallabha** (1479-1531) carried the message to Varanasi.

Indian music Changes constantly occurred in different schools of music within the basic framework of **raga-tala-prabandha** which was well established by the seventh century. From the 13th century the division between the *Hindustani* or the northern system (which included the western and eastern regions as well) and the *Carnatic* or the southern system, became pronounced. The southern school has a more scale-based structure of *raga* whereas the northern school has greater flexibility and thus continued to develop through the centuries. The *tala* too is much more precise. It is also nearly always devotional or didactic where as the northern system also includes non-religious,

Dance, drama & music

everyday themes which are sometimes sensuous. The language that lends itself naturally to the southern system is Telugu and the only bowed instrument that is used to accompany vocal music is the violin, imported from the West but played rather differently.

The fundamental form in **Carnatic music** is the **varnam**. This is like an étude which conforms to phrases and melodic movements of a particular *raga*. They all have lyrics. The complex structure reaches its height in the *kritis* which are usually devotional, particularly in the 18th century with singers like Shyama Shastri and Tyagaraja. Unlike some North Indian musical forms in which the melody became more important than the lyric, *kriti* restored the balance between words and music.

Percussion The unusual southern percussionists' contest takes place during the *Tala Vadya Kacheri* when instrumentalists compete with each other while keeping within the framework of a rhythm and finally come together in a delightful finale.

Dance Bharata Natyam is thought to be the oldest form of classical dance in India. Originating in Tamil Nadu, it is essentially a highly stylized solo feminine dance which combines movement, music and mime with *nritta* (pure dance) and *nritya* (expression), usually on the theme of spiritual love. The opening *alarippu* shows the dancer unfolding her body in strict rhythm and order, accompanied by the *mridangam* (drum) and the singing of the *nattuvanar* (conductor) and the dancer's own ankle bells, while the middle section *varnam* allows her to display her greatest skill and is very demanding, physically and emotionally. The two related dance forms, the *Bhagavata Mela*, performed by men in some important temples and the *Kuravanji*, a dance-opera for women for certain temple festivals also come from Tamil Nadu. Institutions excelling in the teaching of this form are *Kalakshetra*, Chennai, *Darpana*, Ahmadabad, *Rajarajeswar Kala Mandir*, Mumbai, *MS University*, Baroda and *Triveni Kala Sangam*, New Delhi.

South Indian temple architecture Temple building was a comparatively late development in Hindu worship. Long before the first temple was built, shrines were dotted across the land, each with its own mythology. Even the most majestic of South Indian temples have basic features in common with these original shrines, and many of them have simply grown by a process of accretion.

Mythology Most temples today still have versions of the stories which were held to justify their existence in the eyes of early pilgrims. According to David Shulman the story often includes "the (usually miraculous) discovery of the site and the adventures of those important exemplars (such as gods, demons, serpents and men) who were freed from sorrow of one kind or another by worshipping there". The shrine nearly always is claimed to be supreme – better than all others. For example, in a myth, the Goddess **Ganga** herself is forced to worship in a South Indian shrine in order to free herself of the sins deposited by evil-doers who bathe in the river at Benares.

Early architecture Through all its great diversity Hindu temple architecture repeatedly expresses those beliefs shared, though not necessarily expressed, by the millions of Hindus who make visiting temples such a vital and living part of life today. In architecture, as in religious philosophy, the South has derived much from its northern Hindu relations. The Buddhist *chaitya* hall with its apsidal plan had been the common form of most religious shrines up to the time of the Chalukyans in Karnataka, who in the sixth century started experimenting with what the Guptas in the North had already achieved by elaborating the simple square plan of earlier shrines. Developments at

Temple worship

David Shulman gives an excellent idea of the way in which a pilgrim approaches the temple. He writes: "There is often to begin with, the long, uncomfortable journey to the shrine, which may be defined as a form of asceticism, tapas... Once the pilgrim arrives at the shrine, he sees before him the towering gopuras or gates set in the walls that enclose the sacred area. He leaves his shoes outside the gate; he will also usually undergo an initial purification by bathing. Once the pilgrim goes through the gopuram the real journey begins... The tall gopurams of the South Indian temple create a sense of dynamism, of movement away from the gate and towards the centre, which is locked inside the stone heart of the main shrine...".

What do pilgrims hope to achieve by their pilgrimage? Usually there is a practical aim – the worshipper comes into contact with a power that helps him in his ordinary life. By offering his own sacrifice to the god, he hopes that the god will reward him by meeting his wishes – for good health, for a suitable husband or wife, for the birth of a child, for prosperity. As Shulman says: "It is important to realize that no one in Tamil Nadu goes on pilgrimage in order to attain release from this world (moksha). What has happened in the Tamil tradition is that the world-renouncing goal of the ascetic has been redefined as equivalent to bhakti (worship and praise). Pilgrimage came to be a substitute for sannyasa". The Hindu bhakti movements which developed personal worship and praise of a personal Lord, directed the worshipper back to the world in which they live rather than to seek release from it, see also page 526.

Aihole, Badami and Pattadakal in Karnataka led to the divergence of the two styles of Hindu temples and this became obvious in the shape of the spire. In the North, the *sikhara* was a smooth pyramidal structure, rising to a rounded top with a pointed end, while in the South the *vimana* was more like a stepped pyramid, usually square in plan and had at its top a rounded cupola.

The **Dravida** or Dravidian style underwent several changes under the different dynasties that ruled for about 1,000 years from the time of the Pallavas who laid its foundations. In Mahabalipuram, rock-cut cave temples, *mandapas* (small excavated columned halls), and *rathas* (monoliths in the shape of temple chariots) were carved by the early Pallavas. These were followed by structural temples and *bas relief* sculptures on giant rocks. The Ekambaresvara Temple in Kanchipuram shows the evolution of the Dravidian style – the shrine with its pyramidal tower and the separate *mandapa* all within the courtyard with its high enclosure wall made up of cells. Six centuries later the two separate structures were joined by the covered hall (*antarala*). A large subsidiary shrine there, which took the place of an entrance gateway, also hinted at the later *gopuram*.

The **Cholas** did away with the rampant lion pilasters, introducing high relief, half-size sculptures of deities and the gryphon motifs. Their greatest architectural achievements are seen in the early 11th-century temples at Gangaikondacholapuram and at Thanjavur where they built huge pyramidal towers on high vertical bases with exquisitely carved figures in niches on the walls. The Cholas are also remembered for the fine bronzes which adorned their temples.

Development of *gopurams* The **Pandiyas** introduced the practice of building prominent watch towers, the *gopurams* and concentric, often battlemented fortress walls which enclosed the courtyards with shrines. Percy Brown observes that the reason for this change may have been due to the inability of the Pandiyas to structurally alter or remove any insignificant holy shrine which they found to be of no artistic merit, but in order to draw

Tamil Nadu & Chennai

attention to them and give them prominence they constructed the high walls and massive, richly ornamented gateways.

The *gopuram* took its name from the 'cow gate' of the Vedic village, which later became the city gate and finally the monumental temple entrance. This type of tower is distinguished from the *vimana* by its oblong plan at the top which is an elongated vaulted roof with gable ends. It has pronounced sloping sides, usually 65°, so that the section at the top is about half the size of the base. Although the first two storeys are usually built solidly of stone masonry, the rest is of lighter material, usually brick and plaster. You can see examples of Pandiya *gopurams* at Jambukesvara near Tiruchirappalli and in Chidambaram and Tirumalai (see page 139). The Airavatesvara Temple at Darasuram in Thanjavur District built in the 12th century, towards the end of Chola rule under King Rajaraja II, is a more complete example of the period, see page 137. Not only does it have the central temple with its tower but the enclosure also includes a number of smaller shrines. The lion pilasters and the gryphons of the earlier periods reappear here, only to be replaced by horses and dragons in later temples. In the Ramesvaram region on the coast in southern Tamil Nadu, open courtyards, trefoil arches and chariot forms became distinguishing features.

From the 13th century Muslim conquerors penetrated ever deeper into the south, bringing a halt to large scale temple building for 200 years. However by the 15th century the Vijayanagar kings established their Empire across much of South India, building their fortressed city at Hampi. Their temples were carved out in harmony with the rock, the flat-roofed halls having numerous distinctive highly sculpted pillars. Changes in temple design reflected the changes in the ceremonial observances in worship. There was a proliferation of special purpose buildings within the temple enclosure. Around the central temple, a subsidiary shrine was built (usually to the northwest) to house the consort of the main deity and to celebrate their marriage anniversary; a many-pillared open hall with a central altar, or *kalyana mandapa*, made its appearance close to the east entrance. The temples at Kanchipuram, Tadpatri, Srirangam, Lepakshi and Vellore are also in the Vijayanagara style. The development of the temple complex with several shrines to different deities in the courtyard, the tradition of building *gopurams* in each of the four enclosure walls and the remarkable use of the horse motif (and sometimes lions or dragons), mark the Vijayanagara period. The *kalyana mandapas* of the temples at Vellore and Kanchipuram make particular use of hippogryphs in their pillars. In the Srirangam temple it reaches its full expression in the *Seshagiri mandapa* or 'Horse Court'.

17th century After the defeat of Vijayanagar by the Muslim sultans of the Deccan, the Hindu rulers were pushed further South. The Nayakas emerged in the 17th century with their capital at Madurai and continued to build temple complexes with tall *gopurams*. These increased in height to become dominating structures covered profusely with plaster decorations. Madurai and Srirangam have a profusion of defensive walls, lengthy colonnades of the 'thousand pillar' halls and towering *gopurams*. The tall *gopurams* of Vijayanagar and Nayaka periods may have served a strategic purpose, but they moved away from the earlier *Chola* practice of giving the central shrine the tallest tower. The *kalyana mandapa* or marriage hall with a 'hundred' or 'thousand' pillars, and the temple tank with steps on all four sides, were introduced in some southern temples, along with the *Nandi* bull, Siva's 'vehicle', which occupies a prominent position at the entrance to the main Saivite shrine. In some temples you will see the sacrificial altar with a pole which may have small bells attached.

American ice for Madras heat

The first ice arrived in Calcutta from New England in 1833, and followed on the discovery by Frederic Tudor of Boston that ice would remain frozen if covered in sawdust, and transported it around the world. The "ice house" in Madras was built in the early 1840s. The business survived for 30 years, until refrigeration was invented. The building then changed hands several times before becoming the home for a few months of Swami Vivekananda in 1892 hence its modern name, Vivekenanda House.

Government Tamil Nadu took its present form as a result of the States Reorganization Act of 1956. Until 1967 the Assembly was dominated by the Indian National Congress, but after an attempt by the central government to impose Hindi as a national language the Congress Party was routed in 1967 by a regional party, the Dravida Munnetra Kazhagam (the DMK) under its leader CN Annadurai.

Annadurai was almost universally revered in Tamil Nadu. He had helped to convert the original Dravida Kazhagam from its position of atheistic Tamil nationalism, committed to absolute independence for a Tamil state, into a political party within the broad Indian mainstream struggling for social and economic reform while insisting on the primacy of regional Tamil culture. After his death the party split and since then either the **DMK**, or the splinter party, the **All India Anna DMK**, has been in power in the State.

Neither party has any constituency beyond Tamil Nadu and thus at the all India level each has been forced to seek alliances with national parties. From the late 1960s the AIADMK, which controlled the State Assembly for most of the time, has been led by two film stars. The first, **MG Ramachandran**, known lovingly by his initials MGR, was a charismatic figure who even after a stroke which left him paralysed remained the Chief Minister until his death. **Jayalalitha**, his successor and a film actress who had starred in many of MGR's films, became a highly controversial Chief Minister. She and her party were ousted by the DMK in the May 1996 elections and she faced imprisonment and a range of criminal charges. In October 2000, Jayalalitha was sentenced to three years rigorous imprisonment for her role in a corrupt land deal but, with an appeal still to be heard, the saga goes on. The present Chief Minister, M Karunanadhi, is another veteran of Tamil politics. The 1998 Lok Sabha elections provided a major upset when the BJP linked up with Jayalalitha whose AIADMK won 30 of the 39 seats, but it proved a short-lived alliance, a 'marriage of inconvenience' to the BJP.

In the first six months of 2000 the escalating civil war in Sri Lanka raised acute problems for both the Tamil Nadu and the Indian governments, support for the Tamils in Sri Lanka running strongly. While the Indian government wished to prevent the creation of a secessionist Tamil state in Sri Lanka the DMK government of Mr Karunanadhi was more equivocal, and the political situation in the state continued to reflect the uncertainties of the civil war next door.

The economy There are great contrasts between dry farming and

Modern Tamil Nadu

Tamil Nadu & Chennai

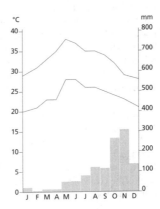

Climate: Chennai
Best time to visit:
Dec-Mar

irrigated agriculture. Irrigation has been practised in the region for over 2,000 years.

There are over 20,000 km of irrigation channels, known in Tamil as 'anicuts'. Rice is the most important crop, Tamil Nadu accounting for over 10% of India's rice production. Sugarcane is also a vital cash crop, as are groundnuts and other oilseeds. Cotton and bananas are also grown for market. In the hills of the Western Ghats tea makes a major contribution to exports and domestic consumption. The hills are also famous for cardamom, pepper, ginger and other spices. Potatoes are widely grown in the Nilgiris for sale in India's big cities. Fishing is increasingly important; a fifth of India's seafood exports, including prawns, crab, squid and oysters, come from Tamil Nadu.

Chennai (Madras மதராஸ்) and the Pallava Country சென்னை

Phone code: 044
Colour map 3, grid A6
Population: 5.36 mn
Altitude: sea level

Despite its role as capital of the Madras Presidency under the British, Madras (Chennai) was always regarded as a much more modest city than either the commercialized Bombay or the heavily industrialized Kolkata. Its sea breezes offered freshness from the otherwise stale and humid heat of its near equatorial location, and it retained a green and shaded cover of trees. Today the impression of relative quiet has been swept aside in its dramatic growth and commercial development, and from its old core between Fort St George and the Harbour it has spread rapidly across the surrounding plain through its industrialized northern suburbs and affluent residential suburbs of the south and west.

Ins & outs   **Getting there** Chennai's international and domestic air terminals are about 12 km from the city centre. Airport buses run a circuit of the main hotels, and include Egmore station; otherwise get a pre-paid taxi or auto-rickshaw. Trains from the north and west come into the Central Station behind the port. Lines from the south terminate at Egmore, which has hotels nearby, but there is pre-paid transport for other destinations. **Getting around** Chennai is very spread out and walking is usually uncomfortably hot so it's best to find an auto. Taxis are comparatively rare and expensive. The bus service is extensive and frequent, but often very crowded.

History   Armenian and Portuguese traders had settled in the San Thome area before the arrival of the British. In 1639, **Francis Day**, a trader with the East India Company, negotiated the grant of a tiny plot of sandy land to the north of the Cooum River as the base for a warehouse or 'factory'. It was completed on 23 April 1640, St George's Day. Its choice was dictated partly by local politics – Francis Day's friendship with Dharmala Ayyappa Nayak provided a useful lever with the Vijayanagar Raja of Chandragiri – but more importantly by the favourable local price of cotton goods.

By 1654 Fort St George had a church and English residences – the 'White Town'. To its north was 'Black Town', referred to locally as Chennaipatnam after Nayak's father. The two towns merged and **Chennaipatnam** grew with the acquisition of neighbouring villages of *Tiru-alli-keni* (Lily Tank) now Triplicane, in 1676. In 1693, Governor Yale (founder of Yale University in the USA) acquired Egmore, Purasawalkam and Tondiarpet from Emperor Aurangzeb, who had by that time extended Moghul power to the far south. In 1746 Madras was captured by the French, to be returned to British control as a result of the Treaty of Aix la Chapelle in 1748. By the middle of the 18th century many other villages such as Nungambakkam, Ennore, Perambur, San Thome and Mylapore (the 'city of the peacock') were added with the help of friendly Nawabs. In 1793 Calcutta became the chief centre of British administration in India, though Madras continued to be the centre of the East India Company's expanding power in South India.

The city

The city is still growing although many services, including water supply and housing, are stretched beyond breaking point. Since Independence an increasing range of heavy and light goods industries have been added to long established cotton textiles and a leather industry. The opening of a new Ford Motor Company plant in Chennai has led some in the city to claim it as "the Detroit of India".

Tamil Nadu & Chennai

Chennai city

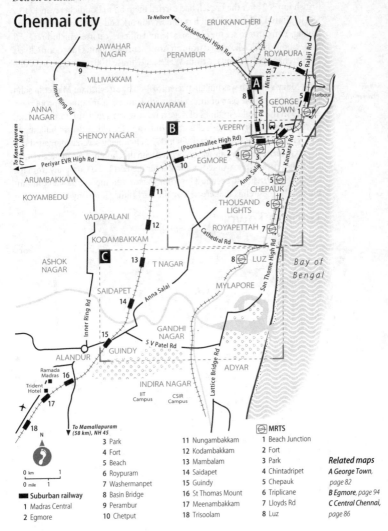

Suburban railway
1 Madras Central
2 Egmore
3 Park
4 Fort
5 Beach
6 Roypuram
7 Washermanpet
8 Basin Bridge
9 Perambur
10 Chetput
11 Nungambakkam
12 Kodambakkam
13 Mambalam
14 Saidapet
15 Guindy
16 St Thomas Mount
17 Meenambakkam
18 Trisoolam

MRTS
1 Beach Junction
2 Fort
3 Park
4 Chintadripet
5 Chepauk
6 Triplicane
7 Lloyds Rd
8 Luz

Related maps
A George Town,
  page 82
B Egmore, page 94
C Central Chennai,
  page 86

Sights

Fort St George

The beginning of the city of Madras was marked by the building of the 'Factory House' with its fortifications on the beach. It was completed by the British in 1654 but was rebuilt several times. The present structure of Fort St George, a fine example of 17th-century British military architecture, was mostly built in 1666. The country's tallest flagstaff, thought to be over 300 years old, stood here. The 24 black **Charnockite** (see page 556) pillars were reclaimed by the British in 1762 after the French had carried them off to Pondicherry in 1746.

The **State Legislative Hall** has fine woodwork and black and white stone paving. You can also see the old barracks and officers' quarters including Lord Clive's house which he rented from an Armenian merchant. One room, Clive's Corner, has small exhibits. Arthur Wellesley's house, 100 m along, is a picturesque ruin.

An excellent booklet about the church is for sale inside

St Mary's church was built between 1678-80 by Streynsham Master in solid masonry to a simple plan of three aisles with semi-circular cannon-proof roofs and 1.3 m thick walls. In times of siege it was used as a military dormitory and store house. The first English church in India and the oldest British building to survive, it was almost entirely rebuilt in 1759 after being severely damaged in a siege. **Governor Elihu Yale** was associated with the church. An American (born to English parents) he worked as a writer for the East India Company from the age of 24 to 39, rising to become Governor. Perhaps the most remarkable monument in the church is that erected by the East India Company to the famous

Tamil Nadu & Chennai (vertical, left margin)

George Town

Related maps
Chennai City,
page 775
Egmore, page 94
Central Chennai,
page 86

missionary **Schwartz**, at one time the intermediary between the British and Haidar Ali. The original black Charnockite font from Pallavaram has been in continuous use since the church was consecrated. Outside the west entrance, the tombstone of Elizabeth Baker is one of the oldest British inscriptions in India.

George Town

Renamed after the future King George V on the occasion of his visit to India in 1905, George Town has long been the centre of Madras's commercial activity. The lawyer Stephen Popham, who was in Madras from 1778-95 was particularly enthusiastic about improving the city's sanitation. Popham laid out what was to become Madras's main commercial street, still known as **Popham's Broadway**.

In Popham's Broadway (Prakasham Road) is the **Wesleyan Church** (1820). In **Armenian Street** to its east is the beautiful ★ **Armenian Church** of the Holy Virgin Mary (1772). Solid walls and massive 3 m high wooden doors conceal the spotless open courtyard inside. On the site of an ancient cemetery, the oldest Armenian tombstone in the courtyard dates from 1663. The East India Company valued the Armenian community for their 'sober, frugal and wise' style of life and they were given the same rights as English settlers in 1688.

Immediately to the north of the Armenian Church is the Roman Catholic Cathedral, **St Mary of the Angels** (1675). The date 1642, inscribed at the entrance to the Church, is when the Capuchin monks built their first church in Madras.

To the east again is **Parry's Corner**, named after the company founded by Thomas Parry in 1790. The group is now controlled by Nattukkottai Chettiars from Ramanathapuram District – see page 131.

The **High Court** (5 km, 1892), is in the Indo-Saracenic style of the late 19th century developed by architects such as **Henry Irwin** (see page 90), who was also responsible for the National Art Gallery. You are allowed to visit the courtrooms in the law courts by using the entrance on the left. A fine example is Court No 13 which has stained glass, fretted wood-work, carved furniture, silvered panels and a painted ceiling. ■ *1045-1345, 1430-1630, Mon-Sat. Contact Registrar for visit and guide.*

The huge red central tower nearly 50 m tall built like a domed minaret to serve as a **lighthouse** can be seen 30 km out at sea. It was in use from 1894 until 1977 when a new one was built on the Marina. You can climb to the top of the lighthouse for a good view. The original **Esplanade Lighthouse**, southeast of the High Court, is in the form of a large Doric pillar which took over from the Fort lighthouse in 1841. It is used as the standard bench mark for Chennai.

Tamil Nadu & Chennai

To the west of the Law Courts is the **Pachaiyappa's Hall** (1850) modelled on the Athenian Temple of Theseus. **Pachaiyappa Mudaliar**, a Hindu, was one of the first Indians to leave a will. Born in 1748 in a destitute family, Pachaiyappa had made a fortune by the age of 21. He left most of his wealth to charity but his will was contested for 47 years after his death in 1794. The trust now administers educational charities across India.

The 19th-century growth of Madras can be traced north from Parry's Corner. **First Line Beach** (North Beach Road), built on reclaimed land in 1814 fronted the beach itself. The **GPO** (1844-84) was designed by Chisholm. The completion of the harbour (1896), transformed the economy of the city.

In the 18th century major commercial expansion took place between First Line Beach and **Mint Street**. The Mint was first opened in 1640, and from the end of the 17th century minted gold coins under licence for the Mughals, though it did not move to Mint Street until 1841-42.

Wall Tax Road (now called **VOC Road**) takes its original name from an unsuccessful plan to raise money by taxation to pay for the defensive wall constructed between 1764-69 to ward off the attacks of Haider Ali.

Central Chennai and the Marina

Triplicane and **Chepauk** contain some of the finest examples of late 19th-century Indo-Saracenic architecture in India, focused on the University of Madras. The Governor of Madras, Mountstuart Elphinstone Grant-Duff (1881-86), decided to develop the Marina, especially as a promenade. Ever since it has been a favourite place for thousands of city dwellers to walk on Sunday evenings. Over a century before that the **Chepauk Palace** had been built for Wallajah Muhammad Ali, Nawab of the Carnatic. It became the focus for a growing Muslim population in the city (see below).

Marina Beach & aquarium
Swimming unattended along Marina beach is dangerous (3 km)

Until the harbour was built at the end of the 19th century the sea washed up close to the present road, but the north drifting current has progressively widened the beach. **Anna Park** is named after the founder of the DMK, CN Annadurai. The **MGR Samadhi**, commemorating **MG Ramachandran**, the film star and charismatic Chief Minister during the 1980s, has become a focus of pilgrimage. The Sunday afternoon **market** on the beach is worth visiting.

University & presidency

The University of Madras (1857) is one of India's oldest modern universities. Chisholm won a competition with his two-storeyed Presidency College (1870), making full use of red brick and 'combining Italianate with Saracenic' styles. The **Senate House** (1874), had a richly carved ceiling and stained glass windows.

Chepauk & Beach Rd

Chepauk Palace (4.5 km) was the former residence of the Nawab of Carnatic. The original four-domed Khalsa Mahal and the Humayun Mahal with a grand *durbar* hall, had a tower added between them in 1855. The original building is now hidden from the road by the modern PWD building, *Ezhilagam*. Immediately behind is the Chepauk **cricket ground** where test matches are played. Lining the Kamaraj Salai (South Beach Road) is a succession of University buildings. Despite its unlikely appearance, **Vivekenanda House** was Madras' first 'ice house' for storing ice imported . On the other side of the beach is the sculpture 'the Triumph of Labour'.

Island & Anna Salai (Mount Rd)

South of Fort St George is the Island, created between 1696 and 1705. First the grounds for a Governor's residence, it later became a military camp, and it has retained its military ownership ever since. In the southwest corner is the

Gymkhana Club. Beyond the Willingdon Bridge is the bronze statue of the former governor Sir Thomas Munro on horseback without stirrups.

Near the Round Thana is the Banqueting Hall of the old Government House, now known as **Rajaji Hall** (1802). Built to mark the British victory over Tipu Sultan, it is in an attractive setting, designed in the Greek temple style.

Wallajah Mosque The 'Big Mosque' was built in 1795 by the Nawab of the Carnatic. There are two slender minarets with golden domes on either side.

Parthasarathi Temple Near the tank, the oldest temple structure in Chennai was built by eighth-century Pallava kings, and later renovated in the 16th by Vijayanagara rulers. Dedicated to Krishna as the royal charioteer, it shows five of Vishnu's 10 incarnations and is the only one dedicated to Parthasarathi. ■ *0600-1200, 1600-2200.*

Chintadripet One of Chennai's earliest suburbs, the densely packed collection of small houses with courtyards, was founded in 1734. It was set up as a weavers' settlement when the East India Company was finding it difficult to get enough good cloth to meet the demand in England. The Tamil words *chinna tari pettai* mean 'small looms village'.

Chintadripet, Egmore & the western inner suburbs

Egmore A bridge across the Cooum at Egmore was opened in 1700. In the late 18th century, the area around Pantheon Road (between the Poonamallee High Road and the Cooum), became the centre of Madras's social and cultural life. Egmore's development, which continued for a century, started with the building of Horden's 'garden house' in 1715.

Pantheon Road The original 'pantheon' (public assembly rooms) which stood here was completely replaced by one of India's National Libraries. The origins of the **Connemara Library** (built 1896) go back to 1662, 'when a bale of calico from Madras was exchanged for books in London'. At the southwest corner of the site stands Irwin's Victoria Memorial Hall, now the ★ **Art Gallery**, which Tillotson describes as one of "the proudest expressions of the Indo-Saracenic movement".

The **museum** here houses one of the world's finest collections of South Indian bronzes (see page 90), very disappointingly displayed, lit and described, but still remarkable. Egmore has a number of other reminders of the Indo-Saracenic period of the 19th and early 20th centuries, the station itself, built in the 1930s, being one of the last.

To the northeast of Egmore station is the splendid ★ **St Andrew's Church**, standing in a spacious compound. Consecrated in 1821, the church still has an active congregation. Apart from the façade which resembles St Martin-in-the-Fields in London, it is essentially circular, 25 m in diameter, and has a magnificent shallow-domed ceiling. You may ask to be allowed to go up the tower.

EVR Periyar Museum and Memorial, EVK Sampath Salai, is a fascinating exposition of the life of the Tamil leader **Periyar EV Ramaswamy**. ■ *Free.*

Nungambakkam today is a prestigious residential and educational area. In the 18th and 19th centuries, the part of town on either side of Anna Salai became the focus for high class residential European settlement. At the end of the 18th century, British administrators and merchants began to arrive in ever larger numbers, and many built splendid houses, including Arthur Wellesley, the future Duke of Wellington. Doveton House is one of Chennai's few remaining 'garden houses'.

Thousand Lights & Nungambakkam

★ **St George's Cathedral** (1816; Church of South India) has a spire over 40 m high. Don't miss the colonial graveyard northeast of the cathedral where banyans grow out of old mausoleums.

Tamil Nadu & Chennai

Central Chennai

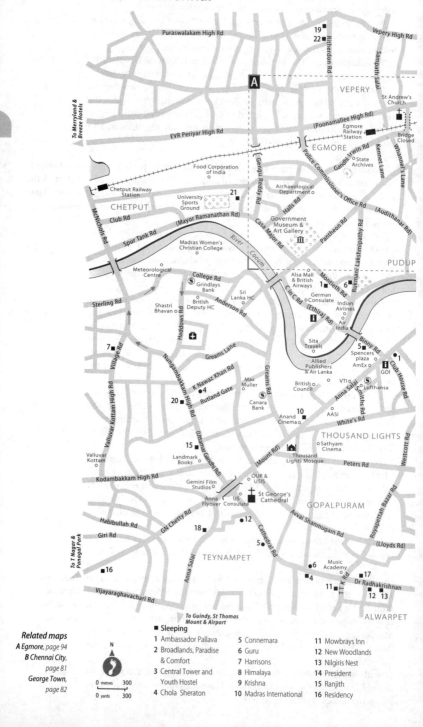

N

0 metres   300
0 yards   300

■ Sleeping
1 Ambassador Pallava
2 Broadlands, Paradise & Comfort
3 Central Tower and Youth Hostel
4 Chola Sheraton

5 Connemara
6 Guru
7 Harrisons
8 Himalaya
9 Krishna
10 Madras International

11 Mowbrays Inn
12 New Woodlands
13 Nilgiris Nest
14 President
15 Ranjith
16 Residency

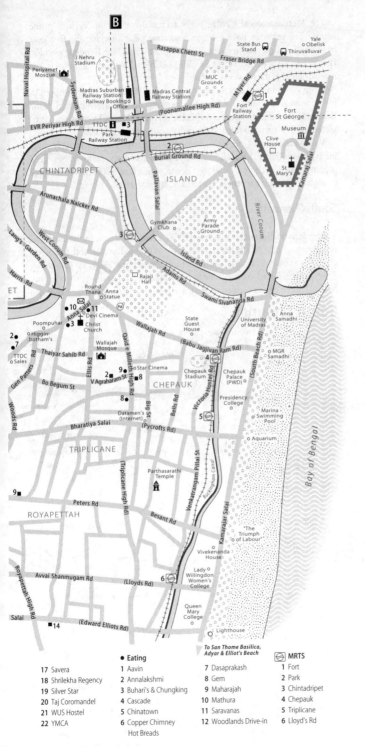

Tamil Nadu & Chennai

17 Savera	**● Eating**	**7** Dasaprakash
18 Shrilekha Regency	**1** Aavin	**8** Gem
19 Silver Star	**2** Annalakshmi	**9** Maharajah
20 Taj Coromandel	**3** Buhari's & Chungking	**10** Mathura
21 WUS Hostel	**4** Cascade	**11** Saravanas
22 YMCA	**5** Chinatown	**12** Woodlands Drive-in
	6 Copper Chimney	
	Hot Breads	

To San Thome Basilica,
Adyar & Elliot's Beach

🖂 MRTS
1 Fort
2 Park
3 Chintadripet
4 Chepauk
5 Triplicane
6 Lloyd's Rd

Tamil Nadu & Chennai

The **Meteorological Centre** plays a crucial role in this cyclone-prone region. The grounds have a commemorative pillar marking the first ever base-line for surveying in India. Its inscription reads "the Geodetic position (Lat 13° 4'3" 0.5N Long 80° 14'54" 20E) of Colonel William Lambton is primary original of the Survey of India".

From that minutely precise beginning spread the extraordinary undertaking of surveying South Asia from the southern tip of Kanniyakumari to the heights of Mount Everest, named after the surveyor **George Everest** who completed the first survey. Here too are India's earliest bench marks.

Valluvarkottam (4 km, 1976), an auditorium in the shape of a temple chariot, is a memorial to Thiruvalluvar (see page 74). Its verses are inscribed on 133 granite slabs. The decorative orange dome, which is reflected in the two large pools in the terrace garden, is a landmark. ■ *0900-1900.*

South Chennai

The present **Basilica of San Thome** (1898), surrounded now by the tenement rehousing scheme of a fishermen's colony, is claimed as one of the very few churches to be built over an apostle's tomb. St Thomas Didymus (Doubting Thomas) is believed to have come to India in AD 52. According to one legend, having landed on the west coast, he travelled across the peninsula, arriving in

South Chennai

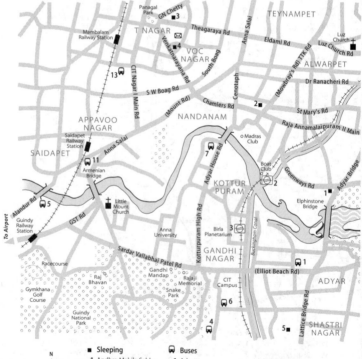

■ **Sleeping**
1 Andhra Mahila Sabha
2 Park Sheraton
3 Parthan
4 Transit House
5 TTDC Youth Hostel

🚌 **Buses**
1 Adyar
2 Anakaputhur
3 Dr Ambedkar Bridge
4 Foreshore Estate
5 Guindy Industrial Estate

6 Indira Nagar
7 Kotturpuram
8 Mandaveli
9 Mylapore

Related Maps
Chennai City, page 81
Central Chennai, page 86

N

0 metres 500
0 yards 250

Mylapore ('town of peacocks') where he lived and preached. To escape persecution he took shelter in Little Mount (see below). An alternative story recalls how he was invited to visit the King Gondophernes in Taxila, where he converted the king and his court before moving to South India. Some claim that his body was ultimately buried in the Italian town of Ortona.

The ★ **Kapaleeswarar Temple** (4 km) is a 16th-century Siva temple with a 40 m *gopuram*, built after the original was destroyed by the Portuguese in 1566. Sacred to Tamil Saivites, non-Hindus are only allowed in the outer courtyard where there are several bronze statues. ■ *0600-1200, 1600-2200.*

The **Luz Church** (1547-82; the date of 1516 in the inscription is probably wrong) is probably the oldest church in Chennai. It was built by the Portuguese in honour of Our Lady of Light. The Tamil name for the church, *Kattu Kovil*, means 'jungle temple', and a story suggests that Portuguese sailors were rescued from a storm by following a light. They traced it on shore, where it disappeared, and on this spot they built the church.

The **Elphinstone Bridge** across the Adyar River was built to provide work during the catastrophic famine in South India in 1876-78. A survey of pollution in the **Adyar River** has suggested that it is 98% effluent. Despite the pollution, the southern banks of the river, in the grounds of the Theosophical Society, have remnants of mangrove, and among the migratory birds which breed on the site are the Kentish plover, the stone curlew, and the white bellied sea-eagle. Olive Ridley turtles breed on the beaches near the mouth of the river and the estuary is home to a wide range of mammals and reptiles.

The **Theosophical Society** is set in large and beautifully quiet gardens. There are several shrines of different faiths and a Serene Garden of Remembrance for Madam Blavatsky and Colonel Olcott who founded the society in New York in 1875 and moved its headquarters to Madras in 1882. The 400-year-old magnificent banyan tree is of particular interest; go past the Nursery (kitchen) garden and look on the left at the central circle, with notes in English. Buildings include the Adyar Library and a Hall of Meditation. ■ *0830-1000, 1400-1600; Sat morning only, closed Sun.*

Kalakshetra, 1 km south, founded by Rukmini Devi Arundale, is a cultural centre for the revival of Indian classical arts and crafts.

Little Mount is where **St Thomas** is believed to have spent some time. The older of the two churches (1551), with its small vaulted chapel, was built by the Portuguese. The modern circular church was built in 1971. St Thomas is believed to have been martyred and bled to death in AD 52 on the **Great Mount**, though others

Tamil Nadu & Chennai

believe that he was accidentally killed by a hunter's arrow. On top of the 90 m high 'mount' is the **Church of Our Lady of Expectation**. The altar marks the spot where, according to legend, Thomas fell.

Some legends suggest that after St Thomas had been martyred on the Little Mount his body was brought back to the beach which had been his home and was buried there. The **Armenian Christians** who came from Persia are believed to have found St Thomas' grave and built a tomb and a church over it in AD 530. The village was called San Thome. Marco Polo in his travels in 1293 recorded the chapel on the seashore and a Nestorian monastery on a hill to the west where the apostle was put to death. In 1523, when the Portuguese started to rebuild the church they discovered the tomb containing the relics consisting of a few bones, a lance head and an earthen pot containing bloodstained earth. The church was replaced by the neo-Gothic structure which has two spires and was granted the status of a basilica in 1956. The relics are kept in the sacristy and can be seen on request. There are 13th-century wall plaques, a modern stained glass window, a 450-year-old Madonna brought from Portugal and a 16th-century stone sundial.

The **Snake Park** at **Guindy** is in the grounds of the Guindy National Park in the Raj Bhavan Estate, and has quite a wide collection of snakes and other reptiles. There is an hourly display from 1000 near the entrance, with a nearly inaudible recording; still "good fun". ■ *0830-1730. Rs 2. Trains run from Egmore (No 23C or Beach station or buses from town centre. There is also a deer park (see under parks and zoos below).*

Museums ★ **Government Museum and Art Gallery**, The Pantheon had been a 'place of public entertainment and balls' in the late 18th century. The museum is a red-brick rotunda surrounded by an Italianate arcade. Set up in 1851 in three buildings: Archaeology, Art and Bronzes. Look for the excellent collection of bronzes and the exhibits of Stone and Iron Age hunting and cooking implements which have been excavated locally. There is also an excellent numismatic collection and sections on botany (500-year-old teak and engineering designs inspired by plants), zoology (18.5 m whale skeleton) and arms and armoury. ■ *0900-1700, closed Fri. Entry Rs 3, camera Rs 20, video Rs 100. Pantheon Rd.*

Archaeology Stone sculptures from the Deccan and the beginnings of Buddhist artistic traditions are featured, including fragments from damaged limestone panels from Amravati, posts and railings from a dismantled stupa, including episodes in the life of Buddha (eg Subduing an elephant, IIIA.15). There are numerous Hindu images from later periods (eg 10th-century sculptures from Kodambalur, 'Siva and the Goddess' illustrating early Chola style).

Bronzes Although in some need of maintenance, one of the largest and finest collection of bronzes are well displayed in the Art Gallery. Among the most striking examples are an 11th-century Nataraja from Tiruvengadu, seated images of Siva and Parvati from Kilaiyur, and large standing figures of Rama, Lakshmana and Sita from Vadakkuppanaiyur. Buddhist bronzes from Nagapattinam have been assigned to Chola and later periods.

The National Art Gallery, in a superb building designed by Henry Irwin, has a good collection of old paintings and sculptures including Tanjore paintings on glass, Rajput and Mughal miniatures, 17th-century Deccan paintings, 11th- and 12th-century handicrafts, metalware and ivory carvings. Fine 13th- and 14th-century bronzes are housed in a separate building at the rear.

The Gallery of Modern Art has a permanent collection of contemporary art with temporary exhibitions on the first floor.

★ **Fort Museum** (within Fort St George). The 18th-century building houses exhibits from 300 years of British Indian history. It includes prints, documents, paintings, sculpture, arms (medieval weapons with instructions on their use) and uniforms. The Indo-French gallery has some Louis XIV furniture and clocks. Clive Corner, which includes letters and photographs, is particularly interesting. Disappointing labelling and display. ■ *0900-1700, closed Fri. Rs 2.*

Development Centre for Musical Instruments, 86 Mundakanni Koil Street, Mylapore. There are ancient and modern instruments which you may touch and play. Of special interest are those reconstructed with the help of ancient literary texts and temple sculptures. **Tamil Isai Sangam** Interesting and rare national collection of folk and classical musical instruments; a few are from abroad. ■ *Raja Annamalai Hall (2nd floor), Esplanade. 1630-2000. Closed Sun.*

Agri-Horticultural Society Gardens, next to the Cathedral, covering about 10 ha. Lawns, trees, flower beds and a collection of *bonsai*. ■ *0800-1200, 1330-1730, closed Thu.* **Guindy Deer Park**, next to Raj Bhavan, has the endangered black buck, white buck, bonnet monkey, civet cat, jackals and many species of birds. ■ *0830-1730, closed Tue.*

Parks & zoos

Excursions

The zoo attempts to provide a natural environment and breed some endangered species. There are 28 species of mammals including a nocturnal animal house, a lion and bison safari park, 61 species of birds and eight species of reptiles. ■ *0800-1700, daily except Tue. Vandalur, 32 km.*

Anna Zoological Park
For Pulicat Lake & the bird sanctuary (Andhra Pradesh) see page 404

On the coast road to Mahabalipuram, 19 km from Chennai, is this village. Started in 1969, the community of artists who live and work here exhibit and sell their paintings, graphics, sculptures, pottery and batik. Occasional dance performances in small open-air theatre. Stop for a short visit. ■ *Daily 0600-2000. T412892.*

Cholamandal Artists' village

Set up by the non-profit making Madras Craft Foundation. It presents the arts and crafts of the four southern states and performance of folk-arts (eg puppet shows) in a setting of traditional 19th- and early 20th-century architecture. This living museum has a crafts shop and restaurant. ■ *One hour guided tour, Rs 100 (Rs 250 foreigners); enquiries T044-4918943. Muttukadu, East Coast Rd, T04114-45303 (21 km).*

Dakshinchitra

Crocodile Bank, 42 km south of Chennai, was set up in 1976 by Romulus Whittaker who was also founder of Guindy Snake Park. Indian and African species are bred in addition to native species of turtle, and it has saved the endangered *gharial* and marsh crocodile. ■ *Entry Rs 5. Cameras Rs 25. Well labelled in English. Allow 30 mins.*

Crocodile Bank

Tours

These are on deluxe coaches and accompanied by a guide. **Tamil Nadu Tourist Development Corporation** (**TTDC**) Departure points and reservations: Sales Counters at 4 EVR Periyar High Road (opposite Central Station), T560294, and at Express Bus Stand near High Court compound, T5341982 (0600-2100). Sales agents: Welcome Tours, 150 Anna Sali (Agarchand Mansions), T8520908.

City sightseeing: **half-day**, daily 0800-1300, 1330-1830. Fort St George, Government Museum (closed on Friday), Valluvar Kottam, Snake Park, Kapaleeswarar Temple, Elliot's Beach and a drive along Marina Beach. Rs 75, a/c Rs 130. **Full-day**, daily 0800-1900. Drive along Marina Beach, Kapaleeswarar Temple, Snake Park, Vallavur Kottam, Museum, Fort St George, St Mary's Church, Birla Planetarium, Muttukadu Boat House and VGP Golden Beach. Rs 135. **Excursions**: Mahabali- puram and Kanchipuram, 0730-1900, Rs 180 (a/c Rs 300) and Tirupati, 0630-2200, Rs 315 (a/c Rs 500). Longer tours cover sites in Tamil Nadu and Karnataka.

ITDC Tours Reservations: 29 Victoria Crescent, C-in-C Road, T8278884. Booking counters at 154 Anna Salai, 0930-1700, Saturday 0900-1300, Sunday closed.

Essentials

Sleeping

Airport Most hotels are 12-15 km from the airport. **L** *Trident*, 1/24 GST Rd, T2344747, F2346699. 166 rooms, useful 12-hour **AL** rate and free airport transfer, restaurants all recommended, elegant garden setting.

Central Chennai Many hotels are strung out within 1 km either side of Anna Salai (Mount Rd). **L** *Chola*
A-E hotels collect an *Sheraton*, 10 Cathedral Rd, T8280101, F8278779. 80 rooms 'boutique hotel', good res-
extra 20-30% tax taurants (including *Peshawari*), airport transfer. **L** *Taj Coromandel*, 17 NH Rd,
T8272827, F8257104. 201 rooms, excellent restaurants, good pool, *MH Taxis*. Recom-
■ *on maps,* mended. Western tour groups dominate. **L** *Connemara* (Taj), Binny's Rd (off Anna
pages, 86, 88 & 94 Salai), T8520123, F8523361. 148 rooms, renovated retaining splendid art deco fea-
Price codes: tures, extremely comfortable, excellent restaurants, bar, good *Giggles* bookshop,
see inside fornt cover heavily booked Dec-Mar. **AL** *Ambassador Pallava*, 53 Montieth Rd, T8554476,
F8554492. 120 rooms, good Chinese restaurant, plush.

A-B *Chennai International*, 693 Anna Salai, T8523411, F8523412. 66 comfortable rooms, quiet and clean (usual hazard of cockroaches), helpful staff, good location. **A-B** *Mowbrays Inn*, 303 TTK Rd, Alwarpet, T4998200, F4984319, mowbrays@md3.vsnl.net.in **B** *President*, Dr Radhakrishnan Rd, T8532211, F8532299, reserve@presiden.com 144 rooms (vary), pool, rather overpriced. **B** *Resi-*
dency, 49 GN Chetty Rd (convenient for airport), T8253434, F8250085. 112 very com-
fortable spacious rooms, 4th floor upwards have good views (9th floor, plush **A** suites), excellent *Ahaar* restaurant (good buffet lunches), exchange, good car hire with knowledgeable drivers, better rooms and service than some higher priced hotels, highly recommended, reserve ahead. **B** *Savera*, 69 Dr Radhakrishnan Rd, T8274700, F8273475. 125 comfortable rooms, good pool (non-residents, Rs 150), older hotel but smart and clean (standard rooms identical to superior!), disaster prone travel desk (ticket confirmation and taxis mis-handled).

D *Broadlands*, 16 Vallabha Agraharam St, T8548131. 50 rooms, a few with shower, dorm (Rs 50), set around lovely shady courtyards, clean with good service, reasonably quiet and extremely popular though some find it over-rated and over-priced, helpful management but operate an outrageous "no-Indians" policy. **D** *Comfort*, 22 Vallabha Agraharam, T8587661, F849671. 40 rooms, some a/c, clean friendly Indian hotel 5 minutes from Marina Beach. **D** *Guru*, 69 Marshalls Rd 500 m from Egmore rly, T/F8554067. Large hotel, fairly clean rooms, (Rs 450+), some a/c, good vegetarian restaurant, no credit cards. **D** *Harrisons*, 154/5 Village Rd, T8275271. Some a/c rooms,

Brahma, Vishnu and the fiery phallus

The Tamil scholar Arunachalam describes the mythical origins of the hill: "Brahma and Vishnu had been quarrelling over who was superior when Siva appeared to them as a linga of fire. Vishnu tried to find its base by digging in the form of a boar while Brahma became a goose and flew towards the top, but neither could find any limit to the linga. They recognized it as a form of Siva, who made the fiery linga into the mountain Tiruvannamalai".

restaurant (South Indian/Chinese), bar. **D** *Himalaya International*, 54 Triplicane High Rd, T8547522. 45 rooms with nice bath, some a/c, modern, welcoming, clean, bright, no food but available from *Hotel Gandhi* next door. **D** *New Woodlands*, 72/75 Radhakrishnan Rd, T8273111, F8260460. 172 spacious rooms (some in 'chalets'), some a/c, restaurant (excellent South Indian), small but pleasant pool (non-residents, Rs 60), unhelpful management reported. **D** *Paradise*, 17/1 Vallabha Agraharam St, T8547542, F8530052. Spacious clean rooms with fans (some with 2!) with shower, good value, very friendly and helpful owners. **D** *Ranjith*, 9 NH Rd, T8270521, F8277688. 51 rooms, some a/c, restaurant (good non-vegetarian continental), excellent and reasonable bar, cool, pleasant and relaxing, travel.

E *Sree Krishna*, 159 Peters Rd, T8522897. 15 rooms, some a/c with bath. **E** YMCA (1), 14 Westcott Rd, Royapettah, T8532158. The **Automobile Association of South India** (Anna Salai) has a guest house for members.

Many hotels (including several good 'budget') are clustered around the station and the EVR Periyar (Poonamallee) High Rd, an auto-rickshaw ride away to the north of the railway line. **C** *Abu Palace* 926 EVR Periyar High Rd, T6412222, F6428091. Plush, well insulated rooms, restaurant, bar, smart business style hotel, concrete fortress-like exterior, huge enclosed lobby. **C** *Breeze*, 850 EVR Periyar High Rd, T6413334, F6413301. 75 rooms, modern, popular. **C** *New Victoria*, 3 Kennet Lane (200 m from station), T8253638, F8250070. 50 a/c rooms, some scruffy, restaurant good value (excellent *Lido* breakfast), bar, quiet, generally good service, ask for 'rupee tariff'.

Egmore

D *Blue Diamond*, 934 EVR Periyar High Rd, T6412244, F6428903. 33 rooms, some a/c, quieter at rear, good a/c restaurant (crowded at peak times), exchange. **D** *Central Tower*, 17 EVR Periyar High Rd (opposite Central Station), T581491, 60 good value rooms (some a/c), good Malabar food (no alcohol). **D** *Pandian*, 9 Kennet Lane, T8252901, F8258459. 90 rooms, some a/c, a/c restaurant (lacks atmosphere), bar, clean but spartan, helpful staff, expensive room service. **D** *Peacock*, 1089 EVR Periyar High Rd, T5322981. 72 rooms some a/c, quieter at rear, restaurant, exchange. Some cheaper **D** hotels on the main road may have a problem with noise except at rear of the building. **D** *Imperial*, 6 Gandhi Irwin Rd, T8250376, F8252030. 80 rooms, some a/c, best at rear, 4 restaurants, good food, reasonable price, bar, friendly. **D** *Ramprasad*, 22 Gandhi Irwin Rd, T8254875. Functional rooms, pleasant roof garden, good a/c vegetarian restaurant, ISTD phones next door. **D** *Rivera*, 943 EVR Periyar High Rd (opposite *Dasaprakash*), T6411845, 6428316. 56 rooms 34 a/c (500-600), good restaurant, exchange. **D** *Udipi Home*, 34 Police Commissioners Office Rd, T8251515. 82 rooms (1-4 beds), some a/c, good vegetarian restaurant, no credit cards. **D** *Vaigai*, 3 Gandhi Irwin Rd, T834959, F835774. 58 rooms, some a/c, restaurant, exchange, good value. **D** *YWCA International Guest House*, 1086 EVR Periyar High Rd, T5324234. Restaurant (rate includes breakfast), 60 rooms, with bath, few a/c, for men and women, small membership fee, popular so book early, excellent value, also *camping ground*, reservations Secretary. Also within the compound **F** *Laharry Transit Hostel*, for women

Many D hotels also have cheaper rooms

Tamil Nadu & Chennai

under 30 only, very cheap and good value. **D-E** *Dasaprakash*, 100 EVR Periyar High Rd, T8255111. 100 rooms, some a/c (quietest in Block B), restaurant (vegetarian), bar, no credit cards, peaceful rooftop gardens. Non-vegetarian food and alcohol not allowed on premises and suggests "No tipping". **E** *Diplomat*, 38-39 Halls Rd, T8253728. Simple but quiet for Egmore.

Kennet Lane budget hotels are often full

E *Embee International*, 12A Whannels Lane, near St John Church, T847537. Noisy but convenient for night buses. **E** *Laxmi Bhavan Lodge*, 16 Kennet Lane, T8254576. Rooms around courtyard in old building, set back in garden. **E** *Masa*, 15/1 Kennet Lane, T8252966, F8251261. 88 clean functional a/c rooms, hot water. **E** *Regent*, 8 Kennet Lane, T8253347. Renovated clean rooms, backyard, friendly. **E** *Satkar*, 65 Ormes Rd (Flowers and Millers Rd junction), T6426304. Spotless rooms with bath, some a/c, good vegetarian *Suryaprakash* restaurant, helpful staff, good value but very noisy. **E** *Silver Star*, 5 Purasawalkam High Rd, T6424414. 38 simple clean rooms set back from road, open air restaurant in courtyard, helpful and friendly staff. **E** *Sri Durga Prasad*, 10/11 Kennet Lane, T8253881. Pleasant old style Indian hotel. **E** *YMCA (1)*, 14 Westcott Rd, Royapettah, and *(2)* at 17 Ritherdon Rd, Vepery, T5322831, where there are **D** rooms

Egmore

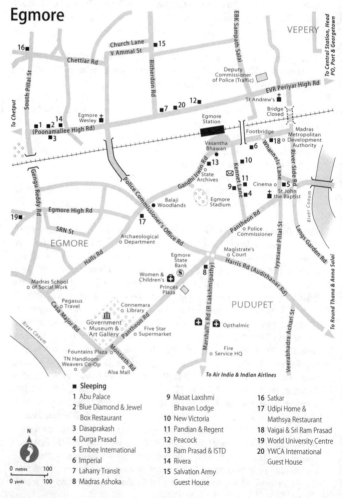

■ **Sleeping**

1 Abu Palace	9 Masat Laxshmi Bhavan Lodge	16 Satkar
2 Blue Diamond & Jewel Box Restaurant	10 New Victoria	17 Udipi Home & Mathsya Restaurant
3 Dasaprakash	11 Pandian & Regent	18 Vaigai & Sri Ram Prasad
4 Durga Prasad	12 Peacock	19 World University Centre
5 Embee International	13 Ram Prasad & ISTD	20 YWCA International Guest House
6 Imperial	14 Rivera	
7 Laharry Transit	15 Salvation Army Guest House	
8 Madras Ashoka		

Street name changes

Mount Road is **Anna Salai**
Poonamallee High Road is **EVR Periyar**
High Road; Mowbray's Road is **TTK Road**

North Beach Road is **Rajaji Salai**
Abbreviations: NH (Nungambakkam
High) Road.

Tamil Nadu & Chennai

with bath. **F** *Railway Retiring Rooms*, T848533. **F** *World University Service*, East Spur
Tank Rd, T8263991. Some rooms with bath, dorm, International Student cards needed,
couples not allowed to share a room, cheap canteen for Indian snacks, value, well
located for Egmore and south central Chennai, reservations: Director. **F** *Youth Hostel*
(YHAI), 2nd Ave, Indira Nagar, T4420233. 44 beds (Rs 14), also campsite.

The heart of the old city and the area round the Central Station and Thiruvalluvar Bus **George Town**
Stand has some budget accommodation. Most are not as good as those in Egmore.
E *Blue Star*, 108 VOC Rd (Wall Tax Rd), T5350001. **E** *Railway Retiring Rooms*, Central
Station, T5353337, some a/c rooms, cheaper dorm. **E** *Sornam International*, 7
Stringer St, T5353061. Rooms with TV, rooftop vegetarian restaurant, large modern
hotel. **E** *Youth Hostel* (TTDC), EVR Park (near Central Rly Station), T589132. Reasonably
quiet. **F** *YMCA*, NSC Bose Rd, T583941, opposite City bus stand.

L-AL *Holiday Inn Crowne Plaza*, 1 GST Rd, T2348976, F4340429. 187 rooms. **L-AL** *Park* **South Chennai**
Sheraton, 132 TTK Rd, T4994101, F4997201. 160 rooms, *Dakshin* Chettinad restaurant,
good pool. **C** *Parthan*, 75 GN Chetty Rd (near Panagal Park), T8241592, F8241591. 29
clean, large, comfortable and quiet rooms, restaurant (Chinese), exchange. Recommended. **D** *Transit House*, 26 Venkataraman St, T Nagar, T4341346. Some a/c rooms,
dorm (Rs 60), snack bar and pleasant garden, no credit cards. **E** *Andhra Mahila Sabha*,
12 D Deshmukh Rd, T4938311. Some **D** a/c rooms, vegetarian restaurant.

Eating

Most are in Central Chennai and are open 1200-1500, 1900-2400. Those serving
non-vegetarian dishes are often more expensive.

Recommended in **hotels**: *Chola Sheraton* Chinese (chef from Beijing) and good roof- **Expensive**
top restaurant, superb views. *Coromandel: Southern Spice* offers very good South ■ *on maps,*
Indian, evening dance recitals, freezing a/c; "exquisite Continental at *Patio*" but *pages, 86, 94 & 88*
pricey, **Golden Dragon** does excellent Chinese. *Trident* Executive lunch, Rs 450.
Connemara: romantic outdoor **Raintree** with good food, atmosphere and ethnic
entertainment but "cavalier service". **Verandah**, poor breakfast, dismally slow service.
Savera's (Ground Floor): excellent Indian, very friendly, helpful service, live Indian
music in the evenings. *Rooftop*, excellent Kashmiri and Mughlai, good views. **Outside**: *Copper Chimney* opposite *Chola Sheraton*. International, a/c, good tandoori,
very clean, pleasant seating. *Kabul's* TTK Rd. Mughlai. Rustic décor, clean, licensed.

Chinese *Cascade*, 15 Khaderi Nawaz Khan Rd. Chinese, Thai, Japanese and Malay. **Mid range**
Chungking, 67 Anna Salai (opposite PO) (1030-2200) where lack of atmosphere (dim
lighting) is compensated for by good food. *China Town*, 74 Cathedral Rd (a/c) and
Dynasty at *Harrison's Hotel*, recommended. *Southern Chinese*, 683 Anna Salai. Thousand Lights (next to Anand Theatre), highly recommended. **Others** *Annalakshmi*,
Anna Salai (opposite LIC). Wholesome, health-restoring offerings, Southeast Asian specialities (profits to charity, run by volunteers). Recommended. *Buhari's*, 83 Anna Salai.
Good Indian. Has a terrace, and dimly lit a/c restaurant, with unusual décor, try crab
curry, egg *rotis* and Muslim dishes; branch in Park Town near Central Station.

Tamil Nadu & Chennai

Dasaprakash, Anna Salai, next to Higginbotham's Bookshop (1200-1445, 1900-2345) and branch at 100 EVR Periyar High Rd. Modern restaurant (buffets Rs 120), also excellent milk shakes. *Gem*, Triplicane High Rd (200 m south of *Broadlands*). Non-vegetarian. Tiny Muslim restaurant. *Jewel Box* in *Blue Diamond Hotel*. Cool a/c, good for breakfasts, snacks and main courses (also Chinese). *Shangrila* in *Chennai International*.

Cheap   **Indian vegetarian** *Balaji Woodlands*, *Vee Yes Hotel*, Egmore. *Maharaja*, Triplicane High Rd, 100 m from *Broadlands*. *Mathura*, Tarapore Towers (opposite *Woodland's*), 2nd Flr, Anna Salai. Lacks style but does good *Udipi* dishes. *Ritz*, *Rivera Hotel*. Wide choice of tasty dishes in clean restaurant. *Saravana* branches (209 NSC Bose Rd), 2 floors. Extremely clean, excellent snacks, fruit juices (try pomegranate!), sweetmeats, all freshly made. *Woodlands Drive-In Restaurant*, 30 Cathedral Rd (0600-2100). Rows of tables, simple, busy, go for breakfast. *Udipi*, 8/9 Anna Salai (near Higginbotham's), good range of snacks; *Udipi Home Mathsya* , 1 Hall's Rd, Egmore. A/c, excellent, wide range of food, friendly management. Highly recommended. *Vasanta Bhavan*, 10 Gandhi Irwin Rd, opposite Egmore station, 1st Flr. Very clean, excellent food, friendly staff, downstairs bakery does delicious sweets.

Cafés &   *Cakes 'n' Bakes*, 22 NH Rd. *Chit Chat*, 557 Anna Salai. *Maratha* in *Trident Hotel*.
fast food   *Snappy*, 74 Cathedral Rd. *Pizza Corner*, NH Rd (near Taj Coromandel). Good value eat-in, take-out or delivered, "just like home". *Aavin*, Anna Salai, near tourist office. Milk bar, ice creams (no seats). *Nala's*, Cathedral Rd, and *Naga's*, Village Rd, do good Indian sweets and savoury snacks.

Bars   It is possible to obtain alcoholic drinks without any difficulty despite local restrictions on sale of alcohol. Regulations change periodically, however, and All India Liquor Permits are available from either an Indian mission or a Govt of India Tourist office abroad or in one of the regional capitals. Try *Hotel Connenmara's* large, bright bar, offering huge tankards of beer, "exceptional 'side-snacks', huge TV; casual clothes accepted".

Entertainment

Cinemas   Show foreign (usually English language) films, are mostly in the centre of town on Anna Salai. They are a/c and quite comfortable and you may appreciate a break on a hot day! **Music and dance**: *Chennai Music Academy* auditoria is the scene of numerous performances of Indian music, dance and theatre, not only during the prestigious 3 week Music Festival from mid-Dec but right through the year; *Sabhas* are membership societies that offer cultural programmes 4 times a month to its members, but occasionally tickets are available at the door. There are several other auditoria: *Raja Annamalai Hall*, *Mylapore Fine Arts Club*, *Narada*, *Brahma and Krishna Gana Sabhas* and the little *Sittraragam*. *Kishkinta*, Tambaram, 4 km, train and courtesy bus (but not worth it).

Sports   **Clubs** Temporary membership at most, sometimes for sports only. *Cosmopolitan Club*, Anna Salai, tennis, billiards, golf, library, bar. *Chennai Boat Club*, Adyar bar. *Chennai Cricket Club*, Chepauk, tennis, swimming, cricket, billiards, bar. *Chennai Gymkhana Club*, Anna Salai, tennis, swimming, cricket, billiards, library, bar. *Chennai Riders Club*, Race View, Race Course, Velachery Rd, riding (including lessons) throughout the year except Jun. Facilities in clubs are for members only, but you may be allowed in on being recommended by a member. Some hotel facilities may be used on payment of a fee. **Golf** At Guindy Race Course. **Swimming** Hotel pools open to non-residents: *Ambassador*, *Savera*, *New Woodlands*. *Chennai Cricket Club* has an excellent pool (less crowded before noon); you need an introduction. Others open to the public are at *Marina Beach* and the *YMCA* pool at Saidapet. Sea bathing is safe at Elliot's Beach, though no longer attractive. **Tennis** Clubs allowing members' guests and temporary members to use courts are Chennai Club, Gymkhana Club, Cricket Club, Cosmopolitan Club, Presidency Club and Lady Willingdon Club. YMCA at Saidapet also has courts.

Festivals

On **January 14**, *Pongal Makara Sankranti*, the harvest thanksgiving, is celebrated all over Tamil Nadu for three days (public holiday). After ritually discarding old clothes and clay pots, festivities begin with cooking the first harvest rice in a special way symbolizing good fortune, and offering it to the Sun god. The second day is devoted to honouring the valuable cattle; cows and bulls are offered special new-rice dishes prepared with jaggery or nuts and green lentils. You will see them decorated with garlands, bells and balloons (!), their long horns painted in bright colours, before being taken out in procession around villages. Often they will pull carts decorated with foliage and flowers and carrying children, accompanied by noisy bands of musicians. On the final day of feasting, it is the turn of the 'workers' to receive thanks (and bonuses) from their employers.

Shopping

Parry's corner and Anna Salai are principal centres. Most shops open Mon-Sat 0900-2000, some close for lunch 1300-1500. Weekly holidays may differ for shops in the same locality. There are often discount sales during the festival seasons of Pongal, Diwali and Christmas. The weekly **Free Ads** (Rs 5, Thu) has listings for second hand cameras, binoculars etc which travellers might want to buy or sell.

Higginbotham's, 814 Anna Salai and F39 Anna Nagar East, near Chintamani Market. **Books** *Landmark*, Apex Plaza, 3 NH Rd, large up-to-date selection, well organized, excellent *Most open* for CDs, cassettes and stationery. *Side Effects*, G17 Eldorado, 112 NH Rd, closes *0900-1900* 1430-1600. Many publishing houses have bookselling departments: *Allied Publishers* (off Anna Salai) and *Oxford Book House* in Cathedral Grounds (Anna Salai) have extensive collections. The *Hotels Adyar Gate, Sindoori* and *Taj Coromandel* have branches of *Danai Bookshops* open 0830-2400. *Giggles* , *Hotel Connemara*, 0930-2100 daily, specializes in all things Indian, helpful, reliable postage service (Rs 100 fee), highly recommended. **Cassettes/CDs**: *Music World*, 1st Flr, Spencer Plaza, Anna Salai, best in town.

South Indian handicrafts (wood carving, inlaid work, sandalwood) at fixed prices from **Crafts** the Government-backed *Victoria Technical Institute*, Anna Salai near *Connemara Hotel*. *Poompuhar*, 818 Anna Salai, specializes in 1st class bronzes. Other Govt Emporia are along Anna Salai *Central Cottage Industries* opposite *Taj Coromandel*, is recommended. Other recommended shops: *Cane & Bamboo*, 26 C-in-C Rd; *Jamal's*, 44 Devraja Mudali St; *Tiffany's*, 2nd Flr, Spencer Plaza (antiques, bric-à-brac); *Kalpa Druma*, 61 Cathedral Rd (opposite *Chola Sheraton*), has attractive selection of wooden toys and panels; *Kalakshetra* at Thiruvanmiyur excels in *kalamkari* and traditional weaving, also good household linen; *New Kashmir Arts*, 111 Anna Salai, for good carpets. *Khazana* at *Taj Coromandel, Habitat*, K Nawaz Khan Rd nearby, and *Vatika* 5 Spur Tank Rd, are good for special, unusual gifts.

Have made shopping easier; most open 0900-2000. *Foodworld* at *Spencers Plaza*, **Department** Anna Salai near *Connemara* offers excellent choice for shopping in comfort. *Five Stars*, **stores** 60 Pantheon Rd, Egmore. *Harringtons*, 99 Harrington Rd, Chetput. *Supermarket*, 112 Davidson St and TNHB Building, Annanagar (closed Fri). *Burma Bazar*, Rajaji Salai, for imports, especially electronic goods, bargain hard.

Tamil Nadu & Chennai

Jewellery Traditional South Indian jewellery is in gold, with diamond and stone setting. 'Chennai Diamond' (zircon), and showy artificial jewellery worn by dancers and stage performers are also sold. Among many, for gold: *Bapalal*, 24/1 Cathedral Rd; *Gem Palace* in *Hotel Adyar Park*, for stone set jewellery.

Fabrics Chennai was founded because of the excellence and cheap prices of the local cotton. Govt *Co-optex* shops stock handloom silks and cottons. *Khadi* stores specialize in handspun and handwoven cotton. *Amrapali* in Fountain Plaza, and Adyar. *Shilpi*; *Urvashi*, TTK Rd, are good for cottons. Look out for excellent Kanchipuram **silk** and **saris**. Recommended for quality and value: *Handloom House*, 7 Rattan Bazar; *Nalli* (opposite Panagal Park) with excellent selection, both in T Nagar. *Rupkala* 191 Anna Salai, good prices, helpful staff.

Tour operators

Cox & Kings, A15 Eldorado Building, Nungambakkam High Rd. *Mercury*, 191 Anna Salai, T8522993, F8520988. *Pegasus*, 1st Flr, 10 Casa Major Rd, Egmore (behind Museums), T8250265, F8257889. *Sita*, 26 C-in-C Rd, T8278861, F8273536. *STIC*, 142 NH Rd, T8271195. *Surya*, 1st Flr, Spencers Plaza, Anna Salai, very efficient, friendly, personal service. *Thomas Cook*, 45 Montieth Rd, opposite *Ambassador Pallava Hotel*. *Welcome*, 150 Anna Salai, near India Tourist Office, T8520908, open 24 hrs.

Transport: local

Auto-rickshaw Three-wheeler scooter taxis take 2 adults and a child, extra passengers negotiable. Usual extra night charge of 25% between 2200-0500. Rs 7 for 1st km. Insist on using the meter. If they refuse or claim theirs doesn't work, walk away; there are plenty available. During the rush hour, however, prices get inflated as most drivers refuse to use the meter; you may be moved, on occasion, to put the meter down yourself! Some drivers take you 'for a ride'. **Cycle-rickshaws** are often no cheaper. Fix the fare first.

Bus The cheap, convenient bus service is not overcrowded and offers a realistic alternative to auto-rickshaws and taxis outside the rush hour (0800-1000, 1700-1900). Make sure you know route numbers as most bus signs are in Tamil (Timetables from major bookshops). Pallavan Transport Corp (PTC), Anna Salai, runs an excellent network of buses from 0500-2300 and a skeleton service through the night. 'M' service on mini-buses are good for the route between Central and Egmore stations and journeys to the suburban rly stations. The 'V' service operates fast buses with fewer stops and have a yellow board with the route number and LSS (Limited Stop Service). PTC has a ½ hourly 'luxury' mini-bus service between Egmore Station, Indian Airlines, Marshalls Rd office and the airports at Meenambakkam picking up passengers from certain hotels (inform time keeper at Egmore in advance, T561284). The fare is about Rs 20. **City routes**: between **Airport-Parry's** via Anna Salai, 18R, 18RR (limited stop); 52, A, B, D, E, G, 55A, 60, A; **Egmore-Central Station/Parry's**, 4B, 9, A, B, 10, 17E, T, K, 28A, M4; **Egmore-Anna Sq** (the Marina), 27, 27B, 29A; **Egmore-Adyar**, 23, A, B, C, E, G, J; **Central Station-EVR Periyar High Rd** (Dasaprakash), 15, B, C, D, G, 50, 53, A, B, C, E, G, K, 71, C; **Parry's/Broadway-Gemini**, 17B, C; **Parrys-St Thomas' Mt**, 18, A, 52, 54C, G, K, T, 55A; **Parry's/Broadway-Adyar**, 19M, 21B, E, F, K; **Anna Sq-Gemini, Guindy**, 25C, E, 45B; **Anna Sq-San Thome**, 12R.

Car hire A/c or ordinary cars with drivers are good value and convenient for sightseeing, especially for short journeys out of the city when shared between 3 and 5 people. Large hotels can arrange, eg *Regency* (Rs 500 per 8 hrs; Rs 750 for Mahabalipuram). **Ganesh Travels**, 36 PCO Rd, T8250066; **Gem**, 2 NH Rd, T8270272; **Hertz**, 426 Anna Salai,

T4330684, F4330014; **TTDC**, 4 EVR Periyar Rd, T560294. **Motor bike hire or purchase Southern Motors**, 282 TTH Rd, T4990784, is a good modern garage with efficient service. The *YWCA* on EVR Periyar High Rd is a good hotel for bikers and has a big shaded garden to park bikes securely.

Yellow-top taxis are increasingly hard to find. Ask a hotel bell-boy to call one and insist on using the meter (ask to see a chart before paying). Some refuse to go a short distance, some a long distance after 2000, or demand a 20% surcharge between 2200-0500. Drivers may ask for 4 or 5 times the metered fare; expect Rs 60-100 for 5 to 7 km. **Taxi**

The Mass Rapid Transit System (1st stage) covers the Beach-Chepauk and Chepauk-Mylapore sections. **MRTS**

Inexpensive and handy, but very crowded at peak times. Stops between Beach Rly Station and Tambaram (every 5 mins in rush hour) include Fort, Park, Egmore, Chetpet, Nungambakkam, Kodambakkam, Mambalam, Saidapet, Guindy, St Thomas Mt. Also serves suburbs of Perambur and Villivakkam. Convenient stop at Trisoolam for the airports, 500m walk from the terminals. **Suburban railway**

Transport: long distance

The **Aringar Anna International airport** (named after CN Annadurai) with 2 terminals, and the **Kamaraj Domestic airport**, are on 1 site at Trisoolam in Meenambakkam, 12 km from the centre. Enquiries, T140, 2343131. Pre-paid taxis from both; to Chennai Central or Egmore, Rs 150-180, 30 mins; Rs 450 to Mahabalipuram. *Aviation Express* coaches to Egmore Station via some hotels (roundabout route, so very slow); Rs 50. Airport, T2346013. Auto-rickshaws to Chennai Central, Rs 100. Suburban Railway: the cheapest way into town, from Trisoolam suburban line station to Egmore and Fort, but trains are often packed. Watch out for International prices for food and drink. **Free Fone**: in the main concourse, after collecting baggage in the international airport, you can use this phone to ring hotels. Railway Bookings 1000-1700. **Air**

    Domestic: *Indian Airlines*, 19 Marshalls Rd, T8555200 (daily, 0800-2000). Reservations, all 24 hrs: T8555209. Mini Booking Offices: 57 Dr Radhakrishnan Rd, T8279799; Umpherson St (near Broadway), T883321; 9 South Bagh Rd, T Nagar, T4347555. Ahmedabad, Bangalore, Bhubaneswar, Kolkata; Coimbatore, Delhi, Goa, Hyderabad; Kochi, Madurai, via Tiruchirappalli; Mumbai, Port Blair and Pune, Puttaparthy, Thiruvananthapuram, Visakhapatnam. *Jet Airways*: 43 Montieth Rd, Egmore, T8555353, airport T2346557, to Kolkata, Kochi, Mumbai, Port Blair, Thiruvananthapuram. *Sahara*, T8263661: Delhi.

    International: *Air India* flies to New York, Kuwait, London, Paris, Bangkok, Kuala Lumpur and Singapore; it is possible to air cargo a motorbike on Air India or MAS to Singapore for approximately $400. *British Airways* flies to London, Singapore. *Air Lanka* to Malaysia. *Saudia*, to some Middle East capitals.

The state highways are reasonably well maintained but the condition of other roads varies. The new East Coast Road (ECR) for Express buses and cars only has helped to cut some journey times, though in 1999-2000 it had an appalling accident rate of nearly one death per day on its one hundred mile stretch. Fast long distance Korean air buses now run on some routes, giving a comfortable ride on air-cushioned suspension. **Bus** Tamil Nadu Govt Express, Parry's, T5341835, offers good connections within the whole region and the service is efficient and inexpensive. Best to take a/c coaches or super deluxe a/c. Buses originate from Express Bus Stand, Esplanade, **Road** picking up from T Nagar, Egmore, Broadway and Basin Bridge. Bookings 0700-2100. Other state and private companies cover the region but you may wish to avoid their video coaches which make listening, if not viewing, compulsory as there are no headphones! Interstate Bus Depot, Broadway Bus Stand handles enquiries and reservations. Computer reservations are now made on long distance routes. **Pallavan Transport Corp (PTC)**, T566063; Reservations: 0430-2100. *Warning*: Beware of children who 'help' you to find your bus in the expectation of a tip; they may not have a clue! Also reports of men in Company uniforms selling tickets which turn out to be invalid; best to buy on the bus. From Tamil Nadu State Bus Stand (Broadway). The listings given are for route number, distance and journey time. **Coimbatore**: No *462*, 500 km; **Chidambaram** and **Nagapattinam**: *326*; **Kanchipuram**: *76B*; **Kanniyakumari**: *282*, 700 km; **Kumbakonum**: *305*, 289 km, 6½ hrs; **Madurai**:*137*, 447 km, 10 hrs; **Mahabalipuram**: *108*, 1½ hrs (*108B* goes via Meenambakkam airport, 2½ hrs) can be very crowded (see page 108); **Nagercoil**: *198*, 682 km, 14 hrs; **Ooty**: *465*, 565 km, 13 hrs; **Pondicherry**, *108*, 106 km, 3 hrs; **Thanjavur**: *323*, 320 km, 8 hrs; **Tiruchirappalli**: *123*, 320 km and Route *124*, 7 hrs; **Tiruvannamalai**: 122, 5 hrs; **Yercaud**: *434*, 360 km, 8 hrs; **Bangalore (via Vellore and Krishnagiri)**: *831*, 360 km, 8 hrs; **Bangalore (via Kolar)**: 350 km, 7½ hrs; **Mysore via Bangalore**: *863*, 497 km, 11 hrs; **Tirupati via Kalahasti**: *802*, 150 km, 3½ hrs. Also several **Andhra Pradesh STC** buses to Tirupati daily. APSTC runs daily buses to many other towns in the state. Bus Stand, Parry's Esplanade, Enquiries, T5340830.

Train Chennai has 2 main stations, **Chennai Central** for broad gauge trains to all parts of India and **Egmore** for metre gauge (and some sections converted to broad gauge). The 2 have a mini-bus link ; taxis take 5 mins. 'Beach Station' is for suburban services. **Chennai Central**: enquiry, T131, reservations, T132, arrivals and departures, T133, then dial train no. Advance Reservations Centre, Southern Rly, is in a separate building in front of suburban station, open 0800-1400, 1415-2000, Sun 0800-1400. You can also order bedding. Indrail Passes and booking facilities for foreigners and NRIs, on the 1st Flr. **Egmore**: enquiry, T135, arrivals and departures, T134. There are also Southern Rly Booking Offices in Mambalam, T4833755, Tambaram and Chennai Beach. Meenambakkam Airport has a Rail Booking Counter. You may reserve 30 days in advance. From **Chennai Central**: **Bangalore**: *Shatabdi Exp*, *2007*, daily except Tue, 0600, 4½ hrs; *Lalbagh Exp*, *2607*, 1615, 5½ hrs; *Brindavan Exp*, *2639* (AC Chair), 0715, 6 hrs; **Coimbatore**, *Shatabdi Exp*, *2023*, 1510, 4½ hrs; **Delhi (ND)**: *Tamil Nadu Exp*, *2621*, 2100, 33½ hrs; *Grand Trunk Exp*, *2615*, 2115, 37½ hrs; **Delhi (HN)**: *Rajdhani Exp*, *2431*, Sat, 1100, 29½ hrs. **Guntakal** (for Hospet) *Chennai-Mumbai Mail*, *6010*, 2220, 9½ hrs; **Hyderabad**: *Charminar Exp*, *7059*, 1810, 14½ hrs; *Chennai-Hyderabad Exp*, *7053* (AC/II), 1600, 15 hrs; **Kochi (Cochin)**: *Chennai-Cochin Exp*, *6041*, 1935, 13½ hrs; *Trivandrum Mail*, *6319*, 1855, 11½ hrs; **Madurai** and **Kanniyakumari**: *Chennai-Kanniyakumari Exp*, *6019*, 1700, 11 hrs plus 6 hrs; **Mettupalayam**: *Nilgiri Exp* *6005*, 2115, 10½ hrs; **Mumbai (VT)**: *Chennai-Mumbai Mail*, *6010*, 2220, 30½ hrs; *Chennai-Mumbai Exp*, *6512*, 1145, 27½ hrs; **Mysore**: *Shatabdi*, daily except Tue, via **Bangalore**, 0600, 7 hrs; **Thiruvananthapuram**: *Trivandrum Mail*, *6319* (AC/II), 1855, 16½ hrs. From **Egmore**: **Kollam (Quilon) via Manamadurai** and **Virudunagar**: *Quilon Mail*, *6105*, 1930, 19½ hrs; **Madurai via Tiruchirapalli**: *Vagai Exp*, *2635*, 1225, 7½ hrs; **Madurai**: *Madurai Exp*, *6719*, 2230, 11½ hrs; via Kodi Rd: *Pandyan Exp*, *6717* (AC/II), 1905, 11½ hrs (this connects with the bus service at Kodaikkanal reaching at midday); **Ramesvaram**: *Ramesvaram Exp*, *6101*, 2050, 16½ hrs; *Sethu Exp*, *6113*, 1805, 14½ hrs; **Tiruchirappalli**: *Pallavan Exp*, *2605*, 1510, 5½ hrs.

Sea Regular passenger ships to the Andaman and Nicobar Islands take 3 days. The *Shipping Corporation of India*, Old Warehouse, opposite Customs House, Rajaji Salai. Also, *Directorate of Shipping Services*, SCI Building, Rajaji Salai, T5226873.

Tickets to the Andaman Islands 1 At 0900 pick a 'letter of intent' to visit the Andamans, and collect details of sailings from the Shipping Corporation of India office. **2** Go to the Foreigners' Registration Office at Shastri Bhavan, and complete an application form for a **permit** and submit it with 2 photos before 1230; pick up at 1700 on the same day (or a day later if the application is submitted after 1230). **3** Next day, take photocopies of your passport identification/Indian Visa pages and also of the Andamans permit, to the SCI office. Pick up a **Ticket** "Order Form", fill it in and queue for a ticket. Women have an advantage when queuing!

Visas are now issued on arrival at Port Blair, see page 192

Directory

Airline offices For domestic airlines see the transport section. Most are open 0930-1730 Mon-Fri, 0930-1300 Sat; *Air India*, 19 Marshalls Rd, T8554477 (0930-1730, avoid 1300-1400), airport T2344927. *Air France*, 43 Montieth Rd, T8554916. *Air Lanka*, 73 Cathedral Rd, T8261535. *British Airways*, Khalili Centre, Montieth Rd, T8554680, Airport T2348282. *Cathay Pacific*, Spencers Plaza, 769 Anna Salai, T8522418. *Gulf Air*, 52 Montieth Rd, T8553091. *KLM*, Hotel Connemara, T8524437. *Kuwait Airways*, 43 Montieth Rd, T8553797. *Lufthansa*, 167 Anna Salai, T8525095. *Malaysian Airlines*, 498 Anna Salai, T4349291. *Qantas*, 112 NH Rd, T8278680. *Singapore Airlines*, 108 Dr Radhakrishna Rd, T8522871. *Saudia*, 560 Anna Salai, T4349666. *Swissair*, 47 Whites Rd, T8526560. General Sales Agents (GSA). *Air Kenya, Garuda Airways, Japan Airlines*, Global Travels, 703 Anna Salai, T8523957. *Alitalia*, 548 Anna Salai, T4349822. *American, Air Canada, Bangladesh Biman, Royal Jordanian* and *TWA*, Thapar House, 43 Montieth Rd, T8569232. *Delta*, Aviation Travels, 47 Whites Rd, T8259655. *Iberian* and *Royal Nepal Airlines*, STIC Travels, 142 NH Rd, T8271195. *Egypt Air* and *Yemen Air*, BAP Travels, 135 Anna Salai, T849913. *Maldive Airways*, Crossworld Tours, 7 Rosy Tower, NH Rd. *Saudia*, Arafaath Travels, 560 Anna Salai, T4349034. *Thai International*, Inter Globe, 144 Kodambakkam High Rd, T8262294.

Banks Most open either 0830-1230 or 1000-1400 on weekdays; am only on Sat. Closed Sun, national holidays and 30 Jun and 31 Dec (foreign exchange dealing may close an hr early). A few big hotels have 24-hr banks. *State Bank of India, Thomas Cook, TT Travels* at International Airport, 24 hrs. *American Express*, G17, Spencer Plaza, Anna Salai, T8523628, F8523615, 0930-1930, offers all foreign exchange and TC services. *Thomas Cook* branches at: 45 Montieth Rd, Egmore. 20 Rajaji Salai. 112 NH Rd, T8274941, Mon-Fri 0930-1830 (closed 1300-1400), Sat 0930-1200. Both recommended. *Madura Travels*, Kennet Lane (near corner of Gandhi Irwin Rd), Egmore, change TCs, good rate. Many banks have branches on Anna Salai, Cathedral, Dr Radhakrishnan and EVR Periyar High Rds. *State Bank of India*, 103 Anna Salai (Foreign Ex in Tower BI at rear, good rate but only encash some TCs). **NB** Some banks have extended hrs: *Indian Overseas*, 473 EVR Periyar High Rd (0830-1530, Sat 0830-1230); *Indian*, EVR Periyar High Rd (near *Hotel Picnic*) (0830-1230, 1600-1800, Sat 0830-1030, 1600-1800). **Visa ATMs** at: *CitiBank*, Anna Salai (24 hrs). Alsa Promenade, Door 149, AA Block, 3rd Ave, Anna Nagar. Pushpa Shoppe, Adyar. 768. *HSBC*, 30 Rajaji Salai. Pushpa Shoppe No 1, Adyar. *Standard Chartered Bank*, 37 Royapettah High Rd. **Credit cards:** in Spencer Plaza, Anna Salai: *American Express*, G17, and others. *Diners Club*, Greenmore, 16 Haddows Rd.

Communications Poste Restante: at the GPO, Rajaji Salai, George Town; other major post offices which accept **Speed Post** Mail are in Anna Salai, Pondy Bazar, T Nagar, Meenambakkam, NH Rd, Flower Bazar and Adyar. Opening times vary, 1st 3 open 0800-2030; **CTO**, Rajaji Salai (near Parry's Corner). Computerized ISTD booths all over town, some open 24 hrs. Beware of con-men claiming to be Sri Lankan refugees pleading payment for a telegram 'home'. **Courier services:** *DHL*, 44/45 Pantheon Rd, Egmore, T8553755, 0930-1800; *Skypak*, 19 Rutland Gate, T8274237; 173 Kodambakkam High Rd, T8274271, 24 hrs. **Directory enquiry:** (national) T183, only from Chennai city itself. Internet: *Cybervision*, off Anna Salai, 64k ISDN; *Datamen's*, 273 Pycrofts Rd, good access, Rs 90 per hr; serves soft drinks. *SRIS*, 1st Flr, F22-A, Spencer Plaza, 769 Anna Salai.

Consulates Most open 0830-1330, Mon-Fri. *Austria*, 115 NH Rd, T8276036. *Belgium*, 97 Anna Salai, T2352336. *Denmark*, 8 Cathedral Rd, T8273399. *Finland*, 742 Anna Salai, T8524141. *France* 16 Haddows Rd, T8266561. *Germany*, 22 C-in-C Rd, T8271747. *Greece* 72 Harrington Rd, T8269194. *Italy*, 19 Rajaji Salai, T5342141. *Japan*, 60 Spur Tank Rd, T8265594. *Malaysia*, 6 Sri Ram Nagar, T4343048. *Mauritius*, 145 Starling Rd, T8271841. *Netherlands*, 64 Armenian St, T584894. *Norway*, 44-45 Rajaji Salai, T517950. *Singapore*, 109 Habibulla Rd, T8276393. *Spain*, 8 Nimmo Rd, San Thome. *Sri Lanka*, 9D Nawab Habibulla Ave, off Anderson Rd, T8276751. *Sweden*, 6 Cathedral Rd, T8275792. *UK*, Deputy High Commission, 24 Anderson Rd, Nungambakkam, T8275130. *USA*, 220 Anna Salai, T8273040.

Tamil Nadu & Chennai

Cultural and language centres *Bharatiya Vidya Bhavan*, 38/39 R E Mada St, T4943450, for Sanskrit. *Hindi Prachar Sabha*, T Nagar, T441824. *International Inst of Tamil Studies*, Central Polytechnic, T412992. Some of the foreign cultural centres have libraries and arrange film shows. *Alliance Française*, 3/4A College Rd, Nungambakkam, T8272650. *American Center*, 561 Anna Salai, library 0930-1800, closed Sun, T8277825. *British Library* 737 Anna Salai, 1000-1900, closed Mon, T852002. *Soviet*, 27 Kasturi Rangan Rd, T4990050. *Max Müeller Bhawan*, 0900-1900, closed Sun, 13 Khadar Nawaz Rd, T8261314.

Medical services Ambulance: *Government*, T102; *St John's Ambulance*, T8264630, 24-hr. **Dental Hospital:** *Govt* T5340411; *All-in-One*, 34 Nowroji Rd, T6411911, 0400-2000, 0900-1200 Sun. **Hospitals & Chemists:** *Apollo Hospital*, 21 Greams Rd, T8277447. *CSI Rainey*, GA Rd, T5951204. *Deviki Hospital*, 148 Luz Church Rd, Mylapore, T4992607. *National Hospital*, 2nd Line Beach Rd, T511405. *SS Day & Night Chemists*, 106D, 1st Main Rd, Anna Nagar.

Tourist offices *Govt of India* (GITO), 154 Anna Salai, T8524785, F8522193, Mon-Fri 0915-1745, Sat until 1300. Domestic Airport Counter, 24 hrs; International Airport Counter, at flight times. *India Tourism Development Corporation* (ITDC), 29 Victoria Crescent, C-in-C Rd, T8278884, 0600-2000, Sun 0600-1400. *Tamil Nadu* (TTDC), 4 EVR Rd (opposite Central Station), T582916, F561385, includes booking of TTDC hotels and tours; Express Bus Stand, T5341982. *TTDC*, 25 Radhakrishnan Rd, T85473 35; Information centres at Central Rly, Gate 2 (Sales Counter on Sun), and Egmore stations, and domestic airport terminal, T2340569, 0700-2300. *Govt of Tamilnadu*, Pangal Building, Saidapet. *State Government Tourist Offices* usually open from 1030-1700 on weekdays (closed Sun and 2nd Sat). *Andaman and Nicobar Islands*, CPWD Campus, KK Nagar, M-78, T4847238. *Kerala*, T8279862.

Useful addresses *Foreigners Registration Office*, Grd Flr, Shastri Bhavan Annexe, 26 Haddows Rd. T8278210, for visa extensions, Mon-Fri 0930-1800.

The Coromandel Coast

Early morning is an excellent time to travel in most places in India, but especially in the South. The air is fresh and cool, the light limpid. Southwards from Chennai on the road to Mahabalipuram, Pondicherry and Cuddalore there are alternating groves of casuarina trees, many recently planted, with coconut and palmyra palms. In January-February, at harvest time, there is also a delightful scent of fresh straw in the air. Paddy, groundnut and sugarcane grow in the fields and grain is often spread out across the road to dry or be threshed by passing traffic.

Mahabalipuram (Mamallapuram) மாமல்லபுரம்

Phone code: 04114
Colour map 2, grid A6
Population: 9,500

Now one of South India's most visited historic sights, Mahabalipuram occupies a stunning position on a rocky outcrop between the beach and a lagoon. The expanding village alongside, with its inviting sandy beach, is a popular haunt of foreign backpackers and there are now plenty of budget hotels and breezy beachside cafés. Mahabalipuram's real claim to fame rests on its ancient history and magnificent rock temples and carvings.

Ins & outs

Getting there Several daily buses from Chennai take about 1½ hours to the bus stand in the centre of the small village. They may stop at hotels north of Mahabalipuram, on the way, otherwise autos wait near the bus stand to ferry you there. **Getting around** Hiring a bike can be fun to get further afield. Beware of con men with "I'm a Sri Lankan refugee" story.

Background The coastal temple town Mahabalipuram is officially known as Mamallapuram after 'Mamalla' (great wrestler), the name given to Narasimhavarman I Pallavamalla, (ruled 630-68). The Pallava ruler made the port famous in the seventh century and was largely responsible for the temples. There are 14 cave temples and nine monolithic *rathas* (shrines in the shape of rathas or chariots), three stone temples and four relief sculptured rock panels. Hawkers now pester visitors near the cave temples and *rathas* and quote highly inflated prices.

A characteristic feature of the temples here was the system of water channels and tanks, drawn from the **Palar River**, which made it particularly suitable as a site of religious worship. The *naga* or serpent cult associated with water worship can be seen given prominence at Bhagiratha's Penance.

Carving in stone is still a living art; stone masons can be heard chipping away from dawn to dusk along the dusty roadsides, while students at the **Government School of Sculpture** near the Bus Stand, continue to practise the skills which flourished centuries ago. ■ *0900-1300, 1400-1830. Closed Tue.*

Sights The best time to walk round the site is early morning, especially for the best light on Bhagiratha's Penance. Allow two hours for a circuit. The paths on the top of the rock are not always clear, but it is difficult to get really lost. You will also need to watch where you step away from the beach.

★ **Bhagiratha's Penance** (Descent of the Ganga, sometimes referred to as **Arjuna's Penance**), is a bas relief sculpted on the face of two enormous adjacent rocks, 29 m long and 7 m high. It shows realistic life-size figures of animals, gods and saints watching the descent of the river from the Himalaya. Bhagiratha, Rama's ancestor, is seen praying for Ganga. A contrived waterfall fed from a collecting chamber above, issues from the natural crack between the two rocks. Some see the figure of an ascetic (on the upper register of the left hand side rock, near the cleft) as representing Arjuna's penance when praying for powers from Siva, though some authorities dispute this. The two large elephants are remarkable and there are also scenes from the fables in the *Panchatantra* and a small shrine to Vishnu. The characteristic system of water channels and tanks, drawn from the Palar River made this a particularly suitable site of religious worship associated with the *naga* (serpent) *cult*.

A path north from 'Bhagiratha's Penance' goes to the double-storeyed rectangular **Ganesh** *ratha* with a highly decorative roof, and two pillars with lions at their base – an architectural feature which was to become significant. The Ganesh image inside is mid-20th century. To the west are the **Valayankuttai** and twin **Pidari** *rathas*. The path continues past the extraordinary, curiously poised, isolated rock, '**Krishna's Butterball**', through some huge boulders at the north end of the hillock to the **Trimurti Temple** caves which have three shrines to Brahma, Vishnu and Siva, the last with a lingam.

Mandapas The 10 *mandapas* are fairly shallow pillared halls or porticos excavated out of the rocky hillside. They provide space for superbly executed sculptures to illustrate tales from mythology, and illustrate the development of the Dravidian (South Indian) temple style.

On the south is a **Durga niche** (AD 630-60), while next door is the '**Gopi's Churn**', a Pallava cistern. Walk back along the ridge, passing 'Krishna's Butterball' on your left and some boulders with evidence of incomplete work. The **Varaha** *Mandapa* (AD 640-74) on the left of the ridge, shows two incarnations of Vishnu – Varaha (boar) and Vamana (dwarf) among scenes with kings and queens. The base forms a narrow receptacle for water for pilgrims to use before entering the temple. From here you can walk to the top of 'Bhagiratha's Penance'.

Tamil Nadu & Chennai

★ The **Krishna Mandapa** (mid-seventh century) has a bas relief scene of Krishna lifting Mount Govardhana to protect a crowd of his kinsmen from the anger of the Rain God, Indra. The realistic portrayal of a cow licking its calf while being milked, is quite remarkable.

The **Kotikal Mandapa** (early seventh century) may be the earliest of the mandapas, roughly carved with a small shrine with no image inside. The **Ramanuja Mandapa** was originally a triple-cell Siva temple, converted later into a Vaishnava temple.

South of the new lighthouse the simple **Dharmaraja cave** (early seventh century) contains three empty shrines. To its west is the **Isvara Temple** (or Old Lighthouse), a truncated Siva temple still standing like a beacon on the highest summit, with a view for miles around. (To the south, across the 'Five Rathas', is the nuclear power station of Kalpakkam; to the west is the flat lagoon and the original port of Mahabalipuram.)

Mahabalipuram

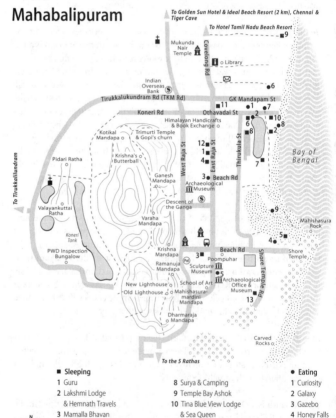

■ Sleeping		● Eating
1 Guru	8 Surya & Camping	1 Curiosity
2 Lakshmi Lodge	9 Temple Bay Ashok	2 Galaxy
& Hemnath Travels	10 Tina Blue View Lodge	3 Gazebo
3 Mamalla Bhavan	& Sea Queen	4 Honey Falls
4 Mamalla Bhavan Annexe	11 Uma Lodge &	5 La Vie en Rose
& Golden Palate	Pumpernickle Bakery	6 Luna Magica
5 New Papillon	12 Veeras	7 Moonrakers
6 Ramkrishna Lodge	13 Youth Hostel & Camping (TTDC)	8 Sea Rock
7 Sea Breeze		9 Sunrise

Coromandel

Tamil Nadu & Chennai

As Hobson-Jobson pointed out, the name Coromandel has been confusingly misinterpreted by many writers, a confusion deepened by early European visitors using the terms Malabar and Coromandel interchangeably! Links have been suggested with apparent authority to such a wide range of meanings as 'black sand', 'the hot country', the 'land of the Kurus', 'the country of cholam (a millet)' or even 'rice fort'. In fact it means 'the realm of the Cholas'. The Coromandel Coast, the plain between Chennai and the Kaveri delta, has been a part of the great heartland of South Indian culture, as several of its most important sites still testify.

Immediately below is the ★ **Mahishasuramardini** *Mandapa* (mid-seventh century) which has particularly fine bas relief and finely carved columns with lion bases. The main sculpture shows the goddess Durga slaying the buffalo demon Mahishasura while another relief shows Vishnu lying under Adishesha, the seven-hooded serpent.

The ★ **Rathas** These mid-seventh century monolithic temples, 1.5 km south of the Old Lighthouse were influenced by Buddhist architecture as they resemble the *vihara* (monastery) and *chaitya* temple hall. They imitate in granite, temple structures that were originally built of wood and are among the oldest examples of their type.

The five Rathas to the south of the hill are named after the Pancha Pandava (five Pandava brothers) in the epic *Mahabharata* and their wife Draupadi. The largest is the domed **Dharmaraja** with numerous images including an interesting Ardhanarishvara (Siva-Parvati) at the rear. The barrel-vaulted **Bhima** nearby has a roof suggestive of a thatched hut, while next to it the dome-shaped ratha **Arjuna** imitates the Dharmaraja. The **Draupadi** ratha, is the smallest and simplest and is again in the form of a thatched hut. The base, now covered by sand, conceals a lion in front which appears to carry it, which suggests that it may be a replica of a portable shrine. Immediately east is a large unfinished *Nandi* (Siva's bull). To its west is the apsidal **Nakula-Sahadeva** ratha with a free-standing elephant nearby. The Bhima and Nakula-Sahadeva follow the oblong plan of the Buddhist *chaitya* hall and are built to two or more storeys, a precursor to the *gopuram*, the elaborate entrance gateway of the Dravidian temple.

The ★ **Shore Temple** The temple by the sea is surrounded by gardens designed according to descriptions of the original layout from ancient texts. The World Heritage Site, is immensely popular with day-trippers and school groups. Built at the end of the seventh century by King Rajasimha, it is unusual for its shrines to both Siva and Vishnu. The sandstone temple has a granite base and a basalt *kalasa* at the very top. Its position on the water's edge, with an east-facing altar designed to catch the rising sun and a stone pillar to hold the beacon for sailors at night, meant that there was no space for a forecourt or entrance gateway. Two additional shrines were built to the west asymmetrically. The second smaller spire adds to the temple's unusual structure. Some of the temple has now been reclaimed from the sea and it seems that in the past the central shrine could have been surrounded by water by the flooding of the outer enclosure. The outer parapet wall has lines of *nandi* (Siva's sacred bull) and lion pilasters.

Five kilometres north of Mahabalipuram, on the coast, is the excavated temple at **Saluvankuppam** which has the **Tiger Cave** mandapa with carvings of tigers' heads. The cave is not signposted from the beach. Secluded and very peaceful – a lovely place for a picnic. On the way you will see the **Mukunda Nayar** Temple.

Suggested reading: *Mahabalipuram* by C Sivaramamurti. 5th ed. New Delhi, Archaeological Survey of India, 1992. *Mahabalipuram and the Pandavas* by Michael Lockwood. Madras, Christian Literature Society, 1982.

Beaches Check about safety of **swimming** in the sea. To avoid hassle and have an undisturbed day by the beach, pay Rs 100 to use the small pool at ITDC *Temple Bay Ashok* or the bigger pool, 1 km north at TTDC *Tamil Nadu Beach Resort*. The **beach** north of the temples towards the *Ashok* and the rocky area behind the Descent of the Ganga are open latrines for the village and badly fouled.

Museums The small **Archaeologicial Museum**, East Raja Street, has granite sculptures and fragments which have been found nearby. **Sculpture Museum**, 0900-1800. Rs 3, Camera Rs 10.

Tours **TTDC**: to Kanchipuram and Mahabalipuram. 0500-1900. Tiring, but good value if you don't mind being rushed. It also includes a stop at the appallingly garish Indian kitsch, *VGP Beach Resort*.

Sleeping
Even modest hotels charge 20% luxury tax

L-AL *Fisherman's Cove* (Taj), Colevong Rd (8 km north), T044304-8253454. 80 rooms, some a/c cottages with seaview, excellent seafood at restaurant right on the beach, beautiful site, very good facilities, ask Reception about "turtle walks". **B-C** *Temple Bay Ashok* (ITDC), on the beach north, T42251, F42257. 50 a/c rooms (poorly maintained), small pool (non-residents Rs 100), pleasant location, poor restaurant. **C** *Golden Sun*, 59 Covelong Rd, 3 km north, T42245, F44444 (Chennai T8241020). 69 a/c cottages, restaurant, bar, exchange, garden, pool, fairly simple but in pleasant surroundings. **C** *Ideal Beach Resort*, Covelong Rd (3½ km north), T42443, F42243, ideal@md2.vsnl.net.in 15 rooms in cottages, some a/c (limited hours), good restaurant, exchange, pool and gardens, clean, comfortable.

D *Sea Breeze* (TTDC), T43035, F43065, vattelco@md3.vsnl.net.in New, clean, spacious, well-furnished rooms (some a/c, Rs 700), pleasant position, direct beach access (dubious swimming), pool in 2000, good food. **D** *Tamil Nadu Beach Resort* (TTDC), T42235, F42268. 48 cottages, some a/c but neglected, damp, restaurants (Indian, Chinese), bar (limited hours), exchange, good pool (gets deep suddenly!) open to non-residents (Rs 75), beautiful setting. **D-E** *Mamalla Bhavan Annexe*, 104 East Raja St, T42260, F42160, mamalla@md3.vsnl.net.in 43 clean, pleasant rooms, 17 a/c, nice balconies, excellent vegetarian restaurant, exchange, travel, spotless, friendly, very good value, highly recommended (some find it lacks atmosphere). **D-E** *Surya*, near beach and tourist office, 1 Thirukula St, T42292, F42992. 12 cottages overlooking small lake (1st floor with balcony dearer), very clean, some a/c, in quiet shaded gardens, a/c restaurant, camping, very knowledgeable, friendly manager. **D-E** *Veeras*, East Raja St, T42288. 16 rooms (10 a/c), clean, well kept, restaurant, bar, quite good value.

E *Erwin Danussi Cottage*, 47 Thirukula St, T42738. Big garden and pleasant rooms. **E** *Lakshmi Lodge*, Othavadai St, T42463. 26 clean rooms, upstairs small but light, downstairs, dark and poor, restaurant with beach view, friendly, popular with backpackers. **E-F** *Mamalla Bhavan* opposite Bus Stand, T42250. 20 rooms, some with bath, clean though rather dark, simple, pleasant, good restaurant. **E-F** *Tina Blue View Lodge*, 1 Othavadai St, T42319, F42511. 25 rooms with bath and balcony, cottages for long term rent, garden. **F** *New Papillon*, off Beach Rd, towards *Sunrise*. Clean but

From thorn scrub to tree planting

On dry land across India a thorn scrub, (Prosopis juliflora), is now very common. Introduced at the turn of the century as a fencing plant to keep cattle off fields by an enthusiastic District Collector, this has run riot. In some areas it is now being used to make charcoal.

On the road between Mahabalipuram and Tirukkalukundram is an experimental tree-planting scheme for tribal women. Much of this reafforestation has been with eucalyptus, introduced to India from Australia a century ago. Such plantations have attracted fierce criticism from some experts, who believe that they take a lot of water from the soil and that they do not supply the products needed by poor people, available from local varieties of trees.

simple rooms, shower (Rs 70), good restaurant upstairs (try muesli). **F** *Ramakrishna Lodge*, 8A Othavadai St, T42431. 31 well kept, clean rooms with fan, shower, Western toilets, no nets (Rs 125), courtyard and roof terrace, friendly, good value (contact Vijay for informal yoga classes). Recommended. **F** *Uma Lodge*, 15 Othavadai St, T42322. 21 rooms, good restaurant above, friendly staff. There are also some cheap guest houses near the Bus Stand and on East Raja St.

Camping: **D-F** *Camping Site* (TTDC), Shore Temple Rd, T42287. 18 cottages (bit run down), dorm beds (Rs 30, theft reported), no nets, snack bar, bar, exchange, well placed but not on beach. *Surya*, 1 TKM Rd, T42239, allows camping.

Expensive In top hotels including *Silver Sands*, 2 km north. The waterfront café is especially attractive in evenings. **Mid-range** *Curiosity*, Othavadai St. Wide range, excellent food, very willing to please. *Gazebo*, East Raja St. Charcoal grilled fish, pleasant seating. *Honey Falls*, Shore Temple Rd. Few tables, served with delicious fish. *La Vie en Rose* upstairs near the Archaeological Office. French. Very good food, 'special teas' (in absence of licence!), friendly French manager. *Moonrakers*, Othavadai St. Pleasant and friendly. Recommended. *Pumpernickel*, 15 Othavadai St. Rooftop above. *Tina Blue View* breezy restaurant, mixed reports (sometimes slow, unfriendly service). *Uma Lodge*. International. A German bakery selling good bread, great cakes, tasty pastas (try yak cheese and lasagne) and Chinese dishes, very friendly, relaxed atmosphere, Nepali run, open Dec-Apr. Recommended. *Village*, near *Surya*. Some outdoor seating in pleasant lakeside position, rustic design, average food, keener to sell beers. **Cheap** *Mamalla Bhavan* and *Annexe*. Good South Indian vegetarian. The former, perhaps the cheapest in town. *Galaxy* Othavadai St. Very friendly. *Sunrise*, Shore Temple Rd. Seafood. Simple, under thatch, serving a wide range of fish.

Eating
Beachside cafés are pleasant for a drink: 'Café 108 Mas' in 'Sea Shore Hotel', 'Sea Rock' & 'Luna Magica'

Dec-early Feb: Six-week *Dance Festival* starting on 25 Dec; at Bhagiratha's (Arjuna's) Penance, Classical 1800-2030, Folk 2030-2100, every Sat, Sun and holidays. Long speeches in Tamil on opening (full-moon) night! **Mar**: *Masi Magam* attracts large crowds of pilgrims. **Apr-May**: *Brahmotsava* lasts for 10 days. **Oct-Nov**: the *Palanquin Festival* is held at the Stalasayana Perumal Temple.

Festivals

Handicrafts shops sell small figures in soapstone and metal. On East Raja St: *Himalayan Handicrafts*, at 21, also has 900 books for exchange. *Hidesign*, at 138. Excellent Western style leather goods, very reasonable. Recommended. *Silver Star*, at 51, T42936. Good tailor. *Wali Crafts*. On Othavadai St: *Art Mart*, 11-G Othavadai St.

Shopping

Hemnath Travels, Othavadai St (next to *Lakshmi Lodge*), T42301.

Tour operators

Tamil Nadu & Chennai

Transport **Local** **Bicycle hire**: from tourist office and shops in East Raja St and hotels, Rs 20 per day. Recommended for Tirukkalukundram – from Dec-Feb a comfortable and very attractive ride. **Long distance** **Car hire**: from tourist office. **Road Bus**: from Chennai also go to Tirukkalukundram and Pondicherry. Nos 19C, 68, 119A. **Taxi**: charge Rs 700-1000 for 1-day excursion from Chennai; Rs 450 to airport. To Pondicherry, Rs 700 (bargain hard). **Train** The nearest station is Chengalpattu, 29 km away with buses to Mahabalipuram, 1 hr.

Directory **Banks** *Indian Overseas Bank*, TKM Rd. *Prithvi Securities*, opposite. Mamalla Bhavan Annexe, change money quickly without commission. **Communications** **Post office**: is on a back street off Covelong Rd (towards the Tourist Office). **Telephone**: several ISD phones on East Raja St. **Libraries** A small library near the Tourist Office has English language dailies. Book exchange at Himalayan Handicrafts. **Tourist offices** *Tamil Nadu*, Covelong Rd (300m north of Othavadai St), T42232, 0945-1745, closed Sat, Sun. 2 TTDC guides available here; others from Chennai. Car and cycle hire possible. The *Archaeological Survey of India*, south of Bus Stand, T42226, has a guide/lecturer (free) available on request.

Tirukkal-ukundram
Colour map 3, grid A5
Population: 23,300

The dramatic potential of hilltop sites for temples is well illustrated 14 km west of Mahabalipuram. A small Siva temple dedicated to Vedagirishvara is on top of the 3,000 million year old rock. About 400 steps take you to the top of the 160 m hill which has good views (and also money conscious priests and 'guides'). Be prepared for a hot barefoot climb, 'donations' at several shrines and Rs 10 for shoe custodian! At midday it is said that you will see two Neophran vultures (*Pharaoh's chickens*) fly down to be fed by the priests – but you may be disappointed. The Bhaktavatsleesvara in town with its *gopuram* (gateway) stands out like a beacon. The tank is considered holy and believed to produce a conch every 12 years. Small shops in the village sell cold drinks.
■ *Getting there: buses from Mahabalipuram take 30 mins or you can hire a bike.*

Sriperumbudur
Population: 13,000

The birthplace of the 11th-century Hindu philosopher **Ramanuja**, is the town where Rajiv Gandhi was assassinated on 21 May 1991. There is a memorial at the site.

★ Kanchipuram காஞ்சீபுரம்

Phone code: 04112
Colour map 7, grid A5
Population: 170,000

One of Hinduism's seven most sacred cities (see page 526), 'the golden city of a thousand temples' dates from the early Cholas in the second century. The main temples' complexes are very spacious and the town itself relatively quiet except for crowds of pilgrims.

History Buddhism is believed to have reached the Kanchipuram area in the third century BC. Successive dynasties made it their capital and built over 100 temples, the first as early as the fourth century. In addition to being a pilgrimage centre, it was a centre of learning, culture and philosophy. Sankaracharya and the Buddhist monk Bodhidharma lived and worked here.

Sights Only a few of the 70 or so scattered **temples** can be seen in a day's visit; most open early, close from 1200-1600; a rickshaw is recommended.

★ **Ekambaresvara Temple** The temple has five enclosures and a 'Thousand-pillared Hall' (actually 540). Dedicated to **Siva** in his ascetic form it was begun by the Pallavas and developed by the Cholas. At the beginning of the 16th century the Vijayanagara king Krishna Deva Raya built the high stone wall which surrounds the temple and the 59 m tall *rajagopuram* (main tower) on which are sculpted several figures of him and his consort.

Tamil Nadu's Tank Country

The Coromandel plains have some spectacular tanks. Some of these shallow reservoirs date back to the Pallava period (6th to 8th centuries), and many were added by the Chola kings. Built in the 8th century they are an invaluable source of irrigation water. Just south of Chengalpattu, bounded by the National Highway to its west, the ancient Chembarambakkam Tank is dammed by a nine kilometre embankment. It is one of South India's most beautiful tanks and the largest in the region but over half the stored water is lost through evaporation.

The main sanctuary has a *lingam* made of earth (Siva as one of the elements) and the story of its origin is told on a carved panel. The teasing Parvati is believed to have unthinkingly covered her husband Siva's eyes for a moment with her hands which resulted in the earth being enveloped in darkness for years. The enraged Siva ordered Parvati to do severe penance during which time she worshipped her husband in the form of an earth *lingam* which she created. When Siva sent a flood to test her, she clung to the lingam with her hands until the waters subsided. Some believe they can see her fingerprints on the *lingam* here. On 18 April each year the sun's rays enters the sanctum though a small square hole. The old mango tree in one of the enclosures is claimed to be 1,000 years old (2,500 according to some) and still bears fruit.

The *Panguni Uthiram Festival* in March-April, see page 77, is the largest and possibly the most atmospheric of Kanchipuram's temples, its historical connections include Clive's Arcot campaign when it served as a fortress.

■ *Small entry fee, cameras Rs 3. Non-Hindus are not allowed into the inner sanctuary.*

★ **Kailasanatha** Built early seventh century. Considered the most beautiful of the town's temples the Kailasanatha Temple was built of sandstone by the Pallava king Narasimha Varman II with the front completed by his son Mahendra III. The outer wall has a dividing wall with a shrine and doorways, separating a large courtyard from a smaller. The unusual enclosure wall has 58 small raised shrines with a *nandi* in most pavilions; some frescoes have survived. The seven shrines in the temple complex have images of different forms of Siva. The intricately carved panels on the walls depict legends about Siva with accompanying text in ancient Grantha script. Extensively restored. Archaeological Survey of India Office has limited opening hours. The festival *Mahashivaratri* is held in February.

Vaikuntha Perumal, eighth century, dedicated to Vishnu. This temple was built by the Pallava king Nandivarman just after the Kailasanatha and illustrates the progress of Dravidian temple architecture. As Percy Brown points out, the two temples (and the Shore Temple at Mahabalipuram) are examples of dressed stones being used for structural temples. Here too the sanctuary is separated from the *mandapa* by an open space. The cloisters are built out of lines of lion pillars. Panels of bas relief accompanied by lines in old Tamil, trace the history of the wars between the Pallavas and Chalukyas. There is an unusual *vimana* (tower) with shrines in three tiers with figures of Vishnu in each.

★**Varadaraja** (Devarajasvami) is 3 km southeast of town. Built by the Vijayanagara kings (circa 16th century), it has superb sculpture in its marriage hall (96 pillars). Note the rings at each corner and the massive flexible chain supposedly carved out of one piece of granite although they are no longer in

Tamil Nadu & Chennai

one piece. The mutilation of the figures and the chains is attributed to the troops of Haider Ali. The main shrine is on an elephant shaped rock, Hastagiri. There are also small shrines in the courtyard with painted roofs. The two tanks in the temple enclosures have granite steps sloping down. ■ *Hindus only are allowed into the sanctum.* **Festivals** *Float Festival* in February and November, *Brahmotsavam* in May, *Garuda Sevai* in June.

Kamakshi Amman Seventh-14th century. It is dedicated to Parvati and is one of the three holiest places of **Shakti** worship, the others being Madurai and Varanasi. There is a shrine to Sri Sankara who founded a monastery. The 'Amai' *mandapa* is beautifully sculpted, but there is little of interest for the non-Hindu to see. ■ *0600-1200, 1600-2030.* Festivals: the annual *'car' festival* when other deities are drawn to this temple in their wooden temple chariots, draws large crowds in February-March.

Weavers From the 16th century silk weavers have used high quality mulberry silk from neighbouring Karnataka, and pure gold thread, to weave in beautiful colours and patterns on their handlooms. Nowadays, about 20,000 work with silk and another 10,000 with cotton. To watch them at work in their spotless huts, contact Weavers' Service Centre, 20 Station Rd, T22530, 1000-1700 Sunday-Thursday; not sales.

Kanchipuram

Jaina Kanchi is just southwest of town but is difficult to find and you will need to ask the way. The two temples worth visiting are **Vardhamana** with beautiful paintings and the smaller **Chandraprabha**.

D-E *Baboo Soorya*, 85 East Raja St (opposite Bus Stand), T22555, F473084, set back off **Sleeping** main road down palm fringed lane. Simple, rather shabby, rooms, some a/c, restaurant, snack bar, cool spacious lobby, friendly staff, quiet. **E** *Sri Rama Lodge*, 20 Nellukkara St, near Bus Stand, T22435. Fairly basic rooms, some a/c with TV, a/c restaurant. **E** *Tamil Nadu* (TTDC), Station Rd, T22553, F22552. Some a/c rooms, dull restaurant. **F** *Raja's Lodge*, 21 Nellukara St, T22603. Very simple rooms, atmospheric green pillared hall. **F** *Sri Krishna Lodge*, 68-A Nellukara St, T22831. 28 good, clean rooms, some with bath, helpful, friendly manager. **F** *Sri Vela*, Station Rd. Clean and good value rooms, restaurant, very good breakfasts.

Cheap Indian vegetarian at: *Baboo Surya*. Good *thalis*. *Sri Rama Lodge* (a/c) and *Sri* **Eating** *Vela*. Good dosas. *Hotel Tamil Nadu*. Reasonable food but is rather gloomy, evenings 1900-2130. *Saravana Bhavan*, next to *Jaybala International*, 504 Gandhi Rd (50 m off the road). "Best in town". Other *thali bhawans* are near the Bus Stand

Silk and cotton fabrics with designs of birds, animals and temples or in plain beautiful **Shopping** colours, sometimes 'shot', are sold by the metre in addition to saris. It is best to buy from Govt shops or Co-operative Society stores. Along Gandhi Rd: *AS Babu Shah*, high quality silks, recommended. *BM Silks*, 23G Yadothagari, Sannathi St (near Rangaswamy Kulam). *Sreenivas*, 135 Thirukatchi Nambi St (Gandhi Rd), recommended.

Local The town is flat and easy to negotiate so the best cheap way to get about is by **Transport** hiring a cycle from near the bus stand or off East Raja St. **Cycle** and **auto-rickshaws** are available for visiting temples. **Long distance** **Road** **Bus**: the bus station in the middle of town with direct Govt Express to Chennai (No 828) 2½ hrs, Bangalore (No 828), Kaniyakumari (No 193), Pondicherry (109 km, No 804) 3½ hrs, and Tiruchirappalli (No 122). For Mahabalipuram (65 km) 3 hrs, direct bus or quicker still take a bus to Chengalpattu (35 km) which are frequent and catch one from there. Very frequent buses to Vellore, other buses go to Tirupati and Tiruttani. **Train** The station, on a branch line, is under a kilometre to the northeast of the bus stand. Trains to Chennai Beach Station (narrow gauge), change at Chengalpattu for suburban line commuter services. Also trains to Arakkonam on the Chennai-Bangalore line.

Banks *State Bank of India*, Gandhi Rd. Amex TCs not accepted; *Indian Overseas Bank*, Gandhi **Directory** Rd. **Communications** Head Post Office, 27 Gandhi Rd. **Tourist office** Tourist information at *Hotel Tamil Nadu*, T22461, 1000-1700.

The **fort** here was built by the Vijayanagar king Thimmu Raya after his defeat **Chengalpattu** at the Battle of Talikota in 1565. After 1687 it was absorbed into the Mughal **(or Chingleput)** Empire. Then in 1750 it was taken by the French, who held it until it was cap- *Phone code: 04144* tured by Clive in 1752; British control being finally established only after the *Colour map 3, grid A5* defeat of Haidar Ali in 1781. Although the fort is now almost totally destroyed *Population: 54,000* (the railway runs through the middle of it), the **Raja Mahal** ('King's Palace') remains. **Sleeping E** *Kanchi*, modern, clean hotel with restaurant, on NH45 at junction with Mahabalipuram Rd.

On the Trichy Road, 87 km from Chennai and 60 km from Mahabalipuram, **Vedanthangal** Vedanthangal sanctuary and Karikili Tank are thought to have existed as a **Bird Sanctuary** protected area for about 250 years. The marshy site, part of which remains submerged in the rainy season, attracts numerous water fowl and provides

Tamil Nadu & Chennai

their main nesting site. It has a small lake and a grove of *Kadappamaram (Barringtonia acutangula)* trees. Visitors (estimated at 30,000 at the beginning of the breeding season) and residents include crested cormorants, night herons, grey pelicans, sand pipers, grey wagtails, open-billed storks, white ibis, egrets, little grebe and purple moorhens. Best season is from November to February for migratory birds which include blue-winged teals, pintails, shovellers. Best time dawn and 1500-1800.

Sleeping A long day-trip from Chennai is possible (58km away); otherwise the very simple **F** *Forest Rest House* has suites of rooms with electricity, bath and running water. The cook will prepare an Indian meal to order. Reservations: Wildlife Warden, DMS Campus, Taynampet, Chennai, T4321471; advance payment expected.

Transport Road From Chennai (75 km) by car or bus from the Broadway Bus Stand, Chennai (only weekends) or one from Mahabalipuram. It is also included in some coach tours. **Train** To Chengalpattu (28 km) and then bus 20 km to sanctuary.

Marakkanam Marakkanam, mentioned in Roman records as an important port in the first century AD, has an ancient Siva temple, with many inscriptions. Immediately inland is the **Kaliveli Tank**, extremely important staging posts and wintering areas for migratory water fowl including over 200 pelicans among the 40,000 shorebirds at the site.

★ Pondicherry பாண்டிச்சேரி (Puducherry)

Phone code: 0413
Colour map 3, grid A5
Population: 401,000
Altitude: sea level

Pondicherry still enjoys a hint of its French colonial atmosphere in the grid pattern streets, distinctive police uniforms and the occasional colonial building. Yet despite its invigorating seafront and relaxing atmosphere the town is visited above all for the Sri Aurobindo Ashram which draws visitors from all over the world.

Ins & outs **Getting there** Buses now take under 4 hours from Chennai on the East Coast Road. Both the State and private bus stands are just west of the town, within walking distance or a short auto-ride from the centre but arrival can be chaotic with hassle from rickshaw drivers. The station on a branch line from Villupuram, which has trains to major destinations, is a few minutes' walk south of the centre. **Getting around** Pondicherry is pleasant to explore on foot, but hiring a bike or moped gives you the freedom to venture further along the coast independently.

History The site of the town has been identified as ancient Vedapuri where **Agastya Muni** (a sage) had his hermitage in 1500 BC. In the first century AD Romans traded from nearby Arikamedu. Colonized by the French (re-named Puducherry), it was voluntarily handed over to the Indian Government in 1954 and became the Union Territory of Pondicherry.

Today, many visitors are attracted by the Ashram founded by Sri Aurobindo and his chief disciple Mirra Alfassa. Sri Aurobindo Ghosh was an early 20th-century Bengali revolutionary and philosopher who struggled for freedom from British colonial power, see page 538. He started the Ashram here to put into practice his ideals of a peaceful community. In this aim he found a lifelong French companion in **Mirra Alfassa**, who became universally known as **the Mother**. After his death in 1950, she continued as the spiritual successor and charismatic figure of Pondicherry until her own death in 1973 at the age of 93. Auroville, 'City of Dawn', was set up in 1968 as a tribute to Sri Aurobindo (see below).

Sri Aurobindo Ashram has its main centre in rue de la Marine. ■ *0800-1200, 1400-1800, free. Meditation: Mon, Tue, Wed, Fri, 1925-1950; in the Playground: Thu, Sun, 1940-2015.* The International Centre is across the road which has occasional films, lectures and other performances (free). The **library** is open daily 0730-1130, 1400-1645.

Ecole Française d'Extrême Orient, nearly 100 years old, has three departments in Pondicherry for Sanskrit, Tamil and Archaeological studies. **The French Institute**, rue St Louis, was set up in 1955 for the study of Indian culture; the Scientific and Technical Section for ecological studies. Superb library overlooking the sea (reference only), many books in French and English. The colonial building is worth seeing.

The French Catholic influence is evident in a number of churches, notably the Jesuit Cathedral (*Notre Dame de la Conception*; 1691-1765). One of the oldest Christian shrines, the 17th-century Chapel of Our Sisters of Cluny is 4 km south at Ariyankuppam (see below).

Serenity Beach, within bike range from the town centre to the north, is much better than the dirty town beaches; very pleasant with few spectators.

Sights *(margin)*

Pondicherry Museum, 2 Rue St Louis, has a good sculpture gallery and a section of archaeological finds from the Roman settlement at Arikamedu. The French gallery charts the history of the colony; includes the four-poster bed in which Dupleix is believed to have slept. Superb collection of snail shells from the Pondicherry region. ■ *1000-1700, except Mon and public holidays. Free.*

Bharati and **Bharatidasan Memorial Museums**. The former is in 20 Eswaran Koil Street where the famous Tamil poet-patriot lived after arriving in 1908 in search of refuge. The latter is in 95 Perumal Koil Street, the home of Kanakasubburatnam who adopted the name meaning disciple of Bharati which has become the second place of literary pilgrimage. **Jawahar Toy Museum**, Goubert Salai, has a small collection of costume dolls (dancers, professions) from different states; a 15 minute diversion. ■ *1000-1700, free.* **Maison Ananda Rangapillai** on Rangapillai Street has material on French India from 1736-60.

Museums *(margin)*

The **Botanical Gardens** (south of City Bus Stand, opened in 1826) are pleasant after some renovation. The **Government (Pondicherry) Park**, laid out with lawns, flower beds and fountains (one at the centre is of Napoleon III period), is in front of the Raj Niwas, the residence of the Lieutenant Governor. The park was originally the site of the first French garrison, Fort Louis, destroyed in 1761 by the British.

Parks *(margin)*

PTDC Sightseeing, Rs 45, Ashram, 0815-1300: Ashram and related departments. Auroville (Matrimandir), 1430.

Tours *(margin)*

Boat trips on a converted fishing boat to see dolphins can be booked through the *Seagulls* restaurant (1100-2300) and Tourist Information Centre, Goubert Salai. February-September, 1000-1100 and 1400-1500, Rs 50 per person (minimum five persons). Special trips, 0600-0800 (advance booking essential), Rs 800 per group of up to 15, Rs 600 for a family. The boat leaves the commercial fishing harbour, 15 minutes' bike ride away; best in early morning for chance to see dolphins. Recommended.

Excursions *(margin)*

Tamil Nadu & Chennai (side margin)

Pondicherry

To Serenity Beach, Auroville & Chennai,
Pondicherry Ashok & Youth Hostel

Sangara Dass St

14

3

7

Sri
Varadaraja
Temple

Thiyagaraja St

Bharatidasan
Museum

Aroma
Clinic

Perumal Koil St

(SV Patel Salai)

Bharati St

Sri
Vedapuriswarar
Temple

Muttu Mariamman Koil St

Eswaran Dharmaraja Koil St

Kamatchi Amman Koil St

Bharati
Museum
Rue

Srl Aurobindo St (Arvindar St)

Calve Supraya Chettiar St

Caltisvaran Koil St

Vysial St

Auro-Kailash @

Amballattadavar Madam St

Mahatma Gandhi Rd

Cathedral St (Mission St)

To Tindivanam
& Chennai

10

Raju
Moped

Poompuhur

Thiaga St

Chemist

Jail

India
Overseas
Bank

Jawaharlal Nehru St

Chemist

6

4

Higginbothams &
Green Connection

Ananda Rangapillai St

Grand Bazar

Vellaja St

Maison Ananda
Rangapillai

Nidarajapayer St (Big Brahmin St)

Anna Salai (West Boulevard)

12

St Theresa St

4

Chinna Vaikal St

Savarirayalu St (Small Brahmin St)

Mahatma Ghandi Rd

Cathedral

Focus Books

Saint Theresa St

Chinna Vaikal St

Canteen St

Marius Xavier St

5

La Porte St

Rue Montorsier

(Anna Salai)

2

Surcouf

To Mofussil Express Bus
Stand & Villupuram

TTC New
Bus Stand

9

Chinna Subraya Billai St

Sports
Ground

Candappa St

Lal Bahadur Shastri St

Kailash
French
Bookshop

(Rue Bussy)

City Bus
Stand

Ignas Mestry St

Yanam Vangadasala Pillar St

Botanical
Gardens

Thillai Mestry St

Bharati St

Jeevandam St

VOC St

Badar Sahib St

Mahatma Gandhi Rd

Ellaman Koil St

Mulla St

Cazivar St

Chanda Sahib St

Ambur Salai

Gingee Salai

Rue Labourdonnais

French
Bookshop

Kuthpa
Mosque

Egilse de
Sacre Coeur
de Jesus

Rajasingh St

Ramaraja St

Subbaiyah Salai

3

Station &
Retiring
Rooms

15

6

Dr Ambedkar Rd

(South Boulevard)

To Sports Complex

N

0 metres 100
0 yards 100

■ **Sleeping**	5 Cottage Guest	9 Les Comptoirs de	15 Tourist Homes
1 Ajantha Guest	House & Auro	L'Inde	16 Villa Helena
House & Roof	Information centre	10 Mass	
Top Restaurant	6 Excursion Centre	11 Park Guest Hotel	● **Eating**
2 Amnivasam	7 Garden House	12 Ram International	1 Ashram Dining
Guest House	8 International	13 Sea Side Guest	Room
3 Anandha Inn	Guest House	House	2 Blue Dragon
4 Aristo Guest House		14 Sriguru	3 Chez Aziz

Ariyankuppam (Arikamedu) is 3 km south. On the bank of the river Ariyankuppam, the fishing village of Virampattinam is believed to be the site of the port of Podouke named by Ptolemy, occupied between the first century BC and AD 200. Coins and other Roman artefacts were found by Sir Mortimer Wheeler in 1945.

Essentials

A-B _Hotel de Orient_. Beautifully renovated old school now a small exclusive hotel with excellent restaurant (French and Indian) run by the Neemrana Group. **B** _Pondicherry Ashok_, Chinnakalapet, T655160, F655140. 20 a/c rooms, mediocre restaurant, exchange 'arbitrary', reported dirty (mouse in room). **B** _Villa Helena_, 14 Suffren St, T226789, F227087, netindia.com.gallery. 5 comfortable rooms with antique furniture around large shady courtyard (1 first floor suite), includes breakfast.

C _Quiet Beach Resort_, 5 km north on highway. New duplex bungalows, right on the beach, nice garden, exclusive but deserted! **C** _Anandha Inn_, 154 Sardar Patel Rd, T330711, F331241, 2 km north of Main Bus Stand. 70 comfortable a/c rooms, business centre, 2 restaurants, best facilities in town. **C** _Les Comptoirs de l'Inde_, 35 rue Dumas, T338934. 5 well furnished rooms, roof terrace. **C-D** _Suguru_, 104 Sardar Patel Rd, T339022, F334377. Good, clean rooms, some a/c, excellent South Indian restaurant, bit noisy. Recommended. **D** _Mass_, Maraimalai Adigal Salai, T337221, F333654, just off the NH45A, near Bus Stand. 35 clean rooms but gloomy (some without windows – the curtain hides a wall!), **C** suites, bar, exchange, helpful staff.

E _Ajantha Guest House_, 22 Goubert Salai (ask for Beach Rd to avoid other _Ajanthas_), T337756. 13 rooms, 4 a/c, some sea-facing, clean rooms, pleasant breezy restaurant (licensed), noisy TV. **E** _Aristo_, 42 Nehru St, T336728. 9 rooms with bath (Rs 200+), front rooms noisy, good restaurant. **E** _Ram International_,

Sleeping
Mission St is now Cathedral St. Western-style hotels are fairly comfortable & have a/c rooms

4 Fortune Bakery
5 Hot Breads & Higginbotham's
6 Indian Coffee House
7 Le Club & Alliance Française
8 Le Transit
9 Penguin & Premier (e-mail)
10 Picnic
11 Rendezvous
12 Satsanga
13 Seagulls
14 Willow Grove Restaurant

212 W Blvd, north of Botanical Gardens, T337230. 53 rooms, some **D** a/c with phone and TV, good restaurant. Govt **E** *Tourist Bungalow*, Uppalam (Dr Ambedkar) Rd, T226376. 12 rooms, some a/c, and VIP suites, in a garden. **F** *Amnivasam Guest House* 47 Montorsier St, T337010. Simple, modest but acceptable. **F** *Balan Guest House*, Vellaja St. Immaculate rooms with bath (Rs 150), clean linen. **F** *Cottage Guest House*, Periarmudaliarchavadi, T338434, on beach, 6 km north of town. Rooms in cottages, French food, bike and motorcycle hire, peaceful, good beach under palm and casuarina trees. **F** *Excursion Centre*, Uppalam Rd. Very cheap bunk-beds in dorm, suitable for groups, south of town, clean and quiet, very good value. Another in Indira Nagar, opposite JIPMER in suburb northwest of the town, T226145. **F** *Palm Beach Cottages*, by Serenity beach, 5 km north of town. Clean huts (Rs 150), concrete beds with mattress, small garden, 5 min walk from beach, friendly staff, excellent food, especially fish, good for bikers but noisy from the highway. **F** *Railway Retiring Rooms* for passengers, quieter than most stations! These are all about 20-30 mins' walk from the centre, best to hire a bicycle. **F** *Youth Hostel*, Solaithandavan Kuppam, T223495, north of town. Dorm beds (Rs 30); close to the sea among fishermen's huts. Bicycle or transport essential.

Ashram guest houses Mainly for official visitors; open to others ('not to hippies'); no alcohol or smoking. They close by 2230 (latecomers may be locked out). Book well in advance, with a day's rate. **E** *Park Guest House*, near Children's Park, T334412, parkgh@auroville.org.in 93 excellent sea-facing rooms (Rs 400), breakfasts, clean, quiet (hear the waves beat agains the breakwater), great garden, reading room, ideal also for long stay. Recommended. **E-F** *International Guest House*, Gingee Salai, near Head Post Office, T336699. 57 very clean and airy rooms, some a/c, huge for the price, very popular so often full. **E-F** *Repos Beach*, 6 km north off the highway. Palm leaf huts on stilts or rooms in a concrete block, only snacks (nearest meals in Auroville), secluded atmosphere, right on the beach, often full. **F** *Garden House*, 136 Akkasamy Madam St (north of town), T40797. Decent, clean rooms (Rs 45 for dbl) with bath (but major bed bug problem and sewer nearby), meals (Rs 20 per day!), quiet, gates locked at 2230.

Near Auroville **F** *Coco Beach Cottage*, East Coast Main Rd, Kottakuppam, opposite the turning for Auroville, T62241. Only 4 rooms, a very friendly and clean little guest house with a popular restaurant.

Eating **Expensive**: *Le Club*, 38 rue Dumas, T339745. French and Continental. Smart, Rs 400 for a splurge, wine Rs 200 glass, opinions differ, "we could have been in a French Bistro!" to 'dearest but not the best', (0730-0930, 1200-1400, 1900-2200). *Le Bistro* (very popular) and *Indochine* are in the garden.

Mid-range: *Aristo*. Good Continental and Indian. Street level and upstairs (rooftop) are recommended. *Blue Dragon*, 30 rue Dumas near the New Pier (south end of Goubert Salai). Chinese. Excellent food, surrounded by antique furniture. *Chez Azis*. Vietnamese. *La Table des Comptoirs*, 45 Romain Rolland St. French. *La Terrasse*, 5 Subbaiyah Salai. Excellent Continental. Good value, huge salads (0830-2200, closed Wed). *Penguin*, 27 rue St Louis (near Raj Bhavan). Good Continental, Indian, Chinese. *Rendezvous*, 30 Suffren St. French and Continental. Attractive, modern, reasonable food (dish Rs 100), overpriced wine, nice roof terrace but slow service (closed during vacations). *Satsanga*, 13 Lal Bahadur Shastri St, T224572. Continental, Indian. Delicious, well presented meals (paté Rs 55, main course R90, wine Rs 200), friendly, helpful English/French speaking staff, French atmosphere with art 'gallery', pleasant outdoor setting. Highly recommended. Foreign students rent rooms too. *Seagulls*, near Children's Park. Continental and others. Large 1st Flr terrace overlooking sea, bit overpriced, bar.

Cheap: *Ashram Dining Hall* north of Govt Place in a French house with a beautiful old façade. Indian vegetarian. Simple, filling, meals (Rs 20 per day) in an unusual setting, seating on cushions at low tables, farm-grown produce, very tasty, brown rice, non-spicy and non-greasy. Highly recommended. *Hot Breads* Ambur Salai. Café. Good burgers, chicken puffs (Rs 35) pizzas, great sandwiches, pastries, shakes (Rs 18) but "tea foul", 0700-2100. *Indian Coffee House*, 41 Nehru St. Real local vegetarian fare throughout the day. *Picnic*, Kamaraj Salai. Vegetarian. *Le Café Pondicherry*, Goubert Salai, by Gandhi statue. Short eats. Pleasant spot, but ordinary fare (daytime). *Ram International*. Excellent vegetarian. *Sea Side Snack Bar*. French. *Willow Grove*, J Nehru St. Reasonably priced Continental, Indian, Chinese, friendly, some rooftop seating.

Bakeries: *Fortune Bakery* 13/9 rue St Thérèse, near Nehru St. Average pastries. *Green Connection*, Nehru St. Sells health food.

Cinema: on Kamaraj Salai and Vallabhai Patel Salai. Ask at Ashram for programmes. **Alliance Française**, 33 rue Dumas. Has a library, organizes French cultural programmes, private restaurant. Register as a temporary member. **Sports complex**: south of the town near the Govt Tourist Home. **Rugby**: Ask for Maurice Saint-Jacques at Lycée Française. **Swimming**: pools in *Hotel Blue Star* and *Calva Bungalow*, Kamaraj Salai open to non-residents for a fee. **Yoga**: *Ananda Ashram* on Yoga Sadhana Beach, 16 Mettu St, Chinamudaliarchavadi, Kottakuppam. They run 1, 3, 6 month courses starting from Jan, Apr, Jul and Oct. **Entertainment**

Feb/Mar: *Masi Magam* On the full moon day of the Tamil month of Masi, pilgrims bathe in the sea when deities from about 40 temples from the surrounding area are taken in colourful procession for a ceremonial immersion. 'Fire walking' sometimes accompanies festivals here. **Festivals**

Dolls of papier-mâché, terracotta and plaster are made and sold at Kosapalayam. Local grass is woven into *Korai* mats. Craftsmen at the Ashram produce marbled silk, hand dyed cloths, rugs, perfumes and incense sticks. **Books**: *Focus*, 204 Cathedral St, good selection of Indian writing in English, cards, stationery, CDs, very helpful. *French Bookshop*, 38 Suffren St. *Kailash French Bookshop*, 87 Lal Bahadur Shastri St, large stock. *Vak*, Nehru St. **Boutiques**: several on Nehru St. Ashram outlets: *Boutique d'Auroville* at no 12, *Auroshree* at no 2D, *Harmonie Boutique*, *Ashram Exhibition Centre*, *Aurocreation* and *Handloom Centre*. Visit the **Sri Aurobindo Handmade paper** 'factory', 44 Sardar Patel Road; shop sells attractive products. **Crafts**: in addition to handicrafts emporia: *Cluny Centre* 46 Romain Rolland St, T/F335668, run by a French order in a lovely colonial house where nuns design and oversee high quality embroidery; *Kalki*, 134 Cathedral St, T39166, produces exceptional printed and painted silk scarves, hangings etc. **Others**: *Market* off MG Rd. Excellent, worth visiting any day but especially on Monday. *Home World* supermarket, 172 Kamaraj Salai. Good toiletries.

Shopping
The shopping areas are along Nehru St & Mahatma Gandhi Rd

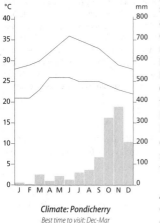

Climate: Pondicherry
Best time to visit: Dec-Mar

Auro Travels, Karikar Building, Nehru St, efficient, quick service. *Sita*, 124 Cathedral St, T336860. **Tour operators**

Tamil Nadu & Chennai

Transport **Local** City **bus**, **cycle-rickshaw** and **auto-rickshaw**: negotiate fare first; bus stands to centre, Rs 20. **Taxi**: particularly along the canal; 4 hrs (50 km) Rs 250, 8 hrs (100 km) Rs 500. *Jupiter Travels*, 170A Anna Salai, has luxury taxis. **Bike/scooter hire**: *Super Snack*, Nehru St opposite Information Centre; *Jaypal*, Gingee Salai; also a hire shop just off Subbaiyah Salai (South Blvd). *Vijay Arya*, 9 Aurobindo St. Daily: cycle, Rs 25, scooter, Rs 120. Well worthwhile as the streets are broad, flat and quiet. Motor bikes for travelling round South India, Rs 250 per day.

Long distance **Road** **Bus**: State Express Bus Stand, NH45A, just west of the traffic circle. T337464; Computerized Reservations: 0700-2100 (helpful staff). **Mofussil (New) Bus Stand**, further W serves all other bus companies. Local Bus Stand: T336919, 0430-1230, 1330-2130. Pondicherry Tourism Corporation (PTC), T337008, 0600-2200, also runs long distance services. Check timings. **Bangalore**: 7½ hrs; **Chidambaram**: frequent buses by all companies, 1½ hrs; **Coimbatore via Salem and Erode**: 8½-9½ hrs; **Gingee**, infrequent, 2 hrs; **Kanniyakumari**: overnight service; **Kannur and Mahé**: 15 hrs; **Karaikal**: 4 hrs; **Chennai**: frequent, under 3 hrs; **Madurai via Tiruchirapalli**: 6½-8 hrs overnight; **Mahabalipuram**: several, about 4 hrs; **Tirupati**: 6½-7 hrs; **Tiruvannamalai (via Villupuram)**: 3-3½ hrs. **Kottakarai**, frequent service from Town Bus Stand. **Car hire**: Round trips to many destinations can be arranged at reasonable rates, e.g return to Bangalore (310 km) Rs 2,000; Chidambaram (74 km), Rs 550; Chennai (166 km), Rs 1000; Mahabalipuram (130 km), Rs 800.**Train** Reservations, T336684, 0800-1400, 1500-1900, Mon-Sat; 0800-1400, Sun. 4 metre-gauge trains (1 hr) daily to **Villupuram** which offers prompt main line connections to Chennai, Madurai, Tiruchirappalli. No *652*, 0510 for Chennai and Madurai; *654*, 0750 for Chennai; *646*, 1615 for Chennai and Tiruchirapalli; *656*, 1920 for *Pandyan Exp 6717* to Tiruchirapalli, Kodai Rd and Madurai; *Quilon Mail 6105* to Tiruchirapalli and Kollam. From **Villupuram**: 4 trains daily for Pondy dep 0510, 0920, 1525, 1825. **NB** The half hourly bus to Villupuram stops 100m from station and connects with trains. Rly Station, Enquiries: 0900-1200, 1500-1800. It is possible to make computerized reservations from Pondy station to any other station, and has a quota on major trains leaving from Chennai Central.

Directory **Banks** *Andhra Bank*, Cathedral St, gives cash against Visa. *State Bank of India*, 5 Suffren St, changes cash and TCs (Amex, Thomas Cook). *UCO Bank*, rue Mahe de Labourdonnais, opposite Govt Park, changes other TCs too, quick and efficient. **Communications** Head Post Office: northwest corner of Govt Place. **CTO**: Rangapillai St. **Internet**: many offices charge around Rs 80 per hr (minimum 30 mins). *Auro-Kailash*, 43A Cathedral St, reliable. *Premier* 45 rue St Louis. **Cultural centres** *French Institute*, rue St Louis, close to the north end of Goubert Salai, and *Alliance Française* at the southern end of Goubert Salai for cultural programmes, 0800-1230, 1500-1800, Mon-Fri. **Embassies & consulates** *French Consulate*, 2 Marine St. **Medical services** *General Hospital*, rue Victor Simone, T336050. *Ashram Dispensary*, Depuis St, near seaside. *Aroma Beauty & Health Clinic*, Perumal Koil St, is recommended. **Tourist offices** *Auroville Information Centre*, Ambur Salai, 12 Nehru St, T339497. *Ashram Reception Service*, Main Building, rue de la Marine, T334836. Useful map. *Pondicherry Tourism* (PTDC), 40 Goubert Salai, T339497, 0845-1300, 1400-1700, daily, town maps, car hire. *Information Bureau*, 19 Goubert Salai. **Useful addresses** *Foreigners' Regional Registration Office*, Goubert Salai.

Auroville ஆரோவில்

Phone code: 41386
Colour map 3, grid A5

Futuristically designed, the layout of the Auroville and its major buildings were to reflect the principles of Sri Aurobindo's philosophy. Far from fully complete, it is nonetheless a striking living experiment.

Ins & outs Either of the 2 roads north from Pondicherry towards Chennai leads to Auroville. Hire a taxi or a scooter to allow you to explore the area at leisure; *La Boutique d'Auroville*, 12 Nehru St, can give directions.

The Mother (see Pondicherry above) had hoped that Auroville would be a major focus for meditation and spiritual regeneration. The Charter says "To live in Auroville one must be a willing servitor of the Divine Consciousness" and describes it as belonging "to humanity as a whole ... the place of an unending education, of constant progress ... a bridge between the past and the future ... a site of material and spiritual researches". Development since 1968 has been very slow. It was planned in the form of a spiral nebula, symbolizing the universality of its faith. The 'city' itself is largely unfinished. **Background**

There are at present about 1,250 Aurovillians drawn mainly from a range of European nations. Designed by a French architect, Auroville has over 50 settlements with names like Sincerity, Shanti (peace), Grace and Verité. Activities include education, 'Green work', alternative technology and handicrafts.

The community at Auroville welcomes visitors who have a genuine interest in the philosophical basis of the community. *Visitor Centre* T622248, F622274, has a map and leaflets, and a café.

The **Matrimandir** (started 1968) at the centre is a 30-m high globe with the lotus bud shaped foundation urn in the Meditation Room with 12 hollow pillars and the centrepiece crystal, said to be the largest in the world, are in place. ■ *Open to visitors 1530-1630 ("you get five seconds to see the crystal"), but to spend time in meditation (1700-1800) go independently.* The garden (*0830-1500*) can be visited within limits. **Bharat Nivas** is a futuristic auditorium to be used for cultural performances with the Secretariat and Boutique nearby. **Sights**

Tours Daily, Rs 30. 0830-1100 from Ashram in Pondicherry, 1430-1745 from Cottage Complex, Ambur Salai, includes Auroville Visitors' Centre, Matri Mandir, a school in New Creation Village. It is better to go independently.

The *Centre Guest House*, T622155 is near the amphitheatre. Rooms for short-stay visitors. New Creation Corner in a 'village', good value Sunday lunch Rs 50, cake Rs 10. **Sleeping & eating**

There are few signs of the town's origins as an **East India Company** trading settlement in 1684, nor of **Fort St David** which was built soon after but destroyed by the French General Lally in 1758. The oldest part of the town, which lies south of Pondicherry, is the commercial centre. **Cuddalore**
Phone code: 04128
Colour map 3, grid A5
Population: 144,000

In the middle is an open maidan, referred to in old records as 'the lawn' or 'the green', and the old Collector's house (1733). The traders of the East India Company set up new suburbs (*pettahs*) for weavers such as Brookespettah. At one time the 'new' town of Tiruppapuliyur was a major Jain centre. The present large temple enshrines the deity Patalesvara, and there are several Chola inscriptions. It has been richly endowed by the **Nattukkottai Chettiars** (see page 131) and houses a silver car and a gold palanquin.

Vellore and the Palar Valley

The broad flat sandy bed of the Palar River runs between the steep-sided northern Tamilnad hill ranges, an intensively irrigated, fertile and densely populated valley cutting through the much poorer and sometimes still wooded high land on either side. The whole valley became the scene of an Anglo-French-Indian contest at the end of the 18th century. Today it is the centre of South India's vitally important leather industry and of intensive agricultural development.

Vellore வேலூர்

Phone code: 0416
Colour map 3, grid A5
Population: 304,700
Altitude: 220 m

The once strategically important centre of Vellore has the air of a busy market town, though its fort and temple are reminders of its historic importance.

The fort is a major attraction, but Vellore is now world famous for its **Christian Medical College Hospital**, founded by the American missionary Ida Scudder in 1900. Started as a one-room dispensary, it extended to a small hospital through American support. Today it is one of the country's largest hospitals with over 1,200 beds and large out-patients' department which caters for over 2,000 patients daily. The college has built a reputation for research in a wide range of tropical diseases. One of its earliest and most lasting programmes has been concerned with leprosy work and there is a rehabilitation centre attached. In recent years it has undertaken a wide ranging programme of social and development work in villages outside the town to back up its medical programmes.

Sights Vijayanagar architecture is beautifully illustrated in the temple at ★ **Vellore Fort**, a perfect example of military architecture and a *jala durga* or water fort. The main rampart of the small fort, believed to have been built by the Vijayanagara kings and dating from the 14th century, is built out of imposing blue granite. It has round towers and huge gateways along its double wall which has Hindu motifs. The moat, still filled with water by a subterranean drain, followed ancient principles of defence with a colony of crocodiles. Defenders could flood the causeways at times of attack. A wooden drawbridge crosses the moat to the southeast. It was the scene of many battles and sieges.

In the 17th century it fell to the Muslim Adil Shahis of Bijapur and then to the Marathas. Vellore came under British control in 1768 who defended it against Haidar Ali in 1782. After the victory in Seringapatnam in 1799, Tipu Sultan's family was imprisoned here and a *sepoy* mutiny of 1806, in which many British and Indian mutineers were killed, left many scars. In the fort is a parade ground, the CSI church, the Temple and two-storeyed *mahals* which are used as Government offices. The moat was refilled and is used for fishing and swimming.

Jalakantesvara Temple (enter from the south) with a 30 m high seven-storeyed granite *gopuram*, has undergone considerable restoration. Inside on the left, the *kalyana mandapa* (wedding hall), one of the most beautiful structures of its kind, has vivid sculptures of dragons and 'hippogryphs' on its pillars. The central pillars show the much older motif of the seated lion, a Pallava symbol from the seventh century, but elaborated to match its Vijayanagar surroundings. Note the impressive stepped entrances and the free hanging chains. Surrounding the temple is a high wall, embossed with small but immaculately carved animal figures. The temple consists of a shrine to Nataraja in the north and a lingam shrine in the west. The *nandi* bull is in the courtyard. Typical giant guardians stand at the door of the main shrine. Although the temple was not touched by the Muslim occupiers of the fort, it was used as a garrison by invading forces and was thus considered desecrated. Since 1981 worship has been resumed and free access is allowed to non-Hindus. The Archaeological Survey of India is in charge.

The easiest way onto the battlements of the fort is to go up the ramp on your right just after passing through the gate. The turret in the northeast corner gives superb views over the town and fort, with an excellent impression of the scale of the fortifications themselves.

There is a small **museum** in the fort. Closed second Saturday every month and Hindu festivals. Interesting collection of wood and stone carvings, sections on anthropology, painting, handicrafts, coins and nature.

Polur Halfway to Tiruvannamalai, 35 km south of Vellore, is the small market town of Polur, famous for its Jain rock carvings. These are found in the Tirumalai temple, which also houses the tallest Jain image in Tamil Nadu. **Excursions**

Ranipet Founded by the Nawab of Arcot in 1771, Ranipet takes its name from the Rani Desingh of Gingee. Her husband, Raja of Gingee, who had refused to pay tribute to the Nawab of the Carnatic, was killed in battle, and his widow performed *sati* on her husband's funeral pyre. The town was established as a mark of respect by the victorious Nawab. It was an important East India Company cantonment. **Sleeping**: E *Hotel Tamil Nadu* (TTDC), T014272-44012, 1-4 bed rooms, dearer a/c double.

Arcot This historically important town just south of Ranipet was formerly the capital of the 18th-century Nawabs of Arcot. Virtually nothing of the old town remains except the Delhi gate, on the banks of the Palar. **Robert Clive** made his reputation here, capturing and then holding the fort during a siege which lasted nearly two months until 15 November 1751.

D *Prince Manor*, 41 Katpadi Rd, T27106, central. Comfortable rooms, very good restaurant. **D** *River View*, New Katpadi Rd, T25251, F25672, 1 km north of town. 31 rooms, some a/c (best on tank side), modern hotel, pleasant inner courtyard with mature palms, 3 good restaurants. **Budget hotels**: several cheap hotels along Babu **Sleeping**

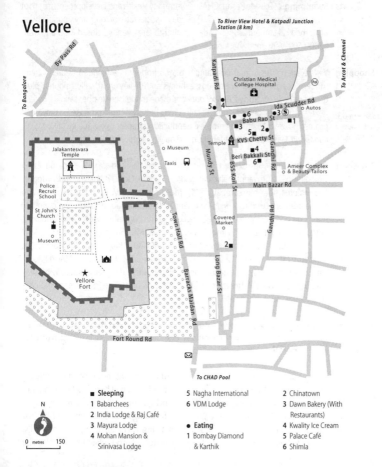

Vellore

To River View Hotel & Katpadi Junction Station (8 km)

Sleeping ■
1 Babarchees
2 India Lodge & Raj Café
3 Mayura Lodge
4 Mohan Mansion & Srinivasa Lodge
5 Nagha International
6 VDM Lodge

Eating ●
1 Bombay Diamond & Karthik
2 Chinatown
3 Dawn Bakery (With Restaurants)
4 Kwality Ice Cream
5 Palace Café
6 Shimla

To CHAD Pool

N

0 metres 150

Rao St and KVS Chetty St cater for families with relatives in the hospital. **F** *Babarchee*, Babu Rao St. Good restaurant (including fast food, pizzas). **F** *India Lodge*, inexpensive rooms and *Raj Café*, good vegetarian restaurant downstairs. **F** *Mayura Lodge*, 85 Babu Rao St, T25488. Clean small rooms, good value. **F** *Mohan Mansion*, 12 Beri Bakkali St, T27083, 15 minutes' walk from bus stand. Small hotel, basic and clean, quieter than others near hospital. **F** *Nagha International Lodge*, 13/A KVS Chetty St, T26731. Some **E** a/c deluxe rooms. **F** *Srinivasa Lodge*, Beri Bakkali St, T26389. Simple and clean. **F** *VDM Lodge*, T24008. Very cheap, pleasant, helpful staff. **F** *YWCA*, in CMC Hospital Ave. Very basic, Indian canteen.

Eating   Several serve South Indian food. *Palace Café*, 21 Katpadi Rd (Indian), 0600-2200. *Hotel Karthik's* vegetarian restaurant is recommended, though not the hotel. *Bombay Diamond* next door, also does good vegetarian. **Ida Scudder Rd**: *Best*, some meals very spicy, nice *parathas*, open 0600 for excellent breakfast. *Geetha* and *Susil*, rooftop or inside, good service and food, reasonable prices. *Shimla*, tandoori, *nan* very good. **Gandhi Rd**: *Chinatown*, a/c, small, friendly (play your own music tapes) – good food and service, very reasonable prices. Recommended. *Nanking* (Chinese). *Dawn Bakery* is recommended for fresh bread and biscuits, wide range of cakes, also sardines, mineral water, fruit juices. Other bakers in Long Bazar.

Sports   **Swimming**: at Hillside Resort, CHAD (Community Health and Development), south of town, excellent private pool, Rs 250 per day (special rate for long stay), popular with CMC medical students. Open early morning to late evening, closed Mon and from 1200-1500. Very good snack bar.

Shopping   Vellore specializes in making 'Karigari' glazed pottery in a range of traditional and *Most of the shops are* modern designs. Vases, water jugs, ashtrays and dishes are usually coloured blue, *along Main Bazar Rd* green and yellow. **Shoes**: *Rolex Footwear* made to measure leather sandals, Rs 120, *& Long Bazar St with* next day. **Tailors**: delivery from all tailors may be slower than promised – may need *a large covered* prompting. *Beauty*, Ameer Complex, Gandhi Rd, cheapest good quality tailoring. *Mr* *market south of* *Kanappan*, Gandhi Rd, very friendly, good quality, a little more expensive. *the bus station*

Transport   **Road Bus**: the Bus Station is off Long Bazar St, east of the Fort. Buses to Tiruchirappalli, Tiruvannamalai, Bangalore, Chennai, Ooty, Thanjavur and Tirupathi. The regional state bus company PATC runs frequent services to Kanchipuram and Bangalore from 0500 (2½ hrs) and Chennai. **Train** Katpadi Junction, the main station, 8 km north of town is on the broad gauge line between Chennai and Bangalore. Buses and rickshaws (Rs 35) into Vellore. **Chennai (MC)**: *Bangalore-Chennai Exp*, 6024 (AC/II), 1200, 2½ hrs; *Brindavan Exp*, 2640 (AC/CC), 1802, 2 hrs; **Bangalore (C)**: *Brindavan Exp*, 2639 (AC/CC), 0903, 4½ hrs; *Chennai-Bangalore Exp*, 6023 (AC/II), 1553, 5 hrs; it is also on the metre gauge line to **Villupuram** to the south, with daily passenger trains to **Tirupathi**, **Tiruvannamalai** and **Pondicherry**. The Cantonment Station is about 1 km south of the GPO.

Directory   **Banks** *Central Bank*, Ida Scudder Rd, east of hospital exit, is at least 10 mins faster at changing TCs than the *State Bank*. **Communications** Post Office: *CMC Hospital* has PO, stamps, takes parcels. **Hospital** *CMC* Ida Scudder Rd, T32102.

Ambur   Ambur is an important centre of the leather tanning industry and the head-
ஆம்பூர் quarters of the Indian Evangelical Lutheran Church. There is a large Muslim
Phone code: 04174 population throughout the Palar valley and a significant Christian minority.
Colour map 3, grid A5
Population: 75,700   To the south and east of the valley are the rising mass of the Javadi Hills. Just
50 km south of Jolarpet is the tiny hill 'resort' of **Yelagiri** (Elagiri), in the Javadi Hills.
The hills themselves are still relatively isolated and populated by tribals. The

hamlet of Yelagiri is at the foot of the hills, but the winding road up to the top gives superb views, and the flat-topped hills have a completely different feel from the plains below. **Sleeping E-F** *Tamil Nadu* (TTDC), a few double rooms.

★ Gingee செஞ்சி

Gingee (pronounced Senjee) has a remarkable 15th-century Vijayanagar fort with much to explore. It is well off the beaten track, very peaceful and in beautiful surroundings.

Phone code: 04145
Colour map 3, grid A5

Getting there Gingee is just off the NH45, between Chennai and Tiruvannamalai, with frequent buses from both, and occasional buses from Pondicherry. **Getting around** Allow at least half a day if you intend to climb the fort, preferably in the morning when it is cooler (only for the fit and healthy). Alternatively, hire a rickshaw.

Ins & outs

The **fort** was intensely contested by successive powers before being captured by an East India Company force in 1762, but by the end of the century it had lost its importance. Although it had Chola foundations, the 'most famous fort in the Carnatic' was almost entirely rebuilt in 1442. It is set on three Charnockite hills, Krishnagiri, Chakklidrug and Rajagiri, all strongly fortified. In places the hills on which the fort stands are sheer cliffs over 150 m high. The highest, **Rajagiri** ('king's hill'), has a south facing overhanging cliff face, on top of which is the citadel. ■ *0900-1700. Gates are locked at 1700.*

Background

The fort, about 3 km west on the Tiruvannamalai road, can be seen from the bus stand. Protected on the north by a deep narrow ravine crossed by a wooden bridge the citadel is approached from the east through a series of defensive lines, two of which have impressive triple arches. In all there are seven gateways, some with large courtyards between them.

Sights

    The inner fort contains two temples and the **Kalyana Mahal**, a square court with a 27 m breezy tower topped by pyramidal roof, surrounded by apartments for the women of the Governor's household. On top of the citadel is a huge cannon and a smooth granite slab known as the **Raja's bathing stone**. An extraordinary stone about 7 m high and balanced precariously on a rock, surrounded by a low circular brick wall, is referred to as the Prisoner's Well. There are fine Vijaynagara temples, granary, barracks and stables and an 'elephant tank'.

    The Archaeological Survey of India Office, just off the main road towards the fort, may have guides to accompany you to the fort. Carry provisions, especially plenty of drinks.

E *Shivasand*, M Gandhi Rd, opposite bus stand, T22218. 21 clean, adequate rooms with bath, 1 dearer a/c, vegetarian restaurant, a/c bar and non vegetarian meals (Indian, Continental), good views of fort from roof, helpful manager. Other cheaper **F** lodges in town.

Sleeping
*Spend a night here
if you can*

Local To visit the fort take a **cycle-rickshaw** from the bus stand to the hills; about Rs 30 for the round trip, including 2 hr wait. **Cycle hire**: from near the bus stand. **Long distance Road Bus**: to/from **Pondicherry**: infrequent direct buses (2 hrs); better via Tindivanam (45 mins). To/from **Tiruvannamalai**, 39 km: several buses (1 hr); ask to be dropped near the fort. TPTC bus 122 to/from **Chennai**.

Transport

★ Tiruvannamalai திருவண்ணாமலை

Phone code: 04175
Colour map 3, grid A5
Population: 119,000

In a striking setting at the foot of the rocky Arunachala Hill Tiruvannamali is one of the holiest towns of Tamil Nadu, and locally considered the home of Siva and his consort Parvati. It is a major pilgrimage centre.

Tamil Nadu & Chennai

Sights One of the largest temples in South India, the ★**Arunachala Temple** (16th and 17th centuries) was built mainly under the patronage of the Vijayanagar kings: its massive *gopurams*, the tallest of which is 66-m high, dominate the centre of the town. It is dedicated to Siva as God incarnate of Fire.

The temple has three sets of walls forming nested rectangles. Built at different periods they illustrate the way in which many Dravidian temples grew by accretion. The east end of each is extended to make a court, and the main entrance is at the east end of the temple. The lower parts of the *gopurams*, built of granite, date from the late Vijyanagar period but have been added to subsequently. The upper 10 storeys and the decoration are of brick and plaster.

There are some remarkable carvings on the *gopurams*. On the outer wall of the east *Gopuram*, for example, Siva is shown in the south corner dancing with an elephant's skin. The design of the temple illustrates the effect in later Dravidian temples of progressive abasement produced by moving from the grandest and greatest of gateways through ever smaller doorways until the very modest inner shrine is reached. Inside the east doorway of the first courtyard is the 1,000-pillared *mandapa* built late in the Vijayanagar period. To the south of the court is a small shrine dedicated to *Subrahmanya*. To the south again is a large tank. The pillars in the mandapa are carved with typically vigorous horses, riders and lion-like *yalis*.

The middle court has four much earlier *gopurams* (mid-14th century), a large columned mandapa and a tank. The innermost court may date from as early as the 11th century and the main sanctuary with carvings of deities is

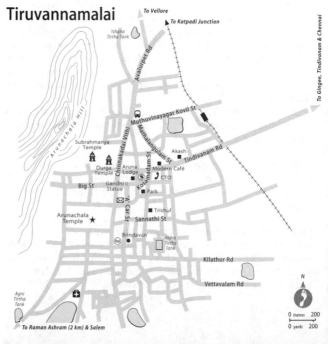

Tiruvannamalai

To Vellore

To Katpadi Junction

To Gingee, Tindivanam & Chennai

Ishana Tirtha Tank

Avalurpet Rd

Muthuvinayagar Kovil St

Mahalangulam St

Chinnakadai Vithi

Subrahmanya Temple

Akash

Tindivanam Rd

Durga Temple

Aruna Lodge

Modern Café

CTO

Big St

Gandhi Statue

Kosamadam St

Park

Car St

Arunachala Temple ★

Trishul

Sannathi St

Brindavan

Indra Tirtha Tank

Kilathur Rd

Vettavalam Rd

Agni Tirtha Tank

To Raman Ashram (2 km) & Salem

N

0 metres 200
0 yards 200

certainly of Chola origin. In the south is *Dakshinamurti*, the west shows *Siva* appearing out of a lingam, and the north has *Brahma*. The outer porch has small shrines to *Ganesh* and *Subrahmanya*. In front of the main shrine are a brass column lamp and the *Nandi* bull.

D *Trishul*, 6 K Mudali St, T22219. 16 clean spacious rooms, 8 a/c, a/c vegetarian restaurant, roof with great temple views. Recommended. **D-E** *Akash*, Tindivanam Rd, T22151. Fairly clean but noisy and run down. **F** *Aruna Lodge*, 82 Kosamadam St, T23291. 24 clean, adequate rooms with bath. **F** *Modern Café*, Tindivanam Rd, T22327. Dark rooms with only camp beds, common bath, old-fashioned, quite clean, very cheap (Rs 20). **F** *Park*, 26 Kosamadam St, T22471. 26 rooms (7 double), east-facing rooms have excellent views of the main temple and hill, light and airy but going downhill. ▸ **Sleeping**

A *thali* lovers paradise with plenty of 'meals' restaurants including *Brindavan* on 'A' Car St; about Rs 10 per meal. A shop in *Modern Café* building sells ultra-pasteurized milk, processed cheese, pasta etc. ▸ **Eating**

Karthikai Deepam Full moon day in **Nov-Dec**. A huge beacon is lit on top of the hill behind the temple. The flames, which can be seen for miles around, are thought of as Siva's lingam of fire, joining the immeasurable depths to the limitless skies. A cattle market is held. ▸ **Festivals**

Local Bicycle hire from near the Bus Stand but not recommended; cycling can be hazardous in this very busy small town. **Long distance** **Road** **Bus**: buses to major cities in Tamil Nadu, Kerala and Karnataka. Local people will point out your bus at the bus stand; you can usually get a seat although they do get crowded. To Gingee, frequent, 1 hr; Chennai, 5 hrs, Rs 30. Pondicherry, 3-3½ hrs. **Train** To **Tirupati** via Vellore, Katpadi and Chittor: *Madurai Tirupati Exp*, *6800*, 2300, 5½ hrs; **Madurai** via Chidambaram, Thanjavur and Tiruchirapalli: *Tirupati Madurai Exp*, *6799*, 2120, 12½ hrs. ▸ **Transport**

Bank *State Bank of India*, Kosamadam St, has foreign exchange facilities on 1st Flr. **Communications** Post Office, 'A' Car St; Central Telegraph Office, Kosamadam St. ▸ **Directory**

Tiruchirappalli திருச்சிராப்பள்ளி and Chettinad

Known as Trichy or Tiruchi for short, Tiruchirappalli is at the head of the fertile Kaveri delta. Its rock fort is visible for miles around, across the flat surrounding plain, but it is its position at the head of the Kaveri delta, and the holy site of Srirangam, which have given it its greatest significance for over 1,000 years.

Phone code: 0431
Colour map 3, grid B5
Population: 711,100
Altitude: 88 m

Getting there **Trichy airport,** about 8 km from the town centre, has flights to Madurai and Chennai and also to Colombo. Well connected by train to major towns, the Junction Railway Station and the two bus stations are right in the centre of the main hotel area, all within walking distance. **Getting around** Much of Trichy is easy to see on foot, but there are plenty of autos and local buses run to the Rock Fort and Srirangam. ▸ **Ins & outs**

Trichy was mentioned by Ptolemy in the second century BC. A Chola fortification from the second century, it came to prominence under the Nayakas from Madurai who built the fort and the town, capitalizing on its strategic position. In legend its name is traced to a three-headed demon Trisiras who terrorized both men and the gods until Siva overpowered him in the place called Tiruchi. ▸ **Background**

Tamil Nadu & Chennai

Cigar making became important between the two World Wars, while the indigenous *bidis* continue to be made, following a tradition started in the 18th century. Trichy is the country's largest centre manufacturing artificial diamonds, having taken over from centres in Switzerland and Burma which provided most of the artificial gems until the Second World War. Jaffersha Street is commonly known as 'Diamond Bazar'. The town is also noted for its high quality string instruments, particularly *veenas* and *violins*.

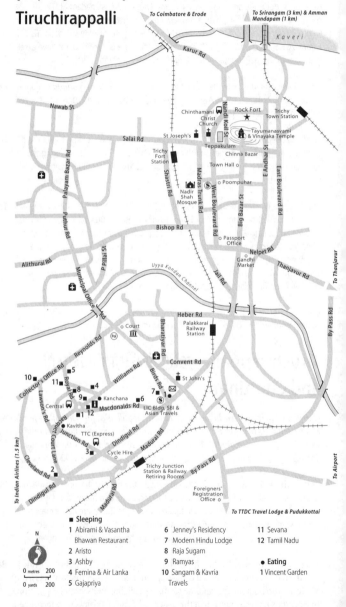

Tiruchirappalli

Tamil Nadu & Chennai

The ★ **Rock Fort** (1660) stands on an 84-metre high rock. The **Vinayaka Temple** (or Ucchi Pillayar Koil), approached from Chinna Bazar, is at the highest point, from which you get marvellous views. You must climb 437 rock cut steps to reach it. The temple itself is disappointing. ■ *0600-2000. Entry Re 1, camera Rs 10, video Rs 50.* On your way up you come to the main 11th-century defence line and the remains of a thousand-pillar hall, destroyed in 1772, at the top of the first flight of steps. Further up is a hundred-pillar hall where civic receptions are held. At the end of the last flight is the **Tayumanasvami Temple**, dedicated to Siva, which has a golden *vimana* and a lingam which is carved out of the rock itself. There are also other seventh-century Pallava cave temples which have beautifully carved pillars and panels.

It is worthwhile discovering the old city on foot, particularly **Big Bazar Street** and **Chinna Bazar**. The Gandhi Market is a colourful vegetable and fruit market.

Teppakulam is a large artificial *tank* surrounded by colourful stalls and a flower market. Among the dozen or so mosques in the town, the **Nadir Shah Mosque** near the Teppakalum and city railway station stands out with its white dome and metal steeple, said to have been built with material taken from a Hindu temple. **St Joseph's College Church** (Church of our Lady of Lourdes), one of several Catholic churches here, designed as a smaller version of the Basilica at Lourdes in France has an unusual sandalwood altar. The 18th-century **Christ Church**, the first English church, is north of the Teppakulam, while the early 19th-century **St John's Church** has a memorial plaque to Bishop Heber, one of India's best known missionary bishops, who died in Trichy in 1826.

Government Museum has a display of sculpture, art, archaeology, handicrafts, numismatics, geology and science. ■ *0900-1230, 1400-1700, closed Fri. Free. Bharatiyar Rd, Cantt.*

Essentials

C *Sangam*, Collector's Office Rd, T464480, F461779. 58 comfortable a/c rooms and restaurants, good breakfast in coffee shop, pleasant bar, exchange, spacious lawns. **B-C** *Jenney's Residency*, 3/14 Macdonalds Rd, T414414, F461451, www.fhraindia.com.hotel.tiruchira palli/jenneys 84 comfortable rooms, most a/c, good restaurant, pool (non-residents Rs 80), excellent travel desk, avoid paying inflated 'dollar price'. **C-D** *Femina*, 14C Williams Rd, T414501, F410615. 116 clean rooms, 70 a/c, vegetarian restaurants, bar, good value, modern 8-storey hotel. **D** *Abirami*, 10 Macdonalds Rd, opposite Central Bus Stand, T460001. 55 rooms, some a/c with bath, good a/c restaurant (vegetarian), exchange. **D** *Ashby*, 17A Junction Rd, opposite Express bus stand, T460652. 11 rooms, 8 a/c, with bath, good restaurants, bar, oldest hotel in town, with Raj character, a bit noisy but excellent friendly staff. **D-E** *Aanand*, 1 VOC Rd (Racquet Court Lane). T415545, F415219. Very clean rooms (hot water, TV), some a/c, in Indian family hotel, excellent *thalis* (Rs 24), busy veg restaurant. **D-E** *Gajapriya*, 2 Royal Rd, T414411, F466456. Good value, clean, modern rooms, some a/c, non-veg restaurant. **D-E** *Ramyas*, 13D/2 Williams Rd, T415128, F412750, near Bus Stand. 75 spotless rooms, some a/c, restaurant, bar. **D-E** *Tamil Nadu* (TTDC), Macdonalds Rd (Cantt) opposite Bus Stand, T414346. 36 rooms (run down), some a/c with bath, restaurant recommended, bar and tourist office. **E** *Sevana*, 5 Royal Rd, Cantt, T41201. 44 rooms, some a/c with bath, a/c restaurant (Indian), bar. **F** *Modern Hindu Lodge*, near SBI, **F** *Rajasugam*, 13b Royal Rd (opp bus stand), T460636. Very noisy but clean. **F** *Railway Retiring Rooms*, some a/c, reputed to be some of the best in India.

Eating **Mid-range** Hotels: *Abirami's*, T460001. A/c vegetarian *Vasantha Bhawan*. *Jenney's Residency*, T461301. Excellent Chinese, Continental. Also *Wild West* bar. *Sangam's*, T464480. Indian, Continental. **Outside hotels:** *Kanchana*, Williams Rd, serves non-vegetarian. *Kavitha*, Junction and Williams Rd corner. A/c. Excellent breakfasts and vegetarian lunch *thalis*; *Skylord*, Municipal Office Rd. *Vincent's*, Dindigul Rd. Very pleasant garden restaurant, wide choice, friendly management. **Cheap** Some good Indian vegetarian restaurants in Chinna Bazar include. *Vasantha Bhawan*, recommended for *thalis* and good service. *Sree Ranga Bhavan*, has local character.

Festivals March: *Festival of Floats* on the Teppakulam when the temple deities are taken out onto the sacred lake on rafts. Several at Srirangam (see below).

Shopping Very 'Indian' with artificial diamonds, toys and bangles on offer. *Khadi Kraft*, Junction Rd, opposite Rly Station. Towards Srirangam temple: *Heritage Arts*, 5 Amma Mandapam Rd, T432113, good bronzes, tribal jewellery, silk selection, astute but not pushy.

Transport **Local Bus**: good City Bus service. From airport Nos 7, 63, 122, 128, take 30 mins. The Central State Bus Stand is across from the tourist office (No 1 Bus passes all the sights). **Taxi**: unmetered taxis, and tourist taxis from *Kavria Travels*, *Hotel Sangam*, Collector's Office Rd, T25202 and **cycle-rickshaws** and **auto-rickshaws**. **Cycle hire**: from Junction Rd near the station.

Long distance Air The airport is 8 km from the centre. *Indian Airlines*, Dindigul Rd, 2 km from Express Bus Stand, T462233, Airport T420563; flies to **Chennai**. *Air Lanka*, 14 Williams Rd, T462551 to **Colombo**. **Road** The bus stands are 1 km from the rly station; TN Govt Express, T460992, Central, T460425. Frequent buses to **Coimbatore** 205 km (5½ hrs), **Kumbakonam** 92 km, **Chennai** (6 hrs), **Madurai** 161 km (3 hrs), **Palani** 152 km (3½ hrs), **Thanjavur** (1½ hrs). Also 2 to **Kanniyakumari** (9 hrs), **Kodai** (5½ hrs) and **Tirupati** (9½ hrs). **Train** Enquiries, T131. **Bangalore**: *Bangalore Exp*, *6531*, 2110, 10½ hrs; **Chengalpattu**: *Quilon Mail*, *6106*, 2335, 6 hrs; **Kollam (via Mamamadurai and Tuticorin)**: *Kollam Mail*, *6105* (AC/II), 0355, 11½ hrs; *6161 Exp*, 1610, 13 hrs; **Chennai (via Thanjavur, Kumbakonam, Chengalpattu and Villupuram)**: *Rameshwaram Exp*, *6102*, 1925, 10½ hrs; **Chennai (ME)**: *Pallavan Exp*, *2606* (AC/II), 0615, 5½ hrs; *Vaigai Exp*, *2636* (AC/CC), 0906, 5½ hrs; **Madurai**: *Vaigai Exp*, *2635* (AC/CC), 1752, 2½ hrs; *Pandyan 6717*, 0300, 3½ hrs; **Mangalore (via Erode, Coimbatore and Kozhikode)**: *Exp*, *6531*, 2050, 16½ hrs; **Pudukkottai and Rameshwaram**: *Chennai-Rameshwaram Exp*, *6101*, 0700, 1 hr and 6½ hrs; **Villupuram (for Pondicherry)**, *Vaigai Exp*, *2636*, 0906, 3 hrs (attractive countryside), plus frequent bus to Pondicherry (1 hr) or another train (4 daily).

Directory **Tourist offices** At *Hotel Tamil Nadu Complex*, 1 Williams Rd, T460136. Mon-Fri, 0945-1745. Also counters at Airport and Junc Station, 0600-2000. **Useful addresses** Bank: *State Bank of India*, Dindigul Rd. **Hospital**: *Govt Hospital*, T24465. **Travel agent**: *Asian Travels*, LIC Building, Cantt, T27660.

Around Trichy

★ **Srirangam** The temple town on the Kaveri, just north of Trichy, is surrounded by seven
Phone code: 0431 concentric walled courtyards, with magnificent gateways and several shrines.
Colour map 3, grid B5 On the way to Srirangam, is an interesting river *ghat* where pilgrims take their
Population: 70,000 ritual bath before entering the temple. ■ *Getting there: Bus No 1 from Trichy or hire a rickshaw.*

Sri Ranganathasvami Temple One of the largest in India and dedicated to Vishnu. The original small temple built by Raja Dharma Varman was enlarged by Chola, Pandiya and Vijayanagara kings. The fact that it faces south, unlike most other Hindu temples, is explained by the legend that Rama intended to present the image of Ranganatha to a temple in Sri Lanka but this was impossible since the deity became fixed here but it still honours the original destination.

The temple, where the Vaishnava reformer **Ramanuja** settled and worshipped, is famous for its superb sculpture, the 21 impressive *gopurams* and its rich collection of temple jewellery. The 'thousand' pillared hall (904 columns) stands beyond the fourth wall, and in the fifth enclosure there is the unusual shrine to Tulukka Nachiyar, the God's Muslim consort. It lacks any grand plan since it was expanded by different rulers, mainly between the 14th and the 17th centuries, each of whom left the central shrine untouched but competed with their predecessors by building further walls with taller *gopurams*. The restoration of the deteriorating granite walls and the unfinished seventh *gopuram* was undertaken with the help of UNESCO and completed in the 1980s. Non-Hindus are not allowed into the sanctuary but can enter the fourth courtyard where the famous sculptures of *gopis* (*Radha's* milk maids) in the Venugopala shrine can be seen. ■ *0615-1300, 1515-2045. A guide is recommended; allow about 2 hrs. Camera, Rs 20, video Rs 70 (Rs 3 for the viewpoint). Shoes must be left outside.*

The **festival** of *Vaikunta Ekadasi*, and associated temple car festival, in December/January draws thousands of pilgrims who witness the transfer of the image of the deity from the inner sanctum under the golden *vimana* to the *mandapa*.

Amma Mandapam Nearby, on the north bank of the Kaveri, this town is a hive of activity. The ghats, where devotees wash, bathe, commit cremated ashes, pray – are interesting to visit, although some may find the dirt and smell overpowering.

So named because a legendary elephant worshipped the lingam, **Tiruvanaik-** Tiruvanaikkaval is 6 km east of Srirangam. It has the architecturally finer **kaval** **Jambukesvara Temple** with its five walls and seven *gopurams*, one of the oldest and largest Siva temples in Tamil Nadu. The unusual lingam under a *jambu* tree always remains under water. There are special festivals in January and the spring. In August *Pancha Piraharam* is celebrated and in *Panguni* the images of Siva and his consort Akhilandesvari exchange their dress.

A major Siva temple in the heart of Vaishnava territory, the Jambukesvara Temple "gives a clearer idea of the Dravidian style at its best", according to Percy Brown, than any other temple in South India. ■ *0600-1300, 1600-2130. Non-Hindus are not allowed into the sanctuary.*

Karur, west of Trichy, may have been the ancient capital of the **Cheras** of the **Karur** Sangam Age. The Amaravati river bed nearby has yielded artefacts including *Phone code: 04324* Roman amphora, Roman and Chera gold and silver coins, portrait figures and *Colour map 3, grid B4* stone inscriptions bearing the Brahmi script. The larger hoards (once as many as 500 silver Roman coins) were found mainly in the 19th century. More recently gold signet rings bearing Tamil inscriptions (in Brahmi) with identifiable personal names have been dated to the first and second century AD. ■ *Getting there: trains from Trichy, 1¾ hrs.*

Tamil Nadu & Chennai

Chettinad

Colour map 3, grid B5

NOTE - train runs from Karur to Trichy

Chettinad, occupying the hot and often dusty coastal plain, south of Trichy, is home to some of South India's wealthiest merchant families. Many of the villages are now semi-deserted but they retain a charm and distinctive style that repays a visit.

The triangle Pudukkottai-Kiranur-Kodumbalur has a number of early Chola and late Pallava monuments containing fine cave sculptures.

There are two small sites just south of Trichy where sculptures can be seen on the way to Chettinad. **Viralimalai** (29 km) is noted for its peacock sanctuary, and a shrine to Subrahmanya (whose divine vehicle is a peacock) on the top of the hill outside the town. It is also known for a dance drama form, the *Viralimalai Kuravanji*, which originated here. **Kodumbalur** has the Moovarkoil where two of the three shrines of the 10th-century temple illustrate the evolution of Dravidian temple architecture. There are some fine sculptures of deities. Now something of a backwater, the village was on the route between the Pandiyan and Chola kingdoms and was once the capital of the Irukkuvel Dynasty. ■ **Getting there:** *Trains run between Trichy and Karaikkudi and there are local buses to the places mentioned. Hire a car if you are short of time.*

Close to **Kiranur** (28 km from Trichy) is the eighth-century Kunnandarkoil cave temple, with the later addition of a Vijayanagar *nritta mandapa* which contains some excellent bronzes. **Narthamalai**, west of the road 6 km further, has important Chola temples including the Vijayalaya Choleesvaram with its circular sanctum, of particular interest in tracing the development of southern temple architecture. In the hills near Narthamalai are some Jain caves.

Pudukkottai

புதுக்கோட்டை
Phone code: 04322
Colour map 3, grid B5
Population: 98,600

Pudukkottai, 50 km from Trichy, was the capital of the former princely state ruled by the Tondaiman Rajas, founded by Raghunatha Raya Tondaiman in 1686. At one entrance to the town is a ceremonial arch raised by the Raja in honour of Queen Victoria's jubilee celebrations. The town's broad streets suggest a planned history – the temple is at the centre, with the old palace and a tank. The new palace is now the District Collector's office.

The rock-cut **Sri Kokarnesvarar Temple** at Thirukokarnam, 5 km north of the railway station, dates from the Pallava period. The natural rock shelters, caves, stone circles, dolmens and Neolithic burial sites show that there was very early human occupation.

The **museum** has a wide range of exhibits, including sections on geology, zoology and the economy as well as sculptures and the arts. The archaeology section has some excellent sculptures from nearby temples. There is a notable carving of Siva as *Dakshinamurti* and some fine bronzes from Pudukkottai itself. ■ *0800-1130, 1400-1700, daily except Mon. Big St, Thirukokarnam 5 km away.*

Sittannavasal (13km) has a Jain cave temple (circa eighth century) with sculptures, where monks took shelter when they fled from persecution in North India. In a shrine and verandah there are some fine frescoes in the Ajanta style and bas-relief carvings. You can also see rock hewn beds of the monks. The *Brahmi* inscriptions date from the second century BC.

Sleeping and eating E *Shivalaya*, Thirumayam Rd by Maternity Hospital (on a side street, just south of town, 1 km east of the Bus Stand), T2864. Basic but clean, good rooms (some a/c), recommended. Very good vegetarian restaurant with excellent service.

Festivals In Jan and Feb bullock races (*manju virattu*) are held in the area.

Transport Road Buses go to Tiruchirappalli, Thanjavur, Madurai, Ramnad, Ramesvaram, and to Sittanavasal (see above). **Train Chennai (ME)**: *Sethu Exp, 6714,* 2007, 9½ hrs; Trichy 1¼ hrs. **Ramesvaram**: *Ramesvaram Exp, 6701,* 0833, 5¾ hrs

Directory Banks *State Bank of India,* East Main St.

Karaikkudi is in the heart of Chettinad with several typical mansions, antique and textile shops. You can visit the local *santhai* (market), craftsmen working in wood and metal, and gold- and silversmiths working in their workshops.

Karaikkudi
Phone code: 04565
Colour map 3, grid B5
Population: 110,500

At **Avudayarkoil**, the Athmanathar temple, has one of the most renowned sites in Tamil cultural history. A legend tells that Manickavaskar, a Pandyan Prime Minister, re-directed money intended for the purchase of horses to build the temple. However, his real fame lies as author of the *Thiruvasakam* ('holy outpourings'), one of the most revered Tamil poetic texts. Completely off the beaten track, the temple has superb sculptures, and is noted for the absence of any images of Siva or Parvati, the main deities, whose empty pedestals are worshipped. The wood carvings on the temple car are notable too.
■ *Getting there: The temple is 12km south east of Arantang; which is 30 km northeast of Karaikkudi.*

Kanadukathan, 5 km north of Karaikkudi, has a number of formerly magnificent mansions, some of them empty except for bats, monkeys – and antique dealers. It has been estimated that the Burma teak and satinwood pillars in just one of the village's Chettiar houses weighed 300 tonnes, often superbly carved. The plaster on the walls is made from a mixture of lime, eggwhite, powdered shells and myrobalan fruit (the astringent fruit of the tree *Phyllantles emblica*), mixed into a paste which, when dried, gave a gleaming finish. Some of these houses were used as weekend retreats. Traditionally in the jewellery and trading business, the **Chettiars** now own a variety of large companies. **Chettinad town**, 11 km north of Karaikkudi, has an impressive 'Palace'.

Sleeping Very few suitable places to stay in the area. In Devakottai, **F** *Nivaas* 1st left from bus station coming from the north, (no sign in English), is basic (no electric sockets), no English spoken. In Karaikkudi: **A** *The Bangala,* Devakottai Rd, Senjai, T Chennai 44-4934912, F4934543, bangala@vsnl.com 8 bright and spacious a/c rooms with period colonial furniture, in a newly restored 1916 bungalow, a 'heritage guest house' of character amidst orchards and palms invoking a privileged life-style on the outskirts of town, authentic Chettinad meals (or Continental), rest stop facilities for day visitors (lunch $15-20).

Transport Road Bus routes link the town with every part of the state. Trichy and Madurai, about 2 hrs, Chennai, 8 hrs. **Train** The *Ramesvaram* and *Sethu Exp* connect Chennai and Ramesvaram with Karaikkudi.

Tamil Nadu & Chennai

Chola Heartland and the Kaveri Delta

★ Thanjavur (Tanjore) தஞ்சாவூர்

Phone code: 04362
Colour map 3, grid B5
Population: 200,200
Altitude: 59 m

Thanjavur's Brihadisvara Temple, a World Heritage Site, is one of the great monuments of South India. In the heart of the lush, rice growing delta of the Kaveri, today the town feels much more like a throbbing rural market centre than a modern commercial or industrial city.

Ins & outs   **Getting there**   Most long distance buses now stop at the New bus stand 4 km south-west of the centre, but there are frequent local buses and autos (Rs 25) to town and the railway station. **Getting around**   It is less than a 15-min walk from the hotels to the Brihadisvara Temple. **Climate**   Summer: Max 37°C, Min 33°C; Winter: Max 24°C, Min 23°C. Annual rainfall: 940 mm.

History   The capital of the great Chola Empire and later of the *Thanjavur* Nayaka and Maratha rulers, the Chola kings built most of Thanjavur's 93 temples. Stein wrote that "The Brihadisvara Temple was built and maintained through the demands by Rajaraja I upon villages throughout the Kaveri Delta, the core of Chola power, as well as from the 'booty in the conquests of Chera, Pandiya.... and Chalukya kings'. The Cholas were great patrons of the arts and while they lavished their wealth to build temples, they encouraged the belief in the divine right of kings, and the practice of donating a part of one's wealth to the temple for spiritual gain.

Sights   ★ **Brihadisvara Temple**. Known as the **'Big Temple'**, is the achievement of the Chola king **Rajaraja I** (ruled AD 985-1012). The magnificent main temple has a 62 m high *vimana* (the tallest in India), topped by a dome carved from an 80 ton block of granite, which needed a 6.5 km ramp to raise it to the top. The attractive gardens, the clean surroundings and well-lit sanctuaries make a visit doubly rewarding.

The entrance is from the east. After crossing the moat you enter through two *gopurams*, the second guarded by two *dvarapalas* typical of the early Chola period, when the gopuras on the outer enclosure walls were dwarfed by the scale of the *vimana* over the main shrine. Shulman has suggested that "the pilgrim's passage toward the central shrine is a form of ascent – as it is in the many shrines built upon hills or mountains. Yet even here the *garbha griha* remains remote". An enormous *Nandi*, carved out of a single block of granite 6 m long, guards the entrance to the sanctuary. According to one of the many myths that revolve around the image of a wounded *Nandin*, the Thanjavur Nandi was growing larger and larger, threatening the temple, until a nail was driven in its back.

The temple, built mainly with large granite blocks, has superb inscriptions and sculptures of Siva, Vishnu and Durga on three sides of the massive plinth. Siva appears in three forms, the dancer with 10 arms, the seated figure with a sword and trident, and Siva bearing a spear. The carvings of dancers showing the 81 different Bharat Natyam poses are the first to record classical dance form in this manner.

The main shrine has a large *lingam*. In the inner courtyard are Chola frescoes on walls prepared with lime plaster, smoothed and polished, then painted while the surface was wet. These were hidden under later Nayaka paintings. Chambers 7 and 9 are well preserved and have fresco paintings of kings, queens and musicians. ■ *0600-1200, 1600-2030*.

The permanent exhibition in the temple complex has reproductions of the paintings and a record of the Archaeological Survey of India's conservation programme. ■ *0900-1200, 1600-2000*. Since music and dance were a vital part of temple life and dancing in the temple would accompany the chanting of the holy scriptures which the community attended, Rajaraja also built two housing colonies nearby to accommodate 400 *devadasis* (temple dancers). Subsidiary shrines were added to the main temple at different periods. The Vijayanagara kings built the Amman shrine, the Nayakas the Subrahmanya shrine and the Marathas the Ganesh shrine.

The Palace Built by the Nayakas in the mid-16th century and later completed by the Marathas, the palace is now partly in ruins. The evidence of its original splendour can be seen in the ornate Durbar Hall. The towers are worth climbing for a good view; one tower has a whale skeleton washed up in Chennai! The **art gallery**, **Sangeeta Mahal** with excellent acoustics, **Saraswati Mahal Library** and the **Tamil University Museum** are here, together with some Government offices.

The **Schwartz Church** (1779) is dedicated to the Danish missionary FC Schwartz who died in 1798. There is a particularly striking marble bas-relief sculpture at the west end of the church by Flaxman of Schwartz on his

Thanjavur

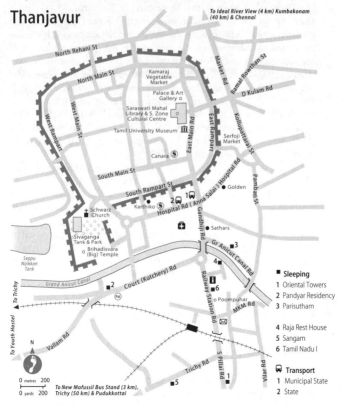

To Ideal River View (4 km) Kumbakonam (40 km) & Chennai

North Rehani St

North Main St

Kamaraj Vegetable Market

Palace & Art Gallery ○

Saraswati Mahal Library & S. Zone Cultural Centre

Tamil University Museum 🏛

West Main St

West Rampart

Market Rd

Ramal Rowthan St

D Kulam Rd

East Rampart

Kollupattarai St

Serfoji Market

Canara ⑤

South Main St

Pambari St

South Rampart St

Karthiko ⑤ 2 1 🚌 Anna Salai) Hospital Rd

Hospital Rd (● Golden

Gandhiji Rd

● Sathars

+ Schwarz Church

Sivaganga Tank & Park

Brihadisvara (Big) Temple ○

Gr Anicut Canal Rd

3 ■

Seppu Naikkan Tank

Grand Anicut Canal

Court (Kutchery) Rd

4 ■

To Trichy ◄

To Youth Hostel

2 ■

Railway Station Rd

i 🛈
6 ■

o Poompuhar

MKM Rd

N

Vallam Rd

S Pillai Rd

Trichy Rd

Villar Rd

1 ■

5 ■

0 metres 200
0 yards 200

To New Mofussil Bus Stand (3 km), Trichy (50 km) & Pudukkottai

■ **Sleeping**
1 Oriental Towers
2 Pandyar Residency
3 Parisutham
4 Raja Rest House
5 Sangam
6 Tamil Nadu I

🚍 **Transport**
1 Municipal State
2 State

Tamil Nadu & Chennai

deathbed, showing him surrounded by the family of Raja Serfoji to whom he was tutor, see page 83.

Tours TTDC *Temple tour* of Thanjavur and surroundings by a/c coach; enquire at Tourist Office. Monday-Friday, 1000-1745.

Museums & libraries ★ **Rajaraja Museum and Nayak Darbar Hall Art Gallery** Large and excellent collection of Chola bronzes (lost wax process) and granite pieces. Look for Bhairava, Umasahita Siva, Kali, Somaskanda and the Rama Lakshmana group. ■ *Thanjavur Palace. 0900-1200, 1500-1800, daily. Rs 3; Camera Rs 5; Video Rs 100.* **Royal Museum**, next to Durbar Hall, is not worth visiting. Quality and maintenance pitiful. **Saraswati Mahal Library** in the palace is one of the country's major reference libraries, having over 40,000 rare books, several first editions and about 8,000 palm leaf manuscripts. ■ *1000-1300, 1330-1730, daily except Wed. Free; scholars only.* **Tamil University Library** Numismatic section and old musical instruments but poorly maintained.

Excursions A visit to **Thiruvaiyaru**, 13 km away, with the Panchanatheswara Siva temple, known for its *Thyagaraja Music Festival*, gives a glimpse of South Indian rural life. Hardly visited by tourists, music connoisseurs arrive in large numbers in January. Performances vary and the often subtle music is marred by loud amplification. The *Car Festival* is in March. ■ *Getting there: Frequent buses from the old bus station, Thanjavur (30 mins, crowded).*

The Thyagaraja Temple (13th-16th century) at **Tiruvarur**, 53 km east of Thanjavur, was an ancient capital founded by the Cholas. The north and west *gopurams* are late additions of the Vijayanagar and Nayaka periods. Just inside the second enclosure wall on the south side is the 10th-century shrine of Achalesvara ('immovable Lord'). The story goes that the king Samatkara "performed *tapas* and, when Siva appeared to him, begged him to be present forever in the holy site". The god promised to remain, immovable, in that place. The king set up a linga, and a voice from heaven announced: "I will dwell eternally in this linga; even its shadow will never move". So the shadow of the Achalesvara linga is ever stationary. Only he who is to die within six months cannot see this marvel. As David Shulman points out, "the miracle is made secure by terror – he who doubts it will die!".

The west facing temple follows the early Chola pattern, with a simple base, pilasters on the walls, a pyramidal tower and a hemispherical roof. The innermost court has two east facing shrines to *Vanmikanatha* and *Thyagaraja*. The former, a 10th century shrine, had most of the external plaster decoration added later. The latter dates from the 13th century.

The original 23 m high old temple chariot needed 10,000 devotees, led by the king, to pull it. Today the chariot is smaller but the car festival remains important. This is also the birthplace of the saint Thyagaraja (1767-1847), one of the three noted composers of Carnatic music.

Sleeping
Even modest hotels charge 20% Luxury Tax

B *Oriental Towers*, 2889 South Pillai Rd, near rly station, T30725, F32770. 164 a/c rooms, some rather narrow and small, but suites spacious, excellent restaurants, bar, pool on top floor, business facilities, basement supermarket ("heaven sent for luxuries like Nescafé, loo paper, tissue etc!"). **B** *Parisutham*, 55 GA Canal Rd, T31801, F30318. 52 a/c rooms in modern hotel (erratic hot water), good restaurants but gloomy bar, lovely pool, exchange (poor rate), friendly, helpful. Recommended. **B-C** *Sangam*, Trichy Rd, T25151, F24895. 54 a/c upgraded rooms, modernized with pool, restaurant, garden. **D** *Pandyar Residency*, Kutchery Rd, near Big Temple, T30574. 63 rooms, some a/c, some overlook temple, restaurant, bar. **D** *Ideal River View Resort*, Vennar Bank, Palli Agraharam (6 km north of centre), T50533, F34933, ideal@md2.vsnl.net.in Clean, comfortable cottages (some a/c) in large grounds, restaurant, boating, peaceful, shuttle to town. Recommended. **D** *Temple Tower*, 20/1A SM Rd, near Flyover, T35125, F33727. Good clean rooms, some a/c, restaurants, bar, lacks atmosphere, indifferent management. **E** *Tamil Nadu I* (TTDC), Gandhiji Rd, 10 minutes' walk from rly, T31421, F31970. Small rooms with bath (no sgl), rather dark, some a/c, in pleasant setting around a cool inner courtyard, simple restaurant, bar, Tourist Office. **F** *Raja Rest House*, behind *Hotel Tamil Nadu*, T30365. 30 basic small rooms (suggest take triple), some in newer building, rooms vary (some grotty), secure, courtyard, quiet, friendly staff. **F** *Youth Hostel*, Medical College Rd, T23597. Dorm (Rs 40).

Mid-range: *Hotel Parisutham*, Gr Anicut Canal Rd. Good North Indian, excellent vegetarian *thalis* ("best of 72 curries"!), service can be slow. **Cheap**: *Karthik*, 73 South Rampart, opposite bus station. Try a traditional vegetarian meal off a banana leaf at lunch time. *Sathars*. Tandoori recommended. Good *thali* s and snacks is veg restaurants on west side of Railway Station Rd between station and Tamil Nadu hotel

Eating

South Zone Cultural Centre, Palace, T31272, organizes programmes in the Big Temple, 2nd and 4th Sat; free. **Bharat Natyam** performances by Guru Herambanathan from a family of dancers, 1/2378 Krishanayar Lane, Ellaiyamman Koil St, T33759. Recommended.

Entertainment

Oct: *Rajaraja Chola's* birth anniversary celebrations.

Festivals

Thanjavur is known for its decorative copper plates with silver and brass relief (repoussé) work, raised "glass" painting, wood carving and bronze and brass casting. Granite carving is being revived by the Government through centres which produce superbly sculpted images. Crafts shops abound in Gandhiji Rd Bazar. **'Antiques'**: *Govinda Rajan's*, 31 Kuthirai Katti St, Karandhai (a few kilometres from town), T30282, is a treasure house of pricey old, and affordable new pieces; artists and craftsmen at work. You may not export any object over 100 years old.

Shopping

Local Unmetered and tourist **taxis**, **cycle-rickshaws** and **auto-rickshaws** and a **city bus** service. **Long distance Air** Tiruchirapalli airport is about 1 hr by car. **Road Bus Old State and Municipal Bus Stand**, south of the fort, for local services. Buses from Kumbakonam stop at the corner before going out to the New Bus Stand; T33455. CRC (Cholan), T32455. **New (Mofussil) Bus Stand** is on Trichy Rd. Daily service to Chidambaram (4 hrs), Kumbakonam (1 hr), Chennai (8 hrs), Madurai (3½ hrs), Pondicherry (6 hrs), Tirupathi, Tiruchirappalli (1½ hrs). Also to Vedaranyam (100 km) for Point Calimere, about hourly, 4-4½ hrs. **Train** Reservations, T31131, 0800-1400, 1500-1700 Mon-Sat; 0800-1400 Sun. **Tiruchirappalli**: *Cholan Exp 6153*, 1800, 1½ hrs; *Chennai Tirunelveli Janata Exp 6179*, 2300, 1½ hrs; **Chennai (ME)**: *Cholan Exp 6154*, 0850, 8½ hrs; *Ramesvaram Exp 6102*, 2040, 9½ hrs.

Transport

Banks *Canara Bank*, South Main St changes TCs; *State Bank of India*, Hospital Rd. **Communications** Head Post and Telegraph Office are off the Rly Station Rd. **Medical services** The *Govt Hospital*, Hospital Rd, south of the old town. **Tourist offices** *Tamil Nadu*, Jawan Bhawan, opposite post office, T33017, 1000-1745, Mon-Fri, very helpful. Also at *Hotel Tamil Nadu*, Gandhiji Rd, T31421, 0800-1100, 1600-2000 except Mon (often closed). **Useful addresses** Police: south of the Big Temple between the canal and the rly, T32200.

Directory

Kumbakonam கும்பகோனம்

Phone code: 0435
Colour map 3, grid B5
Population: 151,000

This very pleasant town, 54 km from Thanjavur, was named from the legend where Siva was said to have broken a kumbh *(water pot) after it was brought here by a great flood. The water from the pot is reputed to have filled the Mahamakam Tank.*

Sights There are 18 temples in the town centre (closed 1200-1630) and a monastery

The temples in this region contain some exceptional pieces of jewellery which can be seen on payment of a small fee

There are 18 temples in the town centre (closed 1200-1630) and a monastery of the Kanchipuram Sankaracharya. The oldest is the **Nagesvara Swami Temple**, a Saivite temple begun in AD 886. The small Nataraja shrine on the right before you reach the main sanctum is designed to look like a chariot being pulled by horses and elephants. Superb statues decorate the outside walls of the inner shrine; Dakshinamurti (exterior south wall), Ardinarisvara (west facing) and Brahma (north) are in the central panels, described as among the best works of sculpture of the Chola period.

Sarangapani is the largest of Kumbakonam's shrines. Dedicated to Vishnu, it is dominated by its 11-storey main *gopuram*, 44 m tall. The Nayaka mandapa, inside the first court, leads through a second, smaller *gopuram* to a further mandapa. On the north is a small vaulted shrine to Lakshmi, Vishnu's consort. The main central shrine is the oldest, dating from the end of the Chola period. In common with a number of other shrines such as those in Chidambaram or distant Konark, it resembles a chariot, with horses and elephants carved in relief. The shrine is covered by a vaulted roof and the walls are richly carved.

The **Kumbesvara Temple** dates mainly from the 17th century and is the largest Siva temple in the town. It has a long colonnaded *mandapa* and a magnificent collection of silver *vahanas* (vehicles) for carrying the deities during festivals. The **Ramasvami Temple** is another Nayaka period building, with beautiful carved rearing horses in its pillared mandapa. The frescoes on the walls depict events from the Ramayana. The Navaratri Festival is observed with great colour.

The **Mahamakam Tank** is visited for a bathe by huge numbers of pilgrims every 12 years, when 'Jupiter passes over the sign of Leo'. It is believed that on the day of the festival nine of India's holiest rivers manifest themselves in the tank, including the Ganga, Yamuna and Narmada.

Sleeping **D-E** *Raya's*, T22545, 28 Head PO Rd, near Tank. Rooms vary, some a/c with bath, TV, restaurant, clean. **E** *ARR*, 21 TSR Big St, T21234. Simple, some a/c rooms with bath. **F** *Pandiyan*, 52 Sarangapani East Sannadi St, T20397. Clean rooms with bath (vary), good restaurant, good value. **F** *PRV Lodge*, 32 Head PO Rd, towards Tank, T21820. Best rooms with bath, restaurant (vegetarian). **F** *Railway Retiring Rooms*, good value.

Festivals *Mahamaha* Feb-Mar every 12 years; next in 2004.

Transport **Local** **Cycle hire**: opposite *New Diamond Lodge*, Nagesvaran North St. **Car hire**: half day for excursions, Rs 400. **Long distance** **Road** **Bus**: TN Govt Express buses to Chennai, No 305, several daily (7½ hrs); half hourly to Thanjavur. **Train** Station 2 km from town centre. **Chennai** (8½-9 hrs), **Chidambaram** (2 hrs), **Thanjavur** (50 mins) and **Tiruchirappalli** (2½ hrs).

Directory **Banks** Changing money is difficult. *State Bank of India*, TSR Big St. **Communications** **Post Office**: near Mahamakam Tank.

Around Kumbakonam

Five kilometres south of Kumbakonam, has the **Airavatesvara Temple**, the third of the great Chola temples after Thanjavur and Gangaikonda-cholapuram, built during the reign of **Rajaraja II** between 1146-72. Originally named Rajarajesvaram, it was re-named after Airavata, Indra's white elephant, who Saivites claimed, worshipped Siva at this temple. Open sunrise to sunset.

The **entrance** is through two gateways. The upper part of the outer *gopuram* has now been lost. A small inner gateway leads to a court where the mainly granite temple stands in the centre. The *gopuram* is supported by beautifully carved *apsaras*. Inside, there are friezes of dancing figures and musicians. The mandapa is best entered from the south – the steps have now gone but the balustrades still show their decoration. Note the elephant, ridden by dwarfs, whose trunk is lost down the jaws of a crocodile.

Architecture The first signs of flower corbelled capitals of the pillars in the mandapa, typical of the later Vijayanagar style, show the development of the late Chola period. The pillars illustrate mythological stories for example 'the penance of Parvati'. The five gods Agni, Indra, Brahma, Vishnu and Vayu in the niches are all shown paying homage to Siva.

The **main mandapa**, completely enclosed and joined to the central shrine, has figures carved in black basalt on the outside. The ceilings are also richly decorated and the pillars have the same flower emblems as in the outer mandapa. The main shrine has some outstanding sculptures; the guardians on the north are particularly fine.

Sculpted door-keepers with massive clubs guard the entrance to the main shrine which has a *Nandi* at the entrance. Some of the niches inside contain superb early Chola sculptures of polished black basalt, including a unique sculpture of Ardhanarisvara with three faces and eight arms, a four-armed Nagaraja and a very unusual sculpture of Siva destroying Narasimha.

The outer walls are also highly decorative. Siva as Dakshinamurti on the south wall, Brahma on the north wall and Siva appearing out of the linga on the

★ **Darasuram**
You can spend a worthwhile afternoon visiting Darasuram first & then Gangaikonda cholapuram (after 1600), by car

Tamil Nadu & Chennai

Kumbakonam

Tamil Nadu & Chennai

 The aphrodisiac betel

Kumbakonam is renowned for the high quality betel vines grown here, the essential raw material for the chewing paan. AVM's Guide to South India sings the praises of "the last item of the meal is a delicacy much sought after by the paan-chewing connoisseurs in South India because it is much too tender, has a pleasing colour and is pleasant to taste. Lovers love it and munch it with relish though unaware of its aphrodisiac property!". See also page 151.

west wall. The inner wall of the encircling walkway (*prakara*) is divided into cells, each originally to house a deity. The corners of the courtyard have been enlarged to make four mandapas, again with beautiful decoration. There is a small **museum** in the north-east corner, but the *nata mandapa* in the northwest corner has an excellent collection of sculptures. Immediately to the west a group of large sculptures represents Siva as a beggar, with a number of attendants.

Swamimalai (3 km from Darasuram, *Phone code*: 0435), one of the abodes of Lord Murugan, is famous for its school of iconography and craftsmen producing Chola style bronzes using the 'lost wax' process. **Sleeping**: **A** *Sterling Swamimalai*, Thimmakkudy, opposite the 'School', T420044, F421705, shr.ibtmd@elnet.ems. vsnl.net.in simple a/c rooms with bath (cramped, dark, minimally furnished), in restored 100-year-old 'heritage' home (inner courtyard, wood carving), traditional vegetarian meals (expensive for non-residents), yoga, meditation, Ayurveda Herbal Health Centre, a "complete experience", recommended but $98 each. **Shopping** *S Rajan*, 107 Main Road, T422886, excellent bronze casting and Tanjore paintings.

★ Gangaikondacholapuram கங்கைக்கொண்டசோழபுரம்

Once the capital of the Chola king Rajendra (1012-44) the town of Gangakondacholapuram (meaning 'The city of the Chola who conquered the Ganga') has now all but disappeared. The temple and the 5 km long 11th-century reservoir embankment survive.

In 1942 Percy Brown wrote "this fine structure now stands in solitary state, except for the mud huts of a village straggling around it, as centuries ago the tide of life receded from these parts, leaving it like a great stranded shell".

The whole site has now been restored. It is well worth visiting. The **temple** which Rajendra built was designed to rival the Brihadisvara temple built by Rajendra's father Rajaraja in Thanjavur. Unlike the *Nandi* in Thanjavur, the huge *Nandi* facing the mandapa and sanctuary inside the compound by the ruined east *gopuram* is not carved out of one block of stone. As in Thanjavur, the mandapa and sanctuary are raised on a high platform, orientated from west to east and climbed by steps. The whole building is over 100 m long and over 40 m wide. Two massive doorkeepers (*dvarapalas*) stand guard at the entrance to the long closed mandapa (the first of the many subsequent mandapas which expanded to 'halls of 1,000 pillars'); the plinth is original. A narrow colonnaded hall (*mukha-mandapa*) links this hall to the shrine. On the east side of this hall are various carvings of Siva such as bestowing grace on Vishnu, who worships him with his lotus-eye, and Kalyanasundara-murti (going out for his marriage attended by goblins) and many others. On the northeast is a large panel, a masterpiece of Chola art, showing Siva blessing Chandikesvara, the steward. Dancing Nataraja is shown in a panelled recess of the southwest corner, Siva within a flaming lingam on the west, and Ganesh on the south. At the centre of the shrine is a huge lingam on a round stand. As in Thanjavur there is a magnificent eighth-tiered, pyramidal *vimana* (tower) above the sanctuary, nearly 55 m high. Unlike the austere straight line of the Thanjavur temple, however, here gentle curves are introduced. Ask the custodian to allow you to look inside (best for light in the morning). Immediately to the north of the mandapa is an excellently carved shrine dedicated to Chandikesvara. To north and south are two shrines dedicated to Kailasanatha with excellent wall sculptures. The small shrine in the southwest corner is to Ganesh. ■ *Getting there: Buses from Chidambaram or Kumbakonam.*

★ Chidambaram சிதம்பரம்

The capital of the Cholas from AD 907 to 1310, the temple town of Chidambaram is 9 km north of the Coleroon River, the northern limit of the Kaveri delta. It is one of Tamil Nadu's most important holy towns. The large bazar is to the west of the main temple and the residential Annamalai University specializing in Tamil studies and Carnatic music, to the southeast of town.

Phone code: 04144
Colour map 3, grid A5
Population: 69,000

The ★ **Nataraja Temple** is dedicated to the dancing Lord Siva, a favourite deity of the Chola kings. One legend surrounding its construction suggests that it was built by 'the golden coloured Emperor', **Hiranya Varna Chakravarti**, who suffered from leprosy. He came to Chidambaram on a pilgrimage from Kashmir in about AD 500. After bathing in the temple tank he was reputed to have recovered from the disease, and as a thanks-offering rebuilt and enlarged the temple. The evening Puja at 1800 is particularly interesting. At each shrine the visitor will be

Sights

Nataraja Temple, Chidambaram

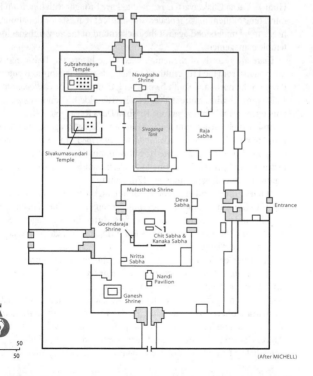

(After MICHELL)

Tamil Nadu & Chennai

☞ *Those who make oblations*

"The Chidambaram temple has never had landed or other endowments, and it belongs to a group of Brahmans called Dikshitars ('those who make oblations') who are held in high regarded by the community, according to the South Arcot District Gazetteer. You may notice that they have the single Brahmin style tuft of hair at the front rather than the back of their heads. They marry only among themselves and ritual here is more like family worship.

Theoretically all the married males have a say in the running of the temple. They support it by going round the district asking for alms and offerings for themselves. Each has his own particular clients, and in return for the alms he receives he undertakes to make offerings at the shrine of his benefactors. From time to time he will send them holy ash or an invitation to a special festival.

20 Dikshitars are always on duty at the temple, each male doing the work which is divided into 20-day rotas. The 20 divide themselves into five parties of four, each of which is on duty for four days at one of the five shrines at which daily Puja is made, sleeps there at night and becomes the owner of the routine offerings of food made at it. Large presents of food are divided among all the Dikshitars. The right to the other oblations is sold by auction every 20 days to one of the Dikshitars at a meeting of the community".

daubed with *vibhuti* (sacred ash) and paste. It is not easy to see some of the sculptures in the interior gloom. You may need patience and persuasive powers if you want to take your own time but it is worth the effort.

Chidambaram is a highly active temple, with Brahmins at every shrine – though they all belong to a local community, unrelated to the 3,000 Brahmins Hiranya Varna Chakravarti is reputed to have brought with him from Kashmir. Some of them make repeated and insistent requests for donations. This needs to be understood against the background of the very unusual form of temple management.

There are records of the temple's existence before the 10th century and inscriptions from the 11th century. On each side are four enormous **gopurams**, those on the north and south being about 45 m high. The east *gopuram* (AD 1250), through which you enter the temple, is the oldest. The north *gopuram* was built by the great Vijayanagar king **Krishna Deva Raya** (1509-30).

Immediately on entering the East Gate is the large **Sivaganga** tank, and the **Raja Sabha**, a 1,000 columned *mandapa* (1595-1685). In the northwest of the compound are temples dedicated to **Subrahmanya** (late 13th century), and to its south the 12th century shrine to Sivakumasundari or Parvati (circa 14th century). The ceiling paintings are 17th century.

At the southern end of this outer compound is what is said to be the largest shrine to **Ganesh** in India. The next inner compound has been filled with colonnades and passageways. In the innermost shrine are two images of Siva, the Nataraja and the lingam. A later Vishnu shrine to Govindaraja was added by the Vijayanagar kings.

The **inner enclosure**, the most sacred, contains four important Sabhas (halls), the **deva sabha**, where the temple managers hold their meetings; the **chit sabha** or *chit ambalam* (from which the temple and the town get their names), meaning the hall of wisdom; the **kanakha sabha**, or golden hall; and the **nritta sabha**, or hall of dancing. Siva is worshipped in the *chit ambalam*, a plain wooden building standing on a stone base, in his form as Lord of the Dance, Nataraja. The area immediately over the deity's head is gold plated. Immediately behind the idol is the focus of the temple's power, the 'Akasa

Lingam', representing the invisible element, 'space', and hence is itself invisible. Known as the 'Chidambaram secret'. A curtain and a long string of golden *bilva* leaves are hung in front of it.

■ *0400-1200. 1630-2100. Enter the temple by the East Gate. Visitors may be asked for donations. Entrance into the inner sanctum is easy on payment of Rs 200.*

C *Afsun Plaza*, 2 VGP (Venugopal Pillai) St, T23312, F21098. New all a/c, high standard (Rs 750), 24 hr check out. **E** *Saradharam*, 19 VGP St, T21336, F22656. 46 basic, clean rooms, 20 a/c, noisy bus station opposite; noisy lift, restaurants, bar, friendly, good value. **D-F** *Tamil Nadu* (TTDC), Railway Feeder Rd, T20056, F20061, reported very dirty. **F** *Ramanathan Mansions*, 127 Bazar St, T22411. 28 rooms with bath, spacious and airy (lights don't always work), quieter than most, away from busy temple area, friendly. **F** *Ramyas Lodge*, South Car St, T23011. 23 clean rooms with bath, 2 a/c, good value. **F** *Sri Nataraj Lodge*, 98 East Car St (150m from temple), T22968. Clean enough rooms (Rs 100), a bit noisy.

Sleeping
Most also do single room rates

Cheap: *Hotels Saradharam*. Good non-vegetarian meals. *Indian Coffee House*, VGP St. Cheap South Indian snacks. *Sree Ganesa Bhavan*, W Car St. South Indian vegetarian. Friendly, helpful staff.

Eating

February/March: *Natyanjali* dance festival for five days starting with *Maha Sivaratri*. **June/July**: *Ani Tirumanjanam* Festival. **December/January**: *Markazhi Tiruvathirai* Festival.

Festivals

Shopping mainly on W Car and Bazar St.

Shopping

Chidambaram

■ Sleeping	**6** Sri Nataraj
1 Afsun Plaza	**7** Tamil Nadu & Youth Hostel
2 Raja Rajan	
3 Ramanathan Mansions	**● Eating**
4 Ramyas Lodge	**1** Indian Coffee House
5 Saradharam	**2** Sree Ganesa Bhavan

N
0 metres 200
0 yards 200

Tamil Nadu & Chennai

Tamil Nadu & Chennai

 Chidambaram – centre of the universe?

One of the most basic ideas of Hinduism "is the identification of a sacred site with the centre or navel of the universe, the spot through which passes the axis connecting the heavens, the earth and the subterranean world of Patala" writes David Shulman. Tillai is the ancient name of Chidambaram, "where Siva performed his dance of joy; so powerful is this dance, which represents the entire cosmic process of creation and dissolution, that it can be performed only at the very centre of the cosmos ... Chidambaram, which sees itself as the heart of the universe, locates an invisible Akasalinga in its innermost sanctum."

The imagery recalls the myth of the origin of the Chidambaram temple itself. The South Arcot District Gazetteer recounts it as follows: "In the forest of Tillai

*was an ancient shrine to **Siva** and another to the Goddess **Kali** which was built where the Nritta Sabha now stands. Siva came down to his shrine to manifest himself to two very fervent devotees there, and Kali objected to his trespassing on her domains. They eventually agreed to settle the question by seeing which could dance the better, it being agreed that the defeated party should leave the site entirely to the winner. Vishnu acted as the umpire, and for a long time the honours were evenly divided. At length Vishnu suggested to Siva that he should do his well known steps in which he danced with one leg high above his head. Kali was unable to imitate or beat this style of dancing, Siva was proclaimed the winner and Kali departed outside the town, where her temple is still to be seen".*

Transport **Road Bus**: chaotic bus station. Daily services to the above cities and to Karaikal (2 hrs), Nagapattinam and Pondicherry (2 hrs). **Train** Reservations T22298, 0800-1200, 1400-1700; Sun 0800-1400. **Chennai**: *Janata Exp, 6180*, 0014, 7 hrs; *Cholan Exp, 6154*, 1122, 6 hrs; **Kumbakonam**: *Janata Exp, 6179*, 1942, 2 hrs continues to **Thanjavur**, 3½ hrs and **Madurai**, 8½ hrs; *Cholan Exp, 6153*, 1519, 1½ hrs, continues to **Thanjavur**, 2½ hrs and **Tiruchirapalli**, 4 hrs.

Directory **Banks** Changing money can be difficult. *City Union Bank*, W Car St has exchange facilities. *Indian Bank*, 64 South Car St, changes cash. **Communications** Post office: Head Post Office, North Car St. branch in railway station. **Tourist offices** At *Hotel Tamil Nadu*, Railway Feeder Rd, T22739.

Around Chidambaram

Pichchavaram There are several places of interest south along the coast. The Pichchavaram Mangroves, 15 km east of Chidambaram at the mouths of the rivers Vellar, Coleroon and Uppanar is the last remaining large area of mangrove forest in Tamil Nadu, spread over 51 islands separated by creeks and protected from the sea by a sand bar. They represent some of the richest mangrove forests in India. The Marine Biological Research Station on the north bank of the Vellar, 10 km away, has a Visitor Reception Centre. Sleeping *Hotel Tamil Nadu* (TTDC). Rooms and dorm, restaurant on opposite bank of the river.

Poompuhar Poompuhar, at the mouth of the **Kaveri**, is a popular excursion among Tamil tourists. As *Kaberis Emporium*, it had trading links with the Romans in the first century AD; it was also visited by Buddhists from the Far East. An important port of the Cholas, later most of the city of *Kaveripoompattinam* (as it was then called) was lost under the sea. Excavations have revealed an ancient planned city. The name Poompuhar has been adopted for Tamil Nadu Government emporia throughout the country. ■ *Getting there: From Chidambaram most require a change at Sirkazhi. From Thanjavur, some direct buses; others involve* change at Mayiladuthurai (24 km). A few buses to Pichchavaram and Tranquebar. There are tourist offices opposite the bus stand, Sirkazhi T39. 0830-2030.

The Danish king Christian IV received permission from Raghunath Nayak of **Tranquebar** Thanjavur to build a fort here (at Tharangampadi) in 1620. The Danish Tranquebar Mission was founded in 1706 and the **Danesborg fort** and the old **church** still survive. The Danes set up the first Tamil printing press, altering the script to make the casting of type easier. The Danish connection resulted in the National Museum of Copenhagen today possessing a remarkable collection of 17th-century Thanjavur paintings and Chola bronzes. There is a **museum** and a good beach. **Suggested reading**: Georgina Harding's *Tranquebar: a season in South India*. London, Hodder and Stoughton, 1993.

Nagapattinam with a Nagaraja temple, was an important port of the Cholas **Nagapattinam** (10-11th century). During the British period it became a prominent Christian *Phone code: 04365* centre and regained its status as a trading port with a new railway connection. Sikkal and Sembian Madevi temples are nearby. **Sleeping**: E *Tamil Nadu* (TTDC), Thonitturai Salai, near railway station, T22389, F40114, 2-6 bedrooms, some a/c, good value.

The coastal sanctuary, half of which is tidal swamp, is famous for its migratory **Point Calimere** water birds. The Great Vedaranyam Salt Swamp (or 'Great Swamp') attracts **Wildlife & Bird** one of the largest colonies of **flamingos** in Asia (5-10,000) especially in **Sanctuary** December and January. Some 243 different bird species have been spotted here. In the spring the green pigeons, rosy pastors, koels, mynahs and barbets can be seen. In the winter vegetable food and insects attract paradise flycatchers, Indian pittas, shrikes, swallows, drongos, minivets, blue jays, woodpeckers and robins among others. Spotted deer, black buck, feral horses and wild boar are also found, as well as reptiles. The swamp supports a major commercial fishing industry. Jeeps can be booked at reception. Exploring on foot is a pleasant alternative to being 'bussed'; ask at reception for a guide. ■ *Open throughout the year. Best season – mid-Dec to Feb. Entry Rs 5, camera Rs 5, video Rs 50.*

Sleeping and eating At **Kodikkarai**: **F** *Poonarai Ilam*, 14 simple rooms with bath *Nov & Dec are busy;* and balcony (Rs 15 per person), caretaker may be able to arrange a meal with advance *advance reservation* notice, intended for foreign visitors, rooms often available; **F** *Calimere Rest House*, 4 *recommended: Wildlife* derelict rooms. Snacks are available from tea shops. At **Vedaranyam**: **F** *PV Thevar* *Warden, 3 Main St,* *Lodge*, 40 North Main St, 50 m from bus station (English sign high up only visible in *Thanjavur* daylight), T50330, 37 basic rooms with bath and fan, can be mosquito-proofed, fairly clean, very friendly owners, good value. Indian vegetarian meals are available in the bazar near the bus stand.

Transport Road Buses via Vedaranyam which has services to/from Thanjavur, Tiruchirapalli, Nagapattinam, Chennai etc. From Thanjavur buses leave the New Bus Stand for **Vedaranyam** (100 km) about hourly (4-4½ hrs); buses and vans from there to Kodikkarai (11 km) which take about 30 mins. **NB** Avoid being dropped at 'Sri Rama's Feet' on the way, near a shrine which is of no special interest.

Tamil Nadu & Chennai

Coimbatore and the Nilgiris

Phone code: 0422
Colour map 3, grid B3
Population: 1.135 mn
Altitude: 425 m

Surrounded by rich agricultural land and within sight of the towering Nilgiri Hills, Coimbatore is high enough to be significantly cooler and pleasanter than the coastal plains. One of South India's most important industrial cities, the development of hydro-electricity from the Pykara Falls in the 1930s led to a cotton boom in Coimbatore. The centre of a rich agricultural area, Coimbatore has a noted agricultural university.

Ins & outs **Getting there** The airport, 12 km from the town centre, has coaches for transfer to some hotels; city buses go to the bus stand. The main Junction station, on the lines to Chennai, Bangalore and Cochin, is in the south of the town while the long distance bus stations are about 1.5 km north. **Getting around** Coimbatore is fairly spread out covered by a good city bus service, including extensive connections from the city station. There are also planty of autos and some taxis.

Coimbatore

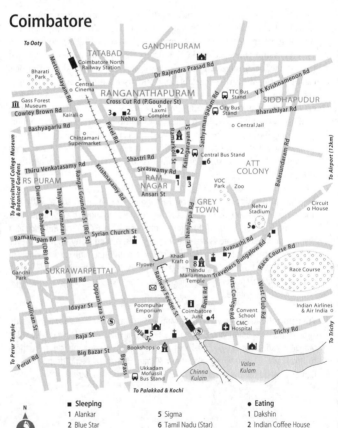

■ Sleeping
1 Alankar
2 Blue Star
3 Heritage Inn, City Tower
& Cloud Nine Restaurant
4 Niligiris Nest
5 Sigma
6 Tamil Nadu (Star)
7 YMCA
8 YWCA

● Eating
1 Dakshin
2 Indian Coffee House
3 Pushpa Bakery
4 Royal Hindu
5 Solai Drive-in

N

0 metres 300
0 yards 300

Coimbatore is at the heart of a region of great historical importance, an area of **Background** contact between the plains of Tamil Nadu to the east, the plateaus of Mysore to the north and the coastal plains of Kerala, reached through the Palakkad gap to the south. The frequency with which the word *palayam* ('encampment') occurs indicates the extent to which this was also a region of conflict between the *Cholas*, the *Pandiyas* and the *Cheras*. Sadly, the city has experienced outbreaks of violence, so enquire about the situation before visiting.

College Museum Special collections of minerals, rocks, insects, pests, fungal **Museums** diseases, snakes, silver and gold medals. Guide service. ■ *0900-1200, 1400-1700, closed Sun and Govt holidays. Tamil Nadu Agricultural Univ.* **Gass Forest Museum** Exhibits of forestry and forest products, library. Worth visiting. ■ *1900-1300, 1400-1630, closed Sun, 2nd Sat and public holidays. 3.5 km north of town.*

The **VOC Park** and **Zoo** are near the Stadium. **Bharati Park**, Main Road, 1 Sai **Parks & zoos** Baba Colony. The Tamil Nadu Agricultural University **Botanical Garden**. On the western edge of Coimbatore, the garden has grown to over 300 ha. Open to the public. It includes formal gardens, such as rose gardens as well as informal areas with a wide variety of flowering trees. ■ *0900-1300, 1500-2000; Bus 1A, 1C, from centre.*

C *Heritage Inn*, 38 Sivaswamy Rd, T231451, F233223. 61 modern, a/c rooms, good **Sleeping** Indian restaurant, good service. **C-D** *City Tower*, Sivaswamy Rd (just off Dr Nanjappa *Many budget hotels in* Rd), Gandhipuram, near bus stand, T230641, F230103. 97 pleasant rooms, some a/c, 2 *the area around the bus* restaurants (rooftop good; ground floor basic), no alcohol, popular with businessmen, *stations & to the east of* very good service. Recommended. **C-D** *Nilgiris Nest*, 739-A Avanashi Rd, T217247, *the rly station* F217131, 2 km rly. 38 a/c rooms, restaurant, bar, dairy farm shop, business facilities, roof garden. Recommended. **D-E** *Alankar*, 10 Sivaswamy Rd, Ramnagar, T235461, F235467. 52 rooms, some a/c with TV, restaurant (beware of overcharging in dining 'special'), dark bar, overpriced. **D-E** *Tamil Nadu* (TTDC), Dr Nanjappa Rd opposite Bus Station, T236312, F236313. 49 rooms, some a/c with TV (charge), restaurant, bar. Recommended. **D-E** *Railway Retiring Rooms*, rooms with bath, some a/c, noisy, **F** dorm off platform 1, restaurant. **E** *Blue Star*, 369 Nehru St, Gandhipuram, T230635. 50 rooms, some a/c with TV, others without window, can be noisy, restaurant, bar. **E** *Shree Shakti*, on Shastri Rd opposite Central Bus Stand, Ramnagar, T234225. Reasonable, clean rooms with attached bath, noisy TV next door can irritate, very handy for buses to Ooty or train connection at Mettupalayam. **E** *YMCA*, Avanashi Rd and **E** *YWCA*, Bank Rd, near Thandu Mariammam temple; don't take guests on Sunday. **F** *Sigma*, Raja St, opposite station, T230341. Simple rooms, friendly.

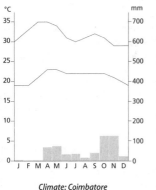

Climate: Coimbatore
Best time to visit: Dec- Mar

Expensive: *Cloud Nine*, *City Tower Hotel*. **Eating** International. Excellent views from rooftop of one of city's tallest buildings, good food and service, nice atmosphere (full of families on Sun evening). **Mid-range**: *China Restaurant*, 410 Trichy Rd. *Dakshin* in *Shree Annapoorna Hotel* Complex, 47 East Arokiasamy Rd, RS Puram. International. Very smart serving good food. *Dasa*. Vegetarian. A/c, good ice creams. *Solai Drive-in*, Nehru Stadium, near VOC

Tamil Nadu & Chennai

Park. Chinese, Indian food. Also good ice creams, drinks. **Cheap**: *Indian Coffee House*, Ramar Koil St. South Indian snacks. *Pushpa Bakery*, Nehru Rd. *Richy Rich*, DB Rd. Good milk shakes. *Royal Hindu*, opposite Junction station. Indian vegetarian.

Entertainment **Cinemas**: Central, Mettupalayam Rd, near Coimbatore North station, shows English films. **Sports Yoga**: *Integral Yoga Institute*, 116 Bashyakaralu Rd (W) off DB Rd, RS Puram. Run by American couple, courses/classes in yoga and meditation – all in English; private lessons on request.

Shopping *Kairali*, off Mettapalayam Rd and *Khadi Kraft*, Dr Nanjappa Rd. Several other shops
Famous for handloom & along the street, handloom in Shukrawarpettai and Gandhipuram, Asoka Plaza, Dr
handicrafts Nanjappa Rd, south of Central Bus Stand, and Lakshmi Complex, Cross Cut Rd. **Books**: *Higginbotham's* and *Pai* in Big Bazar St, behind the station. *Landmark*, has up-to-date titles, many Indian reprints of English publications.

Transport **Local Bus**: City buses run a good service: several connect the bus stations in Gandhipuram with the Junction Rly Station 2 km south. No 20 goes to the airport (Rs 20). **Taxi**: Tourist taxis and yellow top taxis are available at the bus stations, rly station and taxi stands. Rs 2.50 per km; for out-station hill journeys, Rs 3 per km; minimum Rs 30. **Auto-rickshaw**: negotiate fare before journey, minimum Rs 8.

Long distance **Air**: Peelamedu Airport (12 km centre). Transport to town: Cheran Transport airport coach to/from several hotels and the city, Rs 25; taxis Rs 130; auto-rickshaw Rs 85. On Trichy Rd: *Indian Airlines*, T399833, airport T574623, 1000-1300, 1345-1730. **Chennai**; **Kozhikode**; **Mumbai** and **Madurai**. *Jet Airways*: 1055/1 Gowtham Chambers, Avinashi Rd, T212034, airport T575387 to **Mumbai**.

Road **Bus**: 3 main bus stations, off Dr Nanjappa Rd. **City Bus Stand (B1)**, south of Government Express Bus Stand; Reservations 0900-1200, 1600-1800, T227086. **Government Express Bus Stand (B2)**, Cross Cut Rd, T225949. Computerized reservations 0700-2100, T26700. Frequent Government Express buses to Madurai (5 hrs), Chennai (12 hrs), Mysore (6 hrs), Ooty (3 hrs), Tiruchirappalli (5½ hrs). **State Bus Stand (B3)** is further south, on corner of Shastri Rd. SRTC buses to Bangalore and Mysore; Ooty via Mettupalayam (see below for train connection) and Coonoor every 20 mins, 0400-2400, 5 hrs.

Train: Junction Station, enquiries, T132, reservations, T131, 0700-1300, 1400-2030. Bangalore: *Nagercoil-Bangalore Exp*, *6525* (AC/II), 2055, 9½ hrs; **Chennai**: *Shatabdi Exp*, *2024*, 0725, 6½ hrs, best ('Stand by' counter opens at 0600); *Kovai Exp*, *2676* (AC/CC), 1420, 7½ hrs; *Trivandrum-Guwahati Exp*, *2601*, Thu, 2215, 7½ hrs; Kochi (HT): *Tiruchirappalli-Kochi Exp*, *6365*, 0045, 5½ hrs; *Hyderabad-Kochi Exp*, *7030*, 0935, Tue, Fri, Sun, 5½ hrs; *Haora/Patna-Kochi*, *2652/2610* (AC/II), Tue, Sat, Sun, 1315, 5½ hrs; *Guwahati-Kochi*, *2650* (AC/II), Fri, 1315, 5½ hrs; **Madurai** (5½ hrs) and **Ramesvaram** (12 hrs), *Ramesvaram Exp*, daily; *Kanniyakumari Exp*, 13½ hrs; *Madurai Fast Pass*, 0725 and 1335, 5-6 hrs. Other trains: *W Coast Exp (Chennai – Coimbatore – Kozhikode – Bangalore)*, daily to Kozhikode (4½ hrs) and Bangalore (9 hrs). For **Ooty**, train dep 0625 connects with narrow gauge steam train from Mettupalayam. From **Mettupalayam**: to Coimbatore, dep 0815; to Chennai, 1930.

Directory **Banks** Several on Oppankara St. *State Bank of India* and *Bank of Baroda* are on Bank Rd. **Communications** Head Post Office and Telegraph Office, near flyover, Rly Feeder Rd, Fax available. **Medical services** *Govt Hospital*, Trichy Rd. **Tourist offices** At Coimbatore Junction Rly Station, 1000-1800. **Useful addresses** *Automobile Association*, 42 Trichy Rd, T222994. *Travel agent*: *Alooha*, corner near *Heritage Inn*, helpful.

The Blue Mountain Railway

The delightful narrow gauge steam Mountain Railway, in its blue and cream livery, goes from Mettupalayam to Ooty via Coonoor negotiating 16 tunnels and 31 major bridges climbing from 326 m to 2,193 m. It was opened on 15 June 1899. The railway scenes of the 'Marabar Express' in the film of A Passage to India were shot here. The whole four and a half hour (46 km) journey through tea plantations and lush forests is highly recommended for the scenery (First Class front coach for best views). Hillgrove (17 km) a 'watering stop' in the past, and Coonoor (27 km) with its loco shed, have refreshments and clean toilets.

The Blue Mountain train has limited First Class seating and can get very crowded in season, though some trains have a new, more spacious First Class carriage. See Mettupalayam, page 151. For enthusiasts, the more expensive Heritage Steam Chariot with special spacious carriages runs between Ooty and Runneymede picnic area, 23 km away, at weekends (more often in season).

The coal-fired narrow gauge steam locomotive from SLM Winterthur, Switzerland, is the only mountain railway in India with cog-wheel traction. See page 158. **Drawback**: Passengers can be stranded for hours when the engine breaks down; some choose to scramble to the nearest road to flag down a bus.

Around Coimbatore

Perur, 6 km west of the city centre, Perur has one of seven *Kongu Sivalayams*, a temple of great sanctity. The outer buildings were erected by Thirumalai Nayaka of Madurai between 1623-59, but the inner shrine is much older. A remarkable feature is the figure of a *sepoy* (Indian soldier) loading a musket carved on the base of a pillar near the entrance, wearing identical dress to that of Aurangzeb's soldiers at the end of the 17th century. Built between 1623-59, it was desecrated by Tipu Sultan's troops.

Perur
Population: 9,200

Avanashi has a widely visited 13th-century Siva temple (renovated 1756), dedicated to Avinasisvara, noted partly for its colossal *Nandi*. The outer porch of the temple has two stone alligators, each shown vomiting a child. They recall a story which told how a local saint, Sundaramurti Nayanar, interceded on behalf of a child who had been swallowed by an alligator, and the infant was disgorged unhurt.

Avanashi
Phone code: 04296
Colour map 3, grid B3
Population: 17,000

The home of the great Tamil nationalist, social reformer and political leader Periyar EV Ramaswamy Naicker. Today Erode is a busy, hot and dirty industrial railway town. Erode is not a place to stay unless you have to. **C** *Nilgiri's Nest* with modern facilities. **E** *Brindhavan*, 1499 EVN Rd (Mettur Rd), in front of Bus Stand, T61731. Quite good vegetarian restaurant, but bar dingy and "full of gamblers and heavy drinkers".

Erode
Phone code: 0424
Colour map 3, grid A4
Population: 357,400

Haider Ali was reputed to have kept hoards of gold in the 750 m high hill top rock **fort**. There are magnificent views over the Shevaroy Hills and to the Kaveri River. Gruesome events are associated with the fort – certain 'undesirable persons' were rolled down the almost vertical 500 m cliff on the southwest side of the hill. Of the several springs with medicinal properties here, the most famous is the *Maan Sunai* or Deer Spring which is never touched by the sun's rays.

Shankari Drug

Tamil Nadu & Chennai

Bhavani
Phone code: 04256
Colour map 3, grid A4

The town straddling the rocky banks of the Kaveri, is a centre of pilgrimage, especially from Palakkad. The Nayaka Sangamesvara **Temple** at the confluence of the Kaveri and Bhavani has bathing ghats.

Tiruppur
Phone code: 0421
Colour map 3, grid B3
Population: 306,000

Tamil Nadu's textile industry now accounts for 25% of India's cotton textiles, and Tiruppur has become one of India's industrial boom towns. Specializing in knitwear, in the 1990s its output more than doubled, accounting for nearly two-thirds of India's knitwear exports, mostly destined for the US and the European Community. **Sleeping**: **C** *Velan Greenfields*, 41 Kangyam Road, 3 km rly, T30911, F30910, 70 rooms, central a/c, pool, modern business hotel. **E** *India House*, opposite railway station, simple rooms (Rs 300).

Salem சேலம்

Phone code: 0427
Colour map 3, grid A4
Population: 573,700
Altitude: 280 m

Salem is surrounded by hills: the Shevaroy and Nagaramalai Hills to the north, the Jerumumalai Hills to the south, the Godumalai Hills to the east and the Kanjamalai Hills to the west. The busy town, however, has little to offer and it is more pleasant to move on to Yercaud.

Background
Salem is a rapidly growing industrial town, particularly for textiles and metal based industries. The Kanjamalai iron and steel works nearby uses haematite iron ores found nearby (intending visitors should contact the PRO). The old town is on the east bank of the river Manimutheru. On the opposite bank, the Shevapet market, held every Tuesday (Mars' day) attracts large crowds. Along Bazar Street, each evening, cotton carpets made in nearby Bhavani and Komarapalayam are offered for sale.

Sights
Temples here include the **Sukavaneswara** dedicated to Siva (Lord of the Parrot Forest), though an inscription describes him as the 'parrot coloured Lord'.

The **cemetery** next to the Collector's office has some interesting tombstones. To the southeast of the town on a ridge of the Jarugumalai Hills is a highly visible *Naman* painted in *chunam* and ochre. The temple on the nearby hill (1919), is particularly sacred to the weavers' community. 600 steps lead to the top which has excellent views over the town. A huge boulder at the foot of the hill known as **Sanyasi Gundu** has marks believed to be the imprints of the foot and two hands of the saint who stopped the boulder when it came rolling

Salem

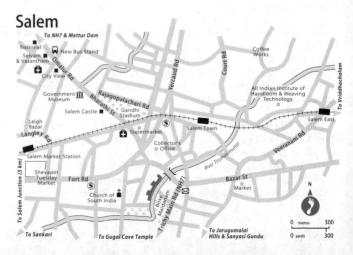

down the hill (the story is similar to one surrounding a Muslim shrine near Attock in Pakistan, where Guru Nanak, the founder of Sikhism, is believed to have left his hand print on a boulder).

Government Museum The largely disappointing collection includes a few Chola bronzes, a portrait of Gandhi by Ramalingam and a library. ■ *Omalur Rd. 0900-1230, 1400-1700; closed Fri, 2nd Sat and holidays.* **Planetarium** in the Government College of Engineering. Fixed shows; apply at the college.

Museums

Built between 1925-34, the **Mettur Dam** is still one of the world's largest. Its reservoir holds three times as much water as the Aswan Dam on the river Nile. The dam is 1.6 km long and 54 m high. There are regular buses from Salem. There are two **F** *Circuit Houses*. Reservations: Sub-Divisional Officer, PWD, Stanley Dam, Sub-Division, PO Mettur Dam.

Excursion

C *Salem Castle*, A-4 Bharati St, Swarnapuri, T448702, F446996, 4 km rly. 64 comfortable, very clean a/c rooms, restaurants (good Chinese but expensive), coffee shop, bar, exchange, pool, rather brash modern hotel. The rest are Indian style. **D** *National*, 8E Omalur Rd, near TVS (3.5 km rly), T212900. 90 rooms, 54 a/c, 10 a/c cottages, restaurant, bar, roof garden, modern, clean. **D** *Vasantham*, Omalur Rd (opposite New Bus Stand), T449356, F447627. Clean rooms. Nearby, **D-E** *City View*, Omalur Rd, T449715, rooms with bath, some a/c, meals, travel. **D-E** *Selvam*, opposite New Bus Stand, T449331. Clean rooms with bath, some a/c, meals. **E** *Apsara*, 19 Car St near rly, T413075. 37 rooms, 3 a/c, restaurant (Indian, Continental), coffee shop, exchange.

Sleeping & eating

Handlooms and jewellery (silver and gold chains) are best buys at *Agrahram*.

Shopping

Air Coimbatore is the nearest airport with commercial services. **Road Bus**: the New Bus Stand is north of the Hospital, off Omalur Rd. Salem is well connected by bus with all major towns in Tamil Nadu, Kerala and South Karnataka. TN Government Express buses, T62960. **Train** Junction is the main Station. Enquiries, T132. Reservations, T131, 0700-1300, 1400- 2030. **Bangalore**: *Kanniyakumari-Bangalore Exp*, 6525 (AC/II), 2055, 8½ hrs; **Chennai**: *Shatabdi Exp*, 2024, 0615, 6½ hrs; *Kovai Exp*, 2676 (AC/CC), 1420, 7½ hrs; **Kochi (HT) (Cochin)**: *Tiruchirappalli-Cochin Exp*, 6365, 0055, 5½ hrs; *Howrah-Cochin*, 2652/2610 (AC/II), Tue, Sun, 1315, 5½ hrs; *Guwahati-Cochin*, 2650 (AC/II), Mon, 1315, 5½ hrs; **Madurai**: *Madurai-Coimbatore-Ramesvaram Fast Pass*, 6115, 2245, 5½ hrs and **Ramesvaram** (11½ hrs). For **Ooty**, train at 0625, connects with narrow gauge steam train from Mettupalayam; dep from **Mettupalayam** at 0745, arrives Ooty at 1205.

Transport

Tourist offices *Tamil Nadu*, Rajaram Nagar, T66449.

Directory

Yercaud ஏற்காடு and the Shevaroy Hills சேர்வராயன் மலை

The beautiful drive up the steep and sharply winding ghat road from Salem quickly brings a sharp freshness to the air as it climbs to over 1500 m. The minor 'resort' has a small artificial **lake** with Anna Park nearby. Some attractive though unsignposted walks start here. The main bazar area with a few dirty and dingy restaurants has little to recommend it. In May there is a special festival focused on the **Shevaroyan Temple**, on top of the third highest peak in the hill range. Many tribal people take part, but access is only possible on foot. Ask for details in the Tamil Nadu Tourist Office in Chennai. Quarry blasting from 0500 to midnight provides unwelcome background noise.

Phone code: 04281
Altitude: 1,515 m
Season: throughout the year, busy Apr-Jun

Tamil Nadu & Chennai

Just outside the town is **Lady's Seat**, which overlooks the ghat road and gives wonderful views across the Salem plains. Near the old Norton Bungalow on the Shevaroyan Temple Road, is another well known local spot, **Bear's Cave**. Formed by two huge boulders, it is occupied by huge colonies of bats. The whole area is full of botanical interest. There is an **Orchidarium-cum-Nursery** and a **Horticultural Research Station**.

Sleeping
Most offer off-season discounts Jan-Mar, Aug-Dec

C *Sterling Resort*, near Lady's Seat, T22700, F22537. 59 rooms (few **B** suites), modern, excellent views. Recommended. **D** *Shevaroys*, Main (Hospital) Rd, near lake, T22288, F22387. 32 rooms, 11 **C** cottages with Western baths, restaurant, bar, good views. **D** *Tamil Nadu* (TTDC), Salem-Yercaud Ghat Rd, near lake, behind Panchayat Office, T22273, F22745. 12 rooms, restaurant, Tourist information, garden. **Budget hotels**: inspect rooms first in those near Bus Stand: **D-E** *Select*, near Bus Stand, T22525. **E** *Hill View*, Main Rd, near Bus Stand, T22446. The view its only recommendation. **F** *Youth Hostel*, dorm bed (Rs 30-45), simple, good value, reservations: Manager or Chennai T830390, F830380.

Transport

Local Bus: no local buses but some from Salem continue through town and connect with nearby villages. **Road** From Salem, buses from Salem Junction station and Municipal Bus Stand, 1 hr.

Directory

Banks Banks with foreign exchange facilities are on Main Rd. **Communications** The Post Office is on the Main Rd. **Medical services** *Govt Hospital*, 1 km from Bus Stand; *Providence Hospital*, on Rd to Lady's Seat. **Tourist offices** Tourist information at *Hotel Tamil Nadu*, T2273.

Namakkal
நாமக்கல்
Phone code: 04286
Colour map 3, grid B4
Population: 45,000

The ruins of this extraordinary hilltop fort, believed to have been built by Tipu Sultan, dominate the busy market town below. Namakkal is equally famous in Tamil Nadu for its Vishnu temple. Opposite the temple is a huge statue of Hanuman worshipping. The district played a leading part in the Indian Independence Movement, and Mahatma Gandhi addressed a huge meeting from the bare rock to the north of the main tank in 1933. Within the shrine of the **Narasimhasvami Temple** are four particularly remarkable Pallava bas-reliefs.

To Hogenakkal
Phone code: 04342

The route north to the district capital of Dharmapuri is the most convenient way of getting to the remote Hogenakkal ('smoke that thunders' in Kannada) Falls on the Kaveri. The point at which the Kaveri takes its last plunge down the plateau edge to the plains, 250 m above sea level can be attractive even in the dry season. Though some find it relaxing, others (especially women alone) can be hassled – "the boats are an absolute rip-off". There is a beautiful forested drive down from Pennargaram to the falls, where the water drops 20 m through a long zig-zag canyon. **Sleeping D** *Tamil Nadu* (TTDC), Pennagaram, T56447, some a/c rooms, with bath, restaurant and *Youth Hostel*, dorm (Rs 40) clean and very good value. Private rooms can be a good alternative – ask around and inspect.

The Nilgiri Ghat Road

The ghat journey up to Coonoor (32 km) is one of the most scenic in South India, giving superb views over the plains below. Between Mettupalayam and the start of the ghat road, there are magnificent groves of tall slender areca nut palms.

Mettupalayam has become the centre for the areca nut trade as well as producing synthetic gems. Areca palms are immensely valuable trees; the nut is used across India wrapped in betel vine leaves – two of the essential ingredients of India's universal after-meal digestive, *paan*. The town is the starting point of the ghat railway line up to Ooty (see page 147). If you take the early morning train you can continue to Mysore by bus from Ooty on the same day, making a very pleasant trip.

Mettupalayam
மேட்டுப்பாளையம்
Phone code: 042254
Colour map 3, grid B3
Population: 63,200

Sleeping and eating Convenient for spending a night before catching the early train to Ooty. **E-F** *Barath Bharan*, 200 m from rly station. Very basic, some with bath and a/c, quiet surroundings. **F** *Surya International*, town centre, fairly clean rooms (Rs 150), rooftop restaurant, often empty, quiet, but characterless. *Karna Hotel* in the bus station is good for *dosas*. **D**, 5 km outside, on the Ooty Rd, is an open air restaurant, clean toilets.

Transport Train The *Nilgiri Exp* from Chennai via Coimbatore, connects with the *Blue Mountain Railway*. From **Chennai** *6605*, 2115, 10½ hrs; to Chennai, *6606*, 1925, 10½ hrs. For those coming from Coimbatore, it is better to arrive in advance at Mettupalayam by bus; this avoids a mad dash at the station from Platform 2 to 1 to catch the connecting train! **Blue Mountain Railway** The first part from Mettupalayam to Coonoor is by **steam**; from there to Ooty by **diesel**. To **Coonoor & Ooty**: *564*, 0745, arr **Coonoor**, 1035, Ooty, 1205 (5½ hrs); return from Ooty, *561*, 1500, arr Coonoor, 1615, Mettupalayam 1835, 3½ hrs (extra services Apr-Jun, dep Mettupalayam 0910, from Ooty, 1400), 1st Class Rs 80, 2nd Class Rs 40. The *Heritage Steam Chariot* runs from Ooty to Runneymede. See also box. **Road** Car to Ooty, 2 hrs.

Coonoor குன்னூர்

Coonoor is smaller and much less developed than Ooty, and enjoys a milder climate. It is a pleasant place to relax, with an interesting market although hotel touts can be unpleasantly pushy on arrival. The picturesque hills around the town are covered in coffee and tea plantations and it is an ideal place for walking.

Phone code: 0423
Colour map 3, grid A3
Population: 52,000
Altitude: 1,800 m

Getting there Most visitors arrive in the Lower Town by train or bus. You need an auto or town bus to go up to Upper Coonoor which has the better hotels 2-3 km away. **Climate** Summer: Max 24°C, Min 14°C; Winter: Max 19°C, Min 9°C. Annual rainfall: 130 cm. Best season: Apr-Jun, Sep-Oct. Clothing: Summer: light woollens, Winter: woollens.

Ins & outs

Sim's Park (mid-19th century). Named in 1874 after JD Sim, a secretary to the Madras Club, the large park in Upper Coonoor on the slopes of a ravine has been developed into a botanical garden partly in the Japanese style. It has over 330 varieties of roses and many gentle monkeys! The Fruit and Vegetable Show is held in May. ■ *0800-1830. Rs 5; Camera Rs 5; Video Rs 25*. Coonoor also has the **Pomological Station** where the State Agricultural Department researches on fruits including persimmon, apricot and pomegranate. The **Pasteur Institute** opposite the main entrance to Sim's Park, established in 1907, researches into rabies and manufactures polio vaccine. ■ *Guided tours on Sat between 1030 and 1115, or with permission of the Director. Contact the United Planters' Association of South India (UPASI), Glenview, to visit tea and coffee plantations.*

Sights

The Wellington barracks (2 km from the town), which are the raison d'être for the town, were built in 1852. It is now the Headquarters of the Indian Defence Services Staff College and also of the Madras Regiment, over 250 years old and the oldest in the Indian Army.

Wellington
Population: 19,600

Tamil Nadu & Chennai

Walks **Lamb's Rock** On a high precipice, 9 km away, has stunning views over the Coimbatore plains and coffee and tea estates on the slopes. **Dolphin's Nose** (12 km) is another 10 km away from which you can see Catherine Falls (several buses 0700-1615). **Droog** (13 km) which has ruins of a 16th-century fort used by Tipu Sultan, requires a 3 km walk (buses 0900, 1345).

Tours **TTDC** from Ooty (reserve in Ooty Tourist Office). Coonoor-Kotagiri Rs 95, six hours; visiting Valley View, Sim's Park, Lamb's Rock, Dolphin's Nose, Kodadu view point.

Sleeping **AL** *Garden Retreat* (Taj), Church Rd, Upper Coonoor, T20021, F32775. 33 rooms, spa-
Most are 3-5 km from cious cottage style and homely (**A** off-season), many with open fires, very well kept,
the station & bus stand good dining room though service can be slow, beautiful gardens, no pool. **C** *Wellington Riga*, Appleby Rd, Cantt, 3 km from town, T30523, F31514. 32 comfort-able rooms in characterless building and 3 cottages with mountain views, tennis, golf, riding. **C-D** *Velan Ritz*, 14 Orange Grove Rd, Bedford, T20484, F30606. Completely rebuilt, 21 rooms, good garden. **D** *Camelia Heights*, Figure of 8 Rd, T080-2281591. Comfortable rooms with views of tea gardens and forests, breakfast. **D** *La Barrier Inn*, Coonoor Club Rd, T32561. 6 spacious, clean rooms with TV and hot water, restaurant serving breakfast only, quiet location.

For paying guest There are also Indian style hotels. **E** *Tamil Nadu* (TTDC), Mt Pleasant, T32813. Simple
accommodation, rooms, restaurant, and *Youth Hostel* dorm (Rs 30-45). **E** *Shree Iswara Lodge*, Ooty Rd,
contact Ms Padmini at Cash Bazar near Bus Stand, T32309. 40 basic, clean rooms, restaurant. **E** *Vivek Tourist*
'Sudharama', Mt *Home*, Upasi Rd, Upper Coonoor, T30658. 60 clean rooms with bath and balcony,
Pleasant, T31933 some **D** with TV, restaurant. **E** *'Wyoming' Guest House* (YWCA), near Hospital. Upper Coonor, T20326. 8 large rooms and 2 dorms (8-bedded), with character, excellent food (no alcohol), garden, friendly, popular, "a superb place to stay", manager quali-fied in alternative therapies (runs clinic and courses). Book ahead.

Eating *The Only Place*, Sim's Park Rd. Simple, homely, good food. *Ramachandra*, 32 Mt Rd. Good service. *Vinayaka*, TDK Pilai Rd. Serves good vegetarian.

Shopping The bazar is full of colour and activity. *Mission Arts and Crafts* and *Spencer's*, Figure of 8 Rd, *Variety Hall*, Jubilee Bridge and *Shanthi Mahal* near the Bus Stand. **Books**: *Issu Book Centre*, Bedford. **Photography**: *Lawndays*, Bedford Circle, offers 1 hour processing.

Transport **Local Taxis**: MB, Belmont, T36207. **Rickshaws**: charge whatever they think they can get, pay RS25 to Bedford from the station. **Long distance Road Bus**: frequent buses to Ooty (every 10 mins from 0530) some via Sim's Park and many via Wellington. Also regular services to Kotagiri and Coimbatore (every 30 mins) through Mettupalayam. **Train**: The *Blue Mountain Railway* runs from Mettupalayam to Coonoor (steam), 3 hrs; continues to Ooty (diesel), 1½ hrs. See Mettupalayam above. The *Heritage Steam Chariot* runs from Ooty to Runneymede beyond Coonoor. See Ooty and page 147.

Directory **Banks** *Travancore bank*, Upper Coonor, (Bedford Circle) changes cash. **Medical services** *Lawley Hospital*, Mt Rd, T31050. **Tour operators** *MB & Co*, Belmont, T30210.

Udhagamandalam (Ooty)

உதகமண்டலம் (ஊட்டி)

Known as the 'Queen of the Blue Mountains', along with Kotagiri and Coonoor nearby, Ooty is famous for its rolling hills covered in pine and eucalyptus forests and its coffee and tea plantations. Developed as a hill station by the British, it is no longer the haven it once was, the centre of town has been heavily built up and can be quite unpleasant in the holiday months of April to June, and again around October. Stay in the outskirts which are still pleasant and quiet.

Phone code: 0423
Colour map 3, grid A3
Population: 85,000
Altitude: 2,286 m

Ins & outs

Getting there Perhaps the only way to arrive in Ooty in style is on the quaint rack and pinion train, when it is running. Alternatively, there are plenty of buses from all over the State and from Mysore. The bus stand is just south of the railway station, close to the bazar and many hotels, but you will need an auto to get to others, up to 3 km away. **Getting about** Ooty is quite spread out and hilly, so autos and taxis are the most practical means of getting about. **Climate**: summer: max 25°C, min 10°C; winter: max 21°C, min 5°C. Best season: Apr-Jun.

History

Near the borders of three southern states, Udhagamandalam had been inhabited by *Toda* tribal people who lived in villages or 'munds' consisting of a handful of huts (see page 73). The original name may come from the Tamil word *votai* (a dwarf bamboo), *kai* (vegetable or unripe fruit), and the Toda word *mund*. Some believe it is 'one-stone-village' in the Toda language. Whatever the origins, the British shortened it to 'Ooty'. Because of its climate they developed it as a summer retreat after John Sullivan, a collector, 'discovered' it. A Government House was built, and the British lifestyle developed with cottages and clubs – tennis, golf, riding – and teas on the lawn. Most of the buildings that survive are sadly very neglected. The Indian Maharajahs followed, built their grand houses and came here to shoot.

Sights

Botanical Gardens There are over 1,000 varieties of plants, shrubs and trees including orchids, ferns, alpines and medicinal plants among beautiful lawns and glass houses, and a 20 million-year-old fossil tree trunk by the small lake. To the east of the garden in a Toda *mund* is the Wood House made of logs. ■ *0800-1800, Rs 25, camera, Rs 50, video Rs 500. 3 km northeast of rly station.* Raj Bhavan is next door. The Annual Flower Show (mainly exotics) is held in the third week of May. The **Rose Garden** 750 m from Charing Cross has over 1,500 varieties of roses. ■ *0800-1800.*

Ooty Lake Built in 1825, the vast irrigation tank has been shrinking for decades and is now only about 2.5 km long. The Tourism Department hires out boats from the Boat House. The lake has become very polluted and is generally rather disappointing. Part of the land which was under water in the 19th century has been reclaimed for the **race course**. ■ *0800-1800, Rs 2, camera Rs 5.*

Raj Bhavan Built by the Duke of Buckingham and Chandos in 1877 when Governor of Chennai, in the style of his family home at Stowe. Now the Raj Bhavan, it is superbly positioned on the Dodabetta Ridge and is approached through the Botanical Gardens. The grounds are very well maintained but may be closed to visitors, as is the building.

Stone House The first bungalow built here by John Sullivan is the residence of the principal of the Government Art College which has its campus opposite.

Kandal Cross Three kilometres west of the railway station is a Roman Catholic shrine considered the 'Jerusalem of the East'. During the clearing of the area as a graveyard in 1927 an enormous 4 m high boulder was found and since then a cross was erected. Now a relic of the True Cross brought to India by an Apostolic delegate is shown to pilgrims every day. The annual feast is in May.

St Stephen's Church Ooty's first church, built in the 1820s in a Gothic style, occupies the site of a Toda temple. Much of the wood is said to be from Tipu Sultan's Lal Bagh Palace in Srirangapatnam. The inside of the church and the graveyard (with its poignant colonial plaques and head stones) at the rear are worth seeing.

Dodabetta About 10 km east of the railway station, off the Kotagiri road, the 'big mountain' reaches 2,638 m, the second highest in the Western Ghats sheltering Coonoor from the southwest monsoons when Ooty gets its heavy rains and vice versa during the northeast Monsoon in October and November. Easily accessible by road – on a clear day you can see as far as the Coimbatore plain and the Mysore plateau. The top is often shrouded in mist. There is a viewing platform at the summit, truly wild and not a 'garden escape'; worth spending an hour there; café serves refreshments. ■ *Getting there: buses from Ooty, 1000-1500. Autos and taxis (Rs 200 round trip) go to the summit.*

Udhagamandalam (Ooty)

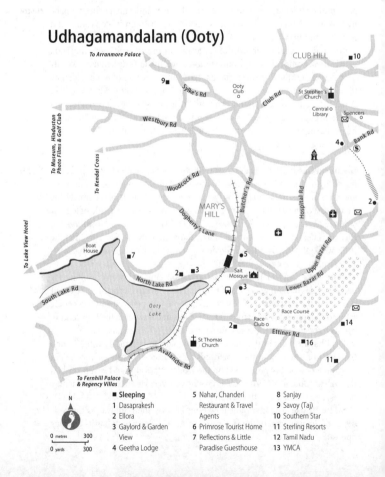

N

0 metres 300
0 yards 300

■ **Sleeping**
1 Dasaprakesh
2 Ellora
3 Gaylord & Garden View
4 Geetha Lodge
5 Nahar, Chanderi Restaurant & Travel Agents
6 Primrose Tourist Home
7 Reflections & Little Paradise Guesthouse
8 Sanjay
9 Savoy (Taj)
10 Southern Star
11 Sterling Resorts
12 Tamil Nadu
13 YMCA

Hiking Hiking or simply **walking** is excellent in the Nilgiris, undisturbed, quiet and interesting. Climbing Dodabetta or Mukurti is hardly a challenge. The longer walks through the *sholas* are best undertaken with a guide. It is possible to see characteristic features of Toda settlements such as *munds* and *boas*, see page 153.

Dodabetta-Snowdon-Ooty walk At "Dodabetta Junction" directly opposite the 3 km road to the summit, is a minor road (later a broad stony track) which a Forest Department signboard advertises as a "green trek" to Ooty. It is a pleasant path which curves gently downhill through a variety of woodland (eucalyptus, conifer, shola) back to Ooty and need take no more than a couple of hours. At about half-way, well after the horticultural research station and shortly before a derelict circular concrete observation platform on the left, a signpost on the right indicates the broad track (initially angled sharply back) through more woodland to Snowdon Peak (2,450m – allow another comfortable each way) where there is a telecom tower and a small open rocky area with views. The original track meanwhile continues for a couple more kilometres before reaching some houses emerging onto a proer road. Turning left for a further kilometre will bring one to St Stephen's Church on the edge of Ooty. You can make a day of it – get transport to Dodabetta in the morning, have refreshments at the summit, and then walk back to Ooty after taking in Snowdon peak.

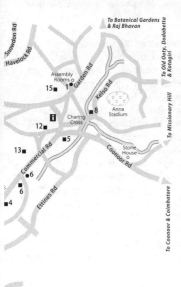

Government Museum and Art Gallery Display of art and sculpture of the Nilgiris. ■ *Mysore Rd, 3 km from Charing Cross. Mon-Thu, 0900-1300, 1400-1700. Free.*

Tours Reservations, TTDC, *Hotel Tamil Nadu*, T44370. Ooty and Mudumalai: Ooty Lake, Dodabetta Peak, Botanical Gardens, Mudumalai Wildlife Sanctuary. Daily 0830-2000. Rs 125. Kotagiri and Coonoor: Kotagiri, Kodanad View Point, Lamb's Rock, Dolphin's Nose, Sim's Park. Daily 0830-1830. Rs 100. *Woodlands Tours*m Race Course Rd, T42551. offers. Ooty and Coonoor: 0930-1730. Rs 100. Stunning views.

Excursions **Mukurti Peak** (36 km) Off the Gudalur road, the 6 km long Mukurti Lake is reached after 26 km. Mukurti Peak, not an easy climb, is to the west. The name suggests a severed nose to describe the peak. The Todas believe that the souls of the dead and the sacrificed buffaloes leap to the next world from this sacred peak. **Sleeping**: Electricity Deparment and Nilgiris Game Association's *Bungalows* are on the south side of the lake, half-way along – you can go fishing and boating. An excellent place to escape for walking and to view the

Tamil Nadu & Chennai

14 YMCA
15 Youth Hostal
16 Woodlands

● **Eating**
1 Hot Breads

2 Kebab Corner
3 Sharma's
4 Shinkow's Chinese
5 Sri Vijaya Vilas
6 Top Café & New
  Tandoor Mahal

occasional wildlife – book early as they are popular. ■ *Getting there: buses from Ooty every 30 minutes from 0630.*

Avalanche The 'avalanche' in 1823 gave the valley its name. It is a beautiful part of the *shola*, 24 km from town, with plenty of rhododendrons, magnolias and orchids and a trout stream running through, and is excellent for walking and superb scenery. Forestry Department *Guest House*, clean with good food; Avalanche Top is 4 km from the bungalow. ■ *Getting there: buses from Ooty, 1110.*

Pykara The river Pykara, 19 km from Ooty, has a dam and power plant. There is breathtaking scenery. The Falls, about 6 km from the bridge on the main road, are best in July though it is very wet then, but they are also worth visiting from August to December. ■ *Getting there: several buses from 0639-2030; or take a car or bicycle.*

Trekking This is difficult to arrange and takes at least a month – four separate permits are needed, any of which can be refused. Treks of up to seven days can be arranged with one month's notice, by the Nilgiris Trekking Association, Kavitha Nilayam, 31-D Bank Road, Ooty, F42572. NR Ayyapan, the President, is very knowledgeable about trekking in the area. Alternatively, contact the Tourist Office, District Forest Offices, N & S Div, Ooty, T44083 or *Nilgiri Wildlife Environment Association*, DFO N Div, Mount Stewart Hills, T43968. One day treks without a permit and overnight camping may also be offered but their success is variable.

Sleeping

Most offer substantial off-season discounts Jul-Mar except during Puja & Christmas. 30% tax in the upper categories. Virtually all have car parking. Winter nights can be bitterly cold; hotel fireplaces often don't work

AL *Savoy* (Taj), 77 Sylkes Rd, T44142, F43318. 40 rooms (**A** off-season), some cottages have fireplaces (no fridge), restaurant (mixed reports), coffee house, lovely gardens, ask Reception for interesting history of hotel, worth visiting. **A** *Holiday Inn (Gem Park)*, Sheddon Rd, T42955, F44302. 95 rooms, modern facilities but poorly managed. **A-B** *Aruna* (Comfort Inn), Gorishola Rd, T44140, F44229. 88 comfortable rooms, 'Victorian' architecture in large landscaped grounds with superb views 'from the point the resort was discovered', 92 rooms. **B** *Monarch*, off Havelock Rd, T44408, F42455. Comfortable rooms, expensive suites, indoor heated pool. **B** *Southern Star* (Merit Inn), 22 Havelock Rd, T43601. 67 rooms, some refurbished, restaurant (over-attentive service), tea garden, good, clean, comfortable, attracts filmstars, bar "closed" but drinks available. **C-D** *Nahar*, 52 A Charing Cross, T42173, F42405. 75 rooms with heaters (ask for newer block), good vegetarian indoors or out. **C-D** *Regency Villa*, 100 m from *Fernhill*, 2 km from bus station, T43097. 18 large rooms (some run down) in former royal hunting lodge, clean and comfortable, food on room service only, woods, tea gardens, riding (see below), very friendly, pleasant, peaceful, good value. Recommended. *Fernhill*. Derelict; no sign of reopening, but you may be allowed to look inside at the ornately gilded/painted ceiling of salon and carved wood panelling in the hall, for a tip of Rs 50.

D *Dasaprakash*, Ettines Rd, T42434. 100 rooms (no shower/bath), near rly and bus station, vegetarian restaurants, coffee shop, exchange, garden, comfortable, quiet location. **D** *Lake View*, W Lake Rd (2 km), T43904, F43579. 123 cottages in large grounds, most without a view, restaurant, bar, isolated. **D** *Nilgiri Woodlands*, Ettines Rd, opposite Race Course, T42451, F42530. 24 rooms (some vast suites), in interesting, old colonial house with verandah, some deluxe, others in cottages, tennis, pleasant location, quiet, comfortable but desperately needing repair so can get very damp, vegetarian restaurant, alcohol on room-service. **D** *Ooty Gate*, Coonoor Rd, few minutes' walk from Charing Cross, T41622, F44258. 85 very clean rooms with bath (some **C** suites), heaters (best at rear with views, quieter), good restaurant (limited off-season), bar (beer Rs 40), recommended for service and value. **D** *Tamil Nadu* (TTDC), Charing Cross, up steps by Tourist Office, T44378, F44369. Rooms and penthouse with good views, restaurant, bar, exchange, pleasant hotel. **D** *YWCA Anandagiri*, Ettines Rd, T42218. Some pleasant cottages, cheap dorm beds, popular with the young, not central, restaurant.

E *Gaylord*, connected to *Garden View*, T42378. Rooms with bath overlook geranium-filled courtyard (could be cleaner, curtains missing), **F** dorm (24 beds), roof-garden restaurant, old tiled bungalow, amazing home-made boiler dispenses hot water! – slow staff. **E** *Primrose Tourist Home*, Commercial Rd, T43848. 18 rooms with bath, dorm, 2 good restaurants, modern building with no views, noisy at times, rates vary according to demand. **E** *Reflections*, North Lake Rd, T43834. 6 rooms (cheaper dorm beds), clean, homely guest house with good views, pleasant dining room serving good food, friendly owners but "not recommended for females travelling alone". **E** *Sanjay*, Charing Cross, T42090. Rooms with spacious balcony, dorm beds (Rs 30-50), restaurant, clean, sometimes noisy at night, excellent room service. Recommended. **E-F** *Garden View*, North Lake Rd, opposite Bus and Rly stations, T43349. 26 good size rooms with bath, deluxe, with better views and hot tap, restaurant, a little tired but clean. **E-F** *Geetha*, Commercial Rd, T44186. 13 very clean rooms, cheap dorm, shared Indian toilet, central but fairly quiet, good value. **E-F** *Youth Hostel* (TTDC) near Tourist Office, T43665. Clean rooms and dorm bed (Rs 30-45), restaurant. **F** *Ellora*, North Lake Rd, T44266. Rooms with bath (Indian toilet) in an old tiled bungalow, a little shabby and unreliable security reported, some rooms have fireplace and old 'Victorian' furniture, garden with lawns overlooking Ooty and lake.

Most budget accommodation is centred around Commercial Rd & Ettines Rd; many are filthy & noisy flea pits which charge inflated rates; few have running hot water (usually supplied in buckets)

Tamil Nadu & Chennai

Expensive: *Savoy*, recommended for relaxed atmosphere and good, not-too-spicy food, buffets more affordable; pleasant coffee house, open all day. **Mid-range**: *New Tandoor Mahal*, Commercial Rd. Smart, serving meat and chicken dishes, good vegetarian curries, beers, but over-zealous waiters. *Regent Villa*. Limited Continental menu, good Indian. Small restaurant with character. *Ritz*. Good food, excellent lemon sodas. **Cheap**: *Blue Hills* Charing Cross. Good value Indian and Continental, non-vegetarian. *Kabab Corner* Commercial Rd. Indian. Good curries and naan, pleasing upmarket, Western décor. *Kaveri*, Charing Cross. Good cakes and savoury snacks but atmosphere nil. *Sharma Bhojanalaya* 12C Lower Bazar. Upstairs, comfortable (padded banquettes!), overlooks race course, good vegetarian lunch *thali* (Rs 40). *Shinkow's*, 42 Commissioner's Rd (near Collector's Office). Authentic Chinese, popular, especially late evening. *Woodlands*. Vegetarian (no alcohol) in pleasant character building. *VK Bakery*, 148 Commercial Rd is recommended for fresh meat and vegetarian patties, bread and cakes. *Nilgiri Dairy Farms* outlets sell quality milk products.

Eating

Bars in larger hotels. 'Southern Star' is recommended, though expensive

The renovated 100-year-old **'Assembly Rooms'**, Garden Rd, T42250, shows films in English. Most of the annual events take place in May – Summer Festival, Dog Show, Flower Show, Vegetable Show in the Botanical Gardens, Boat Race and Pageant on the lake. **Sports** *Gymkhana Club*, T42254, temporary membership; beautifully situated amidst superbly maintained 18-hole golf course. *Lawley Institute*, T42249, for tennis, badminton, billiards. **Boating and rowing** at Ooty Lake. **Riding** from Regency Villa: Rs 500 for 2 hours with 'guide'; good fun but no helmets – worrying when horses gallop! "Wonderful way to see the real Ooty:" – arrive early and ask to see the rooms in the Villa. **Fishing**: good at Avalanche, 25 km away, where there is a trout hatchery; also good at Mukerti, Pykara, Upper Bhavani. Forestry Guest House for overnight accommodation. Licenses for hired tackle from Asst Director of Fisheries, Fishdale, T43946 or TN Fisheries Dev Corp, Bhavanisagar. **Trekking**: see note below. **Yoga**: *Rajayoga Meditation Centre*, 88 Victoria Hall, Ettines Rd.

Entertainment

Jan: Ooty celebrates *Pongal*. **May**: The Annual Flower and Dog Shows in the Botanical Gardens. *Summer Festival* of cultural programmes with stars from all over India.

Festivals

Shopping

Most open 0900-1200, 1500-2000. The smaller shops keep longer hrs

The main areas are Charing Cross, Municipal Market, Upper and Lower Bazar. *Toda Showroom*, Charing Cross, sells silver and tribal shawls. *Kashmir Emporium*, Garden Gate, and *Kashmir House*, Charing Cross, sell Kashmiri goods, but also Toda jewellery. *Variety Hall*, Silver Market, old family firm (1890s) for good range of silk, helpful, accepts credit cards. **Books**: *Higginbotham's*, near Central Library shop better, 1000-1300, 1550-1930.

Tour operators

Blue Mountain, Nahar Complex, Charing Cross, T43650, luxury coach bookings to neighbouring states. *George Hawkes*, 52C Nahar Complex, T42756, for tourist taxis. *Matheson & Bosanquet*, Commercial Rd, next to *Higginbotham's*, T42604, for air tickets. *Sangeetha Travels*, 13 Bharathiyar Complex, Charing Cross, T/F44782 for *Heritage* steam train.

Transport

Good road connections to other towns in the region. Ghat roads have numerous hairpin bends which can have fairly heavy traffic and very bad surfaces at times. The Gudalur road passes through Mudumalai and Bandipur sanctuaries (see page 159). You might see an elephant herd and other wildlife – especially at night. **Local Auto-rickshaws** are unmetered, minimum Rs 7. **Cycle hire**. **Taxis**: minimum charge, about Rs 12.

Long distance Air: Nearest airport, Coimbatore, 105 km. Taxis available. **Road Bus**: *Cheran*, T43970. Frequent buses to **Coonoor** (every 10 mins, 0530-2045), **Coimbatore** (every 20 mins, 0530-2000, 3½ hrs) and **Mettupalayam** (0530-2100, 2 hrs). Also to **Bangalore** (0630-2000), **Mysore** (0800-1530, 3½-5 hrs) and **Kozhikode** (0630-1515), **Chennai** (1630-1830), **Palakkad** (0715-1515), **Palani** (0800-1800). Daily buses to **Kannur** (0915, 2000), **Hassan** (1130, 1500), **Kanniyakumari** (1745), **Kodaikkanal** (0630, 9½ hrs via magnificent route through Palani, Rs 225), **Madikere** (0700, 1100), **Pondicherry** (1700), **Salem** (1300). **NB** Check timings. Several on the short route (36 km) to Masinagudi/Mudumalai, Rs 7, 1½ hrs; a steep and windy but interesting road. **Train**: Rly station, T42246. From Mettupalayam *Blue Mountain* (steam to Coonoor; then diesel to Ooty), *562*, 0745, 5½ hrs; from Ooty, *561*, 1500, 3½ hrs. **Steam** The *Heritage Steam Chariot* to Runneymede runs at weekends (more frequent in season). It departs Ooty 1000, returns 1600 (delayed when engine runs out of steam!). Highly recommended. Tickets include Indian packed lunch: Rs 250, or Rs 500 in Maharaja coach, from *Sangeetha* (listed below) or Ooty rly station. For details, see page 147.

Directory

Banks *State Bank of India* on Bank Rd, deals in foreign exchange. **Communications Post Office**: Head Post Office, Collectorate and Telegraph Office, Town W Circle. **International direct dialling and fax**: Post Office and *Sangeetha*, 13 Bharathiar Building, both at Charing Cross. **Medical services** *Govt Hospital*, Hospital Rd, T42212. **Tourist offices** *Tamil Nadu*, 7/72 Commercial Rd, Super Market, Charing Cross, T43977, lacks efficiency. **Useful addresses** *Police*: T100. *Wildlife Warden*: 1st Flr, Mahalingam Building, T44098, 1000-1300, 1400-1730.

Kotagiri

கோத்தகிரி

Phone code: 04266
Population: 37,800
Altitude: 1,980 m
29 km from Ooty

Kotagiri is the oldest of the three Nilgiri hill resorts and sits on the northeast crest of the plateau overlooking the plains. It has a milder climate than Ooty. The name comes from Kotar-Keri, the street of the *Kotas* who were one of the original hill tribes and have a village to the west of the town (see page 74).

There is a **Handicrafts Centre** of the Women's Welfare Dept. You can visit some scenic spots – St Catherine Falls (8 km) and Elk Falls (7 km), or one of the peaks – Kodanad Viewpoint (16 km) which you reach through the tea estates (also several buses from 0610), or Rangaswamy Pillar which is an isolated rock and the conical Rangaswamy Peak.

Sleeping E *Ramesh Vihar*, T71346. Simple rooms, meals. **E** *Top Hill Lodge*, near Police Station, T71473. Rooms, restaurant, bar. **F** *Blue Star*, next to Bus Station. Rooms with shower and toilet in modern building. **F** *Youth Hostel* (TTDC), signposted beyond bus station. Dorm beds (Rs 35), dirty and crowded with noisy tea-pickers.

Shopping *Kotagiri Co-op Society*, Ramchandra Sq, for Toda embroidery.

Transport Bus: frequent services to/from Coonoor, Mettupalayam Rly Station and Ooty.

From Ooty the road drops through mixed woodland around Naduvattam, **Naduvattam** managed through this century by the Forest Department. Many imported species have been experimented with, including fragrant and medicinal trees such as eucalyptus and chinchona, the bark of which was used for extracting quinine. The road often gives beautiful views, and as with all the hill descents in India the rapid change in altitude quickly brings a sharp increase in temperature. It drops to **Gudalur** and Mudumalai at the base of the hills before crossing the Moyar River, the border with Karnataka, into the Bandipur sanctuary.

★ Mudumalai Wildlife Sanctuary

The sanctuary adjoins Bandipur beyond the Moyar River, its hills (885-1,000 m), ravines, flats and valleys being an extension of the same environment. The park is one of the more popular and is trying to limit numbers of visitors to reduce disturbance to the elephants.

Phone code: 0423
Colour map 3, grid A3

There is a Range Office at Kargudi and a Reception Centre (0630-1800) at Theppakadu **Ins & outs** where buses between Mysore anld Ooty stop. Open through the year, 0630-0900, 1600-1800. Best seasons: Sep-Oct, Mar-May (when the undergrowth dies down, it is easier to see the animals, particularly when they are on the move at dawn). Entrance Rs 5, Camera Rs 5.

The sanctuary has large herds of elephant, gaur, sambar, barking deer, wild **Wildlife** dog, Nilgiri langur, bonnet monkey, wild boar, four-horned antelope and the rarer tiger and leopard, as well as smaller mammals and many birds and reptiles.

   Elephant Camp, south of Theppakadu. Wild elephants are tamed here. Some are bred in captivity and trained to work for the timber industry. You can watch the elephants being fed in the late afternoon, learn about each individual elephant's diet and the specially prepared "cakes" of food. In the wild, elephants forage widely, consuming about 300 kg of green fodder daily, but in captivity they have to adapt to a totally alien lifestyle.

You can hire a jeep (about Rs 6 per km), but must be accompanied by a guide. **Viewing** Most 'Night Safaris' are best avoided – "you go up and down the main road by *The core area is not* jeep". Elephant rides from 0630 and 1600 (Rs 100 per elephant per hour); *open to visitors* check timings and book in advance at the Wildlife Office, Mahalingam Bldg, Coonoor Road, Ooty. They can be fun even though you may not see much wildlife. The 46-seater coach (first come, first served, Rs 25 each) can be noisy with shrieking children. There are *machans* near water holes and salt licks and along the Moyar River. With patience you can see a lot, especially rare and beautiful birds. Trekking in the remoter parts of the forest with guides can be arranged from some lodges (see *Jungle Retreats* below) but remember wild elephants can be dangerous.

Tamil Nadu & Chennai

Sleeping Better near **Masinagudi** which also has restaurants and shops, *Altitude*: 960 m (7 km
Advance booking from Theppakadu). Some in **Bokkapuram**, 3 km further south. Ask private lodges for
essential especially pick-up if arriving by bus at Theppakadu. **C** *Bamboo Banks Farm Guest House*,
during season & at Masinagudi, T56222. 6 clean rooms, 4 in cottages in attractive garden, good food,
weekends birdwatching, riding, jeep. **C** *Jungle Retreat*, Bokkapuram, T/F56469,
peres@giasbg01.vsnl.net.in Large rooms with modern baths, private terrace, superb
views, "wonderful quiet place", friendly relaxed owners (Mr and Mrs Mathias), high
standards, good treks with local guides, elephant rides, Travellers' cheques accepted.
Highly recommended. **C** *Monarch Safari Park*, Bokkapuram, on a hill side, T56326. 14
rooms in twin *machan* huts on stilts with bath (sadly rats enter at night), open-sided
restaurant, cycles, birdwatching, good riding (Rs 150 per hour), some sporting facilities, meditation centre, large grounds, "lovely spot", management slack, friendly if
slow service. **C-D** *Blue Valley Resorts*, Bokkapuram, T56244. 8 comfortable huts (**C**
suites), restaurants, scenic location, wildlife tours. **C-D** *Jungle Hut*, near Bokkapuram,
T56240. 12 clean, simple rooms with bath in 3 stone cottages in valley, good food –
"lovely home cooking", pool, jeep hire, game viewing and treks, very friendly welcome. Recommended. **D** *Forest Hills Farm*, 300 m from *Jungle Hut*, T56216. 6 modern
rooms with bath and views, good food, friendly, game viewing. Recommended.
D *Jungle Trails*, 2 km off Sighur Ghat Rd (23 km from Ooty, ask bus to stop; flat walk,
well marked), T56256. 3 clean rooms in a bungalow, rustic ("bamboo shutters
propped open with poles"), dorm beds (Rs 100), and *machan* good for viewing the
moving tapestry (4 trails and pool visible), meals Rs 200, dedicated to animal watching (quiet after dark; no candles on verandah, no sitting in the garden by moonlight),
Cheetal Walk, 1997 by A Davidas, the owner's father. Recommended. **D-E** *Mountania*,
Masinagudi (500 m from bus stand), T56337. Rooms in cottages (prices vary), "nice
but a bit overpriced", restaurant, jeep tour to waterfalls (Rs 250), easy animal spotting
(evening better than morning). **D-E** *Jain Resorts*, near Chilling Plant Farm, Vazhi
Thottam village, T56318.

Theppakadu: **E** *Tamil Nadu* (TTDC *Youth Hostel*), T56249. 3 rooms, 24 beds in dorm
(Rs 45), restaurant, van for viewing. Several Govt Forest Dept huts charge Rs 80 for
double rooms; reserve in advance through the Wildlife Warden, Mudumalai WLS, 1st
Flr, Mahalingam Bldg, Coonoor Rd, Ooty, T44098 or Wildlife Warden, Kargudi, T26.
Also near the river, *Log House*, 2 rooms, 4 dorm beds (Rs 20), and *Sylvan Lodge*, 4
rooms, recommended. **Kargudi**: *Rest House* and *Annexe*, ask for deluxe rooms;
Abhayaranyam Rest House, 2 rooms and *Annexe*, 2 rooms, recommended. **F Dormi-
tories**: *Peacock*, 50 beds, food excellent; smaller *Minivet* and *Morgan*, 8 and 12 beds.
All, Rs 5 per bed. **Masinagudi**: *Log House*, 5 rooms and *Rest House*, 3 rooms.

Transport **Road** **Bus**: Theppakadu is on the Mysore-Ooty bus route. From **Mysore**, services
from 0615 (1½-2 hrs); last bus to Mysore around 2000. From **Ooty** via Gudalur on a
very winding road (about 2½ hrs); direct 20 km steep road used by buses, under 1 hr.
Few buses between Theppakadu and Masinagudi. **Jeeps**: available at bus stands and
from lodges.

★ Madurai மதுரை and the Vaigai Valley

The river Vaigai, dammed to the west of Madurai and often dry towards the east, runs from the well watered scarp of the ghats to the arid southeastern coast. The area of fertile agricultural land is dotted about with exotically shaped granite mountain ranges such as Nagamalai ("snake hills") and Yanaimalai ("elephant hills"). Spread along the banks of the rocky bed of the Vaigai River, the modern industrial city of Madurai's main claim to fame is as a temple town. It is one of Tamil culture's most vital centres. The temple and bazar at the heart of this very crowded and polluted city can feel quite uncomfortable and overpowering to a Westerner, but is an experience.

Phone code: 0452
Colour map 3, grid B4
Population: 1.094 m
Altitude 100 m

Getting there The airport, 12 km from town, is linked by buses to the city centre, but there are also taxis and autos. The railway station is within easy walking distance of many budget hotels (rickshaw drivers/hotel touts, may tell you otherwise). Hire an auto to reach the few north of the river or the Taj. The main express bus stand is next to the station though there are three others 3-4 km away, with bus links between them. **Getting around** Although very spread out, the centre is very compact and the temple is within easy walking distance of most budget hotels.

Ins & outs

According to legend, drops of nectar fell from Siva's locks on this site, so it was named 'Madhuram' or Madurai, the nectar city. The city's history goes back to the sixth century BC. Ancient Madurai, which traded with Greece and Rome, was a centre of Tamil culture, famous for its writers and poets during the last of the three '*Sangam*' periods (Tamil 'Academies') nearly 2,000 years ago (see page 74). The Pandiyans, a major power from the sixth to the beginning of the 10th century, made Madurai their capital. For the following 300 years, they remained here, although they were subservient to the Cholas who gained control over the area, after which the Pandiyans returned to power. For a short period it became a Sultanate after Malik Kafur completely destroyed the city in 1310. In 1364 it was captured by Hindu Vijayanagar kings, who remained until 1565, after which their local governors the Nayakas asserted their independence.

History

The Nayakas have been seen essentially as warriors, given an official position by the Vijayanagar rulers; though in Sanskrit, the term applied to someone of prominence and leadership. Burton Stein comments, "the history of the Vijayanagara is essentially the history of the great Telugu Nayakas".

The Vijayanagar kings were great builders and preserved and enriched the architectural heritage of the town. The Nayakas laid out the old town in the pattern of a lotus with narrow streets surrounding the Minakshi Temple at the centre. The streets on the four sides of the central temple are named after the festivals which take place in them and give their relative direction, for example South 'Masi' Street, East 'Avanimoola' Street and East 'Chitrai' Street. The greatest of the Nayaka rulers, Thirumalai (ruled 1623-55), built the *gopurams* of the temple. After the Carnatic Wars the British destroyed the fort in 1840, filling in the surrounding moat (now followed by the four Veli streets).

The ★ **Minakshi Temple** is an outstanding example of Vijayanagar temple architecture. Minakshi, the 'fish-eyed goddess' and the consort of Siva, has a temple to the south, and Sundareswarar (Siva), a temple to the west. Since she is the presiding deity the daily ceremonies are first performed in her shrine

Sights

Tamil Nadu & Chennai

and, unlike the practice at other temples, Sundareswarar plays a secondary role. The temple's nine towering *gopurams* stand out with their colourful stucco images of gods, goddesses and animals which are renewed and painted every 12 years. There are about 4,000 granite sculptures on the lower levels. In addition to the Golden Lotus tank and various pillared halls there are five *vimanas* over the sanctuaries. ■ *Inner Temple open 0500-1230, 1600-2130; the sanctuary is open only to Hindus. Camera fee Rs 25, video Rs 70, at South Entrance (valid for multiple entry).*

The main entrance is through a small door of the *Ashta Sakthi Mandapa* (Porch of the eight goddesses) which projects from the wall, south of the eastern *gopuram*. Inside, to the left is the sacred *Tank of the Golden Lotus*, with a lamp in the centre, surrounded by pillared cloisters and steps down to the waters. The Sangam legend speaks of the test that ancient manuscripts had to undergo – they were thrown into the sacred tank, if they sank they were worthless, if they floated they were considered worthy! The north gallery has 17th-century murals, relating 64 miracles said to have been performed by Siva, and the southern has marble inscriptions of the 1,330 couplets of the *Tamil Book of Ethics*. To the west of the tank is the *Oonjal Mandapa*, the pavilion

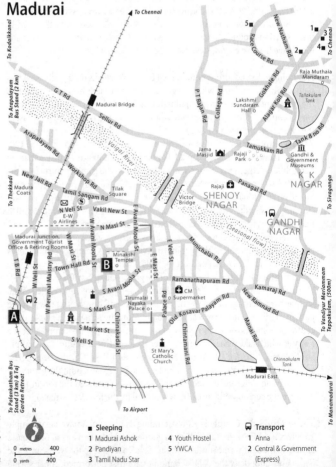

Madurai

Related maps
A *Madurai centre,*
page 167
B *Minashi Temple,*
page 164

0 metres 400
0 yards 400

■ **Sleeping**
1 Madurai Ashok
2 Pandiyan
3 Tamil Nadu Star
4 Youth Hostel
5 YWCA

🚌 **Transport**
1 Anna
2 Central & Government (Express)

leading to the Meenakshi shrine. Here the pillars are carved in the form of the mythical beast *yali* which recurs in temples throughout the region. Golden images of Meenakshi and Sundareswarar are brought to the *oonjal* or swing each Friday evening where they are worshipped. Cages with parrots (Meenakshi's green bird which brings luck) hung from the ceiling of the neighbouring *Kilikootu Mandapam* which is flanked by finely carved columns. The *Meenakshi shrine* with the principal image of the goddess, stands in its own enclosure with smaller shrines around it.

To the north of the tank is another enclosure with smaller *gopurams* on four sides within which is the Sundareswarar shrine guarded by two tall *dwarapalas*. In the northeast corner, the superb sculptures of the divine marriage of Meenakshi and Sundareswarar being blessed by Vishnu and Brahma, and Siva in his 24 forms are in the 19th-century *Kambathadi Mandapa*, around the golden flagstaff.

The *thousand-pillared hall* (mid-16th century) is in the northeast corner of the complex. Near the entrance, the sculpted ceiling has a wheel showing the 60 Tamil years. The 985 exquisitely carved columns include a lady playing the *veena*, a dancing Ganesh, and a gypsy leading a monkey. The **art museum** here exhibits temple art and architecture, fine brass and stone images, friezes and photos (the labelling could be improved). ■ *0600-2000. Re 1, extra camera fee Rs 5 at the door.* Just inside the museum to the right is a cluster of five musical pillars carved out of a single stone. Each pillar produces a different note which vibrates when tapped. Nayaka musicians could play these as an instrument.

The *Nandi* pavilion is to the east and is often occupied by flower sellers. The long *Pudu Mandapa* (New Mandapa), with its beautiful sculptures of *yalis* and Nayaka rulers and their ministers, is outside the enclosure wall, between the east tower and the base of the unfinished *Raya Gopuram* which was planned to be the tallest in the country.

The temple is a hive of activity, with a colourful temple elephant, flower sellers and performances by musicians from 1800-1930, 2100-2200. At 2130 an image of Sundareswarar is carried in procession from the shrine near the east *gopuram* to Minakshi, to 'sleep' by her side, which is returned the next morning. The procession around the temple is led by the elephant and a cow and is well worth watching (Camera fee Rs 25 at the temple office near the South Tower – good views from the top of the South Gate when open). During the day the elephant is on continual duty, 'blessing' visitors with its trunk and then collecting a small offering. (A banana pleases him enormously, but not his keeper!) The flower and vegetable market (north end of East Chitrai Street) is colourful, but watch out for the holes in the floor.

Thirumalai Nayaka Palace Built in 1636 in the Indo-Mughal style, its 15 domes and arches are adorned with stucco work while some of its 240 columns rise to 12 m. Its *Swarga Vilasam* (Celestial Pavilion), an arcaded octagonal structure, is curiously constructed in brick and mortar without any supporting rafters. Special artisans skilled in the use of traditional lime plaster and powdered seashell and quartz have renovated parts. The original complex had a shrine, an armoury, a theatre, royal quarters, a

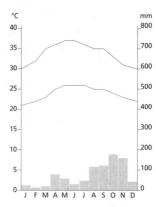

Climate: Madurai
Best time to visit: Dec-Feb

royal bandstand, a harem, a pond and a garden but only about a quarter survives since Thirumalai's grandson removed sections to build another palace in Tiruchirappalli, and the original Ranga Vilasam was destroyed by Muslim invaders. It is a bit run down. ■ *0900-1300, 1400-1700. Bus 17, 17a, 11, 11a.*

Vandiyur Mariammam Teppakulam, to the southeast of town, has a small shrine in its centre where the annual *Float Festival* takes place in January/February. Buses 4 and 4A take 10 minutes from the Bus Stand and Rly Station.

Museums
The best is the excellent **Gandhi Museum**, in the 300 year old Rani Mangammal Palace. It contains an art gallery, memorabilia (Gandhi's *dhoti* when he was shot), traces history of the Independence struggle from 1800, and the 'Quit India' movement. Informative (same management as one at Delhi and equally good), recommended. Also has a Khadi and Village Industries Section and one of South Indian handicrafts. ■ *1000-1300, 1400-1730, daily; free.* Yoga classes, offered daily, 0630. **Government Museum** in the same complex. ■ *1030-1300, 1400-1730, closed Fri. Bus No 1, 2 and 3.* **Thirumalai Nayaka Palace Museum** concentrates on the history of Madurai with galleries on the famous Nayaka king and the art and architecture of Tamil Nadu. Bus No 4. *Sound and Light* show (see Entertainment).

Excursions
Alagar Temple, 20 km to the east of Madurai (Bus 44), is an ancient temple with beautiful sculptures of Vishnu.

Minakshi Temple

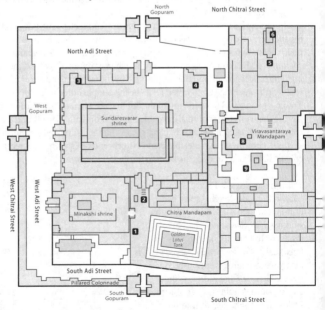

N
Not to scale

1 Killikootu (Parrot Cage) & Oonjal (Swing) Mandapams
2 Subrahmanya Shrine
3 Tamil Sangam College
4 Kambathadi Mandapam
5 Ayirakkal Mandapam, 'Thousand Pillared Hall' & Museum
6 Sabhapati Shrine

TTDC *Temple tour* of Madurai and attractive surroundings by a/c coach; enquire at Tourist Office. Recommended to get an overview. April to June: *Kodaikkanal.* 0700-2100. Also *Ex-Serviceman Travels,* 1 Koodalalagar, Perumal Kovil Street, T730571, *City* half day, 0700, 1500, Rs 110; *Kodaikkanal* or *Ramesvaram,* 0700-1900, Rs 200; overnight to *Kanniyakumari,* 2200-1900, Rs 300; one-way cheaper.

Tours

AL *Garden Retreat* (Taj), Pasumalai Hills, 7 TPK Rd, 5 km southwest of town centre on NH7, T601020, F604004, tgrgm.madu@taj group.ems.vsnl.net.in 30 rooms (some in old colonial house), very attractive gardens, outdoor dining but food average, good bookshop, pool, great views over surrounding country, service poor. **A-B** *Ashok* (ITDC), Alagarkoil Rd, T537531, F537530. 43 musty rooms, pool (open to non-residents), excellent restaurant. **A-B** *Pandiyan,* Race Course, T537091, F533424. 57 rooms, pleasant garden, good restaurant. **C** *Park Plaza,* 114 W Perumal Maistry St, T742114, F743654. Good a/c rooms, excellent restaurant. Recommended. **C-D** *Supreme,* 110 W Perumal Maistry St, T743151, F742637, supreme@md3.vsnl.net.in 69 modern clean rooms, some a/c (Rs 400-800) on 7 floors, **B** suites, good rooftop restaurant (temple views), bar, 24-hour travel, exchange, internet, a bit noisy but good value. **D** *Tamil Nadu II (Star)* (TTDC), Alagarkoil Rd, near Collector's Office, T537462, F583203. 51 rooms, some a/c, good restaurant, bar, exchange, quiet. **D-E** *Taj,* 13a TPK Rd, T730783, F734876, hoteltaj@ maduraionline.com Newish, decent rooms with bath (some noisy), some with a/c and TV Rs 500. **D-E** *Tamil Nadu I,* W Veli St, opposite Express Bus Stand, T547470. 44 rather dark rooms, some **D** a/c, exchange, can be noisy. **E** *Arima,* 4 TB Rd, T603261. 37 rooms, some a/c, modern, simple, clean. **E** *Prem Nivas,* 102 W Perumal Maistry St, T742539. Clean rooms with bath, some **D** a/c, a/c restaurant, basic but good value. **E** *TM Lodge,* 50 W Perumal Maistry St, T741651. 57 rooms (hot water), some a/c, some with TV, very clean and efficient, bookings for rail/bus journeys. **E** *Sree Devi,* W Avani Moola St, T747431. Rooms with bath, some **D** a/c, (avoid noisy ground floor), no meals, some tip-seeking staff, but good value, clean, modern towerblock, superb views of temple gateway from rooftop. **E** *Laxmi Towers,* 40A Perumal Koil South Mada Street, T 734673. Clean, acceptable rooms with bath (Rs 200). **E-F** *Dhanamani,* 20-22 Sunnamukara St, T742703. Nice rooms (some with bath, fan, TV), good roof terrace with temple views, sitting area (8th flr). **E-F** *Railway Retiring Rooms,* Madurai Junction, T540142, 1st Flr above Platform 1. 13 rooms, some a/c, can be very noisy. **E-F** *Ravi Towers,* Town Hall Rd, T741961. Basic, clean, rooms with TV (Rs 205), good value. **F** *KPS,* W Market St. Rooms (hot water), friendly, safe. **F** *Ruby Lodge,* 92W Perumal Maistry St, T543660. Basic, clean, good value, pleasant open-air

Sleeping
20% tax is added by even modest hotels. Auto-rickshaws (about Rs 50) from centre to hotels N of the river

Tamil Nadu & Chennai

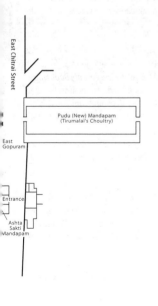

East Chitrai Street

Pudu (New) Mandapam
(Tirumalai's Choultry)

East
Gopuram

Entrance

Ashta
Sakti
Mandapam

7 Musical Pillars
8 Nandi Pavillion
9 Kalyan Mandapam

restaurant next door (limited menu at lunch). **F** *Sangam*, 20 Kakkathoppu St, T743235. Reasonable rooms with bath (Rs 140), hot water on demand, tall block. **F** *Youth Hostel*, MGR Stadium, Race Course, dorm (Rs 40-50).

Eating **Hotels Expensive**: *Park Plaza's**Temple View* rooftop is excellent. **Mid-range**: *Supreme*, a/c restaurant (1700-2400), Indian recommended (try Andhra *thali*), very busy on Sunday evenings, also *Surya*, 7th Flr rooftop (1700-2400) with good views. **Cheap**: *Tamil Nadu II* (*Star*), good, Indian/Chinese. **Outside hotels Cheap**: *Mahal* (a/c), *Amutham* and *Taj*, Town Hall Rd and W Veli St. Indian. Good value *thalis* (Rs 35), friendly. *Muniyandi Vilas*, at *Indo-Ceylon Restaurant*, and other outlets. Non-vegetarian. Try *paratha* and mutton curry. *British Bakery*, W Veli St. Burgers, delicious pizzas, excellent cakes (try apple pie, bread pudding). *Delhiwala Sweets*, W Tower St. Delicious Indian sweets and snacks.

Entertainment **Minakshi Temple**: 'Bed time of the God', 1930-1945, is not to be missed (see 'Sights' above). **Thirumalai Nayaka Palace**: **Sound and Light** show: English 1845-1930; Rs 5 (take mosquito repellent), sadly, "poor, faded tape"; during the day, dance drama and concerts are held in the courtyard. **Sports Yoga**: classes at Gandhi Museum, T481060, 0630, daily.

Festivals **January/February**: At Vandiyur Mariammam Teppakulam. The annual *Float Festival* marks the birth anniversary of Thirumalai Nayaka, who originated it. Many temple deities in silks and jewels, including Minakshi and Sundareswarar, are taken out on a full moon night on floats colourfully decorated with hundreds of oil lamps and flowers. The floats carry them to the central shrine to the accompaniment of music and chanting. The *Jallikattu Festival* (Taming the Bull) is held in January. **April/May**: *Chitrai Festival* The most important at the Minakshi Temple is the 10-day festival which celebrates the marriage of Siva and Minakshi. **August/September**: The *Avanimoolam* is the Coronation Festival of Siva when the image of Lord Sundareswarar is taken out to the river bank dressed as a worker.

Shopping Best buys are textiles, carvings in wood and stone, brass images, jewellery and appliqué work for temple chariots. Most shops are on South Avani Moola St (for jewellery), Town Hall Rd, Masi St and around the Temple. **Books**: *New Century Book House*, Town Hall Rd is recommended; *Higginbotham's Book Exchange* near the temple. **Handicrafts**: 2 good shops in North Chitrai St; *Handicrafts Emporium*, 39-41 Town Hall Rd; *Khadi Gramodoyog Bhandar* and *Surabhi* on W Veli St. **Textiles & Tailors**: market near Pudu Mandapam, next to Minakshi East Gate, sell fabric and is a brilliant place to get clothes made. *Hajee Moosa*, 18 E Chitrai St, tailoring in 8 hrs; 'ready-mades' at *Shabnam*, at No 17. *Femina*, 10 W Chitrai St, is similar (you can take photos of the Minakshi Temple from their rooftop).

Tour operators *Meraj*, 46B Perumal Koil South Mada St; *Siraj*, 19A TPK Rd (opposite Malai Murasu), T739666, F730608 mshersha@md4.vsnl.net.in ticketing, good multilingual guides, cars, internet; *Trade Wings*, 279 North Masi St, T730271. *Window to the World* 167A Vaigai St, Sri Nagar, Iyer Bungalow, T/F683132, Mr Pandian is very helpful, efficient, south India tours, car with excellent driver. Highly recommended.

Transport **Local Bus**: There is a good network within the city and the suburbs. **Taxi/car hire**: Unmetered; 10 hrs/225 km, Rs 450, Rs 675 (a/c); 6 hrs sightseeing, Rs 490 (Rs 750 a/c); 1 hr/10 km, Rs 65, Rs 100 (a/c). *Janakiraman*, 184 North Veli St; *Supreme*, 110 Perumal Maistry St, T743151. **Cycle-rickshaw**: can be persistent; offer about Rs 20 around town; **auto-rickshaw**, Rs 25, bargain first; very predatory.

Tamil Nadu & Chennai

Long distance Air: Airport to city centre (12 km) by Pandiyan coach (calls at top hotels); taxi (Rs 375) or auto-rickshaw (Rs 80). *Indian Airlines*, 7A W Veli St, T741234. 1000-1300, 1400-1700; Airport T670433. **Chennai, Kozhikode, Mumbai**. *Air India*, opposite Rly Station, W Veli St.

Road Bus: State and Private companies (MPTC, PRC) run services to other cities. There are 4 main bus stands. **Govt Express, Mofussil** and **Central (Periyar) Bus Stands**, near W Veli St. Enquiries, T25354, reservations 0700-2100. Rani Mungammal Transport, T33740. Buses for Bangalore (11 hrs), Ernakulam (Kochi), Chennai (10 hrs), Pondicherry (9 hrs), Thiruvananthapuram (8 hrs) etc. **Panagala Tham Pandal**, T43622. Buses to Kumbakonam, Rameswaram (4 hrs), Thanjavur (4 hrs), Tiruchirapalli (2½ hrs) and others. **Arapalayam Bus Stand**, 3 km northwest of centre (Bus route No 7A, auto-rickshaws Rs 20), T603740. Kodai buses leave from here (crowded in peak season, Apr-Jul); 3½ hrs (longer via Palani), Rs 150. Also buses to Bangalore, Coimbatore (5 hrs, change there for Mysore or Ooty), Periyar/Kumili (4 hrs), Salem (5½ hrs). **Palankatham Bus Stand**, 4 km southwest from centre (Bus Route No 7), T600935. Buses for Courtallam (4 hrs), Nagercoil, Tirunelveli, Tuticorin (4 hrs) and South Kerala. **Car** To Kodaikkanal Rs 950 (Rs 1600 a/c), see local transport above.

Train Madurai Junction is the main station: enquiries, T37597, reservations: 1st Class T23535, 2nd Class T33535. 0700-1300, 1330-2000. Foreigners, priority booking through Reservations Officer behind the main booking counters. Left luggage facilities. Pre-paid auto-rickshaw kiosk outside. **Chengalpattu**: *Chennai Exp, 6104*, 2140, 9 hrs; **Chennai** (ME) via Villupuram for **Pondicherry**: *Vaigai Exp, 2636* (AC/CC), 0625, 8½ hrs; *Madurai-Chennai Exp, 6104* (AC/II), 2030, 12 hrs, *Pandiyan, 6718*, 1915, 12 hrs; **Coimbatore**: *Fast Pass, 0776/8*, 0715/1435 (2nd Class only) 6 hrs; **Kollam**: connect

Tamil Nadu & Chennai

Madurai centre

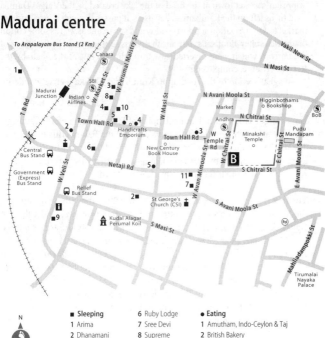

To Arapalayam Bus Stand (2 Km)

Canara Ⓢ

N Masi St

Vakil New St

Madurai Junction

Indian Airlines

SBI Ⓢ

W Market St

W Perumal Maistry St

T B Rd

Town Hall Rd

Handicrafts Emporium

New Century Book House

Netaji Rd

Central Bus Stand

Government (Express) Bus Stand

Relief Bus Stand

W Veli St

W Masi St

Town Hall Rd

Kudal Alagar Perumal Koil

St George's Church (CSI)

S Masi St

N Avani Moola St

Market

Andhra

Higginbothams Bookshop

N Chitrai St

N Chitrai St

Minakshi Temple

W Chitrai St

Temple Rd

W Avani Mimoola St

B

S Chitrai St

S Avani Moola St

Pudu Mandapam

E Chitrai St

E Avani Moola St

BoB Ⓢ

Mahadampokki St

Pol

Tirumalai Nayaka Palace

N

0 metres 200
0 yards 200

■ Sleeping		● Eating
1 Arima	6 Ruby Lodge	1 Amutham, Indo-Ceylon & Taj
2 Dhanamani	7 Sree Devi	2 British Bakery
3 Park Plaza	8 Supreme	3 Delhiwala Sweets
4 Prem Nivas	9 Tamil Nadu	4 Mahal
5 Ravi Towers	10 TM Lodge	5 New Arya Bhavan
	11 YMCA	

with trains from Virudhunagar (see page 180). **Kanniyakumari**: *Chennai-Kanniyakumari Exp, 6721,* 0340, 5½ hrs; **Ramesvaram**: *Coimbatore-Ramesvaram Exp, 6115,* 0600, 4½ hrs, *Pass, 761,* 1355, 5½ hrs; **Thiruvananthapuram**: see Virudhunagar on page 180. **Tiruchirapalli**: several, *Vaigai Exp, 2636,* 0645, 2½ hrs (beautiful countryside); *Pandyan Exp, 6718,* 1935, 3½ hrs.

Directory **Banks** Several on East Avani Moola St. *Andhra Bank*, W Chitral St, accepts credit cards; *Canara Bank* W Veli St, cash Amex and sterling TCs. *Alagendran Finance* 182D N Veli St, good rate for cash $ but not for TCs. **Communications Post office**: the town GPO is at the north end of W Veli St (Scott Rd). In Tallakulam: Head Post Office and Central Telegraph Office, on Gokhale Rd. **Couriers:** *DHL*, T25262. **Medical services** *Christian Mission Hospital*, East Veli St, T22458; *Govt Rajaji Hospital*, Panagal Rd, Goripalayam, T43231; *Grace Kennet Foundation Hospital*, 34 Kennet Rd. **Tourist offices** W Veli St, T34757, 1000-1745, Mon-Fri; useful maps, tours arranged through agents, guides for hire. Madurai Junction Rly Station, Main Hall, T33888, 0630-2030. Airport counter, during flight times.

Around Madurai

Tiruparan-
kunram
Population: 30,000

Almost on the outskirts, south of Madurai, are the Pandiyan rock cut shrines of the eighth century AD, and the much later Nayaka Hindu temple at Tiruparankunram, with a wide range of Hindu gods carved on the walls. The **Subrahmanya cave temple** (AD 773) has a shrine dedicated to Durga, with the figures of Ganesh and Subrahmanya on either side. Other carvings show Siva dancing on the dwarf on the right hand side and Parvati and the *Nandi* with musicians on the left.

Usilampatti &
the Kambam
Valley
Colour map 3, grid B4
Population: 26,400

Usilampatti, west of Madurai, is the starting point of the road up the Kambam Valley to Thekkadi skirting the north end of the Andipatti Hills. At Teni, an important market town at the head of the lake created by the **Vaigai Dam**, a road turns left up the Kambam Valley itself. It passes through a succession of market towns. Irrigation supports paddy and sugarcane as well as some cotton on the rich valley-floor soils. The Suruli River is supplemented by the waters of the Periyar, which were diverted east through the crest of the ghats by the **Periyar scheme**, completed in 1897.

The ghat section of the road up to Kumili and Thekkadi gives wonderful views (see page 262).

Dindigul
திண்டுக்கல்
Phone code: 0451
Colour map 3, grid B4
Population: 182,300
Altitude: 300 m

Now a large market town, Dindigul, north of Madurai, commands a strategic gap between the **Sirumalai Hills** to its east and the **Palani Hills** to the west. The market handles the produce of the Sirumalai Hills, mainly fruit, including a renowned local variety of banana. Dindigul is particularly known for its cheroots. Iron safes and locks are also made in the town.

The fort The massive granite rock towers over 90 m above the plain, offering the Nayakas a vital position to control their western province. Under the first Nayaka kings the near vertical sides were fortified. The Mysore army captured it in 1745 and Haidar Ali was appointed Governor in 1755. He used it as the base from which to capture Madurai itself, and is reputed to have disposed of the prisoners he took by throwing them over the side of the cliff. It was ceded to the British under the Treaty of Seringapatam. There are magnificent views of the town, the valley and the hills on either side from the top of the rock fort. **Our Lady of Dolours Church**, one of several churches in the town, is over 250 years old and was rebuilt in 1970.

Eating Several tea shops and small restaurants near the bus stand include *Cascade Roof Garden* at *Sree Ariya Bhavan*, 19 KHF Building, which serves very good vegetarian.

Transport **Road** **Bus**: good and frequent bus service to Tiruchirappalli, Chennai, Salem and Coimbatore as well as longer distance connections. **Train** **Chennai (ME)**: *Vaigai Exp, 2636* (AC/CC), 0745, 6½ hrs via **Tiruchirappalli**, 1½ hrs; **Madurai**: *Vaigai Exp, 2635* (AC/CC), 1912, 1 hr. Now broad gauge to **Karur**, 2240, 1½ hrs.

★ Kodaikkanal கொடைக்கானல் and the Palani Hills

The climb up the Palanis is 47 km before Kodaikkanal (Kodai) and is one of the most rapid ascents anywhere across the ghats. The views are stunning. In the lower reaches of the climb you look down over the Kambam Valley, the Vaigai Lake and across to the Varushanad Hills beyond. The road twists and winds up through rapidly changing vegetation, but generally wooded slopes to Kodai. Set high in the Palani Hills around a small artificial lake, the town has crisply fresh air even at the height of summer and the beautiful scent of pine and eucalyptus, making it a popular retreat from the southern plains. Today Kodai is a fast growing resort centre.

Phone code: 04542
Colour map 3, grid B4
Population: 27,500
Altitude: 2,343 m

Tamil Nadu & Chennai

Getting there Buses make the long climb from Madurai and other cities to the central bus stand, which is within easy walking distance from most hotels. The nearest station is Kodai Rd. **Getting around** Kodai is small enough to walk around, though for some of the sights it is worth getting an unmetered taxi. **Climate** Best time to visit is late Sep-early Oct. Apr-Jun are high season, avoid May when it is crowded and expensive. The mist can come down any time of the year, especially in the afternoon.

Ins & outs

The lake, created in 1910 by the building of a dam just below the International School (established in 1901), acts as a focus for the town. The 5 km walk around its perimeter gives beautiful and contrasting views across the water and into the surrounding woods.

Background
Kodai is the hill station to visit rather than Ooty

The **Palani Hills** were first surveyed by British administrators in 1821, but the surveyor's report was not published until 1837 – 10 years after Ooty had become the official 'sanitorium' for the British in South India. A proposal to build a sanitorium was made in 1861-2 by Colonel Hamilton, who noted the extremely healthy climate and the lack of disease. Despite the warmth of that recommendation the sanitorium was never built because the site was so difficult to get to. It was the freedom from malaria that was the greatest incentive to opening a hill station there. The American Mission in Madurai, established in 1834, had lost six of their early missionaries within a decade. It looked as if the Sirumalai Hills, at around 1,300 m, might provide a respite from the plains, but it was soon discovered that they were not high enough to eliminate malaria. The first two bungalows were built by June 1845.

The early route was extraordinarily difficult. For 5 km of zig-zag on the steepest section the path was less than 1 m wide, and the average width was only 2 m for the whole journey. Despite the obstacles, the permanent population had reached over 600 by 1883. Seven years later it stood at 1,743. These changes had come about partly because Europeans began to spend their long periods of leave in Kodai, and some civil servants and missionaries retired there rather than to

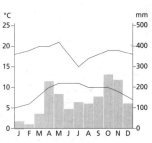

Climate:
Kodaikkanal

Europe. The most influential was Sir Vere Henry Levinge, and in the words of the American geographer Nora Mitchell "it was acclaimed by Europeans and Americans alike that most of the improvements in Kodaikkanal were due to his interest and generosity. He constructed the bund which dammed the stream to form Kodai lake, stocked the lake with fish, and brought up the first boat from Tuticorin. His experiments with foreign varieties of trees, fruits, and flowers have had enduring results as eucalyptus, wattle, and pines are now grown extensively by the forestry department, and pears have become an important export from the hill station. Many of the vegetables he tried are planted today in large quantities in Kodaikkanal and the surrounding villages".

The major transformation came at the turn of the 20th century with the arrival of the car and the bus. The Raja of Pudukkottai (see page 130) had a French car in 1904, but could not use it to get to Kodai because of the lack of a road. Although a new road had been started in 1876, along the line of the present road from Vattalkundu, it was left incomplete because of shortage of funds resulting from the Afghan War in 1876. In 1905 the Trichinopoly Bus Company set up a bus service to Periyakulam, making it possible to do the whole journey from Kodai Road station to Kodai within the hours of daylight. The present road, up 'Law's Ghat' was opened to traffic in 1916.

Sights **Kodaikkanal Lake** covers 24 ha in a star shape surrounded by wooded slopes. The attractive walk around the lake takes between 1 and 1½ hrs. Boating is popular and fishing with permission. The lake, however, is polluted. The view over the plains from **Coaker's Walk** (built by Lieutenant Coaker in the 1870s) is magnificent; on a clear day you can see Madurai. It is reached from a signposted path just above the bazar, 1 km from the Bus Stand.

Kodaikkanal

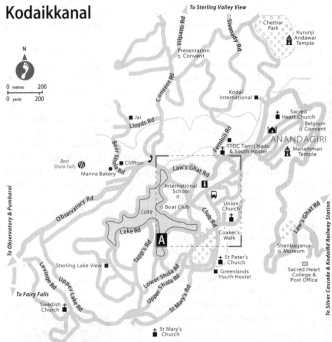

Related maps
A Kodaikkanal centre,
page 173

Kurinji Andavar Temple Northeast of the town, past Chettiar Park, is dedicated to Murugan associated with the *kurinji* flower (*Strobilanthes kunthianus*) that blossoms once in 12 years. There are excellent views of the north and southern plains, including Palani and Vagai Dams. **St Peter's Church** (CSI) built in 1884, has a stained glass window dedicated to Bishop Caldwell. **The International School** has a commanding position on the lakeside, and provides education for children between the ages of 5 and 18 from India and abroad. There is also the Highclere School for Girls and the Bhavan's Gandhi Vidyasram School, founded in 1983, located on the way to Pillar Rocks.

Bear Shola Falls, named because it once attracted bears, is a favourite picnic spot about 2 km from the Bus Stand. These falls and others around Kodai have been reduced to a trickle. **Solar Physical Observatory**, 4 km to the west from the Bus Stand, T40588, was established in 1899 at a height of 2,347 m. ■ *It is open to visitors during the season, 1000-1230, 1900-2100; 1000-1200, Fri.* **Pillar Rocks**, 7 km from the lake, is another striking viewpoint. There are three granite formations over 120 m high. There are over 100 *dolmens* and other megalithic remains that have been discovered in the Palanis, all datable to around the second century AD.

Shenbaganur Museum, the local flora and fauna museum (including 300 orchid species) at the Sacred Heart College, a theological seminary founded in 1895. Small but interesting. It also has some archaeological remains. ■ *1000-1130, 1500-1700. Attractive walk downhill from the town passing waterfalls.*

Museums

Chettiar Park is in the northeast of the town on the way to the Kurinji Andavar Temple. **Bryant Park** on the lakeside is where the annual horticultural show is held in May.

Parks & zoos

Berijam Lake A road runs west past the golf course and Pillar Rocks to Berijam Lake (15 km) which has beautiful views over the lake before running down to it (apply to the District Forest Officer in Kodai). It is better to go to the far end of this lake. A short walk up a shola about 300 m short of the barrier enables you to see and hear a large number of birds and large Malabar squirrels. Those interested in wildlife and trekking in the shola can spend idyllic days at *Bison Wells*, a log hut on the edge of the Kookal Reserve Forest, 25 km from Kodai. Simple accommodation for three, good food, no electricity. Contact George Roshan, a keen conservationist, at 'Camp George', Observatory, Kodaikkanal 624103, T40566, bisonwells@tamilnadumail.com in advance. Apart from timber lorries the road is little used.

Excursions

The road to **Munnar**, one of the most attractive routes in the whole of South India, had been made virtually impassable to cars by the heavy traffic of the timber lorries. A four-wheel drive vehicle was often necessary for the uncomfortable trip across the highest road in peninsular India. At present a concrete barrier at Top Slip has stopped through traffic but the closure has been challenged in the courts.

Trek to Munnar You can walk to Berijam in about four hours and stay at the *Forest Rest House* which is adequate but could be cleaner (Rs 50, but no receipt!). There is a restaurant but no store here. You can continue the next day, by a short cut to **Top Station** (Kerala) in five to six hours, where there is *Forest Hut* and shops and tea stalls selling snacks. There are buses to Munnar (41 km). Contact the Forestry Office, Kodaikkanal for accommodation.

Tamil Nadu & Chennai

Essentials

Sleeping From Apr-Jun prices rocket; 20% tax and service charges can add considerably to the basic price. Most offer good discounts (Jul-Sep, mid-Jan to end-Mar). The majority have a restaurant and rooms with bath down to **D** category; only a few have single rooms. The more expensive hotels are some distance from the centre.

AL-A *Carlton*, Boat Club Rd, T40056, F41170. 90 rooms, fully modernized colonial style hotel, excellent restaurant (try buffet lunch), tennis, golf and boating, superb position on lake, often full in season. **A-B** *Lake View* (Sterling), 44 Gymkhana Rd, T40313. Cottages, modern hotel/apartment complex. **B** *Valley View* (Sterling), Pallangi Rd, Vilpatti, T40635. 39 modern rooms but most without valley view, half-board in season, bit overpriced. **C** *Bala*, 11/49 Woodville Rd (opposite bus station), T41214, F41252, hotelbalakodai@gems.vsnl.net.in. Classy, new, 57 rooms, entrance tucked away in private courtyard. **C** *Kodai International*, Laws Ghat Rd, T40649, F40753. 55 rooms, with bath. **C-D** *Garden Manor*, Lake Rd (10 minute walk from bus), T40461. 7 rooms (including a 4-bed) with sit-out, restaurant (also tables outdoors), good location in pleasant gardens overlooking lake. **C-D** *JS Heritage*, PT Rd, T41323, F40693. 14 clean, comfortably furnished rooms, quiet, friendly and helpful management. **C-D** *Hilltop Towers*, Club Rd, T40413, F40415. 26 modern comfortable rooms, can be noisy but very friendly management, good restaurant. **C-D** *Paradise Inn*, Laws Ghat Rd, T41075, F41024. 40 comfortable rooms with bath, cheaper rooms as good as deluxe.

D *Astoria*, Anna Salai opposite Bus Stand, T40524, astkodai@md4.vsnl.net.in 27 "cramped, stale-smelling", back rooms better furnished (no views), good South Indian vegetarian restaurant downstairs, busy and lively. **D** *Cliffton*, Bear Shola Rd, T40408. 55 large rooms though a bit tatty, many face away from scenic view, quiet location but nothing special, ordinary rooms (no TV) are better value. **D** *Green Acres*, 11/213 Lake Rd. T42384, F43813. Well appointed, clean rooms in pleasant colonial style home, quiet, peaceful. **D** *Jewel*, 7 Rd Junction, T41029. 8 clean well-maintained rooms, 24-hour hot water, good value but on noisy junction. **D** *Tamil Nadu* (TTDC), Fern Hill Rd, T41336, F41340. 15 minutes' walk from Bus Station (away from most interesting walks), restaurant and bar. **D-E** *Anjay*, Anna Salai, T41089, 24 rooms, popular, and **D-E** *Jaya*, behind, T41062, 18 rooms, under same management.

E *Sangeeth*, opposite Bus Stand, T40456. 20 small, very clean rooms with little balconies (hot water), buses silent at night. **E** *Sunrise*, PO Rd. Basic, but clean rooms with bath, front rooms best with excellent views. **E** *Taj Lodge*, Coaker's Walk near the centre has simple rooms in an old building, rustic but popular. On **Anna Salai**: cheap basic lodges, mostly with shared bathroom can charge up to Rs 400 in season depending on demand. Best of these is **E** *Kay Pee Yem Lodge*, T40555 with 16 rooms. *International Tourist Lodge* has rooms with bath.

Youth hostels: **F** *Greenlands Youth Hostel*, St Mary's Rd, Coaker's Walk end, T40899. Very basic rooms, Rs 40 (Rs 50 for non-members) but superb views, pleasant gardens, good dorm and 2 rooms with bath, clean, friendly, walks. **F** *Youth Hostel* (TTDC), Fern Hill Rd, T41336, F41340. Dorm bed (Rs 30-45), reservations: Manager, or Chennai, T830390.

Eating **Expensive** Hotels: *Carlton*, set in very pleasant grounds overlooking lake and Garden Manor. *Tawa*, Hospital Rd, very good Indian. **Mid-range** *Big Belly (formerly JJ's)*, Hospital Rd. For average vegetarian fast food. *Royal Tibet*, J's Heritage Complex, "try noodle soup and beef momos". *Silver Inn*, Hospital Rd. Tamil Nadu (Indian) are recommended. *Tibetan Brothers*, J's Heritage Complex. 1200-2200 (closed 1600-1730) serves excellent Tibetan (vegetarian and non-vegetarian), homely atmosphere, good value. Highly recommended. **Cheap** *Apna Punjab* in 7 Rd (Indian). **Bakery and fast food** *Jacob*, Main Bazar. Vasu, Lake Rd near Telephone Exchange. *Tiny Manna Bakery* on Bear Shola Rd, also serves pizzas and Western vegetarian. *Pastry Corner Anna Salai Bazar* has brown bread and some pastries. The shop next door sells Manna bread. At J's Heritage Complex: *Eco-Nut* good whole foods, brown bread, jams, peanut butter etc (cheese, yoghurts, better and cheaper in *Dairy* across the road). *Hot Breads* for very good pastries. *Philco's Cold Storage*, opposite Kodai International School, for confectionery, cakes, frozen foods, delicatessen. *Kwality Ice Creams*, opposite Kodai International School.

Boating *Boat Club*, T41315, allows daily membership with club facilities. Also from *TTDC boathouse* next door. Both open 0900-1730, similar rates. **Golf** Club, T40323. **Riding** ponies near the Boat House; officially Rs 100 per hour, doubled to include 'guide' (bargaining essential).

Sports

Tamil Nadu & Chennai

Kodaikkanal centre

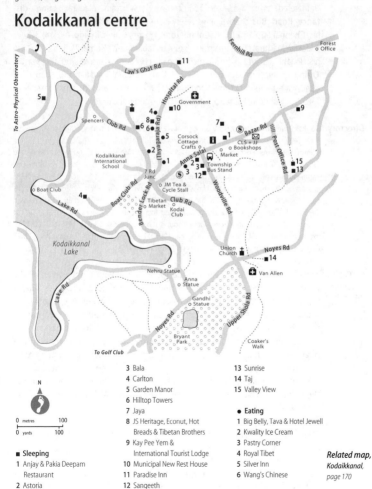

Festivals May: *Summer Tourist Festival*: Boat race, flower show, dog show etc.

Shopping For general toiletries and food, Anna Salai Bazar Rd, near Pastry Corner. The town market, off the bazar, has excellent vegetables. **Books**: *CLS and JJ*, Anna Salai. **Handicrafts**: *Kashmir Handicrafts Centre*, 2 North Shopping Complex, Anna Salai. For shawls, jewellery, brass, walnutwood crafts and 'Numdah' rugs. *Khadi Emporium, Handloom Co-op, Travancore Craft Works*, Post Office Rd. *Govt Sales Emporium* near Township Bus Stand. Only open in season. *Cottage Crafts Shop*, Anna Salai (Council for Social Concerns in Kodai). Volunteer-run, 0900-1230, 1400-1830, Mon-Sat. *Belgian Convent* shop, east of town. Has hand embroidered linen.

Tour operators *Vijay Tours*, near Tourist Information Centre, Anna Salai, T41137, local sights, Rs 70-80 per person. *Sugam*, PO Rd, Upper Coonor, Railway Out Agency.

Transport **Local Bicycle**: can be hired at the top of the Bazar. *JM Tea shop* and cycle hire, at Junction of Club Rd and Anna Salai, good bikes Rs 5 per hr, Rs 50 per day. **Taxi**: Unmetered taxis available. Tourist taxis only from Madurai. **Long distance Road Bus**: check timings; reservations possible. To **Bangalore**, overnight, 12 hrs; **Chennai** (497 km) 12 hrs, **Coimbatore** (171 km) 6 hrs; **Dindigul** (90 km) 3½ hrs, Kodai Rd, **Madurai** (120 km), 0730-1830, 4 hrs, about Rs 25; **Kumili** (Periyar), 1400, 5½ hrs; **Palani** (65 km) 3 hrs; **Tiruchirappalli** (197 km) 5 hrs, during the season. **Train**: Reservations, Jayaraj Hall, Coaker's Walk Rd. **Kodai Road** (04543), 80 km away, is the nearest station. **D** *Tamil Nadu Hotel* (TTDC), 5 mins walk, turn right from station, T38372, overpriced; **F** *Railway Station*, cheap rooms and dorm.

Directory **Banks** *State Bank of India*, Bazar Rd, is painfully slow at changing money; others on Anna Salai, 1000-1400 Mon to Fri, 1000-1200 Sat. *Hotel Tamil Nadu* has an exchange counter. **Communications** **Post office**: Head Post Office on Post Office Rd (parcel post more expensive to 'UK' than to 'Great Britain'!). Others in Main Bazar, Observatory, Lake View, Anantha Giri, Pambapuram and Shenbaganur. **Telephone**: you can make STD calls from the Telephone Exchange, the Boat Club and kiosks. **Medical services** *Van Allan Hospital*, T41273, is recommended. Consultations (non-emergency): 0930-1200, 1530-1630 Mon-Fri. 1000-1200 Sat. Clean and efficient, good doctors (not inclined to prescribe antibiotics unnecessarily). *Govt Hospital*, T41292. **Tourist offices** *Tamil Nadu*, *Rest House*, near Bus Stand, T41675. 1000-1745, except holidays. Helpful staff, maps available. Map of treks available from Forestry Office, Law's Ghat Rd, is useless but they issue permits for Berijam Lake.

Palani
பழனி
Phone code: 04545
Colour map 3, grid B4
Population: 76,000

A highly picturesque route from Udumalpettai to Kochi goes via Munnar, Perumbavur & Aluva

The ghat road to Palani, built in the 1970s in part with money given by the Palani Temple Fund (*devasthanam*), is not heavily used, and gives superb views of the lower Palani Hills. It passes through coffee, orange and banana smallholdings. Interplanting of crops such as pepper is further increasing the yields from what can be highly productive land, even on steep slopes.

The hilltop shrine to **Murugan** (Subrahmanya) is a very important site of pilgrimage. At full moon in January to February pilgrims walk from up to 80 km around and climb the 659 steps up to the shrine. Many carry shoulder-poles with elaborate bamboo or wooden structures on each end, living out the myth which surrounds the origin of the shrine. ■ *Getting there: Buses to Kodai and Madurai (3 hrs)*.

Sleeping D-E *Ganpat Palani*, 103 Poonga Rd, Adivaram, T42294. 48 rooms, some a/c. **D-E** *New Tirupur*, Adivaram, T42303. 88 rooms, some deluxe a/c, a/c vegetarian restaurant. **F** *Modern Home*, Railway Station Rd, T42297. Basic rooms. **Udumalpettai** has **D** *Anamalais Hotel* on 168 Palani Rd, T04252-23569, F24167, with some a/c rooms and bar and pool planned; **F** *Kurinchi Lodge*, opposite Bus Stand, 119 Palani Rd, T24353 has basic rooms with water in buckets.

Pollachi has been an important trading centre for over 2,000 years, as is witnessed by the finds of Roman silver coins bearing the heads of the Emperors Augustus and Tiberias. Today it still occupies an important position on the route from east to west through the Palakkad Gap. It is also the gateway to the small but very attractive sanctuary. **Sleeping**: *Mani's*, T4551, very basic and noisy (opposite truck station).

Pollachi
Phone code: 04259
Population: 127,200
61 km from Madurai

Sheltered by the Neelampathi Ranges on its west and by dense forests, access to the sanctuary is only by public bus. Entry only between 0700 and 1900. The journey traverses the thin scrub of the lowland through bamboo groves around Sethumadai and moist deciduous forests near the reserve itself. Parambikulam itself has rich tropical rain forest. The reserve is particularly rich in birdlife, but also has one of the earliest managed teak forests in the world, going back to 1845. Some of the trees are reputed to be over 400 years old. The sanctuary contains three dams, and the dammed waters are home to a variety of endangered species, including crocodiles, otters and turtles.

Parambikulam Sanctuary
If trekking, beware of leeches

The park (1,400 m), near Pollachi, covers an area of 960 sq km in the western ghats.It is a beautiful, unspoilt forest, rarely visited, except Indian day-trippers. The Reception and Information Centre is at Top Slip. Written permission is needed from District Forest Officer, Pollachi, T25356 (1.5 km out of town on road towards Top Slip).

Anamalai (Indira Gandhi) National Park

Wildlife includes Nilgiri langur, lion-tailed macaque, elephant, *gaur*, tiger, panther, sloth, wild boar, birds (including pied hornbill, drongo, red whiskered *bulbul*, black-headed oriole) and a large number of crocodiles in the Amaravathi reservoir. There is an elephant camp reached by a minibus ride through the forest, but rides can be disappointing.

Viewing Forest Dept vans (for 8), Rs 80. Restricted zone viewing, 0630-1900, 1700-1830. Birdwatching from Kariam Shola watch tower, 2 km from Topslip.

Trekking Routes vary from easy treks to Pandaravara (8 km), Kozhikamuthi (12 km) to Perunkundru peak (32 km) which is demanding. Permits from Range Officer, Topslip. Private guides charge Rs 50 for two.

■ *Open round the year. Best time to visit: Dec-Jun. 0630-1830. Avoid Sun.*

Sleeping and eating F *Forest Rest Houses* at Top Slip, Mt Stuart, Varagaliar, Sethumadai and Amaravathinagar. May only allow 1 night stay. Reservations: District Forest Officer, Coimbatore S Div, Mahalingam Nagar, Pollachi, T04259-2508. The friendly canteen serves good *dosa* and *thalis* for lunch.

Transport Buses from chaotic bus station at Pollachi (for Parambikulam) 0600, 1130, 1500 (check timings); ask for Top Slip, from Perambikulam, 0700, 1300.

To Ramesvaram and Adam's Bridge

Seen from the air the plains of the Vaigai River form one of the most remarkable landscapes in India, for there are over 5,000 tanks, and irrigation has been so widely developed that scarcely a drop of water is wasted. The coastal districts of Ramnad have their own highly distinct economy and society. For the Hindus the sand banks barely concealed in the Palk straights are like giant stepping stones linking India and Sri Lanka, Adam's Bridge. Both Hindu and Muslim communities have long established trading links across the Bay of Bengal – to Malaysia and Southeast Asia and to Sri Lanka. Small towns and villages along the coast such as Kilakkarai have long been associated with smuggling. The civil war in Sri Lanka has made it a sensitive region.

Tamil Nadu & Chennai

Manamadurai
மானாமதுரை
Colour map 3, grid B4
Population: 22,800
45 km

In the **Perumal Temple** Hanuman is enshrined, with the highly unusual feature of a crown on his head, reflecting the local belief that Hanuman was crowned here before leaving for Lanka. According to one account the name of the town is derived from this visit, which in Tamil is described as *Vanara Veera Madurai*, which has been corrupted to become Manamadurai. The crowned Hanuman is enshrined near the entrance of the Vaishnavite Veera Alagar Koil temple on the east bank of the river.

**Ramanatha-
puram**
இராமநாதபுரம்
Phone code: 04567
Colour map 3, grid B5
Population: 52,600
Altitude: 10 m

Ramanathapuram (Ramnad) is now a bustling market town, with shops, restaurants and cinema. The monsoon can cause large areas in town to flood in November-December. The Police Station is very helpful; good English spoken.

Between 1674 and 1710 Raghunatha Setupati built a **fort** of brick and stone nearly 2 km west of the present town. Only the high stone walls and an ornamental gate are still visible. The **Ramalinga Palace** to its north end is open to visitors where the main hall and public rooms are covered with interesting 18th century murals illustrating the epics together with battle scenes fought with the British, who the Setupatis once sided with. The upper chambers display more private royal scenes. The frescoes are being restored over 5 years. **Christ Church** (now CSI) was built by Colonel Martinez, a French Catholic army officer, but handed over and dedicated as a Protestant Church in 1804 under the governorship of Lord William Bentinck.

Sleeping **E** *Velumanickam Lodge* near Police Station has good sized rooms (some a/c) with sofa and armchair, clean, good service. **F** *Traveller's Bungalow* fairly comfortable, 3 rooms. *Aiswaryaa*, Madurai Rd, does good vegetarian meals; also has general stores and a reasonable bakery.

Kilakkarai
கீழக்கரை
Colour map 3, grid B5
Population: 29,800

Meaning simply 'east coast', Kilakkarai's shoreline has been emerging steadily from the sea. The uplift is responsible for converting the living coral into solid rock, and made the link between Ramesvaram and Pamban Island. The majority of the population is Muslim and there are 12 mosques in the town as well as a 16th-century temple dedicated to Siva, and a number of other temples. From 1759 the Setupati chiefs gave the Dutch East India Company permission to trade, and in the following decade the Dutch built a fortified settlement.

The town is particularly famous for its Muslim **pearl divers**. Many are jewel traders, one of the major specialities being the cutting and polishing of chank shells.

Mandapam
Phone code: 04573
Colour map 3, grid B5
Population: 20,400

Mandapam is predominantly a Muslim fishing village, the long Ramesvaram island providing sheltered fishing even during the strong northeast monsoon. The main catch is silverbelly, a non-edible variety of fish converted into fish meal. To the south lie a chain of small coral islands, one of the few coral areas of India. **Kurusadai Islands** west of the Pamban bridge, between the mainland and Ramesvaram, can be reached via Mandapam. They are surrounded by coral reefs and the shallow waters harbour a wealth of marine life of interest to scientists – starfish, crabs, sponges, sea cucumbers, algae and sea cow. Approach the Fisheries Dept for permission to visit.

Central Marine Fisheries Research Institute (CMFRI) has a **museum** and aquarium at Mandapam, which includes seaweeds, corals, sponges, fishes and a pair of live sea cows (*dugongs*). **Sleeping** **E** *Tamil Nadu* (TTDC), T41512, rooms in cottage, dorm bed (Rs 45).

★ Ramesvaram இராமேஸ்வரம்

Ramesvaram normally lapped by waters that are usually a limpid blue, but which can be whipped by cyclones into ferocious storm waves. This is where Rama is believed to have worshipped Siva, and so, a pilgrim to Varanasi is expected to visit Ramesvaram next.

Phone code: 04573
Colour map 3, grid B5
Population: 32,700

Getting there Ramesvaram is connected to Madurai and other centres by regular bus and train services. The bus stand is 2 km from the centre, the railway station 1 km further in and about 1 km southwest of the great temple. **Getting around** Local buses go to the temple where there are a few places to stay.

Ins & outs

The *Ramayana* tells how the monkey king Hanuman built the bridges linking Ramnad to Pamban and Danushkodi (a spot where Rama is believed to have bathed) in order to help rescue Sita from the demon king Ravana. When he returned he was told by the *rishis* that he must purify himself after committing the sin of murdering a Brahmin, for *Ravana* was the son of a Brahmin. To do this he was advised to set up a lingam and worship Siva. The red image of Hanuman north of the main East Gate illustrates this story.

Background

The original shrine long predates the present great Ramesvaram temple. It is one of India's most sacred shrines, being visited by pilgrims from all over India. The temple benefited from enormous donations from the 17th-century *Setupatis* ('guardians of the causeway'), who derived their wealth from the right to levy taxes on crossing to the island. The temple stands on slightly higher ground, surrounded by a freshwater lake.

The **Ramalingesvara (or Ramanathasvami) Temple** was founded by the Cholas but most of the temple was built in the Nayaka period (16th-17th centuries). It is a massive structure, enclosed by a huge rectangular wall with *gopurams* in the middle of three sides. Entrances through the east wall are approached through columned mandapas and the east *gopuram* is on the wall of the inner enclosure rather than the outer wall. Over 45 m high, it was begun in 1640 but left incomplete until recently. The west *gopuram* is comparatively new. In contrast the north and south *gopurams* were built by Keerana Rayar of the Deccan in about AD 1420.

Sights

The most remarkable feature of the temple is its pillared *mandapas*. The longest corridor is over 200 m long. The pillars, nearly 4 m tall, are raised on moulded bases and the shafts decorated with scrollwork and lotus motifs. They give an impression of almost unending perspective, those on the north and south being particularly striking. There are two gateways on the east side which give access to the Parvati and Ramalinga shrines at the centre. The masonry shrine is probably the oldest building on the site, going back to 1173.

On entering the East Gate you see the statue of Hanuman, then the *Nandi* flanked by statues of the Nayaka kings of Madurai, *Visvanatha* and *Krishnama*. The *Sphatikalinga Puja* is performed daily at 0500. Worshippers take a holy bath in the sea in a very calm bay 25 km away, where the waters are believed to wash away their sins. Fishermen occasionally offer to take visitors for a boat ride.

NB Non-Hindus are not allowed beyond the first enclosure. The temple is very commercialized and temple priests aggressively demand donations.

Gandhamadana Parvatam, just over 2 km north of Ramesvaram takes its name from the Sanskrit words *gandha* (fragrance) and *mad* (intoxicate), 'highly fragrant hill'. Dedicated to Rama's feet, this is the spot from which

Tamil Nadu & Chennai

Hanuman is believed to have surveyed the area before taking his leap across the narrow Palk strait to Sri Lanka. You can get an excellent view from the top of the mandapa.

Dhanuskodi, at the tip of the peninsula 20 km to the east of Ramesvaram island, is considered particularly holy. There is a good beach and excellent views. A trip is only recommended for the really hardy – get a local person to accompany. Travel by bus, and then join a pilgrim group on a jeep or lorry for the last desolate few miles.

Sleeping **D-E** *Hotel Tamil Nadu* (TTDC), 14 East Car St, T21277, F21070. 18 rooms (2-6 beds), some a/c, clean with sea-facing balconies, restaurant, bar, sea bathing possible nearby (when calm), exchange; **F** 6-bed dorm (Rs 30); book both well in advance. **D-E** *Maharaja*, 7 Middle St, W of the Temple, T21271, F21247. 30 rooms, some a/c with bath, exchange, temple music broadcast on loudspeakers, otherwise recommended. **D-E** *Venkatesh*, W Car St, T21296. Some a/c rooms, modern. **F** *Swami Ramanatha Tourist Home*, between station and temple, opposite Museum, T21217. Good clean rooms with bath, best budget option. **F** *Railway Retiring Rooms*, T21226, 9 rooms and dorm.

Eating The *Devasthanam Trust* has a canteen opposite the East Gate of the temple. For Indian vegetarian including Gujarati, try *Ashok Bhawan* and *Vasantha Vihar* on W Car St and also at the Central Bus Stand.

Ramesvaram

To Gandhamadhana Parvatham (2 km)

Palk Bay

■ **Sleeping**
1 Maharaja
2 Santhya Lodge
3 Swami Ramanatha
  Tourist Home
4 Tamil Nadu
5 Venkatesh

● **Eating**
1 Ashok Bhawan &
  Vasantha Vihar
2 Devasthanam
  Trust & Cycle Hire

🛕 **Temple**
1 Ramalingesvara

Khadi Kraft, East Car St, close to the temple; *Cottage Industries* Middle St. **Shopping**

Local Bus: Marudhu Pandiyan Transport Corporation (MPTC) covers the town and **Transport** the area around. The Bus Station is 2 km W of the town. You can get a bus from the Rly Station to the Ramalingesvara Temple, to Pamban or to Dhanuskodi (both via the temple). From the temple's east gate to Dhanuskodi roadhead and to Gandhamadana Parvatam, both about every 2 hrs. **Taxi**: a few cars and jeeps are available from the Rly Station and hotels. **Cycle-rickshaw** and **auto-rickshaw** are easily available. You can hire a **bicycle** by the hr from West Car or East Car St.

Long distance Air: Madurai (154 km) has the nearest airport. **Road Bus**: State, MPTC and private bus companies run regular services via Mandapam to several towns nearby. The Central Bus Stand is 2 km from the main temple gate. Govt Express Bus Reservations, North Car St. 0700-2100. Frequent buses to Madurai, 173 km (4½ hrs); Tourist coach (hotel-to-hotel) is better. Daily buses to Pondicherry (12 hrs), Thanjavur, Kanniyakumari 300 km (9 hrs), Chennai 592 km (13 hrs), Ramanathapuram 37 km (1½ hrs), Tiruchendur 205 km, Tiruchirappalli, 258 km (3½ hrs). **Train**: Ramesvaram Rly Station, Enquiries and Reservations, T226. Open 0800-1300, 1330-1730. **Chennai**: *Sethu Exp*, 6114, 1550, 14½ hrs via **Chengalpattu**, 13 hrs; **Coimbatore**: *Coimbatore Fast Pass*, 6116, 1620, 11½ hrs; **Madurai**: *Coimbatore Fast Pass*, 6116, 1620, 5½ hrs; **Tiruchirappalli**: *Ramesvaram Exp*, 6102, 1240, 6½ hrs.

Banks Exchange may prove difficult. **Communications Post offices**: east of temple near Police **Directory** Station and on Mela St towards Bus Station. 0930-1730. **Medical services** *Govt Hospital* near the Rly Station, T21233. *Chemists* in Varthagan St. **Tourist offices** At 14 East Car St, T21371. 1000-1700. Rly Station, T21373, open (with breaks) 0700-2030. *Temple Information*, east side of the temple.

The Cardamom Hills

To the south of Madurai is a series of modest towns in the lee of the southern ranges of the Western Ghats. It is a comfortable day's drive from Madurai to Thiruvanathapuram, either via Tirunelveli or over the ghats, but there are several interesting places on the way if you wish to take your time.

One of 108 sacred Vaishnavite sites, the *gopuram* of the ★ **Vishnu Srivilliputtur Vadabadrasaikoil** in Srivilliputtur towers nearly 60 m. Built of wood, brick நாகர்கோவில் and plaster it comprises 13 storeys excluding the roof. The superstructure is, in *Phone code: 04568* the words of Percy Brown, an "excessively tall composition resembling a hall *Colour map 3, grid B4* with a chaitya roof, elaborately ornamented with a great *suraj mukh* ('sun *Population: 68,500* face') above its gable end and a row of huge pinnacles along its ridge". It has a slightly concave curvature, emphasizing its grace while lessening the feeling of power and strength. There have been increasing signs of stress. By the early 1970s 25 cracks had opened up from the foundations to varying heights. The whole tower is supported on foundations that go no deeper than 2.3 m. The temple car built over 100 years ago takes 3,000 people to pull it.

Sivakasi, 19 km southeast of Srivilliputtur, is famous for modern industries such **Sivakasi** as litho printing, but it is also notorious for the extensive use of child labour in its *Colour map 3, grid B4* match and firework factories. There are over 70 fireworks factories in the town, *Population: 102,100* and most of the *firecrackers* used in India are produced here.

The town originated on the dispersal of the Vijayanagar families after 1565, see **Rajapalayam** page 291. The Western Ghats rise to heights of over 1,200 m immediately behind *Phone code: 04563* the town. Wild elephants still come down through the forests, devastating *Colour map 3, grid B4* farmland. *Population: 114,000*

Tamil Nadu & Chennai

Sleeping and eating F *Bombay Lodge*, 885 Tenkasi Rd, 300 m left out of bus station, T20907. Very clean rooms with Western toilet (cold water), **E** a/c rooms, Indian style, very well run, excellent Indian vegetarian restaurant, good value. Highly recommended.

Transport **Bus**: to Sankaracoil, Rs 5, ½ hr; from there to Kalugumalai, Rs 3, 30 mins. Buses to and from Tenkasi, Rs 10, 2 hrs. **Route** The road over the ghats to Thiruvananthapuram via Shenkottai is narrow and winding, though nowhere particularly steep. It passes through **Puliangudi** (*population*: 54,000) to Tenkasi.

Tenkasi
Phone code: 04633
Colour map 3, grid C3
Population: 55,000

Literally the Kashi (Varanasi) of the South, Tenkasi is the nearest town to the Courtallam Falls (6 km). The temple flagstaff is believed to be 400 years old. From Tenkasi it claims a low pass into the densely forested hills of Kerala. **Sleeping E** *Krishna Tourist Home*, 2 Bus Stand Rd, T23226. Basic though clean and spacious, noisy from being next to the bus station.

Virudhunagar
Population: 70,900
Colour map 3, grid B4

The name Virudhupatti (Hamlet of banners) was changed to Virudhunagar (City of banners) in 1915, and was upgraded to a full municipality in 1957, reflecting the upwardly mobile social status of the town's dominant local caste, the Nadars. Originally low caste toddy tappers, they have established a wide reputation as a dynamic and enterprising group. The powerful Congress leader, Kamaraj Nadar, was chiefly responsible for Mrs Gandhi's selection as Prime Minister.

Sleeping **F** *Amyon Lodge*, 200 m from Bus Stand opposite Police Station. Modern, clean, good value, recommended. Also **Coronation Hotel**.

Transport **Road** **Buses** Go from Madurai (Palankatham), Rs 6. Leave Madurai early morning for Kollam train; get off at Virudhunagar police station and go to the end of the road opposite and turn left; the railway station is about 1 km on the right (take a rickshaw if carrying heavy luggage). **Trains** To Kollam and Thiruvananthapuram go from Platform 3 across the bridge. Good *vadai* and tea on the platform. **Kollam**: *Quilon Mail*, *6161*, 1930, 8½ hrs; *Chennai-Quilon Mail*, *6105*, 0745, 8½ hrs.

Kalugumalai
Colour map 3, grid B4
Population: 13,000

Six kilometres south of Kovilpatti, Kalugumalai (Kazhugumalai) has a profusion of magnificent fifth-century bas-relief Jain figures on a huge rock which are well worth the detour. The Jain temple is to the north of the rock and is easily missed. There is also an unfinished monolithic cave temple to Siva (circa AD 950).

Tuticorin
Phone code: 0461
Colour map 3, grid C4
Population: 284,200

An important industrial port, Tuticorin is also the centre of the pearl fishing industry. Settled originally by the Portuguese in 1540, who were establishing themselves in Ceylon (now Sri Lanka) at the same time, it experienced the same succession of foreign control. The Dutch captured it in 1658 and the East India Company took it over in 1782 for a short period, finally gaining control in 1825. The Portuguese built the most important **church** in the town. Its dedication to Our Lady of the Snows can only have been the result of a strong sense of irony or perhaps of deprivation. Today the Church is the scene of an annual Golden Car Festival every August.

The shallow waters and islands off the southeast coast of Tamil Nadu are an ideal breeding ground for pearl-bearing oysters, which develop in shoals over a four year period. The Department of Fishing monitors the growth of shoals, and announces a pearl fishing season in the appropriate areas. The fishing season lasts for up to five weeks, usually around March. Teams of up to 70 small boats, each with 10 divers, leave the shore at midnight in order to start fishing

Palmyra Palm – the fruitful nut

The road to Tuticorin and the coast from Kovilpatti crosses the startlingly red soils leading to the teri of the coast. Much is just waste, but the **palmyra palm** is everywhere – possibly 10 million in Tirunelveli district alone. They are a vital resource for village economies. The broad fan-shaped leaves were used for writing early Tamil literature, but today they still serve for thatching, fencing, sunshades, basket making and mats. The fibres of the stem are used for making string, rope or brushes. The extremely sweet sap is sometimes drunk fresh, but traditionally it was allowed to ferment into the potent toddy or converted into sugar, or jaggery.

at dawn. The divers work without oxygen, being lowered to the bottom with the help of a weight. Working in pairs to keep watch for sharks or other dangers, the divers normally stay down for up to 80 seconds though some have stayed down for several minutes. Opportunities for pearl fishing are relatively rare, sometimes as infrequently as once in 10 years. The pearl market in Tuticorin is an extraordinary sight when the season is on.

Tirunelveli திருநெல்வேலி and Palayamkottai

*Located on the banks of the **Tamraparni** the only perennial river of the south, Tirunelveli is an attractive market and educational centre surrounded by rice fields irrigated from the river's waters. Rising only 60 km to the east at an altitude of over 1,700 m, the river benefits from both the southwest and the southeast monsoons. It tumbles down to the plains where it is bordered by a narrow strip of rich paddy growing land.*

Population: 233,400
Phone code: 0462
Colour map 3, grid C4
Population: 97,700

Tirunelveli is now joined with the twin settlement of Palayamkottai. It is a market town and one of the oldest Christian centres in Tamil Nadu. St Francis Xavier settled here to begin his ministry in India in the early 16th century, but it has also been a centre of Protestant missionary activity. In 1896 it became the head of an Anglican diocese, now Church of South India.

Background

Kanthimathi Nellaiyappar Temple, a twin temple with the north dedicated to Siva (Nellaiyappar) and the south to Parvati (Kanthi), is worth visiting. Each section has an enclosure over 150 m by 120 m. The temples have sculptures, musical pillars, valuable jewels, a golden lily tank and a 1,000-pillared mandapa. *Car festival* in June/July. **Palayamkottai** has **St John's Church** (Church Missionary Society) with a spire 35 m high, a landmark for miles around. The town produces palm-leaf articles.

Sights
Thousands of pilgrims visit the church during 1-14 Sep

C-E *Aryaas*, 67 Madurai Rd, T339001, F339000. 60 rooms (from Rs 330), a/c (Rs 550) **B** suites, with hot shower, terrace, restaurants (separate vegetarian), bar, open-air rest evenings, modern Indian hotel. Recommended. Several budget hotels are clustered near Junction Rly Station. Rooms usually with Western toilet and shower. Recommended. **D-E** *Barani*, 29 Madurai Rd, T23234. 40 rooms, with hot shower, some a/c, vegetarian restaurants (1 a/c), busy hotel in large, 4-storey modern block. **D-E** *Sri Janakiram*, 30 Madurai Rd, near Bus Stand, T331941, F331522. 70 rooms, with hot shower, some a/c, restaurants, lift, smart, clean, brightly lit. Highly recommended.

Sleeping & eating
Hotels are often full during the wedding season (Apr-Jun). Book ahead or arrive early

Tamil Nadu & Chennai

Tamil Nadu & Chennai

E *Tamil Nadu*, T24268. Has some a/c rooms with bath and a restaurant. **F** *Blue Star*, 36 Madurai Rd, T24495. Rooms with cold shower, **E** a/c, good vegetarian restaurant, Indian style, modern. **F** *Sri Narayan Tourist Lodge*, Trivandrum High Rd (near small bridge), T24451. Rooms with cold shower, Indian toilet, very basic but clean, no English spoken, popular with truck drivers. **F** *Railway Retiring Rooms* and dorm.

Transport   **Local Bus**, **taxi** and **auto-rickshaw** (charge extortionate rates). **Long distance Road Bus**: good bus connections to **Kanniyakumari**, **Thiruvananthapuram**, and to **Madurai**, **Tiruchirappalli** and **Chennai**. For **Courtallam**, go to Tenkasi (Rs 12, 1½ hrs) and take bus to Courtallam (Rs 2, 20 mins). **Train**: **Chennai (ME)**: *Nellai Exp*, *6120* (AC/CC), 1525, 17 hrs. Broad gauge to Chennai (MC): *Kanniyakumari Exp, 6020*, 1740, 15 hrs. Also to **Madurai** and **Kanniyakumari**.

Directory   There are **banks** on Trivandrum High Rd. **Hospital** in High Ground, Palayamkottai. **GPO** is on Trivandrum High Rd.

Around Tirunelveli

Tiruchendur   The town, 50 km east of Tirunelveli, has a famous **shore temple** dedicated to
Phone code: 04639   Subrahmanya (see page 336) and is considered to be one of his six 'abodes'.
Colour map 3, grid C4   There are caves with rock-cut sculptures along the shore. Close by, **Sleeping**
Population: 75,400   **E** *Tamil Nadu* (TTDC), near the temple, T44268, F44658, 4-6 bed rooms, some **D** a/c.

Manapad   This is the predominantly Roman Catholic coastal village, 18 km south of Tiruchendur, where St Francis Xavier is said to have landed and lived in a cave near the headland. The Holy Cross Church (1581) close to the sea is believed to house a fragment of the True Cross from Jerusalem.

Thiruppu-   When the Pandiyan kings were defeated by the Cholas in the 11th century,
damarudur   Rajaraja I and Rajendra I encouraged Chola settlers to migrate to the banks of
(Thiruvidaima-   the Tamraparani. The Chera King Rajasimha built and dedicated the
rudur)   five-storey **Narumbanatha Temple** to Rajendra I in 1036. Standing near the junction with the Ghatana River, 31 km west of Tirunelveli, it was enlarged by the Vijayanagar kings.

Tirunelveli

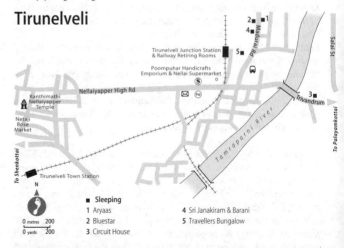

Tirunelveli Junction Station & Railway Retiring Rooms

Poompuhar Handicrafts Emporium & Nellai Supermarket

Nellaiyapper High Rd

Kanthimathi Nellaiyapper Temple

Netaji Bose Market

Tamraparani River

To Shenkottai

Tirunelveli Town Station

To Palayamkottai

Salai St

Madurai Rd

Trivandrum

N

0 metres 200
0 yards 200

■ Sleeping
1 Aryaas
2 Bluestar
3 Circuit House
4 Sri Janakiram & Barani
5 Travellers Bungalow

The east *gopura* dates from this period, and there are superb wood carvings and brightly painted murals on the inner walls of this *gopuram*, largely illustrating myths or scenes from the court. Note the pictures showing an Arab ship carrying horses in the second chamber and the marriage of Minakshi to Sundareshwar (Siva) in the third chamber. Before its defeat in 1565 at Talikota, the Vijayanagar Empire had depended on the flourishing trade in Arab horses to supply its army. The temple, beautifully restored, now stands in a tranquil riverside setting, but may only open early and late in the day for prayers. ■ *Getting there: No direct buses from Tirunelveli; taxis, about Rs 250. The scenic route through the countryside is shorter in distance though longer in time, than the highway.*

The tiny village of **Krishnapuram**, 13 km east of Palayamkottai, is famous for its temple with stunningly executed Nayaka sculptures.

Courtallam, with average temperatures of 22°-23°C, is a very popular health resort, especially during the monsoon. The nine waterfalls (Kuttalam Falls) include the Main Falls where the river Chittar cascades over 92 m. The waters, widely believed to have great curative powers, draws big crowds at the *Saral Festival* in July. "Worth a visit even out of season, when the fall is reduced to a trickle. You can still join the pilgrims in jostling for a bathe under the stream." The tranquil village at the base of forest-clad hills is empty out-of-season when some services close. The Thirukutralanathar Temple contains old inscriptions while the small **Chitra Sabha Temple** nearby, one of five *sabhas* (where Siva as Nataraja is believed to have performed his cosmic dance) contains religious murals.

Courtallam (Kuttalam)
Phone code: 04633

Sleeping and eating Over 30 lodges take in guests. E *Tamil Nadu* (TTDC), T22423. Is recommended, restaurant serves tasty, cheap vegetarian meals. F *Sri Venkateswara*, rooms with Indian toilet, cold water, old-fashioned.

Directory Banks on Main Rd. **Post offices** at bus station and main falls.

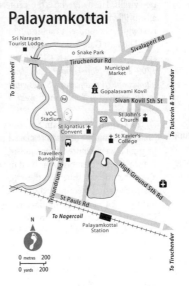

Palayamkottai

Tamil Nadu & Chennai

Tamil Nadu & Chennai

★ Kanniyakumari கன்னியாகுமரி

Phone code: 04652
Colour map 3, grid C4
Population: 17,200

The southernmost point of mainland India and a site that captures the imagination of millions of Hindus, Kanniyakumari occupies a beautiful rocky headland site, though the town itself revolves largely around the pilgrim market selling tacky plastic knick-knacks.

The town

Climate: Temp Summer:
Max 39℃, Min 22℃;
Winter: Max 33℃,
Min 20℃
Annual rainfall:
1,020 mm

Associated with the Goddess Kumari, the virgin, Kanniyakumari (Cape Comorin) has become a busy pilgrimage centre. The memorial to Swami Vivekenanda, on a rocky promontory just over 400 m offshore, now dominates the view. The Bay of Bengal, the Indian Ocean and the Arabian Sea meet here giving spectacular sunrise, sunset and moonrise. In April the sun and the moon appear on the same horizon. The beach sands are of different colours, having been deposited from different directions. Prominent on the beach are the black monazite and red garnet sands.

Sights

The **Kanniyakumari Temple** overlooks the shoreline. The legend tells of the Devi Kanya, one of the incarnations of Parvati, who sought to marry Siva by doing penance. When she was unsuccessful she vowed to remain an unmarried virgin. The deity who is the 'protector of India's shores' has an exceptionally brilliant diamond on her nose ring which is supposed to shine out to sea. The East Gate is opened only on special occasions. ■ *0400-1200, 1700-2000. Non-Hindus are not allowed into the sanctuary. Shoes must be left outside and men must wear a dhoti to enter.*

The **Gandhi Mandapam** Some of Mahatma Gandhi's ashes were placed in public view before immersion in the sea and the memorial was built in a way that the sun shines on the spot where the ashes were placed, on his birthday, 2 October at midday. The **Lighthouse** is closed to visitors.

Vivekananda Memorial, which stands on one of two rocks separated by about 70 m, is about 500 m from the mainland. The Bengali religious leader and philosopher Swami Vivekananda who came here as a simple monk and devotee of the Devi, swam out and sat in long and deep meditation on one of the rocks in 1892. He left inspired to speak on Hinduism at the Parliament of Religions in Chicago, preaching that "the Lord is one, but the sages describe Him differently". He looked on religion as the most powerful instrument of social regeneration and individual development. On his return, he founded the Ramakrishna Mission in

Kanniyakumari

To Trivandrum (NH 47) & Madurai (NH 7)

Vivekanandapuram

Guganathan Temple

Church of Our Lady of Ransom

Main Rd

N Car St

E Car St

Chicken Corner ● S Car St

Kovalam Rd

Lighthouse

Beach Rd

Museum

Toilet

Tamil Nadu Sales Emporium

Shops

Vinayaka Temple

Sravana

Ferry Jetty

Gandhi Mandapam

Kanniyakumari Temple & Kumari Ghat

Vivekananda Rock Memorial

N

0 metres 200
0 yards 200

■ **Sleeping**
1 DKV Lodge
2 Kaveri Lodge
3 Kerala House
4 Lakshmi
5 Madhini
6 NTC Lodge

7 Samudra
8 Sangam & Restaurant
9 Sankar Guesthouse & Vegetarian Restaurant
10 Tamil Nadu Guesthouse
11 Tamil Nadu & Restaurant
12 Youth Hostel

Chennai, which now has spread across the world. The rock was renamed Vivekananda Rock and a memorial was built in 1970. The design of the *mandapa* incorporates different styles of temple architecture from all over India and now also houses a statue of Vivekananda. People also come to see Sri Pada Parai, the 'footprint' of the Devi where she did her penance on the rock (divine footprints are believed to be raised when enshrined on rock), now also enclosed in a newer temple building. Be prepared when grandly ushered into PRO's – they expect a donation of Rs 100 or more! ■ *Daily except Tue, 0700-1100, 1400-1700. Entry Rs 10, Ferry Rs 10, 15 mins (see transport below). Allow 1 hr for the visit. Smoking and eating prohibited. Wear thick socks as you must take off shoes before entering.* A giant 40 m statue of the poet Thiruvalluvar is to be installed on the rock nearby.

Vivekanandapuram An informative photo exhibition, 1 km north, can be reached by an easy walk along the beach though there is no access from that side. The Yoga Kendra there runs courses from June to December. Further north there is a pleasant sandy **beach**, 3½ km along Kovalam Road.

Government Museum Very simple, showing aspects of Indian life. '**Wandering Monk**' Exhibition. ■ *0900-1300, 1400-1700. Main Road, near tourist office.*

Sleeping

Hotels are in heavy demand especially State Tourism hotels on the beach; book well in advance. Better hotels have rooms with attached facilities (cold showers, hot tap & Western toilets)

D *Kerala House* (Kerala Tourism), Beach Rd, T71229. Mainly for government officials, the 3-storey building resembles an aeroplane from the air, 11 rooms, with a view of sunset and sunrise (Sep-Feb), restaurant, exterior looks run down, but attracts VIPs. D *Lakshmi Tourist Home*, East Car St, T71333. Very clean rooms, some a/c with views, Indian WC (Rs 500), restaurant, 24-hour coffee shop, fine views from roof, friendly and helpful staff, but noisy 'when guests arrive at 0400-0500 to see sunrise, and ring loud bells for service!'. D *Madhini*, East Car St, T71787. Rooms with bath and fan (mosquito proof!), some with views, 'garden' restaurant in courtyard (evenings), otherwise excellent food to order. Recommended. D *Samudra*, Sannathi St, T71162. Sea-facing room with bath (prices vary), restaurant, clean, modern. Recommended. D *Tamil Nadu Guest House* (TTDC), Beach Rd, T71424, F71031. 45 rooms, some with bath and some a/c, twin cottages, smaller rooms cheaper, but very slow service.

Most have rooms with fan & cold showers only

E *Kaveri Lodge*, Kovalam Rd, T71288. 30 rooms, clean with bath (**F** off-season) and fan (some 3-4 bedded), good value restaurants nearby. E *NTC Lodge*, Bus Station, Kovalam Rd. Some good, clean rooms with seaview and cheaper dorm (men only), good restaurant, good value. E *Sangam*, Main Rd opposite the post office, T71351. 25 rooms, 2nd Flr at rear quieter, good restaurant downstairs. E *Sankar Guest House*, Main Rd towards Rly station, T71260. Some large seaview rooms with balcony, good vegetarian restaurant. F *DKV Lodge*, good, comfortable rooms. F *Vivekanandapuram*, T71250. Basic rooms and dorm, shower and Indian toilet, well run, safe, friendly, good value. F *Youth Hostel* (TTDC), T71258. Cottage and dorm (Rs 30-45).

Eating

TTDC Restaurant. Looks like a barrack, but excellent non-vegetarian Indian meals. Vegetarian: 2 *Sravanas*, Rock Rd, near Jetty and on Sannathi St, recommended; good *thalis* at *Sangam*, spartan but clean.

Festivals

Chitra Purnima is a special full moon celebration at the temple usually held in the second week of **Apr**. Sunset and moonrise can be seen together. In first week of **Oct** Special *Navarathri* celebrations.

Transport

Local Taxi and **cycle-rickshaw** are available. **Ferry**: to Vivekananda Rock, at least every 30 mins, 0700-1100, 1400-1700; sometimes 2 run continuously. Rs 10. Expect long queues during festivals. **Long distance Road Bus**: Central Bus Station, W of town, about 15 mins' walk from centre, T71285. It has a restaurant, waiting room and *Retiring Rooms* upstairs. There are frequent services to Nagercoil (½ hr), Kovalam and Thiruvananthapuram (2½ hrs) but the journey can be tiring and uncomfortable. Govt Express buses go to other major towns including Chennai (16 hrs), Madurai (6 hrs), Rameswaram (8½ hrs). **Train**: The Station to the north, off the Trivandrum Rd, is large and well organized, T71247. **Chennai** (via Madurai): *Chennai Central Exp*, *6020*, daily 1535, 17 hrs (Madurai 5½ hrs); **Mumbai (VT)**: *Kanniyakumari*, *1082* (AC/II), 0510, 48 hrs; **Thiruvananthapuram**: *Kanniyakumari Bangalore Exp*, *6525*, 0720, 2½ hrs; *Kanniyakumari Exp*, *1082* (AC/II), 0500, 2 hrs.

Directory **Banks** Branches of *Canara Bank*, Main Rd. *State Bank of India*. *State Bank of Travancore*, Beach Rd. **Communications** **Post office:** Head Post Office, Main Rd. Branches at Vivekandandapuram. 1100-1600 and in Sannathi St, 1000-1400.

★ **Suchindram** The temple was founded during the Pandiyan period but was expanded under Thirumalai Nayaka in the 17th century. It was also used later as a sanctuary for the rulers of Travancore to the west and so contains treasures from many kingdoms. One of few temples dedicated to the Hindu Trinity, Brahma, Vishnu and Siva, it is in a rectangular enclosure which you enter through the massive ornate seven-storeyed *gopuram*. North of the temple is a large tank with a small shelter in the middle while round the walls is the typically broad street used for car festivals. Leading to the entrance is a long colonnade with musical pillars and with sculptures of Siva, Parvati, Ganesh and Subrahmanya on the front and a huge Hanuman statue inside. The main sanctuary, with a lingam dates from the ninth century but many of the other structures and sculptures date from the 13th century and after. There are special temple ceremonies at sunset on Friday. Open to non-Hindus; priests acting as guides may expect donations.

Nagercoil
நாகர்கோவில்
Phone code: 04652
Colour map 3, grid C3
Population: 189,500
19 km from
Kanniyakumari

Nagercoil is set with a stunning backcloth of the Western Ghats, reflected from place to place in the broad tanks dotted with lotuses. The landscape begins to feel more like Kerala than Tamil Nadu. It is an important railway junction and bus terminal. It is often a bottleneck filled with lorries so be prepared for delays.

The old town of **Kottar**, now a suburb, was a centre of art, culture and pilgrimage. The **temple** to Nagaraja, after which the town is named, is unique in that although the presiding deity is the Serpent God *Naga*, there are also shrines to Siva and Vishnu as well as images of Jain *Tirthankaras*, Mahavira and Parsvanatha on the pillars. The temple is alive with snakes during some festivals. ■ *0630-0900, 1730-2000.*

Christian missionaries played an important part in the town's development and have left their mark in schools, colleges, hospitals and of course churches of different denominations. There is also a prominent Muslim community in Kottar which is reflected in the closure of shops on Friday, remaining open on Sunday. **Sleeping D** *Rajam*, MS Rd, Vadasery, 2 km rly, T32581, F32589. 32 rooms, some a/c, restaurant, roof garden, exchange, good value. **D** *Parvathi*, T33020. Is similar. ■ *Getting there: The rly station is 3 km from the bus station. Mumbai (VT): Nagercoil-Mumbai Exp, 6340, Fri, 0550, 39½ hrs. Frequent bus connections to Thiruvananthapuram, Kanniyakumari and Madurai.*

★ Padmanabhapuram പന്മനാഭപുരം

Padmanabhapuram, the old palace of the Rajas of Travancore, is beautifully kept and contains some fascinating architecture and paintings.

Padmanabhapuram's name (*Padma*, lotus; *nabha*, navel; *puram*, town) refers **The palace**
to the lotus emerging from the navel of Vishnu. From the ninth century this
part of Tamil Nadu and neighbouring Kerala were governed by the Ay
Dynasty, patrons both of Jainism and Hinduism. However, the land was
always contested by the Cholas, the Pandiyas and the Cheras. By the late 11th
century the new Venadu Dynasty emerged from the Chera rulers of Kerala and
took control of Kanniyakumari District in AD 1125 under Raja Kodai Kerala
Varman. Never a stable kingdom and with varying degrees of territorial control, Travancore State was governed from Padmanab- hapuram between
1590-1790, when the capital was shifted to Thiruvananthapuram. Although
the Rajas of Travancore were Vaishnavite kings, they did not neglect Siva, as
can be seen from various sculptures and paintings in the palace.

The King never officially married and the heir to the throne was his eldest
sister's oldest son. This form of 'matrilineal descent' was characteristic of the
earlier Chera Empire (who ruled for 200 years from the early 12th century).
The palace shows the superb craftsmanship, especially in woodworking, that
has been characteristic of Kerala's art and architecture. There are also some
superb frescoes and excellent stone-sculpted figures.

■ *0900-1700 (last tickets 1630), closed Mon. Entry Rs 5 (accredited guide is
included, but expects a 'donation' after the tour), still camera Rs 5, video Rs 500.
Best at 0900 before coach parties arrive.*

1 *The main entrance* A smooth granite bed (notably cool) is in one corner and
painted mahogany 'musical' ceremonial bows adorn a wall. The carving on the
royal chair is Chinese, illustrating the commercial contact between China and
the Kerala kings. The mahogany ceiling has 90 different flowers carved in rosewood and teak. The metal lamp hangs from a special chain which retains its set
position. **2** *First floor* The durbar hall where the king met with his ministers.
The floor is made of egg-white, jaggery, lime, burnt coconut, charcoal and river
sand, giving a beautiful shiny, hard, black finish. It is very well ventilated with

Plan of Padmanabhapuram Palace

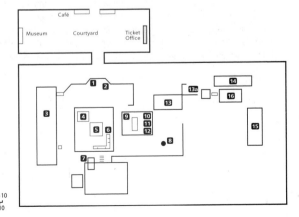

N

0 metres (approx) 10
0 yards (approx) 10

Tamil Nadu & Chennai

wooden slatted surrounds, and has some coloured mica in the windows. Perfumed herbs were placed under the wooden benches. **3** *The dining hall*   An enormous two-storeyed hall (19 m x 85 m) with teak beams, where 2,000 Brahmins were fed for free once daily. The roof, once covered with palm leaves, is now tiled. The walls held oil lamps while downstairs there are cool granite tubs for curds and buttermilk. **4**   The *Thaikottam* – 'Mother palace' – is the original structure built in 1550 with a painted ceiling. There is a *puja* room for the worship of Durga, with a jackfruit tree column; note the moveable pieces in the pendulant flower carved from a single piece of wood. **5**   A small *courtyard* (open to the sky) with ladies' bedrooms overlooking. This is typical of Keralan domestic architecture. There is an *underground secret passage*, which is said to run from another palace 2 km away. **6**   Large urns for pickle (lime, mango, gooseberry) for Brahmins' meals. **7**   Steps down to open-air 'swimming bath'; pulley by window for drawing water. Room above for oil massage. **8**   *Courtyard* The 38 kg stone standing on a pedestal at chest height had to be lifted 101 times consecutively over head as qualification to join the king's army. The potential recruit was watched from room 10. A cool passage leads to **9**   *Treasury* on the ground floor. **10**   *King's bedroom* above has a four-poster medicinal bed of 64 ayurvedic healing woods many presented by the Dutch (note influence on clothing on carved figures; also serpent of Hippocrates at its head). **11**   *King's special bedroom* for fasting times, balcony all round. **12**   *Vishnu's bedroom* (teak beds) vegetable oil tints and frescoes of deities on every wall, two hanging brass lanterns lit continuously since the 18th century. Coconut oil is added twice daily, a cotton wick once a week. The room has a balcony all round. **NB** Rooms **11** and **12** are currently closed for renovation. If you are lucky the guide might open up. **13**   The King's sister's *dressing room* with two hanging beds, Belgian mirrors and pictures of *Krishna*. **13a**   King's sister's *bedroom* and toilets. **14**   Was ladies' quarters, then an *armoury*; a gruesome 'hanging cage' (rather like a suit of armour, but slats of metal) through which eagles tore criminals to death. **15**   A room for scribes and accountants. **16**   Granite *dance hall*; women watched from behind perforated wooden screen. Beautifully carved figures on columns hold oil lamps; note odd fish carvings on ceiling. It is connected to what was once the *Sarasvati* temple.

The outer cyclopean stone wall is fitted together without mortar. It encloses a total area of 75 ha, and the buildings of the palace cover 2 ha.

The *museum* directly opposite the ticket office contains some excellent wooden sculptures and copies of the murals.

Transport   **Road Bus**: regular service to Thiruvananthapuram and Kanniyakumari. Less frequent buses to and from Kovalam. From Kovalam, dep approximately 0940 to Thuckalai. Rickshaw to Padmanabhapuram. Return buses from Thuckalai dep 1445, 1530. **Taxi**: from Kovalam and Thiruvananthapuram including Padmanabhapuram, Suchindram and Kanniyakumari (Tamil Nadu) costs approximately Rs 800.

Andaman and Nicobar Islands

4

Andaman and Nicobar Islands

The Andaman and Nicobar Islands have brilliant tropical flora and are thickly forested with evergreen, deciduous rainforest and tropical trees, with mangrove swamps on the water's edge. Hilly in parts, they have superb palm-fringed, white-sand beaches and coral reefs. The sparkling clear water is excellent for snorkelling with increasing opportunity for fabulous scuba diving for beginners and the experienced. The Andamans are also a bird-watcher's paradise with 242 species recorded and the wildlife includes 58 species of mammals and 83 of reptiles, many endemic as the islands are isolated. It is now, in theory, possible to visit some of the newly opened remoter islands. The islands' aboriginal tribal people are of special interest to anthropologists. Some, like the Jarawas and Sentinelese in the Andamans, have remained isolated and hostile to outsiders even up to the end of the 20th century. Others (eg the Great Andamanese) have interacted with non-tribal settlers for decades and now there are very few left. The Government of India keeps the Primitive Tribal Reserve Areas out of bounds.

Andaman and Nicobar Islands

Background

Entry regulations Foreigners with tourist visas for India are allowed a maximum stay of 30 days on arrival at Port Blair, the capital, by air or sea, but may not visit tribal areas or restricted islands including Nicobar. Foreign tourists may now apply and get a Restricted Area Permit after Registration at Immigration. It is no longer necessary to get a permit in advance; a US$30 (or rupee equivalent) fee is payable in cash only, so come prepared. CID will extend your permit up to a maximum stay of 15 days without difficulty, but only when your initial period of approval is about to expire. Any extension is only valid for stay in Port Blair.

Officially permits allow foreigners to visit and stay overnight in Port Blair, Havelock, Long Island, Neil Island, entire islands of South and Middle Andaman (excluding tribal reserve) Baratang, Rangat, Mayabunder, Diglipur, North Passage Island, Little Andaman Island (excluding tribal reserve), and all islands in Mahatma Gandhi Marine National Park except Boat, Hobay, Twin Island, Tarmugli, Malay and Pluto Island. You can also visit Jolly Buoy, Red Skin (may reopen after crocodile infestation), South Cinque, Mount Harriet and Madhuban, Ross Island, Narcondam, Interview, Brother, Sister and Barren Island during the daytime. In practice, requests to visit remote islands such as Barren, North Passage and Narcondam, which have recently been opened to tourists, are often refused even though ships sail to them. Some dive companies arrange overnight stays on diving courses.

Indians may visit the Andamans and Nicobars without a permit but must obtain a permit for restricted areas on arrival at Car Nicobar or from the Duty Commissioner (Nicobar) at Port Blair.

Foreigners working in the Andamans can get a four month visa but to extend the stay, the person must leave India (not simply the islands) and re-enter with a new visa and permit.

The land
Area: 8,249 sq km
Population: 450,000

The Andaman and Nicobar group comprises about 300 islands formed by a submarine mountain range which divides the Bay of Bengal from the Andaman Sea. The islands lie between latitudes 6° to 14° north (about level with Chennai and longitudes 92°-94° east, a span of 725 km). The land rises to 730 m (Saddle Peak), formed mainly of limestones, sandstones and clays. The Andamans are separated from the Nicobars by a 90 m deep 150 km strait. The Andamans group has 204 islands (26 inhabited) with its three main islands of North, Middle and South, which are separated by mangrove-fringed islets and are together called **Great Andaman**. The **Nicobar Islands** comprise 12 inhabited and seven uninhabited islands including the three groups, **Car Nicobar** in the north, **Camorta** and **Nancowry** in the middle and the largest, **Great Nicobar** in the south.

Wildlife The canopied rain forests harbour 3,000 species of plants including mangroves, epiphytes (130 ferns, 100 orchids), palms, woody climbers, valuable timbers (teak, mahogany, Andaman *paduk*, resistant to termites) and a wide variety of tropical fruit. Marine fauna is particularly diverse including rare species (dugong, grey teal, Estuarine crocodile and marine turtles) and a variety of tropical fish and coral (see MG National Marine Park below).

Climate Tropical. Temperature: 20°C to 32°C. Annual rainfall: 2,540 mm. Monsoons – usually May to mid-September, and November to mid-December (though the first may arrive as early as mid-April, bringing heavy rain on most days). *Best Season*: end-November to mid-April. The

The tribals of Andaman and Nicobar

One story goes that the monkey god Hanuman stopped in the Andamans on his way to Lanka in search of Sita (see page 551), giving the islands his name. They have been inhabited by Aboriginal tribes (some Negrito) for thousands of years but remained unexplored because anyone attempting to land would be attacked. Today there are only a few **Andamanese**, who once inhabited the Great Andamans, some **Onges** in Little Andaman who traditionally painted their naked bodies, the fierce **Jarawas** on South Andaman and the **Sentinelese** on North Sentinel. Car Nicobar (Carnic) is inhabited by the mongoloid **Nicobarese**, the most numerous groups, and **Shompens** who may have been of pre-Dravidian stock, live in Great Nicobar.

Hunting wild pigs, fishing with nets and catching turtles with harpoons from dug-out canoes, the islanders used iron for arrowheads and metal from wrecks for harpoons. Some tribes made pottery but the **Andamanese** particularly were exceptional since they had not discovered fire-making.

The Anthropological Survey of India and the Andaman Administration have been jointly trying to establish friendly contact with the Jarawas and Sentinelese since the 1960s. They consistently repelled groups of explorers with poisoned arrows. More recently, some **Sentinelese** have picked up coconuts (which do not grow on their island) which were left on the beach as a gesture of friendship by anthropologists. In January 1991, Indian anthropologists succeeded in landing on North Sentinel and in February, a few Sentinelese boarded a lifeboat to accept gifts of coconuts. Study groups have made regular visits, removing most of their clothes in order to be accepted. The 400 or so Sentinelese do not appear to have a hierarchical social structure; they are naked, painting their bodies with chalk and ochre and wearing bead and bone ornaments. The **Jarawas** remain in the Tribal Reserve set aside to the west of the Andaman Trunk Road, all along the South and Middle Andamans.

island climate has no extremes, the main contrasts coming with the arrival of the monsoon, and tropical storms in late summer can cause damage.

Lying on the trade route between Burma and India the islands appeared on Ptolemy's second century map and were also recorded by the Chinese traveller I-Tsing in the seventh century. At the end of the 17th century the Mahrathas established a base there to attack the trading British, Dutch and Portuguese ships. Dutch pirates and French Jesuits had made contact with the islands before the Danish East India Company made attempts to evangelize the islands in the mid-18th century. The reputation of ferocity attributed to the Nicobarese may have been partly due to Malay pirates who attacked and killed sailors of any trading vessel that came ashore (some anthropologists believe that in spite of common belief, the aboriginals themselves were not cannibals). The first British attempt to occupy the islands was made in 1788 when the Governor General of India sent Lt Blair (whose name was given to the first port) and although the first convicts were sent there in 1794, it was abandoned within a couple of years.

After the 'First War of Independence' (The 'Mutiny') in 1857 the British gained control of most of the islands and used them as a penal colony for its prisoners (who until then had been sent to Sumatra) right up to Indian Independence, with a short break from 1942-45 when the Japanese occupied Port Blair, Ross Island and the Nicobar islands. However, political prisoners were sent in large numbers only after the completion of the **Cellular Jail** in 1906. The British used it primarily as a penal colony. Each revolt on the mainland

History
The name Kalapani or 'black water' by which the islands were known referred to the blood shed by the nationalists

resulted in the transportation of people from various parts of India, hence the presence of Bengalis, Malayans and Burmese among others. Subhas Chandra Bose, the Indian Nationalist, first raised the Indian tricolour here in 1943.

Culture **People** Sir Arthur Conan Doyle in 1890 described the islanders as "perhaps ... the smallest race upon this earth ... fierce, morose and intractable". In the mid-19th century, the British guessed the tribal population was around 5,000 but the number has been steadily dwindling. Today most of the inhabitants are Indians, Burmese and Malays – some, descendants of the criminals who were transported here. Since the 1950s, refugees from East Pakistan (now Bangladesh), Burma and Indian emigrants from Guyana have settled on the main islands to be followed more recently by Tamils from Sri Lanka. The largest concentration is around the capital, Port Blair, with the majority of the tribal people (about 15% of the population) living in the Nicobars.

Language Hindi, Bengali, Tamil, Malayalam and English are spoken. The **Andamanese language** which bears no resemblance to any other language, uses prefixes and suffixes to indicate the function of a word and is extraordinary in using simply two concepts of number, 'one' and 'greater than one'.

Crafts Shell and exotic woods (for example ebony and teak) crafted for the tourist trade, palm mats and beautiful natural shells are available. However, some people fear that there is a danger of over-exploitation and the sale of some products (including mother-of-pearl jewellery, *paduk*), is now banned.

Modern **Economy** Local seafood (lobsters, prawns and sea fish) is good. Tropical fruit
Andaman like pineapples, a variety of bananas and the extra sweet papaya is plentiful and
& Nicobar the green coconut water very refreshing. Rice is also cultivated.

Resources and industry Tourism is rapidly becoming the Andamans' most important industry and an international airport is scheduled to be ready in 2003. Forests represent an important resource. The government has divided 40% of the forests into Primitive Tribal Reserve areas which are only open to Indian visitors with permits, and the remaining 60% as Protected Areas set aside for timber for export as plywoods, hardwoods and match-woods (a Swedish multinational owns extensive logging rights). Rubber and mahogany have been planted in addition to teak and rosewood which are commercially in demand.

Port Blair

Population: 75,000
Phone code: 03192
Colour map 2, grid C6

Port Blair, the capital, about 1,200 km from Kolkata and Chennai, has only a handful of sights. The small town has changed in the last three decades from one which saw a ship from the mainland once a month if the weather permitted, to a place connected by flights from Chennai and Kolkata several times a week. It now has a hospital, shops, schools and colleges and a few museums, in addition to resort hotels and watersports facilities.

Ins & outs **Getting there** Lamba Line airport, 3 km south of Port Blair, has flights from Kolkata and Chennai. You can get a bus or taxi to town. Ships from the mainland dock at Haddo jetty where you can get taxis but they invariably overcharge. **Getting around** As Port Blair is very small, you can easily see the sights in a couple of days. The compact Aberdeen Village with the Bazar in the town centre has most of the budget hotels, the bus station, shops and offices. Hiring a motor bike or scooter can help to get around as bicycles can be hard work on the hills. Further afield, buses cover sights and towns on the limited road network. Inter-island ferries sail to coastal towns and islands open to visitors which can be far more relaxing than the capital itself.

Sights

The **Cellular Jail** (north of Aberdeen Jetty, 1886-1906) was originally built by the British to house dangerous criminals. Subsequently it was used to place Indian freedom fighters until 1938; it could hold 698 solitary prisoners in small narrow cells. The Japanese used it for their prisoners of war during their occupation from 1942-45. Three of the original seven wings which extended from the central guard tower survive; the jail was renovated in 1998. There is a site **museum**, photographs and lists of 'convicts' held, a 'death house' and the gallows, where you can get an impression of the conditions within the prison in

Port Blair

Andaman & Nicobar Islands

Related maps
A *Port Blair centre*, *page 196*
B *South Andaman and Marine National Park*, *page 205*

■ **Sleeping**
1 Andaman Beach Resort & Waves Restaurant
2 Andaman Teal House
3 ANIIDCO Tourist Home, Megapode Nest & Nicobari Cottages
4 Holiday Resort & Daawath Restaurant
5 Hornbill Nest
6 Municipal Guest House
7 Sinclair Bay

0 metres 500
0 yards 500

the early 1900s and the implements used in torture. ■ *0900-1200, 1400-1700. Entry Rs 5, camera Rs 10, video camera Rs 50. Allow 1 hr.* A well presented 45 minute **Sound and Light** show on prison life in English is shown daily at 1915 (in season), Rs 10 ; highly recommended.

Chatham Saw Mill One of the oldest in Asia, it employs 1,000 workers. Tours take you through the different processes of turning logs into 'seasoned' planks. For tours, report to the Security Office just outside the main gate. Photography is not allowed. The **museum** is listed below. ■ *0630-1430, except Sun (0830 is a good time to arrive to avoid the lunch break). Allow about 1½ hrs.*

The **Mini Zoo** has a small, uninspiring collection in some very old wooden cages with a few specimens of unusual island fauna including a sea crocodile farm. ■ *0800-1700, closed Mon.*

At **Sippighat Farm** (14 km), you can see cash crops such as spices and other plants being propagated. ■ *0600-1100, 1200-1600, daily except Mon.* A watersports complex has been developed nearby (see Sports below).

Viper Island, near Haddo Wharf, is at the mouth of Port Blair harbour where convicts were interned before the Cellular Jail was built. Indian nationals can apply to visit **Dugong Creek** where Onges have been rehabilitated in wooden huts. ■ *Daily boat from Phoenix Bay, 1500.*

Museums **Anthropological Museum** Small but interesting collection of photographs and artefacts, records of exploratory expeditions. Worth visiting. Publications on sale. Comprehensive Research Library on the islands (second floor). A new

Port Blair centre

■ **Sleeping**
1 Abishek
2 Bay Island
3 Bengal KP
4 Central Lodge
5 Jaamathi & New India Café
6 Jagganath Guest House
7 Kavita & Kwality Ice Cream

8 Lakshmi Narayan & Sealord Restaurant
9 Municipal Guest House
10 NK International
11 Raj Nivas
12 Shah & Shah
13 Shompen & Shompen Travels

14 Youth Hostal

● **Eating**
1 Annapoorna Café
2 China Room
3 Chinese
4 Islet
5 New Lighthouse

office and museum complex is expected to open by the end of 2000.
■ *1000-1230, 1400-1600, closed Mon.*

Marine Museum (Samudrika), opposite Andaman Teal House, T32719. Comprehensive collection of corals and shells and display of 350 species of marine life. ■ *0830-1200, 1400-1700, closed Mon. Entry Rs 10. Camera Rs 20. Video camera Rs 40. Allow 30 mins.*

Forest Museum Has unusual local woods including red paduk, satin and marble woods and shows the use of different woods in the timber industry and the methods of lumbering and finishing. ■ *0800-1200, 1430-1700, on working days. Allow 30 mins. Haddo near the Saw Mill.*

City Tour, 0830, 1200, Rs 40. **Corbyn's Cove**, 0830,1700, Rs 40, Chiriya Tapu, 0900, Rs 75. Bus excursions to **Wandoor** for Marine National Park, 0830, Rs 75; via sights, Tuesday-Sunday, 0900, Rs 75. Boat from Wandoor Beach to **Red Skin**, 1000, Rs 55 and to **Jolly Buoy**, Rs 85; also to **Car Nicobar** (closed to foreigners at present). **NB** Cinque Island can only be visited on an organized tour.

Tours
See also ferry details below

A *Bay Island*, Marine Hill, 2 km, T34101, F33389. 48 a/c rooms, imitating local huts (not all have sea view), cool open lounge and restaurant, good gardens but poor tennis court, sea water pool, keen on conservation (discounts to students of 'ecology and conservation'!), far from beach but excellent view across harbour entrance. Highly recommended.

Sleeping
Many offer discounts in low season (Apr-Sep)

B *Peerless Resort*, Corbyn's Cove (4 km), set back from beach, T33463, F33468. 48 rooms, 4 cottages, good *Snack Bar* (see Corbyn's Cove below), pleasant and airy, well kept mature gardens, tennis, beach nearby (take own snorkelling equipment), excellent service, warm atmosphere, free airport transfer but need taxis to town (in daytime, best to wait on beach for one passing), thefts reported. **B-C** *Sinclair Bay View*, South Pt, T32937, F31824. Refurbished resort hotel in elevated location overlooking Ross Island, 24 rooms, some a/c, restaurant, excellent and popular bar, pool, dive centre.

C-D *Shompen*, 2 Middle Pt, T32360, F32425. 40 rooms (noisy in front, windowless and very hot in centre), 15 a/c overpriced, roof-top restaurant, free airport transfer, tours, popular with backpackers, friendly, helpful staff, off-season/long stay discounts. Government **E** *Andaman Teal House*, Delanipur, T32642. 27 cleanish rooms with bath, some a/c (Rs 250-400), comfortable wicker furniture, good views, spacious lounge-restaurant (see Tent hire under Services).

D-E *Abhishek*, Goalghar, T33565, near India Tourist Office, otherwise inconvenient location. Rooms Rs 250-450, friendly, helpful management, good restaurant and bar, snorkel equipment for hire, free transfer (usually meets flights). **D-E** *Lakshmi Narayan*, Aberdeen Bazar, T33953. 16 rooms with bath (some unpleasantly hot), some a/c, good restaurant, central but overpriced (Rs 350-600).

E *Holiday Resort*, Prem Nagar, T30516. Large clean rooms with bath (Rs 200-360), bucket hot water, good restaurant, TV in lounge, helpful manager, stores luggage, evening power cuts. **E** *NK International*, Fore Shore Rd, T33066. 31 very simple rooms (Rs 300), some a/c with bath (Rs 400), few with good view across Phoenix Jetty, functional grey concrete block. **E** *Shah and Shah*, near Aberdeen Bazar, T33696. 23 excellent large clean rooms (Rs 250), huge first floor balcony. Highly recommended. Several basic **F** hotels, some not too clean, give good off-season discounts. **E** *Hornbill Nest*, 10 mins' walk from Corbyn's Cove, T32018. 20 clean rooms, 2-6 beds (Rs 250) on hillside overlooking sea, central open-air lounge and restaurant, transport difficult

Andaman & Nicobar Islands

(stop a 'returning empty' taxis), best for those wanting cheapish shared room near beach but **NB** thefts reported. Reservations: Tourist Office, near Secretariat, T32933, F32656 (Indians pay half). *Central Lodge* Middle Point, Goalghar, set back, T33634. One of the cheapest, some rooms with bath (Rs 80) but often full, camping in garden (Rs 25). *Jagannath*, Moulana Azad Rd, 7 mins from bazar, T33140. 15 clean rooms, some with attached bath and balcony in newer block but no hot water (Rs 150), filtered water, helpful staff. Highly recommended. *Jaimathi*, Moulana Azad Rd, T33457. Large rooms, generally clean but variable standard, good food, helpful staff. *Kavita*, Aberdeen Bazar, opposite CID, T33742. 24 rooms; often has room (Rs 150) when all others full (at time of ship arr/dep), 1 night only. Others popular in Aberdeen Village are *Bengal KP*, T32964 (Rs 150) and *Municipal Guest Houses*, T20696, very basic rooms, *Old* and *New* Rs 20-80. In Delanipur dorm bed Rs 5.

Haddo Hill *Tourist Home Complex* ANIIDCO, T32380. Has a central restaurant, bar and gardens with superb views to the port and Phoenix Bay. **C** *Nicobari Cottages*, T32207. 2 a/c rondavels, mainly for officials. **D** *Megapode Nest*, 25 a/c rooms off central lounge area (no view, Rs 500), short walk from restaurant, large terrace, very peaceful. **D** *Tourist Home*, 18 refurbished rooms attached to the reception area, restaurant, very good value. Reservations for both: New Marine Dry Docks, T32376.

Eating Good seafood is now widely available and even the cheapest hotels offer prawn and crab curries. Larger hotels have a wider selection, but meals (most ingredients imported from the mainland) and drinks can be expensive. Government *Guest Houses* are open to non-residents. All Indian restaurants have excellent fish fry (spiced tuna or mackerel chunks) for under Rs 15. Highly recommended, especially for trips out of Port Blair.

Expensive *Bay Island*, Marine Hill. International. Luxurious surroundings, seafood recommended, lunch buffet Rs 300. *China Room*, Tharg Bagh, T33189. Excellent fish restaurant. Secluded and shaded back yard with mosquito problem at night, very popular so book in advance, main courses Rs 70-120 (great chilli chicken), specials (for example lobster) Rs 200-300, beer Rs 70.

Mid-range *Chinese Restaurant*, Aberdeen Village. Chinese. Owned by Burmese/Punjabi couple is the best in town. Eat in simple outdoor yard, dinner by candlelight (but mosquito problem), freshly prepared with crisp home-grown vegetables, not drenched in oil, soya or tomato sauce, order your own 'specials' the day before from Rs 45. Highly recommended. *Islet*, 1st floor, GB Pant Rd (takeaway downstairs). Indian, Chinese. Relax with a cool beer on the narrow balcony with views across stadium, generous portions but quality overrated, greasy spring rolls, better chilli chicken (Rs 60), off-putting cockroach around table. *Majestic* near bus station. Wide choice, good quality. *New India Café*, next to Hotel Jaimathi. Good Indian, some Western dishes. Great food and prices, Continental breakfast (Rs 55), lobster and other specials often, on request, but very slow service (wait an hour for dinner). *New Lighthouse* opposite *Municipal Guest House*. Indian, Chinese. Wide choice in small open-air café, evening BBQ, closes 2145. *Shompen Rooftop*. Indian, Continental. Limited menu (try *aloo jeera* and *daal*), fish dishes a bit hit-and-miss.

Cheap *Anurod Bakery*, towards Teal House. Sell good cakes, snacks and corn flakes. *Annapurna Café*, Aberdeen Bazar. International. Wide selection, try their different *dosas* and Indian sweets, best place for European style breakfast, a/c rooms, very popular. Highly recommended. *Daawath*, below *Holiday Resort*. Mainly Indian. Good breakfasts and curries (Rs 35-50), avoid Western, service variable. *Kwality* ice cream next door to *Kavita*. *Sea Lord*, 1st floor in *Lakshmi Narayan*. Indian vegetarian. Characterless but good value, tasty meals. *Tillai* behind bus stand. Good South Indian food. *Tourist Home*

Pre-paid Traffic Complaint Cards

Please use these cards to report taxi and rickshaw drivers who refuse to use a meter to take you to your destination etc. In time, this may lea to positive action.

Available from the Inspector, Traffic Branch, Police Station, Aberdeen (opposite Bus Stand), T34472, ext 309.

Complex, Haddo. Indian. Excellent *thali* lunches, try the chicken dishes in the evening. There are several juice bars between the bus stand and clock tower, and stalls selling cheap snacks and fruit between the bus stand and Shah and Shah hotel.

Peerless Beach Resort, Bay Island (vodka and orange, Rs 60) *Shompen* and *Tourist Home Complex, Abishek, Shompen* and have bars. Beer is available at *China Room* (Rs 70), *Islet* and *Chinese Restaurant.* **Wine shops**: 1 behind *Hotel Shah and Shah*, 1 opposite the Syrian Christian church (open till 1930). Beers and spirits from bar below *Shalimar Hotel*, Delanipur (bottle red wine Rs 300, vodka Rs 100).

Bars

Occasional dance performances for tourists. Film of islands' tribal life at govt hotels at 1730. **Swimming**: is excellent. The best spot is the crescent shaped Corbyn's Cove or 1 of the uninhabited islands which tourists may visit for the day. **Watersports**: *Andaman Water Sports Complex*, next to Fisheries Museum, Sippighat, T30769. 0700-1100, 1500-2000. Sailing, paddle boats, wind surfing (Rs 30 per hour), paragliding. Resort hotels have limited equipment, (see Box).

Entertainment

End-February *Island Tourism Festival* for 10 days, with music and dancing from all over India and focusing on local crafts, culture and food.

Festivals

Local curio shops are by the clocktower and opposite the Post Office. *Sagarika Cottage Emporium* next to tourist office. Open 0900-1800, closed Sun. Selection of souvenirs in wood and shell (the government designates areas and limits for collection of shells each year).

Shopping

Island Travel, Aberdeen Bazar, T33358. Indian Airlines, Jet Airways agents, good for excursions, car hire, postcards and exchange. *Sagar Tours*, 7 Krishna Bldg, Haddo, T33704. *Shompen Travels*, Middle Pt, T32452. Local tours, Wandoor to Jolly Buoy/Red Skin ferry.

Tour operators

Local Bicycle: hire from shop between Aberdeen Bazar and the Bus Stop (about Re 1 per hr) but you need to be very fit to manage the hilly island. **Motorbike and scooter hire**: *Prashant Travels*, Phoenix Bay, and next to *Jagannath Hotel*. Newish fleet of motorbikes, Rs 150 per day (Rs 1,000 deposit) return by 1900; scooters, Rs 120; *TSG* (TS Guruswamy), Moulana Azad Rd, near Anthropology Museum, T32894. *GDM*, further up the same road, has good Kinetic Hondas, Rs 200 per day (very good condition, start first time!). **NB** Check insurance papers. Recommended for trips to Wandoor, Chiriya Tapu, Mt Harriet and Corbyn's Cove. **Auto-rickshaw** (new machines) and **taxis**: Central Taxi Stand opposite bus station and by clocktower, Aberdeen Bazar, charge Rs 20 about town, Rs 50 for Corbyn's Bay and Haddo Jetty. They refuse to use meters; overpriced and generally unhelpful.

Transport

The Tourism Festival can cause widespread disruption to plane & boat ticket availability. Make particularly sure you have confirmed reservations. Problems also occur from mid-Apr to mid-May

Long distance Air Transport to town: most buses pass the airport entrance, Rs 2. Taxis should charge Rs 30; fix fare first. Some hotels send taxis. Flights are always fully booked at least a month ahead (earlier for Apr-May). However, because of the strict enforcement of the 30-day stay regulations, officials may find you a seat to fly out

Andaman & Nicobar Islands

Trial by water

"Boarding is chaotic and takes ages; everyone needs a medical before leaving the island to prove they are seaworthy!"

"No alcohol – the bar was closed because inebriated passengers pushed others overboard! Pleasant open lounge deck on top but the pool is rarely used; unfortunately it becomes another place for washing clothes, or to use as a spitoon".

"The MV Akbar (commissioned in 1933), the cheapest option, is in very poor condition, prone to breakdowns and uncomfortable, and is best avoided. 'Bunk class' is acceptable at first but hygiene standards deteriorate after a day ... and

the food may well run out. Films and whale-watching break the monotony!"

"Many budget travellers decided to camp out on the deck ... creating a "zoo" area cordoning off a section as 'foreigners only'. Often they woke up to find a camera flash going off in their face."

"There is little to do on board so take a book, a Walkman and cards. Bunk class is shown a Hindi film each evening, Cabin class gets to see western films (for example Titanic!). There were a lot of dolphins swimming up to the ship, and the sunsets were also great crowd-pullers."

even at the last moment. Get tickets from *Island Travels* for **Jet Airways**, or direct to **Indian Airlines**, and ask the office manager to be placed on the priority waiting list; fare US$195 (under-30s, $140). Book well ahead. You may request your international carrier to get Andaman's tickets, preferably 6 months ahead. Reconfirm on arrival in India, and after you get to Port Blair. Avoid mid-Apr when the summer holiday rush starts. **Indian Airlines**, G55 Middle Pt, behind PO, T33108. Airport T32983. **Chennai**, Mon, Wed, Fri. **Jet Airways** daily to **Chennai**.

Road Bus: Central Bus Station near Aberdeen Bazar serves state and private buses, T32278. Regular service to villages and districts. Bus stops at *Shompen Hotel* and near the airport. A few private buses run between Chatham jetty and the Cellular Jail. **Long distance**: to **Rangat**, 2 private buses daily (6-7 hrs), 1 via Mayabunder at 0420. **Mayabunder** daily dep 0530-0630, Rs 62 (deluxe Rs 100). Buy tickets a day ahead from agents around the bus stand. **For state buses**: Transport office opposite entrance to Phoenix jetty; numbered tickets go on sale at 1400. Long queues, plenty of touts. The *Diglipur Express* is the quickest to the far north, and the only way of reaching Diglipur the same night. Dep 0530, arrive 1930 (Rs 80). Others to Mayabunder miss the last ferry to Kalighat (1630) which connects to Diglipur.

Sea Sailings between **Haddo Jetty**, Port Blair and Kolkata (66 hrs), Chennai (60 hrs), run to a schedule of sorts 3 to 4 times a month. Also Vishakapatnam (56 hrs) once every 2 months. For immigration formalities, see page 192. Tentative schedules for the month are usually available at the end of the previous month; times of departure and arrival appear about a week before in the local papers. Last minute changes are made depending on weather conditions and tides. Tickets are issued 7 days ahead but are not sold on the day of sailing. **NB** They can be difficult to get. Apply with 3 photos to **Shipping Corporation of India**, 2 Supply Rd, near Mosque, T33347, for tickets. Sailing schedules are also available opposite *Lakshmi Narayan Hotel*, Aberdeen Bazar.

The Directorate of Tourism (see above) has a **tourist quota** of 12 bunk class berths for each sailing from Port Blair to Chennai. Put your name down well in advance. A few days before sailing, collect a form which entitles you to claim a berth from the Shipping Corporation of India a day or 2 before ticket go on public sale.

Chennai: Port Trust, near Customs House, Rajaji Salai, and Dy Director of Shipping Services, A & N, T5220841. **Mumbai**: Coastal Passenger Services, Discovery of India Bldg, 5th floor, Nehru Centre, A Besant Rd, Worli, T4931461. **Vishakapatnam** opposite

Port main gate, Banojirow and Pattabhirmayya, T565597. Ships vary but prices are approximately: Deluxe Cabin (2 beds, shower): Rs 3,500 each; 1st/A Class (4 bunks, shower), Rs 2,000; B Class (4/8 berth), Rs 2,300; 2nd Class (for 6), Rs 2,200; a/c dormitory, Rs 1,500 (on MV *Akbar* only); Bunk Class, Rs 830-960. The ships are about 25 to 65 years old! **Facilities**: meals cost Rs 100 (cabin), Rs 50 (bunk) per day but some may not find them suitable. It is best to carry some snacks. A kiosk sells biscuits, cigarettes, mineral water, soft drinks. **Arrival**: disembarkation can be chaotic and a free-for-all. Taxis demand Rs 50 to go anywhere.

Sailings In addition to the mainland service, a bewildering range of inter-island and harbour ferries operate from Port Blair. **Inter-island ferry** most ferries operate from Phoenix Bay Jetty. **NB** Passengers may feel sea-sick! Regular sailings to **Havelock, Neil and Long Islands, Rangat Bay, Mayabunder** and **Aerial Bay** appear in the *Daily Telegrams* newspaper (or ring Shipping Corp of India for times, T33347). There are 2 decks and hawkers sell snacks on board. **Diglipur** via Aerial Bay Jetty, Tue evening and Fri morning Rs 80, 14 hrs. **Havelock** Rs 20, 4 hrs, direct. **Neil**, Wed and Fri, 4 hrs. **Rangat** 4 a week, 7 hrs. There are also less frequent services to the 2 volcanic islands of Narcondam and Barren. **Little Andaman** (Hut Bay), once a week, Rs 20-60, 8 hrs. **NB** Fares are often doubled if tickets are not bought in advance. **Harbour ferry**: from Phoenix Jetty (vehicular only) to Hope Town, Bamboo Flats, Ross Island daily except Wed, 0830, 1000,1230, Rs 15; Cholunga Wharf, Phoenix Bay: Harbour Cruise, Rs 20, 1500-1700, including Viper Island. From Chatham Jetty to Bamboo Flats and Dundas Pt, about hourly, 0600-2025 (2 hrs).

Train Railway Reservations Office, near Secretariat, open 0800-1230 1300-1400. Supposedly separate queues for Kolkata and Chennai, but a total free-for-all in a small building – a sad sight of a crowd behaving badly. Best avoided. Buy tickets in advance on the mainland if possible.

Banks *Island Travels* change currency and TCs. Hotels *Shompen* and *Bay Island* will change TCs if you spend foreign currency there. *State Bank of India* opp bus station. Open 0900-1300, Sat 0900-1100. **Communications** GPO: near centre, by Indian Airlines office. 0700-2200 weekdays, 0800-1800 weekends. CTO for international calls and Fax service. Also several private STD and ISD booths. **NB** Make your important international calls in Port Blair since links from elsewhere on the islands are unreliable. **Internet** is expected in 2000. **Laundry** Near Bazar Taxi stand recommended (Rs 10 for shirt). Quick Passport **photos**, Rs 50 for 4. **Libraries** *State Library*, near *Annapoorna Café*, has a small collection of reference books on the Andamans, useful for identification of corals and fish. Open 1230-1945. **Tent hire** from *Andaman Teal House*, good condition (deposit Rs 2,000-2,500, Rs 40-60 per day). **Tourist offices** *Govt of India*, 2nd Flr (above Super Shoppe), 89 Junglighat main Rd (VIP Rd), T33006. Enthusiastic, knowledgeable officer (printout of local information). *Director of Tourism*, opposite Indian Airlines, T32694, F30933. Register on the Tourist Quota for boats to Kolkata and Chennai. Unhelpful reception desk (notice "Your time is precious, do not waste it here" sums it up!). Poor postcards. Airport counter open at flight times, T32414. *ANIIDCO* (Andaman and Nicobar Islands Integrated Dev Corp), New Marine Dry Docks (first gate after entrance to Phoenix jetty), T33659. Airport counter T32414. Runs *Tourist Home Complex*, Haddo. Screens occasional films about the islands. **Useful addresses** *Fire*, T32101. *Hospital*, T32102. *Police*, T33077. *Deputy Conservator of Forests*, T32816. Helpful. *PWD Office*, between *Shompen Hotel* and *Lighthouse Cinema*, T33050.

Directory

Credit cards are not accepted anywhere in the Andamans. TCs are only changed at Island Travels, Aberdeen Bazar, Port Blair

Andaman & Nicobar Islands

South Andaman and the Marine National Park

Chiriya Tapu Chiriya Tapu, 28 km from Port Blair, at the southern tip of South Andaman, is only an hour by road. Popular for bird watching, it has excellent beaches with good snorkelling. From the bus stop, which has some tea shops, a track past the *Forest Guest House* (not possible to stay here), leads to the first beach. Continue along the trail through the forest for 20 minutes (several smaller trails are ideal for bird watching), until you reach a second beach with very good corals 50 m out; at low tide you can walk a long way.

Sleeping There are excellent camping spots here, with fresh water, in the village set back from the Munda Pahar beach. The trail continues through the forest to a couple of smaller beaches. The corals are not so spectacular along the coastline, but there is a large range of fish.

Transport Buses leave from Port Blair stand at 0500, 0730, 1030, 1200 (1 hr); returns 10 mins after arrivals; last at 1900. It is an easy journey by hired scooter but beware of oncoming traffic; the single-track road has many blind bends.

Corbyn's Cove
(5 km from Port Blair)
Although the only beach close to Port Blair, the cove is only busy at weekends. The water is warm with gentle surf and the white-sand beach is clean and palm fringed. A government Eco-friendly 'Tourist Village' is under way 1.5 km north of the Cove, which should open by 2001.

Eating *Corbyn's Hut* Snack Bar (at *Peerless Beach Resort* listed under Port Blair) serves reasonable food (fish and chips Rs 55), open all day, friendly staff, quick service, good toilets at resort with lockers and changing rooms.

Transport Easiest by taxi (Rs 60); plenty available for return journey.

Mount Harriet
Altitude: 365m
The hill is good for either a morning or a whole day trip but make an early start to avoid the heat. A path through the forest starts by the derelict water viaduct in Hope Town, which joins the surfaced road near the top (excellent vines for would-be-Tarzans here!). Allow 1½ hours to the top. Alternatively, the bus from the jetty stops in Hope Town near the viaduct, or will drop you at the start of the road up the hill with a 4 km walk from here. Near the top of the road lie the ruins of the Chief Commissioner's bungalow, abandoned in 1942. Signs show where the rooms were.

It is also possible to ride a scooter to the top but you will pass the Forest Check Post where national park fees are charged. Entry Rs 10, scooter Rs 10, Camera Rs 25. Video camera Rs 1500. Taking the forest path on foot avoids the check post and fees.

Sleeping *Forest Guest House* (with permission). You can get water and tea from the caretaker. There is an octagonal viewing platform at the top with good views of Ross Island, and a small garden for picnics.

Transport Vehicles must take a **ferry** from Phoenix Bay to Bamboo Flats. Chatham to Hope Town or Bamboo Flats carry foot passengers only (see 'Transport' below); from Bamboo Flats it is a 20 minute walk along the coast to Hope Town. A bus (0600, 0800) runs along this road. For return from Hope Town jetty: 1315, 1415 to Bamboo

Into the deep

There are many excellent locations for snorkelling. The most popular site for a day trip is MG National Marine Park (Wandoor); Chiriya Tapu is very easy to reach from Port Blair. It is best to bring your own mask and snorkel. You may need to pay up to Rs 5,000 as deposit when hiring equipment. Most close from early May during the monsoons.

Scuba diving is a boom business in the Andamans and the number of diving schools is growing. It is difficult to find a cheaper and more beautiful location to learn to dive in the world. For fanatics, longer dive trips can be organized to unexplored sites around the Andamans providing enough people are interested.

The best dive sites for a day trip are in the vicinity of Cinque Island though the Government tax of Rs 1,000 for dives makes it pricey.

Samudra 'Come Dive with Us', T33159, run by Sri Manavi Tukker ("tough instructor"!), and Port Bair Underwater Dive Centre, run by F Jah, affiliated with Peerless Beach Resort, charge Rs 16,000 for a four-day PADI affiliated Open Water course and certificates. Very well organized. You can also get two Open Water dives for Rs 3,200 at the latter.

Andaman Dives opposite Samudra Beach Resort, run by an experienced Swiss diver, Herbert Burvil is well-equipped and efficiently run.

Flats and 1500 to Phoenix Bay; Bamboo Flats to Chatham Jetty: 1520, 1615, 1735, 1830. Taxis charge Rs 320 return to the top from Bamboo Flats jetty. By road alone it is 45 km instead of 15 km.

Black Rocks

Black Rocks (Kalapathar) is 2 km from Mount Harriet and **Madhuban** via Mount Carpenter, 16 km. A signpost marks the start of the nature trail from Mount Harriet which is easy to follow as far as the Black Rocks, the spot where prisoners were pushed to their death. After Black Rocks, the trail is unclear; it is easy to get lost so take a guide if you plan to walk the whole route. The walk back along the rocky coast is uninteresting; you can get a bus 5 km after the lighthouse. **Madhuban Beach** is on the east side where young elephants are trained for forestry; at **Burma Nalla**, 3 km away, they are used for lumbering.

Ross Island

Ross Island was originally developed under the British as the Residence of the Chief Commissioner, and the administrative headquarters. During the Second World War, it was occupied by the Japanese whose legacy is an ugly complex of concrete bunkers which are still intact. The rest of the buildings on the island are ruins with spotted deer living peacefully among them. In many cases the walls are only still standing because of the climbing trees. However, the church in the centre and the Subalterns' club are impressive. The small **museum** by the cafeteria has interesting old photos. The island is officially still under the jurisdiction of the Indian Navy and swimming is not allowed despite the clear enticing waters by the jetty. Open dawn to dusk, except Wednesdays. Entry Rs 10 on arrival; foreigners must sign a registration book. Allow two hours.

Eating A small cafeteria sells cold drinks and biscuits. Take a picnic if you plan to spend the day, and if the cafeteria is shut, try cracking open a fallen coconut. Delicious!

Transport Boats from Phoenix Jetty, 0830, 1030, 1230, 1400, 1500. Take an early boat as later ones get very crowded, especially at weekends. Return boat at 0840, 1040, 1240, 1410, 1640.

The Marine National Park and the Off Islands

About 30 km southwest of Port Blair, the Mahatma Gandhi Marine National Park is well worth visiting. The coral beds and underwater life is exceptional off some of these uninhabited islands.

Ins & outs From Port Blair there are frequent public buses to Wandoor, where from the wooden jetty by the Park Reception Centre, tour boats leave daily at 1000 and return about 1430. Bus, Rs 5 (tour operators charge Rs 90 return!); 0830 bus connects with the 1000 tour. Advance booking is unnecessary. Tickets (boat and entry) are sold at the small kiosk by the bus stop. Jolly Buoy Rs 90 (return), 50 mins; Red Skin, Rs 65, 30 mins.

Background Covering an area of 280 sq km, the park is a group of 15 islands with deep blue waters separating them. It includes Grub, Redskin, Jolly Buoy, Pluto, Boat Island, with Tarmugli to the west, Kalapahar or Rutland to the east and the Twins to the south. It is very rich, not only in marine life but also in the variety of tropical flowers and birds. The dense forests come down to the beach where the mangrove thrives on the water's edge.

Near **Wandoor**, some white-sand beaches strewn with driftwood, provide good snorkelling at high tide for those who miss the tour. The Diving Society, 1 km from the jetty, runs courses (see box). **Alexander Island**, opposite Wandoor jetty, is uninhabited and is covered in dense rain forest. Permission to visit is given to students and for scientific research by the Chief Wildlife Warden, Haddo, Port Blair.

Wildlife There is a rich variety of tropical fauna, including angelfish, green parrot, yellow butterfly, black surgeon and blue damsel fish. There are also silver jacks, squirrel, clown fish and sweetlips as well as sea cucumbers, sea anemones, starfish and a variety of shells – cowries, turbots, conches and the rarer giant clam, as much as a metre wide. It offers excellent opportunities for **watersports**, including snorkelling and scuba diving. There are turtles, sharks and barracudas on the outer reefs and many beautiful corals including brain, finger, mushroom and antler, the colours derived from the algae that thrive in the living coral. **Coral** and **shell** collecting is strictly forbidden.

Viewing Only two islands in the Park are open to tourists – **Jolly Buoy, Red Skin**, as well as **Cinque** (contrary to what you might be told) and it is forbidden to land on any other island or stop overnight within the park. Mask and snorkel hire available here and in Port Blair. Park entry Rs 10.

Tours are arranged depending on demand (minimum 10 people); ask your hotel to enquire. The cost, around Rs 800, covers transport to/from any hotel in Port Blair, park entry fee, simple packed lunch, soft drinks and bottled water. You will be picked up around 0530 and taken to Wandoor Village by boat (3½-4 hours, depending on the tide). This allows a maximum of four hours on the island since boats must return before dark. There are plans to introduce faster boats, starting from Chiriya Tapu, to make it more attractive.

Park information **Jolly Buoy** is a small island at the centre of the park; at low tide you can walk round it in less than one hour. Beach palm umbrellas provide shade while toilets and a changing room are set back from the beach. All rubbish should be placed in the bin provided and returned to the mainland.

Jolly Buoy is an ideal spot for first-time snorkellers. You can view coral and the marine life while still standing or kneeling. For the more experienced, there is a wall 10 m off the beach. When the tide is going out there are very strong currents around the island. There are also scorpion fish.

Red Skin When open to tourists, Red Skin has a limited beach coastline, mostly to the west, with caves to the rocky north and mangrove swamps to the south and east. However, the conditions are ideal for snorkelling; near low tide you can go out 150 m and still be in shallow waters. There are a couple of forest trails and a small freshwater spring; you may occasionally see spotted deer. ■ *Usually only open on Monday. Check at park jetty. Getting there: Both Jolly Buoy and Red Skin can be visited by glass-bottomed boat, allowing 3-4 hrs on the island. Boats from Wandoor Jetty at 1000. Jolly Buoy Rs 83, Red Skin Rs 55.*

Cinque Island is really two hilly islands joined by a permanent sand bar. The sheltered bay here, with very clear water, makes it the best place for snorkelling in the park. Unfortunately, it is a long day trip and expensive to visit, but very worthwhile.

If you walk along the beach to the right of where you land, a forest trail leads you to another excellent beach on the other side of the island where there is a tremendous range of coral. **NB** Only suitable for the experienced since there is no supervision or help at hand on this side. ■ *Getting there: You may only visit Cinque on a trip organized by a tour company (ask any major hotel in town).* **Brothers and Sisters Islands**, a part of the Cinque Group, can only be visited as part of a diving trip.

South Andaman & Marine National Park

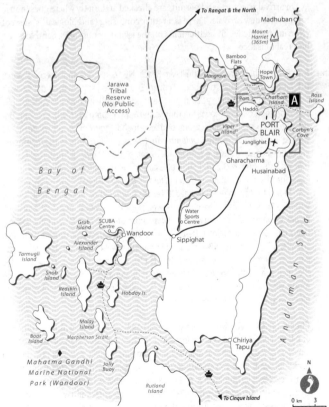

Related map
A Port Blair, page 195

Ritchie's Archipelago

The Archipelago (Outram, E Oringlis, H Lawrence, J Lawrence, Wilson, Peel, Havelock, Neil, Long and Sir Hugh Rose Islands) lies between 20 and 40 km off the east coast of south Andaman and Baratang Islands. Most are inhabited, but only three are open to foreign visitors, **Havelock** (the most popular), **Neil** and **Long Island**. They are much more relaxed, the focus of the government's tourist effort and can be reached by the regular ferry service between Port Blair (Phoenix Jetty) and Rangat Bay (Nimbutala Jetty).

Havelock Island

This beautiful island with pristine white beaches is the government's principal centre for tourist development outside Port Blair. It is the island chosen by most visitors as an escape from Port Blair.

Despite its popularity, you can (as anywhere in the Andamans) very easily escape from other visitors and find your private bit of beach for the day. You can cycle along the road to **Radhnagar** beach (No 7), 11 km to the southwest of the Jetty (No 1), and one of the best in the Andamans. Beach No 3 is 3 km from the jetty, while No 5 is further south.

Festival A week-long *Mela* marking the birth of Subhas Chandra Bose is held in January with special Bengali cultural programmes.

On arrival passports and permits are checked at the jetty where guest house touts pester new arrivals. There is a rather confusing (and illogical) system of referring to beaches and settlements on the island by numbers. Sand flies can be a real nuisance.

Sleeping
Beach camping is not allowed

B-C category huts are being built. At Beach **No 7**, remote and deeply shaded: **B-F** *Jungle Lodge*, small, bamboo, Nicobari 'Eco huts' on stilts, nets, 4 deluxe with wash block (6 more being added), also basic open huts with nets (overpriced at Rs 150), common bath not too clean (public shower on approach road), excellent but pricey food, beer, postcards, promoting 'eco-friendly tourism', good diving (Swiss run). At Beach **No 5**: Govt **B-E** *Dolphin Yatri Niwas*, public bus stops 100 m from the entrance, then walk down a sandy track to campsite, T33238. 18 huts on stilts, very thin walls (Rs 300, 800 and 1,500), pleasant gardens, limited restaurant, no good beach nearby as it is a dumping ground for felled trees cleared for the resort, popular with Indian tourists so reserve ahead. **F** *Tented Camp* rather neglected, tents (better large, Rs 100 with Western toilet and shower; small, Rs 50 with shared wash block 100 m away), limited lunch and dinner *thalis* (order ahead), popular and cheap, very peaceful, closes at first rainfall. Reservation Secretariat, Director of Tourism, Port Blair, T32694, or try Manager. **NB** There is a permanent naval base near this beach. Landings are commonplace. Near the **Jetty** (**No 1**): **F** *MS*, rooms (Rs 200), open-sided thatched huts with floor mattress, net (Rs 150), good food. **F** *Sea View* or *Maya*, 8 rooms vary, some with bath and sea view (Rs 100-200), likely to get shabby (staff are glued to TV), but a good meeting place.

Eating

Cheap Near the Jetty, **No 1**: There are several basic places serving reasonable fish, vegetable and rice dishes. *Das* is the friendliest and best. *Hot Stuff* in town square, (same family as *China Room* in Port Blair) got mixed reports. *MS*, serves wonderful garlic fish (pick your own!). *Women's Co-op Café* does good *thalis*. Beach **No 7**: *Harmony* near the beach, excellent lunch/dinner Rs 60 (delicately spiced huge fish steak, spicy vegetables, chips, dessert) but order before owner's market visit, pots of tea all day (books, cassettes to accompany), very pleasant, great atmosphere, packed in the evening, may have to wait 2 hrs in season so friendly and enterprising Ashok has set up chess, backgammon and carom to maintain a happy, relaxed atmosphere. Highly recommended.

Shopping

Village **No 3** has a good market. *General Stores* has all sorts of camping equipment.

Sport

The *Jungle Lodge*'s **diving school** (better areas and prices than from Port Blair) Swiss run, professional and thoughful, new digital equipment, PADI course Rs 14,000, 2-dive trip with dive master, Rs 2,500. Recommended.

Transport

Two taxis and a jeep drive from the jetty to Beach Nos 3, 5 and 7, Rs 10-30 (varies with number of passengers and luggage). **Local Bikes and scooters**: for hire at Jetty (ask at hotel) or at the paan shop under Susmita Electronics. Also outside *Dolphin Yatri Niwas*. Bikes Rs 35; scooters Rs 125. **Bus**: Regular service from Jetty (No 1) all the way to Radhnagar Beach (No 7), via Village No 3 and *Dolphin Yatri Niwas* (No

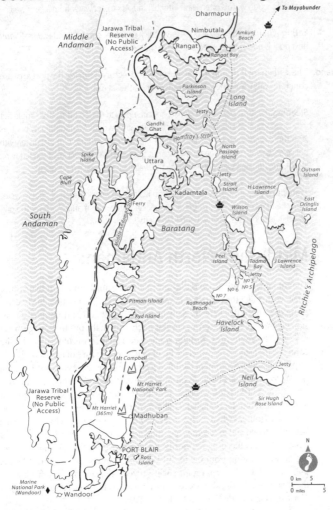

South Andaman & Ritchie's Archipelago

Andaman & Nicobar Islands

5); 2 hourly, 0700-1100, 1500-1900; from No 7, 0600-1000, 1400-1800. Avoid being swamped by school children at 0800 and 1500. **Ferry**: Inter-island, from Phoenix Jetty to Havelock, daily.

Directory **Medical Centre** at No 3. **Internet** at No 7.

Neil Island
40 km from Port Blair

Neil is the smallest island in the Andamans you can stay on. It is very relaxed and attracts fewer visitors than Havelock. The best beach is close to the jetty and you will find shops sell provisions and basic camping gear (except tents, hammocks). ■ *Getting there: To/from Port Blair takes 4 hrs, Rs 9; to Havelock, 2½ hrs, Rs 6.*

Sleeping Govt **E** *Hawabill Nest*, T82630, simple, clean rooms (Rs 400-800 if a/c works) with hot shower, dorm (Rs 75), cook (buy provisions in the market and ask him to prepare meal), snorkel hire; Reservation, Secretariat, Director of Tourism, Port Blair, T32694. *Camping* with permission from PWD, Port Blair, 33050. Beach No 1 is unspoilt and peaceful though visitors often leave litter behind. Ask to get water from a farm well.

Eating *Chand* in the village does great chick pea *daal*, egg rolls and *vadai*s. *Shanti* next door is good too. Bottled water is in short supply.

Long Island

The settlement is dominated by the plywood factory. Outside the port area are concrete walkways; there is no transport on the island.

Sleeping **F** *Forest Dept Guest House*, on path uphill to the left from jetty, simple but very good value. At Lalaji Beach, a 2-hr walk through woods (or get there by boat, Rs 200) there is *camping* by a small coconut plantation. Rs 20 per night (register with police on arrival). Beach lined with coconut trees, and cattle steal any food left lying about. The drinking water quality from the well near the beach is suspect.

Transport Enquire at jetty for ferry to Port Blair via Havelock ; usually 2 boats a week. From Rangat it is possible to get a lumber boat from the mangrove jetty to Long Island (if taking a bus, ask for 'Long Island jetty').

Middle and North Andamans

The Andaman Trunk Road is the only road to the north from Port Blair. Since it passes through the restricted Jawara tribal reserve, it is not possible to drive along this yourself. There are daily buses to Rangat and Mayabunder. Occasionally the more adventurous jawaras hitch a lift on the bus to the edge of the reserve. The route runs through some spectacular forest but sadly, despite controls, there has already been a lot of selective clearance of hard woods.

Although the government has lifted restrictions on where you can visit, until new *Yatri Niwases* are built, accommodation is limited. PWD *Rest Houses*, usually on the outskirts of a village, provide the best accommodation. Ones at Rangat, Mayabunder, Kalighat, Diglipur, Aerial Bay, Kalipur and Long Island are open to tourists when rooms are available. They are clean, well run, often the best place to eat and excellent value (rates are uniform and clearly posted). **NB** Govt and local officials have priority, and they are often full. The housekeeper requires permission from the local PWD officer to release a room. Patience, politeness and a clean appearance helps! If you can plan ahead (difficult given the erratic ferry sailings), reserve in advance at PWD Office between *Shompen Hotel* and Lighthouse Cinema, Port Blair, 33050.

Middle Andaman

It is the only place with a choice of private accommodation for at least 20 visitors. **Amkunj Beach**, 8 km, has little shade left but there is good snorkelling off the rocks at the top end of the beach: from Rangat, take any bus heading for Nimbutala or Mayabunder up to the fork for Rangat Bay, then walk 1 km along track to right just after the heli-pad.

There is a good sandy beach across the road from *Hawksbill Nest*. Ideal for swimming but it is a Wildlife Sanctuary where turtles nest between November-April. In order to step onto the beach permission is needed from the Forest Dept at Rangat, Mayabunder or the Beat Officer at Betapur, 4 km north of *Hawksbill Nest*; entrance fee Rs 10 per day. **NB** Those caught on the beach without permission are promised "an unpleasant experience".

Sleeping E Govt *Hawksbill Nest*, Cutbert Bay, 18 km from Rangat (buses to Mayabunder go past, ask for 'Yatri Niwas'). 8 clean sea-facing rooms (Rs 250, better views on 1st floor), 2 a/c Rs 400, 4-bed dorms (Rs 75), still doing reasonably well. Contact Secretariat, Dir. of Tourism, Port Blair, T32694. **F** *Chandra Mohan Lodge*, blue wooden building on outskirts of town, rundown but friendly staff. Definitely avoid *Krishna*.

Eating Cheap: *Annapurna*, corner of vegetable market (from bus stand, turn left opposite *Krishna Lodge*, then right and left again). Good food. *Darbar Bakery*, near bus stand (on right, at start of road leading to PWD *Rest House*). Good selection.

Transport Road Bus: to **Mayabunder** 0600, connects with ferry to Kalighat at 0930, later bus at 1145; to **Port Blair** *Exp* (B), daily, 0800, 0900 (Rs 33). From **Port Blair** by bus to Rangat there are 2 ferry crossings (Nilambur and Gandhi Ghat). Takes up to 8 hrs to Rangat town, depending on bus connections, ie whether your bus goes on this ferry and/or if bus is waiting on other side at Nilambur. **Sea Ferry**: the jetty is at Rangat Bay (Nimbutala), 7 km from town. To **Port Blair** 0600, 7 hrs, buy tickets (Rs 30) on board. There is an 'Inner' (Creek) and an 'Outer' route, the latter via Strait, Havelock (30 min stop) and Neil islands (see Transport under Port Blair). Lumber boats from Mangrove Jetty go to **Long Island**; **Mayabunder**, 3 per week, 3 hrs.

Directory Banks *State Bank of India*, by the bus stand. **Communications** Post Office: opposite the Police Station.

Mayabunder is the administrative centre for Middle and North Andaman. All amenities are situated along a single road which runs along the brow of a ridge sticking out into the bay; the port is at the north end.

Ask at the Forestry Department next to the PWD *Rest House* for information on places to visit. They are very knowledgeable and helpful and can advise on where you can walk in the forest and how to get there.

You can visit **Karmateng Beach** (25 minutes by bus). A shallow sandy slope over 1 km long, with a few rocks at the north end, it is not so good for snorkelling. Since there is no fresh water nearby, you have to walk back to the road and ask local Karen farmers. A short distance from Karmateng is another idyllic beach popular with foreign tourists at **Gujinala**. You need permission from DFO in Mayabunder or from Beat Officer at Karmateng.

There are several islands in the bay opposite the jetty which can be reached by *dunghy*; ask fishermen and expect to pay Rs 120 for a boat charter for several hours. All offer safe beaches for swimming but there is no good coral. **Avis Island** is a private coconut plantation. You need permission from the Forestry Department to visit.

Rangat

Andaman & Nicobar Islands

Mayabunder
157 km by sea from Port Blair

Sleeping Govt **E** *Swiftlet Nest* away from the beach, overlooking paddy fields (forest not cleared at the beach). 10 good rms (Rs 250), 4 a/c (Rs 400), dorm (Rs 75). T32747. **F** PWD *Rest House*, superb location overlooking Stewart Bay and Sound Island. 5 rms in old block, 8 rms in new, all with bath, good mosquito nets, fans, comfortable and clean, restaurant, excellent food (non-residents order ahead), often full, essential to reserve in Port Blair, excellent value. Avoid **F** *Dhanalakshmi* and *Lakshmi Narayan* with small, dirty rooms (Rs 80). As a last resort, Jetty *Waiting Rooms* provide some shelter and canteen food.

Shopping *Consumer Co-op Stores*, by State Bank has basic provisions. There is a small fruit and vegetable market near the helipad at the other end of the town from the jetty.

Transport Road Bus: Port Blair *Exp* (A) and (C), dep 0600, tickets sold from 1500 the day before, at bus station (2 km from jetty). **Rangat** local bus, 0830, 0915, 1345, 1700. Also some private buses. **Karmateng** Many for beach, 0715, 0900, 1200, 1445, 1700 (return bus approximately 35 mins after these times). **Diglipur** the road is still under construction. **Sea Ferry**: for **Diglipur** take local ferry to Kalighat, or wait for the inter-island ferry from Port Blair which calls here en route to Aerial Bay every 11-12 days. **Kalighat** small sea ferry daily, 0930, 1445, 2½ hrs (Rs 2), is very crowded, with little shade. Private *dunghies* leave at dawn; they can carry 20 people (Rs 20 each) and the occasional scooter; a charter costs Rs 400. **Port Blair** Check outside Asst Commissioner's office near police station for schedules.

Avis Island This tiny island is just east of Mayabunder but its ownership is disputed between the Forestry Dept and The Coconut Society of Mayabunder. To visit, get permission from DCF, Mayabunder, and charter a *dunghy*.

Foreign tourists are also permitted to visit (with permission from DCF, Mayabunder) **Curlew Island**, **Rayhill Island**, **Sound Island**, **Interview Island** and **Mohanpur** on the eastern coast of North Andaman. Tourists are encouraged to destroy illegal deer traps they find.

Interview Island The island which has wild elephants now has a Protected Forest. Day visits can in theory be organized from Mayabunder (20 km). **Sleeping** You may be able to stay overnight at the Forest Dept *Guest House* with 3 rooms; contact DCF, Mayabunder. ■ *Getting there: Since the ferry service was stopped, it can only be visited in a private boat.*

Barren Islands Across to the east from Middle Andaman, Barren has India's only active volcano which erupted in 1991 causing widespread destruction of the island's ecosystem. Smoky fire belches from the side of the crater. It is only possible to visit on a day trip with no landings permitted. Sailings are infrequent and it is essential to get a permit from the tourist office in Port Blair.

North Andaman

Kalighat It is a small settlement at the point where the creek becomes too shallow for the ferry to go any further. Of no particular interest, it still makes a very pleasant and peaceful stopover between Port Blair and the north. You can cross the river by the mangrove footbridge and follow the path up into the forest which is good for bird watching. Sadly you also get a good impression of how many hardwoods are being logged.

You can take a bus to the beach at Ramnagar (11 km). Better still, hire a cycle for Rs 5 per hour and enjoy a very pleasant push, ride, free-wheel, with a refreshing swim at the end as a reward.

Sleeping and eating Only at **F** PWD *Rest House*, on a hill, 2 mins' walk from jetty. 3 rooms (1 for VIPs only), very helpful and friendly housekeeper, excellent vegetable *thalis*, generous portions. There are a few near the jetty. *Viji* has reasonable food. *Bakery* next door.

Transport Local Bus: to **Diglipur** Regular local service (45 mins), 0630, 0800, 1030, 1130, 1400, connect with ferry from Mayabunder. **Sea Ferry**: to **Mayabunder** daily, 0500, 1230, 2 hrs (Rs 3), can get very crowded and virtually no shade; also *Dunghy*, 0600, 2 hrs (Rs 15); or charter a *dunghy* at any time for about Rs 300 (the rate for a full boat).

Previously known as Port Cornwallis, Diglipur is the most northerly commercial centre which foreigners can visit. There is a good market and shops; a special *Mela* is held in January/February which attracts traders. **Diglipur**

Sleeping and eating **E** *Drua*, 15 rooms (Rs 200), but unhelpful manager. **F** *Laxmi*, 4 clean rooms with common bath (Rs 120), friendly, helpful. Recommended. **F** PWD *Rest House*, uphill on right beyond the central bus stand. Meals to order, refuse most foreigners, who must apply in Port Blair to have any chance, strict on checkout at 0800. The **Sports Stadium**, with clean, spacious, guarded area for travellers with immaculate toilets and showers. Recommended. Plenty of snack bars, tea houses and fresh fruit in the market.

North Andaman

Andaman & Nicobar Islands

Transport Bus: to all the surrounding villages and beaches. Regular service to Kalighat, 45 mins (last at 1900) and Aerial Bay (30 mins) which has the occasional boat to Port Blair.

The small fishing village is the last peaceful location before returning to Port Blair. Most of the fish is taken to the market in Diglipur. **Aerial Bay**

Sleeping and eating **F** PWD *Rest House* high up on a hill. 2 rooms, often full when Port Blair boat is sailing, eat at *Mohan*. Also an unmarked wooden hotel on the left, coming into town from Diglipur. Excellent fish is sold near harbour gates; larger fish (tuna and barracuda) in the afternoon (Rs 20-30 per kg). Owner of *Mohan* speaks some English and is helpful, will prepare excellent fish dishes for you, good *thalis*, selection of drinks. A few shops sell basic provisions and there is a small market by the bus stand.

Transport Road Bus: Private and public buses to Diglipur and Kalipur, approximately every hour. **NB** It is not possible to reach Port Blair by bus in 1 day, the furthest one can hope to get is Rangat. **Sea Ferry**: To Mayabunder and

Port Blair (2 sailings a month). The jetty ticket office is not always sure when the next boat is due; better to contact the coastguard tower who have radio contact with Port Blair (no telephone connection with South Andaman). Fare: bunk Rs 47, deck Rs 27 (cabins for Govt officials only); Indian canteen meals. Tickets go on sale the day before departure at the Tehsildar's office, next to Diglipur *Rest House*; to avoid a long wait there, buy on the boat, though you may sometimes have to pay more, and only get a deck ticket.

Smith & Ross Islands From Aerial Bay, you can visit the islands just north where it is possible to camp on pleasant forested beaches. You need permission from the Range Officer (opposite Jetty entrance); open 0700-1400, Monday-Saturday; he doesn't issue permits for Lamia Bay. Ferry: 0600, 1400, Rs 5; or hire a *dunghy*.

Saddle Peak National Park Theoretically 'Lamia Bay Permits' for Saddle Peak and Lamia Bay are available from the Beat Officer in Lamia Bay. However, the path from Lamia Bay to Saddle Peak is very overgrown. **Kalipur** is a small group of farm houses on both sides of the road with a shop and a *Yatri Niwas* a few kilometres south of Aerial Bay. There is a very interesting beach at Kalipur with Saddle Peak as an impressive backdrop, accessible via a small path almost opposite the *Turtle Resort*.

Lamia Bay has a pebble beach south of Kalipur which you can walk to. From the bus stop the road leads straight ahead onto a path which is easy to follow (30 minutes). It is possible to camp under a small round palm-leaf shelter. To the north, there are small bays strewn with large eroded boulders, whilst the beaches to the south lead towards Saddle Peak (730 m), 4½ km away.

Saddle Peak Despite the relatively short distance, the rocky beach, the steep climb, the thick forest and the heat, mean that you need a whole day for the trek, starting early in the morning after camping in Lamia Bay. **NB** Don't attempt the whole trip in a day from Aerial Bay.

Sleeping E-F *Turtle Resort Yatri Niwas*, 8 good rooms Rs 250 (4 a/c, Rs 400), dorm (Rs 75). Clean, very peaceful, on a hillock overlooking paddy fields with thick forests leading up to the Saddle Peak National Park to the south. Though called '*Turtle Resort*', the rooms are named after birds with such unlikely examples as Ostrich and Penguin! Contact T32747.

Transport Buses between Diglipur and Kalipur, via Aerial Bay. From Kalipur: dep 1230, 1330, 1530, 1740, 2015; to Aerial Bay, 25 mins, Rs 2.

Narcondam Island East of North Andaman, this is the most remote island in the group. An extinct craterless volcano, it is covered in luxuriant forest that is the home of the unique Narcondam hornbill (*Rhyticeros narcondami*) and was declared a sanctuary in 1977. It is a bird-watchers paradise though permission to visit is very hard to get and only 24-hour stops are allowed. There are occasional sailings from Aerial Bay.

Little Andaman Island

Malaria is rife This large island lies 120 km (eight hours) south of Port Blair across the Duncan Passage. The main village, **Hut Bay** to the southeast, is 2 km away from the jetty. Heavily deforested during the 1960s and 70s, much of the island has become virtually treeless. Betel, red palm and banana plantations dominate the scenery. It is possible to camp on the large beach in the north of the island (22 km from the jetty), but tourist facilities are virtually non-existent, with only one restaurant next to the *GM Lodge*, and no bottled water so you need to carry everything with you. The long distance makes visiting difficult; women travellers have complained of harassment.

Sleeping F PWD *Rest House*, excellent clean double rooms, no food, rather hostile staff insist on waking guests at 0600 every day; the only alternative is the **F** *GM Lodge*, tiny singles, 1 double.

Nicobar Islands

The names given by travellers and sailors from the east and the west all referred to these islands as the Land of the Naked - Nicobar is derived from the Tamil word nakkavaram. The islands which lay on the trade route to the Far East were visited in the 11th century by the seafaring Cholas during the rule of King Rajendra I who attempted to extend his rule here. Before the British used the Nicobars as a penal territory in the late 19th century, European missionaries (particularly the Danish) made converts during the 17th and 18th centuries but few survived the difficulties of the climate and most died of fever within a year.

The islands, including **Katchal** with a large rubber plantation, **Nancowry** harbour, **Indira Point**, India's southernmost tip and **Campbell Bay** (Great Nicobar), are closed to foreign visitors; Car Nicobar to the north can be visited by Indians with a permit. The significant tribal population live in distinctive huts, which look like large thatched domes which are raised on stilts about 2 m high and are entered through the floor. The Nicobarese enjoy wrestling, fishing, swimming and canoeing but are best known for their love of music. Villages still participate in competitions of traditional unaccompanied singing and dancing which mark every festivity.

Andaman & Nicobar Islands

Kerala

5

Kerala

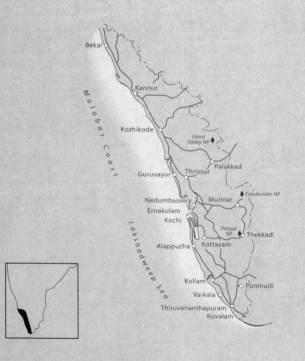

Kerala, South India's most densely populated region has a distinctive charm. From the narrow, coconut-fringed beaches to the still densely forested slopes of the hills inland, Kerala is rich in beautiful landscapes. Despite its busyness and rapidly growing cities, it also has a wonderfully 'getting away from it all' feel. The backwaters beckon the visitor to catch a glimpse of Keralan village life, while festivals are marked by great elephant marches, snake boat races and colourful Kathakali dances. High levels of education and health care have given Kerala an enviable reputation elsewhere in India, and its unique balance of Hindu, Muslim and Christian, sets it apart even from its neighbours Tamil Nadu and Karnataka.

★ *A foot in the door*

  Drift along the backwaters in a punted wooden boat and watch waterside life carry on

  *Arrive early for a **Kathakali** dance performance to see the costumes and watch the make-up*

  *Wander through the spice market in **Fort Kochi**, taking in the Jewish quarter and the **Mattacherry Palace***

  *Take a short walk in the western Ghats from **Munnar** to **Top Station***

  *Relax with an **ayurdevic** massage*

  *Visit the unique snake temple **Mannarsala** near Haripad*

  *Enter into the festival mood at **Thrissur** during Pooram, with elephant processions accompanied by drummers and horn players*

  *Relax at **Varkala beach***

Background

The land
Population: 33 mn
Area: 39,000 sq km

Stretching from some of the highest mountains of the Western Ghats to the lush coastal plain, Kerala encapsulates the rich diversity of western India's coastal landscapes. Its narrow coastal fringe has been raised from the sea in the last one million years. Immediately inland are low, rolling hills of laterite, succeeded by the ancient rocks which form the backbone of the Western Ghats.

Dotted along the edge of the ghats from Ponmudi in the south to Munnar in the centre and Sultan's Battery in the north, Kerala's hill stations experience the full force of the wet monsoon from May to November, often being covered in cloud. The hills offer lovely country for walks and treks.

The state's palm-fringed backwaters along the coastline are a special attraction, see page 242. The Silent Valley National Park in the Western Ghats (restricted entry) has the only substantial area of tropical evergreen rain forest in the country. As forested land is increasingly under threat from soaring land values and growing population the Government legislated in May 2000 to make all ecologically sensitive areas in Kerala the direct responsibility of the state.

Climate Kerala does not have an extended totally dry season characteristic of the rest of India, but is particularly wet from June to September. Maximum temperatures rarely rise above 32°C while minimum temperatures at sea level are never below 20°C.

Wildlife There are two major national parks (Eravikulam/Rajamali and Silent Valley) and a number of small wildlife sanctuaries in the state where you may expect to see wild elephants, the endearing, once-endangered Nilgiri Tahr, langurs and deer. In addition, Kerala has a distinctive and beautiful range of *butterflies*.

History
Early history Although the name Kerala is often widely explained today as meaning "land of coconuts", derived from the Malayalam word "kera" or coconut palm, this is not its origin. '*Keralaputra*' (land of the sons of the Cheras – *putra*, son) was referred to in Asoka's edicts dating from between 273-236 BC, over a thousand years before the Malayalam language of contemporary Kerala took shape. To the Tamils the region was known for centuries as *Seranadu*, again meaning land of the Cheras.

After Asoka's rock inscriptions (273-236 BC) the historical record is sparse. The Romans carried on extensive trade through Kerala, but there are virtually no archaeological remains before the *megalithic monuments* of the second century BC (eg found just north of Kochi). Kerala developed its own distinctive types, most strikingly the so-called hood-stones (*kudaikal*), hat-stones (*topi-kal*) and rock cut tombs. All three have umbrella-like forms, which symbolize authority and power.

Periodically the region had been under Tamil control. The Cheras, who established themselves in the Kuttanad region around Alappuzha as the first Kerala power, continued to use Tamil as the state language up to the seventh century. 200 years separated the ending of the first Chera Dynasty and the emergence of the powerful and prosperous second empire.

The Cheras developed a wide network of trade links in which both the long established Christian community and the Jewish community participated fully. Mahodayapuram (modern Kodangallur) traded from Cordoba in the west to Sumatra in the east. However, the neighbouring Cholas launched several successful attacks against Chera power from AD 985 onwards. When

Chola power itself disintegrated at the end of the 11th century, minor princi-
palities emerged, dominated by a new group, the Nambudiri Brahmans, and
contested for control of the region's vital trade in spices – pepper, ginger, cardamom and cinnamon.

The Zamorin of Calicut Calicut gradually became dominant under the
Zamorin (literally *Lord of the Sea*), who had well established contacts with the
Arab world. By some accounts he was the wealthiest ruler in contemporary
India. He was unable to use these advantages to unite Kerala, and during the
16th century the Portuguese exploited the rivalry of the Raja of Kolattiri with the
Zamorin of Calicut, being granted permission to trade from Kochi in 1499. Over
the following century there was fierce competition and sometimes open warfare
between the Portuguese, bent on eliminating Arab trading competition, and the
Zamorin, whose prosperity depended on that Arab trade. The competition was
encouraged by the rulers of Kochi, in the hope that by keeping the hands of both
tied in conflict their own independence would be strengthened.

After a century of hostility, the **Dutch** arrived on the west coast. The
Zamorin seized the opportunity of gaining external support, and on 11
November 1614 concluded a Treaty giving the Dutch full trading rights. In
1615 the British East India Company was also given the right to trade by the
Zamorin. By 1633 the Dutch had captured all the Portuguese forts of Kollam,
Kodungallur, Purakkad, Kochi and Kannur. The ruler of Kochi rapidly made
friends with the Dutch, in exchange having the new Mattancherry Palace built
for him, and inevitably facing renewed conflict with Calicut as a result.

Travancore and the British In the decade after 1740 Raja Marthanda Varma
succeeded in uniting a number of petty states around Thiruvananthapuram
and led them to a crushing victory over the Dutch in the Battle of Kolachel in
1741. By 1758 the Zamorin of Calicut was forced to withdraw from Kochi, but
the Travancore ruler's reign was brief. In 1766 Haidar Ali had led his cavalry
troops down onto the western coastal plain, and he and his son Tipu Sultan
pushed further and further south with a violence that is still bitterly remembered. In 1789, as Tipu was preparing to launch a final assault on the south of
Travancore, the British attacked him from the east. He withdrew his army
from Kerala and the Zamorin and other Kerala leaders looked to the British to
take control of the forts previously held by Tipu's officers. Tipu Sultan's first
defeat at the hands of Lord Cornwallis led to the Treaty of Seringapatam in
1792, under which Tipu surrendered all his captured territory in the northern
part of Kerala, to direct British rule. Travancore and Kochi became Princely
states under ultimate British authority.

People The distinctiveness of Kerala's cultural identity is reflected in the **Culture**
Brahmin myths of its origin. As Robin Jeffrey has put it, Parasurama, the sixth
incarnation of Vishnu, having been banished from India, was given permission by Varuna, the Lord of the Sea, to reclaim all the land within the throw of
his axe. When Parasaruma threw the axe it fell from Kanniyakumari to
Gokarnam, and as the sea withdrew Kerala was formed. However, the new
land had to be settled, so Parasurama introduced a special race of Brahmins,
the **Nambudris**, to whom he gave all the land and unique customs. He then
brought in – to act as servants and bodyguards for the Nambudris. "He gave
them the matrilineal system of family, and stated that they should have no formal marriage, and that Nair women should always be available to satisfy the
desires of Nambudri men."

Kerala

Matriarchy may have originated in the 10th-century conflict with the Cholas, when the Nairs' vital role as soldiers allowed them to rise in status. The immigrant Nambudri Brahmins had far fewer women than men, so while the eldest sons married Nambudri women other sons married Kshatriya or Nair girls. Krishna Chaitanya suggests that as many Nair and Kshatriya men were slaughtered in the Chola wars there was a surplus of women in all three communities, encouraging the development of a **matrilineal system** in which women controlled family property. Nairs became numerically and politically the dominant force. In the mid 19th century the system was still dominant, as was slavery which was a widespread feature both socially and economically. From 1855, when European missionary pressure encouraged the Travancore government to abolish slavery, Nair dominance weakened. Education spread rapidly, contributing to the belief that qualifications rather than inherited status should determine economic opportunity, and by the beginning of the 20th century literacy in the towns was already higher than in Calcutta and there were over 20 daily newspapers.

Kerala is the first state in India to obtain 100% literacy in some districts and women enjoy a high social status. Yet in the hills are some of India's most primitive tribes, and on the coastal plains there remain too few economic opportunities for the growing population. Very large numbers of Malayalis have emigrated to find work in the Gulf states.

Religion Although Hinduism is now dominant, as much as a quarter of the population is Christian. There is also a large Muslim population. Religious communities have often lived amicably together. There is no conflict between the varying Hindu sects, and most temples have shrines to each of the major Hindu divinities. Christianity, which is thought to have been brought by St Thomas the Apostle to the coast of Kerala at Kodungallur in AD 52, has its own very long tradition. The Portuguese tried to convert the Syrian Christians to Roman Catholicism, but although they established a thriving Catholic Church, the Syrian tradition survived in various forms. The equally large Muslim community traces its origins back to the spread of Islam across the Indian Ocean with Arab traders from the seventh century.

Cuisine Kerala's cuisine reflects its diverse religious traditions, its seaboard location and the ubiquitous presence of the coconut. Uniquely in India, for example, beef is widely eaten, although seafood is far more common. In addition to deep sea fish, prawns, shrimps and crustaceans are prepared in a wide variety of dishes. Coconut based dishes such as *thoran*, a dry fish dish, mixed vegetables chopped very small, herbs and a variety of curry leaves, with *avial*, similar to thoran but cooked in a sauce, are widely eaten. Jack fruit, pineapples, custard apples and a seemingly endless variety of bananas – also play a vital part in many dishes. Rice is the staple cereal, around which in the typical South Indian *thali* will be a range of vegetables, served with *pappadum*, *rasam* (a thin clear pepper water or soup), and *curd*, which is mixed with plain boiled rice to finish off the meal. Traditional meals are eaten with the fingers, and on ceremonial occasions off banana leaves, though more commonly today off large stainless steel plates.

Language Malayalam, the state language, is the most recent of the Dravidian languages, developing from the 13th century with its origin in Sanskrit and the Proto-Dravidian language which also gave rise to Tamil.

Ayurvedic medicine

Ayurveda (science of life/health) is the ancient Hindu system of medicine – a naturalistic system depending on diagnosis of the body's 'humours' (wind, mucus, gall and sometimes, blood) to achieve a balance. In its early form, gods and demons were associated with cures and ailments; treatment was carried out by using herbs, minerals, formic acid (from ant hills) and water, and hence was limited in scope. Ayurveda classified substances and chemical compounds in *the theory of panchabhutas or five 'elements'. It also noted the action of food and drugs on the human body. Ayurvedic massage using aromatic and medicinal oils to tone up the nervous system, has been practised in Kerala for centuries. Interest has been revived in this form of medicine and there are now several centres which include a 'rejuvenation programme'. There are Ayurvedic hospitals in the larger towns in Kerala and elsewhere.*

Dance Kathakali The special dance form of Kerala has its origins in the *Theyyam*, a ritual tribal dance of North Kerala, and *kalaripayattu*, the martial arts practised by the high-caste Nayars, going back 1,000 years. In its present form of sacred dance-drama, Kathakali has evolved over the last 400 years. The performance is usually out of doors, the stage is bare but for a large bronze oil-lamp (now helped by electric lighting), with the drummers on one side and the singers with cymbal and gong, who act as narrators, on the other. The art of mime reaches its peak in these highly stylized performances which always used to last through the night; now they often take just three to four hours. Kathakali is no longer strictly the preserve of the male dancer.

Putting on the elaborate make-up and costumes is very time consuming. The costume consists of a large, billowing skirt, a padded jacket, heavy ornaments and headgear. The make-up is all-important: *Theta* (painted make-up) – *Pacha* (green) characterizing the Good and *Kathi* (knife, shape of a painted 'moustache'), the Villain; *Thadi* (bearded) – white for superhuman *hanumans*, black for the hunter and red for evil and fierce demons; *Kari* (black) signifying demonesses; *Minukku* (shining) 'simple' make-up representing the Gentle and Spiritual. The paints are natural pigments while the stiff 'mask' is created with rice paste and lime. The final application of a flower seed in the lower eyelid results in the red eyes you will see on stage.

This classical dance requires lengthy and hard training to make the body supple, the eyes expressive. 24 *mudras* express the nine emotions of serenity, wonder, kindness, love, valour, fear, contempt, loathing and anger. The gods and mortals play out their roles amid the chaos brought about by human ambition, but the dance ends in peace and harmony restored by the gods.

Every 12 years the North Malabar village communities of Kannur and Kasaragod organize a **Theyyam** festival. The term itself is a corruption of *deivam*, or God. A combination of music and dance, the festival brings together all castes and religions, but is a development of a pre-Hindu cult. Many folk gods and goddesses continue to hold a place in the festival.

Traditionally the dancers were male bonded labourers. Poor performance or any form of insubordination was penalized with a system of fines. 8 to 10 years of training is given to boys to ensure that they learn all the appropriate movements. An informative little booklet on the traditions of the festival by KKN Kurup is available free from the Director of Public Relations, Thiruvananthapuram.

The sensuous **Mohiniyattam**, performed by women, is known as the dance of the charmer or temptress. It evolved through the influence of Tamil dancers who brought Bharata Natyam to the Kerala royal courts. It is performed solo as in Bharata Natyam with a similar core repertoire and musical accompaniments but with the addition of *idakkai*, a percussion instrument. **Tullal**, again peculiar to Kerala, is another classical solo dance form which comes closer to contemporary life, and is marked for its simplicity, wit and humour.

Martial arts **Kalaripayattu**, possibly developed as a form of military training during the 11th-century wars with the Cholas, is still practised in *kalaris* or gymnasia. The four disciplines give training in self-defence and attack. *Maithozhil* comprise exercises to develop fitness, coordination and stamina with high vigorous kicking, followed by squatting the basic movements. *Kolethari* use sticks in training to hit without being hit, while in *Angathari*, swords, spears, shields and daggers are introduced for training in duelling. *Verumkai*, the last discipline, comprises training in unarmed combat.

Kalaripayattu underlay the development of Kathakali and of other Kerala dance forms. The folk dance *Valekali* common during temple festivals, and the Christian *Chavittu-Natakam*, in which dramatic pounding of the feet is a major feature, both derive from the martial art. The Nairs who developed the skills of kalaripayattu also used suicide squads in the wars with the Cholas, and later against the Zamorin of Calicut.

Handicrafts Temples and palaces have excellent carving, and rosewood is still inlaid with other woods, bone or plastics (to replace the traditional ivory). Wooden boxes with brass binding where plain or patterned strips of brass are used for decoration are also made, as are carved models of the 'snake boats'. Kerala produces astonishing *masks* and *theatrical ornaments*, particularly the *Krishnattam* masks which resemble the mask-like make up of the Kathakali dancers. *Conch shells* which are also available in great numbers are carved out in relief.

Modern Kerala **Government** The reorganization of the Indian States in 1956 brought together the Malayalam language area of Kerala into one political unit. With the exception of some of the Kanniyakumari districts now in Tamil Nadu, it comprises all of Travancore, Kochi, Malabar and a part of South Kanara District from Karnataka.

Kerala politics have often been unstable – even turbulent – since the first elections were held in March 1957. They have been dominated by the struggle between the Communist Party (Marxist), the Congress, and various minor parties, and the State government has often been formed by coalitions. Between 1957 and the middle 1980s President's Rule was imposed seven times. In the 1996 State Assembly elections the Congress-led United Democratic Front lost its majority to the left Democratic Front but Congress won 11 of Kerala's 20 Lok Sabha seats in the 1998 election. In mid-2000 the Left Front continued to hold onto power under the Chief Minister E K Nayanar, but with Assembly elections due within the year the parties were jockeying for position again.

Festivals **March-April (Meenam)** and **October-November (Thulam)**: *Arattu* is the closing festival of the 10-day celebrations of the Padmanabhasvami Temple in Thiruvananthapuram in which the deity is processed around the temple inside the fort, and then down to the sea. The former Maharaja of Travancore processes through the east gate of the fort and down to the Sanghumugham Beach, accompanied by six gold clothed elephants. The procession leaves the temple gate at 1700, and returns about 2100.

Useful website www.kerala tourism.com

April-May: *Vishukani* celebrates the start of the rainy season. The fire crackers exploded to ward off evil spirits can be quite terrifyingly loud. On the eve of the festival families place a large bell metal container between two lamps, filled with rice and *Nava Dhanyas* (nine kinds of grain)

NB *The High Court of Kerala has issued a directive banning smoking in public places such as streets, bus stops, railway stations, buses, trains, restaurants etc. Many offenders had to pay Rs 200 in the first few weeks.*

each in a banana leaf cup, a picture of a favourite goddess, cash, jewellery and fruit. This is done in the hope that it will bring prosperity through the year.

August-September: The biggest and most important festival is *Thiruvonam* (*Onam*), a harvest festival, celebrated throughout Kerala in the month of *Chingom*. According to legend it is on the first day that the good Asura king *Mahabali* who once ruled Kerala, comes from exile to visit his beloved people; homes are decorated with flowers in preparation for his visit. *Onam Tourist Week* is a cultural feast of art and folk presentations at 20 venues in Thiruvananthapuram and other major Kerala towns. The four day festival is marked with elephant processions, Kathakali dances, fireworks, water carnivals and *vallam kalli*, the famous snake boat races, at *Aranmula* (see page 244), *Alappuzha*, *Kottayam*, *Kochi* and *Payipad*; early September.

December-January: *Tiruvathira* is exclusively a festival for women, generally unmarried, and is associated with Kamadeva, the god of love. The young women bathe in the temple tank in the morning then return home to dress up and relax. Swings are improvised from trees especially for the day.

The far south

Thiruvananthapuram
തിരുവനന്തപുരം (Trivandrum)

The capital, a pleasant city built over gently rolling coastal land, retains a rural air away from the crowded centre. The imposing Secretariat stands apart from the busy bazar area along the central MG Road. The old fort and the large complex of the Padmanabhasvami Temple are to the south near the bustling bus stand, while the artistic and cultural heart, exemplified by the Museum building, is to the north.

Phone code 0471
Colour map 3, grid C3
Population: 826,250

Getting there The airport is only 15 mins' drive (outside the rush hour) from the town centre. You can easily hire a pre-paid taxi or auto into town, or wait for a local bus. The station and bus termini are at the southern end of town with buses to Kovalam using the stand opposite the fort entrance. Arrival is usually pleasantly unpressurized with no hassle from taxi or rickshaw drivers. **Getting around** The town is quite strung out, though the centre is compact. Buses are usually packed but are very cheap. Autos (or more expensive taxis) are more convenient but you need to bargain.

Ins & outs

Kerala

Thiruvananthapuram (Trivandrum)

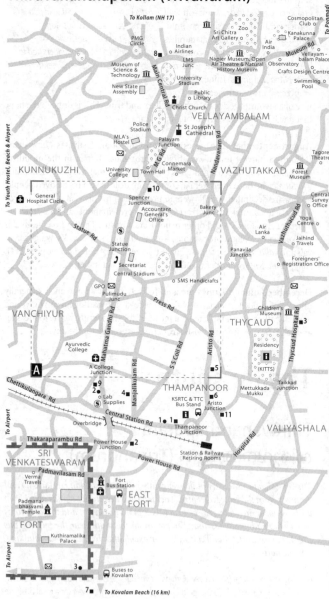

N

| 0 metres | 200 |
| 0 yards | 200 |

■ **Sleeping**
1 Chaithram
2 Fort Manor
3 Government Yatri Niwas
4 Highlands
5 Horizon
6 Jas, Queens & Greenland

7 Luciya Continental
8 Mascot
9 Omkar Lodge & Safari
  Restaurant
10 South Park & Kerala
  Travels

11 Thamburu International

● **Eating**
1 Indian Coffee House
2 Kalandriya
3 Magnet

Thiruvananthapuram became the capital of the Raja of Travancore in 1750 **History**
when the then Raja moved from Padmanabhapuram. The name is derived
from *Tiru Ananta Puram*, the abode of the sacred serpent *Ananta* upon whose
coils Vishnu lies in the main temple.

Sri Padmanabhasvami Temple According to legend, the temple was built in **Sights**
stages to house the statue of Vishnu reclining on the sacred serpent *Ananta*,
which was found in the forest. It was rebuilt in 1733 by Raja Marthanda Varma
who dedicated the whole kingdom, including his rights and possessions, to the
deity. Unusually for Kerala, it is in the Dravidian style with beautiful murals,
sculptures and 368 carved granite pillars which support the main pavilion or
Kulashekhara Mandapa. You can see the seven-storeyed *gopuram* with its
sacred pool from outside; male visitors may wear a dhoti over their trousers to go
inside. Normally open only to Hindus. Permission can sometimes be obtained if
suitably dressed. Kerala Brahmins are often stricter than those in Tamil Nadu.
They have rules of clothing even for male Hindus who must enter wearing only a
white *dhoti*. ■ *0415-0515, 0615-0650, 0815-1000, 1130-1200, 1715-1915.*

   Christ Church (1873, CSI), near Palayam opposite the stadium, known
locally as St Joseph's, was the cantonment church and has some interesting
gravestones; English service at 0730 on Sunday.

   The **Kanakakunnu Palace**, 800 m northeast of the museum, now belongs
to the Government. It is well worth being taken around by the interesting and
knowledgeable guide. **Shankhumukham Beach** near the airport has a stretch
of clean sand, but is unsuitable for sea bathing.

Arts and Crafts Museum (formerly **Napier**), north of city, in park grounds. A **Museums**
spectacular wooden building designed by RF Chisholm in traditional Kerala
style and completed in 1872, it is a landmark (see page 84). It has a famous collection of mainly 8th-18th century South Indian bronzes, mostly from Chola,
Vijayanagar and Nayaka periods; a few Jain and Buddhist sculptures. Also
excellent wood carvings (ceilings, gables and doors of both homes and temples
were usually built of wood and richly decorated). Ivory carvings and Kathakali
costumes also displayed. Printed guide available. Power cuts can be a hazard
when visiting. ■ *1000-1700, Wed 1300-1645, closed Mon. Tickets for complex
from Natural History Museum.*

   Natural History Museum, east of Napier Museum. Ticket covers entry to all
museums and galleries in the complex. Natural history and a small ethnographic
collection. Includes a beautifully made replica of a typical Kerala Nayar wooden
house (*nalukettu*) describing principles of its construction. These houses were
particularly common in North Travancore among wealthy Nayar families. The
Nayars were noted for their
matrilineal pattern of descent.

   Sri Chitra Art Gallery, north of
Napier Museum. Excellent collection of Indian art with examples
from early to modern schools. Paintings by Raja Ravi Verma and works
from Java, Bali, China and Japan,
Mughal and Rajput miniature paintings and Tanjore paintings embellished with semi-precious stones.
Well worth a visit, as is the gallery
devoted to modern art next door.
■ *1000-1700, Wed 1300-1645, closed
Mon & Wed morning. Rs 5.*

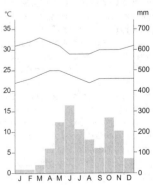

*Climate: Thiruvana
thapuram*
*Best time to visit:
Dec-Mar*

Kuthiramalika Palace Museum The palace of Maharajah Swathi Thirunal Balarama Varma, who was a musician, poet and social reformer is a good example of the Travancore style of architecture with some fine wood carving, and houses an interesting royal collection. ■ *0830-1230, 1530-1730, closed Mon. Near Padmana bhaswami temple, T473952. Foreigners Rs 20. Camera Rs 25.*

Museum of Science and Technology Near the *Mascot Hotel.* ■ *1000-1700, closed Mon. Small entry fee.* **Children's Museum**, Thycaud. Dolls, masks, paintings. ■ *1000-1700.* **Oriental Research Institute** and **Manuscript Library**, University, Kariavattom. Literary treasures including vast collection of palm leaf manuscripts.

Folklore Museum (Koyikkal Palace) at Nedumangad 18 km north of town, in a renovated 15th-century palace, contains old musical instruments, household objects, folk arts and crafts, coins. ■ *0900-1700, closed Mon.*

Parks & zoos **Botanical gardens and zoo** Set in wooded hilly parkland the zoo is spacious and offers delightful shaded walks. It has a wide collection of animals. The Botanical Gardens are here with many trees clearly labelled. Worth a visit. ■ *0900-1645. Closed Mon. Rs 2, Video/cine cameras Rs 5. Entrance at southwest corner of park, 400 m east of Indian Airlines.* Other parks and gardens in the city – around the Secretariat, Gandhi Park, Waterworks Gardens and at Veli Tourist Village. The Aquarium near the beach has closed.

Tours *Kerala Tourism*: from *Hotel Chaithram*, T330031. **1** *City tour*: 0800-1900,
Be prepared for leeches including Kovalam (125 km), Rs 80; **2** *Kanniyakumari*: 0730-2100, including
when walking through Kovalam, Padmanabhapuram and Kanniyakumari (200 km), Rs 150 daily; **3**
the forest particularly *Ponmudi*: 0830-1900, daily, Golden Valley and Ponmudi (125 km), Rs 130.
in the wet season Long tours can be very exhausting; the stops at sites of interest are often very
(see page 58) brief. *Great India Tour Co*, Mullassery Towers, Vanross Square, T331516, offers afternoon city tour among others.

Essentials

Sleeping **B** *Fort Manor (Madison)*, Power House Junction (500 m rly and bus stations), T462222,
See also under Kovalam. F460560. 60 large a/c rooms (erratic hot water) in modern semi-circular tower block,
The centre & rly comfortable restaurant but food unexceptional, no bar but beer smuggled into rooms.
station area have **B** *South Park*, Spencer Junction, MG Rd, T325666, F331861. Central a/c, 82 rooms, some
many cheap hotels, dearer suites, good restaurants, bar, some business facilities, modern 'marble and glass
some excellent value hotel' but pricey. **B-C** *Mascot* (KTDC), Mascot Sq, T318990, F317745, ktdc@vsnl.com 44
■ *on maps* a/c rooms and suites, rather sombre inside, good restaurants, competent without being
Price codes: see inside exciting. **C** *Horizon*, Aristo Rd, T326888. 47 rooms, some **B** a/c, good restaurants (roof-
front cover top on weekend evenings), for breakfast opt for room service, bar, comfortable.
C *Luciya Continental*, East Fort, T463443, F463347. 104 rooms, some a/c, large 'fantasy suites', others very small, good restaurant, exchange, pool. **C** *Pankaj*, MG Rd, opposite Secretariat, T464645, F465020. 50 clean rooms, some a/c, good restaurants, bar, exchange, can be noisy. **C** *Wild Palms* Puthen Rd, 10 minute walk Statue Junction, T/F478992 (London T0181-5342876). 6 rooms in modern guest house (traditional design), spacious, cool, welcoming. **B-D** *Residency Tower*, Press Rd, T332245, F331311, rtower@md2.vsnl.net.in 46 rooms, some a/c, uneven maintenance, good restauran and bar (pleasant and cool). **D** *Chaithram* (Kerala Tourism), Station Rd, T330977. 88 rooms, some **C** a/c, good a/c restaurant, bar, exchange, modern, very clean, next to rly and bus stand, noisy area but good value, often full. **D** *Geeth*, off MG Rd, near GPO, Pulimudu, T471987. 50 rooms, some a/c, rooftop restaurant recommended. **D** *Jas*, Thycaud/Aristo Junction, T324881, F321477. 45 rooms, some **C** a/c, roof-garden restaurant recommended, exchange, quiet, good value. **D** *Thamburu International*, Aristo

Junction, opposite Rly Station, T321974. Pleasant interior, comfortable rooms (some a/c), excellent value, sometimes full.

D-E *Highlands*, Manjalikulam Rd, T333200, F332645. 85 clean, comfortable rooms, some **D** a/c in a tall block, good value. **D-E** *Regency*, Manjalikulam Cross Rd, T330377, F331690. 24-hour hot water, daily change of sheets, friendly staff, acceptable restaurant, Indian business hotel, good value. **D-E** *Navaratna*, YMCA Rd, T331784. 34 rooms, 2 **D** a/c (Rs 280-700) in modern tower block, simple, clean, efficient and helpful, good value. **E** *Pravin Tourist House*, Manjalikulam Rd, 750 m from Thampanoor Rd, T330443. Clean, quiet, no restaurant. **F** *Bhaskara Bhavan Tourist Paradise*, near Ayurvedic College, T330662. 40 rooms, sombre but clean, good value. **F** *Greenland*, near Aristo Junction, T323485, short walk from station and bus. Rooms with bath, very safe, good value. **F** *Omkar Lodge*, MG Rd, opposite SMV School, T478503. 15 clean rooms. Recommended. **F** *Taurus Lodge*, 50 m up narrow path off Statue Rd, T477071. 14 rooms some with bath, some small and dark, could be cleaner but quiet, family run, helpful.

Youth hostels **E-F** *YWCA*, opposite AG's office, Spencer Junction, T446518. Simple, clean, for men too, book ahead. **F** *Yatri Niwas*, Thycaud, T324462. Extremely cheap, very busy. **F** *Youth Hostel* (KTDC), Veli (10 km from centre). Rooms and dorm (Rs 10), very cheap veg lunches, pretty lagoon separated from the sea by a sandbar, surrounded by coconut groves, clean beach, boating, some watersports, good views.

Thiruvananthapuram centre

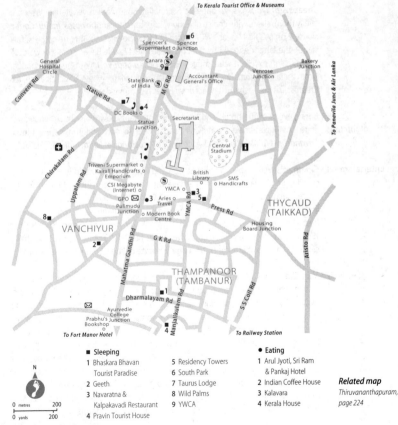

■ Sleeping		● Eating
1 Bhaskara Bhavan Tourist Paradise	5 Residency Towers	1 Arul Jyoti, Sri Ram & Pankaj Hotel
2 Geeth	6 South Park	2 Indian Coffee House
3 Navaratna & Kalpakavadi Restaurant	7 Taurus Lodge	3 Kalavara
4 Pravin Tourist House	8 Wild Palms	4 Kerala House
	9 YWCA	

Related map
Thiruvananthapuram, page 224

Kerala

Kerala

Airport *Asha*, 200m from Airport, T501050. Very handy for early departures, new (therefore clean) rooms with bath (Rs 300).

Eating
● *on maps*

Expensive to mid-range: *Hotels **South Park***. Good tandoori and buffet lunches. *Mascot* . Excellent lunchtime buffet; pleasant, 24-hour Coffee Shop for all types of snacks, all good value, a cool haven at midday! *Pankaj* top floor. Good Indian buffet lunches, excellent views over city. *Residency's **Orion***. Pepper steaks and cocktails recommended. *Coronet*. Dark bar downstairs for refreshing cold beers, while you wait. *Luciya*. Good buffet (outdoor barbecue) and southern dishes, but poor service.

Mid range: *Café Magnet*, Thycaud. Mixed menu. The 'in' place, boring décor but good food, "go early as it runs out, not yet spotted by Westerners (no beer)". *Kalavara*, Press Rd, T331362 Indian, Continental, Chinese fast food (burgers, shakes) takeaway. Food average, slow service but good value buffets in upstairs thatched section with a patch of garden – good ambience, limited views. *Kalpakavadi*, YMCA Rd. Mixed menu. Modern and smart, recommended. *Kerala House*, near Statue Junction. Kerala cuisine. In basement of shopping complex, clean, slow for breakfast but newspaper provided; outside seating in the evening in roadside carpark area, cheaper, colourful and fun to pass the time, even if the food arrives cold; try *neem, kappa* and rice (delicious fish with tapioca), or inexpensive chicken dishes with lots of coconut; *Bakery* in the complex does excellent *samosas* and *puffs*. *Queen's*, Aristo Junction. Indian non-vegetarian. Chilli chicken and chicken fry recommended.

Cheap: *Arul Jyoti*, MG Rd, opposite Secretariat. South Indian vegetarian. With a/c family room, clean, wide choice of good value dishes, try jumbo *dosas*. *Indian Coffee House* 2 on MG Rd (1 near YWCA, north of the Secretariat, another near KSRTC bus stand), the latter designed by the English architect Laurie Baker, spirals upwards – worth seeing, excellent value coffee and snacks. *Kalandriya*, MG Rd, near Overbridge. North Indian. *Sri Rams*, MG Rd. South Indian vegetarian, sweets. Basic, cleanish. *Ice Creams*, just inside the Fort near *Luciya Hotel*, recommended.

Bars & nightclubs

Bars: Several of the hotels and the larger restaurants have bars though increased State govt taxes makes it difficult to get beer in non-govt run hotels. **Clubs**: *Trivandrum Club*, Vazhuthacud. *Automobile Association of South India*, VJT Hall Rd.

Entertainment

Cinemas: several especially near Station and Overbridge Junction on MG Rd some showing English language films. **Kathakali** and other performances, through Tourist Office; **Kalaripayattu**: performances (0400-0700 and 1700-2000), *CVN Kalari*, East Fort, T474182, 0630-0830, watch from balcony, photography with permission only, free; also at Poojapura: *Veera Kerala Marma Kalari*, T330041. **Sport Swimming**: *Waterworks* pool near Museum, entry Rs 2, 0830-1200, 1400-1530, 1815-2000, closed Mon. Also at *Mascot Hotel*. **Yoga**: *Institute of Yogic Culture*, Vazhuthacaud.

Festivals

Mar: *Chandanakuda* at Beemapalli, a shrine on Beach Rd 5 km southwest of the rly station, when local Muslims process to the mosque, holding incense sticks and pots. Marked by sword play, singing, dancing, elephant procession and fireworks. The shrine is dedicated to Beema Bivi, a Muslim woman believed to have divine powers, and the festival is held in her memory. The 10 day festival begins on the first of the Hijra month of Jamadul Akhar (**Mar-Apr**), and comes to a climax on the 10th day. **Mar-Apr** (Meenam) and **Oct-Nov** (Thulam): *Arattu* (see above). **Sep/Oct**: *Navaratri* at the special mandapam in Padmanabhasvami Temple. Several concerts which draw famous musicians. *Thiruvonam week* in **Sep**. Many other fairs and festivals are organized by different agencies throughout the year. **Nov-Mar**: *Nishangandhi Dance Festival*, at weekends when all important classical Indian dance forms are performed by leading artistes at Nishagandhi open-air auditorium, Kanakakkunnu Palace. **Oct**: A similar *Soorya Dance Festival* takes place from 1st-10th.

Shopping areas include the Chalai Bazar, the Connemara market and the Main Rd from Palayam to the East Fort. Usually open 0900 to 2000 (some take a long lunch break). Although ivory goods have now been banned, inlay on wood carving and marquetry using other materials (bone, plastic) continue to flourish, and are the hall-mark of traditional Kerala handicrafts. These and items such as *Kathakali* masks and traditional fabrics can be bought at a number of shops.

Shopping
Ivory carving used to be carried out until restrictions were imposed by the government. Wood carving (sandal & rosewood) continues

    Books: *Current*, and the very modern *DC*, at Statue Junction, Shopping Complex opposite Secretariat. *India Book House, Pai & Co* and *Higginbotham's*, all on MG Rd. *Modern Book Centre*, Pulimudu Junction, MG Rd, excellent range, very helpful knowledgeable owner. *Geeth*, near old GPO. *Prabhu's*, Ayurvedic College Junction, good range. **Camping fuel**: *Laboratory Supplies*, near Ayurvedic College Junction, methyl alcohol for *Trangia* camping stoves. **Clothing and fabric**: shopping centre opposite East Fort Bus stand has a large a/c shop with good selection of silks and saris but not cheap. *Partha's*, towards East Fort, also recommended. *Handloom House*, diagonally across from *Partha's* has an excellent range of fabrics, clothes and export quality *dhur-ries*. The other MG Rd branch near the Overbridge is not as good. *Raymonds*, Karal Kada, East Fort has good men's clothing. *Co-optex*, Temple Rd, good for fabrics and *lungis*. *Khadi* recommended from shops on both sides of MG Rd, south of Pulimudu Junction. *Premier Stationers*, MG Rd, opposite Post Office Rd, are best in town. **Handicrafts**: Govt run *SMSM Handicrafts Emporium* behind the Secretariat, literally 'heaps' of items, wide range, reasonably priced. *Natesan Antique Arts* and *Gift Corner* on MG Rd have high quality goods including old dowry boxes, carved wooden panels from old temple 'cars' or chariots, miniature paintings and bronzes. *Kairali*, opposite the Secretariat in MG Rd, items of banana fibre, coconut, screw pine, mainly utilitarian, also excellent sandalwood carvings and bell-metal lamps, utensils. *Kalanjali*, Palace Garden, across from the Museum. Recommended. *Gram Sree* for excellent village crafts. Also *Spencers* supermarket, MG Rd.

Kerala

Local Auto-rickshaws: charge minimum Rs 5; you may need to bargain for Kovalam, especially in the evening (Rs 70 is fair). **Buses**: City Bus Station, fort, T463029. To **Kovalam**: from East Fort, Platform 9, signed in English, 30 mins, Rs 4. **Car hire**: from agents, Rs 700-800 per day; from *Vacation India*, Pulimudu Junction, T314561; *Southern Travel*, Shasthamangalam, T316850, and tour operators. **Taxis**: from outside *Mascot Hotel* charge about Rs 7 per km; to Kovalam, Rs 175, return Rs 225 (waiting: extra Rs 50 per hr).

Transport
Tell rickshaw drivers which Kovalam beach you want to get to in advance, otherwise they will charge much more when you get there

Long distance Air: The airport is near the beach, 6 km away. Transport to town: by local bus No 14, pre-paid taxi (Rs 85) or auto-rickshaw (about Rs 30, 20 mins). Enquiry, T501424. Confirm international bookings and arrive in good time. Inflated prices at refreshments counter though cheap tea/coffee in the final lounge after 'Security' check. The banks at the airport are outside arrivals. *Johnson & Co* (travel agent) opp Domestic Terminal, T503555, young, enthusiastic executive. **International**: *Indian Airlines*, Mascot Sq, T318288, F501537, (and *Air Lanka*, T501140): to **Colombo** and **Male**. *Air India*, Museum Rd, Velayambalam, T310310, A501426: flies to **London, New York, Frankfurt, Paris** and the Gulf; *Air Maldives*. **Domestic**: *Indian Airlines*: to **Bangalore, Chennai, Delhi, Mumbai**. *Air India*: Mumbai. *Jet Airways*, Akshay Towers, Shashtamangalam, T321018. **Chennai, Mumbai**.

The airport is closed at night so you can't wait overnight, see sleeping

Road Bus: Journeys through heavy traffic can be very uncomfortable and tiring. **Central Bus Station**, near rly station, Thampanoor, T323886. Buses to **Kanniyakumari via Nagercoil** or direct, frequent dep, 2½ hrs; **Kozhikode**, 10 hrs

(*Exp*); **Madurai**, 1230, 6½ hrs; **Thrissur**, 7 hrs (Exp). Buses to **Ernakulam/Kochi** via Alappuzha and Kollam, start early, 5 hrs (*Exp*) or 6½ hrs. You can include a section of the backwaters on the way to Kochi by getting a boat from Kollam (shared taxis there cost Rs 60 each, see below). TNSTC to **Chennai, Coimbatore, Cuddalore, Erode, Kanniyakumari, Madurai** from opposite the Central Rly station.

Train: Central Station, after 1800. Reservations in building adjoining station, T132. Advance, upstairs, open 0700-1300, 1330-1930, Sun 0900-1700; ask to see Chief Reservations Supervisor, Counter 8; surprisingly no "Foreigners' quota". To **Alappuzha**: *Intercity 6342*, 1625, 3 hrs. **Bangalore**: *Kanniyakumari-Bangalore Exp, 6525*, 1020, 19½ hrs. **Kolkata (H)**: *Trivandrum-Guwahati Exp*, 6321 (AC/II), Sat, 1245, 49 hrs; *Trivandrum-Howrah Exp*, 6323, Sat and Sun 1245, 49 hrs. **Ernakulam (Kochi)**: *Intercity, 6342*, 1625, 4 hrs; *Kerala Exp, 2625* (AC/II), 0945, 4¼ hrs. **Kanniyakumari**: 2½ hrs. **Chennai**: *Trivandrum-Guwahati Exp, 6321* (AC/II), Thu, 1245, 18¼ hrs; *Madras Mail, 6320* (AC/II), 1330, 17¾ hrs. **Kollam via Varkala**: 12 trains 0725-2035, 1¼ hrs. **Ernakulam**: 10 trains daily between 0500-2145. **Madgown (Goa)**: *Trivandrum-Nizamuddin Rajdhani Express, 2431*, Sun, 1915, 16¾ hrs. **Mangalore**. *Malabar Exp 6029*, 1740, 16 hrs; *Trivandrum-Mangalore Parsuram Exp, 6349*, 0605, 15 hrs. **Mumbai (VT)**: *Trivandrum Mumbai Exp, 6632*, Fri, 0425, 41 hrs; *Kanniyakumari Exp, 1082* (AC/II), 0725, 45½ hrs via **Ernakulam (Kochi)**, 5¼ hrs. **New Delhi**, *Rajdhani Exp*, Fri, Sat, 31 hrs.

Directory **Airline offices** See Transport above for domestic airlines. *Air Lanka, Maldive Airways*, Spencer Bldg, MG Rd, T322309, and T475541.*Gulf Air*, T501205, and*Kuwait Airways*, National Travel Service, Panavila Junction, T501401. *Saudi Airways*, Arafath Travels, Pattom. **Banks** open 1000-1400, Mon to Fri, and 1000-1200, Sat. *State Bank of India*, near Secretariat; *Canara Bank*, Canara Tower, near Spencer Junction, no hassle cash against Visa, friendly staff. **Visa ATM**: *British Bank*, Vellayambalam. The Airport has banks. **Communications** GPO: with*Poste Restante*, Pulimudu Junc, 0830-1800, efficient. **PO**: north of Secretariat, off MG Rd, is better; Speed Post (computerized; affected by power failures); also PO at Thampanoor, opposite Manjalikulam Rd. **Internet**: *Megabyte*, CSI Building, 3rd and 4th Flrs, MG Rd, Rs 3 per min, email: send Rs 15, receive Rs 10, friendly. *Tandem Communications*, Statue Rd (MG Rd end), good telephone and fax centre; colour photocopying, laser printing. **Central Telegraph office**: Statue Rd, 200m to its north; open 24 hrs, best value internet. **Couriers**: *DHL*, Vellayambalam, T328477. *Corporate Couriers*, Bakery Junction, T329125. **Cultural Centres** *British Library*, near Secretariat with cool reading room, T330716. *Alliance Française*, Vellayambalam, T327776. **Hospitals & medical services** Chemists: many near hospitals; a few near Statue Junction. *Lakshmi Medical Stores*, MG Rd and *Krishna Medicals*, East Fort. **Hospitals**: *General Hospital*, Vanchiyoor, T443874. *Cosmopolitan Hospital*, Maurinja Palayam, T448182. *Ramakrishna Ashrama Hospital*, Sasthamangalam, T322125. Opticians: *Lens & Frames*, Pulimudu Junc, T471354, up to date. **Tour operators** IATA approved agencies include: *Air Travel Enterprises*, MG Rd, near Museum, T323900; *Aries Travel*, Press Rd, T330964, F470159, sivans@giasmd2. vsnl.net.in; *Chalukya*, Vadayakadu, Kunnukzhy, T444618, run unique, expensive tours and treks including 3-day trek through forest staying in bamboo tree-houses and living with bamboo cutters; ends with river rafting return; 2-day elephant or bullock cart 'safari' through village areas, and 3/4-day treks in the hills; very well organized; *Gt India Tour Co*, Mullassery Towers, Vanross Junction, T331422, F330579, reliable but pricey; *Tours India*, PO Box 163, MG Rd, T330437, F331407, knowledgeable, good tailor-made tours. **Tourist offices** Tourist offices are well supplied with leaflets and information sheets and are very helpful. *Kerala Tourism*, Main Office, Park View, opposite Museum, T/F322279, deptour@vsnl.com, www.keralatourism.org. 1000-1700, closed Sun. At airport during flight times and Rly station, 1000-1700, closed Sun; and Thampanoor Central Bus Station. *KTDC*, Central Reservations, Mascot Sq, T318976, F314406, ktdc@vsnl.com Tourist Reception Centre, Thampanoor, near Bus Station, T330031. *PRO*, nr Press Secretariat or Annexe, T468648. *India*, Airport, T451498. **Useful address** **Visa extension**: Foreigners' Regional Registration Office, City Police Commissioner, Residency Rd, Thycaud, T320486; allow up to a week, though it can take less. Open 1000-1700, Mon-Sat.

★ Kovalam കോവളം

Once just a series of sandy bays separated by rocky promontories, deserted except for the scattered fishing villages under the coconut palms, Kovalam is becoming one of the Government's major tourist centres. For 20 years it catered largely for the Western backpacker but now its superb beaches are the focus of package tours from Europe and visitors from all over India.

Phone code: 0471
Colour map 3, grid C3
Population: 25,400

Ins & outs

Getting there Taxis take 30 mins from the airport. Buses from Thiruvananthapuram (see 'Transport' above) stop at Waller Junction, just before Kovalam, just 5 mins walk from the Samudra Beach hotels. After 1.5 km they turn off for the main bus stand at Ashok Hotel gate, 5-10 mins' walk from most southern hotels and cafés. Autos (and taxis) can also get to the beach end of the steep, narrow Lighthouse Road. **Getting around** You can walk the length of beach from the lighthouse end to the north of Samudra beach in about 20 mins. Carry a torch at night. **Best season** Dec-Mar; even at the end of Mar it can get very hot around midday, when only a handful of thatched parasols are usually available.

The beach

There are four main stretches of beach, about 400 m long. A rocky promontory with the Charles Correa designed *Ashok Beach Resort* divides them into north and south sections. The beach immediately to the north of the promontory offers the most sheltered bathing and the clearest water.

The southern beaches are much more populated. Lighthouse Beach is a long line of bars, cafés and vendors selling fruit, clothes, crafts, and unfortunately, drugs. It is still pleasant and quiet by some European holiday beach standards.

There are now lifeguard patrols but you still need to be careful when swimming. The sea can get rough, particularly between April and October with swells of up to 6 m. From May the sea-level rises removing the beach completely in places, and swimming becomes very dangerous.

Excursions

Vizhinjam, 6 km south, the capital of the later *Ay* rulers who dominated South Travancore in the ninth century AD. In the seventh century they had faced constant pressure from the Pandiyans who kept the Ay chieftains under firm control for long periods. There is a typical single-cell rock-cut eighth-century shrine with incomplete relief sculptures of Siva and Parvati on the outside, but now in a poor state and engulfed by tree roots. Today Vizhinjam is the centre of a major fishing industry. Scarcely visited by tourists, it is an easy walk from Kovalam. The traditional boats are rapidly being modernized and the catch is sold all over India, but you can still see the keen interest in the sale of fish, and women taking headloads off to local markets. Take care walking around the beach as some areas are used as toilets.

Padmanabhapuram, the old palace of the Rajas of Travancore, makes an excellent day trip from town or from Kovalam. See page 187.

Essentials

Sleeping
■ *on map, page 232*
Price codes:
see inside front cover

Long power cuts are common, so air-conditioners often do not work. Rooms open to the sea breeze can be an advantage. The area behind the Lighthouse Beach is now full of hotels with a range of rooms from the most basic (Rs 25) to an average of Rs 600 with all facilities. Rates are highly seasonal, particularly in the higher categories. Prices skyrocket in all hotels for the 2-week peak period (20 Dec-10 Jan), though it still pays to bargain. High season: 1-19 Dec, 11 Jan-28 Feb; Season: Mar, Apr, Aug-Nov. Low season discounts as much as 50%.

Kerala

Kovalam Beach

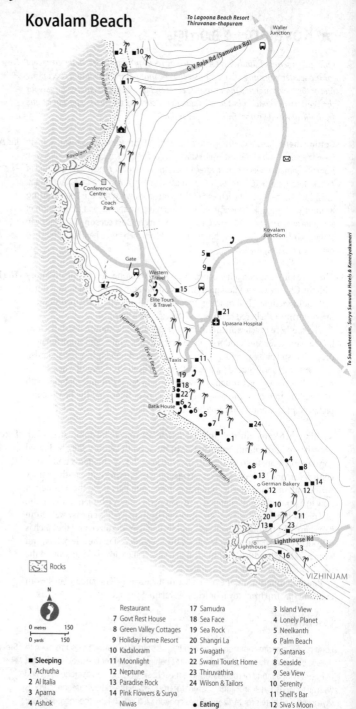

Rocks

N

| 0 metres | 150 |
| 0 yards | 150 |

■ **Sleeping**
1 Achutha
2 Al Italia
3 Aparna
4 Ashok
5 Blue Sea
6 Dwarka & Seashore

Restaurant
7 Govt Rest House
8 Green Valley Cottages
9 Holiday Home Resort
10 Kadaloram
11 Moonlight
12 Neptune
13 Paradise Rock
14 Pink Flowers & Surya
    Niwas
15 Raja
16 Rockholm

17 Samudra
18 Sea Face
19 Sea Rock
20 Shangri La
21 Swagath
22 Swami Tourist Home
23 Thiruvathira
24 Wilson & Tailors

● **Eating**
1 Flamingo & Hawah
2 Garzia & Tailors

3 Island View
4 Lonely Planet
5 Neelkanth
6 Palm Beach
7 Santanas
8 Seaside
9 Sea View
10 Serenity
11 Shell's Bar
12 Siva's Moon
13 Velvet Moon

L-AL *Ashok Beach Resort*, T480101, F481522. In pleasant grounds, poor reports on service and maintenance, 'private' beach area (non-residents pay Rs 90 for beachside facilities including showers, Rs 250 for swimming pool), reasonable ayurvedic massage centre (sometimes deserted). **A** *Samudra*, Samudra Beach, T480089, F480242, Samudra@md3. vsnl.net.in 50 improved rooms, best in new wing facing sea, good pool in sea facing landscaped garden, ayurvedic massage, unremarkable restaurant, mainly package tours, overpriced. **A-B** *Sea Face*, Lighthouse Beach, T481591, F481320. 20 rooms, 12 a/c, excellent restaurant, right on beach, modern, pleasant pool (non-residents pay Rs 175). Recommended.

B *Kadaloram Beach Resort*, GV Raja Rd, T481116, F481115. 16 comfortable rooms (4 a/c), not a 'resort', 5 mins' walk to quiet beach, a bit isolated. **B** *Rockholm*, Lighthouse Rd, T480306, F480607. 17 small rooms (some not clean), hot water after learning "complex tap routine", wonderful position just above lighthouse, good restaurant, good exchange, helpful staff. **B-C** *Moonlight*, inland from beach, T480375. Large modern rooms (few with seaview), bath tub, guaranteed water supply, local and backwater boat trips Rs 500 for 2 people. **B-C** *Swagath* , near Upasana Hospital, 5 minute downhill to beach, T481148, F481150, rajkal@md2.vsnl.net.in 18 spacious, modern rooms (most a/c) on 4 floors, 3 cheaper in 'Row House' much smaller, limited menu restaurant, new pool, friendly and efficient. **C** *Aparna*, Lighthouse Rd, uphill from beach, T480950. 8 rooms with large baths, in modern multi-storey building, clean, private sea-facing terrace, very pleasant. Highly recommended. **C-D** *Al Italia Beach Resort*, Samudra Beach, T480042. 4 simple but modern rooms, secluded beach front (fishermen, early morning), quiet, breezy, shady restaurant, delicious food, friendly service. **C-D** *Blue Sea*, near Telegraph office, T480950, F480490. Simple rooms, attractive chalet and rooftop terrace rooms more expensive but superb views, converted Kerala-style family home in large garden with good pool and service, very pleasant and relaxing. **C-D** *Neptune*, Lighthouse Beach, T480622. 37 rooms, 1 a/c, simple meals, patio garden. **C-D** *Sea Rock*, on the beach, T480422. Clean rooms, sea-facing twice the price (no mosquito nets or wall sockets), restaurant (slow service), avoid laundry. **D-E** *Holiday Home Resort*, Beach Rd (10 mins' walk from sea), T480497, homerest@md3.vsnl.net.in Clean, pleasant rooms and cottages, some a/c (Rs 300-1,000), **F** dorm (Rs 150), good food, beautiful flower garden, internet facility, quiet, friendly, excellent service. Recommended. **D-E** *Thiruvathira*, Lighthouse Rd uphill from beach, T480588. 8 rooms, clean, modern, large, breezy sea-facing terraces, *Anu Massage Centre* for traditional Ayurvedic and 30-day martial arts courses, good value. Recommended.

There are numerous budget cottages and rooms to let. Scouts greet arrivals at bus stand but you may pay considerably more if you use their services. You will find rooms to let, behind bars and restaurants, by walking from the *Sea Rock* towards the lighthouse, and on the Samudra Beach and GV Raja Rd (Samudra Rd). Inexpensive, clean though simple. **D-E** *Wilson Tourist Home*, up path behind Neelkantha, T480051. 20 rooms with bath (Rs 350+), some with Western toilet and hot shower, open-air restaurant, hassle-free exchange all day (accepts Visa), good tailoring, garden, clean, safe, very friendly and well run. Recommended. **E** *Achutha*, Lighthouse Beach. With restaurant, recommended for good clean rooms, 'best bed in India' and good food. **E** *Dwaraka Lodge*, Lighthouse Beach, T480411. 8 clean rooms, some with bath, right on beach, pleasant management, good value. **E** *Paradise Rock*, Lighthouse Rd, T480658. Large rooms, hot showers, close to beach, good views and breeze. **F** *Pink Flowers*, Lighthouse Beach, behind *Neptune*. 4 immaculate rooms with bath (Rs 80+), good location, friendly. **F** *Shangri-La House*, Lighthouse Beach. Attractive setting near beach, restaurant and library. **F** *Surya Nivas*, Lighthouse Beach. 4 very clean rooms with bath, quiet, friendly. **F** *Swami Tourist Home*, with good clean rooms, good food and friendly service.

Hotels near Kovalam: (*phone code: 0471*) **Pozhikkara Beach**: A *Lagoona Beach Resort*, Pachalloor, T480049. 5 km northwest, off the highway, where the backwaters reach the sea, 'backwater' tours in country boats with excellent guide to see coir making, spice garden, tropical plants. **Mulloor**, 6 km south: **B** *Coconut Beach Resort*, T480566, F343349, cocobay@vsnl.com 5 spacious brick/stone cottages on beach, good restaurant, friendly, secluded location in traditional fishing village, next to *Siddharth Ayurvedic and Yoga Centre*. **Pulinkudi**: **L-AL** *Surya Samudra*, 8 km south, Mulloor PO, T480413, F481124. 15 large rooms in old Kerala houses re-assembled and modernized, bathrooms among banana plants (open-above!), no TV, 4 new a/c (no sea view and no mosquitos!), very good food, exclusive (rather cut off from India), secluded beach, stunning setting, popular with Germans. Recommended but overpriced; can book via Toptour GMBH, Piusallee 108, GD-48147 Münster, T251-235559, F235216. **Chowara**, 10 km south: Beach has security staff on duty but hawkers filter through to pester sunbathers. **AL-B** *Somatheeram*, T481600, F480600, soma@md2.vsnl.net.in An ayurvedic health resort, 46 rooms, most in re-assembled Kerala houses with original antique wooden panels, carved doors etc, huge windows with sea views, some modern cottages, yoga by the beach. Low voltage (slow fans, dim lights), gloomy at night. **B-C** *Manatheeram*, next door, T481610, F481611. 30 clean, breezy, beach-facing circular huts, grass screen windows, fans, good showers, good seafood on beach. Specialist ayurvedic treatments at both, massage ($15 per hour).

Eating

Most are along Lighthouse beach

Expensive *Suisse* Stylish venue, unusual menu, very clean, generous portions, personal attention, good atmosphere, enjoyable though the music can get overpowering. Recommended. **Mid-range** *Garzia* Original fish dishes, sizzlers. *Santana* Good atmosphere, music, backgammon, chess and good food (but very slow), open until late. *Rockholm*. International. Very good food, pleasant terrace, beautiful views, especially early morning. *Sea Face*. Breezy raised terrace on the beach by pleasant pool (coconuts above netted for safety!), varied choice, excellent food, versatile fish/ seafood (dearer), friendly and attentive. Recommended. **Cheap**: Towards the lighthouse, a few seafood places display the day's catch (some 1 m long) on metal-top tables for you to select from. Tiger prawns and lobsters are pricey; **avoid** fish on Sun evenings (unlikely to be very fresh). The order of the day is not to rush, service is often slow as tiny kitchens are unable to cope with large numbers! *Achutha*, *Dwaraka* and *Swami* do good tandoori and snacks. *Krishna*. Basic but good *thalis* (the 'cheapest in Kovalam'). *Palm Beach* for good seafood. *Island View*, does good pastas and excellent seafood. *Lonely Planet*, away from beach. Rare vegetarian restaurant. Excellent Indian. Moderately spiced *thalis* recommended, good location overlooking paddy fields and coconut palms. *Roy's*, up from *Sea Rock*. Excellent local Kerala food, very clean, popular with local people. *Sea View*, Hawah Beach, at foot of path from the bus stand. Excellent seafood tandoori. *Seashore*, next to Dwarka. Good à la carte variety (especially pizzas, fish, chicken and toffee dessert), friendly and popular. *Velvet Moon* has fresh fish, except Very good value, great hot apple 'cakes', real baked potatoes, good snacks, friendly, relaxing top floor, getting a bit shabby.

Videos are shown free, nightly at some, often set against poorer food: *Neelkantha* with comfortable seats and a generator to overcome regular power cuts; *Hawah Beach* "where vegetarian dishes taste of fish!" *Shell's Bar* does excellent barbecue fish; *Siva* and *Flamingo* do good tandoori, especially barracuda.

Bars Only a few hotels have licences; *Ashok* and *Samudra* are open to non-residents. Beach restaurants often sell beer; occasionally some spirits.

Kathakali Dance (see page 256), daily at Hotels *Ashok* and *Neptune*, Rs 100. **Sports** **Entertainment** Fishing can readily be arranged through the hotels, as can excursions on traditional catamarans or motor boats. Some near *Ashok Hotel* beach promise corals and beautiful fish just off-shore (do not expect to see very much).

Numerous craft shops, including Kashmiri and Tibetan shops sell a wide range of **Shopping** goods. The majority are clustered around the bus stand at the gate of the *Ashok Hotel* with another group to the south around the lighthouse. It is possible to get good quality paintings, metalwork, woodwork and carpets at reasonable prices. Gems and jewellery are widely available but notoriously difficult to be sure of quality. *Zangsty Gems* on Lighthouse Rd has a good reputation for helpfulness and reliability. **Books**: several bookstalls sell, or 'hire' (Rs 10), English paperbacks. *International Book Centre*, 2nd Beach Rd. **Tailors**: tailoring at short notice is very good value with fabrics available; better than ready mades;*Brother Tailors*, 2nd Beach Rd;*Raja* near Hotel *Surya*; *Suresh* next to *Garzia* Restaurant. Charges vary, about Rs 50-80 per piece.

Local Bus: frequent buses (0540-2100) into East Fort, **Thiruvananthapuram**, from **Transport** bus stand outside *Ashok Hotel* gate (Kovalam beach), fast Rs 4.50, slow 3.30, (30 mins), also picks up from Waller Junction (Main Rd/Samudra beach). From East Fort bus station, auto-rickshaw to town centre, Rs 6, or walk. **NB** Green buses have limited stops; yellow/red buses continue through town up to Museum. **Taxi**: from taxi stand or through *Ashok* or *Samudra Hotels*. One-way to Thiruvananthapuram or airport, Rs 200; station Rs 175; city sights Rs 600; Kanniyakumari, Padmanabhapuram Rs 1,750 (8 hrs); Kochi Rs 2,250 (5 hrs); Kollam Rs 1100; Thekkady Rs 2,650 (6 hrs). **Auto-rickshaw**: to **Thiruvananthapuram**, Rs 70-80, but need to bargain hard. **Bike hire**: from *Voyager*, near Police Station, T4811993. **Long distance Road Bus**: to **Kanniyakumari, Kochi via Kollam (Quilon)** and via **Kottayam, Kollam, Nagercoil, Padmanabhapuram, Varkala, Thodopuzha via Kottayam. Backwaters** Boat trips – see below under Kollam.

There are 3 main points of access to Kovalam's beaches. Remember to specify which, when hiring an auto or taxi

Banks *Central Bank* branch in *Ashok Hotel* (around the corner near the bookshop) changes money **Directory** and TCs for non-residents after 1045. Exchange at *Pournami Handicrafts; Wilson's*, T480051, changes money, any time, no hassle. Best rates (up to 3% higher), however, are at the airport. **Communications** Post Office: inside *Ashok Hotel* gate (closes for lunch). **NB** Check printed prices before paying for calls. Some ISD booths near the bus stand in addition to the Telecommunications Centre just under 1 km away, open 0800-1645.*Western Travel* opposite Bus Stand, until 2200. *Elite Tours*, T481405, 2nd Beach Rd (30m below bus stand), 24-hr ISD from the *Batik House*, Lighthouse Beach. Faxes can be sent from some guest houses/restaurants eg *Santana's*, but can be expensive. **Internet:** Several on Lighthouse Beach: and at *Holiday Home Resort*, Beach Rd. **Hospitals & medical services** Emergency assistance either through your hotel or from the *Govt Hospital* in Thiruvananthapuram. *Upasana Hospital*, near *Ashok Hotel* gate, has experienced English speaking doctor; prompt, personal attention. **Ayurvedic treatment:** Offered by most upmarket resorts (massage about Rs 700). Among many *Medicus* Lighthouse Rd, T 480596, where Dr Babu and his wife have clients returning year after year; similarly, *Vasudeva*, T222510, behind *Neptune Hotel*, is simple but with experienced professionals. **Tour operators** *Visit India*, Lighthouse Rd, T481069, friendly and helpful, exchange, short country-boat backwater tours from Thiruvallam; *Great Indien Travel*, Lighthouse Rd, T481110, F480173, www.keralatours.com Wide range, exchange, eco-friendly beach resort. **Tourist offices** *Kerala Tourism*, T480085, inside *Aihok Hotel* gate, helpful manager but erratic opening hrs.

Kerala

North from Thiruvananthapuram

The coastal and inland routes pass through some beautiful scenery, crossing low rolling hills covered in coconut, jack, eucalyptus, cashew, mangoes, papaya and, under the woodcover, cassava. The lateritic rocks surface from time to time, and there are views of low ranges with a regular succession of rice growing and flat river valleys with wooded slopes. The better-off rice farmers live in the valley bottoms, while up the slope live the much poorer (and mainly Christian) peasantry. Occasional rubber plantations stretch as far down towards the coast as the NH47, but most lie further inland.

Neyyar Dam, Neyyar Wildlife Sanctuary

At the foot of the Western Ghats, 30 km east of Thiruvananthapuram, the Neyyar Sanctuary occupies a beautiful, wooded and hilly landscape, dominated by the peak of Agasthya Malai (1,868 m). The vegetation ranges from grassland to tropical, wet evergreen. Wildlife includes gaur, sloth bear, Nilgiri Tahr, jungle cat, sambar deer, elephants and Nilgiri langur, but the most commonly seen animals are lion-tailed macaques and other monkeys. Tigers and leopards have also been reported. The Neyyar Dam supports a large population of crocodiles and otters; a crocodile farm was set up in 1977 near the administrative complex.

Boating: speed boat for two Rs 100/150; larger boats to view the forests enclosing the lake, Rs 20 each. Mini bus safari Rs 10. If you prefer to trek, get permission from Trivandrum. Details of access from the Chief Conservator of Forests (Wildlife), Forest HQ, Thiruvananthapuram, T62217, or the Assistant Wildlife Warden at Neyyar Dam.

Agasthya Vanam Biological Park
Phone code: 0471

Immediately to the northeast of the Neyyar Wildlife sanctuary a section of dense forest, 'Agasthya Vanam', was set aside in 1992 to recreate biodiversity on a wide scale. The Sivananda *Yoga Vedanta Dhanwantari Ashram*, T290493, F451776, runs yoga and meditation course; highly intensive, only suitable for dedicated devotees of the school, others may find it hard going and heavy on Hinduism and Indian diet. **Sleeping E** *Agasthya House* (Kerala Tourism), opposite viewing tower, near Forest Information Centre, Kattakada, T471-272160, 6 rooms, on the edge of the reservoir, built like a concrete bunker, restaurant, veg and fish lunches (Rs 20-50), beer, views.

Ponmudi
Phone code: 0471
Colour map 3, grid C3
Altitude: 700 m

Ponmudi is the nearest hill station to Thiruvananthapuram (65 km). In a spectacular and peaceful setting, the complex, though basic, serves as a good base for trekking, birdwatching and visiting the nearby minimalist deer park. **Sleeping** Govt **F** *Ponmudi Tourist Resort*, T890230, 24 rooms and 10 cottages, in attractive gardens surrounded by wooded hills, spartan facilities but spacious rooms, restaurant serves limited but reasonable vegetarian meals. There is a KTDC *Restaurant* in the grounds with beer available; also a post office and general stores. ■ *Getting there: Several buses from Central Bus Stand from 0530 until 1630; return from Ponmudi, between 0615 and 1905 (2½ hrs).*

Anjengo
Phone code: 0471
Colour map 3, grid C3
Population: 32,600

Anjengo, north of Thiruvananthapuram, is accessible from Attingal, capital of the Travancore Tamburetti princes until 1758. Initially held by the Portuguese, this massive laterite fort has an English cemetery; the earliest tomb is dated 1704. An English warehouse and trading post had been set up 20 years earlier, but was abandoned in 1810. For a coastline fringed almost along its entire length with coconut palms, it is slightly ironical that Anjengo should mean 'five coconut trees'.

★ Varkala വർക്കല

Varkala has a lovely sea for swimming in and there are still relatively few tourists here though it is rapidly becoming better known. There are mineral water springs on the reddish cliffs and the Papanasam (Pavanacham) Beach is a good place for unwinding.

Phone code: 0472
Colour map 3, grid C3
Population: 39,000

Many find the beach far pleasanter than Kovalam especially since tourists are no longer hassled while swimming or sunbathing. However, some local fishermen and farmers are sometimes unhappy about their arrival, and it is best to dress decently away from the beach. The narrow lanes behind the south cliff are delightful and lead to fishing settlements and totally unspoilt beaches which are worth exploring on foot; just climb over rocks at the bottom of Beach Road. Unfortunately, dynamite fishing is being practised off-shore.

The beach

In the village, a short distance inland, is the attractive south Kerala style **Janardhanaswamy Temple**, a centre for pilgrimage. Largely re-built in the 13th century, the minor shrines are older. The temple is primarily dedicated to Vishnu with subsidiary Saivite shrines outside the main precinct. The *Arattu* festival in March-April draws thousands of pilgrims.

The village

On the cliff top to the north of the temple is the Government *Guest House*, formerly a palace of the Maharajah of Travancore. Behind this were buildings which housed the harems of the Maharajah, but these were sold off at Independence to private owners.

From the northern cliff top there are superb views of the sweeping bay (where you can sometimes spot dolphins), with the Alimood Mosque clearly

Kerala

Varkala

To Edavai (3 km) & Kollam (35 km)

North Cliff

Cliff Rd

To Kera Village Resort

To Railway Station (2.5 km), Sivagiri (3.5 km) & Thiruvananthapuram (50 km)

Helipad

o Nature Cure Centre

Mineral o Springs

Papanasam Beach

Hanuman Temple

Temple Junction

Beach Rd

Janardhanaswamy Temple

To South Cliff

N

| 0 metres | 100 |
| 0 yards | 100 |

■ **Sleeping**

1 Akshay Beach Resort
2 Beach Palace
3 Clafouti
4 Govt Guest House
5 Hill Palace
6 Hill Top Beach Resort
7 JA Tourist Home
8 Mamma Chompos
9 Marine Palace
10 The Palms
11 Panchvadi
12 Sea Shell Resort
13 Sea Spring
14 Taj Garden Retreat

● **Eating**

1 Café Italiano
2 Dreamland
3 Knight Rider
4 Manos & Sunset
5 Oottupura
6 Sea Breeze
7 Sea View
8 Sri Padman

visible in the middle distance. The access road to the north cliff was built to reach the helipad there. *Warning*: Inadequate fencing along the cliff edge with sharp overhangs makes a torch essential at night. Steep paths lead down to the beach but the longer Beach Road is better.

The Nature Cure Hospital, opened in 1983 treats patients entirely by diet and natural cures including hydrotherapy, chromotherapy (natural sunbath with different filters) and mud therapy, each treatment normally lasting 30 minutes.

Sleeping Many people stay with local families near the beach or on the cliff top above. Thefts reported; take care with personal possessions. **AL-A** *Taj Garden Retreat*, 500 m from the beach, T603000. 30 rooms, central a/c, excellent views, beautifully landscaped, pool. **D** *Akshay Beach Resort*, Beach Rd (about 200 m from beach), T602668. 16 very small rooms, some a/c, bright, clean and smart, TV lounge, restaurant. **D** *Hill Top Beach Resort*, north end, T601737. 18 rooms, clean, overlooks beach and bay, very quiet, limited restaurant and slow service. **D** *Panchvadi*, Beach Rd, T600200, F660400. 8 clean rooms (2 luxury) with bath (excellent showers), 24-hour check-in, laundry, Kerala style restaurant planned, good security, friendly helpful staff, close to beach. Recommended.

E *Marine Palace*, Papanasam Beach, on path down from cliff, T603204. 12 rooms (Rs 270+), some **D** a/c in small bungalows (not a palace), good restaurant overlooking beach (slow service), simple, comfortable, great situation, popular with the middle-aged! **E** *Beach Palace*, Beach Rd, T603910. Very basic rooms, good value restaurant, tables set on stilts in small pond. **F** *Govt Guest House* (Kerala Tourism), towards Taj hotel, T602227. 8 rooms, former summer residence of Maharaja, charming appearance but bed bugs (and snoring caretaker!), meals (overpriced, no receipt), individual buildings are better, idyllic and quiet (wooden ceilings, marble floors, big baths, shaded porches (Rs 165), book in advance. **F** *Mamma Chompos*, 100 m beyond *Akshay*. Shared toilet, well-water, good food, picturesque converted Kerala farmhouse, Italian run restaurant. **F** *VTDC Guest House*, opp Govt Guest House. Clean rooms (Rs 200), secretary T667494.

Paying-guest accommodation is available with families if you ask around **North cliff D-E** *Clafouti*, set back, T601414, F600494. Lovely rooms in new house (Rs 500), old house (Rs 200), all tiled baths, very clean, great French bakery though no clafouti in sight! **D-E** *Evergreen Beach Palace*, Thiruvambadi Beach, Kurakkanni, T 603257. New, large clean rooms with bath, non a/c (Rs 400) a/c available, quite smart. **D-E** *Sea Spring*, near Helipad. 9 rooms some with bath and hot water in 3-storey hotel, restaurant, moderate value. **F** *Hill Palace*, further north. Tiny thatched cottages, beautiful views of bay to north. **F** *The Palms*, 7 rooms, built in traditional style with polished coconut wood doors.

Inland E *Kera Village Resort*, Punnamoodu, Guest House Rd, T602337. 28 very basic rooms (some thatched huts) with baths, set in an acre of palms, restaurant, bike hire (5 minute ride to beach), camping, peaceful but a bit overpriced. **E** *Sea Shell Resort*, Cliff Rd, T602381. 7 rooms, 5 cottages with baths, tiled throughout, restaurant, clean, good value. **F** *Ajantha Tourist Home*, Temple Junction, T603684. 16 very clean rooms with bath, very friendly and helpful staff, good restaurant next door. **F** *Anandan Tourist Home*, opposite Rly station, T602135. 32 very cheap rooms, some a/c, restaurant, clean modern building, noisy in early mornings (temple next door), good value. **F** *JA Tourist Home*, Temple Junction, T602453. 11 rooms, modern Indian hotel, good value, also excellent roof restaurant, delicious food, friendly but slow service.

Eating **Mid-range**: Over a dozen pleasant places along the north clifftop, offer fish and seafood. *Clifton*, North Indian. Delicious, prepared fresh to order but slow. *Dreamland Sea Breeze*, *Café Italiano*, good Italian, but pricey (closed 1400-1730). *Knight Rider*, north end. Great seafood. *Manos*, usual menu, popular. *Oottupura*, south end. Excellent vegetarian.*Sunset*. Mainly Continental. Wide choice, special pizzas and home-made pasta, excellent kalamari curry, friendly and amusing staff. **Cheap**: *Sathram* , bus stop, Temple Junction. Excellent (daily changing *thalis* Rs 20), delicious small fish (Rs 10), popular with auto/bus drivers.*Sri Padman*, nearby. Mainly Indian. Good food, excellent Western breakfasts, overlooks temple tank.

Elegance of India and *Mushtaq*, Beach Rd. Kashmiri handicrafts, carpets etc, reported as honest, will safely air-freight carpets etc. **Shopping**

Local Rickshaws and **taxis** from Beach Rd and Helipad. **Motorcycle hire**: next door to *JA Tourist Home*, Temple Junction and *Mamma Home*, Beach Rd. **Long distance Road Bus**: frequent buses to Alappuzha and **Kollam**, and several long distance connections. **Taxi**: to **Thiruvananthapuram**, Rs 350 (1¼ hrs). **Train**: Several daily to coastal towns including **Thiruvananthapuram**, 0447, 0715 then several until 2102 (50 mins). Also to **Kanniyakumari**: 1107, 1400 (3½ hrs); **Kollam**; **Mangalore**, 0651, 1840 (14 hrs). **Transport**

Useful services Bank: *State Bank of Travancore* changes TCs, Visa cards, but will not change cash. **Post office**: next to *Sree Padman*, Temple Junction; ISD phones opposite; also at Maithalam. **Yoga**: *Scientific School of Yoga and Massage*, Altharamoodu, Janardhana Temple, 10-day yoga and massage course (2 classes daily), Rs 500, professionally run by English speaking doctor, T695141. Also **shop** selling ayurvedic oils, soaps, shampoo etc. **Directory**

Kerala

The Backwaters

Kollam (Quilon) കൊല്ലം

Kollam is a shaded town with a compact centre, on the side of the Ashtamudi Lake. At the south end of Kerala's backwaters, it is one of the main centres for boat trips up the canals.

Phone code: 0474
Colour map 3, grid C3
Population: 362,400

Known to Marco Polo (as *Koilum*) its port traded with Phoenicians, Persians, Greeks, Romans and Arabs as well as the Chinese; superb chinaware has been found in the area. Kollam became the capital of the Venad Kingdom in the ninth century. The educated and accomplished king Raja Udaya Marthanda Varma convened a special council at Kollam to introduce a new era. After extensive astronomical calculations the new era was established to start on 15 August AD 825. The town was also associated with the early history of Christianity. **History**

Ashtamudi Lake with coconut palms on its banks and picturesque promontories extends north from the town. You might see some 'Chinese' fishing nets and in wider sections large-sailed dugouts carrying the local coir, copra and cashew. Boats for hire for cruising from the *Kollam Boat Club* or from the *DTPC*, Guest House Compound, T742558. Pedal or rowing boats for two or four persons, Rs 20 per hour each. **Sights**

Tangasseri (Thangassery), 5 km from the town centre, was once a British outpost. The Portuguese Fort Thomas (1503), taken later by the Dutch, formerly dominated the shore, but most of it has now collapsed. There is a ruined belfry in the middle of the Protestant graveyard. Today Tangasseri is little more than a shanty town. The Lighthouse is open from 1530 to 1730. Buses take 15 minutes.

Backwaters
tours
Timings change

Trips for groups of 10, or a 'cruise' for 20 to Alappuzha with a guide. **DTPC**, Ashramam, T742558 dtpcqln@md3.vsnl.net, runs an eight hour 'Luxury' cruise from the jetty near slaughter house (in season), 1000 (timing may alter), Tuesday and Saturday, Rs 150 (ISIC Rs 100); half way (to Alumkadavu;), Rs 100. *En route*, stops may include the longest snake boat in the world, Champakulam, an 11th century black granite Buddha statue at Karumadi, and a coir processing village at Thrikkunnapuzha. However, some travellers say that the only stops are for meals, so check in advance. Some find the trip too long and 'samey'. The DTPC canal trip to Munroe Island village, 0900-1300, Rs 300, is an alternative.

DTPC has a more expensive alternative, the luxury *kettuvallam*, with two bedrooms, a bath and a kitchen hired out for Rs 4,500 for two (full day), traditional Kerala meals are served; overnight trips (24 hours) start at Rs 8,200. The 25 hp outboard engine does about 10 km per hour. You can also hire motor boats for a 'safari cruise' for eight people, Rs 200-300 per hour. Contact DTPC, Soma, T477-261017 or T471-481601. See also Kumarakom.

Sleeping

A *Aquaserene*, Paravoor, 15 mins from town by road/boat, T512410, F 512104, splendid backwaters location, well furnished chalets (some re-assembled Kerala houses with antiques, carved panels, sculptures) with TV, restaurant (superb views) room service by canoe, Ayurvedic massage/treatment, boat rides. **B** *Ashtamudi Resorts*, Chavara South, T882288, F882470. 30 mins by car, 10 mins speed boat, 20 rms in 5 traditional chalets, dearer 'Queens Cottages' and 'King's Palace', all a/c with good views, catamaran trips, an ayurvedic resort. **C** *Palm Lagoon*, Vellimon West, T/F523974. Delightful setting 18 km from town centre on north side of Ashtamudi Lake, can be reached from backwater cruise, attractive thatched cottages, including full board. **C-E** *Sudarsan*, Hospital Rd, Parameswar Nagar, 5 mins from jetty, T744322, F740480. 35 rooms, some a/c with bath (Rs 250), rear quieter, dim a/c restaurant, bar, exchange, backwater trips.

Paying guests through
Prof KRC Nair, Ambadi
Lake Resorts,
Ashramam, T744688

E *Karthika*, Chinnakada, T740106. 40 rooms with bath, some a/c, restaurant, bar, backwater trips arranged, mediocre. **E** *Lake View*, Thoppikadavu, T794669. Near Thevally Bridge (5 km from station; 10 minute walk from small Post Office northwest of town), beautiful position along lakeside, 4 clean, renovated rooms (2 have large balcony) (Rs 275+), lovely garden, good waterside restaurant, bar (occasionally noisy), friendly staff. Recommended. **E** *Shah International*, TB Rd, Chinnakkada, T742362. 72 rooms, some **D** a/c, adequate restaurant, quiet, good value. **E-F** *Yatri Nivas*, Guest House Compound by Ashtamudi Lake, Ashramam, T745538. 15 rooms and 2 6-bed dorm, restaurant, beer, Tourist Office, boating and free boat service from town jetty, ugly block building but clean and good value, cycles for hire, reservations at tourist office, Alappuzha. **F** *Govt Guest House*, Ashramam, T743620. 8 large rooms, simple meals (caretaker overcharges, no receipt given), fine 200-year-old building with garden on edge of lagoon, looks like "a run down Club House in search of a golf course", former British Residency, boating, small pool and park by the lake, full of character, out of the way; can be difficult to get in. **F** *Lakshmi Tourist Home*, Parry Junction, Main Rd, T740167. Some a/c, basic. **F** *Mahalaxmi Lodge*, opposite Bus Station near Ashtamudi Lake, T749440. 7 very small rooms (Rs 90), shared outside toilet, adequate.

Eating

Main St: *Eat N Pack*, near Taluk Office. Excellent value, clean, good choice of dishes, friendly. Recommended. *Indian Coffee House*, Main Rd. Good coffee and non-vegetarian snacks, 0800-2030. *Suprabhatam*, opposite Clock Tower. Adequate, vegetarian.

Festivals

Jan: Kerala Tourism boat race on 19 Jan. **Apr**: colourful 10 day *Vishnu festival* in Asram Temple with procession and fireworks. **Aug-Sep**: Avadayattukotta Temple celebrates a five-day *Ashtami Rohani festival*. *Muharram* too is observed with processions at the town mosque.

Shopping

The main areas are on the Main Rd. *Kairali*, Beach Rd for crafts. *Bishop Jaromnagar Shopping Mall* is modern and handy.

Transport

Local Buses and **auto-rickshaws** are plentiful. **Bikes** for hire. **Long distance Train**: The Junction railway station, T131, is about 3 km east of the boat jetty and bus station. **Chennai (MC)**: *Chennai Mail*, *6320* (AC/II), 1435, 16¼ hrs. **Madurai**: *Quilon Nagore Fast Pass*, *6162* (AC/II), 1220, 9¼ hrs; **Thiruvananthapuram**: *Kerala-Mangala Exp*, *2626* (AC/II), 1450, 2 hrs. **Road Bus**: KSRTC, T752008. Buses every 30 mins to Alappuzha (85 km, 2 hrs) and **Kochi** (140 km, 3½ hrs) and other towns on the coast. Daily bus to **Kumily** village for Periyar National Park (change at Kottayam), 1000, 7 hrs. Also buses to **Kanniyakumari**. Frequent services to **Kochi**, 3 hrs; **Thiruvananthapuram**, 2 hrs. For **Varkala** difficult by bus; take one to Kollambalam and change. However, all southbound trains stop at Varkala.

Kollam

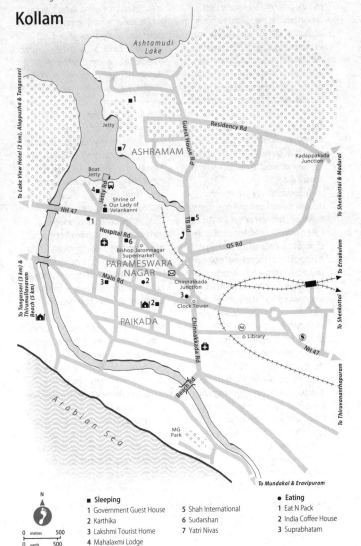

Kerala

■ **Sleeping**
1 Government Guest House
2 Karthika
3 Lakshmi Tourist Home
4 Mahalaxmi Lodge
5 Shah International
6 Sudarshan
7 Yatri Nivas

● **Eating**
1 Eat N Pack
2 India Coffee House
3 Suprabhatam

Kerala

★ Kerala backwaters

The network of rivers, streams, lagoons, canals and tanks that occupies the alluvial plain between the Indian Ocean and the Western Ghats runs the length along the coast from Kollam to Kochi, the northern section known as Kuttanad. It gives an almost uniquely quiet view of Kerala village life, impossible to get simply from the road.

With only two permanent outlets to the sea, one at Kodungallur in the north and the other at Kochi, and a third opening during the southwest monsoon at Thottappally (where a cut was made to let the surplus stagnant freshwater out to sea), Kerala's backwater lagoons are fed by a network of perennial rivers. These flush out the salts between May and September, but seawater rushes in at the end of the monsoon reaching up to 20 km inland. The backwaters become increasingly brackish through the dry season. The alternation between fresh and saltwater has been essential to the backwaters' aquatic life.

Reclamation for agriculture has reduced the surface water area, and the building of a barrier across the Vembanad Lake, north of Kumarakom, and other changes have altered the backwaters' ecology. Most of the original mangrove swamps have now been destroyed; a small residual patch at Kumarakom has limited protection. Many reclaimed areas (plots known as pokkali) are now used alternately for paddy, and fish and shrimp farming. In some parts of Vembanad the population density is four times that on the coastal zone.

On the backwaters' trip you can see how bunds have been built enclosing areas from the main lake. These bunds (often granite and cement) are strengthened by planting coconuts, while electric pumps are used to dry out the normally flooded land. Below the bund the lake is suffering excessive saline flooding, and the reduced exchange between the lakes and the sea has severely worsened pollution. Mass fish kills are reported, and water weed infestation has increased with the excessive use of fertilizers on agricultural land. The dramatic increase in the land value across Kerala has resulted in pressure to put every square centimetre to economic use.

Few of these problems are immediately visible on the backwaters' trip, which can be an idyllic experience. Waterside activities of coir making, toddy tapping, fishing, rice growing along the palm-lined banks and narrow strips of land that separate the waterways, and the constant quiet traffic of vallam (traditional dugouts) are typical. Advantage is taken of the comparatively long rainy season so while coconuts provide a vital economic resource, the land underneath is often intensively cultivated. From the boat you will see papaya, mangoes, jack fruit and cassava (tapioca) growing. Tapioca, only introduced to Kerala in 1920, is very popular since it gives remarkably high yields from lateritic soils that are about 'as fertile as railway ballast'.

Along the backwaters, traditional punted boats or motorized ferries provide one of the most delightful tours in India. The typical journey on a motor boat between Kollam and Alappuzha lasts over eight hours but some people find this too long. A shorter trip is possible, either by doing a round trip from Kollam, or by picking up or getting off the boat closer to Alappuzha (for example Changanacherry or Kottayam). Nearer Kochi too, a quiet half-day can be spent on a traditional dugout or you can have an exclusive upmarket overnight trip in a kettuvallam style houseboat.

Travel tip: even in the coolest times of year this journey during daytime can get very hot. Take a sun hat, sun block and plenty of water. There are stops for refreshments but you should carry some. See Kolam, Alappuzha and Kochi.

Directory

Bank *Bank of Baroda*, Hospital Rd. **Communications** Courier: *DHL*, Jetty Rd. **Internet:** Plenty of competition. **Post:** *Head Post Office*, Parameswara Nagar. Mon-Sat to 2000, Sun to 1800. Speed Post at Chinnakkada. **Tourist offices** DTDC *Govt Guest House* Complex, T/F742558, dtpcqln@md3.vsnl. net.in; also, very helpful counter staff at Ferry jetty; KSRTC Bus station, T745625; Rly station, Plat 4. **Dept of Tourism**, at *Guest House*, T743620. *KTDC*, *Yatri Nivas*, Ashramam, T748638. **Travel:** *World Tours*, Tesson Arcade, T741249.

Kollam to Alappuzha backwaters

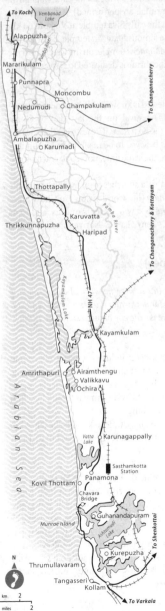

Kollam to Alappuzha

The ashram of Mata Amrithanandamayi, on the backwaters, is sandwiched between the sea and the river, accessible by boat or by road through Kayamkulam or Karungappally. *Darshan* on Thursday and Sunday is attended by large numbers of villagers and Western tourists. Some find the atmosphere disturbing. **Sleeping** Simple rooms (donations expected) and good Western canteen for residents.

Vallikkavu (Amrithapuri)
10 km N of Kollam

Mannarsala has a Nagaraja Temple in the forest. Traditionally Hindu *naga* (serpent) worshippers had temples in serpent groves. Mannarsala is the largest of these in Kerala with "30,000 images" of snake gods along the path and among the trees, and has many snakes living around the temple. Childless women come for special blessing and also return for a 'thanksgiving' ceremony afterwards when the child born to the couple is placed on special scales and gifts in kind equalling the weight are donated. The temple is unusual for its chief priestess.

Mannarsala
32 km before Alappuzha

Haripad has one of Kerala's oldest and most important Subrahmanya temples. The four armed idol is believed to have been found in a river, and the Snake Boat Race at **Payipad** (3 km by bus) for three days commemorates its rescue and subsequent building of the temple. *Jalotsav* during Onam. Boat processions on first two days followed by competitive races on third day; entry by ticket in August and November/December. **Sleeping** *Guest House* on Mankotta Island on the backwaters, large comfortable rooms with bath, well kept, boating, squash.

Haripad

Kerala

Thottapally Squeezed between the backwaters and the sea, and 12 km from Haripad station, Thottapally makes a good stop on a backwaters trip, two hours from Alappuzha. **Sleeping C-D** *Coconut Palms*, Pandavapuram Heritage Village, T836251, idyllic traditional house in shaded compound, on backwaters and 100 m from sea, package deals available including transport from *Aries Travel*, Trivandrum T0471-330964, F470159.

Chengannur
Phone code: 0478
Population: 25,900

Chengannur has a small Narasimha temple dating from the 18th century. The **Mahadeva Temple** uses the base of an older shrine as its *kuttambalam* (a building where dance, music and other rituals are performed). It illustrates the elliptical shape that was found again in the early Siva temple at Vaikom 60 km to the north. In the heart of the town is a famous *Bhagvati* temple, described by the arch over its main entrance as the *Mahadeva* temple, on the west side of the Thiruvanan- thapuram-Aluva road. The shrine is dedicated to Parvati (facing west) and Parameswara (facing east).

Aranmula
10 km from Chengannur

Aranmula has the Parthasarathi Temple and is known for its unique metal mirrors. The *Vallamkali* (or *Uttthrittathi*) festival on the last day of Onam (August-September) is celebrated with the *Boat Race*. The festival celebrates the crossing of the river by Krishna, who is believed to be in all the boats simultaneously, so they are expected to arrive at the same time, not to race each other.

Pathanam-thitta Surrounded by rich forests **Pathanamthitta** stretches from the lowland to the high ranges of the ghats. *Viswadarshanam* (lit. 'world vision'), or the 'Centre for Man and Nature', welcomes visitors to stay in its tents or huts, and to its courses. Contact Viswadar-shanam, Feny Land, Nariyapuram 689513, T0473-350543.

Alappuzha ആലപ്പുഴ (Alleppey)

Phone code: 0477
Colour map 3, grid B2
Population: 264,900

Alappuzha (pronounced Alappoorra) has a large network of canals passing through the town and is a major centre for backwater cruises and the venue for the spectacular 'snake' boat races. There is little else of interest though the people are friendly.

Sights Alappuzha is the headquarters of Kerala's coir industry with some very old warehouses on the canal bank. It is also important for cashew nut processing. The centre of activity is the jetty with the bus stand nearby. Here, in places, the waterways are clogged and completely covered by the rampant water hyacinth with pretty blue flowers which remains a scourge.

St Thomas Church is worth a look if you have time to kill. The beach, 3 km away, is suburban, polluted by oil and with no shade. The 'pier' is out of use. A boating lake has row boats for Rs 15 per hour.

Backwaters tours
Alappuzha is a starting point of backwater boat trips to Kollam, Changanacherry, Kottayam & Kochi

DTPC (District Tourism Promotion Council), Alappuzha, KSRTC Bus Station, T/253308. From August to May, eight-hour cruises depart at 1030, Monday, Wednesday, Friday, Rs 150, with stops for lunch and tea. Half-way cruise to **Alamkadavu**, Rs 100 (ISIC gets reduction) on a local ferry, one-way (29 km) costs Rs 10, from 0500-2100, 2½ hours. Some visitors feel that this trip is so different from the Kollam-Alappuzha trip that it is worth doing both. The journeys in the daytime are more interesting for watching unspoilt village life of Kerala. **Private operators** offer similar trips, sometimes shorter (sometimes only stopping for a swim and lunch).

DTPC have backwater cruises on big country boats (*kettuvallam*). Built in the Keralan style of houseboat, it is punted around the backwaters; moonlit tours on and around the full moon. An overnight tour costs Rs 3,500-5,000 for two, includes meals. The gentle pace and quiet contribute to make this worthwhile, but for one night only as the humidity makes it uncomfortable (no fans).

Casino Group, Kochi T668221, F668001. *Spice Boat Cruise* in similar modified *kettuvallams*, which are idyllic if not luxurious (shaded sit-outs, modern facilities including solar panels for electricity, two double rooms, limited menu, $ 200 per room). Also through **Soma**, opposite the boat jetty, 212 Raiban Annex, T0477-26101n7, soma@md2.vsnl.net.in; **Kumarakom Tourist Village** (KTDC), T0481-524258, F525862, Rs 7,500 (day only), Rs 18,750 (1 night, 2 days).

A *Kayaloram Lake Resort*, Punmamada, on Vembanad lake (4 km; 15 mins by boat from jetty near Punchiri building, behind Canara Bank then 300 m walk), T242040 (or at 'Punchiri', Jetty Rd, T260573, F252918, kayaloram@vsnl.com). 12 Kerala style wood and tile cottages around small inner 'courtyard' with 'open-to-sky' showers ($60 or $84 with meals for 2), pool, backwaters or lake trips, comfortable, very quiet and peaceful. Recommended. **B** *Keraleeyam*, off the Thotampally main road (invloves a short wooded walk), T241468, F251068, mail@keraleeyam.com 1930s 'Heritage home', now attached to an ayurvedic pharmacy, 5 comfortable a/c rooms, pleasant courtyard lawn, Kerala cuisine, excellent ayurvedic centre, boat rides on backwaters, splendid view of boat races in season, homely atmosphere but slow service and uneven a/c reported, larger resort with Ayurvedic spa being added.

Sleeping
All north of Vadai Canal are quieter

C-D *Alleppey Prince*, AS Rd (NH47), 2 km north of centre, T243752, F243758. 30 good, clean rooms, central a/c, very dark bar, pool, luxury boats for backwaters. **D** *Cherukara Nest*, just round the corner from bus station, T251509, F342164,

Alleppuzha (Alleppey)

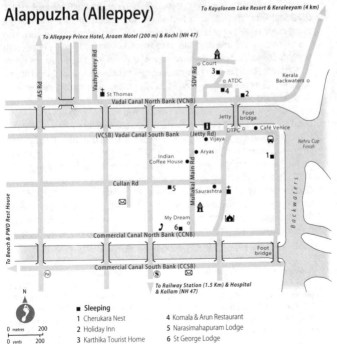

raiyaan@giasmd01.vsnl.net.in. Pleasant traditional home, very clean rooms with bath, very helpful staff, Kerala meals on request. **D-E** *Komala*, near Municipal Maidan, opposite Jetty north of canal, T243631. Some a/c rooms, adequate, very good restaurant, friendly management. Recommended.

E *Holiday Inn*, Vadai Canal North Bank, T242955. Clean, spacious rooms, good value. Recommended. **E** *Tharayil Tourist Home*, 750 m from boat jetty near lake. Some a/c rooms, clean, local furniture. **F** *Narasimhapuram Lodge*, Cullen Rd, T262662. Some a/c rooms, occasional weight-lifting competition with live commentary over loudspeakers! **F** *Karthika Tourist Home*, near Zilla Court, SDV Rd, north of canal, opposite Jetty, T245524. 39 clean, pleasant rooms, some large with baths (but cockroaches), best No 31, helpful and friendly staff, good value. **F** *Araam* (KTDC), AS Rd, near *Prince*, T244460. 2 simple rooms with bath, restaurant. **F** 2 *Railway Retiring Rooms* and snack bar. **F** *Govt Rest House*, Beach Rd, 4 km Bus Stand, T243445. Excellent value, reasonable food (order in advance) but indifferent service, reservations: Dist Collector, Collectorate, Dist HQ, Alappuzha. **F** *St George Lodge*, CCNB Rd, A-5, T251620. 80 basic rooms, some with bath (Rs 55-100), terrace restaurant, good value, popular with backpackers, exchange, book ahead.

Eating **Mid-range**: *Prince Hotel's Vemanad*, International, comfortable a/c, reasonable food, alcohol in bar only. **Cheap**: *Komala*. Excellent South Indian *thalis* and some Chinese. On Mullakal Main Rd: *Aryas*, south of Jetty, good for *idli*, *dosa*, *vadai* etc. Almost opposite, *Indian Coffee House*, does good value, non-vegetarian snacks. *Café Venice*, is just by the DTPC office. *Saurashtra*, vegetarian, ample helpings on banana leaf, locally popular. *Vijaya*, Jetty Rd. Good South Indian vegetarian and Chinese.

Festivals **9-12 Jan**: *Cheruppu* is celebrated in the Mullakal Devi Temple with procession of elephants, music and fireworks. *Champakulam Boat Race* takes place 16 km ferry ride away on 'Moolam' day (check with tourist office). **17-19 Jan**: *Tourism Boat Race*. **Jul**: *DTPC Boat Race* (third Sat) in the backwaters. **Aug**: Second Sat at Punnamadakayal where one of Kerala's most famous boat races is held. The Nehru Cup, inaugurated in 1952, is the largest *Snake Boat Race* in the state. As many as 40 'snake boats', with highly decorated and carved prows, are rowed by several dozen oarsmen before huge crowds. Naval helicopters do mock rescue operations and stunt flying. Entry by ticket; Rs 125 recommended (avoid Rs 60/75 as it gets overcrowded and becomes dangerous and no fun).

Transport **Local** Tourist and other **taxis**, and **auto-rickshaws**. **Boat**: see 'Backwaters' above. DTPC speedboat Rs 400 per hr; others Rs 200 per hr. **Long distance** **Bus**: T252501. Frequent buses to Champakulam; Kochi, 0630-2330, 1½ hrs, Kollam 2½ hrs; Kottayam 1½ hrs; Thiruvananthapuram 3½ hrs. Also to Coimbatore, 0615, 7 hrs. **Ferry**: DTPC, ATDC, Prince and others: to **Champakulam** 9 trips from 0430-2300, 1½ hrs; **Changanacherry**, 3½ hrs; **Chengannur**, 5 hrs etc. **Train**: The station (T253965) is 3 km from the Jetty with occasional buses from there. Trains from **Ernakulam** including the *Intercity 6341*, 0640, 1 hr, which easily allows picking up a backwater cruise from here; to Ernakulam dep 0600 to 1915 (*Intercity 6342*). To **Chennai**: *Alleppey Chennai Exp*, *6042*, 1510, 15 hrs; **Thiruvananthapuram**: *Intercity Exp 6341*, 0745, 3 hrs.

Directory **Bank** *Canara*, opp DTPC, changes most TCs but not cash. **Communications** Head Post office: off Mullakal Rd. **Telegraph Office**: on corner of NH47 and Beach Rd, just over the canal. **Tourist offices** *KTDC*, *Motel Araam*, T244460. *ATDC* (Alappuzha Tourism Dev Corp), Komala Rd, T/F243462, info@atdcaalleppey.com. *DTPC*, KSRTC Bus Station near jetty, T253308, F251720, 0830-2000 (7 days); helpful, good backwaters trips. Also *My Dream Tourist Service*, Cream Korner, Mullackal, T260005.

Around Alappuzha

This quiet, secluded beach until now was only known to the adjoining fishing village. The main village has a thriving cottage industry of coir and jute weaving. **Sleeping A** *Marari Beach Village* (Casino Group), T668221, F668001, casino@vsnl.com 40 well-furnished cottages, some with own pool, comfortable, a/c, local style cottages, good sea food, pool, watersports planned, ayurvedic treatment, yoga, bikes.

Mararikulam
Phone code: 0484
On the coast, 15 km S of Alappuzha

St Mary's Forane Church (Syrian) at this backwaters village dates only from 1870 but is on the site of one going back to AD 427. The English speaking priest is happy to show visitors round. Nearby the *St Thomas Statuary* makes wooden statues of Christ for export round the world. A 2 m statue of Jesus costs approximately US$450. Champakulam is particularly attractive because there is no traffic other than the occasional cycle, and the odd canoe. Visit recommended.

Champakulam
Phone code: 0477
16 km SE of Alappuzha

Sleeping and eating D *Green Palace*, Chempupuram, T736262, F245351, greenpalace@ rediffmail.com 5 rooms in a new co-op effort (Rs 450-750 including Kerala meals and ayurvedic massage), waterside farm.

Transport Take the Alappuzha-Changanacherry bus (every 30 mins) to Moncombu (Rs 4), then rickshaw to Champakulam (4 km, Rs 12). Alappuzha-Edathna ferry leaves at 0615 and 1715 and stops at Champakulam. In **Edathna** you can visit the early Syrian St George's Church.

Kayamkulam, with frequent buses from Alappuzha, has the **Krishnapuram Palace.** Typical of Kerala architecture with gabled roof, dormer windows and narrow corridors, the palace (circa 1740s) is ascribed to Raja Marthanda Varma. It contains a large mural, covering over 5 sq m, relating the story of Gajendra Moksha. The **museum** displays bronzes, sculptures and paintings. **Eating F** *Araam* (KTDC), Alappuzha.

Kayamkulam
47 km S of Alappuzha

Central Malabar

As with several other regional names the name 'Malabar' is an evocative combination of foreign and local elements. Hobson-Jobson has pointed out the Arab connection with the name 'Malabar', applied to the region which the Arabs also knew as the 'Pepper Coast'. Malai is the Dravidian term for mountain, while the suffix bar was applied by Arab sailors to a number of the coastal regions with which they traded such as Zanzibar (the 'Country of the Blacks') and the Kalahbar (the Malay Coast). It is suggested that the word 'bar' indicates both a coast and kingdom.

★ Kochi-Ernakulam കൊച്ചി/എറണാകുളം

Kochi (Cochin), one of South India's most interesting towns, still largely comprises low rise, picturesque buildings. Rich in history, despite rapid recent growth it retains a relaxed, quiet atmosphere once the majority of day-visitors leave. Narrow spits of land and coconut covered islands jut out into the wide, and almost enclosed, bay whose neck is lined with the famous Chinese fishing nets.

Phone code 0484
Colour map 3, grid B2
Population 1.14 mn
(Kochi 583,000,
Ernakulam 558,000)

Today, Kochi's twin town, Ernakulam, is busy and noisy by comparison, a dynamic city with soaring land prices and rapidly industrializing suburbs.

Ins & outs **Getting there** The new Kochi International Airport for Kochi is at Nedumbassery, 36 km away. Ernakulam Junction is the principal railway station, with the main long distance bus station close by. Both are within easy walking distance of some hotels, though pleasanter Fort Kochi is a bus or ferry ride away. **Getting around** During the day, a good ferry service stops at major points around the bay. It is pleasant, cheap and quick. Once in Fort Kochi, the palace and the synagogue in 'Jew Town' are close enough to a jetty but some distance from the other sights eg St Francis Church. Autos and bikes can be hired.

Background From 1795 until India's Independence the long outer sand spit, with its narrow beach leading to the wide bay inland, was under British political control. The inner harbour was in Kochi State, while most of the hinterland was in the separate state of Travancore. The division of political authority delayed development of the harbour facilities until 1920-23, when the approach channel was dredged to allow any ship that could pass through the Suez Canal to dock safely, opening the harbour to modern shipping.

A trading port since at least Roman times, Kochi was on the main trade route between Europe and China. The town is in three main parts. **Fort Kochi** (Fort Cochin) occupies the southern promontory on the seaward side of the bay. **Willingdon Island** was created in the 1920s by dredging the bay to increase the depth of the entrance to the harbour to over 11 m. It is the HQ of the Southern Command of the Indian Navy, and has a naval airport and the railway terminus. Across the causeway from Willingdon Island is **Ernakulam**. Immediately opposite the jetty at Ernakulam is **Bolghatty Island**, and beyond it **Vypeen Island**.

Sights Most of the historic buildings are in **Fort Kochi** with its narrow streets. A plaque in Vasco da Gama Square near the Customs Jetty commemorates the landing of **Vasco da Gama** in 1500. Next to it is the Stromberg Bastion, "one of the seven bastions of Fort Emanuel built in 1767", named after the Portuguese King. Little remains of the old Portuguese fort (founded 1503) except some ruins. Along the sea front are the Chinese fishing nets (see below).

★ **Mattancherry Palace** The palace was built by the Portuguese (circa 1557) as a gift for the Raja of Kochi in exchange for trading rights. In 1663, it was largely rebuilt by the new occupants, the **Dutch**. Built on two floors round a quadrangle with a Bhagavati temple, the plan follows the traditional Kerala pattern known as *nalukettus* ('four buildings') see page 225. To the south of the palace is another temple complex dedicated to **Siva** and **Vishnu**. Although the Palace has exhibits of the Rajas of Kochi (clothes, palanquins, weapons, furniture) the main feature is the series of murals painted on the wooden walls. These are remarkable, matched only by those in the Padmanabhapuram Palace (see page 187). The 'royal bedroom' has low wooden ceilings and walls covered in about 45 late 16th-century paintings illustrating the *Ramayana*, from the beginning to the point of

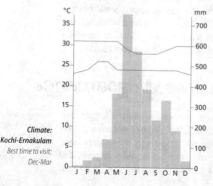

Climate:
Kochi-Ernakulam
Best time to visit:
Dec-Mar

Sita's return from captivity. Every available space is covered with rich red, yellow, black and white; blue and green are used sparingly. To the south of the Coronation Hall, the *kovinithilam* (staircase room) has six 18th-century, large murals including the coronation of Rama; the staircase led downstairs to the women's bedroom on the ground floor. The room to the north has a painting of Vishnu. Other rooms upstairs have more exhibits of the royal house. Two of the women's bedrooms downstairs have 19th century murals with greater detail. They relate Kalidasa's *Kumarasambava* and themes from the *Puranas*. ■ *1000-1700; closed Fri and National holidays. Free (no need to add to the unofficial "collection" bowl at the entrance). Photography is not allowed. Recommended. The imformative ASI booklet by Sivananda Venketarao and Raman Namboodri, 1997, is recommended; Rs 35 (not $3 quoted by staff).*

★ **Jewish Synagogue** (circa 1568) The caretaker will open the Torah scrolls for Jewish visitors. The story of the Kochi Jews is fascinating. For several centuries there were two Jewish communities. The 'black' Jews, who, according to one source, settled here in 587 BC, though some legends trace their origins to King Solomon (1030 BC). The earliest evidence of their presence is a copper inscription dated AD 388 (possibly as much as a century later) by the Prince of Malabar. The 'white' Jews came much later, and eventually in larger numbers, possibly totalling as many as 4,000 at their peak when, with Dutch and subsequently British patronage, they played a pivotal role as trading agents. Speaking fluent Malayalam, they made excellent go-betweens for foreigners seeking to establish contacts. The synagogue of the white Jews is near Mattancherry Palace, at the heart of what is called locally Jew Town, now a fascinating mixture of shops (some selling antiques), warehouses and spice auction rooms. Stepping inside is an extraordinary experience of light and airiness, given partly by the flooring of 18th century blue Cantonese ceramic tiles, hand painted and each one different. In addition to the trade with China, the Jewish community may also have had strong links with Babylonian Jews. It is possible to see the great scrolls of the Old Testament and the copper plates on

Kerala

Fort Kochi detail

Related maps
Kochi-Ernakulam,
page 250
Ernakulan centre,
page 254

which privileges were granted to the Jewish community by the Kochi rulers. Since Indian Independence and the founding of the State of Israel the community has shrunk to half a dozen families. The second Jewish synagogue (in Ernakulam) is deserted. ■ *1000-1200 and 1500-1700, closed Sat and Jewish holidays. Recommended.*

St Francis Church Originally dedicated to Santo Antonio, the patron saint of Portugal, St Francis Church is the first to reflect the new, European influenced tradition. In Fort Kochi, the original wooden structure (circa 1510) was replaced

Kochi (Cochin) & Ernakulam

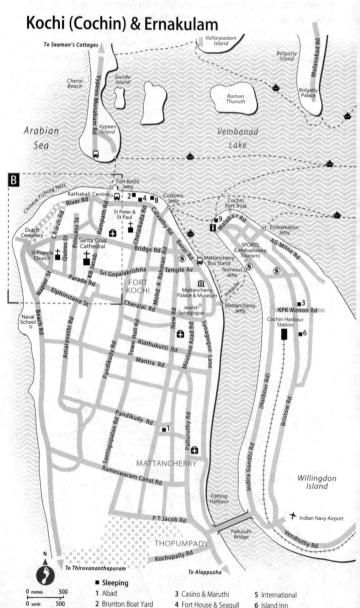

Related maps
A *Ernakulam,*
page 254
B *Fort Kochi,*
page 249

N

0 metres 500
0 yards 500

To Thiruvananthapuram

To Alappuzha

■ **Sleeping**
1 Abad
2 Brunton Boat Yard

3 Casino & Maruthi
4 Fort House & Seagull

5 International
6 Island Inn

by the present stone building (there is no authority for the widely quoted date of 1546). Vasco da Gama died on the site in 1524 and was originally buried in the cemetery. Fourteen years later his body was removed to Portugal. The church was renamed St Francis in 1663, and the Dutch both converted it to a Protestant church and substantially modified it. They retained control until 1795, adding the impressive gable façade at the entrance. In 1804, it became an Anglican church. Inside, the chancel is separated from the nave by a plain arch. The use of the arch is in sharp contrast to traditional Indian use of flat overlapping slabs, or *corbelling*, to produce gateways. In 1949 the congregation joined the Church of South India. ■ *Visiting 0930-1730 Mon-Sat, Sun afternoon. Sun services in English 0800 (except third Sun each month).*

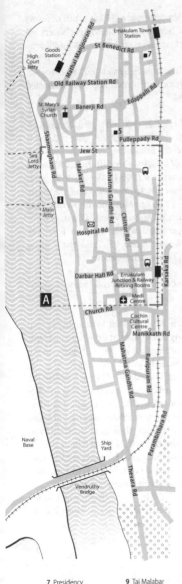

Santa Cruz Cathedral Near St Francis Church, originally built in 1557 by the Portuguese, and used as a warehouse by the British in the 18th century, was rebuilt in the early 20th century. It has lovely carved wooden panels and pulpit, and an interesting graveyard.

★ **Chinese fishing nets** Not unique to Kochi, but uniquely accessible to the short stay visitor, the cantilevered fishing nets line the entrance to the harbour mouth. Chinese traders are believed to have originally introduced them in the late 14th century although, today, parts of the nets are known by Portuguese names. They can best be seen either on the north end of the fort promontory, close to the Fort Kochi bus stand, or from a boat tour of the harbour – they "seem a lot of work for little reward. Are they there to catch fish or tourists?" Occasionally, brazen crows swoop down and remove the few small fish that emerge as the net is hauled out of the water!

Gundu Island On the inshore side of Vypeen island, Gundu is the smallest island in the bay.

Bolghatty Island The 'palace' (circa 1745), set in large gardens and converted into a hotel, was originally built by the Dutch. It became the home of the British Resident at the court of the Raja of Kochi after 1799. There is still some atmosphere of colonial decay which haunted the old building in its premodernized form and gave it much of its charm.

Kerala

7 Presidency

8 Seagull

9 Taj Malabar

Willingdon Island Has become the hub of one of India's busiest ports. The Custom's House and the *Malabar Hotel* are to the north of the naval airport and the rail terminus. You can take a pleasant walk or an inexpensive ferry ride around the lake, though the docks warehouses and truck parks are not very picturesque.

Vypeen Island The Portuguese Azhikotta Fort (the plaque calls it Pallipuram), built around 1503, stands by the police station. You can see cannon holes on the walls of the octagonal fort which was garrisoned by 20 soldiers when it guarded the entrance to the backwaters.

Excursions **Our Lady's Convent** At Palluruthy, Thoppampady (14 km south of town) specializes in high quality needlework lace and embroidery. The sisters are very welcoming and it is an interesting tour (items are for sale). ■ *By appointment only, T230508.*

Raksha Yasmin Manzil, VII/370 Darragh-es-Salaam Rd, Kochangadi, T227707, works with children with physical and mental disabilities. Interested **volunteers** should contact the Principal.

Museums **Parishath Thamburan Museum** In Old Durbar Hall with typical Kerala architecture. Nineteenth century oil paintings, old coins, sculptures, some collections from Kochi royal family. ■ *Darbar Hall Rd, Ernakulam, T369047. 0930-1200 and 1500-1730, closed Mon and National holidays. Free.* **Hill Palace Museum** Royal memorabilia, paintings, carvings, arms. ■ *0900-1230, 1400-1630, closed Mon. Re 1, Rs 3 for car (private buses from Ernakulam). Thripunithura, on the Chottanikkara Rd, 12 km southeast, T857113.* **Museum of Kerala History** Starting with Neolithic man through St Thomas, Vasco da Gama and historical personalities of Kerala are represented with sound and light. ■ *1000-1200, 1400-1600 closed Mon and National holidays, Rs 2. Edappally, Kochi.* **Dutch Palace Museum**, Mattancherry, Fort Kochi. See above.

Parks & zoos *Children's Traffic Park* and *Subhas Park* in Ernakulam and *Nehru Memorial Children's Park* in Fort Kochi.

Tours **KTDC:** Boat tours daily visiting Dutch Palace, Jewish Synagogue, Francis Church, Chinese Fishing Nets, Bolghatty Island. Depart from Sea Lord Jetty, Ernakulam. 0900-1230, 1400-1730; mornings cooler. Rs 70. Highly recommended (see also Transport). **Shorter Sunset Tour**, 1730-1900, Rs 40.

Backwaters VisitIndia, Mr A Edassery, Island Club House, 1st Main Rd, Willingdon Island, T668819, F370073, palicha@giasmd01.vsnl.net.in (attn Visitindia), organizes a delightful boat tour along Kochi's backwaters in a dugout, punted and engine-less through very peaceful shady waterways passing unspoilt villages with toddy tappers, coir making, fishing et cetera; led by an excellent guide. Rs 350 for four hours, depart 0830, 1430, 40 minute drive to jetty; highly recommended. They also have traditional *kettuvallams*; Rs 10,500 (two bedroom) for 24 hours, includes all meals. **Tours India**, Kochi, has similar boats; Ernakulam to Kuttanad backwaters and return. Rs 3,000 per head. **KTDC** Backwater Village tours, T371761, daily from Kuthiathode, 0830-1300, afternoon 1430-1900 (40-minute road transfer), country boat for 8-10, Rs 275. Special moonlight cruise on full moon.

Essentials

Most hotels are in Ernakulam, with a few on Willingdon Island and in Fort Kochi. Book 3 months in advance, for the Christmas period. Be prepared for a serious mosquito problem.

B *Bolghatty Palace*, T355003, F354879, ktdc@vsnl.com Former British Residency, built by Dutch in 1744, in once peaceful grounds (now a Municipal Park), refurbished and upgraded.

Sleeping: Bolghatty Island

AL *Taj Residency*, Marine Drive, T371471, F365576. 109 rooms, good restaurants, pastry shop, all business facilities, commanding views over bay, immaculate, friendly, good value. **B-C** *Avenue Regent*, 39/1796 MG Rd, 500 m from Junction station, T373530, F370129. 53 bright, modern, comfortable rooms, excellent restaurants, business centre, avoid south side rooms especially 408 (horrendous noise from water pump at 0300 and 1900 for an hour), otherwise recommended. **B-C** *Presidency* (Quality Inn), 47 Paramara Rd, T394300, F370222. 47 rooms, deluxe with fridge, central a/c, good restaurant, good service, a bit shabby but recommended. **C** *Abad Plaza* (Best Western), MG Rd, T381122, F370729. 80 a/c rooms, fridge (free soft drinks), on busy main street, best rooms quieter on 5th floor (free breakfast and fitness club), restaurants recommended (no alcohol), good rooftop pool and jacuzzi, good value. Recommended. **C** *Metropolitan*, Chavara Rd, near Juction Station, T352412, F382227. 39 spotlessly clean modern a/c rooms, excellent restaurants and service, excellent value. Recommended.

Sleeping: Ernakulam
■ *on map, page 254*
Price codes: see inside front cover

To capture the atmosphere, stay in Fort Kochi

D *Bharat* (BTH), Durbar Hall Rd near Junction Rly, T353501, F370502, bthekm@md2.vsanl.net.in 92 clean rooms, some spacious a/c, best sea-facing, pleasant a/c restaurant, also excellent lunch *thalis*, exchange, efficient, good value. **D** *Gaanam*, Chitoor Rd (behind *Sangeetha*), T367123. 40 rooms, modern, very clean, free breakfast, good restaurant. **D** *Grand*, MG Rd, T353211. 24 rooms, some a/c, poor restaurant, bar, exchange, garden, comfortable, good value. **D** *Joyland*, Durbar Hall Rd (walking distance of rly station), T367764. 40 modern rooms, some a/c, clean, comfortable, good value, busy area. **D** *Paulson Park*, Carrier Station Rd, south Junction, T382170, F370072. 55 clean, comfortable rooms in modern building, some good value a/c, restaurant, friendly staff. Recommended. **D** *Sealord*, Shanmugham Rd, T352639, F370135. 40 rooms, central a/c, rooftop restaurant.

E *Biju's Tourist Home*, Canon Shed Rd corner, near jetty, T381881. 28 good, renovated, large rooms with bath (hot water), few a/c (Rs 250-400), TV, room service meals, exchange, clean, comfortable, friendly, good value. Recommended. **E** *Luciya*, Stadium Rd, near Bus Station, Ernakulam, T381177. 106 rooms with bath, some a/c, best with balcony, good restaurant and bar, friendly and helpful. **E** *Maple Tourist Home*, opposite Main Boat Jetty, Canon Shed Rd, T355156, F371712. Clean rooms with bath, some **D** a/c, rear ones facing roof garden preferable (Rs 200-400), very quiet. **E** *Piazza Lodge*, Kalathiparambu Rd, near south rly station, T367408, F370136. 33 good rooms (Rs 205), some a/c, clean, quiet, friendly, excellent value. **F** *Hakoba* Shanmugham Rd, T353933. 12 rooms, good sea views from some, clean, friendly, popular. **F** *Modern Guest House*, Market Rd, T352130. Rooms with bath, clean, well-maintained, friendly staff. Recommended. **F** *Railway Retiring Rooms*, T368770. 5 rooms, contact Station Master.

Hotels Expensive: *Taj Residency* plush, "Indian, too highly spiced". **Mid-range**: *Abad Plaza's Regency* for Chinese and seafood lunch buffet, and separate *Canopy* coffee shop for snacks. Good food and service but no alcohol; buffet breakfast (Rs 80) 'all you can eat'; *Avenue Regent*, excellent buffet lunch Rs 150. *Grand*, for Japanese dishes; *International's Mando*, is Goan; *Coq d'Or*, for others. *Sealord's*, rooftop for good fish dishes and Chinese (but check bill for extra taxes). **Cheap**: *Bharat* for very good vegetarian *thalis* and Indian specialities in clean surroundings.

Eating: Ernakulam
● *on maps*

Mid-range: *Bimbi's Southern Star*, Shanmugam Rd. Excellent food, generous portions (Rs 80 main courses, dessert Rs 50). Highly recommended. *Chinese Garden*, off MG Rd. A/c. Authentic Chinese cuisine. *Khyber* serves North Indian meals upstairs.

Pandhal, MG Rd. Keralan, Chinese, Continental. A/c, clean, serving tasty meals, excellent value. Recommended.*Yuvrani*, Jos Junction, MG Rd. Specializes in seafood platters. *Whizz*, Abad Plaza Complex, MG Rd. **Cheap**: *Malabar*, Market Rd. Excellent South Indian but rather gloomy.

Cafés: *Bimbi's*, near Durbar Hall/MG Rd corner. Good fast food. *Ceylon Bake House*, High School Rd. Good variety and quality, excellent service and value, recommended; smaller one in Broadway. *Chariot*, Convent Rd. Good café style meals. *Indian Coffee Houses*, opposite *Bimbi's*; also Park Av and Canon Shed Rd corner. Good coffee and snacks but tediously slow. *Oven*, Shanmugham Rd. Good pizzas and snacks (savoury and sweet). *Snow Ball*, Rajaji Rd, near Muthoot Towers, and *Caravan*, Broadway (south), for ice creams and shakes.

Ernakulam centre

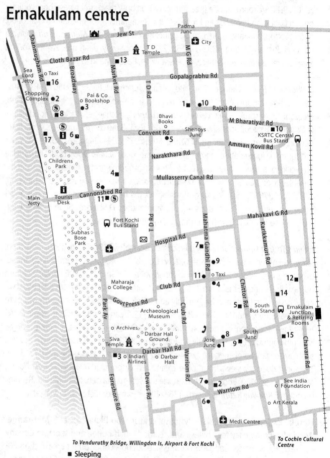

Related maps
Kochi-Ernakulam,
page 250
Fort Kochi, page 249

N

Not to scale

■ **Sleeping**
1 Abad Plaza & Whizz
2 Avenue Regent
3 Bharat Tourist Home
4 Biju's Tourist Home
5 Gaanam
6 Government Rest House
7 Grand
8 Hakoba
9 Joylands
10 Luciya

11 Maple Tourist Home
12 Metropolitan
13 Modern Guesthouse
14 Paulson Park
15 Piazza Lodge
16 Sea Lord
17 Taj Residency

● **Eating**
1 Bimbi's, Khyber & Yuvrani

2 Bimbi's Southern Star
3 Caravan
4 Ceylon Bake House
5 Chariot
6 Chinese Garden
7 Hot Breads
8 Indian Coffee House
9 Pandhal
10 Snowball
11 Woodlands

A *Malabar House Residency*, 1/268 Parade Rd, near St Francis Church, T/F221199, malabar@giasmd01.vsnl.net.in Comfortable rooms in characterful 18th-century colonial house, period furniture, dining pavilion (good Italian, south Indian), tandoori on terrace, minute pool in shaded, grassy courtyard, Ayurvedic treatments, stylish, German/Indian owners. **A-B** *Brunton Boatyard* (Casino), casino@vsnl.com Rooms in boutique hotel overlook the harbour (views – constantly changing tapestry), sympathetic new reconstruction of the original boatyard and a merchant's house around a giant raintree, interesting architecture and furniture (footstools to climb into bed!), good food (see Eating), watch dolphins, honking of ships continue into the night. **A-B** *Fort Heritage*, near Britto School 1/283 Napier St, T/F225233. 10 beautiful, spacious rooms (a/c possible $59), bath tubs, Kerala Christian cuisine and local dishes but very slow service, lovely lawn, sadly inefficient (bookings not honoured). **B-D** *Old Courtyard*, 1/371, Princess Street, T 226302. Beautiful rooms with old wooden furniture overlooking courtyard some with shared balconies (Rs 500-1,500; breakfast included). Western menu and average food but nice relaxed atmosphere, feels like it should cost a lot more.

C-E *Park Avenue*, Princess St corner, T222671, F222186. 25 spotless rooms with bath, some a/c (Rs 350-850), quiet, roof restaurant, marble facing outside. **D** *Abad*, Chullickal, Mattancherry, T228212. 20 comfortable a/c rooms, good restaurant for seafood, coffee shop. **D** *Delight*, Post Office Rd, opposite 'village green', T/F228658. 8 rooms (Rs 700), spotless, stylish, very friendly family run. Highly recommended. **D** *Fort House*, 2/6A Calvathy Rd, T226103, F222066. A few simple rooms (Rs 700) within a walled courtyard with its own little jetty, lovely outlook, excellent food. **D-E** *Seagull*, Calvathy Rd, between the ferry stops, T228128. 8 rooms, some a/c (some damp and dark), good restaurant, exchange, converted old warehouses on the waterside. **E** *Adam's Old Inn*, CC1/430 Burgher St, T/F229495. 8 rooms with bath (Rs 200-350), in old building, meals on roof, helpful. **E** *Elite*, Princess St, T225733. Cheaper rooms long way from toilets, rooms at rear quieter (Rs 350+), cheap restaurant. **E** *Kapithan Inn*, 100m south of Santa Cruz Cathedral, T226560. New, 7 rooms (mosquito-killing wall plug!), clean, pleasant. **F** *Tharavadu Tourist Home*, Quiros St, T226897. 8 clean rooms, with bath, good value.

Expensive: *Brunton Boatyard*. *History Restaurant* revives old recipes of Dutch, Portuguese, Gujarati, British and Malabari merchants, *Terrace Grill* prepares freshly caught fish, informal *Armoury* serves snacks. *Malabar House Residency*. Excellent seafood, authentic Mediterranean and local dishes. **Mid-range**: *Chariot Fort*, Children's Park/Princess Rd corner. Upmarket outdoor café feel, delicious cold coffees and cheese omelettes, expensive but popular. *Fort House* hotel. German/Indian run, in walled courtyard, "the best food ever". *Kashi*, Burgher St, T221769. Healthy salads, good lunches, delicious cakes, herbal teas at "Art café". Limited menu but changes daily, small (5+ tables), good atmosphere, 0830-1830 (Sun 0830-1430), "run by expats, great ambience". Recommended. *Rendezvous Cyber Café*, Burgher St, also serves traditional Kerala and continental. **Cheap**: *Sabala* at *Elite* hotel, popular, pleasant atmosphere (good ice creams opposite). *Seagull*, Calvathy Rd. Good value (Rs 80 buffet lunch), pleasant verandah for drink and dining overlooking harbour. For really original fast food buy your own **fresh fish** when brought in by boat or from the nets, take it over to one of the 'you buy, we cook' stalls on the sea front where they will be grilled or masala fried with chips. Delicious!

E *Seamen's Cottage*, north end of Cherai Beach (Bus from jetty on Vypeen to Devaswamnada Junction (1 hour); then 5 km by rickshaw, Rs 35, to cottage), T489795. 4 small stylish (Rs 300) on a spotless deserted beach, opened by fishermen brothers. Recommended. *Seamen's Cottage*. Good fresh fish, crab, etc. Walk to *Munambam* 1 km away. Very **cheap** basic meals.

Sleeping:
Fort Kochi
■ *on map, page 249*

Far more atmospheric

Eating:
Fort Kochi

Sleeping
& eating:
Vypeen Island

Kerala

Kerala

Sleeping & eating: Willingdon Island	**L-AL** *Taj Malabar*, T666811, F668297, mlbrbc.coc@tajgroup.sprintrpg.ems. vsnl.net, 12 km centre. 97 well furnished rooms, more character in old wing, good restaurants (veg lunch buffet recommended), excellent ambience, *Waterfront Café* for snacks (try *lassi*), good pool, internet, very good service, superb setting with views across water, ferry from Ernakulam. **AL** *Trident* (Oberoi), www.oberoihotels.com. New, 96 rooms overlook landscaped courtyard and pool, low-rise Kerala style building, excellent reputation. **B** *Casino*, T668221, F668001, casino@vsnl,com 70 good rooms, lunch buffet (Rs 250), superb seafood in evening (lobster Rs 1,500 a kg!) but plagued by mosquitos, outdoor pool in large garden. **D** *Island Inn*, Bristow Rd, near rly, T666816, F228013. 32 airy rooms, facing in to courtyard, pleasant atmosphere, very good food. **F** *Maruthi Tourist Home*, next to *Casino*, T666365. 26 rooms, some a/c, Indian style, quite good value if a bit shabby, good vegetarian meals.

■ *on map, page 250*

Entertainment
See maps, page 249, 250 & 254

Daily performances of **Kathakali** Rs 100; you can arrive early to watch the extraordinary make-up being applied. **Ernakulam**: **Art Kerala**, Kannanthodathu Lane, Valanjambalam, T366238, good performance, brief explanations; but best seats 'Reserved' for tour groups. **Cochin Cultural Centre**, Manikath Rd, off Ravipuram Rd, T368183, a/c 'theatre', authentic, English explanations; 1830-1930, make-up 1630, collection of old costumes and reproduced paintings also ayurvedic centre (lectures and treatment). **See India Foundation**, Kalathil Parampil Lane (enter Chittoor Rd south) near Junction station, T369471, Dr Devan's 'interpreted' taste of Kathakali with esoteric English commentary; 1845-2000 (make-up from 1800). **Fort Kochi**: **Kerala Kathakali Centre**, River Rd, New Bus Stand, T221827rustic surroundings but lively performance, enjoyable; 1830-1930 (make-up 1700) but check timing; "main dancer does excellent ayurvedic massage"! **Draavidia**, Jew St. **Musical evenings** with traditional instruments, Rs 100 (take mosquito cream). **Kalaripayattu** performances (0400-0700 and 1700-2000) at ENS Kalari, Nettoor, T809810, Arjuna Kalari, T365440.

Festivals

Jan/Feb: *Ulsavam* at the Siva Temple in Ernakulam for eight days and at Tripunithura Temple in **Nov/Dec**. There are elephant processions each day and folk dance and music performances. **Aug/Sep**: *Onam*.

Shopping
Coir products (eg mats), carvings on rosewood & buffalo horn & models of snake boats

Ernakulam: Several Govt Emporia on MG Rd, include *National Textiles* (another in Banerji Rd). Other shopping areas are in Broadway, Super Bazar, Anand Bazar, Prince St and New Rd. *Curio Palace*, MG Rd, sells gifts. **Antiques**: **Fort Kochi**: In the last 25 years the narrow streets in Jew Town, towards the Synagogue have become popular for 'antique' hunters. About 25 shops have a wide range of both old and new curios with a very pleasant atmosphere for browsing. *Indian Industries*, Princess St, opposite *Elite Hotel*, also recommended. **Books**: **Ernakulam**: *Bhavi Books*, Convent Rd is recommended; *Paico*, Broadway, and Press Club Rd Ernakulam; *Higginbotham's*, Hospital Rd/Chittoor Rd Junction. **Fort Kochi**: *Idiom Books*, VI/183 Synagogue Lane, Jew Town, T224028, very good range on India, travel, fiction, religion, philosophy etc, exchanges second-hand. Another near St Francis Church, Princess St, extensive catalogue/postage worldwide. **Perfumes**: *Dhamdhere*, Pandithan Temple Rd, Mattanchery, T224481, interesting to visit manufacturers who confess many are synthetic (Rs 12), but the sandalwood oil is the real McCoy (Rs 100)!

Transport
Ferries: best way of getting about – faster, cheaper & much more comfortable than buses or autos

Local Ferry: Enquiries, T371761. See also Backwaters Tours above. Ferry stops are clearly named. **Ernakulam**: Main Boat Jetty is 200m from Junction rly station; High Court Jetty for ferries to Bolghatty. **Fort Kochi**: 'Customs' (main stop) with a separate one for Vypeen Island. **Willingdon Island**: 'Embarkation' (north) and 'Terminus' (west). From Ernakulam, to **Bolghatty** public ferry every 20 min, from High Court Jetty, 0600-2200. Ferries do not operate on Sun. Some take bikes/motor bikes. To **Fort Kochi** Customs 0600-2110 (30 mins). To **Willingdon Terminus**: ½-hourly from 0630 to 2110. To **Vypeen Island** via Willingdon Embarkation: ½-hourly, from 0530-2230, 30 mins. To **Mattancherry** 6 from 0710-1740, 30 mins. From Bolghatty to Ernakulam and Fort Kochi, 1745-2000, Rs 50; **speed boat** hire from *Bolghatty Palace*, about Rs 200 to Fort Kochi. From **Fort Kochi** Customs to *Malabar Hotel*, ½-hourly to Vypeen Island, about 2 car ferries per hr. To **Varapusha**, 6 boats, 0740-1500, 2 hrs. **Ferry hire**: motor boat for up to 20, from Sea Lord jetty, book at KTDC office, Rs 200 per hr. You can do a harbour tour and visit Fort Kochi sights in 3 hrs; allow longer for a leisurely visit. KTDC Fort Kochi tour, 0900, 1400, 3½ hrs, Rs 60. **Taxi boats** are faster and more convenient – jetty closer to *Bolghatty Palace*, Rs 20 per head.

Auto-rickshaw: On the whole rickshaw drivers have a reasonably good reputation here. If you have problems, ask police for help. If you are likely to arrive late at night, book a hotel in advance and insist on being taken as some rickshaw drivers take advantage of tourists. **Bus**: Fairly frequent and cheap in Ernakulam. Journeys between Ernakulam, Willingdon and Fort Kochi useful after ferries stop running. **Taxi**: Usually minimum Rs 10 per 3 km. On MG Rd, Ernakulam: Corp Taxi Stand, T361444. Private taxis: **Ensign**, T353080; **Anjali**, Willingdon Isl, T667088; **Ceeyem**, Fort Kochi, T227281. **KTDC**, Shanmugham Rd and **Princy**, T310809, Ernakulam, also offer coach hire.

Rear engined autos: much more comfortable for longer journeys

Long distance Air: New international airport, 36 km away, is clean, hassle-free, T610113. *Classic* shop has a reasonable selection of 'coffee table' books. Transport to town: pre-paid taxis to Fort Kochi, Rs 300. *Indian Airlines*: **Bangalore**, **Chennai** Wed, Fri, Sun, **Delhi** via Goa: **Goa** daily; **Mumbai**. *Jet Airways*: **Mumbai**, daily. **Agatti**.

Road Bus: SRTCs run 'Express' and 'Fast' services from Ernakulam Terminus near Junction Railway station to major cities in the south; computerized reservations not always available. **KSRTC** T360531. To **Alappuzha**, every 20 mins, 1½ hrs, Rs 20; **Devikulam**, 6 hrs, Rs 35; **Kannur**, 7 hrs (Exp), 8½ hrs, Rs 75; **Kottayam**, 2¼ hrs, Rs 30; **Kozhikode**, 5 hrs (Exp), Rs 60, 6½ hrs, Rs 65; **Munnar**, via Aluva, 4 hr, 0630; **Thekkadi** (Kumily) for Periyar, 0630, 6¾ hrs, Rs 65, or take later bus to Kottayam (frequent) which has several daily to Thekkadi; **Thiruvananthapuram**, 5 hrs (Exp), Rs 55, 6½ hrs, Rs 50; **Thrissur**, 1½ hrs (Exp), Rs 25. **Interstate** buses to: **Bangalore** via Kozhikode, Sultan's Battery and Mysore, 0600-2100, night 12 hrs, day 15 hrs, Rs 155-180. **Mysore**, 2000, 10 hrs, Rs 170. **TNSTC**, T372616. To **Coimbatore** via Thrissur and Palakkad, 4¾ hrs (Exp), Rs 60; **Kanniyakumari Exp**, 8 hrs, Rs 90; **Chennai** via Coimbatore, Erode, Salem, 1530, 15 hrs, Rs 160; **Madurai**, via Kottayam, Kumiy, Theni 9 hrs (Exp), Rs 90; **Mysore**, 11 hrs, Rs 130. **Private operators**: from Kalloor and Ernakulam South Bus Stands including *Indira Travels*, DH Rd, T360693 and *SB Travels*, MG Rd, opposite Jos Annexe, T353080, *Princey Tours*, opposite Sealord Hotel, T354712. Overnight coaches to **Bangalore**, 12 hrs, and **Mysore** 10 hrs. To **Kottayam**, every 30 mins, 2 hrs, **Munnar**, 4 hrs. Also to **Chennai** and **Coimbatore**. **Sea**: Cruises to Lakshadweep organized by SPORT, Harbour Rd, Willingdon Island, T340387.

Train: Ernakulam/Kochi (Cochin) is on the broad gauge line joining Thiruvananthapuram to Mangalore, Bangalore and Chennai. Most trains from major cities stop at Ernakulam Junction (the main station) although a few stop at Ernakulam town. Enquiries: Ernakulam Junction, T131. Trains stop at Ernakulam Town station, T353920, when incoming trains bypass Kochi. From Ernakulam Junction to **Alappuzha**: several including *Intercity 6341*, 0640, 1 hr; *Madras-Alleppey 6041*, 0915, 1 hr. **Chennai (MC)**: *Alleppey-Madras Exp, 6042* (AC/II), 1625, 13¾ hrs. **Delhi (ND)**: *Kerala Mangala Exp 2625/2625A* (AC/II), 1435, 48¾ hrs. **Mangalore**: *Thiruvanantha puram-Mangalore Exp, 6349* (AC/CC), 1100, 10 hrs. **Mumbai (VT)**: *Kanniyakumari Exp 1082* (AC/II), 1255, 40½ hrs. **Thiruvananthapuram**: *Vanchinad Exp 6303*, 0550, 4½ hrs; *Venad Exp 6301* (AC/CC), 1715, 5 hrs. From Kochi to **Mumbai (Kurla)**: *Netravati Exp 6636A*, 1720 (from Ernakulam 1740), 36 hrs.

Service to Kochi Harbour Terminus remained suspended in 2000

Kerala

Directory

Airline offices International: *Air India*: MG Rd, T351260, A610050. *British Airways*, T364867. *Cathay Pacific* and *KLM*, T369165. *Japan Airlines*, T350544. *Maldive Airlines*, T351051. *Singapore Airlines* and *Swissair*, T367911. Domestic: *Indian Airlines* and *Alliance Air*, Durbar Hall Rd, near Bharat Hotel, T370242, A610101. *Jet Airways*, Atlantis Junction, Ravipuram, MG Rd, T369423, A610037. **Banks** *Thomas Cook*, Palal Towers, 1st Flr, Right Wing, MG Rd, T369729, Mon-Sat, 0930-1800, foreign exchange and TC refund, very quick service. *Jyotis*, 10, KTDC Shopping Complex, Shanmugam Rd, efficient and friendly. *Union Bank*, Panampilly Nagar, opens Sun. Most banks open till 1500, a few stay open until 1700, and also Sat afternoon for 2 hrs. Several on MG Rd, Shanmugham Rd and on Broadway, Ernakulam including *Chartered*, *Grindlays*. *State Bank of India*. Others in Willingdon Island; Mattancherry Palace Rd, Fort Kochi, and Kochi Rd. **Communications** Post office: Ernakulam Head PO, Hospital Rd, 0830-2000, Sat 0930-1430, Sun 1000-1600, other holidays 1400-1700. Kochi Main PO, Mattancherry (for *Poste Restante*), 0800-2000, Sun 0930-1700; often empty. North End PO, Willingdon Island. **CTO:** (24 hrs) Jos Junction Building, 2nd Flr, MG Rd, Ernakulam; Fax Mon-Sat, 0800-2000; Mattancherry, Kochi. **Internet:** *Rendezvous Cyber Café*, opposite St Mary's School, Burgher St; 1 on road to Synagogue (unreliable connection), around Rs 45 per 30 mins. *Taj Malabar*, Willingdon Island. **Hospitals & medical services** *General Hospital*, Hospital Rd, Ernakulam, T360002 (nearby *Oriental Pharmacy*, Market Rd open 24 hrs). *Govt Hospital*, Fort Kochi, T224444. *Maharaja's Hospital*, Karuvelipady, Kochi, T224561. Ernakulam Private: *Lissie Hospital*, Lissie Junction, T352006. *Lourdes Hospital*, Pachalam, T351507. On MG Rd: *City*, T361809, and *Medical Trust Hospital*, T371852, have 24-hr pharmacies. *City Dental Clinic* T368164. **Tour operators** *Aries*, Hotel Avenue Regent, 39/1796 MG Rd, T353662; *Clipper*, 40/6531 Convent Rd, T364453, F381453, clipcol@md2.vsnl.net.in; *Gt India Tour Co*, Pithru Smarana, Srikandath Rd, Ravipuram, T369246, F351528. On MG Rd. Ernakulam: *Olympus*, South end of MG Rd, near *Little Kingdom* shop, very competent and helpful; *Pioneer Travels*, Bristow Rd, T666148, F668490, pioneer@pner.com Efficient and knowledgeable, can suggest unusual hotels/guest houses. *Indo World Tours*, South end of MG Rd, T354120; *VisitIndia*, for boat trips (see page 252); *TCI*, T351286. **Tourist offices** *Govt of India Tourist Office*, next to *Malabar Hotel*, Willingdon Island, T668352, where you can pick up maps and small booklets, very helpful, 0900-1730, closed Sun. *Guide* rates vary – for up to 4 persons, half day (4 hrs) Rs 50, full day (8 hrs) Rs 100, for journeys outside the city, Rs 50 extra. *KTDC*, Shanmugham Rd, Ernakulam, T353234, helpful accommodation officer, where you can get a small booklet 'Kerala Travel Facts' with useful listings, 0800-1900. Counter at Airport during flight hours. *DTPC*, T361336. *Tourist Desk*, Main Boat Jetty, Ernakulam, T371761, 0900-1800. PJ Verghese helps tourists plan itineraries round Kerala on a voluntary basis, very helpful; maps, Backwaters (country boat) tour, 0900, 1400, 3 hrs, Rs 300, tickets for Alappuzha-Kollam boat trip. **Useful addresses AA:** South India, MG Rd (opposite *Hotel Dwaraka*), T351369. **Tourist Police:** T666076, helps with information of all kinds. **Visa extension:** City Police Commissioner, High Court Ferry Station, Ernakulam, T360700. Foreigners' Regional Registration Office, T352454.

From the coast to Thekkadi

The foothills of the Ghats are intensively cultivated with cash crops, notably rubber, tea, coffee, cardamom and pepper, while the valley bottoms are given over to paddy. Despite very low yields when compared with Malayan rubber production, the area planted to rubber has grown dramatically.

Kottayam കോട്ടയം

Phone code: 0481
Colour map 3, grid B3
Population: 166,000

Kottayam is surrounded by some of the most fertile and beautiful scenery in the state, with hills to its east and backwaters to the west. The compact town centre is noisy, busy and increasingly polluted but the outskirts are much pleasanter.

Background

Kottayam is the main Christian centre in Kerala. The Christians in Kerala largely owed their allegiance to the Orthodox Syrian tradition until the arrival of the Portuguese. After the Inquisition was introduced in 1560 the Portuguese tried to encourage the conversion of Syrian Christians to Roman Catholicism.

Kerala

The Chengannur mystery

K R Vaidyanathan recounts the legend that in repayment of a promise to the sage Agasthya, Siva and Parvati visited him in the southern hills. While there Parvati had her period. The divine couple therefore stayed for 28 days after the "purificatory bath". Vaidyanathan goes on: "Wonder of wonders, even today the deity which is cast in panchaloha gets her periods". He reports that the head priest of the temple describes what happens as follows. The head priest or his assistant "on opening the shrine in the early morning removes the previous day's decoration and hands it over to the attendant along with the white petticoat without looking at it. The attendant examines the dress closely and if there are signs of bleeding sends it to the home of the temple tantri. There the lady of the house scrutinizes the cloth again and confirms the period". He goes on: "The petticoat, after the occurrence, is available for sale to the public. Though the rate fixed by the temple management is only Rs 10, due to its being a rarity it is grabbed by devotees paying hundreds of rupees, booking it well in advance. Among the dignitaries who bought this, we are told, are the late Sir CP Ramaswami Aiyer and ex-President VV Giri".

Vaidyanathan recounts the story of a sceptical British adviser to the Raja of Travancore between 1810-14, Colonel Munro. "When carrying out his duty of checking the temple accounts to regulate their expenses Colonel Munro found expenses relating to replacement of garments soiled by the period. He is reported to have laughed at the naiveté, of the people. How can a metal deity get its periods? he mused. It is not only absurd but obscene he said, and cut out the budget provision with a stroke of his pen. At the same time the goddess had her period. But the Colonel learnt his lesson. His wife started to have heavy bleeding and their children took ill". Fortunately he is reported to have repented of his doubts and ensured the full recovery of all his family.

One of the cruder means was by intercepting ships carrying Syrian bishops and preventing them from joining their churches in Kerala. At the same time efforts were made to train Indian priests, and in 1599 the Thomas Christians were allowed to use the Syriac liturgy. A formal split occurred in the Syrian church in 1665 between the Roman Syrians from the Syrian Christians under their Bishop Mar Gregory. He was a Jacobite, hence the name Jacobite Christians being applied to his branch of the Syrian Church.

Subsequent divisions occurred in the 18th and 19th centuries, but several of the Protestant Syrian churches came back together when the Church of South India was formed in 1947. The town is the centre of Kerala's rubber industry.

Sights Two of the Syrian Orthodox churches, 50 m apart, are on a hillock about 2 km north of town. The 450-year-old **Cheria Palli** ('Small' St Mary's Church) has beautiful vegetable dye mural paintings over the altar. The **Valia Palli** ('Big' St Mary's Church) was built in 1550. Here, two 'Nestorian' crosses are carved on plaques inserted behind two side altars. One has a Pahlavi inscription on it, the other a Syriac. The cross on the left of the altar is the original and may be the oldest Christian artefact in India; the one to the right is a copy. By the altar there is an unusual small triptych of an Indian St George slaying a dragon. Note the interesting Visitors Book 1898-1935 – a paper cutting reports that "the church has attracted many European and native gentlemen of high position". Mass at Valia Palli at 0900 on Sunday, and Cheria Palli at 0730 on Sunday and Wednesday. The Malankara Syrian Church has its headquarters at Devalokam.

Kerala

Sleeping **C** *Anjali* (Casino), KK Rd, 4 km from rly, T563661, F563669, casin@giasmd01.vsnl.net.in 27 rooms with bath, central a/c, good restaurants, exchange (limited). **D** *Vembanad Lake Resort*, near Kodimatha Jetty, 3 km south of town, T564866. Simple rooms in cottages (some a/c), pleasant waterside garden, good houseboat restaurant. **D** *Aida*, MC Rd, 2 km rly, T568391, F568399, aida@md3.vsnl.net.in 40 rooms with bath, some a/c, back quieter, restaurant, bar, clean, pleasant. Recommended. **D** *Green Park*, Kurian Uthup Rd, Nagampadam, T563311. 33 rooms with bath (Rs 400-650), 11 with noisy a/c, non-a/c at back intensely hot even at night, restaurant. **D-E** *Aiswarya* (KTDC), near Thirunakkara Temple. 500 m from jetty, 2 km bus stand, T581256, 30 rooms, some a/c (Rs 300-750), restaurants, beer. **E** *Ambassador*, KK Rd (set back), T563293. 18 rooms, some a/c, pleasant Indian style hotel and comfortable restaurant, bar, exchange, very good value. **F** *Exon*, Paikadas Rd, T564916. Clean, good value. **E** *Pallathaya Tourist Complex*, on the water's edge. 10 rooms 'motel', simple, outdoor restaurant is recommended. **F** *Kaycees Lodge*, YMCA Rd, T563440. Good quality for the price and clean. **F** *Govt Rest House*, on hill 2 km south of town, overlooking flat paddy land. Remarkable late 19th-century building with superb furniture and some original cutlery and tableware, reservations: District Collector, Kottayam or Executive Engineer, PWD Kottayam. **F** *Venad Tourist Complex*, Ancheril Bldg, near State Bus Stand, T561383. Modern building, clean, restaurant. Recommended.

Eating **Mid-range**: *Aida*. Large, uninspried menu, pleasantly cool (though 'chilled' drinks arrive warm!). *Green Park*. International. Reasonable but slow, beers, dinner in mosquito-ridden garden (or in own room for guests). **Cheap**: On TB Rd near the State bus station: *Black Stone*. Good vegetarian, and the dull *Indian Coffee House*. *Mllkshake Bar*, opposite *Blackstone Hotel* do 20 flavours, with or without ice cream.

Shopping Kottayam is a regional shopping centre. Camera services and repairs at *Camera Scan*, Edimariyil Bldg, near Kaycees Lodge, YMCA Rd, T566041.

Transport **Local Auto-rickshaw**: to boat jetty, 2 km. **Long distance Boat**: in summer, backwater boats leave from Kodimatha Jetty; during the monsoons, use the Town Jetty, 3 km southwest of the railway station. Ferries to **Alappuzha**, 0715-1730, 3 hrs; interesting trip but very busy in peak season. **Champakulam**, 1530, 4 hrs; **Mannar**, 1430, 3 hrs (attractive backwaters up to Nedumudi Jetty). To **Champakulam**, 1600, 4 hrs. Alternatively, take ferry from Kumarakom to Muhama village (½-hourly from 0630-2100), 40 mins, and then go to Alappuzha by bus. **Road Bus**: The New Private Bus Station is near the railway station. There are fast and frequent buses to **Thiruvananthapuram**, **Kochi**, **Thekkadi**; also 4 daily to **Madurai**, 7 hrs, 5 to **Munnar**, 5 hrs. The State Bus Station (2 km south) is especially chaotic with often a mad scramble to get on the

Kottayam environs

To Ernakulam · To Angamaly · Vaikom · To Cherthala · To Palai · Thaneer Mukkom Bund · Ettumanoor · Kidangoor · Mannanam · MC Rd · Manarkakad · Kumarakom Tourist Complex · Thirunakkara · KK Rd · Vembanad Lake · Boat Jetty · KOTTAYAM · Kodimatha Jetty · Puthupally · Panachikad · MC Rd · To Thekkady & Sabarimala · Vazhapally · Changanacherry · Vazhoor · Perunna · To Alappuzha · To Thiruvananthapuram

■ Sleeping
1 Aida & Vembanad Lake Resort
2 Aiswarya
3 Ambassador & Anjali
4 Exom
5 Government Rest House
6 Green Park

🚌 Transport
1 New Private
2 State

N

0 km 4
0 miles 4

Thekkadi/Periyar bus. Direct bus dep 0900, 4 hrs; otherwise buses every 2 hrs to **Kumily** between 0900-2250, change at Kumily. The route from Thekkadi to Kottayam is described on page 168, taking 7 hrs over the Thekkadi pass. **Car** hire with driver to Thekkadi, Rs 850, 4 hrs. **Train**: Kollam: *Mangalore-Thiruvananthapuram Exp,* 6350 (AC/CC), 1508, 2¼ hrs; *Vanchinad Exp, 6303,* 0706, 1¾ hrs (and on to Thiruvananthapuram, 3¼ hrs); also *Venad Exp, 6301* (AC/II), Wed, 1834, 3½ hrs.

Tour operators *Concord,* Manorama Junction, GS Rd, T560350. *Seeland,* Padinjarekkara Chambers, KK Rd, T560337. **Useful addresses** *Bank of India,* main branch, and *Hotel Anjali* only change currency and Amex TCs. *Head Post Office,* MC Rd, 0800-2000, 1400-1730 on holidays. *Kerala Tourist office,* Govt Guest House, Nattakom, T562219.

Directory

An old rubber plantation set around the **Vembanad Lake** has been developed by the Tourism Department into a **bird sanctuary**. A path goes through the swamp to the main bird nesting area, while the island in the middle of the lake (*Pathiramanal* – 'midnight sands') can be reached by boat. It is worth hiring a guide for an early morning walk through the sanctuary. Ask at the entrance or at the hotels. ■ *1000-1800. Best season for birdlife Jun-Aug. Getting there: Bus from Kottayam, 30 min, goes to the Kumarakom Tourist Village; auto-rickshaws, Rs 125.*

Kumarakom
Phone code: 0481
Colour map 3, grid B3
16 km from Kottayam

Sleeping and eating **AL-A** *Taj Garden Retreat,* 1/404 (14 km west of Kottayam), T524377, F524371. 19 a/c rooms, in attractive 120 year old 'Bakers' House', sympathetically renovated, newer cottages and a moored houseboat, good meals, an intimate hotel. **AL-A** *Coconut Lagoon* (Casino), T524491, F524373, casino@vsnl.com 37 comfortable century-old *tarawads* (traditional Kerala wooden cottages), some a/c, outdoor restaurant (residents') facing lagoon, good dinner buffet (poor breakfast), good pool, very friendly, ayurvedic massage (Rs 500 per hour), attractive waterside location, spectacular approach by boat (10 mins from road), some find 'sunset cruise' short and disappointing. Both hotels are highly recommended. **A** *Golden Waters* (Tulip), alex@blr.vsnl.net.in Among paddy fields and coconut groves, accessed by boat or paths and bridges, 28 well-furnished, Kerala ethnic cottages on the water, pool, specialist ayurvedic centre. **AL** *Houseboat* (KTDC), unique, idyllic experience on the backwaters at a price. Kerala meals included, Rs 7,500 (day only), Rs 18,750 (1 night, 2 days).

26% taxes added

Kaviyur is noted for the best preserved rock-cut cave in Kerala, dating from the eighth century. The small shrine, dedicated to Siva, is decorated with strikingly well-carved reliefs. The cave has a shrine and *linga*, with a pillared hall immediately in front of it, all aligned east-west. The walls of the pillared entrance hall have reliefs showing either a chieftain or donor of the temple, a bearded ascetic, a four-armed *Ganesh* and at the entrance the two doorkeepers. The chieftain is an impressive, strong-looking figure, standing with arms folded. The temple is a link between the Pandiyan Kingdom of Tamil Nadu and that of southern Kerala, having much in common with temples in Ramanathapuram and Tirunelveli Districts.

Kaviyur
5 km from Thiruvalla,
E of Main Rd

Kottayam to Kumily

The road to the hills rises from the plains, through tropical evergreen forests, rubber and spice plantations, pepper on the low land gives rise to tea and cardamom plantations. It is an interesting drive with superb views down the east side of the Ghats onto the Tamil Nadu plains. You may meet herds of Zebu cattle, buffalo and donkeys being driven from Tamil Nadu to market in Kerala. Above 1,000 m the air freshens and it can be cold. Be prepared for a rapid change in temperature.

Pelai Pelai, off the Kottayam-Thekady road, is known for its rubber estates belonging to the Dominic family (Casino group) and the beautiful 100-year old traditional Kerala plantation bungalow and a 50-year old estate mansion where hot Syrian-Catholic lunches are served. Plantation tours to watch latex collection and packing can be arranged through Brunton Boatyard in Fort Kochi or the Spice Village at Thekady. **Sleeping B** *Estate mansion*, 4 rooms with colonial period Kerala furniture, and a deluxe cottage room in the *Plantation Bungalow*.

Peermade (Peermed, Pirmed)
Phone code: 04869
Colour map 3, grid B3

Peermade is often simply passed through on the way to the much better known wildlife reserve of Periyar 43 km away. Although it is considerably lower than Thekkadi (Periyar), it is surrounded by tea, rubber and cardamom plantations. It can be a pleasant brief halt. **Sleeping** At Pullupara, close to Peermade, is the **B** *Plantation House* a 3-rooms resort, attractive location, friendly service but overpriced; **F** *Govt Guest House*, T32071; **F** *Himarani*, T32288; **F** *Sabala* (KTDC), Kuttikanam, T32250. All basic but acceptable.

★ Sabarimala
Phone code 04739

Many Hindu pilgrims make the journey to the forest shrine dedicated to Sri Aiyappan at Sabarimala (191 km north of Thiruvananthapuram) on a route through Kottayam. Aiyappan is a particularly favoured deity in Kerala and there are growing numbers of devotees. Donations to the shrine rose from Rs 2.4 mn in 1970 to Rs 75 mn in 1986. It is only open on specific occasions: *Mandalam*, 41 days from mid-November to end-December; *Makaravilakku*, mid-January, around Makara Sakranti; *Vishu*, mid-April; *Prathistha* day (May-June); and during the *Onam* festival (August-September).

Reaching the shrine The Erumeli route is the conventional, the most arduous and the most sacred. At Erumeli, thousands of Hindu pilgrims worship at a mosque dedicated to *Vavr* who is regarded as having been a contemporary of Aiyappan, and is worshipped as a deity. From Erumeli it is 60.8 km on foot by track – "a trekker's paradise", passing through Chalakkayam and Pampa. There is then a steep two hours' walk through the jungle to the shrine (914 m). Pilgrims carry their own food, and there are only temporary sheds provided. En route, pilgrims stop at various points, where you can witness interesting ceremonies and share in the beauty of their devotion. An alternative route approaches Sabarimala from Chalakkayam, near Pampa and just 8 km from Sabarimala itself. State buses reach Pampa and this is the easiest and most popular route.

Suggested reading: *The Sabarimala pilgrimage and the Ayyapan cults* by Radhika Sekar (M Banarsidass), and *Pilgrimage to Sabari* by KR Vaidyanathan, 1992 (Bharatiya Vidya Bhavan).

★ Thekkadi തേക്കടി (Periyar National Park)

Phone code: 04863
Area: 777 sq km
Colour map 3, grid B3

Set on an attractive Periyar lake side, significant wildlife sightings in Thekkadi are uncommon, but the beautiful setting attracts over 300,000 visitors a year. The small Kumily village with most of the guest houses and eating places is 3 km above the lake.

Ins & outs **Getting there** Long distance buses reach Thekkadi lakeside via Kumily. **Getting around** Local buses run between Kumily and the lake jetty, or you can hire a bike, share a jeep or take the pleasant walk. 'Cruises' at 0700, 0930, 1130, 1400, 1600. **Climate** Temperature: summer, max 29°C, min 18°C; winter, max 21°C, min 16°C. Annual rainfall: 2,600 mm. Season: Dec-May (best Mar-May), crowded around 14th Jan festival. Clothing: summer, cottons; winter, light woollens.

Kerala

History

In 1895 the lake was created by building a dam which covered 55 sq km of rich forest. A 180-m long tunnel led the water which had flowed into the Arabian Sea east into the *Suruli* and *Vaigai* rivers, irrigating extensive areas of Ramanathapuram and Madurai districts. The 780 sq km sanctuary was created by the old Travancore State government in 1934.

Wildlife

The sanctuary, near the border with Tamil Nadu, is in a beautiful setting and was designated a part of *Project Tiger* in 1973, though tigers are very rarely seen and it is better known for its elephants, which are very likely to be seen until March/April. Most bull elephants here are tuskless (*makhnas*).

Bison, sambar, wild boar and barking deer are fairly common. In addition to 246 species of birds there are 112 species of butterfly. Smaller animals include black Nilgiri langur (seen usually on the tall trees above the jetty booking office), bonnet and lion tailed macaque, Giant and Flying squirrel and otter – "spectacular flight of 'flying foxes' (fruit bats) takes place over *Spice Village* each evening at about 1830".

Viewing
Entry Rs 50 (foreigners)Rs 20 (Indians) for 5 days. Video camera fees Rs 100

Ideal times are dawn and dusk so stay overnight (winter nights can get quite cold), and avoid weekends and holidays. A motor launch trip on the lake is recommended Rs 100. Ask the Wildlife Preservation Officer, Thekkadi, T322027.

The park closes to traffic 1800-0600. The forests have special viewing platforms which you can use if you prefer to walk with a Game Ranger who can act as guide. The three-hour **'trek'**, for only 10 people, 0730, Rs 10 plus Rs 10 for rafts etc. recommended but you need to queue for about an hour outside the office. It is worthwhile but not everybody comes face to face with a herd of elephants. Carry water and beware of leeches. Guides arrange unofficial walking tours privately in the park periphery in the afternoon (not the best time for sportting wildlife); try to assess the guide before signing up. Elephant rides have been suspended. To see the dam, permission is needed from the Executive Engineer, PWD Periyar Project, Tallakulam, PO Madurai. No entry fee.

Kumily village is a good place to find spices, coffee and cashewnuts; check the PMCS outlet.

Sleeping
Book all KTDC hotels well in advance

L *Lake Palace* (KTDC), T322023, F322282 aranyanivas@vsnl.com 6 rooms in interesting building ($198, meals included), restaurant (adequate, uninspired menu) access by free ferry (20 mins) from jetty (last trip 1600), idyllic island setting, superb views,

Periyar Wildlife Sanctuary

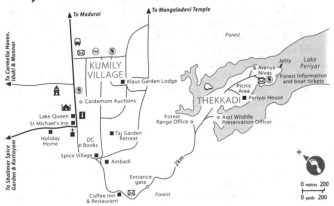

wildlife spotting from lawn, relaxed and informal. **AL-A** *Taj Garden Retreat*, Amalambika Rd, T22273, F322106. 32 well-appointed rooms in thatched, a/c cottages, large windows open to good views, attractive pool, excellent facilities, attentive staff. **AL** *Spice Village* (Casino), Thekkadi-Kumily Rd, T322315, F322317, casin@vsnl.o 52 rooms in cottages with elephant grass thatch (cool and dark with wide eaves), labelled spice garden, good pool, very good restaurant though breakfast/lunch menu limited, chilled beer, excellent ayurvedic massage, forest walk (0730-1130) to see smaller wildlife, luxurious, green, quiet, restful, friendly, excellent service (no individual tipping) tennis and health complex by 2001. Recommended. **A** *Shalimar Spice Garden* Murikkady, 4 km from Kumily, T/F322132. 12 rooms, Swiss-Italian run in inspired style, excellent Italian, south Indian food, pool, ayurvedic flora therapy, water-massage, internet. **A-B** *Carmelia Haven*, Vandanmedu (20 km north on Puliyanmala Rd), on a tea, spice and coconut plantation, T04868-70252. Exclusive and private, with a real tree house 6 m above ground, a cave house 3 m below, and a few discretely spaced cottages in a local style using lots of thatch, excellent open-air restaurant serves delicious Malabari food (try Fish Polichattu). The owners' tea plantation is further ahead at Kailasam on the Munnar road. Tours arranged to tea factory, cardamom processing unit and plantations, treks and boating. Factory fresh tea/cardamom for sale.

B *Aranya Nivas* (KTDC), by lake, T322023, F322282, aranyanivas@vsnl.com 26 rooms (charges vary), interesting old stone building – simple, pleasant restaurant (evening buffet) expensive, new pool but water too cold, poor service and maintenance reported, free boat trips twice a day on lake included, cycle hire, remember park is out-of-bounds after dark. **B** *Cardamom Country* between Kumily and Thekkadi. New, spacious, comfortable cottages, good restaurant, nice pool, friendly staff. **B** *St Michael's Inn*, near Tourist Information, T322355, F322356. Odd wedge-shaped rooms, some a/c, no pool. **C** *Periyar House* (KTDC), 5 minute walk from lake, T322026, F322526. 48 rooms, some with bath (Rs 700 includes meals), simple, very pleasant, clean and comfortable, dorm, reasonable if slightly dingy, buffet meals, strong Goan beer available, pleasant place, good service. **D** *Ambadi*, near Forest Check post (2 km), T322192. Some **C** a/c rooms and cottages, double-storey deluxe units with ornate wood decoration (but "uncomfortable, dangerous stairs, rodents"), basic cottages good value, reasonable restaurant, accepts Visa.

Charming Govt **E** *Forest Rest House*, 3 rooms (sleep on wooden floor, no kitchen; bring sleeping bag, soft mat, net, mosquito cream and food), well placed for walks and watching animals close by at night, Rs 240 including boat transfer. Recommended. In **Kumily village**, 3 km away. **E-F** *Coffee Inn*, 5 minute walk from entrance gate and 3 km from Information centre, T685536. 12 rooms in basic cottages, fan, nets, clean shared baths, lockers, lovely garden with hammocks, popular budget traveller 'hang-out', see eating. **E-F** *Hill Park*, Main St, T685509. 17 rooms with bath, fan, net, friendly helpful staff. **E-F** *Lake Queen*, opposite Tourist Information, T322086, Lakequeen@Thekkady. com Basic rooms, fan, nets, small bath, pleasanter upper floors (Rs 150-300), fairly clean, functional, run by Catholic Diocese (profits to charity). **F** *Holiday Home*, Kottayam Rd, T322016. A large complex of simple cottages with own terrace, good value. **F** *Klaus Garden Rest House*, Rosapukandam, 10 mins uphill from bus stand behind PO, 3rd turn right. Clean, simple rooms, shared toilet/shower, kitchenette, quiet, friendly. **F** *Mickey's*, good new rooms, friendly family, excellent value.

Eating
Hotel restaurants
welcome non-residents

Expensive: *Spice Village*. International. Excellent food and service, 'rustic' décor, fresh garden vegetables, "chef gives demonstration of a dish each night!" **Mid range**: *Coffee Inn*. International. Good food (0700-2200), tables outside under the palms, bonfire in the evening, relaxed and peaceful, friendly.*Máchan Café*. Former Reuters photographer serves the "best coffee and cake here", good atmosphere, art on display. Avoid. *PKN* opposite.

Local Bus: minibuses hourly from Kumily go down to *Aranya Nivas* on the lakeside, Rs 2. At Kumily jeep drivers tell you there is no bus to Thekkadi and charge Rs 50 for the trip; autos charge Rs 25+. On the lake, **motor launches**: 2-hr trips are inexpensive, scheduled every 2 hrs from 0700-1500; tickets sell out in peak season. **Long distance Road Bus**: regular state and private buses run between from Kumily: to **Alappuzha** 1115, **Kochi/Ernakulam** (6 hrs), **Kodaikkanal** (cancelled occasionally), 0630 (5½ hrs), **Thiruvananthapuram**, 285 km (8 hrs). Buses also go from Thekkadi itself (behind Aranya Nivas): to **Kottayam** (0600, 1430); morning to **Madurai**; late afternoon **Kollam** (4½ hrs). KTDC 2-day tours from **Ernakulam**, Sat dep 0730, ret 2000, Rs 120.

Transport

Internet at Shalimar Spice Garden. **Tourist office** At *Aranya Nivas*, Thekkadi, T322023; at Thekkadi Junction, Kumily, T322620. **Useful services** Post office, **bank** and **hospital** at Kumily. Some travellers, particularly women on their own, found shopkeepers here aggressive and intimidating.

Directory

To Munnar and the Palanis

There is a short drive across the undulating and richly cultivated, densely populated lowlands before climbing rapidly up one of South India's most attractive ghat roads.

Vaikom, has the famous Saivite Mahadeva Temple (non-Hindus are not normally allowed inside). The temple has a 12 day festival during the dark lunar fortnight of November-December, the *Ashtami* festival falling on the last night. Deities from neighbouring temples are brought in procession to Vaikom, at midnight they are taken to the elephant stable where the Vaikom deity has been placed earlier in the evening. **Sleeping E** *Kar Thika*, opposite bus station, some a/c rooms, restaurant, clean.

Vaikom
Phone code: 04829
Colour map 3, grid B3
Population: 21,800

Ettumanoor has possibly the wealthiest temple in Kerala. The present Mahadeva Temple was reconstructed in 1542, and is famous for its murals depicting scenes from the Ramayana and the Krishna legends, both inside and outside the *gopuram*. The typical circular shrine with a copper covered conical roof encloses a square sanctuary. The *Arattu* festival in March draws thousands of pilgrims when gold elephant statues are displayed. Just a few of the temple's valuable possessions – they weigh 13 kg.

Ettumanoor

Muvattapuzha is a thriving commercial town and the wholesale centre for pineapples, at the centre of one of the most prosperous agricultural districts of the state. The houses show evidence of the rapid economic growth, partly reflecting the scale of remittances from the Middle East. Each small town centre has distinctive shrines to Christian saints, matched in style by Hindu shrines. At the village of **Meenan Kannan** the road passes a huge statue of the Virgin Mary.

Muvattapuzha

Haritha Farm at Kadalikad offers visitors the chance to stay on an organic farm growing spices and tropical fruit. **Sleeping C** *Haritha*, 150 m north of bus stop, T0485-260216, harithafarms@yahoo.com Clean new cottages, Kerala meals, peaceful and relaxing, interesting village life (Rs 1,200 for two), day visitors (Rs 550 with meals), phone ahead. ■ *Getting there: bus between Muvattapuzha and Thodupuzha stops near the farm (look for arch to Vimala Matha Church); about 2 hrs from Ernakulam.*

Kadalikad
Southeast of Muvattapuzha, 14 kms

Kerala

Thattekad Bird Sanctuary The Kochi-Munnar Road leads from Kothamangalam to the bird sanctuary (20 km) with teak plantations, which is surrounded by the Periyar River which remains shallow most of the year. It attracts water birds and the indigenous Malabar grey hornbill, rose and blue-winged parakeet, egret, heron and mynah, as well as rarer birds like the Ceylon frog-mouth and rose-billed rollers.

Idukki
Population: 10,225

A road runs from Adimali (which has a good *Spice Valley* restaurant) 32 km to the new township of **Idukki**, the heart of a forest reserve and wildlife sanctuary. The name is derived from the word *idukku*, 'gorge', and is taken from the deep gorge through which the river Periyar passes in the district. The township is on the site of the 166 m Idukki Arch Dam (second highest dam in the country). Along with two supplementary dams it retains a lake stretching 50 km. Idukki District now generates over 80% of Kerala's electricity.

Established in 1976, the sanctuary covers 77 sq km of dense tropical forest which is home to very large herds of elephants. At the modest elevation of 450 m to 746 m, it has a variety of important and rare tree species and mammals including tiger and deer. The HQ of the Warden is at **Painu-Vellappara**. **Sleeping F** *Govt Guest House*, T32205; **F** *Idukki Gate*, T52323.

The remainder of the route to Munnar passes through coffee and then tea plantations from the estate of Pullivasal, the site of Kerala's first hydro-electricity project.

★ Munnar മൂന്നാർ

Phone code: 04865
Colour map 3, grid B3
Altitude: 1,520 m

A major centre of Kerala's tea industry and close to Anaimudi, at 2,695 m the highest peak in South India, Munnar is the nearest Kerala comes to a genuine hill station. It is surrounded by about 30 tea estates, among the highest in the world, and forest that is still rich in wildlife, including the reclusive Nilgiri Tahr that continues to survive the increasing commercial use of the hills. The surrounding hills are home to the rare Neelakurunji plant (Strobilanthes), which covers the hills in colour for a month once in 12 years. Despite the appearance of calm the town has witnessed catastrophes, notably the 1924 flood which destroyed the whole settlement.

Ins & outs **Getting there** The easiest access is by bus or taxi from Kochi, but there are daily buses to major towns in Kerala and Tamil Nadu. The state bus stands are in the centre of town but there is another in the bazar. **Getting around** The town is small and pleasant for walking around, though there are autos. It is worth hiring a bike or a jeep for trips out of town. **Climate** The rains from Jun-Sep are very heavy (annual total 2700 mm).

Sights It is possible to visit a working **tea factory**, normally at Mattupetty. Contact the Manager, *Tata Regional Office*, T30561, for information. You can watch tea pickers at work and how tea is processed. Tea is also available for sale.

In the centre of Old Munnar, set on a hill immediately above the road in the centre of town, is **Christ Church**. Rather squat and now blackened by weathering its exterior is unprepossessing, but inside it is a charming small church. Consecrated in 1910 it still contains its original 14 rows of wooden pews. Built to serve the tea estate managers and workers of the High Ranges, the last English language service was held in 1981. Its origins are suggested in several of the memorial plaques on the wall. Sunday services today are in Tamil (0800, when the church is always full) and Malayalam (1000). The Christmas service, which starts at 0430, is particularly special. A zig-zag path up the hill immediately behind the church leads to the small Pioneer cemetery, then through the Indian cemetery to the top.

Mount Carmel Roman Catholic church, the first Catholic Church in the High Ranges, is in Old Munnar on the road up to the Tata General Hospital. The first chapel on the site was founded in 1898 by Fr Alphonse who arrived in Munnar from Spain in 1854. The present church was built by the then Bishop of Vijayapuram in 1938.

Munnar

Mattupetty Lake The lake (*altitude*: **Excursions** 1,700 m, 13 km from Munnar) created by the small hydro-electricity dam is flanked by steep hills and woods. To its south is the Kerala Livestock Development Board's research and cattle breeding centre – formerly the Indo-Swiss dairy project. In a beautiful semi-Alpine setting surrounded for much of the year by lush green fields, the centre offers interesting insights into the practical realities and achievements of cattle breeding in India today. ■ *Visits between 0900-1100, 1400-1530, Rs 5, contact T530389.*

Devikulam (Devikolam) 15 km from Munnar, named after 'the lake of the Goddess', is the last settlement on the road across the Western Ghats to Kodai and Madurai in Tamil Nadu. There are extensive and beautiful views over the highest ranges of the Western Ghats. The alternative shorter route to Kodai via Top Station is often washed out or damaged by heavy logging trucks, and is normally only passable by four-wheel drive vehicles. **Sleeping** New **D-E** *Spring Dale Resort*, T04865-64268, clean rooms (Rs 300-500, dorm Rs 700 for five, heaters Rs 100 extra), good food (but slow to arrive), George Babu arranges trips to the High Ranges, intimate resort with good facilities, recommended.

Top Station, on the border with Tamil Nadu (*altitude*: 2,200 m, 41 km from Munnar), has some of the highest tea estates in India. It is an idyllic spot, with superb views over the Tamil Nadu plains and the edge of the Western Ghats. There are tea and soft drinks (check bottle seals) stalls in the hamlet. Top Station took its name

■ **Sleeping**
1 East End
2 Hill View
3 Misha
4 Poopada Lodge
5 Residency
6 Royal Retreat
7 Sinai Cottages
8 Sree Narayana Lodge

● **Eating**
1 Abad
2 Vegetarian

Kerala

from a ropeway that connected it via Middle Station to Lower Station at the valley bottom. The small town of Bodinayak-kanur (which can be reached on the Devikulam road) lies in the valley.

★ **Eravikulam/Rajamalai National Park** The park, 14 km northeast of Munnar, was set up in 1978 to preserve the endangered Nilgiri Tahr (Nilgiri Ibex) (*Hemitragus hylocrius*). The conservation programme has resulted in the park now supporting the largest population of the species in the world, of nearly 2,000. The sure-footed wild goats live in herds on the steep black rocky slopes of the Anaimudi mountains. They are brownish, have short, flat horns with the male carrying a thick mane, and can be easily seen around the entrance. There are also elephants, sambars, gaurs, macaque and the occasional leopard and tiger. The scenery is magnificent, though the walks into the forest are steep and strenuous.There is an easier well-made paved path from the park entrance following the road immediately below the bare granite outcrop of the Naikundi Hill to the Rajamalai Gap (*altitude*: 1,950 m). **Sleeping** From there it is a one hour walk to the *Forest Rest House*. Overnight visits can be arranged (Rs 200 per night) with permission from the Forest Ranger officer at Devikulam, T530487. ■ *Visitors are allowed in the Rajamala section of the park only. Entry Rs 50, plus Rs 100 per passenger for vehicles taken into the park. Closed during the monsoons.*

Cycling There are some excellent cycle rides around Munnar, not all of them steep. One ride goes up a gentle slope through a beautiful valley 8 km to the Letchmi Estate. There is a *chai* stall at the estate and the road continues to the head of the valley for views down to the forest beyond. A second ride goes to the south end of Munnar and crosses the river by the dam, then takes a right turn through sandalwood and cardamom plantations, again with spectacular views and a tea stall after 4 km. A shorter alternative to this route is to cross the dam and turn left, taking the quiet road north to the *High Range Club* and Munnar.

Sleeping
AM Rd is Alwaye-Munnar Rd

B *Copper Castle*, Kannan Devi Hills, T531201, F530438, copper@md4.vsnl.net.in Delightfully perched on hillside with beautiful views of a cascading stream, good-sized comfortable rooms with attached baths and hot showers, some signs of water seepage in a couple of the rooms, restaurant (good sizzlers), enthusiastic manager who is a fund of information on attractions around Munnar, friendly staff but slow service, jeep safaris/trekking/hand gliding/wilderness camps etc. **B** *Tea Country* (KTDC), new resort outside town, T530969, F530970, ktdc@vsnl.com 43 rooms, good facilities, beautiful views, great walking, own transport essential. **B-C***Eastend* (Edassery), Temple Rd, T530452, F530227. 22 rooms and some cottages (solar heated water), good but expensive restaurant, attractively designed, very clean. Recommended. **C** *Royal Retreat*, Kannan Devan hills, near Bus Stand, T530240. 14 rooms with balcony (views now blocked by *Hill View* next door), colonial bungalow style but with marble and chrome, very good restaurant. Recommended. **C-D** *Residency* (*Issac's*), Top Station Rd, T530501, F530265. 22 rooms with great views, well maintained, canteen-like restaurant but reasonable meals, bar not recommended. **D** *Elysium Gardens*, Top Station Rd, 1.5 km beyond *Residency Hotel*, T530510. Attractive hotel, rooms around central lounge, informal restaurant. **D** *Hill View*, AM Rd, T530567, F530241. 35 clean rooms with bath, some with attractive river views, dorms for 20, 4 storeys, restaurant (slow, items unavailable), exchange, good service, friendly and helpful. **D** *Poopada Guest House*, off AM Rd, T530223. Clean rooms with balconies (Rs 450-600), good restaurant, impressive. **E** *Kannan Devan Hills Club*, on tea estate above town, T530252. Superb views, very good value, quiet. Recommended. **E** *Sinai Cottages*, near *Hill View Hotel* in Tata tea plantation, T530560. Rooms (Rs 350) in

The taming of the Nilgiri Tahr

Visitors to the Rajamalai National Park can thank the patience of the American biologist Clifford G Rice in the early 1980s for the friendliness with which they are greeted by this shyest of wild goats. Spending over two years observing the unique species on the Eravikulam Plateau as part of a PhD research project, he found it impossible to get near enough to them to observe properly. Their reluctance could be put down to over 150 years of exploitation. When the future Duke of Wellington was in hot pursuit of Tipu Sultan in 1795, he made an encampment high in the Annamalai hills. His soldiers marvelled at the beauty of the place – and at the fact that the goats were so tame that it was possible to slaughter them as they walked through the camp. The goats quickly learned to keep as far as possible from people.

The answer to Rice's problem lay in the goats' love of salt, well known by the local tea planters. Concentrating his attention on just one of the groups of tahr he scattered lumps of the crude salt near him and waited hopefully for them to come. It slowly seemed to work, and once he started mixing water to make a salty slush he could scarcely keep them away. Salt continued to be used until 1991 by the forest rangers to ensure that the goats were near the entrance to the park. However, it was found that visitors were also bringing salt to attract the goats, damaging their diet, and the practice has now been discontinued. Today, however, the tahr remain easily approachable and can readily be seen in the park.

colonial house, good views, friendly people, simple. Recommended. **E-F** *Hilltop*, ask Tourist Information, T530616. Basic clean rooms (Rs 175-250), restaurant, travel, friendly; also cottages for Rs 300. **E** *Misha Tourist Home*, Old Bazar, T530376. Dull but clean rooms (Rs 200), 5-bed dorm in Christian guest house. **E-F** *Sree Narayana Tourist Home* (*SN Lodge*), near PO, AM Rd, T530212. 17 modest but clean rooms (Rs 150-300), restaurant, friendly, popular. Recommended.

Mid-range: *Eastend's* The Greens. Very pleasant with glassed-in verandah serving good food, smart. Alternative: very cheap simple meals, if you join the drivers in the eatery 'below stairs' entered from the lower car park! *Royal Retreat*. International. Very pleasant, wide choice. **Cheap**: *Poopada*. Excellent value. *Vegetarian Restaurant* (next to *Misha*) Old Bazar, serves very good meals. *Chicken Shack* in bazar. **Eating**

High Range Club, T530253, charming colonial style planters' club, members only (or with reciprocal arrangements), visit by asking a planter to introduce you; *KDH Club*, for Tata staff, also old-world, visit with permission, excellent pool table. **Entertainment**

Munnar Supply Assoc (MSA), next to tourist information, established 1900, a bit of the old world, where you can get everything; tailors in the bazar can copy your garments in 24 hrs. The newer Main Bazar is to the north. **Shopping**

Local Cycle hire: *Raja*, Rs 40 per day, Rs 20 per half day; from tourist information, Rs 50 per day. *Joy Automobiles*, GH Rd, recommended car mechanics. **Long distance Road Bus**: frequent services to **Mattupetty** (30 mins), **Devikulam** (30 mins), **Adimali** (1 hr) and **Top Station** (1 hr). Daily to **Coimbatore** (6 hrs); **Ernakulam/ Kochi** (4½ hrs); **Kodaikkanal** 0700 via **Udumalpettai**, change for Palani and Kodai. If the Palani-Kodai Rd is closed a further bus goes to Vatalakundu and then Kodai; Kottayam (5 hrs); **Madurai** (5 hrs); **Palani** (4½ hrs); **Thekkadi** (4½ hrs); **Thiruvanantha puram** (9 hrs). **Jeeps/taxis** go to the **Eravikulam National Park**. **Transport**

Kerala

Directory **Banks** *Federal Bank*, near Tata Hospital Rd, very helpful; *State Bank of India*, 1000-1400, Sat 1000-1200. **Communications** The post office is in the centre of the new town. There are several ISD phone booths, but phone connections from Munnar are frequently broken. The nearest ISD phone, when Munnar's phones are out of order, is in Kothamangalam (which has the St Joseph's Hospital), or at night, Muvattupuzha (24 hrs). **Medical services** Excellent *Tata General Hospital*, T530270, on the north edge of town on the Rajamalai Rd. There are several chemists in both the old and new bazar areas. One of the best stocked is among the shops between the Tata Regional Office and the Residency hotel. **Tourist offices** *DTPC*, Old Munnar Bazar, T530679, mainly for booking cycles, Rs 10 per hr, Rs 50 per day; not much information. Try the free *Tourist Information Service*, Main Bazar, opposite bus stop, T530349, Joseph Lype is a mine of invaluable information (small charge for photocopies); arranges accommodation, boats etc.

To Thrissur and Palakkad

One of South India's most important historically strategic routes, the road rises gently to the lowest pass through the Western Ghats along their entire length.

Kalady
Phone code: 04857
Colour map 3, grid B3

Kalady, on the bank of the Periyar River, 45 km from Kochi, is the birthplace of one of India's most influential philosophers, **Sankaracharya**. Living in the eighth century, Sankaracharya founded the school of *advaita* philosophy (see page 525) which spread widely across South India. There are now two shrines in his memory, one to *Dakshinamurti* and the other to the Goddess *Sarada*, open 0530-1230, 1530-2000. The management of the shrines is in the hands of the Math at Sringeri in Karnataka (see page 337). The Adi Sankara Kirti Stambha Mandapam is a nine-storeyed octagonal tower, 46 m high, and details Sri Sankara's life and works and the Shan Maths, or six ways to worship. **Sleeping F** *Sri Sankaracharya New Guest House* which is basic and cheap, T345; **F** *Ramkrishna Mission Guest House.* ■ *0700-1900. Small entry fee. Getting there: Kalady can easily be visited in an afternoon from Kochi or from Aluva by bus (40 mins).*

Angamali
Phone code: 0484
Colour map 3, grid B2

A further 10 km on from Kalady, Amagamali was at one time the seat of one of the most important Syrian bishoprics. According to the Church History of Travancore, the Bishop claimed the ancient title of Metropolitan of India exercising jurisdiction over nearly 1400 churches.

Nearby, and only a rickshaw drive from Angamali, is the noted Jacobite church of Mar Sabore and Afroth at Akapparambu, founded in AD 825. The present building dates from after the arrival of the Portuguese and shows strong Portuguese influence in its exterior design. However, it is particularly noted for its murals, colourfully and simply illustrating stories from the Bible. **Sleeping E** *Mundadan*, Rly Station Junction, T452975, some a/c rooms; **E** *President*, T452985, is cheaper.

Poothamkutty
Phone code: 0484

In the foothills of the ghats and surrounded by a bird sanctuary, is **Thabor** in Poothamkutty, 9 km from Angamali, where "holistic rejuvenation programmes" are offered in a "bio-diverse farm". *Sirius*, Manjaly House, Thabor (Poothamkutty), 451907, F452538, logic@md3.vsnl.net.in Belgian run, 10 rooms (Rs 3,500 each per week) and camping (Rs 2,500), shared facilities, vegetarian meals, no smoking, drugs or alcohol, silence after 2200, guests share the daily chores, bike hire, yoga, "creative workshops" etc. ■ *Getting there: From Kochi or Thrissur to Angamali; there, walk across to the covered Private Bus Stand and take a bus to Poothamkutty (8 km), then follow signs to Sirius or ask for the local auto-rickshaw (Rs 10) from the phone booth. Alternatively from Kochi airport take a taxi (Rs 500).*

Kerala

Thrissur തൃശൂർ (Trichur)

Thrissur (Tiru-siva-perur) is on the west end of the Palakkad gap which runs through the low pass between the Nilgiri and the Palani Hills. The route through the ghats is not scenic but it has been the most important link to the peninsular interior since Roman times. Thrissur has the unique Elephant Owners' Association and is particularly famous for its annual Pooram in April/May.

Phone code: 0487
Colour map 3, grid B2
Population: 275,100

Once the capital of Kochi State, Thrissur was captured by the Zamorin of Calicut and then by the Portuguese and the Dutch. In the 18th century it fell to Tipu Sultan before Raja Rama Varma, 'the architect of the town', came to the throne.

History

Thrissur is built round a hill on which stands the **Vadakkunnathan Temple** and the open green. The town's bearings are given in cardinal directions from this raised 'Round'. The temple is also known as the Rishabhadri or Thenkailasam ('Kailash of the South').

Sights

A predominantly Siva temple, the two circular northern shrines in the complex are dedicated to Vadakkunnathan (Siva) and Sankara Narayana and comprise square sanctuaries surrounded by corridors. They are separated by a small shrine to Ganesh. The round timber roofs are sheathed in metal. To their south is the Rama shrine fronted by an open pillared hall. At the shrine to the Jain Tirthankara Vrishabha, worshippers offer a thread from their clothing, symbolically to cover the saint's nakedness. There are also idols which bear a striking similarity to Buddhist images. The shrine to Sankara Narayana has superb murals depicting stories from the Mahabharata which were apparently renovated in 1731. Subsidiary shrines were added to Ayyappa and Krishna. It is a classic example of the Kerala style of architecture with its special pagoda-like roof richly decorated with fine wood carving. The temple plays a pivotal role in the *Pooram* celebrations (see festivals below). In September/October, there are live performances of Chakyarkothu, a classical art form. There is a small elephant compound attached to the temple. ■ *0400-1030, 1700-2030. Non-Hindus are not permitted inside except during the Pooram festival, when restrictions are lifted.*

The impressive **Lourdes Church** has an interesting underground shrine. The **Town Hall** is a striking building housing an art gallery with murals from other parts of the state.

Archaeological Museum, Town Hall Road, Chembukkavu, T20566 (ask to see the royal chariot). ■ *0900-1500, closed Mon.* Next door, the **Art Museum** has wood carvings, sculptures, an excellent collection of traditional lamps and old jewellery.

Museums

Thrissur Zoo, near the Art Museum, is known for its snake collection. ■ *1500-1715; small entry and camera fee.* Filming only with prior permission of the Director of Museums in Thiruvananthapuram. The **Aquarium** is near Nehru Park; ■ *1500-2000.*

Parks & zoos

Cheruthuruthy, 29 km north of Thrissur near Shornur Junction, is famous for the Kerala Kalamandalam (T0492-622418) on the river bank, which led to a revival of *Kathakali* dancing. It is a centre for teaching music, drama, Mohiniyattam and Ottam Thullal in addition to Kathakali. You can watch training sessions from 0430-0630, 0830-1200 and 1530-1730. All night Kathakali performances: 26 January, 13 March, 15 August, 18 September, 9 November. Closed Saturday, Sunday, public holidays and in April and May.

Excursions

Kerala

Sleeping F *Govt Guest House*, Shornur, T04929-2498, reserve ahead. **F** *PWD Rest House*, here and at Shornur, T2514. ■ *Getting there: frequent private buses from Thrissur northern bus stand (Vadakkechira Bus Stand) go straight to Kalamandalam, about 1 hr.*

Sleeping
Reserve ahead during Pooram, when prices rocket

B Surya, 15 km from town, (8 km from beach), T331347, sureshpr@md3.vsnl.net.in 10 rooms (some a/c) in impressive old building, vegetarian meals, ayurvedic treatments, yoga, all inclusive rate Rs 2000. The mid-range hotels have fairly comfortable, clean rooms, some with a/c restaurants. **D** *Casino*, TB Rd near rly, T424699, F442037, 25 rooms with bath, 11 a/c, restaurant, bar, pastry shop, exchange, lawn. **D** *Elite International*, 22 Chembottil Lane (just south of Round), T421033, F442057. 90 rooms with bath, some a/c, more impressive reception area than rooms (bed bugs reported by some, otherwise fair value), a/c restaurants adequate. **D** *Siddhartha Regency*, Velliyanur/TB Rd, Kokkalai, T424773, F425116. Decent a/c rooms, restaurant, bar. **E** *Alukkas*, Railway Station Rd, T424067, F424073, clean. Comfortable rooms (6 new best), some a/c, good value. Govt **E** *Ramanilayam Guest House*, Palace Rd, T332016. Clean rooms, some a/c (old palace), roof-garden restaurant (meals to order), mainly for officials, ask in advance. **F** *Yatri Nivas* (KTDC), Stadium Rd, Chembukavu, T332333. 19 rooms (1 a/c, Rs 400), snacks. Several cheap hotels on Chembottil Lane and Railway Station Rd.

Eating
Most D hotels have good restaurants

Expensive: *Casino*, is in a large garden with coloured fountains! **Cheap**: On Chembottil Lane: nr *Elite Bharat*, for good South Indian breakfast and lunch. Opposite: *Ming Palace*, very good Chinese (upstairs) and *Yamuna*, an Indian restaurant, very popular, friendly, highly recommended.

Festivals

Jan-Feb: Several temple festivals with elephants involved are held in the surrounding villages which can be as rewarding as the *Pooram*. **End-Mar**: Seven-day *Arratupuzha Festival* at the Ayappa temple, 14 km from Thrissur. On the 5th day the deity processes with nine decorated elephants, while on the 6th day *Pooram* is celebrated with 61 elephants in the temple grounds on a grand scale. **Apr-May**: the magnificent 8-day *Pooram*, a grand festival with elephants, parasols, drums and fireworks should not be missed. **Aug/Sep**: the district also celebrates *Kamdassamkadavu Boat Races* at *Onam*. Also performances of *Pulikali*, unique to Thrissur, when mimers dressed as tigers dance to drumbeats.

Shopping

Cotton spinning, weaving and textile industries, silk saris and brass lamps. Thrissur is also famous for its gold craftsmanship. Kerala handicrafts at *Surabhi*, and shopping areas in north, west and south Rounds, MO Rd, High Rd and MG Rd.

Transport

Local Yellow top **taxis**, **auto-rickshaws** and **buses**. **Car hire** from *Francis*, Round South, T323317. **Long distance Road Bus**: there are 3 bus stands. KSRTC, near rly station, south of 'Round' for long distance and interstate services including several to **Allapuzha** (3½ hrs), **Bangalore** (10 hrs), **Coimbatore** (3 hrs), **Guruvayoor** (1 hr), **Kochi** (2 hrs), **Kozhikode, Chennai** (13 hrs), **Palakkad, Thiruvananthapuram** (7 hrs). **North (Priyadarshini)**, just north of 'Round', buses to Cheruthuruthy, Ottapalam, Palakkad. **Sakthan Thampuran**, 2 km south of 'Round', for frequent private buses to Guruvayoor, Kannur, Kozhikode. **Train**: Kochi (Cochin): *Chennai-Cochin Exp, 6041* (AC/II), 0705, 2 hrs. **Chennai (MC)**: *Alleppey-Chennai Exp, 6042* (AC/II), 1810, 12 hrs; *Trivandrum Chennai Mail, 6320*, 1938, 11¼ hrs; *Cochin-Gorakhpur Exp, 5011* (AC/II), Tue, Thu, Fri, Sun, 1050, 12½ hrs.

Directory

Tourist offices In *Govt Guest House*, Palace Rd, T332300, and opposite Town Hall.

The strategically placed town marks a low point in the ghats (known as the Palakkad Gap). It is the road and rail route from Kerala to Coimbatore and Chennai. The area is notable for tobacco and rice cultivation and processing, and its textile industry. Haidar Ali's old fort here was built in 1766, which the British took in 1790.

Palakkad (Palghat)
Phone code: 0491
Colour map 3, grid B3
Population: 123,300

Sleeping D *Fort Palace*, West Fort Rd, T/F534621. 19 rooms, some good a/c, restaurant, brash imitation turrets. **D** *Garden House* (KTDC), Malampuzha, T815217. Mostly non a/c rooms, pleasant, a/c, Rs 800. **D** *Indraprastha*, English Church Rd, T534641, F534641. 30 rooms, some comfortable, a/c, restaurant, bar, modern building. **D** *Walayar Motels*, Kanjikode West, T866312. 9 km from town centre, 2 km from rly, 10 rooms, some a/c, restaurant, bar. **F** *Kalpaka*, T534631 and **F** *Kalyan*, T534206, both on GB Rd. **At Kodumbu**: **B** *Kairali Ayurvedic Health Resort*, T322553, F322732, www.kairali.com Excellent resort, beautifully landscaped grounds, own dairy and farm, extensive choice of treatments, completent and helpful staff, pool, tennis etc. Recommended.

Transport Road Bus: KSRTC, for long distance; Municipal Bus Stand for Kozhikode, Mannarghat (Silent Valley), Pollachi. **Train** The main Junction station is 5 km northeast of town; enquiries. Also Town Station. **Coimbatore**: *Kerala Exp, 2625* (AC/II), 1750, 1¼ hrs; **Chennai**: *Chennai Exp, 6042* (AC/II), 2000, 10¼ hrs; **Ernakulam Junction**: *Kerala-Mangala Exp, 2626* (AC/II), 0825, 3¼ hrs; **Kochi (Cochin)**: *Guwahati/Howrah Exp, 6314/6316* (AC/II), Wed, Thu, Sun, 1445, 4 hrs. Madgaon (Margao): Netravati Exp 6636, 0545, 14½ hrs. *Ernakulam-Lakshadweep Exp 2617*, 1320, 13½ hrs.

Directory Bank & medical services *State Bank of India*, English Church Rd. **Tourist office** Near Children's Park, T538996.

The park, in the northeast corner of Palakkad District, part of the Nilgiri Biosphere Reserve, is unique as an extraordinary Indian example of almost totally undisturbed rain forest. Tucked away in a remote corner on the border with Tamil Nadu and on the edge of the Nilgiris, *Sairandhri Vanam* (the 'forest in the valley', the name taken from the *Mahabharata*) covering 89 sq km, lies along the Kunthi River valley at an altitude of over 2,000 m. There are over 1,000 species of plants (966 flowering, over 100 orchids, many medicinal plants) and a wide range of animals and birds. Foreigners need a permit to visit. Apply in advance at the Forest Office, Olavakkad, Palakkad Junction; Dr. Mahar Singh, Conservation of Forest Wildlife, Forest Complex, T0492-556393. Access is via Manarkkad (32 km) where there is a very knowledgeable wildlife warden. A Forest Department bus takes visitors around but visibility can be restricted by the very long grass alongside the track. Beware of leaches (wear good walking shoes steeped in insect repellent). **Sleeping** *Forest Rest House* at Murrali.

Silent Valley National Park

The coastal road north

Aluva (Alwaye) is an important industrial town producing chemicals, glass, aluminium, rayon, tyres and fertilizers but the Periyar River on which the town stands is still attractive. During the monsoon, the Periyar can flood dramatically. In 1789 the floods halted the southward march of Tipu Sultan, but though common they are of less historic significance now. **Sleeping D-E** *Periyar*, New By-Pass Rd, T625024. 10 rooms, some a/c, restaurant popular and good, though indifferent management. **E** *Govt Guest House*, T623637. 10 large rooms in an old palace with attractive circular verandah, efficient staff, tourist information, commanding frontage along the very broad river; apply to manager. A ferry runs from the steps which lead down from the guest house to the river but bathing not very enticing.

Aluva
Phone code: 0484
Colour map 3, grid B2
Population: 24,700

Kerala

Kodungallur

Phone code: 0488
Colour map 3, grid B2
Population: 88,700

At one time Kodungallur (Cranganore) was the west coast's major port, and the capital of the Chera king Cheraman Perumal. **Kottapuram**, nearby, is where St Thomas is believed to have landed in AD 52; the commemorative shrine was built in 1952. Kodungallur is also associated by tradition with the arrival of the first Muslims to reach India by sea. Malik-ibn-Dinar is reputed to have built India's first **Juma Masjid** 2 km from town.

It is worth visiting the Tiruvanchikulam Temple and the Portuguese fort. The present mosque has some interesting features. The outer walls have a moulded base similar to that of Brahmanical temples, for example. Muslim festivals are celebrated here on a grand scale.

The Kurumba **Bhagavati Temple** (closed to visitors) on the Ernakulam side of town, commemorates the martyrdom of Kannaki. The temple, which dates from the Chera period, is the focus of Shakti worship; the spectacular and controversial annual *Bharani festival* is held in the Malayalam month of Meenom (March-April). Intoxicated devotees process to the temple singing obscene songs, celebrating the expulsion of 'foreigners' (possibly Buddhists) from the temple. On the first day of the month of Aswathi, pilgrims run madly around the temple compound, watched by spectators. So-called 'oracles', dressed in scarlet, enter the temple in a frenzied and ecstatic state, flailing themselves. Some earlier rituals, such as the sacrifice of cocks, was abandoned under government pressure in 1954, and the whole festival still causes local controversy.

The Syrian orthodox church in **Azikode** blends early Christian architecture in Kerala with surrounding Hindu traditions. Thus the images of Peter and Paul are placed where the *dvarapalas* (door-keepers) of Hindu temples would be found, and the portico in front of the church is for pilgrims.

Sleeping E *Indraprastham*, East Nada, T602678, *Kairali*, TKS Puram, Kottapuram, T602631 and *Polakulath*, North Nada, T602602, are simple but have some a/c rooms. **F** *Parsanthi*, T602939, is more basic. **F** *PWD Resthouse*, contact Dist Collector, Thrissur.

Guruvayur

Phone code: 0487
Colour map 3, grid B2
Population: 118,700

Guruvayur is a heaving pilgrimage centre, filled with stalls and is very lively. The **Sri Krishna Temple** which probably dates from at least the 16th century makes it particulary important. The image of Krishna has four arms with the conch, the discus, the mace and the lotus. One devotee has written that "To millions, *Guruvayurappan* is a living deity who answers all their prayers. It is not only the *gopis* (milkmaids) who yearn for oneness with him, but all men and women who wish to be liberated from *samsara*". The devotional poet MN Bhattathiri composed the famous *Narayaniyam* here.

In the outer enclosure there is a tall gold-plated flagpost and a pillar of lamps. The sanctum sanctorum is in the two-storeyed *srikoil*, with the image of the four-armed Krishna garlanded with pearls and marigolds. Photography of the tank is not allowed.

An unusual feature of the temple at Guruvayur is the timing of the rituals. The sanctum opens at 0300 and closes at 2100. Except between 1300 and 1600, when it is closed, a continuous series of pujas and processions is performed. The darshan at 0300, the *nirnalaya*, when the image is decked out with the previous day's flowers is believed to be particularly auspicious. Non-Hindus are not allowed inside and are not made to feel welcome.

Punnathur Kotta, a fort 4 km away, houses the 40 temple elephants and trains wild ones. Entry Rs 25, interesting insights into traditional animal training (but disappointing for some). Take care; elephants can be dangerous, especially those in 'must'.

Sleeping and eating D *RV Tower*, East Nada, near Manjulal, T555225, F555427, near rly and bus stand. Smart, modern hotel. **D** *Vanamala Kusumam*, South Nada, T556702, F555504. 30 rooms, some comfortable a/c, vegetarian restaurant. **D** *Vyshakh*, near Temple pond, Ring Rd, East Nada, T556188. Comfortable rooms. **D-E** *Nandanam* (KTDC), East Nada, near Garuda Statue and rly station, T556266, F555513. 45 rooms, can be noisy. **F** *Mangalaya* (KTDC), near Sri Krishna Temple, East Nada Gopuram, T554061, F555513. 8 (4/6-bed) rooms, pilgrim hotel. Several *thali* vegetarian restaurants near the temple. Also *Indian Coffee House*, East Nada for good snacks.

D & E hotels have some a/c rooms & cheaper non-a/c; restaurants serve Indian vegetarian meals

Festivals Feb/Mar: *Utsavam*, 10 days of festivities start with an elephant race and continue with colourful elephant processions and performances of Krishattam dances. Details from Kerala Tourist offices. **Nov-Dec**: Five-day *Ekadasi* with performances of *Krishnanattom*, a forerunner of Kathakali – an eight-day drama cycle.

Transport Road: bus station is east of the Sri Krishna Temple and several hotels. Buses to Thrissur (45 mins).

The Palakkad gap has been one of the few relatively easy routes through the ghats for 3,000 years and this area is noted for its wide range of megalithic monuments. Megalithic cultures spread from the Tamil Nadu plains down into Kerala, but developed their own local forms. The small villages of Eyyal, Chovvanur, Kakkad, Porkalam, Kattakampala and Kadamsseri, between Guruvayur and Kunnamkulam have hoodstones, hatstones, dolmens, burial urns and menhirs.

Megalith trail: Guruvayur to Kunnamkulam

Kerala

Chovannur in particular has many *topikals* (hatstones), one of the particularly distinctive Iron Age megalithic remains of Kerala. Nearby **Porkalam** has a wide range of monuments side by side within an area of less than 1 ha. Hoodstones (*kudaikal*) are made of dressed granite and are like a handleless umbrella made of palm leaf used locally. It is shaped into a dome and covers a burial pit. The hatstones, made of dressed laterite, have a circular top stone resting on four pieces of stone placed upright in an almost circular form, looking like a giant mushroom. They did not have any burial chamber.

North Kerala

Kozhikode (Calicut) കോഴിക്കോട്

Kozhikode is a pleasant, if rather anonymous town and is no longer a port though there are still remnants of the trade in spices, copra and coconut oil in the Court Road/Big Bazar Road area. The town beach, though unsuitable for bathing, is pleasant for a stroll.

*Phone code: 0495
Colour map 3, grid B2
Population: 801,200*

Getting there **Karipur airport**, 25 km from the town centre, has connections with several major Indian cities. The station and main bus stand are near the town centre within easy reach of several hotels. **Getting around** Autos are widely available. **Climate** Temperature: summer, max 35°C, min 23°C; winter, max 32°C, min 22°C. Annual rainfall: 2,500 mm. Best season: Nov-Mar.

Ins & outs

Kozhikode (closest pronunciation korli-kodi) was the capital of the Zamorin Rajas. The early 19th-century historian Buchanan-Hamilton recorded: "when

History

Cheruman Perumal had divided Malabar, and had no principality remaining to bestow on the ancestors of the Tamuri, he gave that chief his sword, with all the territory in which a cock crowing at a small temple here could be heard." The romantic derivation of the name Colicudu ('cock crowing'), now Kozhikode, is not unchallenged.

In 1498 **Vasco da Gama** landed at Kappad nearby (see below), starting a turbulent, often violent, century and a half of contact with European powers.

When the Portuguese arrived, Calicut was under the control of the Vijayanagar Empire (see page 345), based in Hampi over 500 km to the north-east. After a decade of violent raids the local Zamorin made peace with the Portuguese and gave them trading rights and the right to build a fort. They remained for over a century. In 1766 the city was threatened by the Muslim Raja from Mysore, Haidar Ali. The Zamorin offered peace but when the offer was rejected, barricaded himself and his family in the palace and burnt it to the ground. Although Haidar Ali soon left, his son Tipu Sultan returned 23 years later and devastated the entire region. British rule was imposed in 1792 by the Treaty of Seringapatam.

Its name during the British period, Calicut, was given to the *calico* cloth, a block printed cotton exported round the world.

The town Today Kozhikode is a major commercial centre for northern Kerala with a strong Arab connection. Its main export today is not spices but workers to the Gulf (the airport has 21 direct flights a week, to the area!). It is also a centre for Kerala's timber industry, boat building is important. There is nothing of Portuguese influence here and little of the former ruling family, the Zamorin Raja. The title however, survives and the current Raja, who succeeded to it in 1998, at the age of 87, lives in a nondescript suburban house. The matrilineal title passes to the oldest male in a vast extended family who is invariably extraordinarily aged! Their palace was burnt down a long time ago – now the site is a park and a tank in the centre of town.

Sights A few interesting wooden mosques are to be found to the west of the town. **Museums Pazhassiraja Museum**: Exhibits include copies of original murals plus bronzes, old coins and models of the different types of megalithic monuments widespread in the area. ■ *5 km on east Hill (Archaeological Department Museum). 1000-1230, 1430-1700, closed Mon.* The **Art Gallery** and **Krishna Menon Museum** (named after the Kerala politician who became a leading left-wing figure in India's post-Independence Congress Government) next door, free. Excellent collection of paintings by Indian artists; also wood and ivory carvings. A section of the museum is dedicated to VK Krishna Menon. ■ *1000-1230, 1430-1700, Mon, Wed afternoon only.*

Excursions **Beypore**, (*phone code*: 0495, 10 km south) once an important port, is where traditional sea-going *Uru* vessels are still built by craftsmen. *Tasara* (Centre for Creative Weaving), North Beypore, T424233, F765653, 7 km from rly station. The craft weaving skills of Tasara are practised and taught in this centre which attracts weavers and painters from around the world; US$500 per week includes eight hours' tuition daily. Tapestries, carpets, innovative and traditional handloom work are for sale.

Kappad (*phone code*: 496, 19 km north) is where Vasco da Gama landed on 27th May 1498 with 170 men and erected a stone pillar to mark a discovery (his first landing) – an old plaque by the approach road to the beach commemorates the event. It is now the site of a small, poor, mainly Muslim, fishing village. Though it is a pleasant spot, the sea is unsuitable for swimming since pollution from Kozhikode filters down this far and the beach itself is used as a toilet by the fishermen. **C** *Kappad Beach Resort*, T683760, F683706, moosa@kappadbeachresort.com 16 rooms in 4 cottages, some a/c, superb views of the sea beating against the rocks, restaurant upstairs has panoramic views (occasional dolphins) but unexciting food, pool, modern facilities, helpful staff, relaxing. There is also a State Tourism *Guest House*.

Malappuram (*phone code*: 0493, 36 km south east of Kozhikode) was the centre of the Moplah rebellion of August 1921 when Muslims rose against both Hindus and the British, still has a large Muslim population. **Sleeping E** *Mahendrapuri*, Main Road, T434201. Contact *Business Lines*, nearby T434044, F435458, for paying guest rooms; they also arrange tours visiting historical sites, teak forests and the Silent Valley. **Eating** KTDC *Changanamkulak*, Nannammukku (halfway, on Thrissur road), is a good lunch stop with cheap, clean but good food.

A *Taj Residency*, PT Usha Rd, near the sea, T765354, F765354. 74 rooms, typical business hotel, gym, good pool, ayurvedic treatment (Coimbatore school). **B** *Malabar Palace*, GH Rd, Manuelsons Junction, T721511, F721594. 52 a/c rooms (*Koran* in every room), excellent a/c restaurant, bar, very helpful Reception. Recommended. **B-D** *Hyson Heritage*, 114 Bank Rd, T766726, F766518. 42 clean, comfortable rooms (Rs

Sleeping
Jail Rd is now Maulana Md Ali Rd, Mavoor Rd is Indira Gandhi Rd

Kerala

Kozhikode (Calicut)

To Ballussery
To Kannur
To Wynad
To Mavoor

Krishna o Menon Museum
Civil Station
Wynad Rd
Co-op
Bypass Rd
Kannur Rd
Gandhi Rd
Joseph Rd
Velayil Rd
Air India
Jet Airways
KSRTC Bus Stand
Indira Gandhi Rd
New Bus Stand
Customs Rd
P T Usha Rd
Exchange at Computer Centre
Red Cross Rd
Government
Convent Rd
Corporation Rd
Cheroty Rd
Bank Rd
AG Rd
Town Hall Rd
CSI Church
Cochin Bakery & Ice Cream
Pavamani Rd
Puthiyara Rd
Market
Manachira
Comtrust
Stadium Rd
Taluk Rd
Court Rd
Taxis
Beach Rd
SM St
GH Rd
Veg Market
Big Bazar Rd
Railway Station
MP Rd
Taxis
Palayam Rd
Old Bus Stand
Veg Market
PC Rd
M M Ali Rd (Jail Rd)
Link Rd
YMCA
Tuli Temple
To Airport & Thrissur

N

0 metres (approx) 300
0 yards (approx) 300

■ **Sleeping**
1 Alakapuri
2 Hyson Heritage
3 Malabar Mansion

4 Malabar Palace & Tom 'n' Jerry
5 NCK Tourist Home & Indian Coffee House

6 Paramount Tower
7 Sea Queen
8 Taj

450+), 49 a/c, in modern wing (Rs 850+), buffet breakfast included, all excellent value, friendly, efficient. Highly recommended. **C** *Paramount Tower*, Town Hall Rd, T722651. 53 rooms, most a/c, restaurants (pleasant rooftop), exchange, modern business hotel. **C-D** *Sea Queen*, Beach Rd, T366604, F365854. 25 rooms, 15 comfortable a/c, good restaurant, bar. **D-E** *Alakapuri*, Maulana Md Ali Rd, T723451, F720219. 31 rooms, some in cottage, some spacious a/c with traditional furniture and bath tubs, good South Indian restaurant, bar, exchange, old guest house with character in attractive garden. **D-E** *Malabar Mansion* (KTDC), SM St, T722391, F721593. 30 rooms, some large a/c in modern block (good range), a/c restaurant, beer. **E** *NCK Tourist Home*, Mavoor Rd, above *India Coffee House*, T723530. 54 rooms, some stuffy, some a/c, with bath, good vegetarian restaurant, good value.

Eating **Mid-range**: *Malabar Palace*, International, a/c, excellent food, efficient service. *Casino*, Bank Rd, good continental food. **Cheap**: *India Coffee Houses* on Kallai and Mavoor Rd but breakfast not recommended, *Woodlands*, Mavoor Rd. **Confectionery and Snacks**: *Mammas & Pappas*, French bakery on Beach Rd, and *Royal Cakes* on Bank Rd. Recommended. *Cochin Bakery & Ice cream* at CSI church, serves hot snacks, fresh daily (1500). Recommended. *Tom 'n' Jerry*, Manuelsons Tower, GH Rd. For delicious ice creams.

Entertainment **Sports Yoga**: Kerala Yogasanam, New Rd. Others in Gandhigram and Maulana Md Ali Rd.

Festivals **Feb**: *Utsavam* at Srikantesvara Temple for seven days during Sivaratri week. Elephant processions, exhibitions, fair and fireworks.

Shopping Local handicrafts are rosewood and buffalo horn carvings, coir products and model snake boats. You can also buy good, export quality shirts. Many are open till 2100. *Comtrust*, South Manachira St, sells handwoven textiles (supplied to *Conran* and *Designer's Guild*); you may be able to watch dyeing and weaving in the factory next door. Working conditions and standard of work are excellent; profit goes to the poor and needy. *Supermarket*, Mavoor Rd. **Books**: *TBS*, next to *Malabar Palace Hotel*, good range, recommended; *Pai*, Kallai Rd.

Transport **Local Tourist taxis**, Palayam, T721854; **auto-rickshaws** and SKS Luxury **Buses** from Maulana Md Ali (Jail) Rd. **Long distance Air**: Airport, T712271. Transport to town: pre-paid taxi Rs 250; but from town Rs 35. *Indian Airlines*, Eroth Centre, Bank Rd, T766243, Airport T766056, flies to **Bangalore**, **Mumbai**, **Coimbatore** (except Fri, Sun), **Goa** (Tue, Thu, Sun), **Chennai**, **Madurai** and Bahrain, Sharjah. *Air India*, Bank Rd. **Mumbai** and Middle East (Abu Dhabi, Dubai, Muscat). *Jet Airways*, 29 Mavoor Rd, T356518, Airport T722375, to **Mumbai**. **Road Bus**: KSRTC, T722771, from Mavoor Rd (near Bank Rd junction) to **Bangalore**, **Thiruvananthapuram** (via Thrissur, Ernakulam, Alappuzha, Kollam), 0630-2200 (10 hrs), **Ooty** (see Waynad below), etc. The **New Bus Stand** is further east on Mavoor Rd for private buses to the north including Kannur. Buses to the south go from the **Old Bus Stand** (Palayam). **Train**: Trains to Mangalore (5 hrs), Ernakulam (4½ hrs), Thiruvananthapuram (9½-10 hrs). Also to Chennai and Coimbatore, and **Goa**, *Netravati Exp 6636*, 0910, 11 hrs, *Ernakulam-Lakshadweep Exp 2617*, 1655, 11 hrs); Mon, *Rajdhani Exp 2431*, 0310, 9 hrs and Mumbai up the Konkan Railway line.

Directory **Airline office** *Air Maldives*, T310181. **Banks** exchange at *SBI*, Bank Rd. *State Bank of Travancore*, YMCA Rd. *Computer Centre*, corner of Mavoor Rd. **Communications** *Head Post Office*, near Mananchira. *Central Telegraph Office*: 24-hr ISD and Fax. **Medical services** *Govt Hospital*, T365367. **Tour operators** *Safiya*, Manuelsons Tower, GH Rd, T723370. Recommended.

Kerala

Gt India Tours, League House, Red Cross Rd, T723727. **Tourist offices** *Kerala Tourism*, Govt *Guest House* and Railway Station. *KTDC*, *Malabar Mansion*, SM St, T722391.

There is a very picturesque journey over the Western Ghats to Mysore, 214 km **Waynad** (5½ hours), or to Ooty, through tea and coffee plantations. The road to **Mysore** goes up through Vayittiri (65 km), Kalpatta (9 km) and Mananthavady (30 km) or Sultan's Battery (25 km). There is also a road to **Ooty** via Gudalur.

Kalpatta is good for a coffee or lunch stop. **Sleeping B** *Green Gates*, T 0493-602001. Scenically located on a hillside amid woods, walking distance of town, modern rooms with a/c, TV and baths (hot showers), disappointing restaurant, sit-outs with views, helpful travel desk arranges trips to caves, wildlife sanctuaries and tribal colonies of Waynad, jungle trekking, walks to remote waterfalls and peaks, fishing. Average service, still new and will take time to feel established. **D-E** *Haritagiri*, T602673. A modern building in the heart of town just off the highway, some a/c rooms, good value but a rather noisy location. **E-F** *PPS Tourist Home*, Pinangode Road, T0493-603431, 25 rooms (Rs 150-275). **Eating** Separate good, clean, cheap *Pankaj* Indian restaurant, varied menu, excellent coffee.

About 3 km before **Mananthavady** (Manantoddy) is the Valliyoorkavu or 'fish pagoda', dedicated to Durga. The tank has sacred carp. In Mananthavady: **Sleeping E-F** *Deluxe Tourist Home*, T0493-540307, comfortable rooms with clean Indian toilets, fairly good restaurant. **E-F** *Elite Tourist Home*, Thalassery Road, T0493-540236, rooms, Indian restaurant.

Sultan's Battery (Sulthan Bathery) to the east of Kalpatta was formerly known as Ganapathivattom, 'the fields of Ganapathi'. In the 18th century, Tipu Sultan built a fort here in the heart of the Waynad coffee and cardamom growing region, but not much of it remains. Some 6 km east of the fort is a natural deep crack in the rock on which four inscriptions have been carved and some rough drawings. **Sleeping D-E** *The Resort*, Gandhi Junction, T0493-620358, some a/c rooms, restaurant. **E-F** *Motel Araam* (KTDC), Cheemal Road, T0493-622150, very basic (two-hour rate, Rs 25). There are several **banks**. ■ *Getting there: the road from Sultan's Battery to Gudalur (Tamil Nadu) is very rough, especially across the border and can 2½ hours by bus.*

North to Kannur (Cannanore)

Mahé, a tiny settlement of just 7 sq km, is still a part of Pondicherry, hence once **Mahé** a 'colony of a colony'. Beautifully positioned on a slight hill overlooking the *Phone code: 04983* river, it was named after M Mahé de Labourdonnais, when he captured it for *Colour map 3, grid A2* the French in 1725. Many still speak French and the very French Church of St *Population: 10,450* Theresa celebrates her feast day on 14-15 October. From the neighbouring hill where the Basel Mission house was built are very attractive views of the Waynad hills inland. Mahé's 'tax haven' type status is evident in cheap beer, alcohol and electrical goods; described by one as "a nightmare full of drunks". The beach to the south of town is dirty; to the north is better though neither are safe for bathing due to undercurrents. **Sleeping E-F** *Arena*, Maidan Rd, T332421. Simple, some a/c rooms. **E-F** *Sara*, Station Rd, T332503. Is similar. **F** *Govt Guest House*, near Govt House. Good rooms, good food.

Once a pretty fishing village with a colourful bazar, some visitors find it lacking **Thalassery** atmosphere and rather dirty and crowded. The seashore is interesting when *Phone code: 0497* the fishermen unload their catch in large baskets and spread them out on mats *Colour map 3, grid A2* to sell, attracting a host of eager birds. *Population: 104,000*

Kerala

Thalassery (Tellicherry) was set up by the British East India Company in 1683 to export pepper and cardamom. In 1708 the Company obtained permission to build a fort which, having survived a siege laid by Haidar Ali, is still standing today on a rocky promontory about 15 m above sea level. Its proud little gateway, raised on a flight of steps, is flanked by colourful mustachioed figures. There are some attractive old buildings, some within the Citadel. The Armenian church is rather shabby now but the Catholic church still thrives though the population is largely *Moplah* (Kerala Muslims).

Sleeping and eating B *Ayisha Manzil*, Court Rd, T231590, moosa@ kappadbeachresort.com A mid-19th century, colonial style heritage home overlooking the sea, family run, 6 massive a/c rooms with carved teak/rosewood furniture and antiques, huge baths, lots of British and Malabari memorabilia (planter's chairs, old clocks, colonial china), elaborate Malabari Muslim meals supervised by the owners (each dish explained in detail), fresh sea food, 'Moplah' mutton biryanis, western/south Indian breakfast, 'temple pond' theme pool, views from terraces, excursions (weaving centre, Kannur fort, Theyyam dancing, plantations etc), hard to find so get directions when booking. **E** *Residency*, T324409. Cleanish rooms, some a/c, modern hotel, courteous service, good value. **F** *Ramdev*, Logan's Rd, T3222666. New, central, clean (Rs 200).

Muzhappilangad Beach, 5 km north, is an unspoilt, beautifully picturesque 4 km stretch of golden sand edged by palm trees at the northern end. **Sleeping** *Beach Resort*, 10 minutes' walk west from the main road bus stand, T833471, three double rooms with baths (Rs 200), halfway along the beach, behind the tree line; no refreshments nearby, but development is likely.

Kannur (Cannanore) കണ്ണൂർ

Phone code: 0497
Colour map 3, grid A2

Kannur stands on raised ground with cliffs at the sea face. The coconut fringed coastline has some attractive beaches nearby.

Sights Kannur, the centre of the Moplah community, a group of Arab descent, was also the capital of the North Kolathiri Rajas for several hundred years. Their palace is at **Chirakkal** (6 km). Fort St Angelo was built out of laterite blocks by the Portuguese in 1505 and taken over by the British in 1790 as their most important military base in the south. At the end of the northwest promontory, in the old cantonment area, it is surrounded by the sea on three sides and a dry ditch on its landward side. The highly picturesque **Moplah town** is round the bay to the south of the fort. The attractive **Payyambalam Beach** is just 2 km away.

Sleeping **B-C** *Kamala International*, SM Rd, 500 m rly, T/F766910. 36 rooms, some a/c, over-
& eating priced. **C** *Mascot Beach Resort*, near Baby Beach, Burnassery (2 km from centre), T708445, F701102. Good rooms overlooking the sea (Rs 750+), **B** suites, wide choice in restaurant, friendly, beautifully located, quiet residential area, book ahead. Recommended. Easily best in town. **D-E** *Yatri Nivas* (KTDC), Thavakkara Rd, near Police Club, T700717. Some a/c rooms, basic. **D-E** *Omar's Inn*, opposite railway station, T706313. Some a/c. **E-F** *High Palace*, near the bus stand.

Transport **Train** T705555. To **Mangalore**: *Mangalore Mail, 6001* (AC/II), 1020, 3 hrs; *Thiruvanantha puram-Mangalore Exp, 6349* (AC/CC), 1805, 3 hrs. **Palakkad**: *Kerala-Mangalore Nizamuddin Exp, 2617*, 1340, 5¼ hrs (and **Coimbatore**, 6¼ hrs); *Chennai Mail, 6002* (AC/CC), 1515, 5 hrs (and to **Chennai (MC)** 15½ hrs); **Goa** *Netravati Exp, 6636*, 1130, 8¾ hrs. Mon. *Rajdhani Exp, 2431*, 0510, 7 hrs. **Road Buses**: T707777. To **Kozhikode** (2½ hrs), **Mangalore** (4½ hrs), **Mysore** (6 hrs).

Tourist offices *Kerala Tourism*, *Govt Guest House*, Payyambalam, T506366. *KTDC*, *Motel Araam*; *DTPC*, T506336.

Kasaragod

Phone code: 0499
Population: 50,100

This is the northernmost town in Kerala. From the bus stand, the walk to the sea through a sprawling residential area (mainly Moplah) takes about 30 minutes. The beach stretching northwards is magnificent and deserted. You can walk a long way before scrambling back to the main road, crossing paddy fields, backwaters, and the Konkan railway line. **Sleeping and eating** Near Municipal Bus Stand: **D-E** *City Tower*, MG Rd, T430562, some a/c rooms (Rs 350+), Chinese and Indian restaurant. **E-F** *Enay Tourist Home*, T421164, 32 rooms, attached bath, good value; **F** *Araam* (KTDC), Thalappadi, Kunjathur, T872960, basic rooms, Tourist Information. *Kafiya Restaurant*, MG Rd (west), modest but very good. ■ *Getting there: Frequent buses to Bekal.*

Bekal

Phone code: 0499
Colour map 3, grid A2
16 km N of Kasaragod

En route, the road passes **Ezhimala** (55 km), with a beach and a hill famous for its ayurvedic herbs. Bekal has an ancient **fort**, the largest and best preserved in Kerala, which gives superb views of the coastline. Originally built by the Kadamba kings, the fort passed under the control of Vijayanagar and of Tipu Sultan before being brought into the hands of the East India Company. ■ *0900-1700.* Just outside the fort is the Sri Mukhyaprana Temple. Drinks and snacks are sold nearby. For *theyyam* and *yakshagana* performances contact the Bekal Tourist Office or Resorts Development Corporation, T736937. Bekal also has a beautiful and still undeveloped **beach** which Kerala Tourism talk of turning into a major resort. **Sleeping D-F** *Holiday Inn*, Poinachi, T490411. Rooms vary, some cottages. **F** *Tourist Rest House*, inside the fort (a long hike from the main road), T772090. 2 rooms, good value, book ahead.

Madikeri A beautiful and relatively little used district road runs inland from Kannur up the ghats to Madikeri (see Karnataka), passing through dense forest.

Lakshadweep, Minicoy and Amindivi Islands

Population: 51,700
225–450 W of Kerala
Area: 39,000 sq km
Total land area: 32 sq km

The islands which are classified as a Union Territory make up the Lakshadweep ('100,000 islands') have superb beaches and beautiful lagoons. There are, despite the name, only 11 inhabited and 11 uninhabited islands making up the group. Minicoy, the southernmost island, is 183 km from Kalpeni, its nearest neighbour. Geologically they are the northernmost extensions of the chain of coral islands that extends from the far south of the Maldives. The atolls are formed of belts of coral rocks almost surrounding semi-circular lagoons, with none more than 4 m above sea level. They are rich in guano, deposits of centuries of bird droppings. The wealth of coral formations (includes black coral) attracts a variety of tropical fish – angel, clown, butterfly, surgeon, sweetlip, snappers and groupers. There are also manta and sting rays, harmless sharks and green and hawkbill turtles. At the right time of the year you may be able to watch them laying eggs, the turtles arrive on the beach at night, each laying 100 to 200 eggs in the holes they make in the sand.

Ins & outs

Getting there You can only visit the islands on a package tour as individuals may not book independently. Lakshadweep Tourism's *Society for Promotion of Recreational Tourism and Sports* (SPORTS) and other Tour operators organize package tours. These are listed below. **Climate** Hottest: Mar-May. Summer, max 35°C, min 25°C; Winter, max 32°C, min 20°C. Annual rainfall: 1,600 mm, southwest monsoon mid-May to Sep. Best season: Oct-Mar when tours are conducted.

Permits Everyone needs a permit, for which you need to provide details of the place and date of birth, passport number, date and place of issue, expiry date (or copy relevant pages of your passport) and four photos; apply two months ahead. If you plan to dive, get a doctor's certificate to prove fitness.

History The islands were mentioned by a first century Greek sailor as a source of tortoise shell which was obtained by the Tamils. He had been taken off course by the monsoon winds and discovered a route from the Arab ports to the peninsular coast by chance. The Cheras, Pandyas and Cholas each tried to control the islands, the last succeeding in the 11th century. However, from the beginning of the 13th century the powerful Muslim family of Kannur, the Arakkals, for a time controlled the islands by appointing administrators. After the Treaty of Srirangapatnam in 1792, the southern group was allowed to be administered by the local chiefs. It was only in 1854 that the British East India Company replaced them by *amins*, chosen from the ruling families on the Laccadive Islands. In 1908 a Resident Administrator in Calicut was given authority over the islands. The islands became a Union Territory in 1956 and were renamed **Lakshadweep** in 1973. The original name meant 'one *lakh* (100,000) islands', and referred to the chain including the Maldives to the south. Minicoy retains its Maldivian character even today.

People Up to the 10th century, Hindus from three castes from the Kannur area settled; the groups are distinguishable even today – *Koya* (land owners), *Malmi* (sailors) and *Melachery* (farmers). With the exception of Minicoy, most of the people speak a sort of Malayalam (the language of Kerala). On Minicoy (*Maliku*) the people speak a language close to Dhivehi (of the Maldives), whose ancestors were Buddhists up to the 12th century. The Moplahs of mixed Indian and Arab descent are nearly all Muslims having been converted around the ninth century. Local legend claims that in the middle of the seventh century, Ubeidulla was shipwrecked on Amini Island on returning from pilgrimage to Mecca, and performed miracles which led the population to convert to his faith.

Agriculture & economy Sea fishing (especially tuna), with coconut production provide the main income for the islanders. Palm trees and jack fruit trees abound. Bananas, grains, pulses and vegetables are also grown. There is also some fruit canning and a small amount of dairy and poultry farming. Tourism is the latest industry to take advantage of the islands' unspoilt beauty.

The islands

Foreign tourists may only visit Bangaram & Kadmat Islands; Indians, Kadmat, Kavaratti, Kalpeni & Minicoy. Thinakkara & Cheriyam are being developed

Kavaratti, the administrative capital, is in the centre of the archipelago. The Ajjara and Jamath mosques (of the 52 on the island) have the best woodcarvings and the former has a particularly good ceiling carved out of driftwood; a well within is believed to have medicinal water. The Aquarium with tropical fish and corals, the lake nearby and the tombs are the other sights. The woodcarving in the Ajjara is by superb local craftsmen and masons. **Sleeping** Dak Bungalow, basic, with two rooms and a rest house with four rooms may be reserved through the Administrator, Union Territory of Lakshadweep, Kozhikode 1. Local food from *dhabas*. There is a bank here.

Some of the other islands in the group are **Andratti (Androth)**, one of the largest which was first to be converted to Islam, and **Agatti**, the only one with an airport (which neighbours Bangaram) and also has a beautiful lagoon and 20-bed *Tourist Complex*.

Barren, desolate and tiny, **Pitti** Island comprises a square reef and sand bank at its south end. It is a crucially important nesting place for terns and has now been listed as a wildlife sanctuary. Conservation groups are pressing for a ban on the planting of trees and the mining of coral, but the main risk to the birds is from local fishermen who collect shells and the terns' eggs for food. Nearby **Cheriam** and **Kalpeni** have suffered most from storm damage.

Bangaram is an uninhabited island where the Casino Group *Island Resort* (see Package Tours below).

Kalpeni, with its group of three smaller uninhabited satellite islands, is surrounded by a lagoon rich in corals, which offers excellent watersport facilities including snorkelling and diving. The raised coral banks on the southeast and eastern shores are remains of a violent storm in 1847; the Moidin Mosque to the south has walls made of coral. The islands are reputedly free from crime – the women dress in wrap-around *lungis* (sarongs), wearing heavy gold ornaments here without fear. Villagers entertain tourists with traditional dances, *Kolkali* and *Parichakkali*, illustrating themes drawn from folk and religious legends and accompanied by music. **Sleeping** On Koomel Bay overlooking Pitti and Tilakam islands, the *Dak Bungalow* and *Tourist Huts* provide accommodation.

Minicoy (Maliku), the southernmost and largest, is interesting because of its unique Maldivian character, having become a part of the archipelago more recently. The people speak *Mahl* similar to *Dhivehi* (the script is written right to left) and follow many of their customs; a few speak Hindi. The ancient seafaring people have been sailing long distances for centuries and the consequential dominance of women may have led Marco Polo to call this a 'female island'. Each of the nine closely knit matrilineal communities lives in an *athir* (village) and is headed by a *Moopan*. The village houses are colourfully furnished with carved wooden furniture. Tuna fishing is a major activity and the island has a cannery and ice storage. The superb lagoon of the palm-fringed crescent shaped island is enclosed by coral reefs. Good views from the top of the 50 m lighthouse built by the British. **Sleeping** *Tourist Huts*.

Lakshadweep islands

The **Amindivi** group consists of the northern islands of **Chetlat**, **Bitra** – the smallest (heavily populated by birds, for a long time a rich source of birds' eggs), **Kiltan** where ships from Aden called en route to Colombo, **Kadmat** and the densely populated **Amini**, rich in coconut palms, which was occupied by the Portuguese. **Kadmat**, an inhabited island 9 km long and only 200 m wide, has a beach and lagoon to the east and west, ideal for swimming and diving. The tourist huts shaded by palms are away from the local village. The Water Sports Institute has experienced qualified instructors. **Sleeping** 10 Executive and Tourist *Cottages* and *Youth Hostel* with dorm for 40.

Package tours Tourism is still in its infancy and facilities are limited on the islands you will be allowed to visit. The relatively expensive package tours (the only way to visit) operate from October-May. **NB** Schedules may change, so allow for extra days when booking onward travel. Most tours are monthly from end-January to mid-May.

Essentials

Lakshadweep Tourism (3 packages): Sports, Willingdon Is, Kochi, T0484-668141, F668155. The 3 options cost Rs 6,000-10,000 per person (student discounts), including transport from Kochi. *Kadmat Water Sports*: 6 days (including 2-day sailing, stay in *Kadmat Cottages* or *hostel*). *Coral Reef*: 5 days to Kavaratti, Kalpeni and Minicoy Islands. *Paradise Island Huts*: 6 days to Kavaratti. *Casino Group*: Willingdon Is, Kochi, T0484-666821, F668001, casino@vsnl.com For foreigners: for the resort only, US$250-280 (for 2), $500-600 for 4, $70-100 extra person (high 21 Dec-20 Jan). *Bangaram Island Resort*: T0484-668221, F668001, casino@vsnl.com 30 rooms (8 deluxe huts for 4), palm-matting walls, tiled floors, with modern facilities, open-sided restaurant (buffet meals, varied menu include local specialities often using fish and coconut), bar, library. Kayaks, catamarans and sailing boats are free. For an extra charge: Scuba diving for beginners and the experienced (equipment for hire); deep sea big game fishing from 1 Oct-15 May – only minimal fishing equipment and boat crew; excursion to 3 neighbouring islands or snorkelling at ship wreck (for 8); glass-bottomed boat (for 4). *Lacca Dives*: An environment conscious, experienced outfit, E 20, Everest, Tardeo, Mumbai, T4942023, F4951644, gen@bom2.vsnl.net.in *Katmad Island Scuba Diving*: US$800, 1 Star CMAS Certificate US$30, Certified diver US$25 per dive; accompanying adult $350, child (under 10) US$165. Travel by ship from Kochi (deck class) included; return air from Kochi or Goa to Agatti, US$300; return helicopter (Agatti-Kadmat), 15 mins, US$60, or local *pablo* boat.

Sleeping Accommodation differs on the islands with **Bangaram** having special facilities. On **Kavaratti** and **Kadmat**, basic tourist cottages resemble local huts with tiled roofs and coconut palm matting walls. Each hut has 1 or 2 bedrooms, mosquito nets, fans and attached baths; electricity is wind or diesel generated.

Eating Meals are served on the beach and are similar to Keralan cuisine using plenty of coconut. Breakfast might be *idlis* or *pooris* with vegetables. Lunch and dinner might be rice and vegetable curry, *sambhar*, meat, chicken or fish curry. Vegetarian meals available on request. Bangaram offers an international menu.

Bars Alcohol is available on board ship and on Bangaram Island (tourists are requested not to carry alcohol).

Sports Windsurfing, scuba diving (Poseidon Neptune School), parasailing, waterskiing and snorkelling. Deep sea fishing (barracuda, sailfish, Yellow-fin, travelly) is possible on local boats with crew; serious anglers bring their own equipment. The satellite islands of Tamakara, Parali I and II can be visited for the day. Package Rs 3,500-9,500 per head, ordinary and deluxe and depending on season. Reservation: *TCI*, MG Rd, Ernakulam, Kochi (opposite Kavitha Theatre), or Mumbai office at Chander Mukhi, Nariman Point, or through *Casino Hotel*, Willingdon Island, Kochi, T0484-666821, F668001, casino@vsnl.com

Air Agatti has a basic airport. *Indian Airlines* by 15-seater Dorniers (baggage allowance, 10 kg): **to/from Kochi**, daily except Tue and Sun; to/from Goa: Tue, Sat. 1¼ hrs, $300 return; transfer by *pablo* boat (15 May-15 Sep). **Casino/Taneja** by 5-seater P68C, twice a week. **Sea** MV *Tippu Sultan* sails from Kochi. 26 passengers in 1st and Exec class have 2 and 4-berth a/c cabins with washbasins, shared toilets, Rs 5,000; 120 passengers in 2nd class in reclining seats in a/c halls, Rs 3,500. Ship anchors 30-45 min away from each island; passengers are ferried from there. Total travel time from Kochi can take up to 30 hrs. **Inter-island transfers** are by helicopter (when available) during monsoons, 15 May-15 Sep (return $60), or by *pablo* boats for 8. **Transport**

Hospitals & medical services Agatti has a medical centre; emergencies on the islands have helicopter back-up. **Tour companies & travel agents** Book at least 2 months ahead (see 'Permits' above). **In** Bangalore: *Clipper Holidays*, T5592023, F5599833, clipper@bangalore.wipro.net.in. **Kolkata:** *Ashok Travels*, T2423254, F2420922; *Mercury*, T2423555, F2423713, both in Everest Bldg, 46 JL Nehru Rd. **Chennai:** *Mercury*, 191 Mount Rd, T044-8522993, F8520988. **Kochi:** *SPORTS*, Indira Gandhi Rd, Willingdon Is, T0484-868387, F668647. **Kozhikode:** *Lakshadweep Travels*, 1 Gandhi Rd, T0495-767596. **Mangalore:** *Lakshadweep Foundation*, KSRM Bldg, Lighthouse Hill, T21969. **Mumbai:** *Lakshadweep Travelinks*, Jermahal 1st Flr, Dhobitalo, T022-2054231, F2089282. **New Delhi:** *ITDC*, Kanishka Plaza, 19 Ashok Rd, T011-3325035, F332495; *SITA*, F-12 Connaught Place, T3311133, F3324652. **Directory**

Kerala

Karnataka

6

Karnataka

Karnataka is the state where South and North most truly meet. The open plateau inland of the Ghats has witnessed a constant succession of influences from the north. Its northern districts saw the rise of architectural styles which shaped the distinctive traditions of Chalukyan and Hoysala temples seen at sites around Pattadakal, Belur and Halebid while the capital of the Vijaynagara kings, Hampi, remains as a haunting reminder of further refinement of temple building. Islam too spread its powerful influence to the southernmost towns and cities leaving its own stamp on Muslim architectural treasures.

Today the state's capital, Bangalore, is one of the most rapidly developing cities in India.

★ *A foot in the door*

*Wallk along the banks of the Tungabhadra River at Hampi to the magnificent **Vitthala Temple***

*Visit **Tipu Sultan's palace** at Srirangapatnam and take a coracle ride on the Kaveri*

*Get up early to enjoy the enchanted atmosphere of some of Hinduism's earliest temples at **Badami***

*Spot a tiger or leopard at **Bandipur** or **Mudumalai National Park***

*Climb the bare granite rock of Sravanabelagola to one of Jainism's holiest shrines, the statue of **Sri Gommateshwara***

*Discover the exquisite sculptures covering the **Chennakesava Temple at Belur** en route for the Jain bastis and **Hoysalesvara Temple of Halebid***

*Stay on a coffee plantation on the forested slopes of the Western Ghats in the **Baba Budan Hills***

Background

The land
Population: 45 mn
Area 192,000 sq km

Karnataka is the source of some of India's greatest rivers

The Western Ghats, called the Malnad or hill country, have beautiful forests with waterfalls and wildlife parks. To the east stretches the Mysore Plateau. Three great rivers originate in the Ghats – the *Kaveri* (or Cauvery, as it is still known in Karnataka), the *Tungabhadra*, and the *Krishna*. Some, like the short westward flowing *Sharavati*, have very impressive waterfalls, Jog Falls being one of the highest in the world. Parts of northern Karnataka are barren, rocky and covered with scrub, but the state has a lush coastline. From Coondapur to Karwar, the beautiful estuaries of the short fast-running rivers flowing west from the Ghats still have mangroves, some still in uniquely good condition, although commercial exploitation seriously threatens their survival.

Interior Karnataka is one of India's most pleasant states to visit during the monsoon

Climate The whole of the west coast is extremely wet from June to September, receiving about 1,500 mm in June and July alone. However, immediately to the east of the Western Ghats rainfall decreases dramatically. Temperatures rise to the low 30s°C between February and June but fall slightly during and after the monsoon. On the plateaus of the south, especially around Bangalore and Mysore, temperatures are moderated by the altitude (generally just under 1,000 m), and night temperatures are pleasantly cool through most of the year. The central and northern parts of the state get considerably hotter in April-May, often exceeding 40°C for days at a time. Although the monsoon rains bring cooler weather, humidity increases sharply. On the coast this can be particularly unpleasant, but it is also noticeable inland.

History
Stone Age settlements were scattered along the major river banks

Early history The region between the *Tungabhadra* and the *Krishna* rivers, was home to some of the earliest settlements in peninsular India, over 500,000 years ago. By the Middle Stone Age there was already a regional division appearing between the black cotton soil area of the north and the granite-quartzite plateau of the south. The division appears between the Krishna and Tungabhadra rivers in the modern districts of *Raichur* and *Bellary*. In the north hunters used pebbles of jasper taken from river beds while quartz tools were developed to the south.

The first agricultural communities of the peninsula have also been identified from what is now northern Karnataka. Radiocarbon datings put the earliest of these settlements at about 3,000 BC, and millets and gram were already widely grown by the first millennium BC. They have remained staple crops ever since.

Early kingdoms played a central role in the development of Hindu culture and architecture

The Dynasties Tradition in Karnataka states that *Chandragupta Maurya*, India's first emperor, became a Jain, renounced all worldly possessions and retired to *Sravanabelagola*. Dynasties, rising both from within the region and outside it, exercised varying degrees of control. The *Western Gangas*, from the 3rd to 11th centuries, and the *Banas* (under the Pallavas), from fourth to ninth centuries, controlled large parts of modern Karnataka. The *Chalukyas* of central Karnataka took some of the lands between the Tungabhadra and Krishna rivers in the sixth century and built great temples in Badami. They and the *Rashtrakutas* tried to unite the plateau and the coastal areas while there were Tamil incursions in the south and east. The break-up of the Tamil Chola Empire allowed new powers in the neighbouring regions to take control. In Karnataka the *Hoysalas* (11th-14th centuries) took advantage of the opportunity, and built the magnificent temples at Belur, Halebid and Somnathpur, symbolizing both their power and their religious authority. Then came the

Sangama and Tuluva kings of the *Vijayanagara* Empire, which reached its peak in the mid-16th century, with Hampi as their capital.

Muslim influence Muhammad bin Tughlaq had attacked northern Karnataka in the 13th century. Even during the Vijayanagar period the Muslim sultanates to the north were extending their influence. The Bidar period (1422-1526, see pages 360 and 358) of *Bahmani rule* was marked by wars with Gujarat and Malwa, continued campaigns against Vijayanagara, and expeditions against Orissa. **Mahmud Gawan**, the Wazir of the Bahmani sultanate, seized Karnataka between 1466 and 1481, and also took Goa, formerly guarded by Vijayanagar kings. By 1530 the kingdom had split into five independent sultanates: **Adil Shahis** of Bijapur, the **Qutb Shahi** of Golconda, the **Imad Shahi** of Ahmadnagar, the *Barid Shahi* of Bidar, and the **Imad Shahi** of Berar. From time to time they still came together to defend common interests, and in 1565 they co-operated to oust the Vijayanagar Raja, but Bijapur and Golconda gathered the lion's share of the spoils and they were rapidly succeeded by the Mughals and then the British.

Muslim influence penetrated from the north in the 15th and 16th centuries

The south experienced a different succession of powers. While the Mughals were preoccupied fighting off the Marathas, the **Wodeyar** rulers of Mysore took Srirangapatnam and then Bangalore. They lost control to **Haidar Ali** in 1761, the opportunist commander-in-chief who with French help extended control and made Srirangapatnam his capital. The Mysore Wars followed and with Haidar Ali's, and then his son Tipu Sultan's death, the **British** re-established rule of the Wodeyars in 1799. The Hindu royal family was still administering Mysore up to the reorganization of the states in the 1950s when the Maharaja was appointed State Governor.

Karnataka's role as a border territory was illustrated in the magnificent architecture of the Chalukyan Dynasty from AD 450 to 650. Here, notably in **Aihole**, were the first stirrings of *Brahman* temple design. A mixture of Jain temples illustrates the contact with the north of India which continued to influence the development of the Dravidian temples which grew alongside them. Visiting this small area of North Karnataka it is possible to see examples in Pattadakal alone of four temples built on North Indian '*Nagari*' principles and six built on South Indian '*Dravida*' lines. Nothing could more clearly illustrate the region's position as a major area of contact. That contact was developed through the Hoysalas four centuries later. In **Belur**, **Halebid** and **Somnathpur**, the star-shaped plan of the base and the shrine, with the bell-shaped tower above and exquisitely crafted exterior and interior surfaces became a hallmark of their temples, a distinctive combination of the two traditions. The Vijayanagara kings advanced temple architecture to blend in with the rocky, boulder-ridden landscape at **Hampi**. Flat-roofed pavilions and intricately carved pillars characterized their style. **Bijapur** has some of the finest Muslim monuments on the Deccan, from the austere style of the Turkish rulers to the refinement in some of the pavilions and the world's second largest dome at the Gol Gumbaz.

Art & architecture
Karnataka was at the crossroads of North and South Indian architectural development

People While the **Lingayats** are the dominant caste group in northern Karnataka, a peasant caste, the **Vokkaligas**, is dominant in the south. Their rivalry still runs through Karnataka politics. Karnataka has its share of tribal people. The nomadic *Lambanis* in the north and west, are among several tribal peoples in the hill regions.

Culture

Karnataka

The medieval Kannada poets had a sharply satirical view

Language and literature Most people speak the Dravidian language *Kannada* (Kanarese) although in the north there has been a lot of intermixture with speakers of Indo-Aryan languages. Kannada has the second oldest Dravidian literary tradition. The earliest classic known is *Kavirajamarga* which dates from the ninth century. A treatise on the writing of poetry, it refers to several earlier works which suggests that the language had been in existence for some centuries. Kannada inscriptions dating from fifth and sixth centuries support this view. Early writings in both Telugu and Kannada owe a lot to Jain influence. Kannada made a distinctive contribution in its very early development of prose writing. From the 10th to the 12th centuries a mixed poetry and prose form was developed by the writers *Pampa*, *Ponna* and *Ranna* – the 'three gems of Kannada literature'. Towards the end of the 12th century the Saivite saint **Basavanna** started a new Hindu renaissance and founded Virosivism. He disliked Brahmins and didn't believe in transmigration of souls; he didn't support child marriages or the veto on widow-remarriage. His sect, the reforming Lingayats, used simple rhythmic prose, the *vachanas*, to spread its teaching. Jordens gives the following example:

> "Oh pay your worship to God now
> before the cheek turns wan, and the neck is wrinkled, and the body shrinks
> before the teeth fall out and the back is bowed, and you are wholly dependent on others
> before you need to lean on a staff, and to raise yourself by your hands on your thighs
> before your beauty is destroyed by age and Death itself arrives.
> Oh now worship Kudala-sangama-deva."

The Hindu-Sanskrit tradition was greatly strengthened by the rise of the Vijayanagar Empire. One of their greatest kings, **Krishna Deva Raya** (ruled 1509-29), was also a poet in Telugu and Sanskrit. From the 16th century onwards Vaishnavism produced a rich crop of devotional songs though after the fall of the Vijayanagar Empire, the quality of literature declined. Muslim power encouraged Hindu art forms almost to go underground, and expressions of Hindu devotion and faith became associated with song and dance for popular entertainment – the *Yakshagana* in Kannada, and the remarkable *Kathakali* in Kerala (see page 221).

Staged theatre was an important part of village culture

Dance, drama and music Open-air folk theatre or *Bayalata* of Karnataka has developed from religious ritual and is performed in honour of the local deity. The plays evolve and are improvised by the actors on an informal stage. The performances usually start at night and often last into the early hours. The famous *Yakshagana* or *Parijata* usually has a single narrator while the other forms of Bayalata have four or five, assisted by a jester. The plots of the *Dasarata* which enacts several stories and *Sannata* which elaborates one theme, are taken loosely from mythology but sometimes highlight real-life incidents and are performed by a company of actors and actresses. There is at least one star singer and dancer in each company and a troupe of dancers who not only perform in these dance-dramas but are also asked to perform at religious festivals and family celebrations.

The *Doddata* is less refined than the *Yakshagana* but both have much in common, beginning with a prayer to the god Ganesh, using verse and prose and drawing from the stories of the epics *Ramayana* and *Mahabharata*. The costumes are very elaborate with fantastic stage effects, loud noises and war cries and vigorous dances. It all amounts to a memorable experience but requires stamina as they continue all night!

Government The 19 districts are grouped into four divisions – Bangalore, Mysore, Belgaum and Gulbarga. The state legislature, which has its assembly hall, the remarkable Vidhana Soudha, in Bangalore, has a legislative assembly of 208 directly elected members and a legislative council of 63 indirectly elected members. The Chief Minister is assisted by a council of ministers.

Modern Karnataka

Assembly elections on 5 October 1999 saw the Congress return to power at the expense of the Janata Dal. Benefiting from being re-united after their earlier splits the Congress defied national trends and reduced the BJP and other parties to the role of a minor opposition. Caste rivalry between Vokkaligas and Lingayats remains a powerful factor in the state's politics, and faction fighting within the parties has been a recurrent theme, so despite its large majority of over half the Assembly's seats the key question is how long the Congress can hold together.

★ Bangalore and the Maidan

Bangalore takes many first time visitors by surprise. The state capital and India's sixth largest city, its reputation as a 'garden city' has survived the dynamic growth of computer and high-tech industries which have given it the reputation as an Indian Silicon Valley. The buzz around Brigade Road's shopping malls, cyber cafés and 'pubs' give it a more modern, open feel than many other Indian cities. Set at an altitude of over 1000 m, its climate adds to its attractions as a place for a relaxing break.

Phone code: 080
Colour map 3, grid A4
Population: 4.09 mn
Altitude: 920 m

Karnataka

Getting there Bangalore's airport is 9 km from the Westernized Mahatma Gandhi/Brigade Road area which has the bigger hotels. There are airport buses, autos and pre-paid taxis into town. 5 km west of MG Road, the main City Station and the busy but well organized bus stations are in Gandhi Nagar with most of the budget accommodation. For hotels in Sivaji Nagar and the MG Road area, it is best to get off at the Cantonment Station. **Getting around** Bangalore is very spread out and you need transport to get around. In the Cubbon Park area in the centre, you will find the tourist office and museums, with MG Road to its east which is very pleasant to wander round with good shops and eating and drinking places. The Old City with its busy bazars is south of the City Station.

Ins & outs

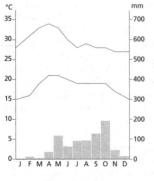

Climate: Bangalore
Best time to visit: Nov-Mar

Kempe Gowda, a Magadi chieftain (1513-69) founded Bangalore (Bengaluru) in 1537, building a mud fort and marking the limits of the city by his four watch towers. His statue stands in front of the City Corporation buildings. It was extended and fortified by **Haidar Ali** and **Tipu Sultan**. When the British gained control after 1799 they installed the *Wodeyar* of Mysore as the ruler and the Rajas developed it into a major city. In 1831 the British took over the administration for a period of 50 years, making it

The city

a spacious garrison town, planting impressive avenues and creating parks, building comfortable bungalows surrounded by beautiful lawns with tennis courts, as well as churches and museums. When the Wodeyars returned they handed over the cantonment area to the British, and only after Independence were the city and cantonment areas amalgamated.

Sights The **Bull Temple** at Basavanagudi in the southwest was built in the Kempe Gowda period in mid-16th century. The monolithic *Nandi* bull is believed to have grown in size and now measures nearly 5 m in height and over 6 m in length! It is made of grey granite polished with a mixture of groundnut oil and charcoal. Nearby is one of Kempe Gowda's four towers.

The **Kempe Gowda Fort** on Krishnarajendra Road, was built of mud in 1537 and was rebuilt in stone two centuries later by Tipu Sultan (not open to the public).

Tipu's Summer Palace to the south was started by Haidar Ali and completed by his son Tipu Sultan in 1789. Based on the Daria Daulat Bagh in Sriranga-patnam, the two-storeyed ornate structure has a substantial amount of wood with walls and ceilings painted in brilliant colours with beautiful carvings. A museum traces the period of Haidar Ali and Tipu Sultan. ■ *0800-1800.*
The **Venkataramanasvami Temple** is in the Dravida style which, when the Wodeyar Dynasty was restored at the end of the 18th century, the new Maharajah is believed to have worshipped in first, before entering the palace.

Bangalore Palace The grand palace of the Mysore Maharajahs, visibly but improbably inspired by Windsor Castle, is only open to the public for a week around 1 November.

Museums **Government Museum**, Kasturba Gandhi Road, Cubbon Park. Opened in 1886, one of the oldest in the country, has 18 galleries including Neolithic finds from the Chandravalli excavations, and from the Indus Valley, especially Moenjodaro antiquities. Also antique jewellery, textiles, coins, art (especially miniature paintings) and geology. ■ *1000-1700, closed Mon. Small entry fee.*
The **Venkatappa Art Gallery** next door, displays the works of the Karnataka painter. **Visveswaraya Industrial and Technological Museum**, Kasturba Gandhi Road, next to Museum. ■ *1000-1700, closed Mon.* The **Trade Centre** next door has a permanent exhibition of what the state produces.

Parks & zoos **Lalbagh Gardens** The superb Botanical Gardens were laid out by Haidar Ali in 1760; Tipu Sultan added a wealth of plants and trees from many countries. There are over 1,800 species of tropical, subtropical and medicinal plants and a Floral Clock. The Glass House holds temporary exhibitions. There is a Kempe Gowda Tower (1537) here. *Flower Shows* in Republic Day (26 January) and Independence Day (15 August) weeks. ■ *0800-2000. Allow 2 hrs.*

Cubbon Park in the Cantonment dates from 1864. Fountains, a bandstand and statues were added, together with official buildings including the High Court, State Library and museums. The **Vidhan Soudha** is a post Independence granite building in the neo-Dravida style which houses the State Legislature and Secretariat; the Cabinet Room has a huge sandalwood door (get permission to see it after office hours). The **Aquarium** on Kasturba Gandhi Road has a good freshwater collection. Outside is a fish restaurant and fresh fish stalls. ■ *Tue-Sun, 0900-1715; Sun 1000-1830. Small fee.*
The ISKCON temple, enshrining the deities Krishna-Balarama and Gaura Nitai, is located on 'Hare Krishna Hill', 1 R Block, Chord Road, Rajaji Nagar, northwest of town. It is a striking architectural blend of traditional and modern. ■ *0700-1300, 1600-2030. Free. Frequent buses from the City Station and Sivaji Nagar.*

Karnataka Tourism tours from Badami House, NR Square, T2275883: *Bangalore City Sightseeing*: Tipu's Palace, Bull Temple, Lalbagh, Ulsoor Lake, Vidhan Soudha, Museums, also stops at Government Emporia. Half-day, 0730-1400 and 1330-1930. Rs 85. Recommended.

Tours
"You may get a lot of temples at the expense of other sites".

There is a large choice of trips out of the city. **1-day** *Sravanabelagola, Belur and Halebid*, Friday, Sunday (except monsoons), 0715-2200, Rs 300; *Mysore* daily, 0715-2245, Rs 220-280 including meals; *Tirupati* , **2-day** Rs 400, **3-day** Rs 630. **3-day** *Tungabhadra Dam and Hampi*, Friday, Rs 675; *Ooty and Mysore*, Monday and Friday, October-January.

Details and prices change, so please check

Whitefield 16 km east of Bangalore on the airport road, Whitefield is known for the Sai Baba Ashram at 'Brindavan'. It also has the International Technical Park, a modern self-contained community of high tech workers.

Excursions

Bannerghatta National Park 21 km south on Anekal Road, has a lion and tiger 'safari' in a caged area, a crocodile and snake farm and offers elephant rides. Picturesque scenery and a temple. ■ *0900-1700, closed Tue. Entry Rs 15; foreigners Rs 150, (some think too high to see "a few big cats in cages"), camera Rs 10, video Rs 50*

Wildlife The 'safari' includes caged tiger, lion, bison, elephant and crocodiles. The park proper also harbours deer, wild boar, leopards (rarely spotted) and a good variety of birds. Viewing is by jeep or bus accompanied by guides; you may see little 20 minutes and photograph even less through the windows. *Mayura Vanashree Restaurant*, T8428542. ■ *Getting there*: *bus No 366 from City Market, 365 from City Bus Stand, 368 from Sivajinagar.*

Essentials

Several hotels are clustered around the MG Rd area near the centre with restaurants, cinemas and shops nearby. **Power cuts** are common so carry a torch (flashlight). Ask for quiet rooms away from the street and not close to generators.

Sleeping
Luxury hotels can add 25% in taxes & charge prohibitive rates for use of pools by non-residents

L *Oberoi*, 37-39 MG Rd, T5585858, F5585960. 130 superb rooms with private sit-outs, attractively landscaped Japanese gardens but disappointing food in garden restaurant. **L** *Taj Residency*, 41/3 MG Rd (Trinity Circle), T5584444, F5584748. 162 rooms, balconies with bougainvilleas, good Indian restaurant, excellent Chinese lunch buffets,bookshop sells foreign newspapers. **L** *West End* (Taj), Race Course Rd, near rly, T2255055, F2200010. 135 rooms, rooms around lawn better than in newer block,*Old World* rooms near entrance "dismal" so view first, superb lawns, excellent outdoor restaurants, pool (non-residents, Rs 500). Highly recommended. **L-AL** *Windsor Manor* (Welcomgroup), 25 Sankey Rd, T2269898, F2264941. 8 km rly, 140 rooms (expensive suites), excellent restaurants (delicious Indian buffet, Chinese "perfect", superb atmosphere, faultless service. Highly recommended. **L-A** *Central Park*, 47 Dickenson Rd, off MG Rd, T5584242, F5588594. 130 rooms, 'American style', very plush, creole and continental food, live jazz Wed-Sat **AL** *Ashok* (ITDC), Kumara Krupa High Grounds (get off at Cantt station if travelling by train), T2269462, F2250033. 187 comfortable rooms (baths could be better), spacious grounds, avoid rooms immediately below *Mandarin Restaurant* for a quiet evening, good pool (non-residents Rs 300), all rather soulless, good service (after tip!). **AL** *Le Meridien* (was *Holiday Inn*), 28 Sankey Rd, T2262233, F2267676. 201 luxury rooms, excellent service.

A *Gateway* (Taj), 66 Residency Rd, T5584545, F5584030. 96 a/c rooms, 6 km rly, excellent South Indian *Karavalli* restaurant (about Rs 300), *Potluck café*. **A** *Kensington Terrace* (Quality Inn), Kensington Rd, T5594666, F5594029. 107 rooms, comfortable, with 'garden' features on terraces, adequate for a city stop. **A** *St Mark's*, 4/1 St Mark's Rd,

■ *on maps, pages 296 & 299 Price codes: see inside front cover*

Karnataka

Bangalore city

Related map
A MG Road,
page 299

■ **Sleeping**
1 Ajantha
2 Ashok
3 Bangalore International
4 Central Park
5 Comfort Inn
6 Geo
7 Harsha

8 Holiday Inn
9 Janardhana
10 Kensington Terrace
11 Mahaveer & Handicrafts
12 Oberoi
13 Pushpamala, Sukh Sagar
& Kamat Café

14 Ramanashree & Noodles
Restaurant
15 Sandhya Lodge
16 Shoba Lodge
17 Taj Residency
18 Taj Westend &
Chalukma Restaurant
19 Vellara

T2279090, F2275700, stmarks@vsnl. com 94 a/c rooms, restaurants, no pool. **A-B** *Ivory Tower*, Penthouse (12th) Flr of Barton Centre, 84 MG Rd, T5589333, F5588697, ivoryhor@satyam.net.in 22 comfortable, spacious rooms (huge beds!), stunning views over city, spotless, excellent value if you like heights, friendly. Recommended. **A-B** *Ramana- shree Comfort*, 16 Raja Rammohan Roy Rd, near Richmond Circle, T2235250 F2221214. 68 rooms (a/c not always effective), Chinese restaurant, friendly service (may give discounts). **A-B** *Vijay Residency*, (Comfort Inn), 18, III Main Rd, near rly and City Bus Station, T2203024, F2281065. 47 very comfortable rooms, good restaurant (no alcohol), very friendly.

B *Bangalore International*, 2A-2B Crescent Rd, T2268011. 72 renovated rooms, restaurant with live music, looks promising. **B** *Nahar Heritage*, 14 St Mark's Rd, T2278731, F2278737. 48 rooms, friendly service, very good restaurant, good value. Recommended. **B-C** *Harsha*, 11 Venkataswamy Naidu Rd (Park Rd), Shivajinagar, T2865566, F2865943. 80 clean rooms, 40 a/c, restaurants, bar, exchange, pool. **B-C** *Highgates*, 33 Church St, T5597172, F5597799. 40 rooms, *Palms* seafood restaurant (gives aphrodisiac rating out of five hearts!), very modern, light airy, pleasant atmosphere, friendly, good value.

C *Algate*, 93 Residency (Brigade Rd crossing), T5594786, algate@blg.vsnl.net.in 30 quiet, a/c rooms, modern. **C** *Rama*, 40/2, Lavelle Rd (off MG Rd) near Cubbon Park, T2273381, F2214857, hotelrama@vsnl. com 55 a/c rooms, restaurant and bar on 1st Flr, good food but 'disco' music, shabby exterior though pleasant inside with good clean rooms, Indian business hotel, good value (breakfast included). **C-D** *Geo*, 11 Devganga Rd (near Richmond Circle), T2220494 F2221993. 71 rooms, modern bath, restaurant slow but reasonable food, clean business hotel. **C-D** *Nilgiris Nest*, 171 Brigade Rd, T5588401, F5582853. 24 rooms, 5 a/c on upper floor, very central, restaurant, exchange, supermarket below, busy

Karnataka

location, clean, comfortable, good value. **D** *Pulikeshi*, 168/29 5th Cross, Gandhinagar, T2269727. 22 very clean rooms, some a/c, very quiet, friendly. Recommended. **B-D** *Woodlands*, 5 Raja Rammohan Roy Rd, T2225111, F2236963. 240 rooms, some a/c and cottages, with attached baths and fridge, good a/c restaurant, bar, coffee shop, exchange, large but pleasant Indian style hotel, good value. **D** *Brindavan*, 40 MG Rd, T5584000. 112 spacious rooms with shower, some **C** a/c, superb *thali* restaurant, fairly quiet, non a/c good value. Recommended.

D-E *Ajantha*, 22A MG Rd (7 km, City rly), T5584321. 62 spacious rooms some a/c and cottages with wc (no showers), restaurant (South Indian vegetarian), very helpful, good information. **E** *Janardhana*, Kumara Krupa High Grounds, T2254444. 58 good size rooms, spartan but clean, restaurant (South Indian), popular Indian business hotel. **D** *Vellara*, 283 Brigade Rd, T5369116. 36 immaculate and spacious rooms with TV (top floor best), excellent value and location. Recommended. **E** *Imperial*, 93-94 Residency Rd.T 5588391. 20 clean rooms with bath, good location, good value. **E** *New Central Lodge*, 56 Infantry Rd, at the Central St end, T5592395. 35 simple, clean enough rooms, some with bath, hot water (0500-1000). In **Gandhi Nagar**: the '*Majestic*' Cinema area is good for budget accommodation. Hotels here are quieter and less likely to be full than on MG Rd. **E** *Mahaveer*, 8/9 Tank Bund Rd, opposite bus station, near City rly station, T2873670, F2870735. 44 smallish rooms, 5 a/c, modern 5-storey hotel, clean, basic, front rooms can be very noisy, larger **D** deluxe rooms at back quieter. **E** *Pushpamala*, 9, 2nd Cross, SC Rd (neon sign stands out above others), T2874010, opposite Bus Station, travel agent. Clean, good value and surprisingly quiet. **E** *Railway Retiring Rooms*, 23 rooms cheaper dorm for passengers in transit. **E** *Sandhya Lodge*, 70 SC Rd. T2874065, F2874064. 100 good, rooms with bath, train reservations **F** *Shoba Lodge*, 5th Main, Gandhinagar, T2263290. Indian toilet and shower/tap, vegetarian restaurant.

Hostels E *YWCA*, 40 Mission Rd, T2277334. Basic rooms with bath, open to both sexes. **E-F** *YMCA* (City), Nrupathunga Rd, near Cubbon Park, T2211848. None too clean, avoid rooms overlooking badminton court, but great atmosphere, excellent café. **F** *YHA Guest House* and Programme Centre. Contact Mr Sridhara, KFC Bldg, 48 Church St, T5585417, F2261468.

Eating
Try the local Kannada chicken & Maddur vada

■ *on maps, pages 296 & 299*

Expensive: *Cosmo*, Magrath Rd. Good "fusion" food, anything from burritos to lamb bourgignon to pad Thai.*Rice Bowl*, Lavelle Rd, T5587417. Chinese, Tibetan. Large portions. *Shezan*, Lavelle Rd (behind *Airlines* Hotel). Steaks highly recommended. *Tycoons*, 83 Infantry Rd, T5591356. International, with garden seating. Recommended. **Mid-range**: Buffet lunches at *Windsor Manor*, *Ashok's* **Mandarin Room** (for Chinese) and the barbecue at the *West End* are recommended.*Amarvathi*, 45/3 Residency Rd. Spicy south Indian.*Blue Fox*, 80 MG Rd, Shrungar Complex. *Chungwah*, 43 Church St. Chinese specialities. *Coconut Grove*, Church St. Varied and good southern menu (Chettinad, Keralan and Kodagan), beers, sit out under shade.*Koshy's*, 39 St Mark's Rd. International, pleasant, old-fashioned, atmospheric, licensed. *Earthen Oven*, 76, Residency Rd. Chicken tikka etc. Minimalist décor – room looks upside down but the food's good. *Kwality's*, 44 Brigade Rd. *Prince's*, 9 Brigade Rd, 1st Flr, with *Knock Out Disco* next door.*Ramanashree Comfort*. Good food especially Chinese at *Noodles*. **Cheap**: *Ballal Residence* Hotel, 74/4 III Cross, Residency Rd, T5597277. Indian, a/c *Palmgrove* serves excellent giant lunch *thalis* Rs 75, "super atmosphere, surrounded by Indian families and businessmen". *Blue Nile*, Church St. Tasty north Indian and tandoori. *Gautam*, 17 Museum Rd. Excellent south Indian veg restaurant and juice bar. Spacious and comfortable.*Rock Garden*, Infantry Rd. Small range of lunches between 1230-1500 for next to nothing *Roomalee*, next to *Highgates Hotel*. Open air, hole-in-the-wall joint. Very good, very cheap *rajma*, *channa* and not much

Karnataka

else. *Sapna*, Residency Rd. Good, quick, clean business lunches but avoid very cold, dark and gloomy a/c Ladies' Room. *Sukh Sagar*, near Majestic Cinema, 6 SM Rd, 3 floors. Each serving different style of food, fresh fruit juice, excellent South Indian *thalis* and Chinese snacks, very clean, modern, a/c. *Tandoor*, 28 MG Rd, for North Indian specialities.

Vegetarian: *Chalukma*, Race Course Rd, by *West End Hotel*. Excellent vegetarian. Many *Darshini* outlets for fresh, cheap south Indian snacks. *Kamat* , near Majestic Cinema. Good range of *thalis*. *Ullas*, MG Rd, 1st Floor verandah restaurant. Very good Indian and Chinese vegetarian, snacks, sweets. Tasty, excellent service, inexpensive and very popular.

M G Road area

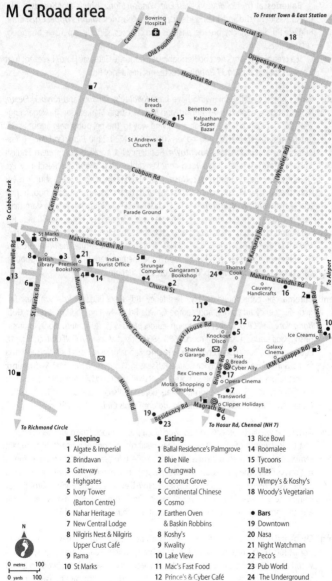

Karnataka

N

| 0 metres | 100 |
| 0 yards | 100 |

■ Sleeping	● Eating	13 Rice Bowl
1 Algate & Imperial	1 Ballal Residence's Palmgrove	14 Roomalee
2 Brindavan	2 Blue Nile	15 Tycoons
3 Gateway	3 Chungwah	16 Ullas
4 Highgates	4 Coconut Grove	17 Wimpy's & Koshy's
5 Ivory Tower	5 Continental Chinese	18 Woody's Vegetarian
(Barton Centre)	6 Cosmo	
6 Nahar Heritage	7 Earthen Oven	● Bars
7 New Central Lodge	& Baskin Robbins	19 Downtown
8 Nilgiris Nest & Nilgiris	8 Koshy's	20 Nasa
Upper Crust Café	9 Kwality	21 Night Watchman
9 Rama	10 Lake View	22 Peco's
10 St Marks	11 Mac's Fast Food	23 Pub World
	12 Prince's & Cyber Café	24 The Underground

Related map
A Bangalore city,
page 296

Cafés and fast food: *Casa Piccola*, Devatha Plaza, 131 Residency Rd. Pizzas, burgers, steaks, ice cream desserts, "excellent food, very good hygiene, European coffee house atmosphere". Highly recommended ('*Raga*' – good gift shop next door). *Indiana Fast Foods*, 9 St Patrick's Complex, Brigade Rd. Serves American fast foods. *Kentucky Fried Chicken*, Brigade Rd, "a great escape from Indian food!", serves vegetarian too, clean, safe ice creams, salads. *Lake View*, MG Rd. Sandwiches, pizza, shakes, ice cream. *Mac's Fast Food*, Church St. Separate section for women and families, disappointing food, cleanish toilets. *Pizza Hut*, Cunningham Rd and *Spencer's Café*, outside Spencer's supermarket, MG Rd. For varied pizzas. *Wimpy* nearby, quite expensive but good (especially vegetarian). *YMCA*, near Cubbon Park, has an excellent cheap a/c café.

Bakeries: at *Taj, Holiday Inn, West End, Windsor Manor* hotels. *Hot Breads*, Infantry Rd, Residency Rd and 44 Brigade Rd. Good for pastries. *Nilgiri's Upper Crust Café*, Brigade Rd. Sells snacks, breads, pastries and cheeses, slightly expensive but good, clean toilets.

Ice cream: The city's best on Residency Rd, opposite Gateway Hotel. Excellent fruit ices and shakes. *Baskin 31 Robbins* icecreams, Residency Rd.

Bars & pubs

Bars open from 1900-2300, but some open 1100-2300

Larger hotels and the following have bars: *Kwality's*, *Tandoor* and *Khyber*, *Fiesta*, MSIL Complex, opposite HAL Airport, and *Napoli*, Gupta Market, Gandhi Nagar. English style pubs once very popular, are giving way to 'theme' pubs; beer about Rs 35; lunches at some from Rs 85. Most open 1000-1430, 1730-2300. *Black Cadillac*, 50 Residency Rd. American style. *Downtown*, Residency Rd. Looks like a modern English pub, nice atmosphere, 2 crowded snooker tables. *Pub World*, 65 Residency Rd. Draught beer, videos, loud music. *Nasa*, 1/4 Church St. Built like a space shuttle (beer from the Fuel Tank), laser show, latest Western dance sounds, videos, loud, trendy (check bill). *Night Watchman*, 46/1 Church St. Excellent nightspot, Tequila slammers, superb music, "you can let your hair down here". *Pecos*, Rest House Rd/Brigade Rd. Small and crowded, great music and vibe, best for Blues. Recommended. *Purple Haxe*, 17/1 Residency, opp Black Cadillac. New style theme venue. *The Underground*, 65 Bluemoon Complex, MG Rd. London Tube theme, draught beer, disco, popular, very good service but turn up 'properly dressed'. Recommended.

Entertainment

Cinema: air conditioned:*Galaxy*, Residency Rd, *Rex*, Brigade Rd, *Santosh*, Brigade-Residency Rd corner, and Kempe Gowda Rd, show English films. **Sports Golf**: *Bangalore Golf Club*, Sankey Rd, foreign visitors pay US$35. New International Championship Golf Course, near the airport. 0600-1800, closed Mon. *KGA Golf Club* charges Rs 200 weekdays, Rs 400 weekends. **Horse racing**: Bangalore is famous for racing and stud farms. *Bangalore Turf Club*, Race Course Rd; season May-Jul and Nov-Mar. **Swimming**: expect to pay Rs 500 for pools in hotels (eg *Ashok, West End,Windsor Manor*). Pools at Corp Office, near Square, Kensington Park Rd, near Ulsoor Lake, Sankey Tank, Sadhiv Nagar, Jayanagar 3rd Block. **Tennis**: *Bangalore Tennis Club*, Cubbon Park.

Festivals

Apr: *Karaga*, Sakti (Mother Goddess) worshipped as Draupadi, the daughter of Fire. To test their strength of character, devotees balance pots on their heads. In the main temple procession, held on a moonlit night, a priest dresses as a woman and carries a pot on his head. The procession includes a number of followers – *Veerakumars* – who wave swords in the air in a vigorous display. **Nov-Dec**: *Kadalekaye Parishe* (Groundnut Fair) at the Bull Temple includes a groundnut eating competition. It marks the harvest and the farmers' first collection is offered to the *Nandi*. Buses 34 and 37.

Shopping

Shops and markets open early and close late (about 2000) though they remain closed from 1300-1600. Local specialities include brass, copper, soapstone statues, sandalwood and rosewood carvings and coloured wood inlay work. Sandalwood oils and soaps, incense sticks, lacquer work, ceramics, carpets. Also fabrics (silk, cotton,

Karnataka

georgette), watches and silver jewellery. On MG Rd (many in Public Utility Bldg): *Central Cottage Emporium*, *Manjusha*, *Cauvery*, and *Shrungar*. *Mota Shopping Complex* on Brigade Rd; *Central Cottage Industries* Cunningham Rd; *Khadi Gramudyog*, Silver Jubilee Park Rd, near City Market; *UP Handlooms*, 8 Mahaveer Shopping Complex, Kempe Gowda Rd; *Raga*, A-13, Devatha Plaza, 131 Residency Rd, for very attractive gifts. **Art**: *Shakshi* gallery, Presidency, 82 St Marks Rd, for contemporary shows. **Books**: *Gangarams*, 72 MG Rd, has a wide ranging and expanding collection. *International Book House*, 97 Residency Rd. *Premier*, 46/1 Church St (and Museum Rd), small, with a good selection of specialist and academic books (best Wodehouse collection anywhere!), helpful owner. **Markets**: to see a colourful local market with plenty of atmosphere, selling fruit, vegetables and flowers, try *City Market* southeast of the station or *Russell Market*, Sivaji Nagar. **Silk and sarees**: *Deepam*, MG Rd, reasonable prices, helpful assistants. *Janardhana*, Unity Bldg, JC Rd. *Karnataka Silks Industries*, Gupta Market, Kempe Gowda Rd. *Mysore Silk Showroom*, Leo Complex, MG Rd. *Vijayalakshmi*, Kempe Gowda Rd, will also make shirts.

Bharat, St Mark's Rd, T2212251. *Clipper Holidays*, 4 Magrath Rd, T5592023, F5599833, clipper@bangalore.wipro.net.in Tours, treks (everything provided), Kerala backwaters etc. Very helpful and efficient. *Indo Asia Tours, 102 Skylark Residency, Wind Tunnel Rd, T5273108, tours may also be abroad. Regal Holidays*, 105/17 8th Cross, RMV Extn, T3314566, F3340171, regal@giasbg01.vsnl.net.in royal connections, culture, wildlife, horse safaris (Rs 4000 a day).*Sita*, St Mark's Rd, T2212826. *Thomas Cook*, 55 MG Rd, T5594168 (foreign exchange and travellers' cheques) and 70 MG Rd (all services), T5586439, F5588036. *Trade Wings*, 48 Lavelle Rd, T2214595, F221161.

Tour operators

Local Auto-rickshaws: metered, widely available, surcharge 15%, ask for card. **Bus**: City buses run a frequent and inexpensive service throughout the city. **Taxis**: at Rly stations **City Taxis**: dial-a-cab service, T5539999, for reliable, prompt pick-up, minimum Rs 30 (about Rs 8 per km). **Private car hire**: firms for city and out-of-town sightseeing. *Cab Service*, Sabari Complex, Residency Rd, T5586121; *Europcar*, T2219502 F2225645. *Hertz* T5599408, F5584759. *Karnataka STDC* (See Directory). About Rs 600-800 for 8 hrs or 80 km; extra km Rs 4-7. Out-of-town, Rs 1,200 (Rs 2,000 a/c).

Transport

Long distance Air: Transport to town: (9-14 km) taxi, 20 mins, Rs 150-200 (pre-paid taxi vans are expensive); auto-rickshaw, Rs 80. KSRTC coach from airport to major hotels, MG Rd and bus station, Rs 40. To airport: special bus leaves from Sivajinagar Stop (near *Hotel Harsha*). *Indian Airlines* and *Alliance Air*, Cauvery Bhavan, Kempe Gowda Rd, T2211914, airport T5266233. **Chennai, Delhi, Goa, Hyderabad, Kochi, Mangalore, Mumbai, Thiruvananthapuram.** *Jet Airways*, 1-4 M Block, Unity Bldg, JC Rd, T2276620, airport T5261926: **Delhi, Hyderabad, Mumbai.** *Sahara*: Church St, T5586976, airport T5262531. Flies twice daily to Delhi and Mumbai. *Air India* flies weekly to **Jakarta**.

Road Bus: **City Bus Station**, opposite the City Rly Station, is extremely busy but well organized. **Central (KSRTC) Bus Station** is just to the south, T2871261. Karnataka (KSRTC), Andhra (APSRTC) and Tamil Nadu (TTC) run efficient, frequent and inexpensive services to all major cities in South India. Frequent service to Mysore (3 hrs); several to Hassan (4 hrs), Hyderabad, Madikeri (6 hrs), Madurai (9 hrs), Mangalore (9 hrs), Ooty (7 hrs), Puttaparthi (4-5 hrs, Rs 65), Tirupati (6½ hrs). Private operators' Deluxe or Ordinary coaches are usually more comfortable though a bit more expensive. They operate from the City and Kalasipalyam Bus Stations.

Video coaches can be noisy & very tiring

Train Pre-paid taxi service available at City Station. Auto-rickshaw to MG Rd, Rs 15. Enquiries and reservations, T132; arrival and departure, T133. City Rly Station, Computerized Advance Reservations in newer building on right of entrance; No 14 is

Karnataka

Karnataka

Foreigners' Counter (also for disabled). If you are booking a ticket for a journey out of the Southern Region go to 1st Flr booking office and join the queue for your region; no special queue for foreigners on the 1st Flr. Cantt Station, T135. Disembark at Cantt Station for some hotels. **Chennai**: *Shatabdi Exp, 2008*, daily except Tue, 1620, 5 hrs; *Lalbagh Exp, 2608*, 0630, 5¼ hrs; *Brindavan Exp 2640* (AC/CC), 1430, 6 hrs; *Bangalore-Chennai Exp 6024* (AC/II), 0815, 7 hrs. **Goa** (Londa): *Bangalore Mumbai Exp, 1018*, Mon, Tue, Sat, 0600, 11 hrs; *Bangalore Miraj Express 6589*, 1930, 11 hrs. **Hospet**: *Hampi Exp, 6592*, 2200, 10 hrs. **Hyderabad/Secunderabad**: *Bangalore Secunderabad Exp, 7086* (AC/II), 1705, 13½ hrs. **Maddur, Srirangapatnam** and **Mysore** *Tipu Express 6206*, 1425, 2½ hrs; or **Mysore**: *Shatabdi Exp*, daily except Tue, 1100, 2 hrs (for a/c, Rs 180). **Mumbai (VT)**: *Udyan Exp 6530* (AC/II), 2030, 24 hrs. **Thiruvananthapuram**: *Kanniyakumari Exp*, 6526 (AC/II), 2000, 18¼ hrs; from Krishnarajapuram, *Rajkot Trivandrum Exp*, 1720, 19½ hrs.

Directory **Airline offices** *Air India*, Unity Bldg, JC Rd, T2277747. At Sunrise Chambers, 22 Ulsoor Rd:*Air France*, T5589397, *Gulf Air*, T5584702,*Kuwait*, T5594243, Royal Jordanian, T5594240, Air Canada, American Airlines, T5585394. *British Airways*, Sophia Complex, St Marks Rd, T2214034. *Cathay Pacific, West End Hotel*, T2259130. *JAL*, 9/1, 2 Residency Rd, T215416. *KLM*, West End Hotel, T2258703. *Lufthansa*, Dickenson Rd, T5588791. *Malaysian*, Richmond Circle, T2213030. *Singapore*, Richmond Rd, T2213833. SwissAir, Richmond Rd, T2211983. **Banks** Usually open 1000-1400, Mon-Fri. *ANZ*, 26, MG Rd.for Visa, ATMs at *Citibank*, Nilgri's Complex, Brigade Rd. Many options for exchange. **Communications** **GPO**: Cubbon Rd near Raj Bhawan, open 1000-1800. *Poste Restante* here, open Mon-Sat, 1030-1600. Brigade Rd and Museum Rd have post and telegraph offices; Museum Rd has a Foreign Post Office, where you can send permissible items abroad. **Internet**: *Cyber Café* on Brigade Rd (near Church St); very good, safe cold coffee, Rs 60 per 30 mins to surf the net/Email. *Cyber Q* Brigade Rd, nr Vellara, with pool tables; *Trans World* 2 Magrath Rd, with coffee shop. **Cultural centres** *Alliance Française*, Millers Tank Bund Rd, off Thimmaiah Rd, opposite station. *British Library*, St Mark's Rd/ Church St corner (Koshy's Bldg), 1030-1830, Tue-Sat. *Max Mueller Bhavan*, 3 Lavalle Rd. *Bharatiya Vidya Bhavan*, Race Course Rd. *Indian Council for Cultural Relations*, 1, 12th Main Rd, Vasanth Nagar. *Karnataka Sangeeta Nataka Academy*, JC Rd. *Palm Leaf Library*, Chamarajpet, 33, V Main Rd. An unusual collection of old leaves which 1 traveller found held his special leaf giving accurate details of his character, past, present, and yet to be tested, future; those arriving here, simply out of curiosity may be disappointed since the custodian may not be able to trace their own special leaf! **Medical services** 24 hr Chemists: at hospitals. *Pancha Shila*, Brigade Rd; *Santoshi*, Mission Rd. **Hospitals**: *Bowring and Lady Curzon Hospital*, Hospital Rd, T5591362, north of Cubbon Park. *Mallya Hospital*, Vittal Mallya Rd, south of Cubbon Park, T2277979, one of the best;*Victoria* opp City Market, T6701150. **Tourist offices** *Govt of India*, KFC Bldg, 48 Church St, T5585417. 1000-1800 Mon-Sat.*Dept of Tourism*, F Block, 1st Flr, Cauvery Bhavan, KG Rd, T2215489, F2272403, dtourism@bir.vsnl.net.in *Karnataka STDC*, 10/4 Kasturba Rd, 2nd Flr, Queen's Circle (near MG Rd Corner), T2212901, infn@kstdcbng.karnataka.nic.in, very helpful and efficient. Also at Badami House, NR Sq, T2275869, F2238016, where tours originate. Tourist Information Counter, 64 St Mark's Rd, T2236854. 0900-1900. City Rly Station Counter, T2870068. 0700-2100. Airport Counter, T5268012. 0700-2030. **Useful addresses** Ambulance: T102; **Visa extensions:** Commissioner of Police, Infantry Rd. *Chief Wildlife Warden*, Aranya Bhavan, 18th Cross, Malleswaram, T3341993.

Around Bangalore

Hesaraghatta Lake
Aalong the NH4 to Tumkur 26 km N from Bangalore

A road follows the right bank of the Arkavati River north to the Hesarghatta lake. The lake now has a boat club with windsurfing facilities. Fishing permits can also be obtained, and there is an Indo-Danish dairy development project which is open to visitors. **Nrityagram** ('Dance Village'), T088-8466312, nearby, won the Rural Architecture Award. It offers courses in classical dance, creative choreography, music, philosophy, mythology and painting. Tours (for groups of four minimum), Rs 500, includes lunch (contact *Clipper* T080-5599032); individuals may walk around with a brochure for Rs 10; accommodation available.

From **Chikballapur**, on the NH7 north of Bangalore, it is 10 km to the granite hill of Nandidurg. Literally 'the fort of Nandi', the place was named after Siva's bull in the **Nandi Hills**. Regarded as a minor hill resort today, Nandidurg was once a summer retreat for **Tipu Sultan**, who thought it would be impossible to capture. Guarded on three sides by almost sheer cliffs, on one side over 300 m high, Tipu massively fortified the western approach. There are superb views from the top. The **Bhoganandisvara Temple** (9th and 16th centuries) at the foot of the hill is an important example of the Nolamba style which had later extensions built during the Vijayanagar period (eg *gopuram* at the entrance). The second gate leads to a colonnaded enclosure with twin Siva shrines. The early style is suggested by the plainness of the walls, but the stone windows have carvings of Nataraj and Durga. The main sanctuary has pyramidal towers and an octagonal roof. **Sleeping** E *Mayura Pine Top* (KSTDC), T78624, contact Manager or KSTDC, Bangalore, T2212901. F *Rest Houses*, reserve through Director of Horticulture, Lalbagh, Bangalore, T5602231. ■ *Getting there: The hills can be visited as a day excursion from Bangalore's Central Bus Stand. Buses from 0830.*

Nandidurg
Phone code: 08156
Population: 47,200
Altitude: 1,418 m

There are two main routes to Mysore. The southern route through *Kanakapura* and *Malvalli* is longer. The more northerly rail and road route is relatively quick. It crosses the open parkland of the Maidan, rising to over 1,200 m. The ancient rocks of some of the oldest granites in India which give reddish or brown soils, often with extraordinary outcropping hills and boulders, provided Merchant and Ivory with the ideal filming location to capture the atmosphere of E M Forster's Barabar Cave for their film of A Passage to India *without the hazards of working in Bihar*.

Routes

Ramanagaram was formerly known as Closepet after Sir Barry Close, the first British resident in Mysore to hold the post after the fall of Tipu Sultan in 1799, and is still often called **Kalispet**, a corruption of its original name. It was established in 1800 to open up previously dense jungle and to help secure the road to Srirangapatnam. It takes its more recent name from the nearby hill, Ramgiri. The name *Closepet* was given to the local granite, which runs in a band 20 km wide due north through Tumkur into Andhra Pradesh, often giving rise to astonishing rock formations. Dry farming predominates on flat land between the bizarre granite boulders, with ragi (*finger millet*), other millets and gram common.

Ramanagaram
50 km SW of Bangalore

Ten kilometres further, entered along the tank bund, Channapatna is a busy market town, known particularly for its lacquer ware. Small dolls with nodding heads are a speciality. Tipu Sultan's religious teacher is buried in one of the two large Muslim tombs just north of the town. The ruined fort (1580) here was built by **Jagadura Rai** who was given land around Channapatna by the Vijayanagar king in gratitude for his military support in defending Penukonda in 1577 – see page 407. In the town centre the *Karnataka Silk Industries* has a showroom; the factory is on the road southwest of the town. **Eating** There are only small tea stalls on the main road in the town centre, where buses stop. The *Kavitha Restaurant*, 10 km south of Channapatna, is quite good.

Channapatna
Phone code: 08113
Population: 55,200

Karnataka

The Western Plateau

The road from Bangalore crosses the open plains of the Western Plateau, intensively cultivated where irrigation is possible from tanks or the occasional well. It is the land of the Vokkaliga caste, the dominant agricultural community of southern Karnataka, longstanding rivals of the reformist Lingayats of the northern districts. Belur and Halebid can be seen in a very long day from Bangalore, but it is better to allow longer if you can and to stay in Hassan overnight.

Nelamangala
Phone code: 08118
Population: 17,600

Nelamangala on the NH4, is an important market town. The Mangalore route passes through the southern end of the Devarayadurga hills (highest point 1,387 m), formed out of the underlying Closepet granites.

Kunigal (*population*: 23,200; *phone code*: 08132), is a bustling town with the stud farm of the Bangalore Turf Club, a college and tile factories.

Yediyur (*phone code*: 08132) is a centre for Saivite pilgrims who come to its Siddhalingeshwara Temple, notably in March-April when the *ratha* (car) festival takes place. The temple has a 12-storey *gopuram*. The town was home of Totada Siddhalinga, a famous religious teacher whose *samadhi* (memorial) is in the temple. You can conveniently visit Belur, Hassan and Halebid from here now, avoiding a long journey from Mysore. **Sleeping and eating** Modern **F** *Mayura Pavitra* (KSTDC) on NH48, T36206, with overnight rooms (Rs 160) and restaurant. Reserve T2215489, F2272403.

Kambadahalli

To see the 10th-century Jain shrines at Kambadahalli which also has a horse stud farm, turn south off the **NH48** towards Nagamangala at Nelligere. The shrines have many features in common with the contemporary Chola temples in Tamil Nadu; clearly defined mouldings on the base, walls divided by pilasters, and shrines with stepped towers rising above them. The *Panchakutu Basti* has three shrines, housing *Adinatha* (the father of *Gommateshwara*) in the south shrine, *Neminatha* in the east and *Santinatha* in the west (note the high relief carvings on the ceiling). There are many excellent sculptures, including a seated Jain figure.

★ Sravanabelagola (Shravanabelgola)

Phone code: 08176
Population: 4120
Altitude: 930 m

The statue of Gommateshwara, sacred to Jains, stands on Vindhyagiri (sometimes known as Indrabetta or Indragiri), rising 150 m above the plain while Chandragiri to the north (also known as Chikka Betta) is just under half that height.

Ins & outs

Direct buses to/from Mysore and Bangalore run in the morning; in the afternoon, change at Channarayapatna. The morning express buses to/from Mysore serve small villages travelling over dusty, though interesting, roads up to Krishnarajapet, then very few stops between there and Mysore. There are also tours from Bangalore.

History

The *Gommateshwara* statue was erected at some time between AD 980 and 983. Just over 17-m high, it represents the saintly prince *Bahubali*, son of the first Tirthankara, after he had gained enlightenment. Having fought a fierce war with his brother *Bharata* over the rights to succession, *Bahubali* accepted defeat when he had won the battle because he recognized its futility. Passing on his kingdom to his defeated brother, Bahubali adopted a life of meditation.

Nearly 700 steps carved in the steep granite slope start near the village tank. **The site**
The path up gives excellent views. There are several small shrines on the way to
the statue on top. In order, these are the *Odeagal Basti*, the *Brahmadeva
Mandapa*, the *Akhanda Bagilu* and the *Siddhara Basti*, all built in the 12th century except the *Brahmadeva Mandapa* which is 200 years older. Several are
intricately carved. It is worth stopping at one about two-thirds of the way up.

The carved statue is nude (possibly as he is a *Digambara* or 'sky clad' Jain)
and captures the tranquillity typical of much Buddhist and Jain art. The depth
of the saint's meditation and withdrawal from the world is suggested by the
spiralling creepers shown growing up his legs and arms, and by the ant hills
and snakes at his feet. He is shown standing on a lotus. While the features are
finely carved, the overall proportions are odd, with greatly enlarged shoulders,
lengthened arms but shortened legs.

Sravanabelagola is often crowded with visitors. Every 12th year it is the
focus for Jain pilgrims from across India to celebrate the *Mastakabhisheka* –
the 'magnificent anointment', or sacred head-anointing ceremony. The night
before the ceremony 1,008 pots – 'kalashas' – holding sacred water are sold by
auction to devotees. The pots are left at the statue's feet overnight, and the following morning the water is poured over the statue's head from specially
erected scaffolding. The water is followed by *ghee*, milk, coconut water, turmeric paste, honey and vermilion powder. Some even sprinkle gold dust.
Unlike many festivals in India, the event is watched by the thousands of devotees in complete silence. The next celebration will be between 2006-2008.

■ *Shoes must be removed. The granite can get extremely hot; thick socks recommended. It can be quite tiring in the heat; dholis are available at the foot of
Indragiri to carry visitors up the steps. Carry water.*

In the town itself is the **Bhandari basti** (1159 and added to later), about 200 m
to the left from the path leading up to the Gommatesvara statue. Inside are 24
images of Tirthankaras in a spacious sanctuary. There are 500 rock-cut steps to
the top of the hill and it takes about 30 minutes to climb. It is safe to leave luggage at the Tourist Office branch at the entrance (closed 1300-1415).

There are 14 shrines on **Chandragiri** and the Mauryan emperor
Chandragupta, who is believed by some to have become a Jain and left his
empire to fast and meditate, is buried here. The temples are all in the Dravidian
style, the Chamundaraya Basti, built in AD 982 being one of the most remarkable. There is a good example of a free-standing pillar or *mana-stambha* in
front of the *Parsvanathasvami Basti*. These pillars, sometimes as high as 15 m,
were placed at the temple entrance. Here, the stepped base with a square
cross-section transforms to a circular section and the column is then topped
by a capital.

All facilities are very basic. **E** *Karnataka Bhavan*, 50 rooms, reserve at Karnataka Tour- **Sleeping**
ism, 9 St Mark's Rd, Bangalore, T579139. **F** *Travellers' Bungalow*, reservations: Chief **& eating**
Exec Officer, Taluk Board, Channarayapatna, Hassan Dist. **F** *Shriyans Prasad*, a pilgrim's guest house at foot of hill. **F** *Vidyananda Nilaya Dharamshala*, closest to the
bus stand, rooms with toilet and fan, "bucket shower", blanket but no sheets, courtyard, good value at Rs 60, reserve through SDJMI Committee, T7223. There are vegetarian cafés and cold drink stalls at the foot of the hill and a canteen at the bus station.

Karnataka

Hassan

Phone code: 08172
Colour map 3, grid A2
Population: 108,500

This pleasant, busy little town, is a good base from which to see Belur and Halebid. Buses pull in at the centre with most hotels within a short walking distance. The railway station is 2 km to the east. The collection in the **District Museum** includes sculpture, paintings, weapons, coins and inscriptions. ■ *0900-1700. Closed Mon & government holidays. Free. Maharaja Park.*

Sleeping **B** *Hassan Ashok* (ITDC), BM Rd, opposite Race Course Rd, 500 m from bus stand, T68731, F67154, hsnashok@bgl.vsnl.net.in 46 comfortable rooms, half a/c, good restaurant, bar (pool table), exchange (poor rate). **D** *Suvarna Regency*, 97 BM Rd (500 m south of bus stand) T64006, F63822. 60 clean rooms (some a/c), modern, swish, good veg restaurant, car hire. Very helpful, efficient, excellent value. Highly recommended. **E** *Amblee Palika*, 4724 Race Course Rd, T67145. 34 rooms (some with TV, balcony), quiet, good value, restaurant, bar, often full. **E** *Residency* (EDR Karigoda), BM Rd (1 km rly), T64506. 30 modern, clean comfortable rooms (western bath), quieter at back, restaurant, hospitable. Recommended. **E-F** *Mahaveer* (Abhiruchi), BM Rd, 250 m south of Bus Stand, T68885. 22 rooms, good restaurant, very clean, quiet, friendly, excellent value. Recommended. **F** *Laxmi Prasanna*, Subhas Sq (opp *New Star*), T68391. Arrogant management, but decent enough rooms if a little run down. Popular veg meals restaurant. **F** *Sanman*, next door to *Laxmi Prasana*, T68024. Standard rooms with bath, bit noisy. **F** *Railway Retiring Room* (2 km from centre). **F** *Vaishnavi Lodge*, Harsha Mahal/Church Rd, T67413. 44 clean, spacious rooms, good vegetarian restaurant.

Eating **Mid-range**: Hotels: *Hassan Ashok*, International. Good food, prompt service. *Suvarna Regency*. Very good South Indian, popular *Golden Gate* bar and restaurant downstairs (T60316). **Cheap**: *Amblee Palika*, good Indian, Chinese, though rundown; Mahaveer's *Abhiruchi* (North Indian, Chinese), **Suruchi**, below, for vegetarians. *GRR*, opposite Bus Stand, for non-veg food and friendly staff. Several cheap South Indian places are grouped around the bus stand: *New Star*, good, non-vegetarian Indian.

Hassan

■ Sleeping
1 Amblee Palika
2 Hassan Ashok
3 Laxmi Prasanna & Sanman
4 Mahaveer, Abhiruchi & Suruchi Restaurant
5 Suvarna Regency
6 Vaishnavi Lodge

● Eating
1 GRR
2 New Star

0 metres 200
0 yards 200

Local Bus: Bus Stand, T68418. **Taxi**: Private Tourist Taxis can be hired from Cauvery Tourist Centre, Race Course Rd, T68026. **Tongas**: are also available. **Long distance Road Bus**: at least hourly to **Belur** from about 0700 (35 km, 1 hr) and **Halebid** from about 0800 (31 km, 1 hr); all very crowded. A few direct to **Sravanabelagola** in the morning (1 hr); alternatively travel to Channarayapatna and change to bus for Sravanabelagola. Also to **Bangalore** about every 30 mins (4½ hrs), **Goa** (14 hrs), **Hampi**, **Madikeri** (3¾ hrs via Kushalnagar), **Mangalore** (5 hrs), **Mysore** hourly (3 hrs). You can reserve seats for the 0730 dep to Hospet (9 hrs). **Train**: Rly Station is 2 km east of centre. Conversion to broad gauge may cause disruption.

Banks *State Bank of Mysore*, Narasimharaja Circle, changes $, £ cash and TCs. **Communications** Post Office: 100m from bus stand. **Medical services** *General Hospital*, Hospital Rd, *Mission Hospital*, Race Course Rd. **Photo shop** next door to Bank of Mysore. **Tourist office** *India*, Vartha Bhavan, BM Rd, T68862. Very helpful.

On the Belur road, the comparatively plain **Lakshmidevi Temple**, built in 1113 in the early Hoysala style, is contemporary with the Belur temple but has virtually no sculpture on the outside. Four shrines lead off a common square mandapa. The northern shrine has an image of *Kali*, followed clockwise by *Mahalakshmi*, *Bhairava* (a form of Siva) and *Bhutanatha*.

Belur & Halebid

The Hoysalas who ruled a large kingdom between the rivers Krishna and the Kaveri, made Belur and Halebid their capital. Great warriors, they also patronized culture and art. The artisans were encouraged to rival each other and even sign their names on their work of art. Steatite gave the sculptors the opportunity to work with intricate detail since the rock is initially comparatively soft when quarried but hardens with exposure to air. The temples, built as prayers for victory in battle, are small but superbly conceived.

On the banks of the Yagachi River, Belur was the first capital of the dynasty. The temples stand in a courtyard with the Chennakesavara (1116) near the centre. One of the earliest of its type it took a century to complete. It celebrated the Hoysala victory over the Cholas at Talakad. Dedicated to *Krishna* it stands in a courtyard surrounded by a rectangular wall, built on a star-shaped platform with an ambulatory. The winged figure of *Garuda*, Vishnu's carrier, guards the entrance, facing the temple with joined palms.

The Chennakesava Temple At first glance the temple is unimpressive because the superstructure has been lost. However, exquisite sculptures cover the exterior with the friezes. The line of 650 elephants (each different) surround the base, with rows of figures and foliage above. The detail of the 38 female figures is perfect. Look at the young musicians and dancers on either side of the main door and the unusual perforated screens between the columns. 10 have typical bold geometrical patterns while the other 10 depict scenes from the *Puranas* in its tracery. Inside superb carving decorates the hand-lathe-turned pillars and the bracket-figures on the ceiling. Each round filigreed pillar is different and bears witness to individual sculptors producing a masterpiece in competition with each other. The unique Narasimha pillar at the centre of the hall is particularly fine and originally could be rotated. The detail is astounding. The jewellery on the figures is hollow and movable and the droplets of water seem to hang at the ends of the dancer's wet hair on a bracket above you. On the platform in front of the shrine is the figure of

Santalesvara dancing in homage to Lord Krishna. The shrine containing a 3 m high black polished deity is occasionally opened for *darshan*. The annual *Car Festival* is held in March-April.

To the west is the **Viranarayana Temple** which has some fine sculpture and smaller shrines around it. It is worth visiting the **Jain Bastis** a few kilometres away although the decoration is incomplete on most.

Sleeping and eating E *Mayura Velapuri* (KSTDC), Temple Rd, T22209 (Bangalore, T2212901). 2 old rooms, 10 newer, clean, spacious with bath (Rs 200), 20-bed dorms (block book), reasonable restaurant (slow service), friendly and obliging staff make up for what it lacks in comfort. **E-F** *Annapoorna*, Temple Rd, T22009. 8 cleanish rooms and restaurant. **E-F** *Vishnu Lodge*, Main Rd, T22263, 27 rooms with bath, some with TV (Rs 50-200), vegetarian restaurnat. **F** *Sri Raghavendra*, right by temple. Cosy rooms (Rs 75-100), homely and friendly. Avoid *Swagath's* rooms. *Prakash*, upstairs, does non-veg, serves cold beer etc in not very salubrious surroundings. *Shankar*, near the temple opposite the bus stand, does vegetarian meals.

Transport **Bus**: the bus stand is about 1 km from the temples. Half-hourly to Hassan (1 hr; last at 2030); to Halebid (30 mins). To Shimoga for Hampi and Jog Falls (4 hrs), 0800, 0845 (check at bus stand); to Mysore (1½ hrs).

★ **Halebid**
Phone code: 08177

History The ancient capital of the Hoysala Empire was founded in the early 11th century as *Dvarasamudra*. It was destroyed by the armies of the Delhi Sultanate in 1311 and 1327, after which it was deserted and later renamed Halebidu or Halebid (Old Capital). Fortunately the great Hoysalesvara Temple survived.

The temples The **Jain bastis** It is worth first visiting the remarkably simple 12th century Jain Bastis at Basthalli about 1 km south. With lathe-turned and multi-faceted columns, several bastis stand in a garden enclosure, which you can walk around and see the dark interiors with carved ceilings. The smaller **Kedaresvara Temple** with some highly polished columns is on a road going south. There are cycles for hourly hire so you can visit these quieter sites, untroubled by the crowds besieging the Hoysalsvara.

The **Hoysalesvara Temple**, set in lawns, has two shrines dedicated to Siva with a *Nandi* bull facing each. The largest of the Hoysala temples, it was started in 1121 but remained unfinished 86 years later. In structure it is similar to the one at Belur, but its superstructure was never completed. There are extraordinary half life-size statues of Hindu deities with minute details, all around the temple. These, and the six bands of sculpture below, show the excellence of the artisans' craft. The lines of elephants at the base, followed by lions and then horsemen, a floral scroll and then most impressive of all, at eye level, stories from the epics and the *Bhagavata Purana*. This frieze relates incidents from the *Ramayana* and *Mahabharata* among them Krishna lifting Mount Govardhana, Rama defeating the demon god Ravana. The friezes above show *yalis* and *hamsa* or geese. Of the original 84 female figures (like the ones at Belur) only 14 remain; over the years, 70 were stolen. ■ *Temples close at 2030. Guides available.*

Archaeological Museum The small museum is on the lawn near the south entrance where the Archaeological Survey of India maintains a gallery of 12th-13th century sculptures, wood carvings, idols, coins and inscriptions. Some sculptures are displayed outside. To the west is a small lake. ■ *1000-1700, closed Fri. No photography.*

Sleeping and eating F *Mayura Shantala* (KSTDC), T73224, Inspection Bungalow compound in nice garden overlooking temple. 4 rooms with fan, nets and bath (Rs 220, 2 better furnished), limited kitchen. Others, plainer but adequate (Rs 150).

£4000 worth of holiday vouchers to be won!

The Different Holiday

exodus

getaway tonight on www.exodus.co.uk

... that can be claimed against any exodus, Peregrine or Gecko's holiday, a choice of around 570 holidays that set industry standards for responsible tourism in 90 countries across seven continents.

exodus

The UK's leading adventurous travel company, with over 25 years' experience in running the most exciting holidays in 80 different countries. We have an unrivalled choice of trips, from a week exploring the hidden corners of Tuscany to a high altitude trek to Everest Base Camp or 3 months travelling across South America. If you want to do something a little different, chances are you'll find it in one of our brochures.

Peregrine

Australia's leading quality adventure travel company, Peregrine aims to explore some of the world's most interesting and inaccessible places. Providing exciting and enjoyable holidays that focus in some depth on the lifestyle, culture, history, wildlife, wilderness and landscapes of areas that are usually quite different to our own. There is an emphasis on the outdoors, using a variety of transport and staying in a range of accommodation, from comfortable hotels to tribal huts.

Gecko's

Gecko's holidays will get you to the best places with the minimum of hassle. They are designed for younger people who like independent travel but don't have the time to organise everything themselves. Be prepared to take the rough with the smooth, these holidays are for active people with a flexible approach to travel.

To enter the competition, simply tear out the postcard and return it to Exodus Travels, 9 Weir Road, London SW12 0LT. Or go to the competition page on www.exodus.co.uk and register online. Two draws will be made, Easter 2001 and Easter 2002, and the winner of each draw will receive £2000 in travel vouchers. The closing date for entry will be 1st March 2002. If you do not wish to receive further information about these holidays, please tick here. ☐ No purchase necessary. Plain paper entries should be sent to the above address. The prize value is non-transferable and there is no cash alternative. Winners must be over 18 years of age and must sign and adhere to operators' standard booking conditions. A list of prizewinners will be available for a period of one month from the draw by writing to the above address. For a full list of terms and conditions please write to the above address or visit our website.

To receive a brochure, please tick the relevant boxes below (maximum number of brochures 2) or telephone (44) 20 8772 3822.

exodus	Peregrine	Gecko's
☐ Walking & Trekking	☐ Himalaya	☐ Egypt, Jordan & Israel
☐ Discovery & Adventure	☐ China	☐ South America
☐ European Destinations	☐ South East Asia	☐ Africa
☐ Overland Journeys	☐ Antarctica	☐ South East Asia
☐ Biking Adventures	☐ Africa	☐ India
☐ Multi Activity	☐ Arctic	

Please give us your details:

Name: ....

Address: ....

....

....

Postcode: ....

e-mail: ....

Which footprint guide did you take this from?

....

exodus
The Different Holiday

getaway tonight on
www.exodus.co.uk

exodus
The Different Holiday

exodus
9 Weir Road
LONDON
SW12 0BR

BUSINESS REPLY SERVICE
Licence No SW4909

2

Transport Bus: The Bus Stand, where you can get good meals, is near the temples. KSRTC buses, half-hourly to Hassan (45 mins) and from there to Bangalore, Mangalore, Mysore. Also direct to Belur (12 km, 1 hr) and from there to Hassan.

Directory Useful services *Canara Bank*, *Post Office*, and a *Photo film* shop.

The direct route from Hassan to Mangalore along the **NH48** is dramatic as it crosses the Western Ghats. There are stunning views. Alternatively, going via Belur a beautiful hill road runs south through the forest to **Sakleshpur** on the NH48. *Sri Durga Darshan* does cheap Indian meals, cold drinks and coffee.

Routes

Chikmagalur, northeast of Belur, means 'younger daughter's town', and according to legend it was the dowry for the younger daughter of a local chieftain. In addition to the Hoysala style **Kodandarama Temple** there are mosques, the moated fort and the St Joseph's Roman Catholic Cathedral.

The town is at the centre of one of India's major **coffee** growing areas. Coffee was first grown in the Baba Budan Hills, just to the north, in 1670; the Central Coffee Research Institute was set up in 1925. The district has curing works for the processing of raw coffee. March-April is the coffee flowering season, a beautiful time of year in the hills.

The road northeast from Chikmagalur to Kadur passes the beautiful tank built by Rukmangada Raya and renovated in 1156 during the Hoysala period at Ayyanakere.

Chikmagalur
Phone code: 08262
Colour map 3, grid A2
Population: 60,800

Sleeping AL *Taj Garden Retreat*, outside town, on a hill side, T30217. 29 luxury a/c rooms in small cottages, pool, good for visiting Belur and Halebid (40 km). Several **F** lodges in town, along Indira Gandhi Rd, include *Quality Inn*, T31257. 20 rooms, restaurant.

North to Jog Falls

Kemmannugundi is a beautiful hill station (1,280 m) with an excellent orchidarium and lovely sunset views. **Sleeping D** *Tourist Home* (KSTDC), book ahead at KSTDC, Bangalore.

Kemmannu-gundi
Colour map 1, grid C3

Bhadravati, an industrial town, is on the edge of the **Baba Bhudan Hills**. Scenically beautiful, the hills are an important source of iron ore and the centre of a major coffee growing region. The Mysore Iron and Steel Co set up a plant here in 1923, making extensive use of charcoal. As a side process it had one of Asia's biggest wood-distillation plants which has expanded into production of ferro-manganese, iron castings and tar products.

Bhadravati
Phone code: 081826
Colour map 1, grid C3
Population: 150,000

A clean and lively town (*population*: 192,600) is useful for a night halt between Hampi to Hassan or Mysore. **Sleeping C** *Jewel*, smart new hotel in town, clean comfortable a/c rooms (Rs 850, accepts Visa), restaurant. Many cheaper.

Shimoga
Phone code: 08182
Colour map 1, grid C2

The falls are a magnificently spectacular sight in the wet season. The 50 km long **Hirebhasgar Reservoir** now regulates the flow of the Sharavati River in order to generate hydro-electricity. The Mysore Power Corporation releases water to the falls every second Sunday from 1000-1800. Often during the monsoon the falls are shrouded in mist. Leeches are a hazard if you walk down to the base of the falls. In the dry season the water is often reduced to a trickle.

There are four falls. The highest is the *Raja*, with a fall of 250 m and a pool below 40 m deep. Next is the *Roarer*, while a short distance to the south is the *Rocket*, which spurts great shafts of water out into the air. In contrast the *Rani*

★ Jog Falls
Phone code: 08186
Colour map 1, grid C2
Population: 13,300
Best time to visit:
late Nov- early-Jan

Karnataka

(once called the White Lady) cascades over the rocks. The walk to the bottom of the falls is well worthwhile for the fit. A walk to the top (not in the monsoons) offering breathtaking views of the river cascading and the valley, is highly recommended. The Inspection Bungalow has excellent views.

No food available at night **Sleeping and eating** Very basic. **F** *Mayura Gerusoppa*, T4732. 10 rooms (Rs 200-300). **F** *Youth Hostel*, Shimoga Rd. Empty rooms (no beds), some dorm beds with dirty bedding. Local families take in guests. Stalls near the falls serve reasonable breakfast and meals during the day.

Transport Road Bus: to/from **Karwar** daily, arriving evening, and leaving Jog in the morning. Other destinations include Sagar, Shimoga for Belur or Hassan (4 hrs), Sirsi (2 hrs). **Goa**: bus to Colva at 1100 is very crowded, 2300 is easier to get a seat on. **Taxi**: to Panaji, Rs 1,500 (6 hrs). **Train** Jog is 16 km from the railway at **Talguppa**. Trains from Bangalore involve a change in Shimoga town.

Gudavi   **Gudavi Bird Sanctuary** is a few kilometres to the east of the road north of Siddapur. A sanctuary since 1985, the 74 ha tank at Gudavi has been home to migratory waterbirds for over 100 years. Heronries with 12 species are established in the smaller southern section while the northern section has many resident and migratory birds.

Mundgod   Lying on the road between Sirsi and Hubli, Mundgod became the home to a Tibetan colony in 1971. The original settlement of 216 monks has now grown to more than 10,000, with three monasteries of Drepung, Ganden and Sera.

The Central Maidan

The NH4 runs from Bangalore to Hubli-Dharwad, Pune and Mumbai across the high open country east of the crest line of the Western Ghats, following one of the main routes for trade and military movement over centuries.

Sivaganga   A small village 5 km south of Dobbspet (40 km northwest of Bangalore), is dominated by the cone-shaped Sivaganga Hill, a granite outcrop which reaches 1,347 m. At the top is the cave shrine to Gangadareshwar (circa AD1400) and a temple to Honna Devi and wonderful panoramic views. It is a steep climb in places but there are steps cut in the rock and a hand rail to help and frequent drinks stalls (allow 4 hours for the return hike). To the north of Dobbspet are the *Devarayadurga Hills* and state forest, covered in quite dense scrub. There are two hilltop temples to Yoganarasimha and Bhoganarasimha (*altitude*: 1,190 m). **Sleeping F** *Mayura Meghadoota* (KSTDC), Devarayadurga, T0816-73400, two rooms (Rs 100).

Siddhaganga   Just north of Kyatasandra on the **NH4** at Siddhaganga, is the Siddhalingeshwara Temple, on a hillock at 1,183 m. Beautifully situated, the temple is an important pilgrimage centre with six shrines at the entrance. The *Matha* near the entrance prepares food for hundreds of pilgrims every day and also offers lodging facilities.

Devaray-   A group of holy sites, 5 km north, is around the fort of Devarayanadurga,
anadurga   including the *Durga Narasimha*, built by the Mysore rajas, a *Hanuman* temple dedicated to Sanjivaraya and the Kumbhi Narasimha temple. Some of the shrines are in caves including the Pada Teertha, one of three sacred ponds. Another cave has statues of *Rama*, *Sita* and *Lakshman*.

Tumkur is an important market town and road junction. About 8 km south-west is the small Dravidian style Kaidala Keshava temple. It contains some striking sculpted stone images, and is associated with the legendary sculptor Jakanachary.

Sibi, northwest of Tumkur on the NH4, has a very attractive Narasimha temple with old terracotta sculptures and wall murals.

Sira has a notable palace and gardens laid out by Dilawar Khan, the Governor of the town appointed by Aurangzeb as he moved south into peninsular India at the end of the 17th century. The Jama Masjid, the tomb of Malik Rihan and the Ibrahim Rauza are all worth seeing.

The town is on the right bank of the river Vedavati. The Teru-Malleshwara Temple has a 14 m-high lamp pillar which holds enough oil for the lamp to be relit only once a year. You can climb the pillar by the slightly projecting steps. There is a very large temple car festival in January-February each year when images of *Siva, Parvati* and *Uma-Maheshwar*, seated on the *nandi*, are pro-cessed through the streets. Some 15 km to the southwest is the Vanivilasapur dam and reservoir. Built at the end of the 19th century it was Mysore's first modern dam, and the lake is in an attractive setting. *Getting there*: local buses run from Hiriyur to Hosdurga.

Molakalmuru is an important centre for making pure silks. The town has an attractive traditional reservoir. It lies approximately 10 km south of **Siddapur**, the site of three Asokan rock edicts. At **Brahmagiri** nearby there are *Asokan edicts* on a large boulder, on the Chinna-Hagari River banks. Discovered in 1891 by B L Rice, they are minor but they represent some of the southernmost discoveries of Asoka's Empire. The northern side of the granite hill has subse-quently revealed evidence of settlements dating from at least five distinct peri-ods. The finds include terracotta beads, pottery, semi-precious stones and metal, and date from early stone age periods up to the Hoysala.

The Megalith periods also underwent successive developments before giv-ing way to the **Andhra culture** when a sophisticated pottery began to make its appearance. Dating of this last period has been made reasonably accurate by the discovery of Roman coins of the Augustan and Tiberian period (minted between 2BC-AD 37) at the neighbouring site of **Chandravalli**.

Chitradurga is at the foot of a group of granite hills, rising to 1,175 m in the south. The *Fort of Seven Rounds* was built in the 17th century by Nayak Poligars, semi-independent landlords who fled south after the collapse of the Vijayanagar Empire in 1565. They were crushed by **Haidar Ali** in 1779 who captured the fort and scattered the population. Haidar Ali replaced the Nayaka's mud fort with stone and **Tipu Sultan** built a palace, mosque, grana-ries and oilpits in it. There are four secret entrances in addition to the 19 gate-ways, and ingenious water tanks which collected rainwater. There are also 14 temples, including a cave temple to the west of the wall. They are placed in an extraordinary jumble of outcropping granite rocks, a similar setting to that of Hampi 300 km to the north. The Hidimbeshwara temple is the oldest temple on the site. There are gold and copper mines just south of the town. **Sleeping** E *Maruthi Inn*, MH Rd, T23474. 21 rooms. E *Roopvani*, Roopvani Rd, T23450. 34 rooms. F *Maurya*, Santhe Bagilu, T24448. 12 rooms, restau-rant. *Getting there:* Buses to Bangalore and Mysore.

Tumkur
Phone code: 0816
Colour map 3, grid A3
Population: 179,500
72 km

Sira
Population: 33,400
Colour map 2, grid C1

Hiriyur
Phone code: 0819312
Colour map 1, grid C3
Population: 37,500
96 km

Molakalmuru
Colour map 1, grid C3
92 km
Altitude: 560 m

Chitradurga
Phone code: 08194
Colour map 1, grid C3
Population: 103,300
Altitude: 976 m

Karnataka

Anekonda Heavy rains have exposed small gold coins here in the past. There is a very small Hoysala temple dedicated to Ishvara which has beautifully worked carvings on the doorways.

Davangere An important market town for cotton, groundnut, sugarcane and millets. The
Phone code: 08192 cotton markets are piled high with huge mounds of snowy white cotton.
Population: 287,000 **Sleeping D-E** *Chetna*, PJ Extension, T28181, 60 rooms, recommended; **F** *Rathna Lodge*, PB Rd.

Harihar **Harihar** now a small industrial town with a *Dak Bungalow*, takes its name
Phone code: 08197 from the combined image, half *Siva*, half *Vishnu*, in the Hoysala style Sri
Population: 66,650 Hariharesvara Temple (1223). This enshrines a 1.3 m image of Harihara. The town is on the right bank of the Tungabhadra River, just below the confluence of its two major tributaries. A local legend attributes the origins of the river to the sweat that flowed down Vishnu's tusks. It formed two streams when he took the form of a boar and engaged in a heroic struggle to rescue the world from the demon *Hiranyaksha*.

Ranibennur Ranibennur, a small market town, has a rocky hill to the south known as Scor-
Population: 67,400 pion Hill. Ranibennur also has a Blackbuck Wildlife Sanctuary. **Sleeping E** *Forest Rest House* (KSTDC), book in advance from KSTDC Bangalore.

Haveri Haveri has one of Karnataka's oldest and best known artificial tanks. Built in
Population: 45,300 1134, the Directory of Indian Wetlands states that the 88 ha tank has a maximum depth of 4 m. It is an important pilgrimage site, thousands of people flocking to it on 14 January every year. It plays an important role in sustaining the rich birdlife of the region, 47 species of waterfowl alone were recorded in 1987.

Hubli-Dharwad

Phone code: 0836 Hubli is a centre for the textile industry and is a major railway junction for
Colour map 1, grid B2 Mumbai, Bangalore and Goa. It also has a big medical school while Dharwad
Population: 647,600 has the State University with a museum, but in themselves the two towns are
Altitude: 600 m not of particular interest. However, they offer an alternative base to Hospet from which to see Dambal and Lakkundi.

Museum **Kannada Research Institute Museum** Collection includes sculpture (notably a *Nataraja*), paintings and manuscripts. ■ *Karnataka University. 1100-1800, closed Tue afternoon and University holidays. Free.*

Excursions **Dandeli Wildlife sanctuary** (75 km) is a **tiger reserve** which also harbours leopard, deer, elephant, gaur, sloth bear and king cobras: with additional routes opening up, sighting of wildlife should improve. From Dandeli a road runs through Ambika Nagar (20 km) to Sykes Point (5 km) which offers breathtaking views of the Kali River. Permission to visit can be obtained from the Electricity Board office at Ambika Nagar. ■ *Entry Rs 15, Rs 150 for foreigners, still camera Rs 10.* **Sleeping C** *Bison River Lodge*, on the banks of the Kali Nadi river (30 km from Dandeli town), attractive, fairly comfortable cottages, bar, rustic, comfortable, sprawling site, scenic location, river rafting, jeep safari, nature walk, T022-6408742, F6458401, www.indianadventures.com. ■ *Getting there: 25 km south along SH95 (off NH4A, near Londa) after passing below Supa Dam which makes a large and beautiful lake north of the park.*

C *Naveen*, Unkal Lake, 5 km north of Hubli on Dharwad Rd, T374501, F372730. 41 modern rooms, **B** suites, exchange, pool. Recommended. **In Dharwad: C-D** *Karishma*, on Pune-Bangalore NH4, T347143. 12 rooms, vegetarian and non-vegetarian restaurant. Recommended. **E** *Royal Palace*, PB Rd and **F** *Railway Retiring Rooms* and dorm. **In Hubli: D** *Kailash*, Lamington Rd, T52235. Some dearer a/c rooms, good food, clean, well run, a bit noisy. **D** *Samrat Ashok*, Lamington Rd (opposite *Kailash*), T362380, F364808. Some good value a/c rooms, restaurant (vegetarian), exchange. **D-E** *Hubli Woodlands*, Keshawpur, T362246. 50 rooms, 6 good a/c with bath, a/c Indian restaurant (dark but clean), bar, good value. **E** *Ajantha*, Station Rd, Jaichamarajnagar, T362216. Large hotel, some rooms with bath, simple dining hall. **E** *Ayodhya*, PB Rd, opposite the town Bus Stand, T366251. 104 rooms, some a/c.

Sleeping

Cheap: *Vishali Lodge* Vijay Rd. Also several clean, modern vegetarian restaurants in town centre.

Eating

Road The main bus stand in Hubli has relocated to 2 km from the centre on the Gokul road. **Buses**: several to **Banagalore** (9 hrs), **Hospet** (3½ hrs), **Panaji** (6 hrs, poor road). Some to **Bijapur** (3-3½ hrs), **Mumbai** (13-14 hrs). **Train** Hubli and Dharwad are on main rail routes with 30 mins between the 2 stations. From Dharwad to **Bangalore**: *Miraj Bangalore Exp, 6590*, 2205, 10¼ hrs. From Hubli to **Gadag**: 1½ hrs. **Bangalore**: *Shatabdi Exp, 2026*, 0500, 7½ hrs. **Mumbai (VT)**: *Hospet Miraj Pass/Koyna Exp, 7301/7308*, 2150, 23 hrs (dep Dharwad 2240). For **Goa (Londa Station)**: *Bangalore Miraj Exp, 6589*, 0530, 1¾ hrs. **Hospet**: *Vijaynagara Exp, 7310*, 1430, 4½ hrs; *Miraj Hospet, 7302*, 0650, 5¼ hrs (and to **Guntakal**: 7¼ hrs). **Secunderabad**: (Change at Guntakal) *Vijaynagara Exp/Venkatadri Exp, 7310/(7598/7604)*, 1430, 20 hrs.

Transport

Internet: in Hubli. **Tourist Office**: Krishna Hotel, Lamington Rd, T362251. **Travel agent**: *Vipra* in *Ashok Hotel*, is helpful.

Directory

Hubli

From Hubli the NH4A keeps close to the railway line to **Londa** (32 km), then down the steep face of the Ghats to **Molem** (35 km) and **Ponda** (37 km). It is a slow and rough journey, particularly between Londa and the Goa border. A better option between Goa and Belgaum is the route through Mapusa, Sawantwadi and Amboli.

Routes

Belgaum

An important border town, Belgaum makes an interesting stop on the Mumbai – Bangalore road or as a trip from Goa. Easily accessible, the crowded market in the centre of town gives a glimpse of India untouched by tourism. With its strategic position in the Deccan plateau, the town had been ruled by many dynasties including the Chalukyas, Rattas, Vijaynagaras, Bahmanis and the Marathas. Most of the monuments date from the early 13th century.

Phone code: 0831
Colour map 1, grid C2
Population: 420,000
Altitude: 770 m

Karnataka

The **fort**, immediately east of the town centre (currently being renovated), though pre-Muslim was rebuilt by Yusuf Adil Shah, the Sultan of Bijapur, in 1481. Inside the **Masjid-i-Sata** (1519), the best of the numerous mosques in Belgaum was built by a captain in the Bijapur army, Azad Khan. Belgaum is also noted for its Jain architecture and sculpture. The late Chalukyan **Kamala Basti** with typical beautifully lathe-turned pillars and a black stone Neminatha sculpture, stands within the fort walls. To the south of the Fort and about 800 m north of the *Hotel Sanman* on the Mumbai-Bangalore by-pass, is a beautifully sculpted Jain temple, which according to an inscription, was built by Malikaryuna. Along the entrance wall are well carved sculptures of musicians.

Burgess has described a further Jain temple which stands in the former Government store yard. The temple has "massive square pillars ... but relieved by floral ornamentations". He comments on the care taken in carving the door leading from the central mandapam. "On the centre of the lintel is a Tirthankar, and above the cornice are four squat human figures." Outside, **Kapileswara**, the oldest Hindu temple is worth visiting.

Sleeping & eating   **D** *Adarsha Palace*, College Rd, T435777, F431022. Small modern and 'personal', some a/c rooms, friendly staff. Recommended. **D** *Milan*, Club Rd (4 km rly), T470555. 45 rooms with bath (hot shower), some a/c, vegetarian restaurant, good value. **E-F** *Mayura Malaprabha* (KSTDC), Ashok Nagar, HUDCO Complex near lake, T470781. 6 simple clean rooms in modern cottages (Rs 190), dorm (Rs 40), restaurant, bar, Tourist Office. **E-F** *Sheetal*, Khade Bazar near bus station, T470222. Cleanish rooms with bath (prices vary), vegetarian restaurant, Indian style, noisy hotel in busy and quite entertaining bazar street. Recommended. The main bus station has a good café.

Transport   **Air** The airport is 10 km from the centre (no flights at present). **Road** There are frequent buses through town between Mumbai and Bangalore. Panaji is approximately 5 hrs by bus, Rs 40. **Train** The station is near the bus stand, 4 km south of the centre; autos available. **Bangalore:** *Miraj Bangalore Exp 6590*, 1845, 13½ hrs. **Mumbai (VT) via Miraj and Pune:** (change at Miraj) *Hubli Miraj Pass/Mahalaxmi Exp 305/1012*, 1655, 15½ hrs (50 min wait at Miraj) and for Pune 10½ hrs. **Goa via Londa**.

★ Mysore and the Southern Maidan

Phone code: 0821
Colour map 3, grid A3
Population: 652,200
Altitude: 776 m

The city of royal palaces, sandalwood and the manufacture of incense sticks, Mysore has a pleasant climate, some beautiful parks and shady avenues, and strolls at a relaxing pace in comparison with its dynamic neighbour Bangalore. The former capital of the princely state, is Karnataka's second largest city.

Ins & outs   **Getting there** The railway station is about 1 km to the northwest of the town centre while the 3 bus stands are all central within easy reach of hotels. **Getting around** Mysore is comfortably compact for walking though there are plenty of autos and buses. **Climate** Summer maximum 28°C; winter maximum 22°C. Rainfall: 74 cm. Best season to visit is Oct (*Dasara Festival*) to Mar, but much more pleasant than on the lower plains throughout the year.

Sights

The City Palace (Amber Vilas), was designed by *Henry Irwin* and built in 1897   **City Palace**
after a fire which burnt down the old wooden palace. It is in the *Indo-Saracenic*
style in grand proportions, with domes, arches and colonnades of carved pillars and shiny marble floors – 'wondrous kitsch'. One of the largest palaces in
the country with some art treasures, it is beautifully restored and maintained
(you might see work in progress). The stained glass, wall paintings, ivory inlaid
doors and the ornate golden throne (now displayed during *Dasara*) are all
remarkable. The fabulous collection of jewels, 'amazing in its extravagance', is
only rarely on display.

Ground Floor Visitors are led through the 'Car Passage' with cannons and carriages to the *Gombe thotti* (Dolls' pavilion). This originally displayed dolls during *dasara* and today houses, in addition, a model of the old palace, European
marble statues and the golden *howdah* (the Maharaja used the battery-operated
red and green bulbs on top of the canopy as 'Stop' and 'Go' signals to the
mahout!). The last is still used during *dasara* but goddess Chamundeshwari
rides on the elephant. The octagonal *Kalyana Mandap* (marriage hall), or Peacock Pavilion, south of the courtyard, has a beautiful stained glass ceiling and
excellent paintings of scenes from the *dasara* and other festivities on 26 canvas
panels. Note the exquisite details, especially of No 19. The Portrait Gallery and
the Period Furniture Room lead off this pavilion.

1st Floor A marble staircase leads to the magnificent *Durbar Hall* (47 m x 13
m), a grand colonnaded hall with lavishly framed paintings by famous Indian
artists. The asbestos-lined ceiling has paintings of Vishnu incarnations. A passage takes you past the beautifully inlaid wood-and-ivory door of the Ganesh
Temple, to the *Amba* (Amber) *Vilas* for private audience (*Diwan-i-Khas*).
This exquisitely decorated hall has three doors. The central silver door depicts
Vishnu's 10 incarnations and the eight *dikpalas* (directional guardians), with
Krishna figures on the reverse (see the tiny Krishna on a leaf, kissing his toes!),
all done in *repoussé* on teak and rosewood. The stained glass (possibly Belgian,
in Art Nouveau style), cast iron pillars from Glasgow, carved wood ceiling,
chandeliers, etched glass windows, the *pietra dura* on the floors and the elegant
colour scheme all add to its grandeur.

    The jewel encrusted **Golden Throne** with its ornate steps, which some like
to attribute to ancient Vedic times, was originally made of figwood decorated
with ivory before it was embellished with gold, silver and jewels. Others trace
its history to 1336 when the Vijaynagar kings 'found' it and they say, passed it
on to the Wodeyars who continue to use it during *dasara*.

■ *Enter by south gate. 1030-1730, Rs 10; cameras must be left in lockers (free),*   *"Tip-seeking guards"*
*you take the key; shoes left. Allow about 1 hr, 2 if you wish to see everything
(worth taking a guide); guidebook, Rs 6. Often very crowded, especially at weekends which can be overwhelming; visitors are channelled through rooms at the
general pace. Downstairs is fairly accessible to the disabled. On Sun nights, government holidays and during festivals, the palace is lit by 50,000 light bulbs; well
worth seeing after 1900.*

Now a museum, the ground floor, with an enclosed courtyard, displays cos-   **Maharaja's**
tumes, musical instruments, children's toys et cetera, and numerous portraits;   **Residence**
the upper floor has a small collection of weapons. Some find it very interesting;
others suggest you avoid the "touristy bazar"! ■ *Open 1000-1830, Rs 10.*

Karnataka

Chamundi Hill The hill immediately to the southeast of the town has a temple to Durga (Chamundeswari) celebrating her victory over the buffalo god. She became the guardian deity of the Wodeyars. Beautiful views on a clear day, otherwise little of interest, though the hill is often crowded with day-trippers and hawkers can be a problem. The giant *Nandi*, carved in 1659 (■ *open 0700-1300,*

Mysore

To Srirangapatnam & Ranganathittoo Bird Sanctuary

To Dasaprakash Paradise Hotel & Bangalore

Pulikeshi Rd

TILAKNAGAR

St Joseph's &
St Philomena's
Cathedral

Mission

Sawdey Rd

Sayaji Rao Rd

Govt House Rd

Railway
Museum

To Mysore University, Green Hotel & Nagarhole

Akbar Rd

Kallama Temple Rd

Ashoka Rd

Church Rd

Medical
College

Irwin Rd

Janata
Bazar

Government
House

Exhibition
Ground

Krishna Rajendra
Hospital

Dhanvantri Rd

St Bartholomew's

Wesley
Cathedral

Vinoba Rd

Devaraja
Market

MG
Square

Clock Tower

Nazarbad Main Rd

Jhansi Lakshmi Bai Rd

Sheshadri Rd

Chamundeswari Rd

KR
Circle

Mirza Rd

Sri Harsha Rd

Statue
Square

(A Victoria Rd)

Hardinge
Circle

B N Rd

Jagan
Mohan
Palace

Chamarajendra
Art Gallery

CTO

Amber
Vilas
City
Palace

Lokranjan Mahal Rd

Racecourse Rd

Ramavilas Rd

CHAMARAJAPURA

Nilgiri Rd

Zoo

Chamaraja Double Rd

Ashram

Dodda
Kere

Narayanashastri Rd

Punjab Bank

Ramanuja Rd

Harishchandra Rd

Vanivilas
Market

Kantaraja Rd

LAKSHMIPURA

Racecourse

To Government Silk Factory

To Bandipur & Ooty

To Oriental Library & Mansa Gangotri (museums)

To Lalitha Mahal Palace Hotel & Bangalore (145 km)

To Chamundi Hill & Nandi Bull

Related map
A *Mysore centre,*
page 319

N

0 metres 300
0 yards 300

Karnataka

1600-1930) is on the motorable road down so it is possible to walk to it along the trail from the top and be picked up by a car later or catch a return bus from the road. If you continue along the trail you will end up having to get a rickshaw back, instead of a bus. ■ *Getting there: City Bus No 185*

The Government **Sandalwood Oil Factory**, T521889, where oil was extracted and incense made. ■ *Mon-Sat 0800-1700, T483651.* **Silk Factory**, Manathavadi Road. Weavers produce Mysore silk saris. ■ *0930-1630, Mon-Sat. T481803.* Good **walks** are possible in the Government House if the guard at the gate allows you in.

Other sights

Chamarajendra Art Gallery at Jaganmohan Palace (1861). Indian Miniature paintings and others, including Ravi Varma and Nicholas Roerich. Also exhibition of ceramics, stone, ivory, sandalwood, antique furniture and old musical instruments. No descriptions or guide book; many items randomly displayed but pleasant atmosphere. ■ *0800-1700. Rs 5. No photography.* The **Technical Institute** produces high class rosewood and sandalwood articles. The **Railway Museum** is small but will interest an enthusiast; includes a royal carriage over 100 years old. ■ *0800-1800. Rs 2, camera Rs 5.* **Folklore Museum**, University of Mysore, Manasa Gangotri. Collection includes weapons, jewellery, folk toys, utensils. Photography with permission of Director. ■ *1030-1730, closed second Sat and Sun. Free.* **Art and Archaeology Museum**, PG Department of Ancient History, University of Mysore, Manasa Gangotri. ■ *1030-1730, closed Sun. Free.* Collection includes antiquities, sculpture, inscriptions, coins. Photography with permission. **Medical College Museum**. Collection includes botanical paintings, charts, models, weapons. ■ *0830-1730. Sun 0800-1300. Free.*

Museums

The **zoo** established in 1892 is in the town centre. The 5 sq km site is well managed with gardens and spacious enclosures; wild animals have been bred in captivity, especially tigers. ■ *0830-1800, Sat-Thu. Rs 10 plus camera charge. Accessible to the disabled.*

Park & zoo

The **Brindavan Gardens** are 19 km from Mysore. The 2 km, rock-filled dam is one of the biggest in India and forms a 130 sq km lake. It was built by Maharaja Krishnaraja Wodeyar to provide continuous water supply for the Sivasamudram Power Station. Some travellers find it disappointing. ■ *Wed (1900-2000), Sat and Sun (1900-2100); very popular with Indian tourists so avoid weekends. Entry Rs 5, still camera Rs 15 (sometimes, extra Rs 20 for photos in the garden), no video cameras. Illuminations.* **Sleeping D** Indrarani near the main gate. Rooms with bath and hot water (Rs 400-650) and balcony. **E** *Mayura Cauvery* (KSTDC), T08236-57252. 14 rooms (Rs 210), may reopen. ■ *Getting there: Bus No 303, from Mysore City Bus Stand, Plat 6, every 30 mins; it is a long walk from the bus/coach stand to the gardens across the dam. It may be difficult to find your tour bus for the return journey.*

Excursions

Sri Mahalingeshwara Temple, 12 km away, is 1 km off the Bhogadi road (right turn after K Hemmanahalli, beyond Mysore University Campus). The 800-year old Hoysala Temple has been carefully restored by local villagers under the supervision of the Archaeological Survey of India. The structure is an authentic replica of the old temple – here, too, the low ceiling encourages humility by forcing the worshipper to bow before the shrine. The surrounding garden has been planted with herbs and saplings, including some rare medicinal trees, and provides a tranquil spot away from the city. ■ *Getting there: taxi or auto-rickshaw.*

Tours KSTDC, *Yatri Nivas*, 2 JLB Road, T423652. Mysore, daily 0730-2030, Rs.110, local sights and Chaumundi Hill, Kukkara Halli Lake, Somanathapura, Srirangapatnam and Brindavan Gardens.*Ooty*: Monday, Thursday, Saturday. 0700-2100. Rs 200. *Belur, Halebid, Sravanabelagola*: Tuesday, Wednesday, Friday, Sunday, 0730-2100, Rs 200 (long and tiring but worth it if you are not travelling to Hassan).

Essentials

Sleeping May is the most important wedding month and so hotels get booked in advance. In
JLB Rd is Jhansi Lakshmi the expensive hotels sales tax on food, luxury tax on rooms and a service charge can
Bai Rd, B-N Rd is increase the bill significantly.
Bangalore-Nilgiri Rd

■ *on maps,* **L+-AL** *Lalitha Mahal Palace* (ITDC), Narasipur Rd, T571265, F571770. 54 rooms
pages 316 & 319 (**A** rooms in turret disappointing), suites ($230-740), built in 1931 for the Maharaja's
Price codes: non-vegetarian, foreign guests, grand setting, old-fashioned (some original baths
see inside front cover with extraordinary spraying system), for nostalgia stay in the old wing, ask to see Vice-roy's suite, attractive pool, but disappointing restaurant. **A** *Rajendra Vilas Palace*, Chamundi Hills, T560690. 29 a/c rooms, including Royal suite, built in 1939 as Maharajah's escape from the city, refurbished, out-of-town hilltop situation attractive but 30 mins to city centre. **A** *Southern Star* (Quality Inn), 13-14 Vinoba Rd, T426426, F421689. 72 luxurious rooms, buffet Rs 200, great pool, helpful, friendly. Recommended. **B** *Ramanashree Comfort*, L-43A Hardinge Circle, T522202, F565781. 68 a/c rooms, 2 good restaurants, spotlessly clean, spacious, airy and light, excellent, but no pool, poor travel desk. **B-C** *Green Hotel* (Chittaranjan Palace), 2270 Vinoba Rd (near Mysore University) on a bus route, T512536, F516139, charities.advisory.trust@ukonline 31 rooms, best are in the palace (unique sympathetic conversion), far more comfortable than 24 in newer block (including 12 simple ground floor rooms), good meals (notify ahead) in cool verandah (no smoking) or on immaculate lawns but noisy road traffic, some find them "anaemic", best garden award ("mosquito-eating fish are now holding their own against the frogs!"), solar heating, hotel auto-rickshaw, profits to charity (environmental and tribal projects), exemplary employment practices hence charming, enthusiastic staff. Highly recommended though away from centre. **B-C** *Metropole*, 5 JLB Rd. Closed indefinitely. **B-C** *Dasaprakash Paradise*, 105 Vivekananda Rd, Yadavgiri, T515655, 2 km north of rly station. 90 rooms, 36 a/c with bath, highly recommended restaurant (vegetarian), very clean, quiet. Recommended.

C-D *Siddharta*, 73/1 Guest House Rd, Nazarabad, T522888, F520692. 105 rooms, some a/c, huge with tubs, good restaurant (Indian vegetarian), exchange, immaculate, well run. **D** *Maurya Palace*,. Sri Harsha Rd, T435912, F429304. 27 rooms, (6 a/c), well furnished and comfortable, well run, good value. **D** *Maurya Residency* T523375, F429304 next door, is a sister hotel with 24 a/c rooms. **D** *Palace Plaza,* 2716 Sri Harsha Rd, T430034, F421070. 27 spacious, comfortable **C** a/c rooms with bath tubs, hot water, some Indian toilets, back much quieter, very clean, modern, good *Dynasty* restaurant (room service when closed), friendly, good value, reserve ahead. Highly recommended. **D** *Viceroy*, Sri Harsha Rd, T424001, F433391. 30 comfortable rooms with phone, some a/c (best have tubs), a/c restaurant (North Indian, Chinese), exchange, travel. **D** *Mayura Hoysala* (KSTDC), 2 JLB Rd, T425349. 20 rooms and a cottage, economy rooms are tatty, no nets, large a/c suites are good value, good restaurant, bar, tourist office (good tours); also **E** *Yatri Nivas*, T423492. 19 small, rather dingy rooms overlooking attractive garden courtyard, dorm (Rs 70), caravan parking and use of WC, showers and possibly electricity.

Karnataka

D-E *Dasaprakash*, Gandhi Sq, T442444. 145 rooms, most with bath, few a/c, clean, fresh-looking, attractive courtyard, quite quiet, rather dark vegetarian restaurant, recommended (resident astro-palmist takes photocopy of palm print to forecast your future, Rs 100-200!). **D-E** *Guptha*, near HPO, 252B Ashoka Rd, T445089. Good range of rooms with hot water, some with a/c, TV, bath tubs, 1 huge with round bed! (Rs 800), room service *thali* Rs 20, fairly quiet, clean, friendly and enthusiastic staff. **D-E** *SCVDS*, Sri Harsha Rd, next to *Park Lane*, T421379, F426297. Decent rooms, few a/c, some rather dreary (Rs 350-700), very friendly. **E** *Ashraya*, Dhanvantri Rd, T427088. 18 rooms, clean and comfortable, South Indian meals. **D-E** *Darshan Palace*, Lokranjan Mahal Rd (between Race Course and zoo, opposite Regency theatre), T520794, F564083. Clean rooms (range of facilities), very quiet, well run, but "staff pester once you use room service". **E** *Govardhan*, Sri Harsha Rd, T431960. 60 rooms, quality varies from small and crumbling to reasonable, some a/c with TV, busy *Gopika* vegetarian restaurant downstairs. **E** *Calinga*, 23 KR Circle (opposite City Bus Stand), T431019. 76 rooms (some with 3-tier cot!) with baths (occasional hot water), Indian toilets, restaurant (Indian vegetarian), fairly basic but clean and popular. **E** *Rajmahal Deluxe*, Jaganmohan Palace Sq. T421196. 26 light and airy rooms with bath, some with balcony, welcoming and helpful. **E** *Ritz*, B-N Rd near Central Bus Station, T422668. Very dark rooms (Rs 300), but pleasant open shaded courtyard, good restaurant. **E** *Sudarshan Lodge*, opposite Jaganmohan Palace, T426718. 44 clean rooms and dorm, quiet, friendly. **E-F** *Indra Bhavan*, Dhanvantri Rd, T423933, F422290. 44 clean rooms with bath, quiet central courtyard, good a/c vegetarian restaurant, spacious and airy, good value. Recommended. **E-F** *Park Lane*, 2720, Sri Harsha Rd, T430400. 8 rooms, some cramped and old-fashioned (1st Flr better), bar, well-kept and friendly, good restaurant but some find music too loud. **F** *Anugraha*, Jus Complex, SR Rd (by S Patel Rd), T430768. Good sized standard, clean rooms, hot water 0600-1000, back

The Gandhi Square area has some Indian style hotels which are clean & good value

Karnataka

Mysore centre

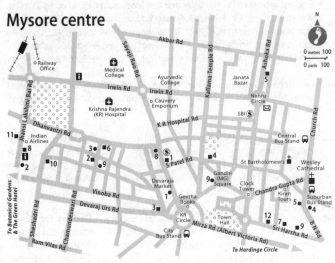

■ **Sleeping**
1 Anugraha
2 Ashraya
3 Calinga
4 Dasaprakash & Veg Restaurant
5 Guptha's
6 Indra Bhavan & Samrat Restaurant
7 Maurya Palace, Mayura Residency & Govardhan
8 Mayura Hoysala, Yatri Nivas & KSTDC Travels
9 Park Lane SCVDS & Palace Plaza
10 Sangeeth
11 Southern Star
12 Viceroy

● **Eating**
1 Bombay Tiffanys
2 Mysore Memories Raintree & Indra Café (at King's Court)
3 Penguin Ice Creams
4 Raghu Niwas
5 Ritz
6 RRR
7 Shilpashri
8 Sri Rama & Ashok Books
9 SR Plantain Leaf

rooms quieter, friendly and helpful. **F** *Kalpana Lodge*, Jaganmohan Palace Sq, T421460. 30 colourful and cosy rooms with bath (Rs 125), good value. **F** *Railway Retiring Rooms*, 7 rooms, 1 a/c, dorm (Rs 30), very good value. **F** *Sangeeth*, 1966 Narayanashastri Rd, near *Udupi Sri Krishan Mandir*, T424693. Rooms with bath, clean Indian style hotel, fairly quiet, near rly, simple South Indian meals. **F** *Youth Hostel* is rather inconvenient, 5 km northwest of city centre.

Eating

■ *on maps, pages 316 & 319*

Best bars are in hotels: 'Lalitha Mahal Palace' & 'Lokranjan Mahal Palace'

Expensive *Ramanashree Comfort* and *Southern Star* hotels are recommended. *Green* – "superb cooking, colourful, subtle, among the best", (see above). **Mid-range** *King's Court's Mysore Memories* and outdoor *Raintree* BBQ are popular. *Park Lane* hotel. Mixed menu. Carefully prepared, excellent food (try *palak paneer*, hot/sour soup) Indian classical music at dinner, attractive shaded courtyard/garden, bar, well run, very busy. Recommended. *Shanghai*, Vinoba Rd. Superb Chinese despite shabby interior. 1100-1500, 1830-2300. *Shilpashri*, Gandhi Sq. Comfortable rooftop, reasonably priced, good food, tourist oriented, chilled beers, but service can be slow. *Durbar*, opposite also has a rooftop bar. **Cheap** *Amaravathi* (*Roopa's*), Hardinge Circle. Excellent, spicy hot Andhra meals on banana leaves. *Jewel Rock* in *Maurya Palace*, Sri Harsha Rd. Dark interior but great chicken tikka and spicy cashewnut chicken, go early to avoid queuing. *Dasaprakash Hotel*, for excellent, as-much-as-you-can-eat vegetarian meals. *Mylari* in *Hotel Mahadeshwara*, Nazarbad Main Rd (ask rickshaw driver), the best *dosas* in town served on a palm leaf (Rs 6), mornings until 1100, "undiscovered by tourists", highly recommended, may have to queue. *Samrat*, Dhanvantri Rd, near *Guptha*, Ashok Rd. Excellent vegetarian *thalis* for Rs 20. *SR Plantain Leaf* (*Chayuka's*), Rajkamal Talkies Rd. Decent veg *thali* s on banana leaf; also tandoori chicken *RRR* near Gandhi Sq. Part a/c, tasty non-veg on plantain leaves. *Ritz*, B-N Rd. Good food and excellent lime-sodas! *Santosh*, near bus station. Excellent value *thalis* (Rs 16). **Cafés and fast food** *Indra Café*, Sayaji Rd. Excellent bhel puri, sev puri etc. *Penguin Ice-cream Parlour*, comfortable sofas shared with local teens listening to Hindi 'pop'.*Raghu Niwas*, B-N Rd, opposite *Ritz*. Does very good breakfasts. *Sri Rama Veg*, 397 Dhanvantri Rd. Serves fast food, good juices. **Sweets** *Bombay Tiffanys*, Devraja Market Building. Try the *Mysore Pak* here.

Entertainment

Two **cinemas** show English language films. **Sports** *Chennai Sports Club*, Lalitha Mahal Palace Rd, just before the hotel. **Swimming** Mysore University has an Olympic-size pool.

Festivals

Mar- Apr: *Temple car festival* with a 15 day fair, at *Nanjangud*, 23 km; *Vairamudi festival* which lasts six days when deities are adorned with three diamond crowns, at *Melkote Temple*, 52 km. **11 Aug**: *Feast of St Philomena*, in Mysore, the statue of the saint is taken out in procession through the city streets ending with a service at the cathedral. **End Sep-early-Oct**: *Dasara*.

Shopping

Books: *Ashok*, Dhanvantri Rd, T435533, excellent selection. **Clothing**: *Craft Emporium* and cloth shops in the middle part of Vinoba Rd are recommended for good selection and good quality. Competent tailors will make up and deliver within a couple of hours. *Badshah's*, 20 Devraj Urs Rd, T429799, beautifully finished salwar-kameez, Mr Yasin speaks good English. For **silks** at reasonable prices, try Sayaji Rao Rd. You can watch machine weaving at *Karnataka Silk Industry's* factory shop on Mananthody Rd, 0730-1130, 1230-1630, Mon-Sat. **Handicrafts**: superb carved figures, sandalwood and rosewood items, silks, incense sticks, handicrafts. The main shopping area is Sayaji Rao Rd. *Cauvery Arts & Crafts Emporium* for sandalwood and rosewood items, 1000-1330, 1500-1930, closed Thu (non-receipt of parcel reported by traveller). *Devaraja Market*, lanes of stalls selling spices, perfumes and much more; good "antique" shop (fixed price) has excellent sandalwood and rosewood items. *Sri*

Karnataka

Lakshmi Fine Arts & Crafts (opposite the zoo) also has a factory shop at 2226 Sawday Rd, Mandi Mohalla. Also recommended are *Shankar* at 12, and *Ganesh* at 532 Dhanvantri Rd. **Photography**: *Classic* 10 Devaraj Urs Rd; *Konika* opposite Central Bus Stand. Many on Dhanvantri and S Patel Rd.

KSE, Hotel Roopa, B-N Rd, T446099, 440947, very competent, recommended. *Kiran*, **Tour operators** 21/1 Chandra Gupta Rd, T436875. *Seagull*, by 8 *Ramanashree Complex*, T529732, F520535, for cars/drivers, flights, wildlife tours etc, helpful. *Siddharta*, 73/1 Guest House Rd, Nazarabad, T444155. *TCI*, Gandhi Sq, T443023. Very pleasant and helpful.

Local   Auto-rickshaw: Easily available. **Car hire**: Travel companies and KSTDC **Transport** about Rs 500 (4 hrs/40 km) for city sightseeing; Rs 850 to include Srirangapatnam and Brindavan. KSE charges Rs 700 for Somnathpur, Srirangapatnam and Bird Sanctuary. **Bus**: City Bus Station, southeast of KR Circle, T425819. To Silk Weaving Centre, Nos 1,2,4 & 8; Brindavan Gardens, No 303; Chamundi Hill, No 201; Srirangapatnam, No 313. Central Bus Station, T529853. Bandipur, Plat 9, Ooty etc, Plat 11.

Long distance   Air: No flights from Mysore at present. *Indian Airlines*, 2 JLB Rd, T421846.

Road   Bus: There are 3 bus stations: **Central**, mainly for long distance SRTC, T520853, **City** for local buses, and **B3 Suburban** and **Private** including Somnathpur. SRTC buses of Karnataka, Tamil Nadu and Kerala run regular daily services between Mysore and other major cities. Check timings. Many private companies near Gandhi Sq operate overnight sleepers and interstate buses which may be faster and marginally less uncomfortable Book ahead for busy routes (eg Hassan). The bus station has a list of buses with reserved places. **Somnathpur**: few from Surburban station, 1 hr direct, or longer via Bannur or T Narasipur. Several buses daily to many towns from **Central** Bus Station. **Bangalore**: every ¼ hr, from non-stop platform. Semi-deluxe, every ¼ hr. **Thiruvananthapuram**: Super-deluxe, 14 hrs.

Train: Advance Computerized Reservations in separate section; ask for foreigners' counter. T131. Enquiries T520103, 0800-2000 (closed 1330-1400); Sun 0800-1400. Left luggage 0600-2200, Rs 3-Rs 6 per day. Tourist Information, telephone and toilets on Plat 1. Taxi counter at entrance. To **Bangalore** (non-stop): *Tippu Exp 6205*, 1120, 2½ hrs; *Shatabdi, 2008*, daily except Tue 1410, 2 hrs (continues to **Chennai** another 5 hrs). **Bangalore** via **Srirangapatnam**, **Mandya** and **Maddur**: *Chamundi Exp 6215*, 0645, 3 hrs; *Nandi Exp 6211*, 1300, 3¼ hrs; *Mysore Tirupati Exp 6213*, 1625, 3¼ hrs; *Kaveri Exp 6221*, 1840, 2¾ hrs. **Chennai**: *Chennai Exp 6221*, 1805, 10½ hrs. **Mumbai**: *Mysore Mumbai Exp 1036*, Mon,Tue, Sat, 0600, 26 hrs.

Banks *State Bank of Mysore*, corner of Sayaji Rao Rd and Sardar Patel Rd. and opposite GPO in **Directory** city centre. *Bank of Baroda*, MG Sq, honours TCs, visa, but unsatisfactory service. **Communications** GPO: on corner of Ashoka Rd and Irwin Rd; *Poste Restante* here. **Central Telegraph Office**: open 24 hrs, is west of Maharajah's Palace. **Internet**: *Coca Cola Cyber Space*, 2 Madvesha Complex, Nazarabad, nr Sri Harsha Rd, T565574; *Cyber Net Corner*, 2/3B Indira Bhavan, Dhanvantri Rd, T446200. *Pepsi Cyber Club*, 413,'Sri Nilaya', 1st Flr, V Shamanna Rd near Agrahara Circle, T538455, F520480. **Medical services** *Medical College*, corner of Irwin and Sayaji Rao Rd. *KR Hospital*, T443300; *Mission Hospital* (Mary Holdsworth), Tilaknagar, in a striking building dating from 1906. **Tourist offices** *Karnataka*, Yatri Nivas, 2 JLB Rd. T423652, efficient; at Old Exhibition Bldg (corner of Irwin Rd), T422096. 1000-1730 (guides available). Counters at Rly Station, T440719 and Bus Stand. **Useful addresses** *Forest Office*, and Project Tiger, Forest Dept, Woodyard, Ashokpuram, T480110, (City Bus No 61).

Karnataka

★ Srirangapatnam

Phone code: 08236
Colour map 3, grid A3
Population: 21,900

Srirangapatnam has played a crucial role in the region since its origins in the 10th century. Occupying an easily fortified island site in the Kaveri River, it has been home to religious reformers and military conquerors, and makes a fascinating day trip from Mysore, 12 km away.

Ins & outs

Getting there Trains and buses between Bangalore and Mysore stop here but arrival can be tiresome with hassle from traders and beggars. **Getting around** The island is over 3 km long and 1 km wide so it is helpful to have an auto or hire a cycle from a shop on the main road.

History

The name comes from the temple of Vishnu Sri Ranganathasvami, which is far older than the fort or the town. The site was frequently a focal point in South India's political development. The fort was built under the Vijayanagar kings in 1454. 150 years later the last Vijayanagar king handed over authority to the Hindu Wodeyars of Mysore, who made it their capital. In the second half of the 18th century it became the capital of **Haidar Ali**, who defended it against the Marathas in 1759, laying the foundations of his expanding power. He was succeeded by his son **Tipu Sultan**, who also used the town as his headquarters.

Colonel Wellesley, the future **Duke of Wellington**, established his military reputation in the battle in which Tipu Sultan was finally killed on 4 May 1799, see page 514 though victory should be more correctly attributed to his brother, the Governor General. Tipu died in exceptionally fierce fighting near the north gate of the fort; the place is marked by a very simple monument. Wellesley was immediately appointed Governor of Srerangapatnam, the start of a further five years, compaigning in India.

Karnataka

Srirangapatnam

The fort had triple fortifications, but the British destroyed most of it. The **Jama Masjid**, built by Tipu Sultan, has delicate minarets, and there are two Hindu **temples**, Narasimha (17th century) and Gangadharesvara (16th century). ■ *0800-1300, 1600-2000*.

Daria Daulat Bagh (Splendour of the Sea), 1 km to the east of the fort, is Tipu's beautiful **summer palace** built in 1784, in its lovely garden. It is "an absolute jewel" with colourful frescoes of battle scenes between the French, British and Mysore armies, ornamental arches and gilded paintings on the teak walls and ceilings which are full of interesting detail. The west wall shows Haidar Ali and Tipu Sultan leading their elephant forces at the battle of Polilur (1780), inflicting a massive defeat on the British. As a result of the battle Colonel Baillie, the defeated British commander, was a prisoner in Srirangapatnam for many years. The murals on the east walls show Tipu offering hospitality to neighbouring princes at various palace durbars. The small museum upstairs has 19th century European paintings and Tipu's belongings. Excellently maintained by the Archaeological Survey of India. ■ *Rs 2, 0900-1700, closed Fri.*

The Gumbaz The family mausoleum (3 km), was built by Tipu in remembrance of his father. Approached through an avenue of cypresses, the ornate white domed Gumbaz contains beautiful ivory-on-wood inlay and Tipu's tiger stripe emblem. Some of his swords and shields are kept here. The tranquil atmosphere is a perfect setting for the elegant and quiet mausoleum which houses the tomb of Haidar Ali in the centre, that of his wife on the east and of Tipu Sultan on the west. ■ *0900-1700, closed Fri.*

Coracles On the banks of the Cauvery, just north of the Lalbagh Palace, is a jetty where six seater coracles are available for river rides. Great fun!

Sights

Daria Daulat Bagh & the Gumbaz are wonderful. The same can not be said of the rickshaw drivers

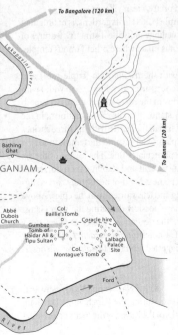

Sleeping

C *Amblee Holiday Resort*, on the Kaveri, T52358, 28 rather deteriorating rooms, billiards, overpriced. **C** *Fort View Resort*, T52777, F53177. 12 upmarket rooms (4 with corner tub!), Rajasthani architecture, huge beds, beautiful shady landscaped gardens, gloomy restaurant (pricey), organic kitchen garden, pool, boating, fishing, no 'fort view', pretentious. **D-E** *Balaji Garden Resort*, Mysore Rd (1 km from Piriyapatna Bridge), T53297. 12 good value cottages (suites) and 28 smallish rooms built with some style around a central courtyard, well furnished, tiled and comfortable, cottages are good value, pool, restaurant. **D** *Mayura River View* (KSTDC), T52114. Beautifully situated on the river, 8 comfortable rooms with sit-outs, 2 a/c (Rs 450-500), good restaurant (Indian, Chinese), really quiet. Next door, **F** *PWD Rest House*, charming former residence of George Harris, very pleasant, basic rooms (Rs 50),but clean and quiet. Book ahead at PWD office near Ranganathaswami Temple, T52051.

Karnataka

Ranganat-hittoo Bird Sanctuary

Some 5 km upstream of Srirangapatnam is the riverine site of the Ranganathittoo Bird Sanctuary, established in 1975. Several rocky islands, some bare while the larger are well wooded, provide excellent habitat for waterbirds. It is a popular tourist site, receiving hundreds of visitors every day. It is possible to go round some of the islands on the river by boat but not to land. Fourteen species of waterbirds use the sanctuary as a breeding ground, most of which begin to breed in June. There is a large colony of fruit bats in trees on the edge of the river and a number of marsh crocodiles between the small islands. ■ *0600-0900, 1600-1800. Entry Rs 15, Rs 150 for foreigners, still camera Rs 10. Best season: Jun-Oct. Getting there: Mysore City Bus 126.*

Mandya
Phone code: 08232
Colour map 3, grid A3
Population: 120,000

Mandya, along the Bangalore road, is an important market town, especially for sugar. It became the centre of the Mysore Sugar Company, which has made refined sugar and spirit since 1930. Tea, coffee, cold drinks and South Indian meals are available in the town centre.

Maddur

Much industrial development is taking place around the town which is on the banks of the river Shimsha. Briefly the HQ of a Vijayanagar Viceroy, Maddur also has two Vaishnava temples. **Eating** *Tiffany's*, Main Rd, 300 m north of rly station (2 km north of town). Simple but superb South and North Indian meals, freshly prepared, very clean. *Mayura Highway* (KSTDC), near bus stand. Clean and airy. ■ *Getting there: See Bangalore and Mysore for trains which stop at Maddur. The town bus stand is on the bypass road.*

★ Somna-thpur
Phone code: 08227

This tiny village, east of Mysore, has one of the best preserved and the only complete one of approximately 80 Hoysala temples in the Mysore region. The drive from Srirangapatnam via Bannur is particularly lovely, passing a couple of lakes through beautiful country and pretty, clean villages.

The small but exquisite **Kesava Temple** (1268) in its gardens, is maintained by the Archaeological Dept. Excellent ceilings show the distinctive features of the late Hoysala style, and here the roof is intact where other famous temples have lost theirs.

The temple has three sanctuaries with the *trikutachala* (triple roof) and stands in the middle of its rectangular courtyard (70 m long, 55 m wide) with cloisters containing 64 cells around it. From the east gateway there is a superb view of the temple with an ambulatory standing on its raised platform, in the form of a 16-pointed star. The pillared hall in the centre with the three shrines to the west give it the form of a cross in plan. Walk around the temple to see the bands of sculptured figures which are particularly fine. The lowest of the six shows a line of elephants, symbolizing strength and stability, then horsemen for speed, followed by a floral scroll. The next band of beautifully carved figures (at eye level) is the most fascinating and tells stories from the epics. Above is the *yali* frieze, the monsters and foliage possibly depicting the river Ganga and uppermost is a line of *hamsa*, the legendary geese. ■ *Open daily 0900-1700. Allow at least 1 hr. KSTDC Canteen in the garden. Getting there: buses from Mysore take 1-1½ hours.* Suggested reading *Hoysalas* by Mishra, is available from the custodian.

Talakad

Talakad is 10 km from Somnathpur. The **Kritti Narayana (Vaidyeshwara) Temple** comes to life once every 12 years during the Panchalinga Darshan, when the temple on the wide sandy banks of the Kaveri is the focus of a colourful and busy festival.

Here, the Kaveri plunges over 100 m into a series of wild and inaccessible gorges (best in July/August). At the top of the falls the river divides around the island of Sivasamudram, the *Barachukki* channel on the east and the *Gaganchukki* on the west. The hydro-electricity project was completed in 1902, the first HEP scheme of any size in India. During the wet season the falls are an impressive sight, water cascading over a wide area in a series of leaps. **Sleeping** *Guest Houses* may be reserved through Executive Engineer, KEB and the PWD at Bluff, Malavalli Taluk, Mandya District. Food to be ordered in advance. Tea stalls available.

★ Sivasa mudram

Jungle Lodges' **B** *Cauvery Fishing Camps* are hidden amid steep hills on the banks of the Cauvery (south of Halagur) it is a peaceful place where mahseer attract anglers. Accomodation is in tents or huts with attached bath. Seperate rates for anglers and non-anglers. Contact Jungle Lodges, T5597025, F5586163, jungle@giasbg 01.vsnl.net.in

Bheemeshwari & Doddamakali

This wildlife sanctuary in a hilly area with deciduous and evergreen trees interspersed with grassland, is southeast of Mysore. The best time for wildlife sighting is November to May. The Soliga tribals pay special respect to an ancient champak tree (*Dodda sampige mara*) believed to be 1,000 year old. The **wildlife** includes panther, elephant, sloth bear, various deer, gaur and tiger as well as 270 species of birds.

Biligiri Rangaswamy
Altitude: 1,000-1,600 m

Sleeping B *Tented Camp*, Kyathadevara. 10 twin bedded tents with modern toilets, simple meals in the open air or at the Maharaja's Hunting Lodge, elephant ride, trekking organized for those staying more than 1 night, contact *Jungle Lodges and Resorts*, T/F5586163.

Transport From Mysore, via Nanjangud (23km) and Chamrajnagar, Nagavalli and Nellore villages. The Ghat Rd starts at the Forest Check Post after passing 2 lakes. The camp (90 km from Mysore) is beyond the second check post.

Bandipur National Park

Bandipur was set up by the Mysore Maharajah in 1931. It has a mixture of subtropical moist and dry deciduous forests (predominantly teak and Anogeissus) and scrubland in the Nilgiri foothills. The wetter areas support rosewood, sandalwood, silk cotton and *jamun*. You should easily spot *gaur*, *chital* (spotted deer), elephant, sambar, flying squirrel and four-horned antelope, but tigers and leopards are rare. Also good variety of birdlife including crested hawk and serpent eagles and tiny-eared owl.

Colour map 3, grid A3
Altitude: 780-1,455 m
Area: 874 sq km

Private cars are not allowed. Jeeps and vans are available through Forestry Department; one hour coach rides (morning and afternoon, 0630-1630), Rs 10 each but other noisy visitors scare away wildlife. Viewing is best from *machans* (raised platforms) near watering places; ask to reserve ahead. Dull coloured clothes are recommended. No elephant rides in the park now; only 30 minute 'joy rides' at 0930; disappointing.

■ *0600-0900, 1600-1800. Entry Rs 15, Rs 150 for foreigners, still camera Rs 10. Best time: Nov-Feb avoiding the hot, dry months. Climate: Temperature range: 30°C- 18°C. Rainfall: 1,000 mm. Buses stop at the main entrance.*

Karnataka

Sleeping

It is important to reserve rooms well in advance; avoid weekends

AL *Bush Betta Wildlife Resort*, 5 km from entrance. 2 dirty jungle huts, lack staff, highly overpriced (foreigners pay double, $200). **B-C** *Tusker Trails*, Mangla Village, 3 km from Bandipur campus. 6 rustic cottages with verandahs around pool with good views, bamboo hut on stilts, nearby 'dam' attracts wildlife, includes meals, entry and park rides. Foreigners pay double. **D** *Jungle Trails*, outside the park, a small guesthouse owned by wildlife enthusiast, simple meals, wildlife viewing from netted porch and *machans* on riverside. **E** *Mayura Prakruti*, at Melkamanahalli nearby, T08229-7301. Simple rooms in cottages (Rs 385) and restaurant under shady trees. **F** *Forest Lodges*, *Guest Houses* with attached baths, and 3 *Wooden Cottages* for 12 in Kakanhalla, Mulehole and Kalkere. A couple of *VIP lodges* – Rajendra I and II, and *Swiss Cottage tents*. Cooks prepare food to order (cooking in rooms prohibited). Also **F** *Venuvihar Lodge*, in beautiful Gopalaswamy Hills (20 km). Meals available but take provisions. Book in advance through Forest Dept, Woodyard, Ashokpuram, Mysore, T480110.

Transport

Bandipur is in Karnataka while the neighbouring park, Mudumalai, is in Tamil Nadu, but they are extensions of the same forest reserve which also stretches west to include the undeveloped Kerala reserve of Waynad. They are on the Mysore to Ooty bus route, about 2½ hrs south from Mysore and 2½ hrs from Ooty. Buses go to and from Mysore (80 km) between 0615-1530.

Coorg (Kodagu) and Nagarhole

Madikeri (Mercara)

Phone code: 08272
Colour map 3, grid A2
Population: 28,800
Altitude: 1,150 m

The capital of Coorg District, Madikeri, is an attractive small town in a beautiful hilly setting surrounded by the forested slopes of the Western Ghats. It promises to become an attractive trekking destination.

Ins & outs

Getting there Coorg is only accessible by road at present although an airport and railway station are planned by 2002. Frequent local and express buses arrive at Madikeri's bus stand from the west coast after a journey through beautiful wooded hills passing small towns and a wildlife sanctuary. From Mysore and Coimbatore an equally pleasant route traverses the Maidan. In winter there is often hill fog at night, making after dark driving dangerous. **Getting around** Madikeri is ideal for walking though you may need to hire an auto on arrival to reach the better hotels. **Climate** Maximum (May) 29°C, Minimum (Jan) 9°C. Annual rainfall: 3,250 mm.

History

Although there were refreneces to the Kodaga people in the Tamil Sangam literature of the second century AD, the earliest Kodaga inscriptions date from the 8th century. After the Vjiayanagar Empire was defeated in 1565 (see page 345) many of their courtiers moved south, establishing regional kingdoms. One of these groups were the Haleri Rajas, members of the Lingayat caste whose leader Virarajendra set up the first Kodaga dynasty at Haleri, 10 km from the present district capital of Madikeri.

The later Kodagu rajas were noted for some bizarre behaviour. Dodda Vira (1780-1809) was reputed to have put most of his relatives to death, a pattern followed by the last king, Vira Raja, before he was forced to abdicate by the British in 1834. In 1852 the last Lingayat ruler of Kodagu, Chikkavirarajendra Wodeyar, became the first Indian prince to sail to England, and the economic character of the State was quickly transformed. Coffee was introduced, becoming the staple crop of the region.

The forests of Kodagu are still home to wild elephants and other wildlife, while the Kodaga people are very proud of the martial traditions and their hospitality. Kodagu also has a highly distinctive cuisine, in which pork curry *(pandi curry)* and rice dumplings *(kadumbuttu)* are particular favourites.

Sights

The **Omkareshwara Temple**, dedicated to both Vishnu and Siva, was built in 1820. The tiled roofs are typical of Kerala Hindu architecture, while the domes show Muslim influence. The **fort** with its three stone gateways, built between 1812-14 by Lingarajendra Wodeyar II, is on high ground dominating the town. It has a small museum in St Mark's Church (■ *1000-1730* where a memorial on the wall includes a First World War Victoria cross to Capt William Leefe Robinson. Several Coorg planters appear to have opted to join the RAF). The fort also encloses the town prison, a temple and a chapel while the palace houses government offices. **Raja's Seat**, 1 km from the bus stand along MG Road, offers panoramic views of mountains and valleys and was a favourite spot of the Rajas at sunset. The **'Rajas' Tombs'** (Gaddige), built in 1820 to the north of the town, are the memorials of Virarajendra and his wife and of Lingarajendra. Although the rajas were Hindu, their commemorative monuments are Muslim in style; Kodagas both bury and cremate their dead. The Friday **Market** near the bus stand, is very colourful as all the local tribal people come to town to sell their produce. It is known locally as 'shandy', a British bastardisation of the Koorg word *shante*, meaning simply market. On Mahadevpet Road, which leads to the Rajas' tombs, is a 250-year-old **Siva temple** with an interesting stone façade. Madikeri has an attractive nine-hole **golf** course.

Fishing

Coorg Wildlife Society (see page 329) can arrange a licence for fishing on the Kaveri river (Rs 500 per day, Rs 1000 weekend). The highlight is the prospect of pulling in a mahseer which can grow up to 45 kg in weight; all fish are returned to the river. This is at Trust Land Estate, Valnoor, near Kushalnagar

Karnataka

Madikeri

After Kim Clark & Lucy Gorman

N

Related map
A Madikeri centre,
Not to scale *page 329*

Karnataka

where there is a lodge but you'll need to carry food. Mr Ponappa has the keys to the lodge and can also issue the licence. Contact Prof MB Madaiah, T08276 76443, or *CWS. Orange County Resort* I is in Dubare Forest (see page 331).

Trekking Madikeri and the surrounding area makes for beautiful walking but if you want to venture further you'll need to take a guide as paths can soon become indistinct and confusing. **Abbi Falls** is a 30-minute rickshaw ride (9 km, Rs 125 round trip including a 30 minute wait) through forests and coffee plantations. It is also an enjoyable walk along a fairly quiet road. The falls themselves are beautiful and well worth the visit – listen for the Malabas Whistling Thrush. You can do a beautiful short trek down the valley and then up and around above the falls before rejoining the main road. Do not attempt it alone since there are no trails and you must depend on your sense of direction along forest paths. *Friends' Tours and Travel*, below Bank of India, College Rd, are recommended for their knowledge and enthusiasm.They do tailor-made treks at about Rs 275 per day per person to include guide, food and accomodation (in temples, schools, huts etc). They have a 'basecamp' at Thalathmane, 4 km from Madikeri, which people can also stay at even if not trekking (basic huts and blankets for Rs 50 each, home cooking from nearby at little extra cost). Contact Mr Raja Shekar on T29974, T29102 (1000-1930) or T25672 (2100-0900). *Coorg Interntional* and *Hotel Cauvery* will also arrange treks.

Sleeping **C** *Capitol Village*, 5 km from town. 13 large, airy rooms, dorm (Rs 150), traditional Keralan building (tiled roof, wooden beams) set in a coffee, cardamom and pepper estate, very quiet, outdoor eating under shady trees (Rs 75-150), rickshaw from town centre Rs 40. Book 10 days in advance through *Hotel Cauvery*, Madikeri. **C** *Coorg International*, Convent Rd, T29390, F28071. 27 large and comfortable rooms, restaurant (wide choice), light, spacious lobby, good facilities including bookshop, pool, health club, tours and trekking. Modern, tastefully decorated and very comfortable, young, enthusiastic and friendly staff. Recommended. **C-D** *Rajdarshan*,116/2 MG Rd, T29142. 25 well laid-out, clean rooms, decent restaurant, fairly plush, modern, with views over town.

Many really cheap hotels are virtually homes for semi-permanent Indian guests

D *Mayura Valley View* (KSTDC), Raja's Seat, T28387. 20 rooms (Rs 450), some with TV (newer rooms better, old dimly lit), good value restaurant, bar, perched on clifftop, outstanding views over town and across rolling forests, appears rundown but rooms are airy though need refurbishing, friendly staff though service can be slow, tranquil and hassle-free, book direct or at Karnataka Tourism, Bangalore, T2212901. **D-E** *Cauvery*, School Rd, T25492. Clean rooms with fans, standard meals. Helpful management, info on surroundings and on trekking (stores luggage). **E** *Amrita*, T23607. Recently opened, resembling something out of a Spanish soap opera, but as yet spotless rooms with bath, restaurant, eager to please staff. **E** *Chitra*, School Rd, T25372, F25191, near bus stand. 31 rooms with western toilets, hot shower, simple but clean, good value, ordinary restaurant, handy bar, helpful and knowledgeable English speaking trekking guide (Mr Muktar); best in its category. **E** *Coorg Side*, Daswal Rd, T25489. 20 clean rooms, hot water (Rs 250), vegetarian canteen, quiet. **E** *East End*, Gen Thimaya Rd, T29996. Darkish rooms but good restaurant (excellent dosas). **E** *Vinayaka Lodge*, 25 m from bus stand, T29830. 50 rooms with bath, hot water buckets (Rs 275), friendly staff, clean and quiet despite unpromising surroundings of open sewer and bus stand.

Eating *Choice*, School Rd. Wide menu (choose tandoori), choice of floors including rooftop. *Udupi Veglands*, opposite fort. Lovely, clean, spacious wooden eatery, delicious and cheap vegetarian *thalis*. *Taj*, College Rd. 'Cheap and best' veg and non-veg, clean and friendly.

Karnataka

Road Bus KSRTC, T26236, frequent express buses to **Bangalore** Plat 4, from 0615 (6 **Transport** hrs); **Chikmagalur; Hassan** (3¾ hrs); **Kannur; Mangalore**, Plat 2, 0530-2400 (3½ hrs); **Mysore** Plat 3 (2½ hrs) via **Kushalnagar** (for Tibetan settlements); **Thalassery**. Daily to **Coimbatore, Kannur, Madurai** 1900, **Mumbai** 0930, **Ooty** 0730, 2030, **Virajpet**. **Private Bus Stand**: *Kamadenu Travels* above Bus Stand, T27024, for *Purnima Travels* bus to **Bangalore**. *Shakti Motor Service* to **Nagarhole** (4½ hrs); **Virajpet**.

Banks *Canara Bank*, Main Rd, accepts some TCs and Visa. **Tourist office** Next to *PWD Travellers'* **Directory** *Bungalow*, Mangalore Rd, T25648. **Useful addresses** *Community Centre*, south of Fort, Main Rd, holds occasional shows, recommended. *Coorg Wildlife Society*, 2 km from GT Circle along Mysore Rd, then 1 km to left), T23505. *Forestry Office*, Aranya Bhavan, Mysore Rd (3 km from town), T25708. *Post Office*, behind Private Bus Stand.

Around Madikeri

Bhagamandala (36 km southwest) The Triveni bathing ghat is at the confluence of the three rivers, Kaveri, Kanike and Suiyothi. Among many small shrines the Bhandeshwara temple, standing in a large stone courtyard surrounded by Keralan-style buildings on all four sides, is particularly striking. You can stay at the temple for a very small charge. ■ *Getting there: half-hourly service from Madikeri's private bus stand from 0630-2000. Also Rama Motors tour bus departs 0830, with 30-min stop.*

Talacauvery (8 km further) This place has been 'developed' so that what was a small temple in the forest is now a disintegrating concrete complex on a barren hillside. Steps lead up from the spring which is the Kaveri's source to the summit of the hill, commanding superb views. The spring is contained in a small and unspectacular pool of brown water. On *Sankaramana Day* in October, Goddess Cauvery is believed to appear – the spring gushes at a particular and foretold moment and thousands come to bathe in the water then. An *ashram* accommodates pilgrims. For the *PWD bungalow*, contact Forestry Dept in Madikeri.

Kakkabe The small town, 35 km from Madikeri, gives access to the highest peak in Coorg, Thandiandamole (1,800 m). Padi Iggutappa nearby is the most important temple in Coorg. **Sleeping** An interesting option is **D-E***Palace Estate*, 2 km south of Kakkabe along Palace Road (rickshaw from Kakkabe Rs 35), a small, traditional farm growing coffee, pepper, cardamom and bananas. Situated close to the late 18th-century Nalnad Palace, a summer hunting lodge of the kings of Coorg, isolated, ideal for walking. Double rooms Rs 350-450, food Rs 100 (unique, interesting local recipes), English speaking guide Rs 150. Reserve ahead, T08272-38446 (Prakash Poovanna) or book through Cauvery Hotel, Madikeri. A similar set-up just 3 km from Palace Estate is **D** *Honey Valley Estate*, Yavakapadi (difficult to get to; jeep access up rough track). Double room Rs 500 in better equipped modern building, bunk room in old house Rs 150, meals Rs 85. Contact Suresh Chengappa T08272- 38339. ■ *Getting there: from Madikeri to Kakkabe, bus at 0630; jeep 1 hr.*

Madikeri centre

After Kim Clark & Lucy Gorman
Not to scale

Hand Post Village

Thirty kilometres from Karapura on the Mysore road is the small town of Hand Post, named by the British during the days of the Raj when it represented the last village accessible before the dense jungle began. So in fear were the locals of what lay beyond, they would venture no further so the British and the maharajas visiting their hunting lodges would have to send a servant, either on foot, horseback or in latter days by car, to pick up any mail. They would travel to Hand Post where the post would literally be handed over.

Virajpet (Virajendrapet) A small place of limited charm, with a few very basic hotels. The area is one of the largest producers of honey in Asia. Irupu Falls are 48 km from Virajpet on the Nagarhole road. A place of pilgrimage, the Sri Rameshwarna temple is said to have been dedicated to Siva by Rama himself on the banks of the Lakshmana Teertha river. It is a picturesque spot and popular with picknickers and gets particularly busy at *Sivaratri*. ■ *Getting there: Buses from Thalasseri north to the important pilgrimage town of Dharamsthala and Kushalnagar to visit the Tibetan settlements.*

Kushalnagar Set in water meadows on the upper reaches of the river Cauvery, the easternmost town in Kodagu has all the marks of the district's distinct identity. It is a very busy town with a market on Tuesdays and quite a transport hub. The State Bank of Mysore here changes Amex or US dollars. **Sleeping and eating** E *Kannika International*, 16 clean, tidy rooms, bucket shower, sit-outs, comfortable sitting area downstairs, restaurant, bar, quiet. *Kwality*, at the bus stand, small, basic rooms, meals. ■ *Getting there: the Bus Stand is for state buses while private buses leave from an area 5 mins walk uphill. To Madikere (Rs 12, 45 mins); Mysore (Rs 25, 1 hr) every 30 min; Virajpet (2 hrs).*

Bylakuppe A large section of forest was made available for the Tibetan refugees (now numbering over 15,000) who settled in the Bylakuppe and have established several monasteries and the Mahayana Buddhist University at **Sera**. They run their own schools and craft workshops and have become self-reliant through farming maize, rice and millet and producing carpets and *thangkas* for sale. You can attend early morning puja at the Sera Gompa (except Tuesdays). This is a good place to meet some of the 4,500 Tibetan monks at Sera and experience their culture. Those interested in visiting other Tibetan villages, a Thursday Tibetan market and monasteries other than Gelugpa, should ask the monks for directions and be prepared to be crammed into a local bus. Hunsur and Kollegal on the way to Mysore have significant Tibetan settlements. Away from the main roads, there is very little traffic so the area around is very pleasant for walking.

Sleeping and eating Bylakuppe has a couple of small hotels on the main road near the bus stand. At Sera **E** *Sera-Jhe Guest House*, T08276 571104, F574672. 24 spotless rooms with bath (hot shower), pleasant ambience, excellent value. Restaurant serving Tibetan, Indian, Chinese (try *momos*) is full of monks at mealtimes. All profits to charitable hospital on camp. Highly recommended.

Transport From **Madikere** or **Virajpet** take a bus to Kushalnagar and a share-rickshaw to **Sera**, the main Tibetan centre. From **Mysore**, take a bus towards Madikeri (via Hunsur), get off at Kushalnagar beyond Bylakuppe bus stand (2 hrs), where there are just tractor repair shops, chicken feed dealers and little else.

Karnataka

The small island reserve in the Kaveri River, 2 km from Kushalnagar, is **Nisargadhama** accessed over a hanging bridge. It consists mostly of bamboo thickets and trees, including sandalwood, and is very good for seeing parakeets, bee eaters and woodpeckers and a variety of butterflies. There is a deer park, pedalo boating, a resident elephant and tall bamboo tree houses for wildlife viewing. The park is very peaceful and pleasant, completely untouched by tourism. ■ *0900-1800. Entry Rs 15, Rs 150 for foreigners, still camera Rs 10.*

Sleeping D-E *Cauvery Nisargadhama*, 8 simple cottages, built largely of bamboo/teak, some with balconies on stilts over the water, electricity (no fan), hot water, peaceful (despite nocturnal rats), but poor canteen food. Contact Forestry Office, Madikeri T08272-26308.

Transport The **bus** from Madikeri passes park gates 2 km before Kushalnagar. A **rickshaw** from Kushalnagar Rs 10.

The reserve forest 15 km from Kushalnagar is notable for its wide variety of **Dubare Forest** birdlife. There is a *Forest Rest House*, an elephant training camp and the possibility of fishing on the Cauvery. Contact Forestry Office in Madikeri, T25708. Near Siddapur, is the B *Orange County Resort*, T/F08274-58481, rhrl@vsnl.com A luxury resort in a great location in 300 acres of coffee and spice plantations, on the banks of the Cauvery. 42 cottages, houseboat, Full facilities, pool, health spa, fishing at Valanoor (18 km), well maintained.

Nagarhole (Rajiv Gandhi) National Park

Nagarhole (meaning snake, streams), once the Maharajas' reserved forest, *Colour map 3, grid A2* became a national park in 1955. Covering gentle hills bordering Kerala, it includes swampland, streams, moist deciduous forest, stands of bamboo and valuable timber in teak and rosewood trees. The Kabini River, which is a tributary of the Kaveri, flows through the deciduous forest where the upper canopy reaches 30 m. The park is accessible both by road and river. A number of tribesmen, particularly Kurumbas (honey-gatherers) who still practise ancient skills, live amongst and care for the elephants. The park also has *gaur* (Indian bison), *dhole* (Indian wild dogs), wild cats, four-horned antelopes, flying squirrels, sloth bears, monkeys, *sambar* deer and panthers – "better sightings than at Mudumalai". Tigers and leopards are sighted infrequently. Many varieties of birds include the rare Malabar *trogon*, great black woodpecker, Indian pitta, pied hornbill, whistling thrush and Green Imperial pigeon. Also waterfowl and reptiles. Savanna fires are common in the grassland areas of the Western Ghats, sometimes caused deliberately to improve grazing, sometimes accidental or natural.

The edge of the dam between March to June during the dry period, makes viewing easier. Jeeps, vans and guides through the Forest Dept. One hour tour at 1715. Viewing from *machans* near waterholes. Trekking is possible with permission (enquire at Hunsur office, T08222-52041 well in advance). You can also visit the Government's *Elephant Training Camp* at Haballa. Organized one hour tours are available on 15 and 26 seater coaches – not particularly suitable vehicles for the purpose.

■ *Main entrance is near Hunsur on the northern side of the Park. Entry Indians Rs 15, foreigners Rs 150, camera Rs 10. The southern entrance is 5 km from Kabini River Lodge at Karapur.*

Karnataka

Sleeping From Sep-Jun, **AL-A** *Kabini River Lodges* (Karnataka Tourism), at Karapur (75 km from Mysore) on reservoir bank, 14 rooms in Mysore Maharajas' 18th-century hunting lodge and bungalow, 6 newer cabins overlooking lake, 5 tents, simple but acceptable, good restaurant, bar, exchange, package includes meals, sailing, rides in buffalo-hide coracles on the Kaveri, jeep/minibus at Nagarhole and Murkal complex, park tour with naturalist, very friendly and professionally run, recommended. **NB** Foreigners pay double. Reservations: in Bangalore, *Jungle Lodges and Resorts*, T5597025, F5586163, jungle@giasbg01.vsnl.net.in, or *Clipper Holidays*, T5592043, F5599833, clipper@bangalore.wipro.net.in **AL-A** *Waterworlds*, 500m away, surrounded on three sides by the Kabini river, T 08228-44421. 6 luxury rooms with sit-outs in a ranchstyle house, exquisitely furnished, beautiful gardens on water's edge, delicious home-cooking, environment conscious (solar power), friendly staff, boating, jeep, ayurvedic massage, gym, swimming, walking, charming, informal atmosphere, peaceful, secluded. Highly recommended. **A** *Jungle Inn*, Veeranahosahalli, at main entrance, T 08222-46022, 52781. 7 well-appointed rooms and 3 dorms, in colonial style lodges, varied meals, boating, elephant rides. *Hammock Leisure Holidays*, T5307963. Forest Dept Rest Houses in the Park: **B** *Cauvery*, 2 rooms; book at T080-3341993, and **B** *Gangotri*, 3 rooms with bath, simple but comfortable, dorm beds (Rs 40), services of cook, book at least 15 days in advance on T0821-480901.

Transport **Road** **Bus**: from Mysore, *Exp*, 3 hrs, Rs 35; Madikere, 4½ hrs. Bangalore, 6 hrs. **NB** For *Kabini River Lodge* and *Waterworlds*, be sure to get the Karapur (not the Nagarhole) bus; *Jungle Lodges* bus leaves Bangalore at 0730, stops in Mysore (around 0930), reaching Kabini around 1230; return bus departs 1315. State bus from Mysore to Karapur. **Train** Nearest, Mysore (96 km). See **Bandipur**, page 325.

Routes From Madikere the road drops quickly down the ghats through rubber, coconut and cocoa plantations, forests and a series of small towns and villages – Samapanje, Subrahmanya and Puttur – on the western coastal fringe around Mangalore.

Mangalore and the West Coast

Phone code: 0824
Colour map 3, grid A2
Population: 425,800

Capital of South Kanara District, the hilly town of Mangalore makes a pleasant, relaxing stop between Goa and Kerala. Rarely visited by Western tourists, it has some interesting churches and decent accommodation.

Ins & outs **Getting there** Bajpe airport is 20 km from town. The Konkan railway has trains from Goa and Mumbai while the old broad gauge goes down the coast to Kozhikode and then inland to Coimbatore. The new Kanakanadi station is 6 km northeast of the City station which is just south of the centre at Hampankatta. The KSRTC Bus Station is 3 km north of the Private Bus Stand in the busy town centre. **Getting around** Although the centre is compact enough to be covered on foot, autos are handy but may refuse to use their meters.

Background In the 14th and 15th centuries Mangalore traded with Persian and Arab merchants and was fought over by the Nayaka princes and the Portuguese. In the 18th century its control was contested by *Haidar Ali* (who made it his centre for shipbuilding) and Tipu Sultan on the one hand, and the British on the other.

The modern port, 10 km north of the town, is now India's ninth largest cargo handling port. Mangalore's economy is dominated by agricultural processing and port-related activities. Imports include tropical timber from Southeast Asia for furniture making, a necessity since India placed major restrictions on its own teak felling. The port handles 75% of India's coffee exports and the bulk of its cashew nuts. The latter are brought from many coastal areas (notably from Kerala, where 90% of India's cashews are grown); the National Cashew Research Centre is inland, at Puttur. Mangalore's other claim to fame is that it produces Ganesh Bidis (the cheap alternative to cigarettes), a few pieces of tobacco wrapped in a leaf tied with thread. The leaf used varies; one being from the Camel's Foot Tree (*Bauhinia*). Mangalorean red clay tiles, used extensively in Southern India are manufactured here.

Sights

St Aloysius College Chapel on Lighthouse Hill is sometimes referred to as the Sistine Chapel of South India. The 19th-century frescoes painted by the Italian trained Jesuit priest Moscheni cover the walls and ceilings in a profusion of scenes, though some might feel the comparison with Michelangelo a little stretched. The town has a sizeable Roman Catholic population (about 20%).

The tile-roofed low structure of the 10th-century **Mangaladevi Temple** is named after a Malabar Princess, Mangala Devi, who may have given her name to Mangalore. The 11th-century **Sri Manjunatha Temple**, 3 km from the centre (a cycle rickshaw ride away), has a rough lingam but its central image of Lokeshwara (968 AD) is a remarkable bronze among several Buddhist images. The **Kadri Caves** in a childrens' 'amusement park' is more a "municipal dump with a horrid zoo".

There are also lakes which have water with medicinal properties, and the Old Lighthouse dating from the 18th century. It is generally believed to have been built by Haider Ali, who built a naval dockyard in Mangalore.

You can take a trip out to the sand bar at the river mouth to watch fascinating boat building and river traffic on the Netravathi River.

Suratkal Beach, 15 km north, is near the promontory on which the new lighthouse stands. A steep path connects the lighthouse to the Sadasiva Temple. The usually quiet beach can get busy on holidays (Bus Nos 40, 41 and 45). Parks are used as a public toilet.

Excursion

Shremmanti Bai Memorial Museum Collection includes archaeology, ethnology, porcelain and wood carvings. ■ *0900-1700. Free.* **Mahatma Gandhi Museum**. Collection includes zoology, anthropology, sculpture, art, coins and manuscripts. Canara High School. ■ *0930-1230, 1400-1730, closed Sun and holidays. Free.*

Museums

Essentials

B-C *Manjarun* (Taj), Old Port Rd, T420420, F420585. 101 rooms, some with sea/river view, restaurant, usual facilities, friendly service. **C-D** *Moti Mahal*, Falnir Rd, T441411, F441011. 90 rooms, 53 a/c, a/c restaurant and bar, coffee shop, pool and poolside BBQ, expanding. **C-D** *Poonja International*, KS Rao Rd, T440171, F441081. 154 rooms, central a/c, wide range of facilities including exchange, spotlessly clean, excellent complimentary buffet breakfast, excellent value. **D-E** *Navaratna Palace*, KS Rao Rd opposite Private Bus Stand, T441104. 72 rooms (Rs 200+), 13 a/c, those at back overlook gardens and plantations, a/c restaurants, bar, exchange, immaculate, very quiet, pleasant, good value. Recommended. **D-E** *Swagath's Panchamahal*, Kodialbail, T 495574. 56 comfortable, clean rooms, good value, very basic restaurant. **E**

Sleeping
12½% luxury tax

karnataka

Dhanyabad, Hampankatta Circle, T440066, F440069. 44 spacious rooms, good value, convenient (open late). **E** *Indraprastha,* Lighthouse Hill Rd, T425750. Good value rooms with bath, helpful staff. **E** *Manorama*, KS Rao Rd, T440306. 60 rooms, some a/c, South Indian restaurant, typical Indian busness hotel. **E** *Railway Retiring Rooms* City Station, 3 good rooms, dorm beds, water cooler, shower, toilet, "outstanding value". **F** *Rupa*, Balmatta Road. T4212771. 69 tatty but airy rooms, friendly staff, best budget category. **F** *Surya*, Greens Compound, Balmatta Rd, T4225736. 18 rooms with bath, set back from road, uninspiring exterior but worth considering for tranquility.

Mangalore

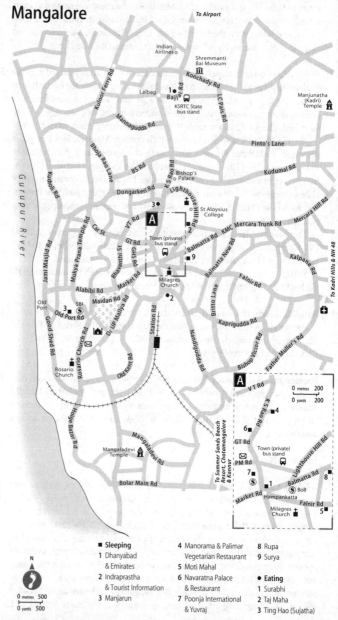

N

0 metres 500
0 yards 500

■ **Sleeping**
1 Dhanyabad
  & Emirates
2 Indraprastha
  & Tourist Information
3 Manjarun

4 Manorama & Palimar
  Vegetarian Restaurant
5 Moti Mahal
6 Navaratna Palace
  & Restaurant
7 Poonja International
  & Yuvraj

8 Rupa
9 Surya

● **Eating**
1 Surabhi
2 Taj Maha
3 Ting Hao (Sujatha)

India's tropical evergreen forest

The Mangalore section of the Ghats is one of the wettest regions of India, still covered in dense tropical forest. Wildlife abounds. Langur monkeys hang in the trees and squat by the roadside. Occasionally King Cobras up to 3 m in length slide across the road. The narrow strip of true tropical evergreen forest – no more than 20 km wide – is rich in varied species. Giant bamboos, often 40 m high, arch gracefully, and even in the dry season the forest feels comparatively cool and damp. Teak, mainly as a plantation crop, and other timbers, plus bamboos, canes, honey and wax are important products. Cashew nuts, introduced by the Portuguese in the 16th century, grow wild and are also cultivated. The nuts are exported and processed for a variety of industrial uses – in paints and varnishes and for caulking boats.

Ullal (10 km south) **C-D** *Summer Sands Beach Resort*, Chotamangalore, T467690. 104 rooms, 49 a/c in cottages and bungalows, some expensive deluxe, restaurant, bar, good pool, imaginatively designed in the local style with a superb beach, watersports, tennis, good value.

Eating

The big hotels have bars

Expensive *Embers* for open-air dinners by the pool at *Manjarun Hotel*. **Mid range** *Yuvraj*, at *Poonja* offers a varied menu. *Yuvraj* restaurant. **Cheap** *Lalith*, Balmatta Road. T426793. Basement restaurant with excellent food, cold beer and friendly service *Surabhi*, opposite KSRTC Bus Station. Tandoori and cold beer, handy if waiting for a night bus. *Taj Mahal*, nearby. Tasty vegetarian meals. *Ting Hao* at *Hotel Sujatha*, KS Rao Rd, dark a/c, does large portions of Chinese/Indian (opens 1800).

Shopping

Market Road, with an excellent range of shops, is good for browsing.

Transport

Local Autorickshaws charge Rs 35 to the Kanakanadi station from the centre, and Rs 25 from KSRTCC Lalbag, Bus Station (higher than the meter charge because of the 'locality').

Long distance Air Bajpe airport is 20 km out of town. Transport from town: taxi, Rs 200; Rs 50 each; coach from *Indian Airlines*, Hathill Complex, Lalbag, T455259. Airport, T752433. To **Chennai** via Bangalore, **Mumbai**. *Jet Airways*: Ram Bhavan Complex, Kodaibail, T440694, airport, T752709. To **Mumbai**.

Road Bus: KSRTC State bus stand, Bajjai Rd, is clean and well-organized. Booking hall at entrance has a computer printout of timetable in English; main indicator board shows different bus categories: red – ordinary; blue – semi-deluxe; green – super-deluxe. (*Exp* buses may be reserved 7 days ahead). **Mysore** and **Bangalore**: 296 km, 7 hrs and 405 km, 9 hrs, ½ hrly from 0600 (route through Madikeri is the most pleasant); trains take 20 hrs. **Chennai** 717 km; **Madurai** 691 km, 16 hrs. **Mumbai**; **Panaji**, 10 hrs.. Numerous private bus companies around the *Taj Mahal* Restaurant, Falnir Road (and a few opposite KSRTC) serve **Bangalore, Bijapur, Goa, Ernakulam, Hampi, Goa, Gokarna, Kochi, Mumbai, Udupi** etc.

Train Central Station has a computerized booking office. **Chennai**, via **Kannur** and **Kozhikode**: *Mangalore Mail 6602* (AC/II), 1115, 18 hrs; *West Coast Exp, 6628*, 1945; **Kollam**: *Malabar Express, 6330*, dep 1620, 14 hrs, and to **Thiruvananthapuram**: also *Parasuram Exp 6350*, 0300; **Madgaon**: 0700, 7 hrs; 2100, 5 hrs. **Mumbai** (Kurla). *Matsyagandha Express 2620*, 2050, 13 hrs. **Palakkad**: *Link Exp 6684*, 0500. From **Kanakanadi Station**: **Mumbai** via Madgaon: *Nethravati 6636*, 1500, 15½hrs. **Madgaon**: *Lakshadeep Exp 2617*, 2330, 5 hrs.

Karnataka

Directory **Bank** *Bank of Baroda*, Balmatta Rd, exchange on Credit Cards. **Communications** Post Office, Panje Mangesh Rd (1st left after *Poonja Arcade*, by petrol station) has Speed Post. Internet:*Frontline*, Ayesha Towers, KS Rao Rd, T441537, Rs 40 per hr. **Photography** *Adlabs*, Lighthouse Hill Rd, opposite the Syndicate Bank **Tourist offices** *Karnataka Hotel Indraprashta* (incomplete building), Lighthouse Hill Rd opp Kasturba Hospital, Gr Flr, T442926, helpful, friendly if limited tourist information. Transport T421692. **Travel agents** *Four Wings*, 2-3 Ganesh Mahal, KS Rao Rd, T440531, F440536. Air tickets, tours, hotels, branches in Bangalore and Udipi. Recommended. *Trade Wings*, Lighthouse Hill Road, T426225, F422004, exchange (TCs, £, $ cash), air, bus, train tickets, hotels, tours etc.

Religious sites in the Ghats

The forested hills of the Western Ghats contain several important religious sites.

Sampanje Sampanje, 26 km from Madikeri, is a very attractive village built in the west coast style. There is a lovely river crossing, and hedges are still common. After a further 4 km the road crosses the Kodagu-South Kanara border to the village of Kalugulli, where there is a coffee shop. The road continues down the valley, lined with mature rubber plantations interspersed with dense forest, and spices such as cloves and cinnamon. The road runs along the right bank of the river Chandragiri through mixed teak and coconut forests.

Sullia Sullia is a village comprising a long and busy street. There are several small
Phone code: 08257 hotels and bars. To the north of the bus stand are the modest *Gopika*, *Supari* and *Annapurna Woodlands* hotels. Four kilometres out of Sullia a right turn leads to the important pilgrimage centre associated with **Subrahmanya**, an ancient Dravidian folk-god known in Tamil as **Murugan**. He was later identi-fied with Skanda, the God of War, but is known by many names and in South India in particular is believed to have power over illness. The shrine in these quiet forested hills marks a spot where the *nagas* (cobras) are believed to have sought Subrahmanya's protection which he provided in local caves. At the shrine he is worshipped in the form of a cobra. There is a huge 150-year-old temple car (*ratha*) which is processed during the November-December fair. There is a *Temple Guest House*, T81224.

Dharmasthala Formerly Kuduma, Dharmasthala is noted for both its shrine to Sri
75 km from Mangalore Manjunatha, and for the catholicity of its management. Served by Madhva Vaishnava priests, the Saivite temple is administered by a Jain trustee. The Jains installed a 12 m-high monolith of *Bahubali* in 1973. The temple is also noted for its free distribution of meals to all visitors and pilgrims. During the festival of *Laksha Deepotsava* 100,000 lamps are lit. Pilgrims bathe in the river Netravathi, 3 km away. The temple authorities run a museum, car museum and aquarium and several charitable trusts. ■ *Darshan for visitors to the shrine: 0630-1300; Darshan and Mahapuja 1900-2000.*

Routes From Beltangadi a minor road runs northwest to **Venur** and **Mudabidri**. Both are famous Jain centres. Venur has a Gommateshwara 12-m statue built in 1604 by Veera Thimanna Ajila IV.

Mudabidri Mudabidri (Moodabidri), sometimes described as the Jain Varanasi, has 18
Population: 25,000 Jain bastis, although Jains themselves are a tiny minority of the population. The 1,000-pillar **Chandranatha Basti** (1429, dedicated on 18 January 1431), also known as Savira Kambada Basti, is a powerful presence in the centre of the town. Three *mandapas* lead to the main sanctuary; they have a series of sloping

tiered roofs, adapted to the heavy monsoon rainfall of the region, and the sanctuary itself is surmounted by a gabled roof. The main entrance, which faces east, opens onto a superb monolithic pillar (*mana-stambha*) in front of the main doorway. The temple has a valuable collection of metal, jewel-encrusted images of Jain tirthankars and superb monolithic columns each, in the Jain tradition, with a different carving. Although such columns are a common feature of Chalukyan architecture, the columns in the Mudabidri temple are extraordinary, being elaborately carved in astonishingly fine detail. There is a 2-m high *panchaloha* (five metal) image of Chandratha.

The Jain *Math* (monastery) 100 m east of the main temple entrance, has a library with some beautiful 12th- and 13th-century palm leaf manuscripts. Booklets on Mudabidri in English, Hindi and Kannada are available. The 17th-century **Chowta Palace**, which is still occupied by descendants of the royal family, is also worth visiting for its beautifully carved wooden pillars, ceilings and screen. **Sleeping F** *Tourist Cottages* (Karnataka Tourism), eight simple rooms.

Karkala has one of the four great monolithic statues of *Gommateshwara* in South India. The 13-m statue (1432) is floodlit.

Karkala
17 km from Mudabidri

Surrounded by dense forests near the ridge of the Western Ghats and the source of the Tunga River, Sringeri is associated with **Sankaracharya**, the seventh-century Advaitin philosopher. He established a monastery here (see page 525) and the leaders of the modern *math* are widely revered by followers of Sankaracharya's philosophy. The **Vidyashankar Temple** has a large courtyard. 12 pillars represent the signs of the zodiac, a huge lion being carved on the front of each; each has a large movable stone ball in its mouth. The pillars are arranged to catch the rays of the sun during the appropriate period of the zodiac. The smaller **Sharada Devi** (Saraswati) **Temple** on the left bank of the Tunga contains a much admired statue of the deity standing on a *Sri Chankra* (a *yantra*). ■ *Getting there: buses link Sringeri with Udupi and Chitradurga and many long distance destinations including Mangalore, Bangalore and Mysore.*

Sringeri
Population: 4,150
Colour map 3, grid A2

Karnataka

Karnataka's Sapphire Coast

Poor transport made the route up the Karnataka's 'sapphire coast' to Goa one of the least travelled scenic routes in India. This is now changing. The Western Ghats are never far away, while the road and the Konkan railway frequently skirt the Arabian Sea in the north passing some magnificent beaches.

Udupi

Udupi (Udipi), one of Karnataka's most important pilgrimage sites, is the birthplace of the 12th-century saint Madhva, who set up eight sannyasi maths (monasteries) in the town (see page 525).

Phone code: 08252
Colour map 3, grid A2
Population: 117,700

Sri Krishna Math, Car Street. According to one legend the statue of *Krishna* once turned to give a low caste devotee *darshan*. The temple complex in the heart of the town is set around a large tank, the *Madhva Sarovar*, into which devotees believe that the Ganga flows every 10 years. There are some attractive *math* buildings with colonnades and arches fronting the temple square. This Hindu temple, like many others, is of far greater religious than architectural importance, and receives a succession of highly placed political leaders.

Udupi – home of 'Brahmin meals ready'

The name of Udupi is associated across South India with authentic Brahmin cooking – which means vegetarian food at its best. But what is authentic Udupi cuisine? Pamela Philipose, writing in the Indian Express, suggests that strictly it is food prepared for temple use prepared by Shivali Brahmins at the Krishna temple. It is therefore not only wholly vegetarian, but it never uses onions or garlic.

Pumpkins and gourds are the essential ingredients, while sambar, which must also contain ground coconut and coconut oil, is its base. Rasam, the spicy pepper water, is compulsory, as are the ingredients jackfruit, heart-shaped colocasia leaves, raw green bananas, mango pickle, red chilli and salt. Adyes (dumplings) ajadinas (dry curries) and chutneys, including one made of the skin of the ridge gourd, are specialities. Favourite dishes are Kosambiri with pickle, coconut chutney and appalam. At least two vegetables will be served, including runner beans, and rice. Sweets include payasa and holige.

Festivals The biennial *Paraya Mahotsava*, on 17/18 January of even-numbered years, when the temple management changes hands (the priest-in-charge heads each of the eight *maths* in turn). *Seven Day Festival* 9-15 January, is marked by an extravagant opening ceremony complete with fire-crackers, dancing elephants, brass band and "eccentric re-enactments of mythical scenes while towering wooden temple cars, illuminated by strip lights followed by noisy portable generators, totter around the square, pulled by dozens of pilgrims".

Sri Ananthasana Temple, where Madhva is believed to have de-materialized while teaching his followers, is in the centre of the temple square. The eight important *maths* are around Car Street: Sode, Puthige and Adamar (south); Pejawar and Palamar (west); Krishna and Shirur (north); and Kaniyur (east). Udupi is almost as well known today as the home of a family of Kanarese Brahmins who have established a chain of coffee houses/hotels across South India.

Sleeping **D** *Kediyoor*, Shiribeedu, near bus stand, T22381. 54 rooms, some a/c, clean, modern, good restaurants. **D-E** *Karavali*, west of the bypass near Malpe turning, T22861. Clean, modern rooms, some a/c, restaurant, bar. **E** *Mallika*, KM St, near Sanskrit College, T21121. 44 rooms (3 more expensive a/c), restaurant, fairly modern and reasonable value. **F** *Kalpana Lodge*, Upendra Bag, T20440, F71112. 62 rooms, some with bath, very cheap. **F** *Sindhur Palace*, Court Rd, near *Mallika*. 30 rooms, T20791, basic but adequate.

Eating *Dwarike*, Car St, facing Temple Sq. Immaculately clean, modern, good service, comfortable, Western and South Indian food, excellent snacks, ice creams.

Transport **Bicycles**: for hire. **Bus**: frequent service to **Mangalore** (1½ hrs). Also mornings and evenings to **Bangalore and Mysore** from 0600; **Hubli** from 0900; **Dharmasthala**, from 0600-0945, 1400-1830; **Mumbai** at 1120, 1520, 1700, 1920.

Directory **Banks** *State Bank of India*, opposite Affan Complex.

Katpadi The small roadside village south of Udupi is famous for its Mangalore *Maliga Maylur* – beautiful flowers widely used for garlands. There are usually women selling the flowers by the roadside.

Five kilometres inland from Udupi has the character of a university campus town. Manipal is famous throughout Karnataka as the centre of **Yakshagana** dance drama, which like Kathakali in Kerala is an all night spectacle. The Rashtrakavi Govind Pai **Museum**, MGM College, has a collection of sculpture, bronze, inscriptions and coins. The Kasturba Medical College has an interesting anatomy museum. **Sleeping and eating** B-C *Valley View International*, T71101, F71327, on campus. 70 good a/c rooms with upmarket facilities, pool. Recommended. D *Green Park*, T70561. 38 rooms, some a/c, restaurant. *JJ's Fast Food*, *Hotel Bhavani*, Parkala Rd. For Western snacks.

Manipal
Phone code: 08252
Colour map 3, grid A2

Malpe is one of the best port sites in southern Karnataka. Across the bay is the island of Darya Bahadurgarh and 5 km to the southwest is **St Mary's Isle**, composed of dramatic hexagonal basalt, where **Vasco da Gama** landed in 1498 and set up a cross. Malpe is an important fishing port today. The fishing village at one end of the beach, and the fish market on the docks are very smelly; the beach too is used as a public toilet in places. If you are prepared for an unpleasant walk or cycle ride, you can reach a deserted sandy beach but there are no facilities so take your own food and water. **Sleeping and eating** E *Silver Sands*, T22223, Thotham Beach (1 km north, hard to find). Eight pleasant cottages, limited menu restaurant, friendly management. Recommended. E *Tourist Home*, half way to Thotham Beach, 4 pleasant, seaside rooms (Rs 250). Beach kiosks nearby. Indian breakfast at the top of the road. Also a large Indian style hotel at main cross roads in town has a bar and restaurant.

Malpe
5 km W of Udupi
Colour map 3, grid A2
Population: 19,000

From Udupi a road goes inland to Sringeri and the Jain temples at Karkal and Mudabidri (see page 336).

Routes

Kundapura, another small port, served the Rajas of Bednur about 50 km inland. The 16th-century Portuguese fort survives. **Sleeping** E *Sharon*, NH17, south of town at junction of bypass and city road, near tourist bus stop, T6623, 54 rooms, some a/c, modern, spacious, airy, non-vegetarian restaurant reported dirty, though vegetarian OK, recommended.

Kundapura
Population: 28,500;
formerly Coondapur

One of the many bullock cart tracks that used to be the chief means of access over the Western Ghats started from Bhatkal. Now only a small town with a predominantly Muslim population, in the 16th century it was the main port of the *Vijayanagar* Empire. It also has two interesting small temples. From the north the Jain *Chandranatha Basti* (17th century) with two buildings linked by a porch, is approached first. The use of stone tiling is a particularly striking reflection of local climatic conditions, and is a feature of the Hindu temple to its south, a 17th-century Vijayanagar temple with typical animal carvings. In the old cemetery of the church is possibly the oldest British memorial in India, inscribed: "Here lyeth the body of George Wye merchant dec. XXXI March Anno Dom NRT Christi Sal Mundi MDCXXXVII, 1637". **Sleeping** F *Seema* and F *Vaibhav Lodge*, very basic, airless rooms, noisy. ■ *Getting there: Direct bus to Jog Falls at 0600 from the bus station (2 hrs). Later buses take 3 hrs.*

Bhatkal
Phone code: 08385
Colour map 1, grid C2
Population: 31,500

Kumta is raised on another laterite plateau, surrounded by green vegetation. Kumta has an excellent *Kamat Restaurant* on the NH17, which crosses the river Haganashini. There are superb views along the river.

Kumta
Population: 26,200

Gokarna

Phone code: 08386
Colour map 1, grid C2

The narrow streets, traditional houses and temples together with its long wide expanse of beach, lure growing numbers of backpackers moving on from Goa who search for an alternative hideaway on the unspoilt beaches to the south. There is a somewhat curious mix of Hindu pilgrims and castaways from the hippy era here. You will also notice tribal women wearing their colourful traditional costume – a cloth held at the neck by bead necklaces, their only pieces of jewellery.

The specially sanctified **temple** here is famous for its Atmalinga, which **Ganesh** is believed to have tricked **Ravana** into putting down on this spot. As Ravana was unable to lift the linga up again, it is called *Mahabala* (the strong one). **Tambraparni Teertha** stream is particularly sacred for casting the ashes of the dead. Today Gokarna is also a centre of Sanskrit learning.

The walk down to Gokarna beach is flanked by pilgrims and *sadhus* begging for alms so come prepared with small change. Walk northwards if you are searching for a quiet stretch of beach.

Most travellers head for the beaches to the south. The superb **Om Beach** shaped like the sacred Hindu symbol, about 3 km south, can be reached by a path from the town temple or by walking over the cliffs and passing the **Kudle** (pronounced Koodlee) Beach which was the first to be 'discovered' by beach campers. Popular with younger travellers, the beach has picturesque views of paddy fields and the Western Ghats. Om Beach can now also be reached by a motorable track which can be accessed from near Mayura Samudra hotel. It is no longer quite the secluded paradise that people came searching for years ago when looking for an alternative Goa. As with Kudle, in season it can get extremely busy and the combination of too many people, shortage of fresh water and the apparant lapse in the standards of hygiene, results in the beaches getting rather dirty. **Half Moon** and **Paradise Beaches** can be reached by continuing to walk over the headlands and are another 2 km or so apart. Here, too long-timers congregate and are catered for in a similar fashion to the other beaches.

Sleeping **Town**: **D-E** *International Gokarna*, T56622. 43 modern rooms (some a/c with bath (Rs 200-600), back quieter and have balconies, restaurant (some food akin to "liquid salt"), bar, and the first lift in Gokarna when it is inaugurated! **E** *Green's 'Om'*, 6-minute walk from bus stand, T56445. 16 rooms with bath, 2 a/c (overpriced), restaurant, chilled beer, not very friendly, exchange (poor rate). **E** *New Prasad Nilaya*, near the Bus Stand, T57135. Spacious rooms with bath (hot water), some colourful balconies, upstairs rooms better, friendly staff. **F** *Mayura Samudra* (KSTDC), 2 km north on hilltop facing the sea, T56236. 3 rooms (Rs 135 double), dining room, garden, helpful staff but quite a trek. **F** *Nimmu Guest House*, near Temple, T56730.15 clean rooms with shared Indian toilets, 5 newest are better value as they are big, bright and catch the breeze, lomited roof space for overspill, garden, laid and friendly. Recommended. **F** *Ramdev Lodge*, 4 simple rooms with bath, cheap. **F** *Shastri's Guest House*, Dasanamath, T56220. 24 rooms with bath, some 3-4 bedded, set back from road, quiet, short walk uphill behind gives superb views of town and sunset, good value. **F** *Vaibhav Nivas*, Ganjigadde off Main St (5 mins walk from bazar), T56714. Family guest house, small rooms (Rs 60+), new annexe with 10 rooms, some with bath (Indian andwestern WC), meals (alas. no "pain-cakes and forage" for breakfast!), taxi, full of travellers from nearby beaches.

Beaches: The usual mud and palm leaf huts with shared facilites charge Rs 30-60 (extra for a mattress). The lack of security in beach huts has prompted the

Karnataka

guesthouses in town to offer to store luggage for a small charge. The exceptions are: at the southern end of *Kudle*: **F** *Shiva Prasad*,with decent brick-built rooms with fan; on *Om*: **F** *Namaste* with acceptable rooms.

Eating

Cheap Cheap vegetarian *thalis* are available near the bus stand and along Main St while shacks at the entrance to the town beach serve up the usual disarray of travellers' favourites.*Pai*, near Vegetable Market does good *masala dosa*. **Vishwa**, on beach, Nepali run, varied menu including Tibetan, large helpings. Icecream parlours abound; try *gudbad* with nuts and fruit. *Prema*, opposite Mahabalesvar temple, now expanded with a large room upstairs, does great fruit salads, ices and *gudbad* and makes its own delicious soft garlic cheese, also popular with westerners for its *thalis*. The southern beaches have their share of *chai* shops and shacks. The only one that stands out is the *Spanish Chai shop* on Kudle, which has clean fresh food including humus and pitta.

Transport

Road KSRTC **buses** provide a good service: **Chaudi** 2 hrs **Karwar** (via Ankola) frequent (1 hrs); **Hospet** 0700, 1425 (10 hrs); **Jog Falls** 0700, 1130 (6 hrs); **Mangalore via Udipi** 0645 (7 hrs); **Panaji** 0800 (5 hrs). **Train** Gokarna Road station is 10 km from the town, 2 km from the NH17; a few rickshaws ferry passengers to and from town but you may have to walk 1 km from the station to the road linking Gokarna and NH17 to find transport. Daily service to Margao (Madgaon) via Chaudi, 1125; to Mangalore 1630.

Directory

Exchange *Pai STD*, opposite *Ramdev Lodge*, changes money.

Routes

From the Hattikari Bridge to Karwar (28 km north) the route runs through alternating sections of forested hills and bays, sometimes with fantastic views. The Kalinadi River estuary has some of the finest stands of mangrove in western India.

Karnataka

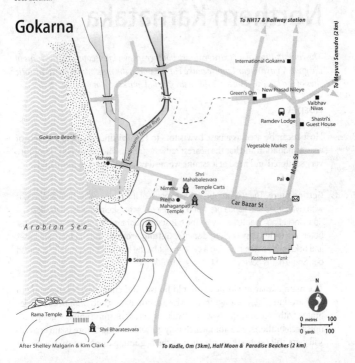

Gokarna

To NH17 & Railway station

To Mayura Samudra (2 km)

International Gokarna ■

Green's Om ■   New Prasad Nileye ■

Vaibhav Nivas ■

Ramdev Lodge ■   Shastri's Guest House ■

Lambrapani Teertha River

Gokarna Beach

Vegetable Market ○

Vishwa ←

Shri Mahabalesvara ⛩

Nimmu ⛩   Temple Carts

Pai ○   Main St

Prema ●   Mahaganpati Temple ⛩

Arabian Sea

Car Bazar St   ✉

Kotitheertha Tank

● Seashore

N

Rama Temple ⛩

Shri Bharatesvara ⛩

After Shelley Malgarin & Kim Clark

0 metres   100
0 yards   100

To Kudle, Om (3km), Half Moon & Paradise Beaches (2 km)

Karwar
Phone code: 08382
Colour map 1, grid C2
Population: 51,000

The administrative headquarters of North Kanara District on the banks of the Kalinadi River, Karwar has a deep-water Naval port protected by five islands. One of these was 'Anjedive' of old, known to sea-farers centuries befor **Vasco da Gama** called at the island in 1498, and the Portuguese built a fort there. It was later used as a Goan penal colony. Since it is now under the control of the Navy it is off-limits to all foreigners. From 1638 to 1752 there was an English settlement here, surviving on the pepper trade. The Portuguese held it for the next 50 years until the old town was destroyed in 1801. Today Karwar, strung out between the port and the estuary, has an unpleasant beach. However, the beaches a little to the south rival those of Goa but are still deserted. Of interest is the hill fort, an octagonal church, and a 300 year old temple.

Sleeping and eating An upmarket hotel is expected to be built here. **D** *Bhadra*, on NH17 (4 km north of Karwar), T25212. 20 rooms, some a/c, lovely views over estuary, restaurant, a modern hotel. A roadside stall outside the hotel serves very good value vegetarian food. **F** *Anand Lodge*, near bus stand, T26156. Rooms with Indian WC, basic. There is an excellent bistro type *Fish Restaurant*, along the street.

Transport Bus: to Jog Falls, 0730 and 1500 (6 hrs). Frequent buses to Palolem, Margao and Panaji, also direct buses to Colva. Buses often full – may have to fight to get on. The road crosses the Kali River (car toll, Rs 5) then reaches the Goa border and check post (8 km north).

Directory Banks *State Bank of India* changes money.

Hampi-Vijayanagara and Northern Karnataka

The combination of an extraordinary boulder strewn landscape and the ruins of the great Vijayanagar Empire make Hampi one of the most atmospheric historic sites of the Deccan. Hospet is the nearest small market town.

Hospet

Phone code: 08394
Colour map 1, grid C3
Population: 135,000
Altitude: 480 m

Hospet can be used as a base by visitors to **Hampi** since it offers a variety of accommodation and has the nearest railway station. The remains at Hampi are very scattered and need at least one whole day, and two to see more fully.

Ins & outs **Getting there** The station, about 500 m north of the town centre, has connections with Hyderabad and Bangalore, but buses offer a better alternative for many destinations, including Goa, 10 hrs away. The bus stand is right in the town centre and most hotels are within easy walking distance. **Getting around** Though there are buses and rickshaws to Hampi, hiring a cycle might be the best option as the site is spread out. Some paths however are too rough to ride on.

The main bazaar in Hospet, with old houses and character, is interesting to walk around. There is a significant Muslim population and *Muharram* is celebrated with vigour with *firewalkers* walking across burning embers along with noisy celebrations, a custom which may go back to long before Islam arrived. Villagers still celebrate events such as the beginning or end of migrations to seasonal feeding grounds of livestock, with huge bonfires. Cattle are driven through such fires to protect them from disease. The archaeologists Allchin and Allchin suggest that Neolithic ash mounds around Hospet could have resulted from similar celebrations over 5,000 years ago.

Excursions

The 2 km **Tungabhadra Dam**, 6 km away, is 49-m high and offers panoramic views. One of the largest masonry dams in the country it was completed in 1953 to provide electricity for irrigation in the surrounding districts. Local buses from Hospet take 15 minutes to the dam. Next door is a deer park, aviary and ornamental gardens, entry Rs 2, recommended. **Sleeping E** *Vaikunta Guest House*, Tungabhadra Dam, T44241. Beautiful hill-top site, but out of town above the dam so own transport needed, usually occupied by officials, book 15 days in advance. At Munirabad, 5 km north of Dam: **F** *Indrabhavan* and **F** *Lake View Guest House*, difficult to reserve. ■ *Getting there: Tourist office coach tours include a visit to the Dam but several local bus services daily do the trip (¼ hr, 6 km).*

Tours

From KSTDC, T21008, and *Malligi* hotel, to Hampi, Rs 75 (lunch extra); 0930-1630. English speaking guide but rather rushed.

Sleeping

Station Rd has been renamed Mahatma Gandhi Rd (MG Rd)

C-F *Malligi*, 6/143 Jambunatha Rd, T28101, F27038, malligihome@hotmail.com Expanded to 150 rooms (Rs 140+), 65 a/c (a/c sometimes inadequate), newer **D** are large rooms with bath (4 **B** suites are overpriced), good restaurant and bar by good covered pool (economy room guests pay Rs 25 for pool), exchange, travel (bus/train tickets Rs 10/25 commission; good Hampi tour Rs 75), local guide books, internet, well-managed, friendly. **D-E** *Karthik*, Pampa Villa, IV Ward, 252/3 Sardar Patel Rd, T24938. Modern, large rooms, some a/c, good a/c restaurant. **D-E** *Priyadarshini*, V/45 Station Rd, near bus station, T28838. Variety of

Karnataka

Hospet

Vijayanagar's Nava Ratri

It is not difficult to imagine the magnificence of the Vijayanagar court or of some of its special occasions. The Mahanavami festival, an annual royal ceremony of the 15th and 16th century was held from mid-September to mid-October. The festival lives on across South India today, often known as Navaratri. Many Persian and Portuguese travellers visited the court when all activity centred around the "House of victory" – the Mahanavami Dibba, and the King's Audience Hall. Now they are just vast granite platforms, which almost certainly carried wooden buildings. Through the festivities the King sometimes shared his throne, or sat at its foot while it was occupied by a richly decorated processional image of the god, while at other times he was alone.

Stein writes: "What was viewed was a combination of great durbar with its offerings of homage and wealth to the King and return of gifts from the King – exchanges of honours; the sacrificial re-consecration of the King's arms – his soldiers, horses, elephants – in which hundreds of thousands of animals were slaughtered; darshana and puja of the King's tutelary – the goddess – as well as his closest kinsmen; and a variety of athletic contests, dancing and singing processions involving the King's women and temple dancers from throughout the realm, and fireworks displays. The focus of these diverse and magnificent entertainments was always the King as glorious and conquering warrior, as the possessor of vast riches lavishly displayed by him and his women (queens and their maids of honour) and distributed to his followers."

rooms, some a/c, extra bed Rs 35, good restaurants. Recommended. **E** *Sandarshan*, MG Rd, T28574. Few a/c rooms with bath (limited hot water). **F** *Mayura Vijayanagara* (KSTDC), TB Dam Rd, 3 km west of centre on bus route, T39270. 21 basic rooms with fans, mosquito nets and bath (Rs 160), simple dining hall serves good *thalis*. **F** *Vishwa*, MG Rd, opposite bus station, away from the road, T27172. Clean rooms (some 4-bed) with bath, *Shanthi* restaurant.

Eating **Mid-price** *Malligi's* open-air *Waves* by pool. Multicuisine. Good food, bar. **Cheap** *Priyadarshini's* vegetarian *thalis* are recommended; also good garden restaurant with bar. Good south Indian meals options at *Shanbhag*, near the bus station. The hotels serve chilled beer.

Transport **Local** From Hospet to/from **Hampi**, travel via Kamalapuram, especially in the rainy season when the slower road to Hampi Bazar which winds through villages, is barely passable. **Bus**: frequent buses to Hampi's two entry points (via Kamalapuram and Museum, Rs 4 and via Hampi Bazar, Rs 3.50), from 0630; last return around 2000. Also from Tungabhadra Dam, 45 mins. **Auto-rickshaws**: to Hampi, demand Rs 150. **Cycle-rickshaw**: from Rly station to Bus Stand about Rs 10. **Cycles** from Hampi Bazar or from *Shanti*. **Taxi/car hire**: KSTDC, T21008, T28537 or from *Malligi Hotel*; about Rs 700 per day (possible to share).

Long distance **Road Bus**: Express bus to/from **Bangalore** (road now upgraded), several from 0700, 10 hrs; **Mysore**, 1830, 10½ hrs (Express buses to Belur/Halebid from both). Services to other sites, eg **Badami** (6 hrs) and **Bijapur** (6 hrs). Overnight Karnataka Tourism luxury coaches to various towns. Direct buses to **Panaji** (Goa); the road is being improved – *Luxury*, 0630 (10½ hrs), State bus, 0830 (reserve a seat in advance); others involve a change in Hubli (4½ hrs). *Paulo Travels Luxury Sleeper* coach from Hotel Priyadarshini, at 1845, Rs 350, daily; *West Coast Sleeper*, from Hotel Shanbhag, 1830, Rs 350; daily (Oct-Mar only); strangers may be expected to share a bunk. It is better to take a train to Londa (under 5 hrs) and get a bus to Madgaon or Panaji (3 hrs).

Train: Bangalore, *Hampi Exp, 6591*, 2010 (via Guntakal, 2½ hrs) 10½ hrs. **Guntakal**: *Vijaynagara Exp, 7310*, 1905, 2½ hrs. **Secunderabad via Guntakal**: *Vijaynagara/ Venkatadri Exp, 7310/7598/7604*, 1905, 14½ hrs (2½ hr wait in Guntakal). For **Belur/ Halebid**: a traveller suggests 1530 train to Hubli (arrive 2000); then 2200 to Ariskere (arrive 0400); walk 5 min to bus station down the main road and get the first bus to Halebid at 0600 (1½ hrs). To **Badami**: via Gadag, 4 hrs.

Banks *State Bank of India*, next to Tourist Office, does not exchange TCs but will change cash (US $ and UK £). *State Bank of Mysore* may oblige. *Monica Travel*, near Bus Station, changes TCs (3% charge). **Communications** Post office: opposite vegetable market. **Telegraph office**: in *Hotel Sandarshan*. **Fax and ISD**: *Essar Area Fax*, beside New Bus Stand, Station Rd. **Tourist Office** *KSTDC*, Old Fire Station, Taluk Office Circle, near Bus Stand, T28537. Free map and leaflets, and sometimes guides for the sites, car hire.

Directory

★ Hampi

Hampi-Vijayanagar is one of India's most remarkable former capital city sites. The rocky outcrops of the peninsula provided the 14th-century Vijayanagar kings with an apparently impregnable hill fortress in which they built a stupendous range of palaces and temples. Although now largely in ruins the site is still hugely impressive.

Phone code: 08394
Colour map 1, grid C3
Altitude: 467 m
Best season: Oct-Mar

Karnataka

Hampi was once the seat of the Vijayanagara Empire and a great centre of Hindu rule for 200 years from its foundation in 1336, although there may have been a settlement in the area as early as 1,000 years before then. The city was enormously wealthy, 'greater than Rome', with a market full of jewels and palaces plated with gold, having held a monopoly of trade in spices and cotton. It was very well fortified and defended by a large army. With the defeat in 1565 at Talikota at the hands of the Deccan Sultans, the city was largely destroyed. Today the stark and barren area of 26 sq km on the right bank of the river Tungabhadra has the ruins of the great empire strewn across it.

Known as the 'The town of victory', Vijayanagara, is 13 km northeast of Hospet town

The site for the capital was chosen for strategic reasons but the craftsmen adopted an ingenious style to blend in their architectural masterpieces with the barren and rocky landscape. Most of the site is early 16th century, built during the 20-year reign of Krishna Deva Raya (1509-1529) with the citadel standing on the bank of the river. Excavations undertaken by the Archaeological Survey of India are still in progress. You enter the area from the west at *Hampi Bazaar* or from the south at *Kamalapuram*. The **tourist office** is located here on the approach to Virupaksha Temple.

The road from the west comes over Hemakuta Hill, overlooking the sacred centre of Vijayanagara, the Virupaksha Temple and the Tungabhadra River to its north. On the hill are two large Ganesh monolithic sculptures and some small temples. Good views at sunset. Climb Matanga Parvat, over the road, early in the morning (around 0530) for a spectacular sunrise.

Sacred Centre
Go in a group and don't carry valuables as muggings have been reported

The road runs down to the village, the once world-famous **market place**. You can now only see the wide pathway running east from the towering **Virupaksha** (*Pampapati*) **Temple** with its nine-storey *gopuram*, to where the bazaar hummed with activity. The temple is still in use; note the interesting paintings on the *mandapam* ceiling. The monkeys here can be aggressive. ■ *Rs 2. 0800-1230, 1500-1830. Before entering the precinct, foreigners are expected to register at the police office on the left.*

Trouble at the Ruins

Over the last few years, there have been incidents of thefts and attacks on foreign visitors to Hampi, and growing concern over the emergence of the rave/party scene which had been drawing large crowds of young travellers to Hampi especially over the Christmas and New Year period. UNESCO has intervened and warned that the World Heritage status of the site will be withdrawn unless the government takes steps to stop illegal activities. Unauthorized guest houses and restaurants in the Hampi Bazar area have been shut down and a state government Task Force has been formed in March 2000 to ensure the restoration of the earlier pleasant atmosphere at the ancient site.

The Riverside You can walk along the river bank (1,500m) to the famous Vitthala Temple. The path is easy and passes several interesting ruins including small 'cave' temples (worthwhile with a guide).

Alternatively, a motorable road skirts the Royal Enclosure to the south, and goes all the way to the Vitthala Temple. On the way back you can visit the **Raghunatha Temple**, on a hill top, for its Dravidian style, quiet atmosphere and excellent view from the rocks above, especially at sunset.

After passing **Achyuta Bazaar**, which leads to the Tiruvengalanatha Temple 400m to the south, the riverside path goes near **Sugriva's Cave**, where it is said that Sita's jewels, dropped as she was abducted by the demon Ravana, were hidden by Sugriva. There are good views of the ancient ruined bridge to the east, and nearby the path continues past the only early period Vaishnavite shrine, the 14th-century **Narasimha Temple**. The **King's balance** is at the end of the path as it approaches the Vitthala Temple. It is said that the rulers were weighed against gold, jewels and food, which were then distributed to Brahmins.

The **Vitthala Temple**, a World Heritage Monument, is dedicated to Vishnu. It stands in a rectangular courtyard, enclosed within high walls. Probably built in the mid-15th century, it is one of the oldest and most intricately carved, with its *gopurams* and *mandapas*. The *Dolotsava mandapa* has 56 superbly sculpted slender pillars which can be struck to produce different musical notes. It has elephants on the balustrades and horses at the entrance. The other two ceremonial *mandapas*, though less finely carved have some interesting carved pillars, eg Krishna hiding in a tree from the *gopis*, a woman using a serpent twisted around a stick to churn a pot of buttermilk. In the courtyard is a superb chariot carved out of granite, the wheels raised off the ground so that they could be revolved!

Krishnapura On the road between the Virupaksha Bazaar and the Citadel, you pass Krishnapura, Hampi's earliest Vaishnava township with a Chariot Street 50m wide and 600m long, which is now a cultivated field. The **Krishna temple** has a very impressive gateway to the east. Just southwest of the Krishna temple is the colossal monolithic statue of Lakshmi Narasimha in the form of a four-armed man-lion with fearsome bulging eyes sheltered under a seven-headed serpent, *Ananta*. It is over 6m high but sadly damaged.

The road south, from the Sacred Centre towards the Royal Enclosure, passes the excavated **Prasanna Virupaksha** (misleadingly named 'underground') **Temple** and interesting watchtowers.

Royal Enclosure At the heart of the Metropolis is the small **Hazara Rama Temple**, the Vaishanava 'chapel royal' (*hazara* meaning 1,000). The outer enclosure wall to the north has five rows of carved friezes while the outer walls of the *mandapa* has three. The episodes from the epic *Ramayana* are told in great detail, starting with the bottom row of the north end of the west *mandapa* wall. The two-storeyed **Lotus Mahal** is in the **Zenana** or ladies' quarter, screened off by its high walls. The watchtower is in ruins but you can see the domed **stables** for 10 elephants with a pavilion in the centre and the guardhouse. Each stable had a wooden beamed ceiling from which chains were attached to the elephants' backs and necks. In the **Durbar Enclosure** is the specially built decorated platform of the **Mahanavami Dibba**, from which the royal family watched the pageants and tournaments during the nine nights of *navaratri* festivities. The 8m-high square platform originally had a covering of bricks, timber and metal but what remains still shows superb carvings of hunting and battle scenes, as well as dancers and musicians.

The exceptional skill of water engineering is displayed in the excavated system of aqueducts, tanks, sluices and canals, which could function today. The 22m square **Pushkarini** is the attractive stepped tank at the centre of the

Hampi - Vijaynagara

enclosure. The road towards Kamalapuram passes the **Queen's Bath**, in the open air, surrounded by a narrow moat, which had scented water filling the bath from lotus shaped fountains. It measures about 15m x 2m and has interesting stucco work around it.

Further reading Longhurst's *Hampi Ruins* recommended; Settar's *Hampi* (both at *Aspirations Bookshop*, Hampi Bazaar).

Museum The **Archaeological Museum** at Kamalapuram has a collection of sculpture, paintings, copper plates and coins. The ASI booklet is on sale. There is a scale model of Hampi in the courtyard. ■ *1000-1700, closed Fri.*

Essentials

Sleeping Mosquitos can be a real problem, especially at dusk – the main bazar is sprayed daily.
Travellers planning to spend more than a day may prefer to stay near the complex **Hampi Bazar** has plenty of character; several basic lodges and more being built. **F** *Mega Lodge*. Small rooms, shared facilities (Rs 120)), good *Shiva* restaurant. **F** *Rahul*, south of the bus stand. Basic sleeping and washing, but clean. **F** *Shanti Guest House*, down path to the right of the temple (signed), T41368. 13 rooms with fans around courtyard, common shower, roof for overspill, very clean and friendly, cycle hire, good cakes (see below). **Kamalapuram**: **E** *Mayura Bhuvaneswari* (KSTDC), 2 km from site, T41574. 32 reasonable rooms (8 a/c) Rs 240-385, fairly clean, poor food, cycle hire.

Eating **Hampi Bazar** **Cheap** *Ganesh* in main street, recommended for *parathas*. *Gopi* for good simple, cheap *thalis* **Manju** family-run, simple but enticing food (apple *parathas*), take-aways for tiffin boxes (will even lend boxes). *Sambhu* opposite *Shanti*, for fresh pasta/noodles and espresso plus all the usual; also bus/train tickets for small commission (better than trying in Hospet), recommended. *Shanti* does good carrot/apple/banana/chocolate cakes to order. *Suresh*, 30m from *Shanti*, down a small alley, very friendly family, made to order so takes a while, but well worth the wait. *Mango Tree* on river bank, 500 m west of the Temple, is relaxed and pleasant.

Kamalapuram *Mayura Bhuvaneswari*, does cheap adequate meals. Snacks are available near the bus stand.

Festivals **Jan-Feb**: Virupaksha *Temple Car festival*. **Nov 3rd-5th** *Hampi Music festival* at Vitthala Temple when hotels get packed.

Shopping *Aspirations Bookshop*, Hampi Bazar, interesting selection (including books on Hampi), postcards, crafts from Aurobindo Ashram, Pondicherry, and soft drinks.

Around Hospet

Gadag Gadag, 23 km away, is an important and typical cotton collection market. CD
Colour map 1, grid B3 Deshpande has described it vividly: "Gadag dominates the southern cotton
Population: 134,100 tract and cotton dominates the town. By the beginning of the picking season
Altitude: 620 m the market bustles with activity and the rest of the town follows the pace; ginning mills and cotton presses lying idle for a long time are now set to work; cotton finds its way out in a well-graded form to Mumbai or for export. By the middle of June this activity is at its zenith, then settles down to a quiet life during the next eight months."

The **cotton market** is well worth a visit. A **Vaishnavite temple** in the northwest corner has a 15-m high *gopuram*. The **fort** at Gadag has a Saivite temple of *Trimbakeshwar*, 'Lord of the Three Peaks', elaborately carved, and an enormous carved bull. An inscription dates the temple at AD 868. The black hornblende pillars in the porch have been smoothed to a remarkable finish with superbly detailed carving, sharp and clear. Behind the main part of the temple is a shrine to Saraswati.

Transport Train To **Bijapur**: *Exp, 1815*, 4¾ hrs; **Guntakal**: at 0030 and 1535, 5 hrs; **Hospet**: 0950, 2 hrs; **Hubli**: 1¾ hrs; **Solapur**: *Golgumbaz Exp 6542*, 2300, 7½ hrs; others at 0330, 0955, 1330.

Directory Useful services Gadag, a railway junction, has tea stalls, cold drinks and simple restaurants and a *Dak Bungalow*.

There are 17 Hindu and Jain **temples** (11th, 12th centuries) at Lakkundi. The **Lakkundi** stone used for the temples in Dambal, Gadag and Lakkundi is schist brought from Dharwad. The sculpture was carried out at the quarry and the near finished work then transported to the temple. In this the method used differed from that in Orissa, for example, where raw stone was moved to the temple site before sculpting. Basements are moulded, walls have pilasters and there is remarkable detail on the ceilings. The late 11th century **Jain basti** is the largest of the temples, with a five-storeyed pyramidal tower and square roof. Especially fine carving is found on the incomplete **Kasivisvesvara Temple**, dating from the 12th century. Both temples are near the tank in the southwest of the town, which is no more than 1 km across. There is a small museum between them.

These towns, 10 km north of Lakkundi, also have temples of the same period. **Kuknur & Ittagi** The **Mahadeva temple** in Ittagi (AD 1112) has similarly finely finished columns with beautifully finished miniature carvings. The **Navalinga** complex, dated at the late ninth century has nine shrines, originally dedicated to female deities. The two gateways are Vijayanagar. The **Kallesvara Temple** (10th century) has a square sanctuary topped by a three-storey tower. Ganes and Durga are enshrined. They represent the transition from a Rashtrakuta style to a Chalukyan style.

Koppal is noted for two impressive **forts**. On the margins of Maratha, **Koppal** Hyderabad and Mysore power, this territory was once under the control of the Nizams of Hyderabad and Koppal was given to Salar Jung, one of the Nizam's nobles, as a *jagir* (a land gift). The upper fort is over 120 m above the plains while the lower one was rebuilt by French engineers when it had been captured by Tipu Sultan from the Marathas. The road continues to Hospet.

Bijapur

Bijapur has some of the finest mosques in the Deccan and retains a pleasant atmosphere with real character. During the reign of Ali Adil Shah I (ruled 1557-79) the citadel was built with its moat as well as palaces and pleasure gardens.

Phone code: 08352
Colour map 1, grid B3
Population: 193,000
Altitude: 550 m

Getting there The railway station is just outside the east wall of the fort under a km **Ins & outs** from the Gol Gumbaz while long distance buses draw in just west of the citadel. Both arrival points are close enough to several hotels. **Getting around** It is easy to walk or cycle round the town. There are also autos.

History The Chalukyas who ruled over Bijapur were overthrown at the end of the 12th century. In the early years of the 14th century the Delhi Sultans took it for a time until the Bahmanis, with their capital in Gulbarga, ruled through a governor in Bijapur who declared independence in 1489 and founded the **Adil Shahi Dynasty**. Of Turkish origin, they held power until 1686. Bijapur has the air of a northern Muslim city with its mausolea, mosques and palaces.

Sights ★ **The Jama Masjid** is one of the finest in the Deccan with a large shallow, onion-shaped dome and arcaded court. It was built by Ali Adil Shah I (ruled 1557-79) during Bijapur's rise to power and displays a classic restraint. The Emperor Aurangzeb added a grand entrance to the Masjid and also had a square painted for each of the 2,250 worshippers that it can accommodate. The **Citadel** with its own wall has few of its grand buildings intact. One is the Durbar Hall, **Gagan Mahal**, open to the north so that the citizens outside were not excluded. It had royal residential quarters on either side. Another worth visiting is the **Jal Manzil** or the water pavilion, a cool sanctuary.

★ **Ibrahim Rauza**, the palatial 17th-century tomb west of the city wall, is beautifully proportioned. It has slender minarets and carved decorative panels with lotus, wheel and cross patterns as well as bold Arabic calligraphy, bearing witness to the tolerance of the Adil Shahi Dynasty towards other religions. Built during the dynasty's most prosperous period when the arts and culture flourished, it also contains the tomb of Ibrahim Adil Shah II (ruled 1580-1626) who had it built for his wife but died first. Near the Rauza is a huge tank, the Taj Bauri, built by Ibrahim II in memory of his wife. The approach is through a giant gateway flanked by two octagonal towers.

Bijapur

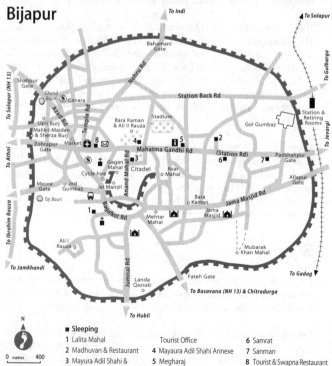

N

0 metres 400

■ **Sleeping**
1 Lalita Mahal
2 Madhuvan & Restaurant
3 Mayura Adil Shahi &

Tourist Office
4 Mayaura Adil Shahi Annexe
5 Megharaj

6 Samrat
7 Sanman
8 Tourist & Swapna Restaurant

Karnataka

Gol Gumbaz The vast whitewashed tomb of Mohammad Adil Shah, buried here with his wife, daughter and favourite court dancer, is the world's second largest dome (unsupported by pillars), and one of its least attractive. Its wide **whispering gallery** carries a message across 38 m which is repeated 11 times. However, noisy crowds make hearing a whisper quite impossible; quietest in early morning. Numerous narrow steps in one of the corner towers, lead to the 3 m wide gallery. The plaster here was made out of eggs, cowdung, grass and jaggery. ■ *0600-1800. Small entry fee, Fri, free.*

There is an excellent view of the city with its walls from the base of the dome

The **Nakkar Khana**, the gate house, is now a Museum. The **Asar Mahal** (c1646) was built with a tank watered by the old conduit system. It was used as a court house and has teak pillars and interesting frescoes in the upper floor. The **Mehtar Mahal** with its delicate minarets and carved stone trellises and brackets supporting the balconies which form a decorative gateway, was supposed to have been built for the palace sweepers.

To the west, **Sherza Burj** (Lion Gate) in the 10 km long fort wall, has the enormous 55 tonne, 4.3 m long, 1.5 m diameter cannon *Malik-i-Maidan* (Ruler of the Plains) on the west. To avoid being deafened the gunner is believed to have dived into the tank off the platform! It was cast in the mid-16th century and was brought back as a prize of war pulled by "400 bullocks, 10 elephants and hundreds of soldiers". Note the muzzle – a lion's head with open jaws with an elephant being crushed to death inside. Inside the city wall, close by, is **Upli Burj**, the 24 m high watch tower on high ground with its long guns and water tanks.

The **Archaeological Museum** in the gatehouse of the Gol Gumbaz has an excellent collection of Chinese porcelain, parchments, paintings, armoury, miniatures, stone sculpture and old Bijapur carpets. ■ *1000-1700, closed Fri. Free.*

Museum

Essentials

B-C *Madhuvan International*, off Station Rd, T25572. Range of rooms, good comfortable a/c but non-a/c cramped, stuffy, dirty and mosquito prone, good veg *thali* restaurant, also served in pleasant garden, beer on room service only. **D-E** *Megharaj*, MG Rd, T21458. 20 cleanish rooms (few a/c), helpful manager, excellent value. **F** *Mayura Adil Shahi* (KSTDC), Anandamahal Rd, near citadel entrance, T20934. Avoid rooms, tourist office; **D** *Annexe* opposite, T20401. 4 acceptable a/c rooms with bath, net (Rs 440), well kept garden. **F** *Lalit Mahal*, near Bus Station, T20761. 64 rooms, those at rear quieter. **F** *Railway Retiring Rooms* and dorm, exceptionally clean, recommended. Nearby **F** *Samrat*, Station Rd, T21620. 31 basic clean rooms with bath, very good vegetarian (beerless) restaurant. **F** *Sanman*, opposite Gol Gumbaz, Station Rd, T21866. 24 simple rooms, noisy in front, popular veg restaurant. **F** *Tourist*, MG Rd by Post Office, T21640. 56 simple rooms with bath, good value.

Sleeping

Swapna, MG Rd, near PO, non-veg and beer upstairs, good vegetarian downstairs.

Eating

Jan: *Siddhesvara Temple festival*. Music festival accompanied by Craft Mela. **Sep**: *Asar Mahal Urs festival* in memory of saints.

Festivals

Handlooms, toys and Lambadi gypsy jewellery.

Shopping

Local Bus: a service runs between the station (2 km east) to west end of town. **Long distance Road** Buses are frequent between Bijapur and **Bidar**, **Hubli**, **Belgaum** and **Solapur** (2-2½ hrs). There are daily services to **Hospet**, **Bangalore** (12 hrs) and **Hyderabad**. Buses to **Badami** get very crowded, 4 hrs; take one to Bagalkot, then a

Transport

Karnataka

minibus to Badami. For **Hospet**, travel via Gadag or Ikal.**Train**: Bangalore, *Hampi Exp*, *6591*, 2030, 10½ hrs, via **Guntakal** (2 hrs). **Secunderabad**: *Vijaynagara/Venkatadri Exp*, *7310/7598/7604*, 1905, 14½ hrs (via Guntakal 2½ hrs, wait 2½ hrs). To get to **Belur/Halebid**: a traveller suggests the 1530 train for Hubli (arr 2000) to catch 2200 to Arsikere (arr 0400); walk 5 mins to bus station down the main Rd and get the 1st bus to Halebid at 0600 (1½ hrs).

Directory **Banks** *State Bank of India* in the citadel, *Canara Bank*, north of market, best for exchange. **Tourist offices** *Mayura Adil Shahi Hotel*, T20359, 1030-1330, 1415-1730, Mon-Sat.

The cradle of Hindu Temple architecture

Although Bijapur became an important Muslim regional capital, its surrounding region has several villages which, nearly 1500 years ago, were centres of Chalukyan power and the hearth of new traditions in Indian temple building. At a major Indian crossroads, the temples at Aihole represent the first finely worked experiments in what were to become distinct North and South Indian temple styles.

Ins & outs **Getting there and around** Since it takes a half day to see Badami, visiting the sites by bus doesn't allow time for Mahakuta. It is well worth hiring a car in Bijapur which allows you to see all the sites quite comfortably in a day. If travelling by bus it is best to visit Badami first, followed by Pattadakal and Aihole. By car it is best to start at Aihole and end at Badami.

★ Aihole

Phone code: 0831 Aihole was the first Chalukyan capital, but the site was developed over a period of more than 600 years from the sixth century AD and includes important Rashtrakuta and Late Chalukyan temples, some dedicated to Jain divinities. It is regarded as the birthplace of Indian temple architectural styles, and the site of the first built temples, as distinct from those carved out of solid rock. Most of the temples were originally dedicated to Vishnu, though a number were subsequently converted into Saivite shrines.

Sights There are about 140 temples – half within the fort walls – illustrating a range of developing styles from Hoysala, Dravida, Jain, Buddhist, Nagara and Rekhanagara. There is little else. All the roads entering Aihole pass numerous temple ruins, but the road into the village from Pattadakal and Bagalkot passes the most important group of temples which would be the normal starting point for a visit. ■ *The main temples are now enclosed in a park. Open sunrise to sunset. Flash photography prohibited.*

Durgigudi Temple The temple is named not after the Goddess Durga but because it is close to the *durga* (fort). Dating from the late seventh century, it has an early *gopuram* structure and semi-circular apse which imitates early Buddhist chaitya halls. It has numerous superb sculptures, a series contained in niches around the ambulatory: walking clockwise they represent Siva and *Nandi*, Narasimha, Vishnu with Garuda, Varaha, Durga and Harihara.

Lad Khan Temple Recent research dates it from approximately AD 700 not from AD 450 as suggested by the first Archaeological Survey of India reports in 1907. This is indicated by the similarity of some of its sculptures to those of the Jambulinga temple at Badami, which has been dated precisely at AD 699. Originally an assembly hall and *kalyana mandapa* (marriage hall) it was named after Lad Khan, a pious Muslim who stayed in the temple at the end of the 19th century. A stone ladder through the roof leads to a shrine with damaged images of Surya, Vishnu and Siva carved on its walls. It bears a striking resemblance to the megalithic caves which were still being excavated in this part of the Deccan at the beginning of the period. The roof gives an excellent view of the village.

Gaudar Gudi Temple Near the Lad Khan temple is this small, rectangular Hindu temple, probably dating from the seventh century. It has a rectangular columned *mandapa*, surrounded on three sides by a corridor for circumambulation. Its roof of stone slabs is an excellent example of North Indian architecture. Beyond the Gaudar Gudi Temple is a small temple decorated with a frieze of pots, followed by a deep well. There are others in various states of repair. To see the most important of the remaining temples you leave the main park. Excavations are in progress, and the boundaries of the park may sometimes be fenced. Turning right out of the main park, the Bagalkot road leads to the **Chikki Temple**. Similar in plan to the Gauda Gudi, this temple has particularly fine carved pillars. The beams which support the platform are also well worth seeing.

Ravan Phadi Cave Temple From the main park entrance turn left to get to the temple, about 300 m from the village. The cave (formerly known as the Brahman) itself is artificial, and the sixth century temple has a variety of carvings of Siva both outside and inside. One is in the *Ardhanarisvara* form (half Siva, half Parvati), another dancing between Parvati and Ganesh. There is a huge lotus carved in the centre of the hall platform. There are two small eighth century temples at the entrance, the one to the northwest dedicated to Vishnu and that to the south, badly weathered, may have been based on an older Dravidian style temple.

The Buddhist Temple There is a plain two-storeyed Buddhist temple on a hill beyond the end of the village on the way to the Meguti Temple. It has a serene smiling Buddha with the Bodhi Tree emerging from his head, on the ceiling of the upper floor. Further uphill is the **Jain temple**, a plain structure lacking the decorations on the plinth, columns and no *gopuram* as on some of the Hindu temples. It has a statue of Mahavira in the shrine within. Climb up through the roof for a good view of Aihole.

The **Meguti Temple** (AD 634) From the Buddhist Temple a path leads down to a terrace, where the left hand route takes you to the foot of some stairs leading to the top of a hill which overlooks the town. This is the site of what is almost certainly the oldest building in Aihole and one of the oldest dated temples in India. Its 634 date is indicated by an inscription by the court poet to the king Ravikirtti. A Dravidian style temple, it is richly decorated on the outside, and although it has elements which suggest Saivite origins, it has an extremely impressive seated Jain figure, possibly Neminath, in the sanctuary which comprises a hall of 16 pillars.

The Kunti Group To visit this group of four Hindu temples (7th-9th centuries) you have to return down to the village. The oldest is in the southeast. The external columns of its *mandapa* are decorated with *mithuna*, or erotic couples. The temple to the northwest has beautifully carved ceiling panels of Siva and Parvati, Vishnu and Brahma. The other two date from the Rashtrakuta period.

Beyond these temples is the **Hucchappayya Math**, dating from the seventh century, which has sculptures of amorous couples and their servants, while the beams inside are beautifully decorated.

Museum **Archaeological Museum** Collection includes early Western Chalukyan sculpture of 7th-8th century. ■ *1000-1700, closed Friday. Free. Photography with permission.*

Sleeping **E** *Tourist Rest House*, T34541, close to the temples. 10 rooms, some with bath (Rs 75), newer annexe in the Durga temple style (Rs 200), simple food on prior notice, peaceful, helpful staff.

Festivals Feb-Mar: *Ramalinga Temple Car Festival.*

★ Pattadakal

On the banks of the Malaprabha River, Pattadakal, a World Heritage Site was the second capital of the Chalukyan kings between the seventh and eighth centuries and the city where the kings were crowned. Ptolemy referred to it as 'Petrigal' in the first century AD. Two of their queens imported sculptors from Kanchipuram.

Sights Most of the temples cluster at the foot of a hill, built out of the pink-tinged gold sandstone, and display a succession of styles of the southern Dravida temple architecture of the Pallavas (even miniature scaled-down models) as well as the North Indian Nagara style, vividly illustrating the region's position at the crossroads of North and South Indian traditions. With one exception the temples are dedicated to Siva. Most of the site is included in the archaeological park. Megalithic monuments dating from the 3rd-4th centuries BC have been found in the area. ■ *Sunrise to sunset.*

Immediately inside the entrance are the very small **Jambulinga** and **Kadasiddheshvara Temples** (eighth century). Now partly ruined, the curved towers survive and the shrine of the Jambulinga Temple houses a figure of the dancing Siva next to Parvati. The gateways are guarded by dvarapalas.

Just to the east is the eighth century **Galaganatha Temple**, again partly damaged, though its curved tower characteristic of North Indian temples is well preserved, including its *amalaka* on top. A relief of Siva killing the demon Andhaka is on the south wall in one of three original porches.

The **Sangamesvara Temple** dating from the reign of Vijayaditya (696-733) is the earliest temple. Although it was never completed it has all the hallmarks of a purely Dravidian style. Beautifully proportioned, the mouldings on the basement and pilasters divide the wall. The main shrine, into which barely any light is allowed to pass, has a corridor for circumambulation, and a lingam inside. Above the sanctuary is a superbly proportioned tower of several storeys.

To the southwest is the late eighth-century North Indian style **Kashi Vishvveshvara Temple**, readily distinguishable by the *nandi* in front of the porch. The interior of the pillared hall is richly sculpted, particularly with scenes of Krishna.

The largest temples, the **Virupaksha** (740-44) with its three-storeyed *vimana* and the **Mallikarjuna** (745), typify the Dravida style, and were built in celebration of the victory of the Chalukyan king Vikramaditya II over the Pallavas at Kanchipuram by his wife, Queen Trailokyamahadevi. The king's death probably accounted for the fact that the Mallikarjuna temple was unfinished, attested by the failure to do more than mark out some of the sculptures. However, the king's victory over the Pallavas enabled him to express his admiration for Pallava architecture by bringing back to Pattadakal one of the chief Pallava architects. The Virupaksha, a Saivite temple, has a sanctuary surrounded by passageways and housing a black polished stone Siva linga. A further Saivite symbol is the huge 2.6-m high chlorite stone *Nandi* at the entrance, contrasting with the pinkish sandstone surrounding it. The three-storeyed tower rises strikingly above the shrine, the outside walls of which, particularly those on the south side, are richly carved. Many show different forms of Vishnu and Siva, including some particularly striking panels which show Siva appearing out of a linga. Note also the beautifully carved columns inside. They are very delicate, depicting episodes from the *Ramayana*, *Mahabharata* and the *Puranas*, as well as giving an insight into the social life of the Chalukyas. Note the ingenuity of the sculptor in making an elephant appear as a buffalo when viewed from a different side.

In the ninth century the Rashtrakutas arrived and built a Jain temple with its two stone elephants a short distance from the centre. The carvings on the temples, particularly on the **Papanatha** near the village which has interesting sculpture on the ceiling and pillars, synthesizes northern and southern architectural styles.

Further reading: *A guide to Pattadakal Temples*, by AM Annigeri, Kannada Research Institute, Dharwad, 1961.

No suitable accommodation; a new restaurant is opening. Stay either in Badami, Aihole (see above) or **Bagalkot** where there is a good **E** *Circuit House* with a/c rooms, 5 km from centre on Bijapur Rd.

Sleeping & eating

Jan: *Nrutytsava* draws many famous dancers and is accompanied by a Craft Mela. Mar-Apr: *Temple car festivals* at Virupaksha and Mallikarjuna temples.

Festivals

Mahakuta

Mahakuta, which was reached by early pilgrims over rocky hills from Badami 5 km away, is a beautiful complex of Chalukyan temples dating from the late seventh century. The superstructures reflect both northern and southern influence and one has an Orissan deul.

The restored temple complex of two dozen shrines dedicated to Siva is built around a large spring-fed tank within an enclosure wall. The old gateway to the southeast has fasting figures of Bhairava and Chamunda. On entering the complex, you pass the *nandi* in front of the older **Mahakutesvara** Temple which has fine scrollwork and figures from the epics carved on the base. Larger Siva figures appear in wall niches, including an *Ardhanarisvara*. The temple is significant in tracing the development of the superstructure which began to externally identify the position of the shrine in Dravidian temples. Here the tower is domelike and octagonal, the tiers supported by tiny 'shrines'. The **Mallikarjuna Temple** on the other side of the tank is similar in structure with fine carvings at the entrance and on the ceiling of the columned *mandapa* inside, depicting Hindu deities and *mithuna* couples. The enclosure has many smaller shrines, some carrying fine wall carvings. Also worth visiting is the **Naganatha** Temple 2 km away.

Temple complex

★ Badami

Badami occupies a dramatic site squeezed in a gorge between two high red sandstone hills. Once called Vatapi, after a demon, Badami was the Chalukyan capital from AD 543-757. The ancient city has several Hindu and Jain temples and a Buddhist cave and remains peaceful and charming. The transcendent beauty of the Hindu cave temples in their spectacular setting warrant a visit.

Phone code: 08357
Colour map 1, grid B3
Population: 15,023
Altitude: 177 m

The village with its busy bazar and a large lake has white-washed houses clustered together along narrow winding lanes up the hillside. There are also scattered remains of 18 stone inscriptions (6th-16th century).

History For a short time in the mid-seventh century the Chalukyas lost control of Badami to the Pallavas and were finally defeated by the Rashtrakutas. They were followed by the Western Chalukyas, the Yadavas, the Vijayanagaras, the Bijapur emperors and the Marathas.

Caves & These are best visited early in the morning. The sites are very popular with
temples monkeys, which can be aggressive, especially if they see food. Take care.

★ The **South Fort** is famous for its cave temples, four of which were cut out of the hill-side in the second half of the sixth century. There are 40 steps to **Cave 1**, the oldest. There are several sculpted figures, including Harihara, Siva and Parvati, and Siva as Nataraja with 18 arms seen in 81 dancing poses. **Cave 2**, a little higher than Cave 1, is guarded by *dvarapalas* (door-keepers). Reliefs of Varaha and Vamana decorate the porch. **Cave 3**, higher still, is dedicated to Vishnu. According to a Kannada inscription (unique in Badami) it was excavated in AD 578. It has numerous sculptures including Narasimha (man-lion), Hari-Hara (Siva-Vishnu), a huge reclining Vishnu and interesting friezes. Frescoes executed in the tempera technique are similar to that used in the Ajanta paintings, and the carved ceilings and brackets. **Cave 4**, probably about 100 years later than the three earlier caves, is the only Jain cave. It has a statue of the seated Parsvanatha with two *dvarapalas* at the entrance. The fort itself above the caves is closed to the public.

The **Buddhist Temple** is in the natural cave near the ancient artificial Bhutanatha Lake (Agasthya Lake), where the mossy green water is considered

Badami

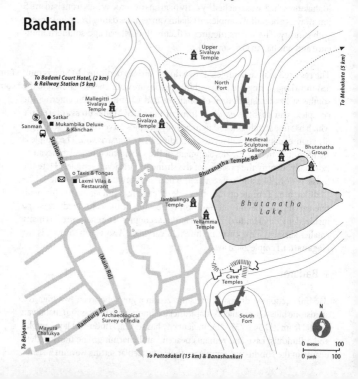

A little man and his 300,000 men

Rizvi quotes the Russian traveller Athanasius Nikhitin writing in the 15th century illustrating the nature of life at the Bahmani Court – the Sultan of Bedar "a little man, 20 years old ... who goes out with 300,000 men of his own troops. The land is overstocked with people, but those in the country are very miserable,

whilst the nobles are extremely opulent and delight in luxury. They want to be carried on their silver beds, preceded by some 20 chargers caparisoned in gold, and followed by 300 men on horseback and 500 on foot, and by horn-men, 10 torchbearers and 10 musicians".

to cure illnesses. The Yellamma Temple has a female deity, while one of the two Saivite temples is to Bhutanatha (God of souls); in this form, Siva appears angry in the dark inner sanctuary.

The seventh-century **Mallegitti Sivalaya Temple**, one of the finest examples of the early southern style, has a small porch, a *mandapa* (hall) and a narrower *vimana* (shrine), which Harle points out is typical of all Early Western Chalukya temples. The slim pilasters on the outer walls are reminders of the period when wooden pillars were essential features of the construction. Statues of Vishnu and Siva decorate the outer walls, while animal friezes appear along the plinth and above the eaves. These are marked by a prominent moulding with a series of purely ornamental small solid pavilions.

Jambulinga Temple This early temple is in the centre of the town near the rickshaw stand. Dating from 699, as attested by an inscription, and now almost hidden by houses, the visible brick tower is a late addition from the Vijayanagar period. Its three chapels, dedicated to Brahma, Vishnu and Siva, contain some fine carving, although the deities are missing and according to Harle the ceiling decoration already shows signs of deteriorating style. The carvings here, especially that of the Nagaraja in the outside porch, have helped to date the Lad Khan temple in Aihole accurately (see above). Opposite the Jambulinga temple is the 10th century Virupaksha Temple.

The **North Fort** temples, mainly seventh century, give an insight into Badami's history. Steep steps, almost 1-m high, take you to 'gun point' at the top of the fort which has remains of large granaries, a treasury and a watchtower. The **Upper Sivalaya Temple**, though damaged, still has some friezes and sculptures depicting Krishna legends.

Dolmens An ancient dolmen site can be reached by an easy hike through interesting countryside; allow 3½ hours. A local English speaking guide Dilawar Badesha at Tipu Nagar charges about Rs 200.

Museum Archaeological Survey's **Medieval Sculpture Gallery**, north of the tank, has fine specimens from Badami, Aihole and Pattadakal and a model of the natural bridge at Sidilinapadi, 5 km away. ■ *1000-1700, closed Fri. Free.*

Sleeping **B** *Badami Court*, Station Rd, T65230, F65207, 2 km from town. 26 clean, modern, though cramped rooms (bath tub), some a/c, average restaurant, new pool and gym, friendly, well-managed, book ahead, only accepts Rupees (poor rate for TCs, if stuck). **C-E** *Mukambika Deluxe*, Station Rd, opposite Bus Stand, T65067, F65106. 6 comfortable rooms with bath, 10 deluxe some with a/c and TV (Rs 250-950), welcoming, helpful, good value. Recommended. Adjoining *Kanchan* has a lively, bar, good food and cheery service. **E-F** *Mayura Chalukya* (KSTDC), 1 km on Ramdurg Rd, T65046. 10 crumbling rooms with baths (Rs 200), 6 new modern cottages, new tourist office, well placed,

No formal money exchange but the hotel Mukambika may be persuaded to change small value TCs

Karnataka

Karnataka

The Deccan's Muslim Contest

*Some of peninsular India's earliest Neolithic settlements are found near the rivers which cross the plateau. The region was a historic battleground between the Hindu Vijayanagar Empire immediately to its south and the Muslim sultanates to the north. The Bahmani Dynasty was the most powerful in the Deccan, ruling from Gulbarga from 1347 until 1422, then making Bidar the capital. The founder, **Ala-ud-Din Bahman Shah**, divided the kingdom into 4 quarters (taraf) and assigned each one to a trusted officer (tarafdar). The Raichur doab (the land between the Krishna and the Tungabhadra rivers) was contested between the Vijayanagara and the Bahmani rulers. In the reign of **Firuz Shah Bahmani** (1397-1422) the 2 powers fought 3 times without disturbing the status quo. Firuz developed **Chaul** and **Abhol** as ports trading in luxury goods not only from the Persian, Arabian, and African coasts, but also (through Egypt) from Europe. Persians, Turks, and Arabs were given a ready welcome by the Bahmanis, ultimately producing conflicts between locals and the foreigners (pardesis).*

in wooded surrounding, basic restaurant, car hire Rs 600 per day (for Aihole, Pattadakal, Mahakuta). **F *Shree Laxmi Vilas***, simple rooms (Rs 100), 3 with balconies with great views back to the temples. Right in the thick of it so interesting if noisy.

Eating *Sanman*, near Bus Stand, has non-vegetarian. *Laxmi Vilas*, near taxi stand, does vegetarian meals. *Dhabas* near the Tonga Stand sell snacks.

Transport **Road Bus:** Few daily to Hospet (6 hrs), very slow and crowded but quite a pleasant journey with lots of stops; Bijapur, 0645-0930 (4 hrs). Several to Pattadakal and Aihole from 0730. Aihole (2 hrs), from there to Pattadakal (1600). Last return bus from Aihole 1715, via Pattadakal. **Car hire**: from Badami with driver for Mahakuta, Aihole and Pattadakal, about Rs 600. **Train** The station is 5 km north (enquire about schedules); frequent buses to town.

Banasankari On the road to Pattadakal there is a village named after the goddess who was believed to have been turned into the lake there. At the temple with its unusual three levels, you can see her rather terrifying black image riding a fierce golden lion. A 20-day fair is held here in January-February.

Hospet to Gulbarga & Bidar

The dry and undulating plains are broken by rocky outcrops giving superb sites for commanding fortresses such as Gulbarga and Bidar.

Shorapur
Population: 30,600
Altitude: 400 m

Shorapur is an attractively sited town surrounded by hills. The fort stands on a hilltop at 567 m. The mid-19th century Venkatappa Nayak, Raja of Shorapur, was one of the few South Indian princes to support the 1857 mutiny against the British. The town is noted for the residence of Col Meadows Taylor, still known for his historical novels, but appointed to Shorapur as Political Agent between 1841-53 when he was responsible for Venkatappa Nayak's education. Meadows' house, 'Taylor's Manzil', has excellent views over the town. The Gopalaswamy shrine is the site of a big annual fair.

Sonthi (**Sannathi**), on the south bank of the Bhima, is an important pilgrimage centre. The Chandralamba Temple was built at an auspicious point on the banks of the Bhima River where it turns briefly from its southerly direction to flow north. Meanders on the rivers of the peninsula had long been valued as settlement sites. Not only do they provide protection on three sides, but water accumulates in the deep area of a meander bend and tends to remain throughout the dry season, making them a source of water for humans and a constant attraction for wildlife.

The **Chandralamba Temple**, probably of Chalukyan origin and dedicated to Siva, has huge *mandapas* on each side of the main entrance, while the inner courtyard enshrines 12 lingas and statues of Mahakali, Mahalakshmi and Saraswati. There are several other temples, and excavations are showing how Sonthi was once an important Buddhist centre, with the remains of stupas and Buddhist sculptures.

The road continues north to **Firuzabad**. On a bend in the Bhima River where it takes a U turn the massive stone fort walls enclose the old city of Firuzabad on the three sides. The **Jama Masjid**, largest of the remaining buildings, lies to the west of the centre behind which was the former palace. Much of the history of the city has yet to be recovered, but stylistically it owes something to influences from central Asia as well as to more local Hindu traditions.

Firuzabad
34 km S of Gulbarga

Gulbarga

Gulbarga was the first capital of the Bahmanis (from 1347-1525). It is also widely known among South Indian Muslims as the home of Saiyid Muhammad Gesu Daraz Chisti (1320-1422) who was instrumental in spreading pious Islamic faith in the Deccan. The annual Urs festival in his memory attracts up to 100,000 people.

Phone code: 08472
Colour map 2, grid B1
Population: 311,000

The most striking remains in the town are the fort, with its citadel and mosque, the Jami Masjid, and the great tombs in its eastern quarter – massive, fortress-like buildings with their distinctive domes over 30 m high.

Sights

The **fort** is just 1 km west of the centre of the present town. Originally built by Ala-ud-din Bahmani, in the 14th century, most of the outer structures and many of the buildings are in ruins although the outer door of the west gate and the *Bala Hissar* (citadel), a massive structure, remain almost intact though the whole is very overgrown. A flight of ruined steps leads up to the entrance in the north wall. Beware of dogs.

★ **Jami Masjid** The whole area of 3,500 sq m is covered by a dome over the *mihrab*, four corner domes and 75 minor domes, making it unique among Indian mosques. It was built by Firoz Shah Bahmani (1397-1432). Similarities with the mosque at Cordoba have contributed to the legend that it was designed by a North African architect from the Moorish court who used the great Spanish mosque as a model.

The **tombs** of the Bahmani sultans are in two groups. One lies 600 m to the west of the fort, the other on the east of the town. The latter have no remaining exterior decoration though the interiors show some evidence of ornamentation. The Dargah of the Chisti saint, **Hazrat Gesu Nawaz** (also known as Khwaja Bande Nawaz), who came to Gulbarga in 1413 during the reign of Firoz Shah Tughlaq, is open to visitors – see page 509. The two-storey tomb with a highly decorated painted dome had a mother of pearl canopy added over the grave. It was probably built during the reign of Mahmud Adil Shah (Firoz Shah Tughlaq's brother), a devoted follower, who gave the saint huge areas of land, and built a college for him. The Dargah library, which has 10,000 books in Urdu, Persian and Arabic, is open to visitors.

The most striking of all the tombs near **Haft Gumbaz**, the eastern group, is that of **Taj-ud-Din Firuz** (1422). Unlike the other tombs it is highly ornamented, with geometrical patterns developed in the masonry. The tombs to the northwest of the fort are those of the earliest Bahmani rulers, while to their north the Dargah to the teacher of the early sultans has a monumental gateway.

Gulbarga

Sleeping **D** *Pariwar*, Humnabad Rd near station, T21522. Some a/c rooms, some good value **E**, tasty vegetarian meals. **D-E** *Mohan*, Station Rd, T20294. 56 rooms, some a/c. **D-E** *Aditya*, Humnabad Rd, T202040. Reasonable rooms, some a/c with bath, good, clean vegetarian restaurant, very good value. Recommended. **F** *Mayura Bahamani* (KSTDC), 10 rooms (Rs 85) is expected to reopen. **F** *Railway Retiring Rooms*.

Transport There are regular train and bus connections to Hyderabad (190 km) and Solapur. **Train** Mumbai (VT): *Udyan Exp, 6530* (AC/II), 0857, 12½ hrs; *Hussainsagar Exp, 7002*, 0928, 11 hrs. **Bangalore**: *Karnataka Exp, 2628* (AC/II), 0220, 11¾ hrs. **Chennai (MC)**: *Chennai Exp, 6063* (AC/II), 0620, 13¾ hrs; *Mumbai Chennai Mail, 6009*, 1145, 18 hrs. **Hyderabad**: *Mumbai-Hyderabad Exp, 7031* (AC/II), 0050, 5¾ hrs; *Hussainsagar Exp, 7001*, 0815, 5½ hrs.

★ Bidar

Phone code: 08357
Colour map 2, grid A1
Population: 130,900
Altitude: 673 m

Bidar's impressive fort is still intact and the town sprawls within and outside its crumbling walls, in places retaining some of its old medieval charm. The palaces and tombs provide some of the finest examples of Muslim architecture in the Deccan.

In & outs **Getting there** The branch railway line is too slow to be of much use. Travel instead by bus from Hyderabad or Gulbarga, both under 4 hrs away, or Bijapur, 8 hrs. The bus stand is 1 km west of the centre.

History The walled fort town, on a red laterite plateau in North Karnataka, once the capital of the **Bahmanis** and the **Barid Shahis**, remained an important centre until it fell to Aurangzeb in 1656 – see page 291. The Bahmani Empire fragmented into four kingdoms, and the ninth Bahmani ruler, **Ahmad Shah I**, shifted his capital from Gulbarga to Bidar in 1424, rebuilding the old Hindu fort to withstand cannon attacks, and enriching the town with beautiful palaces and gardens. With the decline of the Bahmanis, the Barid Shahi Dynasty founded here ruled from 1487 until Bidar was annexed to Bijapur in 1619.

The intermingling of Hindu and Islamic styles has been ascribed to the use of Hindu craftsmen, skilled in temple carving in stone, particularly hornblende, who would have been employed by the succeeding Muslim rulers. They transferred their skill to Muslim monuments, no longer carving human figures, forbidden by Islam, but using the same technique to decorate with geometric patterns, arabesques and calligraphy, wall friezes, niches and borders on the buildings for their masters. The pillars, often of wood, were intricately carved and then painted and burnished with gold to harmonize with the *encaustic* tiles.

The Persian influence in the decorations and tilework may be attributed to the presence of artists and designers from the north, after the mass migration forced by Muhammad-bin-Tughluq, from Delhi to Daulatabad. The preference for brick over stone is evident and in order to create large domes, a light brick was fired using sawdust with clay. The resulting spongy brick was light enough to float!

The **Inner Fort** built by Muhammad Shah out of the red laterite and dark trapstone was later embellished by Ali Barid. The steep hill to the north and east provided natural defence. It was protected to the south and west by a triple moat (now filled). A series of gates and a drawbridge over the moat to the south formed the main entrance from the town. The second gate, the **Sharaza Darwaza** (1503) has tigers carved in bas relief on either side (Shia symbols of Ali as protector), tile decorations on the walls and the *Nakkar Khana* (Drum gallery) above. Beyond this is a large fortified area which brings you to the third gate, the huge **Gumbad Darwaza**, probably built by Ahmad Shah Wali in the 1420s, which shows Persian influence. Note the decorated *gumbad* (dome).

You will see the triple moat to the right and after passing through the gateway, to your left are steps leading to the **Rangin Mahal** (Coloured Palace) where Muhammad Shah moved to, after finding the nearby Shah Burj a safe refuge in 1487 when the Abyssinians attacked. This small palace (an indication of the Bahmanis' declining years) was built by him, elaborately decorated with coloured tiles, later enhanced by Ali Barid with mother-of-pearl inlay on polished black granite walls as well as intricate wood carvings. If locked, ask at the Museum for a key.

The old banyan tree and the **Shahi Matbak** (once a palace, but served as the Royal Kitchens) are to the west, with the **Shahi Hammam** (Royal Baths) next to it, which now houses a small **Museum**. The exhibits include Hindu religious sculptures, stone age implements, cannon balls filled with bits of iron. ■ *0800-1700.*

The **Lal Bagh**, where remains of water channels and a fountain witness to its former glory, and the *zenana*, are opposite the Hammam. The **Sola Khamba** (16 column) or **Zanani Mosque** is to the west (1423). It is the oldest Muslim building in Bidar and one of the largest in the Deccan; the covered courtyards for prayers are exceptional. The adjacent **Tarkash Mahal** (possibly refurbished by the Barid Shahis for the harem), to the south of Lal Bagh, is in ruins but still retains some tilework. From behind the Mosque you can get to the **Gagan Mahal** (Heavenly Palace) which once carried fine decorations and is believed to have allowed the ladies to watch animal fights in the moat below from the back of the double hall. Good view from the roof. The **Diwan-i-Am** (Hall of Public Audience) is to the northwest of the Zenana which once held the 'Takht-i-Firoza' (turquoise throne). Little remains of the splendid tiles and stonework. The black hornblende steps and bases of wooden columns survive, which possibly supported a wooden ceiling. To the north stands the **Takht Mahal** with royal apartments, audience hall and swimming bath. The tile decorations and stone carvings are particularly fine. Good views of the 'lowlands' from the windows of the royal apartment to the west. The steep staircase will take you down to underground chambers.

South of the Royal Apartments is the well which supplied water to the fort palaces through clay pipes. Of the so-called **Hazar** (thousand) **Kothri**, you can only see a few underground rooms and passages which enabled a quick escape to the moat when necessary. Further south, the **Naubat Khana** probably housed the fort commander and the musicians. The road west from the Royal Apartments leads to the encircling Fort Wall (about 10 km) with bastions carrying vast canyons, the one to the northwest being the most impressive. The wall is interrupted by various *darwazas* and *burjes* and gives a view of the moat. You can see the ammunition magazine inside the Mandu Darwaza to the east before returning to the main Fort entrance.

Old town   As you walk south from the fort you can see the ruins of the **Madrassa of Mahmud Gawan** (1472). The great warrior statesman/scholar increased the power and extent of the Bahmani Kingdom and introduced administrative and military reforms, but these cost him his life. His gift to the country of his exile was the fine Madrassa with its valuable collection of manuscripts (see page 291). Once a famous college which attracted Muslim scholars from afar, it was badly damaged by lightning in 1695 and from an accident when Aurangzeb's soldiers used it to store gunpowder. It is a fine example of his native Persian architecture

Bidar

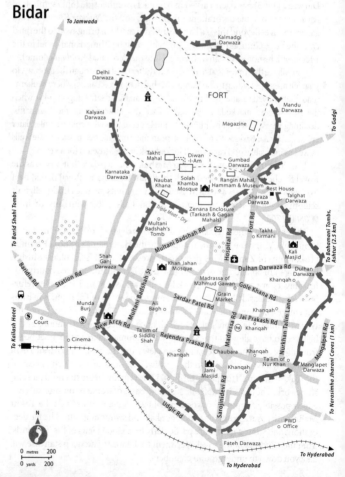

and still bears signs of the once brilliant green, white and yellow tiles which covered the whole façade with swirls of floral patterns and bold calligraphy. Percy Prior points out that lead sheets were used in the foundation, much like a damp-proof course, to reduce moisture damage to the tiles.

The **Chaubara** is a 23 m circular watchtower at the crossroads, south of the town centre (good views from the top). South of this is the **Jami Masjid** (1430) which bears the Barid Shahis' typical chain and pendant motif. The **Kali Masjid** (1694), south of the Talghat Darwaza, is made of black trapstone. It has fine plaster decorations on the vaulted ceiling. There are also a number of **Khanqahs** (monasteries).

To the east of town, outside the walls, are the **Habshi Kot** where the palaces of the important Abyssinians were. From the Police Station, a road leads to the **Narasimha Jharani** underground cave temple (1.5 km). The natural spring requires devotees to wade through water to get to the sanctuary.

The road east from the Dulhan Darwaza, opposite the General Hospital, leads to the eight **Bahmani tombs** at **Ashtur**. These are best seen in the morning when the light is better for viewing the interiors. ■ *0800-1700. The attendant can use a mirror to reflect sunlight but it is best to carry your own flash light.*

The square tombs, with arched arcades all round have bulbous domes. The exteriors have stone carvings and superb coloured tile decoration showing strong Persian influence, while the interiors have coloured paintings with gilding. The tomb of **Ahmad Shah I**, the ninth Bahmani ruler (see above), is impressive with a dome rising to nearly 35 m, and has a particularly fine interior with coloured decorations and calligraphy in the Persian style, highlighted with white borders. To the east and south are minor tombs of his wife and son. The tomb of **Alauddin Shah II** (1458) is possibly the finest. Similar in size to his father's, this has lost its fine painting inside but enough remains of the outer tilework to give an impression of its original magnificence. Some of the tombs were never completed, and that of **'Humayun the Cruel'** was rent apart by lightning, revealing in cross-section the use of light bricks in order to create a large dome. **Muhammad Shah**, who ruled for 36 years, was able to complete his own tomb.

On the way back, is the **Chaukhandi of Hazrat Khalil-Ullah** which is approached by a flight of steps. Most of the tilework has disappeared but you can see the fine carvings at the entrance and on the granite pillars. Hidden behind the entrance doors are the stairs to the roof.

The **Barid Shahi tombs** each of which once stood in its garden, are on the Nanded Road to the west of the old town. That of **Ali Barid** is the most impressive, with the dome rising to over 25 m, with granite carvings, decorative plasterwork and calligraphy and floral patterns on the coloured tiles, which sadly can no longer be seen on the exterior. Here, abandoning the customary *mihrab* on the west wall, Ali Barid chose to have his tomb left open to the elements. A prayer hall, music rooms, a combined tomb for his concubines and a pool fed by an aqueduct are nearby. There are fine carvings on the incomplete tomb to his son **Ibrahim Barid**, to the west. You can also see two sets of granite *ranakhambas* (lit battleposts) which may have been boundary markers. Other tombs show the typical arched niches employed to lighten the heavy walls which have decorative parapets.

The road north from Ali Barid's tomb descends to **Nanak Jhera**, where a *gurdwara* marks the holy place where Sikhs believe a miracle was performed by Guru Nanak (see page 536) and the *jhera* (spring) rose.

No good hotels, but several basic near Bus Station including **D** *Kailash*, T7727, 21 rooms some a/c; **F** *Prince*, Udgir Rd, T5747, 19 rooms. A roadside Punjabi *dhaba* near the junction of NH9 and the Bidar Rd serves very good meals, clean (including toilet at back).

Sleeping & eating

Karnataka

Shopping Excellent *bidriwork* (see page 369) here, where it is said to have originated, particularly shops near the Ta'lim of Siddiq Shah. You can see craftsmen at work in the narrow lanes.

Transport **Local Auto-rickshaws**: are the most convenient. **Long distance Train**: Bidar is on a branch line from Vikarabad to Parbhani Junction.

Raichur

Phone code: 08532
Colour map 2, grid B1
Population: 170,500

The main road from Hospet to Hyderabad passes through the important medieval centre of Raichur, once dominant in the Tungabhadra-Krishna doab but now a dusty peninsula town. An important market town it is in the middle of a cotton growing area. Cotton takes up more than 20% of the sown area, followed by groundnuts.

History For 200 years in the medieval period Raichur dominated the central plateaus. It is still at a crossroads of the regional cultures of Karnataka, Andhra Pradesh and Maharashtra. As Kannada is the dominant language it was allocated to Karnataka after the reorganization of the states in 1956.

Sights The site of the **fort's citadel** at Raichur gives magnificent views over the vast open spaces of the Deccan plateau nearly 100 m below. Built in the mid-14th century Raichur became the first capital of the Bijapur Kingdom when it broke away from the Bahmani Sultans in 1489. Much of the fort itself is now in ruins, but there are some interesting remains.

The north gate is flanked by towers, a carved elephant standing about 40 m away. On the inner walls are some carvings, and a tunnel reputedly built to enable soldiers access to barricade the gate in emergency. Near the west gate is the old palace.

The climb to the citadel begins from near the north gate. In the citadel is a shrine with a row of cells with the Jami Masjid in the east. Its eastern gateway has three domes. The top of the citadel is barely 20 sq m. There are some other interesting buildings in the fort below the hill, including the *Daftar ki Masjid* (Office Mosque), built around 1510 out of masonry removed from Hindu temples. It is one of the earliest mosques in the Deccan to be built in this way, with the bizarre result of producing flat ceilings with pillars carved for Chalukyan temples. The **Ek Minar ki masjid** ('one-minaret mosque') is in the southeast corner of the courtyard. It has a distinctively *Bahmani* style dome.

Sleeping **F** *Laxmi Lodge* at Koppal. **F** *Railway Retiring Rooms* and dorm.

Bichalli Point From Raichur the road runs north to the Krishna River. Just to the west of the road on the south side of the river is the wetland. The Krishna River, slow moving between November and June and with many rocky outcrops and islands, has a good range of resident and migratory waterbirds. The river itself is clear and clean during the dry season and on either side are stands of forest including Bo (*Ficus religiosa*), Acacia and the thorn scrub *Prosopis juliflora*. The banks are covered in grass or cultivated with banana, watermelon and betel leaf. The Directory of Indian Wetlands recorded that duck shooting was common and was a threat to the highly varied birdlife.

Andhra Pradesh

7

Andhra Pradesh

Away from its lush green coastal deltas much of Andhra
Pradesh is rocky, bare and dry. The thin red soils
developed on the ancient rocks of the peninsula support
an often meagre agricultural subsistence, but its capital,
Hyderabad, has become one of India's dynamic
'electronics cities'. Once the centre of the largest Muslim
ruled princely state in India, Hyderabad and its nearby
fort of Golconda are rich in history, but rural Andhra
has its own share of important sites, including the
ancient Buddhist centres of Nagarjunakonda and
Amaravati, and one of India's most important modern
pilgrimage centres, Tirumalai.

★ *A foot in the door*

   Visit the **Tirupati** temple and obtain a darshan
      with ten thousand pilgrims
   Climb **Golconda Fort** at opening time, before the
      crowds arrive, or see the spectacular Sound and
      Light show in the evening
   See one of the great Indian museum collections at
      the **Salar Jung Museum**
   Take a boat acrossthe lake to one of India's oldest
      Buddhist sites at **Nagarjunakonda island**
   Climb the **Vijayanagar Gooty Fort** in southern
      Andhra for spectacular views over the plains
   Walk through the ruins of the medieval city of
      Warrangal

Andhra Pradesh

Background

The land
Population: 78 mn
Area: 275,000 sq km

For much of the year many areas of Andhra look hot, dry and desolate although the great delta of the Krishna and Godavari rivers retains its lush greenness by virtue of their irrigation water. Water is the state's lifeblood, and the great peninsular rivers have a sanctity which reflects their importance The **Godavari**, rising less than 200 km north of Mumbai, is the largest of the peninsular rivers. The **Krishna** rises near **Mahabaleshwar** at an altitude of 1,360 m. After the Ganga these two rivers have the largest watersheds in India, and between them they irrigate nearly 6,000,000 ha of farmland. **Climate** Andhra Pradesh is hot throughout the year. The interior of the state is in the rain shadow of the Western Ghats and receives less rainfall than much of the coast. All regions have most of their rain between June and October, although the south gets the benefit of the retreating monsoon between October and December. Cyclones sweeping across the Bay of Bengal can wreak havoc in the flat coastal districts in November to December.

History The first historical evidence of a people called the 'Andhras' came from Emperor Asoka. The first known Andhra power, the **Satavahanas** encouraged various religious groups including Buddhists. Their capital at Amaravati shows evidence of the great skill of early Andhra artists and builders. Around AD 150 there was also a fine university at Nagarjunakonda.

Vijayanagar In 1323 Warangal, just to the northeast of the present city of Hyderabad, was captured by the armies of Muhammad bin Tughlaq. Muslim expansion further south was prevented for two centuries by the rise of the Vijayanagar Empire, itself crushed at the Battle of Talikota in 1565 by a short-lived federation of Muslim States, and the cultural life it supported had to seek fresh soil.

Muslim states From then on Muslim rulers dominated the politics of central Andhra, **Telangana**. The Bahmani Kingdoms in the region around modern Hyderabad controlled central Telangana in the 16th century. They were even able to keep the Mughals at bay until Aurangzeb finally forced them into submission at the end of the 17th century. **Hyderabad** was the most important centre of Muslim power in central and South India from the 17th to the 19th centuries. It was founded by the fifth in line of an earlier Muslim Dynasty, **Mohammad Quli Qutb Shah**, in 1591. Through his successors Hyderabad became the capital of a Princely State the size of France, ruled by a succession of Muslim Nizams from 1724 till after India's Independence in 1947.

Arrival of the Europeans Through the 18th century British and French traders were spreading their influence up the coast. Increasingly they came into conflict and looked for alliances with regional powers. At the end of the 18th century the British reached an agreement with the **Nizam of Hyderabad** whereby he accepted British support in exchange for recognition of British rights to trade and political control of the coastal districts. Thus Hyderabad retained a measure of independence until 1947 while accepting British suzerainty.

Independence There was doubt as to whether the Princely State would accede to India after Partition. The Nizam of Hyderabad would have liked to join fellow Muslims in the newly created Muslim State of Pakistan. However, political disturbances in 1949 gave the Indian Government the excuse to take direct control, and the state was incorporated into the Indian Union.

People Most of Andhra Pradesh's 78 million people are Dravidians. Over 85% of the population speak Telugu. However, there are important minorities. Tamil is widely spoken in the extreme south, and on the border of Karnataka there are pockets of Kanarese speakers. In **Hyderabad** there are large numbers of Urdu speakers who make up seven percent of AP's population.

Culture

Religion Hyderabad, the capital of modern AP, was the seat of government of the Muslim Nizams. Under their rule many Muslims came to work in the court, from North India and abroad. The Nizam's capital was a highly cosmopolitan centre, drawing extensively on Islamic contacts in North India and in west Asia – notably Persia. Its links with the Islamic world and the long tradition of political power that the Nizams had enjoyed encouraged them to hope that they might gain complete Independence from India in 1947. That option was foreclosed by the Indian Government's decision to remove the Nizam by force in 1948 after a half-hearted insurrection.

Cuisine Andhra food stands out as distinct because of its northern influence and larger number of non-vegetarians. The rule of the Muslim Nawabs for centuries is reflected in the rich, spicy local dishes, especially in the area around the capital. Try *haleem* (spiced pounded wheat with mutton) or *baghara baigan* (stuffed aubergines). Rice and meat *biryani*, *nahari*, *kulcha* and *kababs* have a lot in common with the northern Mughlai cuisine. Vegetarian biryani replaces meat with cashew nuts and sultanas. The growing of hot chillies has led to its liberal use in the food prepared. Good quality locally grown grapes (especially *anab-e-shahi*) or *khobani* (puréed apricots) provide a welcome neutralizing effect.

Craft industries Andhra's **Bidriware** uses dark matt gunmetal (a zinc and copper alloy) with silver damascening in beautiful flowing floral and arabesque patterns and illustrates the Persian influence on Indian motifs. The articles vary from large vases and boxes, jewellery and plates to tiny buttons and cuff links. The name is derived from Bidar in Karnataka and dates back to the Bahmani rulers.

   Toys: Miniature wooden figures, animals, fruit, vegetables and birds are common subjects of *Kondapalli* toys which are known for their bright colours. *Nirmal* toys look more natural and are finished with a herbal extract which gives them a golden sheen, *Tirupati* toys are in a red wood while *Ethikoppaka* toys are finished in coloured lacquer. Andhra also produces fine figurines of deities in sandalwood.

   Jewellery: Hyderabadi jewellers work in gold and precious stones which are often uncut. The craftsmen can often be seen working in the lanes around the Char Minar with shops selling the typical local bangles set with glass to the west. Hyderabadi cultured pearls and silver filigree ware from Karimnagar are another speciality.

   Textiles: The state is famous for **himru** shawls and fabrics produced in cotton/silk mixes with rich woven patterns on a special handloom. Silver or gold threads produce even richer 'brocade' cloth. A young boy often sits with the weavers 'calling out' the intricate pattern. The art of weaving special **ikat** fabrics has been revived through the efforts of the All India Handicrafts Board in the villages of Pochampalli, Chirala, Puttapaka and Koyyalagudem among others. The practice of dyeing the warp and weft threads before weaving in such a way as to

Andhra Pradesh

Early Andhra satire

Although the name Andhra was well known, the Telugu language did not emerge until the 11th century AD. There developed a vigorous literary tradition, not always simply in the hands of the Brahmin priesthood. Two writers dominated. Potana (1400-75) was a poor man who lived in the countryside. His translation of the Bhagavata, immediately popular, combined simple language with deep devotion. Vemana (15th century) was a low caste Saivite, an individualist and a revolutionary. JTF Jordens has pointed out that "His sataka (century) of gnomic verse is known to all Telugus and to most South Indians. His verses bristle with sarcastic attacks on the Brahmins, on polytheism, idolatry, and pilgrimages.

> *The solitariness of a dog! The meditation of a crane!*
> *The chanting of an ass! The bathing of a frog!*
> *Ah, why will ye not try to know your own hearts?*
> *What are you the better for smearing your body with ashes?*
> *Your thoughts should be set on God alone;*
> *For the rest, an ass can wallow in dirt as well as you.*
> *he books that are called the Vedas are like courtesans,*
> *Deluding men, and wholly unfathomable;*
> *But the hidden knowledge of God is like an honourable wife.*
> *He that fasts shall become (in his next birth) a village pig;*
> *He that embraces poverty shall become a beggar;*
> *And he that bows to a stone shall become like a lifeless image".*

produce a pattern, additionally used oil in the process when it was woven into pieces of cloth *Teli rumal* (literally oil kerchief) to be used as garments. Other towns produce their own special weaves.

Kalamkari paintings (*kalam* refers to the pen used) produced in Kalahasti in the extreme south of Andhra, have a distinctive style using indigo and vegetable dyes extracted from turmeric, pomegranate skin et cetera, on cloth. Fabric is patterned through the medium of dye, then glued. The blues stand out markedly from the otherwise dullish ochre colours. Originally designed to tell stories from mythology (Mahabharata and Ramayana), they make good wall hangings. *Pallakollu* and *Masulipatam* were particularly famous for printing and painting of floral designs. In addition hand block printed textiles are also produced.

Carpets: Those produced in Warangal and Eluru and are known as 'Deccan rugs' with designs that reflect a Persian influence.

Modern Andhra Pradesh

Government In 1953 Andhra Pradesh (AP) was created on the basis of the Telugu-speaking districts of Madras Presidency. This was not enough for those who were demanding statehood for a united Telugu-speaking region. One political leader, Potti Sreeramulu, starved himself to death in protest at the government's refusal to grant the demand. Finally, in 1956, AP took its present form. It was the first State to be reorganized when the Indian Government decided to reshape the political map inherited from the British period. In 1956 all Telugu-speaking areas were grouped together in the new State of Andhra Pradesh. This brought together the eastern parts of the old Nizam's territories and the coastal districts which had formerly been in Madras Presidency became the capital of the new state.

AP was regarded as a stronghold of the Congress Party until 1983 when a regional party, the **Telugu Desam**, won a crushing victory in the State Assembly elections. The Assembly elections on 5 October 1999 saw a repeat performance, with the highly regarded Chief Minister N Chandrababu Naidu, being swept back to power in the State Assembly with nearly a two thirds majority. Allied with the BJP in the governing coalition in New Delhi, the Telugu Desam has a reputation for pushing ahead with rapid economic modernisation, particularly visible in Hyderabad, but poverty remains endemic in many rural areas and the extremist violence of the *Naxalite* movement and the Peoples' War Group (PWG) continues to plague some remote districts, especially in the northeast.

★ Hyderabad-Secunderabad and North Central Andhra

The twin cities of Hyderabad-Secunderabad are built on the ancient granites and gneisses of the Peninsula, which outcrop in bizarre shapes on hills in this area and which provide building stone for some of the city's most impressive monuments in the dusty and congested Old City to the south of the Musi River. Within the rocks lie some of the region's most valued resources – gem stones. The Golconda Kingdoms which preceded those of Hyderabad produced magnificent diamonds, probably including the Koh-i-Noor. Wealth today comes increasingly from the burgeoning IT sector, and the city's press suggested re-naming the city Cyberabad in honour of President Bill Clinton's visit in March 2000.

Phone code: 040
Colour map 2, grid B2
Population: 4.28 mn
Altitude: 537 m

Andhra Pradesh

Getting there Begumpet airport is just 6 km from Secunderabad station and 15 km from the Old City which has most of the sights. It is only a short taxi ride to several luxury hotels and to some cheaper options. Secunderabad station, with trains to major cities, is in the Cantonment area, while the Hyderabad City station at Nampally is close to the Abids district, with the majority of budget accommodation. The large Imbli-Ban Bus terminal for long distance buses is on an island in the Musi River, south of Abids. The Jubilee Bus Terminal is in Secunderabad. **Getting around** Autos (or taxis) are the best means of getting about the city north of the Musi and in Secunderabad, but in the congested old quarter you are best off walking, though there are cycle rickshaws.

Ins & outs

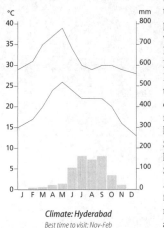

Climate: Hyderabad
Best time to visit: Nov-Feb

Even though Hyderabad's population was always predominantly composed of Telugu-speaking Hindus, it was ruled by a succession of Muslim Nizams from 1724 when the Nizam-ul-Mulk ('Regulator of the Land') **Asaf Jah**, seized power from the Mughal Governor, founding the dynasty that included some of the richest men in the world. Hyderabad had been founded in 1589 by the fifth Sultan of Golconda of an earlier Muslim Dynasty, Muhammad Quli Qutb Shah, under the original name of *Bhagnagar*. The founders were famous for their beautiful 'monuments, mosques and mistresses' and also for their diamond markets.

History
Hyderabad has a large Muslim minority. Occasionally the political situation can become tense & parts of the city put under curfew

Hyderabad stood on the south bank of the river Musi, in a superb military position. During the Asaf Jahi rule it expanded north. Then in the early 19th century, during the reign of Sikander Jah (1803-30), the cantonment of Secunderabad was developed by the British.

Devastating floods and outbreaks of plague at the beginning of the 19th century were followed by programmes of urban renewal initiated by Nizam Osman Ali Khan. A series of new public buildings date from this period including those from 1914-21, under the British architect **Vincent Esch**. Tillotson shows that although the Nizam's family and others had begun to experiment with European styles, Esch himself attempted to build in an Indian style. Some of his major buildings are described here.

The cities Unlike Mughal cities Hyderabad was planned in a grid pattern with enormous arches and the Char Minar was built in 1591 by the Sultan as the city's prime monument. The streets were lined with stone buildings which had shops below and living quarters above.

If you come out through the western arch of the Char Minar you enter Lad Bazar where shops sell the typical Hyderabadi glass embedded bangles, while to the north you will find jewellers including those with pearls, and cloth merchants. To the south the craftsmen in their tiny shops still prepare thin silver 'leaf' by pounding the metal.

Close to the Salar Jung Museum, you can see examples of Asaf Jahi architecture. North of the river are the Asafia State Library and Osmania General Hospital and on the south bank the City College and the High Court. Other typical examples are in the Public Gardens behind the Archaeological Museum, where you will find the Ajanta Pavilion, the elaborate Jubilee Hall, the State Assembly Hall and the Health Museum.

The old city Charminar

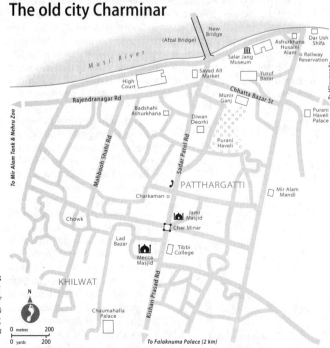

Related maps
A *Hyderabad centre, page 377*
B *Hyderabad & Secunderabad, page 374*

Old City and Char Minar Facing the river is the **High Court**, on the new roads laid out along the Musi's embankments after the great flood, a splendid Mughal-style building in the old Qutb Shahi gardens, Amin Bagh, near the Afzal Ganj Bridge (New Bridge). Vincent Esch's most striking work, it was built in 1916 of local pink granite, with red sandstone carved panels and columns, a large archway and blue-glazed and gold domes, now painted pink. A further recent change is the enclosure of the verandahs. It cost Rs 2mn. The detail is Mughal, but as Tillotson argues the structure and internal form are Western.

Next door to the High Court is Esch's **City College** (1917-20), originally built as the City High School for boys. Built largely of undressed granite, there are some distinctive Indian decorative features including some marble *jalis*. Esch deliberately incorporated Gothic features, calling his style 'Perpendicular Mogul Saracenic'.

One of the oldest imambaras in the country, the Badshahi (Royal) **Ashurkhana**, or house of mourning, built in the Qutb Shahi style at the end of the 16th century, has excellent tile mosaics and wooden columns in the outer chamber, both of which were later additions.

Two hundred metres southeast of the Darus Shafa (hospital) is Asaf Jah's **Purani Haveli** (Old Palace), a vast mansion comprising 11 buildings (closed to the public).

South from the bridge is **Charkaman** with its four arches. The eastern Black Arch was for the Drums, the western led to the palaces, the northern was the Fish Arch and the southern led to the Char Minar.

★ **Char Minar** Sometimes called the Oriental Arc de Triomphe (though certainly not on account of its physical appearance), it was built between 1591 and 1612 by **Sultan Mohammad Quli Qutb Shah** as a showpiece at the centre of his beautiful city; it has become the city's symbol. With its 56 m tall slender minarets with spiral staircases and huge arches on each side (the whole plastered with lime mortar) it stood at the entrance to the palace complex. Now, standing at the centre of a crossroads, it guards the entry to the main bazar. There is a beautiful mosque on the second floor and a large water tank in the middle. Some believe it was built to commemorate the eradication of the plague from the city. There is a special market on Thursday. Illuminations, 1900-2100. **NB** The site is closed to visitors but you can walk under the arches.

★ **Mecca Masjid** immediately to the southwest. The grand mosque was started in 1614 by the sixth **Sultan Abdulla Qutb Shah** and completed by Aurangzeb when he annexed Golconda in 1692. Built of enormous black granite slabs quarried nearby it has tall pillars, stucco decorations and red bricks on its entrance arches believed to have been made from clay from Mecca mixed with red colouring. The vast mosque can accommodate 10,000 at prayers. The tombs of the Asaf Jahi rulers, the Nizams of Hyderabad, are in a roofed enclosure to the left of the courtyard. The **Jama Masjid** was the second mosque built in the old city at the end of the 16th century.

The **Lad Bazar** area has interesting buildings with wood and stone carvings and pink elephant gates. It is at the heart of the Muslim part of the city, so densely packed with people it can be very difficult even to look at the buildings, and some foreign women visitors have found it a bit daunting. You arrive at the **Chowk** which has a mosque and a Victorian Clock Tower. Southeast of the Lad Bazar is the huge complex of the palaces which were built by the different Nizams, including the grand **Chaumahalla Palace** around a quadrangle.

The ★ **Falaknuma Palace** (1873), originally a rich nobleman's house, was built in a mixture of classical and Mughal styles. Bought by the Nizam in 1897, it has a superb interior (particularly the state reception room) with marble, chandeliers and paintings. The palace houses oriental and European treasures,

Andhra Pradesh

Hyderabad & Secunderabad

BEGUMPET

✈ Airport

■ 5

Sardar Patel Rd (SP Rd)

Paradise Garden

■ 13 ⓘ

1

Sir R Ross Rd

■ 4

Begumpet Rd

Begumpet Station

James St Station

12

Amirpet Rd

Hussain Sagar Station

Boat Club

14

(MG Rd)

Walden's Bookshop

Husain Sagar

Road No 2

Sunat Nagar Rd

Rajbhavan Rd

9 ■

Road No 6

BANJARA HILLS

Raj Bhavan

Road No 7

■ 6

Buddha Statue

NH 7

Tank Bund Rd

Road No 10

■ 8

Road No 11

Khairatabad Station

Road No 12

Road No 1

10 ■

KHAIRATABAD

British Library

Secretariat Rd

ⓘ AP Tourism

Nirula's Open House

ITDC Tourist Office ⓘ

■ 4

Himayatnagar

A

Lakdi ka Pul

Public Gardens Rd

Lal Bahadur Stadium

Old MLA Quarters Rd

SAIFABAD

■ 2

Mahatma Gandhi Rd

NAMPALLY

Vidhan Sabha

Abids Rd

Hyderabad City Station & Railway Retiring Rooms

Mukarramjahi Rd

ABIDS

SULTAN BAZAR

Turreba zkha

Residency

ALLAH BANDA

Jawaharlal Nehru Rd

GOSHAMAHAL

BEGUM BAZAR

Maharani Jhansi Rd

Maulvi Alauddin Road

Imbli-Ban Bus Stand

To Golconda & Tombs

Dhulpet Rd

City College Rd

Musli Jang Bridge

New Bridge

Musi River

DHULPET

Golconda Rd

Old Bridge

Rajendranagar Rd

SABZIMANDI

PATTHARGATTI

Bangalore Rd

Char Minar

★

B

Related maps
A Hyderabad centre,
page 377
B Old City Charminar,
page 372

N

0 metres 500
0 yards 500

To Zoo

■ Sleeping	4 Deccan Continental	8 Krishna Oberoi
1 Asrani International	5 Grand Kakatiya	9 Rock Castle
2 Central Court	6 Holiday Inn Krishna	10 Taj Residency &
3 Club View	7 Karan	Golconda

Andhra Pradesh

Gymkhana Grounds
Jubilee Bus Stand
YWCA
Bolaram Rd
Sarojini Devi Rd (SD Rd)
7
Golden Dragon
11
Rashtrapati Rd
Station Rd
Subhash Rd
Secunderabad Station
Library
Mahatma Gandhi Rd
Nampally Bus Stand
Kavadiguda Rd
Indira Park
Chikadpalli Rd
NEHRU NAGAR
City Central Library
Narayanguda Rd
Rd
Vir Savarkar Rd
Kacheguda Station
Maulvi Alauddin Rd
To Race Course
Bhagya Reddy Rd
Rd
OLD MALAKPET
Malakpet Station
Vijayawada Rd
To Raymond's Tomb & Vijayawada
Dabirpura Station

11 Taj Mahal
12 Viceroy
13 Yatri Nivas
14 Youth Hostel

including a collection of jade, crystal and precious stones and a superb library. The spectacular building is closed (being converted into a Taj hotel, opening 2001).

The **Tomb of Michel Raymond** is off the Vijayawada Road, about 3 km from the Oliphant Bridge. The Frenchman joined the second Nizam's army in 1786 as a common soldier and rose to command 15,000 troops. His popularity with the people earned him the combined Muslim-Hindu name 'Moosa Ram', and even today they remember him by holding a commemorative *Urs* fair at his grey granite tomb which is 7 m high and bears the initials 'JR'.

Mir Alam Tank to the southwest of the old city is a large artificial lake. It was built by French engineers under instructions of the grandfather of Salar Jung III and is a popular picnic spot. It is now part of the **Nehru Zoological Park** which is to its north (see page 379).

The **Osmania General Hospital** (1918-21) is the third of Vincent Esch's impressive buildings in Hyderabad. It stands across the river, opposite the High Court. The 200-m long building was one of the largest – and best equipped – hospitals in the world when it was opened. Its Indian context is indicated by decorative detail rather than structural plan. To its east, also on the river, is the imposing **Asafia State Central Library** (1929-34) with its priceless collection of Arabic, Persian and Urdu books and manuscripts. The Library was designed by anonymous architects of the PWD. Tillotson states that "Its main front facing the river is dominated by the huge arch of the entrance portal. This is a powerful and also an original motif: round, rather than the usual pointed form, it is rendered Indian by the mouldings on the intrados and by the *chajja* which sweeps over the top".

The **Public Gardens** in Nampally, north of Hyderabad Station, contain

Hyderabad Centre: The New City

Andhra Pradesh

Andhra Pradesh

some important buildings including the Archaeological Museum and Art Galleries and the State Legislative Assembly (Vidhan Sabha). The **City Railway Station** (1914) was intended by Esch to be pure Mughal in style but built entirely of the most modern material then available – pre-cast, reinforced concrete. It has a wide range of distinctively Indian features – the chhattris of royalty, wide eaves (*chajjas*), and onion domes. The **Naubat Pahad** (Kala Pahad or Neeladri) are two hillocks to the north of the Public Gardens. The Qutb Shahis are believed to have had their proclamations read from the hill tops accompanied by the beating of drums. In 1940 pavilions were built and then a hanging garden was laid out on top of one. The modern, stunning white marble **Venkatesvara Temple** with an intricately carved ceiling which overlooks Husain Sagar, was built on the other by the Birlas, the Marwari business family who have been responsible for building important new Hindu temples in several major cities, including the Laxmi Narayan Temple in New Delhi. Completed in 1976, the images of the deities are South Indian, although the building itself drew craftsmen from the north as well, among them some who claimed to have ancestors who built the Taj Mahal. ■ *0900-1200, 1600-2000, Sun 2030. The temple can be reached by an attractive path about 100 m from the Air India office on Secretariat Rd.*

Vidhan Sabha The massive State Legislative Assembly building, originally the Town Hall, was built by the PWD in 1922. Although Esch had nothing to do with its design, Tillotson records that he greatly admired it for its lightness and coolness, even on the hottest day. He suggests that both the Town Hall and the State Library marked a move away from a Hyderabadi style to a more universal 'Indian' approach to design.

The **Jubilee Hall** (1936), behind the Vidhan Sabha, is another remarkable PWD building, with clear simple lines. Tillotson notes the irony in the fact that official contemporary descriptions of these works claim that they represent the natural redevelopment of a Hyderabadi style, when the PWD architects themselves appear to have been aiming for something more genuinely pan-Islamic.

★ **Husain Sagar** The 16-m deep lake was created in the mid-16th century by building a bund linking Hyderabad and Secunderabad, and was named to mark the gratitude of Ibrahim Quli Qutb Shah to Hussain Shah Wali who helped him recover from his illness. The *bund* is a favourite promenade for the city dwellers. At the far end of the lake is the Nizamia Observatory. The 17.5 m high, 350 tonne granite statue of the Buddha was erected in the lake after years of successive disasters and finally inaugurated by the Dalai Lama in 1993. The tank, fed by streams originating from the Musi River, supplies drinking water to Hyderabad. Although it supports a rich birdlife and is used for fish culturing it receives huge amounts of industrial effluent, agricultural waste and town sewage.

Osmania University, built by the Nizam in 1939, is just outside the city, towards the east. Inaugurated in 1917 in temporary buildings, its sprawling campus with its black granite Arts College combines Moorish and Hindu Kakatiya architectural styles. There is a botanical garden and the **State Archives**.

The Malakpet **Race Course**, south of the river, is one of the major centres of racing in the country and one of the most modern.

Secunderabad has the Mahakali Temple where the *Bonalu* festival is held in June/July.

★ **Salar Jung Museum** Sir Yusuf Ali Salar Jung III was the Wazir (Prime Minister) to the Nizam between 1899-1949, and his collection forms the basis of the modern museum, one of the three national museums in India. Originally housed on the edge of the city in one of the palaces, it was rehoused in a purpose-built if singularly dull and unattractive building just inside the north boundary of the city in 1968. There are informative descriptions of the exhibits in English, Urdu, Hindi and Telugu. The museum is built to a semi-circular plan with the entrance off the reception area. Along the verandah, 19th-century copies of European statuary overlook a small open space.

Hyderabad centre

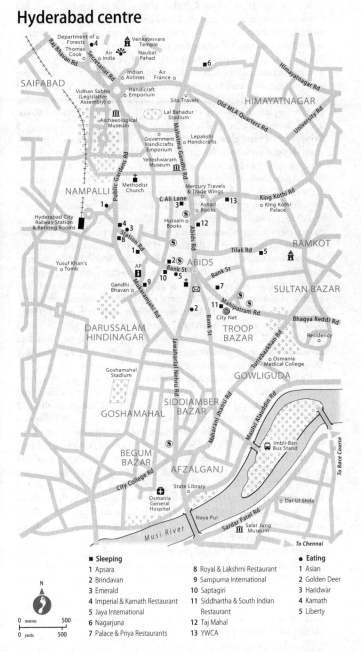

■ Sleeping
1 Apsara
2 Brindavan
3 Emerald
4 Imperial & Kamath Restaurant
5 Jaya International
6 Nagarjuna
7 Palace & Priya Restaurants
8 Royal & Lakshmi Restaurant
9 Sampurna International
10 Saptagiri
11 Siddhartha & South Indian Restaurant
12 Taj Mahal
13 YWCA

● Eating
1 Asian
2 Golden Deer
3 Haridwar
4 Kamath
5 Liberty

Andhra Pradesh

Rooms 1 and **2** are on the left. At the end of verandah turn right to find **3 Indian textiles and bronzes**, houses late Pallava bronzes, seventh century Vishnu (Vijayanagar), some Chola Vaishnavite and Jain images. The earliest is a standing figure of Partha-vananda and a nine-headed cobra over Jaina's head (late eighth century). *Kalamkaris* and *Picchwais* were temple hangings which were used to cover the walls behind the deities (see page 370). *Jain statues* include some of Mahavira from Karnataka and Gujarat. There is a very fine small Tamil Nadu Nataraja (14th century) and a Dancing Nataraja (14th century) performing *Anandatandava* – the five attributes of the Lord: creation, preservation, destruction, salvation and omnipotence. There is an unusual dancing Ganesh from Mysore (15th century). **3a Indian sculpture** *Early development* Stone carving from rock pillars (Asokan edicts), Sungan art developments, abounding with the organic forms of nature, through the Gupta period (Amaravati and Nagarjunakonda had a soft grey limestone, popularly known as *Palna* marble). An early Gupta *Mukhalinga* (third century AD) is given pride of place. **4 Minor arts of South India** Carvings in sandal and rose-wood and temple carving. **6 Printed fabrics and glass** Temple cloths in Rajasthani freehand designs with glued appliqué work, wood block printing and scrolls used as visual aids by itinerant 'preachers' and storytellers; 18th-century Dhaka muslin; some attractive Mughal glass characterized by gilt paint. Through Room 6, the small open space at the end is **7** The small open space on the right with large pots counts as **8** On the right as you retrace your steps are **9, 10, 11 Children's sections**. **12** is a very shallow porch with stags, deer et cetera in glass cabinets; among many crude models are some real collectors' pieces. Possibly the only model flying boat left in the world, brought out by W Bristow in 1939, is in the collection; some show signs of metal-fatigue that attacks pre-war zinc alloy 'Mazah'! **14 Ivory room** Ivory chairs and inlaid tables (Delhi, Mysore, Travancore and Visakhapatnam). The cuckoo clock is a great attraction. **16 Armaments** Amazing variety and quantity of old arms includes 17th century chain mail, blunderbusses, matchlock guns, Persian swords. **15** *Metal ware* Includes excellent examples of Bidri ware, local to the region. **17a Modern Indian painting** (19th and 20th century) with some of Ravi Varma, Abanindranath Tagore, Sunil Prakash. **18 Indian miniatures** Representatives of major schools, Mughal Deccani, Rajasthani, Mewar, Amber and Jain palm leaf manuscripts.

Upstairs: 20 European art A Landseer is perhaps the best in a mediocre collection. European porcelain from Dresden, Sèvres and Wedgewood, Italian and Austrian porcelain and a porcelain mirror, belonging to Marie Antoinette. v **25 Jade** Some outstandingly beautiful Indian and Chinese jade. **26 European bronzes** All 19th century copies of classical sculpture. **28 Clock room** Some bizarre examples, many French. Some English grandmother clocks. **29 Manuscripts** This includes some early Islamic scripts. A ninth century Qu'ran, a script on Unani medicine. No 6 is the oldest in the collection. A copy of the Qu'ran, written in 1288, has signatures of Jahangir, Shah Jahan and Aurangzeb. **31 Far Eastern Porcelain** Sung Dynasty. Celadon, brought to Europe in the 12th century, was replaced by cobalt-derived blue ('Mohammadan blue') from Persia and Baluchistan. **32** *Kashmiri room* **33** *Far Eastern statuary* Various Buddhist sculptures recounting the birth of Buddha at Lumbini.

■ *1000-1715, closed Fri and public holidays. Afzal Ganj. Tape recorded guides at ticket office. Cameras and bags must be left at counter on right; tickets from counters on left. Specialist publications available immediately inside the door. Some rooms are closed from time to time. Allow at least 1½ hours. Free guided tours six times a day at half past the hour, from 1030. It is often difficult to hear what is being said and to see the objects when going round in a group; individual visit recommended.*

Hyderabad Museum Public Gardens. The small museum is next to the Lal **Other museums**
Bahadur Shastri Stadium, 10 minutes by car from Banjara Hills area. Opened in
1930 in the specially built semi-circular building. Sections on prehistoric imple-
ments, sculptures, paintings, inscriptions, illuminated manuscripts, coins,
arms, bidri ware, china, textiles and the crowd-drawing 4,000-year-old Egyptian
mummy. Behind the museum, in the Ajanta Pavilion are life-size copies of
Ajanta frescoes while the Nizam's collection of rare artefacts are housed in the
Jubilee Hall. The Public gardens open daily except Monday. ■ *1030-1700.*
Closed Mon and public holidays. Publications section, but nothing on archaeology!
 Birla Archaeological Museum, Malakpet. Collection of finds from excavations of historic sites, housed in Asman Ghad Palace, 9 km away. ■ *Open
daily.* **Birla Planetarium**, Naubat Pahad. Believed to be 'the most modern
planetarium in the country', Rs 5. **Khazana Museum** On the way to Golconda – stone sculptures (see page 382).

★ **Nehru Zoological Park** occupies 13 ha of a low hilly area with remarkable **Parks & zoos**
boulders. This offers a welcome relief from the bustle of the city, and is a good
introduction to Indian avifauna for birdwatchers new to the country – worth a
visit. The animals are kept in natural surroundings. One of the best zoos in India.
Also a lion safari park and a nocturnal house. The Natural History Museum,
Ancient Life Museum and Prehistoric Animals Park are here. ■ *0900-1800,
closed Mon. Cars Rs 10.* Bus 7Z from Public Garden Road. **Nampally Public
Gardens**, north of the Station, near the Stadium, with lotus ponds is rather
crowded and dirty. **Indira Park**, east of Husain Sagar, is very pleasant.

APTTDC City sightseeing: full day, 0745-1730, Rs 90; unsatisfactory as it allows **Tours**
only an hour at the Fort and includes unimportant sights. *Nagarjunasagar*:
daily to Dam, Museum, Ethipothala Falls and Nagarjunakonda.

Essentials

Hyderabad Banjara Hills, Rd 1, 5 km centre: **AL** *Krishna* (Oberoi), T3392323, **Sleeping**
F3393079. 274 rooms, suites with private pools, 3 restaurants ("too sophisticated for *The city suffers*
light snacks, only available through room-service"), large pool and beautiful gardens, *frequent electric power*
immaculately kept, good bookshop. **AL** *Taj Residency*, T3399999, F3392218. 121 refur- *cuts. Larger hotels*
bished rooms, pleasant restaurant overlooking private lake, excellent local cuisine and *have enough power*
barbecues, tennis, boating. **A-B** *Holiday Inn Krishna*, T3393939, F3392684. 152 rooms, *from their own*
reasonable food but slow service and unfriendly, altogether disappointing. **B** *Central* *generators, but a/c*
Court, Ladki-ka-pul, T233262, F232737, north of station. Modern, comfortable rooms, *& lifts in smaller hotels*
good restaurants. Recommended. **B** *Residency*, Public Garden Rd, T3204060, F3204020. *often do not work.*
95 a/c rooms on 4 floors, polite service, popular with Indians, good vegetarian restau- *Street lighting is also*
rant. **B-C** *Golconda*, Masab Tank, T3320202, F3320404. Modern 150 room hotel. *affected: carry a torch*

 Abids area: **D** *Emerald*, Chirag Ali Lane, T202836, F203902. 69 rooms, central a/c,
good vegetarian restaurant. **D** *Jaya International*, Bank St, T232929. 75 rooms, 18 a/c,
reasonable but no restaurant. **D** *Sampurna International*, Mukaramjahi Rd, T40165.
120 rooms, central a/c, restaurants recommended (especially Indian vegetarian), bar.
D *Taj Mahal*, H-1-999 Abids Rd, corner of King Kothi Rd, set back from junction,
T237988. 69 simple, bright, devoid of insects rooms, 20 a/c with baths, busy restaurant (South Indian vegetarian), roof-garden, room service meals, good value. Recommended. **D** *Siddharth*, Bank St, T590222. Has good rooms, quiet location and good
South Indian food. **D-E** *Brindavan*, 4-1-65 Bank St, near the Circle, T203970. Popular
with good restaurants. **D-E** *Saptagiri*, off Station Rd, T2344601. Modern, clean, some
big rooms with balcony, some a/c, quiet. **D** *Nagarjuna*, 3-6-356 Basheerbagh,
T237201, F236789. 60 rooms, central a/c, restaurants (Mughlai, Chinese), pool, on a

Andhra Pradesh

busy main road. **E** *Rock Castle*, Rd 6, Banjara Hills, T229841. 22 rooms, some a/c in cottages with phone, restaurant, bar, large delightful gardens, lovely location tucked away, has character, helpful manager but sometimes closed for filming, ring in advance. **E** *Royal*, Nampally, T201020, F834439. 43 rooms, acceptable, functional room. Near the Rly Station: *Palace*, Mahipatram Rd, and **F** *Apsara*, Station Rd, T502663. Basic, clean friendly service. **F** *Imperial*, corner of Station and Public Gardens Rd (5 minutes from station), T3202220. Large, clean rooms with bath (Rs 150) bucket hot water, large Indian hotel, helpful, excellent service.

Secunderabad (SD Rd is Sarojinidevi Rd) **L-AL** *Grand Kakatiya* (Welcomgroup), Begumpet, 1.5 km from airport, 189 rooms, T310132, F311045. 181 rooms in modern luxury hotel, few **A** rooms, good restaurants. **A-B** *Ramada Manohar*, by Airport Exit Rd, T819917, F819801, manohar@hd1.vsnl.net.in 135 well designed, sound-proofed rooms, smart, modern business hotel, good value (a meal included) and service. **A-B** *Viceroy*, Tank Bund Rd, T7538383, F7538797, viceroy@hd1.vsnl.net.in 150 a/c rooms, most with fine views of lake, pool, business hotel, good travel desk (airport taxi Rs 160), well located, excellent service. Highly recommended. **B** *Green Park* (Quality Inn), Begumpet, Greenlands Arch, 2.5 km airport, T291919, F291900. 148 rooms, typical modern hotel. **C** *Asrani International*, 1-7-179 MG Rd, T842267, F811529. 65 rooms, good restaurants, bar, exchange. **C** *Baseraa*, 9-1, 167/168 SD Rd, T7703200, F7704745. 75 comfortable a/c rooms, restaurants recommended, bar, exchange. **C-D** *Karan*, 1-2-261/1 SD Rd, T840191, F848343. 44 rooms, central a/c, restaurants, coffee shop, exchange, roof-garden, pleasant position. **D-F** AP Tourism *Yatri Nivas*, SP Rd, T816375. 16 rooms, some a/c (Rs 325-450), 6-bed (Rs 500). **E** *Club View*, 30 Wellington Rd, behind Secunderabad Club, T7845965. New, quiet, spotless, rooms (some **D** a/c) simply appointed, light and airy, pleasant management, meals on room service. Highly recommended. **E** *Taj Mahal*, 88 SD Rd, T812105. Adequate, clean rooms, vegetarian restaurant. Rly Station has **F** *Retiring Rooms*. **F** *Youth Hostel*, near Sailing Club. 2 single rooms, 48 beds in dorms.

Eating **Hyderabad Expensive**: top hotels recommended include *Taj Residency*. *Centre Court*, does good buffet lunches. **Mid-range**: *Residency* hotel's *Madhubani* vegetarian. Lunch buffets popular so à la carte may be slow, try North Indian *thali*. *Golden Deer* a/c, MG Rd. Chinese highly recommended. *Liberty's*, Bank St (Abids). Continental and Chinese. For Hyderabadi, try *Diwan* and *Mughal Durbar*, near High Court. **Cheap**: *Lakshmi*, Nampally, across from rly station. Light meals. *Palace Heights* (8th Flr), Triveni Complex, Abids. *Shan Bagh*, Basheerbagh Rd. Good value. Recommended. **Fast food**: *East and West*, opposite Telephone Bhavan, Saifabad and *Manju Café*, 4-1-873 Tilak Rd. In Himayatnagar Rd, Nirula's *Open House* (corner of Basheerbagh), *Pick 'n' Move*, Amrutha Estates. **Vegetarian Mid-range**: *Haridwar*, Station Rd. Indian. **Cheap**: *Kamat* near rly station, 60/1 Saifabad, Secretariat Rd. Simple, good value.

Secunderabad Expensive (in hotels): *Ramada Manohar*. International. Recommended for service, surroundings and food. *Viceroy*. International. Pleasant atmosphere, excellent preparations. **Mid-range**: *Asrani International* hotel does good Mughlai. *Akbar*, 1-7-190 MG Rd. Hyderabadi. *Baseraa* hotel's Indian vegetarian restaurant is simple; *Mehfil* is dearer and has an international menu and serves alcohol. *China Regency*, Airport Rd, Begumpet. Chinese. *Golden Dragon* near *Park Lane Hotel* off MG Rd. Chinese. *Kwality's*, 103 Park Lane. Mixed menu. *Paradisi Gardens*, 38 Sarojini Devi Rd. Al fresco (or a/c inside), tasty Indian or Chinese takeaway. *Varun*, Begumpet, opposite Police Station. **Cheap**: *Kamat* Sarojini Devi Rd. Vegetarian. Simple surroundings, clean, *thalis*.

Bars Larger hotels have bars.

Sound and Light at Golconda Fort; spectacular (see details below). Some cinemas **Entertainment** show English language films. *Ravindra Bharati* (a/c) regularly stages dance, theatre and music programmes, *Lalit Kala Thoranam*, Public Gardens, hosts art exhibitions and free film shows daily. **Swimming**: *BV Gurumoorthy Pool*, Sardar Patel Rd. Some hotel pools are open to non-residents.

Jan: *Makara Sankranti* (13-15) when houses bring out all their collections of dolls. **Festivals** Mar-Apr: *Ugadi*, New Year in Andhra Pradesh – *Chaitra Sudda Padyami*. *Muharram* and *Ramzan* are celebrated distinctively in Hyderabad.

The *bazar* around the Char Minar with colourful stalls is a fascinating glimpse into the **Shopping** past. Down the alleys, silver craftsmen work in their tiny rooms. **Antiques**: *Govind* *Mukandas*, Bank St. *Humayana* at *Taj Residency*. **Books**: *Akshara*, 8-2-273 Pavani Estates, Road No 2, Banjara Hills, T213906. Excellent collection on all aspects of India in English. *Waldens*, Raj Bhavan Rd, Begumpet, opposite *Blue Moon Hotel*, *Haziq and* *Mohi*, Lal Chowk. Interesting antiquarian bookshop, especially for Arabic and Persian. **Handicrafts**: Govt Emporia: *Nirmal Industries*, Raj Bhavan Rd; *Lepakshi*, and *Coircraft*, Mayur Complex, Gun Foundry; *Cooptex* and several others in Abids; *Khadi*, shops in Sultan Bazar and in Municipal Complex, Rashtrapati Rd, Secunderabad. Others may charge a bit more but may have more attractive items: *Kalanjali*, Hill Fort Rd, opposite Public Gardens, has a large selection of regional crafts of high quality on 3 floors; *Bidri Crafts*, Abids. In Secunderabad: *Jewelbox*, SD Rd, *Baba Handicrafts*, MG Rd. **Jewellery**: especially pearls at *Mangatrai Ramkumar*, *Taj Residency* and Pathergatti, *Sri Jangadamba Pearls*, MG Rd, Secunderabad, *Tibrumal*, Basheerbagh and *Totaram Sagarlal*, Abids.

Most open 1000-1900, some close on Fri

Look for pearls, Bidri ware, crochet work, Kalamkari paintings, himroo and silk saris

Mercury, Public Gardens Rd, T234441, SD Rd, Secunderabad, T830670. *Sita*, 3-5-874 **Tour operators** Hyderguda, T233628, F234223, and 1-2-281 Tirumala, SD Rd, Secunderabad, T849155, F849727. *Thomas Cook*, Saifabad, T222689. *TCI*, 680 Somajiguda, Greenlands Rd, T212722.

Local Auto-rickshaw: (Rs 6 for 2 km) and cheaper cycle rickshaws. **Bicycle hire**: **Transport** easily available (ask for "bicycle taxi" shop), Rs 20 per day but may ask for a large deposit; good for visiting Golconda. **Bus**: City buses are very crowded in rush hrs. Nos 119, 142: Nampally to Golconda Fort. **Car hire**: tourist taxis and luxury cars from AP Tourism, Gagan Vihar, Mukaramjahi Rd, T557531, *Ashok Travels*, Lal Bahadur Stadium, T230766, *Travel Express*, Saifabad, T234035. About Rs 550 per 8 hrs or 80 km, Rs 300 per 4 hrs.

Long distance Air: Transport to town: pre-paid taxi Rs 100-200; metered auto-rickshaw, Rs 40 to Banjara Hills, 30 mins. *Indian Airlines*: opposite Ravindra Bharati, Saifabad, T599333, **Bangalore**; **Chennai**: daily; **Mumbai, Visakhapatnam**. *Jet Airways*, 6-3-1109 Nav Bharat Chambers, Raj Bhavan Rd, T3301222; 201 Gupta Estates, Basheerbagh, T231263. **Bangalore, Mumbai**. *Sahara*, T212767: **Mumbai**.

Road Bus: APSRTC, T513955. The vast **Imbli-Ban Bus Station**, T4614406, is for long distance buses including Srisailam and Nagarjunasagar Dam. Private coaches run services to Aurangabad, Bangalore, Mumbai, Chennai and Tirupati. Reservations: *Royal Lodge*, entrance to Hyderabad Rly Station. Secunderabad has the **Jubilee** Bus Station, T7802203. **Nampally**: buses to Golconda.

Train All trains terminate in Secunderabad. South-Central Enquiries: T131. Reservations (Hyderabad/Secunderabad), T135. From **Hyderabad/Secunderabad** To: **Bangalore**: *Kachiguda Bangalore Exp* (from Secunderabad), *7685* (AC/II), 1805, 16½

Andhra Pradesh

hrs. **Guntakal**: (for Hospet and Hampi), *Dharmavaram Exp, 7609/7505*, 1910, 9¼ hrs; *Venkatadri Exp, 7603/7597*, 1550, 9 hrs. **Chennai (MC)**: *Charminar Exp, 7060* (AC/II), 1840, 14¾ hrs; *Hyderabad Chennai Exp, 7054*, 1545, 14½ hrs. **Mumbai (VT)**: *Hyderabad-Mumbai Exp, 7032*, 2020, 17¼ hrs; *Hussainsagar Exp, 7002*, 1430, 15¾ hrs. **Tirupati**: *Rayalaseema Exp, 7429* (AC/II), 1700, 16 hrs; *Venkatadri Exp, 7603/7597*, 1530, 17¾ hrs. **Vijayawada**: *Godavari Exp, 7008* (AC/II), 1715 (1745 from Secunderabad), 6½ hrs; *Krishna Exp, 7406*, 0500 (0530 from Secunderabad), 8 hrs.

Directory **Airline offices** *Air India*, Samrat Complex, Secretariat Rd, T237243. *Air France*, Nasir Arcade, Secretariat Rd, T236947. *British Airways*, Chapel Rd, T234927. *Cathay Pacific*, 89 SD Rd, Secunderabad, T840234. *Egypt Air*, Safina International, Public Garden Rd, T230778. *KLM*, Gemini Travels, Chapel Rd, T236042. *Lufthansa*, 86 Shantinagar, T220352. *Saudia*, Arafath Travels, Basheerbagh, T238175. *Singapore Airlines* and *Swissair*, Regency Bldg, Begumpet. *Thai*, Chapel Rd, T236042. **Domestic** airlines under Transport below. **Banks** 1000-1400, Mon-Fri,1000-1200, Sat. In Hyderabad, several banks on Bank St, Mahipatram Rd and Mukaramjahi Market and in Secunderabad on Rashtrapati Rd. *Thomas Cook*, Nasir Arcade, 6-1-57, Saifabad, T596521. **Communications** In Hyderabad: **GPO** (with Poste Restante) and **CTO**, Abids. **Internet**: *Cyber Café 209*, 5-8-511/1 Ground Flr, opposite Karimabad, Chirag Ali Lane, Abids, T3205312, a/c, modern, helpful, access Rs 80 per hr with coffee (and *Cue 'n Ball* billiards!) spotless toilets, 1000-2000, Sun 1000-1600. In Secunderabad: **Head PO** in RP Rd and **CTO** on MG Rd. **Cultural centres & libraries** *Alliance Française*, near Planetrium, Naubat Pahad, T220296. *British Library*, Secretariat Rd. *Max Müller Bhavan*, Eden Bagh, Ramkote. *Bharatiya Vidya Bhavan*, King Kothi Rd, T237825. **Medical services** Out-patients usually from 0900-1400. Casualty 24 hrs. *General Hospital* in Nampally, T234344. Newcity (Secunderabad) T7805961. **Tourist offices** *AP*, Tourist Complex, near Secretariat, 0930-1730, tourism@stph.net for tours. *APTTDC Yatri Nivas*, SP Rd, Secunderabad, T843931. Information at Rly Stations and Airport. *India*, Sandozi Building, 26 Himayatnagar, T666877. **Useful addresses** AP Dept of Forests, Public Garden Rd, nr Secretariat (opposite Reserve Bank), provides excellent advice, may help with arrangements to visit wildlife reserves – Asst Conservator of Forests, is very helpful. **Foreigners' Regional Registration Office**, Commissioner of Police, Purani Haveli, Hyderabad, T230191.

Short excursions from Hyderabad

★ **Golconda**
11 km
Open 0900-1630

Golconda, one of the most accessible of great medieval fortresses in India, was the capital of the Qutb Shahi kings who ruled over the area from 1507 to 1687. Nizam-ul-Mulk repossessed it in 1724 and restored it to its former glory for a time. Modern day restorations are being carried out by the Archaeological Survey of India.

The fort
Both the fort and the tombs are popular sites & can get crowded & very noisy after 1000; if you arrive early it is worth asking to be allowed in

Originally built of mud in the 12th century by the **Hindu Kakatiyas**, the fort was reinforced by masonry by the Bahmanis who occupied it from 1363. The massive fort, built on a granite hill, was surrounded by three walls. One encircled the town, another the hill on which the citadel stood and the last joined huge boulders on the high ridge with parts of masonry wall. The citadel's 5 km double wall had 87 bastions with cannons and eight huge gates with outer and inner doors and guardrooms between. Some of the guns of the Qutb Shahis are still there with fortifications at various levels on the way up. Another of India's supposed *underground tunnels* is believed by some to run from a corner of the summit, about 8 km to Gosha Mahal.

The old mint on the road to Golconda is now the **Khazana Museum** (Archaeological Department) which exhibits stone sculptures.

The fort had an ingenious system of laminated clay pipes and huge 'Persian Wheels' to carry water to cool the palace chambers up to the height of 61 m where there were hanging gardens. The famous diamond vault once held the *Koh-i-noor* and the *Hope diamonds*. The fort fell to Emperor Aurangzeb after two attempts, an eight month siege and the help of a Qutb Shahi General who turned traitor. The English traveller Walter Hamilton described it as being almost completely deserted in 1820: "the dungeons being used by the Nizam of Hyderabad as a prison for his worst enemies, among whom were several of his sons and two of his wives".

The **Fateh Darwaza** or Victory Gate at the entrance, made of teak, with a Hindu deity engraved, is studded with iron spikes as a defence against war elephants. The superb acoustics enabled a drum beat or bugle call or even a clap under the canopy of this gate, to be heard by someone at the very top of the palace; it is put to the test by the visiting crowds today. A couple of glass cases display a map and some excavated finds.

Beyond the gate the **Mortuary Bath** on the right has beautiful arches and a crypt-like ceiling; you see the remains of the three-storeyed **armoury** and the women's palaces on the left. About half way up is a large water tank or well and to the north is what was once the most densely populated part of the city. Nearby, the domed store house turned into the **Ramdas Jail** has steps inside that lead up to a platform where there are relief sculptures of deities on the wall, dominated by *Hanuman*. The **Ambar khana** (granary) has a Persian inscription on black basalt stating that it was built between 1626-72. The steps turn around an enormous boulder with a bastion and lead to the top passing the Hindu **Mahakali Temple** on the way. The breezy **Durbar Hall** is on the

Golconda fort

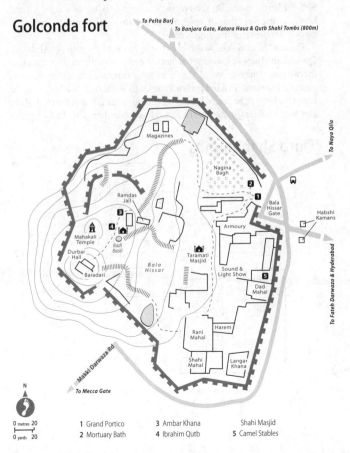

To Pelta Burj
To Banjara Gate, Katora Hauz & Qutb Shahi Tombs (800m)

Magazines

Nagina Bagh

To Naya Qila

Ramdas Jail

Bala Hissar Gate

Armoury

Habshi Kamans

Mahakali Temple

Badi Baoli

Taramati Masjid

Durbar Hall

Bala Hissar

Sound & Light Show

Baradari

Dad Mahal

To Fateh Darwaza & Hyderabad

Makki Darwaza Rd

Rani Mahal

Harem

Shahi Mahal

Langar Khana

To Mecca Gate

N

0 metres 20
0 yards 20

1 Grand Portico
2 Mortuary Bath

3 Ambar Khana
4 Ibrahim Qutb

Shahi Masjid
5 Camel Stables

Andhra Pradesh

summit. It is well worth climbing the stairs to the roof here for good views. The path down is clearly signed to take you on a circular route through the **harem** and **Rani Mahal** with its royal baths, back to the main gate. A welcome chilled drink is available at the 'café' diagonally opposite the gate.

■ *1000-1630, Entry Rs 2. Guides wait at the entrance. Allow 2-3 hrs. Closed on Mon. Excellent Sound & Light show, 1 hr, Nov-Feb 1830; Mar-Oct 1900, English on Wed, Sat and Sun. Tickets at Golconda from 1700, Rs 20 (autorickshaw, about Rs 50, 30 mins); at Yatri Nivas, 1000-1200; a coach trip from there (minimum number needed) departs at 1700 and returns 2015; Rs 45 includes show ticket. Getting there: See Qutb Shahi Tombs.*

★ **Qutb Shahi Tombs**

One road leaves Golconda Fort to the north through the Banjara Gate. 800 m north-northwest of the fort on a low plateau are the **Qutb Shahi Tombs**.

Each tomb of black granite or greenstone with plaster decoration is built on a square or octagonal base with a large onion dome and arches with fine sculptures, inscriptions and remains of glazed decoration. The larger tombs have their own mosque attached which usually comprises an eastward opening hall with a *mihrab* to the west. The sides have inscriptions in beautiful Naksh script, and remnants of the glazed tiles which used to cover them can still be seen in places. The tombs of the rulers were built under their own supervision but fell into disrepair and the gardens ran wild until the end of the 19th century when *Sir Salar Jang* restored them and replanted the gardens. It is now managed and kept in an excellent state of repair by the Archaeological Survey of India. The gardens are being further improved.

The road from Golconda fort goes north, passing **1** the tomb of **Abdullah Qutb Shah** (1626-72) as it approaches the entrance to the tombs, which is at the east gate of the compound. On the left side of the road just outside the compound is **2** the tomb of **Abul Hasan Tana Qutb Shahi** (r 1672-87). He was the last of the kings to be buried here as the final king in the line of the Qutb Shahi Dynasty, Abul Hasan, died in the fort at **Daulatabad** in 1704. To the right of

Qutb Shahi tombs

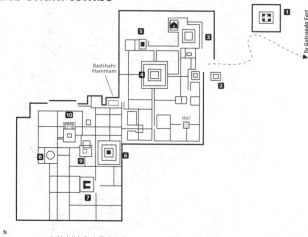

1 Abdullah Qutb Shah
2 Abul Hasan Tana Qutb Shahi
3 Hayat Baksh Begum
4 Muhammad Qutb Shah
5 Pemamati
6 Muhammad Quli Qutb Shah
7 Ibrahim Qutb Shah
8 Kulsum Begum
9 Jamshid Quli Qutb Shah
10 Sultan Quli Qutb Shah

the entrance are **3** the tomb of Princess **Hayat Baksh Begum** (d 1677), the daughter of Ibrahim Qutb Shah, and a smaller mosque, while about 100 m directly ahead is **4** the granite tomb of **Muhammad Qutb Shah** (r 1612-26). Tucked away due north of this tomb is **5** that of **Pemamati**, one of the mistresses of Muhammad Qutb Shah, dating from 1663. The path turns south and west around the tomb of Muhammad Qutb Shah. About 100 m to the south is a tank which is still open. The ramp up and down which the bullocks walked to draw the water is typical of those found in villages across South India where *kavalai* irrigation is practised. The path turns right again from near the corner of the tank and runs west to the oldest structure in the compound, the *Badshahi Hammam*, the 'bath' where the body of the king was washed before burial. You can still see the channels for the water and the special platforms for washing the body. The Badshahi kings were Shi'a Muslims, and the 12 small baths in the Hammam stand symbolically for the two imams revered by the Shi'a community. Next door, a small Archaeological Museum has interesting items in a few glass cases (closed 1300-1400).

To the south of the Hammam is a series of major tombs. The most striking lies due south, **6** the 54 m high mausoleum of **Muhammad Quli Qutb Shah** (ruled 1581-1612), the poet king founder of Baghnagar (Hyderabad). It is appropriate that the man responsible for creating a number of beautiful buildings in Hyderabad should be commemorated by such a remarkable tomb. The underground excavations here have been turned into a Summer House. You can walk right through the tomb and on to **7**, the tomb of the fourth king of the dynasty, **Ibrahim Qutb Shah** (ruled 1550-80), another 100 m to the south. At the west edge of the compound is the octagonal tomb **8** of **Kulsum Begum** (died 1608), granddaughter of Mohammad Quli Qutb Shah. To its east is **9** the tomb of **Jamshid Quli Qutb Shah** (ruled 1543-50), who was responsible for the murder of his 90 year old father and founder of the dynasty, **Sultan Quli Qutb Shah** (ruled 1518-43), **10**. This has the appearance of a two-storey building though it is in fact a single storey structure with no inscription. There are some other small tombs here.

■ *1000-1630 except Fri. Rs 2, camera fee Rs 10, car Rs 10. Allow 2 hrs, or half a day for a leisurely exploration. Inexpensive guidebook available. Getting there: Bus (Nos 119 or 142 from Nampally or 66G from Charminar or 80D from Secunderabad) takes 1 hr to the fort. Nos 123 and 142S go direct from Charminar to the Qutb Shahi Tombs. Autos about Rs 50. Cycling in the early morning is a good option; it is an easy journey.*

Osman Sagar

This was the name given to the 46 sq km reservoir in honour of the last Nizam, constructed at great cost to avoid a repetition of the devastating flooding of the Musi River in 1908. Hyderabad's water supply comes from this lake, also known as **Gandipet**. Very pleasant landscaped gardens and a swimming pool. Guest houses *Sagar Mahal*, T253907, and *Visranti*, dorm (Rs 50); reserved through AP Tourism. It lies 22 km from Hyderabad.

Himayat Sagar

An 85 sq km lake named after the Nizam's eldest son is close to Osman Sagar and can only be reached by a separate road 22 km from Hyderabad. *Dak Bungalow* with a cook available, reservations: Supt Engineer, PWD, Water Works, Gosha Mahal, Hyderabad, T48011.

Vanasthalipuram

The **Deer Park** (Mahavir Harin Vanashtali) is a wildlife sanctuary with spotted deer, black buck, chinkara, wild boar, porcupines and python and over 100 species of birds. ■ *Getting there: 13 km on the Hyderabad-Vijayawada Road.*

Andhra Pradesh

North Central Andhra

All the routes from Hyderabad are off the major tourist track. They are not inaccessible or difficult, though accommodation is often limited and basic, but they are attractive and pleasantly free of traffic.

The route to Nagpur crosses the granite Telangana plateau, with its thin red soils, then across the black Deccan lavas. It passes close to the **Jeedimatla Lake**. This freshwater reservoir was built for irrigation in 1897. Now heavily polluted but waterfowl include grey heron, egret, sandpiper and pariah kite.

Kondapur, 90 km away on the NH7, is the 'town of mounds' with the remains of a great Buddhist complex. Nearly 2,000 coins have been discovered – gold, silver, copper and lead – as well as fine glass beads, coming from as far afield as Rome.

Medak, some 6 km further on, has an extraordinary Gothic style cathedral, complete with stained glass windows and a spire over 60-m high, begun in 1914 and completed 10 years later; it can hold 5,000. Nizam Sagar, a further 30 km northwest, irrigates rice, sugarcane and turmeric.

Kamareddi has important iron ore deposits, in common with several areas immediately to its north.

Nirmal, 56 km along, became famous in the 16th century for its wood painting. Today the painters and craftsmen here are making furniture as well as painting portraits and pageants for which they are more commonly known. Eleven kilometres from Nirmal are the 46-m **Kuntala Falls** on the river Kadam, a tributary of the Godavari, an impressive sight immediately after the monsoon. To the east are the important coal reserves of **Singareni**. Once across the Godavari the focus of economic life is north towards Nagpur.

Adilabad is the last major town before crossing the Penganga into Maharashtra and to **Wardha**, the centre of the Gandhi ashram movement.

★ Warangal

Phone code: 08712
Colour map 2, grid A2
Population: 466,900

The capital of the Kakatiya Empire in the 12th and 13th centuries, Warangal's name is derived from the Orugallu (one stone) Hill, a massive boulder with ancient religious significance which stands where the modern town is situated. Warangal is 156 km northeast of Hyderabad.

History The city, was probably laid out during the reigns of King Ganapatideva (1199-1262) and his daughter Rudrammadevi (until 1294). Warangal was captured by armies from Delhi in 1323, enforcing the payment of tribute. Control of Warangal fluctuated between Hindus and Muslims but between the 14th and 15th centuries it remained in Bahmani hands. Thereafter it repeatedly changed hands, and Michell argues that although the military fortifications were repeatedly strengthened the religious buildings were largely destroyed, including the great Siva temple in the middle of the city. Marco Polo was highly impressed by Warangal's riches, and it is still famous for the remains of its temples, its lakes and wildlife, and for its three circuits of fortifications.

Sights At the centre of the 'fort' is a circular area about 1.2 km in diameter. Most of it is now farmland with houses along the road. Near the centre are the ruins of the original Siva temple. Remains include the beautifully carved stone entrance gateways to the square enclosure, aligned along the cardinal directions and beyond are overturned slabs, smashed columns, brackets and ceiling panels.

Nearby Siva temples are still in use, and to the west is the Khush Mahal, a massive royal hall used by the Muslim Shitab Khan at the beginning of the 16th century for state functions. It may well have been built on the site of earlier palaces, near its geometric centre while some structures in the central area may have been granaries.

From the centre, four routes radiate along the cardinal directions, passing through gateways in the three successive rings of fortification. The innermost ring is made of massive granite blocks, and is up to 6 m high with bastions regularly spaced along the wall. The middle wall is of unfaced packed earth, now eroded, while the outermost circuit, up to 5 m high, is also of earth. The four main roads pass through massive gateways in the inner wall, and there are also incomplete gateways in the second ring of fortifications. Some of the original roads that crossed the city have disappeared.

Michell suggests that the plan of Warangal conforms to early Hindu principles of town planning. **'Swastika towns'**, especially suited to royalty, were achieved following the pattern of concentric circles and swastika of the *yantras* and *mandalas*. They were a miniature representation of the universe, the power of god and king recognized symbolically, and in reality, at the centre.

The Chalukya style '1,000-pillar' Siva *Rudresvar* temple on the slopes of the Hanamakonda (Hanamakonda) Hill, 4 km to the north, has beautiful carvings. It is a low, compact temple, built on several stepped platforms with subsidiary shrines to Vishnu and Surya, rock-cut elephants, a large superbly carved *nandi* in the courtyard and an ancient well where villagers have drawn water for 800 years. There is no sign of the underground passage which is believed to have connected the temple with the fort 11 km away. The Bhadrakali Temple overlooks a shallow lake.

Sleeping Hotels with some a/c rooms on Main Rd, Hanamakonda are 8 km from the rly (bus or auto-rickshaw Rs 30): **D-E** *Ashoka*, T78491. 55 clean rooms, good restaurant, bar, friendly service. **E** *Ratna*, Ponchamma Maidan, T23647. 50 rooms some a/c. **E-F** *Tourist Guest House*, Kazipet Rd opposite Engineering College, 4 km away, T76201. 20 rooms, 6-bed dorm, restaurant. Tourist information. **F** *Vijaya*, 200m from bus and railway. clean rooms with bath, very friendly and helpful, good value. Recommended.

Transport **Train** Many Express trains stop here. **Vijayawada**: *Kerala Exp, 2626* (AC/II), 1204, 3¼ hrs; *GT Exp, 2616* (AC/CC&AC/II), 2032, 3¼ hrs. **Chennai (MC)**: *Tamil Nadu Exp, 2622* (AC/II), 2140, 10¼ hrs; *GT Exp, 2616* (AC/CC&AC/II), 2032, 10½ hrs. **Secunderabad**: *Vijaywada Secunderabad Intercity Exp, 2713*, 0900, 2¼ hrs; *Konark Exp, 1020* (AC/II), 0554, 3¾ hrs; *Golconda Exp, 7201* (AC/CC), 1020, 3½ hrs.

Pakhal, Ethurnagaram & Lakhnavaram Game Sanctuaries The great artificial lakes that are still in use – from the south, Pakhal, Lakhnavaram, Ramappa and Ghanpur – were created as part of the Kakatiya rulers' water management and irrigation schemes in the 12th and 13th centuries. The lakes are fringed with an emerging marsh vegetation and surrounded by extensive grasslands, tropical deciduous forests and some evergreens. The park was set up in 1952, and although it is well established, some of the significant management problems include grazing by domestic livestock and illegal burning.

This is the richest area for wildlife in the state with tiger, panther, hyena, wild dogs, wild boars, gaur, foxes, spotted deer, jackals, muntjacks, sloth bears and pythons. There is also a large variety of waterbirds and fish, otters and alligators in the lakes. Pakhal Lake, 40 km east of Warangal, is particularly important as an undisturbed site well within the sanctuary, while the Laknavaram Lake is 20 km to the north. They are superb for birdwatching (numerous

Andhra Pradesh

migratory birds in winter) and occasional crocodile spottings. Tigers and panthers live deep in the forest but are rarely seen. Forest rangers might show you plaster casts of tiger pug marks.

Kothaguda, about 10 km further, is a Banjara tribal village. It has been subjected to unregulated tree-felling – and also to the activities of political extremists. Permission to visit may be refused.

Sleeping F *Forest Rest House*, APTTDC and F *Sarovihar*. NB Both have been reported as destroyed by political activists. Check with Warangal Tourist Office, T76201.

Transport From Hanamkonda or Warangal Bus Station to Narsampet. Regular bus service from Narsampet to Pakhal Lake or take a taxi.

Palampet

Palampet lies close to the Ramappa Lake. The **Ramappa Temple**, dedicated to Siva as Rudreswara, was built in 1234 and is one of the finest medieval Deccan temples. The black basalt sculpture is excellent (even richer than that at the 1,000-pillar temple) with famous Mandakini figures of female dancers which appear on brackets at the four entrances. The base of the temple has the typical bands of sculpture, the lowest of elephants, the second, a lotus scroll, the third which is the most interesting depicting figures opening a window on the life of the times and finally another floral scroll. There are more fine sculpture inside, some displaying a subtle sense of humour in common with some of the figures outside, and paintings of scenes from the epics on the ceiling. **Sleeping** APTTDC F *Vanavihar Tourist Rest House* nearby, also overlooking the lake, four simple and clean rooms, cook available but bring own provisions. **NB** No bottled water available and mosquito infested, so net essential.

Ghanpur

No hotels or restaurants in the village. Take your own food & drink

Nine kilometres north of Palampet, also has some remarkable 13th-century temples. Now partly ruined, the two main temples and the open *mandapa*, which is surrounded by 18 minor shrines, have some finely sculpted figures and carved brackets. Michell comments that "the basements have sharply cut mouldings; the columns have prominent brackets and are overhung by angled eaves". There are also remains of layered towers "surmounted by hemispherical roofs". The village was within a fort, whose earth wall is still clearly visible.

★ Nagarjunakonda

One of India's richest Buddhist sites, Nagarjunakonda, 150 km southeast of Hyderabad, now lies almost entirely under the lake created by the Nagarjunasagar Dam, completed in 1960. The remains of a highly cultured Buddhist civilization had remained almost undisturbed for 1,600 years until their discovery by AR Saraswati in March 1926. The reconstructed buildings are on a comparatively small scale, in a peaceful setting on top of the hilltop fort, now an island planted with low trees.

History

Phone code: 08680

Rising from the middle of the artificial lake is the Nagarjuna Hill (konda is hill in Telugu) which had been nearly 200 m above the floor of the secluded valley in the northern ranges of the **Nallamalais** ('black hills') which surround the lake on three sides. On the fourth side was the great river **Krishna**, superimposed on the hills as it flows towards the Bay of Bengal.

Early archaeological work showed the remnants of Buddhist monasteries, many limestone sculptures and other remains. The Archaeological Survey carried out a full excavation of the sites for six years before they were covered by the rising waters of the lake. More than 100 distinct sites ranging from the

Andhra Pradesh

prehistoric early stone age period to the late medieval were discovered. Some of the most important remains have been moved and reconstructed on the hilltop fort. These include nine monuments, rebuilt in their original form, and 14 large replicas of the ruins.

The **Ikshvakus** made Nagarjunakonda the centre of extraordinary artistic activity from the third century AD. Inscriptions suggest that their first king, **Chamtamula**, followed the Hindu god of war, **Karttikeya**. However, his sister, **Chamsatri**, supported Buddhism, creating the first Buddhist establishment found at Nagarjunakonda. The support of both Buddhism and Brahmanism side by side throughout the reign of the Ikshvaku rulers encouraged the building of monuments and development of art which reflected both traditions at the same site.

In the mid-fourth century AD the Pallavas pushed north from Tamil Nadu and eclipsed the Ikshvaku Kingdom, reducing Nagarjunakonda to a deserted village. However, during the Chalukya period between the 7th and 12th centuries a Saiva centre was built at Yellaswaram, on the other bank of the Krishna. In the 15th and 16th centuries the hill became a fortress in the contest for supremacy between the Vijayanagar, Bahmani and Gajapati kings. After the fall of the Vijayanagar Empire both the hill and the valley below lost all importance.

Sights

The Ikshvaku's capital was a planned city on the right bank of the Krishna – **Vijayapuri** ('city of victory'). The citadel had rampart walls on three sides with the river on the fourth. The buildings inside including houses, barracks, baths and wells were probably destroyed by a great fire. Most people lived outside the citadel in houses made of rubble bound by mud. An inscription near a goldsmith's house showed that there were guilds of craftsmen – sweet makers, masons, artisans. The nine temples show the earliest developments of Brahmanical temple architecture in South India. The Vishnu temple (AD 278) had two beautifully carved pillars which were recovered from its site. Five temples were dedicated to Siva or Karttikeya. The river bank was dotted with **Brahmanical shrines**. The largest temple complex was nearly 150 sq m, with an apsidal sanctuary, and was clearly a centre of pilgrimage for long after the decline of the Ikshvaku Kingdom.

Nagarjunakonda excavations also revealed some of India's finest early **sculptures** and **memorial pillars**. Over 20 pillars were raised in the memory not just of rulers and nobles but also of artisans and religious leaders. The sculptures represent the final phase of artistic development begun at Amaravati in the second century BC.

The **hill fort** (early 14th century) has remnants of the Vijayanagar culture though the present layout of the fort probably dates from as recently as 1565. The ruins run the entire length of the hill. The main entrance was from the northeast, near where the ferry now lands on the island. In places the walls are still over 6 m high, with regular bastions and six gateways. There are two temples in the east, where the museum now stands.

Further reading: H Sarkar and BN Misra: *Nagarjunakonda*, Archaeological Survey of India, 1987, carries full details.

Museum

Most of the reconstructed buildings are around the museum on the hill fort. Collection of beads, coins, relic caskets and a variety of ornaments, but most importantly sculptures (including a 3 m-high standing Buddha). Also prehistoric and protohistoric remains and several panels and friezes depicting Buddhist scenes. ■ *0900-1600. Closed Fri. The island is 11 km from Vijayapuri. 2 ferries daily from jetty, 0930 and 1330. Other ferries serve APTTDC tours organized locally or from Hyderabad.*

Andhra Pradesh

Toddy tappers

In many villages of South India palm toddy is a common drink. Known locally as karloo this white, fizzy alcoholic drink is made by collecting sap from the palmyra palm. The tapper climbs the tree and cuts the main fronds of the palm, from which the sap is collected in small earthenware pots. This is poured into a *larger pot carried by the toddy tapper on his waist band. If left for a few hours the juice ferments, but it may also be drunk fresh. It is drunk by holding a folded palm leaf to your mouth in both hands while the juice is poured into it as you drink. Nod vigorously when you have had enough!*

Tours AP Tourism's day trip from Hyderabad can be very tiring with 4 hours on a coach each way, but is convenient and cheap. 0630-2130, Rs 190 including lunch. Nagarjunasagar, is a village beside the dam from which boats fery visitors to the temples and museum on the island at 0800, 1200, 1500, the trip taking 1 hour. If you take the first or second boat you have enough time to visit the sights and return on the next boat. You can leave your luggage for a few hours at this pier provided someone is on duty.

Nagarjunasagar

The **Nagarjunasagar Dam** project, completed in 1966, is one of the largest in India. The 124 m high, 1 km long dam is constructed across the Krishna River out of stone masonry. Two of the irrigation tunnels are said to be among the longest in the world.

Sleeping
No Western style, guest houses some mainly for officials

There are no hotels in Najarjunakonda. At Nagarjunasagar: **E** *Soundarya Tourist Annexe* (APTTDC), Hill Colony. 8 decent rooms, a/c or air-cooled. **F** *Project House* (APTTDC), T76240. 25 rooms on ground floor, 18 rooms upstairs cheaper. **F** *River View Rest House* and cottages. Also some on Hill Colony. **F** *Vijaya Vihar Complex*, T76325, 8 a/c rooms, restaurant, reservations: Asst Manager. **F** *Youth Hostel*, 12 rooms, contact Executive Engineer, B & R Hill Colony, T72672, Res 72635.

Directory **Useful services** Banks and **Post Offices** at Hill Colony and Pylon (4 km). State **Tourist Office**, Project House, Hill Colony, T76333 (Office), T2134 (Residence). A guide is available through this office; others from the Hyderabad Tourist Office.

Srisailam Wildlife Sanctuary

Colour map 2, grid B2
Altitude: 200-900 m

The sanctuary, in an area deeply incised by gorges of the Nallamalai hills, has mixed deciduous and bamboo forest as well as semi-desert scrubland in the northeast. There are tiger, leopard, a large colony of Indian pangolins, panther, wild dogs, civet, hyena, jackals, wolves, giant squirrels, crocodiles, lizards, python, vipers, kraits and over 150 species of birds.

Ins & outs At times it is disturbed due to political activists and can be very difficult to get permission to visit. Check latest position with Forest Officer. Temperature range: 42°C to 12°C. Rainfall: 1,500 mm. Best time to visit: Oct-Mar. Worth visiting AP Dept of Forests (see Hyderabad – Useful Addresses). Cars are not permitted in the Tiger Reserve from 2100-0600.

The largest of the State's wildlife sanctuaries is at Srisailam (201 km from Hyderabad) near Nagarjunasagar. The park, named after the reservoir, is

Andhra Pradesh

India's largest tiger reserve covering 3,560 sq km in five neighbouring districts. Project Tiger was started here in 1973. Srisailam also attracts visitors to its **fort** and **temple** (originally, circa second century AD) with one of 12 *jyotirlingas* in the country. It is a small pilgrimage town in the heart of the vast reserve of hilly dry forest. The ancient **Mahakali Temple** on a hill rising from the Nallamalai forest contains a rare *lingam* which draws large crowds of pilgrims daily and especially at *Sivaratri*, see page 405. There is a nature trail signposted 1 km short of Srisailam. Otherwise, you can walk the access road and explore from there. You can arrange for a guide.

F *Saila Vihar* (AP Tourism), 3 *Rest Houses* and **F** *Temple cottages*. Contact Project Tiger HQ, Field Director at Sunnipanta (7 km from Srisailam), for accommodation at *Rest Houses*. Cook will prepare meals. **Sleeping**

Road Buses from Imbli-Ban Bus Station, Hyderabad, about 6 hrs. **Train** Marchelna (13 km). Hire Jeep beforehand. **Transport**

Vijayawada and the Krishna- Godavari Delta

The rice growing delta of the Krishna and Godavari rivers is one of Andhra Pradesh's most prosperous and densely populated regions, and the core region of Andhra culture. The flat coastal plains are fringed with palmyra palms and occasional coconut palms, rice and tobacco. Inland, barely 40% of the land is cultivated. About 120 km to the west of the road south to Chennai run the Vellikonda Ranges, only visible in very clear weather. To the north the ranges of the eastern ghats can often be clearly seen.

Vijayawada

At the head of the Krishna delta, 70 km from the sea, the city is surrounded by bare granite hills. During the hot dry season these radiate heat, and temperatures of over 45°C are not uncommon in April and May. In winter the can be as low as 20°C. The Krishna cuts through a gap less than 1,200-m wide in the bare ridge of gneissic rocks. The Krishna delta canal scheme, one of the earliest major irrigation developments of the British period in South India completed in 1855, now irrigates nearly 1,000,000 ha, banishing famine from the delta and converting it into one of the richest granaries of the country. The dam Prakasam barrage, over 1,000-m long, carries the road and railways. The name of this city, over 2,000 years old, is derived from the goddess Kanakdurga or Vijaya, the presiding deity. There is a temple to her on a hill along the river.

Phone code: 0866
Colour map 2, grid B3
Population: 845,300

There are several sites with caves and temples with inscriptions from the first century AD. The **Mogalarajapuram Temple** has an **Ardhanarisvara** statue which is thought to be the earliest in South India. There are two 1,000-year-old **Jain temples** and the **Hazratbal Mosque** which has a relic of the Prophet Mohammed. The **Qutb Shahi** rulers made Vijayawada an important inland port. It has retained its importance as a commercial town, and has capitalized on its position as the link between the interior and the main north-south route between Chennai and Calcutta. A colossal granite Buddha statue (now in **Sights**

Andhra Pradesh

Guntur) shows that the site was an important Buddhist religious centre even before the seventh century AD, when it was visited by Hiuen Tsang.

Museum **Victoria Jubilee Museum**, Bundar Road. Collection includes sculpture and paintings. ■ *1030-1700 except Fri. Free. Camera Rs 5.*

Excursions **Kondapalli**, 20 km northwest, is a famous toy-making centre. The toys are usually made of light wood and laquered in brilliant colours. Craftsmen can be seen working on carvings of human, animal and religious figures.

A rock temple close to the village of **Sitanagaram** and a five-storeyed Brahman cave temple at **Undavali**, south of Vijaywada, dating from the fifth century, were discovered in 1797. The upper storeys are set back, while the lowest storey has three rows of pillars partly cut out of the rock. They probably date from the same period as the Mamallapuram shore temples. One compartment has a shrine cell with an altar, another has a relief of Vishnu and his wives. There are friezes of geese, elephants and lions. The third storey has a hall over 15 m by 10 m, with a figure of **Vishnu** seated on the snake Ananta. Another shows **Narayana** on the snake Sesha. The top storey has barrel vaulted roofs. To reach the temple, cross the barrage going south out of Vijayawada, then turn right up the course of the river for nearly 3 km beyond and west of Sitanagaram.

Amaravati is 30 km west of Vijaywada was the capital of the medieval Reddi kings of Andhra. Some 1,500 years before they wielded power Amaravati was a great Mahayana Buddhist centre (see page 542). Initially the shrine was dedicated to the Hinayana sect but under Nagarjuna was changed into a Mahayana sanctuary where the Buddha was revered as Amareswara. Its origins go back to the 3rd-2nd centuries BC, though it was enlarged between the 1st-4th centuries AD. Very little remains. Excavations were begun by Colonel Colin Mackenzie in 1797. Subsequently most of the magnificent sculpted friezes, medallions and railings were removed, the majority to the museums at Chennai (see Amaravati Gallery, which has finds from excavations from 1797-1905) and Kolkata. The remainder went to the British Museum, London.

The **Archaeological Museum** on site contains panels, mainly broken, railings and sculptures of the Bodhi Tree (some exquisitely carved), *chakras* and caskets containing relics. There are also pottery, coins, bangles and terracotta. Apart from items excavated since 1905, some exhibits relate to other sites in the Krishna and Visakhapatnam districts. **Sleeping F** *PWD Guest House.* ■ *0900-1700 except Fri, free. Getting there: buses via Guntur of by ferry from Krishneveni Hotel.*

Sleeping **D** *Krishna Residency*, Rajagopalachari Rd, T573197. 39 rooms, some a/c, **C** suites, res-
Bundar Rd is MG Rd taurants. **D** *Ilapuram*, Besant Rd, T571282. 81 large clean rooms, some a/c, **C** suites, restaurants, travel. **D** *Kandhari International*, Bundar Rd, Labbipet, T471311. 73 rooms, some a/c, a/c restaurants. **D** *Raj Towers*, Congress Office Rd, T571311. 50 rooms, some a/c, **C** suites, restaurants, bar, travel. **D** *Swarna Palace*, Eluru Rd, T577222, F572227. 50 rooms, most a/c, restaurants, bar. **D-E** *Mamata*, Eluru Rd (1 km centre), T571251. 59 rooms, most a/c with bath, good a/c restaurants (1 rooftop), bar. **D** *Manorama*, 27-38-61 Bundar Rd (5 minutes from Bus Stand), T571301. 69 rooms, some a/c, a/c restaurants, exchange. **E** *Chaya*, 27-38-1 Governorpet, T578330. 39 rooms, 12 a/c, restaurant (South Indian vegetarian). **E** *Krishnaveni* (AP Tourism), Gopal Reddy Rd (opposite Old Bus Stand), T426382. Clean rooms, restaurant, Tourist office, car hire. **E** *Santhi*, Elluru Rd, T577355. Clean rooms with bath (hot water), good vegetarian restaurant. There are some **F** hotels near the Bus Stand on Bundar Rd and

near the Rly Station. **F** *Sarovar*, Rajagopalachari Rd. Adequate rooms, a/c restaurant. **F** *Railway Retiring Rooms*, the reasonable restaurant opens at 0600.

Kandhari, *Krishna* and *Mamata* hotels are recommended. Garden restaurants are **Eating** very pleasant, especially *Greenlands*, Bhavani Gardens, Labbipet, with 7 huts in lawns.

Watersports and boating: KL Rao Vihara Kendram, Bhavani Island on Prakasham **Entertainment** Barrage Lake offers rowing, canoeing, water scooters, pedal boats. 0930-1830.

Local Kondapalli toys and Machilipatnam Kalamkari paintings are popular. The empo- **Shopping** ria are in MG Rd, Governorpet and Eluru Rd. *Apco*, Besant Rd, *Handicrafts Shop*, *Krishnaveni Motel*, *Lepakshi*, Gandhi Nagar are recommended. **Books**: *Ashok*, oppo- site Maris Stella College, T476966, good collection on India, also English fiction.

Local Auto and **cycle rickshaws**, and **tongas** are available. **Buses**: good network of **Transport** city but overcrowded. **Car hire**: from AP Tourism. **Ferry**: to Bhavani Islands, 0930-1730. **Taxi**: Very few metered yellow-top taxis. **Long distance Road Bus**: SRTC buses to neighbouring states including Chennai (9 hrs). New Bus Stand, Bundar Rd, near Krishna River, has a restaurant and dorm beds. Enquiries T473333. Reserva- tions 24 hrs. **Sea**: Ferry services between *Krishnaveni Hotel* and Amaravati. Daily 0800. Rs 50 return. Book at hotel or at RTC Bus Station. **Train**: Vijayawada is an important junction. Reservations, 0800-1300, 1300-2000; tokens issued 30 mins earlier. **Chennai (MC)**: *Tamil Nadu Exp*, *2622* (AC/CC&AC/II), 0100, 6¾ hrs; *Coromandel Exp*, *2841* (AC/II), 1045, 6¾ hrs. **Delhi (ND)**: *Tamil Nadu Exp*, *2621* (AC/CC&AC/II), 0350, 27 hrs; *Kerala Exp*, *2625* (AC/II), 1035, 28¾ hrs. **Secunderabad**: *Konarak Exp*, *1020* (AC/II), 0240, 6½ hrs. **Hyderabad**: *Godavari Exp*, *7007*, 2305, 7¼ hrs; *Krishna Exp*, *7405*, 8¼ hrs.

Banks *State Bank of India* and others on Babu Rajendra Prasad Rd. **Communications** Head **Directory** Post Office: Kaleswara Rao Rd. **Tourist offices** *AP*, *Hotel Krishnaveni*, T426382, 0600-2000. AP Tourism counter at RTC Bus Stand, Machilipatnam Rd. *Regional Tourist Information*, 3rd Flr, AMC Complex, Governorpet, T477386. **Useful addresses** Foreigners' Regional Registration Office, Superintendent of Police, Bundar Rd.

From Vijayawada the NH5 southwest crosses the barrage (giving magnificent **Guntur** views over the Krishna at sunset) to Guntur, a major commercial town. It lies *Phone code: 0863* at the junction of the ancient charnockite rocks of the Peninsula and the allu- *Colour map 2, grid B3* vium of the coastal plain. It is also a junction for the rail line crossing central AP *Population: 471,000* to Guntakal. In the 18th century it was important as the capital of the region known as the Northern Circars, and was under Muslim rule from 1766 under the Nizam of Hyderabad.

Sleeping D *Vijayakrinshna International*, Collectorate Rd, Nagarampalem, T222221, F223541. 42 rooms, some a/c, restaurant. **D-E** *Sudarsan*, Kothapet, Main Rd, T222681. 28 rooms, some a/c, Indian vegetarian restaurant. **F** *Railway Retiring Rooms*.

Transport Chennai via Vijayawada: *Golconda Exp*, *7201* (AC/CC), 0530, 1 hr, change at Vijayawada (4¼ hrs wait), then *Coromandel Exp*, *2841*, 6¾ hrs (total 12 hrs). **Hospet**: (change at Giddalaur and Guntakal), *7225/7825/7309*, 1810, 14¼ hrs. **Secunderabad**: *Guntur Secunderabad Intercity Exp*, *7005*, 1225, 5 hrs; *Golconda Exp*, *7201* (AC/CC), 0530, 8¼ hrs.

Southwards along the NH5, Nellore is another administrative and commercial **Nellore** town. There are some good South Indian restaurants on the roadside, with *Phone code: 0861* excellent coffee, dosai, idli and puris available near the bus stand. *Colour map 2, grid C3*

Andhra Pradesh

Sleeping D *Shivam International*, 18/1 Achari St, 1 km from rly, T27181, F24471. 40 rooms, some a/c, restaurant. **D-E** *Simhapuri*, Rly Station Rd, T27041. 64 rooms, some a/c, restaurant.

Transport Train Chennai **(MC)**: *Vijaywada Chennai Pinakini Exp, 2711*, 0947, 3¼ hrs; *Navjivan Exp, 6045* (AC/II), daily except Thu, 1402, 3¼ hrs. **Secunderabad**: *Charminar Exp, 7059* (AC/II), 2125, 10¼ hrs. **Vijayawada**: *Navjivan Exp, 2642* (AC/II), daily except Fri, 1239, 4 hrs; *Chennai Vijayawada Pinakini Exp, 2712*, 1704, 4 hrs.

Eluru
Phone code: 08812
Colour map 2, grid B4

From Vijaywada, 63 km northeast along the NH5, Eluru is a trading and administrative centre with little by way of industry apart from carpet making. The nearby **Kolleru Lake** has been a site visited by migrating waterbirds for many years. It was made a sanctuary in 1976.

The natural freshwater lake with an average maximum depth of only 3 m was formed in the geologically recent past in silts deposited by the Krishna and Godavari rivers. It shrinks dramatically in the dry season. Supporting a wide variety of aquatic plants, the State Government has accepted that protective conservationist measures need to be taken if the lake is to survive. Once the largest breeding site for the grey or spotted pelican in the world the breeding colonies disappeared completely by 1974, many pelicans dying from fertilizer poisoning. The lake remains an important wintering area for ducks.

Rajahmundry

Phone code: 0883
Colour map 2, grid B4
Population: 403,700
67 km NE of Eluru

The capital of the Eastern Chalukyas, Rajahmundry was captured by the Muslims from the Vengi kings in 1471, then returned to the Orissan Kingdom in 1512. The Deccan Muslims retook it in 1571 and it was repeatedly the scene of bitter hostilities until being granted to the French in 1753. It is remembered for the poet Nannayya who wrote the first Telugu classic *Andhra Mahabharathamu*. Every 12 years the Pushkaram celebration is held by the river bank. The **Markandaya** and **Kotilingeswara Temples** on the river bank draw pilgrims. Rajahmundry is noted for its carpets and sandalwood products and as a convenient base from which to visit the coastal districts. There are simply economy hotels in the town.

Excursions

Rajahmundry is one of two places where you can divert towards the hills of the Eastern Ghats. The Godavari, 80 km northwest of the town, cuts through a gorge and there is a succession of stunningly beautiful lakes, reminiscent of Scottish lochs rather than India, where you can take boat trips.

Samalkot, east of Rajahmundry, has the small 10th-century Chalukyan Temple which is unusual, being arranged on two levels. A two-storey tower with a dome roof rises above the roof. There is no sculpture on the walls but some of the columns have figures.

Kadiam (one hour drive) has flourished since the earlier 1980s when a social forestry programme helped to set up plant nurseries. Today there are 250 nurseries covering 325 ha employing 600 people. Plants grown for sale, mainly in Delhi and Jaipur, include crotons, hybrid roses, royal and table palms and Ashoka trees. About one million plants are sold monthly and there are spin-offs into pottery.

Museums

Sri Rallabandi Subbarao Government Museum Collection of coins, sculpture, pottery, palm leaf manuscripts and inscriptions. ■ *Godavari Bund Road. 1030-1700. Closed Fri and AP Government holidays. Free. Photography with permission.* **Sri RSR Government Museum**, Ullithota Street. Collection of

Andhra Pradesh

Archaeological material and sculpture. ■ *1030-1700. Closed Fri and Bank holidays. Camera fee Rs 3.*

Train Vijayawada: *Coromandel Exp 2841* (AC/II), 0745, 2¾ hrs; *Chennai Mail, 6003,* 1700, 3 hrs; *Bokaro Alleppey Exp, 8689,* 1515, 4 hrs. **Visakhapatnam**: *Coromandel Exp 2842* (AC/II), 1750, 3¼ hrs; *Chennai Howrah Mail, 6004* (AC/II), 0935, 4 hrs; *East Coast Exp 8046,* 1630, 4 hrs.

Transport

Northeastern Andhra Pradesh

From Vijayawada the NH5 crosses the lush and fertile delta of the Krishna and Godavari to Rajahmundry and then the narrowing coastal plain with the beautiful hills of the Eastern Ghats rising sharply inland. The whole pattern of life contrasts sharply with that to the south. Higher rainfall and a longer wet season, alongside the greater fertility of the alluvial soils, contribute to an air of prosperity. Village house styles are quite different, with thatched roofed cottages and white painted walls, distinctive house types and equally distinctive bullock carts. Rice and sugarcane dominate.

Although the building of dams on both the Krishna and the Godavari has eliminated the catastrophic flooding common until the mid-19th century, it is still prone to cyclones. In 1864 a cyclone claimed over 34,000 lives. The totally flat delta, lying virtually at sea level, was completely engulfed by a tidal wave in 1883 when the volcano of Mount Krakatoa blew up 5,000 km away. Further catastrophic cyclones in 1977 and 1996 caused massive damage and loss of life. You may notice the increasing number of small concrete buildings on raised platforms along the roadside designed to provide temporary shelter to villagers during cyclones.

Check weather forecasts before travelling

The area was brought under Muslim rule by the Golconda kings of the Bahmani Dynasty in 1575 and ceded to the French in 1753. In 1765 the Mughal Emperor granted the whole area to the East India Company, its first major territorial acquisition in India. The region is also the most urbanized part of AP, with a dozen towns with more than 100,000 people. Most are commercial and administrative centres with neither the functions nor the appearance of industrial cities, but they serve as important regional centres for trade, especially in agricultural commodities, and they are the homes of some of the wealthiest and most powerful families in Andhra.

Visakhapatnam

Set in a bay with rocky promontories, Visakhapatnam (Vizag) commands a spectacular position between the Eastern Ghats and the sea. It has become one of India's most rapidly growing cities. Already India's fourth largest port it has developed ship building, oil refining, fertilizer, petro-chemical, sugar refinery and jute industries as well as one of India's newest and largest steel mills. On the Dolphin's Nose, a cliff rising 174 m from the sea, is a lighthouse whose beam can be seen 64 km out to sea.

Phone code: 0891
Colour map 2, grid A5
Population: 1.05 mn

Andhra Pradesh

Its twin town of **Waltair** to the north used to be thought of as a health resort with fine beaches, though increasing atmospheric pollution is a problem. Ramakrishna Beach, along the 8 km Lawson's Bay and below the 300 m Mount Kailasa, 6 km away, is best. Don't swim at the harbour end of the beach.

Sights The **Andhra University** founded in 1926 is in the Uplands area of Waltair. The red stone buildings are built like a fortress and are well laid out on a large campus. The country's major **Ship Building Yard** at Gandhigram makes all types of ocean going vessels – passenger liners, cargo vessels as well as naval ships. The **zoo** to the northeast is large and attempts to avoid cages, keeping its animals in enclosures which are close to their natural habitat.

Each of the three hills here is sacred to a different religion. The Hindu Venkateswara Temple on the Venkateswa Konda was built in 1866 by the European Captain Blackmoor. The Muslims have a mausoleum of the saint Baba Ishaq Madina on the Darga Konda, while the highest Ross Hill has a Roman Catholic Church. A Buddhist relic was discovered at **Dhanipura** nearby.

Simhachalam, 16 km northwest, is noted for its 13th century Varaha Narasimha Temple, set in the Kailasa Hills, which are also noted for their hot springs.

The **Borra Caves** in the nearby limestone hills have stalactites and stalagmites. ■ *0800-1200, 1400-1700.* Here the village stream disappears into the

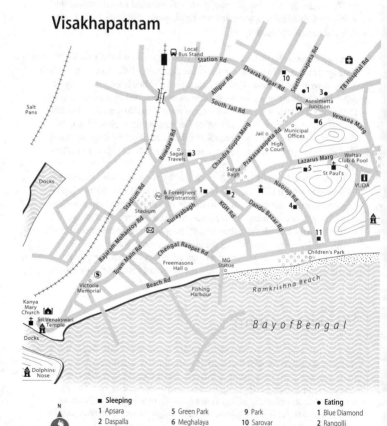

Visakhapatnam

N
Not to scale

● **Sleeping**
1 Apsara
2 Daspalla
3 Dolphin
4 Grand Bay Ravi
5 Green Park
6 Meghalaya
7 Ocean View Inn
8 Palm Beach
9 Park
10 Sarovar
11 Taj Residency

● **Eating**
1 Blue Diamond
2 Rangolli
3 Sarigama

hillside and reappears in the gorge, 90 m below. There is little of tourist interest, but the old part of town between the State Bank and fishing port is interesting with good views of the town and port from Kanya Mary Church, approached by steep steps or gentler concrete road. Trains from Visag.

AP Tourism, RTC Complex. Full day *local sightseeing*, 0830, Rs 75, Araku Valley, 0700, Rs 80. **Tours**

Essentials

AL-A *Taj Residency*, Beach Rd (2 km from centre), T577756, F564370. 95 narrow sea-facing rooms, spacious, light restaurant (pricey but generous), best in town, located at centre of bay, unremarkable public beach across road. **A** *Grand Bay Ravi* (Welcomgroup), 15-1-44 Naoroji Rd, Maharanipeta, T566550, F552804. 104 rooms, fairly new. **B** *Park*, Beach Rd, T554488, F554181. 64 renovated rooms, expensive suites, bookshop, clean pool, well kept gardens, facilities average, slick management, best for direct beach access (beware of rocks when swimming), popular with German and Czech expatriates. **B-C** *Dolphin*, Daba Gardens, T567027, F567555. 147 rooms, popular restaurants, rooftop has good views, live band, highly recommended (reserve ahead), exchange, pool, family run with excellent service, drawback is distance from beach. **C** *Green Park*, Waltair Main Rd, T56444, F563763. Modern business hotel, rooms vary (Rs 750+).

Sleeping
Late night arrivals are quoted high prices by auto-rickshaws to go to the beach. Stay overnight at a simple hotel (walk right from rly station) & move next morning

D *Apsara*, 12-1-17 Waltair Main Rd, T564861. 130 rooms, central a/c, restaurants, bar, exchange, very helpful and friendly staff. **D** *Daspalla*, Surya Bagh, T564825, F562043. 102 rooms (Rs 400+), **C** suites, central a/c, 2 good restaurants (continental and *thalis*), bar, exchange, set back from road, recommended by some, but no late-night check-in. **D-E** *Meghalaya*, Asilametta Junction (5 minute walk from bus, short rickshaw ride from station), T555141, F555824. 65 rooms (Rs 300), some a/c (Rs 400+), dull vegetarian restaurant (non-vegetarian on room service), spacious lobby with murals, pleasant roof garden, friendly and helpful, popular with Indian tourists, good value. Recommended. **D-E** *Ocean View Inn*, Kirlampudi (north end of the beach), T554828, F563234. 48 rooms, some a/c rooms, a/c restaurant, clean and comfortable, location spoilt by high-rise flats, quiet end of town. **D-E** *Palm Beach*, Beach Rd (next to Park), Waltair, T554026. 34 rooms, 30 a/c, restaurant, beer garden, pool, pleasant with shady palm grove but run-down building, recommended for inexpensive beach break.

Andhra Pradesh

Most budget hotels are near the bus station; there are none near the rly

E *Lakshmi*, next to St Joseph's Hospital, Maryland. 10 rooms a/c, some with bath, clean and welcoming, good Indian restaurant. **E** *Saga Lodge*, off Hospital Rd towards beach. Rooms with balcony, some with bath and sea view, no restaurant but very good room service. Recommended. **E** *Viraat*, Indira Gandhi Stadium Rd, Old Bus Stand, T564821. 42 rooms with bath, some a/c, a/c restaurant and bar, exchange. **E** *Railway Retiring Rooms* decent rooms, men's dorm. **F** *Rest House* at Bus Station, good rooms.

Eating Most serve alcohol. Outside hotels there are restaurants on Station Rd. In **Surya Bagh**: *Black Dog* (near Jagdamba Theatre). In Dabagardens: *Delight*, 7-1-43 Kirlampudi, Beach Rd. *Blue Diamond* opposite RTC.

Entertainment **Swimming**: Hotels *Park* and *Palm Beach* are open to non-residents. *Waltair Club* has a pool.

Shopping The main areas are Jagadamba Junction and Waltair Uplands, Main Rd. **Books**: *Ashok*, 13-1-1c St Anthony's Church, Jagadamba Junction, T565995. Good collection on India, also English fiction.

Tour operators *Taj Travels*, *Meghalaya Hotel*, T555141 ext 222, F555824.

Transport **Local Rickshaw**: auto-rickshaws common (offer Rs 2 over meter-charge to make them use a meter); night fares exorbitant. Only cycle rickshaws in the centre. **Ferry**: operates from 0800-1700 between the Harbour and Yarada Hills. You can take one to visit the Dolphin Lighthouse. **Taxi**: at the airport, rly station or from hotels: 5 hrs per 50 km, Rs 300; 10 hrs per 100 km, Rs 550 (higher for a/c).

Long distance **Air**: Airport is 16 km from city centre; Taxi (Rs 120) or auto-rickshaw. Indian Airlines, T565018, Airport, T558221 and *Air India* agent, *Sagar Travel*, 1000-1300, 1345-1700. Daily except Sun to **Hyderabad**; some to **Chennai Mumbai**.

Road **Bus**: Aseelmetta Junction Bus Station is well organized. APSRTC run services to main towns in the state. Enquiries, T565038, reservations 0600-2000. Araku Valley, Guntur (0930, 1545, 2045), Hyderabad (638 km, 1630), Kakinda, Puri (0700), Rajahmundry, Srikakulam, Vijayawada (1945, 2015), Vizianagram (57 km, 0610-2130).

Sea Occasional service to Port Blair in the Andaman Islands, sometimes at short notice. Enquiries: M/s A.V. Banojirow & Co, PO Box 17, opposite Port Main Gate.

Train: Enquiries, T569421. Reservations T546234. 0900-1700. Advance Reservations, left of building (facing it). Computer reservations close 2100, Sun 1400. Counter system avoids crush at ticket window. City Rly Extension Counter at Turner's Chowltry for Reservations. Taxi from centre, Rs 50. **Hyderabad**: *Godavari Exp*, *7007*, 1600, 14¼ hrs; *Konark Exp*, *1020*, 2005, 13½ hrs; *East Coast Exp*, *8045*, 0535, 13½ hrs; *Faluknama Exp 7003*, Tue, Fri, Sun, 2330, 11½ hrs.

Directory **Banks** Several on Surya Bagh. *State Bank of India* is at Old Post Office. **Communications** Head Post Office: Vellum Peta; also at Waltair Rly Station. **Medical services** *Seven Hills*, Rockdale Layout; *King George*, Hospital Rd, Maharani Peta, T564891. *St Joseph's*, Maryland, T562974. **Tourist offices** *AP Tourism*, 1st Flr, Vuda Complex, Siripuram Junction, T554716, 1000-1700, closed Sun and 2nd Sat. Also at Rly Station. Transport Unit, 8 RTC Complex, Dwarka Nagar, T54646. **Useful addresses** Foreigners' Regional Registration Office, SP Police, T562709.

Andhra Pradesh

Tirupati, Tirumalai and the Tamil Borders

★ Tirupati and Tirumalai

The Tirumalai Hills provide a picture-book setting for the famous temple. The main town of Tirupati lies at the bottom of the hill where there are several temples, some centres of pilgrimage in their own right. The seven hills are compared to the seven-headed Serpent God Adisesha who protects the sleeping Vishnu under his hood. The main destination of the 10,000 daily pilgrims is the Sri Venkatesvara Temple in Tirumalai, 18 km away at the top of the ghat road. Tirumalai is remarkably clean and free of beggars.

Phone code:
08574 (Tirupati)
08577 (Tirumalai)
Colour map 2, grid C2
Population: 189,000

Getting there There are flights from Chennai and Hyderabad which arrive at the airport 15 km from Tirupati. The railway station in the town centre has several fast trains from Chennai and other southern towns while the main (central) bus stand is 500 m east of it with express buses from the region. To save time and hassle, buy a through 'Link' ticket to Tirumalai. **Getting around** Buses for Tirumalai leave from stands near the station, but there are also share taxis available. Some choose to join pilgrims for a 4-5 hr walk uphill, starting before dawn to avoid the heat though the path is covered most of the way. Luggage is transported free from the toll gate at the start of the 15 km path and maybe collected from the reception office at in Tirumalai. **Climate** Summer, maximum 40°C, minimum 22°C; Winter, maximum 32°C, minimum 15°C. Annual rainfall: 710 mm, mainly Oct-Dec.

Ins & outs

★ Sri Venkatesvara Temple in **Tirumalai** is believed to have been dedicated by the Vaishnava saint Ramanuja and is known as Balaji in the North and Srinivasa Perumalai in the South. The town of Tirupati, at the base of the hill, was established in approximately AD 1131 under the orders of Ramanuja that the temple functionaries who served in the sacred shrines must live nearby. Although a road runs all the way up the hill to a bus stand at the top, most pilgrims choose to walk up the wooded slope through mango groves and sandalwood forest chanting "Om namo Venkatesaya" or "Govinda, Govinda". Order is maintained by providing 'Q sheds' under which pilgrims assemble. There are two types of queues for *darshan* or special viewing: '*Sarvadarsan*' is open to all, while those who pay for '*Special darshan*' enter by a separate entrance and join a short queue. The actual *darshan* (from 0600-1100) itself lasts a precious second and a half even though the 'day' at the temple may last 21 hours. *Suprabhatam* 0300-0330 (awakening the deity) costs Rs 100; *Tomala Seva* 0330-0415 (flower-offering), Rs 200. Mornings are particularly busy. Mondays and Tuesdays are less crowded.

Sights
Of all India's temples, this draws the largest number of pilgrims

Every day is festival day with shops remaining open 24 hours. Sri Venkatesvara's image is widely seen across South India, in private homes, cars and taxis and in public places, and is instantly recognizable from its black face and covered eyes, shielded so that the deity's piercing gaze may not blind any who look directly at him. In the temple the deity's body is anointed with camphor, saffron and musk. The holy *prasadam* or consecrated sweet is distributed to well over 50,000 pilgrims on festival days.

Sri Venkatesvara is a form of Vishnu. Theoretically the inner shrines of the Tirumalai temple are open only to Hindus. However, foreigners are usually welcome. They are sometimes invited to sign a form to show they sympathize with Hindu beliefs. According to the Tourist Information leaflet "All are welcome. The temple welcomes all devotees regardless of formal religions. The only criterion for admission is faith in God and respect for the temple's conventions and rituals".

The Venkatesvara Temple dates from the 10th century, with later additions. The atmosphere is unlike any other temple in India. Turnstiles control the flow of pilgrims into the main temple complex, which is through an intricately carved *gopuram* on the east wall. Much of the *gopuram* is rebuilt. There are three enclosures. The first, where there are portrait sculptures of the Vijayanagar patrons, include Krishnadeva Raya and his queen and a gold covered pillar. The outer colonnades are in the Vijayanagar style; the gateway leading to the inner enclosure may be of Chola origin. The second enclosure has more shrines, a sacred well and the kitchen. The inner enclosure is opened only once every year. The main temple and shrine is on the west side of the inner enclosure.

The sanctuary (9th-10th centuries), known as 'Ananda Nilayam', has a domed *vimana* entirely covered with gold plate, and gold covered gates. The image in the shrine is a standing Vishnu, richly ornamented with gold and jewels. The 2 m high image stands on a lotus, two of his four arms carry a conch shell and a *chakra* or discus and he wears a diamond crown which is said to be the most precious single ornament in the world. It is flanked by *Sridevi* and *Bhudevi*, Vishnu's consorts. There is a small **museum** with a collection of stone, metal and wooden images (see below).

In **Tirupati** itself the **Govindarajasvami Temple** (16th-17th centuries), is the most widely visited. Built by the Nayakas, the successors to the Vijayanagar Empire, the temple has an impressive outer *gopuram*. Of the three *gopurams* the innermost is also the earliest, dating from the 14th-15th centuries. The main sanctuaries are dedicated to Vishnu and Krishna. The other temple is **Kapilesvarasvami** in a very attractive setting which has a sacred waterfall, Kapila Theertham.

Sri Venkatesvara temple

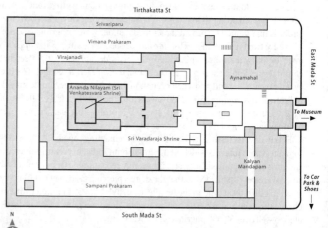

Andhra Pradesh

Tirupati haircuts

Architecturally Sri Venkatesvara Temple is unremarkable, but in other respects is extraordinary. It is probably the wealthiest in India, and the devasthanam (or temple trust) now sponsor a huge range of activities, from the Sri Venkatesvara University at Tirupati to hospitals, orphanages and schools. Its wealth comes largely from its pilgrims, on average over 10,000 a day but at major festivals many times that number. All pilgrims make gifts, and the hundi (offering) box in front of the shrine is stuffed full with notes, gold ornaments and other offerings.

*Another important source of income is the **haircutting service**. Many pilgrims come to Tirupati to seek a special favour – to seek a suitable wife or husband, to have a child, to recover from illness – and it is regarded as auspicious to grow the hair long and then to offer the hair as a sacrifice. You may see many pilgrims fully shaven at the temple when appearing before the deity. Lines of barbers wait for arriving pilgrims. Once, when coaches unloaded their pilgrims, one barber would line up customers and shave one strip of hair off as many heads as possible in order to maximize the number of customers committed to him before he returned and finished off the job! Now, a free numbered ticket and a razor blade can be collected from the public bath hall which pilgrims take to the barber with the same number to claim a free haircut. The hair is collected, washed and softened before being exported to the American and Japanese markets for wig making.*

One kilometre away are strange rock formations in a natural arch, resembling a hood of a serpent, a conch and a discus, thought to have been the source of the idol in the temple. There is a sacred waterfall **Akasa Ganga** 3 km south of the temple. The **Papa Vinasanam Dam** is 5 km north.

Chandragiri (11 km southwest) became the capital of the Vijayanagaras in 1600, after their defeat at the battle of Talikota 35 years earlier. The Palace of Sri Ranga Raya, built in 1639 witnessed the signing by Sri Ranga Raya of the original land grant to the East India Company of Fort St George, but seven years later the fort was captured by Qutb Shahi from Golconda. **The fort** was built on a 180 m high rock where earlier fortifications may date from several hundred years before the Vijayanagar kings took over. You can still see the well preserved fortifications and some palaces and temples. Visit the Rani Mahal and Raja Mahal with its pretty lily pond. Museum, in Raja Mahal, contains Chola and Vijayanagar bronzes.

Tiruchanur, 5 km southeast, has the temple to **Alamelu Manga** (Padmavati Devi), the consort of Venkatesvara, with a Kalyana Mandapa and a temple garden.

Sri Kalahasti or Kalahasti, 36 km northeast of Tirupati, is very attractively sited on the banks of the Svarnamukhi River at the foot of the extreme southern end of the Vellikonda Ranges, known locally as the Kailasa Hills. The town and temple, built in the 16th and 17th centuries, developed largely as a result of the patronage of the Vijayanagar kings. The **Kalahastisvara Temple** dominates the town with its *gopuram* facing the river. It is built in the Dravida style like the famous temple of Tirumalai. The magnificent detached *gopuram* was built by the Vijayanagar Emperor Krishnadeva Raya. Set within high walls with a single entrance to the south, the temple is particularly revered for the white stone Siva lingam in the western shrine, believed to be worshipped by *sri* (spider), *kala* (king cobra) and *hasti* (elephant). The Nayaka style is typified by the columns carved into the shape of rearing animals and the riders. The temple to the Wind God *Vayudeva* is the only one of its kind in India. The bathing

Excursions

Andhra Pradesh

ghats of the Swarnamukhi (golden) River and the temple attract a steady flow of pilgrims.

In addition to its function as a pilgrim centre, the town is known for its *kalamkaris*, the brightly coloured **hand painted textiles** used as temple decoration. There are fine examples in the Salar Jung Museum in Hyderabad, see page 378.

Museums At Tirupati, the TTD **Sri Venkatesvara Museum** of temple art at the Sri Govindarajasvamy Temple compound. ■ *0800-2000. Re 1.*

At Tirumaai, there is an interesting collection of Indian musical instruments at the entrance to the temple. ■ *0800-2000. Re 1.* Sri Venkatesvara University Oriental Research Institute. Collection includes images of stone, wood and metal, pottery, coins, inscriptions. ■ *1000-1630. Free.*

Tours *AP Tourism*, Room 15, Srinivasa Choultry, T20602. Local sightseeing tour starts at the APSRTC Central Bus Stand at 1000. Rs 75. Tirupati (not Venkatesvara), Kalahasti, Tiruchanur, Chandragiri and Srinivasamangapuram. From Chennai to Tirumalai, Rs 300.

Essentials

Sleeping **Tirumalai**: Pilgrims are usually housed in well maintained Temple Trust's *choultries* in Tirumalai which can accommodate about 20,000. They vary from luxury suites and well-furnished cottages to dormitories and unfurnished rooms (some free). Contact PRO, TT Devasthanams, T2753 or Reception Officer 1, T2571. TTD *New Guest House*,

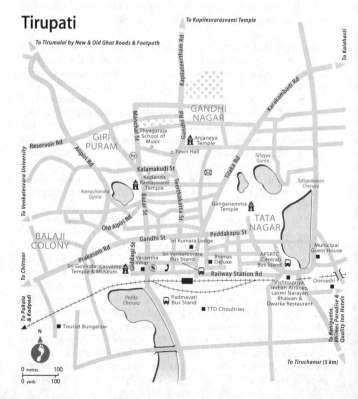

Tirupati

Travellers' Bungalow, *Modi Bhavan*, *Shriniketan*, *India*, *Balakuteeram*, *Padmavati*, *Gokulam Guest Houses* are graded as Deluxe. **D** *Mayura*, 209 TP Area, Pravasi Soudha, T25925, F25911, 65 rooms, some a/c, Indian restaurant, exchange.

Tirupati: C *Guestline Days*, 14-37 Karambadi Rd, 3 km from centre, T28866, F27774. 140 rooms, central a/c, restaurants (including non-vegetarian), bar, pool. **C** *Quality Inn Buss*, Renigunta Rd near Overbridge, T25793, F25846. 72 modern clean a/c rooms, restaurants (including non-vegetarian). **D** *Bhimas Deluxe*, 38 Govindaraja Car St (near rly), T25521, F25471. 60 rooms, 40 a/c, a/c restaurant (Indian), exchange. **D** *Bhimas*, 42 Govindaraja Car St, T20766. 59 clean rooms with bath, some a/c, near rly, restaurant (South Indian vegetarian), roof-garden. **D** *Bhimas Paradise*, 33-37 Renigunta Rd, T25747, F25568. 73 clean rooms, some a/c, pool, garden, good restaurant. The more expensive **D** *Mayura*, 209 TP Area, T25925, F25911. 65 rooms, half a/c, vegetarian restaurant, exchange. **D** *Sri Oorvasi International*, Renigunta Rd, T20202. 78 rooms, some a/c, 1 km rly, restaurant (vegetarian). **D** *Vishnu Priya*, opposite APSRTC Central Bus Stand, T20300. 134 rooms, some a/c, restaurants, exchange (Indian Airlines office). **F** *Kumara Lodge*, near railway station. Decent rooms (Rs 125). **F** *Vasantham Lodge* 141G Car St, near Railway, T20460. Reasonable rooms with bath (Rs 100).

Eating

Outside hotels, vegetarian restaurants including *Laxmi Narayan Bhawan* and *Dwarka*, opposite APSRTC Bus Stand, *Konark* Rly Station Rd, *New Triveni*, 139 TP Area and *Woodlands*, TP Area. Tirupathi-Tirumalai Devasthanam Trust (TTD) provides free vegetarian meals at its guest houses. In Tirumalai particularly, the Trust prohibits non-vegetarian food, alcohol and smoking. Near the TTD Canteen and the APSRTC Bus Stand: *Indian Coffee House* and *Tea Board Restaurant*.

Festivals

May/Jun: *Govind Brahmotsavam*. Sep: *Brahmotsavam* is the most important, especially grand every third year when it is called *Navarathri Brahmotsavam*. On the third day the Temple Car Festival *Rathotsavam* is particularly popular. Many others.

Shopping

Copper and brass idols, produced at **Perumallapalli** village, 8 km away, and wooden toys are sold locally. Try *Poompuhar* on Gandhi Rd and *Lepakshi* in the TP Area.

Transport

Local Bus: service between Tirupati and Tirumalai every 3 mins, 0330-2200. In Tirupati: **Sri Venkatesvara** Bus Stand, opposite Rly Station for passengers with through tickets to Tirumalai; Enquiries: 3rd Choultry, T20132. **Padmavati** Bus Stand in TP Area, T20203; long queues for buses but buying a return ticket from Tirupati (past the rly footbridge) saves time at the ticket queue. The journey up the slow winding hill road – which some find worrying – takes about 45 mins. In **Tirumalai**, arrive at **Kesavanagar** Bus Stand, near Central Reception area, ½ km southeast of temple; walk past canteen and shop. Depart from **Rose Garden** Bus Stand, east of the temple. **Auto-rickshaws**: fixed point-to-point fares; **cycle rickshaws**: negotiable. **Taxi**: tourist taxis through AP Tourism from the Bus Stand and Rly Station to Tirumalai, Rs 600 return, for 5½ hours. Share taxi between Tirupati and Tirumalai, about Rs 65 per person. *Balaji Travels*, 149 TP Area, T24894.

Long distance Air: Transport to town: APSRTC coach to Tirupati (Rs 20) and Tirumalai (Rs 30); taxis Rs 150. *Indian Airlines*, Hotel Vishnupriya opposite Central Bus Stand, T22349. 1000-1730. To **Chennai**: Tue, Thu, Sun and **Hyderabad**: Tue, Thu, Sat. **Road Bus**: Good service through SRTCs from the neighbouring southern states. Chennai 4 hrs, Kanchipuram 3 hrs, Vellore 2½ hrs. **Central Bus Stand** Enquiries: T22333. 24 hr left luggage **Train**: Chennai (MC): *Tirupati Chennai Exp, 6054*, 1005, 3¼ hrs; *Saptagiri Exp, 6058*, 1730, 3¼ hrs. **Mumbai** (VT) via Renigunta: *Tirupati Chennai Exp, 6054*, 1005, ¼ hr, then wait 4¼ hrs, then *Chennai Mumbai Exp, 6572*, 1445, 24¼ hrs

Trains are often delayed. Phone station in advance if catching a night train as it could be delayed until next morning

(total 28¾ hrs). **Mumbai (VT) via Chennai**: *Saptagiri Exp 6058*, 1730, 3¼ hrs, then wait 1¾ hrs, then *Chennai Mumbai Mail, 6010*, 2220, 30½ hrs (total 35¼ hrs). **Guntakal**: *Rayalaseema Exp 7430* (AC/II), 1530, 6½ hrs. **Mysore**: *Tirupati Mysore Exp, 214*, 2200, 12 hrs. **Hyderabad**: *Rayalaseema Exp, 7430* (AC/II), 1530, 16¾ hrs; *Venkatadri Exp, 7598/7604*, 1440, 18¾ hrs (for Secunderabad).

Directory **Banks** Most are on Gandhi St. *State Bank of India*, opposite APSRTC. **Tourist offices** *AP, Regional*, 139 TP Area, near Choultry III, T24306; *AP State* Govindraja Car St, T24818 *APTTDC*, Transport Unit, 12 APSRTC Complex, T25602. *Karnataka Tourism*, Hotel *Mayura Saptagiri* (see above). *TTD Information*, 1 New Choultry, T22777 and at Rly Station and Airport. **Useful addresses** Foreigners' Regional Registration Office, 499 Reddy Colony, T20503.

The Tamil Borders

Pulicat Lake Pulicat Lake on the coast, 50 km north of Chennai, is the second largest saltwater lagoon in India and one of the most important wetlands for migratory shorebirds on the eastern seaboard of India. The northern area has large concentrations of greater flamingos near the islands of Vendadu and Irukkam. There are also many birds of prey. The shallow brackish waters are rich in crustaceans and **Sriharikotta Island** has patches of residual dry evergreen forest. However, the island today is noted for its rocket launching site.

About 20 km north of Suluru is the **Neelapattu Lake**, which was given protected status in 1976 to conserve a large breeding colony of spotbilled pelicans.

Chittoor
Colour map 2, grid C2

Chittoor, on the NH18 southwest of Tirupati, and Palmaner are both on the main route between Chennai and Bangalore. A monument at **Narsingh Rayanpet**, near Chittoor, marks the place where **Haidar Ali** died on 7 December 1782. The cemetery in the town contains a number of striking tombs.

Palmaner
Colour map 2, grid C2

In the 19th century Palmaner, 39 km west of Chittoor, was regarded almost as a hill station. Before the Nilgiris were opened up, officials from Madras and others visited the town to provide a break from the intense heat of the lower plains.

The Arid Western Borders

For much of the way the NH7 from Hyderabad to Bangalore crosses the boulder covered plateau of the ancient peninsular granites and gneisses. On either side reddish or light brown soils are cultivated with millets or rice on the patches of irrigated land.

Kurnool
Phone code: 08518
Colour map 2, grid B1
Altitude: 300 m

Between 1950-56 Kurnool, 214 km southwest of Hyderabad, was capital of the state of Andhra Desa before Hyderabad was chosen as the capital of the new state of Andhra Pradesh in 1956. Located at the junction of the Hindri and Tungabhadra rivers, it was an administrative centre for the Nawabs of Kurnool. Muslim influence is still evident in the **ruined palace** of the Nawabs on the steep bank of the Tungabhadra.

Sleeping **D** *Raja Vihar Deluxe*, Bellary Rd, T20702. 48 rooms, half a/c, a/c Indian restaurants. **D** *Raviprakash*, Railway Station Rd (500 m from rly), T21116. 46 rooms and bungalows, some a/c with baths, restaurants (Indian), lawns.

Andhra Pradesh

Transport Train Kurnool Town to **Chennai (MC)** via Tirupati: *Venkatadri Exp,* *7603/7597*, 2120, 12¼ hrs, 30-min wait, then *Tirupati-Chennai Exp, 6054*, 1005, 3¼ hrs (total 16 hrs). **Guntakal**: *Venkatadri Exp, 7597/7604*, 2120, 3½ hrs. **Secunderabad**: *Tungabhadra Exp 7508/7608* (AC/II), 1430, 5 hrs; *Dharmavaram Exp, 7506/7610*, 2311, 6¼ hrs.

From the main road between Kurnool and Bellary, a 20 km diversion from Aspari goes to the important cotton market town of Adoni, west of Kurnool. After the Battle of Talikota in 1565 Malik Rahman Khan, the Abyssinian, was appointed Governor by the Sultan and remained for 39 years. His tomb on the Talibanda Hill is a pilgrimage centre. The fort was captured by one of Aurangzeb's generals in 1690 after fierce fighting, and in 1740 it fell to the Nizam of Hyderabad, Asaf Jha. Its position at the borders of warring regional powers exposed it to a turbulent history, which culminated in its capture by Tipu Sultan in 1786 and its demolition, ultimately to be returned to the Nizam and then to the British in 1800. The citadel is built on five hills, rising 250 m above the plateau. There is an excellent tank half way up the rocks that is reputed never to run dry and is very pleasant for swimming.

Adoni
Phone code: 08512
Colour map 2, grid B1
Population: 135,700

Sleeping D-E *Rajashri*, Rly Station Rd, T53304, F53308, between station and hill fort. Some a/c rooms, good Indian restaurant. **F** *Tourist*, 300 m from rly. A very cheap "home away from home", built in 1926 by 'cotton baron' in French colonial style, still original building, (trains stop outside to drop passengers!).

Take the minor road north out of Kurnool and after 6 km turn right for Alampur. The early Chalukyan seventh and eighth century **temples** are known as the 'nine Brahma' temples – the **Nava Brahma** – but are dedicated to Siva. They overlook the Tungabhadra River near its confluence with the Krishna. A huge dam built just to the southeast of Kolhapur at the entrance to the Nallamalai hills has created a lake which has threatened the site, now protected by very large embankments. Defended with fortifications, the temples are in very good condition, beautifully carved. The layout conforms to a standard pattern: the sanctuary faces east and is surrounded by a passage and a *mandapam*. Over the sanctuary, the tower is Orissan, capped by an *amalaka*. The **Papanatham** temples have fine stone trelliswork and are dedicated to Yogini (Shakti). Alampur has a small but very good **museum** in the middle of the site.

Alampur
10 km from Kurnool

A longer excursion, 170 km east of Kurnool on the route through Doranala, takes you to this popular site of Saivite pilgrimage on the banks of the Krishna, see page 391. The wooded Nallamalai Hills are home to the *Chenchu* tribes. The township has been built for workers on a massive dam construction project.

Srisailam
Phone code: 085195
Colour map 2, grid B2
Population: 20,900

Srisailam's origins are obscure, and the **Mallikarjuna Temple** (14th century) on a hill, containing one of 12 *jyotirlingas*, has often been attacked and damaged. 300 m long (dated to 1456), the outer face is richly decorated with carved figures. These include a portrait of *Krishna Deva Raya*, the Vijayanagar Emperor who visited the site in 1514. The walls and gates have carvings depicting stories from the epics. Non-Hindus are allowed into the inner sanctuary to witness the daily puja ceremony. To avoid the long queue in the middle of the day, it is best to arrive early – first prayers at 0545. *Mahasivaratri Festival* draws large crowds. Srisailam can also be reached straight from Hyderabad (200 km) across the wide open Telangana Plateau.

Andhra Pradesh

Gandikot Southeast of Kurnool, beyond Nandyal, where a hoard of Roman coins was found in 1932, is Gandikot's 'fort of the gorge'. Built in 1589 at a height of more than 500 m above sea level, it proved far from impregnable, falling in succession to the Golconda kings, to the Nawab of Cuddappah, to Haidar Ali and finally to the British. The remains hang precariously, just to the west of the flat Nandyal Valley through which the Kurnool River flows south to join the Pennar. It is part of a route that has always been strategically significant.

Ahobilam Ahobilam, southeast of Gandikot, is an important Hindu pilgrimage centre. The **temples** are dedicated to *Narasimha*, where according to local legend the man-lion incarnation of Vishnu actually took form to defeat the demon *Hiranyakasipu*. There are two main sets of temple complexes: in town, and in Upper Ahobilam (8 km). In the heart of the limestone region, there are many natural caves, some of which are used for temples. The 14th century shrine in the town of Lower Ahobilam was developed and completed by the Vijayanagar kings. The inner *gopuram*, has been renovated. In Upper Ahobilam the Narasimha Temple has been made in a natural cave. There is also a Vaishnav *Math* here. *Getting there*: local buses connect with Kurnool and Tadpatri.

Routes From Allagadda the road goes southwest and crosses the Cuddappah River (often dry) to Koilkuntla and **Banganapalle**, formerly the capital of a small Muslim princely state and which had some noted diamond mines.

Gooty
Phone code: 08553
Colour map 2, grid C1

Gooty, south of Kurnool, has a dramatic **Vijayanagara Fort** with excellent views on an isolated granite outcrop 300-m high. In the 18th century the fort fell into the hands of a Maratha chief but was captured in 1776 by Haidar Ali after a siege of nine months. Sir Thomas Munro, (Governor of Madras) who died nearby in 1827, has his grave in the cemetery by the path leading up to the Fort though his body was moved to Fort St George in Madras.

The town (4 km from the rly station) is a major crossroads and truck stop. A bypass has taken many of the hundreds of lorries that used to pass through it every day, round its outskirts, leaving it once more as a typically pedestrian-dominated Indian market town.

Sleeping A very basic hotel (with restaurant) is next to the bus stand.

Transport **Train** Guntakal: *Chennai-Mumbai Mail, 6010* (AC/II), 0755, ½ hr; *Chennai-Dadar Exp, 6512* (AC/II), 1803, ½ hr. **Chennai (MC)**: Mumbai *Chennai Exp, 6511* (AC/II), 0802, 8¾ hrs; *Mumbai Chennai Mail, 6009*, 1950, 10 hrs.

Guntakal
Phone code: 08552
Colour map 2, grid C1

Guntakal, 95 km west of Gooty, is an important railway junction with little to attract a tourist. It is en route to Bellary to visit Hampi and Hospet (see page 342). **Sleeping** An excellent value **F** hotel has a South Indian *Restaurant* next door. Local rickshaw drivers will take you there if you have to spend the night.

Transport **Train** Chennai (MC): *Mumbai Chennai Exp, 6511* (AC/II) 0735, 9 hrs; *Chennai Exp, 6063* (AC/II), 1145, 8¼ hrs. **Bangalore**: *Karnataka Exp, 2628* (AC/II), 0800, 6 hrs; *Hampi Exp, 6591* (AC/II), 2330, 7½ hrs. **Hospet**: *Hampi Exp, 6592*, 0455, 2½ hrs; *Vijaynagar Exp 7309*, 0600, 2½ hrs; *Guntakal Hubli Pass, 303*, 2015, 3¾ hrs; *Guntur-Hubli-Amaravati Exp*, 0745, 2½ hrs; *Vijayanagara Exp 7829*, 0300, 2½ hrs. **Secunderabad**: *Venkatadri Exp 7598/7604*, 0015, 9¼ hrs. **Hyderabad**: *Rayalaseema Exp 7430* (AC/II), 2215, 9¾ hrs. **Mumbai (VT)**: *Udyan Exp, 6530* (AC/II), 0255, 17½ hrs; *Chennai Mumbai Mail, 6010* (AC/II), 0820, 20½ hrs. **Goa**: train to Hubli 1st, then by road to Londa (gauge conversion in progress); **Hubli**: *Vijaynagar Exp 7309*, 0600, 7 hrs. **Kochi (HT)**: *Rajkot Cochin Exp*

6337, Tue, 1110, 20¾ hrs; *Rajkot Trivandrum Exp, 6333*, Sun, 1100, 20 hrs (to Ernakulam); *Gandhidham Trivandrum Exp, 6335*, Wed, 1110, 20 hrs.

The first agricultural communities of the peninsula lived around Bellary (now Karnataka). The black cotton soils are pierced by islands of granite hills, and the **Neolithic communities** here lived at roughly the same time as the early Indus Valley civilizations. Radiocarbon datings put the earliest of these settlements at about 3,000 BC. **Ash mounds** have been discovered at four places in this area, close to the confluence of the **Krishna** and **Tungabhadra**, and to the south of Bellary. The mounds are where cattle were herded together; some of the pens are near permanent settlements but others are isolated and look very much like the traps used for catching wild elephants much nearer to the modern period. Evidence from later sites in Karnataka shows that millets and grain were already widely grown by the first millennium BC. They have remained staple crops ever since.

Bellary
Phone code: 08392
Colour map 2, grid C1

Transport To **Gadag**: *Amravathi Exp, 7825*, 0850, 3½ hrs; to **Guntakal**: *Amravathi Exp, 7826*, 1720, 1¼ hrs.

On the eastern edge of a quite distinct geographical region, the Anantapur-Chittoor basins and the hill ranges of Cuddappah. The Seshachamal Hills are clearly visible to your left travelling south from Anantapur. In the hills to the west are deposits of corundum, mica and gold.

Routes

To the left is the railway junction and silk producing town, connected by rail with Tirupati and Katpadi (for Vellore).

Dharmavaram

Puttaparthi, just southeast of Dharmavaram, has the principle Sai Baba Ashram, *Prasanthi Nilayam* (open 0400-2100), which attracts his followers from all over India and some from abroad. The present **Sai Baba** is widely believed to be a reincarnation of the Maharashtrian Sai Baba of Shirdi. He also spends some time at *Whitefields* near Bangalore. The Ashram accommodation is good and open 0800-1900. **Transport Air**: Flights from Chennai and Mumbai were introduced by the former Prime Minister Narasimha Rao, a Sai Baba follower. KSRTC **bus** from Bangalore takes four to five hours.

Puttaparthi

It is possible to climb Penukonda (literally 'big hill') by a steep path that goes to the top. At the base, east of the hill, are huge walls and gateways of the old fortifications. The Jain **Parsvanatha Temple** has a sculpture of Parshvanatha, naked in front of an undulating serpent (11th century) in late Chalukyan style. There are also two granite Hindu temples from the early Vijayanagar period dedicated to Rama and Siva, the mosque of Sher Ali (circa1600), and the **Gagan Mahal** (Ancient Palace). The last has Islamic style arches, plaster decoration and features that are derived from temple architecture.

Penukonda became the headquarters of the districts ceded to the East India Company by the Nizam of Hyderabad in 1800. There is a well carved 10-m high column in the compound of the sub-collector's office. **Sleeping** One very basic hotel near the bus stand.

Penukonda
Phone code: 088196
Population: 17,000
Altitude: 932 m

Approaching Lepakshi (south of Penukonda) from Chilamattur you see a massive sculpture of Siva's bull (*Nandi*), carved out of a granite boulder, 5 m high and 8 m long. This tiny village has a temple of outstanding interest for its murals. The **Virabhadra Temple**, built in 1538 under the Vijayanagar Emperor Achutyadeva Raya, has well preserved sculptures, but the mural paintings are particularly striking, depicting popular legends from the *Puranas*

Lepakshi

Andhra Pradesh

(see page 550) and epics. The "Elegant linework and vibrant colours (mostly browns and ochres) and details of costumes and facial types are of outstanding interest" (Michell). On an outcrop of gneiss, the main temple is entered through two *gopurams* with unfinished brick towers. There are pyramidal brick towers over the main shrine.

Inside are large sculptures of Nataraja on a column while narrative reliefs on the south walls illustrate Siva legends, including Arjuna's penance. The principal sanctuary has a life-size Virabhadra, decked with skulls and carrying weapons, appropriate to this form of Siva, bent on revenge.

Sleeping F *Rest House*, opposite temple. 2 very basic rooms, and a simple restaurant nearby. Alternatively stay in **Hindupur**, where there are several hotels by the State Bus Stand, near some good 'meals' restaurants.

Mumbai

8

Mumbai

Mumbai is India's outward looking, commercial face. Sprawling across seven islands joined into an artificial isthmus, its problems are only matched by the enormous drive which makes it unique as the centre of business, fashion and film-making in modern India.

Daily flights from many parts of the world make Mumbai an attractive alternative entry or departure point for those choosing an 'open-jaw' air ticket. It gives you a chance to see something of India's largest city or perhaps to relax on Goa's legendary sands on the way to or from Karnataka and Kerala.

Ins and outs

Getting there
Phone code: 022
Colour map 1, grid A1
Population: 12.57 mn

Sahar International air terminal is 30 km from Nariman Point, the business heart of the city. The domestic terminals at Santa Cruz are 5 km closer. Pre-paid taxis to the city centre are good value and take between 40 mins and 1½ hrs, depending on traffic but there are also cheaper but slower buses. If you arrive late at night without a hotel booking it is best to stay at one of the hotels near the domestic terminal before going into town early in the morning.

Getting around

Mumbai's sights are spread out and you need transport. Taxis (yellow-top and blue a/c) are metered and generally good value. Autos are only allowed in the suburbs. There are frequent buses on major routes, and the two suburban railway lines are useful out of peak hours on some routes, but get horrendously crowded.

History

Languages:
*Marathi, Gujarati,
Hindi & English.
There is also a sizeable
Tamil-speaking
population*

Hinduism had made its mark on Mumbai long before the Portuguese and then the British transformed it into one of India's great cities. The caves on the island of Elephanta were excavated under the Kalachuris (500-600 AD). Yet still only 350 years ago the area occupied by this great metropolis comprised seven islands inhabited by Koli fishermen (from whom we have the word 'coolies').

The British acquired these marshy and malarial islands as part of the marriage dowry paid by the Portuguese when Catherine of Braganza married Charles II in 1661. Some suggest that Bombay took its English name from the Portuguese *Bom Bahia*, or 'good harbour'. The modern name of Mumbai is derived from the local Koli name for the goddess Parvati, Mumba devi. Four years later, the British took possession of the remaining islands and neighbouring mainland area and in 1668 the East India Company leased the whole area from the crown for £10 sterling per year, which was paid for nearly 50 years.

Today Mumbai has become the hub of India's commercial activity. It has become the home of India's stock exchange and headquarters for many national and international companies and is also a major industrial centre. Mumbai is still growing fast. One third of the population live in its desperately squalid *chawls* of cramped, makeshift and miserable hovels. There are also many thousands of pavement dwellers, yet despite the extreme poverty, Mumbai remains a city of hope for millions.

Sights

**Gateway
of India**
*The area around the
Gateway is popular
among city dwellers for
evening strolls and has a
huge buzz at weekends*

The Indo-Saracenic-style Gateway of India (1927), designed by George Wittet to commemorate the visit of George V and Queen Mary in 1911, is modelled in honey-coloured basalt on 16th-century Gujarati work. The great gateway comprises an archway with halls on each side capable of seating 600 at important receptions. The arch was the point from which the last British regiment serving in

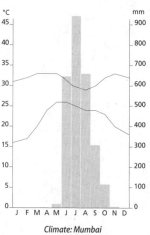

Climate: Mumbai
Best time to visit: Nov-Mar

Mumbai

India signalled the end of the empire when it left on 28 February 1948. Scores of boats depart from here for Elephanta Island, creating a sea-swell which young boys delight in diving into. Hawkers, beggars and the general throng of people all add to the atmosphere.

✴ The **Taj Mahal Hotel** The original red-domed hotel has been adjoined by a modern skyscraper (the *Taj Mahal Inter-Continental*). Jamshedji Tata, a Mumbai Parsi, was behind the enterprise; designed by West Chambers. **Warning** Drug addicts, drunks and prostitutes frequent the area behind the hotel; exercise caution.

The **Bombay Natural History Society** (BNHS), Hornbill House on SB Singh Marg, opposite Regal Cinema, founded over 100 years ago, is dedicated to the conservation of India's flora and fauna. It has an informative PR officer, a shop, wildlife collection and library.

South of the Gateway of India is the crowded southern section of Shahid (liter- **Colaba** ally 'martyr') Bhagat Singh Marg (Colaba Causeway). Sadly, increasing num- bers of beggars target foreign visitors here. The Afghan Memorial **Church of St John the Baptist** (1847-58) is at the northern edge of Colaba itself. Early English in style, with a 58 m spire, it was built to commemorate the soldiers who died in the First Afghan War. Fishermen still unload their catch early in the morning at **Sassoon Dock**, the first wet dock in India; photography is pro- hibited. Beyond the church near the tip of the Colaba promontory lie the **Observatory** and **Old European cemetery** in the naval colony (permission needed to enter; try week days). Frequent buses ply this route.

The area stretching north from Colaba Causeway to Victoria Terminus dates **Central Mumbai** from after 1862, when Sir Bartle Frere became Governor (1862-7). Under his enthusiastic guidance Mumbai became a great civic centre and an extravaganza of Victorian Gothic architecture, modified by Indo-Saracenic influences.

Just behind the Prince of Wales Museum in South Bhagat Singh Marg is **St Andrew's Kirk** (1819), a simple neo-classical church. At the south end of Mahatma Gandhi (MG) Road is the Renaissance style **Institute of Science** (1911) designed by George Wittet. The Institute, which includes a scientific library, a public hall and examination halls, was built with gifts from the Parsi and Jewish communities.

The Oval garden has been restored to a pleasant public garden. On the east side **✴ Pope Paul** of the Pope Paul (Oval) Maidan is the Venetian Gothic style old **Secretariat** **(Oval) Maidan** (1874), 143 m long, with a façade of arcaded verandahs and porticos faced in *The old buildings of* buff-coloured Porbander stone from Gujarat. Decorated with red and blue *the centre are floodlit* basalt, the carvings are in white Hemnagar stone. The University **Convoca-** *after 1900* **tion Hall** (1874) to its north was designed by Sir George Gilbert Scott in a 15th-century French decorated style. Scott also designed the adjacent Univer- sity **Library** and the 79 m high **Rajabai Clocktower** (1870s) next door, based on Giotto's campanile in Florence. The sculpted figures in niches on the exte- rior walls of the tower were designed to represent the castes of India. Originally the clock could chime 12 tunes such as Rule Britannia.

The **High Court** (1871-79), in Early English Gothic style, has a 57 m high central tower flanked by lower octagonal towers topped by the figures of Jus- tice and Mercy. The Venetian Gothic **Public Works Office** (1869-72) is to its north. Opposite, and with its main façade to Vir Nariman Road, is the former General Post Office (1869-72). Now called the **Telegraph Office**, it stands next to the original Telegraph Office adding Romanesque to the extraordinary mixture of European architectural styles. Both buildings are in honey-coloured sandstone from Kurla.

Mumbai

Mehboob Studio
Rangsharda

DHARAVI

Mahim

Mahim Bay

Swatantryaveer Savarkar Marg
Tilak Marg
Gokhale Rd (North)
Gokhale
Ranade Rd
Matunga Road
Sion Road

Sivaji Park

4
Dadar
Matunga

WORLI

7

13

Gokhale Rd (South)
Senapati Bapat Marg
Dadasaheb Phalke
Dr Babasaheb Ambedkar Rd
Wadala

6

Khan A G K Marg
Annie Besant Rd

Elphinstone
Road

Parel
5

Dr Babasaheb Ambedkar Rd
Rafi Ahmed Kidwai Rd

Sewri

8   **16**

*Arabian
Sea*

Dr E Moses Rd

Lower
Parel

Bowling Co

Curry
Rd

Chinchpoli

Cotton
Green

Stadium

Mahalaxmi
Race
Course

Keshavrao Khade Rd

Mahalakshmi

M Azad Rd

NM Joshi Marg

Victoria
Gardens
& Museum

Reay
Road

Barrister Nath Pai Marg

(Reay Rd)

Haji
Ali's
Tomb

Mahalakshmi
Temple

B D Sasi Rd

Benzer

A/C Market

Tardeo Rd

Mumbai
Central

8

Byculla

Sant Savta
Marg

2

Dockyard Rd

Tata Garden

J B
2

10
12
Behram Marg

Jamshedji Jijibhoy Rd

RC
Cathedral

Pyramid &
Crossroads

Kemp's
Corner

15

Christ Church

Grant
Road

4
3

Nana
Chowk

1

Grant Rd (M Shaukat Ali Rd)

Sandhurst
Road

Mani
Bhavan

1   **5**
3

S Patel Rd

Falkland Rd

Chor
Bazar

Masjid

(Frere Rd)

Towers of
Silence

All Saints'
Church

14

11

Charni
Road

Lamington Rd

Walkeshwar Rd

*Chowpatty
Beach*

NSC Bose Rd

Marine
Lines

Mahatma Gandhi Rd

P D'Mello Rd

Walkeshwar
Temple

Raj Bhavan

*Back
Bay*

Marine Drive

Dr Dadabhai Naoroji Rd

CST

Churchgate

Vir Nariman Rd

Madam Cama Rd

Gateway of India

D   **C**

Tata Institute
of Fundamental
Research

World
Trade
Centre

Colaba Woods

Shahid Bhagat Singh Rd

St John's Church

Sassoon dock

Homi Bhabha
Auditorium

Dr N Moos Marg

Roman
Catholic
Church

Observatory

N

0 km   1
0 miles   1

■ **Sleeping**
1 Anukool
2 Heritage
3 Kalpana Palace & Café
  Heaven
4 Midtown Pritam
5 Parklane

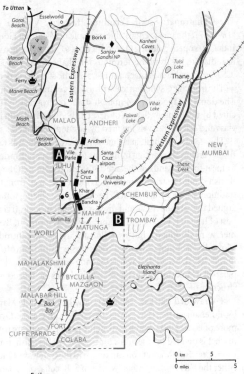

0 km   5
0 miles   5

6 Red Rose

7 Shubhangan, Mayura
& Royal Inn

8 YMCA International

● **Eating**

1 Bombay A1

2 Café Olé & Biscotti

3 China Garden

4 China Town &
Contemporary Arts

5 Chopsticks

6 Copper Chimney

7 Davaat, Mirch Masala,
Moti Mahal, Satranj

8 Flora

9 Goa Portuguesa

10 Kamat

11 New Yorker

12 Only Fish

13 Rashtriya

14 Revival

15 Under the Over

16 Viva Paschim

Horniman Circle From the imposing Horniman Circle, Vir Nariman Road leads to Flora (or Frere) Fountain (1869), now known as **Hutatma Chowk**. Horniman Circle itself was laid out in 1860. On the western edge are the Venetian Gothic **Elphinstone Buildings** (1870) in brown sandstone. The **Cathedral Church of St Thomas** was begun in 1672, opened in 1718, and subject to a number of later additions. Inside are a number of monuments forming a heroic 'Who's Who' of India. The **Custom House** is believed to incorporate a Portuguese barrack block of 1665. Over the entrance is the crest of the East India Company. Parts of the old Portuguese fort's walls can be seen. Many Malabar teak 'East Indiamen' ships were built here.

The Mint (1824-29), built on the Fort rubbish dump, has Ionic columns and a water tank in front of it. The **Town Hall** (1820-3) has been widely admired as one of the best neo-classical buildings in India. The original idea of paired columns was abandoned as being too monumental, and half the columns – imported from Britain – were used at Christ Church, Byculla. The Corinthian interior houses the Assembly Rooms and the Bombay Asiatic Society.

Behind Horniman Circle on the water's edge lies the **Old Castle**. Entry is not permitted. Going north to CST (VT) station you pass the **Port Trust Office** on your right, while a little farther on, to your right, by the station is the **General Post Office** (1909), based on the architecture of Bijapur (Karnataka) in the Indo-Saracenic style.

✳ CST or 'VT' (Victoria Terminus) Station area The **Chhatrapati Sivaji Terminus** (formerly Victoria Terminus or **VT**) (1878-87), the most remarkable example of Victorian Gothic architecture in India, was opened during Queen Victoria's Golden Jubilee year. The first train in India had left from this terminus for Thane in April 1853. Known today as 'CST', over half a million commuters use the station every day.

The frontage is symmetrical with a large central dome flanked by two wings. The dome is capped by a 4 m high statue of Progress by Thomas Earp, executed by the Bombay School of Art. The booking hall with its arcades, stained glass and glazed tiles was inspired by London's St Pancras station.

The station was built at a time when fierce debate was taking place among British architects working in India as to the most appropriate style to develop to meet the demands of the late 19th century boom. One view held that the British should restrict themselves to models derived from the best in western tradition, as the British were to be seen as a 'civilizing force' in India. Others argued that architects should draw on Indian models, trying to bring out the best of Indian tradition and encourage its development. By and large, the former were dominant, but as Tillotson argues, the introduction of Gothic allowed a blending of western traditions with Indian (often Islamic Indian) motifs, which became known as the Indo-Saracenic style. The new giant caterpillar-like walkway with perspex awnings looks incongruous against the gothic structure of 'VT'.

✳ Crawford Market (1865-71), now Jyotiba Phule Market, was designed by Emerson in the 12th-century French Gothic style. Over the entrance is more of Lockwood Kipling's work; the paving stones are from Caithness! The market is divided into sections for fruit, vegetables, fish, mutton and poultry. From Crawford Market you can return to the Gateway of India or take a taxi to either the Victoria and Albert Museum at Byculla, or Malabar Hill.

Marine Drive & Malabar Hill You can do an interesting half-day trip from Churchgate Station, along Marine Drive to the Taraporewala Aquarium, Mani Bhavan (Gandhi Museum), the Babulnath Temple, past the Parsi Towers of Silence to Kamla Nehru Park, the Hanging Gardens and the Jain Temple. If you wish you can go further towards

Malabar Point to get a glimpse of Raj Bhavan and the Walkeshwar Temple, before returning via the Mahalaxmi Temple and Haji Ali's tomb.

★ The **Hanging Gardens** (Pherozeshah Mehta Gardens) immediately south of the Towers of Silence, in the centre of a low hill, are so named since they are located on top of a series of tanks that supply water to Mumbai. The gardens themselves have little of interest but there are good views over the city from the children's park across the road. Snake charmers operate from the roadside.

Nearby is the Church of North India **All Saints' Church** (1882). Across the road from the Hanging Gardens is the **Kamla Nehru Park**, laid out in 1952 and named after the wife of India's first Prime Minister. Very good views over Back Bay.

Museums

✷ **Mahatma Gandhi Museum** (**Mani Bhavan**) This private house, at 19 Laburnum Road, where Mahatma Gandhi used to stay on visits to Mumbai, is now a memorial museum and research library with 20,000 volumes. Well worth a visit. There is a diorama depicting important scenes from Gandhi's life – slides (without mount) are available (Rs 100). The display of photos and letters on the first floor is more interesting, and includes letters Gandhi wrote to Hitler (1939) asking him not to go to war, Roosevelt and Tolstoy, and there are also letters from Einstein and Tolstoy. Cards, pamphlets et cetera at the door. ■ *0930-1800. Rs 3. West of Grant Rd, allow 1 hr.*

✷ **Victoria and Albert Museum** (Bhav Daji Laud Museum) Inspired by the V&A in London and financed by public subscription, it was built in 1872 in a Palladian style. Sir George Birdwood, a noted physician and authority on Indian crafts, became its first curator. The collection covers the history of Mumbai and contains prints, maps and models. ■ *Mon, Tue, Thu, Fri, Sat 1030-1700, Sun 0830-1645, closed Wed. North of Byculla station.*

In front of the Museum is a Clocktower (1865) with four faces (morning, noon, evening and night), and a stone statue of an elephant found by the Portuguese in the harbour. Elephanta Island was named after it. The **Victoria Gardens** are very attractive. A list at the entrance shows which trees are in blossom.

✷ **Prince of Wales Museum** This was designed by George Wittet to commemorate the visit of the Prince of Wales to India in 1905. The dome of glazed tiles has a very Persian and Central Asian flavour.

The **archaeological** section has three main groups: Brahminical, Buddhist and Jain; Prehistoric and Foreign. The Indus Valley section is well displayed. The **art** section includes an excellent collection of Indian miniatures and well displayed *tankhas*. There are also works by Gainsborough, Poussin and Titian as well as Indian silver, jade, tapestries and a collection of arms. The **Natural History** section is based on the collection of the Bombay Natural History Society founded in 1833, and includes dioramas. ■ *Closed Mon. 1015-1730 (Oct-Feb), 1015-1800 (Jul-Sep), 1015-1830 (Mar-Jun). Entry (foreigners) Rs 150. Camera fee Rs 15 (no flash or tripods). Good guide books and reproductions on sale. South end of MG Road.*

✷ **Jehangir Art Gallery** (in the Prince of Wales Museum complex). Mumbai's principal art gallery. The '*Samovar*' café is good for a snack and a drink including chilled beer; pleasant garden-side setting. There are phones and toilets. Temporary members may use the library and attend lectures. **Gallery Chemould** on first floor. ■ *1030-1900, closed Mon.* **National Gallery of Modern Art**, Sir Cowasji Jehangir Hall, opposite Prince of Wales Museum.

Mumbai

Central Mumbai

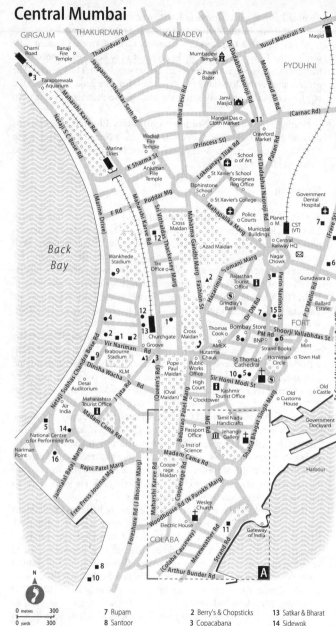

0 metres 300
0 yards 300

■ **Sleeping**
1 Ambassador, Flavours &
  Kamling Restaurant
2 Chateau Windsor
3 City Palace
4 Manama
5 Oberoi Towers & Oberoi
6 Railway

7 Rupam
8 Santoor
9 Sea Green
10 Supreme
11 Taj Mahal & Taj Mahal
   Intercontinental
12 West End

● **Eating**
1 Balwas & Government
  Tourist Office

2 Berry's & Chopsticks
3 Copacabana
4 Geoffrey's
5 George & Croissants
6 Icy Spicey
7 Ideal Corner
8 Mahesh
9 Not Just Jazz by the Bay
10 Piccolo
11 Rajdhani
12 Sapna

13 Satkar & Bharat
14 Sidewok
15 West Coast
16 Woodlands

▲ **Other**
1 Alitalia
2 Bombay Gymkhana
  Club
3 British Airways &
  Croissant

Elephanta Caves

The heavily forested Elephanta Island, often barely visible in the mist from Mumbai only 10 km away, rises out of the bay like a giant whale. The setting is symbolically significant; the sea is the ocean of life, a world of change (Samsara) in which is set an island of spiritual and physical refuge. The 'caves' excavated in the volcanic lava high up the slope of the hill saw Hindu craftsmen over 1,000 years ago, express their view of spiritual truths in massive carvings of extraordinary grace. Sadly a large proportion have been severely damaged, but enough remains to illustrate something of their skill.

Getting there Maharashtra Tourism launches with good guides leave the Gateway of India every 30 mins from 0900 (last one leaves Elephanta at 1730) except during the monsoon from Jun-Sep. The very pleasant journey takes 1½ hrs (Rs 70 return). Reservations, T2026384. Small private boats without guides continue during the monsoon when the seas can be very rough. From the landing place, a 300 m unshaded path along the quayside and then about 110 rough steps lead to the caves at a height of 75 m. The walk along the quay can be avoided when the small train functions (Rs 6). The climb can be trying for some, especially if it is hot, though *Doolies* (chairs carried by porters) are available for Rs 300+ (unnecessary for the reasonably fit). The monkeys can be aggressive. Elephanta is very popular with local day-trippers so avoid the weekend rush. At the start of the climb there are places selling refreshments, as well as lines of stalls with knick-knacks and curios along the way. Maharashtra Tourism normally organizes a festival of classical music and dance on the island in the third week of Feb.

Ins & outs
Early morning is the best time for light and also for avoiding large groups with guides which arrive from around 1000. The caves tend to be quite dark so carry a powerful torch

History

The vast majority of India's 1,200 **cave sites** were created as temples and monasteries between the third century BC and the 10th century AD. Jain, Buddhist and Hindu caves often stand side by side. The temple cave on Elephanta island, dedicated to Siva, was probably excavated during the eighth century by the Rashtrakuta Dynasty which ruled the Deccan from 757 to 973 AD, though the caves may have had earlier Buddhist origins. An earlier name for the island was Garhapuri – city of forts – but the Portuguese renamed it after the colossal sculpted elephants when they captured Mumbai from the Sultan of Gujarat in 1535, and stationed a batallion there. They reportedly used the main pillared cave as a shooting gallery causing some of the damage you see. Muslim and British rulers were not blameless either.

The site

The Entrance Originally there were three entrances and 28 pillars at the site. The entrances on the east and west have subsidiary shrines which may have been excavated and used for different ceremonies. The main entrance is now from the north. At dawn, the rising sun casts its rays on the approach to the main shrine (*garbagriha*), housed in a square structure at the west end of the main hall. On your right is a carving of Siva as Nataraj (see page 532). On the left he appears as Lakulisa in a much damaged carving. Seated on a lotus, the Buddha-like figure is a symbol of the unconscious mind and enlightenment, found also in Orissan temples where Lakulisa played a prominent role in attempting to attract Buddhists back into Hinduism. From the steps at the entrance you can see the *yoni-lingam*, the symbol of the creative power of the deity.

The Main Hall The ribbed columns in the main hall, between 5 m and 6 m high and in a cruciform layout, are topped by a capital. At the corner of each pillar is a dwarf signifying the earth spirit (*gana*), and sometimes the figure of Ganesh (Ganapati). To the right, the main **Linga Shrine** has four entrances, each corresponding to a cardinal point guarded by a *dwarpala*. The sanctum is bare, drawing attention to the *yoni-lingam* which the devotee must walk around clockwise.

Mumbai

The wall panels To the north of the main shrine is **Bhairava killing the demon Andhakasura**. This extraordinarily vivid carving shows Siva at his most fearsome, with a necklace of skulls, crushing the power of Andhaka, the Chief of Darkness. It was held that if he was wounded each drop of his blood would create a new demon. So Siva impaled him with his sword and collected his blood with a cup which he then offered to his wife Shakti. In winter this panel is best seen in the early afternoon.

Opposite, on the south side of the main shrine is the damaged panel of **Kalyan Sundari**, in which Siva stands with Parvati on his right, just before their wedding (normally a Hindu wife stands on her husband's left). She looks down shyly, but her body is drawn to him. Behind Parvati is her father Himalaya and to his left Chandramas, the moon god carrying a gift – *soma*, the food of the gods. On Siva's left is Vishnu and below him Brahma.

At the extreme west end of the temple are **Nataraja** (left) and **Yogisvara Siva** (right). The former shows a beautiful figure of Ganesh above and Parvati on his left. All the other gods watch him. Above his right shoulder is the four-headed God of Creation, Brahma. Below Brahma is the elephant-headed Ganesh.

On the south wall, opposite the entrance are three panels. **Gangadhara** is on the west. The holy River Ganga (Bhagirathi) flowed only in heaven but was brought to earth by her father King Bhagiratha (kneeling at Siva's right foot). Here, Ganga is shown in the centre, flanked by her two tributaries, Yamuna and Saraswati. These three rivers are believed to meet at Allahabad.

To the left of these is the centre piece of the whole temple, the remarkable **Mahesvara**, the Lord of the Universe. Here Siva is five-headed, for the usual triple-headed figure has one face looking into the rock and another on top of his head. Nearly 6 m high, he unites all the functions of creation, preservation and destruction. Some see the head on the left (your right) as representing **Vishnu, the Creator**, while others suggest that it shows a more feminine aspect of Siva. To his right is **Rudra** or Bhairava, with snakes in his hair, a skull to represent ageing from which only Siva is free, and he has a look of anger. The central face is Siva as his true self, **Siva Swarupa**, balancing out creation and destruction. In this mode he is passive and serene, radiating peace and wisdom like the Buddha. His right hand is held up in a calming gesture and in his left hand is a lotus bud.

The panel to the left has the **Ardhanarisvara**. This depicts Siva as the embodiment of male and female, representing wholeness and the harmony of opposites. The female half is relaxed and gentle, the mirror in the hand symbolizing the woman reflecting the man. Siva has his 'vehicle', Nandi on the right.

To the east, opposite the *garbha-griha*, was probably the original entrance. On the south is Siva and Parvati **Playing chaupar on Mount Kailash**. Siva is the faceless figure. Parvati has lost and is sulking but her playful husband persuades her to return to the game. They are surrounded by Nandi, Siva's bull, celestial figures and an ascetic with his begging bowl.

On the north is **Ravana Shaking Mount Kailash** on which Siva is seated. Siva is calm and unperturbed by Ravana's show of brute strength and reassures the frightened Parvati. He pins down Ravana with his toe, who fails to move the mountain and begs Siva's forgiveness which is granted.

The Subsidiary Shrines The larger shrine on the east side has a lingam. There are also damaged images of Karttikeya, Ganesh and the Matrikas.

Tours

City sightseeing
Approved guides from the India tourist office, T2036854

City tour Usually includes visits to The Gateway of India, the Prince of Wales Museum (closed Monday), Jain temple, Hanging Gardens, Kamla Nehru Park and Mani Bhavan (Gandhi Museum).

MTDC, Madam Cama Road, opposite LIC Building, T2026713. **City tour**: daily except Monday, 0900-1300 and 1400-1800, Rs 60. **TCI** offers *Marvellous Mumbai* (a/c coach picks up from hotels), Rs 150. **Fort walk** A heritage walk around CST and Fort area with the Kala Ghoda Association, Army & Navy Building, T2852520; www.artindia.co.in

Elephanta tours from Gateway of India. Boat, 0900-1415, Rs 70 return; reserve at Apollo Bunder, T2026364. If you wish to sightsee independently with a guide, ask at the Tourist Office, T2036854.

Pick up *Mumbai This Fortnight,* an informative free booklet on everything that is hot in the city. Free from larger bookshops and stores.
　Just Dial 888 8888 for free telephonic Yellow Pages service.

Essentials

Most hotels are concentrated in the central area (Marine Drive, Nariman Pt, Apollo Bunder and Colaba). Juhu and Vile Parle (pronounced 'Veelay Parlay') are convenient for late arrivals and early morning departures from the airport. Prices are much higher than elsewhere in India, but there are some moderately priced hotels immediately behind the *Taj Mahal Hotel*. It is difficult to find even dormitory beds under Rs 200. For services in **AL**, **A** and **B** hotels, see page 35. **Hotlink**, India's 1st on-line reservation system, links 300 medium- to top-class hotels, T6152394.

Accommodation in Mumbai is usually very heavily booked. Whenever possible make reservations in advance. If you have not, arrive as early in the day as possible

Juhu Beach (20 km from the centre) used to be quite an attractive and relaxed seaside area but the sea is now polluted. On Sun evenings the beach takes on a fairground atmosphere. Most airport hotels offer free transfer. The Tourist Information Counter at the airport will help to book.

Sleeping: Airport, Juhu Beach & Bandra

Mumbai

Airport **LL-L** *The Leela*, Sahar (near International Terminal), T86363636, F86360606. 460 rooms, excellent restaurants, pricey but excellent. **L-AL** *Orchid*, 70C Nehru Rd, Vile Parle (east), T6100707, F6105974, 5 mins' walk from domestic terminal. Totally refurbished, attractive rooms, 'eco-friendly' (energy saving, recycling etc), *Boulevard*

Mumbai airport & Juhu beach

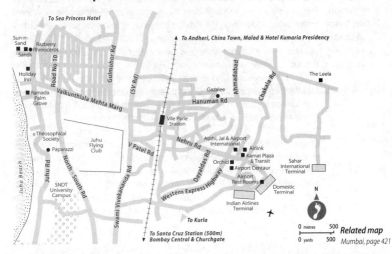

To Sea Princess Hotel

Sun-n-Sand
Razberry
Rhinoceros
Sands
▲ To Andheri, China Town, Malad & Hotel Kumaria Presidency

Holiday Inn
Road No 10
Gulmohor Rd
(SV Rd)
Ahmadabad
The Leela

Ramada Palm Grove
Valkunthlala Mehta Marg
Gazalee
Hanuman Rd
Chakala Rd

Theosophical Society
Juhu Flying Club
Vile Parle Station

Paparazzi
V Patel Rd
Nehru Rd
Atithi, Jal & Airport International
Airlink
Sahar International Terminal

Juhu Beach
North South Rd
SNDT University Campus
Dayaldas Rd
Orchid
Kamat Plaza & Transit
Airport Centaur
Airport Rest Rooms
Domestic Terminal

Pd Juhu
Swami Vivekananda Rd
Western Express Highway
Indian Airlines Terminal
N

To Kurla
✈

0 metres 500
0 yards 500
Related map
Mumbai, page 421

To Santa Cruz Station (500m)
▼ Bombay Central & Churchgate

boasts a '15 minute lightening menu' and good midnight buffet, handy coffee shop. Recommended. **AL** *Centaur Airport*. Definitely avoid. **A-B** *Airlink*, near Domestic Terminal, Vile Parle (E), T6183695, F6105186. Clean, comfortable. **B-C** *Airport International*, 5/6, Nehru Rd, Vile Parle (east), F6141773, near domestic terminal. 27 rooms, modern business hotel, clean, comfortable. **B-C** *Atithi*, 77A Nehru Rd, Vile Parle (east) 7 mins' walk from domestic terminal, T6116124, F6111998. 47 rooms, functional, clean, set meals included, efficient desk, popular. **B-C** *Host Inn*, opposite Marol Fire Brigade, Andheri-Kurla Rd, Andheri (east), near International airport, T8360105, F8391080. Decent, clean rooms, friendly. **B-C** *Jal*, Nehru Rd, Vile Parle (east), T6123820, F6369008. 40 rooms, near domestic terminal. **B-C** *Kumaria Presidency*, Andheri-Kurla Rd, facing International Airport, Andheri (east), T8352601, F8373850. 32 a/c rooms, 24-hr exchange, pool, good value. Recommended. **B-C** *Transit*, off Nehru Rd, Vile Parle (east), T6105812, F6105785. 54 rooms, modern, reasonable "overnight halt" for airport, excellent restaurant (good food and service, draught beer), airport transfer. **D** *Airport Rest Rooms*, old Domestic Terminal, Santa Cruz. For passengers with connecting flights within 24 hrs of arrival, comfortable, clean, but often full, ask at Airport Enquiries.

Bandra LL *Regent*, Land's End, Bandra Bandstand, T6551234, F6512471, buscent. regent@lokhandwalahotels.com City's newest luxury hotel, very spacious and chic, top facilities. **B** *Metro Palace*, Hill Rd, near Bandra station (W), T6427311, F6431932. Convenient, close to domestic airport and shops, good restaurant (see below). **B** *Pali Hills*, 14 Union Park, Pali Hill, Bandra, T6492995. Quiet location, near market, continental restaurant (see below).

Most are under 10 km from the airport

Juhu Beach L-AL *Holiday Inn*, Balraj Sahani Marg, T6204444, F6204452. 190 rooms, 2 pools, courtesy coach to town, reliable. **AL** *Sun-n-Sand*, 39 Juhu Beach, T6201811, F6202170. 118 rooms, best refurbished, comfortable, though cramped poolside, good restaurant. **A** *Citizen*, 960 Juhu Tara Rd, T6117273, F6227270, citizen@bom2. vsnl.net.in Despite unexciting appearance, 45 smallish but very well appointed rooms, suites, efficient airport transfer. Recommended. **B** *Juhu Hotel*, Juhu Tara Rd, T6184014. Spacious comfortable cottage-style rooms, sea-facing lawns, good restaurant (try seafood and Mughlai), soundproofed disco. **B** *Sands*, 39/2 Juhu Beach, T6204511, F6205268. 40 rooms, excellent restaurant. Recommended.

Eating: **Mid-range** *Gazalee*, Kadambari Complex, Hanuman Rd, Vile Parle (E), T8388093.
Airport, Finest coastal cuisine, try stuffed Bombay Duck, and shellfish. *Independence*, at Metro
Juhu Beach Palace Hotel, Bandra, T6427311. Pleasant ambience, wide choice, excellent value buf-
& Bandra fet lunches (Rs 150). *Just around the Corner*, 24th-30th road junction, TPS III, Bandra
Bandra has some (W). Bright casual American style diner. Extensive breakfast menu (0800-1100). Pay by
exciting options the plateful, lots of combination options, excellent salads, low-calorie. *Out of the Blue* , at *Pali Hills*. Steak and fondue, great sizzlers, unusual combinations, flavoured ice teas, flambéed desserts, UV lit inside or outside smoke-free. *Trim with Taste*, 500 Sant Kutir, Linking Rd, Bandra (lane behind KBN department store). Small, spotless, serving unusual health food. Try stuffed idlis, peach and yoghurt smoothies.

Cheap *China Town*, Marol-Maroshi Rd, Andheri (E), excellent Indian, Chinese, wide choice, very friendly. *Crunchy Munchy*, Agarwal Market, next to Vile Parle (E) station. Open-air café serving veg Indian and Mexican mini-meals. Very clean, good service and portions. *Lucky*, 9 SV Rd (Hill Rd junction), Bandra (W). Good Mughlai especially Chicken biriyani and tandooris. *Potpourri* , Carlton Court, Turner/Pali Rd junction, opposite HSBC. Streetside café serving great Italian food and desserts.

A-B *Midtown Pritam*, 20-B Pritam Estates, Senapati Bapat Marg, 2 mins from Dadar station, T4145555, F4143388. 63 rooms, terrace garden. **C** *Sagar*, Nagpada Junction (Bellasin Rd/JB Behram Marg corner), Byculla, T3092727, F3072408. Very clean rooms, good restaurant, friendly. Recommended. **C-D** *Red Rose*, Gokuldas Pasta Rd, (behind Chitra Cinema) Dadar East, T4137843. 31 rooms, some a/c, mostly shared but clean baths, flexible checkout, friendly – "welcoming at 0530 with no booking". Recommended. **D** *Anukool*, 292-8 Maulana Saukat Ali Rd, T392401. 23 rooms, some a/c, good value. **D** *Heritage*, Sant Savta Marg, Byculla, T3714891, F3738844. 84 a/c rooms, restaurant (good Parsi), bar. **D** *Kalpana Palace*, 181 P Bapurao Marg, opposite Daulat Cinema, Grant Rd, T3000846. 30 decent rooms, some a/c. **D** *Railway Retiring Rooms*, Mumbai Central, T3077292. Some a/c with bath. **D-E** *YMCA International House*, 18 YMCA Rd, near Mumbai Central, T3091191. Decent rooms, shared bath, meals included, temp membership Rs 60, deposit Rs 1,300, good value, book 3 months ahead with deposit.

Sleeping:
Dadar, Mumbai Central & Grant Rd area
■ *on map, page 418*
Dadar can be a good option to stay – plenty of restaurants and good trains to Churchgate and CST

Expensive *Biscotti*, Crossroads, Haji Ali, T4955055. Excellent Italian. Wholesome, leisurely dining, try batter-fried calamari, giant prawns in liqueur, flavoured sugar-free soda, zabaglioni, bistro-style complete with fiddler. *Goa Portuguesa*, THK Rd, Mahim. Goan. Authentic dishes, taverna-style with guitarist, try *sungto* (prawn) served between *papads*, *kalwa* (oyster), *teesryo* (shell) and clams, lobsters cooked with tomatoes, onions and spices and *bibinca* to end the meal. *Only Fish*, Hotel Rosewood, J Dadaji Rd, Tulsiwadi, Tardeo, T4940320. Indian regional recipes (including Bengali). Seafood too, small but stylish. *Revival*, Chowpatty Sea Face (near footbridge). Classy, good Indian/Continental buffets and desserts, ices.

Eating:
Dadar, Mumbai Central & Grant Rd area

Mid-range *Bombay A1*, 7 Vadilal A Patel Marg (Grant Rd Junc). Parsi. Cheerful, varied menu, try *Patrani machli*. *Chinatown*, 99 August Kranti Marg. Szechwan, Cantonese, Mandarin. Varied menu (27 soups), upstairs more comfortable. *Copper Chimney*, Dr AB Rd, Worli, T4924488. Indian. Window into kitchen, excellent food from extensive menu, reasonable prices, undiscovered by tourists. *Rajdhani*, Mangaldas Rd, opposite Crawford Market. Indian. An a/c oasis, excellent lunch *thali*, very friendly welcome. *Rashtriya*, Rd leading to Dadar (East) stairway. South Indian vegetarian. Good food and excellent coffee. *Sindhudurg*, RK Vaidya Rd, Dadar. Indian. Try seafood *thali* and fish fry. *Under the Over*, 36 Altamount Rd (by flyover). Bistro like, for Mexican, Creole dishes, sizzlers and rich desserts, reasonably priced, no alcohol. *The Village*, *Poonam Intercontinental,* near Mahalaxmi racecourse. Gujarati. 'Village' setting, sea views, good authentic food. *Viva Paschim*, City View, Dr AB Rd, Worli, T4983636. Quality coastal Maharashtrian. Sunday lunch buffet great value (Rs 225), folk dances at dinner often.

Cheap *Heaven*, corner of Grant Rd/P Bapurao Marg. Very cheap, friendly (eg *aloo matar* Rs 10). *Kamat*, Navrose Mansion, Tardeo Rd. Indian. Very inexpensive *thalis* and veg snacks.

Fast food *Kobe*, Hughes Rd, 12 Sukh Sagar. For Japanese sizzlers. *New Yorker*, 25 Chowpatty Sea Face. Pizzas, sandwiches and Mexican fast food, ice cream. *Swaati*, Tardeo Rd for clean *bhelpuri* and *chaats*.

LL-AL *The Oberoi*, Nariman Pt, T2025757, F2041505. 350 large rooms, the newer Oberoi combining modern technology with period furniture, excellent restaurants. **LL-AL** *Oberoi Towers*, Nariman Pt, T2024343, F2043282. 643 rooms, superb views from higher floors, good buffets, garden pool, excellent shopping complex. Recommended. **L-AL** *Ambassador*, Churchgate Extn, Vir Nariman Rd, T2041131, F2040004. 127 rooms, all facilities, revolving restaurant and pastry shop, slightly run-down feel. **A-B** *West End*, 45 New Marine Lines, T2039121, F2057506. 80 small, pleasant suites

Sleeping:
Central Mumbai (Churchgate, Nariman Point & Marine Drive)
■ *on map, page 418*
*Price codes:
see inside front cover*

but need refurbishing, good restaurant, excellent service, very efficient front desk, well located, good value. Highly recommended. **B-C** *Chateau Windsor Guest House*, 86 Vir Nariman Rd, T2043376, F2851415. 36 rooms (some a/c) vary, some very small and dark, room service for light snacks and drinks, friendly, clean, good value. Recommended. Cash only. **B-C** *Sea Green*, 145 Marine Drive, T/F2822294. 34 rooms, 22 a/c, pleasant breezy informal sitting area. **C-D** *Supreme*, 4 Pandey Rd, near *President*, T2185623. Clean rooms with bath, good service but a little noisy.

Eating:
Central Mumbai

Expensive *Ambassador Hotel's* **Pearl of the Orient**, T2041131. Excellent Chinese, Japanese and Thai. The *Revolving Restaurant* offers stunning views especially at night (for a less expensive stationary view try the bar on the floor above which does simple meals!). *Indian Summer*, 80 Vir Nariman Rd, T2835445. Indian. Excellent food, tasty *kebabs*, interesting modern glass décor, smart dress, reserve. *Santoor*, Maker Arcade, Cuffe Parade, near *President Hotel*, T2182262. North Indian. Small place, Mughlai and Kashmiri specialities: creamy chicken *malai* chop, *chana* Peshawari (*puri* with chickpeas), *Kashmiri soda* made with salt and pepper. *Sidewok*, next to NCPA theatre, T2818132. Interesting southeast Asian/ fusion cuisine. Innovative menu, imaginative cocktails (try non-alcoholic too), surprise entertainment by staff, "longest mosaic mural in Asia", a special, fun dining experience. Reserve.

Mid-range *Berry's*, Vir Nariman Rd, near Churchgate Station, T2875691. North Indian. Tandoori specialities, good *kulfi*, reasonable prices. *Chopsticks*, 90A Vir Nariman Rd, Churchgate, T2832308. Chinese, good, hot and spicy Schezwan. Offering unusual dishes (taro nest, date pancakes, toffee bananas). *Kamling*, 82 Vir Nariman Rd, T2042618. Genuine Cantonese. Simple surroundings, but excellent preparations, try seafood, often busy. *Sapna*, Vir Nariman Rd. Indian, very traditional Mughlai delicacies, bar, some tables outside, attentive service, good value. *Satkar*, Indian Express Building, opposite Churchgate station, T2043259. Indian. Delicious vegetarian, fruit juices and shakes; a/c section more expensive.

Cheap *Balwas*, Maker Bhavan, 3 Sir V Thackersey Marg. Inexpensive, well-prepared food. *Woodlands*, Mittal Chambers, Nariman Pt. South Indian. Excellent *idli* and *dosai* and good *thalis*, busy at lunchtime, closed Sun. *Piccolo Café*, 11A Sir Homi Mody St. Parsi. 0900-1800, closed Sat afternoon and Sun, profits to charity, clean, good *dhansak*.

Cafés and fast food *Croissants*, Vir Nariman Rd, opposite Eros Cinema. Burgers, sandwiches, hot croissants with fillings, ice cream, lively atmosphere. *Fountain*, MG Rd. For sizzlers and apple pie in a café atmosphere.

Sleeping:
CST (VT) & fort
■ *on map, page 418*
price codes:
see inside front cover

C *Grand*, 17 Sprott Rd, Ballard Estate, T2618211, F2626581. 73 a/c rooms, exchange, bookshop, old-fashioned, built around a central courtyard but relaxing. **C-D** *City Palace*, 121 City Terrace (Nagar Chowk), opposite CST Main Gate, T2615515, F2676897. Tiny though spotless rooms (some without window), with bath (Indian WC), some a/c, renovated, modern, room service, good value. Recommended. **D-E** *Manama*, 221 P D'Mello Rd, T2613412. Reasonable rooms, few with bath and a/c, popular. **D-E** *Rupam*, 239 P D'Mello Rd, T2618298. 37 rooms, some a/c with phone, clean, friendly, comfortable beds.

Eating:
CST (VT) & fort

Mid-range *Bharat*, 317 SB Singh Marg, opposite Fort Market, T2618991. Excellent seafood and crab as well as *naans* and *rotis*. *George*, 20 Apollo St (near Horniman Circle). Pleasant quiet atmosphere, faded colonial feel, good service, lunchtime *biriyanis* and *thalis*. *Wall Street*, 68 Hamam St, behind Stock Exchange. Coastal cuisine, excellent seafood, try spicy Malabari prawns, squid green garlic, fish patta. **Cheap** *Ideal Corner*, Hornby View, Gunbow St, Fort, CST. Lunchtime Parsi food and snacks in clean

Washing your dirty linen in public

In Mahalakshmi's municipal dhobi ghats you can see a bewildering range of India's contrasts. The dhobis (washermen and women) deal with a staggeringly large wash every day. Through the apparent chaos, thousands of pieces of clothing, bedsheets and towels are collected from private houses (marked with a tiny indelible ink symbol, unique to that household), logged in a note book, washed in the small cubicles rented out to several washermen each day, and returned to the owners a week later (except during the rains, when the delivery period may be 2 weeks or more). Virtually

nothing seems to get lost, and equally miraculously most clothes survive the beating they receive on the stones, having spent a night soaking in soapy water which looks positively murky. Surrounded by public squalor, the dhobis deal in cleansing all in public. However, their days may be numbered, for washing machines are spreading fast and there are signs that demand for this most traditional of Indian activities is falling.

The area can be unpleasant and dangerous – beggars pester and gangs have been known to stop lone travellers and demand a large 'ransom'.

café. *Icy Spicy*, off PM Rd, next to Fort Central Restaurant. Veg snack bar. Great light meals (from Rs 25), no toilet. *Mahesh Lunch Home*, Sir PM Rd, Fort. Excellent for Mangalorean, Goan and *tandoori* seafood, a/c, bar, very popular. *West Coast*, Rustom Sidhwa Rd, off Sir Perin Nariman Rd. Very good meals. On MG Rd (north end), you can have a good traditional breakfast, often as early as 0600.

L-AL *Fariyas*, 25 off Arthur Bunder Rd, Colaba, T2042911, F2834992. 80 upgraded rooms, good restaurants, 'pub', roof garden, pool (open to non-residents), obliging service. **AL** *Taj Mahal*, the original, with great style and character, 294 rooms, and *Taj Mahal Intercontinental*, Apollo Bunder, T2023366, F2872711. 306 rooms, excellent restaurants (no shorts). *Tanjore* (good *thalis*), Indian dance performance (evenings), open to non-residents (Rs 100, 1 hr). Recommended. **A** *Strand*, 25 PJ Ramchandani Marg, T2882222. Friendly, clean, decent rooms, some with bath and seaview. **B** *Apollo*, 22 Lansdowne Rd, Colaba, behind *Taj*, T2020223, F2871592. 39 rooms, some a/c, best with sea view, excellent, helpful, friendly service. **B** *Diplomat*, 24-26 BK Boman Behram Marg (behind *Taj*), T2021661, F2830000, diplomat@vsnl.com 52 a/c rooms, restaurant, quiet, friendly, relaxed atmosphere, good value. Recommended. **B** *Gulf Flower*, Kamal Mansions, Arthur Bunder Rd, T2833742. Off-putting exterior but modern and clean rooms inside. **B** *Regency Inn*, 18 Landsowne Rd behind Regal Cinema, Colaba, T2020292, T2837757. Spacious a/c rooms, fridge, good value. **B** *Regent*, 8 Ormiston Rd (Best Marg), T2871854. Well furnished a/c rooms, no restaurant but good room service. **B** *Suba Palace*, Apollo Bunder, T2020636, F2020812, just behind *Taj*. Clean, modern, well run. Recommended. **B-C** *Godwin*, 41 Garden Rd, T2841226, F2871592. 48 large, clean, renovated, a/c rooms (upper floors have better views), good restaurant, rooftop garden, very helpful management. Recommended. **B-C** *Shelley's*, 30 PJ Ramchandani Marg, Colaba, T2840229, F2840385. Large comfortable, bright airy a/c rooms, some sea-facing with TV and fridge (more expensive), a 'heritage' building with character, breakfasts only, helpful and friendly owners. Recommended. **C** *Bentley's*, 17 Oliver Rd, off Garden Rd, T2841474, F2871846, bentleyshotel@hotmail.com 37 rooms (some large with bath better value), 4 a/c, breakfast included, young owner, very helpful. **C-D** *YWCA International Centre*, 2nd Flr, 18 Madam Cama Rd (entrance on side), Fort, T2020122, F2020445. For both sexes, 34 clean, pleasant rooms with bath (mostly Rs 600 per person), breakfast and dinner included, temp membership Rs 60 – essential to write in advance with Rs 1,300 deposit. Recommended.

Sleeping: Gateway of India & Colaba
■ *on map, page 426*

Rooms with seaview are more expensive.

Mumbai

Few budget hotels are left in the area charging under Rs 400 though you may get a dormitory bed for Rs 250

D *Lawrence*, Rope Walk Lane, behind Prince of Wales Museum, T2843618. 9 rooms, usually full, very good value. **D** *Sea Shore*, 4th Flr, 1/49 Kamal Mansion, Arthur Bunder Rd, T2874237, F2874238. Has good rooms facing sea (avoid others), clean. Some **E-F** category hotels are clustered around the *Taj Mahal Hotel*: **Salvation Army Red Shield Hostel**, 30 Mereweather Rd, T2841824. Mostly dorm (about Rs 150 including breakfast, Rs 200 including meals), some double rooms (Rs 450, all meals), lockers Rs 30 per item 0800-2200, showers Rs 30, check out 0900, book in advance or arrive early, check in as others check out, recommended as convenient, friendly, best value, could be cleaner.

Gateway of India & Colaba

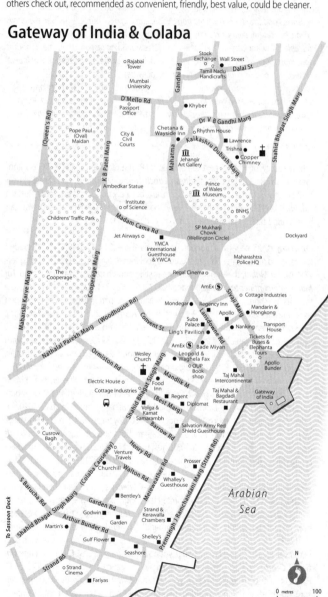

Expensive *Apoorva*, near Horniman Circle, Fort, T2881457. Very good seafood, esp crabs and prawns. *Chetana*, 34 K Dubash Marg, opposite Jahangir Gallery, T2844968. Gujarati, Rajasthani vegetarian. Excellent *thalis*, unique dining experience (also small religious bookshop), reserve. *Copper Chimney*, 18 K Dubash Marg, T2041661. Indian. Subdued lighting and quietly tasteful, excellent North Indian dishes, must reserve. *Excellent Sea*, Ballard Estate, T2668195. Excellent crab, prawn and lobster. *Khyber*, 145 MG Rd, Kala Ghoda, Fort, T2632174. North Indian. For an enjoyable evening in beautiful surroundings (traditional carved furniture, paintings by Hussain, AE Menon), excellent food, especially lobster and *reshmi* chicken kebabs, try *paya* soup (goats' trotters!), outstanding restaurant, reserve. *Ling's Pavilion*, 19/21 KC College Hostel Building, off Colaba Causeway (behind *Taj* and Regal Cinema), T2850023. Stylish décor, good atmosphere and delightful service, colourful menu, seafood specials, generous helpings. Recommended. *Nanking*, Apollo Bunder, T2881638. Chinese. Good choice of very good Cantonese dishes, try Fish ball soup, Pomfret Nanking, Pickled fish, and Beef with watercress. *Trishna*, 7 Rope Walk Lane, behind Kala Ghoda, by Old Synagogue, T2672176. Indian. Good coastline cuisine, seafood, excellent crab. "Swinging, crowded and fun". Highly recommended.

Mid-range *Bagdadi*, Tullock Rd (behind Taj Hotel), T2028027. Mughlai. 1 of the cheapest, first class food, fragrant biryani, delicious chicken (Rs 40), crowded but clean. *Mandarin*, T2023186. Chinese. Excellent food and service (also cold beer).

Cheap *Bade Miyan*, behind Ling's Pavilion. Street side Kebab corner but very clean. Try *baida roti, shammi* and *boti kebabs*. *Kamat Samarambh*, opposite Electric House, SB Singh Marg. Indian vegetarian. Very good *thalis* and snacks, try *chola battura* (*puri* topped with spiced chickpeas). *Martin's*, near Strand Cinema. Goan. Simple, authentic Goan food, excellent seafood and pork *sorpotel*. *Paradise*, Sindh Chambers, Colaba Causeway. Parsi and others. Spotless, excellent *dhansak*; try *Sali boti* (mutton and 'chips'), closed Mon (not a/c).

Cafés and fast food Those serving chilled beer are the craze; prices have gone up and waiters care too much for large tips from tourist groups: *Churchill*, opposite Cusrow Baug, Colaba Causeway, T2844689. Good late breakfasts, continental and steaks served in small a/c café, choice of desserts, ices, shakes, good value. *Leopold's*, Colaba, T2830585. Still full of young backpackers for good Western food and drink (limited Indian veg), friendly but getting expensive. Similar cafés nearby are far better value. *Mondegar*, near Regal Cinema, T2812549. Similar, but a little cheaper. *Wayside Inn*, 38 K Dubash Marg, T2844324. Quaint country inn-style good breakfast menu, average continental but perfect for an afternoon beer in heart of the city, breezy, laid back and leisurely, moderately priced. *Food-Inn* 50 m from Leopold's. Mainly Indian (some western) snacks. Pleasant (a/c upstairs), reasonably priced, friendly service. Recommended. *Kailash Parbat*, 1st Pasta Lane, Colaba. Excellent snacks and *chaats*.

Bars and discos

All major hotels and restaurants have bars, others may only serve beer. Many pubs expect couples Fri-Sun. Most pubs charge Rs 175-250 for a 'pitcher' (bottle); cocktails Rs 75-150.

Gateway *Taj Mahal*, on top floor of the newer building, has excellent all-round views. *Oberoi* too, but all at a price. Taj's *Beyond 1900s*. Exclusive disco, expensive drinks (Rs 330 entry). **Central Mumbai** Ambassador's (Churchgate) *Flavors*. Bright 24-hr coffee shop-resto-bar. Chic, interesting cocktails and starters (PSP prawns, Corn and spinach toast), barbecue buffet lunch (Rs 300-800), happy hour (1800-2000), try

Eating:
Gateway of
India & Colaba
● *on maps*

Expensive

Mumbai

Graveyard (huge) or Flavothon (a shooter race), big screen, DJ (weekends). Fun at a price. *Fire & Ice*, Bowling Co Complex, Phoenix Mills, Lower Parel, T4980444. Disco, night club. The hottest spot in town, latest music, fabulous system, great décor, exotic cocktails and snacks, Rs 400 min; *Silly Point*, there is a casual sports bar, restaurant. A fun place, with unusual cocktails, fusion cuisine, buffets. *Not Just Jazz by the Bay*, 143 Marine Drive, T2851876. Modern chrome and glass, live music (varied), good food menu (great starters, desserts), generous portions, very lively.

Mid-range **Central Mumbai** *Café Olé*, Ground Floor, Cross Roads, Haji Ali, T4955123. Classic sports bar, chrome and glass, interesting menu (some Indianized), try Cactus Passion or Red Ginger (non-al), mini dance floor, DJ at weekends, fun place, affordable drinks. *Copa Cabana*, Dariya Vihar, 39/D Girgaum, Chowpatty, T3680274. Small, playing 70s hits and Latino music, packed at weekends so little space for dancing. *Ghetto*, B Desai Rd (100 m from Mahalakshmi Temple). Western pop from 60s, 70s, 80s, free entry (couples only), neon graffiti. *Geoffreys*, Hotel Marine Plaza, Marine Drive, T2851212. Soft music, relaxing for a drink and a bite, no dancing. **Juhu** *Paparazzi*, opposite Juhu Bus Depot, Juhu Beach Rd, T6602199. Small, cosy disco bar, packed after 2300, drinks and snacks. Closed Mon. *Razzberry Rhinoceros* Juhu Tara Rd, T6184012. Disco, night club. Lots of space for dancing, pool tables, check for live acts.

Cheap Popular bars behind *Taj Mahal Hotel* include *Gokul*.

Entertainment

Art galleries Usually open 1000-1900: Galleries in *Taj Mahal* and *Centaur* hotels. *Aakar* and *Cymroza*, B Desai Rd, T3671983. *JJ School of Art* Dr DN Rd. *Piramal*, NCPA, Nariman Pt. *Pundole*, Hutatma Chowk, T2841837. Several near Kemp's Corner including *Sakshi*, 33 Altmount Rd, run by Synergy Art Foundation.

Sports Swimming: Some hotel pools are open to non-residents. *Breech Candy Club* B Desai Rd, T3612543, for the select set, 2 clean pools including a large one; non-members Rs 250.

Western India has a **Cinema** English language films are shown at *Eros* opposite Churchgate station.
strong creative tradition *Regal*, Colaba and others west of CST station.

Festivals

In addition to the national Hindu and Muslim festivals there are:
    Jan: 1st weekend. *Banganga Classical Music Festival* at Walkeshwar Temple. Magical atmosphere around temple tank with fine musicians taking part; tickets Rs 50-150 (much in demand). **Feb**: *Elephanta Cultural Festival* at the caves. Great ambience. Contact MTDC, T2026713, for tickets Rs 150-200 including launch at 1800. *Kala Ghoda Arts Festival* New annual showcase of all forms of fine arts. T2842520; also weekend fest, mid-Dec to mid-Jan includes food and handicrafts at Rampart Row, Fort. **Mar**: *Jamshed Navroz*, this is New Year's Day for the Parsi followers of the Fasli calendar. The celebrations which include offering prayers at temples, exchanging greetings, alms-giving and feasting at home, date back to Jamshed, the legendary King of Persia. **Jul-Aug**: *Janmashtami*, celebrates the birth of Lord Krishna. Boys and young men form human pyramids and break pots of curd hung up high between buildings. **Aug**: *Coconut Day*, the angry monsoon seas are propitiated by devotees throwing coconuts into the ocean. **Aug-Sep**: *Ganesh Chaturthi* Massive figures of Ganesh are worshipped and immersed in the sea on several days following the festival. **Sep**: *Mount Mary's Feast*, celebrated at St Mary's Church, Bandra. A fair is also held. **Sep-Oct**: *Dasara*, during this nationwide festival, in Mumbai there are group dances by Gujarati women in

all the auditoria. There are also Ramlila celebrations at Chowpatty Beach. *Diwali* (The Festival of Lights) is particularly popular in mercantile Mumbai when the business community celebrate their New Year and open new account books. **25 Dec**: *Christmas*, Christians across Mumbai celebrate the birth of Christ. A pontifical High Mass is held at midnight in the open air at the Cooperage Grounds.

Shopping

Most shops are open 1000-1900 (closed Sun), the bazars sometimes staying open as late as 2100. Mumbai prices are often higher than in other Indian cities and hotel arcades tend to be very pricey but carry good quality select items. Best buys are textiles, particularly tie-and-dye from Gujarat, hand-block printed cottons, Aurangabad and 'Patola' silks, gold bordered saris from Surat and Khambat, handicrafts, jewellery and leather goods. *Crossroads & Pyramid*, Haji Ali, is a shopping centre.

Bazaars: *Crawford Market*, MR Ambedkar Rd (fun for bargain hunting). For a different experience try *Chor (Thieves') Bazaar*, on Maulana Shaukat Ali Rd in central Mumbai, full of finds – from Raj left-overs to precious jewellery. Some claim that the infamous name is unjustified since the original was 'Shor' (noisy) bazaar! On Fri, 'junk' carts sell less expensive 'antiques' and fakes.

Books: *Crossword*, 22 B Desai Rd (near Mahalakshmi Temple), smart, spacious, good selection; *Danai*, 14th Khar Danda Rd is good for books and music; *Nalanda*, *Taj Mahal Hotel*, excellent art books; *Oberoi* bookshop charges higher prices. **Strand Books**, off Sir PM Rd near HMV, T2061994, excellent selection, best deals, shipping (reliable), 20% discount on air freight. **Antiquarian** books and prints: *Jimmy Ollia*, Cumballa Chambers (1st Flr), Cumballa Hill Rd.

Clothes: B Desai Rd, Dr DN Rd, Colaba Causeway shops starting near the *Taj Mahal Hotel*. Cheapest at **Fashion St** opposite Mumbai Gymkhana, South Bhagat Singh Marg, but check quality (often export surplus) and bargain vigorously.

Crafts and textiles: Govt emporia from many states sell good handicrafts and textiles; several at *World Trade Centre*, Cuffe Parade. *Cottage Industries Emporium*, Apollo Bunder. Represents a nationwide selection, especially Kashmiri embroidery, South Indian handicrafts and Rajasthani textiles. New shop at Colaba Causeway, next to BEST, with additional fabrics, ethnic ware, handicrafts. *Khadi and Village Industries*, 286 Dr DN Rd. *Anokhi*, 4B August Kranti Marg, opposite Kumbala Hill Hospital. Good gifts. **Music**: *Groove*, West Wing, 1st Flr, Eros Cinema, Churchgate. Has café. *Hiro*, SP Mehta St. Good Indian classical CDs. *Planet M*, opposite CST station. Also has book/poetry readings, gigs. *Rhythm House*, north of Jehangir Gallery. **Photography**: *Central Camera* near CST station, opp McDonald's. *Camera Care* 225 Commissariat Bldg, next to Handloom House, Dr DN Rd (Olympus); also *Mazda* at 231 (Hasselblad, Metz, Nikon) offers free pick up/delivery, T3004001. *Remedios*, opp Khadi Bhandar, between CST and Flora Fountain, reliable repairs.

Transport: local

Not available in central Mumbai (south of Mahim). Metered; about Rs 7.50 per km, **Auto-rickshaw** revised tariff card held by the driver (x5, in suburbs) 25% extra at night. **Victorias** (horse-drawn carriages), available at Mumbai Central, Chowpatty and Gateway of India. Rates negotiable.

Red BEST (Bombay Electrical Supply Co) buses are available in most parts of Greater **Bus** Mumbai, T4128725. Within the Central Business Dist, buses are marked 'CBD'.

Transport: long distance

Air

There can be long queues at immigration

Sahar International airport, T6329090, 8366700. Left Luggage counter, across the drive from end of Departure terminal, Rs 35 per item. Reports of items left long term being "lost". International Departure Tax, Rs 300 (Rs 150 within South Asia).

Domestic terminals (Santa Cruz) The **new** domestic terminal, exclusively for *Indian Airlines*, is about 400 m from the **old** terminal, used by others. Enquiries: T140, 143; *Indian Airlines*, T8156850, recorded T6114433.

Dispatchers at the airport claim that each taxi can take only 3 passengers. Stand firm as this law is totally disregarded elsewhere

Transport to and from the airport Pre-paid taxis into town, from counter at the exit at the **Sahar** International terminal (ignore taxi touts near the baggage hall). Give the exact area or hotel, and the number of pieces of luggage. Hand the receipt to the driver at the end of the journey. To Nariman Pt or Gateway, about Rs 260, 1 hr. During 'rush hour' it can take 2 hrs. Late at night, taxis take about ½ hr – hair-raising! To Juhu Beach Rs 150. From **Santa Cruz**: metered taxis should charge around the same. **Buses** The red BEST buses connect both terminals with the city. No buses at present to New Mumbai.

Domestic *Indian Airlines*: Air India Building, Nariman Pt, T2876161, to all major cities. *Air India*: flies to **Chennai**; **Hyderabad**; **Thiruvananthapuram**. *Jet Airways*: B1 Amarchand Mansions, Madam Cama Rd, T2855788, airport, T6156666, www.jetairways.com to 39 destinations. *Sahara*: T2882718, airport T6134159: **Goa**.

It is often difficult to get reasonable **accommodation** in Mumbai, particularly late in the evening. Touts are very pushy at both terminals but the hotels they recommend are often appalling. It is worth making your own telephone call to hotels of your choice from the airport. The rest rooms in the old domestic terminal are clean, comfortable (rooms Rs 500, dorm Rs 200); available for those flying within 24 hrs, but are often full; apply to the Airport Manager.

Bus

Maharashtra RTC operates bus services to all the major centres and Dist HQs in the state as well as to Bangalore, Goa, Mangalore and Hyderabad in other states. Information on services from MSRTC, Central Bus Stand, Mumbai Central, T3076622, or Parel Depot, T4374399. Private buses also travel long distance routes. Some long distance buses also leave from Dadar where there are many travel agents. Information and tickets from Dadar Tourist Centre, just outside Dadar station, T4113398.

Car hire

8 hrs or 80 km: Luxury cars, a/c Rs 1,500; Maruti/Ambassador: a/c Rs 1,000, non a/c Rs 800. *Auto Hirers*, 7 Commerce Centre, Tardeo, T4942006; *Blaze*, Colaba, T2020073; *Budget*, T4942644, and *Sai*, Phoenix Mill Compound, Senapati Bapat Marg, Lower Parel, T4942644, F4937524, recommended. *Wheels*, T2822874. Holiday **caravans** with driver, T2024627.

Taxi

Metered yellow-top and a/c blue: easily available. Rs 12 for first km and Rs 12 for each Re 1 on metre. Taxis called by hotel doormen often arrive with meter registering Rs 12. Always get a prepaid taxi at the airport.

Train

Times for trains & planes are published each Sat in the Indian Express newspaper

Suburban electric trains are economical. They start from Churchgate for the west suburbs and CST (VT) for the east suburbs but are often desperately crowded (stay near the door or you may miss your stop!); there are 'Ladies' cars. Trains leaving Mumbai Central often have seats at the terminus but soon fill up. **NB** Avoid peak hours (southbound 0700-1100, northbound 1700-2000), and keep a tight hold on valuables. The difference between 1st and 2nd class is not always obvious although 1st class is 10 times as expensive. Inspectors fine people for travelling in the wrong class.

Mumbai is the HQ of the Central and Western Railways. Central Rly, enquiries, T134/135. **Reservations**: T2659512, 0800-1230, 1300-1630 (Foreigners' Counter opens 0900; best time to go); Western Rly, Churchgate, and Mumbai Central, 0800-1345, 1445-2000. All for 1st Class bookings and Indrail Passes. **Foreign tourists**: Tourist Quota counter on mezzanine floor above tourist office opposite Churchgate Station. Otherwise, queue downstairs at Reservations. Railway Tourist Guides at CST and Churchgate (Bus 138 goes between the two). **NB** For all trains, book as early as possible; sometimes sleeper reservations are possible for same-day travel. CST has TV screens showing availability of seats 3 days in advance. **Indrail Pass holders: confirm return reservations in Mumbai.**

To book trains foreign tourists must have either foreign currency or an encashment certificate

Bangalore: *Udyan Exp 6529*, 0755, 24¼ hrs. **Chennai Central**: *Mumbai-Chennai Mail 6009*, 2320, 30½ hrs; *Dadar-Chennai-Chennai Exp* (from Dadar) *6063*, 1950, 24¼ hrs. **Goa (Margao)** *Madgaon Exp, 0111*, from VT (CST) dep 2240, 11¾ hrs but often 14 hrs (avoid berths 5 and 6); dep Dadar 2255, 10½ hrs, 2 tier a/c Rs 950, 3 tier a/c Rs 512; Return dep Margao 1825; *Netravati Exp* from Kurla: *6635*, 1640, 11¼ hrs (arr 0305 but often late); to get there, suburban trains leave CST every few minutes from platforms 1 and 2 and take 20-30 mins. The Kurla terminus is a 10-minute walk from the suburban line station. **Guntakal**: (for Hospet/Hampi) *Mumbai Chennai Exp 6571*, 1425, 17 hrs. **Kochi**: *Netravati Exp* (from **Kurla** via Konkan) *6635*, 1640, 26¾ hrs. **Secunderabad/Hyderabad**: *Mumbai Hyderabad Exp, 7031*, 2155, 14¼ hrs; *Hussainsagar Exp, 7001*, 2155, 15 hrs. **Thiruvananthapuram**: *Kanniyakumari Exp 1081*, 1535, 44½ hrs.

Directory

Domestic: see 'Transport' above. **International**: *Air India*, 1st Flr, Nariman Pt (Counters also at Taj Mahal Hotel, Centaur Hotel and Santa Cruz), T2024142, Airport T8366767. *Aeroflot*, 241-2, Nirmal Bldg, Nariman Pt. *Alitalia*, Industrial Assur Bldg, Vir Nariman Rd, Churchgate, T2818854, airport T8379657. *Air Canada*, Amarchand Mansions, Madam Cama Rd, T2027632, Airport T6045653. *Air France*, Maker Chamber VI, Nariman Pt, T2029127, Airport T8328070. *Sri Lanka*, Raheja Centre, Nariman Pt, T2833864, Airport T8327050. *Air Mauritius*, Air India Bldg, Nariman Pt, T2811216, Airport T8227123. *Bangladesh Biman*, 199 J Tata Rd, Churchgate, T2824659. *British Airways*, 202-B Vir Nariman Rd, T2820888, weekdays, 0800-1300, 1345-1800. Sat, 0900-1300, airport T8329061. *Canadian Pacific*, Taj Intercontinental, T2029561, airport T8366205. *Continental, Eastern, Iberia* and *MAS*, STIC, Raheja Centre, Nariman Pt, T2846452; also at Raheja Centre, *Japan*, T2874940 *Delta*, Taj Mahal Hotel, T2885660, airport T8349890. *Egypt Air*, 7 J Tata Rd, T2824088. *Emirates*, Mittal Chamber, Nariman Pt, T2871649. *Gulf Air*, Maker Chambers, 5 Nariman Pt, T2021777. *KLM*, 198 J Tata Rd, T2833338. *Kuwait*, 2A Stadium House, 86 Veer Nariman Rd, Churchgate, T2045351, 2047464. *Lufthansa*, Express Towers, Nariman Pt, T2020887. *PIA*, 7 Stadium House, Vir Nariman Rd, T2021373. *Qantas*, 42 Sakhar Bhavan, Nariman Pt, T2020343. *Royal Jordanian*, 199 J Tata Rd, T2824580. *Sabena*, Nirmal Building, Nariman Pt, T2023284. *Saudia*, Express Tower, Nariman Pt, T2020199. *SAS*, 10 Podar House, Marine Dr, T2027083. *Singapore Airlines*, Taj Intercontinental, T2022747. *Swissair*, Maker Chamber VI, 220 Nariman Pt, T2872210. *Thai Airways*, 15 World Trade Centre, Cuffe Parade, T2154597.

Airline offices

Mumbai

Most are open 1000-1400, Mon-Fri, 1000-1200, Sat. Closed on Sun, holidays, 30 Jun, 31 Dec. Best to change money at the airport, at Bureau de Change (upstairs) in Air India Building, Nariman Pt or at *Thomas Cook*, 324 Dr DN Rd, T2048556; also at 102B Maker Tower, 10th Flr, F Block, Cuffe Parade; TCI, Chander Mukhi, Nariman Pt; A/2 Silver Arch, JB Nagar, Andheri; Chembur, Corporate Park Unit No 8, Sion-Trombay Rd; and at International Airport. *ATMs* for VISA card holders using their usual PIN have opened at *British Bank of the Middle East* BBME (16 Vir Nariman Rd); *Citibank* (Air India Building, Nariman Pt, 293 Dr DN Rd); *Hongkong Bank* (52/60 MG Rd, Fort); *Standard Chartered* (81 Ismaili Building, Dr DN Rd, 264 Annie Besant Rd). Also available at other branches across the city. *State Bank of India*, Bombay Samachar Marg (at *Centaur Airport Hotel* until 2200) and Churchgate, behind India Tourist Office, among others. Other foreign and Indian banks have several branches. **Credit Cards**: *American Express*, Lawrence & Mayo Bldg, Dr DN Rd; *Diners Club*,

Banks

Raheja Chambers, 213 Nariman Pt; *Mastercard*, C Wing, Mittal Tower, Nariman Pt; *VISA*, ANZ Grindlays Bank, 90 MG Rd.

Commun-ications   Usually open 1000-1700. Sahar Airport 24 hrs. Post offices all over the city and most 5 star hotels. **GPO:** Nagar Chowk. Mon-Sat, 0900-2000 (*Poste Restante* facilities 0900-1800) and Sun 1000-1730; parcels from 1st Flr, rear of building, 1000-1700 (Mon-Sat); cheap 'parcelling' service on pavement outside. **Central telegraph office:** Hutatma Chowk, Churchgate PO, 'A' Rd. Colaba PO, Colaba Bus Station and also at Mandlik Rd, behind *Taj Mahal Hotel*. Foreign PO, Ballard Pier. Counter at Santa Cruz. **Couriers:** *EMS Speedpost*, GPO, T2621671; *DHL*, Calicut St, Ballard Estate, T2659773; *Skypak*, Jolly Bhavan II, New Marine Lines, T2624746. **Internet:** *British Council*, 'A Wing' 1st Flr, Mittal Tower, Nariman Pt, T2823560, 1000-1745, Tue-Sat. Internet and email services (from Rs 20 per day), excellent library. *Cybercafé*, Waterfield, Bandra. *Infotek* Express Towers, ground floor, Nariman Pt, *Cyber café* with 12 machines, phone, fax etc. *Food Inn Café*, Colaba, 1 machine.

Embassies & consulates   *Australia*, Maker Tower East, 16th Flr, Cuffe Parade, T2181071. *Austria*, Maker Chambers VI, Nariman Pt, T2851066. *France*, Datta Prasad, NG Cross Rd, T4950918. *Germany*, 10th Flr, Hoechst House, Nariman Pt, T2832422. *Indonesia*, 19 Altamount Rd, T3868678. *Israel*, 50 Deshmukh Marg, Kailas, T3862794. *Italy*, Kanchenjunga, 72G Deshmukh Marg, T3804071. *Japan*, 1 ML Dahanukar Marg, T4934310. *Malaysia*, Rahimtoola House, Homji St, T2660056. *Netherlands*, 1 Marine Lines Cross Rd, Churchgate, T2016750. *Philippines*, Sekhar Bhavan, Nariman Pt, T2814103. *Russia*, Nirmal Bldg, Nariman Pt, T2856648. *Spain*, 6 K Dubash Marg, T2874797. *Sri Lanka*, 34 Homi Modi St, T2045861. *Sweden*, 85 Sayani Rd, Prabhadevi, T4212681. *Switzerland*, 102 Maker Chamber IV, 10th Flr, Nariman Pt, T2884564. *Thailand* 43 B Desai Rd, T3631404. *UK*, Maker Chamber IV, Nariman Pt, T2830517. *USA*, Lincoln House, B Desai Rd, T3685483.

Hospitals & medical services   The larger hotels usually have a house doctor, the others invariably have a doctor on call. Ask hotel staff for prompt action. The telephone directory lists hospitals and General Practitioners. *Prince Aly Khan Hospital*, Nesbit Rd near the harbour, T3754343, is recommended. **Chemists:** several open day/night especially opposite Bombay Hospital. *Wordell*, Stadium House, Churchgate; *New Royal Chemist*, New Marine Lines; *Karnik's*, opposite RN Cooper Hospital, Gulmohar Rd.

Shipping offices   *Damania Shipping*, T3743737, F3743740, catamarans suspended since early 1999; *Shipping Corp of India*, Madame Cama Rd, T2026666.

Tour companies & travel agents   Some well established agents: *American Express*, Regal Cinema Building, Colaba, T2046361. *Cox and Kings*, 270-271 Dr DN Rd, T2070314. *Everett*, 1 Regent Chambers, Nariman Pt, T2845339. *Mercury*, 70VB Gandhi Rd, T2024785. *Odati Adventures*, 17/8 Manish Nagar, 4 Bungalows, JP Rd, Andleri (west), T6353861, odati@vsnl.com Unique outdoor activity in the western Ghats; treks, jeep safaris, cycling, rock climbing, waterfall rappelling; 2-10 days. *Sita*, 18 Atlanta, Nariman Pt, T2840666, F2044927. *Thomas Cook*, Cooks Building, Dr DN Rd, T2813454. *Trade Wings*, 30 K Dubash Marg, T2844334. *Space Travels*, 4th Flr, Sir PM Rd, T2864773, for discounted flights and special student offers, Mon-Fri, 1000-1700, Sat 1030-1500. *TCI*, Chandermukhi, Nariman Pt, T2021881. *Venture*, Ground Floor, Abubakar Mansion, South Bhagat Singh Marg, T2021304, F2822803, efficient, helpful and friendly.

Tourist offices   *Govt of India*, 123 M Karve Rd, opposite Churchgate, T2033144, 2032932, F2014496, Mon-Sat 0830-1730 (closed 2nd Sat of month from 1230). Counters open 24 hrs at both airports, and at *Taj Mahal Hotel*, Mon-Sat 0830-1530 (closed 2nd Sat from 1230). Helpful staff who can also issue Liquor Permits; printouts given from computer database of many destinations. *Maharashtra*: CDO Hutments, opposite LIC Building, Madam Cama Rd; Express Towers, 9th Flr, Nariman Pt, T2024482; Information and Booking counters at international and domestic terminals. Also at Koh-i-Noor Rd, near *Pritam Hotel*, Dadar T4143200; CST Rly Station, T2622859. *Goa*, Mumbai Central Station, T3086288.

Useful addresses   **Police Emergency:** T100. **Fire:** T101. **Ambulance:** T102. **Foreigners' Regional Registration Office:** Annex 2, Police Commissioner's Office, Dr DN Rd, near Phule Market, T268111. **Passport Emigration Office:** T4931731.

Goa

Goa

Geographically Goa might look like a South Indian state. Lying well to the south of Hyderabad, for example, it seems to tuck into the south Indian coastline of Karnataka. Yet in many respects it is quite different. Its dominant languages, Marathi and Konkani, are part of the north Indian family of languages, quite unrelated to the Dravidian languages of the four southern states. Its Portuguese history further isolated it from contacts to the south or inland, and the major Indian cultural influences have come from its north. Yet it is today on one of the major routes from Mumbai to the south, the Konkan railway, which has brought Goa to within an eleven hour train journey of Mumbai itself, and yet only the same time again from the borders of Kerala. Thus it makes at attractive stopping point on the way south if you take a flight into Mumbai with the added advantage that it has the best watersports opportunities on mainland India.

Goa

★ ***A foot in the door***

*Stay at the tiny **Tiracol fort**, with its commanding view of the sweeping bays of North Goa*

*See the tomb of St **Francis Xavier** in the Church of Bom Jesus and the other great churches of Old Goa*

*See spices growing in the **Savoi Spice Plantation** and find out how cashew nuts are processed nearby*

*Capture a flavour of life under the Portuguese at a mansion in **Loutolim**, but also discover the indigenous way of life at Ancestral Goa*

*Visit the 18th-century **Shantadurga temple** at Queula, in the unique style of the New Conquests Hindu architecture*

*Relax at the unspoilt southern end of **Palolem** beach*

Background

The land

Population: 1.3 mn
Area: 3,800 sq km

See the Footprint
'Goa Handbook' for
a much fuller
description
of the state

By Indian standards Goa is a tiny state. The coastline on which much of its fame depends is only 97 km long. The north and south of the state are separated by the broad estuaries of the Zuari and Mandovi rivers. Joined at high tide to create an island on which Panaji stands, these short rivers emerge from the high ranges of the Western Ghats less than 50 km from the coast and then glide almost imperceptibly to the sea. Alfonso de Albuquerque grasped the advantages of this island site, large enough to give a secure food-producing base but with a defensible moat, at the same time well placed with respect to the important northwestern sector of the Arabian Sea.

The rich lowland soils have a high mineral content, patches of almost sterile red laterite forming upland areas between the lower lying fertile deltas. Huge reserves of manganese and iron ore have been discovered and mined. While the income derived from this has helped to boost Goa's foreign exchange, it often scars the landscape of the interior and has had a detrimental effect on neighbouring agriculture.

Climate Throughout the year Goa is warm, but its position on the coast means that it never suffers unbearable heat. However, from mid-April until the beginning of the monsoon in mid-June, both the temperature and the humidity rise sharply, making the middle of the day steamy hot. The warm clear and dry weather of its tropical winter stretches from October to March, the best time to visit.

The six weeks of the main monsoon in June-July often come as torrential storms accompanied by lashing winds, while up in the cooler air of the Ghats the hilltops can be in swirling cloud and mist. It is a good time of year for the waterfalls!

Flora and fauna Vegetation None of Goa's original vegetation remains untouched. Its lateritic plateaus are now covered in thin scrub, while the low valleys are normally under intensive rice cultivation, coconut trees dominating many of the lowlands. Inland as the hills rise steeply there are still important areas of dense forest.

In the Mandovi-Zuari estuary Goa also has important mangrove forests, with minor forests remaining along the Chapora, Talpona, Galgibag and Terekhol estuaries.

Wildlife In addition to the animal life typical of the Western Ghats and the coastal lowlands, Goa has a wide range of marine birdlife, notably in some of India's few remaining areas of extensive mangrove forest.

Suggested reading The Forest Dept, Panaji, publishes the booklet *Wildlife Protected Areas of Goa*, which gives details of the parks. *Fish Curry and Rice*, a Goan environmentalists' handbook, is recommended.

History

Early Goa Some identify Goa in the *Mahabharata* as Gomant, where **Vishnu**, reincarnated as Parasurama, shot an arrow from the Western Ghats into the Arabian Sea and with the help of the god of the sea reclaimed the beautiful land of Gomant. **Siva** is also supposed to have stayed in Goa on a visit to bless seven great sages who had performed penance for seven million years. In the *Puranas* the small enclave of low-lying land enclosed by the Ghats is referred to as Govapuri, Gove and Gomant. The ancient Hindu City of Goa was built at the southernmost point of the island. The jungle has taken over and virtually nothing survives.

Contact with the Muslim world Arab geographers knew Goa as Sindabur. Ruled by the Kadamba Dynasty from the second century AD to 1312 and by Muslim invaders from 1312 to 1367, it was then annexed by the Hindu Kingdom of **Vijayanagar** and later conquered by the **Bahmani Dynasty** of Bidar in North Karnataka, who founded Old Goa in 1440. It had already become an important centre for the trade in horses with the Vijayanagar Empire. When the Portuguese arrived, Yusuf Adil Shah, the Muslim King of **Bijapur**, was the ruler. At this time Goa was an important starting point for Mecca-bound pilgrims, as well as continuing to be a centre importing Arab horses and a major market on the west coast of India.

The Portuguese The Portuguese were intent on setting up a string of coastal stations to the Far East in order to control the lucrative spice trade. Goa was the first Portuguese possession in Asia and was taken by **Alfonso de Albuquerque** in March 1510, the city surrendering without a struggle. Three months later Yusuf Adil Shah blockaded it with 60,000 men. In November Albuquerque returned with reinforcements, recaptured the city after a bloody struggle, massacred all the Muslims and appointed a Hindu as Governor.

The Portuguese rarely interfered with local customs except for forbidding the burning of widows (*sati*). At first they employed Hindus as officials and troops. Mutual hostility towards Muslims encouraged links between Goa and the Hindu Kingdom of Vijayanagar. Religion only became an issue when missionary activity in India increased. Franciscans, Dominicans and Jesuits arrived, carrying with them both religious zeal and intolerance. The Inquisition was introduced in 1540 and all evidence of earlier Hindu temples and worship was eradicated from the territories of the "Old Conquests".

Goa became the capital of the Portuguese Empire in the east and was granted the same civic privileges as Lisbon. It reached its greatest splendour between 1575 and 1600, the age of 'Golden Goa', but when the Dutch began to control trade in the Indian Ocean it declined. The fall of the Vijayanagar Empire in 1565 caused the lucrative trade between Goa and the Hindu state to dry up. The Dutch blockaded Goa in 1603 and 1639. They weakened but did not succeed in taking it. It was ravaged by an epidemic in 1635, and manpower was so severely depleted that the Portuguese brought criminals from Lisbon's prisons to maintain their numbers.

Distracted by the Mughals in 1683, the Marathas called off their attack on Goa which remained safe in its isolation, though it was threatened again briefly in 1739. The seat of government was shifted first to Margao (Madgaon) and then in 1759 to Panaji, mainly because of outbreaks of cholera. Between 1695 and 1775 the population of Old Goa dwindled from 20,000 to 1,600 and by the mid-19th century only a few priests and nuns remained.

Independence The Portuguese came under increasing pressure in 1948 and 1949 to cede Goa, Daman and Diu to India. In 1955 *satyagrahis* (non-violent demonstrators) attempted to enter Goa. They were deported but later when larger numbers tried, the Portuguese used force to repel them and some were killed. The problem festered until 1961 when the Indian Army, supported by a naval blockade, marched in and brought to an end 450 years of Portuguese rule. Originally Goa became a Union Territory together with the old Portuguese enclaves of Daman and Diu, but on 30 May 1987 it became a full state of the Indian Union.

The people Despite over four centuries of Portuguese dominance, earlier **Culture** characteristics of Goa's population are still obvious. While during the

Goa

Inquisition the Portuguese made systematic efforts to wipe out all social traces of the earlier Hindu and Muslim cultures, many of their features were simply modified to conform to external Catholic demands.

The visitor's first impression of the religion of Goa's people is likely to be highly misleading. To all appearances the drive from the airport to Panaji or south to any of the coastal resorts might appear to confirm that the state is predominantly Christian. Brilliant white painted churches dominate the centre of nearly every village. Yet while in the area of the Old Conquests tens of thousands of people were indeed converted to Christianity, the Zuari River represents a great divide between Christian and predominantly Hindu Goa. Today about 70% of the state's population is Hindu, and there is also a small but significant Muslim minority.

In the past poverty caused large numbers of Goans to emigrate. Many are found in Mumbai, Mozambique, Natal and elsewhere. Most are of part Portuguese descent and bear Portuguese names like de Silva and Fernandes, a result of Portugal's policy of encouraging inter-marriage (to maintain settler populations in climates that exacted a high toll on Europeans). This intermingling has spread to the church – the complexions of the saints and madonnas are those of South Asia.

Language Portuguese was much more widely spoken in Goa than was English in most of the rest of India, but local languages remained important. The two most significant were *Marathi*, the language of the politically dominant majority of the neighbouring state to the north, and *Konkani*, the language commonly spoken on the coastal districts further south. Konkani has been declared Goa's official language by the state government in early 2000. Yet very few government primary schools teach in Konkani compared with over 800 that use Marathi. Hindi is increasingly spoken. English and Hindi are widely understood in the parts visited by travellers and used on road signs, bus destinations and tourism-related notices. In rural areas, however, Konkani predominates.

Cuisine Although Goan food has similarities with that in the rest of India there are many local specialities. The food in this region is hot, making full use of the small bird's-eye chillies that are grown locally. However, the main tourist centres offer a good range including Western and Chinese dishes.

Common ingredients include rice, coconut and cashew (caju) nuts, pork, beef (which is rare in the rest of India) and a wide variety of seafood. Tavernas with bars are common where you can get a good meal for about Rs 100; expect to pay a lot more in a large hotel. They also serve a range of Indian beers, wines and spirits.

Meat dishes Spicy pork or beef *vindalho*, marinated in garlic, vinegar and chillies is very popular (elsewhere in India 'vindaloo' often refers to a hot, spicy curry). Goa's Christians had no qualms about using pork (not eaten by Muslims and most Hindus). *Chourisso* is Goan sausage made of pork pieces stuffed in tripe, boiled or fried with onions and chillies. It is often eaten stuffed into bread. *Sorpotel*, a highly spiced dish of pickled pig's liver and heart, seasoned with vinegar and tamarind, is perhaps the most famous of Goan meat dishes. One recipe suggests that in addition to other spices you should use 20 dry chillies for 1½ kg of pork plus liver and heart, with four green chillies thrown in for good measure! *Xacutti* (pronounced shakuti), is a hot chicken or meat dish prepared with coconut, pepper and star anise. For *Chicken Cafrial*, the meat is marinated in pepper and garlic and braised over a slow fire.

The standard "fish curry and rice", the common Goan meal, has become a catch phrase. Most beach shacks offer a good choice depending on the day's catch and will usually include preparations of kingfish, tuna, mackerel, prawns and often lobster and shark. *Apa de camarao* is a spicy prawn pie and *reichado* is usually a whole fish, cut in half, and served with a hot *masala* sauce. You will find lobsters, baked oysters, boiled clams and stuffed crabs as specialities. *Bangra* is Goa mackerel and *pomfret* a flat fish; fish *balchao* is a preparation of red masala and onions used as a sauce for prawns or kingfish. A less common dish, not least because it is made without coconut, is *Ambot tik*, a sour curry made with shark, squid or ray and eaten with rice, while *seet corri* uses the ubiquitous coconut. *Kishmar* is ground, dried shrimp used as an accompaniment. Spicy pickles and chutneys (lime, mango, brinjal etc) add to the rich variety of flavours (and have made their way to supermarkets in the West together with vindaloo paste).

Bread and sweets Goan bread is good and there are pleasant European style biscuits. *Unde* is a hard crust round bread, while *kankonn*, hard and crispy and shaped like a bangle is often dunked in tea. *Pole* is like chapatti, often stuffed with vegetables, and Goans prepare their own version of the South Indian *idli*, the *sanaan*. The favourite dessert is *bebinca*, a layered coconut and jaggery delicacy made with egg yolks and nutmeg. Other sweets include *dodol*, a mix of jaggery and coconut with rice flour and nuts, *doce*, which looks like the North Indian *barfi*, *mangada*, a mango jam, and *bolinhas*, small round semolina cakes.

Fruit and nuts Apart from the common coconut and banana and the delicious *alfonso* mangos in season, the extremely rich *jackfruit*, papaya, watermelons and cashew nuts are grown in abundance.

Drinks Despite recent price increases, drinks in Goa remain relatively cheap compared to elsewhere in India. The fermented juice of cashew apples is distilled for the local brew *caju feni* (*fen*, froth) which is strong and potent. Coconut or *palm feni* is made from the sap of the coconut palm. *Feni* (bottle, about Rs 25) is an acquired taste; it is often mixed with soda, salt and lime juice. It can also be taken "on the rocks", as a cocktail or pre-flavoured. 'Port', a very sweet red wine sells for Rs 50-60. Dark rum is cheap ('Old Monk', Rs 80).

January: 6th *Feast of the Three Kings*, celebrated in Cansaulim (Cuelim), Chandor and Reis Magos. See page 457.

February/March: The *Carnival* is a non-religious festival celebrated all over Goa. On the first day (*Fat Saturday*), 'King Momo' leads a colourful procession of floats with competing 'teams' dressed in flamboyant costumes as they wind through the towns' main streets. Dances are held in clubs and hotels through the 4 days and traffic comes to a halt on some streets from time to time. *Mahasivaratri* or *Sivaratri* is celebrated with feasting and fairs at Siva temples, for example Mangesh, Nagesh, Queula and Shiroda.

March: *Shigmotsav* Similar to *Holi*, at full moon, particularly in Panaji, Mapusa, Vasco da Gama and Margao, is accompanied with plenty of music on drums and cymbals. *Procession of all Saints* in Goa Velha, on the Monday of Holy Week.

April: *Feast of Our Lady of Miracles*, Mapusa, on the nearest Sunday, 16 days after Easter. See page 461.

May: 30th *Goa Statehood Day*, when all Government offices and many shops are closed.

June: 13th, *Feast of St Anthony*, with songs requesting the gift of rain. *Feast of St John the Baptist* (*Sao Joao*) (24th). See page 492. *Festival of St Peter* (29th), Fort Aguada, with a pageant on a floating raft.

Festivals
In addition to the major Hindu, Christian & Muslim festivals, Goa celebrates its own special ones. Check dates with the tourist office

Goa

August: *Janmashtami* (birth of Lord *Krishna*) marked with mass bathing in the Mandovi River off Divar Island. *Harvest Festival of Novidade* (different dates from 21st to 27th). The first sheaves of rice are offered to the priests, the Governor and Archbishop, and placed in the Cathedral on the 24th. The festival includes a re-enactment of one of the battles between Albuquerque and the Adil Shah on the lawns of the Lieutenant Governor's Palace.

October: *Narkasur* On the eve of Diwali, Goan Hindus remember the victory of Lord Krishna over the demon Narkasur. In Panaji there are processions. *Fama of Menino Jesus* at Colva (16 October 2000).

December: *Feast of St Francis Xavier* (3rd) at Old Goa. *Liberation Day* (17 December) marking the end of Portuguese colonial rule (public holiday). *Food Festival, Christmas* (25 December). Midnight Mass and family get-togethers involving every community.

Modern Goa

Government The Goa Legislative Assembly has 40 elected members while the state elects three members to the Lok Sabha. Although the Congress has been the largest single party, political life is strongly influenced by the regional issue of the relationship with neighbouring Maharashtra, and the debate over the role of Marathi led to the creation of the Maharashtrawada Gomantak Party (MGP) which was in power in the Union Territory of Goa from 1963 until 1979. Regional issues remain important, but there is now also a strong environmental lobby, in which the Catholic Church plays a prominent part. In the Lok Sabha elections of October 1999 the BJP ousted the Congress, capturing both seats, Mr. Joachim Alemao being the first non-Catholic to represent Marmugao constituency in its history. The BJP's victory in the Lok Sabha elections contrasted with the return to power of the Congress in the Legislative Assembly four months earlier, where the Hindu vote split between the MGP and the BJP, allowing the Congress to win a majority under the leadership of Mr. Luizhnio Faleiro, the current Chief Minister.

Health & safety

Health The sun is hot and burning. Time spent on the beach should be limited; a hat, a high factor sun block and a T-shirt for prolonged swimming, are strongly recommended.

Women travellers in Goa (and in major cities and tourist centres), have increasingly reported harassment from local men who follow and touch them. Cases of rape on beaches have been reported at late night parties so it is best to walk in a large group at night.

Police There have been many cases reported of police harassment. If you hire a motorcycle or car, carry your international Driving licence and vehicle hire and insurance documentation. Police have been suspected of planting drugs on likely looking travellers and then arresting them, hoping for substantial bribes for their release. If you are faced with unlawful detention by the police the best policy is to keep calm and patient. Insist on seeing the senior officer and on reporting the matter to the Chief of Police.

Security Rooms in cheap guest houses are often vulnerable. Use a strong padlock when out and close windows at night. A thief may use a long pole with a hook to 'fish' your posessions out. If you choose to party and leave a house unoccupied, thieves may enter from the roof by removing tiles. It is best to leaves all valuables with a non-partying neighbour if you can.

★ Panaji (Panjim)

Occupying a narrow coastal strip between a low laterite hill – the 'Altinho' – and the mouth of the Mandovi River, Panaji, the capital, still has the feel of quite a small town. There are no great buildings or attractions which would make it a draw for a long stay, but it does retain enough character to warrant a visit. There are very pleasant walks over the Altinho and through the old district of Fontainhas.

Phone code: 0832
Colour map 4, grid B1
Population: 85,200
Airport: 29 km

Getting there From Dabolim airport, across Mormugao Bay, you can get a prepaid taxi or a bus. Most rail travellers arriving by Konkan Railway from Mumbai and the north, or from coastal Karnataka and Kerala, get to Margao, southeast of the capital; from there taxis and buses can get you to Panaji (or to your beach resort). Panaji is the main arrival point for long-distance bus travellers. The state Kadamba buses and private coach terminals are in Patto to the east of town. From there it is a 10 min walk across the footbridge over the Ourem Creek to get to guest houses. The catamaran service from Mumbai remains suspended. **Getting around** Auto-rickshaws are the most convenient means for negotiating the city. Motorcycle rickshaws are cheaper but can be more risky.

Ins & outs
See page 448 for further details

Panaji is the official spelling of the capital city replacing the older Portuguese spelling **Panjim**. It is a smallish town, laid out on a grid pattern overlooked by the **Altinho** (hill) to the south which offered defensive advantages. There were three principal cities in Portuguese Goa: **Old Goa** (Velha Goa), **Panjim** (New Goa) and **Margao**. Panjim was originally a suburb of Old Goa and is built on the left bank of the Mandovi Estuary. It contains the archbishop's palace, a modern port, and government buildings and shops set around a number of plazas.

Background

The riverside boulevard (Devanand Bandodkar Marg) runs from the 'new' Patto bridge, past the jetties, to the formerly open fields of the **Campal**. When Panaji depended on boats for communicating with the rest of Goa as well as with the world beyond, this road was the town's busiest highway. Along it are some of the town's main administrative buildings.

Sights

At the east end is the **Idalcao Palace** of the Adil Shahs, once their castle. The Portuguese rebuilt it in 1615 and until 1759 it was the Viceregal Palace. In 1843 it became the Secretariat, and now houses the Passport Office. Next to it is a striking dark statue of the **Abbé Faria** (1756-1819) looming over a prostrate figure of a woman. Abbé José Custodio de Faria, who made a worldwide reputation as an authority on hypnotism, was born near Calangute and grew up under his father's care. At the age of 15 he travelled to Lisbon – a journey that took over nine months, never to return to Goa. He was given a scholarship to study in Rome where he was ordained a priest in 1780 and later completed his doctoral thesis. He published 'On the Causing of Lucid Sleep' and gave public lectures in Paris on curing little-understood conditions such as

Goa

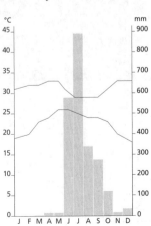

Climate: Panaji
Best time to visit: Dec & Mar

hysteria by the 'magnetizing power' (hypnotism). The character in Dumas' *Count of Monte Christo* may have been based on him.

Further west, almost opposite the wharf are the **library** and public rooms of the **Braganza Institute**. The blue tiled frieze in the entrance, made in 1935, is a 'mythical' representation of the Portuguese colonization of Goa. The tiled panels, about 3 m high, are set against a pale yellow background. They should be read clockwise from the entrance on the left wall. Each picture is set over a verse from the epic poem by the great Portuguese poet Camoes, whose statue stood in front of the Se Cathedral until it was removed by the post-colonial Goa government.

The Institute is also home to the Instituto Vasco da Gama, which was established on 22 November 1871, the anniversary of the date on which Vasco da Gama sailed round the Cape of Good Hope. It was founded to stimulate an interest in culture, science and the arts and has 24 Fellows, who must all be residents of Goa.

Largo da Igreja, the main (Church) square, is south of the Secretariat, dominated by the white-washed **Church of Immaculate Conception** (1541, but subsequently enlarged and rebuilt in 1619), with tall twin towers in the Portuguese Baroque style and modelled on the church at Reis Magos. Its bell, the second largest in Goa, was brought from its original site in the ruined Augustinian monastery in Old Goa.

The domeless **Jama Masjid** (mid-18th century) is near the square. The Hindu **Mahalaxmi Temple** is by the Boca de Vaca (cow's mouth) spring, further up Dr Dada Vaidya Road, on which all these places of worship are situated.

On the eastern promontory, beyond the hill, is the **St Thome** quarter with its traditional 18th and 19th century houses. Across the square is the old **Mint**

Panaji (Panjim)

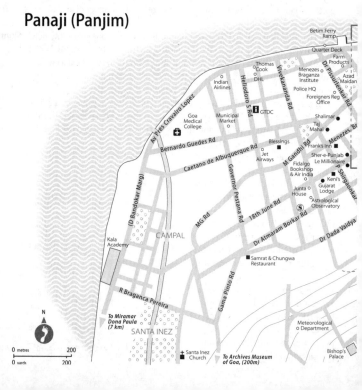

which for many years was used as a telegraph office. **Sebastian Chapel** (1888) retains a quiet charm where old Portuguese houses with their decorative wrought iron balconies have been preserved and is ideal for exploring on foot.

State Archaeological Museum Patto, south of Kadamba Bus Stand, near ADC office. The impressive building contains a disappointingly small collection of religious art and antiquities, both Hindu and Christian, displayed together with sculptures from the Portuguese past. ■ *0930-1300, 1400-1730, Mon-Fri. Free. T226006.* The **Archives Museum**, Ashirwad Building, First floor, Santa Inez. ■ *0930-1300, 1400-1730, Mon-Fri. Free. T226006.* The **Institute Menezes Braganza**. Exhibits include paintings, mainly by European artists of the late 19th and early 20th centuries and Goan artists of the 20th century. There are also sculptures, coins and furniture, the last including a remarkable seven legged rectangular table used for interrogation during the Inquisition. Three legs on one side are carved to represent two lions flanking a central eagle, while the four other legs are carved into the form of human heads. ■ *Mon-Fri 0930-1300, 1400-1745. Dr Pissurlenkar Rd, opposite Azad Maidan.* The **Central Library** here (1832) has a rare collection of religious and other texts.

Museums

Albuquerque's original conquest was of the island of Tiswaldi (now called Ilhas), where Old Goa is situated, plus the neighbouring areas – Bardez (north of the Mandovi), Ponda, Mormugao and Salcete. The coastal provinces formed the heart of the Portuguese territory and are known as the **Old Conquests**. They contain all the important Christian churches. The **New Conquests** cover the remaining peripheral areas which came into Portuguese possession considerably later, either by conquest or treaty. Initially they

Excursions

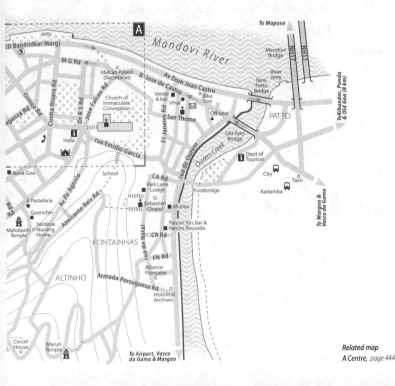

Related map
A Centre, page 444

provided a refuge for not only the peoples driven from the Old Conquest but also their faith. By the time they were absorbed the full intolerant force of the Inquisition had passed. Consequently, the New Conquests did not suffer as much cultural and spiritual devastation. They have a large number of Hindu temples and some mosques.

The Mandovi-Zuari estuary The Mandovi and Zuari estuary is one of the most important mangrove complexes in India, even though today they cover less than 20 hectares. Sea water penetrates a long way inland, especially in the dry season. However, there are approximately 20 species of mangroves, including some rare ones. The species *Kandelia candel* is still common despite being on the verge of extinction elsewhere. The estuary is a spawning ground for crustaceans and molluscs and many species of fish, and is host to huge numbers of migratory birds, especially ducks and shore birds. Jackals, water snakes, bats and marsh crocodiles are common.

Chorao Island and **Dr Salim Ali Bird Sanctuary** which lies opposite Panaji at the confluence of the Mandovi and Mapusa rivers, is now the focus of a range of conservation measures. The bird sanctuary occupies 2 sq km of the west tip of the island along the Mandovi River. The mangrove forests form a protective habitat for coastal fauna and in addition to birds it harbours a large colony of flying foxes, crocodiles, turtles and jackals. Open 1000-1700. Entry Re 1. Best November-February. There is a ferry from Ribandar to Chorao. Local fishermen oblige if asked to take you close to the mangroves; pay no more than Rs 100. Further details from the Wildlife Warden, Forest Dept, Junta House, Panaji.

Carambolim Lake, 12 km east of Panaji between the estuaries of the Mandovi and Zuari, is less than 3 m deep. The lake has been managed for many years, being emptied just before the rains for fishing and refilled through many drains. The water is auctioned every April for its fish although fish numbers have dwindled in recent years. Home to a wide range of varieties of wild

Panaji (Panjim) centre

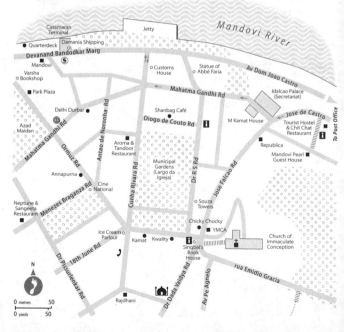

rice, it has remarkably rich concentrations of detoxifying algae, some of which are believed to be responsible for the complete absence of mosquitoes in the area around the lake. The lake has a wide fauna, including 120 species of migratory and local birds, including Siberian pin tail ducks, barbets, woodpeckers, swallows, orioles and drongos.

The **spice plantation** at Savoi Verem offers excellent guided tours illustrating a wide range of spices and other commerically grown fruit and nuts such as pineapples, cashew and areca in a beautiful setting. Details from Goa Tourism, Patto or T340243/340272.

See page 481

Goa Tourism tours can be booked at the *Tourist Hotel*, MG Road, T227103; GTDC, Trianora Apartments, Dr Alvares Costa Road, T226515; Directorate of Tourism, Tourist Home, Patto, T225583; GTDC counters elsewhere including GTDC Tourist Hotels in other towns. The tours which run regularly in season (1 October-16 June) leave from the *Tourist Hotel*, MG Road, T227103. Entrance fees are extra.

Tours

North Goa Tour includes Mapusa, Mayem Lake, beaches Vagator, Anjuna, Calangute, Fort Aguada; **South Goa Tour** includes Old Goa, Loutolim, Margao, Colva, Mormugao, Pilar, Dona Paula, Miramar (with optional river cruise at extra charge); both 0930-1800, Rs 80 (Rs 100, a/c). Similar tours are offered from Margao, Colva, Vasco, Mapusa and Calangute. The **Village Darshan Tour** includes a visit to Savoi Verem spice plantation and Hindu temples at Marcela. 1000-1600, Rs 150 (includes lunch). Two-day **Dudhsagar Special** 1000-1800 (next day) via Old Goa, Bondla Sanctuary, Tambdi Surla. Overnight at Molem. Second Class return train to the Falls the following morning, Rs 350.

River Cruises by launch are organized on the Mandovi River, sometimes with live bands and sing-along entertainment (though no one seems to know the words yet most on board are keen to join in). Evening cruises "corny but pleasant at dusk" are recommended; "all-in-all it's good fun". It is not a "luxury" launch – metal chairs are lined up facing the band and dancers but you are free to wander around on deck. A bar also operates.

The GTDC, Santa Monica Jetty (east of New Patto Bridge): **Sunset Cruise** 1800-1900, Rs 60; **Sundown Cruise** 1915-2015, Rs 60; **Full Moon Pleasure Cruise** (once a month!) 2030-2230, Rs 100 (dinner at extra cost); **Pleasure Cruise** on the Mandovito Aldona includes lunch at a Goan house, 1000-1500, Rs 300.

Essentials

Dabolim airport The new **B** *Hotel Airport*, aimed at business travellers, 28 small but functional a/c rooms, pool. **A-B** *Mandovi*, D Bandodkar Marg, overlooking river, T224405, F225451. 66 large a/c rooms in old hotel, good restaurant, popular pastry shop, pleasant terrace bar, exchange, good bookshop, relaxing but lacks great character. **A-B** *Nova Goa*, T226231, F224958. 118 good a/c rooms with bath, some have fridge and bath tub, cheaper at rear and in annexe occupied by *Golden Goa*, good a/c restaurant and bar, clean, modern, very clean pool, pleasant staff. **B-C** *Park Plaza*, opposite Azad Maidan, T422601, F225635. 37 rooms (power showers!), 28 a/c, a/c bar and restaurant. **C** *Panjim Inn*, E212, 31 Janeiro Rd, Fontainhas, T226523, F228136, panjiminn@goa1.dot.net.in 14 rooms with optional a/c, rooms vary in size and price so inspect first, part in 300-year-old character house kept in traditional style (period furniture, 4-posters), dinner overpriced, but friendly, relaxed.

Sleeping
See Panaji & Panaji Centre maps, pages 442 & 444

Price codes:
See inside front cover

Goa

D *Aroma*, Cunha Rivara Rd, T228310, F224330. Dim public areas, 26 clean rooms some with pleasant outlook, good restaurant, bar. **D** *Manvins*, 4th Floor, Souza Towers, T228305, F223231. 28 good size, clean rooms with excellent views over Municipal Gardens and River Mandovi beyond. Recommended. **D** *Palacio de Goa*, Gama Pinto Rd, T221785, F224155, 18 decent rooms (phone, TV, some 4 or 5-bedded), optional a/c (Rs 150), top floor best for views, restaurant, check-out 0800. **D** *Panjim Pousada*, and opposite it, slightly cheaper sister hotel of *Panjim Inn*. 7 rooms around a permanent gallery in a courtyard, fairly attractive renovation. **D** *Rajdhani*, Dr Atmaram Borkar Rd, T235168. 20 clean rooms with bath, some a/c (Rs 100 extra), in modern Indian business style hotel, good a/c pure vegetarian restaurant (Gujarati, Punjabi, Chinese). **D** *Sona*, Rua de Ourem, near Patto Bridge, T232281, F224425, rajamelvani@hotmail.com 30 clean rooms, some a/c and bath and good views over river. **D-E** *Mayfair and Rohma*, Dr Dada Vaidya Rd, T223317, F230068. Rooms with shower, some a/c with TV, little difference between 'standard' and 'deluxe' (cheaper in *Mayfair* except at Christmas), Goan and Continental restaurant; **D** *Tourist Hotel* (GTDC), near the Secretariat, overlooking the river, T227103. 40 good-size rooms with balcony, some a/c (overpriced at Rs 800), best views from top floor, good open-air restaurant, often full, chaotic reception. **D** *Virashree*, opposite Mahalaxmi Temple, Dr. Dada Vaidya Road, T226656. New (Oct '99), 12 large, comfortable rooms with TV but lacking quality finish (Rs 475). **D-E** *Blessings*, MG Rd, behind Bhatkar House, T224770, F224155, 18 ordinary rooms with TV, two have huge terraces instead of balconies, restaurant, often full.

During high season finding a room can be very difficult especially later in the day

More modest hotels may accommodate a 3rd person in a double room with or without mattress for Rs 50-100

Paying guests: Director of Tourism, T226515 has a list of families

E *Afonso*, near St Sebastian Chapel, Fontainhas, T22239. 8 rooms, pleasant and friendly with bath and hot water in a family-run guest house; **D-E** *Neptune*, Malacca Rd, T224447. 37 very large rooms needing a coat of paint, some **D** a/c, all with bath, friendly but lacks character, good a/c restaurant, good value; **E** *Orav's Guest House*, 31 Janeiro Rd, T426128. 16 pleasant rooms with shower, some with balcony, clean and homely, check-out 0900. Recommended. **E** *Park Lane Lodge*, rua de Natal, near St Sebastian Chapel, Fontainhas, T227154. 8 reasonable rooms (**D** over Christmas), some with bath (Rs 350), clean common shower-room, rambling old house with character "but run by humourless Christian family", verandahs decorated with birdcages and plants in teapots, mediocre food, gates locked at 2230, yet popular with backpackers; **E** *Tourist Home* (GTDC), Patto Bridge, near the Bus Station, T225715. 12 large rooms (3 beds), attached bath, dreary **F** dorm (Rs 50), restaurant. **E-F** *Casa Pinho Lodge*, near St Sebastian Chapel, Fontainhas, simple rooms (Rs 200), dorm, pleasant roof terrace. **F** *Frank's Inn*, 83 Menezes Braganza Rd, T226716. 10 rooms, shared baths, clean; **F** *Venite*, 31 Janeiro Rd, near the Tourist Hostel, T425537. 3 rooms with a common bath in an old colonial house (Rs 100-200), usually full but arrive early as it is worth a try, excellent restaurant (see below). Others nearby (usually rooms belonging to local families), include *Sonia Niwas Guest House*, with 7 rooms with bath.

Eating

Most restaurants here serve some alcohol. Many close between 1500-1900, except for the South Indian & Goan cafés serving snacks

Expensive: *Delhi Darbar*, MG Rd, T222544. Mainly North Indian, traditional Mughlai, varied seafood. A/c, excellent carefully prepared dishes (Rs 80-100 for main), impeccable service (clean toilets), very pleasant, reserve ahead for dinner. *Goenchin*, off Dr Dada Vaidya Rd. Tasty Chinese with spicy seafood (Rs 80-140). *Mandovi*, D Bandodkar Marg. Good seafood and Goan dishes.

Mid-range: *Chungwa*, in *Hotel Samrat*, Dr Dada Vaidya Rd. Authentic dishes (Rs 65-80) cooked by Chinese chef. *Kwality* (Lisbon's) with a bar, Church Square. Chinese and Indian. *Le Millionaire* and bar, Padmavati Towers, 18th June Rd. Good Indian and Chinese. Pleasant atmosphere. *Quarterdeck*, near Betim ferry jetty. Goan. Pleasantly placed on the river bank, live music. *Venite*, 31 Janeiro Rd, near the Tourist Hostel, T225537. Excellent Goan food. Rs 80+ for main dishes, pricier lobsters, heavenly mango juice, arrive early to sit in one of three atmospheric narrow first floor balconies, great ambience, good music, open 0800-2200 (closes in the afternoon and on Sun). Recommended.

Cheap: *Annapurna*, Ormuz Rd. South Indian. Good *thalis* and *dosa* in large, clean eatery upstairs with families relaxing over *chai*. *Goenkar*, MG Rd, near Azad Maidan. Spicy Goan. Good choice of favourites (Rs 35+), popular locally, a/c downstairs, cheaper above. *Kamat*, south of Municipal Gardens. Popular dining hall (a/c upstairs), excellent, *masala dosa* and *thalis* (Rs 30), no alcohol. *Sangeeta*, in *Hotel Neptune*, Malacca Rd. A/c, Rs 40 meals. *Shalimar*, MG Rd. Indian. Wide choice. *Shanbag Café*, opposite Municipal Garden Square, and *Sher-e-Punjab*, 18th June Rd. Generous, spicy, North Indian. *Taj Mahal*, MG Rd, opposite the Press. *Vihar*, R José de Costa. South Indian vegetarian. Well prepared tasty *thalis* and snacks, popular, convenient alternative to *Venite* when it is full.

Bakeries *A Pastelaria*, Dr Dada Vaidya Rd. Good variety of cakes, pastries and breads. *Mandovi Hotel* has a branch too (side entrance). *Simply Delicious* opposite *Hotel Sunrise*, 18th June Road, has appetising cakes and pastries.

Cafés and fast food *Chicky Chocky* near the Church of the Immaculate Conception. Good fast foods.'*Sizzle Point*' for speciality sizzlers. *Eurasia*, Dr Dada Vaidya Rd. Italian. Good pizzas, especially welcome when you are tired of curries.

Bars

There is no dearth of bars in the city. Recommended for rooftop views is *Hotel Mandovi's*, a good place for a chilled beer or wine and for meeting other travellers. *Panjim Inn* is becoming expensive but its large verandah is pleasant. For somewhere more modern and off-beat choose the *Taxi Pub* next to *Hotel Sona*.

Entertainment

A large variety of local drama presentations are performed, many during festivals. *Astronomical Observatory*, 7th Flr, Junta House, 18th June Rd (entrance in Vivekananda Rd) open 14 Nov-31 May, 1900-2100, in clear weather. Rooftop telescope and binoculars, plus enthusiastic volunteers. Worth a visit on a moonless night, and for views over Panaji at sunset. **Sports Soccer** Professional matches are played at the stadium; season Oct-Mar. **Walking**: There are some beautiful walks through the forested areas of Goa. Contact the *Hiking Assoc of Goa*, 6 Anand Niwas, Swami Vivekananda Rd. **Watersports**: for parasailing, windsurfing etc, contact Aqua Sports, Nizari Bhavan, T226960, 2 km from Miramar beach. Some of the bigger beach resorts have windsurfing, sailing, water-skiing, parasailing etc. Diving is possible nearby from *Cidade de Goa*, Vainguinim Beach.

Festivals

In addition to the major festivals: **Feb**: The *Carnival* (three days preceding Lent in Feb/Mar) is somewhat Mediterranean in essence, marked by feasting, colourful processions and floats down streets. **Mar/Apr**: *Feast of Jesus of Nazareth* is celebrated on the first Sun after Easter.**Nov/Dec**: *Food & Culture Festival* at Miramar Beach (see below). **Dec**: *Feast of Our Lady of Immaculate Conception* (8 Dec); a big fair is held.

Shopping
Mapusa & Margao have better Municipal Markets

There are many shops selling cashew nuts and dried fruit. **Books**: *Mandovi Hotel* bookshop has a good range including American news magazines. *Varsha*, near Azad Maidan, carries a wide stock in tiny premises, and is especially good for books on Goa, obscure titles are not displayed but ask knowledgeable staff. **Clothes and textiles**: *Boutiques*, on 18th June Rd. *Government Emporia* and *Khadi Showroom*, Municipal (Communidade) Building, Church Sq, are good value for clothes and fabric. **Handicrafts** include jewellery, particularly malachite set in gold filigree. The bazars are worth browsing through for pottery and copper goods. Some hotel shops have jewellery, rugs and shell carvings. Goa Government handicrafts shops are at the Tourist

Goa

Hotels and the Interstate Terminus. There are other emporia on RS Rd. *Acorn* is near People's School, Patto Footbridge. **Photography**: *Fantasy Studio*, Eldorado. *Souza Paul*, MG Rd. *Central Studio*, Tourist Hostel. *Lisbon Studio*, Church Sq.

Tour operators *Alcon International*, D Bandodkar Marg, T/F232267. Recommended for quick, efficient and friendly flight bookings. *Citizen World Travels*, F/4 Gomes Building, 2nd floor, C Albuquerque Rd, T227087, friendly, helpful, efficient. *Sita*, 101 Rizvi Chambers, 1st floor, C Albuquerque Rd, T221418. *Thomas Cook*, 8 Alcon Chambers, D Bandodkar Marg, 'ferociously efficient' if slightly expensive. *TCI*, "Citicentre", 1st floor, 19 Patto Plaza, T224985.

Transport **Local Auto-rickshaw**: easily available but agree a price beforehand (Rs 15-25). **Motorcycle-taxi**: A bit cheaper. **Tourist taxi**: (white) can be hired from Goa Tourism, Trionora Apts, T223396, about Rs 6 per km. **Private taxi**: charge similar prices. **Share-taxi**: run on certain routes; available near the the ferry wharves, main hotels and market places (maximum 5). **Mapusa** from Panaji, around Rs 10 each.

Bicycle hire: widely available. **Motorcyle hire**: many beach resorts offer these. For tours, contact *Classic Bike Adventure* near New Patto Bridge (see also, Mapusa), T273351, F276124. **Car hire**: *Sai Service* is recommended, 36/1 Alto Porvorim, just north of the Mandovi Bridge; T217065, F217064, or at airport, T514817; at Panaji T223901. They offer a good choice of Maruti cars for self drive, as well as chauffeur driven Marutis and Ambassadors. T217065, F217064. Airport Counter, T514817. *Wheels*, T224304, airport, T512138.

Ferries: flat-bottomed ferries charge a nominal fee to take passengers (and usually vehicles) when rivers are not bridged. *Dona Paula-Mormugao*, fair weather service only, Sep-May, takes 45 mins. Buses meet the ferry on each side. Important ones include: *Panaji-Betim* (the Nehru bridge over the Mandovi supplements the ferry); *Old Goa-Diwar Island*; *Ribandar-Chorao* for Salim Ali Bird Sanctuary; *Siolim-Chopdem* for Arambol and northern beaches; *Keri-Tiracol* for Tiracol fort.

The airport is at Dabolim, see page 483 **Bus**: State Kadamba Transport Corporation (KTC) Luxury and ordinary buses and private buses (often crowded) operate from the Bus Stand in Patto to the east of town, across the Ourem Creek, T222634. Booking 0800-1100, 1400-1630. Tourist Information, 0900-1130, 1330-1700; Sun 0930-1400. The timetable is not strictly kept to as buses often wait until they are full. The minimum fare (for 3 km) is a rupee. Frequent service to **Calangute** direct from Bus Stand 23, 35 mins, Rs 4.50; **Mapusa** 25 mins, Rs 3. Via Cortalim (Zuari bridge) to **Margao** 1 hr, Rs 8; **Vasco** 1 hr, Rs 8. To **Old Goa** (every 10 mins) 25 mins, Rs 2.50, continues to **Ponda** 1 hr, Rs 6.

Long distance Road: NH4A, 17 and 17A pass through Goa. **Mumbai** (582 km), **Bangalore** (570 km), **Mangalore** (371 km), **Pune** (505 km). There are long distance 'Luxury' buses and 'Sleepers', which have separate compartments giving a better chance of some sleep, though bunks are shared. The *Madgaon Express* train is cheaper, quicker and safer than taking the bus. It also allows you to see the lush environment which you cannot on the night bus. **Private operators**: *Laxmi Motors*, near Customs House, T225745; at Cardozo Building, near KTC Bus Stand: *Joy*, G10, T222493, *Paulo*, G1, T223059, *Saraswati*, G11; *Paulo Tours*, Hotel Fidalgo, T226291. **State buses** are run by **Kadamba TC**, **Karnataka RTC**, T225126, 0800-1100, 1400-1700; **Maharashtra RTC**, 0800-1100, 1400-1630. Check times and book in advance at Kadamba Bus Stand. Outside Goa, KTC booking offices: in **Bangalore**: KSRTC Central Bus Stand; **Mumbai**: opposite Azad Maidan, near Cama Hospital; **Pune**: MSRTC, Railway Stand. Buses to **Bangalore**: 1530-1800 (13 hrs), Rs 225; **Belgaum**: 0630-1300 (5 hrs); **Gokarna**; **Hospet**: 0915-1030 (10 hrs), Rs 75; **Hubli** many; **Londa**: 4 hrs on poor road, Rs 50; **Mangalore**: 0615-2030 (10 hrs), Rs 150; **Miraj**: 1030 (10 hrs); **Mumbai**: 1530-1700 (15 hrs), Rs 450 (sleeper), Rs 250; **Mysore**, 1530-1830 (17 hrs), Rs 200; **Pune**: 0615-1900 (12 hrs), Rs 250, Sleeper (Rs 300).

Sea Mumbai: the catamaran service between Panaji and Mumbai remains suspended despite schedules being printed in daily newspapers! The office in Panaji is becoming derelict, while the single catamaran is in a state of disrepair.

Train Rail Bookings, Kadamba Bus Station, 1st floor, T225620, 232169, 0930-1300; 1430-1700. The South Central Railway service on the Vasco-Londa/Belgaum; for details see Transport under Vasco on page 482, and under Madgaon (Margao) below.

Airline offices *Air India*, 18th June Rd, T231101. *British Airways*, 2 Exelsior Chambers, opposite Mangaldeep, MG Rd, T224336. *Indian Airlines & Alliance Air*, Dempo House, D Bandodkar Marg, T224067; *Jet Airways*, Patto, T221472, airport T511005; *Kuwait Airways*, 2 Jesuit House, Dr DR de Souza Rd, Municipal Garden Sq, T224612. *Sahara*, Hotel Fidalgo, 18 June Rd, T230634.

Banks Many private agencies change TCs and cash. *Thomas Cook*, 8 Alcon Chambers, D Bandodkar Marg, T221312. Open 1 Oct-31 Mar, 0930-1800, Mon-Sat, 1000-1700 Sun; Apr-Sept, closed Sun, but open on most Bank Holidays except 16 Jan, 1 May, 15 Aug, 2 Oct. Also good for Thomas Cook drafts; money transfers from any Thomas Cook office in the world within 24 hrs. Recommended. *Wall Street Finance*, MG Rd, opposite Azad Maidan, T225399. *Amex*, at Menezes Air Travel, rua de Ourem, but does not cash TCs. Indian currency against certain credit cards are also given at some banks. *Central Bank*, Nizari Bhavan (against Mastercard); *Andhra Bank*, Dr Atmaram Borkar Rd, opposite EDC House, T223513, accepts Visa, Mastercard, JCB; *Bank of Baroda*, Azad Maidan, accepts Visa and Mastercard, and exchanges up to Rs 5,000 per day. ATM at *HDFC*.

Communications Couriers: *Blue Dart*, T227768. *DHL*, 13, D Bandodkar Marg, T226487. Open 0930-1900, Mon-Sat. *Skypak*, City Business Centre, opposite Jama Masjid, T225199. **GPO:** Old Tobacco Exchange, St Thome, towards Patto Bridge, with Poste Restante on left as you enter. Open Mon-Sat 0930-1730, closed 1300-1400. Many letters are incorrectly pigeon-holed so you can do other travellers a favour by re-sorting any letters you find misplaced. **Telegraph Office:** Dr Atmaram Borkar Rd; also has STD, ISD and trunk services. *Haytechs Communications*, 6 Sujay Apartments, 18th June Rd. **Internet:** *Madhavashram's Cybercafé*, above *Café Real*, MG Rd, T224823, Rs 80 per hr, Rs 2 per min.

Cultural centres *Alliance Française* near Ourem Creek, T223274. *Indo-Portuguese Institute*, E-4 Gharse Towers, opposite Don Bosco School, MG Rd.

High Commissions & consulates *Germany* Hon Consul, c/o Cosme Matias Menezes Group, Rua de Ourem, T223261; *Portugal* 7-B Lake View Colony, Miramar, T224233, F44007; *UK* Agnelo Godinho, House No 189, near the GPO, T226824, F232828.

Medical services *Goa Medical College*, Av PC Lopez, west end of town, T224566, is very busy; also newer College at Bambolim. *CMM Poly Clinic*, Altinho, T225918. *Sardesai Nursing Home*, near Mahalaxmi Temple off Dada Vaidya Rd, T223927, clinic 0800-1330, 1500-1630.

Tourist offices *Government of India*, Municipal Building, Church Sq, T223412. *Goa*, Directorate, Tourist Home, 1st Flr, Patto, T225583, F228819, goatour@goa.goa.nic.in; tours can be booked here but not GTDC accommodation; also Information desk at the Tourist Hostel, T227103, which is chaotic. There are counters at the Kadamba Bus Station, T225620 and Dabolim airport (near Vasco), T512644. Goa Tourism Development Corporation (GTDC), Trionora Apartments, Dr Alvares Costa Rd, T226515, F223926, gtdc@goacom.com, for GTDC accommodation. *Andhra Pradesh*, near *Hotel Sona*; *Karnataka*, Velho Filhos Building, Municipal Garden Sq, T224110. *Kerala*, T232168. *Maharashtra*, near Mahalaxmi Temple. *Tamil Nadu*, Rayu Chambers, Dr AB Rd. **Guides:** for 4 persons, about Rs 250 per 4 hrs, Rs 350 per 8 hrs; excursion allowance Rs 250, overnight, Rs 800, foreign language supplement, Rs 100.

Useful services Ambulance: T223026, T224601. **Fire:** T101, T225500. **Police:** T100; **Tourist Police:** T224757. **Foreigners' Regional Registration Office:** Police Headquarters. **Wildlife:** Chief Wildlife Warden, Conservator's Office, Junta House, 3rd floor, 18th June Rd, T224747, and Deputy Conservator of Forests (Wildlife), 4th floor, T229701, for permits and accommodation in the sanctuaries. **World Wildlife Fund**, Ground Floor, Block B-2, Hillside Apartments, Fontainhas (off 31 January St), T226020, will advise on trekking with a guide in the sanctuaries.

Beaches near Panaji

Miramar
Phone code: 0832

Panaji's seafront boulevard runs south for 3 km along the Mandovi estuary. Miramar is very 'urban' in character, the water is polluted and the beach is not particularly attractive, so it is not an ideal place for a beach holiday. It is however a pleasant drive offering good views over the sea. Most of the hotels are on, or just off, the D Bandodkar Marg (DB Marg), the road to Dona Paula along the coast.

Sleeping C *Blue Bay*, on Caranzalem Beach, T228087, F229735. 12 neat, modern rooms, some a/c, reasonable garden restaurant. **D** *Miramar Beach Resort*, close to the beach, T227754. 60 clean rooms, some a/c, better (and cheaper) rooms in newer wing by shaded groves, good restaurant, best of the GTDC hotels despite chaotic reception. **D-E** *Bela Goa*, T224575, F224155, 11 simple rooms in an uninspiring building, surprisingly light and airy though no balcony, 2 a/c (Rs 900), restaurant, bar, enthusiastic staff. **D** *London Hotel*, T226017. 20 rooms, some a/c better upstairs though not brilliantly maintained, restaurant, bar (pool tables draw large crowds at weekends), roof garden. **F** *Youth Hostel* away from the beach, T225433. 3 rooms (Rs 50 per person), 5 dorms (separate men's and ladies', vacated during the day), maximum 3 nights, YHA members Rs 20, also non-members except in Dec and Jan Rs 40, canteen, 1 day's payment for advance reservation (not always necessary).

Eating Mid-range: *Beach Boogie*, Caranzalem Beach, towards Miramar bus stand. Garden restaurant, varied menu, live music. *Foodland*, Miramar Beach Resort. Good fast food. *Quarterdeck*, near Goa International. Try their South Indian fast food.

Dona Paula

Dona Paula has a small palm fringed beach with casuarina groves and is very peaceful. Fisherfolk turned local vendors sell cheap "seaside goods" testifying to its role as a popular Indian picnic spot.

It is named after a Viceroy's daughter who reputedly jumped from the cliffs when refused permission to marry a fisherman, Gaspar Dias. The low laterite cliff forms a headland joined to the mainland by a short causeway. A ferry crosses over to Vasco.

From the roundabout by the National Oceanography Institute a road runs 600 m up to **Cabo Raj Niwas**, now Raj Bhavan, the State Governor's House. A viewing platform near the entrance gives superb views over the sweep of the coastline across the Mandovi estuary to Fort Aguada.

Watersports at the jetty are restricted to a few mins' ride in a motor boat or on a water scooter. Rs 40. 0900-1830. Popular with domestic visitors but looks hazardous.

Transport Regular **buses** from Panaji to Miramar continue to Dona Paula, Rs 5. A passenger **ferry** which normally crosses over to Vasco (Mormugao) across the bay, was suspended in early 2000.

Directory Hospital: T223026. **Police:** T224488.

Goa

A drop in the ocean

The watersport industry is still a fledgling enterprise and although agents offer a number of options within easy reach of the major resorts, the easiest to arrange are a choice of boat trips.

Popular trips to view **dolphins** are available from most areas, costing between Rs 200-500. John, of John's Boat Trips in Candolim, T277780 (ticket agents at Bom Sucesso and Alma Inn), is a knowledgeable and friendly host with a good understanding of the dolphins. He charges Rs 500, with guaranteed sighting of usually two species, the bottle-nosed and the hump-backed dolphins. The trip includes the option to have a swim near the Aguada prison, plus lunch at a typical Portuguese house on Coco Beach. Other 'Dolphin Watch' trips are reported to just chase the dolphins and return. John also provides fishing trips, snorkelling, boats to the Anjuna Flea Market and a **crocodile spotting** trip, Rs 950. Although there is no guarantee of seeing crocodiles it is still a very pleasant full day excursion. Other agents offer similar trips at varying prices as well as trips to 'Paradise Beach', that is Palolem.

Watersport facilities on the beaches are rare and at present are limited to isolated westerners at various locations with no guarantee that they will be there next year (eg European with the jet ski at Candolim). Splash at Bogmalo seem to be more stable, and parasailing is sometimes available from Candolim and Colva beaches although it is highly erratic. Expect to pay at least Rs 600 for a short parasail. The Taj hotels can arrange these but at a price.

The only recognised **PADI** centre in Goa in early 2000 was the Barracuda Diving India at the Cidade de Goa hotel. Agents offering SCUBA diving should use Barracuda, otherwise safety standards may be questionable. Courses range from 'Discover Scuba Diving' (Rs 3,500) to a two-week 'Divemaster Course' (Rs 25,000). A range of open water dives are offered for experienced divers. The dive shop is open 1000-1700. T221133 ext 5706, F223303, charloo@giasbg01.vsnl.net.in

For those wishing to check for PADI recognised courses in India before arriving, contact PADI International Head Office, Unit 6, Unicorn Park, Whitby Road, Bristol, BS4 4EX. T0117-971 1717, F0117-972 1821, general@padi.co.uk, or PADI Europe, Oberwilerstrasse 3, CH-8442, Hettlingen, Switzerland, T52-304 1414, F52-304 1499, admin@padi.ch

Goa

The beach to the east of Dona Paula on which the Cidade de Goa stands is backed by a part of Tiswadi which the Jesuits enjoyed as highly productive agricultural land. The coastal strip's rich harvests of tropical fruits complemented the fish, crabs, tortoise and shellfish from the sea.

Vainguinim beach

Sleeping **LL-AL** *Cidade de Goa*, 26 km from airport, 7 km from Panaji centre, T221133, F223303, hotelcdg@bom2.vsnl.net.in 210 rooms, 5 restaurants, pool with diving and casino (both open to non-residents), Goa's only PADI course, imaginative development designed by Charles Correa, pleasant and secluded beach but unappealing at low tide. **B** *Swimsea Beach Resort*, Caranzalem Beach, towards Raj Niwas, T227028, F224480. 29 clean, airy, a/c rooms with balconies, sea facing best, pool, very close to black sandy beach. **B** *Villa Sol*, T225852, F224155. 28 rooms with balconies, some a/c, disco/pub "On The Rocks" (literally), good restaurant, small pool, built on high ground so a steep hike back from the beach. **B-C** *O Pescador, Dona Paula Beach Resort*, T227955, F221371, Pescador@goa1.dot.net.in 23 large pleasant rooms in small buildings around a garden, twice as expensive for a/c and sea-facing, small garden restaurant, good pool, own little beach, quiet, pleasant, young friendly management. **B-C** *Prainha Cottages*, T227221, F229959, prainha@bom2.vsnl. net.in 'Madeira cottages' best (a/c, nearer beach and with sea view, Rs 2100), simple but comfortable and quiet, good restaurant, gardens, small pool, secluded (though not particularly clean) beach.

Eating *Cidade de Goa* has several up-market restaurants serving excellent food but at a price. The large sea-front 'coffee house' serves meals all day. *Goan Delicacy*, Hawaii Beach, southeast of National Oceanography roundabout, T224356, tricky to find, overlooking Dona Paula and the sea. Seafood, excellent menu of local dishes (Rs 60-80 main courses), tandoori oven, bar, family-run, very friendly; *O Pescador* with good views over the jetty, serves seafood specialities. There is also a Punjabi *dhaba*.

Entertainment Watersports: *Barracuda Diving* and *Hydro Sports Club*, *Cidade de Goa*, T221133, from near the jetty (see Box below).

Directory Bank You can change money in the larger hotels; otherwise the **State Bank of India**, 1000-1400, Mon-Fri, 1000-1200, Sun, will change TC's.

Bambolim
Police T218551
Off the NH17 south, 8 km from Panaji, Bambolim's dark-sand beach is secluded, free of hawkers and shaded by palms. Goa University is nearby. **Sleeping and eating B** *Bambolim Beach Resort* right on the beach, T230927, F230925. 120 a/c rooms, some seafacing (Rs 1,925), simple but airy with balcony, open-air beach-side restaurant (breakfast included), bar, palm shaded terrace, pool, taxi necessary (usually available), peaceful, isolated spot. *Sand & Sea Restaurant*, down the beach will cook any kind of fish dish ordered (watch out for price quoted though).

Siridao
Close to Bambolim, Siridao is a small secluded beach often good for shells. The *Feast of Jesus of Nazareth* is held on the first Sunday after Easter.

Excursions into the Portuguese past

The road to Old Goa from Panaji passes over the causeway which was built over a swamp in 1633 by the then Viceroy. It is a very attractive ride in the early morning, especially in the winter when mist often hovers over the still waters of the estuary.

Ribandar
At the end of the causeway is the attractive 'preserved village' of Ribandar (pronounced Rai-bunder) or 'Royal Harbour', possibly named after the arrival of the Vijaynagar King in the 14th century. The old houses along the road, however, some substantial and some modest and painted in evocative colours, still conjure up an image of 17th century Portuguese Goa. The **Church to Our Lady of Help** was originally built in 1565 to give thanks for the safe arrival of a Portuguese vessel after a fierce storm at sea. Today the **ferry** is in frequent use for crossing over to Chorao Island for visiting the Salim Ali Bird Sanctuary. It is the shortest route across to Mayem and Bicholim. **Shopping** *Camelot*, House No 139, Fondvem, T234255, 0930-1830, sells good craft, clothing and textiles in contemporary designs – 'stylish and charming'.

★ Old Goa

Phone code: 0832
Colour map 4, grid B1/2
Old Goa (or Velha Goa), on the crest of a low-lying hill on the south bank of the Mandovi, may be regarded as the spiritual heart of Portuguese Goa. Today, it has a melancholy beauty that is revived by a steady flow of tourists and the occasional great pilgrimage to the tomb of St Francis Xavier in the Basilica of Bom Jesus.

Ins & outs
Getting there From Panaji, frequent buses take 15-20 mins (Rs 4). Buses drop you off opposite the Basilica of Bom Jesus; pick up the return bus near the Police Station.

Auto rickshaws charge Rs 25, taxis, Rs 150 return. Slow trains on the Bombay-Managalore line stop at Karmali station, 9 km away. **Getting around** The major monuments are immediately around the Bus Stop and within easy walking distance.

Old Goa owes its origin as a Portuguese capital to **Alfonso de Albuquerque**, and some of its early ecclesiastical development to **St Francis Xavier** who was here in the mid-16th century. However, before the Portuguese arrived it was the second capital of the Bijapur Kingdom but all the buildings of that period have disappeared; only a fragment of the Sultan's palace walls remain. See also Goa Velha, page 456.

Old Goa, enclosed by a fortified wall, had shipyards on the river bank with the administrative and commercial centre nearby. The true centre of the town was filled with magnificent churches. These were built of the local red laterite and basalt with fine white limestone used for decorative detail. The exteriors were coated with lime plaster to protect them from the weather which had to be renewed after each monsoon. When maintenance lapsed, the buildings just crumbled away. The Archaeological Survey of India is responsible for the upkeep of the churches now. **Suggested reading** ASI's inexpensive booklet *Old Goa* by South Rajagopalan, is available from the Archaeological Museum here. An attractive and much more extensive, richly illustrated book is *Goa: A Traveller's Historical and Architectural Guide*, by Anthony Hutt.

Holy Hill Approaching Old Goa from the west, you pass 'Holy Hill' with a **Sights** number of churches. From this site Albuquerque directed the battle against the Adil Shahi forces in 1510. The **Chapel of Our Lady of the Rosary** (1526) belongs to the earliest period of church building. At the time of the conquest of Goa, Portugal was enjoying a period of prosperity under King Manuel I (ruled 1495-1521). The Manueline style, named after him, as seen on the marble cenotaph, borrowed from Iberian decoration and also included local naturalistic motifs and Islamic elements.

Just behind, the **Royal Chapel of St Anthony** (early 17th century) with its unusual semi-circular apsidal front, was restored by the Portuguese in 1961. The ruined **Tower of St Augustine** stands nearby. St Augustine's church

Old Goa

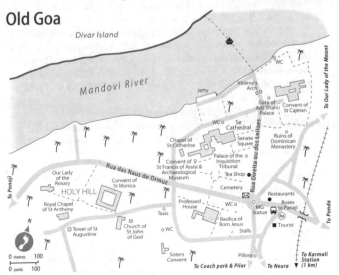

(begun in 1572), once boasted eight chapels, a convent, and an excellent library, once one of the finest in the kingdom. It was abandoned in 1835 due to religious persecution, the vault collapsed in 1842 burying the image, followed by the façade and main tower in 1931. Although it is an uphill hike, it is very evocative and well worth the effort.

Further on is the **Convent of St Monica** (1607-27), the first nunnery in India. The huge three-storey building, built around a sunken central court-yard which contained a formal garden and a church, has, since 1964, been an Institute of Theological Studies. The only other building on the Holy Hill is the **Church and Convent of St John of God** (1685), which was also abandoned in 1835. Descending from the 'Hill' you enter a broad tree-lined plaza. On con-ducted tours this is where you leave your transport and walk.

The tomb lies to the right of the main chancel. There is often a fairly unruly scramble to take a photograph from the best vantage point whilst devotees offer prayers or quietly sing hymns

The **Basilica of Bom** (the Good) **Jesus** (1594-1605) The laterite façade of Bom Jesus is the richest in Goa and also the least Goan in character with a single tower at the east end and unadorned granite decorations. Apart from the elab-orate gilded altars, wooden pulpit and the candy-twist Bernini columns, the interior is very simple. The world renowned church, a World Heritage Site, contains the treasured remains of **St Francis Xavier**, a pupil of Ignatius Loyola who founded the Order of Jesuits (see page 545). In 1613 St Francis' body was brought to the adjoining Professed House (see below) from the College of St Paul. It was moved into the church in 1624, and its present chapel in 1655 where it has remained ever since. St Francis was canonized in 1622. The Order of the Jesuits was suppressed in 1759 and the property confiscated by the state but the church was allowed to continue services, and in 1964 it was raised to a minor basilica. ■ *0900-1230, 1500-1830. No photography, although this appears to be totally ignored by all.*

You can look down onto the tomb from a small window in the art gallery next to the church

The **Tomb of St Francis Xavier** (1696), the gift of one of the last of the Medicis, Cosimo III, was carved by the Florentine sculptor Giovanni Batista Foggini. It is made of marble and jasper, while the casket containing the remains is silver and has three locks, the keys being held by the Governor, Archbishop and Convent Administrator. Initially the saint's body was exposed for viewing on each anniversary of his death but this ceased in 1707. Since 1859, there has been an **Exposition** every 10 to 12 years; the next is in January 2005. The Saint's Feast Day is on 3rd December.

The body of St Francis has suffered much over the years and has been grad-ually reduced by the removal of various parts. One devotee is reputed to have bitten off a toe in 1554 and carried it in her mouth to Lisbon. Part of an arm was sent to Rome in 1615 where it is idolized in the 'Gesu', while a part of the right hand was sent to the Christians in Japan in 1619. In 1890 a toe fell away and is displayed in the Sacristy.

The adjoining **Professed House** for Jesuit fathers is a two-storey building with a typically Mediterranean open courtyard garden. After a fire in 1633 destroyed it, it was only partially rebuilt. It now houses a few Jesuits who run a small college.

The **Se Cathedral**, across the square, is dedicated to **St Catherine**. The largest church in Old Goa, it was built by the Dominicans between 1562-1623. Tuscan in style on the exterior and Corinthian inside, the main façade faces east with the characteristic twin towers (one collapsed in 1776, after being struck by lightning). The remaining tower contains five bells including the Golden Bell which is rung at 0530, 1230 and 1830. The vast interior, divided into a nave and two side aisles, has a granite baptismal font. On each side of the church are four chapels along the aisles. The main altar is superbly gilded and painted, with six further altars in the transept. The marble top table in front of the main altar has been used for the exposition of the relics of St Francis Xavier since 1955 in order to accommodate the vast crowds.

Southwest of the Cathedral are the ruins of the **Palace of the Inquisition**, with dungeons below, where over 16,000 cases were heard between 1561 and 1774. The Inquisition was finally suppressed in 1814.

There are two churches and a museum in the same complex as the Cathedral. The **Church** (and Convent) **of St Francis of Assisi** is a broad vault of a church with two octagonal towers. The floor is paved with tombstones and the walls around the High Altar are decorated with paintings on wood depicting scenes from St Francis' life. The convent was begun by Franciscan friars in 1517, and later restored in 1762-5. The style is Portuguese Gothic. The convent now houses the **Archaeological Museum** (see below under Museums). To the west, **St Catherine's Chapel** was built as an act of gratitude on defeating the forces of Bijapur in 1510. The original mud and thatch church was soon replaced by a stone chapel which in 1534 became the Cathedral (renovated in 1952), and remained so until Se Cathedral was built.

To the northeast of the Cathedral on the road towards the river is **The Viceroy's Arch** (Ribeira dos Viceroys), built at the end of the 16th century to commemorate the centenary of Vasco da Gama's discovery of the sea route to India. His grandson, Francisco da Gama was Viceroy (1597-1600). On the arrival of each new viceroy this would be decorated. The statue of Vasco da Gama was originally surmounted by a gilded statue of St Catherine which was removed during the restoration in 1954 (now in the Museum). Note the strange figures on the back: a lady with a sword and a book (the Bible?) stands above a 'non-believer' awkwardly resting his head on a bent arm! The arch was rebuilt in 1954.

To the east of this lies the splendid domed Baroque Convent and **Church of St Cajetan** (1665), built by Italian friars of the Theatine order, sent to India by Pope Urban III. Shaped like a Greek cross, the church was modelled on St Peter's in Rome. It is rarely visited by groups, and hence more peaceful. There is a well under the dome which the guardian will be pleased to show you.

Beyond is the **Gate of the Fortress of the Adil Shahs**, comprising a lintel supported on moulded pillars mounted on a plinth, probably built by Sabaji, the ruler of Goa before the Muslim conquest of 1471. The now ruined palace was occupied by Adil Shahi sultans of Bijapur, who occupied Goa before the arrival of the Portuguese in 1510. It became the Palace of the Viceroys from 1554 to 1695.

✳ Archaeological Museum and **Portrait Gallery**, Convent of St Francis of **Museums** Assisi. The collection of sculptures covers the period from before the arrival of the Portuguese. Many date from the 12th-13th centuries when Goa came under the rule of the Kadamba Dynasty. The exhibits include 'hero stones' commemorating naval battles and 'sati stones' marking the practice of widow burning. There is also a fine collection of portraits of Portuguese Governors on the first floor which provides an interesting study in the evolution of court dress. ■ *1000-1700, closed Sun. Free. T286133.*

Art Galleries at Se Cathedral and Basilica of Bom Jesus. ■ *0900-1230 (opens 1030 on Sun), 1500-1830, closed Fri and during services. Free.*

Goa Tourism visit to Old Goa (included in the *South Goa* and *Pilgrim Tours*), **Tours** spends a short time visiting the sights. It is better to go by bus or share a taxi to give you time to see Old Goa at leisure.

Goa

Sleeping
& eating
E *Tourist Hotel* (GTDC), near MG (Gandhi) Statue Circle roundabout, T286127. 44 rooms (Rs 220) in a poorly maintained building, mosquito prone (bring a net), adequate for an overnight stay for an early visit of the churches avoiding the crowds, friendly restaurant (limited menu). The tea shop on the place of the Inquisition Tribunal is a good place for cool drinks.

Goa Velha, Pilar and Talaulim

Goa Velha
As Richards says, Goa Velha means "old – being already old when the present-named Old Goa (Velha Goa), was still young and flourishing". Goa Velha, once the centre of international trade along the Zuari, was finally destroyed by the Bahmani Muslims in 1470, although as Gopakapattana or Govapuri it had already suffered from repeated attacks and long term decline due to heavy silting. It is difficult now to spot the exact site. A faded notice board by a cross standing on a pedestal, is the only visible remains. On Monday of Holy Week each year, a colourful *Procession of Saints* starts from St Andrew's Church, just north of the dispersed village.

Pilar
The **Pilar Seminary**, not far from Goa Velha, is on a commanding hilltop site. It was founded by Capuchin monks in 1613, who remained here until 1835. The 17th century Church, dedicated to Our Lady of Pilar still shows faint remains of frescoes on the church walls, and also along the cloisters around the enclosed courtyard of the monastery.

The Carmelites took over and restored the monastery in 1858, but from 1890 it became the headquarters of the Missionary Society of St Francis Xavier. **Father Agnelo de Souza** (1869-1927) who spent 10 years in meditation here before dedicating his life to tireless service, awaits canonization. He is revered and remembered by worshippers at his tomb, especially at services on Thursdays throughout the year.

The museum on the first floor of the seminary, displays some of the finds from the Kadamba period; from the rooftop you can get good views of Mormugao harbour and the Zuari. ■ *1000-1700.*

The more recent extension which houses the present seminary has a small chapel with a fine marble altar and some German stained glass.

■ *Getting there: Buses along the NH17, the Panaji-Margas road, stop nearby at the bottom of the hillock. From there you can walk uphill through the extension of the seminary. It is best to get a taxi, motorbike or bike to get to Talaulim, 4 km north. Drinks and snacks are available near the church.*

Talaulim
Just north of the Pilar Seminary is the ✳ **Church of St Anna** (Santana) at Talaulim by the river Siridado, a tributary of the Zuari. Built around 1695, its elaborate Baroque façade is similar in design (though smaller) to the great Church of St Augustine at Old Goa, of which only part of one tower remains. Once the parish church with a large congregation, it fell into disrepair when Old Goa nearby declined, and had to be refurbished in 1907.

St Anna's feast day (26 July) is celebrated by both communities who come to seek blessing from the mother of the Virgin Mary, whose intervention is traditionally sought by childless couples. It is known popularly as the *Toucheam* (or Cucumber) *Feast* because those who come to pray for a baby boy (*menino*) bring with them a *pepino* (cucumber). Unmarried boys and girls also come to pray for partners bringing with them spoons (*colher*) to plead for wives (*mulher*) and *mung* beans (*urid*) in exchange for husbands (*marido*)!

Chandor, Rachol and Loutolim

There are other excursions which give a variety of insights into the colonial past. These are closer to Margao but can also easily be visited from Panaji or the beaches in central Goa.

Buses from Margao will get you to within walking distance of the sights but it is worth considering a taxi.

Ins & outs

★ Chandor
Phone code: 0832
Colour map 4, grid B2

About 13 km east of Margao (and south of Curtorim), on the site of the 11th-century Kadamba capital of Chandrapur, Chandor is an interesting village. The once navigable tributaries of the Zuari River here allowed trade to flourish with distant Arab ports as early as the seventh century. Even earlier, a fourth century Bhoja king's copperplate inscription dates the existence of an ancient fort which once stood at Chandrapur nearby, taking advantage of the natural defensive moat the two rivers provided.

Today, Chandor is very much a backwater. Succeeding Muslim and Christian rulers destroyed much of Chandor's Hindu past. The **Church of Our Lady of Bethlehem** built in 1645, replaced the principal *Sapta Matrika* (Seven Mothers) temple which was demolished in the previous century. Crowds gather on 6th January each year, for the ★ **Three Kings Festival** at Epiphany, which is similarly celebrated at Reis Magos and Cansaulim (Quelim) in southern Goa. The three villages of Chandor (Cavorim, Guirdolim and Chandor) come together to put on a grand show. Village boys dress up as the Three Kings and process through the village on horseback before arriving at the church.

★ **Menezes Braganza House** Chandor also retains several fine Portuguese mansions. Among them is the enormous Braganza family house which faces one side of the large Church square, about 400 m from the railway station, and receives visitors right through the year. **Luis de Menezes Braganza** was an influential journalist and politician (1878-1938), who not only campaigned for freedom from colonial rule but also became a champion of the less privileged sections of Goan society. The part late- 16th century mansion he inherited (extended in the 18th and 19th), shows the opulent lifestyle of the old Portuguese families who established great plantation estates, still complete with all furniture and effects.

The West Wing, which is better maintained, is owned by Aida de Menezes Bragança. The guided tour by this elderly member of the family is fascinating. She has managed to completely restore the teak ceiling of the 250-year-old library gallery; the old *mareta* wood floor survives since this native Goan timber can withstand water. In the Dining Room, the original polished *argamassa* floor has been replaced by new mosaic though a small section of old tiles have been retained near a window, as an example. There is much carved and inlaid antique furniture and very fine imported china and porcelain. ■ *Donations of Rs 50 per visitor are appreciated; usually open 0900-1800 everyday but it is best to confirm by telephone (T784201). You will find the front door open; go up the stairs and knock on the door on the left.*

The East Wing, occupied by Sr Alvaro de Perreira-Braganza which part mirrors the West Wing, also has some fine carved furniture, where it requires some imagination to conjure up the grand occasions it had witnessed in the past. The family chapel at the back now has a prized relic added to its collection, the decorated nail of St Francis Xavier which had, until recently, been kept guarded, away from public view.

Goa

Loutolim
*Open to visitors by
prior arrangement; ask
at the tourist office*

The small village of Loutolim (Lutolim) has several interesting Goan country houses around it.

Miranda House The Mirandas became wealthy as owners of areca plantations and the garden here still has specimen palms as reminders. Their fine country house built around 1700 is at the end of a rough track which starts near the church square. The house has a typical garden courtyard at the back around which runs the family rooms and bedrooms (note the attractive panelled wood ceilings), protected by shady verandahs. There is also the family chapel with the kitchen and servants' quarters at the far end. The formal reception rooms are to the front lit by equally formal dark wood windows. The grand dining hall upstairs, accessed from the front hall, in turn leads to the large library. The bedroom suite on the other side once offered sanctuary to the Ranes in the 19th century and a defensive gun hole in the wall by a door still serves as a reminder of those uncertain years. The house retains little of the original furniture, but more recently acquired pieces of period artefacts which are now set off by imaginative furnishings in some of the rooms.

Another fine late eighteenth century house in its private compound, the **Salvador Costa House** which is now shared by two descendants, is a little further west from the Square. Here too, the household revolved around a central courtyard at the back, but unlike the Miranda House, a wide welcoming verandah greeted the visitor. The impressively gilded family chapel is still used for daily prayers. Some fine features of its grand past are evident in the original beautifully carved furniture and fine chandeliers.

It is now also possible to visit **Casa Araujo Alvares**, a 200 year old Portuguese mansion, but it is pricey since there is little inside (the Braganza house at Chandor nearby offers more). ■ *1000-1230 and 1500-1800. Rs 100.*

The village has also started attracting visitors to **Ancestral Goa**, a privately developed open-air site designed to illustrate Goa's traditional past. Well worth a visit. Maendra Alvares, an artist/sculptor has devoted considerable time and energy (and finance) to create a unique centre. Great care and research have gone into constructing authentic replicas of old town and village houses and artisans' huts, with an eye to detail when fitting them out with appropriate tools, utensils and artefacts. ■ *0830-1830 daily. Rs 20. Getting there: there is a regular bus to Loutolim from Margao, Rs 5.*

The **fisherman's** shack made out of palm fronds and bamboo with sand and shells on the ground. The **farmer's** house built of mud and laterite blocks, with distinctive small clay tiles on the verandah roof. The **taverna** progresses to being partly white-washed, with larger terracotta "Mangalore tiles" on the roof, a layer of cowdung covers the mud floor. The **landowner's** impressive house shows Portuguese influence in its raised balcao (verandah), plastered walls built of laterite and mortar, clay floor tiles, red cement seats, the family altar, and the use of decorative ceramic wall tiles, slatted wood ceilings and oyster-shell windows.

Various interesting village activities are illustrated from the distillation of the feni liquor from cashew apples in a *bhati*, to the potter and the village violin master. Of particular interest are structures like the Boca da Vaca (the Cow's Mouth') spring, which supplied a community with water, *Sant Kuris* (the wayside Holy Cross) where an annual feast is celebrated, *dhone* (pairs of pillars) on a roadside (possibly rests for heavy loads), and the travellers' "safe passage" *racondar* lamps found under trees at significant points along route.

Set on a hill side in very attractive surroundings, visitors are given a guided tour by well-informed guides who lead you through a socio-historical journey. Parts of the trail are shaded but take a hat. An added attraction is a chance to see a range of Goa's spices and fruit trees. At the top of the site is Maendra Alvares' single-handed achievement "Natural Harmony", a sculpture of Sant Mirabai carved out of a horizontal block of laterite (15 m x 5 m). At the end of the tour, visitors are invited to have a glass of "fresh lime" (not bottled water but safe to drink) and visit a small gift shop with local hand made crafts, pottery, ceramics and paintings. A bakery about 500 m away in a private house sells exceedingly mouth-watering '*Melting moments*' – macaroons made with ground cashew nuts. Ask for directions.

Rachol (pronounced *Rashol*) is set in a fertile valley, vivid green during the wet season and into the New Year, but burnt brown in the summer heat. A stone archway crosses the road marking the entrance, the road coming to an abrupt end in a hamlet by the river bank. The seminary is well worth a visit.

Rachol
Colour map 4, grid B2

The fort There is little evidence of one of Goa's early important forts save a gateway and parts of some walls. Originally Muslim, it was captured by the forces of the Hindu Vijayanagar King in 1520 who then handed it over to the Portuguese who, they hoped, would in turn keep the Muslims at bay. During the Maratha Wars of 1737-9 and the siege that followed, the fort was badly damaged. With the threat of aggression removed, the 100 cannons here were dispersed and most of the buildings gradually disintegrated over the ensuing years.

Rachol Seminary The seminary was established here in 1580 since the site had the protection of the fort (the earlier one at Margao was destroyed by Muslims the previous year). Originally known as the College of All Saints, it was rededicated to **Ignatius Loyola** in 1622. The Rachol complex, principally an ecclesiastical college, also includes a hospital, a primary school, an early printing press which printed the Bible in Konkani and is nearly a self-sufficient community. The seminary was under the Jesuits from 1610 until 1759 when they were expelled, and the 'Oratorians' installed in their place. However, in 1835, when all religious orders lost favour in Portugal they too were removed and the Seminary became the responsibility of the Diocesan Clergy of Goa.

For successive generations the seminary has been the most prestigious centre of education in Goa producing some of Goa's secular as well as religious leaders, and now is a forward-looking institution which trains clergy able to meet the challenges of society today. The vast stone structure is built round a large courtyard. There is an underground cistern which some suggest belonged to an ancient Siva temple here which was destroyed, and an underground passage from the courtyard conjures up images of an escape route through the fort in the precarious years of the 17th and 18th centuries. The seminary also contains large galleries and a famous library of rare books on the first floor.

The church Dating from 1609 it was rebuilt in 1622. The impressive interior, beautifully restored and rich with gilding, has nine altars including one to St Constantine containing his relics, and one with the celebrated Menino Jesus statue (which was considered miraculous when it had been installed in Colva, see page 489). There are many murals in the Seminary and Church. There is a daily service at 0700 to which visitors are welcome. ■ *An attendant will show you round the church and the seminary between 0900-1300, 1430-1700; open to visitors even during term time, though quiet is requested. Free.*

Museum of Christian Art The small, well-kept museum is attached to the seminary but run independently by the Department of Archaeology. Exhibits include Indo-Portuguese sacred art mainly from Goa's churches, convents and Christian homes. The 155 precious items reflect a wealth of workmanship in wood, ivory, silver and gold. ■ *0930-1300, 1400-1700, Rs 5, closed Mon.*

Sleeping and eating Nearby, at Maina-Curtorim village: **C** *Naari*, a guest house for women among cashew groves, not far from the river, bed and breakfast ($160 pw double/$85 single), spacious living space, rooms with bath (hot water), home cooking, garden/terrace, book and pay at least a month ahead, DA/8B Phase 2, DDA Flats, Munrika, New Delhi 110067, T11-6138316, F6187401, naari@del3.vsnl.net.in

Mapusa and North Goa

Bardez and Pernem talukas have a long coastline of wonderful coconut fringed sandy beaches, backed by dunes, and only occasionally interrupted by rocky headland and coves. A string of fishing villages run along the coast. Inland, there are rolling laterite hills covered in open forest. Southern Bardez has saline flood plains which have been managed for centuries through an intricate system of sluice gates. Here salt-tolerant rice varieties co-exist with aquaculture. The Mapusa River was once a transport artery but is no longer so; for its banks have been reclaimed for building and its waters clogged by urban refuse.

★ Mapusa

Phone code: 0832
Colour map 4, grid A1
Population: 31,600

Mapusa (pronounced 'Mahp-sa') is the administrative headquarters of Bardez taluka. It has a busy and colourful Municipal Market, especially interesting on Fridays. The rest of the town is small enough to wander around and observe local activity.

Ins & outs **Getting there** This is an important junction for interstate and local buses to the northern beaches. Buses arrive at the market square opposite the taxi stand, while the State Kadamba Bus Stand is a bit further south. **Getting around** You can walk around the small town and if you should need an auto, Rs 10 should be ample for short hops.

Sights Mapusa stands on a long ridge which runs east-west, with fertile agricultural land occupying the flat valley floor right up to the edge of the town. The name may be derived from the extensive swamps which once covered the area; *maha apsa'* (great swamps).

St Jerome's Church, also known as Milagres Church, **Our Lady of Miracles** (1594), was rebuilt in 1674 and in 1839 after it was destroyed by fire. The small church with its scrolled gable and balconied windows in the façade has a belfry at the rear. The main altar is to Our Lady, and those on the two sides to St John and St Jerome. Note also the interesting wooden ceiling. The Church stands near the site of the Shanteri Temple and so is sacred to Hindus as well. See Local festival below.

The **Maruti temple** was built on the spot of a firecracker shop in the 1840s which had housed a picture and then the silver image of the Monkey God associated with Rama. Followers of Rama would gather in the shop since the Portuguese destroyed all Hindu temples and none was built for nearly three centuries.

C *Green Park*, Mapusa-Panaji Rd, Bypass Junction (2 km from centre), T250667, F252698. 35 modern, comfortable, rooms, quiet, good pool (the only one in town) and restaurants. **D-E** *Satyaheera*, near Maruti Temple, T262949. 34 reasonable rooms (Rs 300), a/c (Rs 600), enclosed rooftop restaurant (shared with mosquitoes and the odd mouse!), bar. *Home stays* arranged by *Siddhartha,* Zed Point, Chandranath Apts, Phase II, BS7, opposite Police Station, T251153, F262076, info@siddharta.de **E** *Mandarin*, near Alankar Cinema, T262579. 21 basic rooms with bath (a/c Rs 400), clean rooftop restaurant. **E** *Tourist Hotel* (GTDC), T262794, at the roundabout. 48 adequate rooms for 2-6, some a/c (Rs 300), reasonable restaurant, beer. **E** *Vilena*, opposite the Municipality, T263115. 14 neat, clean rooms, some a/c, good restaurants, bar, very friendly.

Sleeping
Most check out at 0900

Mid-range: *Vilena*. 2 restaurants (a rooftop and an a/c indoors), serve the best food in town though the music will appeal only to the young! *Mahalaxmi*, Anjuna Rd. A/c, South Indian vegetarian. *Casa Bela*, near Coscar Corner, specializes in Goan food. Opposite, *Moonlight*, Shalini Building, 1st Floor. Good North Indian at lunchtime; rather dark in the evening, used more for drinking than eating. **Cafés and fast food**: *Royal-T*, Shop 96, near the Shakuntala Fountain, Municipal Market, Goan snacks, sweets and spices. Other **cheap stalls** and cafés in the market. From 1630 until late, carts and stalls near the Alankar Cinema, sell popular meat and seafood dishes.

Eating
Little to shout about

Feast of our Lady of Miracles, on the Mon of the 3rd week after **Easter**, the Nossa Senhora de Milagres image is venerated by Christians as well as Hindus who join together to celebrate the feast day of the Saibin. A huge fair and market is held.

Festival

Books: *Ashish Book Centre*, near the KTC Bus Stand. *Other India Bookstore*, 1st floor, St Britto's Apartment, above Mapusa Clinic, T263306, oibs@bom2.vsnl.net.in, different and excellent. **Photography**: *Remy Studios*, Coscar Corner and Shop 8, KTC Bus Stand. **Market**: the Municipal Market, 1130-1530, is well planned and operates all week except Sunday. The colourful and vibrant 'Friday Market' is a must since vendors come from far and wide and there is a lot of activity right into the evening. Open from 0800 to 1800 (though some stalls close much earlier). 0730 to 0800 is best for photography when the light is good and you can capture the local stalls being set up.

Shopping
Beware of pickpockets

Goa

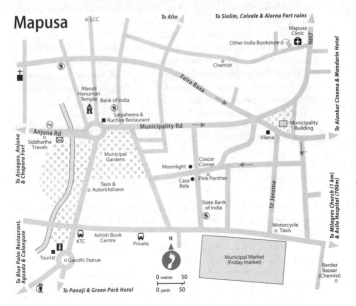

Mapusa

Transport **Local** **Auto-rickshaw**: Calangute, Rs 50. **Bus**: several to Calangute, some continue onto Baga, some go towards Candolim; check before boarding or change at Calangute. Rs 5. To **Panaji**: non-stop mini buses; buy tickets from booth at market entrance. Rs 6. Check times in advance. For the northern beaches buses to Calangute (every 20-30 mins), Rs 4; from there to Aguada or Baga (check before). Also to Vagator and Chapora via Anjuna. **Motorcycle taxi:** to Anjuna or Calangute, about Rs 40, but open to bargaining. **Taxi**: (often shared by up to 5) to Panaji, Rs 70; Calangute/ Baga, Rs 60; Chapora/Siolim, Rs 80. **Car hire**: *Pink Panther*, T263180. **Motorcycle hire**: *Classic Bike Adventure* (Indo-German company) at Casa Tres Amigos, Socol Vado 425, Parra, Assagao, 4 km west (off the Anjuna Rd), T0832-273351, F276124. Reliable bikes and tours. **Long distance** **Bus**: Private operators, lined up opposite the taxi stand, offer near identical routes and rates. To **Bangalore**: 1830, 12 hrs, Rs 250 (Luxury), Rs 450 (Sleeper). **Hampi**: 1800, 11 hrs, Rs 450 (Sleeper). **Mumbai**: 1600, 14 hrs, Rs 250 (luxury), Rs 450 (Sleeper).

Directory **Banks** *Bank of India* opposite Municipal Gardens, changes TCs, cash Visa and Mastercard. 1000-1400 Mon – Fri; 1000-1200 Sat. *State Bank of India* exchanges cash and TCs, 15-20 mins. Foreign exchange on 1st floor, 1000-1600 Mon-Fri, 1000 – 1200 Sat. *Pink Panther Agency* changes Visa and Mastercard Mon-Fri 0900-1700, Sat 0900-1300. **Communications** The **Sub-Post Office** is opposite the Police Station. **Couriers:** *Blue Dart*, T263208. **Internet:** Several across town, well signed. Most charge Rs 90 per hr. Best at *LCC* 3rd Floor, Bhavani Apartments, Rs 15 per 15 mins; 6 terminals, 0700-2130, 7 days a week. **Medical services** *Asilo Hospital*, T262211. **Pharmacies:** including *Drogaria*, near the Swiss Chapel, open 24 hrs; *Mapusa Clinic*, T262350; *Bardez Bazzar*. **Travel agent** *Siddhartha*, Zed Point, Chandranath Apts, Phase II, BS7, opp Police Station, T251153, F262076, info@siddharta.de, arrange special tours, including some for handicapped travellers. **Useful numbers** Ambulance: T262372. **Fire**: T262900. **Police:** T262231. **Tourist Information:** T262390.

★ Northern beaches

Oil and litter washed ashore can be a problem, especially on beaches closer to Panaji

Despite the unending stretch of sand that Goa has as its gift, each section has its own distinctive character. The difference reflects in part the nature of the settlements dotted at intervals behind it. Just north of Panaji is the exclusive resort in **Fort Aguada**. Further along is a relatively quiet strip in **Candolim** and then from **Calangute** to **Baga** the coconut palms come closer to the beach with fishing villages nestled among them. This section has close to 200 beach restaurants open during the season. Across the Baga River, **Anjuna** still draws hundreds to the weekly Flea Market and to its thumping raves and all night parties, though the beach is too rocky for comfortable swimming. The series of secluded beaches quickly empties towards **Chapora**, and in the far north low rocky headlands create a series of small enclosed bays which are not as easily accessible. Some, like **Arambol** near the northern tip of the state, are being 'discovered' and there is talk of further development.

Ins & outs There are buses from Mapusa and Panaji; to Calangate, Anjuna, Chopora and Arambol but some prefer to hire a motorbike or bike to find their stretch of sand.

Reis Magos
Population: 1991 7,500

Reis Magos stands like a watchman facing Panaji across the Mandovi estuary. The small town of some charm is most noted for its 'Royal Fort', built by Don Alfonso de Noronha between 1551 and 1554. In 1703, it was rebuilt; 35 years later it had to face the Maratha onslaught on Bardez and alone with Fort Aguada remained in Portuguese hands.

The Reis Magos **Church** (1555), named after the 'Magi Kings', stands alongside and is one of the early Goan churches which, some believe, was built on the site of a Hindu temple. Dedicated to the three Magi Gaspar, Melchior and Balthazar, the reredos illustrates the story of the Three Kings with a painted wooden panel showing frankincense, myrrh and gold being offered to the baby Jesus.

The Festival of Three Kings accompanied by a big fair is celebrated here as at Chandor on 6 January each year (see page 445).

Sinquerim beach and Fort Aguada

Sinquerim, 13 km from Panaji, is where the Taj Hotel group set up its Hermitage Complex which dominates the headland around the historic Fort Aguada. If you want a long beach walk, the firm sand is uninterrupted all the way north to Baga. It is a good idea to take some water as well as a shirt and hat. Alternatively, buses run along the road 1 km inland behind the main line of sand dunes.

Phone code: 0832
Colour map 4, grid B1

On the northern tip of the Mandovi estuary with the Nerul River to the east, Fort Aguada, considered essential to keep the Dutch Navy at bay, was completed in 1612, the strongest of the Portuguese coastal forts. A large well and a number of springs provided the fort and ships at harbour with drinking water and gave it its name *'aguada'*, meaning watering place. It saw repeated action against the Marathas. The main fortifications with laterite walls, nearly 5 m high and 1.3 m thick, are still intact; the buildings lower down form the Central Jail.

The motorable road up to the plateau passes the small **Church of St Lawrence** (or Linhares Church, 1630-1643). It has an unusual porch with a terrace and balustrades on the towers and parapets.

A 13 m high lighthouse using an oil lamp was added at the top of the fort (84 m above sea level) sometime in the 18th century. In 1864, a new mechanism allowed a rotating beam to be emitted every 30 seconds (one of the first of its kind in Asia). It is supposed to be open from 1030-1730, Rs 3; there are good views from the top. Next to the fort, there is the 'new' 21 m high concrete lighthouse (1975). ■ *1600-1730 (Re 1, no photography).*

Goa

Sleeping

The Taj complex is at the bottom of the hill where sections of the fortification jut out to the sea. **AL** *Aguada Hermitage*, T276201, F276044 (for all 3). Exclusive and extremely luxurious, 20 fully serviced 1- or 2-room villas (US$ 600 peak season drops to $180 in low), few some distance away from main building, each with its own spacious tropical garden, nightclub. **AL-A** *Fort Aguada Beach Resort*, exceptional hotel, superb setting, built into the fort, 120 rooms in 2 wings and some villas with excellent views. Excellent staff. Separate **AL-A** *Holiday Village*, 300 m away. 144 (most a/c), some well designed single 'houses', some in less attractive 2-storey blocks further from the sea ($230 down to $85 in low season), imaginative planning, beautiful gardens of bougainvillea and palms, good restaurants (on beach and on dunes), excellent pool with a water bar and hammocks between palms (better than at the *Resort*), informal, helpful efficient staff. **B-C** *Marbella*, lane left off road to *Aguada Beach Resort*, T275551, F276509. 6 very clean, well decorated rooms (prices vary, best worth the price) in a large Goan house. **D** *Village Belle*, near the *Taj Holiday Village*, T/F276153 vbelle@vsnl.com 8 rooms (Rs 450-Rs 600 a/c), good, cheap restaurant, among palms, 500m from the beach, friendly owners, good value for the area.

Prices vary greatly depending on period (peak 21 Dec-10 Jan, lowest mid Jun-end Sep)

Eating

Expensive *Banyan Tree* at *Taj Holiday Village* entrance for something special. Excellent Thai food in stylish surroundings, wide verandah, water garden (about Rs 500 each). *Beach House* for the "most lavish and complete dinner, served attentively". *Bon Appetit* and *Palm Shade* nearby, are also recommended.

Sports Taj **Sports Complex** with excellent facilities (open to non-residents) at the *Taj Holiday Village*, with a separate access between *Aguada Beach Resort* and the *Holiday Village*. Rs 440 per day for the complex, Rs 330 for the pool (the Arabian Sea is free!). **Tennis** with good markers (Rs 400 per hr); **squash** and **badminton** (Rs 100 for 30 mins); **golf** (Rs 150). A fine **health centre** there offers massage, gym, steam, sauna, all recommended; hairdressers are at hand. **Scuba diving**, **sailing** and **water skiing** Rs 450 per hr; **windsurfing** and (rod) **fishing** Rs 400 per hr; **parasailing** Rs Rs 850; **jet ski** Rs 900.

Candolim

Phone code: 0832 Candolim has the least developed part of the beach north of Aguada. If you wish to be away from the crowds but within reach of good food, try the beach near D'Mello's and Oceanic just north. Candolim has no real centre. The beach itself is long and straight, backed by scrub-covered dunes with little shelter. Some beach shacks now fly Union Jacks, Scottish and English flags and play endless Bob Marley. Some shacks hire out sunbeds for around Rs 50.

Sleeping **Mid-range A** *Whispering Palms*, 300m from beach (looks a bit like a fortress), T276140, F276142, whispering.palms@gnpun.globalnet.ems.vsnl.net.in 66 well-equipped rooms, good restaurant, excellent pool (non residents Rs 150), pleasant garden, mainly packages. **B** *Highland Beach Resort*, T276405, F277881. 205 a/c rooms (Rs 2000 including breakfast), in a rather ugly, sprawling 4-storey complex (completed early 2000), 2 restaurants, package choice, Health /Sports club, pool (non residents Rs 100 per hr). **C** *Aldeia Santa Rita*, towards Aguada, T276868, F276684. 32 rooms with balcony (better upstairs), in colourful 'street' of villas in attractive setting, some a/c (Rs 1,100), good restaurant, bar, very small pool, friendly management. **C** *Costa Nicola*, near the Health Centre (500m from beach), T276343, F277343. 26 clean rooms in very pleasant Goan house, old wing with more character, new wing, restaurant, bar, gentle atmosphere, verandah, pretty garden, pool.

D *Holiday Beach Resort*, short walk to beach, T276088, F276235. 20 clean rooms, some with balcony, rather faded guesthouse, covered terrace restaurant, small pool. **D** *Kamal*, towards Aguada, T276320. 6 large rooms in a fairly new, attractive building, *Fiesta* restaurant (some Italian dishes), pleasant garden, charming owner. **D** *Per Avel*, 100m from beach, T277074. 13 simple rooms (a/c Rs 200 extra), courtyard garden for breakfast, among local family houses, friendly. **D** *Sea Shell Inn*, opposite Canara Bank, Candolim-Aguada Rd, T276131. 8 spotless (Rs 450), comfortable rooms in 2 blocks (one grafted onto an old colonial house with chapel), disappointing restaurant, residents may use pool at *Casa Sea Shell*. **D** *Summerville*, T277075. 15 well kept rooms, breakfast on rooftop, sunbathing terrace. **D** *Xavier*, round the corner from the State Bank. T/F 276911, xavieran@goa1.dot.net.in 10 spacious, well furnished rooms (Rs 500), excellent restaurant (see below), close to beach, friendly. **D-E** *Alexandra Tourist Centre*, Morodvaddo, in lane opposite the Canara Bank, T276097. 12 clean, comfortable rooms, better upstairs (Rs 350-Rs 450), restaurant. **E** *D'Mello's Sea View*, turn at Father Chicho Monteiro Rd (towards Calangute), T277395. 7 rooms (Rs 350), good food (tandoori specials), quiet.

Eating **Mid-range**: *Oceanic* nearby. Spicy, succulent fish grills. *Palms 'n Sand* near the beach. Speciality roast piglet (order the day before). *Stone House*, opposite Octopus Garden. Excellent food, wide choice, good service from friendly young waiters, pleasant music (Blues lapsing into Bob Marley!), boat trips. *Titus Roma Pisa*, Candolim Beach Road. Not just pizzas. Well prepared food, very friendly staff (good place to ask about fishing trips, flea market etc), Soccer Bar for live football, but not rowdy at all, so not just for the younger crowd. Also internet, Rs 90 per hr. *21 Comforts*, further south, now crowded in with other shacks. Good breakfasts for about Rs 75, snacks (seafood, pancakes) and drinks. *Xavier*. Western. Excellent meals, Sunday roasts, (owner/chef spent 30 years in England), very attentive service (and highly efficient hotel cat!). Cocktail Bar ("happy hour" 1800-1900).

John's Boats, T277780, promises 'guaranteed' **dolphin watching**, morning trips start around 0900, Rs 500 (includes meal); see page 451 for details. Occasional **parasailing** is also offered independently on Candolim beach, Rs 600-850 for a 5-min flight.

Entertainment

Medical services *Primary Health Centre*. **Photography** Many outlets do quick processing of holiday snaps; fairly good quality, usually same day (processed at Calangute). *Foto Finish*, next to *Stone House*, stocks slide and black/ white films as well as camera accessories. **Travel agent** *Davidair*, Old Post House, Escrivao, Main Rd, T277000, F276308, davidgoa@goa1.dot.net.in, 0900-1800. Recommended. *Traveland*, Laxmi Apartments, T276773, F276124.

Directory

Calangute

Calangute is the busiest small beachside town with small hotels and guesthouses which are particularly popular with low priced package tours. It has a good beach – no rocks and good swimming.

Phone code: 0832
Colour map 4, grid B1
Population: 11,800

Getting there There are regular buses to Calangute from Mapusa (Rs 4, 20 mins) and Panaji (Rs 5, 35 mins) which arrive at the bus stand near the market towards the beach steps. A few continue to Baga to the north, from the crossroads; others go to Candolim and Fort Aguada. **Getting around** There are plenty of cycles and bikes for hire. On Market days there are boats from Baga to Anjuna (see under Baga).

Ins & outs
16 km from Panaji
10 km from Mapusa

There is little of interest in the town but for a fish market and a hexagonal 'Barbeiria' (barbers shop) near the bus stand at the 'T' junction. Immediately north, the narrower **Baga** beach is lined with fishing boats, nets and village huts. A shallow estuary and little headland separate it from **Anjuna**. The main Baga road has several streets off it giving access to the sea. Village houses take in guests but it is a 500 m walk across hot dunes to the beach.

The beach is reasonable – no rocks and good swimming (but beware of the seaward pulling current) and you won't need to go far to see a large number of fishing boats, tackle and fishermen's huts. Hawkers selling sarongs, offering massages or wishing to tell your fortune can be a constant distraction while licensed shacks line the beach, some offering excellent food and a very pleasant evening atmosphere. Behind the busy beach front, coconut trees still give shade to village houses; some offer private rooms to let, while open space is rapidly being covered by new hotels.

The affluence of this coastal strip also attracts its fair share of out-of-state beggars. At weekends the beach near the tourist resort gets particularly crowded with domestic day trippers (some come in the hope of catching a glimpse of scantily clad foreigners).

The beach & town

Goa

Mid-range B *Goan Heritage*, Gauravaddo, T276253, F276120. 70 large, pleasant rooms but can get stiflingly hot, a/c and fridge (Rs 400 extra), some have sea view, expensive restaurant (others nearby), good pool, beautiful garden, close to beach; B *Paradise Village*, South Calangute, near the beach, T276351, F276155. 83 comfortable rooms in 2-storey chalets, pleasant restaurant (kingfish Rs 90, beer Rs 45), large pool, excellent service and management. B *Villa Goesa*, Cobravaddo, off Baga Rd, T277535, T/F276182. 57 clean rooms, some a/c, excellent restaurant, lovely gardens, pool, quiet, relaxing, friendly owners, long walk from beach. C *Concha Beach Resort*,

Sleeping

Umtavaddo, T/F276056. 13 good sized, clean, comfortable rooms, mosquito nets, best at front with large verandahs, close to beach; **C** *Estrela do Mar*, Calangute-Baga Rd, T276014, 12 clean, well kept rooms with mosquito nets (rare in these parts), size varies, restaurant, pool, pleasant garden, quiet, peaceful, close to beach.

D *Coco Banana*, 5/139A Umtavaddo, back from Calangute beach, T276478, F279068. 6 spotless rooms with nets, airy, light and comfortable, excellent Goan/Swiss owners, very caring and helpful. Recommended. **D** *Golden Eye*, Gauravaddo, T277308, F276187. 26 clean, comfortable rooms (Rs 650), half price singles, right on the beach, excellent beachside restaurant. **D** *Mira*, Umtavaddo, near the Chapel, 10 mins walk from beach, T277342. 17 rooms, restaurant, 24 hr coffeeshop, pool, email facilities. **D** *Tourist Resort* (GTDC), on the beach, near the steps, T276024. 76 basic rooms, some a/c, cheap terrace restaurant, bar, can be noisy. **D** *White House*, Gauravaddo (near *Goan Heritage*), T277938, F276308. 8 rooms with seaview (Rs 500), very pleasant. Among other cheap guest houses in Umtavaddo: **E** *Calangute Beach Resort*, T276063. 16 reasonable rooms, some with bath (Rs 350), restaurant, bar, beach on the

Calangute

To Baga — To Anjuna — To Mapusa

To Mapusa

Ocean Star

Our Lady of Piety

To Mapusa

SBI — BoB

Wall Street — Market

Nikkis — St John's Chapel — Honda Repairs

Taxi — WC — Book Palace — Football Ground — MGM

To St Alex Church & Panaji

UMTAVADDO

Arabian Sea

St Anthony's

Kerkar Art Gallery

GAURAVADDO

To Candolim

Goa

N

0 metres 200
0 yards 200

3 Concha Beach Resort
4 Dona Cristalina
5 Estrela do Mar
6 Goan Heritage
7 Golden Eye
8 Mira
9 Paradise Village
10 Tourist Resort
11 Villa Goesa

■ **Sleeping**
1 Calangute Beach Resort
2 Coco Banana

12 White House

● **Eating**
1 Angelina
2 Delhi Darbar
3 Infanteria
4 Johnny's Shack
5 Little Italy
6 Lobster Pot

7 Master Joel Confectioners
8 Milky Way & Indian Café
9 Oceanic
10 Palm Court
11 Pedro's
12 Tibetan Kitchen

Impact of tourism

Despite the welcomed growth in income that tourism has brought to Calangute and Baga, it has not been an unmixed blessing. For those with memories stretching back 30 years, the area is almost unrecognizable. The huge surge in land values, fuelled by a flow of money from Goans abroad eager to capitalize on the development opportunity, has seen plots covered in concrete flouting all attempts to control or direct, let alone halt, the building boom.

Yet the area most affected by this transformation of a hippy hideout to a global tourist village is small.

Competition for limited ground water has affected some of the villages just inland, and some see its increasing use as threatening to let sea water into the underground supply, putting local people at risk. Others fear even more the cultural change which mass tourism has brought to this spot. It is here that Goa's nightlife is at its most audible (although in 2000 there were rumours of ceilings on decibel levels), a transformation that some local people still find hard to accept. The widespread availability of drugs is both feared and resented by many, just as nude or topless bathing are seen as deeply offensive. Calangute and Baga have become the area of Goa where the tensions between mass tourism and local needs are most exposed. Visitors can help greatly by being aware of the issues and behaving sensitively.

doorstep. **E** *Dona Cristalina*, T279012. 8 clean, simple rooms, some with balcony and sight of the sea (Rs 250-300), discounts for long term stay.

Eating

Expensive *Delhi Darbar*, near the beach towards Baga. Excellent North Indian and fish dishes. Upmarket, candle-lit dinner and dancing. *Little Italy*, 136/1Gauravaddo, behind Kelkar Gallery, away from the beach (mock classical front). T275911. Excellent and authentic Italian (Sicilian chef), pastas and pizzas indoors (a/c) or al fresco. **Mid-range** Near the tourist resort: *Angelina*, near the beach steps. Popular, varied menu (Goan, Tandoori, Italian) and *Cater's*, opposite, raised above the beach, with a large breezy terrace, are recommended. *L'Amour*, beach front terrace, delicious Goan curries. *Pedro's* Gauravaddo beach. Authentic, interesting Tibetan to complement a very smartly printed menu, attentive service. *Johnny's Shack*, seafood, excellent pomfret (Rs 70). *Souza Lobo* in a large shack on the beach, is still popular for seafood. *Tibetan Kitchen*, opposite football ground. Good food, a place to relax. **Bakers** *Infanteria*, near the main crossroads. Recommended for breakfast, baked goodies and snacks all day. *Master Joel Confectioners*, 9 Romano Chambers, opposite the petrol pump. Good Goan specialities. **Cafés** *Milky Way*, inland off Baga Rd. Health foods, ices during the day, French menu 1900-2330, closed off-season. *Indian Café*, behind, serves snacks on a few tables on the verandah of a village home (no fans). Pleasant, cheap, also changes money.

Festivals

The *Youth Fête* (May, second week) attracts Goa's leading musicians and dancers.

Shopping

The asking price in most shops aimed at tourists is highly inflated so be prepared to bargain if you want to pay a realistic price; it is best to look around first before buying. **Books**: *Book Palace*, Beach Rd, near the Bus Stand. There are a number of shops, including a pharmacy, lining the main road.

Transport

Local Bicycles and **motorbikes** for hire from many outlets, eg *JayJays* for bicycles, and a Kinetic Honda repair shop behind *Samir Electricals*, near the petrol station. **Long distance Taxi**: to/from Mapusa about Rs 50, bargain hard.

Directory **Banks** *State Bank of India* changes some TCs but does not accept Visa. *Bank of Baroda* accepts some credit cards, but get there around 1030 and be prepared to spend at least an hour. Also many private dealers offer a convenient and speedy exchange service but offer a poorer rate; *Wall Street*, opposite petrol pump, recommended for quick, efficient and polite service. **Communications** Internet: *Nikki's Internet Café*, T275794, nikkis@goa1.dot.net.in, has 6 terminals, 0900 to midnight, Rs 80 per hr. **Travel agents** Several including *MGM Travels*, Umtavaddo, T/F276073. **Useful services** Police T278284.

Baga

Sandwiched between Calangute and Anjuna, Baga (really the north end of Calangute beach) has more character. Reached either directly along the beach or by the coconut-shaded road slightly inland, parts of Baga still retain something of its more 'distanced' feel, though even here development has been rapid. It has left behind almost completely the hippy past which brought it to prominence.

Although the beach is relatively clean, at high tide the strip is very narrow after accounting for the rows of shacks and fishing boats. It is also far from quiet – with a high concentration of trinket sellers, masseurs and ear cleaners (not hygienic!) who will hassle you for custom at regular intervals. Sun beds are on hire for Rs 50, rising to Rs 100 during the peak season when they are all guaranteed to be occupied.

To the north, you can wade across the attractive estuary at low tide with care, for a pleasant 30-minute walk round the headland leading to Anjuna beach. The ugly concrete bridge across the Baga River adds about 1 km to this walk. Take care when using this bridge at night as there are no lights and not even the full moon can penetrate the excess of concrete.

An Anjuna style "Hippie Market" appears on Saturday evenings when Westerners and local vendors congregate near the headland from around 1700, north of the Baga river, to trade "ethnic" goods.

Sleeping **L** *Nilaya Hermitage*, near Arpora, 3 km inland, T276793, F276792, nilaya@goa1.dot.net 11 superbly and uniquely designed rooms, excellent pool, secluded, peaceful woodland location overlooking Baga headland, health centre, resident French chef during season, really exclusive ($235) and possibly best in Goa. **B** *Casa Portuguesa*, Calangute-Baga Rd, in an old villa with antiques, some tables on the verandah, plenty of atmosphere, good food but reports of small portions and stomach upsets. (Pasta and grilled seafood, thanks to a former Italian chef.)

Many offer big off-season discounts May-Sep; some attract package holidays

Eating **Mid-range** *Bernard's Place* near *CSM*, for Sunday roasts. *Domingo's*, Tito's Road. International. Well cooked and tasty, hygienic (freezes perishables in portions). *Indian Impact*, CSM Rd. Indian. Curries – "as good as Bradford!", *tandoor*, friendly. *Tibetan Friend's Corner*, Sauntovaddo, Tito's Rd (opposite side). End- Oct-Mar, attractive Tibetan decor, good Tibetan music, excellent food, specialities (lobster and tiger praws) when ordered previous day. North, near the river is *Nani's & Rani's*. Friendly, pleasant, good breakfasts. *Sunset*. Pleasant for watching the activities at the river mouth. *St Anthony's*, Goan and seafood. Wide choice. *Two Sisters*. Good muesli, curd and fruit salad.

Bars *Bharat*. Friendly, good for an evening drink. *Tito's*, still attracts a large clientele and is 'the place' for late night drinking (known for Domingo's Pina Colada), packed from 2300 to 0300, entertainment is variable; a/c dance floor now replaced by a cybercafé/games room. Scuffles are not uncommon. *The Cave Pub*, Tito's Rd. European-style pub, good meeting place. Watch out for short measures and sudden price increases.

Shopping **Books**: *Jay-Jays*. Mostly secondhand novels; 50% back if you return the book. Plenty of good quality but over-priced Kashmiri goods in touristy shops.

Bicycles and **motorbikes** are available for hire; ask outside *Brittos* for motorbikes. **Transport**
Boats from the beach to Anjuna Flea market, Rs 50 (one way), avoid in bad weather.
Buses are fairly frequent to/from Mapusa. **Taxi** to/from Mapusa, about Rs 50.

Banks Exchange: just north of Tito's road. **Communications** Internet: every- **Directory**
where; about Rs 2 per min. *Ocean Star Cyber Café*, T276492, oceanstar@india.com,
has 5 terminals. Recommended. **Travel agents** *Lina D'Souza Traveland*, Villa Nova,
Sauntavaddo, T276196, F276308, efficient ticketing.

Baga

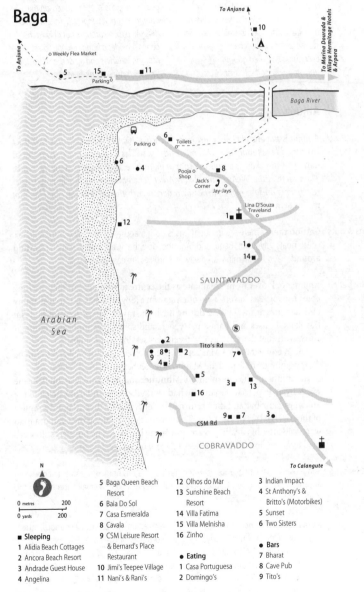

5 Baga Queen Beach Resort	**12** Olhos do Mar	**3** Indian Impact	
6 Baia Do Sol	**13** Sunshine Beach Resort	**4** St Anthony's & Britto's (Motorbikes)	
7 Casa Esmeralda	**14** Villa Fatima	**5** Sunset	
8 Cavala	**15** Villa Melnisha	**6** Two Sisters	
9 CSM Leisure Resort & Bernard's Place Restaurant	**16** Zinho		
	● **Eating**	● **Bars**	
■ **Sleeping**	**1** Casa Portuguesa	**7** Bharat	
1 Alidia Beach Cottages	**2** Domingo's	**8** Cave Pub	
2 Ancora Beach Resort		**9** Tito's	
3 Andrade Guest House	**10** Jimi's Teepee Village		
4 Angelina	**11** Nani's & Rani's		

0 metres 200
0 yards 200

Flea Market

The Wednesday Flea Market is huge and very popular – some find it colourful and worthwhile for jewellery, souvenirs and ethnic clothes. From its origins as an opportunity for foreign travellers to sell personal possessions in order to get on – or get home – the Flea Market has become an all-India market. Kashmiris and Rajasthanis set up stall alongside stallholders from much closer to home. Everything is geared gaudily and unashamedly at the tourist. Haircuts and henna 'tattoos' are on offer, alongside juggling equipment and chocolate cakes. Prices are extortionate compared to other shops. The best time to visit is the early morning (0800) or just before sunset to avoid the midday crowds who jam the approach roads. In the high season the afternoon can get oppressive and it can be difficult to move around, but at least the beach provides a handy escape valve. Many Westerners end up at the Shore Bar for the Wednesday night rave.

Anjuna

Phone code: 0832
Colour map 4, grid A1

Anjuna is still one of Goa's most visited beaches. Beach parties continue to attract crowds and the thump of rave/dance music pervades all the way to Vagator. Even during the day there is a constant roar of motorbikes and scooters along the roads. Then there is the Wednesday Flea Market. The government has imposed strict restrictions on late-night parties in order to curb the unpleasant side-effects of related activities.

Ins & outs   **Getting there**   There are frequent buses from Mapusa and a daily bus from Panaji. Local boats ply from Baga and Arambol for the Wednesday Market. **Getting around**   Baga is a 30 min walk away. Motorbikes are easy to hire.

The beach
Incidents of mugging have been reported, especially on the beach at night

Anjuna took over from Calangute as the centre for hippies but they are long gone, leaving '90s 'ravers' who often stay on a long term basis. The availability of drugs attracts local police during the high season. They carry out raids on travellers' houses and harass partygoers and sometimes innocent motorcyclists. Note that there are several foreigners serving long sentences.

The **Wednesday Flea Market** has become very commercialized so can be disappointing. Some find the Mapusa Market better for local colour.

In Anjuna itself, the splendid **Albuquerque mansion** was built in the 1920s by an expatriate Goan who had worked as a personal physician to the Sultan in Zanzibar and then returned home with a fortune to build a replica of the royal palace of Zanzibar. The coconut groves along the Chapora road were sold after his death and are now being built up. The house is still occupied by his widow and can be viewed from outside.

Sleeping   Some visitors have been robbed when staying in family houses; it is safer to choose an approved hotel or guest house. Good padlocks are sold in a small shop next to the *White Negro Bar* for Rs 150.

AL-A *Laguna Anjuna*, T231999, F420213, www.anjuna-goa.com 22 spacious, attractive apartments in individually designed cotttages with 'Swiss interiors' ($70 for 1-bedroom suite). **C** *Grandpa's Inn*, Gaunwadi, Mapusa Rd, T273271, F274370. 10 comfortable rooms with bath in old Goan house (Rs 800), good restaurant, pool. **D** *Don Joao Resorts*, Sorranto, T274325, F273447, Luzco@bom2.vsnl.net.in 48 large rooms with balcony and fridge (most with kitchenettes), some a/c, restaurant, exchange, small pool, friendly, away from beach; **D** *Sea Wave Inn*, T274455. 5 clean rooms, close to

Tourists welcome?

For some months Goa's new government has been targeting Goa's beach culture. The new Chief Minister Francisco Sardinha followed his announced ban on raves in July 2000 by a decision to close Anjuna flea market. While the decision is being contested as far away as New Delhi, the state's opposition to the backpacking and beach culture which has been a magnet for tens of thousands of visitors from around the world over the last thirty years seems to be hardening. The government, worried about the drug culture that surrounds the beach enclaves, is also resentful that so many of these visitors spend so little money in Goa.

beach, multicuisine restaurant. **D** *White Negro*, near the Church, T273326. 10 rooms with nets (Rs 400-500), good restaurant and bar, very clean.

D-E *Lolita's*, behind Oxford Stores (ask at nearest phone booth), T273289. 5 spacious, clean rooms with fridge and music system (own tapes), some with TV/ air cooler, friendly, secure. **D-E** *Martha's Breakfast Home*, between bus stand and market, T273365. 10 clean, spacious rooms, some newer with verandah (Rs 400), good breakfasts, garden, quiet, peaceful, friendly. **D-E** *Poonam*, near the Bus Stand, T273247. 23 simple, clean rooms with bath (Rs 400-500), some larger for sharing, restaurant. **D-E** *Red Cab Inn*, T274427, F273312. 6 well-designed comfortable, good-value rooms, restaurant ('local entertainment' Mon, 1900). **D** *Tamarind*, Kumarvaddo, 3 km from beach, T274309. 24 rooms, 6 a/c with modern bath in rustic stone cottages, well-managed, excellent restaurant, bar, small pleasant pool, library, pretty garden, 3 dogs and a pet eagle! **E** *Anjuna Beach Resort*, DeMello Vaddo, opposite Albuquerque Mansion, T274433. 14 rooms with bath, balcony, restaurant (breakfast, snacks), bike hire, friendly, secure, quiet, good value. **F** *Manali*, near the bus stand, T274421. 7 basic rooms, shared bath (Rs 125), restaurant, internet, not the friendliest in town. **F** *Zebra Lodging*, inland from St Anthony's. Run down but **camping** possible.

Most budget beachside rooms are occupied by long-stay visitors who pay about Rs 2,000 per month for the most basic

Eating

Anjuna is a vegetarian's paradise with plenty of Western & exotic options

Expensive *Bougainvillea*, at *Grandpa's Inn*. Excellent food, bar (wines, imported beer), in a pretty garden. Recommended. **Mid-range** *German Bakery*, inland from the Flea Market. Outdoors with soft lighting, excellent espresso, capuccino, juice and snacks, 2/3 main courses each night (eg lasagna, tofu-burger). Recommended. *Gregory's*, next to a tennis court. Excellent Continental, especially pizzas (try one with prawns); also tennis! *La Franza* with bar. Good Continental. Pleasant, large verandah overlooking attractive tropical garden. *Xavier's*, St Michaelvaddo, along a windy path, east from the market. **Cheap** *Sea Pearl*. Ideal for breakfast and simple snacks. Good value, pleasant, family run. *Whole Bean Tofu Shop* offers tofu, tempeh and vegetarian snacks. *Bean Me Up*, Soya Station and Salad Bar. Good vegetarian and vegan breakfasts, sandwiches, soups and cakes. All-day vegetarian English, American or Continental breakfasts Rs 80. Open 0830-1700 (maybe later when busy). Closed Wed. Recommended.

Beach parties Locations change every year so if you want to party, you'll soon find out where and when they are. Ask around locally and look out for flyers. Venues are often recognizable by illuminated trees and luminous wall hangings. **NB** It is best to walk there and back in a large group. *Shore Bar*, north of the Flea market, for the après market hoe down. The good sound system complements the fire jugglers' playground; several elderly women set up *chai* stalls with cakes and king-size *rizlas* on sale, making a good profit. *Sonic* is pleasant for a chilled beer at sunset.

Entertainment

Oxford Stores, for groceries, foreign exchange and photo processing. *Orchard Stores*, groceries, toiletries (western brands).

Shopping

Goa

Sport **Bunjee jumping** is offered by a Mumbai based firm with US trained staff, at Rs 500 per go. Safety is a priority with harnesses, carabinas and air bags employed. There are pool tables, a bar, an auditorium for slide/film shows and also beach volleyball. Open 1000-1230 and 1730 until late. **Paragliding** Enterprising foreign long-stayers organize this from season to season. Try *Happy Hours Café*, south Anjuna beach, from 1230-1400; Rs 500 (children welcome), or at the hilltop between Anjuna and Baga. **Windsurfing** boards are sometimes available for hire at the south end of the beach for about Rs 100 per hr, Rs 800 per week.

Transport **Motorcycles** are easy to hire; *Classic Bike Adventure* (Indo-German company) at Casa Tres Amigos, Socol Vado 425, Parra, Assagao, about 5 km east (off the Mapusa Rd), T273351, F262076, recommended for reliable bike hire and tours.

Directory **Banks** *Bank of Baroda*, Mon-Wed, Fri 0930-1330, Sat 0930-1130, accepts most TCs, Visa/Mastercard, 1% commission (min Rs 50); also provide 'Safe Custody Packets'. However, the 'Official' exchange section in *Oxford Stores* is more central, quicker and more efficient. **Communications** *Poste Restante* at Anjuna Post Office, open 1000-1600, Mon-Sat; efficient, parcels are also accepted without a fuss. **Internet** Several guest house and private booths charge about Rs 2 per min; *St Anthony's Store*, next to Post Office, Rs 100 per hr; 0900-2200. **Medical services** *Chemists* opposite Don Joao Resorts. *Health Centre*, T272250. **Travel agents** *MGM*, T274317; *Speedy*, T273266; *Traveland*, near the bus stand, T273207, F217535. **Useful services** *Police* T273233.

Anjuna

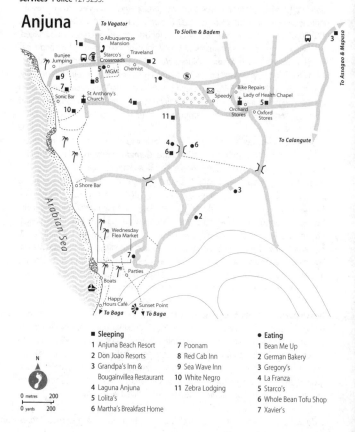

■ **Sleeping**
1 Anjuna Beach Resort
2 Don Joao Resorts
3 Grandpa's Inn &
   Bougainvillea Restaurant
4 Laguna Anjuna
5 Lolita's
6 Martha's Breakfast Home
7 Poonam
8 Red Cab Inn
9 Sea Wave Inn
10 White Negro
11 Zebra Lodging

● **Eating**
1 Bean Me Up
2 German Bakery
3 Gregory's
4 La Franza
5 Starco's
6 Whole Bean Tofu Shop
7 Xavier's

0 metres   200
0 yards   200

Vagator and Chapora

Phone code: 0832
Colour map 4, grid A1
22 km from Panaji

At the north end of Anjuna village, Vagator is an attractive little hamlet with its small bays between rocky headlands shaded by palms. It is quiet and laid back, though it can sometimes get crowded with day trippers. The beach is particularly pleasant in the early morning, but the sea is not always safe for swimming.

Chapora Fort commands the hilltop at the north end of the bay, only a short but steep walk away, immediately above *Sterling Resorts*. Now in ruins, the fort on the south bank of the Chapora River dominates the estuary. It was originally built by Adil Shah. Aurangzeb's son Akbar (not Akbar the Great), plotted his moves against his father in a pact with the Mughal's greatest enemies, the Marathas. The Portuguese built it in its present form in 1717 as a secure refuge for the people of Bardez in the face of Maratha attacks, as well as a defence of the river mouth. Despite the fact that none of the original buildings have survived, the fort remains superbly atmospheric and is well worth a visit. It is quite a climb and normally there are no refreshments save for fruit drinks sold by children at highly inflated prices, so it is worth carrying your own.

Traditional boat building is carried out on the riverside, north of the fort along the estuary mouth at Chapora.

North of Chapora, on the Siolim road, **Badem Church** overlooking the estuary is one of the nicest sunset spots.

Victory House, 549 Coutinho Vaddo, T273564, is an orphanage run by an Englishwoman, Anita Edgar (UK T01803 859094). They collect shoes, clothes, spectacles, books et cetera from charitable departing visitors.

Little Vagator Just south of 'Big' Vagator Beach there are two other small beaches which are more popular with younger travellers who fancy a change from Anjuna. Little Vagator is past the *Disco* party spot, while the very attractive 'Ozran' beach nestles at the bottom of a palm covered cliff. A steep path leads down to the sands where there is a sculpted face of Siva on a rock created by a long-stay visitor in the early 1990s which is partly submerged at high tide – it is a frisbee hang-out. *Getting there:* from *Starco's* restaurant (a well known meeting place in Anjuna) at the junction of Mapusa and Chapora roads, walk, bike or take a bus to Chapora and get off at the stop at the first paved road to the left (west), where there is a board for *Alcove* and *Disco*; the *Alcove* is perched on the rock just above the beach.

Day tourists from Panaji descend on Vagator & Anjuna at about 1100 & leave at about 1700

Goa

B *Sterling Vagator* (partly time-share), T273276, F274376. Attractive setting at the foot of the Fort, 30 well maintained cottages, some poolside (uphill) or in peaceful garden setting with shady *jambul* trees near the beach, restaurants (others 10 mins' walk away), quiet, exchange for residents. **B** *Leoney Resort*, T273634, F274343, romio@goa1.dot.net.in 13 rooms, 3 cottages (Rs 1300), a/c extra Rs 200. Clean, modern, family run, low-key, quiet location, pool, 10 min walk from beach. Several are along the streets leading to the beach from the bus stops: **E** *Abu John's*, 6 small rooms with bath, good restaurant, garden, pleasant, quiet. **E** *Dolrina*, T273382. 13 rooms, most baths shared between 2 rooms, safe, secure, friendly. **E** *Hilltop Motel*, away from the beach, T273665. 14 small rooms, those with bath reasonable, genuine Italian baker. **E-F** *Garden Villa*, T273571. 8 clean rooms (Rs 150-250), some with bath, good value for the area, although away from the beach, restaurant with a decent choice. **F** *Noble Nest*, opposite the Holy Cross Chapel, 274335. 21 rooms, 2 with bath but ample facilities for sharing (Rs 150), basic, but popular, exchange and internet. **F** *Ram Das Swami* restaurant on Little Vagator Beach, allows **camping** but provides no toilets.

Sleeping
Avoid 'Royal Resort'

Eating

Hoards of day trippers congregate around the cafés near the beach

Mid-price: *Alcove* on the cliff above Little Vagator. Smartish, ideal position, excellent food (try fish dishes) plus drinks, pleasant ambience in the evening, sometimes live music. *Mango Tree*, in the village, offers a wide choice of continental favourites. **Cheap**: In **Vagator**: several restaurants line the streets to the beach. Some serve good fresh fish including *Mahalaxmi*. *Primrose Café* serves tasty health foods and also has news of "spontaneous" parties. In **Chapora**: fly-ridden *Scarlet* does good muesli, ice creams and chilled fruity shakes.

Entertainment

Parties: at *Disco Valley* between Vagator and Little Vagator beaches and at *Banyan Tree*, east of Vagator.

Shopping

Books: *Narayan*, small bookstall, sells local newspapers. *Rainbow*, near Victory House Orphanage, buys, sells and exchanges European language books.

Transport

Road: Daily bus from Panaji, 1¼ hrs; frequent from Mapusa to Chapora via Anjuna and Vagator.

Directory

Banks No exchange facilities here except at *Sterling Vagator* (for residents only); nearest is in Anjuna: see above. **Health centre** T262211.

Siolim

Phone code: 0832
Colour map 4, grid A1
Population: 1991 9,700
Pronounced 'Show-lem'

The **Church of St Anthony** dominates the square here. Built in 1606, it replaced an earlier (1568) Franciscan church. St Anthony, the Patron saint of Portugal, is widely venerated throughout the villages of Goa. The high, flat-ceilinged church has a narrow balustraded gallery and Belgian glass chandeliers. The attractive and typically gabled west end has statues of Jesus and St Anthony. **B** *Siolim House*, isabellesood@iname.com, recently renovated 300 year old heritage home, seven large suites. **Ferries** are half-hourly.

Vagator

Safe passage for turtles

Adult turtles come ashore on Morjim beach between October and December, to lay their eggs which hatch after 54 days, usually on the night of the full moon. As soon as a nest is discovered, Forest Department staff put a net over the site and mark it with a flag. When the eggs hatch, the officials escort the hatchlings to the sea to allow them a safe run into the unknowns of the ocean. The nesting sites are patrolled day and night to protect them from the worst of humanity.

Morjim

Morjim lies on the north side of the Chapora River estuary right at its mouth. After crossing the estuary by ferry to Chopdem the coast road runs as a narrow village lane winding along the edge of the estuary giving beautiful views across to Chapora Fort, until it reaches the point where the river meets the sea and the coast turns sharply north. Here the road ends behind the sand dunes. The beach is still clean and idyllic with no more than 50 to 60 daytrippers visiting at the peak of the high season. It has been found to be a **turtle nesting** site. The area is popular for bird watching.

The **Shri Morja Devi Temple** in the village is of special interest because of one of its affiliated shrines dedicated to a Jain guru (Jain dynasties ruled over the region from the sixth to the 10th centuries AD). The month-long *Kalas Utsav*, celebrated every three, five and seven years, closes with a large cultural fair.

Six or seven cheap beach shacks which provide simple food and drink also rent out sunbeds and deckchairs for Rs 50, while palm umbrellas provide the only shade on this long and wide stretch of firm sand.

Asvem

The road from Morjim cuts inland over the low wooded hills to Mandrem village which lies a few kilometres south of Arambol. Just before the village, a road leads down to a deserted but attractive palm-fringed beach.

Sleeping and eating D *Palm Grove* , towards Morjim, 4 tree houses amongst coconut palms very close to the shoreline, simple rooms with fan (Rs 600), bath facilities shared with **F** rooms, occasionally used by package tourists on "Go native" trips, limited menu restaurant. **F** *Beach huts* made of woven palm leaves on concrete, close to the shore line (Rs 150-200 each), shared facilities in nearby *café*. Do not leave valuables in rooms.

Mandrem

Along the road, the fishing and toddy tapping village occupies a beautifully shaded setting. The beach, which is usually deserted, has little shade, but a little to the north is a beautiful little 'island' of sand with coconut palms between the sea and the river. In the **Shri Purchevo Ravalnatha Temple** in the village there is an unusual medieval image of Vishnu's half eagle-half human 'vehicle', Garuda. The crouching Garuda is dressed as a soldier with wings protruding from his back.

Sleeping 5 or 6 **F** *beach shacks* have appeared on the quiet beach. **F** *Village rooms*, usually signed, are rented out to foreigners for up to six months through the winter.

Directory Banks *Canara Bank*, on the main road accepts travellers' cheques but has no facilities for card cash. **Hospital** T230081. **Yoga** (Iyengar) is taught by Sharat Arora, F297375, between Nov and Feb (5 and 10 day courses). Highly recommended.

Goa

Arambol (Harmal)

Phone code: 0832
Colour map 4, grid A1

Arambol (Harmal) is a large, strung out village by the seashore where the main beach is a glorious stretch of curving sand. The once precious quiet of this hidden corner is now broken by a mini building boom and a constant hum of traffic bringing daytrippers. New guest houses signal the end of Arambol as an isolated backwater as they rapidly swallow up the remaining sandy patches between the palms.

Ins & outs

Getting there Many visit Arambol by motorbike from other beaches. There are regular buses to the village from Mapusa and a frequent service from Chopdem which is 12 km away (about 40 mins, Rs 6); the attractive coastal detour via Morjim is slightly longer. The local ferry from Chapora to the south crosses the estuary (Rs 20 each, Rs 40 for a boat). It is then a 2 hr walk through Morjim and Mandrem along the coast. Alternatively, get a bus to Siolim, cross the river by the regular ferry to Chopdem (Rs3) and then pick up a bus or taxi. The bridge across the estuary was half completed in early 2000. **Getting around** You can get a taxi or hire a bike in the village but mind the numerous unmarked speed breakers. On market days there are boats to Anjuna (Rs150).

Village & beach

A sign at the cross roads in the village centre near the bus stop points down to the sea. Shops along the road sell cheap clothes, bags and trinkets but few of these seem to be of Goan origin. To the north, a well-made track runs round the headland past a series of tiny bays to the second quieter beach which is relatively free of beach shacks. There is little shade save for the few sun umbrellas. Here you can walk for miles with starfish being washed up by your feet. Unlike the headlands around Anjuna, the rocks which run into the sea here are basalt, the hexagonal columns tilted almost horizontal but eroded into jagged shapes clearly visible for miles along the coast. There are sulphur pits and a freshwater lake which some visitors use for swimming.

Sleeping

Touts meet newcomers at the bus stand offering rooms close to the main beach for Rs 80-150 (bargaining expected). Others are in a cluster on a parallel road, among trees (so more mosquitoes). Some do not provide bedding. Many rooms lack the security of a hotel compound. Guest houses higher up on the rocky hills charge more but are poorly maintained and there is a distinct smell of sewage. **E** *Ludo*, on the beach road, like a 'Country Club' set back behind a cottage offers massage, 3 **F** basic rooms with fan, cold shower (hot bucket Rs 5), family home, quiet. The tiny **F** *Lakes Paradise* also serves Goan curry and rice.

Eating

There are beach **cafés** all along the main beach and around the headland to the north. Italian food is in vogue. **Mid-range**: *Pirates Cabin*. Indian, succulent *tandoori* grills. **Cheap**: *Double Dutch*, from the beach turn left off the main beach road before *Ganesh Stores* (look for *'i'* for Information). Excellent tea, coffee, imported journals. Closer to the main beach: *Loecke*. Ideal for tea. *Seahorse*, says one, has the "best waiter in India!". *Welcome*, at the end of the road on the sea front. Great muesli. Basic eateries in the village do 'rice plate meals'.

Watersports

For **dolphin trips** or boats to Anjuna, contact *21 Coconuts Inn*, second restaurant on the left after stepping onto the beach; Rs 150 for each. **Paragliding** is also arranged from beach shacks.

Transport

Bike and **taxi hire** from *Welcome Restaurant*.

Directory

Communications The small village *Post Office* is at the 'T' junction, 1.5 km from the beach. **Emergency** Police, T297614. **Medical services** *Chemists*, on the main road; *Health Centre*,

T291249. **Travel agents** *Delight* and *Tara*, in the village, exchange cash and TCs, good for train tickets (Rs100 service charge); also buys bus tickets.

Keri beach, north of Arambol Beach, is a completely unspoilt and rarely visited stretch of sand backed by casuarina trees all the way down to the Arambol highland. It can be reached from the north on foot from the ferry terminal, or from the south by walking round the headland from Arambol. There are dangerous currents near the mouth of the Tiracol estuary so it is best to avoid swimming there; a five-minute walk south along the beach will get you to safer waters.

Keri
Colour map 4, grid A1

Sleeping and eating Forest Department's simple **F** *Keri Forest Rest House*, can be booked through the DCF, North Ponda, T0834 312095. A solitary *restaurant* (limited menu), has 4 very basic **F** rooms with common bath (Rs 70).

The tiny hamlet of Paliem on the edge of the plateau is about 5 km north of Arambol just before the road drops down through dense wooded slopes to Keri and the Tiracol ferry. Its **Vetal** (Betall) **Temple** has charmingly painted designs of the tree of life on its blue exterior wall.

Paliem Village

★ Tiracol

Tiracol (Terekhol), the northernmost tip of Goa (an enclave on the Maharashtra border) has a tiny picturesque fort which is now one of the best positioned coastal hotels in India. The views from here are magnificently atmospheric, looking south to Arambol, Chapora and Fort Aguada. Consider staying two or three nights here to give time to explore the area.

Phone code: 0832
Colour map 4, grid A1

Getting there From **Panaji**, there is a bus around 1130. From **Mapusa**, take a share taxi to Siolim (Rs 8) where you cross the river Chapora by ferry; continue to Keri (Querim) by share taxi, then cross Tiracol River by ferry and walk the remaining 2 km! The Tiracol half-hourly ferry runs between 0600-2130 and takes 15-minutes. Both ferries take cars. From **Dabolim Airport**, pre-paid taxi to Tiracol Fort, Rs 700.

Ins & outs

Goa

Perched on the north side of the Tiracol River estuary, on a piece of high ground, the fort's battlement walls are clearly visible from the Arambol headland. Originally a Maratha fort, it was protected from attacks from the sea, while the walls on the land side rise from a dry moat. It was captured by the Portuguese in 1776 who built the church here which is worth a look. It has a classic Goan façade with an interesting hinged confessional, and was large enough to have catered for the whole village.

The fort

 St Anthony's church inside the tiny fort was built in the early 1750s soon after the Portuguese takeover. It has a classic Goan façade and is just large enough to have catered for the small village. In the courtyard, paved with laterite blocks, stands a modern statue of Christ. Inside, the church has several charming features. The small gallery at the west-end provides space for a harmonium and the choir, while in the body of the church are two old confessional chairs. Too small a church for full scale confessional boxes, two small hinged wooden flaps are pulled out to separate the priest from the penitent, and are tucked back against the wall when not in use. There is a typically decorated altar reredos with St Anthony above. Some of the framed paintings on the walls have deteriorated with time. The *Festival of St Anthony* here is held in May (usually on the second Tuesday), to enable the villagers to attend who would otherwise be away on the conventional festival day of 13 June.

You can explore the fort's battlements and tiny circular turrets which scarcely seem to have been intended for the real business of shooting the enemy. Steps lead down to a terrace on the south side while the north has an open plateau.

Sleeping **B-C** *Tiracol Fort Heritage*, T0831-782240, F782326, tiracol@usa.net 10 rooms in old fort (Rs 800-1750), sympathetically furnished, spacious suites at either end on the 1st floor (number 1 is particularly good with own little tiny terrace), wonderful views, one of Goa's most peaceful and romantic places to stay, limited but tasty menu in the restaurant (in reclaimed dry moat), power cuts can be a problem, birdwatchers' haven, boat trips (dolphins, Redi Beach etc), scooter hire, discounts from 4 May-3 Sep. Non-residents may visit (0900-1800). Recommended. **E** *Hill Rock*, 1 km from the ferry, T02366-68264. Modern, 4 rooms (Rs 210-320) in a family hotel, restaurant, good location overlooking fort and Keri beach but neglected.

Ponda and the Hindu Heartland

Ponda is Goa's smallest taluka. It is also the richest in Goan Hindu religious architecture. Within 5 km of its town centre are some of Goa's most important temples, including the Shri Shantadurga at Queula and the Nagesh Temple near Bandora.

Ponda (Phondya)

Phone code: 0832
Colour map 4, grid B2
Population: 14,700

Once a centre of culture, music, drama and poetry, the area around Ponda, with its group of important Hindu temples, was known as Antruz Mahal. Ponda town is an important transport intersection, where the main road from Margao via Borlim meets the East-West National Highway, NH4A.

Sights The **Safa Mosque** (Shahouri Masjid), the largest of 26 mosques in Goa, was built by Ibrahim 'Ali' Adil Shah in 1560. It has a simple rectangular chamber on a low plinth, with a pointed pitched roof, very much in the local architectural style, but the arches are distinctly Bijapuri. Built of laterite, the lower tier has been quite badly eroded. On the south side is a tank with meherab designs for ritual cleansing. The large gardens and fountains here were destroyed during Portuguese rule. Today the mosque is attractively set off by the low rising forest-covered hills in the background.

Sleeping **D** *Menino*, 100 m east of Bus Stand junction, 1st Flr, T314148, F315026. 20 rooms, some a/c, pleasant, comfortable, good restaurant, totally rebuilt, now an impressive modern hotel, good value. **E** *President*, 1 km east of bus stand, T312287. 11 rooms, basic but clean and reasonable. **E** *Padmavi*, 100m north of bus stand on NH4A, T 312144. 20 large clean rooms, some with bath with TV. At **Farmagudi**, to the north: **C-D** *Atish*, T313224, F313239. 40 comfortable rooms, some a/c (Rs 800), restaurant, pool, gym, good modern hotel, friendly staff. **E** *Farmagudi Tourist Cottages* (GTDC), attractively located though too close to NH4A, T312922. 39 rooms, some a/c, dorm (Rs 50), adequate restaurant with standard government fare (eat at *Atish*).

Eating **Mid-range** Good a/c restaurant at the *Menino* Hotel, pleasant decor, generous main courses (Rs 60), popular, good service, clean toilet. **Cheap** *Kirti*, Nirankal Rd, 2 km

east of centre. Simple but clean a/c room upstairs, reasonable food. *Café Bhonsle*.
Good South Indian snacks, very popular with locals.

Road Buses to Panaji and Bondla via Tisk, but it is best to have your own transport to   **Transport**
see the places nearby.

Hospital *Community Health Centre,* T312115. **Forestry** Deputy Conservator of Forests   **Directory**
(North), T312095.

✴ **Shri Mangesh Temple** To the northwest of Ponda, on the NH17 leading to   **Priol**
Old Goa, the 18th-century Shri Mangesh, set on a wooded hill at Priol just
north of Mardol, is sometimes described as the most important Hindu temple
in Goa. *Jatra* on 25 February. During *Mangesh Jatra* the *rath* (temple car) with
Shri Mangesh is pulled by crowds of attendants.

The Mangesh linga was originally in an ancient temple in Kushatali
(Cortalim in Salcete taluka), across the river. However, after the Inquisition
began in 1561, the deity was carried across the river to Priol. Today the temple
is supported by a large resident community who serve its various functions.

The temple complex is architecturally typical of the highly distinctive Goan
Hindu temple style. The estate on which the temple depends provides a beautiful setting. Note the attractive tank on the left as you approach which is one of
the oldest parts of the site.

The seven-storeyed octagonal *deepmal* in the courtyard is one of the most
famous lamp towers in Goa. Around its base are colourful little 'primitif'
painted images. Lamps are placed in the niches at festivals. The sacred *tulsi
vrindavan* (basil) plant stands nearby.

The *mandapa* (assembly hall) has the typical red tiled steeply pitched roof.
The highest tower with an octagonal drum topped by a dome is over the sanctum. At the entrance to the shrine itself is a beautifully carved wooden door.
19th-century Belgian glass chandeliers hang from the ceiling of the main hall,
usually crowded with pilgrims who make offerings of flowers and coconuts
bought at the entrance. The *nandi* (Siva's bull) is present, as are the silver
dwarpalas (guardian deities) and the additional shrines to Parvati and Ganesh.
The image of the deity is housed behind a highly decorated silver screen.

The **Mahalsa Narayani Temple** is 2 km from Shri Mangesh. *Mahalsa* is a   **Mardol**
Goan form of Vishnu's consort Lakshmi or, according to some, his female
form *Mohini*.

The entrance to the temple complex is through the arch under the
nagarkhana (drum room). There is a seven-storeyed *deepstambha* and in addition a tall brass Garuda pillar which rests on the back of a turtle, acts as a second
lamp tower. The half human-half eagle *Garuda*, Vishnu's vehicle, sits on top.
The 'new' *mandapa* (columned hall) is of concrete, its severity hidden somewhat
under the red tiling, finely carved columns and a series of brightly painted carvings of the 10 *avatars* (incarnations) of Vishnu (see page 180). A decorative
arched gate at the back leads to the peace and cool of the palm-fringed temple
tank. A palanquin procession with the deity marks the *Mardol Jatra*.

The **Nagesh Temple** is 4 km west of Ponda. At Farmagudi junction on the   **Bandora**
NH17, a fork is signposted to Bandora. A narrow winding lane dips down to
the tiny hamlet and its temple to Siva as Nagesh (God of Serpents).

The temple's origin can be established at 1413 by an inscribed tablet here,
though the temple was renewed in the 18th century. The temple tank which is
well stocked with carp, is enclosed by a white-outlined laterite block wall and

Goa

surrounded by shady palms. The five-storey lamp tower near the temple has brightly coloured deities painted in niches just above the base.

The main *mandapa* (assembly hall) has interesting painted woodcarvings illustrating stories from the epics *Ramayana* and *Mahabharata* below the ceiling line, as well as the *Ashtadikpalas*, the eight Directional Guardians (Indra, Agni, Yama, Nirritti, Varuna, Vayu, Kubera and Ishana). The principal deity has the usual *nandi* and in addition there are shrines to Ganesh and Laxmi-Narayan and subsidiary shrines with lingas, in the courtyard.

The *Nagesh Jatra* (normally November) is celebrated at full moon to commemorate Siva's victory.

South of the Nagesh Temple, the **Mahalakshmi Temple** lies in a valley below the road and is thought to be the original form of the deity of the Shakti cult. The sanctuary has an octagonal tower and dome while the side entrances have shallow domes. The stone slab with the Marathi inscription dates from 1413.

Queula (Kavale)
Phone code: 0832

Just 3 km southwest from Ponda's town centre bus stand is one of the largest and most famous of Goa's temples dedicated to ✷ **Shantadurga** (1738), the wife of Siva as the Goddess of Peace. The form of Durga was so named because at the request of Brahma she mediated in a great quarrel between Siva (her husband) and Vishnu, and brought back peace in the Universe. Hence, in the sanctuary she stands between the two other deities. *Jatra* on 15th February.

The temple is set in a picturesque forest clearing on a hillside at Queula and was erected around 1738 by Shahu, a grandson of Sivaji, the great Maratha ruler of the West Deccan. The deity, originally from Quelossim (Queula), had been taken to Ponda 200 years earlier.

Steps lead up to the temple complex which has a very large tank cut into the hillside and a spacious courtyard surrounded by the usual pilgrim hostels and administration offices. The temple has a six-storey *deepstambha* (lamp tower) and subsidiary shrines. The part-gilded *rath* (car) is housed in the compound. The temple, neo-classical in design, has a tall tower over the sanctum. Its two-storey octagonal drum, topped by a dome which has a lantern on top, is an example of the strong influence of church architecture on Goan temple design. The interior of polished marble is lit by many chandeliers. Beyond the hall is the sanctum where the principal deity of Shantadurga, flanked by Siva and Vishnu, is housed behind a silver screen.

Dhavli

Near Ponda, *Hill Billies* Restaurant and Bar, T316317, is also the venue (after temple visits) of an occasional evening of Indian classical dances staged from 1930-2130, followed by a buffet, US$22 (pick-up from Panaji 1500). Contact Passive Active Tourism, T0832-422986, josephb@bom2.vsnl.net.in

★ Savoi Spice Plantation
Colour map 4, grid B2
For information,
T340243

Over 200 years old, it was founded by Mr. Shetye and is still being run by the family. The plantation is focused around a large irrigation tank with beautiful lilies and kingfishers. Being part wetland and part on a hillside allows cultivation of a wide variety of plants and trees. There are grapefruit, areca nut palms (some 150 years old) and coconuts with pepper vines growing up their trunks, soft and hard skin jackfruit which can become giants weighing over 20 kg, and banana plants which can produce 250 bananas from a single flower (one flower is cut off each plant to be eaten as a vegetable delicacy). On the hillside grow pineapples (200,000 fruit are cut between June and September), bamboo, basil, cocoa, wood-apple, mangoes, and the surprising nutmeg which you might mistake for lemons! No space is wasted and the staple tuber *suarn* underground can weigh up to 2 kg. The families employed on the site are housed on the estate and men, women and the older children can be seen working at different seasonal tasks.

Retired employees are encouraged to remain active by producing handicrafts for sale to visitors. You can also buy packets of spices.

The guided tour (Rs 300 for individuals), along shady paths, takes about an hour and includes soft drinks and snacks on arrival, and concludes with lunch and a tot of feni to "give strength" for the return journey to your resort, and the chance to buy packets of spices which make ideal gifts to take home. You will even be offered several cheap, natural alternatives to Viagra, whether you need them or not!

The plantation north of Ponda is reached via Banastari and is 6 km from Savoi. **Buses** run from Ponda (towards Volvoi), and also from Banastari; ask for "Plantation". Taxis ply from the coastal resorts (eg Rs 700 return from Candolim) but travel agents offer competitive rates which include the entrance fee (eg *Day Tripper Tours*, near Kamat Complex, Calangute, Rs 770). Some include a visit to a local cashew nut processing plant. **Transport**

Central Goa

Vasco da Gama

Vasco da Gama (Vasco, in short), is the passenger railway terminus of the Central Goa branch line, and is the industrial heart of modern Goa. It has grown to become Goa's largest town but its only convenience for a visitor is its proximity to the airport.

Phone code: 0832
Colour map 4, grid B1
Population: 91,300

Just 3 km away, Dabolim airport, developed by the Navy, is now shared by domestic and international charter flights from Europe. There are taxis or an airport coach. Alternatively, cheap local buses pass along the main road. Trains via Londa can now bring visitors from the north (eg Delhi, Agra) or the south (Hospet, Bangalore), apart from towns within Goa as far west as Dudhsagar. Panaji is 30 km away. **Tourist offices** At *Tourist Hotel*, T512673. **Getting there**

Part of Baina Beach, the red light district, is notified as a high risk area for HIV

C *La Paz Gardens*, Swatantra Path, T512121, F513302, lapaz.hotel@sma. sprint.rpg.ems.vsnl.net.in 68 rooms, need redecorating, good a/c restaurants (Indian, Chinese, fast food), pleasant bar. **C** *Bismarck*, behind *Auto Service*, T512277, F518524. 22 clean a/c rooms on 3 floors, some with bath tubs or balcony, small pool and terrace at back with an open-air restaurant. **C-D** *Citadel*, near Tourist Hotel, Jose Vaz Rd, T512222, F513036, epson@bom2.vsnl.net.in 42 comfortable rooms, half a/c, restaurant, bar. **C-D** *Maharaja*, FL Gomes Rd, T514075, F512559, mahahotl@goa1.dot.net.in 40 smallish rooms, 18 a/c, Gujarati *thalis*, bar. **E** *Annapurna*, D Deshpande Rd, T513735. 33 clean rooms with bath (Rs 250), good vegetarian food. **E** *Gladstone*, FL Gomes Rd, near railway station, T510005. 18 clean functional rooms, some a/c (Rs 350), restaurant, bar. **E** *Nagina*, D Deshpande Rd, T511670. 21 rooms, some a/c, restaurant serves Goan specialities. **E-F** *Westend*, D Deshpande Rd, T511575. 22 rooms, some a/c, restaurant, bar. **Sleeping**

Mid-range: *Goodyland* near La Paz. Western fast food joint. **Cheap**: *Adarsh*, Swatantra Path, 100m south of railway station. Excellent *masala dosa*. *Ananta* near the Citadel Hotel. Recommended for Indian. *Leads* 300m from station. Indian, Goan, Chinese (no bar), good value. *Nanking* off Swatantra Path. Good value, authentic Chinese. **Eating**

Transport **Road Bus**: from **City Bus Stand** near market, frequent, non-stop service to **Panaji**, and **Margao**, Rs 15, via **Airport**. **Kadamba Bus Stand**, northeast of town, with a helpful information booth, has services to major towns in Goa (not non-stop), and to **Bangalore** via Hubli: 1500, 1645 (15 hrs), Rs 240; **Belgaum**, many, Rs 57; **Hospet**: 1130 (10 hrs) Rs 100; **Hubli** many (6 hrs) Rs 65; **Mangalore**: 1700 (10 hrs) Rs 156; **Mumbai**: 1330 (16 hrs) Rs 325. **NB** Check timetable in advance. **Taxi** to and from Londa, about Rs 1,500.

Trains stop at: **Dabolim** (for the airport and Bogmalo), **Cansaulim**, **Seraulim**, **Majorda** (for the beach), **Madgaon** (Margao) for Colva, Benaulim and the southern beaches, **Chandorgoa**, **Sanvordem**, **Calem**, **Colem (Kolamb)**, **Dudhsagar** (for the waterfalls). **Long distance**: Reservations, T512833. Services via Londa to **Belgaum**, **Bangalore**, **Delhi** via Agra, and with **Hospet (for Hampi)** among others. To **Londa**: by *Goa Exp 2779*, dep 1330, arr 1740; by *Vasco Bangalore Exp 7310*, dep 2110, arr 0120; both 4¼ hrs. To **Bangalore**: by *Vasco Bangalore Exp 7310*, dep 2110, arr 1240, 15½ hrs. To **Delhi (Nizamuddin)**: *Goa Exp 2779*, dep 1330, arr 0645 (after 2 nights), 41¾ hrs. To **Hospet (for Hampi)**: *Amravati Exp 7226*, dep 0505, arr 1525, 10¼ hrs. To **Pune** *Goa Exp 2779*, dep 1330, arr 0400, 15½ hrs.

Vasco da Gama

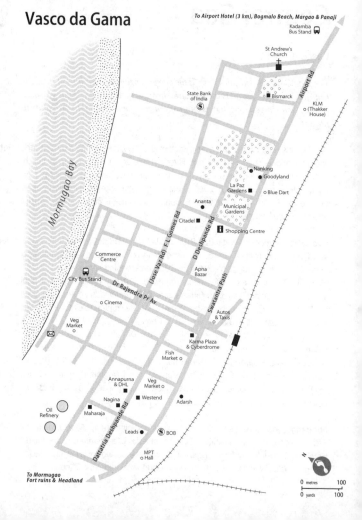

Bogmalo, the nearest beach to the airport (4 km, and a 10 minute drive away) – is small, palm fringed and attractive, yet it is sparsely visited.

Bogmalo
Phone code: 0832

About 2.5 km before reaching Bogmalo, the approach road forks. The right fork continues to Bogmalo whilst the left goes to Hollant Beach (2 km) via Issorcim. Hollant beach is a small rocky cove fringed with coconut palms, with a small section of sandy beach beyond the two bar/ restaurants here. From here, on a clear day, you can view the whole of the beach coastline from Arrosim to Mobor, with Cabo de Rama and the first foothills of the Western Ghats forming an impressive backdrop.

Hollant Beach

Further south, can be reached by going through the village behind the *Park Plaza*. Local fishermen are at hand to ferry passengers to two small islands for about Rs 350 per boat, which can be shared by a group.

Santra Beach

AL-A *Bogmalo Beach Park Plaza*, T513311, F512510, bbppr@goa1.dot.net.in 121 rooms with sea view, palm-shaded poolside, some watersports, ayurvedic centre. **A-B** *Coconut Creek* (new sister hotel of *Joet's*). 20 rooms (10 a/c) in 2-storey cottages, light and airy, pool, mainly packages. **C-D** *Saritas*, T555965, on the beach. 13 clean rooms with bath, some a/c, popular restaurant. **D** *El Mar*, T555329, set back from the beach. 5 clean, large, basic rooms with shower, seafood available. **D** *Joet's Guest House*, right on the beach, T555036, JOETS@goa1.dot.net.in 12 small airy rooms with shower (Rs 500), good restaurant.

Sleeping
Cheaper family guest houses in the village are set back from the beach

The beach cafés near *Bogmalo Beach Park Plaza* are dearer but do excellent seafood. *Joet's*. Good seafood and "very friendly; sun beds on the beach and hammocks among the palms".

Eating

Ritika Bookshop and Boutique, *Bogmalo Beach Park Plaza*'s verandah, a/c, good books and stationery, high quality gifts, good value. **Tailoring**: some beach gift shops offer good quality, made-to-measure cotton and silk jackets and shirts at reasonable prices.

Shopping

Watersports *Splash Watersports* have a shack on the beach, providing parasailing (Rs 850), windsurfing (Rs 400 per hr), water skiing (Rs 500 for 15 mins), trips to nearby island (Rs 1500) etc; during the high season only. *Bogmalo Beach Park Plaza*, T513291, and *Joet's*, T555036, also offer these; diving is possible through the latter. **Museum** *Naval Aviation Museum*, 1 km from beach, on approach road. 1000-1700, closed Mon and public holidays, free. A few rusting examples of old planes.

Entertainment

Dabolim

Goa's airport is south of Panaji, across the Mormugao Bay. There are counters at the airport for car hire, foreign exchange and tourist information, all of which are normally open to meet flights, usually 1230-1530.

Colour map 4, grid B1

Internal flights: *Air India*, T224081, Mumbai; Thiruvananthapuram. *Indian Airlines*, T223826, Reservations 1000-1300, 1400-1600, Airport T0834-512788. Flights to Bangalore, Delhi and Mumbai daily; also Chennai; and from Tiruchirapalli and to Pune. Kochi (flights suspended in early 2000), *Jet Airways*, T221472, Airport T510354, to Mumbai. *Gujarat Airways*, T223730, to Pune. *Sahara*, to Mumbai daily, and Delhi.

Transport

Transport to town: package tour companies and luxury hotels usually arrange courtesy buses for hotel transfer. Other options are to take a taxi, bus or car hire (see Essentials). The pre-paid taxi counter immediately outside the arrivals hall has rates clearly

Goa

displayed (eg Panaji Rs 340 which takes 40 mins; North Goa beaches from Rs 450; Tiracol Rs 750; south Goa beaches from Rs 240; Palolem Rs 700). State your destination at the counter, pay and get a receipt which will give the registration number of your taxi. Keep hold of this receipt until you reach your destination. There is no need to tip the driver since the pre-paid rate is already generous by local standards. The taxi driver may insist that the hotel you have asked for has closed down or is full and will suggest another in order to get a commission from the hotel. To avoid this problem, say that you have a reservation (booking) at the hotel of your choice (even if you don't!). *Indian Airlines* sometimes have a bus for transfer to Panaji to meet their incoming flights (Rs 30), although this was not running in early 2000. The public bus stop on the far side of the roundabout outside the airport gates (left after leaving the Arrivals hall), has regular buses to Vasco da Gama (Rs 3), from where there are connections to all major places in Goa. If you want to go straight to the nearest beach, go to the right of the roundabout, cross the road, and you will find a bus stop for buses to Bogmalo (Rs 3). The possible closure of the Zuari Bridge for repairs may greatly increase the transfer time by road from the airport to Panaji and North Goa via Ponda. The new *Hotel Airport,* 1 km away, is listed under Panaji 'Sleeping'.

Southern Goa

★ Margao

Phone code: 0832
Colour map 4, grid B2
Population: 72,100
33 km from Panaji
30 km from Vasco

Also called Madgaon or Margoa, this is the largest commercial centre after Panaji and the capital of the state's richest and most fertile taluka, Salcete. A pleasant provincial town, it was given the status of a vila *(town) by Royal decree in 1778. The Konkan railway now brings many visitors here as their first port of call, but most head for the beaches, using Margao for an overnight stop for making travel connections.*

Ins & outs **Getting there** The **Konkan Railway** now connects Margao directly with Mumbai and Mangalore; trains to Kerala also use the line. Madgaon station is 1,500 m southeast from the bus stands which are in the Municipal Gardens and the Market area where most of the hotels and restaurants are located. Rickshaws charge Rs 15 to transfer while locals walk the 800 m along the rail line! Those arriving by bus from other states and from North Goa use the New Kadamba (State) bus stand 2 km north of town, but continue to the centre. The central bus stands are for destinations south of Margao (Colva and Benaulim buses leave from the local stand east of the gardens). **Getting around** There are plenty of auto-rickshaws and 8-seater van taxis for hire in addition to city buses.

Sights Tourism has had little impact here. You can still see examples of old Portuguese domestic architecture and some fine churches while also experiencing daily life in a bustling market town going about its business.

The impressive Baroque ✴ **Church of the Holy Spirit** with its classic Goan façade dominates the Old Market (*Feast Day* in June) square, the Largo de Igreja, surrounded by a number of fine town houses. Originally built in 1564 over the ruins of a Hindu temple, it was sacked by Muslims in 1589 and rebuilt in 1675. A remarkable pulpit on the north wall has carvings of the Apostles. The carved reredos is flanked by gold pillars, and there are three Baroque style central pictures. There are statues of St Anthony and of the Blessed Joseph Vaz, kept in glass cabinets in the north aisle near the north transept. In the square is a monumental cross with a mango tree beside it.

Many 18th-century houses, though dilapidated, can be seen, especially in and around Abade Faria Road. The **de Joao Figueiredo House** has a splendid collection of Goan furniture. The **da Silva House** is a fine example of an impressive town house built around 1790 when Inacio da Silva became the Secretary to the Viceroy. No simple pied-a-terre, it was an impressive mansion; it had a long façade with the roof divided into seven separate cropped 'towers'-hence its other name, **Seven Shoulders**. Today, however, only three of these 'towers' remain. The house retains an air of grandeur in its lavishly carved dark rosewood furniture, its gilded mirrors and fine chandeliers. The first floor reception rooms which face the street are lit by large wood and oyster shell windows which are protected by wrought iron balconies. The descendants continue to live in a small wing of the diminished house which has the traditional flower-filled courtyard garden at the back.

Sleeping
Some budget hotels (eg 'Gold Star', 'Green View') don't accept foreigners

C *Nanutel*, Padre Miranda Rd, T733176. F733175, nanutelmrg@nanuindia.com 55 smart rooms, comfortable business hotel, good food, nice pool but unattractive poolside area, bookshop. **D-E** *Goa Woodlands*, ML Furtado Rd, opposite City Bus Stand, T712838, F738732, woodland@goa1.dot.net.in 46 rooms (Rs 270), 18 a/c (Rs 500), clean and spacious with bath, restaurant, bar, popular with businessmen, good value. **D-E** *Tourist Hotel* (GTDC), behind the Municipality, T731996. 69 rooms on 6 floors, a/c better, others cramped, simple restaurant (good vegetable vindaloo), Tourist information, travel desk. **E** *La Flor*, E Carvalho St, T731402. 35 rooms with bath, half a/c, restaurant. **E** *Milan*, Station Rd, T722715. Useful if arriving late by train, good Indian veg restaurant. **E-F** *Poonam*, T732945. 12 good-sized, clean rooms but often full.

Eating
Pork is not usually available

Expensive *Banjara*, T722088. North Indian. Plush but not flashy, a/c, good service, pricey but "food so-so". **Mid-range** *Casa Menino*, LIC Building, Luis Miranda Rd. Goan. Part a/c, with bar. *Chinese Pavilion*, M Menezes Rd (400m west of Municipal Gardens). Chinese. Smart, a/c, good choice. *Food Affair*. North Indian. Basement café, open all day. *Gaylin*, 1 V Valaulikar Rd. Chinese. Tasty hot Szechuan, comfortable a/c. *Longuinhos* near the Municipality. Goan, North Indian. Open all day for meals and snacks, also bar drinks and baked goodies. *Tato*, G-5 Apna Bazar, Complex, V Valaulikar Rd. Excellent vegetarian, a/c upstairs. *Utsav*, Nanutel Hotel. Pleasant, serving a large range of Goan dishes. **Cheap** *Café Margao*. Good South Indian snacks. Four *Kamats* including a/c '*Milan*', Station Rd. Indian vegetarian. Clean and good value *thalis* and snacks. **Bakery** *Baker's Basket* and *Johnny's Cove* at Rangavi Complex, west of Municipal Gardens, have Goan sweets including bebincas.

Shopping

The Old Market was rehoused in the 'New' (Municipal) Market in town. The covered **market** (Mon-Sat, 0800-1300, 1600-2000) is interesting to wander around. It is not at all touristy although holidaymakers come on their shopping trip to avoid paying inflated prices in the beach resorts. To catch a glimpse of the early morning arrivals at the Fish Market head south from the Municipal Building. **Books**: *Golden Heart*, Confident Building, off Abbé Faria Rd, behind the GPO, T726339 (closed 1300-1500). Biggest bookshop in Goa, wide collection, a bit like a warehouse but very helpful staff. Small shop at *Nanutel* hotel. **Handicrafts**: Tourist Hotel shop. *AJ Mavany*, Grace Estate. **Photography**: *Lorenz*, opposite the Municipality. *Wonder Colour Lab*, Garden View Building. **Textiles**: *MS Caro*, Caro Corner, has been in business since 1860, and has an extensive range including 'suiting', and will advise on tailors who can make up garments to order in a few days; some will make near perfect copies of a sample. **Tailor**: *J Vaz*, Martires Dias Rd, near Hari Mandir, T720086. Good quality reliable men's tailor.

Tour operators

Choice Tours, V Valaulikar, Grace Church, T731332; *Paramount Travels*, Luis Miranda Rd (opposite Tourist Hostel), T722150, also exchange.

Goa

Transport **Local Auto-rickshaw**: to Colva, Rs 30; beach, Rs 50. The local **bus** stand is by the municipal gardens. You can usually board buses near the *Kamat Hotel*, southeast of the gardens. To beach, Rs 3. Buses to **Benaulim**, Rs 3; **Cabo de Rama**, 07.30 (2 hrs), Rs 15; **Canacona** and **Palolem**, several; **Colva**, hrly, Rs 4. **Car hire**: Rs 650-900/day or Rs 5,500/week with driver from *Sai Service*, T735772, recommended. **Motorcycle taxis** are also available.

Margao

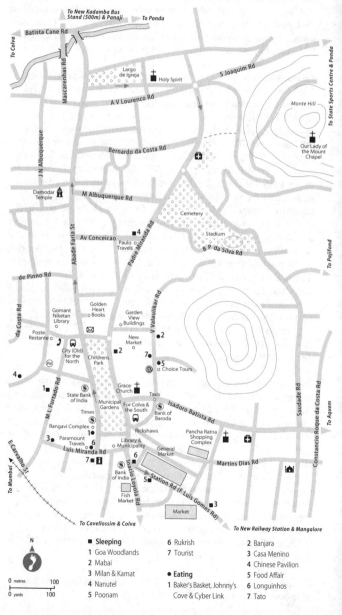

■ **Sleeping**	6 Rukrish	2 Banjara
1 Goa Woodlands	7 Tourist	3 Casa Menino
2 Mabai		4 Chinese Pavilion
3 Milan & Kamat	● **Eating**	5 Food Affair
4 Nanutel	1 Baker's Basket, Johnny's	6 Longuinhos
5 Poonam	Cove & Cyber Link	7 Tato

Long distance Bus The **Kadamba (New) Bus Stand** is 2 km north of town (City buses to the centre, Re 1 or motorcycle taxi Rs 8); buses arriving before 1000 and after 1900, proceed to the centre. **Gokarna**, 1300 daily, Rs 50. **Non-stop KTC buses** to **Panaji**: 1 hr, Rs 15; **Vasco**: Rs 14. Buy tickets from booth at stand number 1. **Private buses** (eg *Paulo*, Metropole Hotel, T721516), Padre Miranda Rd: to **Bangalore**: 1700 (15 hrs), Rs 275; **Mangalore**: 1800, 2130 (8-10 hrs), Rs 140; **Mumbai (Dadar/VT)**: 1400, 1700 (16 hrs), Rs 600 (sleeper); **Pune**: 1700 (13 hrs), Rs 450 (sleeper).

Train Enquiries, T732255. The new station on the broad gauge network is 500 m south of the old station. Most express trains on the Konkan Railway stop at Margao (Madgaon) and a few at Chaudi (Canacona), but they are quite slow. The reservation office on the first floor of the new station is usually quick and efficient, with short queues. Open 0800-1400, 1415-2000, Mon-Sat, 0800-1400, Sun. Tickets for Mumbai and Delhi should be booked well ahead. **NB** Confirm Indrail Pass reservations in Vasco, Mumbai or Mangalore. Useful trains: to **Mumbai (CST)**: *Madgaon Mumbai Exp 0104*, 1230, 10¾ hrs; *0112*, 1815, 12¼ hrs. To **Mumbai Kurla (Tilak)**: *Netravati Exp*, *6636*, 2020, 10¼ hrs. From **Mumbai (CST)**: *Madgaon Exp 0103*, 0515, 11 hrs; *Konkan Kanya Exp 0111*, 2230, 12 hrs (often fully booked a week ahead). To **Ernakulam (Jn)**: *Lakshadweep Exp 2618*, 2115, 14½ hrs. From **Ernakulam (Town)** for Kochi: *Rajdhani Exp 2431*, 2325, 12¼ hrs. To **Thiruvananthapuram (Trivandrum)**: *Rajdhani Exp 2432* (Thu, Fri), 1305, 16¾ hrs (originates in **Delhi (HN)** on Wed, Thu, 1100). From **Trivandrum**: *Rajdhani Exp 2431* (Fri, Sat), 1915, 17 hrs (continues to **Delhi (HN)**, 1215, arr 1350 next day). The broad gauge line between Vasco and **Londa** in Karnataka, runs through Margao and Dudhsagar Falls, connects stations on the line with **Belgaum**. There are services to **Bangalore**, **Delhi via Agra**, and **Hospet (Hampi)** among others. See under Vasco on page 482. The **pre-paid taxi stand** is to the right of the exit; to Margao centre Rs 50, Panaji Rs 422, Colva Rs 115, Palolem Rs 422; **Colva**, Rs 80 (after bargaining). Tourist taxis ask 5 times the price. **Autos** are to the left; to Margao Rs 40; to Colva Rs 70, to Panaji Rs 275 (try bargaining).

Banks *Bank of Baroda*, behind Grace Church; also in Market, Station Rd. *Bank of India*, exchanges cash, TCs, Visa and Mastercard, 0930-1400, 1500-1900, Mon-Fri; 0930-1400 Sat. *State Bank of India*, west of the Municipal Gardens. *Times Bank* (now merged with HDFC), 24 hr ATM for Mastercard, minimum withdrawal Rs 100, maximum Rs 10,000 per day. **NB** Get exchange before visiting beaches to the south where it is more difficult. **Communications** *GPO*, north of Children's Park. *Poste Restante*, near the Telegraph Office, down lane west of Park, 0830-1030 and 1500-1700 Mon-Sat. **Couriers**: *Skypak*, T724777 and *Rau Raje Desprabhu*, near Hotel Mayur, Old Market. **Telephones**: STD (and sometimes fax) at several places in town. **Internet**: *Cyber Link*, Shop 9, Rangavi Complex, inefficient staff. *Cyber Inn*, 105 Karnika Chambers, V Valauliker Rd, T733232, cyberinn@bom2.vsnl.net.in 2 terminals, Rs 3 per min, internet, Rs 60 per hr off-line. **Telephones**: numerous, including New Market, Taxi Stand etc. **Medical services** *JJ Costa Hospital*, Fatorda, T722586. *Hospicio*, T722164. *Holy Spirit Pharmacy*, open 24 hrs. **Tourist offices** GTDC, Tourist Hotel, T722513, 0800-1800 (lunch 1300-1400), daily. **Useful addresses** Ambulance: T722722. Fire: T720168. Police: T722175.

Directory

Goa

★ Southern beaches

*The southern beaches are less distinctive than those of the north. Government regulations have kept all the hotels back from the sea, but the character of the unbroken wide sand nonetheless also varies. The road runs slightly inland, with spurs leading down to the main sections of beach. Some, like **Benaulim** and **Varca** are little more than deserted stretches of dune-backed sand, with isolated fishing hamlets. In contrast **Colva's** all coconut palms come down to the beach edge, shading restaurants and a cluster of hotels and shops. At intervals are some luxurious beach resorts.*

Arossim, These three beaches in Salcete, broad, flat and open, are among the least
Utorda, heavily used. Around the resort hotels there are small clusters of beach shack
Majorda restaurants, and occasional fishing villages scattered under the coconut palms.
Phone code: 0832 One of the distinctive features of this section of coast is the strip of land that
lies between the main series of villages and the dunes which actually front the
sea, used for intensive rice cultivation. The road runs through these villages,
set back between 1 and 2 km from the sea. Old mansions of wealthy families
still standing in the villages include **Utorda House** which is known for its well
kept gardens. The villages from here southwards are noted for the high level of
emigration to the Gulf. Some have returned and invested money in new hotels.

Sleeping Arossim is in deserted north end of the beach stretch. **A** *Heritage Village
Club* (was *Sita*), T754311, F754324, www.sitaresorts.com 100 rooms in large gardens
set around pool. Besides this, a single beach shack offers food and drinks. **Utorda** is 10
mins' walk north of Majorda. **LL** *Kenilworth Beach Resort* (was *Golden Tulip*), T754180,
F754183, kbrgoa@satyam.net.in, www.kenilworth.allindia.com 92 rooms, central a/c,
being completely refurbished and aiming very high, focused on the pool(s) with plenty
of water sports, managed by enthusiastic New Zealander. **Majorda A-B** *Majorda
Beach Resort*, 2 mins' walk from the beach, T754871, F755382. 3 restaurants, pools,
designed on a grand scale with a rather barn-like public area, lush gardens behind, all
very well maintained. **D** *Shalom Guest House*, T754240, shalome81@satyam.net.in 1
large family room (more planned), excellent value.

Betalbatim Betalbatim was named after the main temple to Betal which once stood here; the
Phone code: 0832 deity was moved to Queula near Ponda for safety. There is a pleasant stretch with
some coconut palms and a few casuarinas on the low dunes that separate the seaside from the resort development. Beach bars are 15 minutes' walk away.

Sleeping B-C *Nanu Resorts*, near the beach and open fields, T734950, F734428. 72
comfortable and spacious a/c rooms in 2-storey 'chalet' complex separated by small
patches of green, imaginatively planned and well managed with efficient service,
good restaurant and pool, peaceful (time-share blocks are alongside), very good
value May-Sep. Along Betalbatim Beach road **E** *Baptista*, T720273, 3 simple clean
rooms, kitchen. **E** *Manuela Tourist House*, 1 km from beach. 5 good clean rooms with
bath, TV lounge, food available, secure, quiet. **E** *Ray's Rest Rooms*, T738676. 3 clean
rooms, some a/c, use of kitchen.

Transport Road: Buses from Margao (12 km); motorcycle taxis charge about Rs 30.
Taxis take 20 mins from the airport and under 15 mins from Margao. **Train**: On the
Vasco-Margao line.

Colva

Phone code: 0832 Colva is one of the most popular beaches in southern Goa, though not as devel-
Colour map 4, grid B2 oped or busy as Calangute in the north. The beach has beautiful sand, coconut
palms gently swaying in the breeze and blue waters which can sometimes be
rough and grey-green. However, beach sellers and stray dogs can be a nuisance.
Colva village is a bit scruffy.

Ins & outs **Getting there** From the airport, taxis charge about Rs 250. Those arriving by train at
Margao, 6 km away, can choose between buses, auto-rickshaws and taxis for transfer.

Beach & Teams of fishermen operate all along the coast, from here down to Benaulim to
village the south, with their pitch-boarded boats drawn up on the beach, while

motorized crafts are anchored offshore. They provide added interest and colour and it is worth waking early to watch them haul in their nets. If you are very early you may even be invited out on a boat!

The large **Church of Our Lady of the Miracles** (1581) houses an image of Jesus alleged to have been discovered on the African coast. *Fama of Menino Jesus Jesus* (16 October 2000) is celebrated with a colourful procession and a fair. Near the church, specially blessed lengths of string are sold, as well as replicas of limbs which are offered to the image in thanks for cures effected.

Sleeping
Most hotels are 6-8 km from Margao railway station

B *Sea Coin*, T720892, F710312, seacoin@bom8.vsnl.net.in 32 large comfortable rooms, some a/c, restaurant, but unappealing views. **B** *Vista De Colva*, 4th Ward, T704845, F704983, colmar@satyam.net.in 25 large a/c rooms, restaurant (Goan specialities), small pool, very comfortable new resort. **B-C** *Longuinhos Beach Resort*, on the beach, 1 km from resort centre, T731645, F737588, lbresort@goa1.dot.net.in 50 clean rooms with balcony, 6 a/c, (no TV), good restaurant, near fishermen's huts. **B-C** *William's Resort*, 500m from beach, T721077, F732852. 36 spotless rooms, some a/c, restaurant, large pool (non-residents pay Rs 40), tennis, friendly, good value. **D** *Colva Beach Cottages* (GTDC), near the sea, T721206, T737753. 47 pleasant, clean rooms, few a/c, good restaurant, bar, garden, friendly, secure, popular with Indian tourists. **E** *Colmar*, on the beach (just beyond *Colva Beach Cottages*), T721253. 85 rooms, dearer than similar in area but popular, restaurant (see below), travel desk, motorbike hire, bus to Flea Market (Rs 85), exchange. **E** *Garden Cottages*, behind

Colva

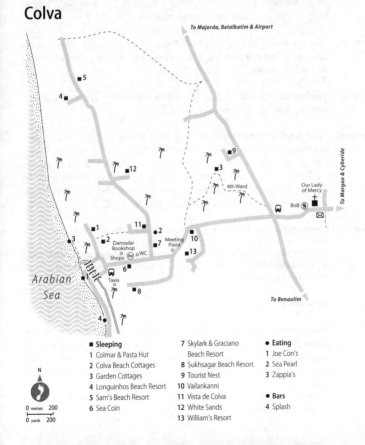

To Majorda, Betalbatim & Airport

4th Ward

Our Lady of Mercy

BoB

To Margao & Cyberide

Arabian Sea

Damodar Bookshop
Shops
WC
Meeting Point
Taxis

To Benaulim

Goa

■ Sleeping
1 Colmar & Pasta Hut
2 Colva Beach Cottages
3 Garden Cottages
4 Longuinhos Beach Resort
5 Sam's Beach Resort
6 Sea Coin
7 Skylark & Graciano Beach Resort
8 Sukhsagar Beach Resort
9 Tourist Nest
10 Vailankanni
11 Vista de Colva
12 White Sands
13 William's Resort

● Eating
1 Joe Con's
2 Sea Pearl
3 Zappia's

● Bars
4 Splash

N

0 metres 200
0 yards 200

Johnny Cool's restaurant, 10 mins from beach. 6 basic rooms with bath (Rs 210), private balcony, pleasant surroundings, quiet, clean, friendly, helpful owner, good value. **F** *Sam's Beach Resort*, 3rd Ward, T735304, 16 clean rooms set around quiet garden courtyard, good value. **E** *Tourist Nest*, 2 km from the sea, T723944. Old Portuguese house, 12 rooms, some with bath (Rs 250), good restaurant, run by two Norwegian women, popular with backpackers. **E** *Vailankanni*, H No 414/2, 4th Ward, near the crossroads, T737747. 10 basic, clean rooms though a bit musty, 5 new flats, friendly family run, good value restaurant. **E** *White Sands*, H No 470, 4th Ward, T720364. 8 clean comfortable rooms in new, family run guest house. **F** *Maria Guest House*, 4th Ward, near beach cafés. 7 rooms, some with bath, very friendly, interesting owners, helpful, car-hire, popular with backpackers, good value. **F** *Romeo's Tourist Cottages*, H No 9, Novo Vaddo, T730942. 2 clean rooms with bath in family guest house, quiet location, 5 mins walk from beach.

Eating **Mid-range**: *Sea Pearl*, 476, 4th Ward. Western. Chef (claimed to have worked for the Queen Mother!) produces excellent fish dishes, roast beef, good desserts, fish pie, good portions, arrive early in season (about 1930), recommended for food and service, also has simple **E** rooms with bath. **Cheap**: Most offer Western food and beer. *China Dragon*, on beach. Mainly Chinese, good food and friendly service. *Joe Con's*, excellent fresh fish and Goan dishes. *Zappia's*, on the beach. Good food and service.

Bars Several beach hotels have bars. *Splash* is 'the' place for music, dancing and late drinking, open all night, trendy, very busy on Sat (full after 2300 on weekdays in season), good cocktails, poor bar snacks – may not appeal to all.

Shopping Small square with usual craft shops – Kashmiri crafts and Karnataka mirror-work are good value. *Damodar* bookshop, near the beach car park, has a good selection of used and new books.

Tour operators *Meeting Point*, opposite, T723338, F732004, for very efficient, reliable travel service, Mon-Sat, 0830-1900 (sometimes even later, if busy).

Transport **Local** **Bicycles** mostly through hotels, Rs 20-25 per day (discounts for long term). **Motorbikes** for hire through most hotels (see also Panaji), Rs 200 per day (less for long term rental), more for Enfields, bargain hard. **Long distance** **Buses** to Margao half-hourly, take 30 mins, Rs 3 (last bus 1915, last return, 2000); motorcycle taxi, Rs 20-25 (bargain hard); auto-rickshaw, Rs 30-40. To **Anjuna** Wed for the Flea Market, bus (through travel agents), dep 0930, return 1730, Rs 90-100.

Directory **Communications** *WorldLinkers* has 24-hr ISD/fax. **Internet**: difficult to work offline in Colva itself as most terminals are used primarily for e-mail. *Cyberide*, 1 km north of crossroads, T735706, single terminal but good for offline work at reasonable rates. *Space Communications*, Beach Rd. 2 terminals, 0900 – 2100, Rs 100 per hr. Avoid *Trans Global Communications*. **Hospital** T722164. **Useful services** Police, T721254.

Benaulim

This is the more tranquil and pleasant end of Colva beach. Even here, tourists can be plagued by fruit and jewellery vendors, as well as drug pushers. If you want to escape their constant attention, hire a bike and cycle some distance south along the beach. The 4 km walk or ride to Colva through idyllic countryside is recommended.

The small **Church of St John the Baptist**, on a hill beyond the village, is worth a visit. See below for *Feast of St John*.

LL *Taj Exotica*, Calvaddo, T705666, F738916. 138 luxurious rooms, deluxe ($165) to Presidential Suites ($450), all facing 800m sea frontage, excellent pool, 9-hole golf, lovely gardens, health club with latest equipment, sumptuously designed by Hawaiian architect. **B** *Royal Palms*, Vasvaddo, T732391, F710617. 50 apartments, some expensive villas, some time-share, restaurant, pool, exchange, travel counter. **C-D** *Carina Beach Resort*, Tambdi-Mati, T734166, F711400. 35 rooms, new wing better with solar powered showers, some a/c (extra Rs 150), light and airy with balcony, restaurant, pool. **C-E** *Camilson's Beach Resort*, Sernabatim, T732781. 15 simple rooms with attached bath (Rs 250-Rs 300), better in new 2-storey building (Rs 800), restaurant, close to the beach. **D** *Failaka*, Adsulim Nagar, near Maria Hall crossing, T734416. 16 clean comfortable rooms with shower (Rs 420), quieter at rear, excellent restaurant, friendly. **D-E** *Palm Grove Cottages*, H No 149, Vasvaddo, T722533, palmgrovecottages@yahoo.com 14 rooms (Rs 250-600), new rooms better with shower and balcony, pleasant palm shaded garden, good food (but slow service).

All along Benaulim Beach Rd, and in the coconut groves on either side, there are numerous rooms available in private houses and "garden cottages", from Rs 50-150 ; south along the beach from *Johncey's* rooms with bath, just off the beach, are Rs 80-100. **E** *Caphina*, Beach Rd, past crossroads, away from road, 8 spotless rooms (Rs 250) on two floors, friendly and helpful owners (if not in, ask at Tansy), good value. **E** *D'Souza Guest House*, T734364. 5 very clean rooms, good food (see below), exchange, garden, friendly family. **E** *O'Palmer Beach Cottages*, T733278. 20 rooms, very close to the beach, has had a recent facelift, internet. **E** *Oshin*, near *Palm Grove*, down a path. Good large rooms with bath, breakfast, friendly manager. **E** *PaulRina Tourist Home*, Beach Rd, T738250. 6 large, airy rooms with balcony (Rs 200), good value. **E** *Rosario's Inn*, Beach Rd, T734167. 28 rooms with bath (Rs 200) in a peaceful setting, popular, restaurant, cycle/motorbike hire. **E** *Tansy*, Beach Rd, T734595. large, very clean rooms with bath (Rs 200), some in cottages, good restaurant (super breakfast), friendly, good value. **E-F** *O Mangueiro*, next to *Carina*, 10 min walk to beach, T734164. 15 rooms (Rs 150-400), including 10 new with bath, very clean, peaceful, safe and friendly. **F** *Caroline*, Beach Rd, T739649. 6 clean, light rooms with bath (Rs 150) in family run guest house. **F** *Casa de Saji*, 5 mins walk from beach, T722937. 5 clean rooms (Rs 150-175), common bath, better with balcony overlooking fields, very quiet. **F** *Priti Kunj*, south of Maria Hall crossing, 15m off the main road, behind church. 4 clean, pleasant rooms, 3 with bath, also large 6-bed rooms in family house, meals to order, helpful owners.

Benaulim

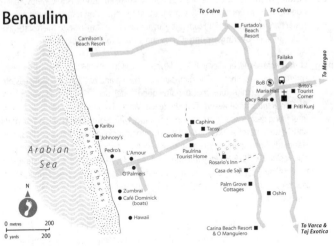

Eating

There are over a dozen places along the beach. Service can be tediously slow during the season. Most close in the monsoons

Cacy Rose, is just off the main road near the bus station. *D'Souza's*. Good juices, lassis and fast food. *Johncey's*, the most popular (not necessarily the best). Varied menu, good seafood, generous portions, *tandoori* recommended (after 1830) but service can be erratic, pleasant atmosphere though (backgammon, scrabble). *Palm Grove*, offers high quality Chinese. *Pedro's*, on the beach. Good seafood and tandoori. Imaginative menu, friendly, the 'in' place to go early to get a table. *Karibu* to the north, and *Hawaii* and *Zumbrai* south along the beach. Good for fresh fish, prawn and lobster. *Tansy* Seafood sizzlers, excellent value at Rs 50. The shop in *O'Palmer's* dispenses good coffee from a machine.

Entertainment

Dolphin watching The trips are scenic and chances of seeing dolphin are high, but it gets very hot (take hat, water and something comfy to sit on). Groups of dolphins here are usually seen swimming near the surface and do not oblige with performing tricks. Boats from *Café Dominick* (signs on the beach) and several others charge about Rs 250. Competition in season is intense, so bargain.

Festivals

Feast of St John the Baptist (*Sao Joao*) (24th Jun) gives thanks for the arrival of the monsoon. Young men wearing crowns of leaves and fruits tour the area singing for gifts. They jump into wells (which are usually full) to commemorate the movement of St John in his mother's womb when she was visited by Mary, the mother of Jesus!

Transport

Bicycle and **scooter** hire, Rs 25 and Rs 150 per day. **Taxis** and **autos** from the beach esplanade near *Pedro's* and at Maria Hall crossing. To/From **Margao**: taxis Rs 70; autos Rs 50; bus Rs 3. **Anjuna** Wed flea market: bus 0930, return 1530, about Rs 90, 2 hrs.

Directory

Bank *Bank of Baroda*, near Maria Hall, best rates (better than at travel agents and STD booths). **Communications** *GK Communications*, Beach Rd. 24 hr phone, money exchange and Internet with 4 terminals, book ahead when very busy, Rs 100 per hr. **Medical services** Late night *Chemists* near the main crossroads.

Varca, Cavelossim and Mobor

Phone code: 0832
Colour map 4,
grid B2/C2

The beaches south of Benaulim, Varca and Cavelossim, are quieter and cleaner than Colva. Further south, Mobor (or Mabor) lies on the narrow peninsula where the river Sal joins the sea.

Ins & outs

Getting there To reach the beaches from Margao, bus journeys to Cavelossim village (18 km) are uncomfortably slow; autos at the bus stand transfer to the resorts. Taxis charge around Rs 180. From Dabolim airport (41-48 km), taxis to the resorts take under an hour. **Getting around** Cycles and scooters are available for hire.

Sleeping

LL-AL *Leela Palace* (Kempinski), Mobor, T746363, F746352, leela.goa@leela. sprintrpg. ems.vsnl.net.in 194 rooms in superb villas and pavilions blending eastern and western architecture, spacious site, good watersports, 9-hole golf, very plush. **AL** *Goa Renaissance Resort*, Fatrade Beach, Varca, T745208, F245225. 202 rooms, interesting design, spacious impressive entrance with beams and arches, watersports and 9-hole golf, miles of white sand beach with no rocks, no mosquitoes or flies, high standards but expensive meals and drinks (little else in vicinity), casino open to non-residents. **AL-A** *Holiday Inn*, Mobor, T746303, F746333, hi.goa@sma.sprintrpg. ems.vsnl.net.in 139 luxurious rooms (prices vary) with shady balconies around a pool and pleasant, part-shaded gardens, health club, tennis, very close to beach, good views of hills.

A-B *Dona Sylvia Resort*, Tamborim, south of Cavelossim, T746321, F748320, Dona_samaria@mailcity.com 176 comfortable rooms, some a/c, low-rise complex with a spacious feel, mainly packages and buffet meals, some watersports (beach a short

Goa

walk away). **B** *Luisa by the Sea*, T/F as *Dona Sylvia*, mainly timeshare but 20 rooms and 8 studios with kitchenette, non a/c, breakfast at *Dona Sylvia*, clean, comfortable, attentive staff. **B** *Resorte de Goa*, Fatrade Beach, Varca, T745066, F745310. 56 rooms and suites in main building, smaller rooms in cottages, remote, idyllic, pleasant pool in large gardens, tennis, clean deserted beach.

C-D *Dona Sa Maria*, Tamborim, 1 km from deserted beach, T745672, F745673, Dona_samaria@mailcity.com. 16 good sized clean rooms in 'villas', good food, pool, family run, very friendly, isolated, quiet (closed Jun-Sep). **D** *Gaffino's*, opposite Dona Sylvia, Mobor, 5 mins walk from beach, T746385. 16 clean, simple rooms with bath on 4 floors, 2 a/c, balconies overlook river or sea (far away), bed and breakfast, personal service, becoming package oriented. **D** *Hippo Cool*, next to *Gaffino's*, T746201. 6 clean, very comfortable rooms with fan (a/c on request) and shower (Rs 400+), restaurant (popular with local people), 5 mins walk from beach, the Almeidas are very helpful. Highly recommended. **D** *Sao Domingos* (was *Edwin's*), opposite Dona Sylvia, T746649. 15 comfortable rooms with fans or a/c and bath, rooftop breakfast area, same owner as *Goan Village* restaurant. **E** *José Holiday Home*, T746127. 10 good clean rooms (Rs 300) with attached bath, some a/c, friendly.

Eating
Mid-range: *River View* in an excellent location next to the river. Wide choice, international menu, good ambience. Dona Sa Maria's, *La Afra* does excellent steaks. Boatmen ferry holidaymakers to *River Sal* at Betul (see below). **Cheap**: Beach shacks offer Goan dishes and seafood at reasonable prices. Around *Dona Sylvia*, several come alive in the evening. *Goan Village*, lane opposite Dona Sylvia. The best here for all cuisines. Others recommended for good food, drink and service in a pleasant atmosphere: *Get Down*, *Mike's Place*, *Shallop* and *Walk In* (limited menu). *Jazz Inn*, 500 m towards Cavelossim. For authentic Goan fish *thalis* (Rs 20), try the first house on the left past the church in Cavelossim if heading north.

Varca to Betul

Entertainment
Dolphin watching: *Betty's Place*, in a Rd opposite the *Holiday Inn*, arranges boat trips for fishing, dolphin viewing as well as trips up river Sal from 1030-1630 (food included), which is recommended.

Transport
Bike hire from *Rocks* outside Dona Sylvia, cycles Rs 10 per hr, Rs 150 a day; scooters Rs 300 a day without petrol, Rs 500 with 7 litres of fuel. **Ferry** crossing, on the river Sal, southeast of Cavelossim.

Directory
Banks *Bank of Baroda* near the church in Cavelossim accepts Visa, Mastercard and TCs, helpful staff, open 0930-1330, Mon-Wed, Fri, Sat.

Betul
Phone code: 0832
Colour map 4, grid C2

Betul, which overlooks the wide estuary, is in an idyllic setting, delightfully shaded by coconut palms, jackfruit,

■ **Sleeping**
1 Dona Sa Maria
2 Dona Sylvia Resort
3 Gaffino's & Hippo Cool
4 Goa Renaissance Resort
5 Holiday Inn
6 José
7 Leela Palace
8 Resorte de Goa
9 Sao Domingos & Goan Village Restaurant

● **Eating**
1 Fish Thalis
2 Jazz Inn
3 River Sal
4 River View
5 Shallop

papaya and banana. Betul is an important fishing village which also depends on coir production and labouring. A walk along the 'jetty' past dozens of many-coloured fishing boats will reveal busy fisherfolk loading fish into baskets or their catch of tiny silvery fish glistening in the sun trapped under spread out nets on the bank. ■ *Getting there: From Cavelossim, the shortest route to Betul is by taking the ferry across the Sal (signposted, just southeast) to Assolna where after a left turn into the village you turn right to join the main road towards Betul. From Margao, the NH17 forks right towards Assolna at Chinchinim.*

Sleeping and eating E *River Sal*, Zuem Velim, on the waterside, T760276. 12 rooms, offers excellent fresh river fish. Boatmen bring holidaymakers from Mobor to eat here in the evening.

★ Cabo de Rama Fort

Phone code: 0832
Colour map 4, grid C2

The whole atmosphere of the fort, untroubled by more than a handful of visitors, creates a sense of history & drama to which only the most unimaginative could fail to respond

Cape Rama is named after the hero of the Hindu epic the *Ramayana*, who is said to have lived there with his wife Sita during their period of exile. The Cape was an obvious site for a fort to any power whose interests might be threatened from the sea. Its origins pre-date the arrival of the Portuguese who captured it in 1763 and used it as a prison too.

The gatehouse, which has been restored, looks rather quaint, with narrow firing slits irregularly spaced like a miniature design by Le Corbusier. The main entrance seems far from impregnable, considering the scale of the fortifications, but note the strategically positioned hole in the wall, pointing straight at the door, behind which a cannon could be stationed.

The outer ramparts are excellently preserved, with several cannons still scattered along their length. Despite the absence of buildings, other than the church, the magnificence of the site gives it an extraordinary atmosphere. There are fine views from several of its major bastions, and you can walk virtually the entire outer length of the fort. From two of the gates it is possible to scramble down to the sea, but great care is needed on the crumbly laterite paths. The most dramatic of the walls is on the landward side, where it rises 10-15 m above the floor of the moat which was dug both to provide laterite blocks from which the fort is constructed, and to create the moat.

The gatehouse is at the lowest point of the whole fort, the ground rising to its highest in the southwest. The view is particularly good to the south in the evening light, across bays stretching down past Palolem to Karnataka easily visible on a clear day. From the highest point and observation post (where a modern but disused and run-down building has been built), there is a 360° view, and the wall then drops down to the north. At its lowest it is only 20 m or so above the sea. At this point of the compound, deeply wooded now, is the source of the Fort's water supply. A huge tank was excavated to a depth of about 10 m, and even today it has water right through the dry season. There are two springs, one of which gives out water through two spouts at different temperatures.

Sleeping & eating Near the fort entrance, these offer meals, drinks and some very basic rooms: *Pinto's Bar*, near the entrance to Fort; *Zina Bar*, next door; *Fernandes' Corner*, a further 200 m.

Transport From Margao, the bus dep at 0730 from southeast corner of the Municipal Gardens (Rs 10, 2 hrs), return at 1200 or later. From Betul (or Palolem), hire a motorcycle.

Agonda beach The beautiful beach mid-way between Cabo de Rama and Palolem is unspoilt with no development. Since it is difficult to get to by local bus and is really only accessible by a scooter or motorbike, there is scarcely a tourist in sight.

Goa

★ Palolem

South of Agonda, the beautiful curve of palm-fringed golden sand is one of the best beaches. The search for the remaining unspoilt idyll brought travellers to Palolem a few years ago but it is no longer a deserted bay. There is a line of beach shacks serving food and drink in the season while the range of accommodation increases with demand.

Phone code: 0832
Colour map 4, grid C2

Getting there Palolem is 3 km from Canacona Junction station, which is now on the Konkan line (*Navratri Express*). From there taxis and auto-rickshaws charge around Rs 25-30 to Palolem beach. There are also several direct buses from Margao which take an hour to Canacona village. You can get off the bus at Canacona Junction (before the village) and walk the 2 km to the beach. **Getting around** You can hire a bicycle from the village for Rs 3 per hr or Rs 25 per day.

Ins & outs

Forty kilometres from Margao via Cuncolim, Palolem is 2 km off the National Highway. The narrow strip of beach has strange rocky outcrops at each end which are known locally as 'Pandava's drums' and 'footprints'. An added attraction here is the freshwater stream to the north, as well as the small Canacona Island which can be reached by a short swim or by wading across at low tide.

Beach

The main beach is to the north with the bulk of the beach shacks, while the relatively smaller southern section has fishermen's huts and some novel accommodation options. The shaded palm tree area is unfortunately becoming increasingly littered. All is worse at weekends when an influx of local trippers bring their picnics, fill the air with loud music and leave behind a pile of garbage and dead whiskey bottles.

D *Bhakti Kutir*, over the hill at the southern end, T643472, F643469. 11 "cabanas", varying sizes, 1 imaginatively and sympathetically built with local materials, all with mosquito nets, common shower and organic toilets, away from the beach and very quiet, emphasizing peace and meditation. Recommended. **E** *Cocohuts*, towards the southern end (moved), T643296, F233298, ppv@goa1.dot.net.in   15 breezy, shaded huts (Rs 300-400) built among palm trees, raised on bamboo stilts, electricity and fan, separate shared toilets on the ground, on the beach, restaurant, now has many imitations. **E** *La Allegro*, T643498. 4 small rooms (Rs 300), basic and fairly bleak but right on the beach, often full. **E** *Palolem Beach Resort*, T/F643054, 9 rooms with bath (Rs 300-400), tents and basic cottages with shared facilities, shower blocks (Rs 200-300), ISD phones, reliable travel service and exchange, friendly, clean, quiet shaded site, book at least a week ahead. Recommended. **E** *Hi-Tide Beach Huts*, on site formally occupied by *Cocohuts*, T643104. 11 huts, possibly the largest of them all, best on stilts at the beach front. **E** *Unic Resort*, away from the sea (about 1km to Colomb Beach), T643059, F739688. 9 clean but uninspiring rooms (Rs 300-350), friendly, good restaurant specialising in seafood, excellent cocktails.

Sleeping
Prices tend to rise on 1 Dec. There may be a shortage of electricity

Behind the line of beach restaurants are thatched bamboo **huts** (Rs 150-300), at ground level instead of being in the trees, all with common bath. Among them: **E** *Ciaran's Camp*, T643477, johnciaran@hotmail.com. 20 good huts on the beach front with restaurant. **F** *Camp Palo*, behind La Allegra, T643173 (ask for Irshad), 13 well built huts (Rs 200) set in a pleasant compound. **F** *Cupid Castle*, Beach Rd, T643326. 8 clean, reasonable rooms (Rs 200), some with attached bath, short walk to the beach, restaurant. **F Rooms** in village houses, very basic facilities ('pig' toilets, unconnected to sewers, are raised on a platform where pigs do the necessary 'cleaning out' below). **F** *Camping*: parking for campers and travellers (Rs 15-20 per day) at *Palolem Beach Resort* and south of *Cocohuts*. Public toilets at the end of the road to the south.

Eating **Mid-price** *Bhakti Kutir*. Tasty western dishes, home grown produce, very pleasant though away from the water's edge. **Cheap** *Nature*, bar and restaurant, away from the beach. Also runs a travel and money exchange service. *Silver Star*, with hammocks in the shade. *Sun & Moon*, T643314. Relocated, now set back from the south end of the beach, under palms. A friendly, popular 'hang-out' with great atmosphere, large helpings of well-cooked Goan food. *Sunset* on the beach and *Rosie's*, near the main road, are recommended.

Entertainment **Dolphin watching** and **fishing** trips are offered by fishermen; mornings between 0830-1230 best. One contact is Dattu Pagi, Boat No 520, four for about Rs 600 for 1½ hr trip. **NB** Take sun-block, shirt, hat and drinking water. You may be able to see some dolphins from the headland to the south of Palolem, just before sunset.

Shopping A good **clothes** shop near Palolem Beach Resort has a friendly owner; not pushy.

Transport **Bus** 6 daily direct buses run between Margao and Chaudi (Canacona, 40 km via Cuncolim), Rs 9. From Chaudi, **taxis** and **auto-rickshaws** charge Rs 25 to Palolem beach. From Palolem, buses for Margao leave at around 0645, 0730, 0930, 1415, 1515, 1630 and take an hour.

Directory **Banks** No bank here, so arrive with enough funds. *Palolem Beach Resort* and *Nature Bar* change foreign currency. **Communications** Post Office: Nearest is at Chaudi. Internet at *Nature Bar* and *Sun & Moon*, Rs 2 per min. **Medical facilities** T643339. **Useful services** Police: T643357.

Chaudi
Colour map 4, grid C2
Population: 10,400

Chaudi (Chauri), also called Canacona (locally pronounced Kannkonn), is a crossroads settlement on the NH17 between Panaji and Karwar in Karnataka. The rail link on the Konkan line has brought the idyllic beaches nearby to the attention of developers. 'Chaudi' the town's main square, has the bus and auto stands, while the large church and high school of **St Tereza of Jesus** (1962) are on the northern edge of town. **Shri Malikarjuna Temple** with 60 auxiliary deities is believed to date from the mid-16th century. The temple 'car' festival in February and *Shigmo* in April attract large crowds.

Sleeping and eating Forest Department's simple **F** *Canacona Forest Rest House*, nearby, can be booked through DCF, South Margao, T0834-735361. *Canacona Palace*, 50 m east of the crossroads, serves good Udupi vegetarian food.

Transport **Buses** run to Palolem and Margao. **Trains** from Canacona Junction 2 km away, to **Ernakulam**, *Netravati Exp 6635*, 0348, 17½ hrs; and to **Mumbai (T)** (Kurla), *6636*, 1936, 11 hrs; **Margao (Madgaon)** 1936, 30 mins.

Directory **Banks** *State Bank of India*, next to Canacona Palace, has no foreign exchange facility. **Communications** *Post Office* is 200m down the highway towards Karnataka. *Internet Café* at Dias Apartment, Nagorcem, at the Agonda Crossing, 1 terminal, Rs 3.50 per min. **Medical services** *Pai Chemists*, is 100m east of the crossroads. **Useful services** *Petrol* from the small house opposite the big tree about 1 km north of the village.

Routes The NH17 continues south (about an hour's bus ride) to the Karnataka border through some beautiful countryside and unspoilt villages. There is a border check post with a barrier across to stop vehicles. **NB** Motorcyclists must carry all documentation.

Across the border there is a marked improvement in the road surface, and the road no longer winds through forest but is relatively wide and straight along the Karnataka coast.

Background

10

498

Background

History

Settlement and early history

South India's earliest settlements go back about half a million years when early Palaeolithic villages were scattered along river banks in Karnataka, Andhra Pradesh and Tamil Nadu. However, cultivation arrived relatively late to South India.

It is impossible to understand this development without reference to events elsewhere in the Indian sub-continent. After the first village communities in South Asia grew up on the arid western fringes of the Indus Plains 10,000 years ago farming spread gradually southwards, reaching Karnataka about 3000 years BC. A series of developments followed. Rock paintings have been found in Andhra Pradesh dating from 2000 BC, and by 1650 BC copper began to be widely used. Gram and millet cultivation was introduced, and cattle, sheep and goats became widespread as domesticated animals. South India's first Iron Age site, Hallur in Karnataka, dates from around 1200BC and from 1000BC the use of iron was common across the whole peninsula.

All these developments appear to have lagged behind their earlier introduction in northwestern India. In the Baluchistan hills of southern Pakistan there is evidence of agricultural settlement as early as 8500 BC. By 3500 BC agriculture had spread throughout the Indus Plains and in the thousand years following there were independent settled villages well to the east of the Indus. At its height the Indus Valley civilization covered as great an area as Egypt or Mesopotamia. However, the culture that developed was distinctively South Asian. The language, which is still untranslated, may well have been an early form of the Dravidian languages which today are found largely in South India.

BC	Northern South Asia	Peninsular India	External events	BC
900,000			Earliest hominids in West Asia First occupation of N China.	450,000
500,000	Lower Palaeolithic sites from NW to the Peninsula; Pre-Soan stone industries in NW.	Earliest Palaeolithic sites - Narmada Valley; Karnataka; Tamil Nadu and Andhra.	Origin of *homo sapiens* in Africa. *Homo sapiens* in East Asia. First human settlement in Americas (Brazil).	150,000 100,000 30,000
10,000	Beginning of Mesolithic period.	Continuous occupation of caves and riverside sites.	Earliest known pottery - Kukui, Japan. Ice Age retreats - Hunter gatherers in Europe.	10,500 8,300
8,000	Firest wheat and barley grown in Indus plains.	Mesolithic.	First domesticated wheat, barley in fertile crescent; first burials in North America.	8,000
7,500	Pottery at Mehrgarh; development of villages.	Increase in range of cereals in Rajasthan.	Agriculture begins in New Guinea.	7,000
6,500	Humped Indian cattle domesticated, farming develops.	Cultivation extends south.	Britain separated from Continental Europe by sea level.	6,500
3,500	Potter's wheel in use. Long distance trade.		Sumeria, Mesopotamia: first urban civilization.	3,500

India from 2000 BC to the Mauryas

In about 2000 BC Moenjo Daro, widely presumed to be the capital of the Indus valley Civilisation, became deserted and within the next 250 years the entire Indus Valley civilization disintegrated. Whatever the causes, some features of Indus Valley culture were carried on by succeeding generations.

From 1500 BC northern India entered the Vedic period. Aryan settlers moved southeast towards the Ganga valley. Classes of rulers *(rajas)* and priests *(brahmins)* began to emerge. Grouped into tribes, conflict was common. In one battle of this period a confederacy of tribes known as the Bharatas defeated another grouping of 10 tribes. They gave their name to the region to the east of the Indus which is the official name for India today – Bharat.

The centre of population and of culture shifted east from the banks of the Indus to the land between the rivers Yamuna and Ganga, the doab (pronounced *doe-ahb*, literally 'two waters'). This region became the heart of emerging Aryan culture, which, from 1500 BC onwards, laid the literary and religious foundations of what ultimately became Hinduism, spreading to embrace the whole of India.

The Vedas The first fruit of this development was the Rig Veda, the first of four Vedas, composed, collected and passed on orally by Brahmin priests from 1300 BC to about 1000 BC. In the later Vedic period, from about 1000 BC to 600 BC, the Sama, Yajur and Artha Vedas show that the Indo-Aryans developed a clear sense of the Ganga-Yamuna *doab* as 'their' territory. Modern Delhi lies just to the west of this region, central both to the development of history and myth in South Asia. Later texts extended the core region from the Himalaya to the Vindhyans and to the Bay of Bengal in the east. Beyond lay the land of mixed peoples and then of barbarians, outside the pale of Aryan society.

From the sixth to the third centuries BC the region from the foothills of the Himalaya across the Ganga plains to the edge of the Peninsula was governed under a variety of kingdoms or Mahajanapadhas – 'great states'. Trade gave rise to the birth of towns in the Ganga plains themselves, many of which have remained occupied

BC	Northern South Asia	Peninsular India	External events	BC
3,000	Incipient urbanization in the Indus plains.	First neolithic settlements in south Deccan (Karnataka). Ash mounds, cattle herding.	First Egyptian state; Egyptian hieroglyphics; walled citadels in Mediterranean Europe.	3,100
2,500	Indus valley civilization cities of Moenjo Daro, Harappa and many others.	Chalcolithic ('copper' age) in Rajasthan; Neolithic continues in south.	Great Pyramid of Khufu China: walled settlements; European Bronze Age begins: hybridization of maize in South America.	2,530 2,500
2,000	Occupation of Moenjo Daro ends.	Chalcolithic in Malwa Plateau, Neolithic ends in south; in Karnataka and Andhra - rock paintings.	Earliest ceramics in Peru. Collapse of Old Kingdom in Egypt. Stonehenge in Britain. Minoan Crete.	2,300 2,150
1,750	Indus Valley civilization ends.	Hill-top sites in south India.	Joseph sold into Egypt - Genesis.	1,750
1,750 1,500	Successors to Indus. Valley. Aryans invade in successive waves. Development of Indo-Aryan language.	Copper Age begins, Neolithic continues; gram and millet cultivation. Hill terracing. Cattle, goats and sheep.	Anatolia: Hittite Empire. New Kingdom in Egypt. First metal working in Peru. First inscriptions in China; Linear B script in Greece, 1650.	1,650 1,570 1,500 1,400

to the present. Varanasi (Benaras) is perhaps the most famous example, but a trade route was established that ran from Taxila (20 km from modern Islamabad in Pakistan) to Rajgir 1,500 km away in what is now Bihar. It was into these kingdoms of the Himalayan foothills and north plains that both Mahavir, founder of Jainism and the Buddha, were born.

The Mauryas

Political developments in the north often left an imprint on South India.

Within a year of the retreat of Alexander the Great's invasion of 326BC, **Chandragupta Maurya** established the first indigenous empire to exercise control over much of the subcontinent. Under his successors that control was extended to all but the extreme south of peninsular India.

Alexander the Great

The centre of political power had shifted steadily east into wetter, more densely forested but also more fertile regions. The Mauryans had their base in the region known as Magadh (now Bihar) and their capital at Pataliputra, near modern Patna. Their power was based on massive military force and a highly efficient, centralized administration. Chandragupta's army may have had as many as 9,000 elephants, 30,000 cavalry and 600,000 infantry. Chandragupta is believed to have been cremated on Chandragiri, a small hiillock in southern Karnataka. Bindusara, his successor, extended the empire south as far as Mysore.

The greatest of the Mauryan emperors, Asoka took power in 272 BC. He inherited a full blown empire, but extended it further by defeating the Kalingans in modern Orissa, before turning his back on war and preaching the virtues of Buddhist pacifism. Asoka's empire stretched from Afghanistan to Assam and from the Himalaya to Mysore. He inherited a structure of government set out by Chandragupta's Prime Minister, **Kautilya**, in a book on the principles of government, the *Arthashastra*. The state maintained itself by raising revenue from taxation – on everything, from agriculture, to gambling and prostitution. He decreed that 'no

Asoka

BC	Northern South Asia	Peninsular India	External events	BC
1,400	Indo-Aryan spread east and south to Ganga – Yamuna doab.	Horses introduced into south. Cave paintings, burials.	Tutankhamun buried in Valley of Kings.	1,337
1,200	Composition of Rig Veda begins?	Iron age sites at Hallur, Karnataka.	Middle America: first urban civilization in Olmec; collapse of Hittite Empire, 1200.	1,200
1,000	Earliest Painted Grey Ware in Upper Ganga Valley; Brahmanas begin to be written.	Iron Age becomes more widespread across Peninsula.	Australia: large stone-built villages; David King of Israel, Kingdom of Kush in Africa.	
800	Mahabharata war – Bhagavad Gita; Aryan invaders reach Bengal. Rise of city states in Ganga plains, based on rice cultivation.		First settlement at Rome. Celtic Iron Age begins in north and east of Alps.	850 800
750		Megalithic grave sites.	Greek city states.	750
700	Upanishads begin to be written; concept of transmigration of souls develops; Panini's Sanskrit grammar.		Iliad composed.	700

Asoka's Empire 250 BC

Rock Edicts ■
Pillar Edicts ▲
Important Sites ○
Boundary of Empire ----

waste land should be occupied and not a tree cut down' without permission, not out of a modern 'green' concern for protecting the forests, but because all were potential sources of revenue for the state. The *sudras* (lowest of Hindu castes) were used as free labour for clearing forest and cultivating new land.

Asoka (described on the edicts as 'the Beloved of the Gods, of Gracious Countenance') left a series of inscriptions on pillars and rocks across the subcontinent. Over most of India these inscriptions were written in *Prakrit*, using the *Brahmi* script. They were unintelligible for over 2,000 years after the decline of the empire until James Prinsep deciphered the Brahmi script in 1837.

BC	Northern South Asia	Peninsular India	External events	BC
600	Northern Black Pottery.		First Latin script; first Greek coins.	600
599			First iron production in China; Zoroastrianism becomes official religion in Persia.	550
563	Mahavir born – founder of Jainism. Gautama Buddha born.			
500	Upanishads finished; Taxila and Charsadda become important towns and trade centres.	Aryans colonize Sri Lanka. Irrigation practised in Sri Lanka.	Wet rice cultivation introduced to Japan.	500
326 321	Alexander at Indus. Chandragupta establishes Mauryan Dynasty.	Megalithic cultures.	Crossbow invented in China.	350

Indo-Aryans and Dravidians – distinct races?

An ancient Tamil myth has long held the Tamils to be the original race in India and Indo-Aryans have similarly cherished a belief in their racial distinctiveness. Recent genetic research suggests that homo sapiens originated in Africa less than 300,000 years ago. Southern and northern Indian types developed distinct genetic characteristics less than 40,000 years ago as they moved out of their central Asian homeland, first into West Asia and then into India, disproving all ideas of racial purity. Early Mediterranean groups form the main component of the Dravidian speakers of the four South Indian states. Later Mediterranean types also seem to have come from the northwest and down the Indus Valley, but more important were the Indo-Aryans, who migrated from the steppes of Central Asia from around 2000 BC. There are recognizable differences in physical type across the subcontinent. People in the south tend to have darker complexions, a lighter build and to be shorter than those in the north. In the northeast many people have Mongoloid features. Numerically tiny groups of Australoid peoples such as the Sentinelese on the Andaman Islands, form exceptions.

Through the edicts Asoka urged all people to follow the code of **dhamma** or dharma – translated by the Indian historian Romila Thapar as 'morality, piety, virtue and social order'. He established a special force of *dhamma* officers to try to enforce the code, which encouraged toleration, non-violence, respect for priests and those in authority and for human dignity.

However, Romila Thapar suggests that the failure to develop any sense of national consciousness, coupled with the massive demands of a highly paid bureaucracy and army, proved beyond the abilities of Asoka's successors to sustain. Within 50 years of Asoka's death in 232 BC the Mauryan Empire had disintegrated and with it the whole structure and spirit of its government.

A period of fragmentation: 185 BC to 300 AD

Beyond the Mauryan Empire other kingdoms had survived in South India. The Satavahanas dominated the central Deccan for over 300 years from about 50 BC. Further south in what is now Tamil Nadu, the early kingdoms of the Cholas and the Pandiyas gave a glimpse of both power and cultural development that was to flower over 1,000 years later. In the centuries following the break up of the Mauryan Empire these kingdoms were in the forefront of developing overseas trade, especially with Greece and Rome. Internal trade also flourished and South Indian traders carried goods to China and Southeast Asia.

Background

BC	Northern South Asia	Peninsular India	External events	BC
300	Sarnath and Sanchi stupas.	First Ajanta caves in original form.	Mayan writing and ceremonial centres established.	300
297	Mauryan power extends to Mysore.			
272-	Asoka's Empire.	Chola Pandiya, Chera kingdoms: earliest Tamil inscriptions.	Ptolemy.	285
232	Death of Asoka.		First towns in Southeast Asia.	250
250	Brahmi script.		Rome captures Spain.	206
185	Shunga Dynasty, centred on Ujjain.	Megalithic cultures in hills of south.	Romans destroy Greek states.	146
100	Kharavela King of Kalingans in Orissa. Final composition of Ramayana.	South Indian trade with Indonesia and Rome. Roman pottery and coins in South India.	Indian religions spread to Southeast Asia. Discovery of monsoon winds Introduction of Julian calendar.	100

The classical period – the Gupta Empire: 319-467 AD

Although the political power of Chandra Gupta and his successors never approached that of his unrelated namesake nearly 650 years before him, the Gupta Empire which was established with his coronation in AD 319 produced developments in every field of Indian culture. Even though their political power was restricted to North India, their influence has been felt profoundly across South Asia to the present.

Geographically the Guptas originated in the same Magadhan region that had given rise to the Mauryan Empire. Extending their power by strategic marriage alliances, Chandra Gupta's empire of Magadh was extended by his son, Samudra Gupta, who took power in AD 335, across North India. He also marched as far south as Kanchipuram in modern Tamil Nadu, but the heartland of the Gupta Empire remained the plains of the Ganga.

Chandra Gupta II reigned for 39 years from AD 376 and was a great patron of the arts. Political power was much less centralized than under the Mauryans and as Thapar points out, collection of land revenue was deputed to officers who were entitled to keep a share of the revenue, rather than to highly paid bureaucrats. Trade with Southeast Asia, Arabia and China all added to royal wealth.

That wealth was distributed to the arts on a previously unheard of scale, but Hindu institutions also benefited and some of the most important features of modern Hinduism date from this time. The sacrifices of Vedic worship were given up in favour of personal devotional worship, known as bhakti. Tantrism, both in its Buddhist and Hindu forms, with its emphasis on the female life force and worship of the Mother Goddess, developed. The focus of worship was increasingly towards a personalized and monotheistic deity, represented in the form of either Siva or Vishnu. The myths of Vishnu's incarnations also arose at this period.

The Brahmins, the priestly caste who were in the key position to mediate change, refocused earlier literature to give shape to the emerging religious philosophy. In their hands the Mahabharata and the Ramayana were transformed from secular epics to religious stories. The excellence of contemporary sculpture both reflected and contributed to an increase in image worship and the growing role of temples as centres of devotion.

Regional kingdoms and cultures

The collapse of Gupta power in the north opened the way for successive smaller kingdoms to assert themselves. In doing so the main outlines of the modern

Background

AD	North India	Peninsular India	External events	AD
		Satavahanas control much of Peninsula up to 300 AD	Rome population of 1 mn; pyramid of the sun at City of Teotihuacan, Mexico.	50
100	Vaishnavism spreads to north and north-west.	Thomas brings Christianity to South India. Tamil Sangram.		
78	Kushan rulers in Northwest followed by Scythians.	Arikamedu – trade with Rome.		68
			Buddhism reaches China. Paper introduced in China; first metal work in Southeast Asia.	100
	Lawbook of Manu Gandharan art.	Mahayana Buddhism spreads. Nagarjunakonda major centre in Andhra Pradesh. First cities on Deccan plateau.	Hadrian's wall in Britain.	125
200	Hinayana/Mahayana Buddhist split.			

regional geography of South Asia began to take clear shape. Regional kingdoms developed, often around comparatively small natural regions.

The southern Deccan was dominated by the Chalukyas from the sixth century up to 750 AD and again in the 11th and 12th centuries. To their south the Pandiyas, Cholas and Pallavas controlled the Dravidian lands of what is now Kerala, Tamil Nadu and coastal Andhra Pradesh. The Pallavas, responsible for building the temples at Mahabalipuram, just south of modern Chennai, flourished in the seventh century. They warded off attacks both from the Rashtrakutas to their north and from the Pandiyas, who controlled the southern deltas of the Vaigai and Tamraparni rivers, with Madurai as their capital.

In the eighth century Kerala began to develop its own regional identity with the rise of the **Kulashekharas** in the Periyar Valley. Caste was a dominating feature of the kingdom's social organization, but with the distinctive twist that the **Nayars**, the most aristocratic of castes, developed a matrilineal system of descent.

It was the **Cholas** who came to dominate the south from the eighth century. Overthrowing the Pallavas, they controlled most of Tamil Nadu, south Karnataka and southern Andhra Pradesh from 850 AD to 1278 AD. They often held the Kerala kings under their control. Under their kings **Rajaraja I** (984-1014) and **Rajendra** (1014-1044) the Cholas also controlled north Sri Lanka, sent naval expeditions to Southeast Asia and successful military campaigns north to the Ganga plains. They lavished endowments on temples and also extended the gifts of land to Brahmins instituted by the Pallavas and Pandiyas. Many thousands of Brahmin priests were brought south to serve in major temples such as those in Chidambaram and Rajendra wished to be remembered above all as the king who brought water from the holy Ganga all the way to his kingdom.

The spread of Islamic power

The Delhi Sultanate

From about 1000 AD the external attacks which inflicted most damage on Rajput wealth and power in northern India came increasingly from the Arabs and Turks. Mahmud of Ghazni raided the Punjab virtually every year between 1000 and 1026, attracted both by the agricultural surpluses and the wealth of India's temples. By launching annual raids during the harvest season, Mahmud financed his struggles in Central Asia and his attacks on the profitable trade conducted along the Silk road between China and the Mediterranean. The enormous wealth in cash, golden images and jewellery of North India's temples drew him back every year and his greed for gold, used to remonetise the economy of the remarkable Ghaznavid Sultanate of Afghanistan, was insatiable. He sacked the wealthy centres of Mathura (UP) in 1017,

Background

AD	North India	Peninsular India	External events	AD
300		Rise of Pallavas.	Classic period of Mayan civilization.	300
319	Chandra Gupta founds Gupta Dynasty (Samudra 335, Chandra II 376, Kumara 415).			
			Constantinople founded.	330
454	Skanda Gupta, the last imperial Gupta, takes power. Dies 467.		End of Roman Empire. Teotihuacan, Mexico, population 200,000.	476 500
540	Gupta rule ends.		Saint Sophia, Constantinople.	532
550		First Chalukya Dynasty, Badami cave temple; last Ajanta paintings.	Buddhism arrives in Japan.	550
578				

Thanesar (Haryana) in 1011, Somnath (Gujarat) in 1024 and Kannauj (UP). He died in 1030, to the Hindus just another *mlechchha* ('impure' or sullied one), as had been the Huns and the Sakas before him. Such raids were never taken seriously as a long term threat by kings further east or south and as the Rajputs continually feuded among themselves the northwest plains became an attractive prey.

Muslim political power was heralded by the raids of Mu'izzu'd Din from 1192 onwards inflicting crushing defeats on Hindu opponents from Gwalior to Benaras. The foundations were then laid for the first extended period of Muslim power, which came under the Delhi sultans.

South India States in the 16th century

Background

AD	North India	Peninsular India	External events	AD
600	Period of small Indian states.	Bhakti movement. Chalukyan Dynasty in west and central Deccan. Pallavas in Tamil Nadu	Death of Mohammad.	632
629	Hiuen Tsang travels			
630	India			
			Buddhism reaches Tibet	645
670	Rajputs become powerful force in northwest.	Mahabalipuram shore temples.		
712	Arabs arrive in Sind.	Nandivarman II in Tamil Nadu. Pandiyas in Madurai.	Muslim invasions of Spain.	711
757				
775		Rashtrakutas dominate central Peninsula. Kailasanath Temple, Ellora. Rise of Cholas.	Charlemagne crowned. Settlement of New Zealand. Cyrillic script developed.	800 850 863

The Delhi Sultanate never achieved the dominating power of earlier empires or of its successor, the Mughal Empire. It exercised political control through crushing military raids, some of which reached deep into the south, and the exaction of tribute from defeated kings, but there was no real attempt to impose central administration. Power depended on maintaining vital lines of communication and trade routes, keeping fortified strongholds and making regional alliances. In the Peninsula to the south, the Deccan, regional powers contested for survival, power and expansion. The Bahmanis were the forerunners of a succession of Muslim dynasties, who sometimes competed with each other and sometimes collaborated against a joint external enemy.

Across West and South India today are the remains of the only major medieval Hindu empire to resist effectively the Muslim advance. The ruins at Hampi in modern Karnataka demonstrate the power of a Hindu coalition that rose to power in the south Deccan in the first half of the 14th century, only to be defeated by its Muslim neighbours in 1565, see page 345.

The Vijayanagar Empire

For over 200 years Vijayanagar ('*city of victory*') kings fought to establish supremacy. It was an empire that, in the words of one Indian historian, made it 'the nearest approach to a war state ever made by a Hindu kingdom'. At times its power reached from Orissa in the northeast to Sri Lanka. In 1390 King Harihara II claimed to have planted a victory pillar in Sri Lanka. Much of modern Tamil Nadu and Andhra Pradesh were added to the core region of Karnataka in the area under Vijayanagar control.

The Mughal Empire

Despite the ability of the Vijayanagar Empire to hold out against local Muslim powers, all regional kingdoms in the south were ultimately brought however fleetingly under Muslim influence through the power of the Mughal Empire. The descendants of conquerors, with the blood of both Tamburlaine (Timur) and Genghis Khan in their veins, the Mughals came to dominate Indian politics from Babur's victory near Delhi in 1526 to Aurangzeb's death in 1707. Their legacy was not only some of the most magnificent architecture in the world, but a profound impact on the culture, society and future politics of South Asia.

Background

AD	North India	Peninsular India	External events	AD
950	Khajuraho temples started.	Rajendra Chola.	Sung Dynasty in China.	979
984		Rajaraja 1st.		
1001	Mahmud of Ghazni raids Indus plains. Rajput dynasties grow.	Chola kings – navies sent to Southeast Asia: Chola bronzes.	Easter Island stone carvings.	1000
1050	Sufism in North India. Rajput dynasties in northwest.		Norman conquest of England.	1066
1110		Rise of Hoysalas	First European universities.	1100
1118	Senas in Bengal			1150
			Angkor Wat, Cambodia; paper making spreads from Muslim world.	
1192	Rajputs defeated by Mu'izzu'd Din.		Srivijaya Kingdom at its height in Java; Angkor Empire at greatest.	1170

Babur (the tiger) Founder of the Mughal Dynasty, Babur was born in Russian Turkestan on 15 February 1483, the fifth direct descendant on the male side of Timur and 13th on the female side from Genghis Khan. He established the Mughal Empire in 1526. but when he died 4 years later, the Empire was still far from secured, but he had not only laid the foundations of political and military power but had also begun to establish courtly traditions of poetry, literature and art which became the hallmark of subsequent Mughal rulers.

Within two generations the Mughals had become fully at home in their Indian environment and brought some radical changes. Babur was charismatic. He ruled by keeping the loyalty of his military chiefs, giving them control of large areas of territory. However, his son Humayun was forced to flee Delhi, only returning to power a year befire his death.

Akbar Akbar, who was to become one of the greatest of India's emperors, was only 13 when he took the throne in 1556. The next 44 years were one of the most remarkable periods of South Asian history, paralleled by the Elizabethan period in England, where Queen Elizabeth I ruled from 1558 to 1603. Although Akbar inherited the throne, it was he who really created the empire. He also gave it many of its distinguishing features.

Through his marriage to a Hindu princess he ensured that Hindus were given honoured positions in government and respect for their religious beliefs and practices. He sustained a passionate interest in art and literature, matched by a determination to create monuments to his empire's political power and he laid the foundations for an artistic and architectural tradition which developed a totally distinctive Indian style. This emerged from the separate elements of Iranian and Indian traditions by a constant process of blending and originality of which he was the chief patron.

But these achievements were only possible because of his political and military gifts. From 1556 until his 18th birthday in 1560 Akbar was served by a prince regent, Bairam Khan. However, already at the age of 15 he had conquered Ajmer and large areas of Central India. He brought Kabul back under Mughal control in the 1580s and established a presence from Kashmir, Sind and Baluchistan in the north and west, to the Godavari River on the border of modern Andhra Pradesh in the south.

It was Akbar who created the administrative structure employed by successive Mughal emperors to sustain their power. Revenue was raised using detailed surveying methods. Rents were fixed according to the quality of the soil in a move which was carried through into British revenue raising systems. Akbar introduced a new standard measure of length and calculated the assessment of tax due on the

Background

AD	North India	Peninsular India	External events	AD
1198	First mosque built in Delhi; Qutb Minar Delhi.		Rise of Hausa city states in West Africa.	1200
1206	Delhi Sultanate established.		Mongols begin conquest of Asia under Genghis Khan.	1206
1206	Turkish 'slave dynasty'.	Pandiyas rise.	First Thai kingdom.	1220
1222				
1230	Iltutmish Sultan of Delhi.	Konark, Sun Temple, Orissa		
1290	Khaljis in Delhi; Jalal ud Din Khalji.		Marco Polo reaches China.	1275
1320-24	Ghiyas ud Din Tughluq.		Black Death spreads from Asia to Europe.	1348
1324-51	Mohammad bin Tughluq.			

basis of a 10 year average of production. Each year the oldest record was dropped out of the calculation, while the average produce for the current year was added. The government's share of the produce was fixed at one quarter.

Akbar deliberately widened his power base by incorporating Rajput princes into the administrative structure and giving them extensive rights in the revenue from land. He abolished the hated tax on non-Muslims (*jizya*)—ultimately reinstated by his strictly orthodox great grandson Aurangzeb—ceased levying taxes on Hindus who went on pilgrimage and ended the practice of forcible conversion to Islam.

Akbar was a patron not just of art but of an extraordinary range of literature. His library contained books on 'biography, theology, comparative religion, science, mathematics, history, astrology, medicine, zoology and anthropology'. Almost hyperactive throughout his life, he required very little sleep, using moments of rest to commission books and works of art.

The influence of his father Humayun's Iranian artists is still clearly evident in the earlier of these works, but the works were not just those of unidentified 'schools' of artists, but of brilliant individuals such as **Basawan** and **Miskin**, unparalleled in their ability to capture animal life. Examples of their work can be seen not just in India, but at major museums in Europe and the United States.

Artistic treasures abound from Akbar's court – paintings, jewellery, weapons – often bringing together material and skills from across the known world. Emeralds were particularly popular, with the religious significance which attaches to the colour green in mystic Islam adding to their attraction. Some came from as far afield as Colombia. Akbar's intellectual interests were extraordinarily catholic. He met the Portuguese Jesuits in 1572 and welcomed them to his court, along with Buddhists, Hindus and Zoroastrians, every year between 1575 and 1582.

Akbar's eclecticism had a purpose, for he was trying to build a focus of loyalty beyond that of caste, social group, region or religion. Like Roman emperors before him, he deliberately cultivated a new religion in which the emperor himself attained divinity, hoping thereby to give the empire a legitimacy which would last. While his religion disappeared with his death, the legitimacy of the Mughals survived another 200 years, long after their real power had almost disappeared.

Akbar died of a stomach illness in 1605. He was succeeded by his son, Prince Salim, who inherited the throne as Emperor Jahangir ('*world seizer*'). He added little to the territory of the empire, consolidating the Mughals' hold on the Himalayan foothills and parts of central India but restricting his innovative energies to pushing back

Jahangir

Background

AD	North India	Peninsular India	External events	AD
1336		Vijayanagar Empire established, Harihara I.		
1347		Ala-ud-Din sets up		
1351-88	Firoz Shah Tughluq.	Bahmani dynasty, independent of Delhi, in Gulbarga.	Ming dynasty in China established.	1368
			Peking the largest city in the world.	1400
1398	Timur sacks Delhi.		Ming sea-going expeditions to Africa.	1405
1412	End of Tughlaq Dynasty.			
1414		Bidar/Bahmani Kingdom in Deccan.		1428
1440	Sayyid Dynasty. Mystic Kabir born in		Aztecs defeat Atzcapatzalco. Incas centralize power.	1438
1451	Benaras. Afghan Lodi Dynasty		Byzantine Empire falls to Ottomans.	1453
1469	established under Bahlul.			
1482	Guru Nanak born in Punjab.	Fall of Bahmanis.	Columbus reaches the Americas; Arabs and Jews expelled from Spain.	1492

frontiers of art rather than of land. By 1622 his Persian wife Nur Jahan effectively controlled the empire but despite her power she was unable to prevent the accession of her least favoured son, Prince Khurram to the throne in 1628. He took the title by by he is now known around the world, Shah Jahan (*Ruler of the World*) and in the following 30 years his reign represented the height of Mughal power.

Shah Jahan The Mughal Empire was under attack in the Deccan and the northwest when Shah Jahan became Emperor. He tried to re-establish and extend Mughal authority in both regions by a combination of military campaigns and skilled diplomacy. He was much more successful in pushing south than he was in consolidating the Mughal hold in Afghanistan and most of the Deccan was brought firmly under Mughal control.

But he too commissioned art, literature and, above all, architectural monuments, on an unparalleled scale. The Taj Mahal may be the most famous of these, but a succession of brilliant achievements can be attributed to his reign.

Aurangzeb The need to expand the area under Mughal control was felt even more strongly by Aurangzeb ('*The jewel in the throne*'), than by his predecessors. He had shown his intellectual gifts in his grandfather's court when held hostage to guarantee Shah Jahan's good behaviour, learning Arabic, Persian, Turkish and Hindi. When he seized power at the age of 40, he needed all his political and military skills to hold on to an unwieldy empire that was in permanent danger of collapse from its own size.

If the empire was to survive, Aurangzeb realized that the resources of the territory he inherited from his father were not enough and thus through a series of campaigns he pushed south, while maintaining his hold on the east and north. For the last 39 years of his reign he was forced to push ever further south, strugging continuously to sustain his power.

The East India Company and the rise of British power

The British were unique among the foreign rulers of India in coming by sea rather than through the northwest and in coming first for trade rather than for military conquest. Some of the great battles that established British power in India were fought in South India, but trade was even more important than military

Background

AD	North India	Peninsular India	External events	AD
1565		Vijayanagar defeated.	Wm Shakespeare born.	1564
		First printing press in Goa.	Dutch East India Co set up.	1566 1602
1603	Guru Granth Sahib compiled.		Tokugawa Shogunate in Japan.	1603
1605	**Jahangir** Emperor.		First permanent English settlement in America.	1607
1608		East India Co base at Surat.	Telescope invented in Holland.	1609
1628	**Shah Jahan** Emperor.		Masjid-i-Shah Mosque in Isfahan.	1616
1632-53	Taj Mahal built.	Fort St George, Madras, founded by East India Co.		1639
			Manchus found Ch'ing Dynasty.	1644
			Tasman 'discovers' New Zealand.	1645
1658	**Aurangzeb** Emperor.		Louis XIV of France - the 'Sun King'.	1653-1715

conquest. The ports that they established – Madras (now Chennai), Bombay (Mumbai) and Calcutta (Kolkata) – became completely new centres of political, economic and social activity. Before them Indian empires had controlled their territories from the land. The British dictated the emerging shape of the economy by controlling sea-borne trade. From the middle of the 19th century railways transformed the economic and political structure of South Asia and it was those three centres of British political control, along with the late addition of Delhi, which became the foci of economic development and political change.

The East India Company in Madras

In its first 90 years of contact with South Asia after the Company set up its first trading post at **Masulipatnam**, on the east coast of India in modern Andhra Pradesh, it had depended almost entirely on trade for its profits. However, in 1701, only 11 years after a British settlement was first established at Calcutta, the Company was given rights to land revenue in Bengal.

The Company was accepted and sometimes welcomed, partly because it offered to bolster the inadequate revenues of the Mughals by exchanging silver bullion for the cloth it bought. However, in the south the Company moved further and faster towards consolidating its political base. Wars between South India's regional factions gave the Company the opportunity to extend their influence by making alliances and offering support to some of these factions in their struggles, which were complicated by the extension to Indian soil of the European contest for power between the French and the British.

The British established effective control over both Bengal and Southeast India in the middle of the 17th century. Robert Clive, who started his East India Company life in Madras with a victory over the French at Arcot,, defeated the new Nawab of Bengal, the 20-year-old Siraj-ud-Daula, in June 1757 at **Plassey** (Palashi), about 100 km north of Calcutta.

Robert Clive

In 1773 Calcutta had already been put in charge of Bombay and Madras. The essential features of British control were mapped out in the next quarter of a

Background

AD	North India	Peninsular India	External events	AD
		Vasco da Gama reaches India.	Inca Empire at its height. Spanish claim Brazil; Safavid Empire founded in Persia.	1498
1500		Vijayanagar dominates South India; Krishnadevraya rules 1509-30.		1500
1506	Sikander Lodi founds Agra.			
		Albuquerque seizes Goa; Nizamshahis establish independent Ahmadnagar sultanate.		1510
1526	Babur defeats Ibrahim Lodi to establish Mughal power in Delhi.		Ottomans capture Syria, Egypt and Arabia.	1516
		Dutch, French, Portuguese and Danish traders.	Spaniards overthrow Aztecs in Mexico.	1519
			Potato introduced to Europe from South America.	1525
1540	Sher Shah forces **Humayun** into exile.			
1542 1555	**Humayun** re-conquers Delhi.	St Francis Xavier reaches Goa.		
1556	**Akbar** Emperor.			

century through the work of **Warren Hastings**, Governor-General from 1774 until 1785 and **Lord Cornwallis** who succeeded and remained in charge until 1793. Cornwallis was responsible for putting Europeans in charge of all the higher levels of revenue collection and administration and for introducing government by the rule of law, making even government officers subject to the courts.

The decline of Muslim power

The extension of East India Company power in the Mughal periphery of India's south and east took place against a background of weakening Mughal power at the centre in Delhi and on the Peninsula. Some of the Muslim kingdoms of the Deccan refused to pay the tribute to the Mughal Empire that had been forced on them after defeats in 1656. This refusal and their alliance with the rising power of Sivaji and his Marathas, had led Aurangzeb to attack the Shi'i-ruled states of Bijapur (1686) and Golconda (1687), in an attempt to reimpose Mughal supremacy.

Sivaji   Sivaji was the son of a Hindu who had served as a small-scale chief in the Muslim ruled state of Bijapur. The weakness of Bijapur encouraged Sivaji to extend his father's area of control and he led a rebellion. The Bijapur general Afzal Khan, sent to put it down, agreed to meet Sivaji in private to reach a settlement. In an act which is still remembered by both Muslims and Marathas, Sivaji embraced him with steel claws attached to his fingers and tore him apart. It was the start of a campaign which took Maratha power as far south as Madurai and to the doors of Delhi and Calcutta.

Sivaji had taken the fratricidal struggle for the succession which brought Aurangzeb to power, as the signal and the opportunity for launching a series of attacks against the Mughals. This in turn brought a riposte from Aurangzeb, once his hold on the centre was secure. However, despite the apparent expansion of his power the seeds of decay were already germinating. Although Sivaji himself died in 1680, Aurangzeb never fully came to terms with the rising power of the Marathas, though he did end their ambitions to form an empire of their own.

Nor was Aurangzeb able to create any wide sense of identity with the Mughals as a legitimate popular power. Instead, under the influence of Sunni Muslim theologians, he retreated into insistence on Islamic purity. He imposed Islamic law, the *sharia*, promoted only Muslims to positions of power and authority, tried to replace Hindu administrators and revenue collectors with Muslims and reimposed the *jizya* tax on all non-Muslims. By the time of his death in 1707 the empire no longer had either the broadness of spirit or the physical means to survive.

AD	North India	Peninsular India	External events	AD
1677		**Shivaji** and Marathas.	Pennsylvania founded.	1681
1690	Calcutta founded.			
1699	Guru Gobind Singh forms Sikh Khalsa.	Regional powers dominate through 18th century: Nawabs of Arcot (1707); Maratha Peshwas (1714); Nizams of Hyderabad (1724).	Chinese occupy Outer Mongolia.	1697
1703	Nawabs of Bengal.		Foundation of St Petersburg, capital of Russian Empire.	1703
1707	Death of Aurangzeb; Mughal rulers continue to rule from Delhi until 1858			
1724	Nawabs of Avadh.			
1739	The Persian Nadir Shah captures Delhi and massacres thousands.			
1757	Battle of Plassey; British power extended from East India.	East India Co strengthens trade and political power through 18th century.	US War of Independence.	1775-8

The decline was postponed briefly by the 5 year reign of Aurangzeb's son. Sixty-three when he acceded to the throne, Bahadur Shah restored some of its faded fortunes. He made agreements with the Marathas and the Rajputs and defeated the Sikhs in Punjab before taking the last Sikh guru into his service.

The decay of the Mughal Empire has been likened to 'a magnificent flower slowly wilting and occasionally dropping a petal, its brilliance fading, its stalk bending ever lower'. Nine emperors succeeded Aurangzeb between his death and the exile of the last Mughal ruler in 1858. It was no accident that it was in that year that the British ended the rule of its East India Company and decreed India to be its Indian empire.

Successive Mughal rulers saw their political control diminish and their territory shrink. **Nasir ud Din Mohammad Shah**, known as Rangila ('*the pleasure loving*'), who reigned between 1719 and 1748, presided over a continued flowering of art and music, but a disintegration of political power. Hyderabad, Bengal and Oudh (the region to the east of Delhi) became effectively independent states; the Marathas dominated large tracts of Central India, the Jats captured Agra, the Sikhs controlled Punjab.

Mohammad Shah remained in his capital of Delhi, resigning himself to enjoying what Carey Welch has called "the conventional triad of joys: the wine was excellent, as were the women and for him the song was especially rewarding". The idyll was rudely shattered by the invasion of **Nadir Shah** in 1739, an Iranian marauder who slaughtered thousands in Delhi and carried off priceless Mughal treasures, including the Peacock Throne.

The Maratha confederacy

Nadir Shah's invasion was a flash in the pan. Of far greater substance was the development through the 18th century of the power of the **Maratha confederacy**. They were unique in India in uniting different castes and classes in a nationalist fervour for the region of Maharashtra. As Spear has pointed out, when the Mughals ceded the central district of Malwa, the Marathas were able to pour through the gap created between the Nizam of Hyderabad's territories in the south and the area remaining under Mughal control in the north. They rapidly occupied Orissa in the east and raided Bengal.

By 1750 they had reached the gates of Delhi. When Delhi collapsed to Afghan invaders in 1756-57 the Mughal minister called on the Marathas for help. Yet again Panipat proved to be a decisive battlefield, the Marathas being heavily defeated by the Afghan forces on 13 January 1761. However Ahmad Shah was forced to retreat to Afghanistan by his own rebellious troops demanding 2 years arrears of pay, leaving a power vacuum.

The Maratha confederacy dissolved into five independent powers, with whom the incoming British were able to deal separately. The door to the north was open.

The East India Company's push for power

In the century and a half that followed the death of Aurangzeb, the **British East India Company** extended its economic and political influence into the heart of India. As the Mughal Empire lost its power India fell into many smaller states. The Company undertook to protect the rulers of several of these states from external attack by stationing British troops in their territory. In exchange for this service the rulers paid subsidies to the Company. As the British historian Christopher Bayly has pointed out, the cure was usually worse than the disease and the cost of the payments to the Company crippled the local ruler. The British extended their territory through the 18th century as successive regional powers were annexed and brought under direct Company rule.

Progress to direct British control was uneven and often opposed. The Sikhs in Punjab, the Marathas in the west and the Mysore sultans in the south, fiercely contested British advances. **Haidar Ali** and **Tipu Sultan**, who had built a wealthy kingdom in the Mysore region, resisted attempts to incorporate them. Tipu was finally killed in 1799 at the battle of Srirangapatnam, an island fort in the Kaveri River just north of Mysore, where Arthur Wellesley, later the Duke of Wellington, began to make his military reputation.

The Marathas were not defeated until the war of 1816-18, a defeat which had to wait until Napoleon was defeated in Europe and the British could turn their wholehearted attention once again to the Indian scene. Even then the defeat owed as much to internal faction fighting as to the power of the British-led army. Only the northwest of the subcontinent remained beyond British control until well into the 19th century.

In 1818 India's economy was in ruins and its political structures destroyed. Irrigation works and road systems had fallen into decay and gangs terrorized the countryside. The peace and stability of the Mughal period had long since passed. Between 1818 and 1857 there was a succession of local and uncoordinated revolts in different parts of India. Some were bought off, some put down by military force.

A period of reforms

While existing political systems were collapsing, the first half of the 19th century was also a period of radical social change in the territories governed by the East India Company. **Lord William Bentinck** became Governor-General at a time when England was entering a period of major reform. In 1828 he banned the burning of widows on the funeral pyres of their husbands (**sati**) and then moved to suppress **thuggee** (the ritual murder and robbery carried out in the name of the goddess Kali). But his most far reaching change was to introduce education in English.

The resolution of 7 March 1835 stated that "the great objects of the British government ought to be the promotion of European literature and science" promising funds to impart "to the native population the knowledge of English literature and science through the medium of the English language". Out of this concern were born new educational institutions such as the Calcutta Medical College. From the late 1830s massive new engineering projects began to be taken up; first canals, then railways.

The innovations stimulated change and change contributed to the growing unease with the British presence, particularly under the Governor-Generalship of the Marquess of Dalhousie (1848-56). The development of the telegraph, railways and new roads, three universities and the extension of massive new canal irrigation projects in North India seemed to threaten traditional society, a risk increased by the annexation of Indian states to bring them under direct British rule. The most important of these was Oudh.

The Rebellion

Out of the growing discontent and widespread economic difficulties came the Rebellion or 'Mutiny' of 1857 (now widely known as the First War of Independence). Appalling scenes of butchery and reprisals marked the struggle, which was only put down by troops from outside. None of the major Indian princes took the side of the rebels, and South India was almost entirely unaffected.

Background

Mahatma Gandhi

Gandhi was asked by a journalist when he was on a visit to Europe what he thought of Western civilization. He paused and then replied: "It would be very nice, wouldn't it". The answer illustrated just one facet of his extraordinarily complex character. A westernized, English educated lawyer, who had lived outside India from his youth to middle age, he preached the general acceptance of some of the doctrines he had grown to respect in his childhood, which stemmed from deep Indian traditions – notably ahimsa, or non-violence. From 1921 he gave up his Western style of dress and adopted the hand spun dhoti worn by poor Indian villagers, giving rise to Churchill's jibe that he was a 'naked fakir' (holy man). Yet if he was a thorn in the British flesh, he was also fiercely critical of many aspects of traditional Hindu society. He preached against the discrimination of

the caste system which still dominated life for the overwhelming majority of Hindus. Through the 1920s much of his work was based on writing for the weekly newspaper Young India, which became The Harijan in 1932. The change in name symbolized his commitment to improving the status of the outcastes, Harijan (person of God) being coined to replace the term outcaste. Often despised by the British in India he succeeded in gaining the reluctant respect and ultimately outright admiration of many. His death at the hands of an extreme Hindu chauvinist in January 1948 was a final testimony to the ambiguity of his achievements: successful in contributing so much to achieving India's Independence, yet failing to resolve some of the bitter communal legacies which he gave his life to overcome.

The Period of Empire

The 1857 rebellion marked the end not only of the Mughal Empire but also of the East India Company, for the British Government in London took overall control in 1858. Yet within 30 years a movement for self-government had begun and there were the first signs of a demand among the new western educated Èlite that political rights be awarded to match the sense of Indian national identity.

The Indian National Congress

The movement for independence went through a series of steps. The creation of the Indian National Congress in 1885 was the first all-India political institution and was to become the key vehicle of demands for independence. However, the educated Muslim Èlite of what is now Uttar Pradesh saw a threat to Muslim rights, power and identity in the emergence of democratic institutions which gave Hindus, with their built-in natural majority, significant advantages. Sir Sayyid Ahmad Khan, who had founded a Muslim University at Aligarh in 1877, advised Muslims against joining the Congress, seeing it as a vehicle for Hindu and especially Bengali, nationalism.

The Muslim League

The educated Muslim community of North India remained deeply suspicious of the Congress, making up less than 8 of those attending its conferences between 1900-1920. Muslims from UP created the All-India Muslim League in 1906. However, the demands of the Muslim League were not always opposed to those of the Congress. In 1916 it concluded the Lucknow Pact with the Congress, in which the Congress won Muslim support for self-government, in exchange for the recognition that there would be separate constituencies for Muslims. The nature of the future Independent India was still far from clear, however. The British conceded the principle of self-government in 1918, but however radical the reforms would have seemed 5 years earlier they already fell far short of heightened Indian expectations.

Background

Mahatma Gandhi

Into a tense atmosphere Mohandas Karamchand Gandhi returned to India in 1915 after 20 years practising as a lawyer in South Africa. On his return the Bengali Nobel Laureate poet, Rabindranath Tagore, had dubbed him 'Mahatma' – Great Soul. The name became his. He arrived as the government of India was being given new powers by the British parliament to try political cases without a jury and to give provincial governments the right to imprison politicians without trial. In opposition to this legislation Gandhi proposed to call a *hartal*, when all activity would cease for a day, a form of protest still in widespread use. Such protests took place across India, often accompanied by riots.

On 13 April 1919 a huge gathering took place in the enclosed space of Jallianwala Bagh in Amritsar It had been prohibited by the government and General Dyer ordered troops to fire on the people without warning, killing 379 and injuring at least a further 1,200. It marked the turning point in relations with Britain and the rise of Gandhi to the key position of leadership in the struggle for complete independence.

The thrust for Independence

Through the 1920s Gandhi developed concepts and political programmes that were to become the hallmark of India's Independence struggle. Rejecting the 1919 reforms Gandhi preached the doctrine of *swaraj*, or self rule, developing an idea he first published in a leaflet in 1909. He saw swaraj not just as political independence from a foreign ruler but, in Judith Brown's words, as made up of three elements: "It was a state of being that had to be created from the roots upwards, by the regeneration of individuals and their realization of their true spiritual being ... unity among all religions; the eradication of Untouchability; and the practice of *swadeshi*." Swadeshi was not simply dependence on Indian products rather than foreign imports, but a deliberate move to a simple life style, hence his emphasis on hand spinning as a daily routine.

Ultimately political Independence was to be achieved not by violent rebellion but by *satyagraha* – a "truth force" which implied a willingness to suffer through non-violent resistance to injustice. This gave birth to Gandhi's advocacy of "non-cooperation" as a key political weapon and brought together Gandhi's commitment to matching political goals and moral means. Although the political achievements of Gandhi's programme continues to be strongly debated the struggles of the 1920s established his position as a key figure in the Independence movement.

In 1930 the Congress declared that 26 January would be Independence day – still celebrated as Republic Day in India today. The Leader of the Muslim League, Mohammad Iqbal, took the opportunity of his address to the League in the same year to suggest the formation of a Muslim state within an Indian Federation. Also in 1930 a Muslim student in Cambridge, **Chaudhuri Rahmat Ali**, coined a name for the new Muslim state – **PAKISTAN**. The letters were to stand 'P' for Punjab, 'A' for Afghania, 'K' for Kashmir, 'S' for Sind with the suffix '*stan*', Persian for country. The idea still had little real shape however and waited on developments of the late 1930s and 1940s to bear fruit.

By the end of second world war the positions of the Muslim League, now under the leadership of **Mohammad Ali Jinnah** and the Congress led by Jawaharlal Nehru, were irreconcilable. While major questions of the definition of separate territories for a Muslim and non-Muslim state remained to be answered, it was clear to General Wavell, the British Viceroy through the last years of the War, that there was no alternative but to accept that independence would have to be given on the basis of separate states.

Independence and Partition

One of the main difficulties for the Muslims was that they made up only a fifth of the total population. Although there were regions both in the northwest and the east where they formed the majority, Muslims were also scattered throughout India. It was therefore impossible to define a simple territorial division which would provide a state to match Jinnah's claim of a '*two-nation theory*'. On 20 February 1947,

Background

The Indian flag

In 1921, the All Indian Congress considered a red and green flag to represent the two dominant religious groups (Hindu and Muslim); Gandhi suggested white be added to represent the other communities, as well as the charka (spinning wheel) symbolizing the Swadeshi movement, now centred in the party flag.

In 1931, the Indian National Congress adopted the tricolor as the national flag. This was intended to have no communal significance. The deep saffron denoted 'Courage and Sacrifice', the white 'Truth and Peace' and dark green 'Faith and Chivalry'. On the white stripe, the Dharma chakra represented the Buddhist Wheel of Law from Asoka's Lion capital at Sarnath.

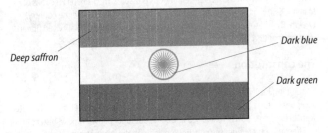

Deep saffron

Dark blue

Dark green

the British Labour Government announced its decision to replace Lord Wavell as Viceroy with Lord Mountbatten, who was to oversee the transfer of power to new independent governments. It set a deadline of June 1948 for British withdrawal. The announcement of a firm date made the Indian politicians even less willing to compromise and the resulting division satisfied no one.

When Independence arrived – on 15 August for India and the 14 August for Pakistan, because Indian astrologers deemed the 15th to be the most auspicious moment – many questions remained unanswered. Several key Princely States had still not decided firmly to which country they would accede. Kashmir was the most important of these, with results that have lasted to the present day. Yet 40 million Muslims, including many in South India, retained their Indian nationality, part of a Mulsim community that now totals about 120 million.

Modern India

India, with over 1 billion people in 2001, is the second most populated country in the world after China. That population size reflects the long history of human occupation and the fact that an astonishingly high proportion of India's land is relatively fertile. Sixty percent of India's surface area is cultivated today, compared with about 10 in China and 20 in the United States.

Although the birth rate has fallen steadily over the last 40 years, initially death rates fell faster and the rate of population increase has continued to be above 2 – or 18 million – a year. Today nearly 30 of the population lives in towns and cities have grown dramatically. In 1971, 109 million people lived in towns and cities. The figure grew to nearly 300 million in 1999. South India has seen particularly rpid progress compared with the north in both health and education. In both Kerala and Tamil Nadu birth rates have fallen to match death rates so that population stability has been reached, and Kerala calims 100% literacy.

Background

Politics and institutions

South Indian politics has always marched to its own music. Regional movements have played a major part in state level givernment, especially in Tamil Nadu and Andhra Pradesh, where national parties like the Congress have struggled to form working partnerships with regional parties to help form a majority in India's central Parliament, or Lok Sabha.

In the years since independence, striking political achievements have been made. With the 2 year exception of 1975-77, when Mrs Gandhi imposed a state of emergency in which all political activity was banned, India has sustained a democratic system in the face of tremendous pressures. The General Elections of March 1998, which involved an electorate of over 400 million, were the country's twelfth. Their results produced a minority government which only survived fifteen months, resulting in the thirteenth general election in September 1999.

The constitution

Establishing itself as a sovereign democratic republic, the Indian parliament accepted Nehru's advocacy of a secular constitution. The President is formally vested with all executive powers exercised under the authority of the Prime Minister.

Effective power under the constitution lies with the Prime Minister and Cabinet, following the British model. In practice there have been long periods when the

South Asia in 1947

States, Agencies & Protectorates

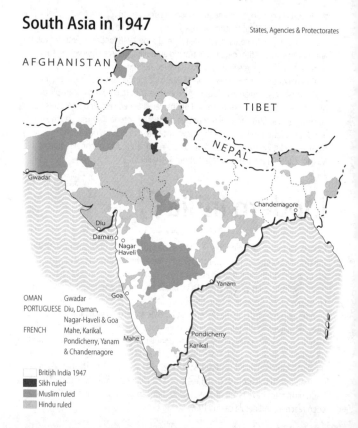

AFGHANISTAN

TIBET

NEPAL

Gwadar

Chandernagore

Diu
Daman
Nagar
Haveli

Yanam

OMAN	Gwadar
PORTUGUESE	Diu, Daman, Nagar-Haveli & Goa
FRENCH	Mahe, Karikal, Pondicherry, Yanam & Chandernagore

Goa

Mahe

Pondicherry

Karikal

British India 1947
Sikh ruled
Muslim ruled
Hindu ruled

Background

Prime Ministers and Presidents since 1947

Date	Prime Minister	Date	President
1947-64	Jawaharlal Nehru	1948-50	C Rajagopalachari
1964-66	Lal Bahadur Shastri	1950-62	Rajendra Prasad
1966-77	Indira Gandhi	1962-67	S Radhakrishnan
1977-79	Morarji Desai	1967-69	Zakir Hussain
1979-80	Charan Singh	1969-74	V V Giri
1980-84	Indira Gandhi	1974-77	Fakhruddin Ali Ahmed
1984-89	Rajiv Gandhi	1977-82	Neelam Sanjiva Reddy
1989-90	VP Singh	1982-87	Giani Zail Singh
1990-91	S Chandrasekhar	1987-1992	R Venkataraman
1991- 96	PV Narasimha Rao	1992-97	Shankar Dayal Sharma
1996 (May)	Atal Behari Vaypayee	1997	K R Narayanan
1996-1997 (May)	H D Deve Gowda	1997-1998 (May)	Inder Kumar Gujral
1998	Atal Behari Vajpayee		

Prime Minister has been completely dominant. In principle parliament chooses the Prime Minister. The Parliament has a lower house (the *Lok Sabha*, or 'house of the people') and an upper house (the *Rajya Sabha* – Council of States). The former is made up of directly elected representatives from the 543 parliamentary constituencies (plus two nominated members from the Anglo-Indian community), the latter of a mixture of members elected by an electoral college and of nominated members. Constitutional amendments require a two-thirds majority in both houses.

India's federal constitution devolves certain powers to elected state assemblies. Each state has a Governor who acts as its official head. Many states also have two chambers, the upper generally called the Rajya Sabha and the lower (often called the Vidhan Sabha) being of directly elected representatives. In practice many of the state assemblies have had a totally different political complexion from that of the Lok Sabha. Regional parties have played a more prominent role, though in many states central government has dictated both the leadership and policy of state assemblies.

States & Union Territories

Union territories are administered by the President "acting to such an extent as he thinks fit". In practice Union territories have varying forms of self-government. Pondicherry has a legislative Assembly and Council of Ministers. The 69th Amendment to the Constitution in 1991 provided for a legislative assembly and council of Ministers for Delhi, elections for which were held in December 1993. The Assemblies of Union Territories have more restricted powers of legislation than full states. Some Union Territories, such as Andaman and Nicobar Islands and Lakshadweep, have elected bodies known as Pradesh Councils. These councils have the right to discuss and make recommendations on matters relating to their territories.

Secularism

One of the key features of India's constitution is its secular principle. This is not based on the absence of religious belief, but on the commitment to guarantee freedom of religious belief and practice to all groups in Indian society. Some see the

Background

commitment to a secular constitution as under increasing challenge, especially from the Hindu nationalism of the Bharatiya Janata Party, the BJP. The BJP persuaded a number of regional parties to join it in government after the 1998 and 1999 elections, appearing to move away from its narrowly defined conception of a Hindu state. The BJP is torn between the narrowly defined Hindu beliefs of its core support and the electoral demands of an enormously varied population.

The judiciary India's Supreme Court has similar but somewhat weaker powers to those of the United States. The judiciary has remained effectively independent of the government except under the Emergency between 1975-77.

The civil service India continued to use the small but highly professional administrative service inherited from the British period. Renamed the Indian Administrative Service (IAS), it continues to exercise remarkable influence across the country. The administration of many aspects of central and regional government is in the hands of this Élite body, who act largely by the constitutional rules which bind them as servants of the state. Many Indians accept the continuing efficiency and high calibre of the top ranking officers in the administration while believing that the bureaucratic system as a whole has been overtaken by widespread corruption.

The police India's police service is divided into a series of groups, numbering nearly 1 million. While the top ranks of the Indian Police Service are comparable to the IAS, lower levels are extremely poorly trained and very low paid. In addition to the domestic police force there are special groups: the Border Security Force, Central Reserve Police and others. They may be armed with modern weapons and are called in for special duties.

The armed forces Unlike its immediate neighbours India has never had military rule. It has approximately 1 million men in the army – one of the largest armed forces in the world. Although they have remained out of politics the armed services have been used increasingly frequently to put down civil unrest especially in Kashmir, where there are currently around 400,000 troops.

The Congress Party For over forty years Indian national politics was dominated by the Congress Party. Its strength in the Lok Sabha often overstated the volume of its support in the country, however and state governments have frequently been formed by parties – and interests – only weakly represented at the centre.

The Congress won overall majorities in seven of the ten general elections held before the 1996 election, although in no election did the Congress obtain more than 50 of the popular vote. It was defeated only in 1977 and in 1989 when the Opposition parties united against it. In the latter election it still gained the largest number of seats, though not enough to form a government on its own and it was unable to find allies.

The Congress had built its broad based support partly by championing the causes of the poor, the backward castes and the minorities. It regained power in mid-1991 in the wake of Rajiv Gandhi's assassination at Sriperumbudur, in Tamil Nadu, and under the leadership of Narasimha Rao, who came from Andhra Pradesh, it succeeded in governing for its full 5-year term, introducing the most radical economic reform programme since Independence. In 1998 it lost support across India, and its power base in the South is generally severely weakened.

The Non-Congress Parties Political activity outside the Congress can seem bewilderingly complex. There are no genuinely national parties. The only alternative governments to the Congress have been formed by coalitions of regional and ideologically based parties. Parties of the left – Communist and Socialist – have never broken out of their narrow regional bases.

The **Communist Party of India** split into two factions in 1964, with the Communist Party of India Marxist (**CPM**) ultimately taking power in West Bengal and Kerala.

At the right of the political spectrum, the **Jan Sangh** was seen as a party of right wing Hindu nationalism but was almost entirely a north Indian party. The most organized political force outside the Congress, the Jan Sangh merged with the **Janata Party** for the elections of 1977. After the collapse of that government it re-formed itself as the **Bharatiya Janata Party** (BJP). In 1990-91 it developed a powerful campaign focusing on reviving Hindu identity against the minorities. The elections of 1991 showed it to be the most powerful single challenger to the Congress in North India. In the decade that followed it became the most powerful opponent of the Congress across northern India and established a sries of footholds and alliances in the South, enabling it to become the most important national alternative to the Congress through the 1990s.

Elsewhere a succession of regional parties dominated politics in several key states. The most important were Tamil Nadu and Andhra Pradesh in the south. In Tamil Nadu power has alternated since 1967 between the **Dravida Munnetra Kazhagam** (the DMK) and a faction which split from it, the All India Anna DMK, named after one of the earliest leaders of the Dravidian political movement, CN Annadurai ('Anna'). In Andhra Pradesh, the **Telugu Desam**, currently under the leadership of the cyber whizz-kid of South India, Chandrababu Naidu, offered a similar regional alternative to Congress rule.

In early 1998 national elections saw the BJP return as the largest single party in India, though without an overall majority, and still with a sparse representation in most of South India. This time however they were able to forge some previously impossible alliances with regional parties and they formed the new government under the Prime Ministership of Atal Behari Vajpayee. The emergence of Sonia Gandhi as an effective campaigner for the Congress in the Assembly elections and her subsequent election as Congress Party President, suggested that the Nehru-Gandhi dynasty may not yet be dead in Indian political life. However, the autumn 1999 election results confirmed the BJP government in power at the head of a broad coalition, the National Democratic Alliance (NDA) under the Prime Ministerhip of Atal Behari Vajpayee, and appeared to offer the prospect of a more extended period of political stability.

Recent developments

State level politics in South India is dominated by the affairs of the State Legislative Assemblies. With a wide range of powers, these reflect the social and historic traditions of the different major linguistic regions. Politics and films get mixed up as the stars of one medium have traded places with those of the other. Film stars have been leading politicians rights across the south, charismatic strs such as M.G. Ramachandran in Tamil Nadu or N.T. Rama Rao in Andhra Pradesh enjoying a massive following of worshipping fans.

Background

Economy

Although agriculture now accounts for less than 30 of India's GDP, it remains the most important single economic activity. More than half India's people depend directly on agriculture and its success has a crucial effect on the remainder of the economy.

Agriculture

South Indian agriculture is enormously varied, reflecting the widely different conditions of climate, soil and relief. Cereal farming dominates most areas. Rice is by far India's most important single foodgrain, concentrated in the wetter regions of the east and south. Production has more than doubled in the last 20 years and 1999-2000 saw production reach record levels.

Other cereal crops – sorghum and the millets – predominate in the drier areas, though both are grown under irrigated conditions in South India. In addition to its cereals and a range of pulses, South India produces important crops of tea, cotton and sugar cane. All have seen significant growth, tea and cotton manufacturers making important contributions to export earnings.

Between independence and the late 1960s most of the increase in India's agricultural output came from extending the cultivated area. About 60% of India's total area is now cultivated. In the last 20 years increasingly intensive use of land through greater irrigation and use of fertilizer, pesticides and high yielding varieties of seeds (HYVs) has allowed growth to continue. The area under irrigation has risen to over 35% in 2000, while fertilizer use has increased 25 times since 1961. Indian agriculture is dominated by small holdings. Only 20% of the land is farmed in units of more than 10 ha (compared with 31 20 years ago), while nearly 60% of farms are less than 1 ha. While the "Green Revolution" – the package of practices designed to increase farm output – has had its opponents, it has now transformed the agricultural productivity of many regions of India, allowing a population twice the size of that thirty years ago to be fed without recourse to imports or aid. Much of this has been achieved as the result of seed breeding and agricultural research in India's own agricultural research institutions.

Resources & industry

South India has extensive resources of iron ore, lignite, and some other minerals. Very imited oil and gas reserves have been discovered off the South Indian coast, and the South also has one nuclear power station just south of Chennai.

India's Five Year Plans

In the early 1950s India embarked on a programme of planned industrial development. Borrowing planning concepts from the Soviet Union, the government tried to stimulate development through massive investment in the public sector, imposing a system of tight controls on foreign ownership of capital in India and playing a highly interventionist role in all aspects of economic policy. The private sector was allowed to continue to operate in agriculture and in a wide range of 'non-essential' industrial sectors.

Although significant achievements were made in the first two Five Year Plans (1951-56, 1956-61), the Third Five Year Plan failed catastrophically. Agriculture was particularly hard hit by three poor monsoons. After a period of dependence on foreign aid at the end of the 1960s, the economy started moving forward again. The 'Green Revolution' enabled Indian agriculture to increase production faster than demand and through the 1980s it was producing surplus foodgrains, enabling it to build up reserves.

Industrial development continued to lag behind expectations, however. Although India returned to the programme of Five Year Plans (in 2000 it was nearing the end of the Ninth Plan), central control has been progressively loosened. Indira Gandhi began to move towards liberalizing imports and foreign investment. Rajiv Gandhi pursued this policy much more strongly in the first 2 years of his government, although many vested interests saw their protected status at risk and the programme slowed to a halt. The Government of Narasimha Rao inherited a foreign exchange and inflation crisis in July 1991 and in its first 2 years in office renewed the effort to encourage foreign investment and liberalization of controls, including making the Rupee partially convertible in March 1993. Defence spending has been cut from 3.8% to about 3% of GNP though the Government reversed this trend in August 1999. In 2000 the economy had re-established growth with single figure inflation. Foreign exchange reserves were at an all time high in mid 2000 and inward investment also registered significant increases.

South India today has a far more diversified industrial base than seemed imaginable at Independence. It produces goods, from aeroplanes and rockets to watches and computers, from industrial and transport machinery to textiles and consumer goods. South India is particularly noted for the speed of its development of computer based technologies. Hyderabad and Bangalore have attracted visits from both Bill Gates and Bill Clinton, and South India;s computer industries now have world reach. According to the London Financial Times since the early 1990s India has become one of the world's leading centres for software development. With over two million Indians already on the net in 2000 and an expected 5 million by the end of 2001, India is rapidly transforming itself into a computer based society. Yet despite the economic successes, many in India claim that the weaknesses remain profound. Perhaps half of the population continues to live in absolute poverty and despite surplus grain production many still lack an adequate diet.

Achievements & problems

While India's industrial economy is producing a range of modern products, many are still uncompetitive on world markets. Furthermore, critics within India increasingly argue that goods are made in factories that often fail to observe basic safety and health rules and that emit enormous pollution into the environment. On top of that, the industrial expansion barely seems to have touched the problems of unemployment. Employment in India's organized industry has risen from 12 million in 1961 to over 28 million in 2001, yet during the same period the number of registered unemployed rose from 1.6 million to over 36 million.

Religion

It is impossible to write briefly about religion in India without greatly oversimplifying. Over 80% of Indians are Hindu, but there are significant minorities. Muslims number about 120 million and there are over 23 million Christians, 18 million Sikhs, 6 million Buddhists and a number of other religious groups. In the south the balance is rather different, for while there are only tiny numbers of Sikhs or Buddhists, Christianity is relatively strong, especially in Kerala and some districts of Tamil Nadu. One of the most persistent features of Indian religious and social life is the caste system. This has undergone substantial changes since Independence, especially in towns and cities, but most people in India are still clearly identified as a member of a particular caste group. The Government has introduced measures to help the backward, or 'scheduled' castes, though in recent years this has produced a major political backlash.

Hinduism

It has always been easier to define Hinduism by what it is not than by what it is. Indeed, the name 'Hindu' was given by foreigners to the peoples of the subcontinent who did not profess the other major faiths, such as Muslims or Christians. The beliefs and practices of modern Hinduism began to take shape in the centuries on either side of the birth of Christ. But while some aspects of modern Hinduism can be traced back more than 2,000 years before that, other features are recent. Hinduism has undergone major changes both in belief and practice, originating from outside as well as from within. As early as the sixth century BC the Buddhists and Jains had tried to reform the religion of Vedism (or Brahmanism) which had been dominant in some parts of South Asia for 500 years.

Key ideas

A number of ideas run like a thread through Hinduism. According to the great Indian philosopher and former President of India, S Radhakrishnan, religion for the Hindu "is not an idea but a power, not an intellectual proposition but a life conviction. Religion is consciousness of ultimate reality, not a theory about God".

Some Hindu scholars and philosophers talk of Hinduism as one religious and cultural tradition, in which the enormous variety of belief and practice can ultimately be interpreted as interwoven in a common view of the world. Yet there is no Hindu organization, like a church, with the authority to define belief or establish official practice. There are spiritual leaders and philosophers who are widely revered and there is an enormous range of literature that is treated as sacred. Not all Hindu groups believe in a single supreme God. In view of these characteristics, many authorities argue that it is misleading to think of Hinduism as a religion at all.

Be that as it may, the evidence of the living importance of Hinduism is visible across India. Hindu philosophy and practice has also touched many of those who belong to other religious traditions, particularly in terms of social institutions such as caste.

Darshan One of Hinduism's recurring themes is 'vision', 'sight' or 'view' – **darshan**. Applied to the different philosophical systems themselves, such as *yoga* or *vedanta*, 'darshan' is also used to describe the sight of the deity that worshippers hope to gain when they visit a temple or shrine hoping for the sight of a 'guru' (teacher). Equally it may apply to the religious insight gained through meditation or prayer.

The four Many Hindus also accept that there are four major human goals; material prosperity
human goals (*artha*), the satisfaction of desires (*kama*) and performing the duties laid down according to your position in life (*dharma*). Beyond those is the goal of achieving liberation from the endless cycle of rebirths into which everyone is locked (*moksha*). It is to the search for liberation that the major schools of Indian philosophy have devoted most attention. Together with dharma, it is basic to Hindu thought.

The Mahabharata lists 10 embodiments of **dharma**: good name, truth, self-control, cleanness of mind and body, simplicity, endurance, resoluteness of character, giving and sharing, austerities and continence. In *dharmic* thinking these are inseparable from five patterns of behaviour: non-violence, an attitude of equality, peace and tranquillity, lack of aggression and cruelty and absence of envy. Dharma, an essentially secular concept, represents the order inherent in human life.

Karma The idea of *karma*, 'the effect of former actions', is central to achieving liberation. As C Rajagopalachari put it: "Every act has its appointed effect, whether the act be thought, word or deed. The cause holds the effect, so to say, in its womb. If we reflect deeply and objectively, the entire world will be found to obey unalterable laws. That is the doctrine of karma".

Rebirth The belief in the transmigration of souls (*samsara*) in a never-ending cycle of rebirth has been Hinduism's most distinctive and important contribution to Indian culture. The earliest reference to the belief is found in one of the Upanishads, around the seventh century BC, at about the same time as the doctrine of karma made its first appearance. By the late Upanishads it was universally accepted and in Buddhism and Jainism it is never questioned.

Ahimsa AL Basham pointed out that belief in transmigration must have encouraged a further distinctive doctrine, that of non-violence or non-injury – *ahimsa*. The belief in rebirth meant that all living things and creatures of the spirit – people, devils, gods, animals, even worms – possessed the same essential soul. One inscription

The four stages of life

Popular Hindu belief holds that an ideal life has four stages: that of the student, the householder, the forest dweller and the wandering dependent or beggar (sannyasi). These stages represent the phases through which an individual learns of life's goals and of the means of achieving them.

One of the most striking sights today is that of the saffron clad sannyasi (sadhu) seeking gifts of food and money to support himself in the final stage of his life. There may have been sadhus even before the Aryans arrived. Today, most of these have given up material possessions, carrying only a strip of cloth, a danda (staff), a crutch to support the chin during achal (meditation), prayer beads, a fan to ward off evil spirits, a water pot, a drinking vessel, which may be a human skull and a begging bowl. You may see one, almost naked, covered in ashes, on a city street.

threatens that anyone who interferes with the rights of Brahmins to land given to them by the king will 'suffer rebirth for 80,000 years as a worm in dung'. Belief in the cycle of rebirth was essential to give such a threat any weight!

Schools of philosophy

It is common now to talk of six major schools of Hindu philosophy. Nyaya, Vaisheshika, Sankhya, Yoga, Purvamimansa and Vedanta.

Yoga

Yoga, can be traced back to at least the third century AD. It seeks a synthesis of the spirit, the soul and the flesh and is concerned with systems of meditation and self denial that lead to the realization of the Divine within oneself and can ultimately release one from the cycle of rebirth.

Vedanta

These are literally the final parts of the Vedic literature, the Upanishads. The basic texts also include the Brahmasutra of Badrayana, written about the first century AD and the most important of all, the Bhagavad-Gita, which is a part of the epic the Mahabharata. There are many interpretations of these basic texts. Three are given here.

Advaita Vedanta holds that there is no division between the cosmic force or principle, Brahman and the individual Self, atman (also referred to as 'soul'). The fact that we appear to see different and separate individuals is simply a result of ignorance. This is termed maya (illusion), but Vedanta philosophy does not suggest that the world in which we live is an illusion. Jnana (knowledge) is held as the key to understanding the full and real unity of Self and Brahman. Shankaracharya, born at Kalady in modern Kerala, in the seventh century AD, is the best known Advaitin Hindu philosopher. He argued that there was no individual Self or soul separate from the creative force of the universe, or Brahman and that it was impossible to achieve liberation (moksha), through meditation and devotional worship, which he saw as signs of remaining on a lower level and of being unprepared for true liberation.

Vishishtadvaita The 12th-century philosopher, Ramanuja, repudiated such ideas. He transformed the idea of God from an impersonal force to a personal God and viewed both the Self and the World as real but only as part of the whole. In contrast to Shankaracharya's view, Ramanuja saw bhakti (devotion) as of central importance to achieving liberation and service to the Lord as the highest goal of life.

Dvaita Vedanta The 14th-century philosopher Madhva believed that Brahman, the Self and the World are completely distinct. Worship of God is a key means of achieving liberation.

Background

Karma – an eye to the future

According to the doctrine of karma, every person, animal or god has a being or 'self' which has existed without beginning. Every action, except those that are done without any consideration of the results, leaves an indelible mark on that 'self', carried forward into the next life.

The overall character of the imprint on each person's 'self' determines three features of the next life: the nature of his next birth (animal, human or god), the kind of family he will be born into if human and the length of the next life. Finally, it controls the good or bad experiences that the self will experience. However, it does not imply a fatalistic belief that the nature of action in this life is unimportant. Rather, it suggests that the path followed by the individual in the present life is vital to the nature of its next life and ultimately to the chance of gaining release from this world.

Worship

As S Radhakrishnan puts it, for millions of Hindus: "It does not matter what conception of God we adopt so long as we keep up a perpetual search after truth".

Puja For most Hindus today worship ('performing puja') is an integral part of their faith. The great majority of Hindu homes will have a shrine to one of the gods of the Hindu pantheon. Individuals and families will often visit shrines or temples and on special occasions will travel long distances to particularly holy places such as Benaras or Puri. Such sites may have temples dedicated to a major deity but will always have numerous other shrines in the vicinity dedicated to other favourite gods.

Acts of devotion are often aimed at the granting of favours and the meeting of urgent needs for this life – good health, finding a suitable wife or husband, the birth of a son, prosperity and good fortune. In this respect the popular devotion of simple pilgrims of all faiths in South Asia is remarkably similar when they visit shrines, whether Hindu, Buddhist or Jain temples, the tombs of Muslim saints or even churches such as Bom Jesus in Goa, where St Francis Xavier lies entombed.

Puja involves making an offering to God and *darshan* (having a view of the deity). Hindu worship is generally, though not always, an act performed by individuals. Thus Hindu temples may be little more than a shrine in the middle of the street, tended by a priest and visited at special times when a darshan of the resident God can be obtained. When it has been consecrated, the **image**, if exactly made, becomes the channel for the godhead to work. According to KM Sen "in popular Hinduism, God is worshipped in different forms" showing "a particular attachment to a particular figure in Hindu mythology". Images are, FranÁoise Bernier quotes "something before the eyes that fixes the mind".

Holy places Certain rivers and towns are particularly sacred to Hindus. Thus there are seven holy rivers – the Ganga, Yamuna, Indus and mythical Sarasvati in the north and the Narmada, Godavari and Kaveri in the Peninsula. There are also seven holy places – Haridwar, Mathura, Ayodhya and Varanasi, again in the north, Ujjain, Dwarka and Kanchipuram to the south. In addition to these seven holy places there are four holy abodes: Badrinath, Puri and Ramesvaram, with Dwarka in modern Gujarat having the unique distinction of being both a holy abode and a holy place.

Rituals & festivals The temple rituals often follow through the cycle of day and night, as well as yearly lifecycles. The priests may wake the deity from sleep, bathe, clothe and feed it. Worshippers will be invited to share in this process by bringing offerings of clothes and food. Gifts of money will usually be made and in some temples there is a charge levied for taking up positions in front of the deity in order to obtain a darshan at the appropriate times.

Every temple has its special festivals. At festival times you can see villagers walking in small groups, brightly dressed and often high spirited, sometimes as far as 80-100 km.

Hindu Deities

Today three Gods are widely seen as all-powerful: Brahma, Vishnu and Siva. Their functions and character are not readily separated. While Brahma is regarded as the ultimate source of creation, Siva also has a creative role alongside his function as destroyer. Vishnu in contrast is seen as the preserver or protector of the universe. Vishnu and Siva are widely represented (where Brahma is not) and have come to be seen as the most powerful and important. Their followers are referred to as Vaishnavite and Shaivites respectively and numerically they form the two largest sects in India.

Popularly Brahma is interpreted as the Creator in a trinity, alongside Vishnu as **Brahma** Preserver and Siva as Destroyer. In the literal sense the name Brahma is the masculine and personalized form of the neuter word Brahman.

In the early Vedic writing, *Brahman* represented the universal and impersonal principle which governed the Universe. Gradually, as Vedic philosophy moved towards a monotheistic interpretation of the universe and its origins, this impersonal power was increasingly personalized. In the Upanishads, Brahman was seen as a universal and elemental creative spirit. Brahma, described in early myths as having been born from a golden egg and then to have created the Earth, assumed the identity of the earlier Vedic deity Prajapati and became identified as the creator.

Some of the early Brahma myths were later taken over by the Vishnu cult. For example in one story Brahma was believed to have rescued the earth from a flood by taking the form of a fish or a tortoise and in another he became a boar, raising the Earth above the flood waters on his tusk. All these images were later associated with Vishnu.

By the fourth and fifth centuries AD, the height of the classical period of Hinduism, Brahma was seen as one of the trinity of Gods – *Trimurti* – in which Vishnu, Siva and Brahma represented three forms of the unmanifested supreme being. It is from Brahma that Hindu cosmology takes its structure. The basic cycle through which the whole cosmos passes is described as one day in the life of Brahma – the *kalpa*. It equals 4,320 million years, with an equally long night. One year of Brahma's life – a cosmic year – lasts 360 days and nights. The universe is expected to last for 100 years of Brahma's life, who is currently believed to be 51 years old.

By the sixth century AD Brahma worship had effectively ceased (before the great period of temple building), which accounts for the fact that there are remarkably few temples dedicated to Brahma. Nonetheless images of Brahma are found in most temples. Characteristically he is shown with four faces, a fifth having been destroyed by the fire from Siva's third eye. In his four arms he usually holds a copy of the Vedas, a sceptre and a water jug or a bow. He is accompanied by the goose, symbolizing knowledge.

Seen by some Hindus as the 'active power' of Brahma, popularly thought of as his **Sarasvati** consort, Sarasvati has survived into the modern Hindu world as a far more important figure than Brahma himself. In popular worship Sarasvati represents the goddess of education and learning, worshipped in schools and colleges with gifts of fruit, flowers and incense. She represents 'the word' itself, which began to be deified as part of the process of the writing of the Vedas, which ascribed magical power to words. The development of her identity represented the rebirth of the concept of a

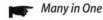 *Many in One*

One of the reasons why Hindu faith is often confusing to the outsider is that as a whole it has many elements which appear mutually self-contradictory but which are tolerated or reconciled by Hindus as different facets of the ultimate Truth. Such tolerance is particularly evident in the attitude of Hindus to the nature of divinity. C Rajagopalachari writes that a distinction that marks Hinduism sharply from the monotheistic faiths is that "the philosophy of Hinduism has taught and trained the Hindu devotee to see and worship the Supreme Being in all the idols that are worshipped, with a clarity of understanding and an intensity of vision that would surprise the people of other faiths. The Divine Mind governing the Universe, be it as Mother or Father, has infinite aspects and the devotee approaches him or her, or both, in any of the many aspects as he may be led to do according to the mood and the psychological need of the hour."

mother goddess, which had been strong in the Indus Valley Civilization over 1,000 years before and which may have been continued in popular ideas through the worship of female spirits.

In addition to her role as Brahma's wife, Sarasvati is also variously seen as the wife of Vishnu and Manu or as Daksha's daughter, among other interpretations. Normally white coloured, riding on a swan and carrying a book, she is often shown playing a vina. She may have many arms and heads, representing her role as patron of all the sciences and arts.

Vishnu Vishnu is seen as the God with the human face. From the second century a new and passionate devotional worship of Vishnu's incarnation as Krishna developed in the South. By 1,000 AD Vaishnavism had spread across South India and it became closely associated with the devotional form of Hinduism preached by **Ramanuja**, whose followers spread the worship of Vishnu and his 10 successive incarnations in animal and human form. For Vaishnavites, God took these different forms in order to save the world from impending disaster. AL Basham has summarized the 10 incarnations (see Table).

Rama and Krishna By far the most influential incarnations of Vishnu are those in which he was believed to take recognizable human form, especially as Rama (twice) and Krishna. As the Prince of Ayodhya, history and myth blend, for Rama was probably a chief who lived in the eighth or seventh century BC.

Although Rama is now seen as an earlier incarnation of Vishnu than Krishna, he came to be regarded as divine very late, probably after the Muslim invasions of the 12th century AD. The story has become part of the cultures of Southeast Asia.

Rama (or Ram – pronounced to rhyme with *calm*) is a powerful figure in contemporary India. His supposed birthplace at Ayodhya became the focus of fierce disputes between Hindus and Muslims in the early 1990's.

Krishna is worshipped extremely widely as perhaps the most human of the gods. His advice on the battlefield of the Mahabharata is one of the major sources of guidance for the rules of daily living for many Hindus today.

Lakshmi Commonly represented as Vishnu's wife, Lakshmi is widely worshipped as the goddess of wealth. Earlier representations of Vishnu's consorts portrayed her as Sridevi, often shown in statues on Vishnu's right, while Bhudevi, also known as Prithvi, who represented the earth, was on his left. Lakshmi is popularly shown in her own right as standing on a lotus flower, although eight forms of Lakshmi are recognized.

Background

How Sarasvati turned Brahma's head

Masson-Oursel recounts one myth that explains how Brahma came to have five heads. "Brahma first formed woman from his own immaculate substance and she was known as Sarasvati, Savitri, Gayatri or Brahmani. When he saw this lovely girl emerge from his own body Brahma fell in love with her. Sarasvati moved to his right to avoid his gaze, but a head immediately sprang up from the god. And when

Sarasvati turned to the left and then behind him, two new heads emerged. She darted towards heaven and a fifth head was formed. Brahma then said to his daughter, 'Let us beget all kinds of living things, men, Suras and Asuras'. Hearing these words Sarasvati returned to earth, Brahma wedded her and they retired to a secret place where they remained together for a hundred (divine) years".

Hanuman The Ramayana tells how Hanuman, Rama's faithful servant, went across India and finally into the demon Ravana's forest home of Lanka at the head of his monkey army in search of the abducted Sita. He used his powers to jump the sea channel separating India from Sri Lanka and managed after a series of heroic and magical feats to find and rescue his master's wife. Whatever form he is shown in, he remains almost instantly recognizable.

Professor Wendy Doniger O'Flaherty argues that "Siva is in many ways the most **Siva** uniquely Indian god of them all". She argues that the key to the myths through which his character is understood, lies in the explicit ambiguity of Siva as the great ascetic and at the same time as the erotic force of the universe.

Siva is interpreted as both creator and destroyer, the power through whom the universe evolves. He lives on Mount Kailasa with his wife **Parvati** (also known as **Uma, Sati, Kali** and **Durga**) and two sons, the elephant-headed Ganesh and the 6-headed Karttikeya, known in South India as Subrahmanya. To many contemporary Hindus they form a model of sorts for family life. In sculptural representations Siva is normally accompanied by his 'vehicle', the bull (*nandi* or *nandin*).

Siva is also represented in Shaivite temples throughout India by the linga, literally meaning 'sign' or 'mark', but referring in this context to the sign of gender or phallus and *yoni*. On the one hand a symbol of energy, fertility and potency, as Siva's symbol it also represents the yogic power of sexual abstinence and penance. The linga has become the most important symbol of the cult of Siva. O'Flaherty suggests that the worship of the linga of Siva can be traced back to the pre-Vedic societies of the Indus Valley civilization (c2000 BC), but that it first appears in Hindu iconography in the second century BC.

From that time a wide variety of myths appeared to explain the origin of linga worship. The myths surrounding the 12 **jyotirlinga** (linga of light) found at centres like Ujjain go back to the second century BC and were developed in order to explain and justify linga worship.

Siva's alternative names Although Siva is not seen as having a series of rebirths, like Vishnu, he none the less appears in very many forms representing different aspects of his varied powers. Some of the more common are:

Chandrasekhara The moon (*chandra*) symboilizes the powers of creation and destruction.

Mahadeva The representation of Siva as the god of supreme power, which came relatively late into Hindu thought, shown as the linga in combination with the *yoni*, or female genitalia.

Background

Hindu Deities

Deity	Association	Relationship
Brahma	Creator	One of Trinity
Sarasvati	Education and culture, "the word"	Wife of Brahma
Siva	Creator/destroyer	One of Trinity
Bhairava	Fierce aspect of Siva	
Parvati (Uma)	Benevolent aspect of female divine power	Consort of Siva, mother of Ganesh
Kali	The energy that destroys	Consort of Siva
Durga	In fighting attitude	Consort of Siva
Ganesh/ Ganapati	God of good beginnings, clearer of obstacles	Son of Siva
Skanda (Karttikkeya, Murugan, Subrahmanya)	God of War/ bringer of disease	Son of Siva and Ganga
Vishnu	Preserver	One of Trinity arms, club and sword (or
Prithvi/ Bhudevi	Goddess of Earth	Wife of Vishnu
Lakshmi	Goddess of Wealth	Wife of Vishnu and fruit
Agni	God of Fire	
Indra	Rain, lightning and thunder	
Ravana	King of the demons	

Background

Krishna, eighth incarnation of Vishnu

Vishnu, Preserver of the Universe

Ardhanarisvara, the male/female form of Siva

Durga, Mother-goddess, destroyer of demons

Attributes	Vehicle
4 heads, 4 arms, upper left holds water pot and rosary or sacrificial spoon, sacred thread across left shoulder	Hamsa (goose/swan)
Two or more arms, vina, lotus, plam leaves, rosary	Hamsa
Linga; Rudra, matted hair, 3 eyes, drum, fire, deer, trident; Nataraja, Lord of the Dance	Bull - Nandi
Trident, sword, noose, naked, snakes, garland of skulls, dishevelled hair, carrying destructive weapons	Dog
2 arms when shown with Siva, 4 when on her own, blue lily in right hand, left hand hangs down	Lion
Trident, noose, human skulls, sword, shield, black colour	Lion
4 arms, conch, disc, bow, arrow, bell, sword, shield	Lion or tiger
Goad, noose, broken tusk, fruits	Rat/ mouse/ shrew
6 heads, 12 arms, spear, arrow, sword, discus, noose cock, bow, shield, conch and plough	Peacock
4 arms, high crown, discus and conch in upper mythical eagle right hand in abhaya gesture, left holds pomegranate, left leg on treasure pot	Garuda -
Seated or standing on red lotus, 4 hands, lotuses, vessel	Lotus
Sacred thread, axe, wood, bellows, torch, sacrificial spoon	2-headed ram
Bow, thunderbolt, lances	
10 heads, 20 arms, bow and arrow	

Siva as Nataraj

Ganesh, bringer of prosperity

Parvati, wife of Siva

Kali, the "black" Mother-goddess

Vishnu's ten incarnations

Name	Form	Story
1 Matsya	Fish	Vishnu took the form of a fish to rescue Manu (the first man), his family and the Vedas from a flood.
2 Kurma	Tortoise	Vishnu became a tortoise to rescue all the treasures lost in the flood, including the divine nectar (Amrita) with which the gods preserved their youth. The gods put Mount Kailasa on the tortoise's back and when he reached the bottom of the ocean they twisted the divine snake round the mountain. They then churned the ocean with the mountain by pulling the snake
3 Varaha	Boar	Vishnu appeared again to raise the earth from the ocean's floor where it had been thrown by a demon, Hiranyaksa. The story probably developed from a non-Aryan cult of a sacred pig.
4 Narasimha	Half-man, half lion	Having persuaded Brahma to promise that he could not be killed either by day or night, by god, man or beast, the demon Hiranyakasipu then terrorized everybody. When the gods pleaded for help, Vishnu appeared at sunset, when it was neither day nor night, in the form of a half man and half lion and killed the demon.
5 Vamana	A dwarf	Bali, a demon, achieved supernatural power by asceticism. To protect the world Vishnu appeared before him in the form of a dwarf and asked him a favour. Bali granted Vishnu as much land as he could cover in three strides. Vishnu then became a giant, covering the earth in three strides. He left only hell to the demon.
6 Parasurama	Rama with the axe	Vishnu was incarnated as the son of a Brahmin, Jamadagni as Parasurama and killed the wicked king for robbing his father. The king's sons then killed Jamadagni and in revenge Parasurama destroyed all male kshatriyas, 21 times in succession.
7 Rama	The Prince of Ayodhya	As told in the Ramayana, Vishnu came in the form of Rama to rescue the world from the dark demon, Ravana. His wife Sita is the model of patient faithfulness while Hanuman, is the monkey-faced god and Rama's helper.
8 Krishna	Charioteer of Arjuma Many forms	Krishna meets almost every human need, from the mischievous child, the playful boy, the amorous youth to the Divine.
9 The Buddha		Probably incorporated into the Hindu pantheon in order to discredit the Buddhists, dominant in some parts of India until the 6th century AD. An early Hindu interpretation suggests that Vishnu took incarnation as Buddha to show compassion for animals and to end sacrifice.
10 Kalki	Riding on a horse	Vishnu's arrival will accompany the final destruction of this present age, Kaliyuga, judging the wicked and rewarding the good.

Nataraja, the Lord of the Cosmic Dance. The story is based on a legend in which Siva and Vishnu went to the forest to overcome 10,000 heretics. In their anger the heretics attacked Siva first by sending a tiger, then a snake and thirdly a fierce black dwarf with a club. Siva killed the tiger, tamed the snake and wore it like a garland and then put his foot on the dwarf and performed a dance of such power that the dwarf and the heretics acknowledged Siva as the Lord.

Rudra Siva's early prototype, who may date back to the Indus Valley Civilization.

Virabhadra Siva created Virabhadra to avenge himself on his wife Sati's father, Daksha, who had insulted Siva by not inviting him to a special sacrifice. Sati attended the ceremony against Siva's wishes and when she heard her father grossly abusing Siva she committed suicide by jumping into the sacrificial fire. This act gave rise to the term *sati* (*suttee*, a word which simply means a good or virtuous woman). Recorded in the *Vedas*, the self immolation of a woman on her husband's funeral pyre probably did not become accepted practice until the early centuries BC. Even then it was mainly restricted to those of the kshatriya caste.

Nandi Siva's vehicle, the bull, is one of the most widespread of sacred symbols of the ancient world and may represent a link with Rudra, who was sometimes represented as a bull in pre-Hindu India. Strength and virility are key attributes and pilgrims to Siva temples will often touch the Nandi's testicles on their way into the shrine.

Ganesh

Ganesh is one of Hinduism's most popular gods. He is seen as the great clearer of obstacles. Shown at gateways and on door lintels with his elephant head and pot belly, his image is revered across India. Meetings, functions and special family gatherings will often start with prayers to Ganesh and any new venture, from the opening of a building to inaugurating a company, will not be deemed complete without a Ganesh puja.

Shakti, The Mother Goddess

Shakti is a female divinity often worshipped in the form of Siva's wife Durga or Kali. As Durga she agreed to do battle with Mahish, an *asura* (demon) who threatened to dethrone the gods. Many sculptures and paintings illustrate the story in which, during the terrifying struggle which ensued, the demon changed into a buffalo, an elephant and a giant with 1,000 arms. Durga, clutching weapons in each of her ten hands, eventually emerges victorious. As Kali ('black') the mother goddess takes on her most fearsome form and character. Fighting with the chief of the demons, she was forced to use every weapon in her armoury, but every drop of blood that she drew became 1,000 new giants just as strong as he. The only way she could win was by drinking the blood of all her enemies. Having succeeded she was so elated that her dance of triumph threatened the earth. Ignoring the pleas of the gods to stop, she even threw her husband Siva to the ground and trampled over him, until she realized to her shame what she had done. She is always shown with a sword in one hand, the severed head of the giant in another, two corpses for earrings and a necklace of human skulls. She is often shown standing with one foot on the body and the other on the leg of Siva.

The worship of female goddesses developed into the widely practised form of devotional worship called Tantrism. Goddesses such as Kali became the focus of worship which often involved practices that flew in the face of wider Hindu moral and legal codes. Animal and even human sacrifices and ritual sexual intercourse were part of Tantric belief and practice, the evidence for which may still be seen in the art and sculpture of some major temples. Tantric practice affected both Hinduism and Buddhism from the eighth century AD; its influence is shown vividly in the sculptures of Khajuraho and Konark and in the distinctive Hindu and Buddhist practices of the Kathmandu Valley in Nepal.

Skanda

The God of War, Skanda (known as Murugan in Tamil Nadu and by other regional names) became known as the son of Siva and Parvati. One legend suggests that he was conceived by the Goddess Ganga from Siva's seed.

Gods of the warrior caste

Modern Hinduism has brought into its pantheon over many generations gods who were worshipped by the earlier pre-Hindu Aryan civilizations. The most important is **Indra**, often shown as the god of rain, thunder and lightning. To the early Aryans, Indra destroyed demons in battle, the most important being his victory over Vritra, 'the Obstructor'. By this victory Indra released waters from the clouds, allowing the earth to become fertile. To the early Vedic writers the clouds of the southwest

Background

monsoon were seen as hostile, determined to keep their precious treasure of water to themselves and only releasing it when forced to by a greater power. Indra, carrying a bow in one hand, a thunderbolt in another and lances in the others and riding on his vehicle Airavata, the elephant, is thus the Lord of Heaven. His wife is the relatively insignificant **Indrani**.

Mitra and **Varuna** have the power both of gods and demons. Their role is to sustain order, Mitra taking responsibility for friendship and Varuna for oaths and as they have to keep watch for 24 hours a day Mitra has become the god of the day or the sun, Varuna the god of the moon.

Agni, the god of fire, is a god whose origins lie with the priestly caste rather than with the kshatriyas, or warriors. He was seen in the Vedas as being born from the rubbing together of two pieces of dead wood and as Masson-Oursel writes "the poets marvel at the sight of a being so alive leaping from dry dead wood. His very growth is miraculous". Riding on a ram, wearing a sacred thread, he is often shown with flames leaping from his mouth and he carries an axe, wood, bellows or a fan, a torch and a sacrificial spoon, for he is the god of ritual fire.

Soma The juice of the soma plant, the nectar of the gods guaranteeing eternal life, Soma is also a deity taking many forms. Born from the churning of the ocean of milk in later stories Soma was identified with the moon. The golden haired and golden skinned god **Savitri** is an intermediary with the great power to forgive sin and as king of heaven he gives the gods their immortality. **Surya**, the god of the sun, fittingly of overpowering splendour is often described as being dark red, sitting on a red lotus or riding a chariot pulled by the seven horses of the dawn (representing the days of the week). **Usha**, sometimes referred to as Surya's wife, is the goddess of the dawn, daughter of Heaven and sister of the night. She rides in a chariot drawn by cows or horses.

Devas & Asuras In Hindu popular mythology the world is also populated by innumerable gods and demons, with a somewhat uncertain dividing line between them. Both have great power and moral character and there are frequent conflicts and battles between them.

The **Rakshasas** form another category of semi-divine beings devoted to performing magic. Although they are not themselves evil, they are destined to cause havoc and evil in the real world.

The **Nagas** and **Naginis** The multiple-hooded cobra head often seen in sculptures represents the fabulous snake gods the Nagas, though they may often be shown in other forms, even human. In South India it is particularly common to find statues of divine Nagas being worshipped. They are usually placed on uncultivated ground under trees in the hope and belief, as Masson-Oursel puts it, that "if the snakes have their own domain left to them they are more likely to spare human beings". The Nagas and their wives, the Naginis, are often the agents of death in mythical stories.

Hindu Society

Dharma is seen as the most important of the objectives of individual and social life. But what were the obligations imposed by dharma? Hindu law givers, such as those who compiled the code of Manu (AD 100-300), laid down rules of family conduct and social obligations related to the institutions of caste and jati which were beginning to take shape at the same time.

Caste Although the word caste was given by the Portuguese in the 15th century AD, the main feature of the system emerged at the end of the Vedic period. Two terms – varna and jati – are used in India itself and have come to be used interchangeably and confusingly with the word caste.

Worship of Siva's linga

Worship of Siva's linga – the phallic symbol of fertility, power and creativeness – is universal across India. Its origins lie in the creation myths of the Hindu trinity and in the struggle for supremacy between the different Hindu sects. Saivite myths illustrate the supreme power of Siva and the variety of ways in which Brahma and Vishnu were compelled to acknowledge his supreme power.

One such story tells how Siva, Vishnu and Brahma emerged from the ocean, whereupon Vishnu and Brahma begged him to perform creation. Siva agreed – but then to their consternation disappeared for 1,000 celestial years. They became so worried by the lack of creation that Vishnu told Brahma to create, so he produced everything that could lead to happiness. However, no sooner had Brahma filled the universe with beings than Siva reappeared. Incensed by the usurping of his power by Brahma, Siva decided to destroy everything with a flame from his

mouth so that he could create afresh.

As the fire threatened to consume everything Brahma acknowledged Siva's total power and pleaded with him to spare the creation that Brahma had brought forth. "But what shall I do with all my excess power?" "Send it to the sun," replied Brahma, "for as you are the lord of the sun we may all live together in the sun's energy."

Siva agreed, but said to Brahma "What use is this linga if I cannot use it to create?" So he broke off his linga and threw it to the ground. The linga broke through the earth and went right into the sky. Vishnu looked for the end of it below and Brahma for the top, but neither could find the end. Then a voice from the sky said "If the linga of the god with braided hair is worshipped, it will grant all desires that are longed for in the heart." When Brahma and Vishnu heard this, they and all the divinities worshipped the linga with devotion."

Varna, which literally means colour, had a fourfold division. By 600 BC this had become a standard means of classifying the population. The fair-skinned Aryans distinguished themselves from the darker skinned earlier inhabitants. The priestly varna, the Brahmins, were seen as coming from the mouth of Brahma; the Kshatriyas (or Rajputs as they are commonly called in Northwest India) were warriors, coming from Brahma's arms; the Vaishyas, a trading community, came from Brahma's thighs and the Sudras, classified as agriculturalists, from his feet. Relegated beyond the pale of civilized Hindu society were the untouchables or outcastes, who were left with the jobs which were regarded as impure, usually associated with dealing with the dead (human or animal) or with excrement.

Jati Many Brahmins and Rajputs are conscious of their varna status, but the great majority of Indians do not put themselves into one of the four varna categories, but into a jati group. There are thousands of different jatis across the country. None of the groups regard themselves as equal in status to any other, but all are part of local or regional hierarchies. These are not organized in any institutional sense and traditionally there was no formal record of caste status. While individuals found it impossible to change caste or to move up the social scale, groups would sometimes try to gain recognition as higher caste by adopting practices of the Brahmins such as becoming vegetarians. Many used to be identified with particular activities and occupations used to be hereditary. Caste membership is decided simply by birth. Although you can be evicted from your caste by your fellow members, usually for disobedience to caste rules such as over marriage, you cannot join another caste and technically you become an outcaste.

Right up until Independence in 1947 such punishment was a drastic penalty for disobeying one's dharmic duty. In many areas all avenues into normal life could be

Auspicious signs

Some of Hinduism's sacred symbols are thought to have originated in the Aryan religion of the Vedic period.

Om The Primordial sound of the universe, 'Om' (or more correctly the three-in-one 'Aum') is the Supreme syllable. It is the opening and sometimes closing, chant for Hindu prayers. Some attribute the three constituents to the Hindu triad of Brahmka, Vishnu and Siva. It is believed to be the cosmic sound of Creation which encompasses all states from wakefulness to deep sleep and though it is the essence of all sound, it is outside our hearing.

Svastika Representing the Sun and it's energy, the svastika usually appears on doors or walls of temples, in red, the colour associated with good fortune and luck. The term derived from the Sanskrit 'svasti' is repeated in Hindu chants. The arms of the symbol point in the cardinal directionswhich may reflect the ancient practice of lighting fire sticks in the four directions. When the svastika appears to rotate clockwise it symbolizes positive creative energy of the sun; the anti-clockwise svastika, symbolizing the autumn/winter sun, is considered unlucky.

Six-pointed star The intersecting triangles in the 'Star of David' symbol represents Spirit and Matter held in balnce. A central dot signifies a particle of Divinity. Incorporated as a decorative element in some Muslim buildings such as Humayun's Tomb in Delhi.

Lotus The 'padma' or 'kamal' flower with it's many petals appears not only in art and architecture but also in association with gods and godesses. Some deities are seen holding one, others are portrayed seated or standing on the flower, or as with Padmanabha it appears from Vishnu's navel. The lotus represents purity, peace and beauty, a symbol also shared by Buddhists and Jains and as in nature stands away and above the impure, murky water from which it emerges. In architecture, the lotus motif occurs frequently and often represented in the base and capitals of columns.

Om

Svastika

Six-pointed star

Lotus

blocked, families would disregard outcaste members and it could even be impossible for the outcaste to continue to work within the locality.

The Dalits Gandhi spearheaded his campaign for independence from British colonial rule with a powerful campaign to abolish the disabilities imposed by the caste system. Coining the term *Harijan* (meaning 'person of God'), which he gave to all former outcastes, Gandhi demanded that discrimination on the grounds of caste be outlawed. Lists – or 'schedules' – of backward castes were drawn up during the early part of this century in order to provide positive help to such groups. The term itself has now been widely rejected by many former outcastes as paternalistic and as implying an adherence to Hindu beliefs which some explicitly reject and today many argue passionately for the use of the secular term 'dalits' – the 'oppressed'.

Affirmative action Since 1947 the Indian government has extended its positive discrimination (a form of affirmative action) to scheduled castes and scheduled tribes, particularly through reserving up to 30 of jobs in government-run institutions and in further education, leading to professional qualifications for these groups and members of the scheduled castes are now found in important positions throughout

Background

The sacred thread

The highest three varnas were classified as "twice born" and could wear the sacred thread symbolizing their status. The age at which the initiation ceremony (upanayana) for the upper caste child was carried out, varied according to class – 8 for a Brahmin, 11 for a Kshatriya and 12 for a Vaishya.

The boy, dressed like an ascetic and holding a staff in his hand, would have the sacred thread (yajnopavita) placed over his right shoulder and under his left arm. A cord of three threads, each of nine twisted strands, it was made of cotton for Brahmans, hemp for Kshatriyas or wool for Vaishyas. It was – and is – regarded as a great sin to remove it.

The Brahmin who officiated would whisper a verse from the Rig Veda in the boy's ear, the Gayatri mantra. Addressed to the old solar god Savitr, the holiest of holy passages, the Gayatri can only be spoken by the three higher classes. AL Basham translated it as: "Let us think on the lovely splendour of the god Savitr, that he may inspire our minds".

the economy. Furthermore, most of the obvious forms of social discrimination, particularly rules which prohibit eating or drinking with members of lower castes, or from plates and cups that have been touched by them, have disappeared. Yet caste remains an extremely important aspect of India's social structures.

Marriage, which is still generally arranged by members of all religious communities, continues to be dictated almost entirely by caste and clan rules. Even in cities, where traditional means of arranging marriages have often broken down and where many people resort to advertising for marriage partners in the columns of the Sunday newspapers, caste is frequently stated as a requirement. Marriage is generally seen as an alliance between two families. Great efforts are made to match caste, social status and economic position, although the rules which govern eligibility vary from region to region. In some groups marriage between even first cousins is common, while among others marriage between any branch of the same clan is strictly prohibited.

Caste also remains an explosive political issue. Attempts to improve the social and economic position of harijans and what are termed 'other backward castes' (OBCs) continues to cause sometimes violent conflict.

Hindu reform movements

Hinduism today is a more self-conscious religious and political force than it was even at Independence in 1947. Reform movements of modern Hinduism can be traced back at least to the early years of the 19th century. These movements were unique in Hinduism's history in putting the importance of political ideas on the same level as strictly religious thinking and in interrelating them.

In the 19th-century English education and European literature and modern scientific thought, alongside the religious ideas of Christian missionaries, all became powerful influences on the newly emerging western educated Hindu opinion. That opinion was challenged to re-examine inherited Hindu beliefs and practice.

Some reform movements have had regional importance. Two of these originated, like the **Brahmo Samaj**, in Bengal. The **Ramakrishna Mission** was named after a temple priest in the Kali temple in Calcutta, Ramakrishna (1834-1886), who was a great mystic, preaching the basic doctrine that 'all religions are true'. He believed that the best religion for any individual was that into which he or she was born. One of his followers, **Vivekenanda**, became the founder of the Ramakrishna Mission, which has been an important vehicle of social and religious reform, notably in Bengal.

Aurobindo Ghose (1872-1950) links the great reformers from the 19th century with the post-Independence period. Educated in English – and for 14 years in England itself – he developed the idea of India as 'the Mother', a concept linked with the pre-Hindu idea of Sakti, or the Mother Goddess. For him 'nationalism was religion'. After imprisonment in 1908 he retired to Pondicherry, where his ashram became a focus of an Indian and international movement (see page 112).

The Hindu calendar While for its secular life India follows the Gregorian calendar, for Hindus, much of religious and personal life follows the Hindu calendar (see also Festivals). This is based on the lunar cycle of 29 days, but the clever bit comes in the way it is synchronized with the 365I day Gregorian solar calendar of the west by the addition of an 'extra month' (*adhik maas*), every 2 -3 years.

Hindus follow two distinct eras. The *Vikrama Samvat* which began in 57 BC (and is followed in Goa), and the *Salivahan Saka* which dates from 78 AD and has been the official Indian calendar since 1957. The *Saka* new year starts on 22 March and has the same length as the Gregorian calendar. In most of South India (except Tamil Nadu) the New Year is celebrated in the first month, *Chaitra* (corresponding to March-April). In North India (and Tamil Nadu) it is celebrated in the second month of *Vaisakh*.

The year itself is divided into two, the first six solar months being when the sun 'moves' north, known as the *Makar Sankranti* (which is marked by special festivals), and the second half when it moves south, the *Karka Sankranti*. The first begins in January and the second in June. The 29 day lunar month with its 'dark' (*Krishna*) and 'bright' (*Shukla*) halves based on the new (*Amavasya*) and full moons (*Purnima*), are named after the 12 constellations, and total a 354 day year. The day itself is divided into eight *praharas* of three hours each and the year into six seasons: *Vasant* (spring), *Grishha* (summer), *Varsha* (rains), *Sharat* (early autumn), *Hemanta* (late autumn), *Shishir* (winter).

Hindu & corresponding Gregorian calendar months

Chaitra	March-April	*Ashwin*	September-October
Vaishakh	April-May	*Kartik*	October-November
Jyeshtha	May-June	*Margashirsha*	November-December
Aashadh	June-July	*Poush*	December-January
Shravan	July-August	*Magh*	January-February
Bhadra	August-September	*Phalgun*	February-March

Islam

Islam is a highly visible presence in India today. Even after partition in 1947 over 40 million Muslims remained in India and today there are just over 120 million. It is the most recent of imported religions. Islamic contact with India was first made around 636 AD and then by the navies of the Arab Mohammad al Qasim in 710-712 AD. These conquerors of Sindh made very few converts, although they did have to develop a legal recognition for the status of non-Muslims in a Muslim-ruled state. From the creation of the Delhi Sultanate in 1206, by Turkish rather than Arab power, Islam became a permanent living religion in India.

The victory of the Turkish ruler of Ghazni over the Rajputs in AD 1192 established a 500 year period of Muslim power in India. The contact between the courts of the new rulers and the indigenous Hindu populations produced innovative developments in art and architecture, language and literature. Hindus and Hindu culture were profoundly affected by the spread and exercise of Muslim political power, but Islam too underwent major modifications in response to the new social and religious context in which the Muslim rulers found themselves.

Islam in South India

Not all Muslim contact was by land through the passes of Afghanistan or Baluchistan. In the Deccan of South India, where the power of the Delhi-based empires was always much weaker than in the northern plains, a succession of Muslim-ruled states maintained strong contact with Arab communities through trade.

From the 15th century to the 18th century much of South India was ruled under independent Muslim kings. Hyderabad, for example, developed a distinctive cultural and artistic life, drawing on a mixed population of Indian Muslims and Hindus, Turks, Persians, Arabs and Africans (see page 371). Until the Mughals conquered the Deccan kingdoms in 1687, Hyderabad was one of the great centres of Arab learning outside the Middle East, a link maintained through trade across the Arabian Sea with Egypt, Yemen and Iraq.

The early Muslim rulers looked to the Turkish ruling class and to the Arab caliphs for their legitimacy and to the Turkish Èlite for their cultural authority. From the middle of the 13th century, when the Mongols crushed the Arab caliphate, the Delhi sultans were left on their own to exercise Islamic authority in India. From then onwards the main external influences were from Persia. Small numbers of migrants, mainly the skilled and the educated, continued to flow into the Indian courts. Periodically their numbers were augmented by refugees from Mongol repression in the regions to India's northwest as the Delhi Sultanate provided a refuge for craftsmen and artists from the territories the Mongols had conquered from Lahore westwards.

Muslims only became a majority of the South Asian population in the plains of the Indus and west Punjab and in parts of Bengal. Elsewhere they formed important minorities, and where there was already a densely populated, Hindu region, little attempt was made to achieve converts.

Muslim populations

In some areas Muslim society shared many of the characteristic features of the Hindu society from which the majority of them came. Many of the Muslim migrants from Iran or Turkey, the Èlite **Ashraf** communities, continued to identify with the Islamic Èlites from which they traced their descent. They held high military and civil posts in imperial service. In sharp contrast, many of the non-Ashraf Muslim communities in the towns and cities were organized in social groups very much like the jatis of their neighbouring Hindu communities. While the Èlites followed Islamic practices close to those based on the Qur'an as interpreted by scholars, the poorer, less literate communities followed devotional and pietistic forms of Islam. The distinction is still very clear today and the importance of veneration of the saints can be seen at tombs and shrines across Pakistan, India and Bangladesh.

The beliefs of Islam (which means 'submission to God') could apparently scarcely be more different from those of Hinduism. Islam, often described as having "five pillars" of faith (see box) has a fundamental creed; 'There is no God but God; and Mohammad is the Prophet of God' (La Illaha illa 'Ilah Mohammad Rasulu 'Ilah). One book, the Qur'an, is the supreme authority on Islamic teaching and faith. Islam preaches the belief in bodily resurrection after death and in the reality of heaven and hell.

Muslim beliefs

The idea of heaven as paradise is pre-Islamic. Alexander the Great is believed to have brought the word into Greek from Persia, where he used it to describe the walled Persian gardens that were found even three centuries before the birth of Christ. For Muslims, Paradise is believed to be filled with sensuous delights and pleasures, while hell is a place of eternal terror and torture, which is the certain fate of all who deny the unity of God.

Background

👉 *The five pillars of Islam*

In addition to the belief that there is one God and that Mohammed is his prophet, there are four further obligatory requirements imposed on Muslims. Daily prayers are prescribed at daybreak, noon, afternoon, sunset and nightfall. Muslims must give alms to the poor. They must observe a strict fast during the month of Ramadan. They must not eat or drink between sunrise and sunset. Lastly, they should attempt the pilgrimage to the Ka'aba in Mecca, known as the Hajj. Those who have done so are entitled to the prefix

Hajji before their name.

Islamic rules differ from Hindu practice in several other aspects of daily life. Muslims are strictly forbidden to drink alcohol (though some suggest that this prohibition is restricted to the use of fermented grape juice, that is wine, it is commonly accepted to apply to all alcohol). Eating pork, or any meat from an animal not killed by draining its blood while alive, is also prohibited. Meat prepared in the appropriate way is called Halal. Finally, usury (charging interest on loans) and games of chance are forbidden.

Islam has no priesthood. The authority of Imams derives from social custom and from their authority to interpret the scriptures, rather than from a defined status within the Islamic community. Islam also prohibits any distinction on the basis of race or colour and most Muslims believe it is wrong to represent the human figure. It is often thought, inaccurately, that this ban stems from the Qur'an itself. In fact it probably has its origins in the belief of Mohammad that images were likely to be turned into idols.

Muslim Sects During the first century after Mohammad's death Islam split in to two sects which were divided on political and religious grounds, the Shi'is and Sunni's. The religious basis for the division lay in the interpretation of verses in the Qur'an and of traditional sayings of Mohammad, the Hadis. Both sects venerate the Qur'an but have different *Hadis*. They also have different views as to Mohammad's successor.

The **Sunnis** – always the majority in South Asia – believe that Mohammad did not appoint a successor and that Abu Bak'r, Omar and Othman were the first three caliphs (or vice-regents) after Mohammad's death. Ali, whom the Sunni's count as the fourth caliph, is regarded as the first legitimate caliph by the Shi'is, who consider Abu Bak'r and Omar to be usurpers. While the Sunni's believe in the principle of election of caliphs, Shi'is believe that although Mohammad is the last prophet there is a continuing need for intermediaries between God and man. Such intermediaries are termed Imams and they base both their law and religious practice on the teaching of the Imams.

The two major divisions are marked by further sub-divisions. The Sunni Muslims in India have followers of the Hanafi, Shafei, Maliki and Hanbali groups, named after their leaders. Numerically one of the smallest groups in South Asia is that of the Ismailis, who regard their leader, the Aga Khan, as their spiritual head.

From the Mughal emperors, who enjoyed an unparalleled degree of political power, down to the poorest peasant farmers of Bengal, Muslims in India have found different ways of adjusting to their Hindu environment. Some have reacted by accepting or even incorporating features of Hindu belief and practice in their own. Akbar, the most eclectic of Mughal emperors, went as far as banning activities like cow slaughter which were offensive to Hindus and celebrated Hindu festivals in court.

In contrast, the later Mughal Emperor, Aurangzeb, pursued a far more hostile approach to Hindus and Hinduism, trying to point up the distinctiveness of Islam and denying the validity of Hindu religious beliefs. That attitude generally became stronger in the 20th century, related to the growing sense of the Muslim's minority position within South Asia and the fear of being subjected to Hindu rule. It was a fear that led to the creation of the separate Muslim majority state of Pakistan in 1947 and which still permeates political as well as religious attitudes across South Asia.

Background

The Islamic Calendar

The calendar begins on 16 July 622 AD, the date of the Prophet's migration from Mecca to Medina, the Hijra, hence AH (Anno Hejirae). *Murray's Handbook for travellers in India* gave a wonderfully precise method of calculating the current date in the Christian year from the AH date: "To correlate the Hijra year with the Christian year, express the former in years and decimals of a year, multiply by .970225, add 621.54 and the total will correspond exactly with the Christian year".

The Muslim year is divided into 12 lunar months, totalling 354 or 355 days, hence Islamic festivals usually move 11 days earlier each year according to the solar (Gregorian) calendar. The first month of the year is *Moharram*, followed by *Safar*, *Rabi-ul-Awwal, Rabi-ul-Sani, Jumada-ul-Awwal, Jumada-ul-Sani, Rajab, Shaban, Ramadan, Shawwal, Ziquad* and *Zilhaj.*

Buddhism

India was the home of Buddhism, which had its roots in the early Hinduism, or Brahmanism, of its time. Today it is practised only on the margins of the subcontinent, from Ladakh, Nepal and Bhutan in the north to Sri Lanka in the south, where it is the religion of the majority Sinhalese community.

India's Buddhist significance is now mainly as the home for the extraordinarily beautiful artistic and architectural remnants of what was for several centuries the region's dominant religion.

India has sites of great significance for Buddhists around the world. Some say that the Buddha himself spoke of the four places his followers should visit. **Lumbini**, the Buddha's birthplace, is in the Nepali foothills, near the present border with India. **Bodh Gaya**, where he attained what Buddhists term his 'supreme enlightenment', is about 80 km south of the modern Indian city of Patna; the deer park at **Sarnath**, where he preached his first sermon and set in motion the Wheel of the Law, is just outside Varanasi; and **Kushinagara**, where he died at the age of 80, is 50 km east of Gorakhpur. There were four other sacred places of pilgrimage – **Rajgir**, where he tamed a wild elephant; **Vaishali**, where a monkey offered him honey; **Sravasti**, associated with his great miracle; and **Sankasya**, where he descended from heaven. The eight significant events associated with the holy places are repeatedly represented in Buddhist art

The Buddha's Life

Siddharta Gautama, who came to be given the title of the Buddha – the Enlightened One – was born a prince into the warrior caste in about 563 BC. He was married at the age of 16 and his wife had a son. When he reached the age of 29 he left home and wandered as a beggar and ascetic. After about 6 years he spent some time in Bodh Gaya. Sitting under the Bo tree, meditating, he was tempted by the demon Mara, with all the desires of the world. Resisting these temptations, he received enlightenment. These scenes are common motifs of Buddhist art.

The next landmark was the preaching of his first sermon on 'The Foundation of Righteousness' in the deer park near Benaras. By the time he died the Buddha had established a small band of monks and nuns known as the *Sangha* and had followers across North India. His body was cremated and the ashes, regarded as precious relics, were divided among the peoples to whom he had preached.

After the Buddha's death

From the Buddha's death, or *parinirvana*, to the destruction of Nalanda (the last Buddhist stronghold in India) in 1197 AD, Buddhism in India went through three phases. These are often referred to as Hinayana, Mahayana and Vajrayana, though they were not mutually exclusive, being followed simultaneously in different regions.

The Buddha's Four Noble Truths

The Buddha preached Four Noble Truths: that life is painful; that suffering is caused by ignorance and desire; that beyond the suffering of life there is a state which cannot be described but which he termed nirvana; and that nirvana can be reached by following an eightfold path.

The concept of nirvana is often understood in the west in an entirely negative sense – that of 'non-being'. The word has the rough meaning of 'blow

out' or 'extinguish', meaning to blow out the fires of greed, lust and desire. In a more positive sense it has been described by one Buddhist scholar as "the state of absolute illumination, supreme bliss, infinite love and compassion, unshakeable serenity and unrestricted spiritual freedom". The essential elements of the eightfold path are the perfection of wisdom, morality and meditation.

Hinayana The Hinayana or Lesser Way insists on a monastic way of life as the only path to the personal goal of *nirvana* (see box page 542) achieved through an austere life. Divided into many schools, the only surviving Hinayana tradition is the **Theravada** Buddhism, which was taken to Sri Lanka by the Emperor Asoka's son Mahinda, where it became the state religion.

Mahayana In contrast to the Hinayana schools, the followers of the Mahayana school (the Great Way) believed in the possibility of salvation for all. They practised a far more devotional form of meditation and new figures came to play a prominent part in their beliefs and their worship – the **Bodhisattvas**, saints who were predestined to reach the state of enlightenment through thousands of rebirths. They aspired to Buddhahood, however, not for their own sake but for the sake of all living things. The Buddha is believed to have passed through numerous existences in preparation for his final mission. Mahayana Buddhism became dominant over most of South Asia and its influence is evidenced in Buddhist art from Gandhara in north Pakistan to Ajanta in Central India and Sigiriya in Sri Lanka.

Vajrayana The Diamond Way resembles magic and yoga in some of its beliefs. The ideal of Vajrayana Buddhists is to be 'so fully in harmony with the cosmos as to be able to manipulate the cosmic forces within and outside himself'. It had developed in the north of India by the seventh century AD, matching the parallel growth of Hindu Tantrism.

Buddhism's The decline of Buddhism in India probably stemmed as much from the growing
decline similarity in the practice of Hinduism and Buddhism as from direct attacks. Mahayana Buddhism, with its reverence for Bodhisattvas and its devotional character, was more and more difficult to distinguish from the revivalist Hinduism characteristic of several parts of North India from the seventh to the 12th centuries AD. The Muslim conquest dealt the final death blow, being accompanied by the large scale slaughter of monks and the destruction of monasteries. Without their institutional support Buddhism faded away.

Jainism

Like Buddhism, Jainism started as a reform movement of the Brahmanic religious beliefs of the sixth century BC. Its founder was a widely revered saint and ascetic, Vardhamma, who became known as **Mahavir** – 'great hero'. Mahavir was born in the same border region of India and Nepal as the Buddha, just 50 km north of

The Jain spiritual journey

The two Jain sects differ chiefly on the nature of proper ascetic practices. The Svetambara monks wear white robes and carry a staff, some wooden pots and a woollen mop for sweeping the path in front of them, wool being the softest material available and the least likely to hurt any living thing swept away. The highest level of Digambara monks will completely naked, although the lower levels will wear a covering over their genitalia. They carry a waterpot made of a gourd and peacock feathers to sweep the ground before they sit.

Jains believe that the spiritual journey of the soul is divided into 14 stages, moving from bondage and ignorance to the final destruction of all karma and the complete fulfilment of the soul. The object throughout is to prevent the addition of new karma to the soul, which comes mainly through passion and attachment to the world. Bearing the pains of the world cheerfully contributes to the destruction of karma.

modern Patna, probably in 599 BC. Thus he was about 35 years older than the Buddha. His family, also royal, were followers of an ascetic saint, Parsvanatha, who according to Jain tradition had lived 200 years previously.

Mahavir's life story is embellished with legends, but there is no doubt that he left his royal home for a life of the strict ascetic. He is believed to have received enlightenment after 12 years of rigorous hardship, penance and meditation. Afterwards he travelled and preached for 30 years, stopping only in the rainy season. He died aged 72 in 527 BC. His death was commemorated by a special lamp festival in the region of Bihar, which Jains claim is the basis of the now-common Hindu festival of lights, Diwali.

Unlike Buddhism, Jainism never spread beyond India, but it has survived continuously into modern India, claiming 4 million adherents. In part this may be because Jain beliefs have much in common with puritanical forms of Hinduism and are greatly respected and admired. Some Jain ideas, such as vegetarianism and reverence for all life, are widely recognized by Hindus as highly commendable, even by those who do not share other Jain beliefs. The value Jains place on non-violence has contributed to their importance in business and commerce, as they regard nearly all occupations except banking and commerce as violent. The 18 m high free-standing statue of Gommateshvara at Sravana Belgola near Mysore (built about 983 AD) is just one outstanding example of the contribution of Jain art to India's heritage.

Jains (from the word Jina, literally meaning 'descendants of conquerors') believe that there are two fundamental principles, the living (*jiva*) and the non-living (*ajiva*). The essence of Jain belief is that all life is sacred and that every living entity, even the smallest insect, has within it an indestructible and immortal soul. Jains developed the view of ahimsa – often translated as 'non-violence', but better perhaps as 'non-harming'. Ahimsa was the basis for the entire scheme of Jain values and ethics and alternative codes of practice were defined for householders and for ascetics.

Jain beliefs

The five vows may be taken both by monks and by lay people: not to harm any living beings (Jains must practise strict vegetarianism—and even some vegetables, such as potatoes and onions, are believed to have microscopic souls); to speak the truth; not to steal; to give up sexual relations and practice complete chastity; to give up all possessions—for the *Digambara* sect that includes clothes.

Celibacy is necessary to combat physical desire. Jains also regard the manner of dying as extremely important. Although suicide is deeply opposed, vows of fasting to death voluntarily may be regarded as earning merit in the proper context. Mahavir himself is believed to have died of self-starvation, near Rajgir in modern Bihar.

Background

In principle the objectives for both lay and ascetic Jains is the same and many lay Jains pass through the stage of being a householder and then accept the stricter practices of the monks. The essence of all the rules is to avoid intentional injury, which is the worst of all sins. Like Hindus, the Jains believe in *karma*, by which the evil effects of earlier deeds leave an indelible impurity on the soul. This impurity will remain through endless rebirths unless burned off by extreme penances.

Jain sects Jains have two main sects, whose origins can be traced back to the fourth century BC. The more numerous **Svetambaras** – the 'white clad' – concentrated more in eastern and western India, separated from the **Digambaras** – or 'sky-clad'– who often go naked. The Digambaras may well have been forced to move south by drought and famine in the northern region of the Deccan and they are now concentrated in the south of India.

Unlike Buddhists, Jains accept the idea of God, but not as a creator of the universe. They see him in the lives of the 24 **Tirthankaras** (prophets, or literally 'makers of fords' – a reference to their role in building crossing points for the spiritual journey over the river of life), or leaders of Jainism, whose lives are recounted in the Kalpsutra – the third century BC book of ritual for the Svetambaras. Mahavir is regarded as the last of these great spiritual leaders. Much Jain art details stories from these accounts and the Tirthankaras play a similar role for Jains as the Bodhisattvas do for Mahayana Buddhists.

Sikhism

Guru Nanak, the founder of the religion was born just west of Lahore and grew up in what is now the Pakistani town of Sultanpur. His followers, the Sikhs, (derived from the Sanskrit word for 'disciples') form perhaps one of India's most recognizable groups. Beards and turbans give them a very distinctive presence and although they represent less than 2 of the population they are both politically and economically significant.

Christianity

There are about 23 million Christians in India. Christianity ranks third in terms of religious affiliation after Hinduism and Islam and there are Christian congregations in all the major towns of India.

The great majority of the Protestant Christians in India are now members of the Church of South India, formed from the major Protestant denominations in 1947.. Together they account for approximately half the total number of Christians. Roman Catholics make up the majority of the rest. Many of the church congregations, both in towns and villages, are active centres of Christian worship.

Origins Some of the churches owe their origin either to the modern missionary movement of the late 18th century onwards, or to the colonial presence of the European powers. However, Christians probably arrived in India during the first century after the birth of Christ. There is evidence that one of Christ's Apostles, **Thomas**, reached India in 52 AD, only 20 years after Christ was crucified. He settled in Malabar and then expanded his missionary work to China. It is widely believed that he was martyred in Tamil Nadu on his return to India in 72 AD and is buried in Mylapore, in the suburbs of modern Madras. St Thomas' Mount, a small rocky hill just north of Madras airport, takes its name from him. Today there is still a church of Thomas Christians in Kerala.

The spread of Christianity

The spread of Roman Catholicism was uneven, but was much stronger in the south. Jesuits concentrated their missionary efforts on work among the high caste Hindus, the most striking example of which was that of Robert de Nobili, who followed a Brahmin way of life in Madurai for many years.

Both the Roman Catholic and subsequently the Protestant denominations struggled to come to terms with the caste system. By the late 18th century the Roman Catholic church had moved substantially to abolishing discrimination on grounds of caste, a pattern which the main Protestant communities tried to follow. The American Mission in Madurai, for example, instituted 'agap, meals', or 'love feasts', to which Christians of all castes were invited to eat meals together cooked by members of low castes.

The Syrian church

Kerala was linked directly with the Middle East, when Syrian Christians embarked on a major missionary movement in the sixth century AD. The Thomas Christians have forms of worship that show very strong influence of the Syrian church and they still retain a Syriac order of service. They remained a close knit community, coming to terms with the prevailing caste system by maintaining strict social rules very similar to those of the surrounding upper caste Hindus. They lived in an area restricted to what is now Kerala, where trade with the Middle East, which some centuries later was to bring Muslims to the same region, remained active.

Roman Catholicism

The third major development took place with the arrival of the Portuguese. The Jesuit St Francis Xavier landed in Goa in 1542 and in 1557 Goa was made an Archbishopric (see page 454). Goa today bears rich testimony to the Portuguese influence on community life and on church building. They set up the first printing press in India in 1566 and began to print books in Tamil and other Dravidian languages by the end of the 16th century.

Northern missions

The nature and the influence of Christian missionary activity in North India were different. There are far fewer Christians in North India than in the south, but Protestant missions in Bengal from the end of the 18th century had a profound influence on cultural and religious development. On 9 November 1793 the Baptist missionary **William Carey** reached the Hugli River. Although he went to India to preach, he had wide-ranging interests, notably in languages and education and the work of 19th-century missions rapidly widened to cover educational and medical work as well. The influence of Christian missions in education and medical work was greater than as a proselytizing force. Education in Christian schools stimulated reformist movements in Hinduism itself and mission hospitals supplemented government-run hospitals, particularly in remote rural areas. Some of these Christian-run hospitals, such as that at Vellore, continue to provide high class medical care alongside Government-run and private medical services.

Christian beliefs

Christian theology had its roots in Judaism, with its belief in one God, the eternal Creator of the universe. Judaism saw the Jewish people as the vehicle for God's salvation, the 'chosen people of God' and pointed to a time when God would send his Saviour, or Messiah. Jesus, whom Christians believe was 'the Christ' or Messiah, was born in the village of Bethlehem, some 20 km south of Jerusalem. Very little is known of his early life except that he was brought up in a devout Jewish family. At the age of 29 or 30 he gathered a small group of followers and began to preach in the region between the Dead Sea and the Sea of Galilee. Two years later he was crucified in Jerusalem by the authorities on the charge of blasphemy – that he claimed to be the son of God.

Background

Christians believe that all people live in a state of sin, in the sense that they are separated from God and fail to do his will. They believe that God is personal, 'like a father'. As God's son, Jesus accepted the cost of that separation and sinfulness himself through his death on the cross. Christians believe that Jesus was raised from the dead on the third day after he was crucified and that he appeared to his closest followers. They believe that his spirit continues to live today and that he makes it possible for people to come back to God.

The New Testament of the Bible, which, alongside the Old Testament, is the text to which Christians refer as the ultimate scriptural authority, consists of four 'Gospels' (meaning 'good news') and a series of letters by several early Christians referring to the nature of the Christian life.

Christian worship Although Christians are encouraged to worship individually as well as together, most forms of Christian worship centre on the gathering of the church congregation for praise, prayer and the preaching of God's word, which usually takes verses from the Bible as its starting point. Different denominations place varying emphases on the main elements of worship, but in most church services today the congregation will take part in singing hymns (songs of praise), prayers will be led by the minister, priest or a member of the congregation, readings from the Bible will be given and a sermon preached. For many Christians the most important service is the act of Holy Communion (Protestant) or Mass (Catholic) which celebrates the death and resurrection of Jesus in sharing bread and wine, which are held to represent Christ's body and blood given to save people from their sin. Although Christian services may be held daily in some churches most Christian congregations in India meet for worship on Sunday, and services are held in all the local languages. In most cities some churches also have services in English. They are open to all.

Denominations Between the second and the fourth centuries AD there were numerous debates about the interpretation of Christian doctrine, sometimes resulting in the formation of specific groups focussing on particular interpretations of faith. One such group was that of the Nestorian Christians, who played a major part in the theology of the Syrian Church in Kerala. They regarded the Syrian patriarch of the East their spiritual head and followed the Nestorian tradition that there were two distinct natures in Christ, the divine and human. The Roman Catholic church believes that Christ declared that his disciple Peter should be the first spiritual head of the Church and that his successors should lead the Church on earth. Modern Catholic churches still recognize the spiritual authority of the Pope and cardinals.

The reformation which took place in Europe from the 16th century onwards resulted in the creation of the Protestant churches, which became dominant in several European countries. They reasserted the authority of the Bible over that of the church. A number of new denominations were created. The reunification of the church which has taken significant steps since 1947 has progressed faster in South Asia than in most other parts of the world.

Zoroastrianism

The first Zoroastrians arrived on the west coast of India in the mid-eighth century AD, forced out from their native Iran by persecution of the invading Islamic Arabs. Until 1477 they lost all contact with Iran and then for nearly 300 years maintained contact with Persian Zoroastrians through a continuous exchange of letters. They became known by their now much more familiar name, the **Parsis** (or Persians).

Although they are a tiny minority (approximately 100,000), even in the cities where they are concentrated, they have been a prominent economic and social influence, especially in West India. Parsis adopted westernized customs and dress and took to the new economic opportunities that came with colonial industrialization. Families in West India such as the Tatas continue to be among India's leading industrialists, just part of a community that in recent generations has spread to Europe and north America.

Origins

Zoroastrians trace their beliefs to the prophet Zarathustra, who lived in Northeast Iran around the seventh or sixth century BC. His place and even date of birth are uncertain, but he almost certainly enjoyed the patronage of the father of Darius the Great. The passage of Alexander the Great through Iran severely weakened support for Zoroastrianism, but between the sixth century BC and the seventh century AD it was the major religion of peoples living from North India to central Turkey. The spread of Islam reduced the number of Zoroastrians dramatically and forced those who did not retreat to the desert to emigrate.

Culture

Language

The graffiti written on the walls of any Indian city bear witness to the number of major languages spoken across the country, many with their own distinct scripts. In all the states of South India a Dravidian language predominates, in contrast to North and West India where Indo-Aryan languages – the easternmost group of the Indo-European family – is most common. Sir William Jones, the great 19th-century scholar, discovered the close links between Sanskrit (the basis of nearly all North Indian languages) German and Greek. He showed that they all must have originated in the common heartland of Central Asia, being carried west, south and east by the nomadic tribes who shaped so much of the subsequent history of both Europe and Asia. Sanskrit has left its mark on all major Indian laguages, though in recent years there have been persistent efforts to remove them from Tamil.

Sanskrit

As the pastoralists from Central Asia moved into South Asia from 2000 BC onwards, the Indo-Aryan languages they spoke were gradually modified. **Sanskrit** developed from this process, emerging as the dominant classical language of India by the sixth century BC, when it was classified in the grammar of **Panini**. It remained the language of the educated until about AD 1000, though it had ceased to be in common use several centuries earlier. The Muslims brought Persian into South Asia as the language of the rulers, where it became the language of the numerically tiny but politically powerful Élite.

Hindi & Urdu

The most striking example of Muslim influence on the earlier Indo-European languages is that of the two most important languages of India and Pakistan, Hindi and Urdu respectively. Hindi is increasingly commonly used as a lingua franca in many parts of India, though it is very rarely heard in Tamil Nadu. Urdu, written from right to left in the flowing Perso-Arabic script, is widely spoken among the Muslim population of towns and cities in the South.

The Dravidian languages

One of the major language families of South Asia today, Dravidian, has been in India since before the arrival of the Indo-Aryans. Four of South Asia's major living languages belong to this family group – Tamil, Telugu, Kannada and Malayalam, spoken in Tamil

Background

What's in a word?

Can you spot the Indian connection?

A number of words below originated from an Indian language. See page 596 to find out which.

Pete and Liz were having a party in their bungalow by the sea and they had been blowing up balloons and getting the punch warmed up. The rain was coming down in buckets, just like the monsoon, and from their verandah they saw the dinghies and catamarans race back to shore, one nearly crashing its prow against the breakwater.

They had planned to have mulligatawney soup with plenty of pepper for a starter. Rice and curry was always a success and the mango chutney would go down well, they thought. But they had none in the house so Pete, still in his dungarees and sandals, grabbed some cash and dashed out to the village shop.

The calico and chinz curtains had been drawn and little Harry was in his pyjamas ready for bed. The door bell rang. The first guest had already arrived carrying a special box of cheroots!

Nadu (and northern Sri Lanka) Andhra Pradesh, Karnataka and Kerala respectively.

Each has its own script. All the Dravidian languages were influenced by the prevalence of Sanskrit as the language of the ruling and educated Élite. There have been recent attempts to rid Tamil of its Sanskrit elements and to recapture the supposed purity of a literature that stretches back to the early centuries BC. Kannada and Telugu were clearly established by AD 1000, while Malayalam, which started as a dialect of Tamil, did not develop its fully distinct form until the 13th century. Today the four main Dravidian languages are spoken by nearly 200 million people.

Scripts

It is impossible to spend even a short time in India or the other countries of South Asia without coming across several of the different scripts that are used. The earliest ancestor of scripts in use today was **Brahmi**, in which Asoka's famous inscriptions were written in the third century BC. Written from left to right, a separate symbol represented each different sound.

Dravidian scripts The Dravidian languages were written originally on leaves of the palmyra palm. Cutting the letters on the hard palm leaf made particular demands which had their impact on the forms of the letters adopted. The letters became rounded because they were carved with a stylus. This was held stationary while the leaf was turned. The southern scripts were carried overseas, contributing to the form of the non-Dravidian languages of Thai, Burmese and Cambodian.

Devanagari For about a thousand years the major script of northern India has been the Nagari or Devanagari, which means literally the script of the 'city of the gods'. Hindi, Nepali and Marathi join Sanskrit in their use of Devanagari. The Muslim rulers developed a right to left script based on Persian and Arabic. Hindi is used for place names on sign boards right across India

Numerals Many of the Indian alphabets have their own notation for numerals. This is not without irony, for what in the western world are called 'Arabic' numerals are in fact of Indian origin. In some parts of South Asia local numerical symbols are still in use, but by and large you will find that the Arabic number symbols familiar in Europe and the West are common.

Yes Yes: the body language of common speech

Body language often carries it own message. In South India strong agreement is often indicated by a repetition of Yes!

Yes!, accompanied by a vigorous shaking of the head from side to side, the opposite of its normal meaning in western cultures.

The role of English

English now plays an important role across India. It is widely spoken in towns and cities and even in quite remote villages it is usually not difficult to find someone who speaks at least a little English. Other European languages are almost completely unknown. The accent in which English is spoken is often affected strongly by the mother tongue of the speaker and there have been changes in common grammar which sometimes make it sound unusual. Many of these changes have become standard Indian English usage, as valid as any other varieties of English used around the world.

Literature

Sanskrit was the first all-India language. Its literature has had a fundamental influence on the religious, social and political life of the entire region. Its early literature was memorized and recited. The hymns of the Rig Veda probably did not reach its final form until about the sixth century BC, but the earliest parts of which may go back as far as 1300 BC – approximately the period of the fall of Mycenean Greece in Europe.

The Vedas

The Rig Veda is a collection of 1,028 hymns, not all directly religious. Its main function was to provide orders of worship for priests responsible for the sacrifices which were central to the religion of the Indo-Aryans. Two later texts, the Yajurveda and the Samaveda, served the same purpose. A fourth, the Atharvaveda, is largely a collection of magic spells.

Central to the Vedic literature was a belief in the importance of sacrifice. At some time after 1000 BC a second category of Vedic literature, the Brahmanas, began to take shape. Story telling developed as a means to interpret the significance of sacrifice. The most famous and the most important of these were the Upanishads, probably written at some time between the seventh and fifth centuries BC.

The Brahmanas

The Brahmanas gave their name to the religion emerging between the eighth and sixth centuries BC, Brahmanism, the ancestor of Hinduism. Two of it's texts remain the best known and most widely revered epic compositions in South Asia, the Mahabharata and the Ramayana.

The Mahabharata

Dating the Mahabharata

The details of the great battle recounted in the Mahabharata are unclear. Tradition puts its date at precisely 3102 BC, the start of the present era and names the author of the poem as a sage, Vyasa. Evidence suggests however that the battle was fought around 800 BC, at **Kurukshetra**. It was another 400 years before priests began to write the stories down, a process which was not complete until 400 AD. The Mahabharata was probably an attempt by the warrior class, the Kshatriyas, to merge

Background

their brand of popular religion with the ideas of Brahmanism. The original version was about 3,000 stanzas long, but it now contains over 100,000 – eight times as long as Homer's Iliad and the Odyssey put together.

Good & evil The battle was seen as a war of the forces of good and evil, the **Pandavas** being interpreted as gods and the **Kauravas** as devils. The arguments were elaborated and expanded until about the fourth century AD by which time, as Shackle says, "Brahmanism had absorbed and set its own mark on the religious ideas of the epic and Hinduism had come into being". A comparatively late addition to the Mahabharata, the Bhagavad-Gita is the most widely read and revered text among Hindus in South Asia today.

The Ramayana

Valmiki is thought of in India as the author of the second great Indian epic, the Ramayana, though no more is known of his identity than is known of Homer's. Like the Mahabharata, it underwent several stages of development before it reached its final version of 48,000 lines.

Sanskrit Literature

Sanskrit was always the language of the court and the Élite. Other languages replaced it in common speech by the third century BC, but it remained in restricted use for over 1,000 years after that period. The remarkable Sanskrit grammar of Panini helped to establish grammar as one of the six disciplines essential to understanding the Vedas properly and to conducting Vedic rituals. The other five were phonetics, etymology, meter, ritual practice and astronomy. Sanskrit literature continued to be written in the counts until the Muslim's replaced it with Persian, long after it had ceased to be a language of spoken communication. One of India's greatest poets, **Kalidasa**, contributed to the development of Sanskrit as the language of learning and the arts.

Vatsyana's Kamasutra not only explores the diversity of physical love but sheds light on social customs. In architecture the Nagara and Dravida styles were first developed. The Brahmins also produced theses on philosophy and on the structure of society, but these had the negative effect of contributing to the extreme rigidity of the caste system which became apparent from this period onwards.

Literally 'stories of ancient times', the Puranas are about Brahma, Vishnu and Siva. Although some of the stories may relate to real events that occurred as early as 1500 BC, they were not compiled until the fifth century AD. Margaret and James Stutley record the belief that "during the destruction of the world at the end of the age, Hayagriva is said to have saved the Puranas. A summary of the original work is now preserved in Heaven!"

The stories are often the only source of information about the period immediately following the early Vedas. Each Purana was intended to deal with five themes: "the creation of the world (sarga); its destruction and recreation (pratisarga); the genealogy of gods and patriarchs (vamsa); the reigns and periods of the Manus (manvantaras); and the history of the solar and lunar dynasties".

The Muslim influence

Persian In the first three decades of the 10th century AD Mahmud of Ghazni carried Muslim power into India. For considerable periods until the 18th century, Persian became the language of the courts. Classical Persian was the dominant influence, with Iran as its country of origin and Shiraz its main cultural centre, but India developed its own Persian-based style. Two poets stood out at the end of the 13th century AD,

The story of Rama

Under Brahmin influence, **Rama** *was transformed from the human prince of the early versions into the divine figure of the final story. Rama, the 'jewel of the solar kings', became deified as an incarnation of Vishnu. The story tells how Rama was banished from his father's kingdom. In a journey that took him as far as Sri Lanka, accompanied by his wife Sita and helper and friend Hanuman (the monkey-faced God depicted in many Indian temples, shrines and posters), Rama finally fought the king* **Ravana**, *again changed in late versions into a demon. Rama's rescue of Sita was interpreted as the Aryan triumph over the barbarians. The epic is widely seen as South Asia's first literary poem and is known and recited in all Hindu communities.*

Ravana, demon king of Lanka

when Muslim rulers had established a sultanate in Delhi, Amir Khusrau, who lived from 1253 to 1325 and the mystic Amir Hasan, who died about AD 1328.

The most notable of the Mughal sponsors of literature, Akbar (1556-1605) was himself illiterate. Babur left one of the most remarkable political autobiographies of any generation, the Babur-nama (History of Babur), written in Turki and translated into Persian. His grandson Akbar commissioned a biography, the Akbar-nama, which reflected his interest in all the world's religions. His son Jahangir left his memoirs, the Tuzuk-i Jahangiri, in Persian. They have been described as intimate and spontaneous and showing an insatiable interest in things, events and people.

Turki

The Colonial Period

Persian was already in decline during the reign of the last great Muslim Emperor, **Aurangzeb** and as the British extended their political power so the role of English grew. There is now a very wide Indian literature accessible in English, which has thus become the latest of the languages to be used across the whole of South Asia.

In the 19th century English became a vehicle for developing nationalist ideals. However, notably in the work of **Rabindranath Tagore**, it became a medium for religious and philosophical prose and for a developing poetry. Tagore himself won the Nobel Prize for Literature in 1913 for his translation into English of his own work, Gitanjali. Leading South Asian philosophers of the 20th century have written major works in English, including not only MK Gandhi and Jawaharlal Nehru, the two leading figures in India's Independence movement, but S Radhakrishnan, Aurobindo Ghose and Sarojini Naidu, who all added to the depth of Indian literature in English.

Some suggestions for reading are listed in Essentials. In addition, several South Asian regional languages have their own long traditions of both religious and secular literature which are discussed in the relevant sections of this Handbook.

Background

Science

The science of early India

By about 500 BC Indian texts illustrated the calculation of the **calendar**, although the system itself almost certainly goes back to the eighth or ninth century BC. The year was divided into 27 *nakshatras*, or fortnights, years being calculated on a mixture of lunar and solar counting.

Views of the universe

Early Indian views of the universe were based on the square and the cube. The earth was seen as a square, one corner south, rising like a pyramid in a series of square terraces with its peak, the mythical Mount Meru. The sun moved round the top of Mount Meru in a square orbit and the square orbits of the planets were at successive planes above the orbit of the sun. These were seen therefore as forming a second pyramid of planetary movement. Mount Meru was central to all early Indian schools of thought, Hindu, Buddhist and Jain.

However, about 200 BC the Jains transformed the view of the universe based on squares by replacing the idea of square orbits with that of the circle. The earth was shown as a circular disc, with Mount Meru rising from its centre and the Pole Star directly above it.

Technology

The only copy of Kautiliya's treatise on government (which was only discovered in 1909) dates from about 100 BC. It describes the **weapons** technology of catapults, incendiary missiles and the use of elephants, but it is also evident that gunpowder was unknown. Large scale **irrigation** works were developed, though the earliest examples of large tanks may be those of the Sri Lankan King Panduwasa at Anuradhapura, built in 504 BC. During the Gupta period dramatic progress was made in **metallurgy**, evidenced in the extraordinarily pure iron pillar which can be seen in the Qutb Minar in Delhi.

Mathematics

Conceptions of the universe and the mathematical and geometrical ideas that accompanied them were comparatively advanced in South Asia by the time of the Mauryan Empire and were put to use in the rules developed for building temple altars. Indians were using the concept of zero and decimal points in the Gupta period. Furthermore in AD 499, just after the demise of the Gupta Empire, the astronomer Aryabhatta calculated Pi as 3.1416 and the length of the solar year as 365.358 days. He also postulated that the earth was a sphere rotating on its own axis and revolving around the sun and that the earth's shadow falling on the moon caused lunar eclipses.

The development of science in India was not restricted to the Gupta court. In South India, Tamil kings developed extensive contact with Roman and Greek thinkers during the first four centuries of the Christian era. Babylonian methods used for astronomy in Greece remained current in Tamil Nadu until very recent times. The basic texts of astronomy (the Surya Siddhanta) were completed by AD 400.

Architecture

Hindu Temple Buildings

The principles of religious building were laid down by priests in the *Sastras*. Every aspect of Hindu, Jain and Buddhist religious building is identified with conceptions of the structure of the universe. This applies as much to the process of building – the timing of which must be undertaken at astrologically propitious times – as to the formal layout of the buildings. The cardinal directions of north, south, east and west are the basic fix on which buildings are planned. George Michell suggests that in addition to the cardinal directions, number is also critical to the design of the religious building. The key to the ultimate scale of the building is derived from the measurements of the sanctuary at its heart.

Indian temples were nearly always built to a clear and universal design, which had built into it philosophical understandings of the universe. This cosmology, of an infinite number of universes, isolated from each other in space, proceeds by imagining various possibilities as to its nature. Its centre is seen as dominated by **Mt Meru** which keeps earth and heaven apart. The concept of *separation* is crucial to Hindu thought and social practice. Continents, rivers and oceans occupy concentric rings around the mountain, while the stars encircle the mountain in another plane. Humans live on the continent of **Jambudvipa**, characterized by the rose apple tree (*jambu*).

Mandalas The Sastras show plans of this continent, organized in concentric rings and entered at the cardinal points. This type of diagram was known as a **mandala**. Such a geometric scheme could be subdivided into almost limitless small compartments, each of which could be designated as having special properties or be devoted to a particular deity. The centre of the mandala would be the seat of the major god. Mandalas provided the ground rules for the building of stupas and temples across India and gave the key to the symbolic meaning attached to every aspect of religious buildings.

The focal point of the temple, its sanctuary, was the home of the presiding deity, the 'womb-chamber' (*garbhagriha*). A series of doorways, in large temples leading through a succession of buildings, allowed the worshipper to move towards the final encounter with the deity to obtain *darshan* – a sight of the god. Both Buddhist and Hindu worship encourage the worshipper to walk clockwise around the shrine, performing *pradakshina*.

Temple design

The elevations are symbolic representations of the home of the gods. Mountain peaks such as Kailasa are common names for the most prominent of the towers. In north and East Indian temples the tallest of these towers rises above the *garbagriha* itself, symbolizing the meeting of earth and heaven in the person of the enshrined deity. In later South Indian temples the gateways to the temple come to overpower the central tower. In both, the basic structure is embellished with sculpture. When first built this would usually have been plastered and painted and often covered in gems. In contrast to the extraordinary profusion of colour and life on the outside, the interior is dark and cramped but here it is believed, lies the true centre of divine power.

Buddhist and Hindu architecture probably began with wooden building, for the rock carving and cave excavated temples show clear evidence of copying styles which must have been developed first in wooden buildings. The third to second century BC caves of the Buddhists were followed in the seventh and eighth centuries AD by free standing but rock-cut temples such as those at Mahabalipuram (see page 102). They were subsequently replaced by temples built entirely out of assembled material, usually stone. By the 13th century AD most of India's most remarkable Hindu temples had been built, from the Chola temples of the south to the Khajuraho temples of the north Peninsula. Only the flowering of Vijayanagar architecture in South India produced continuing development, culminating in the Meenakshi Temple in Madurai (see page 161).

Temple development

Muslim religious architecture

Although the Muslims adapted many Hindu features, they also brought totally new forms. Their most outstanding contribution, dominating the architecture of many North Indian cities, are the mosques and tomb complexes (*dargah*). The use of brickwork was widespread and they brought with them from Persia the principle of constructing the true arch. Muslim architects succeeded in producing a variety of domed structures, often incorporating distinctively Hindu features such as the surmounting finial. By the end of the great period of Muslim building in 1707, the Muslims had added magnificent forts and palaces to their religious structures, a statement of power as well as of aesthetic taste.

European buildings

Nearly two centuries of architectural stagnation and decline followed the demise of Mughal power. The Portuguese built a series of remarkable churches in Goa that owed nothing to local traditions and everything to Baroque developments in Europe. Not until the end of the Victorian period, when British imperial ambitions were at their height, did the British colonial impact on public rather than domestic architecture begin to be felt. Fierce arguments divided British architects as to the merits of indigenous design. The ultimate plan for New Delhi was carried out by men who had little time for Hindu architecture and believed themselves to be on a civilizing mission. Others at the end of the 19th century wanted to recapture and enhance a tradition for which they had great respect. They have left a series of buildings, both in formerly British ruled territory and in the Princely States, which illustrate this concern through the development of what became known as the Indo-Saracenic style.

Music and dance

Music Indian music can trace its origins to the metrical hymns and chants of the Vedas, in which the production of sound according to strict rules was understood to be vital to the continuing order of the Universe. Through more than 3,000 years of development and a range of regional schools, India's musical tradition has been handed on almost entirely by ear. The chants of the **Rig Veda** developed into songs in the **Sama Veda** and music found expression in every sphere of life, reflecting the cycle of seasons and the rhythm of work.

Background

Over the centuries the original three notes, which were sung strictly in descending order, were extended to five and then seven and developed to allow freedom to move up and down the scale. The scale increased to 12 with the addition of flats and sharps and finally to 22 with the further subdivision of semitones. Books of musical rules go back at least as far as the third century AD. Classical music was totally intertwined with dance and drama, an interweaving reflected in the term *sangita*.

At some point after the Muslim influence made itself felt in the north. North and South Indian styles diverged, to become Carnatic (Karnatak) music in the south and Hindustani music in the north. However, they still share important common features: *svara* (pitch), *raga* (the melodic structure) and *tala* or *talam* (metre).

Changes constantly occurred in different schools of music within the basic framework of **raga-tala-prabandha** which was well established by the seventh century. From the 13th century the division between the *Hindustani* or the northern system (which included the western and eastern regions as well) and the *Carnatic* or the southern system, became pronounced. The southern school has a more scale-based structure of *raga* whereas the northern school has greater flexibility and thus continued to develop through the centuries. The *tala* too is much more precise. It is also nearly always devotional or didactic where as the northern system also includes non-religious, everyday themes which are sometimes sensuous. The language that lends itself naturally to the southern system is Telugu and the only bowed instrument that is used to accompany vocal music is the violin, imported from the West but played rather differently.

The big screen

The hugely popular Indian film industry comes mainly out of the tradition of larger-than-life productions with familiar story lines performed as escapist entertainment for the community. The stars lead fantasy lives as they enjoy cult status with a following of millions. It is not surprising that should they choose to turn their hand to politics, they find instant support in an unquestioning, adoring electorate. The experience of a Bollywood or Tamil film is not to be missed - at least once in your life. Television has made a visit to a cinema redundant though it's always easy to find one in any sizeable town; the gaudy posters dominate every street scene. Be prepared for a long sitting with a standard story line, set characters and lots of action as the typical multi-million rupee blockbusters attempt to provide something to please everybody. Marathon melodramas consist of slapstick comedy contrasted with tear-jerking tragedy, a liberal sprinkling of moralizing with a tortuous disentangling of the knots tied by the heroes, heroines, villains and their extended families. The usual ingredients are the same: shrill "film music", unoriginal songs mouthed to the voice of playback artistes, hip-jerking dancing by suggestively clad figures which lack all subtlety when it comes to sexual innuendo, honeymooning couples before a backdrop of snowy mountains, car chases and violent disasters - these will keep you enthralled for hours. Each southern state is prolific in its output. The power of the cinema is particulary obvious in Tamil Nadu which has been led, until recently, by two Chief Ministers, MG Ramachandran and his successor Jayalalitha, who captured the public's loyalty through their screen performances. On a serious note, there are ample examples of truly brilliant works by world-class Indian film makers (Satyajit Ray, Rithwik Ghatak, Shyam Benegal, Aparna Roy to name a few) but they are not usually box office successes or made for popular consumption so they have to be sought out.

The essential structure of a melody is known as a **raga** which usually has five to seven notes and can have as many as nine (or even 12 in mixed ragas). The music is improvised by the performer within certain governing rules and although theoretically thousands of ragas are possible, only around a hundred are commonly performed. Ragas have become associated with particular moods and specific times of the day. Music festivals often include all night sessions to allow performers a wider choice of repertoire.

Carnatic (Karnatak) music

Contemporary South Indian music is traced back to Tyagaraja (1759-1847), Svami Shastri (1763-1827) and Dikshitar (1775-1835), three musicians who lived and worked in Thanjavur. They are still referred to as 'the Trinity'. Their music placed more emphasis on extended compositions than Hindustani music.

Perhaps the best known South Indian instrument is the stringed *vina*, the flute being commonly used for accompaniment along with the violin. An oboe-like instrument called the *nagasvaram* has a wooden mouthpiece and evolved from the snake charmer's *pangi* with two bamboo or metal pipes which have holes. In addition to the drums, *tavil*, the unusual *ghatam*, a round clay pot which has the open neck pressed against the player's stomach while he strikes and taps with his hands, wrists and fingers.

Dance & music festivals

Many cities hold annual festivals, particularly during winter months. See page 54. Some important ones are: **January**: *Thyagaraja Festival,* Tiruvayyaru, near Thanjavur; *Siddheswara Temple Festival,* Bijapur; *Nrutytsava,* Pattadakal.
January-February: *Mamallapuram Nritya Utsav,* Mahabalipuram. **February-March**: *Sivaratri Natyanjali Utsav,* Chidambaram. **October-November**: *Hampi Utsav of*

Background

Vijaynagar, Hampi; *Shanmukhananda*, Mumbai. **October-March**: *Nishagandhi Nritya Utsav*, Thiruvananthapuram. **November**: *Sangeet Sanmelan*, Chennai; *Sur-Singar Festival*, Mumbai. **December**: *Music Academy Festival and Tamil Isa Sangam*, Chennai.

Dance   The rules for classical dance were laid down in the Natya shastra in the second century BC, which is still one of the bases for modern dance forms. The most common sources for Indian dance are the epics, but there are three essential aspects of the dance itself, Nritta (pure dance), Nrittya (emotional expression) and Natya (drama). The religious influence in dance was exemplified by the tradition of temple dancers, *devadasis*, girls and women who were dedicated to the deity in major temples. In South India there were thousands of *devadasis* associated with temple worship, though the practice fell into disrepute and was banned in independent India. Various dance forms (for example Bharat Natyam, Kathakali, Mohinyattam) developed in the southern states.

There are specific folk dance traditions which are widely performed during festivals.

Land and environment

Geography

The origins of India's landscapes

Only 100 million years ago the Indian Peninsula of which South India is a part was still attached to the great land mass of what geologists call 'Pangaea' alongside South Africa, Australia and Antarctica. Then as the great plates on which the earth's southern continents stood broke up, the Indian Plate started its dramatic shift northwards, eventually colliding with the Asian plate. As the Indian Plate continues to get pushed under the Tibetan Plateau so the Himalaya continue to rise.

The crystalline rocks of the Peninsula are some of the oldest in the world, the **Charnockites** – named after the founder of Kolkata an enthusiastic amateur geologist, Job Charnock – being over 3,100 million years old. Over 60 million years ago a mass of volcanic lava welled up through cracks in the earth's surface and covered some 500,000 sq km including northern Karnataka.

The fault line which severed India from Africa was marked by a north-south ridge of mountains, known today as the Western Ghats, set back from the sea by a coastal plain which is never more than 80 km wide. In the south, the Nilgiris and Palanis are over 2,500 m high.

From the crest line of the **Western Ghats**, the Peninsula slopes generally eastwards, interrupted on its eastern edge by the much more broken groups of hills sometimes referred to as the **Eastern Ghats**. The east flowing rivers have created flat alluvial deltas which have been the basis of successive peninsular kingdoms.

Climate

South India lies well to the south of the Tropic of Cancer. Although much of South India has a climate which ranges fro very warm to hot it is much cooler in the hills. There are also huge contrasts in rainfall, largely reflecting the influence of the Western Ghats, which lie astride the thrust of the monsoon winds..

Background

The term monsoon refers to the wind reversal which replaces the dry northeasterlies, characteristic of winter and spring, with the very warm and wet southwesterlies of the summer. Many myths surround the onset of the monsoon. In fact its arrival is as variable as is the amount of rain which it brings. What makes the Indian monsoon quite exceptional is not its regularity but the depth of moist air which passes over the subcontinent. Over South India, for example, the highly unstable moist airflow is over 6,000 m thick compared with only 2,000 m over Japan, giving rise to the bursts of torrential rain which mark out the wet season.

Winter

In winter high pressure builds up over Central Asia. Most of India is protected from the cold northeast monsoon winds that result by the massive bulk of the Himalaya and daytime temperatures rise sharply in the sun. To the south the winter temperatures have minimum of around 20°C. The winter is a dry season through nearly all of India.

Summer

From March onwards as the sun passes overhead much of South India on the plains is almost unbearably hot. Temperatures are generally over 40°C though it never gets as hot as in North India. It is a time of year to get up to the hills. At the end of May the upper air westerly jet stream, which controls the atmospheric system over the Indo-Gangetic plains through the winter, suddenly breaks down. It re-forms to the north of Tibet, thus allowing very moist southwesterlies to sweep across South India and the Bay of Bengal.

Rainfall

Mean annual maximum precipitation (mm)

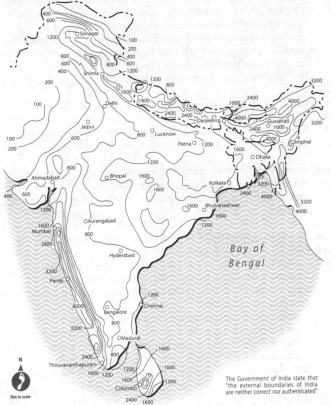

The Government of India state that "the external boundaries of India are neither correct nor authenticated"

The wet seasons

Travel can be seriously disrupted during the monsoon seasons. Be prepared for delays

The monsoon seasons in South India differ from the rest of India. In Kerala, Karnataka and much of inland Andhra Pradesh the main rainy season comes between June and September, as in the rest of India, However in coastal Tamil Nadu and Andhra Pradesh it is the season of the so-called retreating monsoon, between October and December, which brings the heaviest rainfall. The wet season brings an enveloping dampness which makes it very difficult to keep things dry. If you are travelling in the wetter parts of India during the monsoon you need to be prepared for extended periods of torrential rain. However, many parts of India receive a total of under 1,000 mm a year, mainly in the form of heavy isolated showers.

Storms

Some regions of India suffer major storms. Cyclones may hit the east coast causing enormous damage and loss of life, the risk being greatest between the end of October and early December.

Humidity

The coastal regions have humidity levels above 70% for most of the year which can be very uncomfortable. However, sea breezes often bring some relief on the coast itself. Moving north and inland, between December-May humidity drops sharply, often falling as low as 20% during the daytime.

Flora and fauna

Vegetation

India's tropical location and its position astride the wet monsoonal winds ensured that 16 different forest types were represented in India. The most widespread was tropical dry deciduous forest. Areas with more than 1,700 mm of rainfall had tropical moist deciduous, semi-evergreen or wet evergreen forest, while much of the remainder had types ranging from tropical dry deciduous woodland to dry alpine scrub, found at high altitudes. However, today forest cover has been reduced to about 13 of the surface area, mainly the result of the great demand for wood as a fuel.

Deciduous forest

Two types of deciduous tree remain particularly important, **Sal** (*Shorea robusta*), now found mainly in eastern India and **teak** (*Tectona grandis*). Most teak today has been planted. Both are resistant to burning, which helped to protect them where man used fire as a means of clearing the forest. See also box below.

Tropical rainforest

In wetter areas, particularly along the Western Ghats, you can still find **tropical wet evergreen forest**, but even these are now extensively managed. Across the drier areas of the peninsula heavy grazing has reduced the forest cover to little more than thorn scrub.

Mountain forests & grassland

At between 1,000-2,000 m in the eastern hill ranges of India and in Bhutan, for example, wet hill forest includes evergreen oaks and chestnuts. Further west in the foothills of the Himalaya are belts of subtropical pine at roughly the same altitudes. Deodars (*Cedrus deodarus*) form large stands and moist temperate forest, with pines, cedars, firs and spruce, is dominant, giving many of the valleys a beautifully fresh, alpine feel.

Between 3,000-4,000 m alpine forest predominates. Rhododendron are often mixed with other forest types. Birch, juniper, poplars and pine are widespread.

There are several varieties of coarse grassland along the southern edge of the Terai and alpine grasses are important for grazing above altitudes of 2,000 m. A totally distinctive grassland is the bamboo (*Dendo calamus*) region of the eastern Himalaya.

Background

Green gold – India's rare forest resources

India's forests have always been a rich source of products of great economic value. Commercial pressures are also taking their toll. Indian rosewood, much favoured for its use in high quality furniture making, is now restricted to very limited areas in South India. The fragrant sandalwood, still a favourite medium for carving small images of Hindu deities, is so valuable that its exploitation is totally controlled by the government.

Trees

Flowering trees

Many Indian trees are planted along roadsides to provide shade and they often also produce beautiful flowers. The **Silk Cotton Tree** (*Bombax ceiba*), up to 25 m in height, is one of the most dramatic. The pale greyish bark of this buttressed tree usually bears conical spines. It has wide spreading branches and keeps its leaves for most of the year. The flowers, which appear when the tree is leafless, are cup-shaped, with curling, rather fleshy red petals up to 12 cm long while the fruit produce the fine, silky cotton which gives it its name.

Other common trees with red or orange flowers include the Dhak (also called the 'Flame of the forest' or *Palas*), the Gulmohur, the Indian coral tree and the Tulip tree. The smallish (6 m) deciduous **Dhak** (*Butea monosperma*), has light grey bark and a gnarled, twisted trunk and thick, leathery leaves. The large, bright orange and sweet pea-shaped flowers appear on leafless branches. The 8-9 m high umbrella-shaped **Gulmohur** (*Delonix regia*), a native of Madagascar, is grown as a shade tree in towns. The fiery coloured flowers make a magnificent display after the tree has shed its feathery leaves. The scarlet flowers of the **Indian Coral Tree** (*Erythrina indica*) also appear when its branches with thorny bark are leafless. The tall **Tulip Tree** (*Spathodea campanulata*) (not to be confused with the North American one) has a straight, darkish brown, slender trunk. It is usually evergreen except in the drier parts of India. The scarlet bell-shaped, tulip-like, flowers grow in profusion at the ends of the branches from November to March.

Often seen along roadsides the **Jacaranda** (*Jacaranda mimosaefolia*), has attractive feathery foliage and purple-blue thimble-shaped flowers up to 40 mm long. When not in flower it resembles a Gulmohur, but differs in its general shape. The valuable **Tamarind** (*Tamarindus indica*), with a short straight trunk and a spreading crown, often grows along the roadside. An evergreen with feathery leaves, it bears small clusters of yellow and red flowers. The noticeable fruit pods are long, curved and swollen at intervals. In parts of India, the rights to the fruit are auctioned off annually for up to Rs 4,000 (US$100) per tree.

Of these trees the Silk cotton, the Dhak and the Indian coral are native to India. Others were introduced mostly during the last century: the Tulip tree from East Africa, the Jacaranda from Brazil and the Tamarind, possibly from Africa.

Fruit trees

The familiar apple, plum, apricot and cherry grow in the cool upland areas of India. In the warmer plains tropical fruits flourish. The large, spreading **Mango** (*Mangifera indica*) bears the delicious, distinctively shaped fruit that comes in hundreds of varieties. The evergreen **Jackfruit** (*Artocarpus heterophyllus*) has dark green leathery leaves. The huge fruit (up to 90 cm long and 40 cm thick), growing from a short stem directly off the trunk and branches, has a rough, almost prickly, skin and is almost sickly sweet. The **Banana** plant (*Musa*), actually a gigantic herb (up to 5 m high) arising from an underground stem, has large leaves which grow directly off the trunk. Each purplish

Background

flower produces bunches of up to 100 bananas. The **Papaya** (*Carica papaya*) grows to about 4 m with the large hand-shaped leaves clustered near the top. Only the female tree bears the fruit, which hang close to the trunk just below the leaves.

Palm trees   **Coconut Palms** (*Cocos nucifera*) are extremely common all round the coast of India. It has tall (15-25 m), slender, unbranched trunks, feathery leaves and large green or golden fruit with soft white flesh filled with milky water, so different from the brown fibre-covered inner nut which makes its way to Europe. The 10-15 m high **Palmyra palms** (*Borassus flabellifer*), indigenous to South and East India, have very distinctive fan-like leaves, as much as 150 cm across. The fruit, which is smaller than a coconut, is round, almost black and very shiny. The **Betel Nut Palm** (*Areca catechu*) resembles the coconut palm, its slender trunk bearing ring marks left by fallen leaf stems. The smooth, round nuts, only about 3 cm across, grow in large hanging bunches. **Wild Date Palms** (*Phoenix sylvestris*), originally came from North Africa. About 20-25 m tall, the trunks are also marked with the ring bases of the leaves which drop off. The distinctive leaflets which stick out from the central vein give the leaf a spiky appearance. Bunches of dates are only borne by the female tree.

All these palm trees are of considerable **commercial importance**. From the fruit alone the coconut palm produces coir from the outer husk, copra from the fleshy kernel from which coconut oil or coconut butter is extracted, in addition to the desiccated coconut and coconut milk. The sap is fermented to a drink called toddy. A similar drink is produced from the sap of the wild date and the palmyra palms which are also important for sugar production. The fruit of the betel nut palm is wrapped in a special leaf and chewed. The trunks and leaves of all the palms are widely used in building and thatching.

Other trees   Of all Indian trees the **Banyan** (*Ficus benghalensis*) is probably the best known. It is planted by temples, in villages and along roads. The seeds often germinate in the cracks of old walls, the growing roots splitting the wall apart. If it grows in the bark of another tree, it sends down roots towards the ground. As it grows, more roots appear from the branches, until the original host tree is surrounded by a 'cage' which eventually strangles it.

Related to the banyan, the **Pipal** or Peepul (*Ficus religiosa*), also cracks open walls and strangles other trees with its roots. With a smooth grey bark, it too is commonly found near temples and shrines. You can distinguish it from the banyan by the absence of aerial roots and its large, heart shaped leaf with a point tapering into a pronounced 'tail'. It bears abundant 'figs' of a purplish tinge about 1 cm across.

The **Ashok** or **Mast** (*Polyalthia longifolia*) is a tall evergreen which can reach 15 m or more in height. One variety, often seen in avenues, is trimmed and tapers towards the top. The leaves are long, slender and shiny and narrow to a long point.

Acacia trees with their feathery leaves are fairly common in the drier parts of India. The best known is the **Babul** (*Acacia arabica*) with a rough, dark bark. The leaves have long silvery white thorns at the base and consist of many leaflets while the flowers grow in golden balls about 1 cm across.

The **Eucalyptus** or **Gum Tree** (*Eucalyptus grandis*), introduced from Australia in the 19th century, is now widespread and is planted near villages to provide both shade and firewood. There are various forms but all may be readily recognized by their height, their characteristic long, thin leaves which have a pleasant fresh smell and the colourful peeling bark.

The wispy **Casuarina** (*Casuarina*) grows in poor sandy soil, especially on the coast and on village waste land. It has the typical leaves of a pine tree and the cones are small and prickly to walk on. It is said to attract lightning during a thunder storm.

Bamboo (*Bambusa*) strictly speaking is a grass which can vary in size from small ornamental clumps to the enormous wild plant whose stems are so strong and thick that they are used for construction and for scaffolding and as pipes in rural irrigation schemes.

Flowering plants

Common in the Himalaya is the beautiful flowering shrub or tree, which can be as tall as 12 m, the **Rhododendron** which is indigenous to this region. In the wild the commonest colour of the flowers is crimson, but other colours, such as pale purple occur too. From March to May the flowers are very noticeable on the hill sides. Another common wild flowering shrub is **Lantana**. This is a fairly small untidy looking bush with rough, toothed oval leaves, which grow in pairs on the square and prickly stem. The flowers grow together in a flattened head, the ones near the middle being usually yellowish, while those at the rim are pink, pale purple or orange. The fruit is a shiny black berry.

Many other flowering plants are cultivated in parks, gardens and roadside verges. The attractive **Frangipani** (*Plumeria acutifolia*) has a rather crooked trunk and stubby branches, which if broken give out a white milky juice which can be irritating to the skin. The big, leathery leaves taper to a point at each end and have noticeable parallel veins. The sweetly scented waxy flowers are white, pale yellow or pink. The **Bougainvillea** grows as a dense bush or climber with small oval leaves and rather long thorns. The brightly coloured part (which can be pinkish-purple, crimson, orange, yellow et cetera) which appears like a flower is not formed of petals, which are quite small and undistinguished, but by large papery bracts.

The unusual shape of the **Hibiscus**. The trumpet shaped flower as much as 7 or 8 cm across, has a very long 'tongue' growing out from the centre and varies in colour from scarlet to yellow or white. The leaves are somewhat oval or heart shaped with jagged edges. In municipal flowerbeds the commonest planted flower is probably the **Canna Lily**. It has large leaves which are either green or bronzed and lots of large bright red or yellow flowers. The plant can be more than 1 m high.

On many ponds and tanks the floating plants of the **Lotus** (*Nelumbo nucifera*) and the **Water Hyacinth** (*Eichornia crassipes*) are seen. Lotus flowers which rise on stalks above the water can be white, pink or a deep red and up to 25 cm across. The very large leaves either float on the surface or rise above the water. Many dwarf varieties are cultivated. The rather fleshy leaves and lilac flowers of the water hyacinth float to form a dense carpet, often clogging the waterways.

Crops

Of India's enormous variety, the single most widespread crop is **rice** (commonly *Orysa indica*). This forms the most important staple in South and East India, though other cereals and some root crops are also important elsewhere. The rice plant grows in flooded fields called *paddies* and virtually all planting or harvesting is done by hand. Millets are favoured in drier areas inland, while wheat is the most important crop in the northwest.

There are many different sorts of millet, but the ones most often seen are finger millet, pearl millet (bajra) and sorghum (jowar). **Finger millet**, commonly known as ragi (*Eleusine corocana*), is so-called because the ear has several spikes which radiate out, a bit like the fingers of a hand. Usually less than 1 m high, it is grown extensively in the south. Both **pearl millet** (*Pennisetum typhoideum*, known as *bajra* in the north and *cumbu* in Tamil Nadu) and **sorghum** (*Sorghum vulgare*, known as *jowar* in the north and *cholam* in the south) and look superficially similar to the more familiar maize though each can be easily distinguished when the seed heads appear. Pearl millet, mainly grown in the north, has a tall single spike which gives it its other name of bulrush millet. The sorghum bears an open ear at the top of the plant.

Background

👉 *Shining in silk*

Silk has been woven in India for 3,500 years. The belief that the hard to obtain natural fibre was pure, combined with its luxurious feel and rich natural colour led to its importance and its association with religious ritual and ceremonial occasions.

Mulberry silk was probably imported into India from China but wild silks were grown in the Northeastern Hills long before this. In South India, silk has been produced and woven to provide temple deities, and the dancers who served them, with the richest of garments in beautifully vibrant colours emblazoned with gold and silver zari threads.

As early as the 10th century, Tamil Nadu traded in silk with China, but it was Tipu Sultan who spurred Karnataka to produce it commercially in the late 18th century. Karnataka produces about 65% of the country's silk, some of which makes its way to other parts of the country, for example, Varanasi. The typical heavy South Indian silks were once sold by weight. The soft silk made of untwisted yarn is particularly prized for its texture and is ideal for saris. The weaving is still done on handlooms although the vegetables dyes of old have been universally replaced by chemicals.

The sari is 6 yards or 5.5 m in length which has a border along both edges and ends with a distinctive section which hangs over the shoulder, called a pallu. The combination of colours, the width of the border, the patterns and motifs used, all go to make a sari distinctive. Each region (and sometimes, specific towns), produces its own particular style of design, instantly recognizable, and often inspired by beauty in nature, geometric checks, stripes and circles, and also the distinctive temple tower patterns used along the border often in strikingly contrasting colours. They invariably demonstrate mastery of technical skills which have been handed down through generations and it is not surprising that it takes a weaver several weeks to complete each piece on the loom.

The fabric is coveted for its looks, feel and quality and so for any special occasion, silk is the natural choice. Despite rising prices, the demand for it remains, although for the vast majority of the country's population, a family can only afford to buy just one silk sari for a bride for her wedding day.

Another staple grown fairly widely is **cassava** or **tapioca** (*Manihot esculenta*). This is a straight-stemmed bush some 2 m high with dark green leaves divided into thin 'fingers'. The part that is eaten is the root. Cassava is traditionally a famine or reserve crop, because the root can stay in the ground a long time without spoiling and be harvested when needed – a sort of living larder.

To some people India is the home of **tea** (*Camellia sinensis*) which is a very important cash crop. It is grown on a commercial scale in tea gardens in areas of high rainfall, often in highland regions. Over 90 comes from Assam and West Bengal in the Northeast and Tamil Nadu and Kerala in the South. Left to itself tea grows into a tree 10 m tall. In the tea gardens it is pruned to waist height for the convenience of the tea pluckers and forms flat topped bushes, with shiny bright green oval leaves.

Coffee (*Coffea*) is not as widely grown as tea, but high quality arabica is an important crop in parts of South India. Coffee is also a bush, with fairly long, shiny dark green leaves. The white, sweet smelling flowers, which yield the coffee berry, grow in groups along the stems. The coffee berries start off green and turn red when ripe.

Sugar cane (*Saccharum*) is another commercially important crop. This looks like a large grass which stands up to 3 m tall. The crude brown sugar is sold as jaggery and has a flavour of molasses.

Pineapples (*Ananas comosus*) are often grown under trees, for example under coconut palms on the coast. The pineapple fruit grows out of the middle of a rosette of long, spiky leaves.

Of the many spices grown in India, the two climbers pepper and vanilla and the grass-like cardamom are the ones most often seen. The **pepper** vine (*Piper Nigrum*) is indigenous to India where it grows in the warm moist regions. As it is a vine it needs support such as a trellis or a tree. It is frequently planted up against the betel nut palm and appears as a leafy vine with almost heart-shaped leaves. The peppercorns cluster along hanging spikes and are red when ripe. Both black and white pepper is produced from the same plant, the difference being in the processing.

Vanilla (*Vanilla planifolium*), which belongs to the orchid family, also grows up trees for support and attaches itself to the bark by small roots. It is native to South America, but grows well in India in areas of high rainfall. It is a rather fleshy looking plant, with white flowers and long slender pods.

Cardamom (*Elettaria cardomomum*) is another spice native to India and is planted usually under shade. It grows well in highland areas such as Sikkim and the Western Ghats. It is a herbaceous plant looking rather like a big clump of grass, with long leafy shoots springing out of the ground as much as 2-3 m in height. The white flowers grow on separate shoots which can be upright, but usually sprawl on the ground. It is from these flowers that the seed bearing capsules grow.

The **cashew nut** tree (*Anacardium occidentale*) was introduced into India, but now grows wild as well as being cultivated. It is a medium sized tree with bright green, shiny, rounded leaves. The nut grows on a fleshy fruit called a cashew apple and hangs down below this. **Cotton** (*Gossypium*) is important in parts of the west and south. The cotton bush is a small knee-high bush and the cotton boll appears after the flower has withered. This splits when ripe to show the white cotton lint inside.

The **castor oil** plant (*Ricinus Communis*) is cultivated as a cash crop and is planted in small holdings among other crops and along roads and paths. It is a handsome plant up to about 2 m in height, with very large leaves which are divided into some 12 'fingers'. The young stems are reddish and shiny. The well known castor oil is extracted from the bean which is a mottled brown in colour.

Wildlife

India has an extremely rich and varied wildlife, though many species only survive in very restricted environments.

Conservation

Alarmed by the rapid loss of wildlife habitat the Indian Government established the first conservation measures in 1972, followed by the setting up of national parks and reserves. Some 25,000 sq km were set aside in 1973 for Project Tiger. Now tigers are reported to be increasing steadily in several of the game reserves. The same is true of other, less well known species. Their natural habitat has been destroyed both by people and by domesticated animals (there are some 250 million cattle and 50 million sheep and goats). There are now nearly 70 national parks across India as a whole and 330 sanctuaries in addition to programmes of afforestation and coastline preservation. Most parks and sanctuaries are open from October-March; those in the northeast are closed from April-September.

The animals

Of the three Indian big cats the Asiatic lion is virtually confined to a single reserve. The other two, the tiger and leopard, occasionally occur outside. The **tiger** (*Panthera tigris*), which prefers to live in fairly dense cover, is most likely to be glimpsed as it

The big cats

Project Tiger

At one time the tiger roamed freely throughout the sub-continent and at the beginning of this century the estimated population was 40,000 animals. Gradually, due mainly to increased pressure on its habitat by human encroachment and resulting destruction of the habitat, the numbers of this beautiful animal dwindled to fewer than 2,000 in 1972. This was the low point and alarmed at the approaching extinction of the tiger, concerned individuals with the backing of the Government and the World Wildlife Fund, set up Project Tiger in 1973. Initially 9 parks were set up to protect the tiger and this was expanded over the years. However, despite encouraging signs in the first decade the latest tiger census suggests that there are still fewer than 2,500.

lies in long grass or in dappled shadow. The **leopard** or **panther** as it is often called in India (*Panthera pardus*), is far more numerous than the tiger, but is even more elusive. The all black form is not uncommon in areas of higher rainfall such as the Western Ghats and Northeast India, though the typical form is seen more often.

Elephant & rhino The **Indian elephant** (*Elephas maximus*) has been domesticated for centuries and today it is still used as a beast of burden. In the wild it inhabits hilly country with forest and bamboo, where it lives in herds which can number as many as 50 or more individuals. They are adaptable animals and can live in all sorts of forest, except those in the dry areas. Wild elephants are mainly confined to reserves, but occasionally move out into cultivation, where they cause great damage.

Deer, antelope, oxen & their relatives Once widespread, these animals are now largely confined to the reserves. The male deer (stags) carry antlers which are branched, each 'spike' on the antler being called a tine. Antelopes and oxen, on the other hand, have horns which are not branched.

Deer There are several deer species in India, mainly confined to very restricted ranges. Three species are quite common. The largest and one of the most widespread, is the magnificent **sambar** (*Cervus unicolor*) which can be up to 150 cm at the shoulder. It has a noticeably shaggy coat, which varies in colour from brown with a yellowish or grey tinge through to dark, almost black, in the older stags. The sambar is often found on wooded hillsides and lives in groups of up to 10 or so, though solitary individuals are also seen.

The much smaller **chital** or **spotted deer** (*Axis axis*), only about 90 cm tall, are seen in herds of 20 or so, in grassy areas. The bright rufous coat spotted with white is unmistakable; the stags carry antlers with three tines.

The **nilgai** or **blue bull** (*Boselaphus tragocamelus*) is about 140 cm at the shoulder and is rather horse-like, with a sloping back. The male has a dark grey coat, while the female is sandy coloured. Both sexes have two white marks on the cheek, white throats and a white ring just above each hoof. The male carries short, forward-curving horns and has a tuft of long black hairs on the front of the neck. They occur in small herds on grassy plains and scrub land.

Oxen The commonest member of the oxen group is the **Asiatic wild buffalo** or water buffalo (*Bubalus bubalis*). About 170 cm at the shoulder, the wild buffalo, which can be aggressive, occurs in herds on grassy plains and swamps near rivers and lakes. The black coat and wide-spreading curved horns, carried by both sexes, are distinctive.

The **Indian bison** or **gaur** (*Bos gaurus*) can be up to 200 cm at the shoulder with a heavy muscular ridge across it. Both sexes carry curved horns. The young gaur is a light sandy colour, which darkens with age, the old bulls being nearly black with

Elephants – a future in the wild?

Elephants are both the most striking of the mammals and the most economically important. The Indian elephant (Elephas maximas), smaller than the African, is the world's second largest land mammal. Unlike the African elephant, the male rarely reaches a height of over 3 m; it also has smaller ears. Other distinguishing features include the high domed forehead, the rounded shape of the back and the smooth trunk with a single 'finger' at the end. Also the female is often tuskless or bears small ones called tushes and even the male is sometimes tuskless (makhnas). The Indian elephant has 5 nails on its front feet and 4 on the back (compared to the African's 4 and 3 respectively). There are approximately 6,500 elephants living in the wild in

northern West Bengal, Assam and Bhutan. There are a further 2,000 in Central India and 6,000 in the three South Indian states of Kerala, Tamil Nadu and Karnataka. There are plans for a new elephant reserve on the borders of Bhutan and India.

The loss of habitat has made wild elephants an increasing danger to humans and about 300 people are killed every year by wild elephants, mainly in the North-east. The tribal people have developed skilled techniques for capturing and training wild elephants, which have been domesticated in India for about 5,000 years. They need a lot of feeding – about 18 hours a day. Working elephants are fed on a special diet, by hand straight at the mouth and they eat between 100 and 300 kilograms per day.

pale sandy coloured 'socks' and a pale forehead. Basically hill animals, they live in forests and bamboo clumps and emerge from the trees to graze.

Others The **wild boar** (*Sus scrofa*) has mainly black body and a pig-like head; the hairs thicken down the spine to form a sort of mane. A mature male stands 90 cm at the shoulder and, unlike the female, bears tusks. The young are striped. Quite widespread, they often cause great destruction among crops.

One of the most important scavengers of the open countryside, the **striped hyena** (*Hyena hyena*) usually comes out at night. It is about 90 cm at the shoulder with a large head with a noticeable crest of hairs along its sloping back.

The **common giant flying squirrel** are common in the larger forests of India, except in the northeast (*Petaurista petaurista*). The body can be 45 cm long and the tail another 50 cm. They glide from tree to tree using a membrane stretching from front leg to back leg which acts like a parachute

The **common langur** (*Presbytis entellus*), 75 cm, is a long-tailed monkey with a distinctive black face, hands and feet. Usually a forest dweller, it is found almost throughout India. The Nilgiri langur (Presbytis johni) is slightly taller at 80 cm, with glossy balck hair and a yellowish brown head. Females have a clearly visible patch of white hair on the inside of their thighs. The Nilgiri langur has made the dense evergreen sholas its major habitat, but the beauty of its fur has sadly made it prized by hunters. The **lion tailed macaque** (*Macaca mulatta*), 50-60 cm, has a striking mane of grey hair, a glossy black coat and a tufted tail – hence its name. It lives in the higher hills in herds of up to 20, and the male's voice is said to sound almost human, but it is yet another endangered species..

In towns & villages

Palm squirrels are very common. The **five-striped** (*Funambulus pennanti*) and the **three-striped palm squirrel** (*Funambulus palmarum*), are both about the same size (30 cm long, about half of which is tail). The five-striped is usually seen in towns.

The two bats most commonly seen in towns differ enormously in size. The larger so-called **flying fox** (*Pteropus giganteus*) has a wing span of 120 cm. These

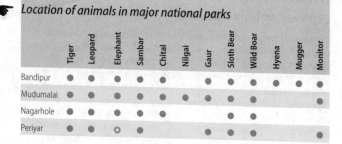

Location of animals in major national parks

	Tiger	Leopard	Elephant	Sambar	Chital	Nilgai	Gaur	Sloth Bear	Wild Boar	Hyena	Mugger	Monitor
Bandipur	●	●	●	●	●		●	●	●	●	●	●
Mudumalai	●	●	●	●	●		●	●	●			●
Nagarhole	●	●	●	●			●		●			
Periyar	●	●	✿	●			●	●	●			●

● good place to see this species   ✿ hard ground Barasingha

fruit-eating bats, found throughout, except in the driest areas, roost in large noisy colonies where they look like folded umbrellas hanging from the trees. In the evening they can be seen leaving the roost with slow measured wing beats. The much smaller **Indian pipistrelle** (*Pipistrellus coromandra*), with a wing span of about 15 cm, is an insect eater. It comes into the house at dusk, roosting under eaves and has a fast, erratic flight.

The **jackal** (*Canis aureus*), a lone scavenger in towns and villages, looks like a cross between a dog and a fox and varies in colour from shades of brown through to black. The bushy tail has a dark tip.

The **common mongoose** (*Herpestes edwardsi*) lives in scrub and open jungle. It kills snakes, but will also take rats, mice and chicken. Tawny coloured with a grey grizzled tinge, it is about 90 cm in length, of which half is pale-tipped tail.

The **sloth bear** (*Melursus ursinus*), about 75 cm at the shoulder, lives in broken forest, but may be seen on a lead accompanying a street entertainer who makes it 'dance' to music as a part of an act. They have a long snout, a pendulous lower lip and a shaggy black coat with a yellowish V-shaped mark on the chest.

If you take a boat trip look out for the **common dolphin** (Delphinus delphis> as they comes to the surface to breathe.

Birds

Town & village birds

Some birds perform a useful function scavenging and clearing refuse. One of the most widespread is the brown **pariah kite** (*Milvus migrans*, 65 cm). The more handsome chestnut and white **brahminy kite** (*Haliastur indus*, 48 cm) is largely confined to the waterside. The common brown **white-backed vulture** (*Gyps bengalensis*, 90 cm) looks ungainly and has a bare and scrawny head and neck. The smaller **scavenger vulture** (*Neophron percnopterus*, 65 cm) is mainly white, but often has dirty looking plumage and the bare head and neck of all vultures. In flight its wedge-shaped tail and black and white colouring are characteristic.

The **house crow** (*Corvus splendens*, 45 cm) on the other hand is a very smart looking bird with a grey body and black tail, wings, face and throat. It occurs in almost every town and village in India. The **jungle crow** (*Corvus macrorhynchos*, 50 cm) originally a bird of the countryside has started to move into populated areas and in the hill stations tends to replace the house crow. Unlike the house crow it is a glossy black all over and has a much deeper, hoarser caw.

The **feral pigeon**, or **blue rock dove** (*Columba livia*, 32 cm), found throughout the world, is generally a slaty grey in colour. It invariably has two dark bars on the wing and a white rump. The **little brown dove** (*Streptopelia senegalensis*, 25 cm) is bluey grey and brown above, with a pink head and underparts and a speckled pattern on the

Background

neck. The **collared dove** (*Streptopelia decaocto*, 30 cm) with a distinct half collar on the back of its neck, is common, especially in the drier parts of India.

Bulbuls are common in gardens and parks. The **red-vented bulbul** (*Pycnonotus cafer*, 20 cm), a mainly brown bird, can be identified by the slight crest and a bright red patch under the tail. The **house sparrow** (*Passer domesticus*, 15 cm) can be seen in towns throughout the mainland. The ubiquitous **common myna** (*Acridotheres tristis*, 22 cm), feeds on lawns, especially after rain or watering. Look for the white under the tail and the bare yellow skin around the eye, yellow bill and legs and in flight the large white wing patch.

A less common, but more striking bird also seen feeding in open spaces, is the **hoopoe** (*Upupa epops*, 30 cm), easily identified by its sandy plumage with black and white stripes and long thin curved bill. The marvellous fan-shaped crest is sometimes raised. Finally there is a member of the cuckoo family which is heard more often than seen. The **koel** (*Eudynamys scolopacea*, 42 cm), is commonly heard during the hot weather – kuoo-kuoo-kuoo, the double note starts off low and flute-like, rises in pitch and intensity, then suddenly stops, only to start all over again. The male is all black with a greenish bill and a red eye; the female streaked and barred.

The *jheels* (marshes or swamps) of India form one of the richest bird habitats in the world. Cormorants abound; the commonest, the **little cormorant** (*Phalacrocorax niger*, 50 cm) is found on most inland waters. An almost entirely black bird with just a little white on the throat, it has a long tail and a hooked bill. The **coot** (*Fulica atra*, 40 cm), another common black bird, seen especially in winter has a noticeable white shield on the forehead.

The magnificent **sarus crane** (*Grus antigone*, 150 cm) is one of India's tallest birds. It is widespread all year round across northern India, almost invariably in pairs. The bare red head and long red legs combined with its height and grey plumage make it easy to identify. The commonest migrant crane is probably the **common crane** (*Grus grus*, 120 cm), present only in winter, often in large flocks. It has mainly grey plumage with a black head and neck. There is a white streak running down the side of the neck and above the eye is a tuft of red feathers.

The **openbill stork** (*Anastomus oscitans*, 80 cm) and the **painted stork** (*Ibis leucocephalus*, 100 cm) are common too and are spotted breeding in large colonies. The former is white with black wing feathers and a curiously shaped bill. The latter mainly white, has a pinkish tinge on the back and dark marks on the wings and a broken black band on the lower chest. The bare yellow face and yellow down-curved bill are conspicuous.

By almost every swamp, ditch or rice paddy up to about 1,200 m you will see the **paddy bird** (*Ardeola grayii*, 45 cm). An inconspicuous, buff-coloured bird, it is easily overlooked as it stands hunched up by the waterside. As soon as it takes off, its white wings and rump make it very noticeable. The **bronze-winged jacana** (*Metopidius indicus*, 27 cm) has very long toes which enable it to walk on the floating leaves of water-lilies and there is a noticeable white streak over and above the eye. Village ponds often have their resident bird.

The commonest and most widespread of the Indian kingfishers is the jewel-like **common kingfisher** (*Alcedo atthis*, 18 cm). With its brilliant blue upperparts and orange breast it is usually seen perched on a twig or a reed beside the water.

The **cattle egret** (*Bubulcus ibis*, 50 cm), a small white heron, is usually seen near herds of cattle, frequently perched on the backs of the animals. Equal in height to the sarus crane is the impressive, but ugly **adjutant stork** (*Leptopilos dubius*, 150 cm). This often dishevelled bird is a scavenger and is thus seen near rubbish dumps

Water & waterside birds

Open grassland, light woodland & cultivated land

Background

and carcasses. It has a naked red head and neck, a huge bill and a large fleshy pouch which hangs down the front of the neck.

The **rose-ringed parakeet** (*Psittacula krameri*, 40 cm) is found throughout India up to about 1,500 m while the **pied myna** (*Sturnus contra*, 23 cm) is restricted to northern and central India. The rose-ringed parakeet often forms huge flocks, an impressive sight coming in to roost. The long tail is noticeable both in flight and when the bird is perched. They can be very destructive to crops, but are attractive birds which are frequently kept as pets. The pied myna, with its smart black and white plumage is conspicuous, usually in small flocks in grazing land or cultivation. It feeds on the ground and on village rubbish dumps. The all black **drongo** (*Dicrurus adsimilis*, 30 cm) is almost invariably seen perched on telegraph wires or bare branches. Its distinctively forked tail makes it easy to identify.

Weaver birds are a family of mainly yellow birds, all remarkable for the intricate nests they build. The most widespread is the **baya weaver** (*Ploceus philippinus*, 15cm) which nest in large colonies, often near villages. The male in the breeding season combines a black face and throat with a contrasting yellow top of the head and the yellow breast band. In the non-breeding season both sexes are brownish sparrow-like birds.

Hill birds Land above about 1,500 m supports a distinct range of species, although some birds, such as the ubiquitous **common myna**, are found in the highlands as well as in the lower lying terrain.

The highland equivalent of the red-vented bulbul is the **white-cheeked bulbul** (*Pycnonotus leucogenys*, 20 cm) which is found in gardens and woodland in the Himalaya up to about 2,500 m and as far south as Bombay. It has white underparts with a yellow patch under the tail. The black head and white cheek patches are distinctive. The crest varies in length and is most prominent in birds found in Kashmir, where it is very common in gardens. The **red-whiskered bulbul** (*Pycnonotus jocosus*, 20 cm) is widespread in the Himalaya and the hills of South India up to about 2,500 m. Its pronounced pointed crest, which is sometimes so long that it flops forward towards the bill, white underparts and red and white 'whiskers' serve to distinguish it. It has a red patch under the tail.

In the summer the delightful **verditer flycatcher** (*Muscicapa thalassina*, 15 cm) is a common breeding bird in the Himalaya up to about 3,000 m. It is tame and confiding, often builds its nest on verandahs and is seen perching on telegraph wires. In winter it is much more widely distributed throughout the country. It is an active little bird which flicks its tail up and down in a characteristic manner. The male is all bright blue green with somewhat darker wings and a black patch in front of the eyes. The female is similar, but duller.

Another species associated with man is the **white wagtail** (*Motacilla alba*, 21 cm), very common in the Himalayan summer up to about 3,000 m. It is always found near water, by streams and lakes, on floating vegetation and among the house boats in Kashmir. Its black and white plumage and constantly wagging tail make it easy to identify.

Yet another species common in Kashmir and in other Himalayan hill stations is the **red-billed blue magpie** (*Urocissa erythrorhyncha*, 65 cm). With a long tail and pale blue plumage, contrasting with its black head, it is usually seen in small flocks as it flies from tree to tree. This is not so much a garden bird, but prefers tea gardens, open woodland and cultivation.

Jungle fowl and pheasants The highlands of India, especially the Himalaya, are the home of the ancestors of domestic hens and also of numerous beautiful pheasants. These are mainly forest dwellers and are not easy to see as they tend to be shy and wary of man.

Last but not least, mention must be made of India's national bird, the magnificent and well-known **Peafowl** (*Pavo cristatus*, male 210 cm, female 100 cm), which is more commonly known as the peacock. Semi-domesticated birds are commonly seen and heard around towns and villages, especially in the northwest of India. In the wild it favours hilly jungles and dense scrub.

Reptiles and amphibians

India is famous for its reptiles, especially its snakes which feature in many stories and legends. In reality, snakes keep out of the way of people. One of the most common is the **Indian rock python** (*Python molurus*) a 'constrictor' which kills it's prey by suffocation. Usually about 4 m in length, they can be much longer. Their docile nature make them favourites of snake handlers.

The other large snakes favoured by street entertainers are cobras. The various species all have a hood which is spread when the snake draws itself up to strike. They are all highly venomous and the snake charmers prudently de-fang them to render them harmless. The best known is probably the **spectacled cobra** (*Naja naja*), which has a mark like a pair of spectacles on the back of its hood. The largest venomous snake in the world is the **king cobra** (*Ophiophagus hannah*) which is 5 m in length. It is usually brown, but can vary from cream to black and lacks the spectacle marks of the other. In their natural state cobras are generally inhabitants of forest regions.

Equally venomous, but much smaller, the **common krait** (*Bungarus caeruleus*) is just over 1 m in length. The slender, shiny, blue-black snake has thin white bands which can sometimes be almost indiscernible. They are found all over the country except in the northeast where the cannibalistic **banded krait** with bold yellowish and black bands have virtually eradicated them.

In houses everywhere you cannot fail to see the **gecko** (*Hemidactylus*). This small harmless, primitive lizard is active after dark. It lives in houses behind pictures and curtain rails and at night emerges to run across the walls and ceilings to hunt the night flying insects which form its main prey. It is not usually more than about 14 cm long, with a curiously transparent, pale yellowish brown body. At the other end of the scale is the **monitor lizard** (*Varanus*), which can grow to 2 m in length. They can vary from a colourful black and yellow, to plain or speckled brown. They live in different habitats from cultivation and scrub to waterside places and desert.

The most widespread crocodile is the freshwater **mugger** or Marsh crocodile (*Crocodilus palustrus*) which grows to 3-4 m in length. The only similar fresh water species is the **gharial** (*Gavialis gangeticus*) which lives in large, fast flowing rivers. Twice the length of the mugger, it is a fish-eating crocodile with a long thin snout and, in the case of the male, an extraordinary bulbous growth on the end of the snout. The enormous, aggressive **estuarine** or **saltwater crocodile** (*Crocodilus porosus*) is now restricted to the brackish waters of the Sundarbans, on the east coast and in the Andaman and Nicobar Islands. It grows to 7 m in length and is much sleeker looking than the rather docile mugger.

Background

Footnotes

11

Footnotes

Glossary

Words in *italics* are common elements of words, often making up part of a place name

A

aarti (arati) Hindu worship with lamps

abacus square or rectangular table resting on top of a pillar

abad peopled

acanthus thick-leaved plant, common decoration on pillars, esp Greek

achalam hill (Tamil)

acharya religious teacher

agarbathi incense

Agastya legendary sage who brought the Vedas to South India

Agni Vedic fire divinity, intermediary between gods and men; guardian of the Southeast

ahimsa non-harming, non-violence

alinda verandah

ambulatory processional path

amla/amalaka circular ribbed pattern (based on a gourd) at the top of a temple tower

amrita ambrosia; drink of immortality

ananda joy

Ananda the Buddha's chief disciple

Ananta a huge snake on whose coils Vishnu rests

anda literally 'egg', spherical part of the stupa

Andhaka demon killed by Siva

anicut irrigation channel (Tamil)

anna (ana) one sixteenth of a rupee (still occasionally referred to)

antarala vestibule, chamber in front of shrine or cella

antechamber chamber in front of the sanctuary

apsara celestial nymph

apse semi-circular plan, as in apse of a church

arabesque ornamental decoration with intertwining lines

aram pleasure garden

architrave horizontal beam across posts or gateways

ardha mandapam chamber in front of main hall of temple

Ardhanarisvara Siva represented as half-male and half-female

Arjuna hero of the Mahabharata, to whom Krishna delivered the Bhagavad Gita

arrack alcoholic spirit fermented from potatoes or grain

aru river (Tamil)

Aruna charioteer of Surya, the Sun God; Red

Aryans literally 'noble' (Sanskrit); prehistoric peoples who settled in Persia and North India

asana a seat or throne (Buddha's) pose

ashram hermitage or retreat

Ashta Matrikas The eight mother goddesses who attended on Siva or Skanda

astanah threshold

atman philosophical concept of universal soul or spirit

atrium court open to the sky in the centre In modern architecture, enclosed in glass

avatara 'descent'; incarnation of a divinity

ayacut irrigation command area (Tamil)

ayah nursemaid, especially for children

B

baba old man

babu clerk

bada cubical portion of a temple up to the roof or spire

badlands eroded landscape

bagh garden

bahadur title, meaning 'the brave'

baksheesh tip 'bribe'

baluster (balustrade) a small column supporting a handrail

bandh a strike

Bangla (Bangaldar) curved roof, based on thatched roofs in Bengal

banian vest

baoli or vav rectangular well surrounded by steps

baradari literally 'twelve pillared', a pavilion with columns

barrel-vault semi-cylindrical shaped roof or ceiling

bas-relief carving of low projection

basement lower part of walls, usually with decorated mouldings

basti Jain temple

bazar market

bedi (vedi) altar/platform for reading holy texts

begum Muslim princess/woman's courtesy title

beki circular stone below the amla in the finial of a roof

belvedere summer house; small room on a house roof

bhadra flat face of the sikhara (tower)

Bhagavad-Gita Song of the Lord; section of the Mahabharata

Bhagiratha the king who prayed to Ganga to descend to earth

bhai brother

Bhairava Siva, the Fearful

bhakti adoration of a deity

bhang Indian hemp

Bharata half-brother of Rama

bhavan building or house

bhikku Buddhist monk

Bhima Pandava hero of the Mahabharata, famous for his strength

Bhimsen Deity worshipped for his strength and courage

bhogamandapa the refectory hall of a temple

bhumi literally earth; a horizontal moulding of a sikhara

bidi (beedi) tobacco leaf cigarette

bigha measure of land – normally about one-third of an acre

bo-tree (or Bodhi) *Ficus religiosa*, pipal tree associated with the Buddha

Bodhisattva Enlightened One, destined to become Buddha

bodi tuft of hair on back of the shaven head (also *tikki*)

Brahma Universal self-existing power; Creator in the Hindu Triad.

Brahmachari religious student, accepting rigorous discipline (eg chastity)

Brahman (Brahmin) highest Hindu (and Jain) caste of priests

Brahmanism ancient Indian religion, precursor of modern Hinduism

Buddha The Enlightened One; founder of Buddhism

bund an embankment

bundh (literally closed) a strike

burj tower or bastion

burqa (burkha) over-dress worn by Muslim women observing purdah

bustee slum

C

cantonment planned military or civil area in town

capital upper part of a column

caryatid sculptured human female figure used as a support for columns

catamaran log raft, logs (*maram*) tied (*kattu*) together (Tamil)

cave temple rock-cut shrine or monastery

cella small chamber, compartment for the image of a deity

cenotaph commemorative monument, usually an open domed pavilion

chadar sheet worn as clothing

chai tea

chaitya large arched opening in the façade of a hall or Buddhist temple

chajja overhanging cornice or eaves

chakra sacred Buddhist wheel of the law; also Vishnu's discus

Chamunda terrifying form of the goddess Durga

Chandra Moon; a planetary deity

chapatti unleavened Indian bread cooked on a griddle

chaprassi messenger or orderly usually wearing a badge

char sand-bank or island in a river

char bagh formal Mughal garden, divided into quarters

char bangla (char-chala) 'four temples' in Bengal, built like huts

charan foot print

charka spinning wheel

charpai 'four legs' – wooden frame string bed

chatt(r)a ceremonial umbrella on stupa (Buddhist)

chauki recessed space between pillars; entrance

chaukidar (chowkidar) night-watchman; guard

chaultri (choultry) travellers' rest house (Telugu)

chaumukha Jain sanctuary with a quadruple image, approached through four doorways

chauri fly-whisk, symbol for royalty

chauth 25% tax raised for revenue by Marathas

cheri outcaste settlement; slum (Tamil Nadu)

chhatri umbrella shaped dome or pavilion

chhetri (kshatriya) Hindu warrior caste

chit sabha hall of wisdom (Tamil)

chitrakar picture maker

chlorite soft greenish stone that hardens on exposure

choli blouse

chowk (chauk) a block; open place in a city where the market is held

chunam lime plaster or stucco made from burnt seashells

circumambulation clockwise movement around a shrine

clerestory upper section of the walls of a building which allows light in

cloister passage usually around an open square

coir fibre from coconut husk

corbel horizontal block supporting a vertical structure or covering an opening

cornice horizontal band at the top of a wall

crenellated having battlements

crewel work chain stitching

crore 10 million

cupola small dome

curvilinear gently curving shape, generally of a tower

cusp,

cusped projecting point between small sections of an arch

D

daal lentils, pulses

dacoit bandit

dada (dadu) grandfather; elder brother

dado part of a pedestal between its base and cornice

dahi yoghurt

dais raised platform

dak bungalow rest house for officials

dak post

dakini sorceress

Dakshineshvara Lord of the South; name of Siva

dan gift

dandi wooden 'seat' carried by bearers

darbar (durbar) a royal gathering

dargah a Muslim tomb complex

darshan (darshana) viewing of a deity

darwaza gateway, door

Dasara (dassara/dussehra/dassehra) 10 day festival (Sep-Oct)

Dasaratha King of Ayodhya and father of Rama

Dattatraya syncretistic deity; an incarnation of Vishnu, a teacher of Siva, or a cousin of the Buddha

daulat khana treasury

dentil small block used as part of a cornice

dervish member of Muslim brotherhood, committed to poverty

deval memorial pavilion built to mark royal funeral pyre

devala temple or shrine (Buddhist or Hindu)

devasthanam temple trust

Devi Goddess; later, the Supreme Goddess

dhansak Parsi dish made with lentils

dharamshala (dharmsala) pilgrims' rest-house

dharma moral and religious duty

dharmachakra wheel of 'moral' law (Buddhist)

dhobi washerman

dhol drums

dholi (dhooli) swinging chair on a pole, carried by bearers

dhoti loose loincloth worn by Indian men

dhyana meditation

digambara literally 'sky-clad' Jain sect in which the monks go naked

dighi village pond (Bengal)

dikka raised platform around ablution tank

dikpala guardian of one of the cardinal directions mostly appearing in a group of eight

dikshitar person who makes oblations or offerings

dipdan lamp pillar

distributary river that flows away from main channel

divan (diwan) smoking-room; also a chief minister

Diwali festival of lights (Oct-Nov)

diwan-i-am hall of public audience

diwan-i-khas hall of private audience

diwan chief financial minister

doab interfluve, land between two rivers

dokra tribal name for lost wax metal casting (cire perdu)

dosai (dosa) thin pancake

double dome composed of an inner and outer shell of masonry

Draupadi wife-in-common of the five Pandava brothers in the Mahabharata

drug (*durg*) fort (Tamil, Telugu)

dry masonry stones laid without mortar

duar (dwar) door, gateway

Durga principal goddess of the Shakti cult

durrie (dhurrie) thick handloom rug

durwan watchman

dvarpala doorkeeper

dvipa lamp-column, generally of stone or brass-covered wood

F

faience coloured tilework, earthenware or porcelain

fakir Muslim religious mendicant

fan-light fan-shaped window over door

fenestration with windows or openings

filigree ornamental work or delicate tracery

finial emblem at the summit of a stupa, tower, dome, or at the end of a parapet

firman edict or grant issued by a sovereign

foliation ornamental design derived from foliage

frieze horizontal band of figures or decorative designs

G

gable end of an angled roof

gaddi throne

gadi/gari car, cart, train

gali (galli) lane; an alley

gana child figures in art

Gandharva semi-divine flying figure; celestial musician

Ganesh (Ganapati) elephant-headed son of Siva and Parvati

Ganga goddess personifying the Ganga river

ganj market

ganja Indian hemp

gaon village

garbhagriha literally `womb-chamber'; a temple sanctuary

garh fort

Garuda Mythical eagle, half-human Vishnu's vehicle

Gauri `Fair One'; Parvati

Gaurishankara Siva with Parvati

ghagra (ghongra) long flared skirt

ghanta bell

ghat hill range, hill road; landing place; steps on the river bank

ghazal Urdu lyric poetry/love songs, often erotic

ghee clarified butter for cooking

gherao industrial action, surrounding home or office of politician or industrial manager

giri hill

Gita

Govinda Jayadeva's poem of the Krishnalila

godown warehouse

gola conical-shaped storehouse

gompa Tibetan Buddhist monastery

Gopala (Govinda) cowherd; a name of Krishna

Gopis cowherd girls; milk maids who played with Krishna

gopuram towered gateway in South Indian temples

Gorakhnath historically, an 11th-century yogi who founded a Saivite cult; an incarnation of Siva

gram chick pea, pulse

gram village; gramadan, gift of village

gudi temple (Karnataka)

gumbaz (gumbad) dome

gumpha monastery, cave temple

gur palm sugar

guru teacher; spiritual leader, Sikh religious leader

gurudwara (literally `entrance to the house of God'); Sikh religious complex

H

Haj (Hajj) annual Muslim pilgrimage to Mecca

hakim judge; a physician (usually Muslim)

halwa a special sweet meat

hammam Turkish bath

handi Punjabi dish cooked in a pot

Hanuman Monkey devotee of Rama; bringer of success to armies

Hara (Hara Siddhi) Siva

harem women's quarters (Muslim), from `haram', Arabic for `forbidden by law'

Hari Vishnu Harihara, Vishnu- Siva as a single divinity

Hariti goddess of prosperity and patroness of children, consort of Kubera

harmika the finial of a stupa in the form of a pedestal where the shaft of the honorific umbrella was set

hartal general strike

Hasan the murdered eldest son of Ali, commemorated at Muharram

hat (haat) market

hathi pol elephant gate

hathi (hati) elephant

havildar army sergeant

hindola swing

hippogryph fabulous griffin-like creature with body of a horse

Hiranyakashipu Demon king killed by Narasimha

hiti a water channel; a bath or tank with water spouts

Holi spring festival (Feb-Mar)

hookah `hubble bubble' or smoking vase

howdah seat on elephant's back, sometimes canopied

hundi temple offering

Hussain the second murdered son of Ali, commemorated at Muharram

huzra a Muslim tomb chamber

hypostyle hall with pillars

E

eave overhang that shelters a porch or verandah

ek the number 1, a symbol of unity

ekka one horse carriage

epigraph carved inscription

eri tank (Tamil)

I

lat pillar, column

icon statue or image of worship

Id principal Muslim festivals

Idgah open space for the Id prayers

idli steamed rice cake (Tamil)

ikat `resist-dyed' woven fabric

imam Muslim religious leader

Indra King of the gods; God of rain; guardian of the East

Ishana Guardian of the North East

Ishvara Lord; Siva

iwan main arch in mosque

J

jadu magic

jaga
mohan audience hall or ante-chamber of an Orissan temple

Jagadambi literally Mother of the World; Parvati

jagati railed parapet

jaggery brown sugar, made from palm sap

jahaz ship; building in form of ship

jala durga water fort

jali literally `net'; any lattice or perforated pattern

jamb vertical side slab of doorway

Jambudvipa Continent of the Rose-Apple Tree; the earth

Jami masjid (Jama, Jumma) Friday mosque, for congregational worship

Jamuna Hindu goddess who rides a tortoise; river

Janaka Father of Sita

jangha broad band of sculpture on the outside of the temple wall

jarokha balcony

jataka
stories accounts of the previous lives of the Buddha

jawab literally `answer,' a building which duplicates another to provide symmetry

jawan army recruit, soldier

jaya stambha victory tower

jheel (jhil) lake; a marsh; a swamp

jhilmil projecting canopy over a window or door opening

-ji (jee) honorific suffix added to names out of reverence and/or politeness; also abbreviated `yes' (Hindi/Urdu)

jihad striving in the way of god; holy war by Muslims against non-believers

Jogini mystical goddess

Jyotirlinga luminous energy of Siva manifested at 12 holy places, miraculously formed lingams

K

kabalai (kavalai) well irrigation using bullock power (Tamil Nadu)

kabigan folk debate in verse

kachcha man's `under-shorts' (one of five Sikh symbols)

kacheri (kutchery) a court; an office for public business

kadal wooden bridge (Kashmir)

kadhi savoury yoghurt curry (Gujarat/North India)

kadu forest (Tamil)

Kailasa mountain home of Siva

kalamkari special painted cotton hanging from Andhra

kalasha pot-like finial of a tower

Kali literally `black'; terrifying form of the goddess Durga, wearing a necklace of skulls/heads

Kalki future incarnation of Vishnu on horseback

kalyanamandapa marriage hall

kameez women's shirt

kanga comb (one of five Sikh symbols)

kankar limestone pieces, used for road making

kapok the silk cotton tree

kara steel bracelet (one of five Sikh symbols)

karma impurity resulting from past misdeeds

Kartikkeya (Kartik) Son of Siva, God of war

kati-roll Muslim snack of meat rolled in a `paratha' bread

keep tower of a fort, stronghold

kere tank (Kanarese)

keystone central wedge-shaped block in a masonry arch

khadi woven cotton cloth made from home-spun cotton (or silk) yarn

khal creek; a canal

khana suffix for room/office/place; also food or meal

khanqah Muslim (Sufi) hospice

kharif monsoon season crop

kheda enclosure in which wild elephants are caught; elephant depot

khondalite crudely grained basalt

kirpan sabre, dagger (one of five Sikh symbols)

kirti-stambha `pillar of fame,' free standing pillar in front of temple

kohl antimony, used as eye shadow

konda hill (Telugu)

kot (kota/kottai/kotte) fort

kothi house

kotla citadel

kovil (koil) temple (Tamil)

Krishna Eighth incarnation of Vishnu

kritis South Indian devotional music

Kubera Chief yaksha; keeper of the treasures of the earth, Guardian of the North

kulam tank or pond (Tamil)

kumar a young man

Kumari Virgin; Durga

kumbha a vase-like motif, pot

Kumbhayog auspicious time for bathing to wash away sins

kumhar (kumar) potter

kund lake, well or pool

kundan jewellery setting of uncut gems (Rajasthan)

kuppam hamlet (Tamil)

kurta Punjabi shirt

kurti-kanchali small blouse

kutcha (cutcha/kacha) raw; crude; unpaved; built with sun-dried bricks

kwabgah bedroom; literally `palace of dreams'

L

lakh 100,000

Lakshmana younger brother of Rama

Lakshmi Goddess of wealth and good fortune, consort of Vishnu

Lakulisha founder of the Pashupata sect, believed to be an incarnation of Siva

lassi iced yoghurt drink

lath monolithic pillar

lathi bamboo stick with metal bindings, used by police

lena cave, usually a rock-cut sanctuary

lingam (linga) Siva as the phallic emblem

lintel horizontal beam over doorway

liwan cloisters of a mosque

Lokeshwar `Lord of the World', Avalokiteshwara to Buddhists and form of Siva to Hindus

lunette semicircular window opening

lungi wrapped-around loin cloth, normally checked

M

madrassa Islamic theological school or college

mahamandapam large enclosed hall in front of main shrine

maha great

Mahabharata Sanskrit epic about the battle between the Pandavas and Kauravas

Mahabodhi Great Enlightenment of Buddha

Mahadeva literally `Great Lord'; Siva

mahal palace, grand building

mahant head of a monastery

maharaja great king

maharana Rajput clan head

maharani great queen

maharishi (Maharshi) literally `great teacher'

Mahavira literally `Great Hero'; last of the 24 Tirthankaras, founder of Jainism

Mahayana The Greater Vehicle; form of Buddhism practised in East Asia, Tibet and Nepal

Mahesha (Maheshvara) Great Lord; Siva

Mahisha Buffalo demon killed by Durga

mahout elephant driver/keeper

mahseer large freshwater fish found especially in Himalayan rivers

maidan large open grassy area in a town

Maitreya the future Buddha

makara crocodile-shaped mythical creature symbolizing the river Ganga

makhan butter

malai hill (Tamil)

mali gardener

Manasa Snake goddess; Sakti

manastambha free-standing pillar in front of temple

mandala geometric diagram symbolizing the structure of the Universe

mandalam region, tract of country (Tamil)

mandapa columned hall preceding the temple sanctuary

mandi market

mandir temple

mani (mani wall) stones with sacred inscriptions at Buddhist sites

mantra chant for meditation by Hindus and Buddhists

maqbara chamber of a Muslim tomb

Mara Tempter, who sent his daughters (and soldiers) to disturb the Buddha's meditation

marg wide roadway

masjid literally `place of prostration'; mosque

mata mother

math Hindu or Jain monastery

maulana scholar (Muslim)

maulvi religious teacher (Muslim)

maund measure of weight about 20 kilos

mausoleum large tomb building

maya illusion

medallion circle or part-circle framing a figure or decorative motif

meena enamel work

mela festival or fair, usually Hindu

memsahib married European woman, term used mainly before Independence

Meru mountain supporting the heavens

mihrab niche in the western wall of a mosque

mimbar pulpit in mosque

Minakshi literally `fish-eyed'; Parvati

minar (minaret) slender tower of a mosque

mitthai Indian sweets

mithuna couple in sexual embrace

mofussil the country as distinct from the town

Mohammad `the praised'; The Prophet; founder of Islam

moksha salvation, enlightenment; literally `release'

monolith single block of stone shaped into a pillar

mouza (mowza) village; a parcel of land having a separate name in the revenue records

mridangam barrel-shaped drum (musical)

muballigh second prayer leader

mudra symbolic hand gesture

muezzin mosque official who calls the faithful to prayer

Muharram period of mourning in remembrance of Hasan and Hussain, two murdered sons of Ali

mukha mandapa, hall for shrine

mullah religious teacher (Muslim)

mund Toda village

mural wall decoration

musalla prayer mat

muthi measure equal to `a handful'

N

nadi river

nadu region, country (Tamil)

Naga (nagi/nagini) Snake deity; associated with fertility and protection

nagara city, sometimes capital

nakkar khana (naggar or naubat khana) drum house; arched structure or gateway for musicians

nal staircase

nal mandapa porch over a staircase

nallah (nullah) ditch, channel

namaaz Muslim prayers, worship

namaste common Hindu greeting (with joined palms) translated as: `I salute all divine qualities in you'

namda rug

Nandi a bull, Siva's vehicle and a symbol of fertility

nara durg large fort built on a flat plain

Narayana Vishnu as the creator of life

nata mandapa (nat-mandir; nritya sala) dancing hall in a temple

Nataraja Siva, Lord of the cosmic dance

nath literally `place' eg Amarnath

natya the art of dance

nautch display by dancing girls

navagraha nine planets, represented usually on the lintel or architrave of the front door of a temple

navaranga central hall of temple

navaratri literally `9 nights'; name of the Dasara festival

nawab prince, wealthy Muslim, sometimes used as a title

niche wall recess containing a sculpted image or emblem, mostly framed by a pair of pilasters

nirvana enlightenment; literally `extinguished'

niwas small palace

nritya pure dance

O

obelisk tapering and usually monolithic stone shaft

ogee form of moulding or arch comprising a double curved line made up of a concave and convex part

oriel projecting window

P

pada foot or base

padam dance which tells a story

padma lotus flower, Padmasana, lotus seat; posture of meditating figures

pagoda tall structure in several stories

pahar hill

paisa (poisa) one hundredth of a rupee

palanquin covered litter for one, carried on poles

palayam minor kingdom (Tamil)

pali language of Buddhist scriptures

palli village

pan leaf of the betel vine; sliced areca nut, lime and other ingredients wrapped in leaf for chewing

panchayat a 'council of five'; a government system of elected councils

pandal marquee made of bamboo and cloth

pandas temple priests

pandit teacher or wise man; a Sanskrit scholar

pankah (punkha) fan, formerly pulled by a cord

parapet wall extending above the roof

pargana sub-division of a district usually comprising many villages; a fiscal unit

Parinirvana the Buddha's state prior to nirvana, shown usually as a reclining figure

parishads political division of group of villages

Parsi (Parsee) Zoroastrians who fled from Iran to West India in the eighth century to avoid persecution

parterre level space in a garden occupied by flowerbeds

Parvati daughter of the Mountain; Siva's consort

pashmina fine wool from a mountain goat

Pashupati literally Lord of the Beasts; Siva

pata painted hanging scroll

patan town or city (Sanskrit)

patel village headman

patina green film that covers materials exposed to the air

pattachitra specially painted cloth (especially Orissan)

pau measure for vegetables and fruit equal to 250 grams

paya soup

pediment mouldings, often in a triangular formation above an opening or niche

pendant hanging, a motif depicted upside down

peon servant, messenger (from Portuguese peao)

peristyle range of columns surrounding a court or temple

Persian wheel well irrigation system using bucket lift

pettah suburbs, outskirts of town (Tamil: pettai)

pice (old form) 1/100th of a rupee

picottah water lift using horizontal pole pivoted on vertical pole (Tamil Nadu)

pida (pitha) basement

pietra dura inlaid mosaic of hard, semi-precious stones

pilaster ornamental small column, with capital and bracket

pinjra lattice work

pipal Ficus religiosa, the Bodhi tree

pir Muslim holy man

pitha base, pedestal

pithasthana place of pilgrimage

podium stone bench; low pedestal wall

pol fortified gateway

porch covered entrance to a shrine or hall, generally open and with columns

portico space enclosed between columns

pradakshina patha processional passage

prakaram open courtyard

pralaya the end of the world

prasadam consecrated temple food

prayag confluence considered sacred by Hindus

puja ritual offerings to the gods; worship (Hindu)

pujari worshipper; one who performs puja (Hindu)

pukka literally 'ripe' or 'finished'; reliable; solidly built

punya merit earned through actions and religious devotion (Buddhist)

Puranas literally 'the old' Sanskrit sacred poems

purdah seclusion of Muslim women from public view (literally curtains)

pushkarani sacred pool or tank

Q

qabr Muslim grave

qibla direction for Muslim prayer

qila fort

Quran holy Muslim scriptures

R

rabi winter/spring season crop

Radha Krishna's favourite consort

raj rule or government

raja king, ruler (variations include rao, rawal)

rajbari palaces of a small kingdom

Rakshakas Earth spirits

Rama Seventh incarnation of Vishnu

Ramayana Sanskrit epic – the story of Rama

Ramazan (Ramadan) Muslim month of fasting

rana warrior (Nepal)

rangamandapa painted hall or theatre

rani queen

rath chariot or temple car

Ravana Demon king of Lanka; kidnapper of Sita

rawal head priest

rekha curvilinear portion of a spire or sikhara (rekha deul, sanctuary, curved tower of an Orissan temple)

reredos screen behind an altar

rickshaw 3-wheeled bicycle-powered (or 2-wheeled hand-powered) vehicle

Rig (Rg) Veda oldest and most sacred of the Vedas

rishi 'seer'; inspired poet, philosopher

rumal handkerchief, specially painted in Chamba (Himachal Pradesh)

rupee unit of currency in India

ryot (rayat/raiyat) a subject; a cultivator; a farmer

S

sabha columned hall (sabha mandapa, assembly hall)

sabzi vegetables, vegetable curry

sadar (sadr/saddar) chief, main especially Sikh

sadhu ascetic; religious mendicant, holy man

sagar lake; reservoir

sahib title of address, like 'sir'

sahn open courtyard of a mosque

Saiva (Shaiva) the cult of Siva

sal (sala) a hall

sal hardwood tree of the lower slopes of Himalayan foothills

salaam literally `peace'; greeting (Muslim)

salwar (shalwar) loose trousers

samadh(i) literally concentrated thought, meditation; a funerary memorial

sambar lentil and vegetable soup dish, accompanying main meal (Tamil)

samsara transmigrati on of the soul

samudra large tank or inland sea

sangam junction of rivers

sangarama monaster y

sangha ascetic order founded by Buddha

sangrahalaya rest-ho use for Jain pilgrims

sankha (shankha) the conch shell (symbolically held by Vishnu)

sanyasi wandering ascetic; final stage in the ideal life of a man

sarai caravansarai, halting place

saranghi small four-stringed viola shaped from a single piece of wood

Saraswati wife of Brahma and goddess of knowledge

sarkar the government; the state; a writer; an accountant

sarod Indian stringed musical instrument

sarvodaya uplift, improvement of all

sati (suttee) a virtuous woman; act of self-immolation on a husband's funeral pyre

Sati wife of Siva who destroyed herself by fire

satyagraha 'truth force'; passive resistance

sayid title (Muslim)

schist grey or green finely grained stone

seer (ser) weight (about 1 kg)

sepoy (sepai) Indian soldier, private

serow a wild Himalayan antelope

seth merchant, businessman

seva voluntary service

shahtush very fine wool from the Tibetan antelope

Shakti Energy; female divinity often associated with Siva

shala barrel-vaulted roof

shalagrama stone containing fossils worshipped as a form of Vishnu

shaman doctor/priest , using magic, exorcist

shamiana cloth canopy

Shankara Siva

sharia corpus of Muslim theological law

shastras ancient texts defining temple architecture

shastri religious title (Hindu)

sheesh mahal palace apartment with mirror work

shehnai (shahnai) Indian wind instrument like an oboe

sherwani knee-lengt h coat for men

Shesha (Sesha) serpent who supports Vishnu

shikar hunting

shisham a valuable building timber

sikhara (shikhara) curved temple tower or spire

shloka (sloka) Sanskrit sacred verse

shola patch of forest or wood (Tamil)

sileh khana armoury

sindur vermilion powder used in temple ritual; married women mark their hair parting with it (East India)

singh (sinha) lion; Rajput caste name adopted by Sikhs

sinha stambha lion pillar

sirdar a guide who leads trekking groups

Sita Rama's wife, heroine of the Ramayana epic

sitar classical stringed musical instrument with a gourd for soundbox

Siva (Shiva) The Destroyer in the Hindu triad of Gods

Sivaratri literally `Siva's night'; a festival (Feb-Mar)

Skanda the Hindu god of war; Kartikkeya

soma sacred drink mentioned in the Vedas

spandrel triangular space between the curve of an arch and the square enclosing it

squinch arch across an interior angle

sri (shri) honorific title, often used for `Mr'; repeated as sign of great respect

sridhara pillar with octagonal shaft and square base

stalactite system of vaulting, remotely resembling stalactite formations in a cave

stambha free-standin g column or pillar, often for a lamp or figure

steatite finely grained grey mineral

stele upright, inscribed slab used as a gravestone

sthan place (suffix)

stucco plasterwork

stupa hemispheric Buddhist funerary mound

stylobate base on which a colonnade is placed

Subrahmanya Skand a, one of Siva's sons; Kartikkeya in South India

sudra lowest of the Hindu castes

sufi Muslim mystic; sufism, Muslim mystic worship

sultan Muslim prince (sultana, wife of sultan)

Surya Sun; Sun God

svami (swami) holy man; a suffix for temple deities

svastika (swastika) auspicious Hindu/ Buddhist cross-like sign

swadeshi home made goods

swaraj home rule

swatantra freedom

syce groom, attendant who follows a horseman

T

tabla a pair of drums

tahr wild goat

tahsildar revenue collector

taikhana undergroun d apartments

takht throne

talao (tal, talar) water tank

taluk administrative subdivision of a district

tamasha spectacle; festive celebration

tandava (dance) of Siva

tank lake dug for irrigation; a masonry-lined temple pool with stepped sides

tapas (tapasya) ascetic meditative self-denial

Tara literally `star'; a goddess

tatties cane or grass screens used for shade

Teej Hindu festival

tempera distemper; method of mural painting by means of a `body,' such as white pigment

tempo three-wheeler vehicle

teri soil formed from wind blown sand (Tamil Nadu)

terracotta burnt clay used as building material

thakur high Hindu caste

thali South and West Indian vegetarian meal

thana a police jurisdiction; police station

tiffin snack, light meal

tika (tilak) vermilion powder, auspicious mark on the forehead; often decorative

tikka tender pieces of meat, marinated and barbecued

tillana abstract dance

tirtha ford, bathing place, holy spot (Sanskrit)

Tirthankara literally `ford-maker'; title given to 24 religious 'teachers', worshipped by Jains

tonga two-wheeled horse carriage

topi (topee) pith helmet

torana gateway; two posts with an architrave

tottam garden (Tamil)

tribhanga triple-bended pose for standing figures

Trimurti the Hindu Triad, Brahma, Vishnu and Siva

tripolia triple gateway

trisul the trident chief symbol of the god Siva

triveni triple-braided

tulsi sacred basil plant

tympanum triangular space within cornices

Uma Siva's consort in one of her many forms

untouchable 'outcast es', with whom contact of any kind was believed by high caste Hindus to be defiling

Upanishads ancient Sanskrit philosophical texts, part of the Vedas

ur village (Tamil)

usta painted camel leather goods

ustad master

uttarayana northward s

vahana 'vehicle' of the deity

vaisya the `middle-class' caste of merchants and farmers

Valmiki sage, author of the Ramayana epic

Vamana dwarf incarnation of Vishnu

vana grove, forest

Varaha boar incarnation of Vishnu

varam village (Tamil)

varna 'colour'; social division of Hindus into Brahmin, Kshatriya, Vaishya and Sudra

varnam South Indian musical etude, conforming to a raga

Varuna Guardian of the West, accompanied by Makara (see above)

Vayu Wind god; Guardian of the North-West

Veda (Vedic) oldest known Hindu religious texts

vedi (bedi) altar, also a wall or screen

verandah enlarged porch in front of a hall

vihara Buddhist or Jain monastery with cells around a courtyard

vilas house or pleasure palace

vimana towered sanctuary containing the cell in which the deity is enshrined

vina plucked stringed instrument, relative of sitar

Vishnu a principal Hindu deity; the Preserver (and Creator)

vyala (yali) leogryph, mythical lion-like sculpture

-wallah suffix often used with a occupational name, eg rickshaw-wallah

wazir chief minister of a raja (from Turkish 'vizier')

yagya (yajna) major ceremonial sacrifice

Yaksha (Yakshi) a demi-god, associated with nature

yali see vyala

Yama God of death, judge of the living

yantra magical diagram used in meditation; instrument

yatra pilgrimage

yoga school of philosophy stressing mental and physical disciplines; yogi

yoni a hole symbolising female sexuality; vagina

zamindar a landlord granted income under the Mughals

zari silver and gold thread used in weaving or embroidery

zenana segregated women's apartments

Useful words and phrases: Tamil

general greeting	*vanakkam*
Thank you/no thank you	*nandri*
Excuse me, sorry, pardon	*mannikkavum*
Yes/no	*ām/illai*
never mind/thats all right	*paruvai illai*
please	*thayavu seithu*
What is your name?	*ungaludaya peyr enna*
My name is...	*ennudaya peyr*
How are you?	*ningal eppadi irukkirirgal?*
I am well, thanks	*nan nantraga irrukkirain*
Not very well	*paruvayillai*
Do you speak English?	*ningal angilam kathappirgala*

Shopping

How much is this?	*ithan vilai enna?*
That will be 20 rupees	*athan vilai irupatha rupa*
Please make it a bit cheaper!	*thayavu seithu konjam kuraikavuam!*

The hotel

What is the room charge?	*arayin vilai enna?*
May I see the room please?	*thayavu seithu arayai parka mudiyama?*
Is there an a/c room?	*kulir sathana arai irrukkatha?*
Is there hot water?	*sudu thanir irukkuma?*
...a bathroom?	*oru kuliyal arai...?*
...a fan/mosquito net?	*katotra sathanam/kosu valai...?*
Please clean the room	*thayavu seithu arayai suththap paduthava*
This is OK	*ithuru seri*
Bill please	*bill tharavum*

Travel

Where's the railway station?	*station enge?*
When does the Chennai bus leave?	*eppa Chennai bus pogum?*
How much is it to Madurai?	*Madurai poga evalavu?*
Will you go to Madurai for 10 rupees?	*paththu rupavitku Madurai poga mudiyami?*
left/right	*idathu/valathu*
straight on	*naerakapogavum*
nearby	*aruqil*
Please wait here	*thayavu seithu ingu nitkavum*
Please come here at 8	*thayavu seithu ingu ettu*
stop	*nivuthu*

Time and days

right now	*ippoh*
morning	*kalai*
afternoon	*pitpagal*
evening	*malai*
night	*iravu*
today	*indru*
tomorrow/yesterday	*nalai/naetru*
day	*thinam*
week	*vaaram*
month	*maatham*

Sunday	*gnatruk kilamai*
Monday	*thinkat kilamai*
Tuesday	*sevai kilamai*
Wednesday	*puthan kilamai*
Thursday	*viyalak kilamai*
Friday	*velli kilamai*
Saturday	*sanik kilamai*

Numbers

1	*ontru*	10	*pattu*
2	*erantru*	20	*erupathu*
3	*moontru*	30	*muppathu*
4	*nangu*	40	*natpathu*
5	*ainthu*	50	*ompathu*
6	*aru*	100/200	*nooru/irunooru*
7	*aelu*	1000/2000	*aiyuram/iranda*
8	*ettu*		*iuram*
9	*onpathu*		

Basic vocabulary

Some English words are widely used, often alongside Tamil equivalents, such as, airport, bank, bathroom, bus, embassy, ferry, hospital, hotel, restaurant, station, stamp, taxi, ticket, train (though often pronounced a little differently).

		ferry	*padagu*
		hospital	*aspathri*
		hot (temp)	*ushnamana*
		hotel/restaurant	*sapathu*
		viduthi juice	*saru*
		open	*thira*
airport	*agaya vimana nilayam*	road	*pathai*
		room	*arai*
bank	*vungi*	shop	*kadi*
bathroom	*kulikkum arai*	sick (ill)	*viyathi*
café/food stall	*unavu kadai*	stamp	*muththirai*
chemist	*marunthu kadai*	station	*nilayam*
clean	*suththam*	this	*ithu*
closed	*moodu*	that	*athu*
cold	*kulir*	ticket	*anumati situ*
dirty	*alukku*	train	*rayil*
embassy	*thootharalayam*	water	*thannir*
excellent	*miga nallathu*	when	*eppa?*
		where?	*enge?*

Useful words and phrases: Malayalan

á as un ah
ó as in oh

ú as in oo

Hello, good morning, goodbye	*namaskaram*
Thank you/no thank you	*nandi/nanni*
Excuse me, sorry	*kshamikku*
yes/no	*athe/alla*
never mind/that's all right	*saramilla/kuzhapamillá*
What is your name?	*ningalude perendhannu?*
My name is	*ende (ente) peru ...... ennanu*
Pardon?	*onnukoodi parayammó?*
How are you?	*ningalku sughamanó*
I am well, thanks, and you?	*anikku sughamanu. Thangalkkó*
Not very well	*anikku nalla sughamillá*
Where is the ...?	*... avidayannu?*
Who is ......?	*...... arannu?*

Eating out - food and menus

Cooking in South India remains distinctive in the frequent use of some ingredients such as coconut in various forms, *umbalakada* the powdered dry Maldive fish used to flavour curries as well as the different ways in which rice is prepared like *appa* and *pittu*.

The Dutch and Portuguese have also influenced South India's cuisine. Festive *lamprais* and *frikkadels*, the small, crumbed and fried meat or fish balls. The influence is more obvious in confectionary and desserts using eggs, as in *breudher* the 'Christmas cake' or *wattapallam*, as well as flaky pastries like *foguete* or the cashew-filled *bolo folhado*.

A typical South Indian '**rice and curry** meal' would include a couple of different curries and *sambols*, some chutney and pickles, and would be eaten with the fingers of the right hand, however, you may get a spoon to eat the meal. It is quite usual to ask for second helpings of whatever you fancy. For variety rice may be replaced by hoppers, pittu or rotty on occasions.

A rough guide as to how hot the curry is - *Kiri* are fairly mild 'white' curry prepared with coconut milk; *Badun* prepared with freshly roasted spice are drier, 'black' and hotter; *Rathu* the 'red' curries are hottest, with plenty of dried red-chilli (rathu miris) powder added.

Spices which are grown locally and which attracted sea-faring traders to the island, are liberally used in the kitchen - cardamom, cinnamon, cloves, fenugreek and pepper etc, as well as the typical cumin, coriander and turmeric.

Coconut is plentiful and appears in various forms or during cooking or serving - coconut oil, coconut 'milk' (strained infusion) to cook with or prepare a batter, grated coconut, small pieces of kernel - even the shell is used as a ladle. Molee are mild curries with a creamy coconut milk gravy. As a drink, King Coconut water (*thambili*) is safe and refreshing. The unfermented palm sap produces thelija, the fermented toddy and the distilled arrack.

Pronounce

a - as in ah	**u** as oo in book
i - as in bee	**o** - as in oh

Nasalized vowels are shown as an- un- etc

Note These marks to help with pronunciation do not appear in the main text.

Basic Vocabulary

	Tamil
bread	*rotti/pān*
butter	*butter/vennai*
(too much) chilli	*kāram*
drink	*kudi*
egg	*muttai*
fish	*min*
fruit	*palam*
food	*unavu*

jaggery	*sini/vellam*
juice	*sâru*
meat	*iraichchi*
oil	*ennai*
pepper	*milagu*
pulses (beans, lentils)	*thâniyam*
rice	*arisi*
salt	*uppu*
savoury	*suvai*
spices	*milagu*
sweetmeats	*inippu pondangal*
treacle	*pâni*
vegetables	*kai kari vagaigal*
water	*thanneer*

Fruit

banana	*valaippalam*
cashew	*muruthivi*
coconut	*thengali*
green coconut	*pachcha niramulla thengai*
mango	*mampalam*
papaya	*pappa palam*
pineapple	*annasi*

Vegetables

aubergine	*kathirikai*
beans (green)	*avarai*
cabbage	*muttaikosu*
gourd (green)	*pudalankai*
mushrooms	*kalân*
okra	*vendikkai*
onion	*venkayam*
pea	*pattani*
pepper	*kâram*
potato	*uruka kilangu*
spinach	*pasali*
tomato	*thakkali*

Meat, fish and seafood

chicken	*koli*
crab	*nandu*
pork	*pantri*
prawns	*irâl*

Ordering a meal in a restaurant (Tamil)

Please show the menu	*thayavu seithu thinpandangal patti tharavum*
No chillis please	*kâram vendâm*
... sugar/milk/ice	*sini/pâl/ice*
A bottle of mineral water please	*oru pothal soda panam tharavum*

Eating out

Eating out is normally cheap and safe but menus can be dauntingly long and full of unfamiliar names. North Indian dishes are nearly universal. Outside their home states regional dishes are normally only served in specialist restaurants.

Methods of preparation

Many items on restaurant menus are named according to well-known methods of preparation, roughly equivalent to terms such as 'Provençal' or 'sauté'.

bhoona *in a thick, fairly spicy sauce*

chops *minced meat, fish or vegetables, covered with mashed potato, crumbed and fried*

cutlet *minced meat, fish, vegetables formed into flat rounds or ovals, crumbed and fried (eg prawn cutlet, flattened king prawn)*

do piaza *with onions (added twice during cooking)*

dumphuk *steam baked*

jhāl frāzi *spicy, hot sauce with tomatoes and chillies*

Kashmiri *cooked with mild spices, ground almonds and yoghurt, often with fruit*

kebab *skewered (or minced and shaped) meat or fish; a dry spicy dish cooked on a fire*

kìma *minced meat (usually 'mutton')*

kofta *minced meat or vegetable balls*

korma *in fairly mild rich sauce using cream /yoghurt*

masālā *marinated in spices (fairly hot)*

Madras *hot*

makhani *in butter rich sauce*

molī *South Indian dishes cooked in coconut milk and green chilli sauce*

Mughlai *rich North Indian style*

Nargisi *dish using boiled eggs*

navratan curry *('9 jewels') colourful mixed vegetables and fruit in mild sauce*

Peshwari *rich with dried fruit and nuts (Northwest Indian)*

tandoori *baked in a tandoor (special clay oven) or one imitating it*

tikka *marinated meat pieces, baked quite dry*

vindaloo *hot and sour Goan meat dish using vinegar*

Ordering a meal

A **thāli** *for which you might pay Rs 15 (in small dhabas) to Rs 50, is usually the cheapest way of eating; the menu is fixed but refills are normally offered. You will be expected to eat with your fingers although a spoon is usually available. When ordering from a menu, you might like to try some 'bread' and/or rice, a vegetable and/or meat curry, bhāji, dāl, raita and pāpad. It is perfectly acceptable to order as little as some bread or rice and a vegetable dish or dāl. Sweets are an extra. Gulāb jāmun, rashmalāi and kulfi are popular.*

Some typical dishes

Coastal and riverine areas often have a wide range of specialist seafood.

aloo gosht *potato and mutton stew*

aloo gobi *dry potato and cauliflower with cumin*

aloo, matar, kumbhi *potato, peas, mushrooms in a dryish mildly spicy sauce*

bhindi bhaji *lady's fingers fried with onions and mild spices*

boti kebab *marinated pieces of meat, skewered and cooked over a fire*

dāl makhani *lentils cooked with butter*

dum aloo *potato curry with a spicy yoghurt, tomato and onion sauce*

kìma mattar *mince meat with peas*

matar panīr *curd cheese cubes with peas and spices (and often tomatoes)*

murgh massāllam *chicken in rich creamy marinade of yoghurt, spices and herbs with nuts*

Nargisi kofta *boiled eggs covered in minced lamb, cooked in a thick sauce*

rogan josh *rich, mutton/ beef pieces in creamy, red sauce*

sāg gosht *mutton and spinach*

sāg panīr *(pālak panīr) Drained curd sautéd with chopped spinach in mild spices*

shabdeg *a special Mughlai mutton dish with vegetables eg turnips*

yakhni *lamb stew*

Rice

bhāt/sādā chāwal   plain boiled rice
biriyāni   partially cooked rice layered over meat and baked with saffron.
khichari   rice and lentils cooked with turmeric and other spices
pulao/ pilau   fried (and then boiled) rice cooked with spices (cloves, cardamom, cinnamon) with dried fruit, nuts or vegetables. Sometimes cooked with meat, like a biriyāni

Roti – breads

chapāti (phoolka, roti)   thin, plain, wholemeal unleavened bread cooked on a tawa (griddle), usually made from ātā (wheat flour). Makkai-ki-roti is with maize flour. Soft, thicker version of poori, made with white flour
nān   oven baked (traditionally in a tandoor) white flour leavened bread often large and triangular; sometimes stuffed with almonds and dried fruit
parāthā   fried bread layered with ghī (sometimes cooked with egg or stuffed with potatoes)
poori   thin deep-fried, puffed rounds of flour

Accompaniments

achār   pickles (usually spicy and preserved in oil)
appalam   (South India) similar to pappadom, often smaller, made with unspiced gram flour
chutnī   often fruit or tomato, freshly prepared, sweet and mildly spiced
dahī   plain yoghurt
namak   salt
papad, pappadom   deep fried, pulse flour wafer rounds
raita   yoghurt with shredded cucumber, pinapple or other fruit, or bundi (tiny batter balls)
rasam   clear peppery South Indian soup/ drink
sambhar   lentil based preparation, thicker than rasam, served with South Indian meals, along with coconut chutney and pickles

Sweets

These are often made with reduced/ thickened milk, drained curd cheese or powdered lentils and nuts. They are sometimes covered with a flimsy sheet of decorative, edible silver leaf

barfi   fudge-like rectangles/diamonds
khīr, payasam, paesh   thickened milk rice/vermicelli pudding
gājar halwa   dry sweet made with thickened milk, carrots and spice
gulāb jāmun   dark fried spongy balls, soaked in syrup
halwa   rich sweet made from cereal, fruit, vegetable, nuts and sugar
kulfi   cone-shaped Indian ice cream with pistachhios/almonds, uneven in texture
jalebi   spirals of fried batter soaked in syrup
laddoo   lentil based batter 'grains' shaped into orange rounds
rasgulla (roshgulla)   balls of curd in clear syrup
rasmalāi   spongy curd rounds, soaked in sweetened cream and garnished with pistachio nuts
sandesh   dry sweet made of curd cheese
shāhi tukrā   pieces of fried bread soaked in syrup and creamy thickened milk then sprinkled with nuts
srikhand   West Indian sweet made with curds, sometimes eaten with fried puris

Snacks

bhāji, pakora   vegetable fritters (onions, potatoes, cauliflower, aubergine etc) deep-fried in batter
chāt   sweet and sour cubed fruit and vegetables flavoured with tamarind paste and chillis
chanā choor, chioora ('Bombay mix') lentil and flattened rice snacks mixed with nuts and dried fruit
dosai   South Indian pancake made with rice and lentil flour; served with a mild potato and onion filling (masala dosai) or without (ravai or plain dosai)
idli   steamed South Indian rice cakes, a bland breakfast food given flavour by its spiced accompaniments
kachori   fried pastry rounds stuffed with spiced lentil/ peas/ potato filling
namkīn   savoury pastry bits
samosā   cooked vegetable or meat wrapped in pastry circle into 'triangles' and deep fried
utthappam   thick South Indian rice and lentil flour pancake cooked with spices/onions/tomatoes

vadai *deep fried, small savoury lentil 'doughnut' rings. Dahi vada - similar rounds in yoghurt*

Drinks
chai *tea boiled with milk and sugar*
doodh *milk*
kāfi *ground fresh coffee boiled with milk and sugar*
lassi *cool drink made with yoghurt and water, salted or sweetened*
nimboo pāni *refreshing drink made with fresh lime and water, chilled bottled water, added salt or sugar syrup but avoid ice. Also, fresh lime soda*
pāni *water*

Index

Footnotes

Shorts

Map index

What's in a word? - the answers

balloon Marathi *balyanw*, originally a rowing vessel, canoe or dugout.

bungalow *Bangala house* - from the style of houses built by the British in Bengal

calico from Calicut in Kerala

cash Sanskrit *karsha* - " a weight of silver or gold". But probably from the Tamil *kasu* - through Portuguese into English

catamaran Tamil ***kattu maram*** -raft of 3 or 4 logs lashed together to make a wooden fishing boat

cheroot Tamil *shuruttu* - a roll of tobacco

chintz Hindi *chint*, Sanskrit *chitra* - variegated/ speckled picture - then Portuguese *chita*.

curry Tamil *kari* meaning sauce. The Kanarese form *karil* was adopted by the Portuguese

dinghy Bengali - *dingi* - a small boat or skiff, sometimes a canoe.

door Sanskrit - and thence into many other languages -*duar*

dungaree Telugu - *dangidi* - a coarse cotton cloth

mango Tamil - ***man kai*** the unripe fruit, the tree being *mamarum* and the ripe fruit *mampalam*".

monsoon Not an Indian word, but derived from the Arabic *mausim*, meaning season.

mulligatawny Tamil - *milagu tannir* - pepper-water

pepper Sanskrit - *pippali*, the long pepper, not the black pepper. The name was transferred to the black variety in error by traders.

prow Malayalam - *paru* - a boat - largely made of cane

punch Hindi, Marathi - *panch* - literally "five" - the ingredients being arrack, sugar, lime juice, spice and water.

pyjamas Hindi *pae - jammas* - literally leg-clothing.

rice Tamil *arisi* , 'rice deprived of its husk'. - the root of the Greek, the Latin name *Oryza sativa*, into Italian *risi*, then English

sandals Sanskrit - çandala

veranda Portuguese probably, though found in various Indian languages.

Will you help us?

*We try as hard as we can to make each Footprint
Handbook as up-to-date and accurate as possible but, of
course, things always change. Many people write to us -
with corrections, new information, or simply comments.*

*If you want to let us know about an experience or
adventure - hair-raising or mundane, good or bad,
exciting or boring or simply something rather special -
we would be delighted to hear from you. Please give us as
precise information as possible, quoting the edition
number (you'll find it on the front cover) and page
number of the Handbook you are using.*

*Your help will be greatly appreciated, especially by
other travellers. In return we will send you details about
our special guidebook offer.*

email Footprint at:
sind1_online@footprintbooks.com

or write to:
Elizabeth Taylor
Footprint Handbooks
6 Riverside Court
Lower Bristol Road
Bath BA2 3DZ
UK

Footnotes

Sales & distribution

Footprint Handbooks
6 Riverside Court
Lower Bristol Road
Bath BA2 3DZ England
T 01225 469141
F 01225 469461
discover
@footprintbooks.com

Australia
Peribo Pty
58 Beaumont Road
Mt Kuring-Gai
NSW 2080
T 02 9457 0011
F 02 9457 0022

Austria
Freytag-Berndt Artaria
Kohlmarkt 9
A-1010 Wien
T 01533 2094
F 01533 8685

Freytag-Berndt
Sporgasse 29
A-8010 Graz
T 0316 818230
F 3016 818230-30

Belgium
Craenen BVBA
Mechelsesteenweg 633
B-3020 Herent
T 016 23 90 90
F 016 23 97 11

Waterstones
The English Bookshop
Blvd Adolphe Max 71-75
B-1000 Brussels
T 02 219 5034

Canada
Ulysses Travel Publications
4176 rue Saint-Denis
Montréal
Québec H2W 2M5
T 514 843 9882
F 514 843 9448

Europe
Bill Bailey
16 Devon Square
Newton Abbott
Devon TQ12 2HR. UK
T 01626 331079
F 01626 331080

Denmark
Nordisk Korthandel
Studiestraede 26-30 B
DK-1455 Copenhagen K
T 3338 2638
F 3338 2648

Scanvik Books
Esplanaden 8B
DK-1263 Copenhagen K
T 3312 7766
F 3391 2882

Finland
Akateeminen Kirjakauppa
Keskuskatu 1
FIN-00100 Helsinki
T 09 121 4151
F 09 121 4441

Suomalainen Kirjakauppa
Koivuvaarankuja 2
01640 Vantaa 64
F 09 852751

France
FNAC – major branches

L'Astrolabe
46 rue de Provence
F-75009 Paris 9e
T 01 42 85 42 95
F 01 45 75 92 51

VILO Diffusion
25 rue Ginoux
F-75015 Paris
T 01 45 77 08 05
F 01 45 79 97 15

Germany
GeoCenter ILH
Schockenriedstrasse 44
D-70565 Stuttgart
T 0711 781 94610
F 0711 781 94654

Brettschneider
Feldkirchnerstrasse 2
D-85551 Heimstetten
T 089 990 20330
F 089 990 20331

Geobuch
Rosental 6
D-80331 München
T 089 265030
F 089 263713

Gleumes
Hohenstaufenring 47-51
D-50674 Köln
T 0221 215650

Globetrotter Ausrustungen
Wiesendamm 1
D-22305 Hamburg
T040 679 66190
F 040 679 66183

Dr Götze
Bleichenbrücke 9
D-2000 Hamburg 1
T 040 3031 1009-0

Hugendubel Buchhandlung
Nymphenburgerstrasse 25
D-80335 München
T 089 238 9412
F 089 550 1853

Kiepert Buchhandlung
Hardenbergstrasse 4-5
D-10623 Berlin 12
T 030 311 880
F 030 311 88120

Greece
GC Eleftheroudakis
17 Panepistemiou
Athens 105 64
T 01 331 4180-83
F 01 323 9821

India
India Book Distributors
1007/1008 Arcadia
195 Nariman Point
Mumbai 400 021
T 91 22 282 5220
F 91 22 287 2531

Israel
Eco Trips
8 Tverya Street
Tel Aviv 63144
T 03 528 4113
F 03 528 8269

For a fuller list, see www.footprintbooks.com

Italy
Librimport
Via Biondelli 9
I-20141 Milano
T 02 8950 1422
F 02 8950 2811

Libreria del Viaggiatore
Via dell Pelegrino 78
I-00186 Roma
T/F 06 688 01048

Netherlands
Nilsson & Lamm bv
Postbus 195
Pampuslaan 212
N-1380 AD Weesp
T 0294 494949
F 0294 494455

Waterstones
Kalverstraat 152
1012 XE Amsterdam
T 020 638 3821

New Zealand
Auckland Map Centre
Dymocks

Norway
Schibsteds Forlag A/S
Akersgata 32 - 5th Floor
Postboks 1178 Sentrum
N-0107 Oslo
T 22 86 30 00
F 22 42 54 92

Tanum
Karl Johansgate 37-41
PO Box 1177 Sentrum
N-0107 Oslo 1
T 22 41 11 00
F 22 33 32 75

Olaf Norlis
Universitetsgt 24
N-1062 Oslo
T 22 00 43 00

Pakistan
Pak-American Commercial
Hamid Chambers
Zaib-un Nisa Street
Saddar, PO Box 7359
Karachi
T 21 566 0418
F 21 568 3611

South Africa
Faradawn CC
PO Box 1903
Saxonwold 2132
T 011 885 1787
F 011 885 1829

South America
Humphrys Roberts
Associates
Caixa Postal 801-0
Ag. Jardim da Gloria
06700-970 Cotia SP
Brazil
T 011 492 4496
F 011 492 6896

Southeast Asia
APA Publications
38 Joo Koon Road
Singapore 628990
T 865 1600
F 861 6438

In Hong Kong, Malaysia,
Singapore and Thailand:
MPH, Kinokuniya, Times

Spain
Altaïr
C/Balmes 69
08007 Barcelona
T 933 233062
F 934 512559

Altaïr
Gaztambide 31
28015 Madrid
T 0915 435300
F 0915 443498

Libros de Viaje
C/Serrano no 41
28001 Madrid
T 01 91 577 9899
F 01 91 577 5756

Il Corte Inglés – major
branches

Sweden
Hedengrens Bokhandel
PO Box 5509
S-11485 Stockholm
T 08 611 5132

Kart Centrum
Vasagatan 16
S-11120 Stockholm
T 08 411 1697

Kartforlaget
Skolgangen 10
S-80183 Gavle
T 026 633000
F 026 124204

Lantmateriet Kartbutiken
Kungsgatan 74
S-11122 Stockholm
T 08 202 303
F 08 202 711

Switzerland
Office du Livre OLF
ZI3, Corminboeuf
CH-1701 Fribourg
T 026 467 5111
F 026 467 5666

Schweizer Buchzentrum
Postfach
CH-4601 Olten
T 062 209 2525
F 062 209 2627

Travel Bookshop
Rindermarkt 20
Postfach 216
CH-8001 Zürich
T 01 252 3883
F 01 252 3832

Tanzania
A Novel Idea
The Slipway
PO Box 76513
Dar es Salaam
T/F 051 601088

USA
NTC/ Contemporary
4255 West Touhy Avenue
Lincolnwood
Illinois 60646-1975
T 847 679 5500
F 847 679 2494

Barnes & Noble, Borders,
specialist travel bookstores

What the papers say

"Who should pack the Footprint guides – people who want to escape the crowd."
The Observer

"Footprint can be depended on for accurate travel information and for imparting a deep sense of respect for the lands and people they cover."
World News

"Footprint Handbooks, the best of the best."
Le Monde, Paris

"The guides for intelligent, independently-minded souls of any age or budget."
Indie Traveller

"Intelligently written, amazingly accurate and bang up-to-date. Footprint have combined nearly 80 years experience with a stunning new format to bring us guidebooks that leave the competition standing."
John Pilkington, writer and broadcaster

Mail order
Available worldwide in bookshops and on-line. Footprint travel guides can also be ordered directly from us in Bath, via our website **www.footprintbooks.com** or from the address on the imprint page of this book.

Advertisers

Pettitts are the leading specialists in arranging quality tailor-made journeys throughout the Indian Subcontinent and the rest of Asia. We can help you plan your 'holiday of a lifetime', and provide a flexible, professional and fast service.

INDIA
NEPAL
SRI LANKA
PAKISTAN
CHINA
THAILAND
LAOS
VIETNAM
CAMBODIA
BALI
BURMA
SABAH
SARAWAK

For our brochures
call **01892 515966** 24 hours

www.pettitts.co.uk
email: pettitts@centrenet.co.uk

Calverley Travel Ltd. ABTA V5041 / ATOL 2841

SLEEPING BEAUTY

fairy Tale
HOLIDAY'S

Wake your body, mind and soul with the healing touch of Ayurveda. Come, holiday
in a land handpicked by the National Geographic Traveler as one of the ten paradises
in the world. And kiss all your cares away.

www.keralatourism.org Email: deptour@vsnl.com Fax: ++91-471-322279 Kerala Tourism Park View Trivandrum 695 033 Kerala India

kerala
God's Own Country

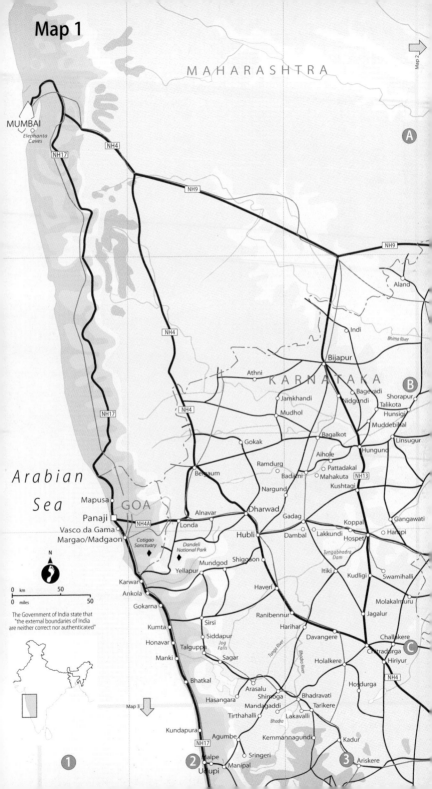

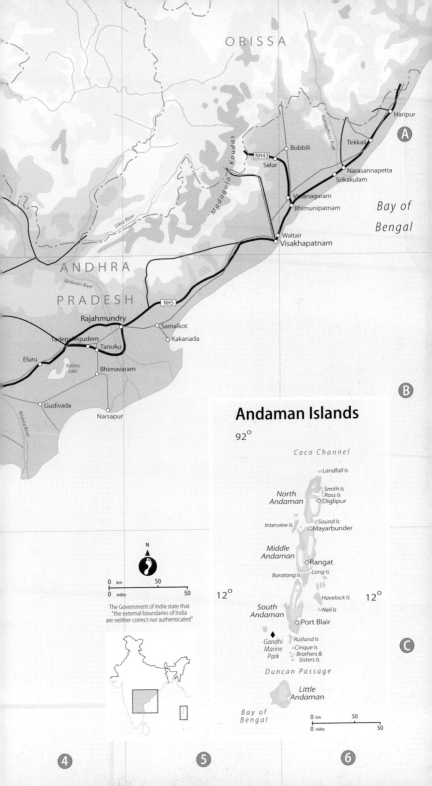

ORISSA

Haripur

Tekkali

Bobbili

Narasannapetta

Srikakulam

Salur

NH43

Vizianagaram

Bhimunipatnam

Waltair

Visakhapatnam

*Bay of
Bengal*

ANDHRA

Godavari River

PRADESH

NH5

Rajahmundry

Samalkot

Kakanada

Tadepalligudem

Tanuku

Eluru

*Kolleru
Lake*

Bhimavaram

Gudivada

Narsapur

N

0 km 50

0 miles 50

The Government of India state that
"the external boundaries of India
are neither correct nor authenticated"

Andaman Islands

92°

Coco Channel

Landfall Is

North
Andaman

Smith Is
Ross Is
Diglipur

Interview Is

Sound Is
Mayarbunder

Middle
Andaman

Rangat

Long Is

Baratang Is

12°

12°

South
Andaman

Havelock Is

Neil Is

Port Blair

Gandhi
Marine
Park

Rutland Is
Cinque Is
*Brothers &
Sisters Is*

Duncan Passage

Little
Andaman

*Bay of
Bengal*

0 km 50

0 miles 50

4   5   6

A

B

C

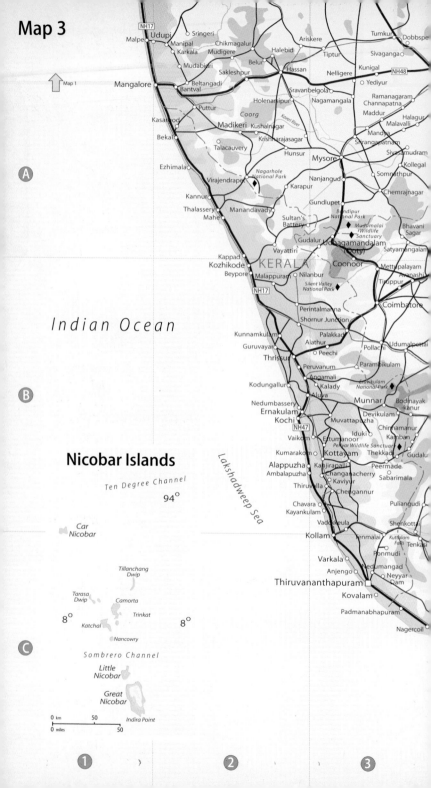

Map 3

NH17

Malpe • Udupi • Sringeri
Manipal
Karkala • Chikmagalur • Ariskere • Tumkur • Dobbspe
Mudabidri • Mudigere • Halebid • Tiptur • Sivaganga
Beltangadi • Saklespur • Belur • Nelligere • Kunigal • NH48
Mangalore • Bantval • Hassan • Yediyur
• Puttur • Holenarsipur • Ramanagaram
• Nagamangala • Channapatna
Kasargod • Madikeri • Kushalnagar • Maddur • Halagur
Bekal • Coorg • Krishnarajasagar • Malavalli
• Talacauvery • Krishnarajasagar • Mandya • Sivasamudram
Ezhimala • Hunsur • Mysore • Kollegal
Virajendrapet • Nagarhole • Nanjangud • Somnathpur
National Park • Karapur • Chemrajnagar
Kannur • Manandavady • Gundlupet • Bhavani
Thalassery • Sultan's • Bandipur • Sagar
Mahe • Battery • National Park • Mudumalai • Satyamangalam
• Gudalur • Wildlife • Sanctuary • Udagamandalam
Kappad • Vayattiri • Ooty • Coonoor • Mettupalayam
Kozhikode • KERALA • Avanashi
Beypore • Malappuram • Nilanbur • Tiruppur
NH17 • Silent Valley • Coimbatore
National Park
• Perintalmanna
• Shornur Junction
Kunnamkulam • Palakkad
Guruvayan • Alathur • Udumalpettai
• Peechi • Pollachi
Thrissur • Parambikulam
• Peruvanum
Kodungallur • Angamali • Eravikulam
• Kalady • National Park
Nedumbassery • Aluva • Munnar • Bodinayak-
Ernakulam • Devikulam • kanur
Kochi • Muvattupuzha • Chinnamanur
NH47 • Ertumanoor • Iduki • Kamban
Vaikom • Kottayam • Thekkad • Gudalu
Kumarakom • Periyar Wildlife Sanctuary
Alappuzha • Kanjirapalli • Peermade
Ambalapuzha • Changanacherry • Sabarimala
Thiruvalla • Kaviyur
• Chengannur
Chavara • Puliangudi
Kayankulam • Shenkottai
Vadakkeula • Kuttalam • Tenkasi
Kollam • Tenmali • Falls
• Ponmudi
Varkala • Nedumangad
Anjengo • Neyyar
Thiruvananthapuram • Dam
Kovalam
Padmanabhapuram
Nagercoil

Indian Ocean

Lakshadweep Sea

Nicobar Islands

Ten Degree Channel

94°

Car Nicobar

Tillanchang Dwip

Tarasa Dwip • *Camorta*
Trinkat
8° • *Katchal* • 8°
Nancowry

Sombrero Channel

Little Nicobar

Great Nicobar

0 km 50
0 miles 50 • *Indira Point*

Ⓐ Ⓑ Ⓒ
① ② ③

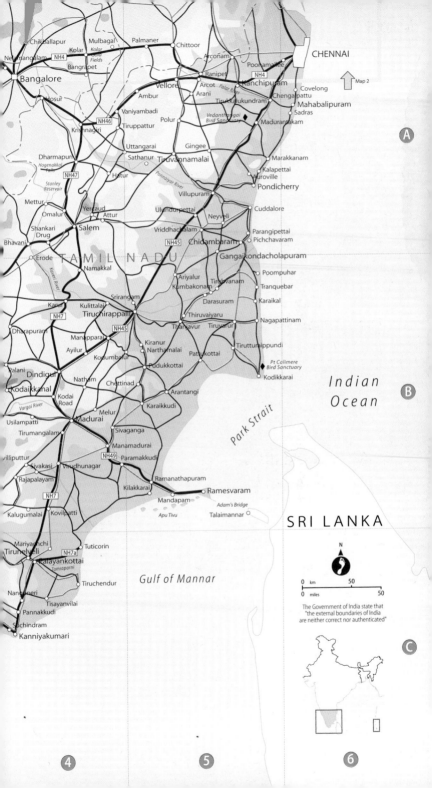

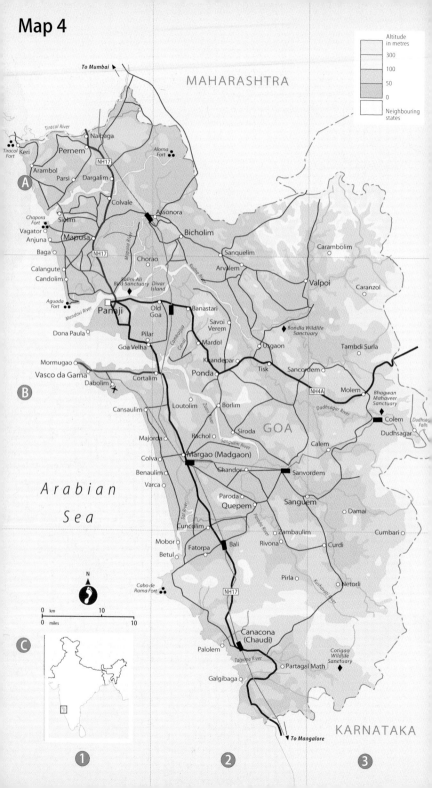

Acknowledgements

We record our warmest thanks to a number of people who helped us to update this new edition. We are particularly grateful to our researchers for their painstaking efforts and their wholehearted commitment to the Handbook.
We are particularly indebted to:

Kim Clark and Lucy Gorman, London, for their detailed feedback on Karnataka; Cyrus Dadachanji, Mumbai, who completely revised Mumbai; Ian Large, Antwerp, who travelled extensively through Goa and parts of Kerala to carry out an exhaustive update and Anil Mulchandani, Ahmadabad, for his thorough contribution to coastal Kerala.

We have a host of other travellers to thank for their generous help in amending, updating and correcting information and sharing their experiences or ideas for improvement in the hope that fellow travellers will benefit. Our warmest thanks to all who wrote to us during the year.

We would like to give a special mention for particularly detailed and informative letters from: Lynne Anderson, Cornhill on Tweed, England; JD Saul, London, England; Roger Vogler, USA; Simon Watson Taylor, England; Steve Scott, Blackpool, England; Achim Köhler, Isernhagen, Germany. A special thanks also to Catherine Lewis for making careful corrections to a large section of the handbook.

Paul Andrews, England; Jose Augustine, Thiruvananthapuram, India; Klaus Behrendt, Stuttgart, Germany; Anne-Marie Berg, Lund, Sweden; Claire Bonham-Carter, London, England; Regine Bossert; Boy en Marielle; Andy Brody; Deirdre Coffey; Russell Cohen; JeanClaude Colla, Lugano, Switzerland; Catherine Comte; Sudarshan Das, Balasore, India; Colonel PS Davis, Papplewick, England; Dr Richard Davis, Newcastle/Tyne, England; Fred H DeVinney, Oakland, Ca, USA; Wilfred Dierick, Netherlands; Remco Dubbeldam, Rotterdam, Holland; Steve Edgerton, De Haan, Belgium; Offer Eshel, Israel; Dr Puran Ganeriwala, Stafford, England; Dirk Geeroms, Belgium; Jim Giles, London, England; Claudia Glaeser, Switzerland; Dr Travers Grant, Rusper, England; Dr and Mrs Robin Harrod; John Heap, Harrogate, England; Cathy Hillman, Epsom, England; Alasdair Hind, Edinburgh, Scotland; Gordon Hoehne, Braunschweig, Germany; Jos Holzer, Nijmegen, The Netherlands; Barry Hughes, Edinburgh, Scotland; Penny and Geoffrey Hughes, Baginton, England; David Hunt, Lewes, England; Bijo Jacob, Thiruvananthapuram, India; Aditya Jalan, Patna, India; John J Jones; Maike Juta, Düsseldorf, Germany; Jessica Kaekkeboom, Enschede, The Netherlands; Seth Kasten; Dr. Ditza Kempler, Tel Aviv, Israel; Anton Keulaars, Tamil Nadu; Johann Kokoschinegg, Graz, Austria; Armin Kowarsch, Ternitz, Austria; Christian Kuendig, Maennedorf, Switzerland; Catherine Lewis; Rupert Lory, Sydney, Australia; Roy McKenzie, South Africa; Sarah McKibber, NY, USA; Valentina Maffei, Rome, Italy; Arabind Menon, Trivandrum, India; Katrin Mueller, Germany; Arthur Murray; Bernice Nikijuluw; Keith Oberg; Hazel Orchard, Hove, England; Donella Perkins; Jesper Pettersen, Oslo, Norway; Eric Pezet; GE Quinan, Harrow-on-the-Hill, England; Hannah Satz, Jerusalem, Israel; Caroline Schmutz, Switzerland; Steve Scott, Blackpool, England; Nanneke Seegers, Netherlands; Michael and Diana Seymour, Grantham, England; Darren Shepherd, Tenbury Well, England; Dr Cornelius Sigglekow; PN Sripada, Hospet, India; Dinah Swayne, London, England; Amy Taylor, Healdsburg, CA, USA; Tom K Tolk, Düsseldorf, Germany; Emerick W Toth, Bandon, Republic of Ireland; Rosanne Trottier; BL Underwood, Colchester; Ana Maria Uribe; Jan Vergauwe; Sandra Vick, Edinburgh, Scotland; Andrew Whitehead, London, England; Will Wyatt; Peter Yore, Kells, Ireland.

Robert and Roma Bradnock

Robert went to India overland in 1966, as a research student at Cambridge, to spend a year in South India and travel widely across the country. That journey was the first of many visits, living and working throughout the sub-continent. Since joining the School of Oriental and African Studies in 1968, where he is now head of the Department of Geography, he has carried out and supervised research covering the whole region. As an international authority he comments on South Asian current affairs across the world and lectures extensively in Britain and Europe.

A Bengali by birth, Roma was brought up in Kolkata (Calcutta), where, after graduating, she worked as a librarian. Her travels across the sub-continent had started early but to widen her horizons she went to Europe, and England subsequently became her home. Her work with Footprint started with the South Asian Handbook 1992 while her daughters were growing up. In addition to the India Handbook she and her husband now write the Footprint Sri Lanka and Goa Handbooks and the soon to be published handbooks on Rajasthan and Gujarat, Indian Himalaya and South India. They return to the sub-continent each year to research and seek out yet unexplored corners.